Modern REAL ESTATE Practice in Georgia

THIRD EDITION

Fillmore W. Galaty
Wellington J. Allaway
Robert C. Kyle
Mark Schneider, Consulting Editor

President: Dr. Andrew Temte
Executive Director, Real Estate Education: Melissa Kleeman-Moy
Development Editor: Adam Bissen

MODERN REAL ESTATE PRACTICE IN GEORGIA THIRD EDITION

Published by DF Institute, Inc., d/b/a Dearborn Real Estate Education
332 Front St. S., Suite 501
La Crosse, WI 54601

Printed in the United States of America
First revision, May 2017

ISBN: 978-1-4754-2902-2
PPN: 1511-5503

Contents

UNIT 26

Financing and Closing Residential Transactions 647

UNIT 27

Real Estate Commission and License Law 715

Preface

Since it first appeared in 1959, *Modern Real Estate Practice* has set the industry standard for real estate education. Whether preparing for a state licensing examination, fulfilling a college or university requirement, looking for specific guidance about buying a home or investment property, or simply expanding your understanding of this fascinating field, you can rely on *Modern Real Estate Practice*, the recognized authority for accurate and comprehensive information presented in a user-friendly format.

Just as today's real estate market is challenging and complex, today's real estate students are increasingly sophisticated and demand a high level of expertise and efficiency. This third edition of *Modern Real Estate Practice in Georgia* meets those expectations. In response to expanding state licensing requirements and the growing body of laws that govern the practice of real estate, this edition contains revisions and new features designed to make it an even more effective tool, no matter what your goal may be.

SPECIAL FEATURES

This update to *Modern Real Estate Practice* retains the successful features developed for previous editions to reflect the rapid pace of change in the real estate industry.

Quick Math Reference Inside the front and back covers of the book is a great time-saving reference tool: the most frequently used real estate math equations.

Math Concepts Throughout the book, helpful math hints and answers to commonly asked math questions appear at point of use to help you understand examples in real estate that require math computations.

Math FAQs This section at the end of the book provides additional math hints and solutions to commonly asked math questions to help you understand basic math concepts and apply them to examples in real estate.

In Practice Throughout the text, there are examples of how the concepts discussed are carried out in everyday real estate practice.

Directory of State Licensing Agencies and Statutes An internet address for every state licensing agency, as well as a link to the state's real estate licensing law, is provided in the appendix. State real estate regulatory agencies typically provide state statutes, real estate regulations, required forms, and other useful information.

Other Internet Resources Throughout the text, *Modern Real Estate Practice* helps connect the student to internet resources by identifying relevant websites whenever appropriate. The student can access the many government and professional association websites that are continually expanded to provide historical, as well as current, information.

Glossary The glossary features definitions of all key terms, as well as definitions of other important real estate the terms used in the text. It also includes page references that indicate where the terms are defined or explained in the text.

Margin Notes Notes in the margins direct students' attention to important vocabulary terms, concepts, and study tips, as well as internet resources included in the text. The margin notes also help students locate issues for review and serve as memory prompts for more efficient and effective studying.

UNIT FEATURES

Learning Objectives Each unit begins with a list of the unit goals that will help the reader anticipate the unit content.

Key Terms Key terms appear at the beginning of each unit. This feature not only alerts the student on the important vocabulary words that should be noted as the text is read but also helps the student to study and review.

Key Point Reviews At the end of each unit is a summary of the most essential content covered in that unit.

Unit Quizzes Demanding fact-pattern problems encourage students to not just memorize but to also understand and apply information. This approach gives students valuable practice in these important test-taking and exam-preparation skills. The questions have been carefully designed to follow the style and content of the most widely used testing services and to demonstrate the types of questions that students will likely encounter on state licensing exams. The answer key includes specific page references to the text.

The fundamental goal of *Modern Real Estate Practice in Georgia, Third Edition*, is to help readers understand the dynamics of the real estate industry by providing the critical information needed to pass a licensing examination, buy or sell property, or establish a real estate career.

STRUCTURE

The first 22 units of this textbook cover those general principles common to the practice of real estate in most every state. Units 23 through 27 examine how these long established fundamentals apply in Georgia. Here, readers will discover how statutory guidelines and local customs impact real estate ownership, brokerage relationships, contractual documents, residential financing, and transactional closings. As the five units in this state-specific section of the text are self-contained, each may serve independently as a topic review or offer additional perspective to traditional real estate practice. Considered as a whole, consulting editor Mark Schneider intends these units to provide a narrative structure allowing a reader to follow a Georgia licensee's role in a real estate transaction from start to finish.

A FINAL NOTE

With the publication of *Modern Real Estate Practice in Georgia, Third Edition*, we think it is fair to consider the book a classic. For more than two generations, this book has provided readers accurate and comprehensive real estate information, but we continue to ask, "What can we do to make a great book even better?"

With this edition, we provide clear, concise content that complements the collective voice of the original authors, while emphasizing contemporary issues such as fair housing, client representation, financing, and the environment. The text provides a balance between key teaching points and the material needed to round out a quality real estate education.

Please let us know what you think of this edition by emailing us at contentinquiries@dearborn.com.

Thank you for your help as you join the ranks of successful *Modern Real Estate Practice* users.

— The Publisher

Acknowledgments

Like a real estate transaction, this book is the product of teamwork and cooperation among professionals. We would like to express our gratitude and appreciation to the instructors and other real estate professionals whose invaluable suggestions and advice help *Modern Real Estate Practice* remain the industry's leading real estate text. Whether they responded to instructor surveys, provided reviews and suggestions for improving the previous edition, or reviewed the manuscript for this edition, the participation of these professionals—and their willingness to share their expertise—is greatly appreciated.

REVIEWERS

Valleri J. Crabtree, JD, CLU, Independent Consultant

Sam Martin, President, SamTheTutuor.com, Inc.

Ben C. Scheible, Esq., Truckee Meadows Community College, Reno, Nevada, and Ben C. Scheible Seminars

Marie S. Spodek, DREI, Professional Real Estate Solutions

Each new edition of *Modern Real Estate Practice* builds on earlier editions. We gratefully acknowledge the many real estate professionals and others who have contributed to prior editions of this book.

Robert H. Allen, National Real Estate Institute

Penny Alston, Wardley Real Estate School

Jean Anglin, Chattanooga State Community College

Jim Anselmi, Academy Real Estate School

Christopher O. Ashe, Learning Unlimited Doris Barrell, DSB Seminars

Donald R. Bates, Mountain Empire Community College

Thomas E. Battle, Center for Real Estate Education and Research

E. E. Bayliss III, Ford Fairfax Community College

Tom Bowen, Professional School of Real Estate

Paul Boyter, CRS, GRI, McColly School of Real Estate

Dianna Brouthers, Homefinders of America

Thomas Bull, McColly School of Real Estate

Virgil V. Bullis, Sr., Delaware Tech

Leona Busby, Long & Foster Institute of Real Estate

Chuck Byers, Professional Marketing Concepts

Marie Callas, Iowa Association of REALTORS®

Alice W. Cater, Lamar University Institute of Technology

Peter J. Certo, Gabelli School of Business

Charles Civer, Scottsdale Community College

Richard J. Clemmer, D&D School of Real Estate

Ginny Commins, Windermere Education

Kay Knox Crawford, Continual Learning Institute

David Dean, Litchfield County Real Estate School

Gregory Dunn, U.S. Books, Inc.

John Eaton, Ocean School of Real Estate

Dr. Kenneth W. Edwards, GRI, Linn-Benton Community College

Stephen Etzel, Kaplan Professional Schools, Texas

William B. Frost, Weichert Real Estate School

Katherine J. Gandy, Spokane Falls Community College and American Business and Professions Institute

Richard Garnitz, Kelley Academy of Real Estate

Michael Craig Glazer, Ivy Tech State College

Ignacio Gonzales, Mendocino Community College, Ukiah, California

Helen L. Grant, Moseley-Flint Schools of Real Estate, Inc.

Edward A. Guinane, Real Estate School of Siouxland

Randall S. Guttery, PhD, CLU, CLFC, Associate Dean and Professor of Finance and Real Estate, University of North Texas

Terry Hastings, Ridgefield Adult Education

Terry Hayes, Real Estate Brokerage Education

Arthur W. Heinbuch, Allied Institutes of Real Estate

Ray Henry, Arizona Institute of Real Estate

Mary Hibbler-Kee, Bess Technical College/UAB Options

Russell S. Hicks, The Real Estate School

Carl R. Hurst, Hurst Education Center

Diana T. Jacob-Rouhoff, Northwestern State University of Louisiana and Lincoln Graduate Center

F. Jeffrey Keil, J. Sargeant Reynolds Community College

John H. Kilroy, Jefferson County Board of Education

Rick Knowles, Capital Real Estate Training

Dr. Corbet J. Lamkin, Southern Arkansas University

Allen Lamont, Lamont School of Real Estate

Craig Larabee, Larabee School of Real Estate

George W. Lawrence, Master Instructor Faculty, California Association of REALTORS®

Jerome D. Levine, Tunxis Community-Technical College

Richard S. Linkemer, American School of Real Estate, Ltd.

Joyce Magee, Genesee Community College

Denise M. Mancini, J.W. Riker

Charline Mason, Charline Mason Seminars Unlimited

John D. Mathis III, Kaplan Real Estate Education

Peggy Ann McConnochie, Alaska Coastal Homes, Inc.

Paul McLaughlin, Esquire

Thomas L. Meyer, Cape Girardeau School of Real Estate

Coad Miller, Central Nebraska Community College

J. Leo Milotte, CRB, CRS, GRI, Milotte Associates Real Estate School

John R. Morgan, Morgan Testing Services

Monte Needler, Ivy Tech State College

Edward Neeley, Russell & Jeffcoat Real Estate Institute of Training & Education

Robert Neuwoehner, Heartland School of Real Estate

Jessie L. Newman, Grempler Real Estate Institute

Judith A. Nolde, JD, Content Consultant

Mary M. Otis, Northern Virginia Association of REALTORS®

Katherine Pancak, University of Connecticut

Andrew G. Pappas, Capital Community Technical College/Manchester Community Technical College

Joyce D. Remsburg, Trident Technical College

Walter L. Rice, Quality Workshops

John D. Rinehart, CRB, CRS, GRI, The Real Estate Institute of York County, Inc.

Robbie Robison, Allegany College

Kathy Roosa, Kathy Roosa School of Real Estate

Jay Rose, Esq., Tucker School of Real Estate

Phyllis Rudnick, CRS, GRI, Annex Real Estate School

Susann Shadley, Eastern Idaho Technical College

Don Shrum, The Real Estate School, Houston

Sherry Steele, Kaplan Professional Schools, Colorado

Bill Standiford, Ed Smith School of Real Estate

Allan R. Stevenson, GRI, CRB, Frostburg State University

Rita Stuckart, Jack White Real Estate School

Wayne A. Tarter, Greenville Tech

Dennis Tosh, FNC, Inc.

Ruth A. Vella, Omega Real Estate School

Howard E. Walker, Nashville School of Real Estate

Darline C. Waring, Charleston Trident Association of REALTORS®

Cynthia L. Weber, ABC Real Estate School

Donald Dwight Wells, Troy State University

Brenda S. White, Brenda White School of Real Estate

John P. Wiedemer, Houston Community College

Don W. Williams, Alabama Courses in Real Estate—ACRE

Judith B. Wolk, Charleston Trident Association of REALTORS®

Jerry L. Wooten, Tucker School of Real Estate

John Wright, Iowa Real Estate School of Cedar Rapids

UNIT 1

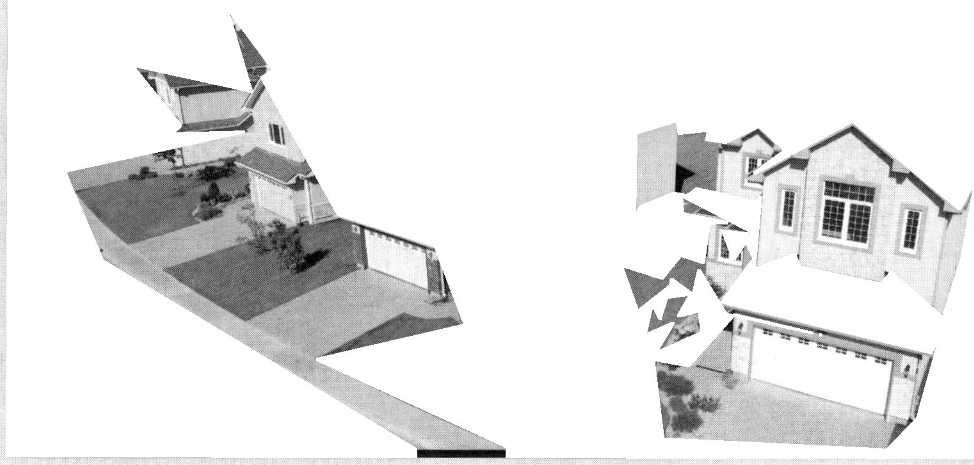

Introduction to the Real Estate Business

■ **LEARNING OBJECTIVES** *When you have finished reading this unit, you will be able to*

- **list and describe** the various careers available in the real estate industry;
- **discuss** the role of primary professional organizations, including the services and designations they offer the real estate practitioner and the ethical codes they establish;
- **list and describe** the different classifications and characteristics of real property;
- **explain** the factors which influence and affect supply and demand in the real estate market; and
- **define** the following *key terms*:

associate licensee	market	salesperson
broker	real estate licensee	supply and demand
code of ethics	sales associate	

OVERVIEW

Real estate transactions are taking place all around us, all the time. When a commercial leasing company rents space in a mall, or the owner of a building rents an apartment, it's a real estate transaction. The most common transaction is the purchase of a home, whether by a first-time buyer, by someone seeking a larger or smaller place to live or a second home, or by an investor interested in the property's income-producing potential. Consumers of real estate services thus include buyers and sellers of homes, tenants and landlords, investors, and developers. Nearly everyone, at some time, is involved in a real estate transaction.

All this adds up to big business—complex transactions that involve trillions of dollars each year in the United States. The services of millions of highly trained individuals are required: attorneys, bankers, trust company representatives, abstract and title insurance company agents, architects, surveyors, accountants, tax experts, and many others, in addition to buyers and sellers. All these people depend on the skills and knowledge of licensed real estate professionals.

REAL ESTATE: A BUSINESS OF MANY SPECIALIZATIONS

Despite the size and complexity of the real estate business, many people think of it as a business of real estate brokers and real estate salespeople only. Actually, the real estate industry is much broader than that. Appraisal, property management, financing, subdivision and development, home inspection, counseling, and education are all separate businesses within the real estate field. To succeed in a complex industry, every real estate professional must have a basic knowledge of these specialized areas.

Brokerage

Brokerage is the business of bringing people together in a real estate transaction. A licensed real estate broker acts as a point of contact between two or more people in negotiating the sale, purchase, or rental of property. A **broker** is defined as a person or company licensed to buy, sell, exchange, or lease real property for others and to charge a fee for these services. A licensed real estate **salesperson** is employed by or associated with the broker to perform brokerage activities on behalf of or for the broker, and may also be referred to as a **sales associate** or **associate licensee**.

A **real estate licensee** is a person who has satisfied the requirements of a licensing agency, as authorized by state legislation. The requirements include course hours or work experience and passing a state-mandated real estate exam. In some states, every real estate licensee is a broker, but only a managing broker may employ other licensees to act as sales associates, and the managing broker is responsible for the sales associates' conduct. Check the laws in your state to see which terms are used for licensees.

Appraisal

Appraisal is the process of developing an opinion of a property's market value, based on established methods and the *appraiser's* professional judgment. Although brokers should have some understanding of the valuation process and, in some circumstances, may even be asked to estimate the price at which a property is likely to sell, lenders require a professional appraisal for most transactions. Appraisers must have detailed knowledge of the methods of valuation. Appraisers must be not only licensed or certified for many federally related transactions but also licensed or certified in many states to be involved in transactions that are not federally related. The Appraisal Institute, www.appraisalinstitute.org, is the largest trade association of real estate appraisers.

Property Management

A *property manager* is a person or company hired to maintain and manage property on behalf of the property owner. By hiring a property manager, the owner is relieved of day-to-day management tasks, such as finding new tenants, collecting rents, finishing or altering space for tenants, ordering repairs, and generally maintaining the property. The scope of the manager's work depends on the terms of the management agreement—the employment contract between the owner and the manager. Whatever tasks are specified, the basic responsibility of the property manager is to protect the owner's investment and maximize the return on that investment. Depending on the size of the property and/or the scope of the work required, the property manager may need a real estate license or a property management license that is issued by the state in which the property is located. The Building Owners and Managers Association International, www.boma.org, provides useful resources for both owners and managers.

www.boma.org

Financing

Financing is the business of providing the funds that make real estate transactions possible. Most transactions are financed by a loan that is secured by a mortgage or deed of trust on the property purchased. Individuals involved in financing real estate may work in commercial banks, thrifts (which include savings associations), and credit unions, as well as mortgage banking and mortgage brokerage companies.

Subdivision and Development

Subdivision is the dividing of a single property into smaller parcels. *Development* involves the construction of improvements that benefit the land. These improvements may be either on-site or off-site. Off-site improvements, such as water lines and storm sewers, are made on public lands to serve the new development. On-site improvements, such as new homes or swimming pools, are made on individual parcels. While subdivision and development normally are related, they are independent processes that can occur separately.

Home Inspection

www.ashi.org
www.nahi.org

Home inspection is a profession that combines a practitioner's interest in real estate with skills and training in the construction trades. Many states have recognized the importance of a thorough home inspection by a competent, well-trained inspector by instituting home inspector licensing requirements that include education, training, examinations, and ongoing coursework. The American Society of Home Inspectors, www.ashi.org and the National Association of Home Inspectors, www.nahi.org, are both trade groups for home inspection professionals.

A professional home inspector conducts a thorough visual survey of a property's structure, systems, and site conditions and prepares an analytical report that is valuable to both purchasers and homeowners. The inspector examines the property from the chimney to the basement, being alert to deterioration, water intrusion, mechanical, or other observable problems. Often, the home inspection leads to a recommendation for additional examination when warranted by a property condition, such as evidence of mold damage or insect infestation. Cautious consumers, especially those who live in states in which *caveat emptor* (buyer beware) is the law, are relying more and more on the inspector's report to help them make purchase decisions. Frequently, a real estate sales contract will be contingent (conditioned) upon the inspector's report.

Counseling

Counseling involves providing clients with competent independent advice based on sound professional judgment. A real estate counselor helps clients choose among the various alternatives involved in purchasing, using, or investing in property. A counselor's role is to furnish clients with the information needed to make informed decisions. Professional real estate counselors must have a high degree of industry expertise.

Education

Real estate education is available to both practitioners and consumers. Colleges and universities, private schools, and trade organizations all conduct real estate courses and seminars covering topics from the principles of a prelicensing program to the technical aspects of tax and exchange law. State licensing laws establish the minimum educational requirements for obtaining—and keeping—a real estate license. Continuing education helps ensure that licensees keep their skills and knowledge current.

Other Areas

Many other professionals are involved in real estate, including lawyers who specialize in this area of practice, land-use planners employed by state and local agencies, and tax assessors.

PROFESSIONAL ORGANIZATIONS AND ETHICS

www.realtor.org

Many trade organizations serve the real estate business. Some of them have already been mentioned. The largest is the National Association of REALTORS® (NAR), whose website is www.realtor.org. NAR is composed of state, regional, and local associations. NAR also sponsors various affiliated organizations that offer professional designations to brokers, salespersons, appraisers, and others who complete required courses in areas of special interest. Members of NAR are entitled to be known as REALTORS® or REALTOR-ASSOCIATES®.

NAR Affiliates

www.cre.org
www.ccim.com
www.irem.org
www.rliland.com
www.crb.com
www.crs.com
www.realtor.org
www.crs.com
www.sior.com
www.wcr.org

NAR has many affiliated institutes, societies, and councils that are available to members who wish to increase their knowledge of a specialized area of real estate practice and earn the accompanying designation. These include the following:

- Counselors of Real Estate (CRE) www.cre.org
- Commercial Investment Real Estate Institute (CIREI) www.ccim.com
- Institute of Real Estate Management (IREM) www.irem.org
- REALTORS® Land Institute (RLI) www.rliland.com
- Certified Real Estate Brokerage Manager (CRB) www.crb.com
- Certified Residential Specialist (CRS) www.crs.com
- Graduate, REALTOR® Institute (GRI) www.realtor.org
- Council of Residential Specialists (CRS) www.crs.com

- Society of Industrial and Office REALTORS® (SIOR) www.sior.com
- Women's Council of REALTORS® (WCR) www.wcr.org

Other professional associations are mentioned throughout the text.

Professional Ethics

Professional conduct involves more than just complying with the law. In real estate, state licensing laws establish what activities are illegal and, therefore, prohibited. Merely complying with the letter of the law may not be enough: real estate professionals may perform legally yet not ethically. *Ethics* refers to a system of moral principles, rules, and standards of conduct. These moral principles do two things:

- They establish standards for integrity and competence in dealing with consumers of an industry's services.
- They define a code of conduct for relations within the industry among its professionals.

Code of Ethics

One way that many organizations address ethics among their members or in their respective businesses is by adopting codes of professional conduct. A **code of ethics** is a written system of standards for ethical conduct. The code contains statements designed to advise, guide, and regulate behavior. To be effective, a code of ethics must be specific by dictating rules that either prohibit or demand certain behavior. By including sanctions for violators, a code of ethics becomes more effective.

REALTORS® are expected to subscribe to NAR's Code of Ethics. NAR has established procedures for professional standards committees at the local, state, and national levels of the organization to administer compliance to the Code of Ethics. Practical applications of the articles of the code are known as Standards of Practice. The NAR Code of Ethics contains practical applications of business ethics.

www.nareb.com

The National Association of Real Estate Brokers (NAREB), whose members are known as *Realtists*, also adheres to a Code of Ethics. NAREB arose out of the early days of the civil rights movement as an association of racial minority real estate brokers in response to the conditions and abuses that eventually gave rise to fair housing laws. Today, NAREB remains dedicated to equal housing opportunity and can be found at www.nareb.com.

Many other professional organizations in the real estate industry have codes of ethics as well. In addition, many state real estate commissions are required by law to establish codes or canons of ethical behavior for licensees in their state.

TYPES OF REAL PROPERTY

Six Categories of Real Property

- Residential
- Commercial
- Mixed use
- Industrial
- Agricultural
- Special purpose

Just as there are areas of specialization within the real estate industry, there are different types of property in which to specialize. Real estate can be classified as

- *residential*— all property used for single-family or multifamily housing, whether in urban, suburban, or rural areas;
- *commercial*— business property, including office space, shopping centers, stores, theaters, hotels, and parking facilities;
- *mixed use*— property that allows for two uses, commercial and residential, in the same building;
- *industrial*— warehouses, factories, land in industrial districts, and power plants;
- *agricultural*— farms, timberland, ranches, and orchards; or
- *special purpose*— privately owned properties, such as places of worship, schools, and cemeteries, as well as publicly held properties, such as schools, municipal service buildings, and parks.

The market for each type of real property can be divided into three main functions: buying, selling, and leasing.

IN PRACTICE Although it is possible for a single real estate firm or an individual real estate professional to perform all the services and handle all classes of property discussed here (unless restricted by a state's license law), this is rarely done. A variety of services may be available within the same real estate firm in small towns, but most firms and professionals specialize to some degree.

Home Ownership

People buy homes for a variety of reasons. To many people, home ownership is a sign of financial stability. A home is an investment that can appreciate in value, especially over many years of ownership. Even when a loan is necessary to be able to afford the purchase of a home, the interest paid on the loan usually is a deduction from federal income tax. Home ownership also offers benefits that may be less tangible but no less valuable, such as pride, security, and a sense of belonging to a community.

Types of Housing

Some housing types are innovative uses of real estate while also incorporating various ownership concepts. These different forms of housing respond to the demands of a diverse marketplace.

The *single-family detached house* has been one of the most popular housing types, although it has been adapted in urban areas to take the form of the row house that may share a wall with an adjoining property. Often, multistory residences in cities like New York and Chicago have one or more separate living units on each floor, offering the possibility of an owner-occupied building that also provides rental income.

The *apartment building* was the response to housing demand in crowded urban areas. Modern highrise structures can offer residents many amenities. In the suburbs, multifamily housing has taken advantage of greater availability of large tracts of affordable land. An *apartment complex* is made up of a group of apartment buildings with a varying number of units in each building. The buildings may be lowrise or highrise, and the complex may include parking, security, clubhouse, swimming pool, tennis court, and even a golf course.

Condo = conventional ownership; deed

Co-op = proprietary lease

The *condominium* is a popular form of residential ownership, offering the security of owning property without the care and maintenance responsibilities a house demands. It is also a popular ownership option in areas where property values make single-family building ownership inaccessible to many people. A condominium owner owns an individual unit and also shares ownership with other unit owners of common facilities (called *common elements*), such as halls, elevators, reception area, main entrance security system, and surrounding grounds, which may include a swimming pool, clubhouse, tennis court, or other amenities. Management and maintenance of building exteriors and common facilities are provided by the governing association, typically making use of a management company and outside contractors, with expenses paid out of monthly *assessments* charged to owners. While condos are often apartment-style homes, this ownership form includes single-family and even commercial properties.

A *cooperative* also has units that share common walls and facilities within a larger building. The owners do not own the units; instead, each owner owns shares in a corporation that holds title to the real estate. Each shareholder receives a *proprietary lease* to a specified unit in the building. Like condominium unit owners, cooperative shareholders pay their share of the building's expenses.

Planned unit developments (PUDs), sometimes called *master-planned communities*, might consist entirely of residences, but they can also serve to merge such diverse land uses as housing, recreation, and commercial units into one self-contained development. PUDs are planned under special zoning ordinances. These ordinances often permit maximum use of open space by reducing lot sizes and street areas. Owners do not have direct ownership interest in the common areas. A community association is formed to maintain these areas, with fees for expenses collected from the owners. A PUD may be a small development of just a few homes or an entire planned city.

Highrise developments, sometimes called *mixed-use developments* (MUDs), combine office space, stores, theaters, and apartment units into a single vertical community. MUDs are usually self-contained and may offer laundry facilities, restaurants, food stores, beauty parlors, barbershops, swimming pools, and other attractive and convenient features.

Converted-use properties are factories, warehouses, office buildings, hotels, schools, churches, and other structures that have been converted to residential use. Developers often find renovation of such properties more aesthetically and economically appealing than demolishing a perfectly sound structure to build something new. An abandoned warehouse may be transformed into luxury loft condominium units; an out-of-date hotel may be renovated to create an apartment building; and an unused factory may be recycled into a profitable shopping mall.

Factory-built housing was once the often-derided *mobile home*, the most temporary of residences. Today, what are termed *manufactured homes* are permanent installations built to federal specifications, providing principal residences or vacation homes. The relatively low production cost of assembly-line-type construction in factories unaffected by the elements, coupled with the increased living space available in newer models, makes such homes an attractive option for both manufacturers and buyers. Increased sales have resulted in growing numbers of manufactured home parks that offer complete residential environments with permanent community facilities, as well as semi-permanent foundations and hookups for gas, water, and electricity.

Another type of factory-built housing is the *modular home* with components that are assembled at a building site on a prepared foundation. Workers finish the structure and connect plumbing and wiring. Entire developments can be built at a fraction of the time and cost of conventional stick-built construction.

THE REAL ESTATE MARKET

A **market** is a place where goods can be bought and sold. A market may be a specific physical place, such as a shopping mall. It also may be a vast, complex, economic system for moving goods and services throughout the world. In either case, the function of a market is to provide a setting in which supply and demand can establish market value, making it advantageous for buyers and sellers to trade.

Supply and Demand

When supply increases and demand remains stable, prices go down.

When demand increases and supply remains stable, prices go up.

Prices for goods and services in the market are established by the operation of **supply and demand**. The supply is the quantity of goods or services that can be sold at a given price. In the real estate market, the supply is made up of residential and commercial land and structures. Demand refers to the quantity of goods or services that consumers are willing and able to buy at a given price. In the real estate market, the number of homebuyers and businesses seeking to buy property can vary greatly depending on general economic conditions.

When supply and demand are roughly balanced, prices are stable and there is neither inflation (prices increasing) or deflation (prices decreasing). When supply increases and demand fails to increase commensurately, prices go down; when demand increases and supply fails to increase sufficiently to satisfy that demand, prices go up. Greater supply means producers need to attract more buyers, so they lower prices. Greater demand means producers can raise their prices because buyers compete for the product.

IN PRACTICE In 30 years in real estate, broker B has seen supply and demand in action many times. When a computer retailer relocated its distribution center to B's town 10 years ago, more than 100 families were interested in the 60 houses for sale at the time. Those sellers received multiple offers, and most sold their homes for more than the asking prices. On the other hand, 10 years before that, when the nearby naval base closed and 500 civilian jobs were transferred to other parts of the country, it seemed that every other house in town was for sale. There were plenty of sales, but prices were lower than they had been in many years.

Supply and Demand in the Real Estate Market Two characteristics of real estate govern the way the market reacts to the pressures of supply and demand: uniqueness and immobility. *Uniqueness* means that, no matter how identical they may appear, no two parcels of real estate are ever exactly alike; each occupies its own unique geographic location. *Immobility* refers to the fact that property cannot be relocated to satisfy demand where supply is low, nor can buyers always relocate to areas with greater supply. For these reasons, real estate markets are local markets. Each geographic area has different types of real estate and different conditions that drive prices. In these well-defined areas, real estate offices can keep track of the types of property that are in demand, as well as the properties that are available to meet that demand.

IN PRACTICE Technological advances and market changes have enabled real estate professionals to track trends and conditions that affect their local markets. Computers, the internet, smartphones, digital cameras, e-fax technology, and global positioning systems are just a few of an ever-expanding gallery of tools that help real estate practitioners stay on top of their markets.

Because of real estate's uniqueness and immobility, the market generally adjusts slowly to the forces of supply and demand. Though a home offered for sale can be withdrawn in response to low demand and high supply, it is just as likely that oversupply will result in lower prices. When supply is low, on the other hand, a high demand may not be met immediately because development and construction are lengthy processes. As a result, development tends to occur in uneven spurts of activity.

Even when supply and demand can be forecast with some accuracy, natural disasters such as hurricanes and earthquakes can disrupt market trends. Similarly, a sudden change in the national financial market, a local event such as a business closure, or a regional disruption caused by storm damage can dramatically disrupt a seemingly stable market.

Factors Affecting Supply

Factors affecting real estate supply are

- labor force, construction, and material costs;
- government controls and financial policies; and
- local government factors.

Factors that tend to affect the supply side of the real estate market's supply and demand balance include labor force availability, construction and material costs, and governmental controls and financial policies.

Labor Force, Construction, and Material Costs A shortage of skilled labor or building materials or an increase in the cost of materials can decrease the amount of new construction. High transfer costs, such as taxes and construction permit fees, can also discourage development. Increased construction costs may be passed along to buyers and tenants in the form of higher sales prices and increased rents that can further slow the market.

Governmental Controls and Monetary Policy The government's monetary policy can have a substantial impact on the real estate market. The Federal Reserve Board (the Fed) establishes a discount rate of interest for the money it lends to commercial banks. That discount rate has a direct impact on the interest rates the banks charge to borrowers, which in turn plays a significant part in people's ability to buy homes. The Federal Housing Administration (FHA) and the Government National Mortgage Association (Ginnie Mae) can also affect the amount of money available to lenders for mortgage loans.

Even apart from financing concerns, virtually any government action has some effect on the real estate market. For instance, federal environmental regulations may increase or decrease the supply and value of land in a local market. Real estate taxation is one of the primary sources of revenue for local governments. Policies on taxation of real estate can have either positive or negative effects. While high taxes may deter investors, tax incentives may attract new businesses and industries and bring increased employment and expanded residential real estate markets.

Local governments also influence supply. Land-use controls, building codes, and zoning ordinances help shape the character of a community and control the use of land. Careful planning can help stabilize, and even increase, real estate values.

Factors Affecting Demand

Factors affecting real estate demand are

- population,
- demographics, and
- employment and wage levels.

Factors that tend to affect the demand side of the real estate market include population, demographics, and employment and wage levels.

Population Because shelter is a basic human need, the demand for housing grows with the population. Although the total population of the country continues to rise, the demand for real estate increases faster in some areas than in others. In some locations, growth has ceased altogether or the population has declined. This may be due to economic changes (such as business closings), social concerns (such as the quality of schools or a desire for more open space), or population changes (such as population shifts from colder to warmer climates). The result can be a drop in demand for real estate in one area, which may be matched by increased demand elsewhere.

Demographics The study and description of a population is called *demographics*. The population of a community is a major factor in determining the quantity and type of housing in that community. The number of occupants per household and their ages, the ratio of adults to children, the number of retirees, family income, and lifestyle are all demographic factors that contribute to the amount and type of housing needed.

IN PRACTICE *Niche marketing* is the phrase used to refer to the targeted marketing of specific demographic populations. For example, as baby boomers age and look for retirement housing, their need or demand is considered a niche market. At the same time, fair housing laws prohibit discriminatory practices against protected classes of individuals.

Employment and Wage Levels Decisions about whether to buy or rent and how much to spend on housing are closely related to income. When job opportunities are scarce or wage levels low, demand for real estate usually drops. The market might, in fact, be affected drastically by a single major employer moving in or shutting down. Real estate professionals should stay informed about the business plans of local employers.

As you have seen, the real estate market depends on a variety of economic forces, such as interest rates and employment levels. To be successful, real estate professionals must follow economic trends and anticipate where those trends will lead. How people use their income depends on consumer confidence, which is based not only on perceived job security but also on the availability of credit and the impact of inflation. General trends in the economy, such as the availability of mortgage money and the rate of inflation, will influence people's spending decisions.

KEY POINT REVIEW

Real estate brokerage is the business of bringing people together in a real estate transaction conducted by a **real estate broker** who is a person or company licensed to buy, sell, exchange, or lease real property for others for compensation, or by a **real estate salesperson (sales associate)** who conducts brokerage activities on behalf of the broker.

Appraisal is the process of developing an opinion of a property's value (typically, market value) based on established methods and an appraiser's professional judgment. Licensing or certification is required for many federally related transactions, and many states require licensing or certification for other transactions as well.

Property management is conducted by a **property manager**, a person or company hired to maintain and manage property on behalf of the property owner. The property manager's scope of work depends on a **management agreement**, and the basic responsibility of the property manager is to protect the owner's investment while maximizing the owner's financial return.

Financing is the business of providing the funds that make real estate transactions possible through loans secured by a mortgage or deed of trust on the property, with funding provided by commercial banks, thrifts (which include savings associations), credit unions, mortgage bankers, and mortgage brokerage companies.

Subdivision and development involve splitting a single property into smaller parcels (subdividing) and constructing improvements on the land (development).

Home inspection is of interest to both purchasers and homeowners, and an inspection report will show results of a thorough survey of observable property conditions. A state license may be required of a home inspector.

Real estate counseling involves independent advice based on sound professional judgment regarding how to buy, sell, or invest in property.

Types of real property include **residential**, **commercial**, **mixed use**, **industrial**, **agricultural**, and **special purpose**, which can be privately or publically held.

The **real estate market** reflects the principle of **supply and demand**, influenced by the **uniqueness** and **immobility** of parcels of real estate. When the supply increases relative to demand, prices go down, and when demand increases relative to supply, prices go up.

The factors affecting the **supply** of real estate include labor force availability, construction and material costs, government controls (environmental restrictions, land use policies, building codes, zoning), and monetary policy that impacts interest rates and the money supply.

The factors affecting the **demand** for real estate include population, demographics, and employment and wage levels.

UNIT 1 QUIZ

1. A professional opinion of a property's market value, based on established methods and using trained judgment, is performed by a
   a. real estate attorney.
   b. real estate appraiser.
   c. real estate counselor.
   d. home inspector.

2. In general, when the supply of a certain commodity increases,
   a. price tends to rise.
   b. price tends to drop.
   c. demand for it tends to rise.
   d. demand for it tends to drop.

3. Which factor primarily affects supply in the real estate market?
   a. Population
   b. Demographics
   c. Employment
   d. Governmental monetary policy

4. Which factor is *MOST* likely to influence demand for real estate?
   a. Number of real estate professionals in the area
   b. Number of full-time real estate professionals in the area
   c. Wage levels and employment opportunities
   d. Price of new homes being built in the area

5. Property management, appraisal, financing, and development are all examples of
   a. factors affecting demand.
   b. specializations within the real estate industry.
   c. non–real estate professions.
   d. activities requiring broker management and supervision.

6. A REALTOR® is *BEST* described as an individual who is
   a. a real estate professional who acts as a point of contact between two or more people in negotiating the sale, purchase, or rental of property.
   b. any real estate professional who assists buyers, sellers, landlords, or tenants in any real estate transaction.
   c. a member of the National Association of Real Estate Brokers who specializes in residential properties.
   d. a real estate licensee and a member of the National Association of REALTORS® (NAR).

7. A major manufacturer of automobiles announces that it will relocate one of its factories, along with 2,000 employees, to a small town. What effect will this announcement *MOST* likely have on the small town's housing market?
   a. Houses will likely become less expensive.
   b. Houses will likely become more expensive.
   c. Because the announcement involves an issue of demographics, not of supply and demand, housing prices will stay the same.
   d. The announcement involves an industrial property; residential housing will not be affected.

8. A real estate professional who has several years of experience in the industry decided to retire from actively marketing properties. Now this person helps clients choose among the various alternatives involved in purchasing, using, or investing in property. What is this person's profession?
   a. Real estate counselor
   b. Real estate appraiser
   c. Real estate educator
   d. REALTOR®

9. The words *broker* and *REALTOR®* are
   a. interchangeable.
   b. different categories of membership in the National Association of REALTORS®.
   c. different titles offered by separate professional organizations.
   d. not necessarily related; a broker is a real estate licensee, and a REALTOR® is a real estate licensee who is a member of the National Association of REALTORS®.

10. Schools would be considered part of which real estate classification?
    a. Special-purpose
    b. Industrial
    c. Commercial
    d. Residential

11. When demand for a commodity decreases and supply remains the same,
    a. price tends to rise.
    b. price tends to fall.
    c. price is not affected.
    d. the market becomes stagnant.

12. A licensed real estate professional acting as a point of contact between two or more people in negotiating the sale, rental, or purchase of a property is known as a(n)
    a. sales affiliate.
    b. broker.
    c. property inspector.
    d. appraiser.

13. An increase in the following would affect supply *EXCEPT*
    a. population.
    b. construction costs.
    c. governmental controls.
    d. the labor force.

14. All of the following are categories of the uses of real property *EXCEPT*
    a. residential.
    b. developmental.
    c. agricultural.
    d. industrial.

15. All of the following would affect demand *EXCEPT*
    a. population.
    b. demographics.
    c. wage levels.
    d. monetary policy.

16. All of the following affect how quickly the forces of supply and demand work *EXCEPT*
    a. a property's specific geographic location.
    b. immobility of a property.
    c. degree of standardization of the property's price.
    d. uniqueness of a property.

17. A real estate professional who performs a visual survey of a property's structure and prepares a report for a purchaser or an owner is
    a. an educator.
    b. an appraiser.
    c. a property manager.
    d. a home inspector.

18. When the supply of a commodity decreases while demand remains the same, price tends to
    a. rise.
    b. drop.
    c. be unaffected.
    d. go in the direction of supply.

19. A person or company responsible for maintaining a client's property and maximizing the return on the client's investment is serving as
    a. a rental agent.
    b. a building maintenance specialist.
    c. a property manager.
    d. an investment counselor.

20. Detailed information about the age, education, behavior, and other characteristics of members of a population group is called
    a. population analysis.
    b. demographics.
    c. family lifestyles.
    d. household data.

Real Property and the Law

LEARNING OBJECTIVES *When you have finished reading this unit, you will be able to*

- **discuss** the concepts of land and ownership rights in real property;
- **distinguish** between real and personal property and the differences in transferring ownership and title;
- **describe and explain** the basic economic and physical characteristics of real property;
- **discuss** the limitations of the real estate professional under the law; and
- **define** the following *key terms*:

accession
accretion
air rights
annexation
appurtenance
area preference
avulsion
bundle of legal rights
chattel
emblements
erosion
fixture
improvement
land
littoral rights
manufactured housing
nonhomogeneity
personal property
prior appropriation
real estate
real property
riparian rights
severance
situs
subsurface rights
surface rights
trade fixture
water rights

OVERVIEW

Real estate is a market like any other. Real property is the product, and the real estate professional is the salesperson. As any successful salesperson will tell you, product knowledge is the key to success. The real estate professional needs to know enough about the product to be able to educate and guide clients and customers, whether they are buyers, sellers, renters, or investors. The real estate professional is dealing with a product that involves very specific and often very complicated legal issues, making in-depth knowledge of those matters a must. Here you will learn about the fundamental principles of the product that is at the heart of every real estate transaction.

LAND, REAL ESTATE, AND REAL PROPERTY

The words *land*, *real estate*, and *real property* are often used interchangeably. To most people, they mean the same thing. Strictly speaking, however, the terms refer to different aspects of ownership interests in land. To fully understand the nature of real estate and the laws that affect it, real estate professionals must be aware of the subtle yet important differences in meaning of these words.

Land

For the real estate professional, land is more than just a handful of dirt. **Land** is defined as the earth's surface extending downward to the center of the earth and upward to infinity. Land includes naturally attached objects, such as trees, as well as bodies of water found on or under it. (*See* Figure 2.1.)

FIGURE 2.1: Land, Real Estate, and Real Property

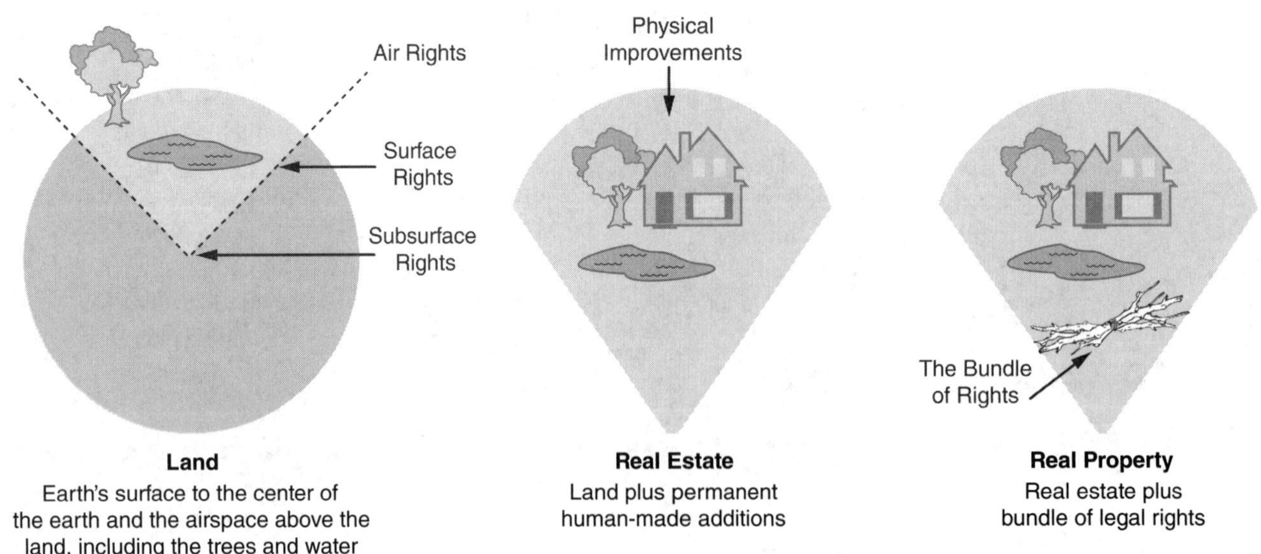

Land thus includes not only the surface of the earth, with the boulders and plants found on it, but also the underlying soil. It includes the *subsurface*, the minerals and substances that lie far below the earth's surface as well as the *airspace*, the air above the earth, all the way into space. Most of the surface of the earth, of course, is not land at all, but water. Federal, state, and local laws govern the ownership and use of the wetter parts of the earth, including oceans, lakes, and rivers. Private contracts, as well as laws and regulations, can also limit ownership and use rights in the surface, subsurface, and airspace of land.

Real Estate

Real estate is defined as land plus all human-made improvements to the land that are permanently attached (annexed) to it. (*See* Figure 2.1.)

An **improvement** to land can be any artificial thing attached on or below ground, such as a building, fence, water line or sewer pipe, as well as growing things that are made part of the landscaping.

Real Property

Real property is defined as the interests, benefits, and rights that are automatically included in the ownership of real estate. (*See* Figure 2.1.) In many states, the terms *real estate* and *real property* are synonymous, and are used to refer to both the physical property and the rights of ownership, while other states still make the distinction.

Traditionally, ownership rights of real property are described as a **bundle of legal rights**. These rights include the

- right of possession,
- right to control the property within the framework of the law,
- right of enjoyment (to use the property in any legal manner),
- right of exclusion (to keep others from entering or using the property), and
- right of disposition (to sell, will, transfer, or otherwise dispose of or encumber the property).

The concept of a bundle of rights comes from old English law. In the Middle Ages, a seller transferred property by giving the purchaser a handful of earth or a bundle of bound sticks from a tree on the property. After accepting the bundle, the purchaser became the owner of the tree from which the sticks came and the land to which the tree was attached. Because the rights of ownership (like the sticks) can be separated and individually transferred, the sticks became symbolic of those rights. (*See* Figure 2.2.)

Title to Real Property The word *title*, as it relates to real property (real estate), has two meanings: (1) the right to or ownership of the property, including the owner's bundle of legal rights; and (2) evidence of that ownership by a deed. Title refers to *ownership* of the property, not to a printed document. The document by which the owner transfers title to the property is the deed.

FIGURE 2.2: The Bundle of Legal Rights

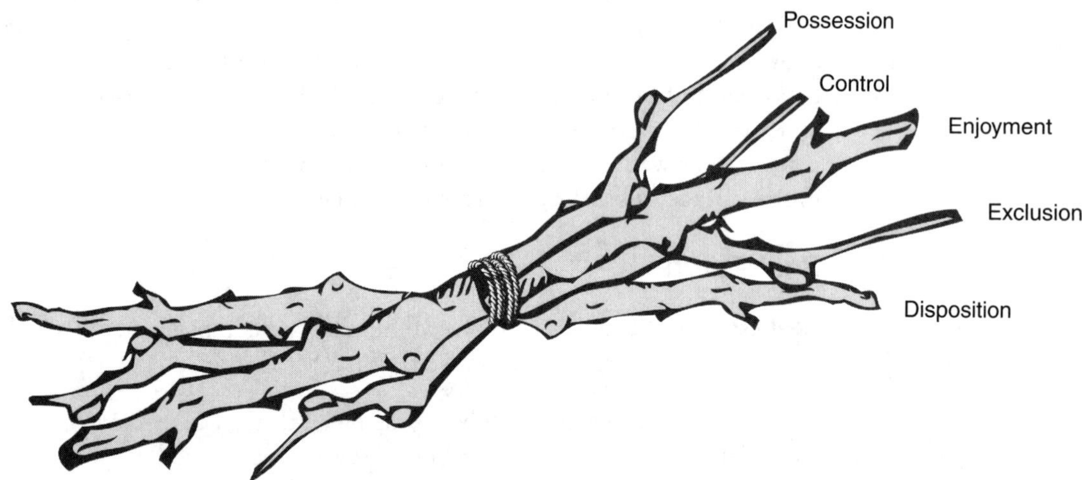

Real property is often coupled with the word *appurtenance*. An **appurtenance** (something that is transferred with or "runs with" the land) is a right or privilege associated with the property, although not necessarily a physical part of it. Typical appurtenances include parking spaces in multiunit buildings, easements, water rights, and other improvements. An appurtenance is connected to the property, and ownership of the appurtenance normally transfers to the new owner when the property is sold.

IN PRACTICE When people talk about buying or selling homes, office buildings, and land, they usually call these things real estate. For all practical purposes, the term *real estate* is synonymous with *real property* as defined here. Thus, in everyday usage, *real estate* includes the legal rights of ownership specified in the definition of real property. Sometimes people use the term *realty* instead.

Surface, Subsurface, and Air Rights

Surface Rights Ownership rights in a parcel of real estate that are limited to the surface of the earth are called **surface rights**.

Subsurface Rights The rights to the natural resources below the earth's surface are called **subsurface rights**. An owner may transfer subsurface rights without transferring surface rights, and vice versa. In oil-producing states, real estate is commonly transferred without including the rights to minerals found below ground level. Recently, natural gas found in shale rock beneath the surface that is removed in the process called hydraulic fracturing ("fracking") has become economical and created new interest in subsurface rights in many states. Fracking also has resulted in environmental concerns.

IN PRACTICE A landowner sells the rights to any oil and gas found beneath the owned farmland to an oil company. Later, the same landowner sells the remaining interests (the surface, air, and limited subsurface rights) to a buyer, reserving the rights to any coal that may be found. This buyer sells the remaining land to yet another buyer but retains the farmhouse, stable, and pasture. After these sales, four parties have ownership interests in the same real estate: (1) the original landowner owns all the coal; (2) the oil company owns all the oil and gas; (3) the first buyer owns the farmhouse, stable, and pasture; and (4) the second buyer owns the rights to the remaining real estate. (*See* Figure 2.3.)

Air Rights The rights to use the space above the earth may be sold or leased independently, provided the rights have not been limited by law. **Air rights** can be an important part of real estate, particularly in large cities, where the air rights over railroad tracks must be purchased or leased to construct office buildings, such as the MetLife Building (formerly the PanAm Building) in New York City and One Prudential Plaza (formerly the Prudential Building) in Chicago. To construct such a building, the developer must purchase not only the air rights but also numerous small portions of the land's surface for the building's foundation supports.

FIGURE 2.3: Surface and Subsurface Rights

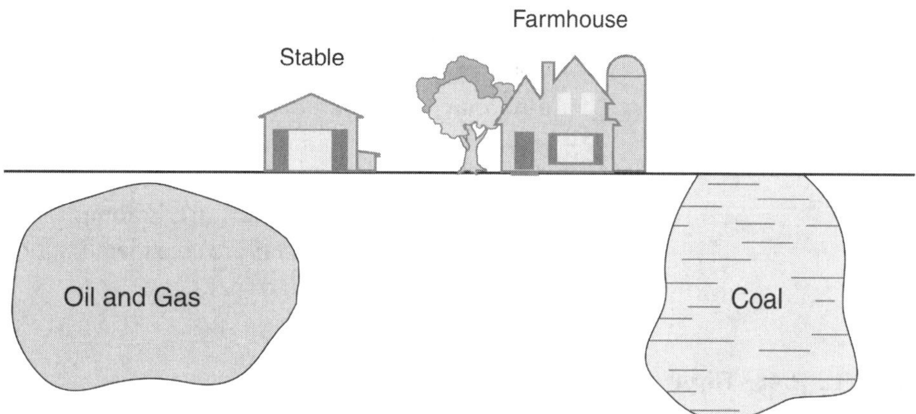

Before air travel was possible, a property's air rights were considered unlimited, extending upward into the farthest reaches of outer space. Now that air travel is common, however, the federal government, through laws, regulations, and court decisions, has put limits on air rights. Today, reasonable interference with these rights is permitted, such as that necessary for aircraft (and presumably spacecraft), as long as the owner's right to use and occupy the land is not unduly lessened. Government and airport authorities often purchase adjacent air rights to provide approach patterns for air traffic.

With the continuing development of solar power, air rights—and, more specifically, light or solar rights—are being closely examined by the courts. A new high-rise building that blocks sunlight from a smaller existing building may be found to be interfering with the smaller building's right to sunlight, particularly if systems in the smaller building are solar powered. Air and solar rights are regulated by state and local laws and regulations.

Water Rights

Water rights are common-law (historical) or statutory rights held by owners of land adjacent to rivers, lakes, or oceans and are restrictions on the rights of land ownership. Water rights are particularly important in arid western states, where water is a scarce and valuable public commodity, but are also of concern in agricultural areas and population centers.

Whether for agricultural, recreational, or other purposes, waterfront real estate has always been desirable. Each state has strict laws that govern the ownership and use of water as well as the adjacent land. The laws vary among the states, but all are closely linked to climactic and topographical conditions. Where water is plentiful, states may rely on the simple parameters set by the common-law doctrines of riparian and littoral rights. Where water is scarce, a state may control all but limited domestic use of water, according to the doctrine of prior appropriation.

Riparian Rights Common-law rights granted to owners of land along the course of a river, stream, or similar flowing body of water are called **riparian rights**. Although riparian rights are governed by laws that vary from state to state, they generally include the unrestricted right to use the water. As a rule, the only limitation on the owner's use is that such use cannot interrupt or alter the flow of the water or contaminate it in any way. In addition, an owner of land that borders a nonnavigable waterway, (i.e., a body of water unsuitable for commercial boat traffic) owns the land under the water to the exact center of the waterway. Land adjoining commercially navigable rivers, on the other hand, is usually owned to the water's edge, with the state holding title to the submerged land. (*See* Figure 2.4.) Navigable waters are considered public highways in which the public has an easement or right to travel.

FIGURE 2.4: Riparian Rights

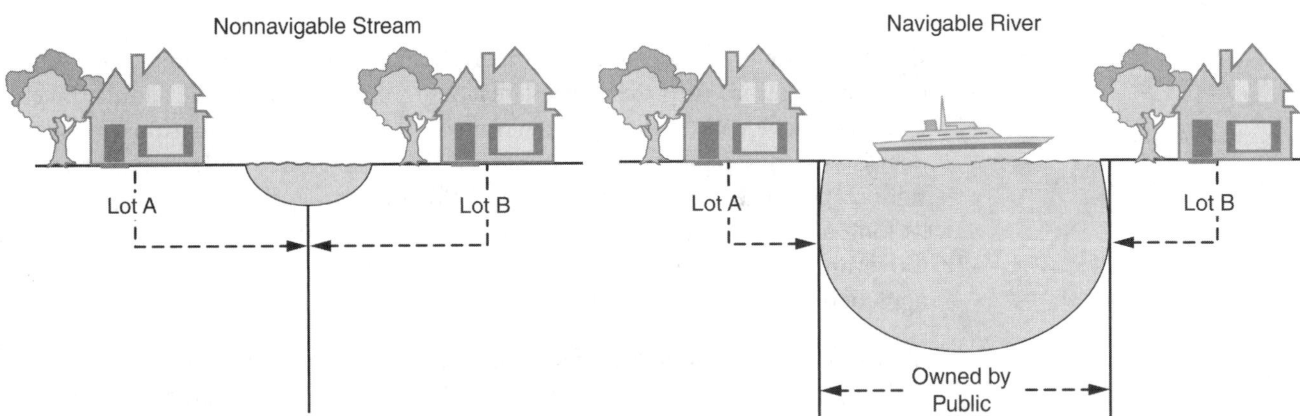

Littoral Rights Closely related to riparian rights are the **littoral rights** of owners whose land borders commercially navigable lakes, seas, and oceans. Owners with littoral rights enjoy unrestricted use of available waters but own the land adjacent to the water only up to the average high-water mark. All land below this point is owned by the government.

In some states, riparian and littoral rights are appurtenant to (run with) the land and cannot be retained when the property is sold. The right to use the water belongs to whoever owns the bordering land and that right cannot be retained by a former owner after the land is sold.

Accretion, Erosion, and Avulsion The amount of land an individual owns may be affected by the natural action of water. An owner is entitled to all land created through **accretion**—increases in the land resulting from the deposit of soil by the water's action.

On the other hand, an owner may lose land through the action of the elements. **Erosion** is the gradual and sometimes imperceptible wearing away of the land by natural forces, such as wind, rain, and flowing water. Fortunately, erosion usually takes hundreds or even thousands of years to have any noticeable effect on a person's property. Flash floods or heavy winds, however, can increase the speed of erosion.

If erosion is a slow natural process, avulsion is its opposite. **Avulsion** is the sudden removal of soil by an act of nature. It is an event that causes the loss of land in a much less subtle manner than erosion. An earthquake or a mudslide, for instance, can cause an individual's landholding to become much smaller very quickly.

Doctrine of Prior Appropriation In states where water is scarce, ownership and use of water are often determined by the doctrine of **prior appropriation.** Under this doctrine, the right to use any water, with the exception of limited domestic use, is controlled by the state rather than by the landowner adjacent to the water.

To secure water rights in prior appropriation states, a landowner must demonstrate to a state agency that the owner's plans are for *beneficial* use, such as crop irrigation. If the state's requirements are met, the landowner receives a permit to use a specified amount of water for the limited purpose of the beneficial use. Although statutes governing prior appropriation vary from state to state, the priority of water rights is usually determined by the oldest recorded permit date.

Under some state laws, water rights, once granted, attach to the land of the permit holder. The permit holder may sell a water right to another party; however, issuance of a water permit does not grant access to the water source. All access rights-of-way over the land of another (easements) must be obtained from the property owner.

REAL PROPERTY VERSUS PERSONAL PROPERTY

Property may be classified as either real or personal. **Personal property**, sometimes called personalty, is all the property that can be owned and that does not fit the definition of real property. An important distinction between the two is that personal property is movable. Items of personal property, also called **chattels**, include such tangibles as chairs, tables, clothing, money, bonds, and bank accounts.

Factory-Built Housing

Factory-built housing is defined as dwellings that are not constructed at the site but are built off-site and trucked to a building lot where they are installed or assembled. Factory-built housing includes modular, panelized, precut, and mobile homes. Use of the term *mobile homes* was phased out with the passage of the National Manufactured Housing Construction and Safety Standards Act of 1976, when manufactured homes became federally regulated. **Manufactured housing** is that which is built specifically to the standards of the Department of Housing and Urban Development (HUD), although the term *mobile home* is still commonly used. Most states have agencies that administer and enforce the federal regulations for manufactured housing. State and local building codes regulate www.manufacturedhousing.org

the construction and installation of other types of factory-built housing. A useful resource is the Manufactured Housing Institute, www.manufacturedhousing.org.

The distinction between real and personal property is not always obvious. Factory-built components are found in virtually every building and become part of the real estate once installed. Manufactured housing may be considered personal property, even though its mobility may be limited to a single trip to a park or development to be hooked up to utilities. Any type of factory-built or manufactured housing may, however, be considered real property if it becomes permanently affixed to the land. The distinction is generally one of state law. Real estate professionals should be familiar with local laws before attempting to sell factory-built housing of any type.

Plants

The legal term for plants that do not require annual cultivation (such as trees and shrubbery) is *fructus naturales* (fruits of nature); plant or crops that require annual cultivation are legally known as **emblements** or *fructus industriales* (fruits of industry).

Trees and crops generally fall into one of two classes: (1) Trees, perennial shrubbery, and grasses that do not require annual cultivation are known as *fructus naturales*. These items are considered real estate. (2) Annually cultivated crops such as fruit, vegetables, and grain are known as **emblements**, or *fructus industriales*, and are generally considered personal property. The current owner or tenant is entitled to harvest the crops that result from that individual's labor. For example, when farmland is sold, the seller won't have to dig up growing corn plants and haul them away unless the sales contract says so. The young corn remains on the land. The seller may come back and harvest the corn when it's ready. Perennial crops, such as orchards or vineyards, are not personal property and so transfer with the land.

An item of real property can become personal property by **severance**, which is the act of separating it from the land. For example, a growing tree is part of the land until the owner cuts it down, literally severing it from the property. Similarly, an apple becomes personal property once it is picked from a tree.

It is also possible to change personal property into real property through the process known as **annexation**. For example, if a landowner buys cement, stones, and sand and mixes them into concrete to construct a sidewalk across the land, the landowner has converted personal property (cement, stones, and sand) into real property (a sidewalk).

Real estate professionals need to know whether property is real or personal. An important distinction arises, for instance, when the property is transferred from one owner to another. Real property is conveyed by deed, while personal property is conveyed by a bill of sale or receipt.

Classifications of Fixtures

In considering the differences between real and personal property, it is necessary to distinguish between a fixture and personal property.

Fixtures A **fixture** is personal property that has been so attached to land or a building that, by law, it becomes part of the real property. Examples of fixtures are heating systems, elevator equipment in highrise buildings, radiators, kitchen cabinets, light fixtures, and plumbing. Almost any item that has been added as a permanent part of a building is considered a fixture.

During the course of time, the same materials may change their classification as real or personal property several times, depending on their use and location.

Legal tests of a fixture:

- Method of annexation
- Adaptability of item to land's use
- Relationship of parties
- Intention in placing item on the land
- Agreement of the parties

Legal Tests of a Fixture In determining whether an item is a fixture, and thus part of the real estate, courts use the following five basic tests, which can be remembered by the acronym *MARIA*:

- *Method of annexation:* How *permanent* is the method of attachment? Can the item be removed without causing damage to the surrounding property, or can any damage caused by the removal be easily repaired?
- *Adaptability of the item for the land's ordinary use:* Is the item being *used* as real property or personal property? For example, a refrigerator is usually considered personal property. However, if a refrigerator has been adapted to match the kitchen cabinetry, it may be considered a fixture.
- *Relationship of the parties:* In general, a court will favor a tenant over a landlord, and a buyer over a seller.
- *Intention of the person in placing the item on the land:* This should be the most important consideration, but the actions of the tenant may not be consistent with the tenant's earlier intention. If an installation is intended to be temporary, it should not be attached in a way that appears to be permanent.
- *Agreement of the parties:* Have the parties agreed on whether the item is real or personal property in the provisions of an offer to purchase or lease?

Although these tests may seem simple, court decisions have been complex and inconsistent. Property that appears to be permanently affixed has sometimes been ruled to be personal property, while property that seems removable has been ruled a fixture. It is important not only for an owner to clarify what is to be sold with the real estate at the very beginning of the sales process but also for a tenant to make certain that items installed for personal use be removable at the conclusion of the lease term.

IN PRACTICE At the time a property is listed, the seller and the listing agent should discuss which items to include in the sale. Any item that would usually be considered part of the real property (such as a light fixture) should be clearly labeled as remaining with the owner and so noted on any promotional materials, including property listing forms. Most importantly, the written sales contract between the buyer and the seller should specifically list all articles that are being included in the sale, as well as those that are being excluded from it, particularly if any doubt exists as to whether the items are personal property or fixtures (for instance, built-in bookcases, chandeliers, ceiling fans, or exotic shrubbery). This specificity will avoid a misunderstanding between the parties that might result in the collapse of the transaction and an expensive lawsuit. The most commonly disputed items between buyers and sellers are draperies, light fixtures, and appliances.

Trade Fixtures A special category of fixtures includes property used in the course of business. An article owned by a tenant, attached to a rented space or building, and used in conducting a business is a **trade fixture**, or a chattel fixture. Some examples of trade fixtures are hydraulic lifts in an auto repair shop, lanes and pin-setting equipment in a bowling alley, and dining booths in a restaurant. Agricultural fixtures, such as chicken coops and tool sheds, are also included in this category. Trade fixtures must be removed on or before the last day the property is rented. The tenant is responsible for any damage caused by the removal of a trade fixture. Trade fixtures that are not removed become the real property of the landlord. Acquiring the property in this way is known as **accession** (this is related to the legal principle of *constructive annexation*).

IN PRACTICE A pizza parlor leases space in a small shopping center, and the restaurateur bolts a large iron oven to the floor of the unit. When the pizza parlor goes out of business or relocates, the restaurateur will be able to remove the pizza oven if the bolt holes in the floor can be repaired. The oven is a trade fixture. On the other hand, if the pizza oven was brought into the restaurant in pieces, welded together, and set in concrete, the restaurateur might not be able to remove it without causing structural damage. In that case, the oven might become a fixture and the real property of the building owner.

Trade fixtures differ from other fixtures in the following ways:

- Fixtures belong to the owner of the real estate, but trade fixtures are usually owned and installed by a tenant for the tenant's use.
- Fixtures are considered a permanent part of a building, but trade fixtures are removable. Trade fixtures may be attached to a building so they appear to be fixtures.

In general, fixtures are real property, so they are included in any sale or mortgage. Trade fixtures, however, are considered personal property and are not included in the sale or mortgage of real estate, except by special agreement.

CHARACTERISTICS OF REAL PROPERTY

Real property possesses seven basic characteristics that define its nature and affect its use. These characteristics fall into two broad categories—economic and physical.

Economic Characteristics

Four Economic Characteristics of Real Estate

- Scarcity
- Improvements
- Permanence of investment
- Area preference or situs

The four economic characteristics of land that affect its value as a product in the marketplace are scarcity, improvements, permanence of investment, and area preference.

Scarcity We usually do not consider land a rare commodity, but only about a quarter of the earth's surface is dry land; the rest is water. The total supply of land, then, is not limitless. While a considerable amount of land has not been developed, the supply in a given location that is suitable for a particular use is finite. There is also value in leaving land in its natural condition to preserve species that might otherwise be extinguished, as well as to benefit the earth's environment overall.

Improvements Building an improvement on one parcel of land can affect the land's value and use, as well as that of neighboring tracts and whole communities. For example, constructing a new shopping center or selecting a site for a nuclear power plant or toxic waste dump can dramatically change the value of land in a large area.

Permanence of Investment The capital and labor used to build an improvement represent a large fixed investment. Although even a well-built structure can be razed to make way for a newer building, improvements such as drainage, electricity, water, and sewerage remain. The return on such investments tends to be long term and relatively stable.

Area Preference Also known as **situs** ("place"), **area preference** is commonly referred to as "location, location, location." This economic characteristic refers not only to geography but also to the preference for a specific area. Area preference is based on several factors, such as convenience, reputation, and history. It is the unique quality of these preferences that results in the different price points for similar properties. Location is often considered the single most important economic characteristic of land.

IN PRACTICE A river runs through a town, dividing it more or less in half. Houses on the north side of the river sell for an average of $170,000. On the south side of the river, identical houses sell for more than $200,000. The two areas have equally desirable amenities, but the south side of the river provides a somewhat better view of the downtown area to the east, which may account for the price differential.

Physical Characteristics

Three Physical Characteristics of Land

- Immobility
- Indestructibility
- Uniqueness

Land has three physical characteristics: immobility, indestructibility, and uniqueness.

Immobility It is true that some of the substances of land are removable and that topography can be changed, but the geographic location of any given parcel of land can never be changed. It is fixed and therefore immobile.

Indestructibility Land is considered indestructible, even though it is subject to both natural and human forces. Land can be denuded of vegetation by strip mining, paved over for a highway or building, or eroded by a flood or dust storm. The geographic location will still remain, whatever its condition. This permanence of land, coupled with the long-term nature of most improvements, tends to stabilize investments in real property.

The fact that land is indestructible does not, however, change the fact that the improvements on land depreciate and can become obsolete, which may dramatically reduce the land's value. This gradual depreciation should not be confused with the knowledge that the economic desirability of a given location can change.

Uniqueness Uniqueness, which is also known as **nonhomogeneity**, is the concept that no two parcels of property are exactly the same or in the same location. The characteristics of each property, no matter how small, differ from those of every other, and each property has its own geographic coordinates. An individual parcel has no substitute because each is unique.

LAWS AFFECTING REAL ESTATE

Laws Affecting Real Estate

- Contract law
- General property law
- Agency law
- Real estate license law
- Federal, state, and local laws and regulations (e.g., consumer protection, environmental, tax, land use, and zoning)

The unique nature of real estate has given rise to an equally unique set of laws and rights. Even the simplest real estate transaction involves a body of complex laws. Real estate professionals must have a clear and accurate understanding of the laws that affect real estate.

The specific areas of law that are important to the real estate professional include contract law, general property law, agency law, and the specific state real estate license law. Federal laws and regulations, such as those involving consumer protection and the environment, as well as federal, state, and local tax laws, also play an important role in real estate transactions. State and local land-use and zoning laws have a significant effect on the practice of real estate, too.

Real estate professionals can't be experts in all areas of real estate law, but they should know and understand some basic principles. Perhaps most important is the ability to recognize problems that should be referred to a competent attorney. Only attorneys are trained and licensed to prepare documents defining or transferring rights in property and to give advice on matters of law. Although real estate professionals may be permitted in their states to provide contract forms and other documents to clients and customers, under no circumstances may real estate professionals act as attorneys unless they are also licensed attorneys representing clients in that capacity.

Real Estate License Laws

Because real estate professionals handle transactions that involve the most expensive purchase most consumers will ever make, the need for regulation of licensees' activities has long been recognized. The purpose of real estate license laws is to protect the public from fraud, dishonesty, and incompetence in real estate transactions. All 50 states, the District of Columbia, and all Canadian provinces have passed laws that require real estate brokers and their sales associates to be licensed. Although state license laws are similar in many respects, they differ in some details, such as the amount and type of prelicensing education required.

KEY POINT REVIEW

Land includes the earth's **surface**, its **subsurface** extending downward to the center of the earth, and the **air space** above the surface. **Subsurface rights** include mineral rights and other natural resources that can be leased or sold separately from surface rights. **Air rights** can be sold separately from surface rights and have limitations to enable air travel. **Water rights** can be held by owners of land adjacent to rivers, lakes, or oceans.

Land includes things naturally attached to it, such as trees and crops that do not need cultivation (*fructus naturales*), and perennial crops, orchards, and vineyards (*fructus industriales*).

Real estate includes the land as well as all things permanently attached or annexed to the land, both by nature and by humans.

Real property includes the interests, benefits, and rights that are automatically included in the ownership of unimproved land and real estate.

The **bundle of legal rights** includes the rights of possession, control, enjoyment, exclusion, and disposition.

Title is the right to ownership of real property and the evidence of ownership provided by a written document, called a deed, by which title is transferred.

An **appurtenance** is a right or privilege associated with real property in some way, such as a parking space in a multiunit building, an easement, or water rights, and is normally conveyed to the new owner when the property is sold.

Water rights are determined by common law and statute and include **riparian rights**, which belong to owners of land along a flowing body of water, and **littoral rights**, which belong to owners of land that borders a commercially navigable lake, sea, or ocean. The doctrine of **prior appropriation** is followed in some states and provides that water use, aside from limited domestic use, is controlled by the state rather than the landowner adjacent to the water; to use water, the landowner must demonstrate a beneficial use of the water, such as for irrigation of crops.

Personal property (chattel) includes

- movable items, such as a chair or a sofa;
- **emblements** (*fructus industriales*), annual plantings or crops of grains, vegetables, and fruit;
- items of real property that can become personal property by **severance**;
- items of personal property that can become real property by **annexation** (such as construction materials); and
- factory-built homes, including **manufactured homes**, that can be personal property unless **permanently affixed** to land.

A **fixture** is personal property that has been affixed to the land or to a building so that by law it becomes part of the real property. The legal tests for a fixture include **MARIA**: the method of **annexation**, **adaptability** of the thing for the land's ordinary use, **relationship** of the parties, **intent** in placing the item on the land, and **agreement** of the parties.

Trade fixtures include property attached to the structure but used in the course of business, and can be **personal property**, if removed by the tenant and the premises are returned to original condition before the lease expires; or real property, if left behind by the tenant. The landlord can acquire this type of property by **accession**.

The **characteristics of land** are both economic and physical. **Economic** characteristics of land include scarcity, improvements, permanence of the investment, and area preference (situs). **Physical** characteristics of land include immobility, indestructibility, and nonhomogeneity (uniqueness).

State laws that affect real estate include those on contracts, property, agency, and real estate licensing. There are state and local land-use and zoning laws, as well as federal and state laws concerning consumer protection, the environment, and taxation.

UNIT 2 QUIZ

1. Real estate generally includes all the following *EXCEPT*
   a. trees.
   b. air rights.
   c. annual crops.
   d. mineral rights.

2. A woman rents space in a commercial building where she operates a bookstore. In the bookstore, she has installed large reading tables fastened to the walls and bookshelves that create aisles from the front of the store to the back. These shelves are bolted to both the ceiling and the floor. Which of the following *BEST* characterizes the contents of the bookstore?
   a. The shelves and tables are trade fixtures and will transfer when the property owner sells the building.
   b. The shelves and tables are trade fixtures and may properly be removed by the woman before her lease expires, and the tenant would be responsible to the landlord for any damage that their removal caused to the premises.
   c. Because the woman is a tenant, the shelves and tables are fixtures and may not be removed except with the building owner's permission.
   d. Because the shelves and tables are attached to the building, they are treated the same as other fixtures.

3. The term *nonhomogeneity* refers to
   a. scarcity.
   b. immobility.
   c. uniqueness.
   d. indestructibility.

4. Another term for *personal property* is
   a. realty.
   b. fixtures.
   c. chattels.
   d. fructus naturales.

5. A property owner wants to use water from a river that runs through the property to irrigate a potato field. To do so, the owner is required by state law to submit an application to the Department of Water Resources describing in detail the plan for beneficial use of the water. If the department approves the owner's application, it will issue a permit allowing a limited amount of river water to be diverted onto the property. Based on these facts, it can be assumed that this property owner's state relies on which rule of law?
   a. Riparian rights
   b. Littoral rights
   c. Doctrine of prior appropriation
   d. Doctrine of highest and best use

6. A man inherited a piece of vacant land, removed and sold all the topsoil, limestone, and gravel. At his death, he left the property to his daughter. Which is *TRUE?*
   a. The daughter inherits nothing because the property no longer exists.
   b. The daughter inherits the property as is.
   c. The daughter owns the gravel, limestone, and topsoil, no matter where it is.
   d. The man's estate must restore the property to its original condition.

7. In determining whether an item is real or personal property, a court would *NOT* consider which of the following?
   a. The cost of the item when it was purchased
   b. Whether its removal would cause severe damage to the real estate
   c. Whether the item is clearly adapted to the real estate
   d. Any relevant agreement of the parties in their contract of sale

8. Which of the following is a physical characteristic of land?
   a. Indestructibility
   b. Improvements
   c. Area preference
   d. Scarcity

9. Which of the following describes the act by which real property can be converted into personal property?
   a. Severance
   b. Accession
   c. Conversion
   d. Attachment

10. While moving into a newly purchased home, the buyer discovered that the seller had taken the ceiling fan that hung over the dining room table. The seller had not indicated that the ceiling fan would be removed, and the contract did not address this issue. Which statement is *TRUE?*
   a. Ceiling fans are usually considered real estate.
   b. The ceiling fan belongs to the seller.
   c. Ceiling fans are considered trade fixtures.
   d. Ceiling fans are considered personal property.

11. A buyer purchased a parcel of land and immediately sold the mineral rights to an oil company. The buyer gave up which of the following?
   a. Air rights
   b. Surface rights
   c. Subsurface rights
   d. Occupancy rights

12. A truckload of lumber that a homeowner purchased has been left in the driveway for use in building a porch. The lumber is considered
   a. real property.
   b. personal property.
   c. a chattel that is real property.
   d. a trade or chattel fixture.

13. Method of annexation, adaptation to real estate, and agreement between the parties are the legal tests for determining whether an item is
   a. a trade fixture or personal property.
   b. real property or real estate.
   c. a fixture or personal property.
   d. an improvement.

14. Parking spaces in multiunit buildings, water rights, and similar things of value that convey with property are classified as
   a. covenants.
   b. emblements.
   c. chattels.
   d. appurtenances.

15. A paint company purchases a large tract of scenic forest land and builds several tin shacks there to store used turpentine and other items. Which statement is *TRUE?*
   a. The company's action constitutes improvement of the property.
   b. The chemicals are considered appurtenances.
   c. The tin shacks are considered trade fixtures.
   d. Altering the property in order to store waste is not included in the bundle of legal rights.

16. A property owner's land is located along the banks of a river. This owner's water rights are called
   a. littoral rights.
   b. prior appropriation rights.
   c. riparian rights.
   d. hereditaments.

17. A property owner's bundle of legal rights entitles the owner to do all of the following *EXCEPT*
   a. sell the property to a neighbor.
   b. exclude utility meter readers.
   c. erect No Trespassing signs.
   d. enjoy profits from its ownership.

18. According to law, a trade fixture is usually treated as
   a. a fixture.
   b. an easement.
   c. personalty.
   d. a license.

19. A buyer is interested in a house that fits most of her needs, but it is located in a busy area where she is not sure she wants to live. Her concern about the property's location is called

a. physical deterioration.
b. area preference.
c. permanence of investment.
d. immobility.

20. Which of the following is considered personal property?

a. Wood-burning fireplace
b. Awnings
c. Bathtub
d. Patio furniture

UNIT

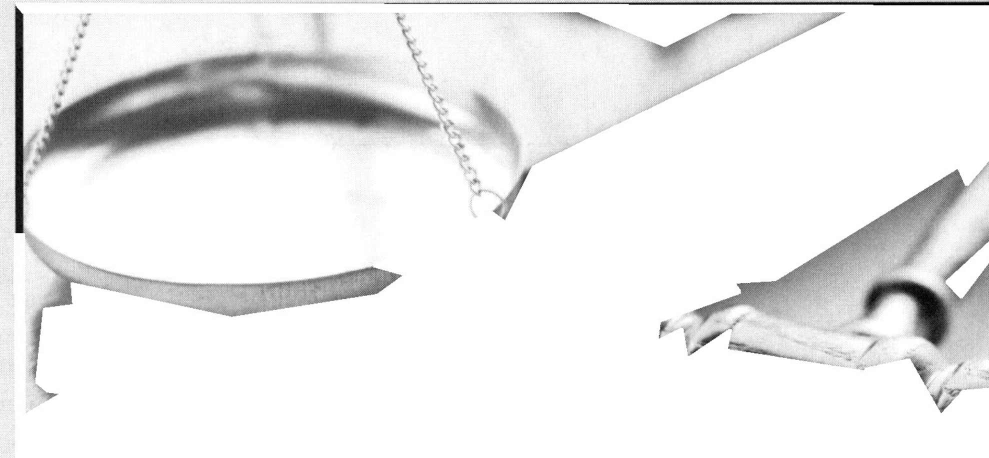

Fair Housing

LEARNING OBJECTIVES

When you have finished reading this unit, you will be able to

- **explain** the significance of the Civil Rights Act of 1866 and the constitutional legal framework as they relate to and affect the equal opportunity in housing;
- **describe and explain** the various federal laws which protect Americans from unfair housing practices;
- **describe** blockbusting, steering, redlining, and other abusive housing practices;
- **list** the various recourses available to the aggrieved person who believes illegal discrimination has occurred including acts against real estate professionals;
- **describe** the importance of real estate professionals understanding and complying with fair housing laws; and
- **define** the following *key terms:*

administrative law judge (ALJ)
Americans with Disabilities Act (ADA)
blockbusting
Civil Rights Act of 1866
conciliation
Department of Housing and Urban Development (HUD)
Fair Housing Act
Fair Housing Amendments Act
Housing for Older Persons Act (HOPA)
redlining
steering
Title VIII of the Civil Rights Act of 1968

OVERVIEW

Real estate professionals and their clients and customers reflect the wide diversity of America's population. The ability to buy or rent a home allows an individual or family to achieve and maintain a satisfying lifestyle. Housing discrimination takes its toll on its immediate victims, and it also reflects poorly on the society that allows it to exist. Even when legal action is required to correct abuses, the end result benefits all. Understanding and working within the context of fair housing laws is critical to creating and maintaining a vibrant and ultimately profitable real estate market for everyone. We will examine the history of federal fair housing legislation and court decisions, but state and local laws may provide even greater recognition of opportunities to work against the many forms of discrimination. Later, we will also consider the fair lending practices that help make financing available for home purchasers on an equitable basis.

EQUAL OPPORTUNITY IN HOUSING

The civil rights laws that affect the real estate industry recognize the importance of having the opportunity to live where one chooses. Federal, state, and local fair housing or equal opportunity laws affect every phase of a real estate transaction, from listing to closing. Together, they help ensure that housing is not denied on the basis of an individual's race, nationality, religion, or other characteristic specified in the law.

While the passage of laws may establish a code for public conduct, centuries of discriminatory practices and attitudes, reinforced by public and private conduct, are not so easily changed. Just as real estate professionals must not allow their own prejudices to interfere with the ethical and legal conduct of their profession, they must not allow discriminatory attitudes of property owners or property seekers to affect compliance with fair housing laws. Complying with fair housing laws is not always easy because it requires thoughtful consideration of both one's own actions and those of others. In addition to obeying the law and "doing the right thing," it is important to remember that failure to comply with fair housing laws not only subjects a real estate professional to both civil and criminal penalties but also constitutes grounds for disciplinary action by the licensing authority.

IN PRACTICE Real estate professionals must have a thorough knowledge of federal, state, and local fair housing laws. State and local laws may be broader than the federal requirements by providing protections for more classes of persons and may be applicable to all real property transactions, not just the residential transactions that are the focus of federal law. State and local licensing rules may provide for fines, and state penalties may include suspension or revocation of an offender's license for violation of any fair housing law.

The Civil Rights Act of 1866

The federal government's effort to end discrimination in the provision of housing began with the passage of the **Civil Rights Act of 1866**. The law prohibits discrimination based on race in every property transaction but was largely ignored.

Housing was not the only area subject to discrimination. The U.S. Supreme Court's 1896 decision in *Plessy v. Ferguson*, which involved segregated railway cars, upheld racial segregation in public facilities—the "separate but equal" doctrine. A series of court decisions and federal laws between 1948 and 1968 attempted to address inequities in the provision of public housing and other services that were the result of *Plessy*. Only certain aspects of the housing market, such as federally funded housing programs, could be addressed, however.

The U.S. Supreme Court did eventually issue decisions that rejected racial discrimination. In 1954, *Plessy* was overturned by the Court's decision in *Brown v. Board of Education*, which held that separate schools for black and white students were inherently unconstitutional. Finally, in 1968, the Court, in *Jones v. Mayer*, held that there was a constitutional basis for the Civil Rights Act of 1866 in the 13th Amendment to the U.S. Constitution, which prohibits slavery. The 1866 law prohibits all racial discrimination in the sale or rental of publicly or privately held property, without exception, whether facilitated by a real estate professional or sold or rented by the owner. Where race is involved, no exceptions apply.

In subsequent cases, the U.S. Supreme Court has expanded the definition of the term *race* to include ancestral and ethnic characteristics, including certain physical, cultural, or linguistic traits that are shared by a group with a common national origin. These rulings are significant because discrimination on the basis of race, as it is now defined, allows a complaint to be brought under the provisions of the Civil Rights Act of 1866.

IN PRACTICE A real estate professional is not obligated to provide ethnic-diversity information to homebuyers. At issue in a 2001 case from Ohio, *Hannah v. Sibcy Cline Realtors*, was whether a real estate professional had the fiduciary duty to (1) inform a client whether a neighborhood was ethnically diverse or (2) direct the client to resources that provided such information. The court concluded that while real estate professionals might choose to provide such information to clients or direct clients to resources about the ethnic diversity of a particular area, the real estate professionals do so at their own risk and there is no fiduciary duty to do so. The risk, of course, is that the real estate professional might be accused of illegally steering a client to a particular neighborhood based on the racial, ethnic, or other protected characteristics of its residents. Steering is discussed in more detail later.

The 1866 Civil Rights Act applies only to racial discrimination, but 1968 also saw passage of Title VIII of the Civil Rights Act of 1968, which we know as the Fair Housing Act. The Fair Housing Act prohibits specific discriminatory practices throughout the real estate industry.

FAIR HOUSING ACT

The Fair Housing Act prohibits discrimination based on

- race,
- color,
- national origin,
- religion,
- sex,
- familial status, or
- disability.

Title VIII of the Civil Rights Act of 1968, as amended by the Housing and Community Development Act of 1974 and the **Fair Housing Amendments Act** of 1988, is the **Fair Housing Act**. It prohibits discrimination in housing based on

- race,
- color,
- national origin,
- religion,
- sex,
- familial status, or
- disability.

The Fair Housing Act also prohibits discrimination against individuals because of their association with persons in the protected classes.

The Fair Housing Act originally prohibited discrimination based on race, color, religion, or national origin. The Housing and Community Development Act added sex to the list of protected classes, and the Fair Housing Amendments Act added disability and familial status (i.e., households with children), although an exception was made for certain housing intended for persons age 55 or older. The amended act also changed the penalties for violations of the law, making them more severe and added the right to seek damages, such as those for noneconomic injuries (humiliation, embarrassment, inconvenience, and mental anguish).

Housing for Older Persons Act (HOPA)

In 1995, Congress passed the **Housing for Older Persons Act (HOPA)**, which repealed the requirement that housing intended for those age 55 or older have "significant facilities and services" designed for seniors. HOPA still requires that at least 80% of occupied units have one person age 55 or older living in them. The act prohibits the awarding of monetary damages against those who, in good faith, reasonably believed that property designated as housing for older persons was exempt from familial status provisions of the Fair Housing Act.

www.hud.gov

The Fair Housing Act is administered by the **Department of Housing and Urban Development (HUD),** and information on fair housing can be found by going to www.hud.gov and entering "fair housing" in the search box at the top of the page. HUD has established rules and regulations that further interpret the practices affected by the law. In addition, HUD distributes an equal housing opportunity poster. (*See* Figure 3.1.) The poster declares that the office in which it is displayed promises to adhere to the Fair Housing Act and pledges support for affirmative marketing and advertising programs.

IN PRACTICE When HUD investigates a real estate broker for discriminatory practices, it may consider failure to prominently display the equal housing opportunity poster in the broker's place of business as evidence of discrimination. If a real estate brokerage is accused of a fair housing violation and has not displayed the poster, the burden of proof may shift from the complainant (the party alleging discrimination) to the broker. This means that the broker would have to prove that there had been no act of discrimination rather than the complainant proving that there had been an act of discrimination.

FIGURE 3.1: Equal Opportunity Housing Poster

U.S. Department of Housing and Urban Development

We Do Business in Accordance With the Federal Fair Housing Law

(The Fair Housing Amendments Act of 1988)

It is Illegal to Discriminate Against Any Person Because of Race, Color, Religion, Sex, Handicap, Familial Status, or National Origin

- In the sale or rental of housing or residential lots
- In advertising the sale or rental of housing
- In the financing of housing
- In the provision of real estate brokerage services
- In the appraisal of housing
- Blockbusting is also illegal

Anyone who feels he or she has been discriminated against may file a complaint of housing discrimination:
1-800-669-9777 (Toll Free)
1-800-927-9275 (TDD)

U.S. Department of Housing and Urban Development
Assistant Secretary for Fair Housing and Equal Opportunity
Washington, D.C. 20410

Previous editions are obsolete

form HUD-928.1A (2/2003)

Definitions

HUD's regulations provide specific definitions that clarify the scope of the Fair Housing Act.

Dwelling The regulations define a *dwelling* as any building or part of a building designed for occupancy as a residence by one or more families. This includes a single-family house, a condominium, a cooperative, and manufactured or other factory-built housing, as well as vacant land on which any of these structures will be built.

Family/Familial Status A family can be as small as a single individual. *Familial status* is defined as one or more individuals under age 18 living with a parent or guardian. It also includes a woman who is pregnant and anyone who is in the process of assuming custody of a child under age 18. Housing that qualifies for older people is exempt. Otherwise, single or multifamily housing must be made available to families with children under the same terms and conditions applied to anyone else. It is illegal to advertise properties as being for adults only or to indicate a preference for a certain number of children. Landlords and condominiums/cooperatives cannot restrict the number of occupants with the intent of eliminating families with children. Any occupancy standards must be based on objective factors, such as sanitation or safety.

IN PRACTICE An elderly tenant was terminally ill and requested that no children be allowed in the vacant apartment next door because the children's noise would make the situation more difficult. The owner of the apartment building agreed and refused to rent that unit to families with children. Although the intent was to make things easier for a dying tenant, the owner was nonetheless found to have violated the Fair Housing Act by discriminating on the basis of familial status.

Disability A *disability* is included in the Fair Housing Act as a *handicap*, although the word *disability* is now the preferred term. A disability is a physical or mental impairment that substantially limits one or more of a person's major life activities and includes having a record of having such an impairment, or being regarded as having such an impairment, even if one does not exist. It is unlawful to discriminate against prospective buyers or tenants on the basis of disability. Persons who have AIDS are protected by fair housing laws under this classification. The classification does not include current, illegal use of or addiction to a controlled substance, as defined in the Controlled Substances Act.

IN PRACTICE Just as the federal Fair Housing Act's protection of persons with a disability does not include those who are current users of illegal or controlled substances, it also does not extend to individuals who have been convicted of the illegal manufacture or distribution of a controlled substance. The law does prohibit discrimination against those who are participating in addiction recovery programs; for instance, a landlord could lawfully discriminate against a cocaine addict but not against someone who is in a drug recovery program.

Landlords must make reasonable accommodations to existing policies, practices, or services to permit persons with disabilities to have equal enjoyment of the premises. It would be reasonable to expect a landlord to permit a support animal (such as a guide dog) in a normally no-pets building or to provide a designated parking space in a generally unreserved lot for a person with a disability.

People with disabilities must be permitted to make necessary, reasonable modifications to the premises at their own expense. Such modifications might include lowering door handles or installing bath rails to accommodate a person in a wheelchair. Failure to permit reasonable modification constitutes illegal discrimination.

The law recognizes that some reasonable modifications might make a rental property undesirable to the general population. In such a case, the landlord is allowed to require that the property be restored to its previous condition when the lease period ends, aside from reasonable wear and tear. Where it is necessary to ensure with reasonable certainty that funds will be available to pay for the restorations at the end of the tenancy, the landlord may negotiate, as part of a restoration agreement, a provision requiring that the tenant pay into an interest-bearing escrow account, over a reasonable period, a reasonable amount of money not to exceed the cost of the restorations. The interest in the account accrues to the benefit of the tenant. A landlord may not increase the required security deposit for a person with a disability, however.

The law does not prohibit restricting occupancy exclusively to persons with a disability in dwellings that are designed specifically for their accommodation.

In newly constructed multifamily buildings with an elevator and four or more units, the public and common areas must be accessible to persons with a disability, and doors and hallways must be wide enough for wheelchairs. The entrance to each unit must be accessible, as well as the light switches, electrical outlets, thermostats, and other environmental controls. A person using a wheelchair should be able to use the kitchen and bathroom; bathroom walls should be reinforced to accommodate later installation of grab bars. Ground-floor units must meet these requirements in buildings that do not have an elevator. Real estate professionals should be aware that state and local laws may have stricter standards.

Exemptions to the Fair Housing Act

The federal Fair Housing Act covers most housing but does exempt

- owner-occupied buildings with no more than four units,
- single-family housing sold or rented without the use of a real estate professional, and
- housing operated by organizations and private clubs that limit occupancy to members.

The rental of rooms or units in an owner-occupied building of no more than four units is exempt from the Fair Housing Act.

The sale or rental of a single-family home is exempt from the Fair Housing Act when the transaction meets all of the following conditions:

- The home is owned by an individual who does not own more than three such homes at one time (and who does not sell more than one every two years).
- A real estate professional is <u>not</u> involved in the transaction.
- Discriminatory advertising is not used.

Housing owned by a religious organization may be restricted to people of the same religion if membership in the organization is not restricted on the basis of race, color, or national origin. A private club that is not open to the public may restrict the rental or occupancy of lodgings that it owns to its members, as long as the lodgings are not operated commercially. Membership in a private club must be open to people of all races, colors, and national origins.

IN PRACTICE The Metropolitan Club accepts members who have graduated from Grandiose University, a private institution. At its building in downtown Metropolis, the club has some sleeping rooms that it makes available to members at a nominal cost for no more than a one-week stay every year. Because the rooms are provided as a member convenience and not operated as a commercial venture, their use can be limited to members of the Metropolitan Club.

The Fair Housing Act does not require that housing be made available to an individual whose tenancy would constitute a direct threat to the health or safety of other individuals or would result in substantial physical damage to the property of others.

Housing for Older Persons As mentioned earlier, while the Fair Housing Act protects families with children, the Housing for Older Persons Act (HOPA) provides that certain properties can be restricted to occupancy by older persons. Housing intended for persons age 62 or older or housing occupied by at least one person 55 years of age or older per unit (where 80% of the units are occupied by individuals 55 or older) is exempt from the familial status protection. Such "senior housing" typically will allow temporary occupancy by younger visitors, such as permitting overnight visits for up to two weeks per year.

Americans with Disabilities Act

www.ada.gov

Although the **Americans with Disabilities Act (ADA)** is not a housing law, it still has a significant effect on the real estate industry. ADA requires reasonable accommodations in employment and access to goods, services, and public buildings. The law is important because real estate professionals are often employers, and their offices are public spaces. ADA's goal is to enable individuals with disabilities to become part of the economic and social mainstream of society. Information can be found online at www.ada.gov.

Title I of ADA requires that employers, including real estate professionals, make *reasonable accommodations* that enable an individual with a disability to perform essential job functions. Reasonable accommodations include making the work site accessible, restructuring a job, providing part-time or flexible work schedules, and modifying equipment that is used on the job. The provisions of the ADA apply to any employer with 15 or more employees.

Title III of ADA requires that individuals with disabilities have full accessibility to businesses, goods, and public services. As a result, building owners and managers of commercial spaces must be constantly alert to ensure that obstacles are removed. The Americans with Disabilities Act Accessibility Guidelines (ADAAG) contain detailed specifications for designing parking spaces, curb ramps, elevators, drinking fountains, toilet facilities, and directional signs to ensure maximum accessibility. Unless a real estate professional is a qualified ADA expert, it is best to advise commercial clients to seek the services of an attorney, an architect, or a consultant who specializes in ADA issues.

IN PRACTICE In 1999, the U.S. Supreme Court strictly limited the definition of *persons with disabilities* protected by the ADA. As a result, ADA excludes individuals whose disability, such as nearsightedness, can be corrected. In 2002, the U.S. Supreme Court narrowed the definition even further by stating that in determining whether a person has a disability, you may ask whether the impairment prevents or restricts the person from performing tasks that are ordinarily of central importance to daily life.

ADA and the Fair Housing Act ADA exempts from its requirements:

- property that is covered by the Fair Housing Act, which already prohibits discrimination on the basis of disability, and
- property that is exempt from coverage by the Fair Housing Act, such as housing for those age 55 or older.

Some properties are subject to both laws. For example, in an apartment complex, the rental office is a place of public accommodation. As such, it is covered by ADA and must be accessible to persons with a disability at the owner's expense. Individual rental units would be covered by the Fair Housing Act. A tenant who wished to modify the unit to make it accessible would be responsible for the cost.

Issues of housing and disability discrimination are often litigated in the courts. For example, in *Wells v. State Manufactured Homes*, a 2005 case before the U.S. District Court, District of Maine, the landlord ordered the owner of a manufactured housing unit to move from the community because he claimed she violated the no-pets provision of her rental agreement. The landlord refused to make a reasonable accommodation for the owner's emotional disability by permitting her to keep a dog. She filed suit under the ADA and Fair Housing Act. The court held that there was no violation of the Fair Housing Act or the ADA. The court said she failed to establish that her mental impairment substantially limited a major life activity and so did not meet the definition of a disability under ADA.

IN PRACTICE Real estate professionals need a general knowledge of ADA's provisions in dealing with clients and customers. It is necessary for a real estate broker's workplace and employment policies to comply with the law. Amendments to ADA are periodically introduced in the U.S. Congress, and it is important to be aware of changes in the law. Real estate professionals who are building managers must ensure that the properties managed are legally accessible. ADA compliance questions also may arise with regard to a client's property listed for sale or lease. Unless the real estate professional is a qualified ADA expert, it is best to advise commercial clients to seek the services of an attorney, architect, or consultant who specializes in ADA issues.

FAIR HOUSING PRACTICES

For fair housing and other civil rights laws to accomplish their goal of prohibiting discrimination, real estate professionals must apply them routinely. Compliance also means that real estate professionals avoid violating not only the law but also the ethical standards of the profession. The following discussion examines legal and ethical issues that continue to confront real estate professionals.

Blockbusting

Blockbusting is the act of encouraging people to sell or rent their homes by claiming that the entry of a protected class of people into the neighborhood will have some sort of negative impact on property values. Blockbusting was a common practice during the 1950s and 1960s when unscrupulous real estate professionals profited by fueling "white flight" from cities to suburbs. Any message from a real estate professional, however subtle, that property should be sold or rented because the neighborhood is "undergoing changes" is considered blockbusting. It is illegal to assert that the presence of certain persons will cause property values to decline, crime or antisocial behavior to increase, or the quality of schools to suffer.

A critical element in blockbusting, according to HUD, is the profit motive. A property owner may be intimidated into selling a property at a depressed price to the blockbuster, who in turn sells the property to another person at a higher price. Another term for this activity is *panic selling*. To avoid accusations of blockbusting, real estate professionals should use good judgment when choosing locations and methods for marketing their services and soliciting listings.

Steering

Steering is the channeling of homeseekers to particular neighborhoods or discouraging potential buyers from considering some areas. In the rental process, steering occurs when the landlord puts members of a protected class on a certain floor or building. Another form of steering occurs when the landlord tells a prospective tenant that no vacancy exists when, in fact, there is a vacancy. When the misstatement is made on the basis of a protected class, the prospect is steered away from that building. In any case, it is an illegal limitation of a purchaser's or renter's options.

Advertising

www.hud.gov/offices/fheo/library/part109.pdf

Advertisements of property for sale or rent may not include language indicating a preference or limitation. No exception to this rule exists, regardless of how subtle the choice of words. HUD's regulations include the types of language that are considered discriminatory. One such regulation can be found at www.hud.gov/offices/fheo/library/part109.pdf. Figure 3.2 shows some examples of language that is permitted and language that is considered discriminatory and not permitted. An advertisement that is gender specific, such as "female roommate sought," is allowed as long as the advertiser seeks to share living quarters with someone of the same gender. The media used for promoting property or real estate services cannot target one population to the exclusion of others. The selective use of media, whether by language or geography, may have discriminatory impact. For instance, advertising property only in a Korean-language newspaper tends to discriminate against non-Koreans. Similarly, limiting advertising to a cable television channel available only to white suburbanites may be construed as a discriminatory act. If an advertisement appears in general-circulation media as well, however, it may be legal.

FIGURE 3.2: HUD's Advertising Guidelines

Category	Rule	Permitted	Not Permitted
Race Color National origin	No discriminatory limitation/ preference may be expressed	"master bedroom" "good neighborhood"	"exclusive neighborhood" "English-speaking only"
Religion	No religious preference/ limitation	"chapel on premises" "kosher meals available" "Merry Christmas"	"no Muslims" "nice Christian family" "near great Catholic school"
Sex	No explicit preference based on sex	"mother-in-law suite" "master bedroom" "female roommate sought"	"great bachelor pad" "wife's dream kitchen"
Disability	No exclusions or limitations based on disability	"wheelchair ramp" "walk to shopping"	"no wheelchairs" "able-bodied tenants only"
Familial status	No preference or limitation based on family size or nature	"two-bedroom" "family room" "quiet neighborhood"	"married couple only" "no more than two children" "empty nester's dream house"
Photographs or illustrations of people	People should be clearly representative and nonexclusive	Illustrations showing multiple ethnicities, family groups, singles, etc.	Illustrations showing only individuals in ethnic dress, African American families, mature white adults, etc.

IN PRACTICE The Fair Housing Council of Oregon filed a complaint against a local multiple listing service (MLS), charging that the phrase "adults only over 40" was included in the "Remarks" section of a condominium listing. While the condominium association's bylaws actually did contain the (illegal) age restriction, the Fair Housing Council argued that including the phrase in the listing constituted discrimination against families with children in violation of the Fair Housing Act. The MLS paid $30,000 to settle with HUD, $20,000 of which went to support the antidiscrimination efforts of the Fair Housing Council of Oregon. The MLS also agreed to conduct regular computerized searches of its database for 67 different discriminatory words and phrases.

Appraising

Those who prepare appraisals or any statements of valuation—whether formal or informal, oral or written (including a comparative market analysis prepared by a real estate professional)—may consider any factors that affect value. Race, color, religion, national origin, sex, disability, and familial status are factors that may not be considered, however.

Redlining

The practice of refusing to make mortgage loans or issue insurance policies in specific areas for reasons other than the economic qualifications of the applicants is known as **redlining**. Redlining refers to literally drawing a line around particular areas. This practice is often a major contributor to the deterioration of older neighborhoods. Redlining is frequently based on racial grounds rather than on any real objection to an applicant's creditworthiness. The federal Fair Housing Act prohibits discrimination in mortgage lending and covers not only the actions of primary lenders but also activities in the secondary mortgage market. A lending institution, however, can refuse a loan solely on sound economic grounds.

Intent and Effect

If an owner or real estate professional purposely sets out to engage in blockbusting, steering, or other unfair activities, the intent to discriminate is obvious. However, owners and real estate professionals must examine their activities and policies carefully to determine whether they have unintentional discriminatory effects. Whenever policies or practices result in unequal treatment of people in the protected classes, they are considered discriminatory, regardless of any innocent intent. This "effects" test is applied by regulatory agencies to determine whether an individual has been discriminated against.

Response to Concerns of Terrorism

In response to the concern of future terrorist attacks, landlords and property managers have been developing new security procedures. These procedures have focused on protecting buildings and residents. Landlords and property managers are also educating residents on signs of possible terrorist activity and how and where to report it. At the same time, landlords and property managers need to ensure that their procedures and education do not infringe on the fair housing rights of others.

For screening and rental procedures, it is unlawful to screen housing applicants on the basis of race, color, religion, sex, national origin, disability, or familial status. According to HUD, landlords and property managers have been inquiring about whether they can screen applicants on the basis of citizenship status. The Fair Housing Act does not specifically prohibit discrimination based solely on a person's citizenship status. Therefore, asking applicants for citizenship documentation or immigration status papers during the screening process does not violate the Fair Housing Act. For many years, the federal government has been asking for these documents in screening applicants for federally assisted housing. HUD provides a specific procedure for collecting and verifying citizenship papers.

IN PRACTICE During an interview with a landlord, a woman mentions that she left her native country to study at the local university. The landlord is concerned about the woman's visa and whether it will expire during the lease term. The landlord asks the woman for documentation to determine how long she can legally live in the United States. The landlord asks for this information, regardless of her race or national origin. The landlord has not violated the Fair Housing Act.

ENFORCEMENT OF THE FAIR HOUSING ACT

The federal Fair Housing Act is administered by the Office of Fair Housing and Equal Opportunity under the direction of the secretary of HUD. Any aggrieved person who believes illegal discrimination has occurred may file a complaint with HUD within one year of the alleged act. HUD also may initiate its own complaint. Complaints may be reported to the Office of Fair Housing and Equal Opportunity, Department of Housing and Urban Development, Washington, DC 20410, or to the Office of Fair Housing and Equal Opportunity in care of the nearest HUD regional office. Complaints may also be submitted directly to HUD using an online form available on the HUD website.

Upon receiving a complaint, HUD initiates an investigation. Within 100 days of the filing of the complaint, HUD either determines that reasonable cause exists to bring a charge of illegal discrimination or dismisses the complaint. During this investigation period, HUD can attempt to resolve the dispute informally through conciliation. **Conciliation** is the resolution of a complaint by obtaining assurance that the person against whom the complaint was filed (the respondent) will remedy any violation that may have occurred. The respondent further agrees to take steps to eliminate or prevent discriminatory practices in the future. If necessary, these agreements can be enforced through civil action.

The aggrieved person has the right to seek relief through administrative proceedings. An administrative proceeding is a hearing held before an **administrative law judge (ALJ)**. An ALJ has the authority to award actual damages to an aggrieved party and, if it is believed the public interest will be served, to impose a monetary penalty. The penalty can range from up to $16,000 for a first offense to $70,000 for a third violation within seven years. The ALJ also has the authority to issue an injunction to order the offender to either do something (such as rent an apartment to the complaining party), or refrain from doing something (such as acting in a discriminatory manner).

The parties may elect civil action in federal court at any time within two years of the discriminatory act. For cases heard in federal court, unlimited punitive damages can be awarded in addition to actual damages. The court can also issue injunctions.

www.justice.gov

www.justice.gov/crt/about/hce/whatnew.php

The attorney general, upon finding reasonable cause to believe that any person or group is engaged in a pattern or practice of resistance to the full enjoyment of any of the rights granted by the federal fair housing laws, may file a civil action in any federal district court. Civil penalties may result in an amount not to exceed $50,000 for a first violation and an amount not to exceed $100,000 for second and subsequent violations. The U.S. Department of Justice is at www.justice.gov. Recent cases can be found at www.justice.gov/crt/about/hce/whatnew.php.

Complaints brought under the Civil Rights Act of 1866 are taken directly to federal courts. The only time limit for action is a state's statute of limitations for torts (injuries one individual inflicts on another).

IN PRACTICE In July 2009, HUD charged a landlord and the real estate company with two separate acts of housing discrimination for refusing to rent to families with children. Not only was their initial ad discriminatory—"This is an immaculate, spacious three-bedroom house for rent. ... No cats, dogs, or children please"—but when two different families with children called, the agent refused to show the home to them stating that "the owner would not rent to families with children." (*Colon v. Bill, Wetherbee*, and others).

State and Local Enforcement Agencies

Many states and municipalities have their own fair housing laws. If a state or local law is substantially equivalent to the federal law, all complaints filed with HUD are referred to the local enforcement agency. To be considered substantially equivalent, the local law and its related regulations must contain prohibitions comparable to those in the federal law. In addition, the state or locality must show that its local enforcement agency takes sufficient affirmative action in processing and investigating complaints and in finding remedies for discriminatory practices.

All real estate professionals should be aware of their states' fair housing laws, as well as applicable local ordinances.

Threats or Acts of Violence

Working in real estate is not generally considered dangerous, but some real estate professionals may find themselves the targets of threats or violence merely for complying with fair housing laws. The Fair Housing Act protects the rights of those who seek the benefits of the fair housing laws. It also protects owners and real estate professionals who aid or encourage the enjoyment of fair housing rights. Threats, coercion, and intimidation are punishable by criminal action. In such a case, the victim should report the incident immediately to law enforcement officials.

IMPLICATIONS FOR REAL ESTATE PROFESSIONALS

The real estate industry is largely responsible for creating and maintaining an open housing market. Real estate professionals are a community's real estate experts. With the privilege of profiting from real estate transactions comes the social and legal responsibilities to ensure that everyone's civil rights are protected. Establishing relationships with community and fair housing groups to discuss common concerns and find solutions to problems is a worthwhile activity. Real estate professionals who actively work to improve their community will earn a reputation for being concerned citizens, which may well translate into a larger consumer base.

Consequences

Fair housing is the law. The consequences for anyone who violates the law are serious. In addition to the financial penalties, the livelihood of a real estate professional may be in jeopardy if the license is suspended or revoked. That the offense was unintentional is no defense. Real estate professionals must scrutinize their practices and be particularly careful not to fall victim to clients or customers who expect them to discriminate.

KEY POINT REVIEW

Equal opportunity in housing is intended to create a marketplace in which persons of similar financial means have a similar range of housing choices. Equal opportunity laws apply to owners, real estate professionals, apartment management companies, real estate organizations, lending agencies, builders, and developers.

The **Civil Rights Act of 1866** prohibits all racial discrimination in real estate transactions, with no exceptions, and was upheld in *Jones v. Mayer* in 1968.

Race has been defined by the U.S. Supreme Court to include ancestral and ethnic characteristics, including certain physical, cultural, or linguistic traits that are shared by a group with a common national origin.

The **federal Fair Housing Act** is Title VIII of the **Civil Rights Act of 1968**, as amended, and prohibits discrimination in housing based on **race, color, national origin, religion, sex, familial status**, or **disability**. The Fair Housing Act does not prohibit discrimination based solely on a person's citizenship status. Illegal activities include steering, blockbusting, and redlining.

The **Housing and Community Development Act of 1974** added **sex** to the list of protected classes. The **Fair Housing Amendments Act of 1988** added **disability** and **familial status** to the protected classes. The Fair Housing Act is administered by HUD, which established rules and regulations to further clarify the law, and created the Equal Housing Opportunity poster.

Exemptions from the Fair Housing Act (but not the Civil Rights Act of 1866) include

- rentals in **owner-occupied buildings** with no more than four units;
- housing operated by organizations and private clubs that limit occupancy to members; and
- the sale or rental of a **single-family home** when fewer than three homes are owned by an **individual**, discriminatory advertising is not used, and a real estate professional is not involved in the transaction.

The **Housing for Older Persons Act of 1995 (HOPA)** repealed facilities and services requirements for housing intended for persons age 55 or older. The law prohibits an award of monetary damages against those who reasonably rely in good faith on property designated as housing for older persons as being exempt from familial status provisions of the Fair Housing Act.

Housing is **exempt** from familial status protection if it is restricted to persons **age 62** or older, or if 80% of the units are occupied by persons **age 55** or older.

Familial status extends fair housing protections to families with children, meaning a family including a woman who is pregnant or in which one or more individuals under the age of 18 live with either a parent or a guardian.

A **disability** is a physical or mental impairment that substantially limits one or more of an individual's major life activities. A person with AIDS is considered disabled but the law does not protect individuals who are current users of illegal or controlled substances or who have been convicted of the illegal manufacture or distribution of a controlled substance. The law does protect an individual who is participating in an addiction recovery program. Reasonable modifications to property to make it usable by an individual with a disability must be allowed, but the individual must return the property to its former condition on vacating it.

The **Americans with Disabilities Act (ADA)** prohibits discrimination in employment and public accommodations. Access to facilities and services in commercial properties must be provided when **reasonably achievable** in existing buildings, with higher standards for new construction/remodeling. Exempt properties include those covered by federal fair housing laws.

HUD enforces the Fair Housing Act. A complaint must be brought within one year of the alleged act of discrimination. Within 100 days of filing a complaint that is not referred by HUD to a local enforcement agency, HUD dismisses or goes forward with a charge of illegal discrimination. Conciliation is the resolution of a complaint within 100 days of filing when a respondent promises to remedy any violation.

A complaint brought to HUD may be heard by an **administrative law judge (ALJ)**, with remedies that may include a fine or injunction. A civil action may be brought in federal court by the complainant within two years of the alleged discriminatory act. The attorney general may bring a civil action in federal court.

Complaints under the Civil Rights Act of 1866 go directly to federal court.

Real estate professionals must act legally, doing their part to avoid discriminatory practices.

UNIT 3 QUIZ

1. Under the Fair Housing Act, which action is legally permitted?
   a. Advertising property for sale only to a special group
   b. Altering the terms of a loan for a member of a protected class
   c. Refusing to make a mortgage loan to a member of a protected class because of a poor credit history
   d. Telling a member of a protected class that an apartment has been rented when in fact it has not

2. Complaints relating to the Civil Rights Act of 1866
   a. must be taken directly to federal courts.
   b. are no longer reviewed in the courts.
   c. are handled by HUD.
   d. are handled by state enforcement agencies.

3. Why is the Civil Rights Act of 1866 unique?
   a. It has been broadened to protect the aged.
   b. It adds welfare recipients as a protected class.
   c. It contains "choose your neighbor" provisions.
   d. It provides no exceptions that would permit racial discrimination.

4. A real estate professional said to a homeowner, "I hear *they're* moving in. There goes the neighborhood! Better put your house on the market before values drop!" This is an example of what illegal practice?
   a. Steering
   b. Blockbusting
   c. Redlining
   d. Fraudulent advertising

5. The act of directing homeseekers toward or away from particular areas, either to maintain or to change the character of the neighborhood, is
   a. blockbusting.
   b. redlining.
   c. steering.
   d. permitted under the Fair Housing Act of 1968.

6. A lender's refusal to lend money to potential homeowners attempting to purchase properties located in predominantly Latino neighborhoods is known as
   a. redlining.
   b. blockbusting.
   c. steering.
   d. prequalifying.

7. All of the following would be permitted under the federal Fair Housing Act *EXCEPT*
   a. an expensive club in New York renting rooms only to members who are graduates of a particular university.
   b. the owner of a 20-unit residential apartment building renting to men only.
   c. a Catholic convent refusing to furnish housing for a Jewish man.
   d. an owner refusing to rent the other side of the duplex in which she lives to a family with children.

8. It is illegal for a lending institution to refuse to make a residential real estate loan in a particular area only because of the
   a. questionable economic situation of the applicant.
   b. physical location of the property.
   c. applicant not being of legal age.
   d. deteriorated condition of the premises.

9. Which agency, upon receiving a complaint regarding a Fair Housing Act violation, investigates?
   a. HUD
   b. HOPA
   c. DOJ
   d. ADA

10. Housing that qualifies for exemption from familial status provisions
    a. includes housing intended for persons 50 or older.
    b. includes a restriction that 80% of the units be occupied by persons 55 or older.
    c. is not permitted under the federal Fair Housing Act.
    d. is permitted for owner-occupied buildings with four or more units.

11. Which statement describes the Supreme Court's decision in the case of *Jones v. Alfred H. Mayer Company*?
    a. Racial discrimination is prohibited by any party in the sale or rental of real estate.
    b. Sales by individual residential homeowners are exempted, provided the owners do not use real estate professionals.
    c. Laws against discrimination apply only to federally related transactions.
    d. Persons with disabilities are a protected class.

12. After a real estate professional takes a sale listing of a residence, the owners specify that they will not sell the home to any Asian family. The real estate professional should do which of the following?
    a. Advertise the property exclusively in Asian-language newspapers.
    b. Explain to the owners that the instruction violates federal law and that the real estate professional cannot comply with it.
    c. Abide by the owners' directions despite the fact that they conflict with the fair housing laws.
    d. Require that the owners sign a separate legal document stating the additional instruction as an add-on to the listing agreement.

13. The fine for a first violation of the federal Fair Housing Act could be as much as
    a. $100,000.
    b. $37,500.
    c. $65,000.
    d. $16,000.

14. A single man with two small children has been told by a real estate professional that homes for sale in a condominium complex are available only to married couples with no children. Which statement is *TRUE*?
    a. Because a single-parent family can be disruptive if the parent provides little supervision of the children, the condominium is permitted to discriminate against the family under the principle of rational basis.
    b. Condominium complexes are exempt from the fair housing laws and can therefore restrict children.
    c. The man may file a complaint alleging discrimination on the basis of familial status.
    d. Restrictive covenants in a condominium take precedence over the fair housing laws.

15. The following ad appeared in the newspaper: "For sale: 4 BR brick home; Redwood School District; excellent Elm Street location; short walk to St. John's Church; and right on the bus line. Move-in condition; priced to sell." Which statement is *TRUE*?
    a. The ad describes the property for sale and is very appropriate.
    b. The fair housing laws do not apply to newspaper advertising.
    c. The ad should state that the property is available to families with children.
    d. The ad should not mention St. John's Church.

16. A discrimination suit may be filed in federal court by
    a. a person aggrieved by racial discrimination.
    b. the Department of Housing and Urban Development.
    c. the state or county nondiscrimination officer.
    d. the Federal Housing Administration.

17. The federal Fair Housing Act does *NOT* prohibit
    a. blockbusting.
    b. discriminatory advertising.
    c. redlining.
    d. discriminating on the basis of marital status.

18. Which of the following is legal?

a. Charging a family with children a higher security deposit than those with no children
b. Requiring a person with a disability to establish an escrow account for the costs to restore a property after it has been modified
c. Picturing only white people in a brochure as the "happy residents" in a housing development
d. Refusing to sell a house to a person who has a history of mental illness

19. The landlord's lease prohibits tenants from altering the property in any way. A young woman who uses a wheelchair cannot maneuver over the doorstep into her apartment by herself. In addition, she cannot access the bathroom facilities in her wheelchair. Which of the following is *TRUE*?

a. The landlord is responsible for making all apartments accessible to people with disabilities.
b. The tenant cannot remedy these conditions because of the terms of the lease.
c. The landlord should not have rented this apartment to the tenant.
d. The tenant is entitled to make the necessary alterations.

20. The provisions of the federal Fair Housing Act apply

a. in all states.
b. in those states that have ratified the act, but not in other states.
c. only in those states that do not have substantially equivalent laws.
d. only in those states that do not have specific state fair housing laws.

Unit 4: Interests in Real Estate

LEARNING OBJECTIVES *When you have finished reading this unit, you will be able to*

- **identify and describe** the various types of estates;
- **explain** the difference between liens and all other types of encumbrances;
- **explain** the limitations of private property rights for the welfare of the public; and
- **define** the following *key terms*:

condemnation
covenants, conditions, and restrictions (CC&Rs)
deed restrictions
easement
easement appurtenant
easement by necessity
easement by prescription
easement in gross
eminent domain
encroachment
encumbrance
escheat
estate in land
fee simple
fee simple absolute
fee simple defeasible
fee simple determinable
fee simple subject to a condition subsequent
freehold estate
future interest
homestead
inverse condemnation
legal life estate
license
lien
life estate
police power
pur autre vie
remainder interest
reversionary interest
taking
taxation

OVERVIEW

Ownership of a parcel of real estate includes all or some of the bundle of rights, depending on the type of interest a person holds in the property. Even the most complete ownership the law allows may be limited by public and private restrictions. These restrictions are intended to ensure that one owner's use and enjoyment of the property owned does not interfere with others' use and enjoyment of their property or with the welfare of the general public. For example, a zoning ordinance might not allow a convenience store to be built in a residential neighborhood, a condo association bylaw might prohibit rental of a unit without board approval, and an easement allowing neighbors to use a property owner's private beach might deter a future buyer of the property.

ESTATES IN LAND

An **estate in land** defines the degree, quantity, nature, and extent of an owner's interest in real property. Many types of estate exist, but not all *interests* in real estate are *estates*. To be an estate in land, an interest must allow possession, meaning the holding and enjoyment of the property either now or in the future, and must be measured according to time. Historically, estates in land have been classified primarily by their length of time of possession.

A *freehold estate* is an ownership interest that continues for an indefinite period.

A freehold estate lasts for an indeterminable length of time, such as for a lifetime or forever. A freehold estate can be a *fee simple estate* that continues for an indefinite period and may be passed along to the owner's heirs. A freehold estate can also be a *life estate* that is held only for the lifetime of a person (who may not be the holder of the life estate) and ends when that individual dies. There are various types of freehold estates, which are illustrated in Figure 4.1 and discussed in the next section.

FIGURE 4.1: Freehold Estates

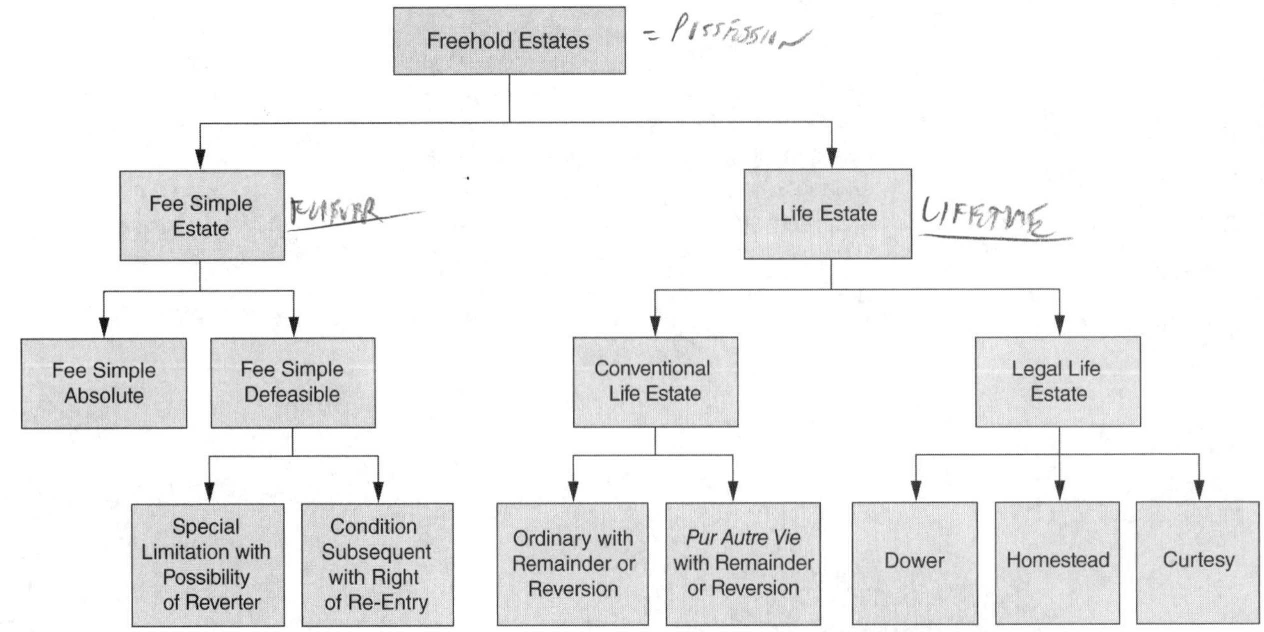

A nonfreehold estate is one for which the length of time of the property's use can be determined. A nonfreehold estate is commonly referred to as a *leasehold estate*.

Fee Simple Estate

A **fee simple** estate, or **fee simple absolute**, is the highest interest in real estate recognized by law. Fee simple ownership is ownership in which the holder is entitled to all rights to the property by law. This estate is intended to run forever. Upon the death of the owner of a fee simple estate, the property interest passes to

- the decedent's co-owner, if there is one and the co-ownership was accompanied by a right of survivorship;
- the person or persons specified in the decedent's will (the devisees); or
- if the decedent has left no will, to the person or persons designated by the state's law of intestate succession.

The right to use a fee simple estate is limited only by public and private restrictions, such as zoning laws and restrictive covenants.

Fee Simple Defeasible A **fee simple defeasible** estate is a qualified fee estate that is subject to the occurrence or nonoccurrence of some specified event. There are two categories of defeasible estate: *fee simple determinable* and *fee simple subject to a condition subsequent*.

A **fee simple determinable** is a fee simple defeasible estate that may be inherited. This estate is qualified by a special limitation (which is an occurrence or event). The language used to distinguish a special limitation—words such as *so long as* or *while* or *during* —is the key to creating this special limitation. The former owner retains a *possibility of reverter*, which is an interest that can be transferred to someone else. If the limitation is violated, the holder of the possibility of reverter (or heir or successor) can reacquire full ownership with no need to bring a legal action in court. The title is automatically transferred to the person who holds the possibility of reverter.

IN PRACTICE When an owner gives land to a church, *so long as the land is used for only religious purposes*, it is known as a fee simple determinable. The church has the full bundle of rights possessed by a property owner, but one of the "sticks" in the bundle has a special feature. If the church ever decides to use the land for a nonreligious purpose, the holder of the possibility of reverter obtains title without going to court.

Fee simple *determinable*:
"So long as"
"While"
"During"
Fee simple subject to a condition subsequent:
"on condition that"

With a **fee simple subject to a condition subsequent**, an owner gives real estate *on condition of* ownership, which means there is a difference in the way the estate will terminate if there is a violation of the condition. With a fee simple subject to a condition subsequent, the estate does not automatically terminate upon violation of the condition of ownership. The owner (or the owner's heir or successor) has the right of reentry but must bring a legal action in court to assert this right.

IN PRACTICE Land given *on the condition that* there be no consumption of alcohol on the premises is a fee simple subject to a condition subsequent. If alcohol is consumed on the property, the former owner (or the owner's heir or successor) has the right to reacquire full ownership. It will be necessary for that person to go to court to assert that right.

In the defeasible fee estates, the *possibility of reverter* (fee simple determinable) or *right of entry* (fee simple subject to a condition subsequent) will only be possible at some time in the future, and may never take effect. Each of those rights thus is considered a **future interest**.

Life Estate

A **life estate** is a freehold estate limited in duration to either the life of the holder of the estate or the life of some other designated person or persons.

Unlike other freehold estates, a life estate based on the life of the holder of the estate is not inheritable. It passes to the future owner according to the provisions by which the life estate was created.

The holder of a life estate is called a *life tenant*. A life tenant is not a renter like a tenant associated with a lease. A life tenant is entitled to the rights of ownership and can benefit from both possession and ordinary use, and profits arising from ownership, just as if the individual were a fee simple owner. The life tenant's ownership may be sold, mortgaged, or leased, but it is always subject to the finite limitation of the life estate.

Pur Autre Vie A life estate may also be based on the lifetime of a person other than the life tenant. Although a life estate is not considered an estate of inheritance, a life estate **pur autre vie** (for the life of another) provides for inheritance of the property right by the life tenant's heirs, but the right exists only until the death of the identified person or persons. A life estate pur autre vie is often created for people who are physically or mentally incapacitated in the hope of providing incentive for someone to care for them. More than one person could be identified as the measuring life; for instance, a life estate could be granted to a surviving brother by a deceased property owner for the life of the surviving brother's children. As long as one of the children survives, the life estate is in control of the life tenant or the life tenant's successor.

Remainder and Reversion The fee simple owner who creates a life estate must plan for its future ownership. When the life estate ends, it is replaced by a fee simple estate. The future owner of the fee simple estate may be designated in one of two ways:

- **Remainder interest**— The creator of the life estate may name a *remainderman* as the person to whom the property will pass when the life estate ends.
- **Reversionary interest**— The creator of the life estate may choose not to name a remainderman. In that case, ownership returns to the original owner upon the end of the life estate.

Legal Life Estate A **legal life estate** is not created by a property owner, but rather is established by state law. It becomes effective automatically when certain events occur. *Dower, curtesy*, and *homestead* are the legal life estates currently used in some states.

Dower and curtesy provide a nonowning spouse with a means of support after the death of the owning spouse. *Dower* is the life estate of a wife in the real estate of her deceased husband. *Curtesy* is a life estate of a husband in the real estate of his deceased wife. (In some states, the terms are used interchangeably.)

States that recognize dower and curtesy typically provide that the nonowning spouse has a lifetime right to a one-half or one-third interest in the real estate, even if the owning spouse wills the estate to others. The surviving spouse benefits because the property cannot be conveyed with clear title until the life estate interest is released; the surviving spouse may release the claim to the property when the value of the interest is paid. Because a nonowning spouse might claim an interest in the future, both spouses should sign the proper documents when real estate is conveyed. The signature of the nonowning spouse would be needed to release any *potential* interest in the property being transferred.

Most states have abolished the common law concepts of dower and curtesy in favor of the Uniform Probate Code (UPC). The UPC gives a surviving spouse the right to an elective share on the death of the other spouse, if the surviving spouse is not satisfied with the decedent's disposition of the property by will. Community property states do not use dower and curtesy.

A **homestead** is a legal life estate in real estate occupied as the family home. In effect, the home (or at least some part of it) is protected from most creditors during the occupant's lifetime. In states that have homestead exemption laws, a portion of the land or value of the property occupied as the family home is exempt from certain judgments for debts, such as charge accounts and personal loans, but not a mortgage for the purchase or improvement of the property. If a debt is secured by the property, including funds advanced under a home equity line of credit, the property cannot be exempt from a judgment on that debt. The homestead also is not protected from real estate taxes billed against the property.

In some states, all that is required to establish a homestead is for the head of a household (who may be a single person) to own or lease the premises occupied by the family as a residence. In other states, the family is required by statute to record a notice of homestead rights. A family can have only one homestead at a time.

How does the homestead exemption actually work? In most states, the homestead exemption merely reserves a certain amount of money for the family in the event of a court sale. In a few states, however, the entire homestead is protected. Once a sale occurs (where permitted), any debts secured by the home (a mortgage, unpaid taxes, or mechanics' liens, for instance) will be paid from the proceeds. Then the family will receive the amount reserved by the homestead exemption. Finally, whatever remains will be applied to the family's unsecured debts.

www.law.cornell.edu/lii/get_the_law

More information on estates in land can be found at the site of Cornell University Law School's Legal Information Institute, www.law.cornell.edu/lii/get_the_law, by entering "real property" in the search engine at the top of the page.

ENCUMBRANCES

An **encumbrance** is a type of interest in real estate that does not rise to the level of ownership or possession, yet still gives an individual, business, or other entity some degree of use or control of the property. This section covers

- easements and licenses, which permit a limited use of property;
- private restrictions found in property deeds, which cannot impose an illegal requirement;

- liens, which give notice of a claim against the property; and
- encroachments, which can result if a neighboring improvement extends over a property boundary.

Liens

A **lien** is a charge against property that provides security for a debt or an obligation of the property owner. If the obligation is not repaid, the lienholder is entitled to have the debt satisfied from the proceeds of a court-ordered or forced sale of the debtor's property. Real estate taxes, mortgages, judgments, and mechanics' liens all represent possible liens against an owner's real estate.

Private Restrictions on the Use of Real Estate

Private restrictions that affect the use of real estate are often found in the deed that conveys title to the property. Once placed in the deed by a previous owner, a **deed restriction** will run with the land, limiting the use of the property by the current owner, as well as future owners to whom the property is subsequently transferred.

A deed restriction cannot violate any law, such as a fair housing law, by attempting to prohibit certain property transfers. A deed restriction that would attempt to do so would be illegal and thus unenforceable.

Covenants, conditions, and restrictions (CC&Rs) are used by a subdivision developer to maintain specific standards in a subdivision, such as by requiring adherence to certain architectural or design specifications for improvements. CC&Rs are detailed in the original development plans for the subdivision that are filed in the public record in the county where the property is located, and they are referred to (incorporated by reference) in the deeds to individual properties in the subdivision. Future purchasers of the property should be given a copy of the CC&Rs and should make review of the CC&Rs a condition of the purchase. The restrictions can be enforced by the developer as long as the developer maintains an interest in any part of the development, and then by any of the subsequent property owners.

Easements

An **easement** is the right to use the land of another for a particular purpose. It may exist in any portion of the real estate, including the airspace above or a right-of-way across the land.

An **easement appurtenant** is attached to the ownership of real estate and allows the owner of that property the use of a neighbor's land. For an easement appurtenant to exist, two adjacent parcels of land must be owned by two different parties. The parcel that benefits from the easement is known as the *dominant tenement*; the parcel over which the easement runs is known as the *servient tenement*. (See Figure 4.2.)

FIGURE 4.2: Easement Appurtenant

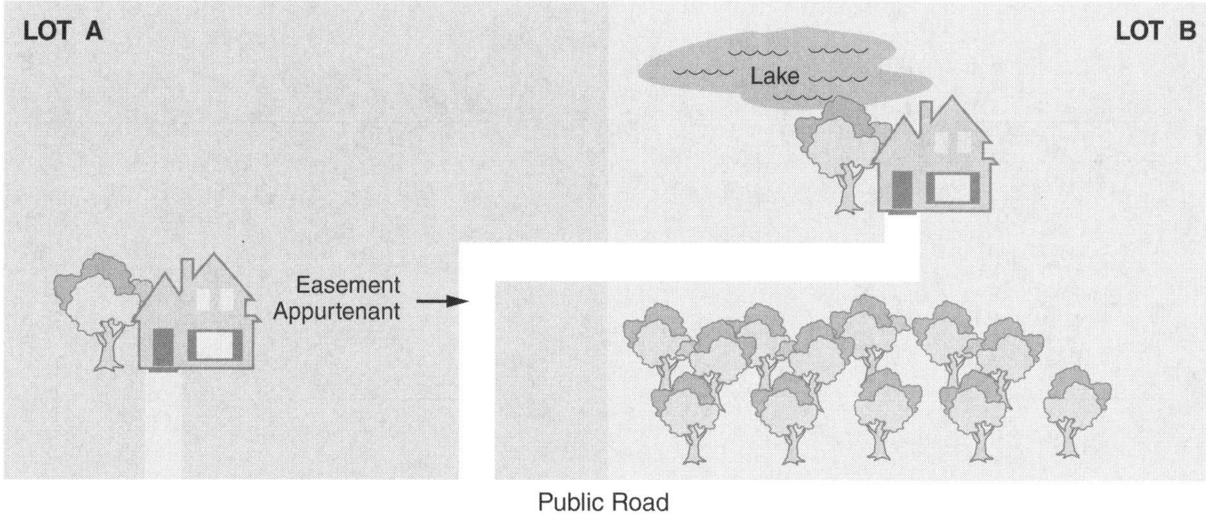

The owner of Lot B has an easement appurtenant across Lot A to gain access to his property from the public road. Lot B is dominant, and Lot A is servient.

An easement appurtenant is part of the dominant tenement. If the dominant tenement is conveyed to another party, the easement transfers with the title. This type of easement will run with the land. It is an encumbrance on the servient property and will transfer with the dominant tenement forever, unless the holder of the dominant tenement legally releases the right or it is terminated in one of the ways that are discussed later in this section. The easement will terminate, for instance, if the owner of the dominant tenement also becomes the owner of the servient tenement (or vice versa). Because the same person then owns both properties, there is no need for the easement to exist.

A *party wall* can be an exterior wall of a building that straddles the boundary line between two lots, or it can be a shared partition wall between two connected properties. The individual lot owners own the half of the wall on their lot, and each has an easement appurtenant in the other half of the wall. The reciprocal interest of each owner in the property of the other is often referred to as a *cross easement*. A written party wall agreement must be used to create the easement rights. Expenses to build and maintain the wall are usually shared. A fence built on the lot line is treated the same as a wall. A party driveway shared by and partly on the land of adjoining owners should be created by written agreement and specify responsibility for maintenance and expenses.

An **easement in gross** is an individual or company interest in or right to use someone else's land. (*See* Figure 4.3.) A railroad's right-of-way is an easement in gross, as are the rights-of-way of utility easements (such as for a pipeline or power line). Commercial easements in gross may be assigned, conveyed, and inherited. Personal easements in gross are usually not assignable. Generally, a personal easement in gross terminates on the death of the easement owner.

FIGURE 4.3: Easement in Gross

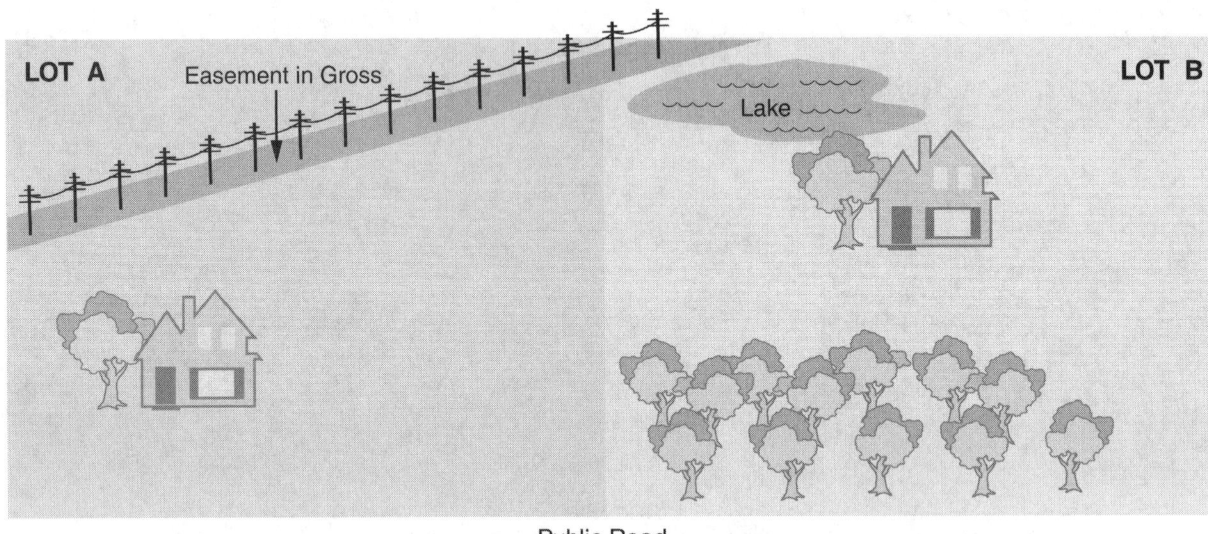

The utility company has an easement in gross across both parcels of land for its power lines.

Creating an Easement An easement is created by a written agreement between the parties that establishes the easement right. The creation of an easement always involves two separate parties; one party owns the land over which the easement runs and the other party benefits from the easement. Two other ways for an easement to be created are by means of an *easement by necessity* and *easement by prescription.*

Easement by Necessity An easement that is created when an owner sells a parcel of land that has no legal access to a street or public way except over the seller's remaining land is an **easement by necessity**. An easement by necessity is created by court order based on the principle that owners must have the right to enter and exit their land—the right of *ingress* (*enter*) and *egress* (*exit*); they cannot be landlocked. Remember, this form of easement is called an easement by *necessity*; it is not merely for convenience.

Easement by Prescription If the claimant has made use of another's land for a certain period of time as defined by state law, an **easement by prescription**, or a *prescriptive easement*, may be acquired. The prescriptive period generally runs from 10 to 21 years. The claimant's use must have been continuous, nonexclusive (the owner isn't excluded from using that part of the property), and without the owner's permission. The use must be visible, open, and notorious, and the owner must have been able to learn of it.

The concept of *tacking* provides that successive periods of continuous occupation by different parties may be combined (tacked) to reach the required total number of years necessary to establish a claim for a prescriptive easement. To tack on one person's possession to that of another, the parties must have been *successors in interest*, such as a deceased individual and the deceased's heir, a landlord and a tenant, or a seller and a buyer.

IN PRACTICE A property is located in a state with a prescriptive period of 20 years. For the past 22 years, the neighbor to the east has driven across the property's front yard several times a day to reach her garage from a more comfortable angle. The neighbor has an *easement by prescription.*

For 25 years, the neighbor to the west has driven across this same front yard two or three times a year to reach his property when he is in a hurry. This neighbor does not have an easement by prescription because the use was not continuous.

For 15 years, the neighbor to the north parked a car on the same property, next to the garage. Six years ago, the house to the north was sold to a person who continued to park a car next to the garage of the adjoining property. Last year, the buyer acquired an *easement by prescription* through *tacking.*

Terminating an Easement An easement terminates

- when the need no longer exists,
- when the owner of either the dominant or the servient tenement becomes sole owner of both properties,
- by the release of the right of easement to the owner of the servient tenement,
- by the abandonment of the easement (the intention of the parties is the determining factor), or
- by the nonuse of a prescriptive easement.

Note that an easement may not automatically terminate for these reasons. Certain legal steps may be required.

Licenses

A **license** is a personal privilege to enter the land of another for a specific purpose. A license differs from an easement in that it can be terminated or canceled by the owner of the property. If the right to use another's property is given orally or informally, it generally is considered to be a license rather than an easement. A license ends with the death of either party or with the sale of the land.

Encroachments

When a building, fence, or driveway illegally extends beyond the boundaries of the land of its owner or legal building lines, an **encroachment** occurs. An encroachment is usually disclosed by either a physical inspection of the property or a limited survey. If a building encroaches on adjoining land, the neighbor may be able to either recover damages or secure removal of the portion of the building that encroaches. An encroachment that exceeds the state's prescriptive period, however, may give rise to an easement by prescription.

Lis Pendens

A *lis pendens* (Latin for *litigation pending*) is a notice filed in the public record of a pending legal action affecting the title to or possession of property. While it does not have a physical effect on property, the lis pendens creates a "cloud on the title" to the property, which may prevent the property from being sold or further encumbered. Recording of a lis pendens should act as an incentive to the property owner to resolve the underlying dispute. When the matter is resolved, the party who filed the lis pendens will record a release to clear the title. If the lis pendens has been recorded without adequate evidence of a bona fide dispute, the property owner can have the lis pendens expunged.

GOVERNMENTAL POWERS

Memory Tip

Four Governmental Powers

Police power

Eminent domain

Taxation

Escheat

Individual ownership rights are subject to certain powers, or rights, held by federal, state, and local governments. These limitations on the ownership of real estate are imposed for the general welfare of the community and, therefore, supersede the rights or interests of the individual. Government powers include police power, eminent domain, taxation, and escheat, which can be remembered by the acronym PETE.

Police Power

Every state has the power to enact legislation to preserve order, protect the public health and safety, and promote the general welfare of its citizens. That authority is known as a state's **police power**. The state's authority is passed on to municipalities and counties through legislation called enabling acts. What is identified as being in the public interest can vary considerably from state to state and region to region. The police power of government is used to enact environmental protection laws, zoning ordinances, and building codes. These include the regulations that govern the use, maximum occupancy, size, location, and construction of real estate.

The government's power to regulate land use is not absolute. A law or regulation must be uniform and nondiscriminatory on its face, even though in practice it may operate to the advantage or disadvantage of a particular owner or owners.

IN PRACTICE A large area of previously undeveloped land consists of 27 different parcels and is located near the location of a new highway. The land is incorporated into the city limits of Cedar City. The city council conducts the appropriate public hearings on the use of the land and ultimately decides to zone most of the area for residential use and a smaller section for commercial use. Because of its proximity to the highway, the commercially zoned area will keep heavy traffic away from the residential area. Years earlier, all the land was farm land and similarly valued. As a result of the zoning, however, a parcel zoned for commercial use will most likely become far more valuable than a similarly sized parcel zoned for residential use.

Eminent Domain

Eminent domain is the government's right to acquire private property for public use; **condemnation** is the actual process of taking property.

Eminent domain is the right of the government to acquire privately owned real estate for public use. **Condemnation** is the process by which the government exercises this right, by either judicial or administrative proceedings.

Generally, states delegate their power of eminent domain to cities and counties or public entities for public services. For example, a public housing authority might take privately owned land to build low-income housing, or the state's land-clearance commission or redevelopment authority could use the power of eminent domain to allow construction of a new sports arena. If there were no other feasible way to do so, a railway, utility company, or state highway department might acquire farmland to extend railroad tracks, bring electricity to a remote new development, or build a highway.

Taking The concept of the **taking** of property for public use is found in the Fifth Amendment to the U.S. Constitution, which reads, "[N]or shall private property be taken for public use, without just compensation," meaning that when land is taken for public use through the government's power of eminent domain, the owner must be compensated fairly. The rights of the owner of the property also are to be protected by due process of law, as set out in the Fifth and Fourteenth Amendments to the U.S. Constitution. Ideally, the public agency and the owner of the property in question agree on compensation through direct negotiation, and the government purchases the property for a price considered fair by the owner. In some cases, the owner may simply dedicate the property to the government as a site for a school, park, or another beneficial use. If the owner's consent cannot be obtained, the government agency can initiate condemnation proceedings to acquire the property on payment of just compensation to the owner.

In the past, the proposed use for taking property was to be for the public good. However, in June 2005, the U.S. Supreme Court in *Kelo v. City of New London* significantly changed the definition of public use. The court held that local governments can condemn homes and businesses for economic development purposes, even when a private developer is a beneficiary.

In *Kelo*, the city invoked a state statute that authorized the use of eminent domain to promote economic development. The Supreme Court decision leaves it to the states to establish rules that cities must follow when exercising eminent domain powers. *Kelo* caused an uproar when it was decided, and in response, many state legislatures acted to impose a narrower definition of *public use* in eminent domain proceedings to ensure that property would be taken only for public purposes as more commonly understood—roads, bridges, schools, municipal facilities, and so on—and not for commercial endeavors.

Inverse condemnation is an action brought by a property owner seeking just compensation for land adjacent to land used for a public purpose when the property's use and value have been diminished. For example, property along a newly constructed highway that could not have been anticipated by nearby property owners may be considered inversely condemned. While the property itself was not used in constructing the highway, the property value may be significantly diminished due to the construction of the highway close to the property. The property owner may bring an inverse condemnation action to be compensated for the loss in value.

It is sometimes very difficult to determine what level of compensation is fair in a particular situation. The compensation may be negotiated between the owner and the government, or the owner may seek a court judgment setting the amount after presentation of evidence of value.

IN PRACTICE One method used to determine just compensation is the before-and-after method. This method is used primarily where a portion of an owner's property is seized for public use. The value of the owner's remaining property after the taking is subtracted from the value of the whole parcel before the taking. The result is the total amount of compensation due to the owner.

www.realtor.org

Articles on eminent domain, as well as information on current cases, can be found by going to the website of the National Association of REALTORS®, www.realtor.org, and entering "eminent domain" in the search engine at the top of the page.

Taxation

Taxation is a charge on real estate to raise funds to finance the operation of government facilities and services. Taxes on real estate include

- annual real property taxes assessed by local and area governmental entities to support school districts, transportation districts, and utility districts;
- taxes on profit realized by individuals and corporations on the sale of real property; and
- special fees that may be levied to finance special projects, such as road or utility installation.

Imposition of real property taxes may be accompanied by an automatic lien on the taxed property. Nonpayment of any of these taxes may allow the taxing body to enforce its lien rights in the property.

Escheat

Escheat is a process by which the state may acquire privately owned real or personal property. State laws provide for ownership to transfer, or **escheat,** to the state when an owner dies and leaves no heirs (as defined by the law) and there is no will or living trust instrument that directs how the real estate is to be distributed. In some states, real property escheats to the county where the land is located; in other states, it becomes the property of the state. Escheat is intended to prevent property from being ownerless or abandoned.

KEY POINT REVIEW

A **freehold estate** lasts for an indeterminable length of time. **Fee simple** is the highest estate recognized by law. **Fee simple defeasible** is an estate that is qualified because it is subject to the occurrence or nonoccurrence of a specified event. A **life estate** is based on the lifetime of the life tenant or someone else **(pur autre vie)**.

An **encumbrance** is a claim, charge, or liability that attaches to real estate. A **lien** is a charge against property that provides security for a debt or obligation of the property owner. **Covenants, conditions, and restrictions (CC&Rs)** are private limitations on the use of land.

An **easement** is a right to use the land of another. An easement is usually created by written agreement between the parties. An **easement appurtenant** is said to run with the land when title is transferred. The **dominant tenement** benefits from the easement, which runs over the **servient tenement**.

An **easement in gross** is an individual or company interest in or right to use another's land. An **easement by necessity** arises when land has no access to a street or public way. An **easement by prescription** is acquired when a claimant has used another's land for the period required by law. The use must be continuous, nonexclusive, visible, open, and notorious.

An easement is **terminated** when the need for it no longer exists, when the owner of either the dominant or servient tenement becomes the owner of both, when the owner of a dominant tenement **releases** the right of easement to the owner of the servient tenement, if the easement is **abandoned**, or by the **nonuse** of a prescriptive easement.

A license is a personal privilege to enter the land of another for a specific purpose.

An encroachment occurs when all or part of a structure illegally intrudes on the land of another or beyond legal building lines.

A **lis pendens** gives notice of litigation in progress that may affect title to property.

Government powers can be recalled by using the acronym PETE. **Police power** is the state's authority, passed down to counties and municipalities through enabling acts, to legislate to preserve order, protect the public health and safety, and promote the general welfare of citizens. **Eminent domain** is the government's right to acquire privately owned real estate for a public or economically beneficial use through condemnation. **Taxation** can include a charge on real estate to raise funds to meet public needs. **Escheat** occurs when the state takes control of property after the owner dies leaving no will or lawful heirs.

When a **taking** of property occurs, the Fifth Amendment to the U.S. Constitution requires that the owner be given just compensation. A property owner may claim compensation under **inverse condemnation** if an adjacent public land use diminishes the value of the owner's property but the property has not been condemned for public use.

UNIT 4 QUIZ

1. The right of a government body to take ownership of real estate for public use is called
   a. escheat.
   b. eminent domain.
   c. condemnation.
   d. police power.

2. One who has ownership rights of real estate that could continue forever and which provide that no other person can claim to be the owner of or have any ownership control over the property has
   a. fee simple interest.
   b. life estate.
   c. determinable fee.
   d. condition subsequent.

3. A woman owned the fee simple title to a vacant lot adjacent to a hospital and was persuaded to make a gift of the lot. She wanted to have some control over its use, so her attorney prepared her a deed to convey ownership of the lot to the hospital "so long as it is used for hospital purposes." After completion of the gift, the hospital will own a
   a. fee simple absolute estate.
   b. license.
   c. fee simple determinable.
   d. leasehold estate.

4. Your neighbors use your driveway to reach their garage, which is on their property. Your attorney explains that ownership of the neighbors' real estate includes an easement appurtenant giving them the right to do this. Your property is the
   a. leasehold interest.
   b. dominant tenement.
   c. servient tenement.
   d. license property.

5. A license is an example of a(n)
   a. easement appurtenant.
   b. encroachment.
   c. personal privilege.
   d. restriction.

6. An easement appurtenant
   a. terminates with the sale of the property.
   b. is a right-of-way for a utility company.
   c. is revocable.
   d. runs with the land.

7. A property on Main Street that was formerly a retail store will become the site of a new city hall, made possible by the government's power of
   a. escheat.
   b. possibility of reverter.
   c. eminent domain.
   d. taxation.

8. Which of the following is *NOT* an example of governmental power?
   a. Remainder
   b. Police power
   c. Eminent domain
   d. Taxation

9. A property owner who has the legal right to use a neighbor's land holds a(n)
   a. estate in land.
   b. easement.
   c. police power.
   d. encroachment.

10. Which of the following is a legal life estate?
    a. Leasehold
    b. Fee simple absolute
    c. Homestead
    d. Determinable fee

11. An owner conveys ownership of his residence to his church but reserves for himself a life estate in the residence. The future interest held by the church is a
    a. pur autre vie.
    b. remainder.
    c. reversion.
    d. leasehold.

12. An owner has a fence on his property. By mistake, the fence extends one foot over the lot line onto a neighbor's property. The fence is an example of a(n)
    a. license.
    b. encroachment.
    c. easement by necessity.
    d. easement by prescription.

13. A homeowner may be allowed certain protection from judgments of creditors as a result of the state's
    a. littoral rights.
    b. curtesy rights.
    c. homestead rights.
    d. dower rights.

14. A person has permission from a property owner to hike on the owner's property during the autumn months. The hiker has
    a. an easement by necessity.
    b. an easement by condemnation.
    c. riparian rights.
    d. a license.

15. A homestead is a legal life estate in real estate that is
    a. leased by renters.
    b. occupied as the family home.
    c. used as a vacation home.
    d. a secondary residence.

16. Because a homeowner failed to pay the real estate taxes on time, the taxing authority imposed a claim against the homeowner's property. This claim is known as a(n)
    a. deed restriction.
    b. lien.
    c. easement.
    d. reversionary interest.

17. The type of easement that is a right-of-way for a utility company's power lines is a(n)
    a. easement in gross.
    b. easement by necessity.
    c. easement by prescription.
    d. nonassignable easement.

18. The process by which government takes control of a property after the owner dies without a will or lawful heirs is
    a. escheat.
    b. lis pendens.
    c. condemnation.
    d. taxation.

19. A landowner has divided much of his land into smaller parcels and has recently sold a tract near a nature preserve that is landlocked and cannot be entered except through one of the other tracts. The buyer of that property will probably be granted what type of easement by court action?
    a. Easement by necessity
    b. Easement in gross
    c. Easement by prescription
    d. Easement by condemnation

20. All of the following will terminate an easement *EXCEPT*
    a. when the need no longer exists.
    b. nonuse of a prescriptive easement.
    c. abandonment of easement.
    d. release of the right of easement to the dominant tenement.

5 UNIT

Forms of Real Estate Ownership

LEARNING OBJECTIVES

When you have finished reading this unit, you will be able to

- **define and explain** the distinction between ownership in severalty and co-ownership;
- **describe** the various forms of co-ownership in real estate;
- **describe** the key elements of trusts, partnerships, corporations, and LLCs;
- **identify and describe** the types of property ownership for common-interest properties; and
- **define** the following *key terms:*

common elements
community property
condominium
cooperative
co-ownership
corporation
general partnership
joint tenancy
limited liability company (LLC)
limited partnership
partition
partnership
PITT
right of survivorship
separate property
severalty
tenancy by the entirety
tenancy in common (TIC)
time-share
town house
trust

OVERVIEW

Real estate buyers must determine the type of ownership that best fits their needs. The choice of ownership will affect the ability to transfer the real estate in the future and has tax implications as well. While real estate professionals should be able to identify the basic forms of ownership available, it is up to the prospective buyer to explore the options and make a decision, most likely with the advice of an attorney.

Although the forms of ownership available are controlled by state law, real estate may be held in one of three basic ways. They include ownership in severalty (one owner), co-ownership (more than one owner), and ownership by a trust (property held for the benefit of another).

OWNERSHIP IN SEVERALTY

Ownership in **severalty** occurs when property is owned by one individual, corporation, or other entity. The term comes from the fact that a sole owner is *severed* or *cut off* from other owners. The owner in severalty has sole rights to the property and sole discretion to sell, will, lease, or otherwise transfer part or all of the ownership rights to another person.

IN PRACTICE Rohan has inherited a condominium from his parents. Rohan owns the property in severalty, making him the sole owner of the condominium, entitled to all of the rights of ownership.

Co-Ownership

When title to a parcel of real estate is held by two or more individuals, those parties are called co-owners or concurrent owners. Most states commonly recognize various forms of **co-ownership**. Individuals may co-own property as tenants in common or joint tenants. In some states, if co-owners are married or in a recognized civil union, they may co-own property as tenants by the entirety or as community property.

FORMS OF CO-OWNERSHIP

Forms of Co-Ownership

- Tenancy in common (TIC)
- Joint tenancy
- Tenancy by the entirety
- Community property

During the lifetime of the co-owners, there may be no apparent difference between the various types of ownership. Only when the property is conveyed, or when one of the owners dies, will the differences become apparent.

Tenancy in Common

A parcel of real estate may be owned by two or more people as tenants in common. In a **tenancy in common (TIC)**, each tenant holds an *undivided interest* in the property. The co-owners have *unity of possession*, meaning that each owner is entitled to possession and use of the entire property, even though each holds only a fractional ownership interest. If there are two co-owners of a property, for instance, and no other division is specified in the deed conveying the property, each owns a one-half interest. It is the ownership interest, not the property, that is divided.

The deed creating a tenancy in common may or may not state the fractional interest held by each co-owner. If no fractions are stated, the tenants are presumed to hold equal shares; for example, if five people hold title, each owns an undivided one-fifth interest. Each of the shares can also be held by a couple, whether married or in a civil union.

Because the co-owners own separate interests, they can sell, convey, mortgage, or transfer their individual interests in the TIC without the consent of the other co-owners. A share owned by a married couple can be transferred only with the agreement of both parties.

No individual tenant may transfer the ownership of the entire property. When one co-owner dies, the tenant's undivided interest passes according to the decedent's will, to the heirs identified by statute if there is no will, or by the terms of the decedent's living trust, if one was established prior to death. (*See* Figure 5.1.)

FIGURE 5.1: Tenancy in Common

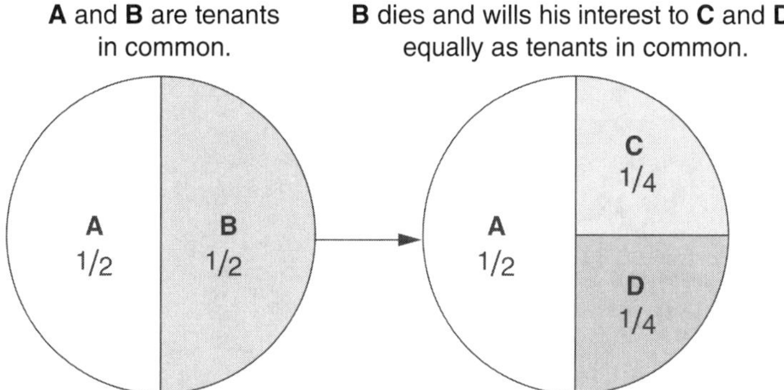

When two or more single individuals or couples acquire title to real estate and the form of ownership is not indicated, the new owners are usually determined to have acquired title as tenants in common. The TIC has become popular in expensive urban areas because it allows a multi-family dwelling to be sold to multiple owners without the need to convert the entire property to the condominium form of ownership, which may entail a lengthy and expensive approval process. The downside of a co-owner's TIC interest is that it may not be as easy to sell as property held in a different form of ownership. Formation of a TIC requires use of an attorney to clarify the terms of ownership.

IN PRACTICE The problem of owning the right to use an entire property, but having only a fractional ownership interest, usually is resolved by agreement of the co-tenants to specify the part of the property that each will use individually and the part of the property that will be shared. In a residential property with three units, for instance, if there are three TIC interests, each co-tenant may, by agreement of all three, occupy a specified unit, with all three having the right to use all other areas, such as a basement storage space or outdoor space. The agreement should also specify how responsibility for property maintenance, expenses, and taxes is to be shared. Unless all three units are very comparable, this is where any differences may be equalized, with the co-tenant who enjoys the use of the largest or most desirable unit paying a larger portion of the expenses.

Joint Tenancy

Most states recognize some form of **joint tenancy** in property owned by two or more people, whether married or unmarried.

The distinguishing feature of a joint tenancy is the **right of survivorship**. Upon the death of a joint tenant, the deceased's interest transfers directly to the surviving joint tenant or tenants. Essentially, there is one less owner. No formal legal action is required, although the death certificate of the deceased owner should be made part of the public record and a copy retained by the surviving owner(s).

If there are only two joint tenants, the death of one of the owners terminates the joint tenancy. If there are three or more joint tenants, at each successive joint tenant's death, the surviving owners acquire the deceased's interest. In either case, the last survivor takes title in severalty and has all the rights of sole ownership, including the right to pass the property to any heirs. (*See* Figure 5.2.)

FIGURE 5.2: Joint Tenancy With Right of Survivorship

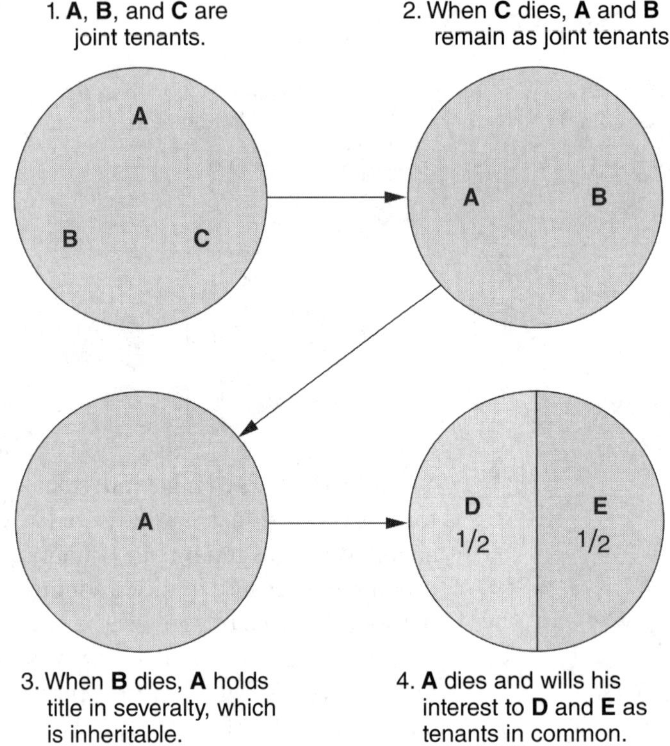

IN PRACTICE The form under which title to property will be taken should be discussed with an attorney. Remember that real estate professionals may not give legal advice or engage in the practice of law.

Creating a Joint Tenancy A joint tenancy can be created only by the intentional act of conveying a deed or giving the property by will or living trust. It cannot be implied or created by operation of law. The instrument must specifically state the parties' intention to create a joint tenancy, and the parties must be explicitly identified as joint tenants.

Memory Tip

The four unities necessary to create a joint tenancy may be remembered as **PITT**:

- **P**ossession
- **I**nterest
- **T**ime
- **T**itle

To create a joint tenancy, four elements or unities are needed, which can be remembered as PITT: possession, interest, time, and title.

- Unity of *possession*—all joint tenants hold an undivided right to possession.
- Unity of *interest*—all joint tenants hold an equal ownership interest.
- Unity of *time*—all joint tenants acquire their interests at the same time.
- Unity of *title*—all joint tenants acquire their interests by the same document.

The four requirements or unities are met when the right to possession of a property is acquired by all of the joint owners by means of a single instrument that conveys an equal, undivided interest to all of them, stipulating that they are to be joint owners with the right of survivorship. In some states, identifying the owners as "joint owners" automatically includes the right of survivorship, but use of the wording "with right of survivorship" makes the meaning explicit. Use of a single instrument necessarily means that the right of ownership is conveyed to all of the joint owners at the same time.

Terminating a Joint Tenancy A joint tenancy is destroyed when any one of the four unities of joint tenancy is terminated. Unless prohibited by state law, joint tenants are free to convey their individual interest in the jointly held property, but doing so destroys the unities of time and title as to that interest. This means that the new owner cannot be a joint tenant, but instead is a tenant in common. If there were only two joint tenants to begin with, the joint tenancy is terminated. If the joint tenancy had more than two owners to begin with, and one of them conveys that interest, there will still be a joint tenancy, but only as to the interests held by the remaining joint tenants; the new owner is a tenant in common.

IN PRACTICE Sisters A, B, and C hold title to their family home as joint tenants. Sister A conveys her interest to her son, D; D then owns an undivided one-third interest in the property as a tenant in common with B and C, who continue to own their undivided two-thirds interest as joint tenants. (*See* Figure 5.3.) The difference in the form of ownership means that, unless B and C also convey their separate interests, on the death of either B or C, the surviving sister will be a tenant in common with D, but with a two-thirds interest to D's one-third interest. On the death of the last sister, that sister's share of the TIC will transfer by will or as provided by statute. Unless D is the person to whom the ownership is transferred, D will be a tenant in common with the new owner but D will still have only a one-third interest in the property.

FIGURE 5.3: Combination of Tenancies

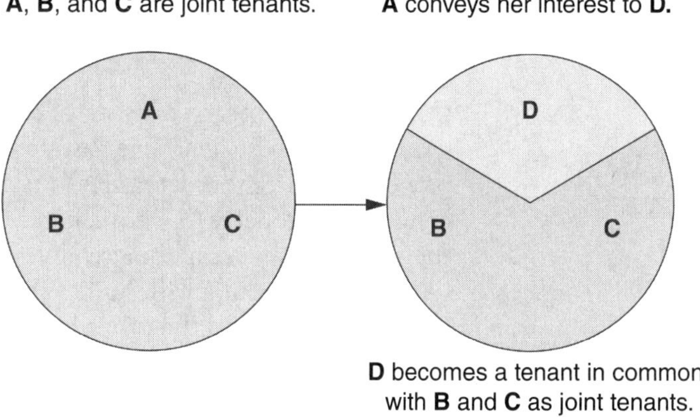

Termination of Co-Ownership by Partition Suit

Partition is a legal way to dissolve the relationship between co-owners of real estate when the parties do not voluntarily agree to its termination. If the court determines that the property cannot be divided physically into separate parcels without destroying its value, the court will order the real estate sold. The proceeds of the sale will then be divided among the co-owners according to their fractional interests.

Ownership by Married Couples

Tenancy by the entirety is a special form of co-ownership used in some states that allows a spouse to inherit the other spouse's ownership interest upon death. In this form of ownership, each spouse has an equal, undivided interest in the property. (The term *entirety* refers to the fact that the owners are considered one indivisible unit because early common law viewed a married couple as one legal person.) Spouses who are tenants by the entirety have the right of survivorship. During their lives, they can convey title only by a deed signed by both parties. One party cannot convey a one-half interest, and generally they have no right to partition or divide the property.

Community Property Rights **Community property** laws are based on the idea that spouses, rather than merging into one entity, are equal partners in the marriage. Under community property laws, any property acquired during a marriage is considered to be obtained by mutual effort. Today, nine states uphold this concept. Although community property law varies widely among these states, all of them recognize two kinds of property: separate property and community property.

Separate property generally is real or personal property that was owned solely by either spouse before the marriage, acquired by gift or inheritance by one spouse during the marriage, or purchased with separate funds during the marriage. Any income earned from a spouse's separate property remains part of that spouse's separate property. Separate property can be mortgaged or conveyed by the owning spouse without the signature of the nonowning spouse.

IN PRACTICE A spouse who wishes to maintain the character of separate property must be careful not to *commingle* funds that are separate with funds that belong to the community. If the proceeds of the sale of separate property are placed in a community property bank account, for instance, they may thereafter be considered community funds.

Community property consists of real and personal property acquired by either spouse during the marriage. Any conveyance or encumbrance of community property requires the signatures of *both* spouses. Spouses can will their half of the community property to whomever they desire, but upon the death of one spouse, the surviving spouse automatically owns one-half of the remaining property. If a spouse dies without a will, half of the community property already belongs to the surviving spouse and the other half is inherited by the surviving spouse or by the decedent's other heirs, depending on state law. Community property does *not* provide the automatic right of survivorship that joint tenancy does.

Figure 5.4 lists the forms of co-ownership and summarizes how property is held and conveyed under each form.

FIGURE 5.4: Forms of Co-Ownership

Form of Co-Ownership	Property Held	Property Conveyed
Tenancy in Common	Each tenant holds a fractional undivided interest with unity of possession only.	The tenants can convey or will their individual interest, but not the entire interest.
Joint Tenancy	Unity of ownership. Created by intentional act; unities of possession, interest, time, title.	Right of survivorship; cannot be conveyed to heirs.
Tenants by the Entirety	Spouses each have equal undivided interest in property.	Right of survivorship; conveys by deed signed by both parties. One party can't convey one-half interest.
Community Property	Spouses are equal partners in marriage. Real or personal property acquired during marriage is community property.	Conveyance requires signature of both spouses. No right of survivorship; when one spouse dies, survivor owns one-half of community property. Other one-half is distributed according to will or, if no will, according to state law.

TRUSTS AND BUSINESS ORGANIZATIONS

A **trust** is a device by which one person transfers ownership of property to someone else to hold or manage for the benefit of a third party. Perhaps a grandfather wishes to ensure the college education of his granddaughter. He can transfer an amount sufficient to cover the granddaughter's tuition and expenses to a trust account that will be held by his bank, with his daughter—the grandchild's mother—named as trustee of the account. The mother can be directed to use the funds in the account to pay for the grandchild's college tuition. In this case, the grandfather is the *trustor*—the person who creates the trust. The granddaughter is the *beneficiary*—the person who benefits from the trust. The mother is the *trustee*—the party who holds legal title to the property and is entrusted with carrying out the trustor's instructions regarding the purpose of the trust. The trustee is in the role of a *fiduciary*, a person who acts in confidence or trust and has a special legal relationship with the beneficiary. The trustee's power and authority are limited by the terms of the trust agreement. A trust can be established during the trustor's lifetime, or by will to take effect at the trustor's death.

IN PRACTICE The legal and tax implications of setting up a trust are complex and vary widely from state to state. Attorneys and tax experts should always be consulted on the subject of trusts.

Most states allow real estate to be held in trust. Depending on the type of trust and its purpose, the trustor, trustee, and beneficiary can all be either people or legal entities, such as corporations. Trust companies are corporations set up for this specific purpose.

Real estate can be owned under living or testamentary trusts and land trusts. It can also be held by investors in a *real estate investment trust (REIT)*.

Living and Testamentary Trusts

Property owners may provide for their own financial care or for that of their family by establishing a trust. The trust may be created by agreement during the property owner's lifetime (a *living trust*) or established by will after the owner's death (a *testamentary trust*). (Note that neither of these is related to the so-called living will, which deals with the right to refuse medical treatment.)

The person who creates the trust conveys real or personal property to a trustee (usually a corporate trustee), with the understanding that the trustee will assume certain duties. These duties may include the care and investment of the trust assets to produce an income. After paying the trust's operating expenses and trustee's fees, the income is paid to or used for the benefit of the beneficiary. The trust may continue for the beneficiary's lifetime, or the assets may be distributed when the beneficiary reaches a certain age or when other conditions are met.

In recent years, living trusts have become a major estate planning tool used to minimize the time and costs of probate. In a living trust, the property owner (trustor, grantor, or settler) transfers ownership of real and personal property to a trustee. The trustee is often the trustor. In this way, the owner continues to control the assets of the trust. The trustee may transfer property into and out of the trust, subject to the trust agreement. Upon the death of the trustee, the property passes to the beneficiary or beneficiaries without the need for probate. In the case of community property, the spouses may transfer real and personal property into a trust and name themselves as joint trustees with rights of survivorship. Upon the death of the surviving trustee, the estate is distributed to the beneficiary or beneficiaries.

Land Trusts

Real estate is the only asset of a *land trust*. As in all trusts, the property is conveyed to a trustee, and the beneficial interest belongs to the beneficiary. In the case of a land trust, however, the beneficiary is usually also the trustor. While the beneficial interest is personal property, the beneficiary retains management and control of the real property and has the right of possession as well as the right to any income produced by the property or proceeds from its sale. Land trusts are frequently created for the conservation of farmland, forests and other wildlife habitats, coastal land, and scenic vistas.

One of the distinguishing characteristics of a land trust is that the public records usually do not name the beneficiary. A land trust may be used for secrecy when assembling separate parcels. There are other benefits as well. A beneficial interest can be transferred by *assignment*, making the formalities of a deed unnecessary. The beneficial interest in property can be pledged as security for a loan without having a mortgage recorded. Because the beneficiary's interest is personal, it passes at the beneficiary's death under the laws of the state in which the beneficiary resided. If the deceased owned property in several states, additional probate costs and inheritance taxes can be avoided.

A land trust ordinarily continues for a definite term, such as 20 years. If the beneficiary does not extend the trust term when it expires, the trustee is usually obligated to sell the real estate and return the net proceeds to the beneficiary.

Ownership of Real Estate by Business Organizations

A business organization is a legal entity that exists independently of its members. Ownership by a business organization makes it possible for many people to hold an interest in the same parcel of real estate. Investors may be organized to finance a real estate project in various ways. Some provide for the real estate to be owned by the entity; others provide for direct ownership by the investors.

Partnership A **partnership** is an association of two or more persons who carry on a business for profit as co-owners. In a **general partnership**, all the partners participate in the operation and management of the business and share full liability for business losses and obligations. A **limited partnership** consists of one or more general partners, as well as limited partners. The business is run by the general partner or partners. The limited partners are not legally permitted to participate, with the result that each can be held liable for business losses only to the amount invested. The limited partnership is a popular method of organizing investors because it permits investors with small amounts of capital to participate in large real estate projects with minimum personal risk.

If a partner in a general partnership dies, withdraws, or goes bankrupt, the traditional common law result would be to dissolve the partnership, which could be reorganized as a partnership of the surviving partners in order to conduct business. Nearly every state has now adopted the *Uniform Partnership Act*, which provides for the continuation of the existing business even under these circumstances.

In a limited partnership, the partnership agreement may provide for the continuation of the organization after the death or withdrawal of one of the partners.

Corporations A **corporation** is a legal entity—an artificial person—created under the authority of the laws of the state from which it receives its charter. A corporation is managed and operated by its board of directors, who are selected by the owners of the corporation—its shareholders The members of the board of directors then usually select the officers who are responsible for the day-to-day operation of the corporation. The corporate charter sets forth the powers of the corporation, including its ability to buy and sell real estate (based on a resolution by the board of directors). Because the corporation is a legal entity, it can own real estate in *severalty* or as a *tenant in common* with other natural or artificial persons. Some corporations are permitted by their charters to purchase real estate for any purpose; others are limited to purchasing only the land necessary to fulfill the entities' corporate purposes.

As a legal entity, a corporation continues to exist until it is formally dissolved. The death of one of the officers or directors does not affect title to property owned by the corporation.

Limited Liability Companies The **limited liability company (LLC)** is a relatively recent form of business organization in this country, becoming popular only since about 1980, although it has been used in Europe for over a century. An LLC combines the most attractive features of limited partnerships and corporations. The members of an LLC enjoy the limited liability offered by a corporate form of ownership. In addition, the LLC offers the tax advantages of a partnership—income flows directly to the member of the LLC, instead of being subject to the double taxation of a corporation, with income taxed when received by the corporation, and then taxed again when received as dividends by the shareholders. In addition, the LLC offers a flexible management structure without the complicated requirements of a corporation or the restrictions of a limited partnership. The structure and methods of establishing a new LLC, or of converting an existing entity to the LLC form, vary from state to state.

CONDOMINIUMS, COOPERATIVES, AND TIME-SHARES

A growing urban population, diverse lifestyles, changing family structures, and heightened mobility have created a demand for new forms of property ownership. Condominiums, cooperatives, and time-share arrangements are three types of property ownership that have arisen in residential, commercial, and industrial markets to address changing real estate needs.

See Figure 5.5 for a comparison chart of these types of property ownership.

FIGURE 5.5: Three Types of Property Ownership

Type	Condominium	Cooperative	Time-Share
Description	Single units are located in lowrise and highrise complexes, as town houses or stand-alone units.	Single units are located in lowrise and highrise complexes.	Multiple purchasers buy interests in real estate—usually resort or hotel property. Each purchaser has right to use unit for set time each year or a number of usage points.
Ownership	Owners have fee title to interior space of units and share title to common areas.	Tenants own shares in a corporation, partnership, or trust that holds title to the building. Tenants have proprietary leases and the right to occupy their respective units.	Time-share estate is a fee simple interest. Time-share use agreement is personal property that expires after a specified time period.
Transfer	Single units are transferred by deed, will, or living trust.	Shares are personal property. Shareholders may sell or transfer shares. Transfer of shares may be restricted by bylaws.	An interest in a time-share estate may be conveyed by deed or will by the owner. An interest in time-share use is personal property that may or may not be transferable according to the contract.
Governance (in Addition to State Law)	Declaration of condominium and board of directors elected by homeowners	Bylaws of the corporation and board of directors elected by shareholders	Developer

Condominium Ownership

The **condominium** form of ownership is used throughout the United States. Condominium laws, often called horizontal property acts, have been enacted in every state. Under these laws, the owner of each unit holds a fee simple title to the unit. The individual unit owners also own a specified share of the undivided interest in the remainder of the building and land, known as **common elements.** Common elements typically include such items as land, courtyards, lobbies, the exterior structure, hallways, elevators, stairways, and the roof, as well as recreational facilities such as swimming pools, tennis courts, and golf courses. (*See* Figure 5.6.) Balconies and patios used exclusively by individual units but which must comply with restrictive covenants (such as those regarding use, furnishings, and maintenance) are called limited common elements. Unit owners own the common elements as *tenants in common*, although state law usually provides that condominium unit owners do not have the same right to partition that other tenants in common have.

FIGURE 5.6: Condominium Ownership

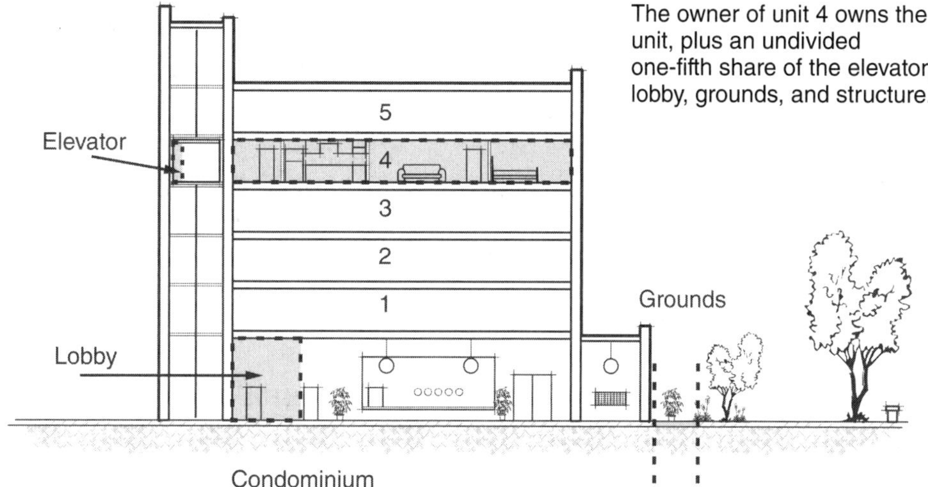

Condominium ownership is not restricted to highrise buildings. Lowrises, **town houses** that share a wall, and detached structures can all be condominiums.

Owning a condominium Once a property is established as a condominium, each unit becomes a separate parcel of real estate that is owned in fee simple and may be held by one or more persons in any type of ownership or tenancy recognized by state law. A condominium unit may be mortgaged like any other parcel of real estate, although the condominium project will be required to meet lender requirements. The unit can usually be sold or transferred to whomever the owner chooses, unless the condominium association provides for a *right of first refusal.* In that case, the owner is required to offer the unit at the same price to the other owners in the condominium or the association before accepting an outside purchase offer.

Real estate taxes are assessed and collected on each unit as an individual property. Default in the payment of taxes or a mortgage loan by one unit owner may result in a foreclosure sale of that owner's unit. An owner's default, however, does not affect the other unit owners.

IN PRACTICE Before buying a condominium, the buyer should do as much background research as possible. Consideration of association fees and rules is critical to understanding all the ramifications of condominium ownership.

Operation and Administration The condominium property is administered by a homeowners association (HOA), which is made up of unit owners. The association may be governed by a board of directors or another elected entity, and it may manage the property on its own or hire a property manager.

The association must enforce any rules it adopts regarding the operation and use of the property. The association is responsible for the maintenance, repair, cleaning, and sanitation of the common elements and structural portions of the property. It must also maintain fire, extended-coverage, and liability insurance.

The expenses of maintaining and operating the condominium building are paid by the unit owners in the form of fees and assessments. Both fees and assessments are imposed and collected by the homeowners association. Recurring fees (called

HOA fees) are paid by each unit owner. The fees may be due monthly, quarterly, semiannually, or annually, depending on the provisions of the bylaws. If fees are not paid, the association may seek a court-ordered judgment to have the delinquent owner's unit sold to cover the outstanding amount or place a lien on the property. In some states, the association can pursue a foreclosure without first obtaining a court order.

Assessments are special payments required of unit owners to address some specific expense, such as a new roof. Assessments are structured like condo fees: Owners of larger units pay proportionately higher assessments than smaller units. The relative ownership shares are established by the developer prior to the sale of the units.

Cooperative Ownership

In a **cooperative**, a corporation holds title to the land and the building. The corporation then offers shares of stock to prospective tenants. The price the corporation sets for each apartment becomes the price of the stock. The purchaser becomes a shareholder in the corporation by virtue of stock ownership and receives a proprietary lease to the apartment for the life of the corporation. Because stock is personal property, the cooperative tenant-owners do not own real estate, as is the case with condominiums. Instead, they own an interest in a corporation that has only one asset: the building.

Operation and Management The operation and management of a cooperative are determined by the corporation's bylaws. Through their control of the corporation, the shareholders of a cooperative control the property and its operation. They elect officers and directors who are responsible for operating the corporation and its real estate assets. Individual shareholders are obligated to abide by the corporation's bylaws.

An important issue in most cooperatives is the method by which shares in the corporation may be transferred to new owners. For instance, the bylaws may require that the board of directors approve any prospective shareholders. In some cooperatives, a tenant-owner must sell the stock back to the corporation at the original purchase price so that the corporation realizes any profits when the shares are resold.

IN PRACTICE In often publicized events, a well-known celebrity attempts to purchase a unit in a cooperative apartment building and is blocked by the cooperative's board. In refusing to allow a celebrity to purchase shares, the board may cite the unwanted publicity and media attention other tenants might suffer.

Unlike a condominium association, which has the authority to impose a lien on the title owned by someone who defaults on maintenance payments, the burden of any defaulted payment in a cooperative falls on the remaining shareholders. Each shareholder is affected by the financial ability of the others. For this reason, approval of prospective tenants by the board of directors will include financial evaluation. If the corporation is unable to make mortgage and tax payments because of shareholder defaults, the property might be sold by court order in a foreclosure suit. This would destroy the interests of all shareholders, including those who have paid their assessments.

Advantages Cooperative ownership, despite its risks, has become more desirable in recent years for several reasons. Lending institutions view the shares of stock as acceptable collateral for financing and the availability of financing expands the transferability of shares beyond wealthy cash buyers. As a tenant-owner, rather than a tenant who pays rent to a landlord, the shareholder has some control over the property. Tenants in cooperatives also enjoy certain income tax advantages. The IRS treats ownership of a cooperative as it does a fee simple interest in a single-family home or condominium in regard to deductibility of loan interest and property taxes, and homesellers' tax exclusions. Finally, owners enjoy freedom from maintenance chores.

IN PRACTICE The laws in some states may prohibit real estate professionals or brokerages from listing or selling cooperative interests because the owners own only personal property. Individuals who participate in these transactions may need a securities license appropriate for the type of cooperative interest involved.

Time-Share Ownership

Time-share ownership permits multiple purchasers to buy relatively small interests in real estate, typically resort properties. Each purchaser receives the right to occupy the facilities for a certain period. A *time-share estate* includes a real property interest in a specified unit for a particular period of the year, or it can be a designated share of ownership of the property expressed as a fractional interest or number of points. A *time-share use* is a contract right under which the developer owns the real estate. The owner of the time-share use has the right to occupy the facilities for the designated period each year, but only for a certain number of years. At the end of that time, the owner's rights in the property terminate.

The right to transfer the period of occupancy—or even exchange the period of use between properties that are part of the same exchange organization—can make time-share ownership attractive. High development and marketing costs have made time-shares an expensive form of property ownership, however, as evidenced by the discounts offered for resales of time-share interests on various internet sites. Maintenance costs are an ongoing expense, even if the time-share is not used in a given year.

Membership camping may be offered in a form similar to a time-share use. The owner purchases the right to use the developer's facilities, which usually consist of an open area with minimal improvements (such as camper and trailer hookups and restrooms). Normally, the owner is not limited to a specific time for using the property; use is limited only by weather and access.

IN PRACTICE The laws governing the development and sale of time-share units are complex and vary substantially from state to state. In addition, the sale of time-share properties may be subject to federal securities laws, as well as a state's real estate commission oversight. In many states, time-share properties are now subject to subdivision requirements. Several states have adopted versions of the *Model Real Estate Time-Share Act*, drafted by the National Conference of Commissioners on Uniform State Laws. The model act contains provisions for the management and termination of time-share units and also provides consumer protections for purchasers of time-shares.

KEY POINT REVIEW

Ownership in severalty is ownership by one individual, who may be an artificial person, such as a corporation.

Co-ownership by two or more individuals may take one of four forms, depending on the state in which the property is located. In a **tenancy in common (TIC)**, each tenant holds an undivided fractional interest and co-owners have unity of possession. Each interest can be sold, conveyed, mortgaged, or transferred, and will be passed by will or state law when a co-owner dies. A legal action called **partition** can be brought by one or more of the tenants in common to force division or sale of the property.

In a **joint tenancy**, there are four unities (PITT): unity of **possession**, unity of *interest*, unity of **time**, and unity of **title**. Joint tenants enjoy the **right of survivorship**, which means that, on the death of a joint tenant, that tenant's interest passes to the other joint tenant or tenants.

A joint tenancy can be terminated by **death** of all but one joint tenant, who then owns the property in severalty; **conveyance** of a joint tenant's interest, but only as to that interest if there were more than two joint tenants originally; or **partition**, the legal action to force division or sale of the property.

Some states recognize a **tenancy by the entirety**, which is available only to spouses and which carries a right of survivorship. Property held by a tenancy by the entirety can be conveyed only by both spouses.

Community property, currently recognized by nine states, is property acquired during marriage that is not separate property and requires agreement of both spouses to be conveyed. **Separate property** is property owned by one spouse before marriage, or acquired by one spouse during marriage by gift, inheritance, or with the proceeds of separate property. On the death of a spouse, that spouse's half of the community property is distributed according to the deceased's will or by state law.

A **trust** is a legal arrangement in which property is transferred by the **trustor**, the person creating the trust, to a **trustee**, to be held for the identified **beneficiary**. The trustee acts as a **fiduciary** in carrying out the wishes of the trustor.

In a **land trust**, the beneficiary is also the trustor, but the public record will not identify the beneficiary.

A **partnership** is an association of two or more persons who carry on a business for profit as co-owners in a general or a limited partnership, as provided by state law.

In a **general partnership**, all partners **participate** in operation and management, and partners share **full liability** for business losses and obligations.

A **limited partnership** has both general partners and limited partners. The **general partners** run the business. **Limited partners** do not participate in running the business and are liable for business losses only up to the amount of the individual's investment.

A **limited liability company (LLC)** may be permitted by state law and offers its members the benefits of the limited liability of a corporation, the tax advantages of a partnership, and a flexible management structure.

A **condominium** owner holds fee simple title to the airspace of a unit, as well as an undivided share in the remainder of the building and land, known as the **common elements**, which may be referenced in what are called **horizontal property acts**.

Common elements are owned by condominium unit owners as tenants in common. The condominium is administered by a **homeowners association** of unit owners that may decide to hire an outside property management firm. **Maintenance** of common elements is funded by **fees** charged to each unit owner.

Condominium unit owners have no right to partition common elements. Individual condominium units may be mortgaged; default on a mortgage payment does not affect other unit owners. The condominium association may have a **right of first refusal** when a unit owner wants to sell.

In a **cooperative**, title to the land and the building is held by a corporation, which sells shares of stock to prospective tenants. A purchaser of stock becomes a **shareholder** in the corporation and receives a **proprietary lease** to the apartment for the life of the corporation. The stock is owned as personal property and not real estate.

A **lender** may accept stock in a cooperative as collateral for financing, which expands the pool of potential owners. The IRS treats a cooperative the same as a house or condominium for tax purposes.

A **time-share** permits the sale of an **estate** or **use** interest that allows occupancy of a property during a specific period of time, typically weekly. **Time-share** ownership permits multiple purchasers to buy interests in real estate, a form of ownership most commonly found with resort property.

The **Model Real Estate Time-Share Act** deals with time-share management and protections for purchasers of units.

UNIT 5 QUIZ

1. The four unities of possession, interest, time, and title are associated with which of the following?
   a. Community property
   b. Severalty ownership
   c. Tenants in common
   d. Joint tenancy
2. A parcel of property was purchased by two friends. The deed they received from the seller at closing transferred the property without further explanation. The two friends took title as which of the following?
   a. Joint tenants
   b. Tenants in common
   c. Tenants by the entirety
   d. Community property owners
3. Three people are joint tenants with rights of survivorship in a tract of land. One owner conveys his interest to a friend. Which statement is *TRUE*?
   a. The other two owners remain joint tenants.
   b. The new owner has severalty ownership.
   c. They all become tenants in common.
   d. They all become joint tenants.
4. A man owns one of 20 units in fee simple, along with a 5% ownership share in the parking facilities, recreation center, and grounds. What kind of property does he own?
   a. Cooperative
   b. Condominium
   c. Time-share
   d. Land trust
5. A trust is a legal arrangement in which property is held for the benefit of a third party by a(n)
   a. beneficiary.
   b. trustor.
   c. trustee.
   d. attorney-in-fact.
6. According to some states, any real property that either spouse owns at the time of marriage remains separate property. Further, any real property acquired by either spouse during the marriage (except by gift or inheritance of with the proceeds of separate property) belongs to both of them equally. What is this form of ownership called?
   a. Partnership
   b. Joint tenancy
   c. Tenancy by the entirety
   d. Community property
7. Three women were concurrent owners of a parcel of real estate. When one of the women died, her interest, according to her will, became part of the estate. The deceased was a
   a. joint tenant.
   b. tenant in common.
   c. tenant by the entirety.
   d. severalty owner.
8. A legal arrangement under which the title to real property is held to protect the interests of a beneficiary is a
   a. trust.
   b. corporation.
   c. limited partnership.
   d. general partnership.
9. A person lives in an apartment building. The land and structures are owned by a corporation, with one mortgage loan securing the entire property. Like the other residents, this person owns stock in the corporation and has a lease to the apartment. This type of ownership is called
   a. condominium.
   b. planned unit development.
   c. time-share.
   d. cooperative.

10. An owner purchased an interest in a house in Beachfront. The owner is entitled to the right of possession only between July 10 and August 4 of each year. Which of the following is *MOST* likely the type of ownership that has been purchased?
   a. Cooperative
   b. Condominium
   c. Time-share
   d. Partnership

11. A corporation is a legal entity, recognized as an artificial person. Property owned solely by the corporation is owned in
   a. trust.
   b. partnership.
   c. severalty.
   d. survivorship tenancy.

12. Which of the following refers to ownership by one person?
   a. Tenancy by the entirety
   b. Community property
   c. Tenancy in common
   d. Severalty

13. A married couple co-owns a farm and has the right of survivorship. This arrangement is *MOST* likely
   a. severalty ownership.
   b. community property.
   c. a tenancy in common.
   d. an estate by the entirety.

14. The real property interest that takes the form of personal property is the
   a. ownership in severalty.
   b. cooperative unit ownership.
   c. condominium unit ownership.
   d. tenancy in common.

15. Two people are co-owners of a small office building with the right of survivorship. One of the co-owners dies intestate and leaves nothing to be distributed to his heirs. Which of the following would explain why the surviving co-owner acquired the deceased's interest?
   a. Severalty
   b. Joint tenancy
   c. Community property
   d. Condominium

16. Which of the following is *MOST* likely evidence of ownership in a cooperative?
   a. Tax bill for an individual unit
   b. Existence of a reverter clause
   c. Shareholder's stock
   d. Right of first refusal

17. An ownership interest that can be an estate interest or a right of use is a
   a. leasehold.
   b. time-share.
   c. condominium.
   d. cooperative.

18. Which statement applies to both joint tenancy and tenancy by the entirety?
   a. There is no right to file a partition suit.
   b. The last survivor becomes a severalty owner.
   c. A deed signed by one owner will convey a fractional interest.
   d. A deed will not convey any interest unless signed by both spouses.

19. Which of the following is *NOT* a form of co-ownership?
   a. Tenancy in common
   b. Ownership in severalty
   c. Tenancy by the entirety
   d. Community property

20. If property is held by two or more owners as joint tenants, the interest of a deceased co-owner will be passed to the
   a. surviving owner or owners.
   b. heirs of the deceased.
   c. state, under the law of escheat.
   d. trust under which the property was owned.

Land Description

LEARNING OBJECTIVES *When you have finished reading this unit, you will be able to*

- **identify and explain** the methods used for describing real estate;
- **explain** the process involved in identifying and measuring property rights including those above and below the surface; and
- **define** the following *key terms:*

air lots	metes-and-bounds method	rectangular (government) survey system
base lines	monuments	sections
benchmarks	plat map	survey
datum	point of beginning (POB)	tiers
legal description	principal meridians	township lines
lot-and-block (recorded plat) method	ranges	townships

OVERVIEW

A street address, while usually enough to find the location of a property or building, is not precise enough to define the perimeter of a parcel of land in a way that excludes all other parcels. A street address will not indicate how large the property is, or where it begins and ends. The description of the property must be *legally sufficient* —that is, the property must be described in a way that will enable a sales contract, deed, or mortgage document to be legally enforceable.

A **legal description** is a detailed way of describing a parcel of land for documents such as deeds and mortgages that will be accepted in a court of law. The description is based on information collected through a **survey**—the process by which boundaries are measured by calculating the dimensions and area to determine the exact location of a piece of land. Courts have stated that a description is *legally sufficient* if it allows a surveyor to *locate* the parcel. In this context, *locate* means that the surveyor must be able to define the exact boundaries of the property. Several alternative systems of identification have been developed to express a legal description of real estate.

METHODS OF DESCRIBING REAL ESTATE

There are three basic methods currently used to describe real estate:

- Metes and bounds
- Rectangular (or government) survey
- Lot and block (recorded plat)

Although each method can be used independently, the methods may be combined in some situations. Some states use only one method; others use all three. About 10 states, including Hawaii and Colorado, have properties that are identified by means of a Torrens certificate, which is issued and guaranteed by the state. The Torrens system was created by Robert Torrens in Australia in 1858. Because of the expense involved in verifying a property description before issuing a certificate, the Torrens system was not widely adopted in this country, but it is still popular in Australia, New Zealand, and Canada.

www.fgdc.gov/ngac
www.fgdc.gov

Today, technology allows for greater precision both in land measurement and recordkeeping. The use of a satellite-based geographic information system (GIS) to locate land boundaries and objects with amazing accuracy and the use of computer-assisted design (CAD) programs to create maps have created a new era in land description. The National Geospatial Advisory Committee, www.fgdc.gov/ngac, was created in 1994 to coordinate geographic data acquisition and access. The Federal Bureau of Land Management and the USDA Forest Service were charged in 1998 with the task of developing the National Integrated Land System (NILS) in cooperation with states, counties, and private industry. Recognizing the need for consistent standards of data collection and use, the Cadastral Data Content Standard was created by the Federal Geographic Data Committee, www.fgdc.gov, to integrate information found in publicly available land records. The NILS is being designed to be compatible with land descriptions utilizing both the metes-and-bounds method and the rectangular survey system.

Metes-and-Bounds Method

The **metes-and-bounds method** of land description is the oldest found in the United States, and it was used in the original 13 colonies, as well as in those states that were being settled while the rectangular survey system was being developed. *Metes* means to measure, and *bounds* means linear directions. The method relies on a property's physical features to determine the boundaries and measurements of the parcel. A metes-and-bounds description starts at a designated place on the parcel, called the **point of beginning (POB)**. The POB is also the point at which the description ends. From there, the surveyor proceeds around the property's boundaries. The boundaries are recorded by referring to linear measurements, natural and artificial landmarks (called *monuments*), and directions. A metes-and-bounds description always ends back at the POB so that the tract being described is completely enclosed.

Monuments **Monuments** are fixed objects used to identify the POB, all corners of the parcel or ends of boundary segments, and the location of intersecting boundaries. In colonial times, a monument might have been a natural object such as a stone, a large tree, a lake, or a stream. It also may have been a street, a fence, or other marker. Today, monuments are iron pins or concrete posts placed by the U.S. Army Corps of Engineers, other government departments, or trained private surveyors. Measurements often include the words *more or less* because the location of the monuments is more important than the distances between them. The actual distance between monuments takes precedence over any linear measurements in the description. Because monuments can be moved, surveyors give their final metes-and-bounds reference in terms of cardinal points and distance. They include the statement "to the point of beginning (POB)" to ensure closure and to remove questions if an error in footage prevents closure.

An example of a historical metes-and-bounds description of a parcel of land (pictured in Figure 6.1) follows:

> A tract of land located in Red Skull, Boone County, Virginia, described as follows: Beginning at the intersection of the east line of Jones Road and the south line of Skull Drive; then east along the south line of Skull Drive 200 feet; then south 15° east 216.5 feet, more or less, to the center thread of Red Skull Creek then northwesterly along the center line of said creek to its intersection with the east line of Jones Road; then north 105 feet, more or less, along the east line of Jones Road to the point of beginning.

FIGURE 6.1: Metes-and-Bounds Tract

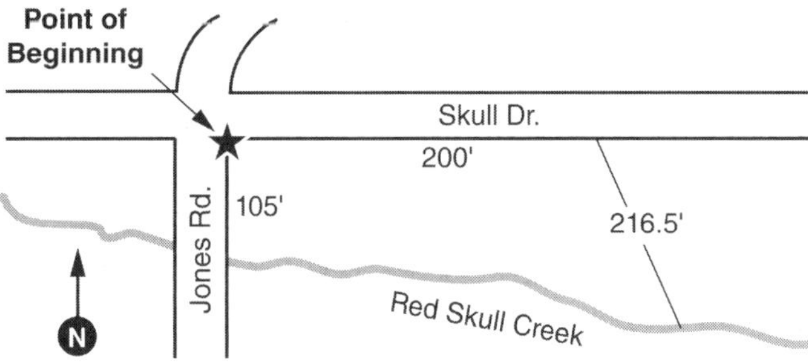

When used to describe property within a town or city, a metes-and-bounds description may begin as follows:

> Beginning at a point on the southerly side of Kent Street, 100 feet easterly from the corner formed by the intersection of the southerly side of Kent Street and the easterly side of Broadway; then . . .

In this description, the POB is given by reference to the corner intersection. *Again, the description must close by returning to the POB.*

An example of a technically assisted metes-and-bounds description follows:

> Beginning at a point (POB) on the North side of Newberry Street 100.50 feet East from the corner formed by the intersection of the East boundary of Peter Road and the North boundary of Newberry Street; then East 90 degrees, 15 minutes, 200.22 feet; then North 1

degree, 3 minutes, 2 seconds 300 feet; then West 89 degrees, 10 minutes, 3 seconds, 200.05 feet; then direct to the POB.

Metes-and-bounds descriptions are complicated. They can be difficult to understand when they include detailed compass directions or concave and convex lines. Sometimes the lines are curved on an arc or radius that becomes part of the description. Natural deterioration or destruction of the monuments in a description can make boundaries difficult to identify.

Technological advances, such as the use of computers, lasers, satellites, and global positioning systems, have meant a resurgence in property descriptions using points of reference or metes-and-bounds descriptions.

Rectangular (Government) Survey System

The **rectangular survey system**, sometimes called the *government survey system*, was established by Congress in 1785 to standardize the description of land acquired by the newly formed federal government. By dividing the land into rectangles, the survey provided land descriptions by describing the rectangle(s) in which the land was located. The system is based on two sets of intersecting lines: principal meridians and base lines. The **principal meridians** run north and south, and the **base lines** run east and west. Both are located by reference to degrees of longitude and latitude. Each principal meridian has a name or number and is crossed by a base line. Each principal meridian and its corresponding base line are used to survey a definite area of land, indicated on the map by boundary lines. There are 37 principal meridians in the United States and each is referenced by a name or meridian number.

Each principal meridian describes only specific areas of land by boundaries. No parcel of land is described by reference to more than one principal meridian. The meridian used may not necessarily be the nearest one.

Tiers Lines running east and west, *parallel to the base line* and six miles apart, are called **township lines**. (*See* Figure 6.2.) They form strips of land called **tiers**. Think of these tiers as being like the tiers of a wedding cake. The tiers are designated by consecutive numbers north or south of the base line. For instance, the strip of land between 6 and 12 miles north of a base line is Township 2 North.

FIGURE 6.2: Township Lines

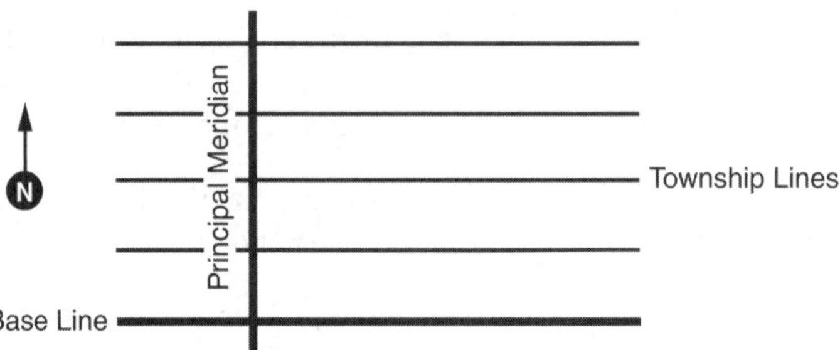

Ranges The land on either side of a principal meridian is divided into six-mile-wide strips by lines that run north and south, *parallel to the meridian*. These north-south strips of land are called **ranges**. (*See* Figure 6.3.) They are designated by consecutive numbers east or west of the principal meridian. For example, Range 3 East would be a strip of land between 12 and 18 miles east of its principal meridian.

FIGURE 6.3: Range Lines

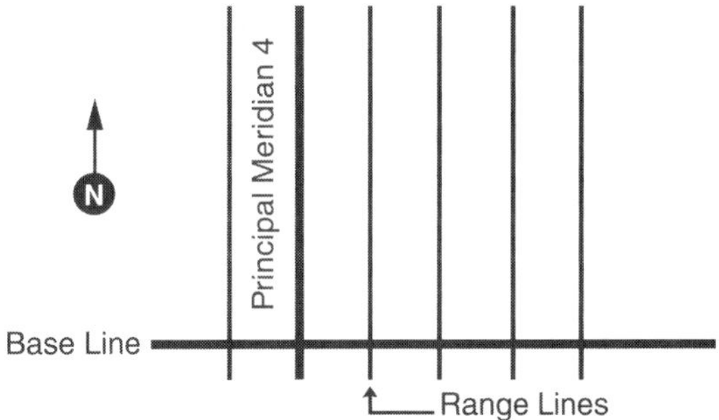

The directions of township and range lines, and tiers and ranges, may be easily remembered by thinking of the words this way:

Township lines
Range lines

Townships When the horizontal township lines and the vertical range lines intersect, they form squares, or **townships**, that are the basic units of the rectangular survey system. (*See* Figure 6.4.) A township is 6 miles square and contains 36 square miles (23,040 *acres*).

Each township is given a legal description. A township's description includes the

- designation of the tier in which the township is located,
- designation of the range, and
- name or number of the principal meridian for that area.

FIGURE 6.4: Townships in the Rectangular Survey System

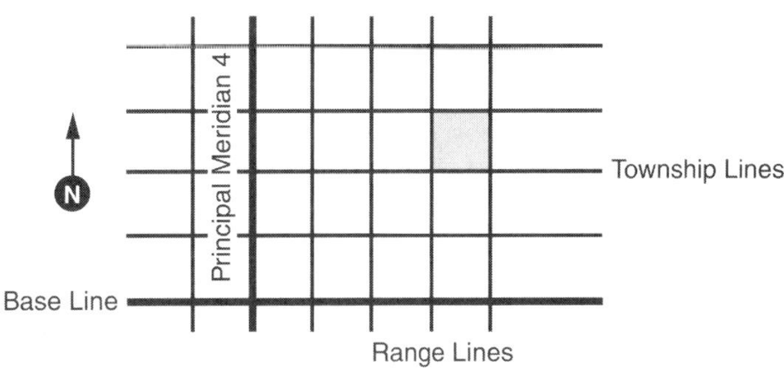

IN PRACTICE In Figure 6.4, the shaded township is described as Township 3 North, Range 4 East of the Fourth Principal Meridian. This township is in the third tier north of the base line, and in the fourth range east of the principal meridian. Finally, reference is made to the principal meridian because the land being described is within the boundary of land surveyed from that meridian. This description is abbreviated as *T3N, R4E 4th Principal Meridian.*

Townships are numbered the same way a field is plowed. Remember: *right to left, left to right, right to left,* and so on.

Sections Townships are subdivided into sections and subsections called halves and quarters, which can be further divided. Each township contains 36 **sections**. Each section is one square mile or 640 acres, with 43,560 square feet in each acre. Sections are numbered 1 through 36, as shown in Figure 6.5. Section 1 is always in the northeast, or upper right-hand, corner. The numbering proceeds right to left to the upper left-hand corner. From there, the numbers drop down to the next tier and continue from left to right, then back from right to left. By law, each

Section 16 was set aside for school purposes, and the sale or rental proceeds from this land were originally available for township school use. The schoolhouse was usually located in this section so it would be centrally located for all the students in the township. As a result, Section 16 is commonly called a *school section*.

FIGURE 6.5: Sections in a Township

N

6	5	4	3	2	1
7	8	9	10	11	12
18	17	16	15	14	13
19	20	21	22	23	24
30	29	28	27	26	25
31	32	33	34	35	36

W E

S

Sections are divided into *halves* (320 acres) and *quarters* (160 acres). In turn, each of those parts is further divided into halves and quarters. The southeast quarter of a section, which is a 160-acre tract, is abbreviated SE¼. The SE¼ of SE¼ of SE¼ of Section 1 would be a 10-acre square in the lower right-hand corner of Section 1. (*See* Figure 6.6; the old measurements in chains and rods are defined in Figure 6.8.)

FIGURE 6.6: A Section

5,280 Feet
1,320 20 Chains
1,320 20 Chains
2,640 40 Chains 160 Rods
2,640
W¹/2 of NW¹/4 (80 Acres)
E¹/2 of NW¹/4 (80 Acres)
NE¹/4 (160 Acres)
1,320
NW¹/4 of SW¹/4 (40 Acres)
NE¹/4 of SW¹/4 (40 Acres)
N¹/2 of NW¹/4 of SE¹/4 (20 Acres)
W¹/2 of NE¹/4 of SE¹/4 (20 Acres)
20 Acres
1 Furlong
20 Acres
1,320
SW¹/4 of SW¹/4 (40 Acres)
40 Acres
(10 Acres) (10 Acres)
5 Acres
5 Acres
5 Acs.
5 Acs.
SE¹/4 of SE¹/4 of SE¹/4 10 Acres
660 Feet
660 Feet
80 Rods
440 Yards

The rectangular survey system sometimes uses a shorthand method in its descriptions. For instance, a comma may be used in place of the word *of*: SE¼, SE¼, SE¼,

> **Math Shortcut**
>
> To calculate acres in a rectangular survey system description, multiply all the denominators and divide that number into 640 acres. For instance, the SE¼ of SE¼ of SE¼ of Section 1 = 4 × 4 × 4 = 64; 640 ÷ 64 = 10 acres.

Section 1. It is possible to combine portions of a section, such as NE¼ of SW¼ and N½ of NW¼ of SE¼ of Section 1, which could also be written NE¼, SW¼; N½, NW¼, SE¼ of Section 1. A semicolon means *and*. Because of the semicolon in this description, the area is 60 acres.

Reading a Rectangular Survey Description To determine the location and size of a property described in the rectangular or government survey style, *start at the end* and work backward to the beginning, *reading from right to left*. For example, consider the following description (*see* Figure 6.6):

> The S½ of the NW¼ of the SE¼ of Section 11, Township 8 North, Range 6 West of the Fourth Principal Meridian.

To locate this tract of land from the citation alone, first search for the fourth principal meridian on a map of the United States and note its base line. Then, on a regional map, find the township in which the property is located by counting six range strips west of the fourth principal meridian and eight townships north of its corresponding base line. After locating Section 11, divide the section into quarters. Then divide the SE¼ into quarters, and then the NW¼ of that into halves. The S½ of that NW¼ contains the property in question.

Legal descriptions should always include the name of the county and the state in which the land is located because meridians often relate to more than one state and occasionally relate to two base lines. For example, the description "the southwest quarter of Section 10, Township 4 North, Range 1 West of the Fourth Principal Meridian" could refer to land in either Illinois or Wisconsin.

Metes-and-Bounds Descriptions Within the Rectangular Survey System Land in states that use the rectangular survey system may also require a metes-and-bounds description. This usually occurs in one of three situations: (1) when describing an irregular tract; (2) when a tract is too small to be described by quarter-sections; or (3) when a tract does not follow the lot or block lines of a recorded subdivision or section, quarter-section lines, or other fractional section lines.

Lot-and-Block Method

The third type of legal description is the **lot-and-block (recorded plat) method**. This system uses lot and block numbers referred to in a **plat map** filed in the public records of the county where the land is located. The plat map is a map of a town, a section, or a subdivision, indicating the location and boundaries of individual properties. The lot-and-block method is used mostly in subdivisions and urban areas.

A lot-and-block survey is performed in two steps. First, a large parcel of land is described either by the metes-and-bounds method or by a rectangular survey. Once this large parcel is surveyed, it is broken into smaller parcels. As a result, a lot-and-block description always refers to a prior metes-and-bounds or rectangular survey description. For each parcel described under the lot-and-block system, the *lot* refers to the numerical designation of any particular parcel. The *block* refers to the name of the subdivision under which the map is recorded. The block reference is drawn from the early 1900s, when a city block was the most common type of subdivided property.

The lot-and-block system starts with the preparation of a *subdivision plat* by a licensed surveyor or engineer. (*See* Figure 6.7.) On this plat, the land is divided into numbered or lettered lots and blocks, and streets or access roads for public use are indicated. Lot sizes and street details must be described completely and must comply with all local ordinances and requirements. When properly signed and approved, the subdivision plat is recorded in the county in which the land is located. The plat becomes part of the legal description. In describing a lot from a recorded subdivision plat, three identifiers are used:

1. Lot and block number
2. Name or number of the subdivision plat
3. Name of the county and state

FIGURE 6.7: Subdivision Plat Map of Block A

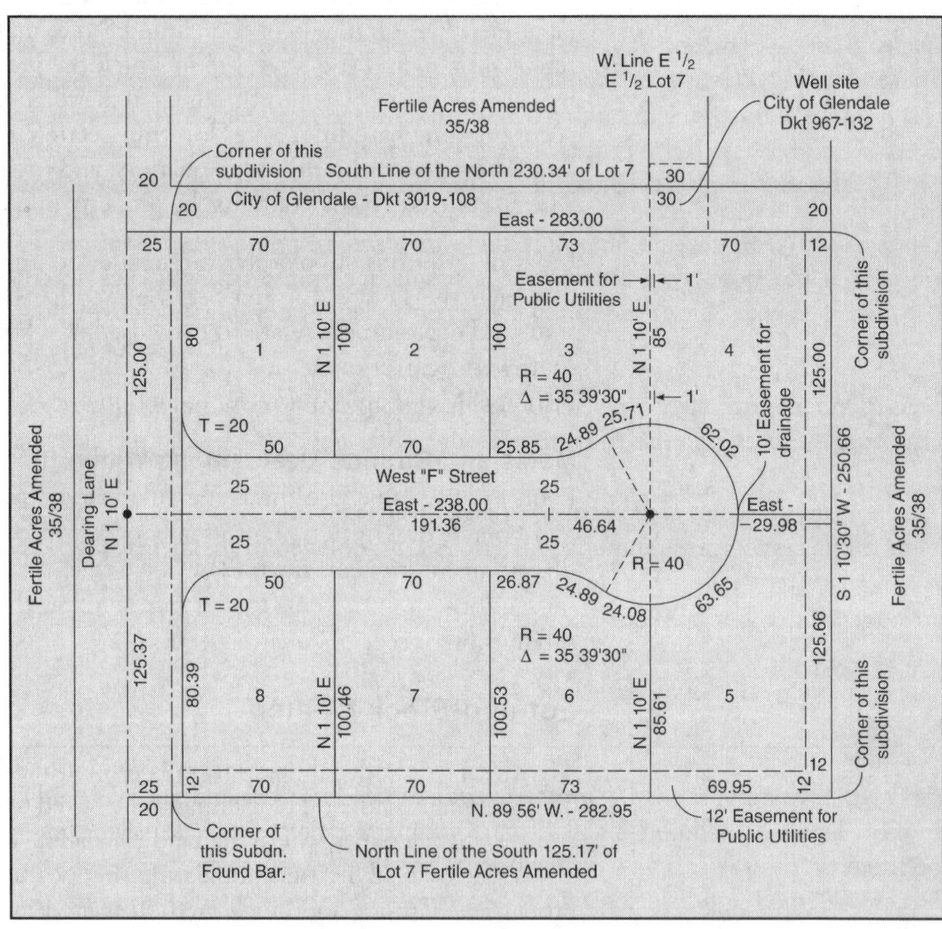

The following is an example of a lot-and-block description:

> Lot 71, Happy Valley Estates 2, located in a portion of the southeast quarter of Section 23, Township 7 North, Range 4 East of the Seward Principal Meridian in ____ County, ____ [state].

To locate this parcel, one would start with the map of the Seward principal meridian to identify the township and range reference, then consult the township map of Township 7 North, Range 4 East, and the section map of Section 23. From there, one would look at the quarter-section map of the southeast quarter. The quarter-section map would refer to the plat map for the subdivision known as the second unit (second parcel subdivided) under the name of Happy Valley Estates.

Some lot-and-block descriptions are not dependent on the government survey system and may refer simply to the plat recorded in the land records of the county.

THE SURVEY: MEASURING PROPERTY RIGHTS

Legal descriptions should not be altered or combined without adequate information from a surveyor or title attorney. A licensed surveyor is trained and authorized to locate and determine the legal description of any parcel of land. The surveyor does this by preparing two documents: a survey and a survey sketch. The *survey* states the property's legal description. The *survey sketch* shows the location and dimensions of the parcel. When a survey also shows the location, size, and shape of buildings on the lot, it is referred to as a *spot survey*.

Legal descriptions should be copied with extreme care. An incorrectly worded legal description in a sales contract may result in a conveyance of more or less land than the parties intended. For example, damages suffered from an incorrect description could be extensive if buildings and improvements need to be moved because the land upon which the improvements were made is not owned. Often, even punctuation is extremely critical. Title problems can arise for the buyer who seeks to convey the property at a future date. Even if the contract can be corrected before the sale is closed, the real estate professional risks losing a commission and may be held liable for damages suffered by an injured party because of an improperly worded legal description.

Real estate professionals should be aware of the types of surveys and their uses recognized by state law or local custom. Not all surveys include surveyor liability and warranties of accuracy. An improvement location certificate (ILC), for instance, may be sufficient for some purposes but is not a full survey. It is prepared in a shorter time frame and at less cost, and provides the location of structures and improvements, easements, and any encroachments in relation to property boundaries.

www.nsps.us.com

The National Society of Professional Surveyors provides useful information for real estate professionals and consumers at www.nsps.us.com, including links to state associations and other affiliated organizations.

IN PRACTICE Because legal descriptions, once recorded, affect ownership of real estate, they should be prepared only by a professional surveyor. Real estate professionals who copy legal descriptions create potential risks for themselves and their clients and customers. The better practice is to refer to a reliable document, such as the deed that transferred the property to the current owner, for a full and accurate legal description.

Measuring Elevations

Just as surface rights must be identified, surveyed, and described, so must rights to the property above the earth's surface. Recall that *land* includes the space above the ground. In the same way that land may be measured and divided into parcels, the air may be divided. The owner may subdivide the air space above the land into **air lots**. Air lots are composed of the airspace within specific boundaries located over a parcel of land.

The *condominium laws* passed in all states require that a registered land surveyor prepare a plat map that shows the elevations of floor and ceiling surfaces and the vertical boundaries of each unit with reference to an official *datum* (discussed in the next section). A unit's floor, for instance, might be 60 feet above the datum and its ceiling, 69 feet. Typically, a separate plat is prepared for each floor in the condominium building.

The following is an example of the legal description of a condominium apartment unit that includes a fractional share of the common elements of the building and land:

> UNIT _____, Level ___, as delineated on survey of the following described parcel of real estate (hereinafter referred to as Development Parcel): The north 99 feet of the west ½ of Block 4 (except that part, if any, taken and used for street), in Sutton's Division Number 5 in the east ½ of the southeast ¼ of Section 24, Township 3 South, Range 68 West of the Sixth Principal Meridian, in Denver County, Colorado, which survey is attached as Exhibit A to Declaration made by Colorado National Bank as Trustee under Trust No. 1250, recorded in the Recorder's Office of Denver County, Colorado, as Document No. 475637; together with an undivided _____% interest in said Development Parcel (excepting from said Development Parcel all the property and space comprising all the units thereof as defined and set forth in said Declaration and Survey).

Subsurface rights can be legally described in the same manner as air rights, but they are measured *below* the datum rather than above it. Subsurface rights are used not only for coal mining, petroleum drilling, and utility line location but also for multistory condominiums—both residential and commercial—that have several floors below ground level.

Datum

www.usgs.gov

A **datum** is a point, line, or surface from which elevations are measured or indicated. For the purpose of the United States Geological Survey (USGS), *datum* is defined as the mean sea level at New York Harbor. But virtually all large cities have local official datum that is used instead of the USGS datum. A surveyor would use a datum in determining the height of a structure or establishing the grade of a street. USGS has information on a variety of climate, land use, and environmental issues, as well as a state site locator, www.usgs.gov.

Monuments Monuments are traditionally used to mark surface measurements between points. A monument could be a marker set in concrete, a piece of steel-reinforcing bar (rebar), a metal pipe driven into the soil, or simply a wooden stake stuck in the dirt. Because such items are subject to the whims of nature and vandals, their accuracy is sometimes suspect. As a result, surveyors rely most heavily on benchmarks to mark their work accurately and permanently.

Benchmarks are monuments that have been established as permanent reference points throughout the United States. They are usually embossed brass markers set into solid concrete or asphalt bases. While used to some degree for surface measurements, their principal reference use is for marking datums.

IN PRACTICE All large cities have established a local official datum used in place of the USGS datum. For instance, the official datum for Chicago is known as the *Chicago City Datum.* It is a horizontal plane that corresponds to the low-water level of Lake Michigan in 1847 (the year in which the datum was established) and is considered to be at zero elevation. Although a surveyor's measurement of elevation based on the USGS datum will differ from one computed according to a local datum, it can be translated to an elevation based on the USGS.

FIGURE 6.8: Units of Land Measurement

Unit	Measurement
mile	5,280 feet; 1,760 yards; 320 rods
furlong	220 yards; 660 feet; 40 rods; 10 chains
chain	66 feet; 4 rods; 100 links
rod	16.5 feet; 5.50 yards
square mile	640 acres (5,280 × 5,280 = 27,878,400 ÷ 43,560)
acre	43,560 square feet
cubic yard	27 cubic feet
square yard	9 square feet
square foot	144 square inches

Land Units and Measurements

It is important to understand land units and measurements because they are integral parts of legal descriptions. Some historical measurements are listed in Figure 6.8. Today, the terms *rods* and *chains* are not often used.

MATH CONCEPTS

Land Acquisition Costs

To calculate the cost of purchasing land, use the same unit in which the cost is given. Costs quoted per square foot must be multiplied by the proper number of square feet; costs quoted per acre must be multiplied by the proper number of acres; and so on.

To calculate the cost of a parcel of land of three acres at $1.10 per square foot, convert the acreage to square feet before multiplying:

43,560 square feet per acre × 3 acres = 130,680 square feet

130,680 square feet × $1.10 per square foot = $143,748

To calculate the cost of a parcel of land of 17,500 square feet at $60,000 per acre, convert the cost per acre into the cost per square foot before multiplying by the number of square feet in the parcel:

$60,000 per acre ÷ 43,560 square feet per acre = $1.38 (rounded) per square foot

17,500 square feet × $1.38 per square foot = $24,150

KEY POINT REVIEW

Three methods of legal description of land are the metes-and-bounds method, rectangular survey system, and lot-and-block system. The National Integrated Land System is being developed by the federal government to coordinate the land descriptions found in public records, making use of the accuracy in determining and recording property boundaries that is possible with current technology.

The **metes-and-bounds method** measures distances (**metes**), starting from a **point of beginning (POB)**, and following compass directions or angles (**bounds**) to arrive back at the point of beginning. **Monuments** (fixed objects or markers) identify the POB and corners or places where the boundary line changes direction.

The **rectangular survey system (government survey system)** divides land into rectangles called **townships**, measured from the intersection of a **principal meridian** and **base line**, and referenced by degrees of longitude and latitude. **Township lines** within a section run east to west parallel to the base line, six miles apart; **range lines** run north to south parallel to and counted from the principal meridian, six miles apart. Rows of townships are called **tiers** and columns of townships are called **ranges**. A township is divided into 36 **sections** of one square mile (640 acres) each and run from right to left, then left to right, starting at section 1 at the northeast corner of the township and ending at section 36 at the southeast corner of the township.

The **lot-and-block (recorded plat) method** divides a **subdivision** into **block** and **lot** (individual parcel) **numbers** and references all data in a subdivision **plat map,** noting lot sizes, street names, and other required information that is **approved** by the governing body, and filed **in public records** of the county where the land is located.

Survey preparation includes both a **legal description** and a **survey sketch**. A less precise analysis, found in the improvement location certificate (ILC), may be used. The legal description must be included by reference or transcribed **exactly** as written to avoid future problems over incorrect boundaries.

Elevations must be measured if **air lots** above the surface or **subsurface rights below the datum** are to be described and conveyed. Distances are noted as above or below datum, defined by U.S. Geological Survey (USGS) as **mean sea level at New York Harbor**, making use of permanent **benchmarks** that are established throughout the United States and are often based on a **local official datum,** and noting **monuments** marking surface measurements between points.

The most common units of **land measurement** include the

- **mile** of 5,280 feet,
- **acre** of 43,560 square feet (approximately 207 × 207 feet), and
- **square mile** of 640 acres (a section).

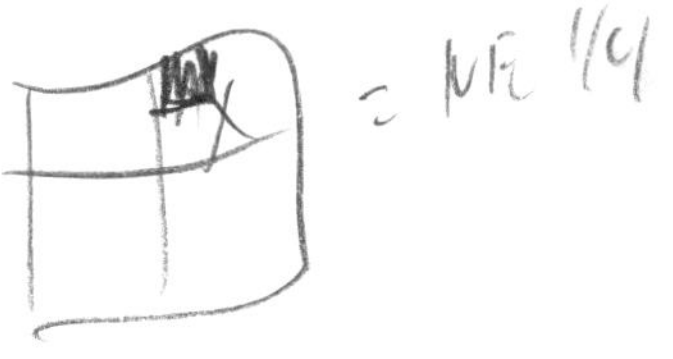

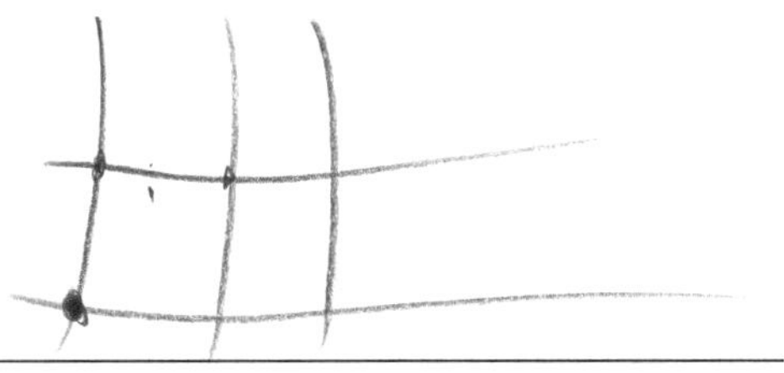

UNIT 6 QUIZ

1. What is the proper description of this shaded area of a section using the rectangular survey system?

   a. SW¼ of the NE¼ and the N½ of the SE¼ of the SW¼
   b. N½ of the NE¼ of the SW¼ and the SE¼ of the NW¼
   c. SW¼ of the SE¼ of the NW¼ and the N½ of the NE¼ of the SW¼
   d. S½ of the SW¼ of the NE¼ and the NE¼ of the NW¼ of the SE¼

2. When surveying land, a surveyor refers to the principal meridian that is

   a. nearest the land being surveyed.
   b. in the same state as the land being surveyed.
   c. not more than 40 townships or 15 ranges distant from the land being surveyed.
   d. within the rectangular survey system area in which the land being surveyed is located.

3. The N½ of the SW¼ of a section contains how many acres?

   a. 20
   b. 40
   c. 60
   d. 80

4. In describing real estate, the method that may use a property's physical features to determine boundaries and measurements is

   a. rectangular survey.
   b. metes and bounds.
   c. government survey.
   d. lot and block.

Questions 5 through 8 refer to the following illustration of one complete township and parts of the adjacent townships.

Section 1

A B
D C

5. The section marked A is which of the following?

   a. School section
   b. Section 31
   c. Section 36
   d. Government lot

6. Which of the following is Section 6?

   a. A
   b. B
   c. C
   d. D

7. The section directly below C is

   a. Section 7.
   b. Section 12.
   c. Section 25.
   d. Section 30.

8. Which of the following is Section D?

   a. Section 1
   b. Section 6
   c. Section 31
   d. Section 36

9. Which of these shaded areas of a section depicts the NE¼ of the SE¼ of the SW¼?

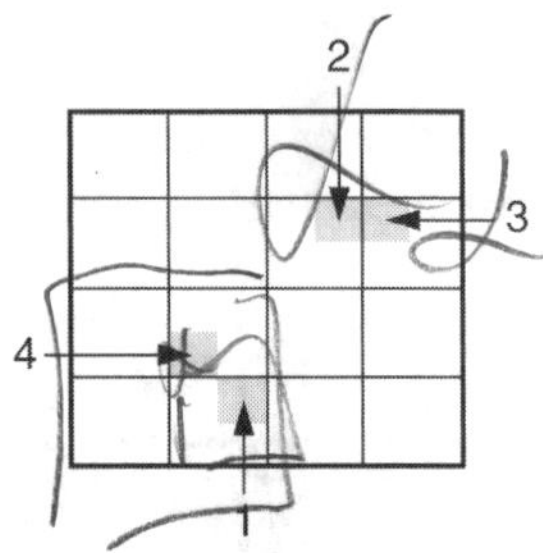

a. Area 1
b. Area 2
c. Area 3
d. Area 4

10. A buyer purchased a half-acre parcel for $2.15 per square foot. What was the selling price of the parcel?

a. $774
b. $46,827
c. $1,376
d. $93,654

11. How many acres are contained in the tract described as "beginning at the NW corner of the SW¼, then south along the west line to the SW corner of the section, then east along the south line of the section 2,640 feet, more or less, to the SE corner of the said SW¼, then in a straight line to the POB"?

a. 80 acres
b. 90 acres
c. 100 acres
d. 160 acres

12. If a farm described as "the NW¼ of the SE¼ of Section 10, Township 2 North, Range 3 West of the 6th. P.M." sold for $4,500 an acre, what was the total sales price?

a. $45,000
b. $90,000
c. $135,000
d. $180,000

13. As a legal description, "the northwest ¼ of the southwest ¼ of Section 6, Township 4 North, Range 7 West" is defective because it contains no reference to

a. lot numbers.
b. boundary lines.
c. a principal meridian.
d. a record of survey.

14. A man buys 4.5 acres of land for $78,400. An adjoining owner wants to purchase a strip of this land measuring 150 feet by 100 feet. What should this strip cost the adjoining owner if the owner sells it for the same price per square foot he originally paid for it?

a. $3,000
b. $6,000
c. $7,800
d. $9,400

15. Which of the following are *NOT* basic components of a metes-and-bounds description?

a. Tangible and intangible monuments
b. Base lines, principal meridians, and townships
c. Degrees, minutes, and seconds
d. Points of beginning

16. A property contains 10 acres. How many lots of not less than 50 feet by 100 feet can be subdivided from the property if 26,000 square feet were dedicated for roads?

a. 80
b. 81
c. 82
d. 83

17. A parcel of land is 400 feet by 640 feet. The parcel is cut in half diagonally by a stream. How many acres are in each half of the parcel?

a. 2.75
b. 2.94
c. 5.51
d. 5.88

18. What is the shortest distance between Section 1 and Section 36 in the same township?

a. Three miles
b. Four miles
c. Five miles
d. Six miles

19. In any township, what is the number of the section designated as the school section?

a. 1
b. 16
c. 25
d. 36

20. The *LEAST* specific method for identifying real property is

a. rectangular survey.
b. metes and bounds.
c. street address.
d. lot and block.

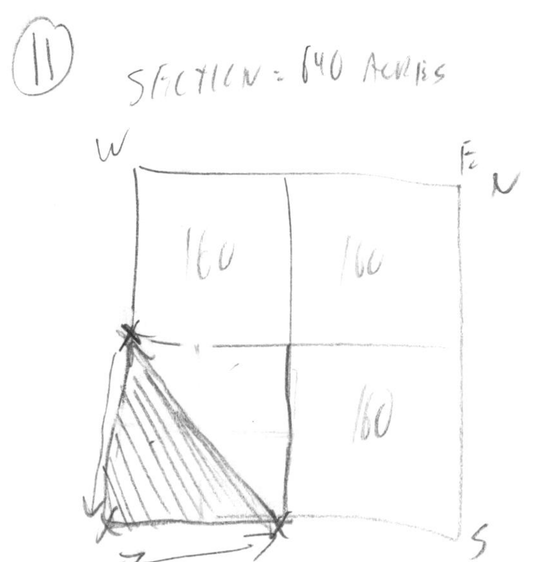

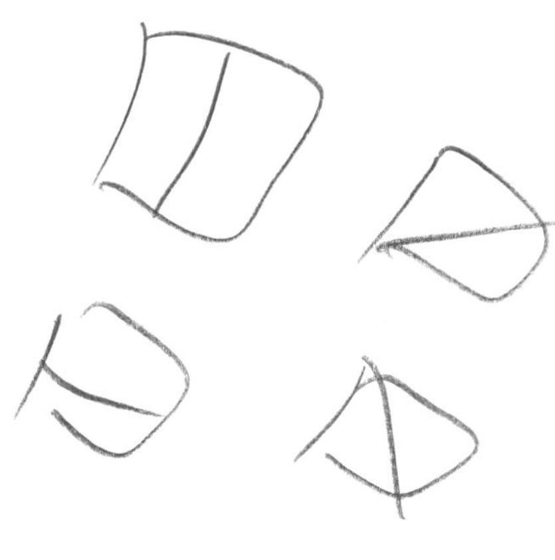

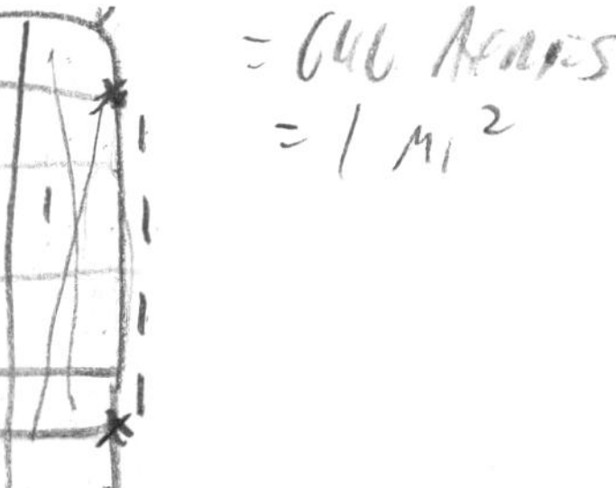

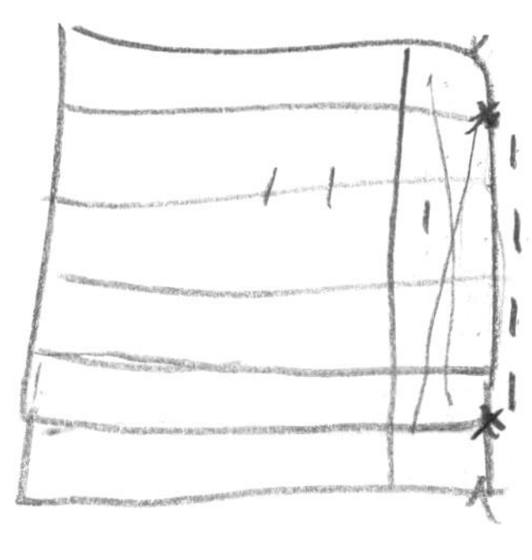

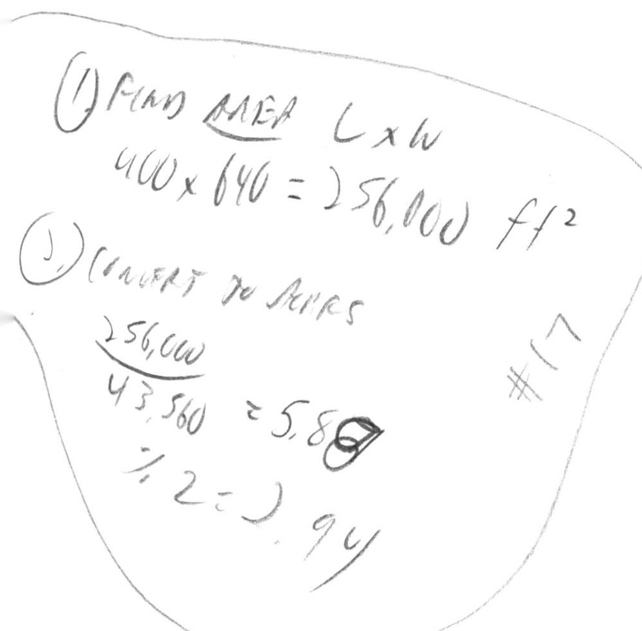

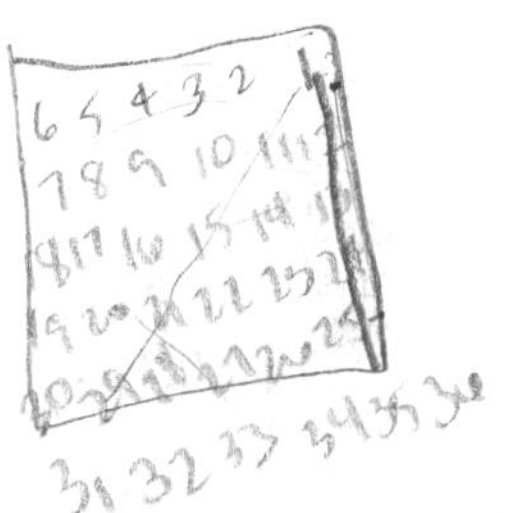

UNIT 7

Transfer of Title

LEARNING OBJECTIVES

When you have finished reading this unit, you will be able to

- **describe** the fundamental concepts of *title* as it relates to the ownership of land, and the processes and instruments used to apply these concepts;
- **describe** the circumstances and conditions which may provide for the involuntary transfer of title;
- **explain** testate, intestate, wills, and the probate process; and
- **define** the following *key terms*:

acknowledgment	granting clause	special warranty deed
adverse possession	grantor	testate
bargain and sale deed	habendum clause	testator
deed	intestate	title
deed of trust	involuntary alienation	transfer tax
devise	probate	trustee's deed
general warranty deed	quitclaim deed	voluntary alienation
grantee	reconveyance deed	will

OVERVIEW

Transfer of title is an aspect of the real estate transaction generally handled by lawyers and title companies. Nonetheless, as with other legal aspects of the transaction, a real estate professional who is aware of the fundamentals of deeds and title issues will better understand the transaction and will know what kind of questions to ask. An informed real estate professional will be able to alert consumers to to the need for legal advice to avoid potential title problems.

TITLE CONCEPTS

The term *title* has two functions. **Title** to real estate means the *right to or ownership of the land*; it represents the owner's bundle of legal rights. Title also serves as *evidence* of that ownership. A person who holds the title, if challenged in court, would be able to recover or retain ownership or possession of a parcel of real estate. Unlike the title to a motor vehicle, which is a document that transfers ownership, title to real estate is a way of referring to ownership but is not an actual printed document. There is one exception to that general rule, however. In states that recognize a Torrens certificate, it is the certificate itself that provides evidence of ownership.

Real estate may be transferred voluntarily by sale or gift. Alternatively, it may be transferred involuntarily by operation of law. Real estate may be transferred while the owner lives or, after the owner dies, either by will or as provided by state law if the owner died without leaving a will.

Voluntary Alienation

A **grantor** conveys property to a grantee.

A **grantee** receives property from a grantor.

A **deed** is the instrument that conveys property from grantor to grantee.

Voluntary alienation is the legal term for the transfer of title during the property owner's lifetime. An owner may transfer title by making a gift or by selling the property. (As will be discussed later, the actions of a property owner can also determine the disposition of the property on the owner's death.)

A **deed** is a document by which an owner of real estate conveys the right, title, or interest owned in the parcel of real estate to someone else. The statute of frauds, found in all states, requires that all deeds be in writing. The owner who transfers the property is referred to as the **grantor**, and the person who receives the property is called the **grantee**. A deed is executed (signed) by the grantor. The terms are easier to remember if you keep in mind that the grant<u>or</u> is the property <u>o</u>wne<u>r</u>. Figure 7.1 lists a number of terms that appear throughout the text that can be remembered in the same way.

FIGURE 7.1: Remembering Legal Terminology: "OR" Versus "EE"

Product	Property Owner or Person Giving the Right	Recipient
Devise	Devisor	Devisee
Deed	Grantor	Grantee
Legacy	Legator	Legatee
Lease	Lessor	Lessee
Mortgage	Mortgagor	Mortgagee
Offer	Offeror makes the offer	Offeree
Option	Optionor	Optionee
Sublease	Sublessor, who is the original lessee	Sublessee
Trust	Trustor	Trustee

Requirements for a Valid Deed

Although formal requirements vary, a valid deed generally must contain the following elements:

- Grantor who has the legal competency to execute the deed
- Grantee named with reasonable certainty to be identified
- Statement of consideration (usually required for recording of the deed)
- Granting clause (words of conveyance)
- Habendum clause, which defines the ownership right received by the grantee
- Accurate legal description of the property conveyed
- Any relevant exceptions or reservations
- Acknowledgment (notarization) of the signature of the grantor
- Delivery of the deed and acceptance by the grantee to pass title

A deed may include a description of any *limitations* on the conveyance of a full fee simple estate and a statement of any *exceptions and reservations* (also known as *"subject to" clauses*) that affect title to the property.

IN PRACTICE The deed to each property in a subdivision that is subject to covenants, conditions, and restrictions (CC&Rs) will include a reference to the recorded document that sets out all of the limitations on the property's use.

Grantor A grantor must be of lawful age, usually at least 18 years old. A deed executed by a minor is generally *voidable*. After reaching legal adult age, the minor can choose to treat the deed as a valid conveyance or can have the conveyance recognized as of no legal effect by a court.

A grantor also must be *legally competent* (of *sound mind*). Generally, any grantor who can understand the action being undertaken is viewed as mentally capable of executing a valid deed. A deed executed by someone who was mentally impaired at the time is voidable, but it is not automatically *void* (of no legal effect). If, however, the grantor has been judged legally incompetent, the deed will be void. Real estate owned by someone who is legally incompetent can be conveyed only with a court's approval.

The grantor's name must be spelled correctly and consistently throughout the deed. If the grantor's name has changed since the title was acquired, as when a person's name is changed following marriage, both names should be shown—for example, "Mary Smith, formerly Mary Jones."

Grantee To be valid, a deed must name a grantee. The grantee must be specifically named so that the person to whom the property is being conveyed can be readily identified from the deed itself.

IN PRACTICE Olive Burbank wanted to convey Whiteacre to her nephew, Joseph Mara. In the deed, Olive wrote the following words of conveyance: "I, Olive Burbank, hereby convey to Joseph all my interest in Whiteacre." The only problem was that Olive also had a son named Joseph, a cousin Joseph, and a neighbor Joseph. The grantee's identity could not be discerned from the deed itself. Olive should have conveyed Whiteacre "to my nephew, Joseph Mara."

If more than one grantee is involved, the granting clause should specify their individual rights in the property. For instance, the clause might state that the grantees will take title as joint tenants or tenants in common. This is especially important when specific wording is necessary to create a joint tenancy.

Consideration A valid deed must contain a clause acknowledging that the grantor has received some form of consideration; that is, something in return for deeding the described property to the grantee. Generally, the amount of consideration is stated in dollars. When a deed conveys real estate as a gift to a relative, love and affection may be sufficient consideration. In most states, it is customary to recite a nominal consideration, such as "$10 and other good and valuable consideration."

Granting clause A deed must contain a **granting clause**, or words of conveyance, that states the grantor's intention to convey the property. Depending on the type of deed and the obligations agreed to by the grantor, the wording would be similar to one of the following:

- "I, *JKL*, convey and warrant . . ."
- "I, *JKL*, remise, release, alienate, and convey . . ."
- "I, *JKL*, grant, bargain, and sell . . ."
- "I, *JKL*, remise, release, and quitclaim . . ."

A deed that conveys the grantor's entire fee simple interest usually contains wording such as "to *ABC* and to her heirs and assigns forever." If less than the grantor's complete fee simple interest is conveyed, such as a life estate, the wording must indicate that less than a full interest is being conveyed—for example, "to *ABC* for the duration of her natural life."

Habendum Clause When it is necessary to define or explain the ownership to be enjoyed by the grantee, a **habendum clause** may follow the granting clause. The habendum clause begins with the words *to have and to hold*. Its provisions must agree with those stated in the granting clause. For example, if a grantor conveys a time-share interest or an interest less than fee simple absolute, the habendum clause would specify the owner's rights as well as how those rights are limited (a specific time frame or certain prohibited activities, for instance).

Legal Description of Real Estate To conform to the intent of the grantor, a deed must contain an accurate legal description of the real estate conveyed. Land is considered adequately described if a professional surveyor can locate the property and accurately mark its boundaries using the description.

Exceptions and Reservations A deed may specifically note any encumbrances, reservations, or limitations that affect the title being conveyed. This might include such things as restrictions and easements that run with the land. In addition to citing existing encumbrances, a grantor may reserve some right in the land, such as an easement, for the grantor's use. A grantor may also place certain restrictions on a grantee's use of the property. Developers often restrict the number of houses that may be built on each lot in a subdivision. Such private restrictions must be stated in the deed or contained in a previously recorded document, such as the subdivider's master deed, that is expressly referred to in the deed. Many of these deed restrictions have time limits and often include renewal clauses.

Signature of Grantor To be valid, a deed must be signed by all grantors named in the deed. Some states also require witnesses to or notarization of the grantor's signature, as described below.

Most states permit someone with a *power of attorney* (written specific authority) to sign legal documents for a grantor. The person having power of attorney has written authority to execute and sign one or more legal instruments for another person. The power of attorney will be a special power of attorney if it is created only for a specific act or acts. A general power of attorney provides authority to carry out all of the business dealings of the person giving it. The person with power of attorney does not have to be an attorney-at-law, but could be. Usually, the power of attorney must be recorded in the county where the property is located.

IN PRACTICE A power of attorney can be a great convenience when all of the co-owners of a property are not available to convey title at the required time. A spouse who is out of the country, for instance, can give a special power of attorney to the other spouse so that property can be conveyed when required.

In some states, a grantor's spouse is required to sign any deed of conveyance to waive any marital or homestead rights. This requirement varies according to state law and depends on the manner in which title to real estate is held.

Many states still require a seal (or simply the word *seal*) to be written or printed after an individual grantor's signature. The corporate seal may be required of a corporate grantor.

Acknowledgment An **acknowledgment** is a formal declaration under oath that the person who signs a written document does so *voluntarily* and that the signature is genuine. The declaration is made before a registered notary public or an authorized public officer, such as a judge, justice of the peace, or some other person as prescribed by state law. An acknowledgment usually states that the person signing the deed or other document is known to the officer or has produced sufficient identification to prevent a forgery. After verifying the individual's identity, the notary public will also sign and stamp the document, which allows it to be recorded.

An acknowledgment (that is, a formal declaration before a notary public) is not essential to the validity of a deed unless it is required by state statute; however, a deed that is not acknowledged may not be legally sufficient for certain purposes. In most states, for instance, an unacknowledged deed is not eligible for recording—an important act that puts the world on notice as to who owns the property.

Transfer of title requires both delivery and acceptance of the deed.

Delivery and Acceptance A title is not considered transferred until the deed to the property is actually delivered to and accepted by the grantee. The grantor may deliver the deed to the grantee personally or through a third party.

Title is said to *pass* only when a deed is delivered and accepted. The effective date of the transfer of title from the grantor to the grantee is the date of delivery of the deed itself. Delivery and acceptance are usually presumed if the deed has been examined and registered by the county clerk.

IN PRACTICE Is there ever a time when someone would refuse a property deed? It's possible. For instance, when property is contaminated by hazardous materials, the owner may find that no one wants to buy the property, and no one wants it even as a gift. A deed attempting to convey such property can be refused by the potential grantee.

Execution of Corporate Deeds

Although state laws governing a corporation's right to convey real estate vary, two basic rules must be followed:

- A corporation can convey real estate only by the authority defined in its bylaws or on the basis of a resolution passed by its board of directors. If all or a substantial portion of a corporation's real estate is being conveyed, usually a resolution authorizing the sale must be secured from the shareholders.
- A deed conveying corporation-owned real estate can be signed only by an authorized officer.

Rules pertaining to not-for-profit corporations vary even more widely. Because the legal requirements must be followed exactly, an attorney should be consulted for all corporate conveyances.

Types of Deeds

A deed can take several forms, depending on the extent of the grantor's promises to the grantee. Regardless of any guarantees the deed offers, the grantee will want assurance that the grantor has the right to offer what the deed purports to convey. To obtain this protection, grantees commonly seek evidence of title.

The most common deeds are the following:

- General warranty deed
- Special warranty deed
- Bargain and sale deed
- Quitclaim deed
- Deed of trust
- Reconveyance deed
- Trustee's deed
- Deed executed pursuant to a court order

General Warranty Deed

- Covenant of seisin
- Covenant against encumbrances
- Covenant of further assurance
- Covenant of quiet enjoyment
- Covenant of warranty forever

General Warranty Deed A **general warranty deed** provides the greatest protection to the buyer because the grantor is legally bound by certain covenants (promises) or warranties. In most states, the warranties are implied by the use of certain words specified by statute. In some states, the grantor's warranties are expressly written into the deed itself. Each state law should be examined, but some of the specific phrases include *convey and warrant* or *warrant generally*. The basic warranties are as follows:

- *Covenant of seisin*: The grantor warrants that he or she owns the property and has the right to convey title to it. The grantee may recover damages up to the full purchase price if this covenant is broken.
- *Covenant against encumbrances*: The grantor warrants that the property is free from liens or encumbrances, except for any specifically stated in the deed. Encumbrances generally include mortgages, mechanics' liens, and easements. If this covenant is breached, the grantee may sue for the cost of removing the encumbrances.
- *Covenant of further assurances*: The grantor promises to obtain and deliver any instrument needed to make the title good. For example, if the grantor's spouse has failed to sign away dower rights, the grantor must deliver a quitclaim deed (discussed below) to clear the title.

- *Covenant of quiet enjoyment*: The grantor guarantees that the grantee's title will be good against any third party who might bring a court action to establish superior title to the property. If the grantee's title is found to be inferior, the grantor is liable for damages; that is, the grantor will pay the grantee if the title is not good.
- *Covenant of warranty forever*: The grantor promises to compensate the grantee for the loss sustained if the title fails at any time in the future.

These covenants in a general warranty deed are not limited to matters that occurred during the time the grantor owned the property; they extend back to its origins. The grantor defends the title against defects the grantor created as well as defects created by *all those who previously held title*.

Special Warranty Deed

- Warranty that grantor received title
- Warranty that property was unencumbered by grantor

Special Warranty Deed A **special warranty deed** contains two basic warranties:

- That the grantor received title
- That the property was not encumbered during the time the grantor held title, except as otherwise noted in the deed

In effect, the grantor defends the title against the grantor's actions, but not those of earlier owners of the property. The granting clause generally contains these words: "Grantor remises, releases, alienates, and conveys." The grantor may include additional warranties, but they must be specifically stated in the deed. In areas where a special warranty deed is in common use, the purchase of title insurance typically is viewed as providing adequate additional protection to the grantee.

A special warranty deed may be used by fiduciaries such as trustees, executors, and corporations. A special warranty deed is appropriate for fiduciaries because they lack the authority to warrant against acts of predecessors in title (the former owners). A fiduciary may hold title for a limited time without having a personal interest in the proceeds. Sometimes a special warranty deed is used by a grantor who has acquired title at a tax sale.

Bargain and Sale Deed

- Implication that grantor holds title and possession

Bargain and Sale Deed A **bargain and sale deed** contains no express warranties against encumbrances, but it does *imply* that the grantor holds title and possession of the property. The granting clause usually states a person's or entity's name and the phrase *grants and releases* or *grants, bargains, and sells*. Because the warranty is not specifically stated, the grantee has little legal recourse if title defects appear later. In some areas, this deed is used in foreclosures and tax sales. The buyer should purchase title insurance, if it is not provided by the seller.

A covenant against encumbrances initiated by the grantor may be added to a standard bargain and sale deed to create a *bargain and sale deed with covenant against the grantor's acts*. This deed is equivalent to a special warranty deed. Warranties used in general warranty deeds may be inserted in a bargain and sale deed to give the grantee similar protection.

Quitclaim Deed

- Used primarily to convey less than fee simple or to cure a title defect

Quitclaim Deed A **quitclaim deed** provides the grantee with the least protection of any deed. It carries *no covenants or warranties* and generally conveys only whatever interest the grantor may have when the deed is delivered. If the grantor has no interest, the grantee will acquire nothing and will have no right of warranty claim against the grantor. A quitclaim deed can convey title as effectively as a warranty deed if the grantor has good title when the deed is delivered, but it provides none of the guarantees of a warranty deed. Through a quitclaim deed, the grantor only *remises, releases, and quitclaims* the grantor's interest in the property, if any.

A quitclaim deed is usually the only type of deed used to convey less than a fee simple estate. This is because a quitclaim deed conveys only the grantor's right, title, or interest without any warranty that the grantor has any right, title, or interest.

A quitclaim deed is frequently used to cure a title defect, called a *cloud on the title*. For example, if the name of the grantee is misspelled on a warranty deed filed in the public record, a quitclaim deed with the correct spelling may be executed to the grantee to perfect the title.

A quitclaim deed is also used when a grantor has apparently *inherited* property but it is not certain that the decedent's title was valid. A warranty deed from the grantor in such an instance would oblige the grantor to warrant good title, while a quitclaim deed would convey only the grantor's interest, whatever it may be.

One of the most common uses of the quitclaim deed is for a simple transfer of property from one family member or co-owner to another.

IN PRACTICE A quitclaim deed is frequently used when real property is part of a divorce settlement. Because the parties are familiar with the property and its history, they will agree to a transfer of title without the usual protections afforded by a warranty deed, which would be demanded in a transaction between unrelated parties.

Deed of Trust

Conveyance from trustor to trustee

Deed of Trust A **deed of trust** (or *deed in trust* in some states) is the means by which a *trustor* conveys real estate to a *trustee* for the benefit of a *beneficiary*. The real estate is held by the trustee to fulfill the purpose of the trust. (*See* Figure 7.2.)

FIGURE 7.2: Trust Deeds

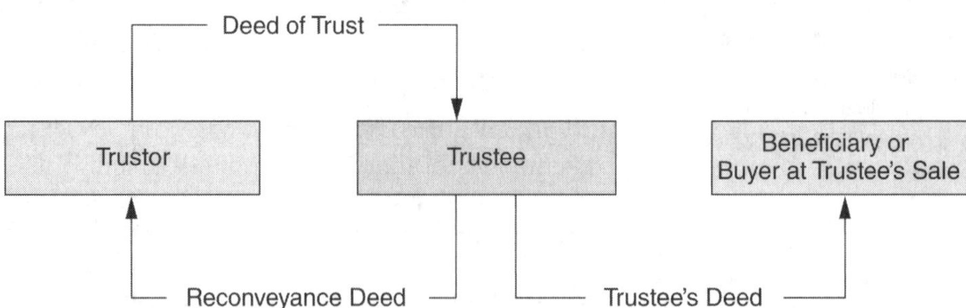

Reconveyance Deed

Conveyance from trustee back to trustor

Reconveyance Deed A **reconveyance deed** is used by a trustee to return title to the trustor. For example, when a loan secured by a deed of trust has been fully paid, the beneficiary notifies the trustee. The trustee then conveys the property back to the trustor. As with any document of title, a reconveyance deed should be recorded to prevent title problems in the future. In a "lien theory" state in which a deed of trust is treated as creating a lien on property, rather than transferring title, a document called a *satisfaction of mortgage* fulfills this same purpose.

Trustee's Deed

Conveyance from trustee to third party

Trustee's Deed A deed executed by a trustee is a **trustee's deed**. It is used when a trustee conveys real estate held in the trust to anyone other than the trustor. The trustee's deed must state that the trustee is executing the instrument in accordance with the powers and authority granted by the trust instrument.

Deed Executed Pursuant to a Court Order Executors' and administrators' deeds, masters' deeds, sheriffs' deeds, and many others are all deeds executed pursuant to a court order. These deeds are established by state statute and are used to convey title to property that is transferred by will or by court order. The form of the deed must conform to the laws of the state in which the property is located.

One common characteristic of deeds executed pursuant to court order is that the *full consideration* is usually stated in the deed. Instead of "$10 and other valuable consideration," for example, the deed would list the actual sales price.

Transfer Tax Stamps

Many states have enacted laws providing for a state **transfer tax** (also referred to in some states as a *grantor's tax*) on conveyances of real estate. In these states, the tax is usually payable when the deed is recorded. In some states, the taxpayer purchases *stamps* from the recorder of the county in which the deed is recorded and the stamps must be affixed to the deed before it can be recorded. In other states, the clerk of the court or county recorder simply collects the appropriate transfer tax amount in accordance with state and local law.

The transfer tax may be paid by either the seller or the buyer, or split between them, depending on local custom or agreement in the sales contract. The actual *tax rate* varies and may be imposed at the state, county, and/or city level. For example, the rate might be calculated as $1.10 for every $1,000 of the sales price, as $0.55 for every $500 of the sales price, or as a simple percentage of the sales price.

MATH CONCEPTS

Calculating Transfer Taxes

A state has a transfer tax of $1.50 for each $500 (or fraction of $500) of the sales price of any parcel of real estate. The transfer tax is to be paid by the seller. To calculate the transfer tax due in the sale of a $300,000 house, use the following two steps:

Value ÷ dollar amount per taxable unit = taxable units

Taxable units × rate per unit = tax

In this example:

$300,000 ÷ $500 = 600 taxable units

600 × $1.50 = $900

The seller in this transaction must pay a transfer tax of $900 to the state.

In many states, a *transfer declaration form* (or *transfer statement* or *affidavit of real property value*) must be signed by both the buyer and the seller or their real estate professionals. The transfer declaration states

- the full sales price of the property;
- its legal description;
- the type of improvement;
- the address, date, and type of deed; and
- whether the transfer is between relatives or in accordance with a court order.

Certain deeds may be *exempted* from the tax, such as the following:

- Gifts of real estate
- Deeds not made in connection with a sale (such as a change in the form of co-ownership)
- Conveyances to, from, or between government bodies
- Deeds by charitable, religious, or educational institutions
- Deeds securing debts or releasing property as security for a debt
- Partitions
- Tax deeds
- Deeds pursuant to mergers of corporations
- Deeds from subsidiary to parent corporations for cancellations of stock

INVOLUNTARY ALIENATION

Title to property may be transferred without the owner's consent by **involuntary alienation**. (*See* Figure 7.3.) Involuntary transfers are usually carried out by operation of law—such as by condemnation, foreclosure of a mortgage loan, or a sale to satisfy delinquent tax or mortgage liens. When a person dies **intestate** (without a valid will), the title to the real estate passes to the heirs identified in the state's law of *intestate succession*. If no heirs can be identified or found, the state will acquire the property by the state's power of *escheat*. Land may be acquired through the process of accretion or actually lost through erosion. Other acts of nature, such as earthquakes, hurricanes, sinkholes, and mudslides, may also change or destroy a landowner's property.

FIGURE 7.3: Involuntary Alienation

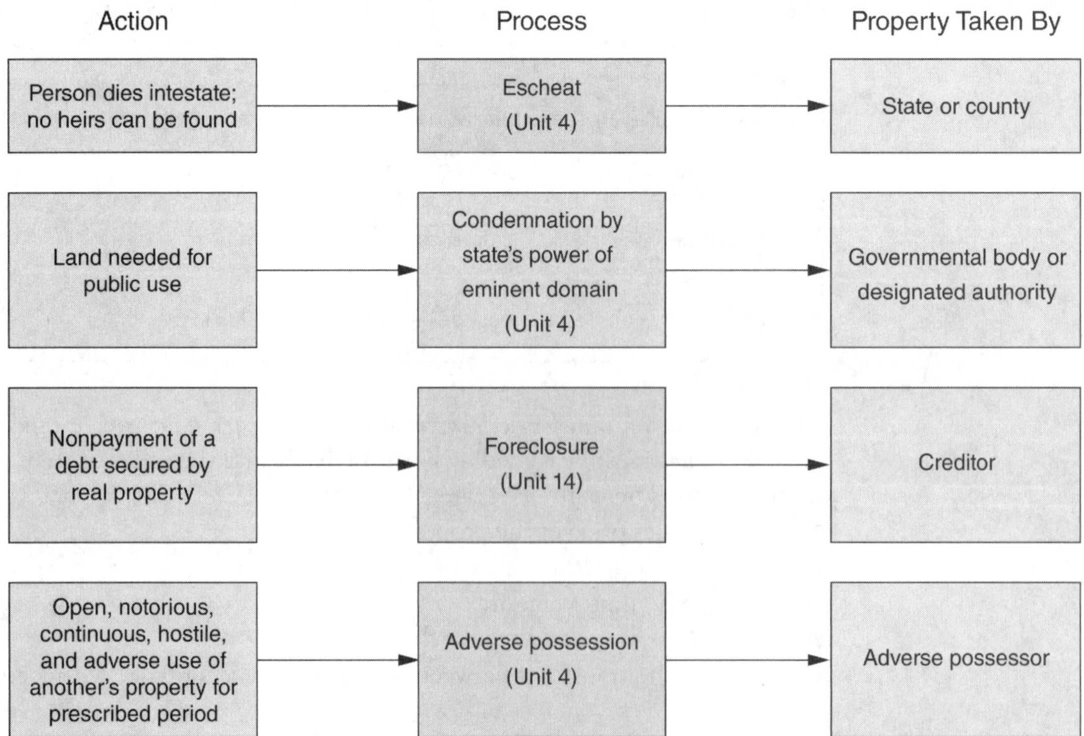

Adverse Possession

Adverse possession is another means of involuntary transfer. An individual who makes a claim to certain property, takes exclusive possession of it by excluding the true owner and any other title claimants, and (most important) uses it, may take title away from an owner who fails to use or inspect the property for a period of years. The law recognizes that the use of land is an important function of its ownership.

Adverse possession must be ONCHA:

- Open
- Notorious
- Continuous
- Hostile
- Adverse

Usually the possession by the claimant must have the following characteristics, which can be remembered as ONCHA. The property use must be

- *open*—obvious to anyone who looks,
- *notorious*—known by others,
- *continuous*—uninterrupted,
- *hostile*—without the true owner's consent, and
- *adverse*—against the true owner's right of possession.

The necessary period of uninterrupted possession is a matter of state law. The statutory periods range from as few as 5 years in some states to as many as 30 years in others. A shorter time period may be accompanied by the requirement for the adverse possessor to make all property tax payments. A state may allow subsequent adverse owners to *tack* their years of possession together to create the necessary period of adverse use. A subsequent adverse owner usually must take possession under a claim of right, or *color of title*, such as a deed from the prior adverse owner that purports to convey ownership of the property.

To claim legal title, the adverse possessor normally files an action in court to receive undisputed title.

IN PRACTICE Acquiring title to property by a claim of adverse possession is not a common occurrence. Usually, a claim arises when the titleholder isn't paying attention to the property, which may happen when the owner does not live nearby or if the property is bequeathed to someone who doesn't visit the property. A homeowner who thoughtfully cares for a neighboring vacant property may be tempted to think of applying the concept of adverse possession. Keep in mind, however, that the right of adverse possession is a statutory right. State requirements must be followed carefully to ensure the successful transfer of title. Those who think they might make such a claim should not wait until the end of the statutory period to consult an attorney; doing so early in the process will ensure that all the statutory requirements are met.

CONVEYANCE OF A DECEDENT'S PROPERTY

A person who dies **testate** has prepared a will indicating how his or her real and personal property will be disposed of at the time of death. As discussed earlier, when a person dies **intestate** (without a valid will), real estate and personal property pass to the decedent's heirs according to the state's *statute of descent and distribution*. In effect, the state makes a will for an intestate decedent.

When a person dies, ownership of real estate passes to

- the co-owner by virtue of a joint tenancy with right of survivorship or a tenancy by the entirety;
- the party or parties named in a valid will; or
- the statutory heirs determined by the state's law of descent and distribution.

Title to property held in joint tenancy with right of survivorship or in tenancy by the entirety needs no court action for title to pass, but the death certificate should be filed so that it becomes part of the record of property ownership.

When title passes by will or descent, the estate must go through a judicial process called **probate** in which the successor to the property title will be recognized; usually, claims against the estate must be satisfied before the designated individual(s) can take possession of the property. The party named in a will could be the trustee of either an existing trust or a *testamentary trust* established by the will.

Transfer of Title by Will

A **will** is made by a property owner to convey title to real and personal property after the owner's death. This type of property transfer differs from a deed, which *must* be delivered during the lifetime of the grantor and that conveys a present interest in property. While the **testator**, the person who makes a will, is alive, any property included in the will can still be conveyed by the owner. The parties named in a will have no rights or interests as long as the party who made the will is alive; they acquire interest or title only after the owner's death.

Only property owned by the testator at the time of the testator's death may be transferred by will. The gift of real property by will is known as a **devise**, and a person who receives real property by will is known as a *devisee*. The will can also include a bequest of a legacy, which is a gift of personal property.

For title to pass to the devisees, state laws require that, on the death of a testator, the will be filed with the court and probated. *Probate* is the formal judicial process for verifying the validity of a will and accounting for the decedent's assets, and is discussed below. The process can take several months—or considerably longer—to complete before the estate is *settled*.

A will cannot supersede the state laws of dower, curtesy, and homestead, which were enacted to protect the inheritance rights of a surviving spouse in certain real property owned by the decedent. In most states, the surviving spouse is further protected by a statute that provides for certain personal property of the decedent to go to the surviving spouse if the will does not provide the minimum statutory inheritance. In either case, the surviving spouse must decide whether or not to contest the will.

Legal Requirements for Making a Will A will must be prepared and executed according to the laws of the state in which the testator resides. If the testator owns property in any other state, the will should also comply with the laws of the state in which the real estate is located.

A testator must have legal capacity to make a will. There are no rigid tests to determine legal capacity. Usually, a person must be of *legal age* and of *sound mind*. Legal age varies from state to state. To demonstrate sound mind, the testator must have sufficient mental capacity to understand the nature and extent of the property the testator owns. A testator must also understand that the described property will go to those persons named in the will, who may or may not be the testator's natural heirs—those persons identified by the state law of descent and distribution. The drawing of a will must be a voluntary act, free of any undue influence by other people.

In most states, a written will must be signed by its testator before two or more witnesses, who must also sign the document. The witnesses should not be individuals who are named in the will as recipients of any property. Some states still recognize oral (*nuncupative*) wills or entirely handwritten (*holographic*) wills. Other states do not permit real property to be conveyed by anything other than a formally witnessed, written will.

While living, a testator may alter a will at any time. Any modification or addition to a previously executed will is contained in a separate document called a *codicil*, which must comply with state law to be valid.

Transfer of Title by Descent

Under a state's statute of descent and distribution, the primary **heirs** of the deceased are the surviving spouse and children by birth or adoption, but the statute will also identify other close blood relatives in the event that the decedent has no surviving spouse or children, including parents, brothers, sisters, aunts, uncles, and, in some cases, first and second cousins. The right to inherit under laws of descent varies from state to state, and the property of someone who dies intestate is distributed according to the laws of the state in which the property is located. Figure 7.4 illustrates how a state's statute of descent and distribution might provide for an intestate's estate. The specific persons entitled to property, and the various percentages involved, vary from state to state. A real estate professional should never try to determine descent or ownership without consulting legal counsel.

FIGURE 7.4: Sample Statutory Distributions

Decedent Status	Family Status	How Property Passes
Married, surviving spouse[1]	No children No other relatives	100% to surviving spouse
Married, surviving spouse	Children	50% to surviving spouse 50% shared by children or descendants of deceased child
Married, no surviving spouse	Children	Children share equally, with descendants of a deceased child taking their parent's share
Unmarried, no children	Relatives	100% to father or mother, brothers or sisters, or other relatives (such as grandparents or great-grandparents; uncles or aunts; nieces or nephews; first or second cousins) in order of priority
	No relatives or heirs as defined by state law	100% to state by escheat

[1] Some states allow the decedent's spouse the right to elect a life estate of dower or curtesy in place of the share provided for in the law of descent.

Probate

Probate is a formal judicial process. Probate proceedings take place in the county *in which the decedent last resided.* If the decedent owned real estate in another county, probate would occur in that county as well.

The person who has possession of the will presents it for filing with the court. The court is responsible for determining that the will meets the statutory requirements for its form and execution. If the will was modified or if more than one will exists, the court will decide how these documents should be probated.

The probate court acts on its own volition as well as through the *executor* named in the will or an *administrator* or personal representative appointed by the court if there is no will, or the will fails to name an executor. The court

- publishes required notices of the pending probate;
- proves or confirms the validity of the will, including ruling on any challenges to the will;
- determines the precise assets in the estate of the deceased person; and
- identifies the people to whom the estate's assets are to pass.

The purpose of probate is to properly allocate and distribute the assets of the deceased. All assets must be accounted for, and the decedent's debts must be satisfied before any property is distributed to the heirs. In addition, applicable federal estate taxes and state inheritance taxes must be paid before any distribution. The laws of each state govern probate proceedings as well as the functions of the individuals appointed by will or the court to administer the decedent's affairs. The specific persons entitled to property, and the various percentages involved, vary from state to state.

IN PRACTICE A real estate broker entering into a listing agreement with the executor or administrator of an estate in probate should be aware that the amount of commission is approved by the court and that the commission is payable only from the proceeds of the sale. The real estate broker will not be able to collect a commission unless the court approves the sale.

In some states, the probate process is not unduly cumbersome, but in other states, it can be lengthy and expensive. One way in which property owners can avoid the delay and expense of probate is by establishing a *living trust* while still living and transferring title to real and personal property to the trust. In a revocable living trust, the person establishing the trust is the trustor as well as the trustee and the terms of the trust can be changed at any time (or terminated) during the life of the trustor. On the trustor's death, the trust need not go through a probate proceeding as title automatically passes to the beneficiary named in the trust.

There are many more details to creation of a living trust, more than be covered adequately here. The advice of an attorney should be sought to create the trust, to successfully transfer property to it, and to file the necessary documentation on the death of the trustor. It is important that all of the trustor's property be transferred to the trust, or part of the estate will still have to go through probate. The living trust also has no effect on the value of the estate for estate tax purposes.

KEY POINT REVIEW

Title is the right to or ownership of land, and can also be evidence of that ownership.

Voluntary alienation is the transfer of title to real estate by **gift** or **sale** during one's life, using some form of **deed**. To create a valid deed, the **grantor** (person who transfers title) must be of legal age and legally competent to execute (sign) the deed. A deed executed by a **minor** is **voidable**. The **grantee** must be identifiable with sufficient certainty.

Consideration (payment) of some form must be stated to record a deed. **The granting clause** (words of conveyance) must be used. The **habendum clause** defines the ownership interest taken by the grantee. An accurate **legal description** of the property conveyed is essential. **Exceptions** or **reservations** to the full transfer of all of the rights of ownership must be noted.

The signature of the grantor(s) must be **acknowledged** by a notary public or other official authorized by the state in which the property is located. Finally, there must be a **delivery** of the deed **and its acceptance** by the grantee.

Types of deeds include the **general warranty deed**, which provides the greatest protection to the grantee and includes the **covenant of seisin, covenant against encumbrances, covenant of further assurances, covenant of quiet enjoyment,** and **covenant of warranty forever**.

The **special warranty deed** includes the warranties that the grantor received title and that the property was not encumbered during the time the grantor held title, except as otherwise noted.

The **bargain and sale deed** implies that the grantor holds title and possession of the property, but there are no express warranties against encumbrances.

The **quitclaim deed** provides the least protection of any deed as it carries no covenants or warranties, and conveys only whatever interest the grantor may have when the deed is delivered.

With a **deed of trust**, a **trustor** conveys real estate to a **trustee** for the benefit of a **beneficiary**. A **reconveyance deed** is used by the trustee to return title to the trustor, but a **trustee's deed** conveys the property to someone other than the trustor. There may also be a **deed executed pursuant to a court order**.

Transfer tax stamps may be required to record a deed.

Involuntary alienation (transfer) of title to property is usually by operation of law. **Using the government's power of eminent domain,** property can be taken for a public purpose, with just compensation paid to the owner. In a **foreclosure,** property is taken by a creditor for nonpayment of a debt secured by real property. **In the process called escheat,** property is taken by the state when no heirs of the deceased can be found.

Property can be acquired by adverse possession when someone who is not the lawful owner takes exclusive possession of the property for the length of time specified by state law in a way that is ONCHA: **open, notorious, continuous, hostile**, and **adverse to the interest of the true owner**.

Transfer of title by will occurs when someone dies **testate** (leaving a valid will, prepared as required by state law). A will takes effect only after death and can be changed by **codicil** or revoked while the **testator** is still alive.

A **devise** is a gift of real property by will to the **devisee**. A **bequest** or **legacy** is a gift of personal property.

To pass title to property on death, a will must be **filed with the court** and **probated**.

Wills cannot supersede state laws protecting inheritance rights of a surviving spouse (**dower** or **curtesy**, or benefits granted by homestead laws).

Transfer of title under a state's **statute of descent and distribution** occurs when a person dies **intestate** (without a valid will). The laws of the state where real property is **located** govern property distribution.

UNIT 7 QUIZ

1. The basic requirements for a valid conveyance are governed by
   a. state law.
   b. local custom.
   c. national law.
   d. the law of descent.

2. Every deed must be signed by the
   a. grantor.
   b. grantee.
   c. grantor and grantee.
   d. devisee.

3. A 15-year-old boy recently inherited many parcels of real estate from his late father and has decided to sell one of them. If the boy enters into a deed conveying his interest in the property to a purchaser, such a conveyance would be
   a. valid.
   b. void.
   c. invalid.
   d. voidable.

4. A form authorizing one person to execute documents for another is called a
   a. power of attorney.
   b. release deed.
   c. quitclaim deed.
   d. power to represent.

5. The grantee receives greatest protection with what type of deed?
   a. Quitclaim
   b. General warranty
   c. Bargain and sale with covenant
   d. Executor's

6. Party Y receives a deed from party X. The granting clause of the deed states, "I hereby remise, release, alienate, and convey to Y the following real property." What type of deed has Y received?
   a. Special warranty
   b. Quitclaim
   c. General warranty
   d. Bargain and sale

7. Under the covenant of quiet enjoyment, grantors
   a. promise to obtain and deliver any instrument needed to make the title good.
   b. warrant that the property is free from liens and encumbrances.
   c. warrant that he or she is the owner and has the right to convey title to the property.
   d. ensure that the title will be good against the title claims of third parties.

8. Which type of deed merely implies but does *NOT* specifically warrant that the grantor holds good title to the property?
   a. Special warranty
   b. Bargain and sale
   c. Quitclaim
   d. Trust deed

9. Step 1: A decided to convey a house to B.

   Step 2: A signed a deed transferring title to B.

   Step 3: A gave the signed deed to B, who accepted it.

   Step 4: B took the deed to the county recorder's office and had it recorded.

   At which step did title to the house actually transfer or pass to B?
   a. Step 1
   b. Step 2
   c. Step 3
   d. Step 4

10. P signed a deed transferring ownership of P's house to Q. To provide evidence that P's signature was genuine, P executed a declaration before a notary. This declaration is known as an
    a. affidavit.
    b. acknowledgment.
    c. affirmation.
    d. estoppel.

11. Title to real estate may be transferred during a person's lifetime by
    a. devise.
    b. descent.
    c. involuntary alienation.
    d. escheat.

12. A woman bought acreage in a distant county, never went to see the acreage, and did not use the ground. A man moved his mobile home onto the land, had a water well drilled, and lived there for 22 years. The man may become the owner of the land if he has complied with the state law regarding
   a. requirements for a valid conveyance.
   b. adverse possession.
   c. avulsion.
   d. voluntary alienation.

13. Eminent domain and escheat are two examples of
   a. voluntary alienation.
   b. adverse possession.
   c. transfers of title by descent.
   d. involuntary alienation.

14. A deed contains a promise that the title conveyed is good and a promise to obtain and deliver any documents necessary to ensure good title. This deed contains an example of which covenant?
   a. Further assurances
   b. Seisin
   c. Quiet enjoyment
   d. Warranty forever

15. A deed contains a guarantee that the grantor will compensate the grantee for any loss resulting from the title's failure in the future. This is an example of which covenant?
   a. Warranty forever
   b. Further assurance
   c. Quiet enjoyment
   d. Seisin

16. A person who has died without a valid will has died
   a. testate.
   b. in valid conveyance.
   c. intestate.
   d. under the acknowledgment clause.

17. Title to real estate can be transferred upon death by what type of document?
   a. Warranty deed
   b. Special warranty deed
   c. Quitclaim deed
   d. Will

18. An owner of real estate was declared legally incompetent and was committed to a state mental institution. While institutionalized, the owner wrote and executed a will. The owner died while still institutionalized and was survived by a spouse and three children. The real estate will pass
   a. to the owner's spouse.
   b. to the heirs mentioned in the owner's will.
   c. according to the state laws of descent.
   d. to the state.

19. Generally, where does a probate proceeding involving real property take place?
   a. Only in the county in which the property is located
   b. Only in the county in which the decedent resided
   c. In both the county where the decedent resided and the county in which the property is located
   d. In the county in which the executor or the beneficiary resides

20. A deed states that the grantors are conveying all their rights and interests to the grantees to have and to hold. This is communicated in the
   a. acknowledgment clause.
   b. restriction clause.
   c. covenant of seisin.
   d. habendum clause.

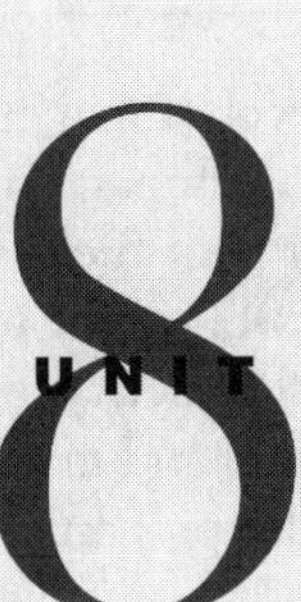

Title Records

LEARNING OBJECTIVES

When you have finished reading this unit, you will be able to

- **explain** the public recordation system and its importance to the title insurer;
- **explain** the benefits of title insurance and the difference between an owner's policy and a lender's policy; and
- **define** the following *key terms*:

abstract of title	chain of title	subrogation
action to quiet title	constructive notice	title insurance
actual notice	marketable title	title search
attorney's opinion of title	priority	Torrens system
certificate of title	recording	

OVERVIEW

Public records are open to anyone interested in a particular property. A review of the records will reveal the documents, claims, and other details that affect the property's ownership. A prospective buyer, for example, needs to be sure that the seller can convey good title to the property. If the property is subject to any liens or other encumbrances, a prospective buyer or lender needs to know. An attorney or title company typically performs a search of the public records to ensure that good title is being conveyed. A real estate professional should understand what is in the public record and what the searchers may find.

PUBLIC RECORDS

Public records contain detailed information about each parcel of real estate in a city or county. These records are crucial in establishing ownership, giving notice of encumbrances, and establishing priority of liens. They protect the interests of real estate owners, taxing bodies, creditors, and the general public. The real estate recording system includes written documents that affect title, such as deeds and mortgages. Public records regarding taxes, judgments, probate, and marriage also may offer important information about the title to a particular property.

Depending on the jurisdiction in which property is located, the public records are maintained by

- recorders of deeds,
- county clerks,
- county treasurers,
- city clerks,
- collectors, and
- clerks of court.

IN PRACTICE Prospective buyers rarely search public records for evidence of title or encumbrances themselves. Instead, *title companies,* attorneys, and lenders conduct the searches. Real estate professionals should not perform title searches for their clients or customers, even if qualified to do so, because of conflict of interest concerns.

Recording

In most states, written documents that affect land *must be recorded in the county where the land is located.*

Recording is the act of placing documents in the public record. The specific rules for recording documents are a matter of state law. Although the details may vary, all recording acts essentially provide that any written document that affects any estate, right, title, or interest in land must be recorded in the county (or, in some states, the town) where the land is located to serve as public notice. This way, anyone interested in the title to a parcel of property will know where to look to discover the various interests of all other parties. Recording acts also generally give legal priority to those interests recorded first—the *first in time, first in right* or *first come, first served* principle. There are exceptions to this principle, such as liens for property taxes, special assessments, and delinquent amounts owed to the Internal Revenue Service.

To be *eligible for recording,* a document must be drawn and executed according to state law. For instance, a state may require that the parties' names be typed below their signatures or that the document be acknowledged before a notary public. In some states, the document must be witnessed. Others require that the name of the person who prepared the document appear on it. States may have specific rules about the size of documents and the color and quality of paper they are printed on. Electronic recording by computer or fax is permitted in a growing number of localities. Some states require a certificate of real estate value and the payment of current property taxes due for recording.

Notice

Anyone with an interest in a parcel of real estate can take certain steps, called *giving notice*, to ensure that the existence of the interest is made available to the public. The two basic types of notice that can be given are **constructive notice** and **actual notice**.

Constructive notice is the legal presumption that information has been obtained by an individual through due diligence. A document placed in the public record serves as notice to the world of an individual's right or interest in the property. Physical possession of property also serves as constructive notice of the right of the person in possession. Because the information or evidence is readily available to the world, a prospective purchaser or lender is responsible for discovering the interest and is presumed to have done so.

Actual notice means not only that information of an interest in property is available but also that someone is actually aware of it. An individual who has searched the public records or inspected the property has actual notice of what is contained in the records or obvious from the property inspection. If it can be proved that an individual has had actual notice of a property right, that person cannot use a lack of constructive notice (such as an unrecorded deed) to justify a claim.

Priority

Priority refers to the order of when documents or liens were recorded. Many complicated situations can affect the priority of rights in a parcel of real estate—who received a property interest first, who recorded the interest first, who was in possession first, or who had actual or constructive notice. How the courts rule in any situation depends, of course, on the specific facts of the case. These are strictly legal questions that should be referred to the parties' attorneys.

IN PRACTICE Buyer A purchased a property from seller B and received a deed. Buyer A did not record the deed but took possession of the property in June. In November, B sold the same property to buyer C who received a deed, which C promptly recorded. C never inspected the property to determine if someone was in possession of it. In this case, by taking possession of the property, A has the superior right to the property even though A did not record the deed.

Unrecorded Documents

Certain types of liens are not recorded. Real estate taxes and special assessments are liens on specific parcels of real estate and are not usually recorded until after the taxes or assessments are past due, although some states create a lien right in unpaid taxes from the beginning of the period for which tax is owed. Inheritance taxes and franchise taxes, where applicable, are statutory liens and are placed against all real estate owned by a decedent at the time of death or by a corporation at the time the franchise taxes became a lien. Like real estate taxes, they are not recorded.

Notice of these liens must be gained from sources other than the recorder's office. Evidence of the payment of real estate taxes, special assessments, municipal utilities, and other taxes can be gathered from the tax collector's office, paid tax receipts, and letters from municipalities. Creative measures are often required to get information about *off the record* liens.

Chain of Title

The **chain of title** is the record of a property's ownership. Beginning with the earliest owner, a title may pass to many individuals. Because the grantee of the first deed to the property will become the grantor of the next transfer of title, each owner is linked to the next so that a chain is formed. In same way, the title can be worked backward by searching for the record in which the present grantor of the property right received title as the grantee. An unbroken chain of title thus can be traced through conveyances from the present owner back to the earliest recorded owner, and then forward from the earliest recorded owner to the present owner. The chain of title does not include liens and encumbrances or any other document not directly related to ownership.

If ownership cannot be traced through an unbroken chain, a gap in the chain of title or *cloud on the title* is said to exist. In such a case, it is necessary to establish ownership by a court action called an **action to quiet title**. For instance, legal action might be required if a grantor acquired title under one name and conveyed it under another name. Evidence will be presented in court to prove that the grantee in the first transfer is the grantor in the second transfer.

IN PRACTICE There may be a forged deed in the chain of title, which means that no subsequent grantee, even though innocent of the forgery, acquired legal title. In an action to quiet title brought by an individual currently living on the property and claiming title many years after the forgery, the individual may claim the right of ownership by virtue of adverse possession. Legal title could be acquired by adverse possession even in the case of an invalid document in the chain of title if there were the necessary years of property occupancy (typically, a higher requirement if a forgery has occurred) accompanied by the "color of title" provided by what appeared to each successive owner to be a valid deed.

Title Search and Abstract of Title

A **title search** is an examination of the public records to determine whether any defects exist in the chain of title. The records of the conveyances of ownership are examined, beginning with the present owner. Then the title is traced backward to its origin (or 40 to 60 years or some definite period of time, depending on state statute). The time beyond which the title must be searched can be limited in states that have adopted the Marketable Title Act. These states recognize that a review of the same records from, say, the 1800s, over and over again for each conveyance is not a productive use of time or money. This law also extinguishes certain interests and cures certain defects arising before the root of the title is found—the conveyance that establishes the source of the chain of title.

Other public records are examined to identify wills, judicial proceedings, and other encumbrances that may affect title. These include a variety of taxes, special assessments, and other recorded liens.

A full **abstract of title** is a summary report of what the title search found in the public records. The person who prepares this report is called an *abstractor*. The abstractor searches all the public records and then summarizes the various events and proceedings that affected the title throughout its history. The report begins with the original grant (or root) and then provides a chronological list of recorded instruments. All recorded liens and encumbrances are included, along with their current status. A list of all of the public records examined is also provided as evidence of the scope of the search.

IN PRACTICE An abstract of title is a condensed history of those items that can be found in public records. It does not reveal such items as encroachments or forgeries or any interests or conveyances that have not been recorded.

Marketable Title

Under the terms of the typical real estate sales contract, the seller is required to deliver to the buyer **marketable title** to the property—that is, title that is acceptable to a reasonably prudent person and which will not subject the buyer to litigation. To be marketable, a title must

- disclose no serious defects and not depend on doubtful questions of law or fact to prove its validity;
- not expose a purchaser to the hazard of litigation or threaten the quiet enjoyment of the property; and
- convince a reasonably well-informed and prudent purchaser, acting on business principles and with knowledge of the facts and their legal significance, that the purchaser could sell or mortgage the property at a later time.

Although a title that does not meet these requirements still can be transferred, it contains certain defects that may limit or restrict its ownership. A buyer cannot be forced to accept a conveyance that is materially different from the one bargained for in the sales contract, but questions of marketable title must be raised by a buyer *before acceptance of the deed.* Once a buyer has accepted a deed with unmarketable title, the only available legal recourse may be to sue the seller under any covenants of warranty contained in the deed.

In some states, a preliminary title search is conducted as soon as an offer to purchase has been accepted. In fact, it may be customary to include a contingency in the sales contract that gives the buyer the right to review and approve the title report before proceeding with the purchase. A preliminary title report also benefits the seller by giving the seller an early opportunity to cure title defects.

PROOF OF OWNERSHIP

Proof of ownership is evidence that title is marketable. A deed by itself is not considered sufficient evidence of ownership. Even though a warranty deed conveys the grantor's interest, it contains no proof of the condition of the grantor's title at the time of the conveyance. The grantee needs assurance that ownership is actually being acquired and that the title is marketable. A certificate of title, title insurance, or a Torrens certificate is commonly used to prove ownership.

Certificate of Title

A **certificate of title** is a statement of opinion of the title's status on the date the certificate is issued. *A certificate of title is not a guarantee of ownership.* Rather, it certifies the condition of the title based on an examination of the public records—a title search. The certificate may be prepared by a title company, licensed abstractor, or attorney. An owner, mortgage lender, or buyer may request the certificate.

Although a certificate of title is used as evidence of ownership, it is not perfect. Unrecorded liens or rights of parties in possession cannot be discovered by a search of the public records. Hidden defects, such as transfers involving forged documents, incorrect marital information, incompetent parties, minors, or fraud, cannot be detected. A certificate offers no defense against these defects because they are unknown. The person who prepares the certificate is liable only for negligence in preparing the certificate.

IN PRACTICE You earlier learned about the phrase *color of title*. Title may be conveyed in a transaction by a written instrument (such as a deed or will) that is actually inadequate to legally transfer ownership, whether because it was incorrectly executed or because it was executed by someone who did not, in fact, hold title in the first place. State law will specify how title may be perfected (made legally valid) in the event that there is a defect in the title.

An abstract and **attorney's opinion of title** are used in some areas of the country as evidence of title. It is an opinion of the status of the title based on a review of the abstract. Similar to a certificate of title, the opinion of title does not protect against defects that cannot be discovered from the public records. Many buyers purchase title insurance to defend the title from these defects.

Title Insurance

Title insurance is a contract under which the policyholder is protected from losses arising from defects in the title. A title insurance company determines whether the title is insurable, based on a review of the public records. If so, a policy is issued. Unlike other insurance policies that insure against *future losses*, title insurance protects the insured from an event that occurred *before* the policy was issued. Title insurance is considered the best defense of title: the title insurance company will defend any lawsuit based on an insurable defect and pay claims if the title proves to be defective.

After examining the public records, the title company usually issues what may be called a preliminary report of title or a commitment to issue a title policy. This describes the type of policy that will be issued and includes

- the name of the insured party;
- the legal description of the real estate;
- the estate or interest covered;
- conditions and stipulations under which the policy is issued; and
- a schedule of all exceptions, including encumbrances and defects found in the public records and any known unrecorded defects.

The premium for the policy is paid once, at closing. The maximum loss for which the company may be liable cannot exceed the face amount of the policy (unless the amount of coverage has been extended by use of an inflation rider). When a title company makes a payment to settle a claim covered by a policy, the company generally acquires the right to any remedy or damages available to the insured. This right is called **subrogation.**

Coverage Exactly which defects the title company will defend depends on the type of policy. (*See* Figure 8.1.) A standard coverage policy normally insures the title as it is known from the public records. In addition, the standard policy insures against such hidden defects as forged documents, conveyances by incompetent grantors, incorrect marital statements, and improperly delivered deeds.

FIGURE 8.1: Owner's Title Insurance Policy

Standard Coverage	Extended Coverage	Not Covered by Either Policy
Defects found in public records Forged documents Incompetent grantors Incorrect marital statements Improperly delivered deeds	Standard coverage plus defects discoverable through the following: ■ Property inspection, including unrecorded rights of persons in possession ■ Examination of survey ■ Unrecorded liens not known by policyholder	Defects and liens listed in policy Defects known to buyer Changes in land use brought about by zoning ordinances

Extended coverage as provided by an *American Land Title Association (ALTA) policy* includes the protections of a standard policy plus additional protections. An extended policy protects the homeowner against defects that may be discovered by inspection of the property: rights of parties in possession, examination of a survey, and certain unrecorded liens. Most real estate sales contracts will include a requirement that an ALTA policy be provided.

Title insurance does not offer guaranteed protection against all defects. A title company will not insure a bad title or offer protection against defects that clearly appear in a title search. The policy generally lists certain uninsurable losses, called exclusions. These exclusions typically include zoning ordinances, restrictive covenants, easements, certain water rights, and current taxes and special assessments.

IN PRACTICE Certain conditions that have been discovered in the title examination, such as encroachments or property improvements that violate zoning requirements (building setback requirements, for example), as well as existing oil and gas leases, will also be excluded from coverage. A defect may be so severe that the title insurance company will refuse to issue a policy, creating an insurmountable obstacle to completing a transaction.

Types of Policies The different types of title insurance policies depend on who is named as the insured. An *owner's policy* is issued for the benefit of the owner (new buyer) and the owner's heirs or devisees and is issued for the property's purchase price. A lender's policy (mortgagee policy) is issued for the benefit of the mortgage lender and the amount of the mortgage loan will determine the amount of the coverage.

The Torrens System

As described previously, the **Torrens system** is a legal registration system used to verify ownership of real estate. Where it is recognized, registration in the Torrens system provides evidence of title without the need for an additional search of the public records. Under the Torrens system, an owner of real property submits a written application to register a title. The application is submitted to the court clerk of the county in which the real estate is located. If the applicant proves ownership, the court enters an order to register the real estate. The registrar of titles is directed to issue a certificate of title. The original Torrens certificate of title in the registrar's office reveals the owner of the land and all mortgages, judgments, and similar liens. It does not, however, reveal federal or state taxes and some other items. The Torrens title system of registration relies on the physical title document itself; a person acquires title only when it is registered.

KEY POINT REVIEW

Constructive notice of a document is assumed when **due diligence** (such as a search of public records and inspection of the property) would reveal its existence. **Actual notice** means that an individual has **direct knowledge** of documents in the public records and facts revealed by an inspection of the property.

To serve as **constructive notice**, and provide **priority** over subsequent documents, a **written document** that affects an **estate**, **right**, **title**, or **interest** in **land** must be **drafted** and **executed** according to state law (**recording acts**) and must be **recorded** in the **public records** that are maintained by the designated **official**, such as the recorder of deeds, county clerk, or city clerk, in the **county** (or city) in which the **property is located**.

Public records are typically **searched** by **title companies** that provide **title insurance** to prospective purchasers based on what the search reveals.

Unrecorded documents that may affect title, such as a tax lien, may not be recorded immediately, yet are still given priority by law and require a search of tax records and other sources.

The **chain of title** is a record of property ownership, but it does not include liens and other encumbrances. A **gap** in the chain or other dispute of ownership creates a **cloud on the title**, which is resolved by a **suit to quiet title**.

An **abstract of title**, prepared by an **abstractor** or an **attorney**, is a **summary** report of what the title search reveals. It includes all **recorded liens and encumbrances** and lists **records searched** but does not indicate forgeries and interests that are unrecorded or could be discovered by property inspection.

A **marketable title** is one that a reasonably well-informed and prudent purchaser would accept because it does **not have serious defects** and does not rely on doubtful questions of law or fact to prove its validity, so that it does not expose the purchaser to litigation or threaten the purchaser's **quiet enjoyment** of the property.

Title insurance is issued as an **owner's policy** or **mortgagee's policy** and protects the insured from losses arising from defects in title and hidden defects, but it also identifies **exclusions** from coverage that typically include readily apparent title defects, zoning, and others.

The **Torrens system** provides a **certificate of title** issued by the county clerk that requires no further search to validate.

UNIT 8 QUIZ

1. A title search in the public records may be conducted by
   a. anyone.
   b. attorneys and abstractors only.
   c. attorneys, abstractors, and real estate professionals only.
   d. anyone who obtains a court order under the Freedom of Information Act.

2. Which statement *BEST* explains why instruments affecting real estate are recorded?
   a. Recording gives constructive notice to the world of the rights and interests claimed in the identified parcel of real estate.
   b. Failing to record will void the transfer.
   c. The instruments must be recorded to comply with the terms of the statute of frauds.
   d. Recording proves the execution of the instrument.

3. A purchaser went to the county building to check the recorder's records, which showed that the seller was the grantee in the last recorded deed and that no mortgage was on record against the property. The purchaser may assume which of the following?
   a. All taxes are paid and no judgments are outstanding.
   b. The seller has good title.
   c. The seller did not mortgage the property.
   d. No one else is occupying the property.

4. The date and time a document was recorded help establish which of the following?
   a. Priority
   b. Abstract of title
   c. Subrogation
   d. Marketable title

5. A buyer bought a house, received a deed, and moved into the residence but neglected to record the document. One week later, the seller died and the heirs in another city, unaware that the property had been sold, conveyed title to a relative, who recorded the deed. Who owns the property?
   a. The buyer
   b. The relative
   c. The seller's heirs
   d. Both the buyer and the relative

6. A property with encumbrances that will outlast the closing
   a. cannot be sold.
   b. can be sold only if title insurance is provided.
   c. cannot have a deed recorded without a survey.
   d. can be sold if a buyer agrees to take it subject to the encumbrances.

7. Which of the following would *NOT* be acceptable evidence of ownership?
   a. Attorney's opinion
   b. Title insurance policy
   c. Abstract
   d. Deed to the current owner signed by the last seller

8. Chain of title is *MOST* accurately defined as
   a. a history of all documents and legal proceedings affecting a specific parcel of land.
   b. a report of the contents of the public record regarding a particular property.
   c. an instrument or document that protects the insured parties (subject to specific exceptions) against defects in the record of a property's ownership.
   d. the examination of the record and hidden risks such as forgeries, undisclosed heirs, errors in the public records, and so on.

9. A seller delivered title to a buyer at closing. A title search had disclosed no serious defects, and the title did not appear to be based on doubtful questions of law or fact or to expose the buyer to possible litigation. The seller's title did not appear to present a threat to the buyer's quiet enjoyment, and the title insurance policy provided was sufficient to convince a reasonably well-informed person that the property could be resold. The title conveyed would commonly be referred to as a(n)
   a. certificate of title.
   b. abstract of title.
   c. marketable title.
   d. attorney's opinion of title.

10. The person who prepares an abstract of title for a parcel of real estate
   a. searches the public records and then summarizes the events and proceedings that affect title.
   b. insures the condition of the title.
   c. inspects the property.
   d. issues title insurance.

11. Homeowners are frantic because they want to sell their property and the deed is missing. Which of the following is *TRUE*?
   a. They may need to sue for quiet title.
   b. They must buy title insurance.
   c. They do not need the original deed if it has been recorded.
   d. They should execute a replacement deed to themselves.

12. Mortgagee title policies protect which parties against loss?
   a. Buyers
   b. Sellers
   c. Lenders
   d. Buyers and lenders

13. Which of the following are traditionally covered by a standard title insurance policy?
   a. Unrecorded rights of persons in possession
   b. Improperly delivered deeds
   c. Changes in land use because of zoning ordinances
   d. Unrecorded liens not known to the policyholder

14. A written summary of the history of all conveyances and legal proceedings affecting a specific parcel of real estate is called a(n)
   a. adjustment of title.
   b. certificate of title.
   c. abstract of title.
   d. title insurance policy.

15. Which of the following is *NOT* covered by a standard title insurance policy?
   a. Forged documents
   b. Incorrect marital statements
   c. Unrecorded rights of parties in possession
   d. Incompetent grantors

16. Documents referred to as title evidence include
   a. policies of title insurance.
   b. general warranty deeds.
   c. security agreements.
   d. special warranty deeds.

17. All of the following are true regarding public records *EXCEPT*
   a. they give notice of encumbrances.
   b. they establish priority of liens.
   c. they guarantee marketable title.
   d. they provide constructive notice of interests in the identified property.

18. A sells a portion of property to B. B promptly records the deed in the appropriate county office. If A tries to sell the same portion of property to C, which of the following statements is *TRUE*?
   a. C has been given constructive notice of the prior sale because B promptly recorded the deed.
   b. C has been given actual notice of the prior sale because B promptly recorded the deed.
   c. Because C's purchase of the property is the more recent, it will have priority over B's interest, regardless of when B recorded the deed.
   d. Because C purchased the property from its rightful owner, C is presumed by law to be aware of B's prior interest.

19. The *BEST* reason for a buyer to obtain title insurance is

a. that the mortgage lender requires it.
b. to ensure that the seller can deliver marketable title.
c. to ensure that the abstractor has prepared a complete summary of title.
d. to pay future liens that may be filed.

20. A mortgagee received a title insurance policy on the property a buyer is pledging as security for the mortgage loan. Which of the following is *TRUE*?

a. The policy is issued for the benefit of the buyer.
b. The policy guarantees that the buyer's equity will be protected.
c. The amount of coverage is commensurate with the loan amount.
d. The amount of coverage increases as the borrower grows older.

Real Estate Brokerage

LEARNING OBJECTIVES *When you have finished reading this unit, you will be able to*

- **describe** the fundamentals of real estate brokerage and licensing laws;
- **describe** the purpose and basic elements of antitrust laws including price fixing, boycotts, and allocation of markets;
- **explain** how real estate professionals should use technology in real estate practice to comply with laws and ethical standards; and
- **define** the following *key terms:*

antitrust laws
boycott
brokerage
commission
disclaimers
electronic contracting
Electronic Signatures in Global and National Commerce Act (E-Sign)
employee
independent contractor
Internet Data Exchange (IDX) policy
managing broker
minimum level of services
multiple listing service (MLS)
National Do Not Call Registry
price-fixing
procuring cause
ready, willing, and able buyer
Uniform Electronic Transactions Act (UETA)

OVERVIEW

Real estate is an industry driven by small businesses. Most brokerages are not giant national companies, and even those that are members of large franchises are still small businesses at heart, run locally to serve what is essentially a local market. Within a brokerage, no matter how large or small it is, each real estate professional has his own business. To be successful, a real estate professional has to not only know the product—real estate—but also how to run a business. Economics is part of running any operation, as are personnel decisions, such as how many people to hire and in what capacity. What positions are needed? How do you find the right people to fill those jobs? Who's your competition? The answers to these questions are not easy ones, but a successful real estate professional needs to think like a businessperson.

BROKERAGE AND REAL ESTATE LICENSE LAWS

www.arello.org

All 50 states, the District of Columbia, and all Canadian provinces license and regulate the activities of real estate professionals. While the laws share a common purpose, the details vary from state to state. Information on state laws and regulations can be found at the websites listed in the appendix. Another good source of information on current laws is the Association of Real Estate License Law Officials (ARELLO), www.arello.gov. In addition to individual states, ARELLO's membership includes governing bodies from countries around the globe.

Purpose of License Laws

Real estate license laws protect the public by ensuring a standard of competence and professionalism in the real estate industry. The laws achieve this goal by

- establishing basic requirements for obtaining a real estate license and, in most cases, requiring continuing education to keep a license;
- defining which activities require licensing;
- describing the acceptable standards of conduct and practice for licensees; and
- enforcing those standards through a disciplinary system.

The purpose of these laws is not merely to regulate the real estate industry. Their main objective is to make sure that the rights of purchasers, sellers, tenants, and owners are protected from unscrupulous or negligent practices. The laws are not intended to prevent licensees from conducting their businesses successfully or to interfere in legitimate transactions. Laws cannot guarantee that fair and honest dealing will always prevail in the business of real estate, but by establishing minimum levels of education and standards of behavior, these laws provide a base line for behavior and competency upon which an ethical marketplace can be nurtured and built.

Each state has a licensing authority—a commission, department, division, board, and/or agency—for real estate professionals. This authority has the power to issue licenses, make real estate information available to licensees and the public, and enforce the statutory real estate law.

Each licensing authority has also adopted a set of administrative regulations that administer the statutory law and set operating guidelines for licensees. The regulations have the same force and effect as statutory law, though if they conflict, the statute will prevail. Both regulations and statutory law are usually enforced through fines and the denial, suspension, or revocation of licenses. Civil and criminal court actions also can be brought against violators in some serious cases.

IN PRACTICE Each state's real estate license laws and the regulations of its real estate commission, board, or other body establish the framework for all of a licensee's activities. It is vital that licensees have a clear and comprehensive understanding of their state's laws and regulations for purposes of the licensing examination, as well as to ensure that the licensee's practice of real estate is both legal and successful. This is especially true for a licensee who holds a license in another state by reciprocity (reciprocal agreement of the states) and who may not have been required to take a special course or examination.

Real Estate Brokerage

Brokerage is simply the business of bringing parties together. A *real estate broker* is licensed to buy, sell, exchange, or lease real property for others and to charge a fee for those services. A broker may be an *agent* for a client, or broker and client may decide on a different form of representation, if allowed by state law.

A licensed brokerage business may take many forms, as permitted by state law. It may be a sole proprietorship, a corporation, a limited liability company, or a partnership with another real estate broker. The business may be independent of other businesses, or it may be part of a regional or national franchise organization. The business may consist of a single office or multiple branches. A real estate brokerage may specialize in one kind of transaction or service, or it may offer a variety of services. For licensing purposes, the brokerage must have a physical address, but it's most important marketing presence may be its website.

No matter what form it takes, a real estate brokerage has the same demands, expenses, and rewards as any other small business. A real estate broker faces the same challenges as an entrepreneur in any other industry. In addition to mastering the complexities of real estate transactions, the real estate broker must be able to handle the day-to-day details of running a business and set effective policies for every aspect of the brokerage operation:

- Maintaining space and equipment
- Hiring licensed real estate professionals, as well as unlicensed support staff
- Determining compensation
- Directing staff
- Implementing procedures for licensees to follow in carrying out activities permitted by the state's real estate license laws and regulations

IN PRACTICE A broker should always advise the parties to a real estate transaction to secure legal counsel to protect their interests. Although real estate professionals may bring buyers and sellers together and, in most states, may fill in preprinted blank purchase agreement forms, only an attorney may offer legal advice or prepare legal documents. Real estate professionals who are not attorneys are prohibited from practicing law.

Relationship of Broker and Sales Associate

Although brokerage firms vary widely in size, few brokers today perform their duties without the assistance of other licensed individuals. A *sales associate* might be licensed as a real estate salesperson or be a licensed real estate broker who simply chooses to work for another broker rather than set up an independent brokerage office. This section looks at the relationship of broker and sales associate.

In the traditional definition, a real estate *salesperson* is licensed to perform real estate activities on behalf of a licensed real estate broker. The broker for whom the salesperson works is called the *employing broker*, and both will be subject to the terms of an *employment agreement*, even when the salesperson is an *independent contractor* for tax and other purposes. The distinction is discussed in the next section; regardless of the salesperson's status for tax purposes, the broker is fully responsible for the actions performed in the course of the real estate business by all persons licensed under the broker, which is why the sales associate can never be an independent contractor for purposes of the licensing law.

From now on, we will use the term *sales associate* when we refer to a licensed individual employed by a broker. When we refer to a *broker*, we will mean an employing broker.

A sales associate can carry out *only* those responsibilities delegated by the employing broker and can receive compensation *only* from that broker. As an agent of the broker, the sales associate has no authority to make contracts with or receive compensation from any other party. The agency relationship also makes the broker liable for the acts of a sales associate that fall within the scope of the employment agreement.

The complexity of the real estate business and the emphasis on protection of consumer rights has led many states to require that all real estate professionals be licensed as real estate brokers. Even with increased educational requirements, however, the practicalities of running a real estate brokerage require that one broker be identified as the managing or supervising broker. A **managing broker**, who may also be called the supervising broker, is responsible for supervision of the real estate professionals who act on behalf of the brokerage. In a one-office firm, the managing broker may be the broker under whose license the firm has been created. In a larger company, every branch office of the brokerage typically will be required to designate a managing broker for that office location, and the managing broker may be required to live within a certain number of miles of the office. To qualify for the role of managing broker and maintain that status, the real estate professional may have to meet specific education requirements. Note that not all states use the same terminology to refer to managing brokers, brokers, and sales associates. Check your state for the specific language used.

IN PRACTICE The sales associate must always be supervised by a managing broker. The managing broker cannot delegate office supervision of sales associates to an unlicensed person, although state law should provide for a temporary transfer of the duties of the managing broker to another licensed broker.

Independent Contractor Versus Employee The employment agreement between a broker and sales associate should define the nature, obligations, and responsibilities of the relationship. State license laws generally make it clear that a broker is responsible for the acts of the sales associates employed by the brokerage (the traditional employer-employee relationship). This is true regardless of whether a sales associate is considered an employee or an independent contractor for income tax purposes, which will affect the broker's legal obligation to pay and withhold taxes from the sales associate's earnings.

In other businesses, an employer can exercise certain controls over workers who are considered employees and not independent contractors. An employer may require an **employee** to follow rules governing working hours, office routine, attendance at sales meetings, assignment of sales quotas, and adherence to dress codes. An employer is required by the federal government to withhold Social Security taxes and income taxes from wages paid to employees. The employer is also required to pay unemployment compensation taxes on wages paid to one or more employees, as defined by state and federal laws. In addition, employees might receive benefits such as health insurance, profit-sharing plans, and workers' compensation.

In most businesses, the employer's relationship with a person who is an **independent contractor** is very different. As the term implies, an independent contractor operates with more independence than an employee, and the employer may not exercise the same degree of control over an independent contractor's activities. Independent contractors are responsible for paying their own income and Social Security taxes and receive nothing from the employer that could be construed as an employee benefit, such as health insurance or paid vacation time.

Special rules apply when a real estate broker employs other real estate professionals to act on the broker's behalf. Under state license law, the broker is responsible for supervising the business activities of the sales associate and is liable for the actions of the sales associate. The broker's sales associate thus is treated as an employee of the broker, even though the employment agreement between sales associate and broker treats the sales associate as an independent contractor for tax purposes.

Confusion over the nature of the independent contractor status of a real estate sales associate has prompted the Internal Revenue Service (IRS) to issue specific rules to clarify the employer-employee relationship in a real estate office. Under the *qualified real estate agent* category set out in the Internal Revenue Code (26 U.S.C. 3508), the following three requirements must be met for a sales associate to establish a nonemployee status with the employing broker for tax purposes:

- The individual must have a current real estate license.
- The individual must have a written contract with the broker that specifies that the individual will not be treated as an employee for federal tax purposes.
- A substantial portion of the individual's income as a real estate professional must be based on sales production or other output and not on the number of hours worked.

IN PRACTICE Broker K has nine sales associates, all of whom are nonemployees for federal and state tax purposes. To make sure that there is no question of the status of the sales associates, each is compensated based solely on the amount of sales activity generated. None receives an hourly wage or is required to work a certain number of hours per week.

Real Estate Assistant

A real estate assistant (also known as a personal assistant or professional assistant) can be a combination office manager, marketer, organizer, and facilitator who has a fundamental understanding of the real estate industry. The assistant can be a staff member working for more than one real estate professional but often works for a specific sales associate. The assistant might be required to have a real estate license, depending on the tasks performed. The extent to which the assistant can help the real estate broker or sales associate with transactions will be determined by the state licensing law and regulations. An unlicensed assistant generally may perform duties that include clerical tasks, office management, website development and maintenance, and production of marketing pieces, but with little direct contact with consumers. A licensed assistant, on the other hand, can also set up and host open houses and assist in all aspects of a real estate transaction, including day-to-day contact with consumers.

Most states have very specific rules about what a licensed assistant and an unlicensed assistant may do and how they can be compensated. Usually, an unlicensed personal assistant working for a sales associate can be paid by the sales associate, but a licensed personal assistant working for a sales associate must be paid by the employing broker. For purposes of the real estate licensing laws and regulations, both the sales associate and licensed personal assistant are under the supervision of the employing broker.

IN PRACTICE A sales associate considering hiring a personal assistant must understand state requirements. The parameters of the relationship should be clear both to the sales associate and the person hired to act as a personal assistant. Even an unlicensed individual could incur liability under the state licensing law, especially if that person conducts activities that require a real estate license.

Broker's Compensation

The broker's compensation is specified in the contract with the client. The real estate license law (or statute of frauds) usually will require that there be a written agreement to establish the compensation to be paid. Compensation can be in the form of a **commission** or broker's fee (computed as a percentage of the total sales price), a flat fee, or an hourly rate. The amount of a broker's commission is negotiable in every case. Even subtle attempts to impose uniform commission rates in an area are clearly a violation of state and federal laws. Nevertheless, a broker may set the minimum rate acceptable for that broker's firm; the client is free to work with a different broker if the rate is deemed unacceptable by the client. The important point is for broker and client to agree on a rate before any form of representation is established.

The broker's compensation will also be affected by the participation in the transaction of a broker from another firm, who may be representing one of the parties. Brokers have long realized that the marketing of a property is enhanced when the largest possible number of real estate professionals are aware of the availability of the property and can show it to their clients. Membership in a **multiple listing service (MLS)** provides that marketing opportunity, and the rules of the MLS set out the terms under which brokers agree to *cooperate* in a transaction, including the sharing of the compensation earned.

A commission is considered earned when the work for which the real estate broker was hired has been accomplished. This most likely is different from the time at which the commission is paid; most sales commissions are payable when the sale is consummated by *delivery and acceptance* of the seller's deed. This provision is generally included in the agreement between seller and broker.

To be entitled to receive compensation from a real estate sales transaction, an individual must be

- a licensed real estate broker,
- employed by the buyer or seller under a valid contract, and
- the procuring cause of the sale.

To be a **procuring cause**, the broker or the broker's sales associate must have started an uninterrupted chain of events that resulted in a sale.

To be considered the **procuring cause** of a sale, the broker must have started or caused an uninterrupted chain of events that resulted in the sale. For example, procuring cause may include activities such as conducting an open house, placing an advertisement in the local real estate advertising magazine, making the property listing available on the internet, and showing the house to the buyer. A broker (or a sales associate of the broker) who causes or completes such a course of action without a contract or without having been promised payment is a volunteer and may not legally claim compensation.

A **ready, willing, and able buyer** is one who is prepared to buy on the seller's terms and is ready to complete the transaction.

Once a seller accepts an offer from a ready, willing, and able buyer, the real estate broker is entitled to a commission. A **ready, willing, and able buyer** is one who is prepared to buy on the seller's terms and is ready to take positive steps toward consummation of the transaction. A court may prevent the real estate broker from receiving a commission if the real estate broker knew the buyer was unable to perform. If the transaction is not consummated, the real estate broker may still be entitled to a commission if the seller

- has a change of mind and refuses to sell,
- has a spouse who refuses to sign the deed,
- has a title with uncorrected defects,
- committed fraud with respect to the transaction,
- is unable to deliver possession within a reasonable time,
- insists on terms not in the listing (e.g., the right to restrict the use of the property), or
- has a mutual agreement with the buyer to cancel the transaction.

Sales Associate's Compensation

The amount of compensation a sales associate receives is set by mutual agreement between the broker and the sales associate. A broker may agree to pay a fixed salary, but usually the compensation is a share of the commissions from transactions originated by the sales associate. In some cases, the sales associate may draw from an account against earned shares of commissions, providing a minimal level of regular income. Some brokers require sales associates to pay all or part of the expenses of advertising listed properties.

Some firms have adopted a 100% commission plan in which each sales associate pays a monthly service charge to the broker to cover the cost of office space, telephone, and supervision in return for keeping 100% of the commissions from the sales the sales associate negotiates. Sales associates on a 100% commission plan pay all of their individual business expenses, such as the salary of a personal assistant or the costs associated with development and maintenance of the sales associate's website.

Other firms have *graduated commission splits* based on a sales associate's achieving specified production goals. For instance, a broker might agree to split commissions 50/50 up to a $25,000 sales associate's share, 60/40 for shares from $25,000 to $30,000, and so on. Commission splits could go up to 80/20 or 90/10, particularly for high producers.

No matter how the sales associate's compensation is structured, as a rule only the employing real estate broker can pay it. In a transaction involving two firms, the entire commission is received by the broker representing the party who pays the commission, and the agreed-upon share of the commission is paid to the cooperating broker. Each broker then pays any employed sales associate who took part in the transaction the amount due to that person.

The method and amount of the compensation received by the sales associate also does not affect the broker's responsibility for the conduct of the sales associate. The real estate license law will always make the broker liable for acts of the sales associate performed in the course of business.

MATH CONCEPTS

Sharing Commissions

A commission might be shared by many people: the broker and sales associate working for the seller, as well as the broker and sales associate working for the buyer. A diagram may help you determine which real estate professional is entitled to receive what amount of the total commission. For example, a sales associate took a listing on a $289,000 house at a 5% commission rate. A sales associate employed by a different firm found the buyer for the property. If the property sold for the listed price, the seller's broker and the buyer's broker shared the commission equally, and the buyer's broker kept 45% of the shared commission, how much did the sales associate employed by the buyer's broker receive?

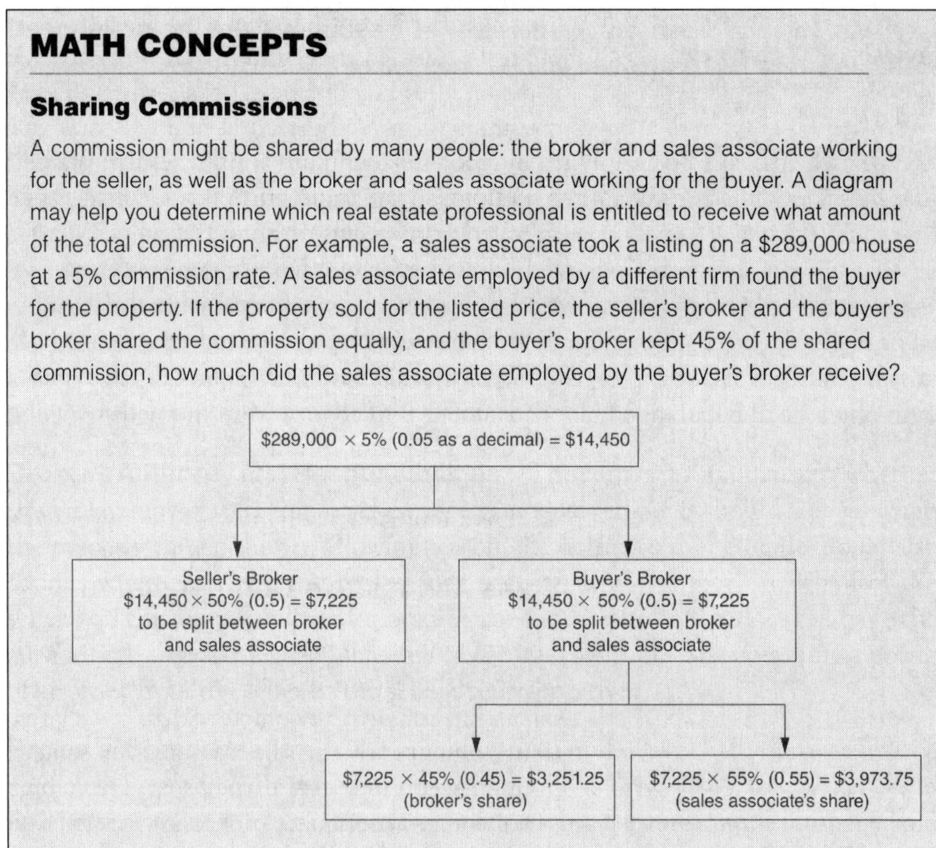

Fee for Service

One of the more notable impacts of the internet is that it has allowed buyers and sellers to have tremendous access to information about the real estate market, as well as individual properties. The average consumer today is much more knowledgeable about real estate matters, including financing and legal issues, and is accustomed to finding information quickly.

Successful real estate professionals understand and encourage consumers' exploration of the vast resources of the internet but can also identify the services a real estate professional provides and underscore the value of those services. One way in which that can be done is by explaining the tasks that can be performed by a real estate professional as a bundle of services. The next step is to be willing to unbundle those services, customizing the service offered by making a range of options available to the real estate consumer. For example, a real estate professional may want to offer a seller the following services, as permitted by state law:

- Helping the seller prepare the property for sale
- Performing a comparative market analysis (CMA) to assist the seller in pricing the property
- Assisting with marketing the property using the MLS and websites
- Locating and screening a buyer
- Helping fill in the blanks of a sales agreement
- Assisting with negotiations
- Being available to assist with the closing of the transaction

Other services can be directed toward buyers. For example, a real estate professional may offer a buyer the following services, as permitted by state law:

- Working out the economics of renting versus owning
- Helping a buyer with a mortgage preapproval
- Consulting on a buyer's desired location
- Visiting properties with a buyer and checking property information
- Helping fill in the blanks of an offer to purchase
- Assisting with negotiations
- Being available to assist with the closing of the transaction

The range of services offered must always comply with state law, particularly those that may be viewed as the unlicensed practice of law. Some states also require a **minimum level of services** to be provided, covered in the next section, making it important that the real estate professional understand the law and be able to explain it to a prospective client.

Many real estate professionals use either an hourly rate or a flat fee for particular services. The *fee-for-service* concept can create marketing opportunities for specific services, such as preparing a property for sale, but can also lead to a recognition by the consumer of the value of the real estate professional's knowledge and expertise.

Real estate professionals may also want to develop their own lists of services for sellers and buyers, as well as a specific list of services to help people who decide to sell their own home, known as *for sale by owners* (FSBOs). Again, state law may dictate what the real estate professional can offer. In any event, the property owner should be clear as to the level of representation being offered and how it will affect the services the owner can expect to receive.

Communicating with consumers to identify their real estate needs is key to developing a successful real estate business. It is ultimately the broker who decides whether an unbundling of services is good for the firm.

IN PRACTICE A buyer wants to buy a house without contracting with a broker but needs help writing an offer. The buyer asks a broker friend to write an offer to purchase, and they agree on the terms of the work. If state law permits, the broker can discuss the terms of the offer with the buyer, help the buyer complete an offer-to-purchase form, and charge the buyer a set fee for the service.

Minimum Level of Services

A growing number of brokerages offer limited-service listing agreements. The real estate broker may offer no services other than that of listing a property in the MLS. When sellers enter into this kind of agreement, they are essentially representing themselves, accepting communications from prospective buyers, showing the property, and perhaps hiring an attorney to assist with completing a transaction. If questions emerge during the negotiation or completion of such a transaction, the seller may turn to the real estate professional working for the buyer for answers, which can put the real estate professional in an awkward position or, worse, involve the real estate professional in an unethical or even illegal position if even an implication that the real estate professional has worked on behalf of both parties to the transaction without their informed consent is present.

In response to this potential problem, some states have enacted legislation defining an exclusive brokerage agreement. Other states have proposed regulations that define the minimum level of services a consumer should expect from a real estate professional.

For example, one state now requires all exclusive brokerage agreements to specify that the broker—through one or more sponsored sales associates—must, at a minimum,

- accept delivery of and present offers and counteroffers to the client;
- assist the client in developing, negotiating, and presenting offers and counteroffers; and
- answer the client's questions about offers, counteroffers, and contingencies.

ANTITRUST LAWS

Antitrust violations include
- price-fixing,
- the group boycott,
- allocation of customers,
- allocation of markets, and
- tie-in agreements.

The real estate industry is subject to **antitrust laws**. At the federal level, the Sherman Antitrust Act provides specific penalties for a number of illegal business activities. Each state also has its own antitrust laws. These laws prohibit monopolies and any contracts, combinations, and conspiracies among competitors that unreasonably restrain trade—that is, behaviors that interfere with the free flow of goods and services in a competitive marketplace. The most common antitrust violations are price-fixing, the group boycott, allocation of customers or markets, and tie-in agreements.

Price-Fixing

Price-fixing is a practice in which competitors agree to set prices or other terms and conditions for products or services rather than letting competition in the open market establish those prices. In real estate, price-fixing occurs when competing brokers agree to set sales commissions, fees, or management rates. Price-fixing is illegal. Real estate brokers must independently determine commission rates or fees for their own firms only. These decisions must be based on a broker's business judgment and revenue requirements. A broker may discuss commissions and fees with real estate professionals who are affiliated with the same brokerage but must not discuss compensation issues with anyone from another real estate firm.

Trade groups, such as associations of REALTORS®, multiple listing services, and other professional organizations, may neither set fees or commission splits, nor deny membership to a real estate broker based on the fees that the broker charges. In fact, no discussion of commissions or fees should ever take place at *any* gathering of two or more real estate professionals from different brokerages.

The challenge for real estate professionals is to avoid even the impression of price-fixing. Hinting to prospective clients that there is a "going rate" of commission or a "normal" fee implies that rates are, in fact, standardized. The broker and sales associates must make it clear to clients that the rate stated is only what that brokerage charges.

Group Boycott

A group **boycott** occurs when two or more businesses conspire against another business or agree to withhold their patronage to reduce competition. A group boycott is illegal under antitrust laws.

The most recent example of this type of violation has occurred when traditional full-service brokers have conspired to destroy a competitor's firm by not showing that firm's listings. The competitor may be a so-called discount broker or one who offers unbundled services under the fee-for-service concept discussed earlier. Obviously, if such a scheme succeeds, it diminishes consumer choices by limiting the availability of property.

Allocation of Customers or Markets

Allocation of customers or markets involves an agreement between real estate brokers to divide their markets and refrain from competing for each other's business. Allocations may be made on a geographic basis, with real estate brokers agreeing to specific territories within which they will operate exclusively. The division may also occur by markets, such as by price range or category of housing. These agreements result in reduced competition.

Tie-in Agreements

Finally, *tie-in agreements* (also known as *tying agreements*) are agreements to sell one product only if the buyer purchases another product as well. The sale of the first (desired) product is *tied* to the purchase of a second (less desirable) product. In the real estate business, this can occur if, for instance, a broker will agree to list a seller's home for sale only if the seller agrees to be represented by the broker in the purchase of a new home.

Penalties

The penalties for violating antitrust laws are severe. Under the federal Sherman Antitrust Act, the penalty for fixing prices or allocating markets is a maximum $1 million fine and 10 years in prison. For corporations, the penalty may be as high as $100 million. An individual who has suffered a loss because of an antitrust violation may sue for treble damages—three times the actual damages sustained.

In addition, the injured party may recover the cost of the suit, which includes reasonable attorney fees.

TECHNOLOGY IN REAL ESTATE PRACTICE

Most real estate agencies have websites that provide access to extraordinary databases for property and other searches. Trade associations and MLSs form the backbone for much of this information. The National Association of REALTORS® has adopted an **Internet Data Exchange (IDX) policy** that allows all MLS members to have equal rights to display MLS data, while also respecting the rights of the property owner and the real estate broker who represents the property owner to market a property as they wish. A *blanket opt-out* provision provides that those MLS participants interested in keeping their listings from competitors' websites cannot then display other real estate brokers' listings. Real estate brokers who opt out of displaying their listings on competitors' websites can, at the direction of a seller, make an exception and display the seller's property on the MLS website. The NAR IDX policy, which is updated often, can be found at www.realtor.org/topics/internet-data-exchange-idx/policy.

www.realtor.org/topics/internet-data-exchange-idx/policy

While the internet can provide a vast amount of information, much of that information is unverified or comes from questionable sources. Many real estate websites, particularly those that provide links to other sources, have **disclaimers** to indicate that the material on the site is solely for informational purposes and that no warranties or representations have been made. When information is taken from the internet, the source should be one that is known to be reliable.

www.realtor.com
www.zillow.com
www.trulia.com
www.nahb.org

NAR has a property search site available at www.realtor.com, providing consumers access to millions of property listings. Other sites that provide information on current property listings, as well as information on property sales and taxes are www.zillow.com and www.trulia.com. The National Association of Home Builders, www.nahb.org, provides data on new home construction, building materials costs, and building permits issued.

Real estate professionals can purchase website management tools to help with their marketing efforts. These tools help assess the effectiveness of internet marketing by providing statistics on the number of people visiting the site, the most visited pages of the site, the page used to enter and exit the site, and the operating system and browser used by visitors, among other data.

Communication in a Digital Age

The use of the internet as a means of communication has continued to expand. Just when the latest program or device gains popularity, a new one emerges to eclipse it.

Smartphones The telephone no longer requires a landline that limits its use to a single location. The mobile phone has rapidly evolved from the expensive and clumsy apparatus of the early 1980s to today's sleek smartphone that can also serve as a *personal digital assistant (PDA)* and be used for internet access. Touchscreen tablet devices can allow telephone conversations and video conferencing via one of the available software applications.

Email/Texting Email and texting, its cell phone equivalent, have made communication between real estate professionals and consumers more efficient. Email is an excellent opportunity for the ongoing marketing of a business. Contact information should be kept up to date and appear in every message. State licensing regulations may specify the information that should be provided in every client or customer communication, including electronic communications. Laws against unwanted email messages are discussed later, in the section on prohibited communications.

In communicating with clients or consumers via email, the best practice is to use the subject line in a useful and helpful manner, avoid spelling errors, respond promptly to all email messages, be specific and brief, and pay attention to the size of any file attachments. Never send unsolicited email messages.

The same type of recommendations apply to text messages, which are rapidly overtaking email as the preferred method of client contact. Be clear while being concise, making sure that the subject of the message isn't lost, and avoid too many text message acronyms. State law may require that all communications by real estate professionals include their name, address, license number, and (for a sales associate) the name of the employing broker.

Social Media

www.facebook.com

www.twitter.com

www.linkedin.com

Social Media The latest methods of communicating via the internet include Facebook, www.facebook.com, which allows users to post a page of information and receive and send messages from identified friends. The popularity of a Facebook page or posting can be measured by the number of users who indicate by clicking on an icon that they like it. A real estate professional can establish a presence on Facebook but should always be mindful that information available to the public imposes a level of restraint on comments and photos posted to avoid embarrassment or even potential liability.

Twitter, www.twitter.com, allows users to post short messages called tweets of no more than 140 characters that can be read by others who follow that user. Tweets can be a useful and entertaining way of gathering comments from a number of people on a variety of issues, from politics to entertainment.

LinkedIn, www.linkedin.com, emphasizes business networking by allowing users to post brief resumes and to join groups of those who share similar interests. When users update their information, members of their groups receive those updates. Users can also post announcements or messages to members of their groups, allowing others to post comments or responses in return.

Internet Advertising

State laws vary regarding internet advertising. It is important for you to check your own state's laws before engaging in advertising and other marketing activities on the internet. In addition to NAR's Internet Data Exchange policy, internet advertising laws and regulations frequently include the following stipulations:

- All electronic communication by a real estate professional must include the professional's name, office address, and broker affiliation.
- Real estate professionals must disclose their license status on each page of a website that contains an advertisement.
- The listing of only a sales associate's name without the sponsoring broker's name in an advertisement is prohibited.
- An advertisement must be a true, current representation of the information it contains and not be misleading.

Electronic Contracting

The legal requirements for a contract will be discussed later, but it is worth noting here that technology and the internet have significantly changed the way in which real estate transactions are performed. **Electronic contracting** is a growing part of real estate practice because it quickly and efficiently integrates information in a real estate transaction between clients, lenders, and title and closing agents. The transactions are conducted through email or fax and can save both time and money.

Two federal acts govern electronic contracting: the **Uniform Electronic Transactions Act (UETA)** and the **Electronic Signatures in Global and National Commerce Act (E-Sign)**.

www.uniformlaws.org

The Uniform Electronic Transactions Act (UETA) was created by the National Conference of Commissioners on Uniform State Laws, www.uniformlaws.org. At present, UETA has been adopted by all but three states (Illinois, New York, and Washington). The law sets forth basic rules for entering an enforceable contract using electronic means. The primary purpose of UETA is to remove barriers in electronic commerce that would otherwise prevent enforceability of contracts. UETA validates and effectuates electronic records and signatures in a procedural manner and is intended to complement a state's digital signature statute, but it does not in any way require parties to use electronic means. UETA's four key provisions are the following:

- A contract cannot be denied its legal effect just because an electronic record was used.
- A record or signature cannot be denied its legal effect just because it is in an electronic format.
- If a state's law requires a signature on a contract, an electronic signature is sufficient.
- If a state's law requires a written record, an electronic record is sufficient.

The Electronic Signatures in Global and National Commerce Act (E-Sign) was passed by Congress in 2000. E-Sign functions as the electronic transactions law in states that have not enacted UETA, and some sections of E-Sign apply to states that have enacted UETA. The purpose of E-Sign is to make contracts (including signatures) and records legally enforceable, regardless of the medium in which they are created. For example, contracts formed using email or transmitted electronically rather than by paper have the same legal significance as those formed on paper.

IN PRACTICE When entering into a residential sales agreement, it is important for the parties to feel comfortable with and clearly communicate the method chosen for transacting the agreement, whether by paper and ink or by email.

Prohibited Communications

Businesses must comply with a variety of prohibitions intended to protect consumers from the intrusions of unwanted communications.

In 2003, federal do-not-call legislation was signed into law, and the Do Not Call Improvement Act of 2007 further strengthened the protections available to consumers. Real estate professionals must comply with the provisions of the **National Do Not Call Registry**, which is managed by the Federal Trade

Commission (FTC). The registry is a list of telephone numbers from consumers who have indicated their preference to limit the telemarketing calls they receive. The registry applies to any plan, program, or campaign to sell goods or services through interstate phone calls. The registry does not limit calls by political organizations, charities, collection agencies, or telephone surveyors. The law does apply to a for-profit telemarketer, even if the telemarketer is working for a nonprofit organization. Information for consumers and businesses can be found at www.donotcall.gov.

www.donotcall.gov

Telemarketers and sellers are required to search the registry at least once every 31 days and drop registered consumer phone numbers from their call lists. Normal business relationships are still possible. Real estate professionals may call consumers with whom they have an established business relationship for up to 18 months after the consumer's last purchase, delivery, or payment, even if the consumer is listed on the National Do Not Call Registry. Also, a real estate professional may call a consumer for up to three months after the consumer makes an inquiry or submits an application. Note that if a consumer asks a company not to call, despite the presence of an established business relationship, the company must abide by the consumer's request, which stays in effect permanently.

Even though the federal legislation applies to interstate telephone calls, most states also have do-not-call rules or regulations that apply to in-state calls. It is important to keep up to date with state laws regarding do-not-call policies, as well as the national law.

www.fcc.gov/guides/fax-advertising

Similar federal and state laws apply to marketing and business communications by fax and email. The Telephone Consumer Protection Act (TCPA), Junk Fax Prevention Act, and rules of the Federal Communications Commission (FCC) prohibit most unsolicited fax advertisements. There is an exemption for faxes sent as part of an established business relationship. More information can be found at www.fcc.gov/guides/fax-advertising.

www.business.ftc.gov/documents/bus61-can-spam-act-compliance-guide-business

Junk emails (spam) are prohibited by the federal Controlling the Assault of Non-Solicited Pornography and Marketing Act of 2003, known as the CAN-SPAM Act. An important feature of this law, which applies to commercial electronic mail messages, is that email solicitations must include a means by which the recipient can "unsubscribe" from future messages. A compliance guide for businesses is available at www.business.ftc.gov/documents/bus61-can-spam-act-compliance-guide-business.

www.business.ftc.gov/privacy-and-security/childrens-privacy

The most recent restrictions on the use of the internet, including mobile apps and ad networks, went into effect on July 1, 2013, as part of the ongoing Children's Online Privacy Protection Act (COPPA). COPPA requires the posting of a privacy policy and limits the personal information that can be collected from children younger than 13, even if a website or app is directed toward a general audience. Details of the law can be obtained at www.business.ftc.gov/privacy-and-security/childrens-privacy.

KEY POINT REVIEW

All 50 states, Canadian provinces, and the District of Columbia have real estate license laws and rules with the force and effect of law that establish basic requirements for obtaining a real estate license, define which activities require licensing, and enforce standards through a disciplinary system.

A real estate **broker** is licensed to buy, sell, exchange, or lease real property for others for a fee and may operate as a sole proprietorship, partnership, corporation, or limited liability company.

The real estate **brokerage** may be independent or part of a regional or national franchise.

A real estate **sales associate** is a salesperson or broker who is licensed to perform real estate activities **only** on behalf of a licensed real estate broker. The **broker-employer** is liable for the actions of the **sales associate** within the scope of the **employment agreement** or as provided by state law.

An **independent contractor** is an employee who usually receives a commission, with no withholding for Social Security, income tax, and other purposes and has the freedom to set hours and accomplish goals. A real estate broker always has liability and supervisory responsibilities for the real estate related work activities of a sales associate.

An **employee** may receive salary in lieu of or in addition to commission; may receive benefits, such as health insurance, profit-sharing, and workers' compensation; and has an employer who is required to withhold Social Security, income taxes, and other applicable federal and state taxes from earnings. The employer sets hours, duties, and other specifics of the employee's day-to-day work and remains liable for related work activities of the employee.

There are Internal Revenue Service (IRS) requirements for a **qualified real estate agent** to be treated as a **nonemployee** for tax purposes.

A real estate **assistant** may be a licensed employee of the employing broker who is compensated by the broker, or, if unlicensed, is paid by either the sales associate or broker and is limited in the activities that can be undertaken.

A broker's **compensation** can be a **commission** based on a property's sales price, a **flat fee**, or an **hourly rate**.

A broker's **commission** is earned when the seller accepts an offer from a **ready, willing, and able buyer** prepared to buy on the seller's terms and ready to take positive steps toward consummation of the transaction.

A sales associate's compensation is set by mutual agreement of the employing broker and the sales associate.

Fee for services means that a broker's compensation is based on charges for separate activities that the client desires (unbundling of services). Some states now require **minimum services** to be offered by the broker.

Antitrust laws are both state and federal (**Sherman Antitrust Act**) and prohibit **monopolies**, and contracts, combinations, and conspiracies that unreasonably restrain trade, including

- **price-fixing,**
- **group boycott,**
- **allocation of customers or markets**, and
- **tie-in agreements** (tying agreements) that force customers to purchase a product when only another was wanted.

Under the Sherman Antitrust Act, antitrust violators face up to a $1 million fine and 10 years in prison, with corporate fines as high as $100 million. In a civil suit, the successful plaintiff may recover triple damages plus attorney's fees and costs.

The **Internet Data Exchange (IDX) policy** of the National Association of REALTORS® allows members to limit the internet distribution of listing information. Overall, the **internet** is invaluable for communication, research, marketing, and advertising of a brokerage and includes the use of email, websites, and social networking, all of which must be conducted in compliance with applicable federal and state laws.

Electronic contracting must take into account the **Uniform Electronic Transactions Act (UETA)**, which has been adopted in most states and the **Electronic Signatures in Global and National Commerce Act (E-Sign)**, which functions as the **electronic transactions** law in states that have not enacted UETA and makes contracts (including signatures) and records legally enforceable, regardless of the medium in which they are created.

Do-not-call legislation is found at federal and state levels. The **National Do Not Call Registry** (regulated by the **Federal Trade Commission**) lists telephone numbers of consumers who have asked to be registered and prohibits interstate calls to those numbers to sell goods or services.

Many states provide their own do-not-call legislation for in-state calls. Other prohibited communications include those defined in the laws regulating junk faxes, as well as the **CAN-SPAM Act**.

Restrictions on collection of information from children younger than 13 by means of the internet, including mobile apps, are specified in **COPPA**, the **Children's Online Privacy Protection Act**.

UNIT 9 QUIZ

1. Which statement *BEST* explains this sentence: "To recover a commission for brokerage services, a broker must *be employed* as the agent of the client"?
   a. The broker must work in a real estate office.
   b. The client must make an express or implied agreement to pay a commission to the broker.
   c. The broker must express an interest in representing the client.
   d. The broker must have a salesperson employed in the office.

2. Sales associates who are paid in a lump sum and who are personally responsible for paying their own taxes are probably treated for tax purposes as
   a. employees.
   b. buyer's agents.
   c. independent contractors.
   d. transactional brokers.

3. A sales associate's contract with her broker states that she is not an employee. In the past year, less than half her income was commission, with the rest an hourly wage paid by the broker. The IRS would classify her as
   a. self-employed.
   b. an employee.
   c. an independent contractor.
   d. a part-time real estate salesperson.

4. When acting as an employee rather than an independent contractor, a sales associate may be obligated to
   a. list properties in his or her own name.
   b. work set hours.
   c. accept a commission from another broker.
   d. advertise property on his or her own behalf.

5. Terry is the personal assistant of a real estate sales associate. Terry must be paid by the broker who employs the sales associate. This means that
   a. Terry has a real estate license.
   b. the sales associate doesn't make very much money.
   c. Terry is a part-time employee.
   d. ultimate responsibility for Terry's conduct in the performance of work-related activities lies with the sales associate.

6. A broker would have the right to dictate which of the following to an independent contractor?
   a. Number of hours the person would have to work
   b. Work schedule the person would have to follow
   c. Sales meetings the person would need to attend
   d. Conduct in compliance with statutory law and regulations

7. Two real estate professionals were found guilty of conspiring with each other to allocate real estate brokerage markets. A seller suffered a $90,000 loss because of their activities. If the seller brings a civil suit against the two real estate professionals, what can the seller expect to recover?
   a. Nothing, because a civil suit cannot be brought for damages resulting from antitrust activities
   b. Only $90,000—the amount of actual damages the seller suffered
   c. Actual damages plus attorney's fees and costs
   d. $270,000 plus attorney's fees and costs

8. Two sales associates who work for the same firm agree to divide their town into a northern region and a southern region; one sales associate will handle listings in the north, and the other will handle listings in the south. Which statement is *TRUE*?
   a. The agreement does not violate antitrust laws.
   b. The agreement constitutes illegal price-fixing.
   c. The two sales associates have violated the Sherman Antitrust Act and are liable for treble damages.
   d. The two sales associates are guilty of a group boycott with regard to other sales associates in their firm.

9. A state has recently updated its *Rules and Regulations for the Real Estate Profession*. Assuming this state is like all others, which statement is *TRUE* regarding this publication?
   a. The rules and regulations are state laws enacted by the legislature.
   b. The rules and regulations do not have the same force and effect as the statutory license law.
   c. The rules and regulations have the same force and effect as the license law itself.
   d. The rules and regulations are not enforceable against real estate professionals.

10. After a particularly challenging transaction finally closes, the client gives a sales associate a check for $500 "for all your extra work." Which statement is accurate?
   a. Such compensation is irregular but appropriate for the sales associate to accept.
   b. The sales associate may receive compensation only from the broker.
   c. The sales associate should accept the check and deposit it immediately in a special escrow account.
   d. The sales associate's broker is entitled to 80% of the check.

11. A broker has established the following office policy: "All listings taken by any sales associate of this real estate brokerage must include compensation based on a 7% commission. No lower commission rate is acceptable." If the broker attempts to impose this uniform commission requirement, which statement is *TRUE*?
   a. A homeowner may sue the broker for violating the antitrust law's prohibition against price-fixing.
   b. The sales associates of the brokerage will not be bound by the requirement and may negotiate any commission rate they choose.
   c. The broker must present the uniform commission policy to the local professional association for approval.
   d. The broker may, as a matter of office policy, legally set the minimum commission rate acceptable for the firm.

12. A real estate company has adopted a 100% commission plan. The monthly desk rent required of sales associates is $1,500, payable on the last day of the month. In August, a sales associate closed a transaction that earned a commission of $11,370 and a second transaction that earned a commission of $6,875. The sales associate's additional expenses for the month were $2,170. How much of the total monthly income did the sales associate keep?
   a. $14,575
   b. $16,075
   c. $16,745
   d. $18,245

13. A sales associate took a listing on a house that sold for $329,985. The commission rate was 5%. A sales associate employed by another broker found the buyer. The seller's broker received 60% of the commission on the sale; the buyer's broker received 40%. If the seller's broker kept 30% and paid the seller's sales associate the remainder, how much did the seller's sales associate earn on this sale?
   a. $4,346.85
   b. $5,774.74
   c. $6,929.68
   d. $8,249.00

14. On the sale of any property, a sales associate's compensation is based on the total commission paid to the broker. The sales associate receives 30% of the first $2,500, 40% of the next amount between $2,500 and $7,500, and 50% of any remaining amount exceeding $7,500. If a property sells for $234,500 and the broker's commission rate is 6.5%, what is the sales associate's total compensation?
    a. $5,847.00
    b. $6,621.25
    c. $6,871.25
    d. $7,621.25

15. The federal law that makes contracts originated, negotiated, and executed over a combination of computer and cell phone enforceable is
    a. CAN-SPAM.
    b. Junk Fax Prevention Act.
    c. COPPA.
    d. UETA.

16. The amount of commission paid to a sales associate is determined by
    a. state law.
    b. the local real estate board.
    c. mutual agreement with the broker.
    d. mutual agreement with the client.

17. A broker was accused of violating antitrust laws. Of the following, the broker was MOST likely accused of
    a. not having an equal housing opportunity sign in the office window.
    b. undisclosed dual agency.
    c. price-fixing.
    d. dealing in unlicensed exchange services.

18. A real estate broker was responsible for a chain of events that resulted in the sale of a client's property. This is called
    a. pro forma.
    b. procuring cause.
    c. private offering.
    d. proffered offer.

19. A sales associate wants to be classified by the IRS as a qualified real estate agent—the equivalent of holding independent contractor status for tax purposes. The sales associate must meet all of the following requirements *EXCEPT*
    a. receive substantially all income from the brokerage based on production, not time worked.
    b. perform all work unsupervised by the managing broker.
    c. hold a current real estate license.
    d. have a written agreement with the broker stating that the sales associate will not be treated as an employee for federal tax purposes.

20. A real estate sales associate, classified by the IRS as an independent contractor, receives
    a. a monthly salary or hourly wage.
    b. company-provided health insurance.
    c. a company-provided automobile.
    d. a negotiated share of commissions on transactions.

UNIT 10

Real Estate Agency

LEARNING OBJECTIVES *When you have finished reading this unit, you should be able to*

- **explain** agency concepts and terminology;
- **explain** the difference between express and implied agency;
- **define** the types of agency and identify which, if any, are involved in real estate practice;
- **describe and explain** an agent's duties to third-party customers, especially regarding misstatements, misrepresentation, and potential fraud; and
- **define** the following *key terms*:

agency
agent
buyer representation agreement
buyer's agent
client
customer
designated agency
designated agent
dual agency
express agency
express agreement
fiduciary
fiduciary relationship
fraud
general agent
implied agency
implied agreement
latent defect
law of agency
listing agreement
negligent misrepresentation
nonagent
principal
puffing
single agency
special agent
transaction broker
universal agent

OVERVIEW

The relationship between a real estate professional and the parties involved in a real estate transaction is not a simple one. A real estate professional can represent a client as an **agent**, but in addition to the parties' assumptions and expectations, the real estate professional acts as a **fiduciary** and is subject to a wide range of legal and ethical requirements designed to protect the seller, the buyer, and the transaction itself. There are other **agency** relationships in the real estate business, including that of sales associate to the employing broker. We will look at the possible agency relationships in a real estate transaction, as well as other types of relationships that can be established.

HISTORY OF AGENCY

Agency relationships in real estate transactions are governed by three kinds of law, which have been mentioned earlier, including

- *common law*, the rules established by tradition and court decisions;
- *statutory law*, the laws enacted by the legislature; and
- *administrative law*, the rules and regulations created by real estate commissions and departments, as authorized by the legislature.

The fundamentals of agency law have remained largely unchanged for hundreds of years, but the nature of real estate brokerage services, particularly those provided in residential sales transactions, has changed significantly in the last half-century.

In the 1950s, the common law doctrine of *caveat emptor* ("let the buyer beware") that came to the United States as a legacy of British rule was the norm; buyers were pretty much on their own. It should have been clear that the real estate broker represented the seller's interests, but buyers often failed to realize that fact.

In the 1960s, the way that buyers and sellers were brought together in real estate transactions began to change. Brokers started to share information about properties they listed, which often resulted in two brokers cooperating to sell a property. The brokers formalized this exchange of information by creating the multiple listing service (MLS). The MLS expedited sales by increasing a single property's exposure to more brokers, and thus more potential buyers. Because it generated more sales, the MLS quickly became a widely used industry service. But one thing remained the same: both brokers still represented the seller's interest. Because two different brokers would take part in a transaction, it was even less apparent to the buyer that the obligation of both was to work on behalf of the seller.

While sellers benefited from this arrangement, buyers eventually came to question whether their interests were being protected. By the early 1990s, buyers began to demand that they be represented, too. They came to expect not only accurate, factual information but also objective advice, particularly in the face of increasingly complex real estate transactions. As a result, state laws and regulations (and subsequently, MLS rules) were changed to allow a broker to represent a buyer and share in the commission paid to the seller's broker. Buyers have learned to view the real estate professional as the expert on whom they can rely for guidance, and a large percentage of sales contracts are now written by buyer agents.

A real estate broker must comply with the laws and regulations regarding all aspects of a transaction, but an increasing number of brokers are choosing to represent buyers exclusively, just as some brokers prefer to represent sellers. In any case, brokers also must decide how they will cooperate with other brokers, in compliance with the rules of the MLS.

The relationship of a real estate broker and consumer may not be an agency relationship, and other forms of representation that are recognized by state laws will be discussed here. Even as the elements of real estate practice change, however, the underlying assumptions that govern an agency relationship remain intact. Those assumptions are discussed next.

Definitions

An **agent** is a person authorized to act on behalf of the **principal** in dealings with a **third person**.

The **law of agency,** whether expressed in the common law or statutes, typically includes the following definitions:

- **Agent**—the individual who is authorized and consents to represent the interests of another person in dealings with a third person. The sales associates of a real estate broker act as agents (representatives) of the broker. In a real estate transaction, a firm's broker may be the agent of a client and will share this responsibility with the sales associates who work for the firm. As agents of the broker the sales associates thus have the same relationship to a client of the firm that the broker does. If the broker is an agent of a seller, for instance, a sales associate also acts as agent of the seller unless some other provision is made.
- **Principal**—the individual who hires the agent and delegates to that agent the responsibility of representing the principal's interests. In a real estate transaction in which an agency relationship is established, the principal is the buyer or the seller or the landlord or the tenant. The broker is the principal in dealings with sales associates.
- **Agency**—the fiduciary relationship between the principal and the agent by which the agent is authorized to represent the principal in one or more transactions.
- **Fiduciary**—the relationship in which the agent is held in a position of special trust and confidence by the principal.
- **Client**—the principal in a real estate transaction for whom a real estate broker acts as agent. The term *client* is also used when a broker represents someone in a relationship other than an agency.
- **Customer**—the third party or nonrepresented consumer who is not a principal but for whom some level of service may be provided and who is entitled to fairness and honesty. The customer may be represented by a separate agent.
- **Nonagent**—(also referred to as a *facilitator*, *intermediary*, *transactional broker*, *transaction coordinator*, or *contract broker*) someone who works with a buyer and a seller (or a landlord and a tenant), assisting one or both parties with the transaction without representing either party's interests. Nonagents are often subject to specific statutory responsibilities. A broker may be considered a nonagent when dealing with a customer (someone other than the person the broker represents).

IN PRACTICE The general discussion here involves the concepts and principles that govern traditional common law agency relationships. Many states have passed agency legislation that supersedes the common law of agency.

Many agency statutes make the common law duties a matter of statutory law rather than (or in addition to) creating totally new legal relationships. While we are providing an overview of current agency laws, a real estate professional should be familiar with the specific terms of any agency statute adopted by the legislature of the state in which the real estate professional does business. The websites listed in the appendix provide access to statutory law, as well as the rules and regulations of each state's real estate licensing agency.

A **single agent** works *for* the principal and *with* the customer.

In what is termed a *single agency* relationship, the agent represents only one of the parties to a transaction, and there is a distinction between the level of services that the agent provides to the *client* the agent represents and those services that the agent provides to the other party, who is the *customer*. The client is the principal to whom the agent gives advice and counsel. The agent is entrusted with certain *confidential information* and has *fiduciary responsibilities* (discussed in greater detail later) to the principal. The client can expect full disclosure of all relevant information learned by the agent. In contrast, the *customer* is entitled to factual information and fair and honest dealings as a consumer but does not receive advice and counsel or have an expectation that information disclosed to the agent will remain confidential. The agent works *for* the principal and *with* the customer. This means that the agent supports and defends the principal's interests, not the customer's.

The relationship between the principal and agent must be *consensual*—that is, the principal *delegates* authority, and the agent *consents* to act. The parties must agree to form the relationship.

Just as the agent owes certain duties to the principal, the principal has responsibilities toward the agent. The principal's primary duties are to comply with the agency agreement and cooperate with the reasonable expectations of the agent—that is, the principal must not hinder the agent and must deal with the agent in good faith. The principal also must compensate the agent according to the terms of the agency agreement.

CREATION OF AGENCY

Later, you will learn about the legal requirements to create a contractual relationship, along with descriptions of the varieties of contracts that are part of a real estate transaction. Here, some of the elements of an agreement to create an agency relationship are discussed.

An agency relationship may be created by an oral or written agreement between the parties, which is an **express agency**. An agency relationship may also result from the parties' behavior by an **implied agency**.

Express Agency

The principal and the agent may enter into a contract, or an **express agreement**, in which the parties formally express their intention to establish an agency and state its terms and conditions. The agreement may be either oral or written, unless a written agreement is required by law. The employment agreement of broker and sales associate must be in writing.

An agency relationship between a real estate seller and a broker is generally created by a written employment contract, commonly called a **listing agreement** (*seller representation agreement*), which authorizes the broker to find a buyer or a tenant for the owner's property. Although a written listing agreement is usually preferred, some states consider an oral agreement binding in some circumstances, although an exclusive representation agreement must be in writing in order to be enforced in court.

An express agency relationship between a buyer and a broker is created by a **buyer representation agreement**. Similar to a listing agreement, the buyer representation agreement stipulates the activities and responsibilities the buyer expects from the broker in finding the appropriate property for purchase or rent.

Implied Agency

An agency may also be created by **implied agreement**. This occurs when the parties act as though they have mutually consented to an agency, even if they have not entered into a formal agency agreement. While neither the real estate professional nor the represented party may have consciously planned to create an agency relationship, they can create one *unintentionally*, *inadvertently*, or *accidentally* by their actions. If the existence of an agency relationship becomes the focus of a legal action, the real estate professional may be in a lose-lose position. If an agency relationship can be shown to have been intended, legal responsibilities may be imposed on the real estate professional even in the absence of a written agency agreement. The real estate professional may also be denied compensation on the grounds that there is no written agreement, as required by law.

IN PRACTICE Prospective buyers enter a real estate office asking to see a property listed with another brokerage. A real estate sales associate immediately calls the sellers' representative and makes an appointment to show the property. Without having the prospective buyers sign a written representation agreement, the sales associate drives them to the house. The intent of the parties to create an agency relationship can be inferred from the actions of the sales associate.

Even though real estate professionals might be required to disclose their agency status, consumers often find it difficult to understand the complexities of the law of agency. Buyers can easily assume that when they contact a real estate sales associate in order to be shown a property, the real estate sales associate becomes their agent, even though, under the listing contract on the property, the real estate sales associate (through the broker) legally represents the seller. An implied agency with the buyer can result if the words and conduct of the sales associate do not dispel this assumption, which may lead to the creation of an illegal undisclosed dual agency (discussed later). Some states prohibit the creation of agency implied by conduct.

Compensation

In a real estate transaction, *the source of compensation does not determine agency*. An agent does not necessarily represent the person who pays the agent's commission. In fact, agency can exist even if no fee is involved (called a *gratuitous agency*).

The seller's agency agreement may allow the seller's broker to make use of the services of other real estate professionals in the broker's firm, as well as other real estate professionals who are part of the broker's MLS. Under such an arrangement, the compensation for a cooperating broker will be paid by the seller's broker out of the commission paid by the seller. A **buyer's agent** could instead be paid directly by the buyer. Any written agency agreement (with seller or buyer) should state how the agent is to be compensated, after all the alternatives are discussed with the client.

Remember, a real estate sales associate can only receive compensation from the sales associate's employing broker.

Fiduciary Responsibilities

The agency agreement between a broker and client usually authorizes the broker to act on the principal's behalf. The agent's **fiduciary relationship** of trust and confidence means that the real estate broker owes the principal certain duties. These duties are not simply moral or ethical, they are the law—the common law of agency and/or the statutory law governing real estate transactions. Under the common law of agency, an agent owes the principal the six duties of *care*, *obedience*, *loyalty*, *disclosure*, *accounting*, and *confidentiality*, which can be remembered as COLD-AC.

Memory Tip

The six common-law fiduciary duties of an agent are COLD-AC:

Care

Obedience

Loyalty

Disclosure

Accounting

Confidentiality

Care Agents must exercise a reasonable degree of care while transacting the business entrusted to them by principals. Principals expect the agent's skill and expertise in real estate matters to be superior to that of the average person. The most fundamental way in which an agent exercises care is to use that skill and knowledge on a principal's behalf. The agent should know all facts pertinent to the principal's affairs, such as the physical characteristics of the property being transferred and the type of financing being used.

If the agent represents the seller, care and skill include helping the seller arrive at an appropriate and realistic listing price, discovering and disclosing facts that affect the seller, and properly presenting, as allowed by law, the contracts and other documents that the seller signs. It also means making reasonable efforts to market the property, such as advertising and holding open houses, and helping the seller evaluate the terms and conditions of offers to purchase.

A real estate broker who represents the buyer is expected to help the buyer locate suitable property and evaluate property values and neighborhood and property conditions, and complete offers and counteroffers, as allowed by law, with the buyer's interest in mind.

A representative who does not make a reasonable effort to properly represent the interests of the principal may be found negligent by a court of law. The representative is liable to the principal for any loss resulting from the representative's negligence or carelessness.

IN PRACTICE Because real estate firms have, under the law, exposure to liability in what is ordinarily a very expensive and complex transaction, some brokers purchase what is known as *errors and omissions* (E&O) *insurance*. Similar to malpractice insurance in the medical and legal fields, E&O policies cover liability for errors and negligence in the listing and selling activities of a real estate broker and often the broker's sales associates. Some E&O insurance companies also offer policies directly to individual sales associates.

Licensing laws in several states now require E&O insurance for brokers and, in some cases, for individual sales associates as well. No insurance policy will protect a real estate professional from a lawsuit or prosecution arising from criminal acts. Insurance companies normally exclude coverage for fraud and violations of civil rights and antitrust laws.

Obedience The fiduciary relationship obligates an agent to act in good faith at all times, obeying the principal's lawful instructions in accordance with the contract. That obedience is not absolute, however. The agent may not obey instructions that are unlawful or unethical. On the other hand, an agent who exceeds the authority assigned in the contract will be liable for any losses that the principal suffers as a result.

Loyalty The duty of loyalty requires that the agent place the principal's interests above those of all others, including the agent's own self-interest. The agent must be particularly sensitive to any possible conflicts of interest. Because the agent may not act out of self-interest, the negotiation of a sales contract must be conducted without regard to how much the agent will earn in commission. All states forbid agents to buy property listed with them for their own accounts or for accounts in which they have a personal interest without first disclosing that interest and receiving the principal's consent. Neither real estate brokers nor real estate sales associates may sell property in which they have a personal interest without informing the purchaser of that interest.

Disclosure It is the agent's duty to keep the principal informed of all facts or information that might affect a transaction. The *duty of disclosure* includes relevant information or *material facts* that the agent knows or in some cases what the agent should have known.

The real estate agent is obligated to discover facts that a reasonable person would feel are important in choosing a course of action, regardless of whether those facts are favorable or unfavorable to the principal's position. The agent may be held liable for damages for failing to disclose such information. Depending on state law, information that must be disclosed could include

- the identity of prospective purchasers, which may include any relationships the purchasers might have with the agent (such as when the agent or a relative of the agent is a purchaser);
- the purchaser's ability to complete the sale or offer a higher price;
- any interest or prospective interest the agent has in the buyer or the buyer's business (such as the broker's agreement to manage the property after it is purchased); and
- an incorrect market value of the property.

A seller's real estate agent is also expected (and required under many states' laws) to disclose information about known material defects in the property to prospective buyers. This may appear to violate the agent's duty of loyalty to the seller, but this requirement falls under the broader duty to serve the general public and can protect the agent from claims of misrepresentation.

In turn, the buyer's agent must disclose deficiencies of a property and the sales contract provisions and financing that may affect the buyer's decision to purchase. The buyer's agent would suggest the lowest price the buyer should pay based on comparable values, regardless of the listing price. If known, the agent would also disclose how long a property has been listed and why the owner is selling, because such information would affect the buyer's ability to negotiate the lowest purchase price. If the agent represents the seller, of course, disclosure of any of this information without the seller's permission would violate the agent's fiduciary duty to the seller.

Other disclosures are discussed later.

IN PRACTICE Selling a property "as is" does not negate provisions already in the contract. If sellers truly mean "as is," they amend any printed provisions existing in the contract that relate to the condition of systems and appliances. The seller must still comply with state laws regarding disclosure of the condition of the property, and selling a property "as is" does not affect the buyer's right to request an inspection of the property. A buyer is free to accept a property in its current condition but has the right to know what that condition is.

Accounting The agent must be able to report the status of all funds received from or on behalf of the principal. Most state laws require that a real estate professional give accurate copies of all documents to all affected parties and keep copies on file for a specified period. Most license laws also require monies to be deposited into an escrow account immediately, or within a specified time. Commingling client monies with personal or general business funds is strictly illegal. *Conversion* is the illegal use of such entrusted money.

Confidentiality Confidentiality is a key element of fiduciary duties. An agent may not disclose the principal's personal information—for example, the principal's financial condition. If the principal is the seller, the agent may not reveal such things as willingness to accept less than the listing price or urgency to sell, unless the principal has authorized the disclosure, and often the authorization must be in writing. If the principal is the buyer, the agent may not disclose the buyer's willingness to pay a higher price, the buyer's tight moving schedule, or other buyer facts that might affect the principal's bargaining position.

The information that must be kept confidential can change if the business relationship changes, such as when a seller's agent becomes a disclosed dual agent, because the broker is now also representing the buyer.

Depending upon state law, the duty of confidentiality could terminate on conclusion of the agency relationship, or it could extend for a number of years, or forever. Under the NAR Code of Ethics, the duty of confidentiality does not expire. Anything a REALTOR® learns about a client that can be considered confidential must remain confidential forever. Check your state's laws for guidance in dealing with confidentiality issues.

TYPES OF AGENCY RELATIONSHIPS

An agency relationship can be classified based on the extent of the agent's authority. An agent's authority to represent the principal can be broad, or it can include only a certain type of activity or a specific transaction.

A **universal agent** is a person empowered to do anything the principal could do personally. The universal agent's authority to act on behalf of the principal is virtually unlimited. A court appointed guardian, for instance, will have the authority granted by the court, which can include caring for both the person and the property of the guardian's ward—the individual who is the subject of the guardianship. A real estate professional typically does not have this scope of authority in a real estate transaction.

A **general agent** represents the principal in certain business matters *generally*; a **special agent** represents the principal only for *specified transactions*, such as the sale of a house.

A **general agent** may represent the principal in a broad range of matters related to a particular business or activity. The general agent may, for example, bind the principal to any contract within the scope of the agent's authority. An entertainer may employ more than one general agent—an agent to find work, as well as a business manager to hire and supervise staff and make other arrangements. A *property manager* hired by the owner of income-producing property is typically a general agent for the owner. A real estate sales associate usually is a general agent of the employing broker.

A **special agent**, or *limited agent*, is authorized to represent the principal in one specific act or business transaction only. A real estate broker is usually a special agent. If hired by a seller, the broker is limited to finding a ready, willing, and able buyer for the seller's property. A special agent for a buyer would have the limited responsibility of finding a property that fits the buyer's criteria. As a special agent, the real estate broker may not bind the principal to any contract.

Disclosure of Agency

Real estate professionals are required to disclose the parties they represent. Understanding the scope of the service a party can expect from the agent allows consumers to make an informed decision about whether to seek their own representation.

Mandatory agency disclosure laws now exist in every state. These laws stipulate when, how, and to whom disclosures must be made. They may, for instance, dictate that a particular type of written form be used. The laws might state what information a real estate professional must provide to gain informed consent where disclosed dual agency is permitted. The laws might require that all agency alternatives be explained, including the brokerage firm's policies regarding the firm's services. Frequently, printed brochures outlining agency alternatives are available to a firm's clients and customers.

Whether or not the law requires it, real estate professionals should explain to both buyers and sellers what agency alternatives exist. Good business practice is to make the disclosure of agency before any confidential information is disclosed about an individual's motivation or financial situation. (*See* Figure 10.1.)

FIGURE 10.1: Agency Disclosure Form

AGENCY RELATIONSHIPS IN REAL ESTATE TRANSACTIONS

Page 1

<u>MINNESOTA LAW REQUIRES</u> that early in any relationship, real estate brokers or salespersons discuss with consumers what type of agency representation or relationship they desire.[1] The available options are listed below. This is **not** a contract. **This is an agency disclosure form only. If you desire representation you must enter into a written contract, according to state law** (a listing contract or a buyer/tenant representation contract). Until such time as you choose to enter into a written contract for representation, you will be treated as a customer and will not receive any representation from the broker or salesperson. The broker or salesperson will be acting as a Facilitator (see paragraph V on page two (2)), unless the broker or salesperson is representing another party, as described below.

ACKNOWLEDGMENT: I/We acknowledge that I/we have been presented with the below-described options. I/We understand that until I/we have signed a representation contract, I/we am/are not represented by the broker/salesperson. I/We understand that written consent is required for a dual agency relationship.

THIS IS A DISCLOSURE ONLY, NOT A CONTRACT FOR REPRESENTATION.

(Signature)	(Date)	(Signature)	(Date)

I. **Seller's/Landlord's Broker:** A broker who lists a property, or a salesperson who is licensed to the listing broker, represents the Seller/Landlord and acts on behalf of the Seller/Landlord. A Seller's/Landlord's broker owes to the Seller/Landlord the fiduciary duties described on page two (2).[2] The broker must also disclose to the Buyer material facts as defined in MN Statute 82.68, Subd. 3, of which the broker is aware that could adversely and significantly affect the Buyer's use or enjoyment of the property. (MN Statute 82.68, Subd. 3 does not apply to rental/lease transactions.) If a broker or salesperson working with a Buyer/Tenant as a customer is representing the Seller/Landlord, he or she must act in the Seller's/Landlord's best interest and must tell the Seller/Landlord any information disclosed to him or her, except confidential information acquired in a facilitator relationship (see paragraph V on page two (2)). In that case, the Buyer/Tenant will not be represented and will not receive advice and counsel from the broker or salesperson.

II. **Subagent:** A broker or salesperson who is working with a Buyer/Tenant but represents the Seller/Landlord. In this case, the Buyer/Tenant is the broker's customer and is not represented by that broker. If a broker or salesperson working with a Buyer/Tenant as a customer is representing the Seller/Landlord, he or she must act in the Seller's/Landlord's best interest and must tell the Seller/Landlord any information that is disclosed to him or her. In that case, the Buyer/Tenant will not be represented and will not receive advice and counsel from the broker or salesperson.

III. **Buyer's/Tenant's Broker:** A Buyer/Tenant may enter into an agreement for the broker or salesperson to represent and act on behalf of the Buyer/Tenant. The broker may represent the Buyer/Tenant only, and not the Seller/Landlord, even if he or she is being paid in whole or in part by the Seller/Landlord. A Buyer's/Tenant's broker owes to the Buyer/Tenant the fiduciary duties described on page two (2).[2] The broker must disclose to the Buyer material facts as defined in MN Statute 82.68, Subd. 3, of which the broker is aware that could adversely and significantly affect the Buyer's use or enjoyment of the property. (MN Statute 82.68, Subd. 3 does not apply to rental/lease transactions.) If a broker or salesperson working with a Seller/Landlord as a customer is representing the Buyer/Tenant, he or she must act in the Buyer's/Tenant's best interest and must tell the Buyer/Tenant any information disclosed to him or her, except confidential information acquired in a facilitator relationship (see paragraph V on page two (2)). In that case, the Seller/Landlord will not be represented and will not receive advice and counsel from the broker or salesperson.

______ (initial) ______ (initial) *I have had the opportunity to review the "Notice Regarding Predatory Offender Information" on page two. (2)*

MN:AGCYDICS-1 (11/10)

FIGURE 10.1: Agency Disclosure Form (continued)

AGENCY RELATIONSHIPS IN REAL ESTATE TRANSACTIONS

Page 2

IV. **Dual Agency - Broker Representing both Seller/Landlord and Buyer/Tenant:** Dual agency occurs when one broker or salesperson represents both parties to a transaction, or when two salespersons licensed to the same broker each represent a party to the transaction. Dual agency requires the informed consent of all parties, and means that the broker and salesperson owe the same duties to the Seller/Landlord and the Buyer/Tenant. This role limits the level of representation the broker and salesperson can provide, and prohibits them from acting exclusively for either party. In a dual agency, confidential information about price, terms and motivation for pursuing a transaction will be kept confidential unless one party instructs the broker or salesperson in writing to disclose specific information about him or her. Other information will be shared. Dual agents may not advocate for one party to the detriment of the other.[3]

Within the limitations described above, dual agents owe to both Seller/Landlord and Buyer/Tenant the fiduciary duties described below.[2] Dual agents must disclose to Buyers material facts as defined in MN Statute 82.68, Subd. 3, of which the broker is aware that could adversely and significantly affect the Buyer's use or enjoyment of the property. (MN Statute 82.68, Subd. 3 does not apply to rental/lease transactions.)

V. **Facilitator:** A broker or salesperson who performs services for a Buyer/Tenant, a Seller/Landlord or both but does not represent either in a fiduciary capacity as a Buyer's/Tenant's Broker, Seller's/Landlord's Broker or Dual Agent. **THE FACILITATOR BROKER OR SALESPERSON DOES NOT OWE ANY PARTY ANY OF THE FIDUCIARY DUTIES LISTED BELOW, EXCEPT CONFIDENTIALITY, UNLESS THOSE DUTIES ARE INCLUDED IN A WRITTEN FACILITATOR SERVICES AGREEMENT.** The facilitator broker or salesperson owes the duty of confidentiality to the party but owes no other duty to the party except those duties required by law or contained in a written facilitator services agreement, if any. In the event a facilitator broker or salesperson working with a Buyer/Tenant shows a property listed by the facilitator broker or salesperson, then the facilitator broker or salesperson must act as a Seller's/Landlord's Broker (see paragraph I on page one (1)). In the event a facilitator broker or salesperson, working with a Seller/Landlord, accepts a showing of the property by a Buyer/Tenant being represented by the facilitator broker or salesperson, then the facilitator broker or salesperson must act as a Buyer's/Tenant's Broker (see paragraph III on page one (1)).

---

[1] This disclosure is required by law in any transaction involving property occupied or intended to be occupied by one to four families as their residence.

[2] The fiduciary duties mentioned above are listed below and have the following meanings:
Loyalty - broker/salesperson will act only in client(s)' best interest.
Obedience - broker/salesperson will carry out all client(s)' lawful instructions.
Disclosure - broker/salesperson will disclose to client(s) all material facts of which broker/salesperson has knowledge which might reasonably affect the client(s)' use and enjoyment of the property.
Confidentiality - broker/salesperson will keep client(s)' confidences unless required by law to disclose specific information (such as disclosure of material facts to Buyers).
Reasonable Care - broker/salesperson will use reasonable care in performing duties as an agent.
Accounting - broker/salesperson will account to client(s) for all client(s)' money and property received as agent.

[3] If Seller(s)/Landlord(s) decide(s) not to agree to a dual agency relationship, Seller(s)/Landlord(s) may give up the opportunity to sell/lease the property to Buyer(s)/Tenant(s) represented by the broker/salesperson. If Buyer(s)/Tenant(s) decide(s) not to agree to a dual agency relationship, Buyer(s)/Tenant(s) may give up the opportunity to purchase/lease properties listed by the broker.

NOTICE REGARDING PREDATORY OFFENDER INFORMATION: Information regarding the predatory offender registry and persons registered with the predatory offender registry under MN Statute 243.166 may be obtained by contacting the local law enforcement offices in the community where the property is located, or the Minnesota Department of Corrections at (651) 361-7200, or from the Department of Corrections Web site at www.corr.state.mn.us.

MN:AGCYDISC-2 (11/10)

Single Agency

In **single agency**, the agent represents only one party to a transaction. The real estate agent must provide fiduciary common law or statutory duties exclusively to one principal within the transaction (who may be *either* the buyer or the seller—or the landlord or the tenant). The customer is the party not represented by the agent. (*See* Figure 10.2.)

While a single agency broker may represent both sellers and buyers (or landlords and tenants) in separate transactions, that broker cannot represent both the buyer and the seller (or the landlord and the tenant) in the same transaction and remain a single agent. Single agency thus avoids conflicts and results in client-based service and loyalty to only one principal in any transaction. On the other hand, it necessarily limits the broker's client base by ruling out the sale of in-house listings to prospective buyers.

Another agency relationship that involves one principal and one agent is the relationship between a real estate broker and a sales associate of that broker. The employing broker is the principal, and the sales associate is authorized to conduct real estate business only as an agent of the employing broker. The sales associate owes the broker the same fiduciary duties that the broker owes to the client—the broker's principal. The sales associate owes those fiduciary duties to the client as well because, as the agent of the broker, the sales associate is the *subagent* of the client.

Seller Representation If a seller enters a listing agreement with a broker to market the seller's real estate, the broker becomes an *agent* of the seller; the seller is the *principal*, the broker's *client*. The broker is obligated to deal honestly with all parties in the transaction and act within the licensing law. The broker is strictly accountable to the principal. The listing contract, the document that usually forms the agency relationship of broker and seller, typically authorizes the broker to use the services of sales associates employed by the broker, as well as the services of other cooperating brokers in marketing the seller's real estate.

FIGURE 10.2: Single Agency

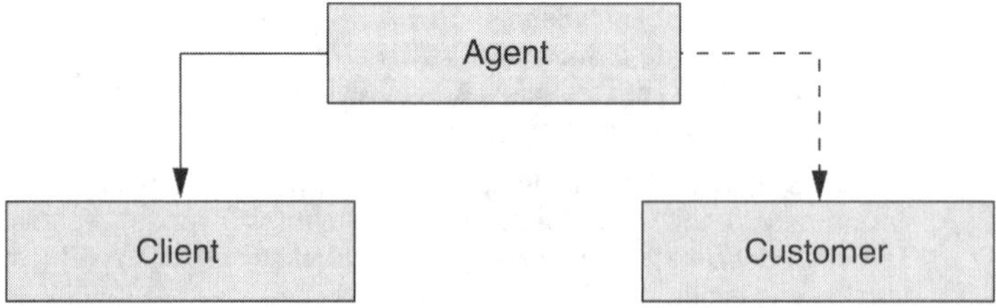

Buyer Representation A buyer who contracts with a broker to locate property and represent the buyer's interests in a transaction is the *principal*—the broker's client. The broker, as *agent*, is strictly accountable to the buyer.

Although it has been customary in commercial transactions, *buyer agency* is relatively new to residential practice but is quickly becoming a popular area of expertise. Real estate commissions or boards across the country have developed rules and procedures to regulate the buyer's agent. Local real estate associations have developed agency representation forms and other materials specifically for the buyer's agent. Professional organizations offer assistance, certification, training, and networking opportunities.

A buyer agency relationship is established in the same way as any other agency relationship: by contract or agreement. The buyer's agent may receive a flat fee or a share of the commission or both, depending on the terms of the agency agreement.

Property Management An owner may employ a broker to market, lease, maintain, or manage the owner's property. Such an arrangement is known as *property management*. The broker is made the agent of the property owner through a property management agreement. As in any other agency relationship, the broker has a fiduciary or statutory responsibility to the client-owner. Sometimes, an owner may employ a broker for the sole purpose of marketing the property to prospective tenants. In this case, the broker's responsibility is limited to finding suitable tenants for the owner's property. Some states recognize a special real estate license for those who exclusively handle property rentals.

A broker can also represent the tenant of either residential or commercial property. A knowledgeable real estate broker is an important resource for a transferred employee needing suitable housing, as well as for the owner of a business seeking to find a larger (or smaller) property or expand to an additional location.

Dual Agency

In **dual agency**, the agent represents two principals in the same transaction. Dual agency requires equal loyalty to two different principals at the same time—a high burden that means neither principal has the full, undivided loyalty of the agent. Dual agency arises, for example, when a real estate broker is the agent of both the seller and the buyer. The broker's sales associates, as agents of the broker, also have fiduciary or statutory responsibilities to the same principals. The challenge is to fulfill these fiduciary obligations to one principal without compromising the interests of the other. While practical methods of ensuring fairness and equal representation may exist, it should be noted that a dual agent can never fully represent either party's interests because the duty of undivided loyalty cannot be shown to both principals at the same time. Similarly, it is impossible to maintain both confidentiality and full disclosure to parties whose interests are in opposition. (*See* Figure 10.3.)

FIGURE 10.3: Dual Agency

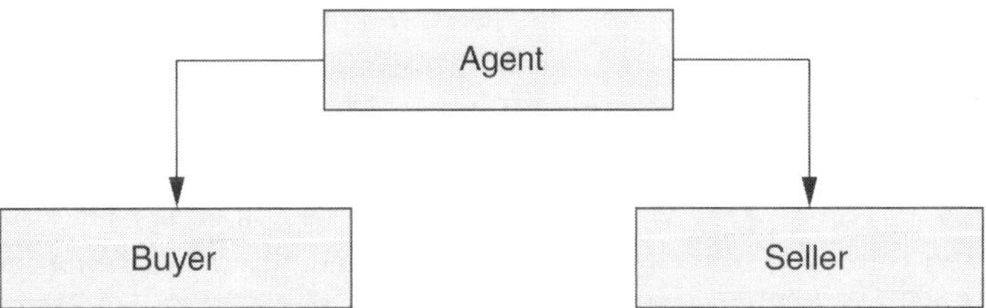

Because of the risks inherent in dual agency—ranging from conflicts of interest to outright abuse of trust—the practice is illegal in some states. In those states where dual agency is permitted, all parties must consent to the arrangement, usually (and always preferably) in writing.

Disclosed Dual Agency Although a conflict of interest still exists, disclosure is intended to minimize the risk for the broker. The disclosure alerts the principals that they might have to assume greater responsibility for protecting their interests than they would if they had independent representation. Because the duties of disclosure and confidentiality are sometimes limited by mutual agreement, they must be carefully explained to the parties in order to establish informed consent.

IN PRACTICE A real estate broker is the agent for the owner of a condominium. A prospective buyer comes into the broker's office and asks her to represent him in a search for a single-family home on a large lot. After several weeks of activity, including two offers unsuccessfully negotiated by the broker, the prospective buyer decides to make an offer on a condominium that he has seen on the broker's website. He tells the broker that he wants to make an offer and asks for the broker's advice on a likely price range. The broker is now in the difficult position of potentially being a dual agent. The broker explains what would be her role as a dual agent—to both the condo seller and the prospective buyer. Both agree that she should represent both of them and both sign the agency disclosure form required by the state. The broker now represents both the seller (who naturally is interested in receiving the highest possible price for his condominium) and the buyer (who is interested in making a successful low offer).

Undisclosed Dual Agency A broker may not intend to create a dual agency. It might occur *unintentionally* or *inadvertently*. Sometimes the cause is carelessness. Other times, a sales associate does not fully understand the fiduciary responsibilities of agency. Some sales associates lose sight of other responsibilities when they focus intensely on bringing buyers and sellers together. For instance, a sales associate representing the seller might suggest to a buyer that the seller will accept less than the listing price. Or the same sales associate might promise to persuade the seller to accept an offer that is in the buyer's best interests. Giving a buyer any specific advice on how much to offer can lead the buyer to believe that the sales associate represents the buyer's interests and is acting as the buyer's advocate.

Any of these actions can create an **implied agency** with the buyer and violate the duties of loyalty and confidentiality to the principal-seller. Because neither party has been informed of the situation and given the opportunity to seek separate representation, the interests of both are jeopardized. This undisclosed dual agency violates licensing laws. It can result in the rescission of the sales contract, forfeiture of a commission, a lawsuit for damages, and possible license problems.

IN PRACTICE In the situation described earlier, if the broker doesn't tell the prospective buyer that she represents the seller of the property, she will be an undisclosed dual agent. The broker has two options. First, knowing the prospective buyer's comfortable financial situation and intense desire for the property, she might choose not to tell the buyer about the dual agency situation. Instead, she could tell him that the condominium's owner will accept nothing less than the full asking price. While this will ensure that the broker receives the maximum possible commission, it will also subject her to severe penalties for violating the state's licensing laws. Alternatively, she can disclose her relationship with the seller, and then she has several options. She could work out a dual agency agreement with both parties in which she legally represents both parties' interests. She could refer the buyer to another broker, enabling her to avoid even the appearance of a conflict of interest. She could also leave the buyer unrepresented.

Designated agency, also called *assigned agency* or *appointed agency*, is available in some states to accommodate an *in-house* sale in which two sales associates of the same broker are involved. The broker designates one sales associate to represent the seller and another sales associate to represent the buyer. Thus, a **designated agent**, or designated representative, is the only sales associate in the company who has a fiduciary responsibility toward the principal. When one sales associate in the company is a designated agent, the other sales associates are free to represent (through the broker) the other party in a transaction. Disclosure of the designated agent status of the sales associates to both parties is required, as is the consent of both parties to the arrangement.

Nonagency

A **nonagent** (also called a **transaction broker**, *facilitator*, *transaction coordinator*, or *contract broker*) is not an agent of either party. A nonagent's job is simply to help both the buyer and the seller with the necessary paperwork and formalities involved in transferring ownership of real property—what may be referred to as *ministerial acts*.

The nonagent is expected to treat all parties honestly and competently, to locate qualified buyers or suitable properties, to help the parties arrive at mutually acceptable terms without acting on behalf of either side, and to assist in the closing of the transaction. The nonagent is equally responsible to both parties and must disclose known defects in a property; however, the nonagent may not negotiate on behalf of either the buyer or the seller and must not disclose confidential information to either party. The buyer and the seller negotiate the sale without the services of the real estate agent(s), though one or both parties may be represented by an attorney during that process.

Termination of Agency

An agency may be terminated for any of the following reasons:

- Completion, performance, or fulfillment of the purpose for which the agency was created
- Death or incapacity of either party
- Destruction or condemnation of the property
- Expiration of the terms of the agency
- Mutual agreement by all parties to cancel the contract
- Breach by one of the parties
- By operation of law, as in bankruptcy of the principal (bankruptcy terminates the agency contract and title to the property transfers to a court-appointed receiver)

An agency coupled with an interest cannot be revoked by the principal acting alone, and it is not terminated upon the principal's death. An agency coupled with an interest will occur, for example, when a real estate agent is made a part-owner of a property that is the subject of a transaction.

Even though an agency relationship has terminated, the fiduciary responsibilities of the agent, such as the duty of confidentiality, might continue.

CUSTOMER-LEVEL SERVICES

An agent owes a **customer** the duties of *reasonable care and skill, honest and fair dealing,* and *disclosure of known facts* about the property.

Even though an agent's primary responsibility is to the principal, the agent also has duties to third parties. When working with a third party, or **customer,** a real estate professional is responsible for adhering to state and federal consumer protection laws, as well as the ethical requirements imposed by professional associations and state regulators. In addition, the real estate professional's duties to the customer typically include

- reasonable care and skill in performance,
- honest and fair dealing, and
- disclosure of all facts that the real estate professional knows or should reasonably be expected to know that materially affect the value or desirability of the property.

Opinion Versus Fact

Real estate brokers and sales associates must always be careful about the statements they make. They must be sure that the consumer understands whether a statement is an opinion or a fact. Statements of opinion are permissible if not made carelessly and there is no intention to deceive.

Statements of fact, however, must be accurate. Exaggeration of a property's benefits is called **puffing.** While puffing is legal, real estate professionals must ensure that none of their statements can be interpreted as fraudulent. For REALTORS®, puffing is considered unethical even if it is legal. **Fraud** is the intentional misrepresentation of a material fact in such a way as to harm or take advantage of another person. That includes not only making false statements about a property but also intentionally concealing or failing to disclose important facts when there is a duty to disclose.

IN PRACTICE While showing a potential buyer an average-looking house, the sales associate described even its plainest features as "charming" and "beautiful." Because the statements were obviously the sales associate's personal opinions designed to encourage a positive feeling about the property (or puff it up), the truth of the statements is not an issue.

The misrepresentation or omission does not have to be intentional to result in real estate professional liability. A **negligent misrepresentation** occurs when the real estate professional should have known that a statement about a material fact was false. A real estate professional's lack of awareness of an issue is no excuse. A misrepresentation due to the professional's carelessness will make the professional culpable (subject to liability). If the buyer relies on the real estate professional's statement, the professional will be liable for any damages that result. Similarly, a real estate professional who accidentally fails to perform some act—for instance, forgetting to deliver a counteroffer—may be liable for damages that result from such a negligent omission. Simple negligence can result in an accidental misrepresentation and, while some damages may result, they may be covered by the real estate professional's errors and omissions insurance.

Disclosures

As part of the recent trend for more consumer protection for purchasers, many states have enacted statutes requiring the disclosure of known adverse property conditions to prospective buyers. Generally, these apply to sellers of residential properties, often for those of one to four dwelling units. Prepurchased structural inspections, termite infestation reports, or other protective documentation may also be used. The actual disclosures that sellers are required to make vary according to each state's law.

Environmental Hazards Disclosure of environmental health hazards, which can render properties unusable for the buyer's intended purpose, may be required. For instance, federal law requires the disclosure of lead-based paint hazards. Frequently, the buyer or the buyer's mortgage lender requests inspections or tests to determine the presence or level of risk.

IN PRACTICE Real estate professionals are encouraged to obtain advice from state and local authorities responsible for environmental regulation whenever the following conditions might be present: toxic-waste dumping; underground storage tanks; contaminated soil or water; nearby chemical or nuclear facilities; and health hazards such as radon, asbestos, and lead paint.

Property Conditions In residential transactions involving property of up to four units, the seller typically has a duty to disclose any known defects that threaten structural soundness or personal safety. A **latent defect** is a hidden structural defect that would not be discovered by ordinary inspection. Buyers may cancel the sales contract or receive damages when a seller fails to reveal known latent defects. The courts also have decided in favor of the buyer when the seller neglected to reveal violations of zoning or building codes. Increasingly, however, there is a growing trend of not only the right but the responsibility of the buyer to discover any material problems with the property. Some states allow the seller to provide a nondisclosure statement to the buyer that places the burden of discovering any adverse property conditions on the buyer.

In addition to the seller's duty in most states to disclose known latent defects, in some states, the agent has an independent duty to conduct a reasonably competent and diligent inspection of the property. It is the real estate professional's duty to discover any material facts that may affect the property's value or desirability, whether or not they are known to or disclosed by the seller. Any such material facts discovered by the real estate professional must be disclosed to prospective buyers. If the real estate professional should have known about a substantial defect that is detected later by the buyer, the real estate professional may be liable to the buyer for any damages resulting from that defect.

IN PRACTICE A broker knew that a house had been built on a landfill. A few days after the house was listed, one of the broker's salespeople noticed that the living room floor was uneven and sagging in places. In some states, both the broker and the salesperson have a duty to conduct further investigations into the structural soundness of the property. (See *Easton v. Strassburger*, 152 Cal. App. 3d 90, a 1984 California case.) In other states, no such duty exists, but the broker and the salesperson would have the duty of discussing the issue with the seller and advising the buyer to have an inspection performed. They cannot simply ignore the problem or place throw rugs over particularly bad spots and hope buyers won't look underneath. If the seller refuses to disclose the problem, then the broker should refuse the listing.

Stigmatized Properties Stigmatized properties are those that society has found undesirable because of events that occurred there or because of proximity of the property to a known nuisance. A common stigma is a criminal event, such as a homicide, illegal drug manufacturing, gang-related activity, or a suicide. Properties have even been stigmatized by rumors that they are haunted. Because of the potential liability to a real estate professional for inadequately researching and disclosing material facts concerning a property's condition, real estate professionals should be fully aware of any relevant state laws.

IN PRACTICE A broker was asked by a potential buyer if a particular neighborhood was safe. The broker knew that the area was experiencing a skyrocketing rate of violent crime but assured the buyer that no problem existed. The broker also neglected to inform the buyer that the lot next to the house the buyer was considering had been sold to a waste disposal company for use as a toxic dump. Both might be examples of fraudulent misrepresentation.

Some states have laws regarding the disclosure of information about such properties, designed to protect sellers, real estate professionals, and local property values against a baseless psychological reaction. In other states, the real estate professional's responsibility may be difficult to define because the issue is not a physical defect but merely a perception that a property is undesirable. Many states provide greater statutory direction to real estate professionals by identifying stigmas that are not considered material facts and that therefore do not require disclosure. Federal law may also provide guidance.

IN PRACTICE A disclosure that a property's previous owner or occupant died of AIDS or was HIV positive constitutes illegal discrimination against a person with a disability under the federal Fair Housing Act and therefore should never be revealed. State law may provide the same prohibition.

www.fbi.gov/scams-safety/registry

Megan's Law The federal legislation known as Megan's Law promotes the establishment of state registration systems to maintain residential information on every person who kidnaps children, commits sexual crimes against children, or commits sexually violent crimes. Upon release from prison, offenders must register their name with state authorities and indicate where they will be residing, and also inform authorities of a change of residence. The Federal Bureau of Investigation (FBI) maintains an internet site, www.fbi.gov/scams-safety/registry, which provides online access to every state's offender registry.

Megan's Law affects a real estate professional's duty of disclosure. In accordance with state law, a real estate professional may need to request that a customer sign a form that includes information on where the customer may obtain information about the sex offender registry. Depending on the state, a real estate professional may be required to disclose information regarding a released offender if the real estate professional is aware that officials have informed individuals, groups, or the public that a sex offender resides in a particular area. Megan's Law, in effect, creates another category of stigmatized property.

KEY POINT REVIEW

Real estate agency relationships are governed by **common law**, which is established by tradition and court decisions, and **statutory law**, which is passed by state legislatures and other governing bodies.

An **agent** is hired by a principal to act on the principal's behalf. **Agency** is the fiduciary relationship in which the agent is held in a position of special trust and confidence by the principal. In a real estate transaction, the **principal** is the **client**. A **customer** is the nonrepresented party for whom some level of service is provided and who is entitled to fairness and honesty.

A **nonagent** (also known as a **facilitator**, **intermediary**, **transaction broker**, **transaction coordinator**, or **contract broker**) assists one or both parties with the transaction without representing either party's interests and often is subject to specific statutory responsibilities.

The relationship between principal and agent must be **consensual**. As **express agency** is based on an express agreement between agent and principal, while an **implied agency** will be created when the actions of the parties indicate that they have mutually consented to an agency. The source of the agent's **compensation** does not determine the agency, because the agent may be compensated by someone other than the client, or the agency may exist even if no compensation is involved—a **gratuitous agency**.

An agent has a **fiduciary relationship** of trust and confidence with the principal. The six common-law fiduciary duties can be remembered as **COLD-AC**, which is an acronym for the following:

- **Care**—An agent must exercise a reasonable degree of care in transacting the principal's business.
- **Obedience**—An agent must act in good faith at all times, with obedience toward the principal's lawful instructions, in accordance with the agency agreement.
- **Loyalty**—An agent must place the principal's interests above those of all others, including the agent's own interests.
- **Disclosure**—An agent is duty-bound to inform the principal of certain relevant facts concerning the transaction, particularly those mandated by state law.
- **Accounting**—An agent must be able to report the status of all funds received from or on behalf of the principal.
- **Confidentiality**—An agent owes the principal confidentiality in carrying out agency obligations.

A **universal agent** is empowered to do anything the principal could do personally.

A **general agent** represents the principal in a broad range of matters.

A **special agent** represents the principal in one specific act or business transaction only, under detailed instruction.

A **single agency** is one in which an agent represents only one party in a transaction. A real estate broker becomes an agent of the seller by entering into a listing agreement for the seller's property. The seller's broker markets the seller's property to potential buyers and performs other services to find a buyer who is ready, willing, and able to purchase on the price and terms set out by the seller in the listing agreement. A **buyer's broker** represents a buyer as an agent to find property that meets the buyer's specifications, as set out in the **buyer representation agreement**.

A **dual agency** is one in which an agent represents two principals in the same transaction. Dual agency, where allowed by state law, requires the **informed consent** of both principals. An **undisclosed dual agency**, which may occur inadvertently, can result in rescission of the sales contract, forfeiture of a commission, a lawsuit for damages, and possibly license suspension or revocation.

A **designated agent** (or **designated representative**) is a sales associate authorized by the broker to represent one party to a transaction, while a different sales associate in the same firm represents the other party to the transaction.

Termination of agency may be accomplished by the

- completion, performance, or fulfillment of purpose of agency;
- destruction or condemnation of the property;
- expiration of the terms of the agency;
- mutual agreement of all parties to the contract;
- breach by one of the parties, who may be liable for damages; or
- operation of law, as in the bankruptcy of the principal.

An **agency coupled with an interest** cannot be revoked by the principal or terminated upon the principal's death.

Statements to clients and customers should be clearly identified as **opinion** or **fact**. **Puffing** is legal exaggeration of a property's benefits, while **fraud** is the intentional misrepresentation of a material fact to harm or take advantage of another person.

A **negligent misrepresentation** occurs when a real estate professional **should have known** that a statement about a material fact was false and the real estate professional's misrepresentation was due to culpable (careless) negligence rather than simple (accidental) negligence.

The **seller** of residential property may have the duty to disclose any known **latent** (i.e., hidden) **defects** that threaten a building's structural soundness or an occupant's personal safety. In some states, an agent has an independent duty to conduct a **reasonably competent and diligent inspection** of the property and to disclose defects to prospective buyers. Disclosure of environmental hazards may be required.

Stigmatized properties may require an agent to consult an attorney. **Megan's Law** requires states to make available to the public information about how they can determine where persons convicted of sexual offenses live in the community.

UNIT 10 QUIZ

1. In a real estate transaction, the term *fiduciary* typically refers to the
   a. sale of real property.
   b. people who give someone else the legal power to act on their behalf.
   c. person who has legal power to act on behalf of another.
   d. agent's relationship to the principal.

2. The relationship between real estate broker and seller is generally what type of agency?
   a. Special
   b. General
   c. Implied
   d. Universal

3. Which statement is *TRUE* of a real estate broker acting as the agent of the seller?
   a. The broker is obligated to render loyalty to the seller.
   b. The broker can disclose confidential information about the seller to a buyer if it increases the likelihood of a sale.
   c. The broker can agree to a change in price without the seller's approval.
   d. The broker can accept a commission from the buyer without the seller's approval.

4. A real estate broker lists a woman's home for sale for $189,500. Later that same day, a man comes into the broker's office and asks for general information about homes for sale in the $130,000 to $140,000 price range but refuses representation by the broker's company at this time. Based on these facts, which statement is *TRUE*?
   a. Both the woman and the man are the broker's customers.
   b. The woman is the broker's client; the man is a customer.
   c. The broker owes fiduciary duties to both the woman and the man.
   d. If the man later asks for buyer representation by the broker's firm, he cannot have it because of the firm's earlier agreement with the woman.

5. In a dual agency situation, a broker may represent both the seller and the buyer in the same transaction if
   a. the broker informs either the buyer or the seller of this fact.
   b. the buyer and the seller are related by blood or marriage.
   c. both parties consent in writing to the dual agency.
   d. both parties are represented by attorneys.

6. Which event will terminate an agency in a broker-seller relationship?
   a. The broker discovers that the market value of the property is such that an adequate commission will not be earned.
   b. The owner declares personal bankruptcy.
   c. The owner abandons the property.
   d. The broker appoints other brokers to help sell the property.

7. Designated agency is *MOST* likely to occur when
   a. there is a client-buyer and a customer-seller.
   b. the seller and the buyer are represented by different companies.
   c. both the buyer and the seller are customers.
   d. the buyer and the seller are represented by the same company.

8. A real estate broker hired by an owner to sell a parcel of real estate must comply with
   a. the common law of agency in the state in which the property owner lives.
   b. a prospective buyer's instructions.
   c. the concept of caveat emptor.
   d. all lawful instructions of the owner.

9. Which of the following is *NOT* a valid reason to terminate an agency relationship?
   a. The agent found a home for a buyer to purchase, and the sale closed.
   b. The property was condemned.
   c. The buyer wanted to work with a new agent, but the terms of agency had not yet expired and the current agent did not agree to terminate.
   d. The buyer went bankrupt.

10. A seller tells his agent in confidence that he must sell fast and may accept less than the list price. The agent tells a buyer the seller will accept up to $5,000 less than the list price. Which is *TRUE*?

   a. The agent has not violated any agency responsibilities to the seller.
   b. The agent should have disclosed this information, regardless of its accuracy.
   c. Disclosure was improper and possibly illegal, regardless of the agent's motive.
   d. The relationship between the agent and the seller ends automatically if the purchaser submits an offer.

11. A buyer who is a client of the broker wants to purchase a house that the broker has listed. Which statement is *TRUE*?

   a. The broker may proceed to write an offer on the property and submit it.
   b. The broker should refer the buyer to another broker to negotiate the sale.
   c. The seller and the buyer must be informed of the situation and agree in writing to the broker's representing both of them.
   d. The buyer should not have been shown a house listed by the broker.

12. What does the phrase *the law of agency is a common law doctrine* mean?

   a. It is a legal doctrine that is not unusual.
   b. It is one of the rules of society enacted by legislatures and other governing bodies.
   c. It is part of a body of law established by tradition and court decisions.
   d. It may not be superseded by statutory law.

13. A broker helps a buyer and a seller with paperwork but does not represent either party. This relationship is

   a. dual agency.
   b. prohibited in all states because a broker must always represent one party.
   c. a transactional brokerage.
   d. a designated agency.

14. A real estate sales associate represents a buyer. At their first meeting, the buyer reveals plans to operate a dog-grooming business out of the purchased house. The sales associate did not check the local zoning ordinances to determine in which parts of town such a business could be conducted. Which common law duty did the sales associate violate?

   a. Care
   b. Obedience
   c. Loyalty
   d. Disclosure

15. A broker tells a buyer, "This home has the most beautiful river view." In fact, the view includes the river and the back of a shopping center. Which is *TRUE*?

   a. The broker has committed fraud.
   b. The broker is guilty of negligent misrepresentation.
   c. The broker is guilty of intentional misrepresentation.
   d. The broker is merely puffing.

16. A real estate broker's responsibility to keep the principal informed of all the facts that might affect a transaction is the duty of

   a. care.
   b. disclosure.
   c. obedience.
   d. accounting.

17. Which of the following is considered dual agency?

   a. A broker acting for both parties in the same transaction
   b. Two brokerage companies cooperating with each other
   c. A broker representing more than one principal
   d. A broker listing a property and then, after it is relisted with another broker, selling the same property

18. The relationship of broker to client in an agency relationship is that of

   a. a trustee.
   b. a subagent.
   c. a fiduciary.
   d. an attorney-in-fact.

19. A real estate broker acting as the agent of the seller

a. must promote and safeguard the seller's best interests.
b. can disclose the seller's minimum price.
c. should present to the seller only the highest offer for the property.
d. can accept an offer on behalf of the seller.

20. A broker is permitted to represent both the seller and the buyer in the same transaction when

a. the principals are not aware of such action.
b. the broker is a subagent rather than the agent of the seller.
c. commissions are collected from both parties.
d. both parties have been informed and agree in writing to the dual representation.

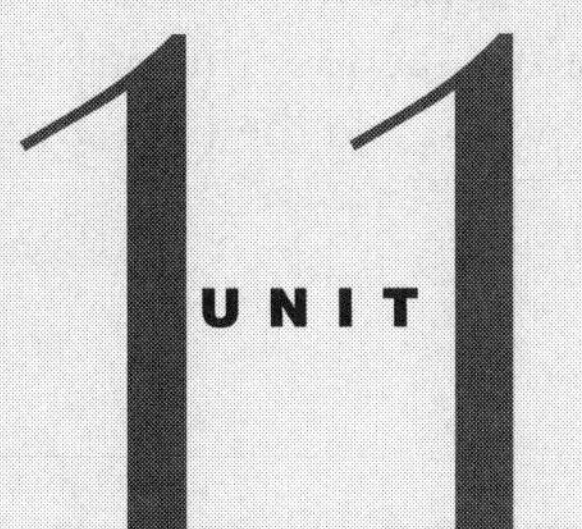

Unit 11: Client Representation Agreements

■ **LEARNING OBJECTIVES** *When you have finished reading this unit, you will be able to*

- **describe** the different types of listing agreements and causes for termination;
- **describe** the listing presentation and the information needed for a listing agreement;
- **identify and explain** the listing agreement terms and the responsibilities of both parties;
- **describe** the types of buyer representation agreements and causes for termination; and
- **define** the following *key terms*:

buyer representation agreement
comparative market analysis (CMA)
exclusive agency listing
exclusive buyer representation agreement
exclusive right-to-sell listing
multiple listing service (MLS)
net listing
open listing

OVERVIEW

A variety of contracts are used throughout the typical real estate transaction, including the agreement between a broker and a sales associate; the terms by which the broker makes use of the multiple listing system; the contract that allows the broker to list property for sale; the agreement by which a buyer makes use of the services of a broker; the sales contract that set out the terms of the transaction; and the escrow, title insurance, and other agreements that are required to complete the transaction.

You have already learned about the employment agreement between broker and sales associate. Here, we look at the agreements by which a broker can be employed to act for a seller or a buyer. The sales contract between seller and buyer, the documents that are needed for the closing of the transaction, the property management agreement between broker and property owner, and the tenant representation agreement will be covered later.

REPRESENTING THE SELLER

The employment contract between a broker and a seller is commonly called the *listing agreement.* It is a contract for the professional services of the real estate broker by which the broker is authorized to represent the principal (and the principal's real estate) to consumers. That authorization includes obtaining and submitting offers for the property. As previously discussed, the real estate sales associate's authority to provide brokerage services originates with the broker. Even though the real estate sales associate may perform most, if not all, of the listing services, the listing remains with the broker, who is responsible for the conduct of the sales associate.

Types of Listing Agreements

Exclusive Right-to-Sell Listing

- One authorized listing broker receives a commission.
- Seller pays listing broker regardless of who sells the property.

The type of listing agreement used by broker and client determines the rights and obligations of the parties. A listing agreement can be *exclusive* to one broker or made available to multiple brokers. *All states require that an exclusive listing agreement be in writing to be enforceable in court.* (*See* Figure 11.1.)

Exclusive Right-to-Sell Listing In an **exclusive right-to-sell listing**, one broker is employed as the seller's sole representative. The broker is given the exclusive right, or authorization, to market the seller's property. If the property is sold while the listing agreement is in effect, the seller must pay the broker a commission, *regardless of who sells the property*. In other words, if the seller finds a buyer, with or without the broker's assistance, the seller *still* must pay the broker a commission.

FIGURE 11.1: Types of Listing Agreements

Exclusive Right to Sell	Exclusive Agency	Open Listing
Seller employs one broker	Seller employs one broker	Seller employs multiple brokers
Listing broker is paid regardless of who sells the property.	Listing broker is paid only if procuring cause of sale.	Only successful listing broker is paid.
	Seller retains the right to sell without obligation to listing broker.	Seller retains the right to sell without obligation to any listing broker.

Sellers benefit from this form of agreement because the broker feels freer to spend time and money actively marketing the property, making a timely and profitable sale more likely. From the broker's perspective, an exclusive right-to-sell listing offers the greatest opportunity to receive a commission. Because of the protection it offers the broker, many brokers have an office policy that sales associates may only take exclusive right-to-sell listings.

Exclusive Agency Listing
- There is one authorized agent.
- Broker receives a commission only if the procuring cause.
- Seller retains the right to sell without obligation.

Exclusive Agency Listing In an **exclusive agency listing**, one broker is authorized to act as the exclusive agent of the principal, but *the seller retains the right to sell the property without the obligation to pay the broker*. When a request is made by a property owner for this type of agreement, the broker would, understandably, be very reluctant to list the property. The request usually means that the seller is reasonably confident of having the contacts needed to be able to sell the property directly and is only listing the property with a broker to show that the offer to sell is sincere. For the broker, this type of listing is very risky and somewhat odd because the broker is placed in the position of expending time and money to market the property only to be in competition with the client to find a buyer.

Open Listing
- There are multiple agents.
- Only the selling agent is entitled to a commission.
- Seller retains the right to sell independently without obligation.

Open Listing In an **open listing** (also known in some areas as a *nonexclusive listing*), the seller retains the right to employ any number of brokers as agents. The listing brokers market the property simultaneously, and the seller is obligated to pay a commission only to the listing broker who successfully produces a ready, willing, and able buyer. If the seller personally sells the property without the aid of any of the listing brokers, the seller is not obligated to pay a commission to any of them.

The terms of an open listing must be negotiated and should be in writing to protect the successful listing broker's ability to collect an agreed-on fee from the seller. An offer to purchase brought to the seller by a buyer's broker should specify the commission or fee to be paid to the buyer's broker out of the sale proceeds, unless the buyer has agreed to compensate the broker by a separate commission or fee.

In a **net listing**, the broker is entitled to any amount exceeding the seller's stated net proceeds.

Net Listing A **net listing** provision specifies that the seller will receive a net amount of money from any sale, with the excess going to the listing broker as commission. The broker is free to offer the property at any price greater than that net amount. Because a net listing can create a conflict of interest between the broker's fiduciary responsibility to the seller and the broker's profit motive, it is illegal in many states and discouraged in others.

Listings Involving Cooperating Brokers

A *multiple listing clause* may be included in an exclusive listing. It is used by brokers who are members of the **multiple listing service (MLS)**. As previously discussed, the MLS is a marketing organization whose broker members make their own exclusive listings available through other brokers who participate in the MLS and gain access to other brokers' listed properties as well. The broker must have the written consent of the seller (which is provided by including the multiple listing clause in the listing agreement) to include the property in an MLS.

The MLS offers advantages to brokers, sellers, and buyers. Brokers develop a sizable inventory of properties and are assured at least a portion of the sales commission if a listing the broker places in the MLS is sold by a participating broker or if the broker sells another broker's listing. Property owners benefit because properties are exposed to a larger market and buyers benefit because they gain access to a wide variety of properties.

The contractual obligations among the member brokers of an MLS vary widely. Most MLSs require that a broker turn over new listings to the service within a specific, fairly short period of time after the broker obtains the listing. The length of time during which the listing broker can offer a property exclusively without notifying the other member brokers varies. Some MLSs permit a broker up to five days before the listing must be submitted to the service.

Under the provisions of most MLSs, a participating broker makes a unilateral offer of cooperation and compensation to other member brokers. The offer is accepted when a *cooperating broker* brings a buyer to the seller and a sale takes place. The cooperating broker typically may choose to work on the seller's behalf as a subagent who bears the same fiduciary responsibilities to the seller as the seller's broker, or the cooperating broker may work as the representative of the buyer. Whether the cooperating broker acts as a subagent of the seller, a *buyer's representative*, or in some other capacity permitted by state law, all initial communication about a buyer's interest in a listed property is broker to broker through the MLS.

IN PRACTICE Technology has enhanced the benefits of MLS membership. In addition to providing instant access to information about the status of listed properties, MLSs often offer a broad range of other useful information about mortgage loans, real estate taxes and assessments, and municipalities and school districts. Access to the MLS database of active, pending, sold, and expired listings is especially helpful to the real estate professional who needs to suggest an appropriate range of listing prices for a particular property. Computer-assisted searches also help buyers select properties that best meet their needs.

Termination of Seller Representation

The success of a contract to represent a property seller depends on the broker's professional efforts. Because the broker's services are unique, the agreement to list property for sale cannot be assigned to another broker without the principal's written consent. The property owner cannot force the broker to perform, but the broker's failure to work diligently toward fulfilling the contract's terms constitutes a breach of the listing agreement. If the listing is canceled by the broker, the seller may be entitled to sue the broker for damages.

On the other hand, a property owner could be liable for damages to the broker by refusing to cooperate with the broker's reasonable requests, such as not allowing the broker to show the property to prospective buyers or refusing to proceed with an accepted sales contract.

A broker's agreement to represent a property seller may be terminated for the following reasons:

- The agreement's purpose is fulfilled by the transfer of title to the buyer.
- The agreement's term expires.
- The property is destroyed, or its use is changed by some force outside the owner's control, such as a zoning change or condemnation by eminent domain.
- Title to the property is transferred by operation of law, as in the case of the owner's bankruptcy or foreclosure.
- The broker and the seller mutually agree to cancel the agreement.
- Either the broker or the seller breaches the agreement, such as by the seller's refusal to consider an offer or the broker's refusal to present an offer to the seller.
- Either the broker or the seller dies or becomes incapacitated. If a sales associate dies or becomes incapacitated, the agreement is still valid.

Expiration of Listing Period

All exclusive listings should specify a definite period during which the broker is to be employed. In most states, failing to specify a definite termination date in a listing is grounds for the suspension or revocation of a real estate license.

Legislatures and courts also have prohibited or discouraged the use in exclusive listings of *automatic extension clauses*, such as a clause providing for a base period of 90 days that "continues thereafter until terminated by either party hereto by 30 days' notice in writing." Extension clauses are illegal in some states, and many listing contract forms specifically provide (as may be required by law) that there can be no automatic extension of the agreement. Some courts have held that an extension clause actually creates an open listing rather than an exclusive agency agreement.

Safety clause

Some listing contracts contain a *broker protection clause*. This clause provides that the property owner will pay the listing broker a commission if, within a specified number of days after the listing expires, the owner transfers the property to someone the broker originally introduced to the owner. This clause protects a broker from losing a commission in the event that the transaction is not completed (and, perhaps, is intentionally delayed) until after the listing expires.

THE LISTING PRESENTATION

The first opportunity that a property owner has to learn what a real estate brokerage can do to bring about a sale of the owner's property typically is in a *listing presentation* made by a sales associate of the broker. The sales associate will describe the marketing efforts that the brokerage will make to bring about a sale of the property as quickly as possible.

Before signing a contract that will go to the broker for review and signature, the sales associate and prospective seller will discuss a variety of issues. The property owner's main concerns typically are the selling price of the property and the net proceeds. The sales associate should already have performed a **comparative market analysis (CMA)** and should be prepared to discuss the range of value in which the property is likely to fall, as well as the charges that will affect the amount that the seller will receive. The CMA is not a formal appraisal, which must meet the separate licensing and other requirements, but instead looks at properties on the market that are similar to the property the seller owns in size, location, and amenities. A comparative market analysis is also referred to as a competitive market analysis. The sales associate, by examining MLS data, can consider the asking prices of properties currently available, as well as the sales prices of properties that have sold recently and the asking prices on property listings that have expired without a sale being achieved. All of this information should make it easier for the seller to decide on a suitable asking price for the subject property.

Common questions property owners may ask include "How quickly will the property sell?" and "What services will the broker provide during the listing period?" The property owner will also want to know whether the property's condition is suitable for showing to prospective buyers, or if certain improvements should be made. This is the sales associate's opportunity to explain the various types of listing agreements, the ramifications of different agency relationships, the marketing services the broker provides, and the other services, such as "staging" the property to make it as attractive as possible, that could be used to help market the property effectively. At the end of this discussion, the seller should have an idea of what is involved in the sale process and should feel comfortable with the decision to list with the broker.

The sales associate will also have questions for the property owner. Before the listing agreement is signed, the seller should provide comprehensive information about the property and indicate any personal concerns about the sale process. Based on this information, the broker can accept the listing with confidence that the seller's goals can be met in a profitable manner for both parties.

Information Needed for a Listing Agreement

Obtaining as many facts as possible about the property ensures that most contingencies can be anticipated. This is particularly important when the listing will be shared with other brokers through the MLS and those real estate professionals must rely on the information taken by the sales associate acting for the listing broker.

The information needed for a listing agreement generally includes the

- names and relationship, if any, of the owners;
- street address and legal description of the property;
- size, type, age, and construction of improvements;
- number of rooms and their sizes;
- dimensions of the lot;
- existing loans, including the name and address of each lender, the type of loan, the loan number, the loan balance, the interest rate, the monthly payment of principal, interest, taxes, and insurance (PITI), whether the loan may be assumed by the buyer and under what circumstances, whether the loan may be prepaid without penalty, and whether or not the lender has approved a *short sale* (one in which the sales price may be less than the amount of the outstanding loan balance) and, if so, whether the seller will incur a personal debt for the difference;
- possibility of seller financing;
- amount of any outstanding special assessments and whether they will be paid by the seller or assumed by the buyer;
- zoning classification of the property;
- current (or most recent year's) property taxes;
- neighborhood amenities (e.g., schools, parks and recreation areas, places of worship, and public transportation);
- real property, if any, to be removed from the premises by the seller and any personal property to be included in the sale for the buyer (both the listing contract and the subsequent purchase contract should be explicit on these points);
- any additional information that would make the property more appealing and marketable; and
- required disclosures regarding property condition.

Disclosures

Most states have enacted laws requiring that real estate professionals disclose whose interests they legally represent. It is important that the seller be informed of the company's policies regarding single agency, subagency, buyer agency, dual agency, and any other forms of representation allowed by state law.

The residential property owner must also disclose the property's condition, as required by law in most states. Property condition disclosures cover a wide range of structural, mechanical, and other conditions that a prospective purchaser should know about in order to make an informed decision. Frequently, state law requires that the property owner complete a standardized form that may require the owner to indicate the condition of specific property features, such as heating and plumbing systems. A real estate professional should always caution a property owner to make truthful disclosures to avoid litigation arising from fraudulent or careless misrepresentations.

THE LISTING CONTRACT

Real estate firms, local and state trade associations, and other groups have worked with their attorneys to draft standardized listing contracts that meet the needs of real estate brokers and their clients, and also comply with the laws and regulations that define acceptable business practices. In some states, independent publishers sell a variety of contract forms that are drafted to meet legal requirements. Even if all the contract wording is not mandated by law, many parts of the agreement may have to use specific wording and appear in a mandated type font and size so that they are clear and conspicuous.

Because contract terms often appear mysterious to the untrained consumer, most states specifically allow a real estate professional to go over the terms of a preprinted contract with a client without risking an accusation of the unlawful practice of law. Figure 11.2 is a sample exclusive right-to-sell listing agreement. It is provided as an example only; many state-specific or regional forms are available online. In addition, many states make available handbooks and other reference materials for real estate professionals, as well as consumers that explain real estate transaction contracts and obligations. Each state real estate agency's website is listed in the appendix.

FIGURE 11.2: Sample Listing Agreement

This form provided to Kaplan Real Estate Education by the Minnesota Association of REALTORS® and is intended for educational purposes only.

LISTING CONTRACT: EXCLUSIVE RIGHT TO SELL

Date ______________________

Page 1 of __________ pages

DEFINITIONS: This Contract involves the property located at ______________________, legally described as ______________________ ______________________("Property").

Seller is ______________________("Seller").

Broker is ______________________("Broker").
(Real Estate Company Name)

This Contract starts on ____________, 20 ____, and ends at 11:59 p.m. on ____________, 20 ____.

This Contract may only be canceled by written mutual agreement of the parties.

PRICE: Seller offers the Property for sale for the price of $ ______________, upon the following terms: ______________________.

LISTING: Seller gives Broker the exclusive right to sell the Property. In exchange, Broker agrees to list and market the Property for sale. Broker may place a "For Sale" sign and a lock box with keys on the Property, unless prohibited by governing authority. Seller understands this Contract DOES NOT give Broker authority to rent or manage the Property. Seller understands Broker may be a member of a Multiple Listing Service ("MLS"), and if Broker is a member of MLS, and where available, Broker may give information to the MLS concerning the Property. Broker may place information on the Internet concerning the Property, including sold information (except as limited in the *Internet Display Options* Form). If Broker sells the Property, Broker may notify the MLS and member REALTORS® of the price and terms of the sale. Seller acknowledges that neither Broker, the MLS, the Minnesota Association of REALTORS®, nor any other broker is insuring Seller or occupant against theft, loss or vandalism.

(Initial)

_______ (Seller) _______ (Seller) Seller acknowledges that Seller has received and has had the opportunity to review the *Internet Display Options* Form.

LISTED FOR LEASE: The Property ☐ **IS** ☐ **IS NOT** currently listed for lease. If **IS**, the listing broker is
(Check one.)
______________________. If **IS NOT**, Seller ☐ **MAY** ☐ **MAY NOT** list the Property for lease during the terms of this Contract with another broker.
(Check one.)

Nothing in this Contract shall prohibit Broker and Seller from entering into a listing agreement for the lease of this Property upon terms acceptable to both parties.

SELLER'S OBLIGATION: Seller shall notify Broker of relevant information important to the sale of the Property. Seller shall cooperate with Broker in selling the Property. Seller shall promptly inform Broker about all inquiries Seller receives about the Property. Seller agrees to provide and pay for any inspections and reports required by any governmental authority. Seller agrees to provide unit owners' association documents, if required. Seller shall remain responsible for security, maintenance, utilities and insurance during the term of this Contract, and for safekeeping, securing and/or concealing any valuable personal property during Property showings or open houses. Seller shall surrender any abstract of title and a copy of any owner's title insurance policy for this Property, if in Seller's possession or control, to buyer or buyer's designated title service provider. Seller shall take all actions necessary to convey marketable title by the date of closing as agreed to in a purchase agreement. Seller shall sign all documents necessary to transfer to buyer marketable title to the Property. Seller has the full legal right to sell the Property.

Seller authorizes Broker, and any other broker authorized by Broker, to preview and show the Property at reasonable times and upon reasonable notice and agrees to commit no act which might tend to obstruct Broker's performance hereunder. If the Property is occupied by someone other than Seller, Seller shall comply with Minnesota law and any applicable lease provisions of an existing lease and provide tenant with proper notice in advance of any Property showing.

FIGURE 11.2: Sample Listing Agreement (continued)

LISTING CONTRACT: EXCLUSIVE RIGHT TO SELL

Page 2

Property located at ____.

SELLER CONTENT LICENSE: In the event Seller provides content, including, but not limited to, any photos or videos of the Property ("Seller Content") to Broker, Seller grants to Broker a nonexclusive, perpetual, world-wide, transferable, royalty free license to sub-license (including through multiple tiers), reproduce, distribute, display, perform and create derivate works of the Seller Content. Seller represents and warrants that Seller has authority to provide Seller Content and Seller Content does not violate any restrictions regarding use including any third-party intellectual property rights or laws. Seller agrees to execute any further documents that are necessary to effect this license.

NOTICE: THE COMPENSATION FOR THE SALE, LEASE, RENTAL OR MANAGEMENT OF REAL PROPERTY SHALL BE DETERMINED BETWEEN EACH INDIVIDUAL BROKER AND THE BROKER'S CLIENT.

BROKER'S COMPENSATION:

Seller agrees to pay Broker a retainer fee of $ ____________________ at the commencement of this Contract, which fee should be kept by Broker whether or not Seller sells the Property. The retainer fee will apply toward satisfaction of any obligation to compensate Broker.

Seller shall pay Broker, as Broker's compensation, ______________ percent (%) of the selling price or $ __________________________, whichever is greater, if Seller sells or agrees to sell the Property during the term of this Contract.

Other: ____

In addition, if before this Contract expires Broker presents a buyer who is willing and able to buy the Property at the price and terms required in this Contract, but Seller refuses to sell, Seller shall still pay Broker the same compensation. Seller agrees to pay Broker's compensation whether Broker, Seller or anyone sells the Property. Seller hereby permits Broker to share part of Broker's compensation with other real estate brokers, including brokers representing only the buyer. Seller agrees to pay Broker's compensation in full upon the happening of any of the following events:

1. the closing of the sale;
2. Seller's refusal to close the sale; or
3. Seller's refusal to sell at the price and terms specified above.

If, within ________ days *(not to exceed six (6) months)* after the expiration of this Contract, Seller sells or agrees to sell the Property to anyone who:

1. during this Contract made inquiry of Seller about the Property and Seller did not tell Broker about the inquiry; or
2. during this Contract made an affirmative showing of interest in the Property by responding to an advertisement, or by contacting Broker or the licensee involved, or was physically shown the Property by Broker and whose name and address is on a written list Broker gives to Seller within 72 hours after the expiration of this Contract;

then Seller shall still pay Broker the compensation noted herein, even if Seller sells the Property without Broker's assistance. Seller understands that Seller does not have to pay Broker's compensation if Seller signs another valid listing contract or facilitator services agreement for this Property after the expiration or cancellation of this Contract, under which Seller is obligated to compensate another licensed real estate broker.

To secure the payment of Broker's compensation, Seller hereby assigns to Broker the gross proceeds from the sale of the Property in an amount equal to the compensation due to Broker under this Contract.

COMPENSATION DISCLOSURE: Broker's compensation to cooperating brokers shall be as specified in the MLS unless Broker notifies Seller otherwise in writing.

CLOSING SERVICES:

NOTICE: THE REAL ESTATE BROKER, LICENSEE REPRESENTING OR ASSISTING SELLER OR REAL ESTATE CLOSING AGENT HAS NOT EXPRESSED AND, UNDER APPLICABLE STATE LAW, MAY NOT EXPRESS OPINIONS REGARDING THE LEGAL EFFECT OF THE CLOSING DOCUMENTS OR OF THE CLOSING ITSELF.

After a purchase agreement for the Property is signed, arrangements must be made to close the transaction. Seller understands that no one can require Seller to use a particular person in connection with a real estate closing and that Seller may arrange for a qualified closing agent or Seller's attorney to conduct the closing.

FIGURE 11.2: Sample Listing Agreement (continued)

LISTING CONTRACT: EXCLUSIVE RIGHT TO SELL

Page 3

Property located at ____.

Seller's choice for closing services. *(Initial one.)*

_______ (Seller) _______ (Seller) Seller wishes to have Broker arrange for the closing.

_______ (Seller) _______ (Seller) Seller shall arrange for a qualified closing agent or Seller's attorney to conduct the closing.

ADDITIONAL COSTS: Seller acknowledges that Seller may be required to pay certain closing costs, which may effectively reduce the proceeds from the sale.

Seller understands that mortgage financing services are usually paid for by buyer; however, certain insured government loans may require Seller to pay a portion of the fees for the mortgage loan. Seller understands that Seller shall not be required to pay the financing fees on any mortgage without giving Seller's written consent.

WARRANTY: There are warranty programs available for some properties which warrant the performance of certain components of a property, which warranty programs Seller may wish to investigate prior to the sale of the Property.

AGENCY REPRESENTATION: If a buyer represented by Broker wishes to buy the Seller's Property, a dual agency will be created. This means that Broker will represent both the Seller and the buyer, and owe the same duties to the buyer that Broker owes to the Seller. This conflict of interest will prohibit Broker from advocating exclusively on the Seller's behalf. Dual agency will limit the level of representation Broker can provide. If a dual agency should arise, the Seller will need to agree that confidential information about price, terms, and motivation will still be kept confidential unless the Seller instructs Broker in writing to disclose specific information about the Seller. All other information will be shared. Broker cannot act as a dual agent unless both the Seller and the buyer agree to it. By agreeing to a possible dual agency, the Seller will be giving up the right to exclusive representation in an in-house transaction. However, if the Seller should decide not to agree to a possible dual agency, and the Seller wants Broker to represent the Seller, the Seller may give up the opportunity to sell the Property to buyers represented by Broker.

<u>Seller's Instructions to Broker:</u>

Having read and understood this information about dual agency, Seller now instructs Broker as follows:

☐ Seller will agree to a dual agency representation and will consider offers made by buyers represented by Broker.

☐ Seller will not agree to a dual agency representation and will not consider offers made by buyers represented by Broker.

Real Estate Company Name: ____

Seller: ______________________________

By: ______________________________ (Licensee) Seller: ______________________________

Date: ______________________________

OTHER POTENTIAL SELLERS: Seller understands that Broker may list other properties during the term of this Contract. Seller consents to Broker representing or assisting such other potential sellers before, during and after the expiration of this Contract.

PREVIOUS AGENCY RELATIONSHIPS: Broker or licensee representing or assisting Seller may have had a previous agency relationship with a potential buyer of Seller's Property. Seller acknowledges that Seller's Broker or licensee representing or assisting Seller is legally required to keep information regarding the ultimate price and terms the buyer would accept and the motivation for buying confidential, if known.

INDEMNIFICATION: Broker will rely on the accuracy of the information Seller provides to Broker. Seller agrees to indemnify and hold harmless Broker from and against any and all claims, liability, damage or loss arising from any misrepresentation, misstatement, omission of fact or breach of a promise by Seller. Seller agrees to indemnify and hold harmless Broker from any and all claims or liability related to damage or loss to the Property or its contents, or any injury to persons in connection with the marketing of the Property. Indemnification by Seller shall not apply if the damage, loss or injury is the result of the gross negligence or willful misconduct of the Broker.

MN:LC:ERS-3 (8/13)

FIGURE 11.2: Sample Listing Agreement (continued)

LISTING CONTRACT: EXCLUSIVE RIGHT TO SELL

Page 4

Property located at ____.

CERTIFICATION INDIVIDUAL TRANSFEROR: Section 1445 of the Internal Revenue Code provides that a transferee (buyer) of a U.S. real property interest must be notified in writing and must withhold tax if the transferor (Seller) is a foreign person and the sale price exceeds $300,000. In the event transferor (Seller) is a foreign person and the sale price exceeds $300,000, requirements of the 1980 Foreign Investment in Real Property Tax Act (FIRPTA) will be fulfilled.

Seller(s) states and acknowledges the following: Seller is a citizen of the United States or, if a corporation, partnership or other business entity, duly incorporated in the United States or, if a partnership or business entity, formed and governed by the laws of the United States: ☐ Yes ☐ No

If "No," please state country of citizenship, incorporation or the like: ______________________

Under the penalties of perjury Seller declares that Seller has examined this certification and, to the best of Seller's knowledge and belief, it is true, correct and complete.

FAIR HOUSING NOTICE: Seller understands that Seller shall not refuse to sell, or discriminate in the terms, conditions or privileges of sale, to any person due to his/her race, color, creed, religion, national origin, sex, marital status, status with regard to public assistance, handicap (whether physical or mental), sexual orientation or family status. Seller understands further that local ordinances may include other protected classes.

ADDITIONAL NOTICES AND TERMS: As of this date Seller has not received notices from any municipality, government agency or unit owners' association about the Property that Seller has not informed Broker about in writing. Seller agrees to promptly inform Broker, in writing, of any notices of such type that Seller receives during the term of this Contract.

This shall serve as Seller's written notice granting Broker permission to obtain mortgage information (e.g., mortgage balance, interest rate, payoff and/or assumption figures) regarding any existing financing on the Property. A copy of this document shall be as valid as the original.

ELECTRONIC SIGNATURES: The parties agree the electronic signature of any party on any document related to this transaction constitute valid, binding signatures.

CONSENT FOR COMMUNICATION: Seller authorizes Broker and its representatives to contact Seller by mail, phone, fax, e-mail or other means of communication during the term of this Agreement and anytime thereafter.

OTHER: ____

____

____

____.

ACCEPTED BY: ____
(Real Estate Company Name)

BY: ____
(Licensee) (Date)

ACCEPTED BY: ______________________ (Seller)

ACCEPTED BY: ______________________ (Seller)

______________________ (Date) ______________________ (Date)

______________________ (Address) ______________________ (Address)

______________________ (Phone) ______________________ (Phone)

______________________ (E-mail Address) ______________________ (E-mail Address)

THIS IS A LEGALLY BINDING CONTRACT BETWEEN SELLER AND BROKER.
IF YOU DESIRE LEGAL OR TAX ADVICE, CONSULT AN APPROPRIATE PROFESSIONAL.

Listing Agreement Provisions

Regardless of which type of listing agreement is used, the same considerations arise in most real estate transactions. Even though all listing contracts require similar information, real estate professionals should review the specific forms used in their areas and refer to their states' laws for any specific requirements.

Names of All Parties to the Contract Anyone who has an ownership interest in the property must be identified and should sign the listing to validate it. If the property has co-owners, that fact should be clearly established. If one or more of the co-owners is married, the spouse's consent and signature on the contract to release any marital rights is required in most states. If the property is in the possession of a tenant, that should be disclosed (along with the terms of the tenancy), and instructions should be included on how the property is to be shown to prospective buyers.

Brokerage Firm The brokerage company name, the employing broker, and if applicable, the sales associate taking the listing must all be identified, even though the sales associate only acts on behalf of the broker and is not a party to the agreement.

Description of the Premises In addition to the street address, the legal description, lot size, and tax parcel number may be required for future purchase offers.

Listing Price This is the proposed sales price and is also called the *asking price*. This usually is a starting point for negotiation rather than the amount that will actually be agreed upon in the eventual purchase contract. What the seller will receive is the actual sales price, although the seller's proceeds usually will be reduced by unpaid real estate taxes, special assessments, mortgage debts, seller closing costs, brokerage fee, and any other outstanding obligations. If this is to be a short sale, the approval of the current lienholder(s) of any debts secured by the seller's property must be sought, and that fact should be included in all marketing.

Broker's Authority and Responsibilities The contract should specify whether the broker may place a sign on the property and advertise; it should address when the property can be shown, allowing reasonable notice to the seller. It should also address whether or not the broker may accept earnest money on behalf of the seller, and the responsibilities for holding the funds. The broker does not have the authority to sign any legal documents or contracts without first obtaining a power of attorney from the seller or the seller's representative.

Broker's Compensation The circumstances under which the broker will be paid must be specifically stated in the contract. The broker's compensation could be a percentage of the sales price (commission) or a flat rate, and it is usually paid at closing directly by the seller or the party handling the closing. The seller must also indicate whether the compensation may be shared with a cooperating broker.

MATH CONCEPTS

Calculating Sales Price, Commission, and Net to Seller

When a property sells, the sales price equals 100% of the money being transferred. If a broker is to receive a 5% commission, 95% will remain for the seller's other expenses and equity. To calculate a commission using a sales price of $325,000 and a commission rate of 5%, multiply the sales price by the commission rate:

$325,000 × 5% = $325,000 × 0.05 = $16,250 commission

To calculate a sales price using a commission of $16,250 and a commission rate of 6%, divide the commission by the commission rate:

$16,250 ÷ 6% = $16,250 ÷ 0.06 = $270,833 sales price

To calculate a commission rate using a commission of $8,200 and a sales price of $164,000, divide the commission by the sales price:

$8,200 ÷ $164,000 = 0.05, or 5% commission rate

To calculate the net to the seller using a sales price of $125,000 and a commission rate of 4%, multiply the sales price by 100% minus the commission rate:

$125,000 × (100% – 4%) = $125,000 × (96%) = $125,000 × 0.96 = $120,000

The same result can be achieved by calculating the commission ($125,000 × 0.04 = $5,000) and deducting it from the sales price ($125,000 – $5,000 = $120,000); however, this involves unnecessary extra calculations.

$$\frac{\text{commission}}{\text{sales price} \times \text{commission rate}}$$

Real Property and Personal Property Any personal property that will be included in the sale of the real estate must be explicitly identified. Items of real property that the seller expects to remove at the time of the sale must be specified as well. Some items that may later become points of negotiation might include major appliances, swimming pool and spa equipment, fireplace accessories, storage sheds, window treatments, stacked firewood, and stored heating oil.

Leased Equipment It must be determined if leased equipment—security system, cable television boxes, water softener, special antenna—will be left with the property. If so, the seller is responsible for notifying the equipment's lessor of the change of property ownership.

Proposed Dates for Closing and Buyer's Possession These dates should be based on an anticipated closing date. The listing agreement should allow adequate time for the paperwork involved (including the buyer's qualification for any financing) and the move-in date to be arranged by the seller and the buyer. A short sale means that the lienholder(s) must approve the transaction, possibly at several stages, which will add at least several months to the closing process.

Closing An attorney, title company, or escrow company should be considered and retained as soon as possible and may be required by state law. A designated party will be needed to complete the paperwork, disburse the funds, and file the proper forms, such as documents to be recorded and documents to be sent to the IRS.

Evidence of Ownership A warranty deed, title insurance policy, abstract of title with an attorney's opinion, or other documentation customary in the area will be used for proof of title.

Encumbrances All liens will be paid in full by the seller or be assumed by the buyer at the closing.

Home Warranty Program To make the property more desirable to potential buyers, the seller may agree at the time of the listing to purchase a home warranty when a sale closes to cover the property's plumbing, electrical, and heating systems, water heaters, duct work, and major appliances. (Of course, the buyer may purchase a home warranty at closing if the seller doesn't offer or agree to do so.)

Termination of the Contract A contract should provide a way for the parties to terminate the agreement and should specify under what circumstances the contract can be terminated. Under certain circumstances, an agreement can be canceled if the seller arbitrarily refuses to sell or cooperate.

Broker Protection Clause Brokers may be well advised to protect their interests against possible fraud or a reluctant buyer's change of heart. Usually, the contract will include a period of time during which the broker will be entitled to a fee if a sale is closed with someone who was introduced to the seller by the broker while the contract was in effect.

Warranties by the Owner The owner is responsible for certain assurances and disclosures. Is the property suitable for its intended purpose? Does it comply with the appropriate zoning and building codes? Will it be transferred to the buyer in essentially the same condition as it was originally presented, considering repairs or alterations to be made as provided for in a purchase contract? Are there any known defects that should be revealed to a prospective buyer?

Indemnification (Hold Harmless) Wording The seller and the broker may agree to hold each other harmless (i.e., not to sue one another) for any incorrect information supplied by one to the other. Indemnification may be offered, regardless of whether the inaccuracies are intentional or unintentional.

Nondiscrimination (Equal Opportunity) Wording The seller must understand that the property will be shown and offered without regard to the race, color, religion, national origin, familial status, sex, or disability of the prospective buyer. Refer to state and local fair housing laws for a complete listing of protected classes in your area. There are also federal, state, and local laws that prohibit discrimination in lending and other aspects of a real estate transaction.

Antitrust Wording The contract should state that all fees have been negotiated between the seller and the broker; to do otherwise is a violation of antitrust laws.

Signatures of the Parties All parties identified in the contract must sign the contract, including all individuals who have a legal interest in the property.

Date the Contract Is Signed This date may be different from the date the contract actually becomes effective. For example, a sales associate may take the listing and, in some states, then must have the broker sign the contract to accept employment under its terms.

REPRESENTING THE BUYER

Like a listing agreement, a **buyer representation agreement** is an employment contract. In this case, the broker is employed by the buyer and the purpose of the agreement is to find a suitable property. The type of representation will determine the relationship of broker and client. Although the term *buyer agency* may be used to refer to any type of buyer-broker relationship, in some states the buyer and the broker can also establish a relationship that is less than agency. State law will define the nature of the buyer-broker relationship.

An agency agreement will give the buyer a degree of representation possible only in a fiduciary relationship. A broker acting as the agent of the buyer must protect the buyer's interests at all points in the transaction.

Buyer Representation Provisions

A number of topics must be discussed by broker (typically acting through a sales associate) and buyer before they sign a buyer representation agreement. For instance, a sales associate should make the same disclosures to a prospective buyer that would be made to a prospective seller in a listing presentation. The sales associate should explain the types of representation available and the parties' rights and responsibilities under each. The specific services provided to a buyer-client should be clearly explained.

In an **exclusive buyer representation agreement**, the buyer works with only one broker, although the broker is free to represent other buyer clients. If the representation is not exclusive, the buyer can work with two or more brokers, which may create a problem if more than one broker suggests the same property to the buyer. A *nonexclusive representation* may work if the buyer is considering a purchase in more than one geographic area; each broker's familiarity with a particular area will help find the property or properties that best match the buyer's needs.

Figure 11.4 is a sample exclusive buyer representation agreement. As noted earlier, examples of state, regional, and local contract forms may be available online for your state.

Compensation issues should be addressed, whatever the type of representation. The buyer's broker may be compensated in the form of a flat fee for services, an hourly rate, a percentage of the purchase price, or some combination of those methods. The broker may require a *retainer fee* at the time the agreement is signed to cover initial expenses. The retainer may be applied as a credit toward any fees due at the closing. As in any brokerage agreement, the source of compensation does not determine the relationship of the parties. A buyer's broker may be compensated by either the buyer or (through the listing broker) the seller. Issues of compensation are always negotiable.

Figure 11.3 lists the obligations owed to a buyer by the broker who works for the buyer, as well as the obligations owed to a buyer by the broker who works for the seller. While many of the responsibilities are the same, there are distinct differences that direct the actions of the seller's and buyer's representatives.

FIGURE 11.3: Obligations of Real Estate Broker to Buyer

Broker Works for Seller	Broker Works for Buyer
Responsibilities	
Be honest with buyer but responsible to seller, including duty of skill and care to promote and safeguard seller's best interests	Be fair with seller but responsible to buyer, including duty of skill and care to promote and safeguard buyer's best interests
Earnest Money Deposit	
Collect amount sufficient to protect seller	Suggest deposit sufficient to indicate sincerity in offer; put money in interest-bearing account if required by state law
Seller Financing	
Encourage financing terms and contract provisions favorable to seller, such as (1) due-on-sale clause, (2) deficiency judgment, (3) secured note. If a corporate buyer, suggest seller require personal guaranty	Suggest terms in best interests of buyer, such as low down payment, deferred interest, long maturity date, no due-on-sale clause, long grace period, security interest limited to the real property (nonrecourse)
Property Condition	
Require seller to fill out all disclosure forms	Require that seller sign property condition statement and confirm representations of condition; require soil and termite inspections, if appropriate; look for negative features and use them to negotiate better price and terms
Documents	
Give buyer a copy of important documents, such as mortgage to be assumed, declaration of restrictions, title report, condominium bylaws	Research and explain significant portions of important documents affecting transaction, such as prepayment penalties, subordination, right of first refusal; refer buyer to expert advisers when appropriate
Negotiation	
Use negotiating strategy and bargaining talents in seller's best interests	Use negotiating strategy and bargaining talents in buyer's best interests
Showing	
Show buyer properties in which broker's commission is protected, such as in-house or MLS-listed properties. Pick best times to show properties. Emphasize attributes and amenities	Search for best properties for buyer to inspect, widening marketplace to for-sale-by-owner properties, lender-owned (REO) properties, probate sales, unlisted properties. View properties at different times to find negative features, such as evening noise, afternoon sun, traffic congestion
Property Goals	
Find a buyer whose stated objectives match the seller's property on the seller's price and terms	Counsel buyer as to developing accurate objectives; may find that buyer who wants apartment building might be better off with duplex at half the price or that buyer looking for vacant lot would benefit more from investment in improved property
Offers	
Transmit all offers to seller. Consult with seller about possible action steps (e.g., accept offer, counteroffer, reject offer)	Help buyer prepare strongest offer at least risk to buyer
Possession Dates	
Consider best date for seller in terms of moving out, notice to existing tenants, impact on insurance, risk of loss provision	Consider best date for buyer in terms of moving in, storage, favorable risk of loss provision if fire destroys property before closing
Default	
Discuss remedies upon default by either party. Point out to seller any attempt by buyer to limit liability (nonrecourse; deposit money as liquidated damages)	Consider having seller pay buyer's expenses and cancellation charges if seller defaults

FIGURE 11.3: Obligations of Real Estate Broker to Buyer (continued)

Broker Works for Seller	Broker Works for Buyer
Efficiency	
As listing broker, expend much time and effort in helping seller sell property	Broker's role is to assist buyer in locating and acquiring best property, not to sell buyer a particular property
Appraisal	
No duty to disclose low appraisal or fact broker sold similar unit yesterday for $10,000 less	Review comparable sales from buyer's perspective

Termination of Buyer Representation

Just as with a contract to represent a property seller, the success of a contract to represent a property buyer depends on the broker's professional efforts; the agreement to find a suitable property for the buyer cannot be assigned to another broker without the buyer's written consent. The prospective buyer cannot force the broker to perform, but the broker's failure to work diligently toward fulfilling the contract's terms constitutes a breach of the buyer representation agreement. If the agreement is canceled by the broker, the buyer may be entitled to sue the broker for damages. The buyer could be liable for damages to the broker by refusing to cooperate with the broker's reasonable requests, such as viewing property that the broker has located or refusing to proceed with an accepted sales contract.

A broker's agreement to represent a property buyer may be terminated for the following reasons:

- The agreement's purpose is fulfilled by the transfer of title to the buyer.
- The agreement's term expires.
- The broker and the buyer mutually agree to cancel the agreement.
- Either the broker or the buyer breaches the terms of the agreement, such as by the buyer failing to pay an agreed-upon retainer fee to the broker.
- Either the broker or the buyer dies or becomes incapacitated. If a sales associate dies or becomes incapacitated, the agreement is still valid.

If a transaction fails to be completed through no fault of the buyer or the buyer's broker, the representation will survive, provided the agreement's term has not expired.

FIGURE 11.4: Sample Buyer Representation Agreement

This form provided to Kaplan Real Estate Education by the Minnesota Association of REALTORS® and is intended for educational purposes only.

BUYER REPRESENTATION CONTRACT: EXCLUSIVE

This form approved by the Minnesota Association of REALTORS®, which disclaims any liability arising out of use or misuse of this form.

Date ______________________________

Page 1 of __________ pages

DEFINITIONS: Buyer is ______________________________ ("Buyer").

Broker is ______________________________ ("Broker").
(Real Estate Company Name)

Buyer gives Broker the exclusive right to locate and/or to assist in negotiations for the purchase, exchange of or option to purchase ("Purchase") property at a price and with terms acceptable to Buyer. This Contract starts on ______________, 20______, and ends at 11:59 p.m. on ______________, 20______.

This Contract may only be canceled by written mutual agreement of the parties.

BROKER'S OBLIGATION: Broker shall make a reasonable effort to locate property acceptable to Buyer. Broker shall use professional knowledge and skills to assist in negotiations for the Purchase of property. Broker shall assist Buyer throughout the transaction. Broker shall act in Buyer's best interest at all times, subject to any limitations imposed by law or dual agency. Broker shall comply with all applicable fair housing and nondiscrimination regulations.

BUYER'S OBLIGATION: Buyer shall work exclusively with Broker for the Purchase of property. Buyer shall promptly furnish to Broker accurate and relevant personal financial information to ascertain Buyer's ability to Purchase property, if requested. Buyer shall cooperate with Broker in finding a property to Purchase. After a purchase agreement has been accepted by seller, Buyer is legally obligated to Purchase the property. If Buyer refuses to close the Purchase for any reason other than the failure of seller to perform, subject to relevant contingencies, Buyer shall pay Broker all compensation due under this Contract.

NOTICE: THE COMPENSATION FOR THE PURCHASE, LEASE, RENTAL OR MANAGEMENT OF REAL PROPERTY SHALL BE DETERMINED BETWEEN EACH INDIVIDUAL BROKER AND THE BROKER'S CLIENT.

BROKER'S COMPENSATION: *(Fill in all blanks.):*
If Buyer, or any other person acting on Buyer's behalf, agrees to Purchase any property during the term of this Contract, the following compensation will apply.

1. Buyer agrees to pay Broker a retainer fee of $ ______________ at the commencement of this Contract, which fee shall be kept by Broker whether or not Buyer Purchases property. The retainer fee shall apply toward satisfaction of any obligation to compensate Broker.
2. Buyer shall pay Broker, as Broker's compensation, __________ percent (%) of the selling price or $ ______________________, whichever is greater, when Buyer closes the Purchase, if:

   A: Buyer Purchases or agrees to Purchase a property before the expiration of this Contract, even if Buyer does not use Broker's services; or

   B: within ________ days *(not to exceed six (6) months)* after the expiration of this Contract, Buyer Purchases property which either Broker or licensee representing or assisting Buyer has physically shown Buyer or in which Buyer has made an affirmative showing of interest to Broker or licensee representing or assisting Buyer before the expiration of this Contract, as long as Broker has identified this property on a written list Broker gives to Buyer within 72 hours after the expiration of this Contract.

Broker is authorized to negotiate and receive compensation paid by seller, or broker representing or assisting seller, if Broker informs Buyer in writing before Buyer signs an offer to Purchase the property. Any compensation accepted by Broker from seller, or broker representing or assisting seller, ☐ **SHALL** ☐ **SHALL NOT** reduce any obligation of Buyer
(Check one.)
to pay the compensation by the amount received by seller or broker.

Buyer understands that Buyer does not have to pay Broker's compensation if Buyer signs another valid buyer representation contract or facilitator services agreement after the expiration or cancellation of this Contract, under which Buyer is obligated to compensate another licensed real estate broker.

FIGURE 11.4: Sample Buyer Representation Agreement (continued)

BUYER REPRESENTATION CONTRACT: EXCLUSIVE

Page 2

CAUTION: BUYER'S ACTIONS IN LOCATING A PROPERTY MAY AFFECT PAYMENT OF COMPENSATION BY SELLER(S) AND MAY THEREFORE OBLIGATE BUYER TO PAY ALL OR PART OF THE COMPENSATION IN CASH AT CLOSING. FOR EXAMPLE: THE ACT OF GOING THROUGH AN OPEN HOUSE UNACCOMPANIED BY BUYER'S BROKER OR LICENSEE REPRESENTING OR ASSISTING BUYER; OR SIGNING A PURCHASE AGREEMENT THROUGH ANOTHER BROKER OR WITH OWNER (FOR SALE BY OWNER) MAY REQUIRE BUYER'S PAYMENT OF THE FULL COMPENSATION TO BUYER'S BROKER.

GENERAL NATURE OF PROPERTY: (Including the following property types: existing, new construction or to-be-built.) *(Check all that apply.)*

☐ Commercial/Industrial ☐ Farm ☐ Recreation
☐ Residential/Investment ☐ Residential/Personal ☐ Vacant Land

CLOSING SERVICES:

NOTICE: THE REAL ESTATE BROKER, LICENSEE REPRESENTING OR ASSISTING BUYER OR REAL ESTATE CLOSING AGENT HAS NOT EXPRESSED AND, UNDER APPLICABLE STATE LAW, MAY NOT EXPRESS OPINIONS REGARDING THE LEGAL EFFECT OF THE CLOSING DOCUMENTS OR OF THE CLOSING ITSELF.

After a purchase agreement for the property is signed, arrangements must be made to close the transaction. Buyer understands that no one can require Buyer to use a particular person in connection with a real estate closing and that Buyer may arrange for a qualified closing agent or Buyer's attorney to conduct the closing.

Buyer's choice for closing services. *(Initial one.)*

______ (Buyer) ______ (Buyer) Buyer wishes to have Broker arrange for the closing.

______ (Buyer) ______ (Buyer) Buyer shall arrange for a qualified closing agent or Buyer's attorney to conduct the closing.

ADDITIONAL COSTS: Buyer acknowledges that Buyer may be required to pay certain closing costs, which may effectively increase the cash outlay at closing.

PRIVATE INSPECTION/WARRANTY: Broker recommends that Buyer obtain a private home inspection to satisfy himself/herself with the physical condition of the property. Furthermore, there are warranty programs available for some properties which warrant the performance of certain components of a property, which warranty programs Buyer may wish to investigate prior to the Purchase of any specific property.

AGENCY REPRESENTATION: If the Buyer chooses to Purchase a property listed by Broker, a dual agency will be created. This means that Broker will represent both the Buyer and the seller, and owe the same duties to the seller that Broker owes to the Buyer. This conflict of interest will prohibit Broker from advocating exclusively on the Buyer's behalf. Dual agency will limit the level of representation Broker can provide. If a dual agency should arise, the Buyer will need to agree that confidential information about price, terms and motivation will still be kept confidential unless the Buyer instructs Broker in writing to disclose specific information about the Buyer. All other information will be shared. Broker cannot act as a dual agent unless both the Buyer and the seller agree to it. By agreeing to a possible dual agency, the Buyer will be giving up the right to exclusive representation in an in-house transaction. However, if the Buyer should decide not to agree to a possible dual agency, and the Buyer wants Broker to represent the Buyer, the Buyer may give up the opportunity to Purchase the properties listed by Broker.

Buyer's Instructions to Broker:

Having read and understood this information about dual agency, Buyer now instructs Broker as follows:

☐ Buyer will agree to a dual agency representation and will consider properties listed by Broker.

☐ Buyer will not agree to a dual agency representation and will not consider properties listed by Broker.

Real Estate Company Name: ____________________

Buyer: ____________________

By: ____________________ (Licensee) Buyer: ____________________

Date: ____________________

FIGURE 11.4: Sample Buyer Representation Agreement (continued)

BUYER REPRESENTATION CONTRACT: EXCLUSIVE

Page 3

OTHER POTENTIAL BUYERS: Buyer understands that other potential buyers may consider and/or make offers to purchase through Broker the same or similar properties as Buyer is seeking to Purchase. Buyer consents to Broker representing such other potential buyers before, during and after the expiration of this Contract.

PREVIOUS AGENCY RELATIONSHIPS: Broker or licensee representing or assisting Buyer may have had a previous agency relationship with a seller of a property Buyer is interested in Purchasing. Buyer acknowledges that Buyer's Broker or licensee representing or assisting Buyer is legally required to keep information regarding the ultimate price and terms the seller would accept and the motivation for selling confidential, if known.

NOTICE REGARDING PREDATORY OFFENDER INFORMATION: Information regarding the predatory offender registry and persons registered with the predatory offender registry under MN Statute 243.166 may be obtained by contacting the local law enforcement offices in the community where the property is located or the Minnesota Department of Corrections at (651) 361-7200, or from the Department of Corrections web site at www.corr.state.mn.us.

ELECTRONIC SIGNATURES: The parties agree the electronic signature of any party on any document related to this transaction constitute valid, binding signatures.

CONSENT FOR COMMUNICATION: Buyer authorizes Broker and its representatives to contact Buyer by mail, phone, fax, e-mail or other means of communication during the term of this Contract and any time thereafter.

OTHER: ______________________________

ACCEPTED BY: ______________________________
(Real Estate Company Name)

BY: ______________________________
(Licensee) (Date)

ACCEPTED BY: ______________________ **ACCEPTED BY:** ______________________
(Buyer) (Buyer)

______________________ ______________________
(Date) (Date)

______________________ ______________________
(Address) (Address)

______________________ ______________________
(Phone) (Phone)

______________________ ______________________
(E-mail Address) (E-mail Address)

THIS IS A LEGALLY BINDING CONTRACT BETWEEN BUYER AND BROKER.
IF YOU DESIRE LEGAL OR TAX ADVICE, CONSULT AN APPROPRIATE PROFESSIONAL.

KEY POINT REVIEW

A **listing agreement** is an **employment contract** between a real estate broker and a property seller. In all states, an **exclusive listing agreement** must be in writing to be enforceable in court. The broker is a **special agent** of the seller.

As an **agent**, the **broker** is authorized to represent the **principal** and the principal's real estate to consumers. A real estate **salesperson** is a **general agent** of the broker and can carry out listing services only in the name of and under the supervision of the broker.

In an **exclusive right-to-sell listing**, **one broker** is appointed as the seller's **sole** agent, and if the property is sold while the listing is in effect, the broker is entitled to a commission, no matter who sells the property.

An **exclusive agency listing** authorizes **one broker** to act as the **sole** agent of the seller but allows the **seller** to retain the right to sell the property without obligation of payment to the broker.

In an **open listing** (also known as a **nonexclusive listing**), the seller retains the right to employ **any** number of brokers; the seller is obligated to pay a commission **only** to the broker who successfully produces a **ready, willing, and able buyer**; and the seller is not obligated to pay a commission if the seller personally sells the property without the aid of any broker.

A **net listing** in which the excess over the seller's desired net from the sale is paid to the broker as compensation may be prohibited by state law.

A **multiple listing clause** permits cooperation with other brokers in the **multiple listing service (MLS)**.

An **agreement to represent a seller** may be **terminated** when

- the agreement's **purpose** is fulfilled,
- the agreement's **term expires**,
- the property is **destroyed**,
- **title** to the property is transferred by operation of law (e.g., bankruptcy),
- the broker and the seller **mutually agree** to end the agreement,
- either the broker or the seller **breaches** the contract, or
- either party **dies** or becomes **incapacitated**.

All **exclusive listings** should have a **definite termination date** and should not have an automatic extension provision.

The **broker protection clause** preserves a broker's right to compensation if, within a certain number of days after the listing agreement expires, the owner transfers the property to a purchaser who was brought to the seller by the listing broker.

The **listing presentation** is usually made by a sales associate of the broker and is the job interview with a prospective client—the property owner. The sales associate presents information about the firm, the market, and how the firm can provide the best service to the owner. The sales associate also makes a **comparative market analysis (CMA)** to help the seller have a realistic idea of the price range in which the subject property falls. Both sales associate and property owner should be clear on their expectations before agreeing to a listing.

A **listing agreement** will identify the property owner(s) and the property, describe the property improvements, list any loans held by the owner and their current status, itemize loan and other payments on the property, and provide the details of a short sale, if the lender is willing to accept one.

Disclosures of agency relationships and property condition are important consumer safeguards and may be required by state law.

The listing agreement must specify any **personal property** that will be included in the sale of the real estate, as well as any **fixtures** or other items that will be excluded from the sale. **Leased equipment** also should be identified.

The seller may make a **home warranty** policy available for the buyer.

A **buyer representation agreement** is an employment contract in which a prospective property buyer employs a broker for the purpose of finding a suitable property. State law may specify the type of agreement that is available to the broker when representing a buyer. In an **agency** relationship, the broker will have a **fiduciary** responsibility to the buyer. In an **exclusive buyer representation** agreement, the buyer works with only one broker, but the broker is free to represent other buyer clients.

The buyer's broker will be **compensated** by a retainer, a flat fee for services, an hourly rate, a percentage of the purchase price, or some combination of these methods.

In any brokerage relationship, the **source of compensation** does not determine the relationship of the parties and compensation is always negotiable.

Buyer representation is **terminated** when

- the agreement's purpose is **fulfilled**,
- the agreement's **term expires**,
- broker and buyer **mutually agree** to cancel the agreement,
- broker or buyer **breaches** the terms of the agreement, or
- broker or buyer **dies** or becomes **incapacitated**.

UNIT 11 QUIZ

1. A property listing taken by a real estate sales associate is technically an employment agreement between the seller and the
   a. broker.
   b. local multiple listing service.
   c. sales associate.
   d. sales associate and broker together.

2. Which of the following is a similarity between an exclusive agency listing and an exclusive right-to-sell listing?
   a. Under each, the seller retains the right to sell the real estate without the broker's help and without paying the broker a commission.
   b. Under each, the seller authorizes only one particular sales associate to show the property.
   c. Both types of listings give the responsibility of representing the seller to one broker only.
   d. Both types of listings are open listings.

3. The listing agreement on a residential property states that it expires on May 2. Which event would terminate the listing before that date?
   a. The agreement is renewed before May 2.
   b. The owner becomes ill on April 29.
   c. On April 15, the owner and agent cancel the agreement.
   d. The house is destroyed by fire on May 3.

4. A seller listed a property with a broker under an exclusive agency listing agreement. If the seller finds a buyer, the seller will owe the broker
   a. no commission.
   b. the full commission.
   c. a partial commission.
   d. only reimbursement for the broker's costs.

5. A broker sold a residence for $485,000 and received $26,675 as commission in accordance with the terms of the listing agreement. What was the broker's commission rate?
   a. 5%
   b. 5.5%
   c. 6%
   d. 6.5%

6. Under a brokerage agreement with a property owner, the broker is entitled to sell the property for any price, as long as the seller receives $85,000. The broker may keep any amount over $85,000 as a commission. This type of listing might be illegal and is called a(n)
   a. exclusive right-to-sell listing.
   b. exclusive agency listing.
   c. open listing.
   d. net listing.

7. Which of the following is a similarity between an open listing and an exclusive agency listing?
   a. Under each, the seller avoids paying the broker a commission if the seller sells the property to someone the broker did not procure.
   b. Each grants a commission to any broker who procures a buyer for the seller's property.
   c. Under each, the broker earns a commission regardless of who sells the property, as long as it is sold within the listing period.
   d. Each grants the exclusive right to sell to whatever broker produces a buyer for the seller's property.

8. The final decision on a property's asking price should be made by the
   a. seller's broker.
   b. appraised value.
   c. seller.
   d. seller's attorney.

9. Which statement is *TRUE* of a listing agreement?
   a. It is an employment contract for the professional services of the broker.
   b. It obligates the seller to transfer the property if the broker procures a ready, willing, and able buyer.
   c. It obligates the broker to work diligently for both the seller and the buyer.
   d. It automatically binds the owner, the broker, and the MLS to its agreed provisions.

10. A broker sold a property that was owned by a bank that had acquired it through foreclosure, and the broker received a 6.5% commission. The broker gave the listing sales associate $3,575, which was 30% of the firm's commission. What was the selling price of the property?

a. $55,000
b. $95,775
c. $152,580
d. $183,333

11. A seller hired a broker under the terms of an open listing agreement. While that agreement was still in effect, the seller—without informing the first broker—hired another broker from a separate firm under an exclusive right-to-sell listing for the same property. If the first broker produces a buyer for the property whose offer the seller accepts, the seller must pay a full commission to

a. only the first broker.
b. only the second broker.
c. both brokers.
d. neither broker.

12. A seller listed her residence with a broker. The broker brought an offer at full price and terms of the listing agreement from a buyer who is ready, willing, and able to pay cash for the property, but the seller rejected the buyer's offer. In this situation, the seller

a. must sell her property.
b. owes a commission to the broker.
c. is liable to the buyer for specific performance.
d. is liable to the buyer for compensatory damages.

13. A buyer signed an agreement with a broker to compensate the broker even if the buyer purchases the property from a relative. This is called an

a. open buyer representation agreement.
b. exclusive agency buyer representation agreement.
c. exclusive buyer representation agreement.
d. invalid agreement.

14. A prospective buyer signs an agreement with a broker to find a property for the buyer, and the buyer agrees to work only with that broker. While this agreement is in effect,

a. only one sales associate of the broker can work with the buyer.
b. the broker can represent other buyers.
c. the broker cannot show the buyer a property that is listed by the broker.
d. the sales associate working with the buyer cannot work with other buyers.

15. A seller sold property to a neighbor without the services of a real estate broker; however, the seller still owes a broker a commission because the seller signed

a. an exclusive agency listing agreement.
b. an open listing agreement.
c. an exclusive right-to-sell listing agreement.
d. a net listing agreement.

16. Most states require that a real estate listing agreement contain

a. a multiple listing service (MLS) clause.
b. a definite contract termination date.
c. an automatic extension clause.
d. a broker protection clause.

17. Which type of listing is prohibited in some states?

a. Exclusive right to sell
b. Net listing
c. Buyer representation
d. Open listing

18. By executing a listing agreement with a seller, a real estate broker becomes

a. a procuring cause.
b. obligated to open a special trust account.
c. the agent of the seller.
d. responsible for sharing the commission.

19. The provision in a contract with a property seller that gives additional authority to the broker and obligates the broker to alert other brokers to the availability of the property is a(n)

a. joint listing clause.
b. multiple listing clause.
c. net listing clause.
d. open listing clause.

20. All of the following reasons are valid bases for terminating a buyer representation agreement *EXCEPT*

a. purchase of a property.
b. death of the sales associate who worked with the buyer.
c. agreement of the parties.
d. death of the broker.

UNIT 12

Real Estate Contracts

LEARNING OBJECTIVES *When you have finished reading this unit, you will be able to*

- **describe** the essential elements of contracts;
- **explain** the various means by which a contract may be enforced, terminated, assigned, or replaced;
- **describe** the primary written agreements and forms used in real estate sales and leasing; and
- **define** the following *key terms*:

addendum
amendment
assignment
bilateral contract
breach of contract
consideration
contingencies
contract
counteroffer
disclosure
earnest money
enforceable contract
executed contract
executory contract
express contract
implied contract
land contract
liquidated damages
novation
offer and acceptance
option
owner financing
purchase money mortgage
rescission
statute of frauds
suit for specific performance
"time is of the essence"
unenforceable contract
unilateral contract
valid contract
void contract
voidable contract

OVERVIEW

Various types of contracts have already been mentioned, but now you will learn about all the legal requirements for contract formation, performance, and termination. The real estate market is driven by contracts. Both seller and buyer representation agreements are contracts. Options are contracts—and an offer is the first half of a sales contract. Leases and management agreements are contracts. Every aspect of the real estate business involves contracts, and everyone involved in a real estate transaction—even those who are not real estate professionals—should understand what a contract means. A real estate professional must know not only what a contract means but also how one is created, what is required of the parties to the contract, and how the contract is concluded.

CONTRACT LAW

A **contract** is a voluntary promise between two competent parties to *perform* (or *not perform*) some legal act in exchange for consideration.

A **contract** is a voluntary agreement or promise between legally competent parties, supported by legal consideration, to perform (or refrain from performing) some legal act. The definition may be easier to understand if its various parts are examined separately.

A contract must be

- *voluntary*—no one may be forced into a contract;
- *an agreement or a promise*—a contract is essentially a promise or set of promises;
- made by *legally competent parties*—the parties must be viewed by the law as capable of making a legally binding promise;
- supported by lawful *consideration*—a contract must be supported by something of value that induces a party to enter into the contract; and
- for a *legal act*—a contract is invalid if it attempts to have an illegal objective.

Real estate professionals use many types of contracts and agreements to carry out their responsibilities to sellers, buyers, landlords, tenants, and the general public. The area of law that governs such agreements is known as *contract law*.

IN PRACTICE Real estate professionals may be permitted by state law to use contract forms drafted by attorneys and provided by their trade associations or employing brokers. A real estate professional cannot practice law unless also licensed as an attorney. The parties to a transaction, including buyer, seller, landlord, and tenant, always have the option of hiring their own attorney and should never be discouraged from doing so.

Express and Implied Contracts

A contract is either express or implied. In an **express contract**, the parties state the terms and show their intentions in words, either oral or written. Most real estate contracts are express contracts and are written. In an **implied contract**, the agreement of the parties is demonstrated by their acts and conduct.

Real estate representation agreements should be written in order to comply with the state's real estate law. Exclusive representation agreements must always be written to be enforceable. In addition, the state will probably have a **statute of frauds** requiring certain contracts, such as real estate sales or lease agreements, to be in writing. In any of those cases, only a written agreement can be enforced in a court of law.

Bilateral and Unilateral Contracts

Bilateral contract:

Bi means *two*—must have two promises.

Unilateral contract:

Uni means *one*—has only one promise.

Contracts are classified as either bilateral or unilateral. In a **bilateral contract**, both parties promise to do something; one promise is given in exchange for another. A real estate sales contract is a bilateral contract because the seller promises to sell a parcel of real estate and transfer title to the property to the buyer, who promises to pay a certain sum of money or other lawful consideration for the property. An exclusive right-to-sell listing contract is a bilateral contract.

A **unilateral contract**, on the other hand, is a one-sided agreement. One party makes a promise in order to entice a second party to do something. The offer made in a unilateral contract is usually accepted by the performance of the party to whom the offer is made. The second party is not legally obligated to act, but if the second party does comply, the first party is obligated to keep the promise.

IN PRACTICE A brokerage lists a property for sale with the multiple listing service. Any other broker who is part of the multiple listing service may or may not bring a buyer to the listing broker. The offer by the listing broker to share compensation with a cooperating broker is an offer for a unilateral contract. The brokers who receive the offer are not obligated to bring a buyer to the listing broker, but if a cooperating broker does produce a buyer, the listing broker is obligated to share the compensation on the transaction on the terms specified.

Executed and Executory Contracts

A contract is either executed or executory, depending on whether the agreement has been completed or some obligation under the agreement has yet to be performed. An **executed contract** is one in which all parties have fulfilled their promises; the contract has been performed. The term *executed* is also used to refer to the signing of a contract. An **executory contract** exists when one or both parties still have an act to perform. A sales contract is an executory contract from the time it is signed until closing; ownership has not yet changed hands, and the seller has not received the sales price. At closing, when the contract terms have been met, the sales contract is executed.

Figure 12.1 highlights the issues involved in the formation of a contract.

FIGURE 12.1: Contract Issues

Essential Elements	Classification	Discharge
offer and acceptance	valid, void, voidable	performance
consideration	enforceable, unenforceable	breach
legal purpose	express, implied	remedies (damages, specific performance, rescission)
consent	unilateral, bilateral	
legal capacity	executory, executed	

Creation of a Valid Contract

A contract must meet certain minimum requirements to be considered legally valid. The following are the essential elements of a contract.

Offer and Acceptance In a real estate sales transaction, the sales contract sets out the offer by the buyer that is accepted by the seller. This is known as **offer and acceptance.** The person who makes the offer is the *offeror*. The person to whom an offer is made is the *offeree*. This requirement is also called *mutual assent*. It means that there must be a meeting of the minds; that is, there must be complete agreement between the parties about the purpose and terms of the contract. Courts look to the objective intent of the parties to determine whether they intended to enter into a binding agreement. Most states require that the terms and conditions of the sales contract be in writing. The wording of the contract must express all the agreed terms and must be clearly understood by the parties.

Elements of a Contract

- Offer and acceptance
- Consideration
- Legally competent parties
- Consent
- Legal purpose

An *offer* is a promise made by one party, requesting something in exchange for that promise. The offer is made with the intention that the offeror will be bound to the terms if the offer is accepted. The terms of the offer must be definite and specific and must be communicated to the offeree.

An *acceptance* is a promise by the offeree to be bound by the exact terms proposed by the offeror. The acceptance must be communicated to the offeror. Proposing any deviation from the terms of the offer is considered a rejection of the original offer. The changed offer is known as a *counteroffer* and is explained more fully later. The counteroffer must be accepted for a contract to exist.

Besides being *terminated* by a counteroffer, an offer can be terminated if the offeree fails to accept it before expiration of the time stated in the offer. An offer also may be terminated by the offeree's outright rejection of it.

The offeror may revoke the offer at any time before acceptance. This *revocation* must be communicated to the offeree by the offeror, either directly or through the parties' agents. The offer is revoked if the offeree learns of the revocation and observes the offeror acting in a manner that indicates that the offer no longer exists. For example, if a buyer gives a seller three days to accept an offer and on the third day the buyer's agent calls the seller's agent and revokes the offer, the offer is terminated.

Consideration The contract must be based on consideration. **Consideration** is something of legal value offered by one party and accepted by another as an inducement to perform or to refrain from performing some act. Consideration is some interest or benefit accruing to one party, or some loss or responsibility by the other party. There should be a statement of the promised consideration in a contract to show that something of value will be given in exchange for the promise of the transfer of the described property, even if the amount of the consideration is yet to be determined. For example, a contract to purchase 300 acres of land could state that the consideration is the promise to pay the appraised value of the land as of a certain date.

Consideration must be *good and valuable* between the parties. The courts usually do not inquire into the adequacy of consideration. Adequate consideration could be a promise of love and affection or it could be a substantial sum of money.

Anything that has been bargained for and exchanged is legally sufficient to satisfy the requirement for consideration. The only requirements are that the parties agree and that no undue influence or fraud has occurred.

Consent A contract must be entered into by consent as a free and voluntary act of each party. Each party must be able to make a prudent and knowledgeable decision without undue influence. A mistake, misrepresentation, fraud, undue influence, or duress would deprive a person of that ability. If any of these circumstances is present, there is no valid offer and acceptance and the contract is voidable by the injured party. If the other party were to sue for breach, the injured party could use lack of voluntary assent as a defense.

Legal Purpose A contract must be for a legal purpose—that is, even with all the other elements (consent, competent parties, consideration, and offer and acceptance), the contract must have a legal reason for existence. A contract for an illegal purpose or for the performance of an act against public policy is not a valid contract.

Legally Competent Parties All parties to the contract must have legal capacity, meaning they must be of legal age and have enough mental capacity to understand the nature or consequences of their actions in the contract. In most states, 18 is the age of contractual capacity. If it is discovered that a party is not legally competent, the contract is voidable at the option of the person who lacks competency.

A contract may be

- valid—has all legal elements;
- void—lacks one or more elements and has no legal force or effect;
- voidable—has all legal elements on its face, but it may be rescinded or disaffirmed; or
- unenforceable—appears to have all legal elements but cannot be enforced in court.

Validity of a Contract

A contract can be described as valid, void, voidable, or unenforceable, depending on the circumstances.

A **valid contract** meets all the essential elements that make it legally sufficient, or enforceable, and is binding in a court of law.

A **void contract** has no legal force or effect because it lacks some or all the essential elements of a contract. A contract that is void was never a legal contract. For example, the use of a forged name in a listing contract would make the contract void.

A **voidable contract** appears on the surface to be valid, but it may be rescinded or disaffirmed by one or both parties based on some legal principle. A voidable contract is considered by the courts to be valid if the party who has the option to disaffirm the agreement does not do so within a period of time. A contract with a minor, for instance, is voidable. A contract entered into by a mentally ill person is usually voidable during the mental illness and for a reasonable period after the person is cured. If a contract was made under duress, with misrepresentation, under the influence, and with intent to defraud, it is also voidable.

IN PRACTICE Mental capacity to enter into a contract is not the same as medical sanity. The test is whether the individual in question is capable of understanding his actions. A person may suffer from a mental illness but clearly understand the significance of his actions. Such psychological questions require consultation with experts.

An **enforceable contract** meets all the elements of a valid contract, including compliance with any applicable statute of frauds or other law that requires it to be in writing and signed by the parties. An **unenforceable contract** may also appear on the surface to be valid; however, neither party can sue the other to force performance. For example, an oral agreement for the sale of a parcel of real estate would be unenforceable; the defaulting party could not be taken to court and forced to perform. There is, however, a distinction between a suit to force performance and a suit for damages, which may be possible even with an oral agreement. An unenforceable contract is still said to be *valid as between the parties*. This means that once the agreement is fully executed by the transfer of the deed and purchase price, satisfying both parties, neither has reason to initiate a lawsuit to force performance.

DISCHARGE OF CONTRACTS

A contract is *discharged* when the agreement is terminated. A contract terminates when it has been completely performed, with all its terms fulfilled, but a contract may be terminated for another reason, such as a party's breach or default.

Performance of a Contract

Each party to a contract has certain rights and duties to fulfill. The question of when a contract must be performed is an important factor. Many contracts call for a specific time by which the agreed acts must be completely performed. Some contracts provide that **"time is of the essence"** which means that each of the elements of the contract must be performed within the specified time. A party who fails to perform an obligation under the contract on time is liable for breach of contract.

IN PRACTICE When a *time is of the essence* clause is used in a contract, the parties should consult an attorney. The ramifications of a breach of a contract in which *time is of the essence* can be significant; for example, a buyer might lose escrow funds, or the seller might lose the right to enforce the contract.

When a contract does not specify a deadline for performance, the acts it requires should be performed within a reasonable time. The interpretation of what constitutes a reasonable time depends on the situation. Courts can declare a contract invalid because the contract did not contain a time or date for performance.

Assignment

Assignment refers to a transfer of rights or duties under a contract. Generally rights and obligations may be assigned to a third party as long as they do not involve a contract for personal services. Obligations may be delegated, but the original party remains liable unless specifically released. Many contracts have a clause that will either allow or forbid assignment.

IN PRACTICE A homeowner signs an exclusive right-to-sell agreement with a broker. Because the contract is for the services that the particular broker will provide, the broker cannot assign the agreement to a different broker.

Novation

Assignment = Substitution of parties

Novation = Substitution of a new contract

Substitution of a new contract for an existing contract is called **novation**. The new agreement may be between the same parties, or a new party may be substituted for either (this is *novation* of the parties). The parties' intent must be to discharge the old obligation. For instance, when a real estate purchaser assumes the seller's existing mortgage loan, the lender may choose to release the seller and substitute the buyer as the party primarily liable for the mortgage debt. Or when there are many changes to a real estate contract and it is faxed, scanned, or otherwise re-transmitted several times, that it becomes illegible. Novation occurs when a new, clear contract with all the accepted changes is signed by all the parties.

Breach of Contract

A contract may be terminated if it is breached by one of the parties. A **breach of contract** is a violation of any of the terms or conditions of a contract. A seller who fails to deliver title to the buyer breaches a sales contract. The breaching or defaulting party assumes certain burdens, and the nondefaulting party has certain legal and/or equitable remedies.

If the seller breaches a real estate sales contract, the buyer may sue for *specific performance* unless the contract specifically states otherwise. In a **suit for specific performance**, the buyer asks the court to force the seller to go through with the sale and transfer the property as previously agreed. The buyer may choose to sue for damages, in which case the seller is asked to pay for any costs and hardships suffered by the buyer as a result of the seller's breach.

If the buyer defaults, the seller can sue for damages or sue for the purchase price. A suit for the purchase price is an action for damages, but it has the same result as a suit for specific performance: The seller tenders the deed and the buyer is required to pay the agreed price.

The contract may limit the remedies available to the parties. A *liquidated damages* clause in a real estate purchase contract specifies the amount of money to which the seller is entitled if the buyer breaches the contract. The liquidated damages in the event that the buyer defaults may be specified as the buyer's earnest money deposit (down payment), although in some states, the amount of liquidated damages is limited to a specific percentage of the purchase price—say, 3%—even if the buyer has made a down payment for a larger amount.

Statute of Limitations Every state limits the time during which parties to a contract may bring a legal action, or lawsuit, to enforce their rights. The statute of limitations varies for different legal actions, and any rights not enforced within the applicable time period are lost.

Other Reasons for Termination

A contract may also be discharged or terminated when any of the following occurs:

- *Partial performance of the terms, along with a written acceptance* by the party for whom acts have not been done or to whom money is owed. If the parties agree that the work performed is close enough to completion, for example, they can agree that the contract is discharged even if some minor elements remain unperformed.

- *Substantial performance*, in which one party has substantially performed on the contract but does not complete all the details exactly as the contract requires. Such performance may be enough to force payment, with certain adjustments for any damages suffered by the other party. For example, if a newly constructed addition to a home is finished except for polishing the brass doorknobs, the contractor is entitled to the final payment.
- *Impossibility of performance*, in which an unforeseen circumstance has made an act required by the contract impossible or impracticable. Sometimes, a contract will cover a contingency, such as the destruction of property to be transferred. At other times, an event will occur that makes fulfillment of the contract terms a practical impossibility, such as when a buyer is laid off and can no longer afford to complete the purchase.
- *Mutual agreement* of the parties to cancel the contract. Cancellation by one party will terminate a contract but does not automatically return the parties to their original position, unless provided by law (such as the right of cancellation that accompanies some consumer contracts) or by the terms of the agreement.
- *Operation of law*, such as in the voiding of a contract by a minor, or as a result of fraud, or because a contract was altered without the written consent of all parties involved. **Rescission** returns the parties to their original positions before the contract, so any monies or property exchanged must be returned. Rescission is normally a contractual remedy for a breach, but a contract may also be rescinded by the mutual agreement of the parties.

IN PRACTICE If a contract contains any ambiguity, the court will generally interpret the agreement against the party who prepared it. In a contract between a business and a consumer, the court will tend to favor the consumer unless it can be shown that the consumer signed the contract with full knowledge of and consent to its terms.

CONTRACTS USED IN THE REAL ESTATE BUSINESS

The written agreements most commonly used by real estate professionals are

- client representation agreements,
- real estate sales contracts,
- options,
- escrow agreements,
- property management agreements,
- leases, and
- owner financing contracts, such as land contracts or contracts for deed.

We will now discuss real estate sales contracts, options to purchase real estate, and owner financing contracts. Owner financing contracts, escrow agreements, leases, and property management agreements will be covered later.

Use of Contract Forms

The practice of law includes preparing legal documents, such as deeds and mortgages, and offering advice on legal matters. A real estate professional who is not a licensed attorney cannot practice law. Nevertheless, many states have specific guidelines for when and how real estate professionals may assist consumers with contract preparation. These guidelines, which specify the activities that are not considered the practice of law or which can be performed by non-attorneys, are created by state real estate officials, court decisions, or statutes. Often, brokerage representation agreements, agency and property disclosure forms, and parts of residential property sales agreements must comply word for word with statutory language.

A real estate professional also may be permitted to fill in the blanks on other preprinted documents, such as those created by bar associations, real estate trade associations, and attorneys for real estate firms, as directed by the client. No separate fee may be charged for completing the forms.

The parties to a real estate transaction always should be advised to have sales contracts and other legal documents examined by their lawyers before they sign them to ensure that the agreements accurately reflect their intentions. When preprinted forms do not sufficiently cover special provisions in a transaction, the parties should have an attorney draft an appropriate contract.

IN PRACTICE Real estate professionals should always be aware of the source of any preprinted document, particularly those that have not come from the state, a trade association, or their employer's attorney and have not been approved by the firm. The forms made available by a national publishing company, for instance, may or may not be state-specific, and should always be shown to and approved by the firm, acting on the advice of counsel, before being used. Just because a preprinted form is available doesn't mean that the real estate professional should offer it to a client.

Sales Contracts

A real estate sales contract contains the complete agreement between a buyer of a parcel of real estate and its seller. It establishes the legal rights and obligations of buyer and seller. Depending upon the area, the contract may be referred to as an offer to purchase, a contract of purchase and sale, a purchase agreement, an earnest money agreement, or a deposit receipt.

In addition to the essential elements of a contract, a real estate sales contract will include

- the sales price and terms;
- an adequate description of the property and improvements;
- a statement of the kind and condition of the title and the form of deed to be delivered by the seller;
- the kind of title evidence required, who will provide it, and how many defects in the title will be eliminated; and
- a statement of all the terms of the agreement between the parties, including any contingencies—conditions that must be met to successfully complete the transaction.

Offer The real estate sales agreement is an offer to purchase real estate when it has been prepared, signed by the prospective buyer, and communicated to the seller. Typically, the buyer's offer is presented by the buyer or the buyer's representative to the seller or the seller's representative. If either party is represented by a real estate professional, the real estate professional must be the one who sends or receives communications on behalf of the client. If the buyer's offer is accepted by the seller and the seller signs the document, it becomes a sales contract.

A **counteroffer** is a *new* offer; it rejects the original offer.

Counteroffer As mentioned earlier, any change by the seller to the terms proposed by the buyer creates a **counteroffer**. The original offer ceases to exist because the seller has rejected it. The buyer may accept or reject the seller's counteroffer. If the buyer desires, the process may continue by making another counteroffer. Any change in the last offer results in a new counteroffer until either the parties reach agreement or one party walks away.

An offer or counteroffer *may be withdrawn at any time before it has been accepted*, even if the person making the offer or counteroffer agreed to keep the offer open for a set period.

Acceptance If the seller agrees to the original offer or a later counteroffer *exactly* as it is made and signs the document, the offer has been accepted and a contract is formed. The seller's representative advises the buyer (through the buyer's representative, if there is one) of the seller's acceptance and a copy of the contract is provided to each party. The next step is the approval of the parties' attorneys, if the contract calls for it.

An offer is not considered accepted until the person making the offer has been notified of the other party's acceptance. When the parties communicate through a representative or at a distance, questions may arise regarding whether an acceptance, rejection, or counteroffer has occurred. Though current technology allows for fast communication, a signed agreement that is scanned and sent by email or faxed, for instance, would not necessarily constitute adequate communication. All offers, acceptances, or other responses should be transmitted as soon as possible and acknowledged by the recipient to avoid later questions of proper communication.

Binder In some states, and particularly when a transaction involves commercial or industrial property, a buyer's offer may be presented in a shorter document known as a *binder*, or *letter of intent*, instead of a complete sales contract. The binder states the essential terms of the offer and acknowledges that the buyer's representative has received the buyer's deposit. A more formal and complete contract of sale is drawn up by an attorney once the seller accepts and signs the binder. A binder is useful when the details of the transaction are too complex for the standard sales contract form.

Earnest Money Deposits It is customary, although not essential, for a purchaser to provide a deposit when making an offer to purchase real estate. This deposit, usually in the form of a check, is called **earnest money**. The earnest money deposit is evidence of the buyer's intention to carry out the terms of the contract in good faith. The amount of the deposit is a matter to be agreed on by the parties but typically is an amount sufficient to

- discourage the buyer from defaulting,
- compensate the seller for taking the property off the market, and
- cover any expenses the seller might incur if the buyer defaults.

In many states, the earnest money check is given to the seller's agent on acceptance of the offer to purchase by the seller. When the disposition of the funds has been determined, they will be placed in an escrow account according to the terms of the escrow agreement, the contract between the buyer, the seller, and the escrow holder that sets forth the rights and responsibilities of each. The escrow holder will collect and then disburse the funds and documents that are necessary to close the transaction.

If there is a delay in presentation of an offer or negotiations are lengthy, most states require that earnest money be deposited in a broker's escrow or trust account, where it is held until the offer to purchase is accepted or rejected. The escrow account must be separate from the broker's business or personal account. A separate escrow account does not have to be opened for each earnest money deposit received; all deposits may be kept in one account. A broker must maintain full, complete, and accurate records of all earnest money deposits. The broker's (and any involved sales associate's) real estate license may be revoked or suspended if deposits are not managed properly. In some areas, it is customary for deposits to be held in escrow by the seller's attorney. If the offer is not accepted, the earnest money deposit is immediately returned to the would-be buyer. If the offer is accepted, the funds are delivered to the escrow holder according to the terms of the escrow agreement.

Equitable Title When a buyer signs a contract to purchase real estate that is accepted by the seller, the buyer does not immediately receive title to the land. Title transfers only upon delivery and acceptance of a deed. After both buyer and seller have executed a sales contract, however, the buyer acquires an interest in the land known as *equitable title*. A person who holds equitable title has rights that vary from state to state. Equitable title may give the buyer an insurable interest in the property.

Destruction of Premises In some states, once the sales contract is signed by both parties, the buyer assumes the risk of any damage to the property that may occur before closing the contract. In other states, laws and court decisions have placed the risk of loss on the seller. The Uniform Vendor and Purchaser Risk Act, which has been adopted by some states, specifically provides that the seller bear any loss that occurs before the title passes or the buyer takes possession.

Liquidated Damages To simplify matters in the event that one party breaches a contract, the parties may agree on a certain amount of money that will compensate the nonbreaching party. Such money is called **liquidated damages**. If a sales contract specifies that the earnest money deposit is to serve as liquidated damages in the event that the buyer defaults, the seller will be entitled to keep the deposit if the buyer refuses to perform without good reason. The seller who keeps a deposit as liquidated damages may not sue for any further damages if the contract provides that the deposit is the seller's sole remedy (usually, the purpose of liquidated damages). State law may limit the amount of the deposit that can be retained as liquidated damages.

Provisions of a Sales Contract

All real estate sales contracts contain a number of provisions, or clauses. Most sales contracts include the following information:

- Purchaser's name and a statement of the purchaser's obligation to purchase the property, sometimes including how the purchaser intends to take title
- Adequate description of the property, such as the street address; while a street address is adequate to describe most residential properties in a sales contract, it is not adequate for the legal description that will be included in the deed
- Seller's name and a statement of the type of deed the seller agrees to provide, including any covenants, conditions, and restrictions

- Purchase price and how the purchaser intends to pay for the property, including earnest money deposits, additional cash from the purchaser, and the conditions of any anticipated mortgage financing
- Identification of the closing or settlement agent and closing or settlement instructions
- Date for the closing of the transaction and the transfer of possession of the property to the purchaser
- Title evidence that will be satisfactory to the buyer
- Method by which real estate taxes, rents, fuel costs, and other expenses are to be prorated
- Outcome of the contract should the property be damaged or destroyed between the time of signing and the closing date
- Liquidated damages, specific performance, or other statement of remedies available in the event of default
- Contingencies or conditions of the sale
- Personal property to be left with the premises for the purchaser (such as major appliances or lawn and garden equipment)
- Fixtures or other items that could be considered part of the real property that are to be removed by the seller before the closing (such as a chandelier or storage shed)
- Transfer of any applicable warranties on items such as heating and cooling systems or built-in appliances
- Identification of any leased equipment that must be transferred to the purchaser or returned to the lessor (such as security system, cable television boxes, and water softener)
- Transfer or payment of any outstanding special assessments
- Purchaser's right to inspect the property shortly before the closing or settlement (often called the final walk-through)
- Documents to be provided by each party and when and where they will be delivered
- Dated signatures of all parties; in some states, the seller's nonowning spouse may be required to release potential marital or homestead rights. In most states, an agency disclosure statement that indicates the form of representation provided by the real estate professional(s)

Contingencies

Conditions that must be satisfied before a sales contract is fully enforceable are **contingencies**. The contract clause that provides a contingency will include the following three elements:

- The action necessary to satisfy the contingency
- The time frame within which the action must be performed
- The party who is responsible for paying any costs involved

The most common contingencies are as follows:

- A *mortgage contingency* protects the buyer's earnest money in the event that the buyer is unable to secure a mortgage on the property.
- An *inspection contingency* provides that the buyer may obtain certain inspections of the property and may cancel the contract if the inspections indicate an unsatisfactory or unsafe property condition. Inspections may include those for wood-boring insects, lead-based paint, structural and mechanical

systems, sewage facilities, and radon or other toxic materials. Buyer and seller can usually come to an agreement on any work indicated by a property inspection, and the party responsible for paying for the work.

- A *property sale contingency* protects a buyer who has to sell a home in order to buy the seller's property. This provision protects the buyer from owning two homes at the same time and also helps ensure the availability of cash for the purchase.
- A *lienholder approval*, if the contract is a short sale.

The seller may insist on an *escape clause*, which permits the seller to continue to market the property until all the buyer's contingencies have been satisfied or removed. The buyer may retain the right to eliminate the contingencies if the seller receives a more favorable offer. (Note that contingencies create a *voidable contract* ; if the contingencies are rejected or not satisfied, the contract is void.)

IN PRACTICE The real estate professional should avoid recommending sources for any inspection or testing services. If a buyer suffers any injury as a result of a provider's negligence, the real estate professional might also be named in any lawsuit. The better practice is to give the client the names of several professionals who offer high-quality services. In addition, a real estate professional who receives any compensation or reward from a source they recommend to a client must disclose such an arrangement to the client. Real estate professionals must never receive compensation from an attorney or a lender.

Amendments and Addendums

A change or modification to the existing content of a contract is an **amendment.** An amendment can also be a change to the existing words or provisions in a preprinted contract form. Amendments to the contract form must be separately initialed or signed by all parties prior to or at the time that the contract is signed.

Even after there is agreement on the contract terms and the contract has been signed by both parties, there may be a need to change one of the contract provisions. If that happens, a separate agreement stipulating the changed provision can be executed by the parties.

IN PRACTICE Seller and buyer have agreed to a sales contract that provides for a closing (completion of the transaction) in 60 days. In the next few weeks, it becomes obvious that, because of a backlog in the lender's underwriting department, a closing in 60 days will not be possible. The parties agree to amend the contract by allowing for 30 more days within which to complete the contract terms, executing a document that changes the provision requiring closing "within 60 days of contract acceptance" to "within 90 days of contract acceptance."

An **addendum** is any provision added to an existing contract that may change or be an addition to the content of the original. An addendum includes the original contract's provisions *by reference*, meaning the addendum mentions the original contract and must be signed by all parties. For example, an addendum might be an agreement to split the cost of repairing certain items discovered in a home inspection.

Disclosures Many states have enacted mandatory property condition disclosure laws, which help consumers make informed decisions. **Disclosure** of property conditions may be included as part of a sales contract or may be required in a separate document that is presented to the buyer before an offer to purchase is made. Many states require separate forms for disclosing environmental problems. In addition, disclosure of the real estate professional's agency relationship may also be required by state law.

Options

An **option** is a contract by which an optionor (generally an owner) gives an optionee (a prospective purchaser or tenant) the right to buy or lease the owner's property at a fixed price within a certain period of time. The optionee pays a fee as consideration for the option right. The optionee must then decide whether to exercise the option right or allow the option to expire. An option is enforceable by the optionee only (a unilateral contract). Options must contain all the elements of a valid contract.

A common application of an option is a lease that includes an option for the tenant to purchase the property. Options on commercial real estate frequently depend on some specific conditions being fulfilled, such as obtaining a zoning change or a building permit. The optionee may be obligated to exercise the option if the optionor has expended resources and money to see that conditions specified in the option are met. Similar terms could also be included in a sales contract.

Owner Financing Contracts

A traditional lender does not always have to be involved in the financing of a real estate purchase. With **owner financing**, the seller provides credit for all or part of the funds that will allow the buyer to move forward with the transaction.

A real estate sale can be made under a **land contract**, also called a *contract for deed*, a *contract of sale*, a *bond for title*, an *installment contract*, a *land sales contract*, or *articles of agreement for warranty deed*. Under a typical land contract, the owner/seller (also known as the *vendor*) retains legal title. The buyer, or the vendee, takes possession and gets equitable title to the property. The buyer agrees to give the seller a down payment and pay regular monthly installments of principal and interest over a number of years. The buyer also agrees to pay real estate taxes, insurance premiums, repairs, and upkeep on the property. Although the buyer obtains possession under the land contract, in its oldest form the seller is not obligated to execute and deliver a deed to the buyer until the terms of the contract have been satisfied—that is, all payments due to the seller have been made. This frequently occurs when the buyer has made enough payments to obtain a mortgage loan and pay off the contract balance. Although a land contract is usually assumable by subsequent purchasers, it generally must be approved by the seller.

IN PRACTICE State legislatures and courts have recognized the harsh result that may occur if a buyer under a land contract breaches the terms of the contract by missing a single payment, even after many years of fulfilling the terms of the agreement. Depending on the state, the buyer under a land contract may have an equitable interest in the property after as little as one year of successfully making contract payments. This means that the statutory requirements for a foreclosure must be followed if the vendor wants to take back the property, and also that the defaulting vendee is entitled to a share of the proceeds of a forced sale.

The seller who finances a sale can also make use of a **purchase money mortgage** in which the buyer receives title to the property but places a security interest on it—the mortgage—in favor of the seller. The terms of the mortgage will dictate how it can be foreclosed in the event that the buyer defaults on the purchase. The ways in which a mortgage can be foreclosed are covered later.

There is another way in which a property owner can help a buyer complete a transaction. If the buyer cannot obtain all the money needed for the purchase from a traditional lender, the seller may be willing to "take back a second" by holding part of the debt as a second mortgage. The lender will still have the priority interest in the property in the event that the buyer defaults, but the seller will have a secondary interest. This can be a very useful tool if the buyer has an insufficient down payment, provided the lender is made aware of and approves the arrangement.

KEY POINT REVIEW

A **valid contract** is a voluntary agreement based on the consent of the parties to the agreement. An offer by one party (**offeror**) is accepted by the other (**offeree**). A contract can be **revoked** by the offeror up to the time of acceptance. The parties must be of **legal age** and able to understand the **nature or consequences** of their actions. The contract must be supported by **consideration**—something of value, which could be love and affection—and must have a **legal act** as its objective.

A contract may be **express** (in words) or **implied** by the conduct of parties and may be required to be **in writing** to be **enforceable** in a court of law. A contract may be **bilateral** (having obligations on both sides) or **unilateral** (a promise by one side that can be accepted by performance of the other side). A contract may be **executed** (all parties have fulfilled their promises) or **executory** (one or both parties still have an act to perform).

A contract is **voidable** if it may be **rescinded** or **disaffirmed** by one or both parties. A contract with a minor is *voidable*. A contract is **void** if one of the essential elements is missing. If a mistake, misrepresentation, fraud, undue influence, or duress occurs, there is no mutual consent or meeting of the minds, which means that an essential element of the contract is missing and the contract is *void.*

A contract may be **discharged** (completed) by

- **performance**, which completes the contract terms;
- **partial performance**, if agreeable to both parties;
- **substantial performance**, depending on circumstances;
- **impossibility of performance** (required acts cannot be legally accomplished); **assignment** (transfer of rights to **assignee** or **delegation** of duties, if allowed by the contract);
- **novation** (substitutes a new contract or party for the original);
- **breach** by one of the parties without legal cause, in which case a **liquidated damages clause** may specify the amount the seller will receive if the buyer defaults;
- failure to enforce contract within **statute of limitations;**
- **mutual agreement** of the parties;
- **operation of law**, as when a contract is void from inception;
- **rescission**, which returns the parties to their original pre-contract positions, so any property or funds that have been transferred must be returned; or
- **cancellation,** which also is a termination of the contract.

Real estate contracts usually may be completed by real estate professionals, as provided by state law. **Real estate professionals who are not licensed attorneys may not practice law**. Preprinted contract forms may be prepared by trade association, firm attorneys, or as mandated by state law.

The written agreements most often used by real estate professionals are **client representation agreements, sales contracts, options, escrow agreements, property management agreements, leases**, and **owner financing agreements**, such as land contracts or contracts for deed.

A real estate sales contract is usually accompanied by an **earnest money deposit**, which may be held in a broker's **escrow** or **trust account** until an escrow is arranged to complete a property purchase or the funds are returned to the would-be buyer if there is no sales agreement.

The sales contract usually will identify the **parties** and the **property** that is the subject of the transaction, indicate the amount that the buyer is including with the offer to serve as **earnest money**, how the buyer intends to **finance** the purchase, who will serve as the **closing agent** for the transaction, when the transaction is to **close** and **possession** of the property delivered to the buyer, **fixtures** or other items on the property that are not part of the sale, **personal property** of the seller that will be included in the sale, **inspections** that will be made by the buyer, **seller disclosures** that are required by law, and other provisions.

The **contingencies** included in a sales contract allow the buyer to have an attorney review the contract, secure financing, conduct necessary inspections, and perform other activities.

Amendments and **addendums** can be used to alter the terms of a preprinted contract during the negotiation of the sale or to include additional terms after the contract has been signed by the parties.

An **option** allows the **optionor** (owner) to give the **optionee** the right to purchase the property at a later date at the price fixed in the **option agreement**.

Owner financing can assist a buyer by providing a credit for some or all of the purchase price. A **land contract**, also known as a **contract for deed, bond for title, installment contract**, **land sales contract**, or **articles of agreement for warranty deed**, must comply with state law. With a **purchase money mortgage**, the buyer receives title to the property immediately but places a security interest on the property in favor of the seller.

UNIT 12 QUIZ

1. A legally enforceable agreement under which both parties promise to do something for each other is called
   a. an escrow agreement.
   b. a legal pledge.
   c. a bilateral contract.
   d. an option agreement.

2. A person approaches an owner and says, "I'd like to buy your house." The owner says, "Sure," and they agree on a price. What kind of contract is this?
   a. Implied
   b. Unenforceable
   c. Void
   d. No contract

3. A contract is said to be bilateral if
   a. one of the parties is a minor.
   b. the contract has yet to be fully performed.
   c. only one party to the agreement is bound to act.
   d. both parties to the contract exchange binding promises.

4. During the period of time after a real estate sales contract is signed, but before title actually passes, the status of the contract is
   a. voidable.
   b. executory.
   c. unilateral.
   d. implied.

5. A contract for the sale of real estate that does not state the consideration and provides no basis on which the consideration could be determined is considered
   a. voidable.
   b. executory.
   c. void.
   d. enforceable.

6. A buyer and a seller sign a contract to purchase. The seller backs out, and the buyer sues for specific performance. What is the buyer seeking in this lawsuit?
   a. Money damages
   b. New contract
   c. Deficiency judgment
   d. Transfer of the property

7. In a preprinted sales contract, several words were crossed out or inserted by the parties. To eliminate future controversy as to whether the changes were made before or after the contract was signed, the usual procedure is to
   a. write a letter to each party listing the changes.
   b. have each party write a letter to the other approving the changes.
   c. redraw the entire contract.
   d. have both parties initial or sign in the margin near each change.

8. A buyer makes an offer on a seller's house and the seller accepts. Both parties sign the sales contract. At this point, the buyer has what type of title to the property?
   a. Equitable
   b. Voidable
   c. Escrow
   d. Contract

9. The sales contract says the buyer will purchase only if an attorney approves the sale by the following Saturday. The attorney's approval is a
   a. contingency.
   b. reservation.
   c. warranty.
   d. consideration.

10. A real estate professional uses earnest money placed in the company trust account to pay for the rent owed on the real estate professional's office. Using escrow funds for this purpose is
   a. illegal unless the client has approved the expenditure.
   b. legal if the trust account is reimbursed by the end of the calendar month.
   c. legal if the seller gives consent in writing.
   d. illegal.

11. An option to purchase binds which of the following parties?
   a. Buyer only
   b. Seller only
   c. Neither buyer nor seller
   d. Both buyer and seller

12. A buyer and a seller enter into a real estate sales contract. Under the contract's terms, the buyer will pay the seller $500 a month for 10 years. The seller will continue to hold legal title, while the buyer will live in the home and pay all real estate taxes, insurance premiums, and regular upkeep costs. What kind of contract do the buyer and seller have?
   a. Option contract
   b. Contract for mortgage
   c. Unilateral contract
   d. Land sales contract

13. The purchaser of real estate under an installment contract
   a. generally pays no interest charge.
   b. receives title immediately.
   c. is not required to pay property taxes for the duration of the contract.
   d. has only an equitable interest in the property's title.

14. Under the statute of frauds, all contracts for the sale of real estate must be
   a. originated by a real estate professional.
   b. on preprinted forms.
   c. in writing to be enforceable.
   d. accompanied by earnest money deposits.

15. If, upon the receipt of an offer to purchase a property, the seller makes a counteroffer, the prospective buyer is
   a. bound by the original offer.
   b. bound to accept the counteroffer.
   c. bound by whichever offer is lower.
   d. relieved of the original offer.

16. A buyer makes an offer to purchase certain property listed with a real estate professional and leaves an escrow deposit with the real estate professional to show good faith. The real estate professional should
   a. immediately apply the deposit to the listing expenses.
   b. put the deposit in an account, as provided by state law.
   c. give the deposit to the seller when the offer is presented.
   d. put the deposit in the real estate professional's personal checking account.

17. While suffering from a mental illness that caused delusions, hallucinations, and loss of memory, a person signed a contract to purchase real estate. Which statement regarding the contract to purchase is *TRUE*?
   a. The contract is voidable.
   b. The contract is void.
   c. The contract lacks consent.
   d. The contract is fully valid and enforceable.

18. A real estate professional has found a buyer for a seller's home. The buyer has indicated in writing a willingness to buy the property for $1,000 less than the asking price and has deposited $5,000 in earnest money with the real estate professional. The seller is out of town for the weekend, and the real estate professional has been unable to inform the seller of the signed document. At this point, the buyer has
   a. a voidable contract.
   b. an offer.
   c. an executory agreement.
   d. an implied contract.

19. A buyer and a seller agree on a purchase price of $200,000 for a house. The contract contains a clause stating that "time is of the essence." Which statement is *TRUE*?

a. The closing must take place within a reasonable period before the stated date.
b. A "time is of the essence" clause is not binding on either party.
c. The closing date must be stated as a particular calendar date, and not simply as a formula, such as "two weeks after loan approval."
d. If the closing date passes and no closing takes place, the contract may be rescinded by the party who was ready to settle on the scheduled date.

20. A buyer signs a contract under which he is given the right to purchase a property for $130,000 anytime in the next six months. The buyer pays the current owner $500 at the time that contract is signed. Which of the following *BEST* describes this agreement?

a. Contingency
b. Option
c. Installment
d. Sales

land contract

AKA: contract for deed
or
installment contract

Buyer is paying seller in installments

Real Estate Taxes and Other Liens

LEARNING OBJECTIVES *When you have finished reading this unit, you will be able to*

- **describe** the characteristics of statutory and equitable liens;
- **describe** and explain general taxes and special assessment taxes;
- **describe and explain** real property liens, including judgments and taxes, as well as the protection and limitations they offer the respective parties; and
- **define** the following *key terms*:

ad valorem tax
assessment equalization factor
equitable lien
equitable right of redemption
estate tax
general lien
general real estate tax
inheritance tax
involuntary lien
judgment
junior lien
lien
mechanic's lien
mill
mortgage lien
special assessment
specific lien
statutory lien
statutory right of redemption
subordination agreement
tax lien
tax sale
vendor's lien
voluntary lien
writ of attachment

OVERVIEW

The ownership of real estate is subject to certain obligations imposed by state and local governments, usually in the form of taxes that become a *lien* against the property. A creditor or a court can also place a claim against property to secure payment for a debt or other obligation. The ability to place a lien on property helps provide assurance to governments, lenders, homeowners associations, and those who provide work or services to improve property that the property owner will meet financial obligations incurred by virtue of owning the property.

LIENS

A **lien** is a charge or claim against a person's property made to enforce the payment of money. Whenever someone borrows money, the lender generally requires some form of *security*. Security (also called *collateral*) is something of value that the borrower promises to give the lender if the borrower fails to repay the debt. When the lender's security is in the form of real estate, the security interest is called a mortgage lien. Property can thus be used to ensure payment for work performed, material provided, or debts incurred.

Liens are not limited to security for borrowed money. Liens can be enforced against property by a government agency for payment of property tax owed by the owner. A lien also can be used to force the payment of an assessment or other special charge.

All liens are encumbrances, but not all encumbrances are liens.

A lien represents an interest in ownership, but it does not constitute actual ownership of the property. It is an encumbrance on the owner's title. An *encumbrance* is any charge or claim that attaches to real property and lessens its value or impairs its use. An encumbrance does not necessarily prevent the transfer or conveyance of the property, but because an encumbrance is attached to the property, it transfers along with it. Liens differ from other encumbrances because they are financial or monetary in nature and attach to the property because of a debt. Other encumbrances may be physical in nature and may affect the owner's use of the property, such as easements or encroachments.

If a lien is not paid in the allotted time, the lienholder may foreclose on the lien, potentially forcing the sale of the property as set out by state law. Depending on how the lien was created, a lienholder may be required to initiate a legal action to force the sale of the property or acquire title. In other cases, the sale of the property can take place without a court hearing. The debt is paid out of the proceeds of the sale; any remaining amount goes to the debtor.

Types of Liens

Memory Tip

Four ways to create a lien (VISE):

- **V**oluntary
- **I**nvoluntary
- **S**tatutory
- **E**quitable

There are many different types of liens. (*See* Figure 13.1.) One way that liens are classified is by how they are created. A **voluntary lien** is created intentionally by the property owner's action, such as when someone takes out a mortgage loan. An **involuntary lien** is not a matter of choice; it is created by law and may be either statutory or equitable. A **statutory lien** is created by statute. A real estate **tax lien**, for example, is an involuntary, statutory lien. It exists without any action by the property owner. An **equitable lien** arises out of common law. A court-ordered judgment that requires a debtor to pay the balance on a delinquent charge account, and which can be filed in the county where the debtor owns property, would create an involuntary, equitable lien on the debtor's real estate.

FIGURE 13.1: Types of Liens

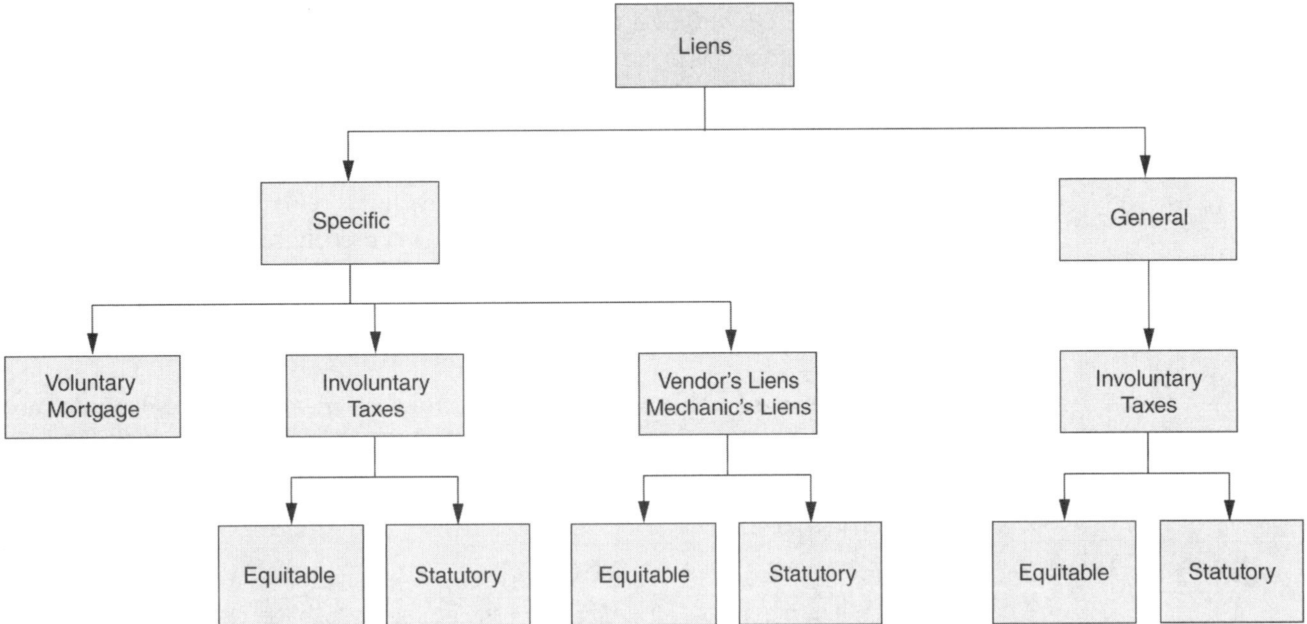

Liens may be classified according to the type of property involved. **General liens** affect all the property, both real and personal, of a debtor. This includes judgments, estate and inheritance taxes, decedent's debts, corporate franchise taxes, and Internal Revenue Service taxes. A lien on real estate differs from a lien on personal property. A lien attaches to real property *at the moment it is filed and recorded*. In contrast, a lien does not attach to personal property *until the personal property is seized*.

Specific liens are secured by specific property and affect only that particular property. Specific liens on real estate include vendors' liens, mechanics' liens, mortgage liens, real estate tax liens, and liens for special assessments and utilities. A **vendor's lien** is a lien belonging to the vendor (seller) for the unpaid purchase price of the property, when the vendor has not taken any other lien or security, such as a mortgage, beyond the personal obligation of the purchaser. Vendors' liens in real estate are uncommon and arise out of the use of owner financing to sell property.

Effect of Lien on Title

The existence of a lien does not necessarily prevent a property owner from transferring title to someone else. The lien might reduce the value of the real estate because few buyers will take on the risk of a property that has a lien on it. Because the lien attaches to the property, not the property owner, a new owner might lose the property if the creditors take court action to enforce payment. Once in place, a lien *runs with the land* and will bind all successive owners until the lien is paid or settled and title is cleared by the filing of a *release of lien* by the lienholder.

IN PRACTICE A buyer should insist on a title search before closing a real estate transaction so that any recorded liens are revealed. If liens are present, the buyer may decide to purchase at a lower price or at better terms, require that the liens be removed, or refuse to complete the purchase.

Priority of liens *Priority of liens* refers to the order in which claims against the property will be *satisfied* if the property is sold by the debtor. In general, the rule for priority of liens is *first to record, first in right (priority)*. In accordance with state law, the priority of payment typically is established by the date the liens are placed in the public record of the county in which the property is located. If the holder of the first lien to be recorded forecloses on that lien, the proceeds of the property sale are used to pay that lien; if there are any funds remaining, the holder of any other lien is paid, with the former property owner receiving anything that remains after all lien holders are paid off. The holder of a **junior lien** (one that comes after an earlier lien) can foreclose on that lien, but the property will still be subject to the lien or liens with higher priority.

There are some notable exceptions to this rule. For instance, real estate taxes and special assessments generally take priority over all other liens, regardless of the order in which the liens are recorded. This means that outstanding real estate taxes and special assessments are paid first from the proceeds of a court-ordered sale.

IN PRACTICE It is important for a creditor to have the highest lien priority because it will mean that the creditor will be paid first if it becomes necessary to bring about a forced sale of the debtor's property. A creditor in the second or later position may receive little or nothing from the sale.

Subordination agreements are written agreements between lienholders to change the priority of mortgage, judgment, and other liens. Under a subordination agreement, the holder of a superior or prior lien agrees to permit a later lienholder's interest to take precedence.

IN PRACTICE The seller of a vacant parcel of land often finances the purchase for a builder, claiming the first lien priority, but will then agree to subordinate that interest to the interest of the lender who provides financing for the construction of a home on the lot. The construction lender will insist on having first lien priority but, because the overall property value will be increased by the improvements made to it, the seller of the land is willing to bear the risk that, in the event of a forced sale of the property, the proceeds of the sale will be sufficient to cover both liens.

REAL ESTATE TAX LIENS

There are two types of real estate taxes: general real estate taxes and special assessments or improvement taxes. Both are levied against specific parcels of property and automatically become liens on those properties.

The ownership of real estate is subject to certain governmental powers. One of these is the right of state and local governments to impose (levy) taxes to pay for their functions. Because the location of real estate is permanently fixed, the government can levy taxes with a high degree of certainty that the taxes will be collected. The annual taxes levied on real estate in most states usually have priority over previously recorded liens and may be enforced by a court-ordered sale.

Ad Valorem Tax

The **general real estate tax** is an **ad valorem tax**. *Ad valorem* is Latin for "according to value." Ad valorem taxes are based on the value of the property being taxed and are specific, involuntary, statutory liens. Real estate property taxes are a favored source of revenue for local governments because real estate cannot be hidden and is relatively easy to value. Property taxes pay for a wide range of government services and programs, including those of

- states;
- counties;
- cities, towns, boroughs, and villages;
- school districts (local elementary and high schools, publicly funded junior colleges, and community colleges);
- drainage districts;
- hospital districts;
- water districts;
- sanitary districts;
- transportation districts; and
- parks, forest preserves, and recreation districts.

Exemptions From General Taxes Most state laws exempt certain real estate from taxation. Such property must be used for tax-exempt purposes, as defined in the statutes. The most common exempt properties are owned by

- cities,
- various municipal organizations (such as schools, parks, and playgrounds),
- state and federal governments,
- religious and charitable organizations,
- hospitals, and
- educational institutions.

Many state laws also allow special exemptions to reduce real estate tax bills for certain property owners or land uses. For instance, senior citizens, veterans, and persons with a disability are frequently granted reductions in the *assessed values* of their homes. In some states, low-income seniors may request a property tax freeze on the principal residence, which means that the tax assessed will not increase during the remaining years of the senior's ownership and use of the property. In an effort to stem the recent record number of home foreclosures, some states have subsidized low-income homeowners' tax bills, without regard to the owners' ages.

Some state and local governments offer real estate tax reductions to attract industries and sports franchises. Many states also offer tax reductions for agricultural land.

Assessment Real estate is valued for tax purposes by county or township assessors or appraisers. This official valuation process is called *assessment*. A property's assessed value is generally based on the sales prices of comparable properties, although practices may vary. Land values may be assessed separately from buildings or other improvements, and different valuation methods may be used for different types of property. State law may provide for property to be periodically reassessed.

Sometimes, a property owner believes that an error was made in determining the assessed property value—usually that the assessment is too high in comparison with the assessments of neighboring properties. Such owners may present their objections to a local board of appeal or board of review. A protest or appeal regarding a tax assessment may ultimately be taken to court.

Equalization In some jurisdictions, when it is necessary to correct inequalities in statewide tax assessments, an **assessment equalization factor** is used to achieve uniformity. An equalization factor may be applied to raise or lower assessments in a particular district or county. The assessed value of each property in the area is multiplied by the equalization factor and the tax rate is then applied to the equalized assessment.

Tax Rates The process of arriving at a real estate tax rate begins with the adoption of a budget by each taxing district. Each budget covers the financial requirements of the taxing body for the coming fiscal year. The fiscal year may be the January through December calendar year or some other 12-month period designated by statute. The budget must include an estimate of all expenditures for the year.

The next step is appropriation, which means that a taxing body authorizes the expenditure of funds and provides for the sources of the funding. Appropriation generally involves the adoption of an ordinance or the passage of a law that states the specific terms of the proposed taxation. Some states require voter approval of any real property tax increase.

After appropriation or approval by voters, the amount to be raised from the general real estate tax is imposed on property owners through a *tax levy*. A tax levy is the formal action taken to impose the tax, usually by a vote of the taxing district's governing body.

The tax rate for each taxing body is determined by state law or computed separately. Unless the tax rate has already been determined by state law, the total monies needed for the coming fiscal year are divided by the total assessments of all real estate located within the taxing body's jurisdiction.

The tax rate may be stated in a number of ways. In many areas, it is expressed in mills. A **mill** is 1⁄1000 of a dollar, or $0.001. The tax rate may be expressed as a mills-per-dollar ratio—for instance, in dollars per hundred or in dollars per thousand. A tax rate of 0.032, or 3.2%, could be expressed as 32 mills, or $3.20 per $100 of assessed value or $32 per $1,000 of assessed value.

IN PRACTICE An easy way to recall the value of a mill is to remember that there are 10 mills in a penny.

Tax Bills A property owner's tax bill is computed by applying the tax rate to the assessed valuation of the property.

IN PRACTICE A property is assessed for tax purposes at $160,000. At a tax rate of 3%, or 30 mills, the tax owed on the property is $4,800 ($160,000 × 0.03). If an equalization factor of 120% is used, the computation is in two steps: $160,000 × 1.20 = $192,000, and $192,000 × 0.03 = $5,760. The tax owed on the property is $5,760.

The due dates for tax payments (also called the penalty dates) are set by statute. Taxes may be payable in 2 installments (semiannually), 4 installments (quarterly), or 12 installments (monthly). In some areas, taxes become due at the beginning of the current tax year and must be paid in advance (e.g., the year 2015 taxes must be paid at the beginning of 2014). In other areas, taxes are payable during the year after the taxes are levied (e.g., 2015 taxes are paid throughout 2015). In some states, taxes are paid one year in arrears, and you cannot pay any portion of the ad valorem taxes during the current year (e.g., 2014 taxes could not be paid until the tax books open in 2015). In still other areas, a partial payment is due in the year the tax is imposed, with the balance due in the following year (e.g., 2015 taxes are payable partly during 2015 and partly during 2016).

Some states offer discounts and monthly payment plans to encourage prompt payment of real property taxes. Penalties, typically in the form of monthly interest charges on overdue taxes, are added to all taxes that are not paid when due.

Enforcement of Tax Liens Real estate taxes must be valid to be enforceable. That means they must be charged properly, must be used for a legal purpose, and must be applied equitably to all property. As previously mentioned, tax liens usually are given priority over all other liens against a property. Real estate taxes that have remained delinquent for the statutory period can be collected through a **tax sale** of the property. While the methods and details of the various states' tax sale procedures differ substantially, the results are the same.

A tax sale is usually held according to a published notice after a court has rendered a judgment for overdue taxes, penalties, and administrative costs and has ordered that the property be sold. A tax sale is advertised in local newspapers, and a notice of sale is posted on the affected property. The county sheriff or other public official then holds a public sale of the property. Because a specific amount of delinquent tax and penalty must be collected, the purchaser at a tax sale must pay at least that amount. A *certificate of sale* is usually given to the highest bidder when that bidder pays the delinquent tax amount in cash. The certificate of sale gives the holder the right to take possession of the property.

The holder of the certificate of sale may be required to wait for a while after the sale to receive the deed to the property. Some states grant a period of redemption after the tax sale. In this case, the defaulted owner (or the defaulted owner's creditors) may redeem the property by paying the amount collected at the tax sale plus interest and charges (including any taxes levied since the sale). This is known as a **statutory right of redemption**. If the property is not redeemed within the statutory period, the certificate holder can apply for a *tax deed (sheriff's deed)*. The quality of the title conveyed by a tax deed varies from state to state.

In some states, the delinquent taxpayer may redeem the property anytime before the tax sale. The taxpayer exercises this **equitable right of redemption** by paying the delinquent taxes plus interest and charges (any court costs or attorney's fees). An owner who does not exercise this right may force a sale.

Special Assessments and Local Improvement District Taxes

A **special assessment** is a tax charged on real estate to fund public improvements to the property, and it creates a lien for the amount of the assessment on the property. Property owners in the improvement area are required to pay for the improvements because their properties benefit directly from them. For example, the construction of paved streets, curbs, gutters, sidewalks, storm sewers, or street lighting increases the value of properties that benefit from them. The additional tax paid by the homeowner of those properties covers the cost of the improvements.

A special assessment is generally paid in equal annual installments over a period of years. The first installment is usually due during the year following the public authority's approval of the assessment. The first bill includes one year's interest on the property owner's share of the entire assessment. Subsequent bills include one year's interest on the unpaid balance. Property owners have the right to prepay any or all installments to avoid future interest charges.

For large-scale improvement projects such as streets, sidewalks, and water or sewer construction, a local improvement district (LID) may be created. An LID is a specific geographical area formed by a group of property owners working together to fund needed capital improvements. LID taxation is simply a financing method available for the design and construction of public improvements.

In some parts of the country, strict subdivision regulations and LIDs have just about eliminated special assessments. Most items for which assessments have traditionally been levied are now required to be installed at the time of construction as a condition of a subdivision's approval.

OTHER LIENS ON REAL PROPERTY

In addition to real estate tax and special assessment liens, a variety of other liens may be charged against real property.

Mortgage Lien

A **mortgage lien** is a voluntary lien on real estate given to a lender by a borrower as security for a real estate loan. It becomes a lien on real property when the lender records the documents in the county where the property is located. Lenders generally require a preferred lien, called a first mortgage lien. This means that no other liens against the property (aside from real estate taxes) can take priority over the mortgage lien. As mentioned earlier, subsequent liens are referred to as junior liens.

Mechanic's Lien

A **mechanic's lien** is a specific, involuntary lien that gives security to persons or companies that perform labor or furnish material to improve real property. A mechanic's lien is available to contractors, subcontractors, architects, equipment lessors, surveyors, laborers, and other providers. This type of lien is filed when the owner has not fully paid for the work or when the general contractor has been compensated but has not paid the subcontractors or suppliers of materials. Statutes in some states prohibit subcontractors from placing liens directly on certain types of property, such as owner-occupied residences. While laws regarding mechanics' liens vary from state to state, there are many similarities.

To be entitled to a mechanic's lien, the person who did the work must have had a contract with the owner or the owner's authorized representative, such as a general contractor. A person claiming a mechanic's lien must file a notice of lien in the public record of the county where the property is located within a certain time after the work has been completed. A lien waiver is required for a contractor to receive a payment from the owner's construction loan. Once the work is completed and accounts paid, the owner will ask for a release or satisfaction of lien to be filed to clear the property title.

According to state law, priority of a mechanic's lien may be established as of the date the construction began or materials were first furnished; the date the work was completed; the date the individual subcontractor's work was either commenced or completed; the date the contract was signed or work was ordered; or the date a notice of the lien was recorded, filed, posted, or served. In some states, mechanics' liens may be given priority over previously recorded liens, such as mortgages.

If improvements that were not ordered by the property owner have commenced, the property owner should execute a document called a *notice of nonresponsibility* to be relieved from possible mechanics' liens. By posting this notice in some conspicuous place on the property and recording a verified copy of it in the public record within the time specified by statute, the owner gives notice that he or she is not responsible for the work done. This may prevent the filing of mechanics' liens on the property.

IN PRACTICE In most states, a mechanic's lien takes priority from the time it attaches, even though a claimant's notice of lien will not be filed in the public record until sometime later. A prospective purchaser of property that has been recently constructed, altered, or repaired should be cautious about possible unrecorded mechanics' liens against the property.

Judgment

A **judgment** is a decree issued by a court. When the decree establishes the amount a debtor owes and provides for money to be awarded, it is called a *money judgment*. These often result from damages caused to one person by another person through a wrongful act, breach of contract, or nonpayment of a debt.

A judgment is a general, involuntary, equitable lien on both real and personal property owned by the debtor. A judgment is not the same as a mortgage because no specific parcel of real estate was given as security at the time the debt was created. A lien automatically covers only property located within the county in which the judgment is issued, so a notice of the lien must be filed in any county to which a creditor wishes to extend the lien coverage. Judgments expire after a number of years but, in some states, can be renewed indefinitely by the judgment creditor.

To enforce a judgment, the creditor must obtain a *writ of execution* from the court. A writ of execution directs the sheriff to seize and sell as much of the debtor's property as is necessary to pay both the debt and the expenses of the sale. A judgment does not become a lien against the personal property of a debtor until the creditor orders the sheriff to assess the property and the charge is actually made.

A judgment lien's priority is established by one or a combination of the following (as provided by state law):

- Date the judgment was entered by the court
- Date the judgment was filed in the recorder's office
- Date a writ of execution was issued

When real property is sold to satisfy a debt, the debtor should demand a legal document known as a *satisfaction of judgment* (or *satisfaction piece*). Filing the satisfaction of judgment clears the record of the lien. In those states using a deed of trust, a deed of reconveyance must be filed with either the clerk of the court or, in some states, the recorder of deeds.

Lis Pendens There is often a considerable delay between the time a lawsuit is filed and the time final judgment is rendered. When any suit that affects title to or possession of real estate is filed, a special notice, known as a lis pendens is recorded. A lis pendens is not itself a lien, but rather notice of a possible future lien. Recording a lis pendens notifies prospective purchasers and lenders that there is a potential claim against the property. It also establishes a priority for the later lien. The lien is backdated to the recording date of the lis pendens.

Attachment To prevent a debtor from conveying title to previously unsecured real estate while a court suit is being decided, a creditor may seek a **writ of attachment**. A writ of attachment is a court order against the property of another person that directs the sheriff or other officer of the court to seize or take control of a property. By this writ, the court retains custody of the property until the suit concludes. Most *attachments* arise from an action for payment of an unsecured debt. For example, a plaintiff in a lawsuit may attach a defendant's property to gain a security interest in order to foreclose the property or to prevent the defendant from disposing of property that may be needed to pay a judgment.

Estate and Inheritance Tax Liens

Federal **estate taxes** and state **inheritance taxes** (as well as the debts of decedents) are general, statutory, involuntary liens that encumber a deceased person's real and personal property. These taxes and debts are normally paid or cleared in probate court proceedings.

Lien for Municipal Utilities

Municipalities often have the right to impose a specific, equitable, involuntary lien on the property of an owner who refuses to pay bills for municipal utility services.

Bail Bond Lien

A real estate owner who is charged with a crime that will result in a trial may post bail in the form of real estate rather than cash. The execution and recording of such a bail bond creates a specific, statutory, voluntary lien against the owner's real estate. If the accused fails to appear in court, the lien may be enforced by the sheriff or another court officer.

Corporation Franchise Tax Lien

State governments generally levy a corporation franchise tax on corporations as a condition of allowing them to do business in the state. Such a tax is a general, statutory, involuntary lien on all real and personal property owned by the corporation.

IRS Tax Lien

A federal tax lien, or *Internal Revenue Service (IRS) tax lien*, results from a person's failure to pay any portion of federal taxes, such as income and withholding taxes. A federal tax lien is a general, statutory, involuntary lien on all real and personal property held by the delinquent taxpayer. Its priority, however, is based on the date of filing or recording; it does not supersede previously recorded liens. The same rules apply to most state income tax liens. Information on federal tax liens can be found at www.irs.gov.

www.irs.gov

KEY POINT REVIEW

A **lien** is a claim of a creditor or taxing authority against the **real property** of a debtor that is used as **security** to ensure repayment of the debt.

A lien is not an ownership interest in real estate; it is an **encumbrance** that transfers with it (**runs with the land**) and lessens its value or impairs its use because it binds all successive owners until paid and cleared. If a debtor **defaults** in payment of a debt secured by property, the **lienholder** can force the **sale** of the property, or **acquire title**.

Creation of a lien may be **voluntary**, if it is created by action of the property owner, such as a mortgage or **involuntary**, if it is created without the property owner's express permission. It may also be **statutory**, if it is permitted by statute, or **equitable**, if it is granted by a court.

A **general lien** affects all of a debtor's property, both real and personal; examples are judgments, estate and inheritance taxes, decedent's debts, corporate franchise taxes, and federal income taxes. A **specific lien** affects only identified property; examples include a vendor's lien, mortgage lien, real estate tax lien, and lien for special assessments and utilities.

Priority of liens determines the order in which claims will be **satisfied** (paid off). Generally, the first lien to be recorded will take priority, but real estate taxes and special assessments usually take priority over all other liens. If a junior lien is foreclosed, the property is still subject to prior liens. A **subordination agreement** between lienholders can be used to change the order of priority.

Real estate taxes are *ad valorem* taxes based on the value of the property taxed. They create specific, involuntary, statutory liens that are levied by states, counties, municipalities, and school and other districts. Exemptions are available for certain property uses, reductions in tax are available for homeowners, senior, veterans, and those with a disability. Certain land uses may also qualify for a reduction in property tax.

Property **assessments** (valuations) are conducted by county or township tax **assessors** or appraisers. **Assessed value** is generally based on sales prices of comparable properties. **An equalization factor** may be applied to correct inequalities in statewide tax assessments.

The **tax rate** for each taxing body is computed separately and may be expressed in **mills**. A mill is 1/1000 of a dollar, or $0.001. Mills may be shown as dollars per hundred or thousand dollars of assessed value.

Delinquent taxes can be collected through a **tax sale** following statutory notice requirements. The **taxpayer** usually has **equitable right of redemption** any time before a tax sale. The state may allow a **statutory right of redemption** following a tax sale. If there are **no bidders** at the tax sale, the property may be forfeited to the state.

Special assessments are levied and create a lien on property that benefits from public improvements, such as properties located in a **local improvement district (LID)**, and are always specific and statutory, but may be voluntary or involuntary, and are usually paid in annual installments over a period of years.

A **mortgage lien** is a voluntary lien given to a lender by a borrower as security for a real estate loan. The lien takes effect when the lender **records** the documents in the county where the property is located. A **first mortgage lien** on a property, when recorded, has **priority** over other liens (except for tax liens); subsequent liens are **junior liens**.

A **mechanic's lien** is a specific, involuntary lien that gives a security interest in real property to persons or companies that perform labor or furnish material to improve the property. A mechanic's lien is **filed** when an **owner** has not fully paid for work or the **general contractor** has been compensated but has not paid subcontractors or suppliers of materials.

In some states, a mechanic's lien has priority over previously recorded liens such as mortgages. A property owner who did not order improvements that are being made should execute, post, and record a **notice of nonresponsibility** to be relieved from possible lien claims.

A **judgment**, a decree issued by a court, is a general, involuntary, equitable lien on both real and personal property owned by a debtor and must be filed in **every county** in which the judgment debtor owns property.

While a lawsuit is pending, a **lis pendens** can be filed to give notice of an action pending relating to the title or possession of real property and establish priority of the claimant, and a **writ of attachment** can be sought from the court to authorize the sheriff to seize the property that the debtor may attempt to transfer. A **writ of execution** can be obtained from the court to enforce a judgment.

Estate and inheritance tax liens are general, statutory, involuntary liens that encumber a deceased person's real and personal property and are normally paid or cleared in a probate proceeding.

A **lien for municipal utilities** is a specific, equitable, involuntary lien on the property of the owner who refuses to pay bills for municipal utility services.

A **corporation franchise tax lien** is a general, statutory, involuntary lien on real and personal property owned by the corporation.

An **IRS tax lien** is a general, statutory, involuntary lien on all real and personal property held by a delinquent taxpayer; it does not supersede previously recorded liens (which is also true of most state income tax liens).

UNIT 13 QUIZ

1. Which lien affects all real and personal property of a debtor?
   a. Specific
   b. Voluntary
   c. Involuntary
   d. General
2. Priority of liens refers to which of the following?
   a. Order in which a debtor assumes responsibility for payment of obligations
   b. Order in which liens will be paid if property is sold to satisfy a debt
   c. Dates liens are filed for record
   d. Fact that specific liens have greater priority than general liens
3. A lien on real estate made to secure payment for a specific municipal improvement project is which of the following?
   a. Mechanic's lien
   b. Special assessment lien
   c. Ad valorem
   d. Utility lien
4. Which of the following is classified as a general lien?
   a. Mechanic's lien
   b. Bail bond lien
   c. Judgment
   d. Real estate taxes
5. Which lien usually would be given highest priority in disbursing funds from a foreclosure sale?
   a. Mortgage dated last year
   b. Real estate taxes due
   c. Mechanic's lien for work started before the mortgage was made
   d. Judgment rendered the day before foreclosure
6. A specific parcel of real estate has a market value of $160,000 and is assessed for tax purposes at 75% of market value. The tax rate for the county in which the property is located is 40 mills. The tax bill will be
   a. $6,400.
   b. $5,000.
   c. $5,200.
   d. $4,800.
7. Which tax targets homeowners in particular?
   a. Personal property tax
   b. Franchise tax
   c. Real property tax
   d. Luxury tax
8. A mechanic's lien claim arises when a contractor has performed work or provided material to improve a parcel of real estate on the owner's order and the work has not been paid for. Such a contractor has a right to
   a. tear out the work.
   b. record a notice of the lien.
   c. record a notice of the lien and file a court suit within the time required by state law.
   d. have personal property of the owner sold to satisfy the lien.
9. What is the annual real estate tax on a property valued at $135,000 and assessed for tax purposes at $47,250, with an equalization factor of 125%, when the tax rate is 25 mills?
   a. $945
   b. $1,181
   c. $1,418
   d. $1,477
10. Which of the following is a voluntary, specific lien?
    a. IRS tax lien
    b. Mechanic's lien
    c. Mortgage lien
    d. Seller's lien

11. A seller sold a buyer a parcel of real estate. Title has passed, but to date the buyer has not paid the purchase price in full, as originally agreed. If the seller wants to force payment, which remedy is the seller entitled to seek?
   a. Attachment
   b. Mechanic's lien
   c. Lis pendens
   d. Judgment

12. A general contractor recently filed suit against a homeowner for nonpayment. The contractor now learns that the homeowner has listed the property for sale with a real estate professional. In this situation, which of the following will the contractor's attorney use to protect the contractor's interest?
   a. Seller's lien
   b. Buyer's lien
   c. Assessment
   d. Lis pendens

13. Which statement *MOST* accurately describes special assessment liens?
   a. They are general liens.
   b. They are paid on a monthly basis.
   c. They take priority over mechanics' liens.
   d. They cannot be prepaid in full without penalty.

14. Which of the following creates a lien on real estate?
   a. Easement running with the land
   b. Unpaid mortgage loan
   c. License
   d. Encroachment

15. Which statement is *TRUE* of both a mortgage lien and a judgment lien?
   a. It must be entered by the court.
   b. It involves a debtor-creditor relationship.
   c. It is a general lien.
   d. It is an involuntary lien.

16. A mechanic's lien would be available to all of the following *EXCEPT*
   a. subcontractors.
   b. contractors.
   c. surveyors.
   d. real estate professionals.

17. The right of a defaulted taxpayer to recover property before its sale for unpaid taxes is the
   a. statutory right of reinstatement.
   b. equitable right of appeal.
   c. statutory right of assessment.
   d. equitable right of redemption.

18. Which of the following is a specific, involuntary, statutory lien?
   a. Real estate tax lien
   b. Income tax lien
   c. Estate tax lien
   d. Judgment lien

19. General real estate taxes levied for the operation of the government are
   a. assessment taxes.
   b. ad valorem taxes.
   c. special taxes.
   d. improvement taxes.

20. All of the following probably would be exempt from real estate taxes *EXCEPT*
   a. public hospitals.
   b. golf courses operated by the park district.
   c. synagogues and churches.
   d. apartment buildings.

Real Estate Financing

LEARNING OBJECTIVES

When you have finished reading this unit, you will be able to

- **describe** the various aspects of housing affordability, including mortgage terms, ability to pay, and investment and tax considerations;
- **describe** the terms, conditions, and use of the promissory note;
- **explain** the elements and use of security instruments, and describe the mortgage deed of trust and the roles, rights, and obligations of the parties involved;
- **describe** the various types of real estate financing;
- **explain** the distinction between a judicial foreclosure and a non-judicial foreclosure, and the process involved in each;
- **describe** the various consumer protections related to homeownership; and
- **define** the following *key terms*:

acceleration clause
adjustable-rate mortgage (ARM)
alienation clause
amortized loan
assumption of mortgage
balloon payment
beneficiary
Comprehensive Loss Underwriting Exchange (CLUE)
debt to income (DTI)
deed in lieu of foreclosure
deed of reconveyance
deed of trust
defeasance clause
deficiency judgment
discount points
equity
foreclosure
growing-equity mortgage
homeowners insurance
hypothecation
index
interest
interest-only loan
lien theory
loan origination fee
loan-to-value ratio (LTV)
margin
mortgage
mortgagee
mortgagor
negative amortization
negotiable instrument
note
novation
PITI (principal, interest, taxes, and insurance)
prepayment penalty
promissory note
release deed
reverse mortgage
satisfaction of mortgage
short sale
straight loan
"subject to"
title theory
trustor
usury

OVERVIEW

In the United States, relatively few homes that are to be owner-occupied are purchased for cash. Most such homes are bought with borrowed money, and a huge lending industry has been built to service the financial requirements of homebuyers. Here, we will examine housing affordability—what it takes to purchase a home, and whether the investment is manageable. We then look at the ways in which real estate is financed. We conclude with a discussion of homeowners property insurance, an essential element to loan approval. Later, you will examine the many ways in which government programs and assistance help both home buyers and lenders.

IN PRACTICE A real estate professional should refer a prospective buyer to a lender to be preapproved for a loan prior to showing properties to the buyer. It is important for the real estate professional to be knowledgeable about real estate financing programs and products in order to provide quality service, especially when representing a buyer, but it is also important for the buyer to be realistic about the type and amount of financing that the buyer can acquire.

HOUSING AFFORDABILITY

Congress, state legislatures, and local governments work diligently to increase the affordability of housing. Because more homeowners mean more business opportunities, real estate and related industry groups have a vital interest in ensuring affordable housing for all segments of the population. At the start of this century, creative financing, low-interest loans, interest-only loans, and flexible lending standards helped initiate housing loans to an ever-broader pool of borrowers, including many in the "subprime" housing market who would not have qualified for a housing loan otherwise. As a result, according to the U.S. Bureau of the Census, by June of 2004, 69.2% of households were homeowners. By 2012, however, many borrowers had defaulted and a record number of foreclosures meant that real estate prices fell precipitously. In addition, a recessionary period was in effect and unemployment had risen, making matters even worse both for homeowners in distress and those who would otherwise have entered the housing market. By 2015, most areas of the country saw an increase in sales and property values; however, for many, those increases were modest, and the overall rate of homeownership continued to decline. According to the Joint Center for Housing Studies of Harvard University, www.jchs.harvard.edu, the homeownership rate for 2014 was 64.5%. This rate dropped to 63.7% in the first quarter of 2015, making it the lowest quarterly rate of homeownership since early 1993.

www.jchs.harvard.edu

Certainly, not everyone wants to or should own a home. Home ownership involves substantial commitment and responsibility. People whose work requires frequent moves or whose financial position is uncertain particularly benefit from renting. Renting also provides more leisure time by freeing tenants from management and maintenance.

Those who choose home ownership over renting must evaluate many factors before they decide to purchase property. And the purchasing decision must be weighed carefully in light of each individual's financial circumstances.

The decision to buy or to rent property involves considering

- how long a person wants to live in a particular area,
- a person's financial situation,
- housing affordability,
- current mortgage interest rates,
- tax consequences of owning versus renting property, and
- what might happen to home prices and tax laws in the future.

Mortgage Terms

Mortgage terms and payment plans are two of the biggest factors when deciding whether to own or rent a home. Although many loan programs of the past are no longer offered or are offered only to highly qualified borrowers, mortgages on less stringent terms are still available to those who qualify. The Federal Housing Administration (FHA) and the U.S. Department of Veterans Affairs (VA), for example, have programs with low down payments and lower credit score requirements, although they, too, have tightened lending standards in recent years.

Ownership Expenses and Ability to Pay

The basic costs of owning a home are **PITI**—
Principal,
Interest,
Taxes, and
Insurance

Home ownership involves many expenses, including utility costs, such as electricity, natural gas, heating oil, water, trash removal, and sewer charges, in addition to routine maintenance and repairs. Owners also must pay real estate taxes, buy property insurance, and repay (with interest) the mortgage loan used to purchase the property—what lenders refer to as **PITI (principal, interest, taxes, and insurance)**.

www.equifax.com
www.experian.com
www.transunion.com

To determine what a prospective buyer can afford, most home mortgage lenders use an automated (computerized) underwriting system that considers various factors, including the loan applicant's credit report and credit score. There are three major credit reporting companies in the United States: Equifax (www.equifax.com), Experian (www.experian.com), and TransUnion (www.transunion.com).

Checking Your Credit Report

The *credit report* is important in acquiring a loan for a home or other major purchase, obtaining a credit card, being approved for a lease, and even in acquiring a new job. Because of its significance to the consumer in so many ways, the federal government requires each of the major credit reporting companies to make a free copy of the report available annually to every consumer for whom a report is available. The free reports can be obtained at www.annualcreditreport.com. (Don't be confused by similarly named sites that charge for this service.) Because each of the credit reporting agencies is required to comply with the law, the consumer can request a free report every four months from a different company each time, making it possible to monitor one's credit status on a regular basis.

www.myfico.com/CreditEducation/articles

A *credit score* is prepared by a credit reporting company and is based on a consumer's past history of credit use, including income, outstanding loans, number of credit accounts open, outstanding credit lines, number of accounts opened and closed, payment history, and credit inquiries. The credit score, often called the FICO score because it can be created from software developed by Fair Isaac and Company, can range from a low of 300 to a high of 850, the best score. Lenders will require a minimum credit score for a loan, often dependent on whether or not the lender will sell the mortgage after initiating it or the borrower is making use of a government-sponsored program, such as those of FHA and VA. More information on the FICO score is at www.myfico.com/CreditEducation/articles.

Lenders generally look at a loan applicant's percentage of **debt to income (DTI)**. A homebuyer who is able to provide at least 10% of the purchase price as a down payment, for instance, could be expected to incur a monthly PITI payment of no more than 28% of the borrower's gross (pretax) monthly income. Monthly payments on all debts—normally including long-term debt such as car payments, student loans, or other mortgages—would be expected to not exceed 36% of gross monthly income. Expenses such as insurance premiums, utilities, and routine medical care would not be included in the 36% figure but would be expected to be covered by the remaining 64% of the buyer's monthly income. The formula can vary, depending on the type of loan program and the borrower's earnings, credit history, number of dependents, and other factors. The borrower's credit score now plays a key role in the lending decision, though the debt-to-income ratio is still important.

IN PRACTICE A prospective homebuyer wants to know how much house she can afford to buy. The buyer has a gross monthly income of $5,000. If the required down payment can be made, the buyer's allowable housing expense may be calculated as follows:

$5,000 gross monthly income × 28% = $1,400 total housing expense allowed

$5,000 gross monthly income × 36% = $1,800 total housing and other debt expense allowed

If actual monthly non-housing debts exceed 8% of gross income (36%–28%), and the borrower is unable to reduce that amount, the monthly payment must be lowered proportionately because the debts and housing payment combined cannot exceed 36% of gross monthly income. Lower debts would not result in a higher allowable housing payment, but would be considered a factor for approval.

Investment Considerations

Purchasing a home can offer financial advantages to a buyer, provided the marketplace cooperates. First, if the property's value increases, an eventual sale of the property might bring in more money than the owner's purchase price. Second, as the total mortgage debt is reduced through monthly payments that include part of the principal owed, the owner's actual ownership interest in the property increases. The difference between the market value of the property and the amount still owed on it is the homeowner's **equity** in the property. The equity can be borrowed against in future or realized on a sale of the property. A homeowner's mortgage payments thus help to build personal net worth. The third financial advantage of home ownership may be the tax deductions available to the homeowner for mortgage interest and property tax, if those deductions total more than the amount of the applicable standard deduction. Finally, part of the profit made on the sale of a principal residence is not taxed at all.

Tax deductions Homeowners may deduct from their gross income

- mortgage <u>interest</u> payments on first and second homes (for mortgage balances below $1 million, or $500,000 if married filing separately, as well as home equity loans on those dwellings of no more than a combined $100,000),

- real estate taxes (but not interest paid on overdue taxes),
- certain loan origination fees,
- loan discount points (whether paid by the buyer or the seller), and
- loan prepayment penalties.

Other Tax Benefits When a married couple who file a joint tax return sell a principal residence, up to $500,000 in profit (sales price minus purchase price) can be excluded from capital gains tax. A taxpayer who files singly is entitled to a $250,000 exclusion. The exclusion may be used repeatedly, as long as the homeowner has both owned and occupied the property as the principal residence for at least two of the past five years.

A first-time homebuyer may make a penalty-free withdrawal from a tax-deferred individual retirement account (IRA) for the down payment on a home, although the withdrawal is still subject to income tax in that year. The limit on the withdrawal is $10,000 and the amount withdrawn must be spent entirely within 120 days on a down payment to avoid any penalty.

Other tax incentives, such as a tax credit for part of the purchase price, also are offered by the federal government from time to time to encourage homebuying. In addition, many states have their own programs meant to encourage home ownership.

Real estate purchases purely for investment purposes (property that is not to be owner-occupied) offer their own tax and other incentives.

PROMISSORY NOTE

The purchase of a home usually requires borrowing a substantial amount or all of the purchase price. In exchange for a lender providing the needed funds, the borrower promises to repay the debt with interest.

The **promissory note**, called the *note* or *financing instrument*, is a borrower's personal promise to repay a debt according to the agreed terms. A promissory note executed by a borrower (the *maker* or *payor*) is a contract with the lender (the *payee*). The note generally states the amount of the debt, the time and method of payment, and the rate of interest. When signed by the borrower and other necessary parties, the note becomes a legally enforceable and fully negotiable instrument of debt. When the terms of the note are satisfied, the debt is discharged. If the terms of the note are not met, the lender may choose to sue to collect on the note or to foreclose on any property that was used as security for the debt. A note could also be unsecured, if there is no collateral provided for the debt.

A **note** is a **negotiable instrument**, similar to a check or bank draft. The payee who holds the note may transfer the right to receive payment to a third party in one of two ways:

- By signing the instrument over (that is, by *assigning* it) to the third party
- By delivering the instrument to the third party

IN PRACTICE Most home loans are sold by the lenders who have made them, which is useful because it means that more funds are made available for future borrowers. Home loans are bought and sold in the *secondary mortgage market*.

Interest

Interest is a charge for the use of money, expressed as a percentage of the remaining balance of the loan. A lender charges interest on the principal (amount borrowed that has not yet been repaid) over the term of the loan, usually monthly. Interest may be due at either the end or the beginning of each payment period. Payments made at the end of a period are known as payments *in arrears*. This payment method is the general practice, and home loans often call for end-of-period payments due on the first of the following month. Payments may also be made at the beginning of each period and are known as payments *in advance*. Whether interest is charged in arrears or in advance is specified in the note. This distinction is important if the property is sold before the debt is repaid in full.

MATH CONCEPTS

Determining Interest

Interest is the cost of using money. The amount of interest paid is determined by the agreed annual interest rate, the amount of money borrowed (loan amount) or the amount of money still owed (loan balance), and the period of time the money is held. When a lender grants a loan for real estate, the **loan-to-value ratio (LTV)** is the percentage of the sales price or appraised value, whichever is less, that the lender is willing to lend.

loan amount		
sales price or appraised value (whichever is less)	X	loan-to-value ratio (LTV)

Sales price or appraised value (whichever is less) × loan-to-value ratio (LTV) = **loan amount**

Loan amount ÷ loan-to-value ratio (LTV) = **sales price** or **appraised value** (whichever is less)

annual interest		
loan amount (principal)	X	annual interest rate

Loan amount (principal) × annual interest rate = **annual interest**

Annual interest ÷ annual interest rate = **loan amount (principal)**

Annual interest ÷ loan amount (principal) = **annual interest rate**

For example, a parcel of rural land sold for $335,200. The lender approved a 90% loan at 4.5% for 30 years. The appraised value on this parcel was $335,500. How much interest is paid to the lender in the first monthly payment?

loan amount		
$335,200 sales price	X	90%

$335,200 × 90% = $301,680 loan

annual interest		
$301,680 loan amount	X	4.5%

$301,680 × 4.5% = $13,575.60 annual interest

$13,575.60 annual interest ÷ 12 months = $1,131.30 monthly interest

$1,131.30 interest in the first monthly payment is the answer.

Usury Charging interest in excess of the maximum rate allowed by law is called **usury**. To protect consumers from unscrupulous lenders, many states have enacted laws limiting the interest rate that may be charged on loans. In some states, the legal maximum rate is a fixed amount. In others, it is a floating interest rate, which is adjusted up or down at specific intervals based on a specified economic standard, such as the prime lending rate or the rate of return on government bonds. In some states, a lender that makes a usurious loan is permitted to collect the borrowed money, but only at the legal rate of interest. In others, a usurious lender may lose the right to collect any interest or may lose the entire amount of the loan in addition to the interest.

As of March 31, 1980, federal law *exempts* federally related residential first mortgage loans made after that date from state usury laws. A federally related transaction is one that involves a federally chartered or insured lending institution or an agency of the federal government. Because federal law always preempts state law on the same subject, the federal law means that most home loans are not subject to state usury protections. Private lenders are still subject to state usury laws, however.

Loan Origination Fee

The processing of a mortgage application is known as *loan origination*. When a home loan is originated, a **loan origination fee**, or transfer fee, is charged by most lenders to cover the expenses involved in generating the loan. These expenses include the loan officer's salary, paperwork, and the lender's other costs of doing business. A loan origination fee is not prepaid interest; rather, it is a charge that must be paid to the lender. The loan origination fee will vary, depending on how competitive a lender chooses to be, but typically is about 1% of the loan amount.

IN PRACTICE Because many real estate loans are made by private loan companies that may not be covered by federal regulations, it is important that borrowers insist on receiving a statement in advance from their lender that clearly states the total amount of the loan closing costs and the effective interest rate, in order to avoid unpleasant surprises at closing.

Discount Points

Discount points are used to increase the lender's *yield* (rate of return) on its investment. For example, the interest rate that a lender charges for a loan might be less than the yield an investor demands. To make up the difference, the lender charges the borrower discount points. The number of points charged depends on two factors:

- The difference between the loan's stated interest rate and the yield required by the lender
- How long the lender expects it will take the borrower to pay off the loan

A **point** is 1% of the amount being borrowed; it is not 1% of the purchase price.

For borrowers, one discount point equals 1% of the loan amount (not purchase price) and is charged as prepaid interest at the closing. For instance, three discount points charged on a \$100,000 loan would be \$3,000, which is \$100,000 × 3%, or \$100,000 × 0.03. If a house sells for \$100,000 and the borrower seeks an \$80,000 loan, each point would be \$800, *not* \$1,000. In some cases, however, the points in a new acquisition may be paid in cash at closing by the buyer (or, of course, by the seller on the buyer's behalf) rather than being financed as part of the total loan amount.

To determine how many points are charged on a loan, divide the total dollar amount of the points by the amount of the loan. For example, if the loan amount is $350,000 and the charge for points is $9,275, how many points are being charged?

$9,275 ÷ $350,000 = 0.0265 or 2.65% or 2.65 points

Prepayment Penalty

Most mortgage loans are paid in installments over a long period of time. As a result, the total interest paid by the borrower may add up to more than the principal amount of the loan. That does not come as a surprise to the lender; the total amount of accrued interest is carefully calculated during the origination phase to determine the profitability of each loan. If the borrower repays the loan before the end of the term, the lender collects less than the anticipated interest. For this reason, some mortgage notes contain a *prepayment clause*. This clause requires that the borrower pay a **prepayment penalty** against the unearned portion of the interest for any payments made ahead of schedule, typically during the first years of the loan. This gives the lender the assurance of a certain level of income earned on the loan.

Lenders may not charge prepayment penalties on mortgage loans insured or guaranteed by the federal government or on those loans that have been sold on the secondary mortgage market to one of the government-sponsored enterprises that will be discussed later.

SECURITY INSTRUMENT

Mortgage loans are secured loans. Mortgage loans have two parts: the debt itself and the security for the debt. When a property is mortgaged, the owner must *execute* (sign) two separate instruments—the financing instrument that creates the debt and the security instrument that specifies the property that the debtor will use as collateral for the debt. The financing instrument is the promissory note (discussed earlier), which states the amount owed. Depending on the state, the security instrument will take the form of either a mortgage or a deed of trust, though both are commonly referred to as a mortgage, and will specify the property used to secure the loan. A mortgage creates a lien on the property; the deed of trust actually transfers legal title from the borrower to a third party to hold on behalf of the lender while the borrower's debt is still outstanding. This section looks at the differences in how each form of security interest is created and how each is enforced.

A basic principle of property law is that no one can convey more than he actually owns. This principle also applies to a mortgage. The owner of a fee simple estate can mortgage the fee. The owner of a leasehold or subleasehold can mortgage that leasehold interest. The owner of a condominium unit can mortgage the fee interest in the condominium. Even the owner of a cooperative unit may be able to offer that property interest (the owner's stock in the underlying corporation) as security for a loan.

Hypothecation

In mortgage lending practice, a borrower is required to make specific real property security (collateral) for the loan. In the process called **hypothecation**, the debtor retains the right of possession and control of the secured property, while the creditor receives an equitable right in the property. The right to foreclose on the property in the event a borrower defaults is contained in the security agreement, which takes the form of either a mortgage or a deed of trust, as discussed next.

Mortgage

A **mortgage** is a lien on the real property of a debtor. The borrower, or **mortgagor**, receives a loan and in return gives a promissory note and mortgage to the lender, called the **mortgagee**. The mortgage is a voluntary, specific lien. If the debtor defaults, the lender can sue on the note and foreclose on the mortgage. When the loan is paid in full, the mortgagee issues a document called a **satisfaction of mortgage**, which can be filed in the public record as evidence of the removal of the security interest, which would otherwise continue to be an encumbrance on the ownership interest of the borrower. The judicial process for foreclosure of a mortgage depends on state law and on whether the state treats the mortgage as a lien or as a conveyance of some part of the title to the property.

In a mortgage or **lien theory** state, the mortgagor retains both legal and equitable title to property that serves as security for a debt. The mortgagee has a lien on the property but the mortgage is nothing more than collateral for the loan. If the mortgagor defaults, the mortgagee must go through a formal foreclosure proceeding in court to obtain legal title. If the foreclosure is approved by the court, the property is offered for sale at public auction, and the funds from the sale are used to pay the balance of the remaining debt. In some states, a defaulting mortgagor may *redeem* (buy back) the property during a certain period after the sale, the *statutory right of redemption*. A borrower who fails to redeem the property during that time loses the property irrevocably. *See* Figure 14.1 for a diagram of how a mortgage works.

FIGURE 14.1: Mortgages

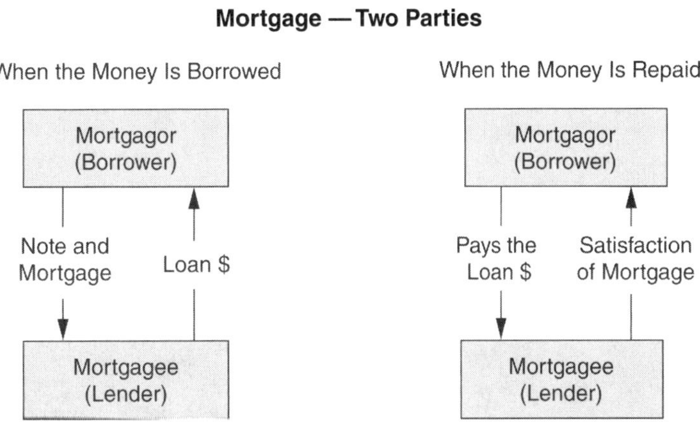

Deed of Trust

In some states, lenders prefer to use a three-party security instrument known as a **deed of trust**. A trust deed conveys bare legal title (naked title)—that is, title without the right of possession—from the borrower to a third party, called the *trustee*. The trustee holds legal title on behalf of the lender, the holder of the promissory note, who is known as the **beneficiary**. On full payment of the underlying debt, the lender/beneficiary notifies the trustee, who returns legal title to the trustor.

In a deed of trust or **title theory** state, then, the mortgagor actually conveys *legal title* to the mortgagee (or some other designated individual) and retains *equitable title* and the right of possession. Legal title is returned to the mortgagor only when the debt is paid in full (or some other obligation is performed). In effect, because the lender holds legal title, the lender has the right to immediate possession of the real estate and rents from the mortgaged property if the mortgagor defaults.

The deed of trust establishes the actions that the trustee may take if the borrower, the **trustor**, defaults under any of the deed of trust terms. In states where deeds of trust are generally preferred, foreclosure procedures for default, which must comply with state law, are usually simpler and faster than for mortgage loans. On notification of the borrower's default, the trustee is authorized to sell the secured property, providing the proceeds to the beneficiary, the lender. If the sale proceeds are greater than the amount owed on the debt, the borrower receives the difference, less penalty fees and court costs.

Usually, the lender chooses the trustee and reserves the right to substitute trustees in the event of the trustee's death or dismissal. State law usually dictates who may serve as trustee. Although the deed of trust is particularly popular in certain states, it is used all over the country. *See* Figure 14.2 for a diagram of how a deed of trust works.

FIGURE 14.2: Deeds of Trust

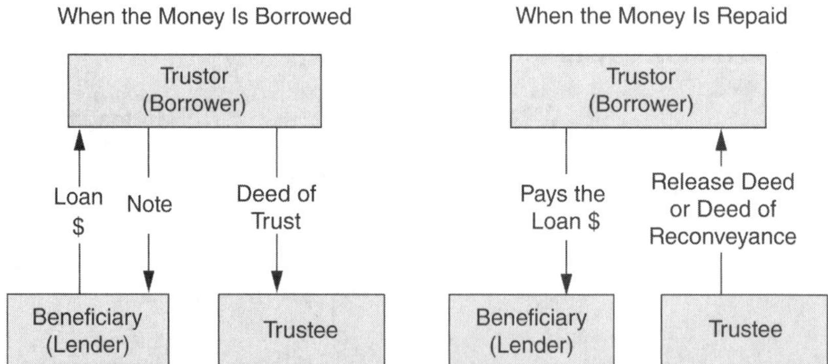

IN PRACTICE In the financing of a commercial or industrial real estate venture that involves a large loan and several lenders, the borrower generally executes a single deed of trust to secure as many notes as necessary. Sometimes a large note will be secured by multiple parcels of real property, as in a subdivision, and there will be a separate security instrument for each parcel.

A mortgage or deed of trust must clearly establish that the property is security for a debt, identify the lender and the borrower, and include an accurate legal description of the property. Both instruments incorporate the terms of the promissory note by reference, which coordinates the note and security instrument, and both should be signed by all parties who have an interest in the real estate.

IN PRACTICE In reality, the differences between the parties' rights in a lien theory state and those in a title theory state are more technical than actual. Regardless of the theory practiced in any particular state, all borrowers and lenders observe the same general requirements to protect themselves in a loan transaction. As with any contract, the parties must be legally competent, their signatures valid and attested, and adequate consideration exchanged.

Duties of the Borrower

The borrower—whether a mortgagor or a trustor—is required to fulfill certain obligations created by the mortgage or deed of trust. These usually include the following:

- Payment of the debt in accordance with the terms of the promissory note
- Payment of all real estate taxes on the property used as security
- Maintenance of adequate insurance to protect the lender in the event that the property is destroyed or damaged by fire, windstorm, or other hazard
- Maintenance of the property in good repair at all times
- Receipt of lender authorization before making any major alterations on the property

Failure to meet any of these obligations can result in a borrower's default. The loan documents may, however, provide for a grace period (such as 30 days) during which the borrower can meet the obligation and cure the default. If the borrower does not do so, the lender has the right to take the steps described next.

Provisions for Default

The mortgage or deed of trust typically includes an **acceleration clause** to assist the lender in foreclosure. If a borrower defaults, the lender has the right to accelerate the maturity of the debt. This means the lender may declare the *entire* principal balance due and payable *immediately*. Without an acceleration clause, the lender would have to sue the borrower every time a payment was overdue.

Other provisions in a mortgage or deed of trust enable the lender to take care of the property in the event of the borrower's negligence or default. If the borrower does not pay taxes or insurance premiums, or fails to make necessary repairs on the property, the lender may step in and do so. The lender has the power to protect the security (the real estate).

IN PRACTICE In financing a real estate sale, a lender will seldom accept an unsecured promissory note because there would be no backup for the loan. If a borrower defaulted, the lender would be forced to sue for a money judgment. In the meantime, the debtor might dispose of the property and hide assets. In some states, a money judgment cannot be used to foreclose on a debtor's personal residence. Because of these, and other reasons, lenders prefer a security interest in real property.

Assignment of the Mortgage

As noted earlier, a promissory note usually is a negotiable instrument. This means that, without changing the provisions of the contract, the note may be sold to a third party, such as an investor or another mortgage company. The original mortgagee (the *assignor*) endorses the note to the third party (the *assignee*) and executes an *assignment* of mortgage. The assignee becomes the new owner of the debt and security instrument. When the debt is paid in full (or satisfied), the assignee is required to execute the document that releases the security interest.

Release of the Mortgage Lien or Deed of Trust

When all loan payments have been made and the promissory note has been paid in full, the borrower will want the public record to show that the debt has been satisfied and that the lender is divested of all rights conveyed under the mortgage or deed of trust. By the provisions of the **defeasance clause** in the financing instrument, the lender is required to execute a **satisfaction of mortgage** (also known as a *release* or *discharge*) when the note has been fully paid. This document returns to the borrower all interest in the real estate originally conveyed to the lender. Entering this release in the public record shows that the debt has been removed from the property.

When a real estate loan secured by a deed of trust has been completely repaid, the beneficiary must make a written request that the trustee convey the title to the property back to the grantor. The trustee executes and delivers a *deed of reconveyance* (sometimes called a **release deed**) to the trustor. The deed to the trustor conveys the same rights and powers that the trustee was given under the deed of trust. It should include a notarized acknowledgment and be recorded in the public records of the county in which the property is located.

If the mortgage or deed of trust has been assigned, the satisfaction of mortgage or reconveyance deed must be executed and recorded by the assignee or mortgagee.

Tax and Insurance Reserves

As discussed previously, many lenders require that borrowers provide a reserve fund to meet future real estate taxes and property insurance premiums. This fund is called an *impound* or *escrow account*. When the mortgage or deed of trust loan is made, the borrower starts the reserve by depositing funds to cover the amount of unpaid real estate taxes. If a new insurance policy has just been purchased, the insurance premium reserve will be started with the deposit of one-twelfth of the insurance premium liability. The borrower's monthly loan payments will include PITI: principal, interest, taxes, and insurance. Other costs also may be included, such as flood insurance. Federal regulations limit the total amount of reserves that a lender may require.

Flood Insurance Reserves The National Flood Insurance Reform Act of 1994 imposes certain mandatory obligations on lenders and loan servicers to set aside (*escrow*) funds for flood insurance on new loans for property in flood-prone areas. This means that if a lender or servicer discovers that a secured property is in a flood hazard area, it must notify the borrower. The borrower then has 45 days to purchase flood insurance. If the borrower fails to procure flood insurance, the lender must purchase the insurance on the borrower's behalf. The cost of the insurance may be charged back to the borrower. More information on flood insurance, which can be a critical part of home ownership, is provided later.

Buying "Subject to" or Assuming a Seller's Mortgage or Deed of Trust

When a person purchases real estate that has an outstanding mortgage or deed of trust, the buyer may take the property in one of two ways. The property may be purchased **"subject to"** the mortgage or deed of trust, or by **assumption of mortgage**, in which the buyer assumes the mortgage or deed of trust and agrees to pay the debt. This technical distinction becomes important if the buyer defaults and the mortgage or deed of trust is foreclosed.

When the property is sold *subject to* the mortgage, the buyer is not personally obligated to pay the debt in full. The buyer takes title to the real estate knowing that she must make payments on the existing loan. Upon default, the lender forecloses and the property is sold by court order to pay the debt. If the sale does not pay off the entire debt, the purchaser is not liable for the difference. In some circumstances, however, the original seller might continue to be liable.

In contrast, a buyer who purchases a property and assumes the seller's debt becomes personally obligated for the payment of the entire debt. If a seller wants to be completely free of the original mortgage loan, the seller(s), buyer(s), and lender must execute a **novation** agreement in writing. The novation makes the buyer solely responsible for any default on the loan. The original borrower (seller) is freed of any liability for the loan.

The existence of a lien does not prevent the transfer of property; however, when a secured loan is assumed, the mortgagee or beneficiary must approve the assumption and any release of liability of the original mortgagor or trustor. Because a loan may not be assumed without lender approval, the lending institution would require the assumer to qualify financially, and many lending institutions charge a transfer fee to cover the costs of changing the records. This charge can be paid by either the buyer or the seller.

Alienation Clause The lender may want to prevent a future purchaser of the property from being able to assume the loan, particularly if the original interest rate is low. For this reason, most lenders include an **alienation clause** (also known as a *resale clause*, *due-on-sale clause*, or *call clause*) in the note. An alienation clause provides that when the property is sold, the lender may either declare the entire debt due immediately or permit the buyer to assume the loan at an interest rate acceptable to the lender. Land contracts that involve a due-on-sale clause also limit the assumption of the contract.

Recording a Mortgage or Deed of Trust

The mortgage document or deed of trust must be recorded in the recorder's office of the county in which the real estate is located. Recording gives constructive notice to the world of the borrower's obligations. Recording also establishes the lien's priority. If the property is registered in the Torrens system, notice of the lien must be entered on the original Torrens certificate.

Priority of a Mortgage or Deed of Trust

Priority of mortgages and other liens normally is determined by the order in which they were recorded. A mortgage or deed of trust on land that has no prior mortgage lien is a *first mortgage* or *first deed of trust*. If the owner later executes another loan for additional funds, the new loan becomes a *second mortgage* or *second deed of trust* (or a *junior lien*) when it is recorded. Second loans represent greater risk to the lender, and they usually have a higher interest rate.

In the event that a second lien has a higher amount than the first, the lender may require a *subordination agreement*, in which the first lender subordinates or lowers its lien position to that of the second lender. To be valid, both lenders must sign the agreement.

TYPES OF LOANS

Real estate can be financed in a variety of ways. The most popular forms of financing are discussed next. Most provide for some form of *amortization*, with each payment including part of the loan principal, so that the entire principal is paid off by the end of the loan term. The first type of loan discussed does not include part of the principal in the regular payments, however.

Straight Loan

A **straight loan** (also known as a *term loan* or **interest-only loan**) essentially divides the loan into two amounts to be paid off separately. The borrower makes periodic payments of interest only, followed by the payment of the principal *in full at the end of the term*. Straight loans were once the only form of home loan available, but are now generally used for home improvements and second mortgages rather than for residential first mortgage loans. A loan may provide for interest-only payments in the beginning years, to make payments affordable.

Amortized Loan

Unlike a straight loan payment, each payment in an **amortized loan** partially pays off both principal and interest. Most mortgage and deed of trust loans are amortized loans. The word *amortize* literally means to kill off. The loan is paid off slowly, over time, in regular periodic payments that include both principal and interest over a term of years. The payment period usually ranges from 10 to 30 years. At the end of the loan term, the full amount of the principal and all interest due is reduced to zero. Such loans are known as *direct reduction loans*.

The most frequently used mortgage payment plan is the *fully amortized loan*, or *level-payment loan*. The mortgagor pays a *constant amount*, usually monthly. The lender credits each payment first to the interest due, then to the principal amount of the loan. As a result, while each payment remains the same, the portion applied to repayment of the principal grows and the interest due declines as the unpaid balance of the loan is reduced. If the borrower pays additional amounts that are applied directly to the principal, the loan will amortize more quickly. This benefits the borrower, who will then pay less interest if the loan is paid off before the end of its term.

Unfortunately, some mortgage loans allow options that might increase, rather than reduce, the outstanding loan balance. Such *negative amortization* is discussed in the next section.

If you know what the monthly payment and interest rates are, you can determine the amount of the constant payment of an amortized loan from a prepared mortgage payment book or a mortgage factor chart. The mortgage factor chart indicates the amount of monthly payment per $1,000 of loan, depending on the term and interest rate. This factor is multiplied by the number of thousands (and fractions of thousands) of the amount borrowed.

IN PRACTICE Financial calculators can accurately perform most of the standard mortgage lending calculations, and most commercial lenders provide mortgage calculators on their websites. Nonetheless, it is valuable to understand how the calculations are performed.

Adjustable-Rate Mortgage (ARM)

The **adjustable-rate mortgage (ARM)** begins at one rate of interest, then fluctuates up or down during the loan term, based on a specified economic indicator. Because the interest rate may change, the mortgagor's loan payment may change. Details of how and when the interest rate will change are included in the note. Common components of an ARM include the following:

- The **index** is an economic indicator that is used to adjust the interest rate in the loan. Most indexes are tied to U.S. Treasury securities. The adjustment period establishes how often the rate may be changed, which could be monthly, quarterly, or annually. If interest rates are going up, the longest adjustment period benefits the borrower. If interest rates are going down, the borrower benefits from a shorter adjustment period.
- Usually, the interest rate is the index rate plus a premium, called the **margin**. The margin represents the lender's cost of doing business.
- *Rate caps* limit the amount the interest rate may change. Most ARMs have two types of rate caps—periodic and life-of-the-loan (or aggregate). A periodic rate cap limits the amount the rate may increase over a stated term, usually a year. A life-of-the-loan rate cap limits the amount the rate may increase over the entire life of the loan.

The mortgagor can be protected from unaffordable individual payments by a *payment cap*. The payment cap sets a maximum amount for payments, but the difference between the payment made and the full payment amount will be added to the remaining mortgage balance. The amount of the loan actually increases (instead of decreasing) in the process called **negative amortization**. If property values do not increase as anticipated, or the borrower can no longer afford to make mortgage payments, negative amortization can result in the borrower owing more than the property is worth—the unhappy situation of being *under water*. The *option* ARM that allowed negative amortization as one of the borrower's choices was a contributing factor to many of the foreclosures that suppressed the housing market in many parts of the country.

The lender may offer a conversion option that permits the mortgagor to convert from an adjustable-rate to a fixed-rate loan at certain intervals during the life of the mortgage.

Growing-Equity Mortgage

A **growing-equity mortgage** is also called a *rapid-payoff mortgage*. The growing-equity mortgage uses a fixed interest rate, but payments of principal are increased according to an index or schedule. The total payment thus increases, and the loan is paid off more quickly. A growing-equity mortgage is most frequently used when the borrower's income is expected to keep pace with the increasing loan payments.

MATH CONCEPTS

The Mortgage Amortization Triangle

If you know the monthly payment and interest rate on a loan, you can easily track how much of each month's payment is being applied toward principal and how much is applied toward interest.

Always begin with the top box and follow the direction of the arrows to perform the calculations described in each box for each month's calculation. Your result will show how much of a given month's mortgage payment goes to pay principal and what portion pays interest on the loan to the lender. For instance, if you wanted to see how much the loan principal would be reduced after three months, you would "go around the triangle" three times.

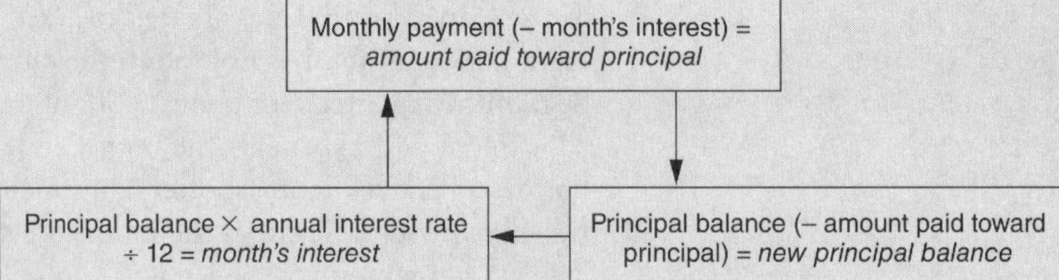

For example, using the Mortgage Factor Chart in Figure 14.3, assume a 15-year mortgage loan for $150,000 at a 3.75% annual interest rate and a monthly payment of $1,090.50 (150,000 ÷ 1,000 × 7.27 = $1,090.50). You can see how the triangle can help you determine the amount of principal and interest in each payment for the first two months of the loan (shown in each box as "1" and "2").

The principal balance on the loan at the end of the second month (the beginning of the third month) 148,754.56.

What is the principal balance on this loan at the end of the third month?

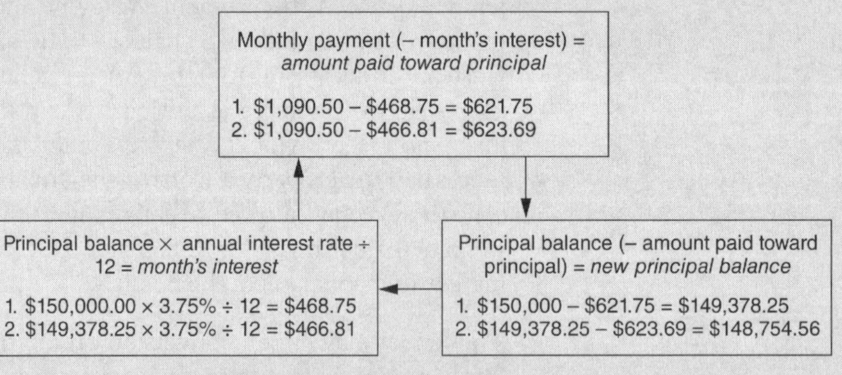

Solution

Step 1: $148,754.56 × 3.75% ÷ 12 = $464.86

Step 2: $1,090.50 – $464.86 = $625.64

Step 3: $148,754.56 – $625.64 = $148,128.92

Principal balance at the end of the third month is $148,128.92

FIGURE 14.3: Mortgage Factor Chart

How To Use This Chart

To use this chart, start by finding the appropriate interest rate. Then follow that row over to the column for the appropriate loan term. This number is the *interest rate factor* required each month to amortize a $1,000 loan. To calculate the principal and interest (PI) payment, multiply the interest rate factor by the number of 1,000s in the total loan.

For example, if the interest rate is 6% for a term of 30 years, the interest rate factor is 6.00. If the total loan is $200,000, the loan contains 200 1,000s. Therefore, 200 × 6.00 = $1,200 PI.

Rate	Term 15 Years	Term 30 Years
3	6.91	4.22
3 1/8	6.97	4.28
3 1/4	7.03	4.35
3 3/8	7.09	4.42
3 1/2	7.15	4.49
3 5/8	7.21	4.56
3 3/4	7.27	4.63
3 7/8	7.33	4.70
4	7.40	4.77
4 1/8	7.46	4.85
4 1/4	7.52	4.92
4 3/8	7.59	4.99
4 1/2	7.65	5.07
4 5/8	7.71	5.14
4 3/4	7.78	5.22
4 7/8	7.84	5.29
5	7.91	5.37
5 1/8	7.97	5.44
5 1/4	8.04	5.52
5 3/8	8.10	5.60
5 1/2	8.17	5.68
5 5/8	8.24	5.76
5 3/4	8.30	5.84
5 7/8	8.37	5.92

Rate	Term 15 Years	Term 30 Years
6	8.44	6.00
6 1/8	8.51	6.08
6 1/4	8.57	6.16
6 3/8	8.64	6.24
6 1/2	8.71	6.32
6 5/8	8.78	6.40
6 3/4	8.85	6.49
6 7/8	8.92	6.57
7	8.98	6.65
7 1/8	9.06	6.74
7 1/4	9.12	6.82
7 3/8	9.20	6.91
7 1/2	9.27	6.99
7 5/8	9.34	7.08
7 3/4	9.41	7.16
7 7/8	9.48	7.25
8	9.56	7.34
8 1/8	9.63	7.43
8 1/4	9.71	7.52
8 3/8	9.78	7.61
8 1/2	9.85	7.69
8 5/5	9.93	7.78
8 3/4	10.00	7.87
8 7/8	10.07	7.96
9	10.15	8.05

Balloon Payment Loan

When the periodic payments on a loan are not enough to fully pay off the principal of the loan by the time the final payment is due, the final payment will be larger than the others. State law will provide the definition, but typically a **balloon payment** is a final payment that is at least twice the amount of any other payment. The loan will be considered a *partially amortized loan* because some of the principal has been paid, with some still owed at the end of the term.

It is frequently assumed that if payments are made promptly, the lender will extend the balloon payment for another limited term. The lender, however, is not legally obligated to grant this extension and can require payment in full when the note is due.

Reverse Mortgage

A **reverse mortgage** allows a homeowner aged 62 or older to borrow money against the equity built up in the home. With a reverse mortgage, the homeowner's equity diminishes as the loan amount increases. The money may be used for any purpose and the borrower decides if the funds will be paid out in a lump sum, fixed monthly payments, an open line of credit, or another option. The borrower is charged a fixed rate of interest and no payments are due until the property is sold or the borrow defaults (perhaps by failing to maintain the property), moves, or dies. With the recent recession and volatility of the stock market, the reverse mortgage has become a popular method of providing more income while allowing the homeowner to remain in the home. It is important to remember, however, that the usual property tax, insurance, maintenance, and utility costs must still be paid by the homeowner, and these may be more substantial than the income produced by the reverse mortgage. Also, with the equity in the home reduced, the homeowner will have fewer resources on which to draw in the event that a move to an assisted-living facility or nursing home becomes necessary.

The most popular reverse mortgages are those insured by FHA.

FORECLOSURE

When a borrower defaults on any required payment or fails to fulfill any of the other obligations set forth in the mortgage or deed of trust, the lender's rights can be enforced through foreclosure. **Foreclosure** is a legal procedure in which property pledged as security for a debt is sold to satisfy the debt. Any unpaid lienholder, regardless of priority position, can initiate foreclosure proceedings; however, foreclosure of a junior lien means that the liens with higher priority remain in place and the buyer takes title subject to those liens. The foreclosure of a lien with highest priority brings the rights of the parties and all junior lienholders to a conclusion. It passes title to the person holding the mortgage document, the beneficiary of a deed of trust, or a third party who purchases the property at a *foreclosure sale*. The property is sold *free of the foreclosing mortgage and all junior liens*.

The purchaser on foreclosure of a debt secured by real property could be the mortgagee—the lender—and the property then becomes part of the lender's *REO (real estate owned)* portfolio. The lender then becomes responsible for maintaining the property and paying the expenses of ownership, including property taxes.

IN PRACTICE Institutional lenders are not in the business of managing property, so they try to minimize their REO portfolios, but dealing with an institutional seller can be a frustrating experience. In some areas, a prospective buyer should be prepared for a much longer than usual time for acceptance of an offer to purchase as well as a lengthy period before the sale is closed, during which there may be repeated requests from the seller that must be addressed. In other areas, the volume of REO sales has prompted lenders to expedite the sale process. In any event, an attractive sales price may make the purchase of an REO property worth any aggravation.

Methods of Foreclosure

There are three general types of foreclosure proceedings—judicial, nonjudicial, and strict foreclosure. The specific provisions and procedures depend on state law.

Judicial Foreclosure Judicial foreclosure allows the property to be sold by court order after the mortgagee has given sufficient public notice. When a borrower defaults, the lender may *accelerate* the due date of the remaining principal balance, along with all overdue monthly payments and interest, penalties, and administrative costs. The lender's attorney can then file a suit to foreclose the lien. After presentation of the facts in court, if the court grants the request, the property is ordered sold. A public sale is advertised and held, and the real estate is sold to the highest bidder.

Nonjudicial Foreclosure Some states allow nonjudicial foreclosure procedures to be used when the security instrument contains a *power-of-sale clause*. In nonjudicial foreclosure, no court action is required. In those states that recognize deed of trust loans, the beneficiary is generally given the power of sale, which is conducted by the trustee. Some states allow a similar power of sale to be used with a mortgage loan, if specified in the terms of the mortgage.

To institute a nonjudicial foreclosure, the trustee or mortgagee will send a notice of default to the borrower indicating the amount that must be paid to make the debt current, as well as the action that will be taken if the required payment is not made. If the borrower fails to *cure* the default within the specified time, the next step will be the sending of a notice of foreclosure to the borrower, indicating when and where the property will be sold at public auction. The notice of foreclosure will be recorded within a designated period to give notice to the public of the intended auction. The notice is generally provided by newspaper advertisements that state the total amount due and the date of the public sale. After selling the property, the trustee or mortgagee may be required to file a notice of sale or affidavit of foreclosure.

Strict Foreclosure In some states, a lender may acquire mortgaged property through a *strict foreclosure* process. First, appropriate notice must be given to the delinquent borrower. Once the proper papers have been prepared and recorded, the court establishes a deadline for the balance of the defaulted debt to be paid in full. If the borrower does not pay off the loan by that date, the court simply awards full legal title to the lender. No sale takes place. Strict foreclosure is more common when personal property is used to secure a debt.

Deed in Lieu of Foreclosure

As an alternative to foreclosure, a lender may be willing to accept a **deed in lieu of foreclosure** from the borrower. This is sometimes known as a *friendly foreclosure* because it is carried out by mutual agreement rather than by lawsuit. The disadvantage of the deed in lieu of foreclosure to the lender is that it does not eliminate junior liens. In a foreclosure action, all junior liens are eliminated. Also, by accepting a deed in lieu of foreclosure, the lender usually loses any rights pertaining to FHA or private mortgage insurance or VA guarantees. Finally, a deed in lieu of foreclosure is still considered an adverse element in the borrower's credit history.

Redemption

Most states give defaulting borrowers a chance to redeem their property through the *equitable right of redemption.* If, after default but before the foreclosure sale, the borrower (or any other person who has an interest in the real estate, such as another creditor) pays the lender the amount in default, plus costs, the debt will be reinstated. In some cases, the person who redeems may be required to repay the accelerated loan in full. If some person other than the mortgagor or trustor redeems the real estate, the borrower becomes responsible to that person for the amount of the redemption.

Certain states also allow defaulted borrowers a period in which to redeem their real estate after the sale. During this period (which may be as long as one year), the borrower has a *statutory right of redemption.* The mortgagor who can raise the necessary funds to redeem the property within the statutory period pays the redemption money to the court. Because the debt was paid from the proceeds of the sale, the borrower can take possession free and clear of the former defaulted loan. The court may appoint a receiver to take charge of the property, collect rents, and pay operating expenses during the redemption period. (*See* Figure 14.4.)

Deed to Purchaser at Sale

If redemption is not made, or if state law does not provide for a redemption period, the successful bidder at the sale receives a deed to the real estate. Officials such as a sheriff, an officer of the court, or a trustee executes this deed to the purchaser to *convey whatever title the borrower had.*

FIGURE 14.4: Redemption

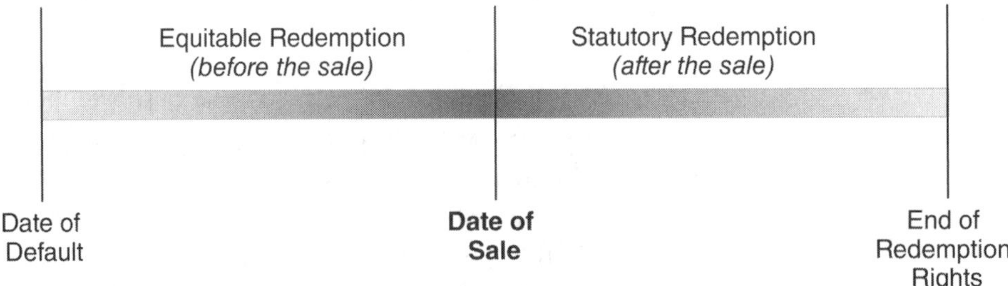

Deficiency Judgment

The foreclosure sale may not produce enough cash to pay the loan balance in full after deducting expenses and accrued unpaid interest. In that case, the mortgagee may be entitled to a *personal judgment* against the borrower for the unpaid balance. Such a judgment is a **deficiency judgment**. It may also be obtained against any endorsers or guarantors of the note and against any owners of the mortgaged property who assumed the debt by written agreement. If any money remains from the foreclosure sale after paying the debt and any other liens (such as a second mortgage or a mechanic's lien), expenses, and interest, those proceeds are paid to the borrower.

Some states prohibit a deficiency judgment on a purchase money loan for the borrower's principal residence. A lender could decide not to pursue a deficiency judgment, even though entitled to one, but the defaulting borrower could then be faced with the situation described in "Short Sale."

Short Sale

Since 2008, many parts of the country have experienced a severe drop in market values of all kinds of real estate. While the market has improved somewhat in many places, a prospective property seller may still be faced with a proposed sales price that is less than the amount outstanding on the seller's mortgage debt. In such a situation, the lender may permit a **short sale** in which the sales price is less than the remaining indebtedness. The best practice if a short sale is sought is to contact the lender before marketing the property to determine whether or not the short sale would be accepted and, if so, how low a sales price the lender would be willing to approve.

The listing of a property for which a short sale has been approved should always disclose that fact. The lender will expect to approve the sales contract negotiated by buyer and seller and will also be informed of the progress of the transaction, giving final approval before the closing. Lender approvals will add several months or longer to the closing of the transaction, and the buyer should be aware of the lengthy period before the transaction can be completed. This might be acceptable to a buyer who is satisfied that the sales price is worth the wait; another buyer might not be able to wait that long.

A lender's willingness to approve a short sale may result in forgiveness of part of the borrower's debt. Of course, the seller in such a position has probably already lost a great deal of equity in the property as a result of its diminished market value and does not feel much sympathy for the lender. As the final blow to the seller, however, the forgiveness of part of the seller's mortgage debt has been considered by the IRS to be income to the seller/borrower and thus subject to income tax. The widespread dismay at this outcome resulted in the passage by Congress of the Mortgage Debt Relief Act of 2007. The law allows a taxpayer to exclude from income the forgiveness of part of the mortgage debt on the taxpayer's principal residence on a sale of the property, restructuring of an existing mortgage loan, or foreclosure of a mortgage loan. Subsequent legislation, including the American Taxpayer Relief Act of 2012, extended this provision through December 31, 2013.

CONSUMER PROTECTIONS

http://files.consumerfinance.gov/f/201312_cfpb_mortgagerules.pdf

www.consumerfinance.gov

As directed by the Wall Street Reform and Consumer Protection Act of 2010 (Dodd-Frank), the Consumer Financial Protection Bureau (CFPB) issued new mortgage disclosure rules that took effect January 10, 2014. A consumer information pamphlet, which was released in January 2013, is at http://files.consumerfinance.gov/f/201312_cfpb_mortgagerules.pdf. The pamphlet explains information that the mortgage lender must provide to the borrower and also provides contact information for the borrower to initiate a complaint if the lender is not following the rules. The lender must

- provide billing information in writing;
- give the borrower two months' warning if an adjustable-rate mortgage will have a rate change;

- promptly credit the borrower's payments;
- respond quickly when the borrower asks about paying off the loan;
- not charge for insurance the borrower doesn't need, or over-charge for insurance the lender provides if the borrower fails to do so ("force-placed insurance");
- quickly resolve complaints, generally within 30 to 45 business days, and share information;
- have and follow good customer service policies and procedures;
- contact the borrower to help when the borrower is having trouble making payments;
- work with the borrower, if the borrower is having trouble paying the mortgage, before starting or continuing foreclosure; and
- allow the borrower to seek review of the decision about a loan workout request.

The CFPB also created two new forms to be provided to the borrower after the loan application and before the close of the transaction. These forms are discussed later.

Homeowners Insurance

A home is usually the biggest purchase many people ever make. Most homeowners see the importance of protecting their investment by insuring it. A lender will require that a homeowner obtain insurance when the loan is secured by the property. While owners can purchase individual policies that insure against destruction of property by fire or windstorm, injury to others, and theft of personal property, most buy a **homeowners insurance** policy to cover all these risks.

Coverage and Claims The most common homeowners policy is called a *basic form*. The basic form provides property coverage against

- fire and lightning,
- glass breakage,
- windstorm and hail,
- explosion,
- riot and civil commotion,
- damage by aircraft,
- damage from vehicles,
- damage from smoke,
- vandalism and malicious mischief,
- theft, and
- loss of property removed from the premises when it is endangered by fire or other perils.

Broad-form homeowners insurance covers

- falling objects;
- damage due to the weight of ice, snow, or sleet;
- collapse of all or part of the building;
- bursting, cracking, burning, or bulging of a steam or water heating system or of appliances used to heat water;
- accidental discharge, leakage, or overflow of water or steam from within a plumbing, heating, or air-conditioning system;

- freezing of plumbing, heating, and air-conditioning systems and domestic appliances; and
- damage to electrical appliances, devices, fixtures, and wiring from short circuits or other accidentally generated currents.

Additional insurance is available to cover almost all possible perils. Special apartment and condominium policies generally provide fire and windstorm, theft, and public *liability coverage* for injuries or losses sustained within the unit, but they usually do not cover losses or damages to the structure. The basic structure is insured by either the landlord or the condominium owners association.

Most homeowners insurance policies contain a *coinsurance clause*. This provision usually requires that the owner maintain insurance equal to a specified percentage (usually 80%) of the *replacement cost* of the dwelling (not including the price of the land). An owner who has this type of policy may make a claim for the full cost of the repair or replacement of the damaged property without deduction for depreciation or annual wear and tear.

IN PRACTICE A homeowner's insurance policy is for 80% of the replacement cost of the home, or $80,000. The home is valued at $100,000, and the land is valued at $40,000. The homeowner sustains $30,000 in fire damage to the house. The homeowner can make a claim for the full cost of the repair or replacement of the damaged property without a deduction for depreciation. If the owner has insurance of only $70,000, the claim will be handled in one of two ways. The owner will receive either actual cash value (replacement cost of $30,000 less depreciation cost of say $3,000, or $27,000), or the claim will be prorated by dividing the percentage of replacement cost actually covered (0.70) by the policy's minimum coverage requirement (0.80). So, 0.70 divided by 0.80 equals 0.875, and $30,000 multiplied by 0.875 equals $26,250.

http://oci.wi.gov/pub_list/pi-207.htm

Comprehensive Loss Underwriting Exchange The **Comprehensive Loss Underwriting Exchange (CLUE)** is a database of consumer claims history that enables insurance companies to access prior claims information in the underwriting and rating process. The database contains up to five years of personal property claims history. The reports include policy information such as name, date of birth, policy number, and claim information date (date and type of loss, amounts paid, and description of property covered). More information about the CLUE report, and how one can be obtained, is at http://oci.wi.gov/pub_list/pi-207.htm.

IN PRACTICE Water-related problems have emerged in some properties over time. In particular, significant problems can occur with synthetic stucco exterior finishes and mold. The exterior insulating finishing system (EIFS) is a highly effective moisture barrier that also tends to seal in moisture—trapping water in the home's walls, which can result in massive wood rot. Frequently, the effects of the rotting cannot be seen until the damage is extensive and sometimes irreparable. Homeowners who suspect that EIFS was used on their home and is causing damage should have the property inspected. Some insurance companies refuse to cover homes with EIFS exteriors, and class action lawsuits have been brought against builders by distressed homeowners.

Federal Flood Insurance Program

The National Flood Insurance Act of 1968 was enacted by Congress to help owners of property in flood-prone areas by subsidizing flood insurance and by taking land-use and land-control measures to improve future management for floodplain areas. The Federal Emergency Management Agency (FEMA) administers the National Flood Insurance Program. The Army Corps of Engineers has prepared maps that identify specific flood-prone areas throughout the country. To finance property with federally related mortgage loans, owners in flood-prone areas must obtain flood insurance.

In flood-prone areas identified as *special flood hazard areas* (*SFHAs*), flood insurance is required on all types of buildings—residential, commercial, industrial, and agricultural—used as security for a federally related mortgage loan. The insurance must cover either the value of the property or the amount of the mortgage loan, subject to the maximum limits available. Policies are written annually and can be purchased from any licensed property insurance broker, the National Flood Insurance Program (NFIP), or the designated servicing companies in each state. A borrower who can produce a survey showing that the lowest part of the building is located above the 100-year flood mark may be exempted from the flood insurance requirement, even if the property is in a flood-prone area. A flood insurance premium reduction is available for communities that participate in NFIP's voluntary Community Rating system (CRS) by taking floodplain management steps to reduce flood losses, facilitating accurate insurance ratings, and promoting awareness of flood insurance issues.

Even when it is not required, flood insurance should be considered for all properties in coastal states subject to hurricanes and in any state through which major rivers run. The cost of flood insurance will increase the property owner's expenses, which will be taken into consideration by the lender when making a financing decision. Higher expenses mean that a borrower will qualify for a lower loan amount, or may be charged a higher interest rate, but a lower interest rate will be no comfort if the property suffers unexpected flood damage.

IN PRACTICE A flood insurance policy is separate from a homeowners insurance policy, which many property owners fail to realize until it is too late. Flood insurance is not retroactive; it must be purchased before a disaster occurs. Flood insurance is not effective until 30 days after it is purchased, unless the lender requires it.

Flood Insurance: What's Covered and What's Not

FEMA defines a flood as "a general and temporary condition of partial or complete inundation of two or more acres of normally dry land or two or more properties from

- an overflow of inland or tidal waves,
- an unusual and rapid accumulation or runoff of surface waters,
- mudflows or mudslides on the surface of normally dry land, or
- the collapse of land along the shore of a body of water (under certain conditions)."

The physical damage to a building or personal property "directly" caused by a flood is covered by flood insurance policies. For example, damage from sewer backups is covered if it results directly from flooding. Flood policies exclude coverage for losses such as swimming pools, cars, money, animals, groundcover, or underground systems.

www.fema.gov/national-flood-insurance-program

Policies are of two types: replacement cost value (RCV) or actual cost value (ACV). Deductibles and premiums vary accordingly. More information is at www.fema.gov/national-flood-insurance-program.

IN PRACTICE Massive losses in the NFIP due to the Mississippi River floods in 1993 caused Congress to pass laws that greatly increase the number of properties that are required to be covered by the NFIP. This requirement not only results in higher expenses for the property buyers in those areas but may also negatively affect property values; nevertheless, the important resource offered by the insurance can determine whether or not an area recovers after a disaster. Real estate professionals should be aware of identified flood areas to alert buyers; an appraisal should also indicate whether or not a property is located in a floodplain.

KEY POINT REVIEW

Home affordability is a goal of both governments and businesses. Past attempts to broaden home mortgage lending standards resulted in a record number of defaulting borrowers. The true cost of home ownership—from down payment to **PITI (principal, interest, taxes, and insurance)** and utility and maintenance costs—must be considered to determine whether it is a desirable alternative to renting a home. A prospective borrower's **credit report**, **credit score**, and **percentage of debt to income (DTI)** will be considered by a lender. There may be **tax benefits** to home ownership, but all factors should be considered. The difference between the amount owed on a property and its current market value is the property owner's **equity**.

A **mortgage loan** will require two instruments: the **financing instrument** and the **security instrument**. A **promissory note**, as a financing instrument, is a contract with a lender that sets out the terms under which a borrower promises to repay a debt. A promissory note is a **negotiable instrument** that can be transferred to a third party.

Interest is a charge for the use of money; charging an excessive rate of interest is called **usury**. **Discount points** are a percentage of a loan amount and are charged by a lender to increase the lender's yield on its investment. Most home loans are not subject to state usury protections because they are **federally related** and thus exempted from state usury laws. A mortgage loan may include a **prepayment penalty**.

A home mortgage loan is **secured** by the borrower's real property in the process called **hypothecation**. The borrower retains the right of possession and control of the property. The security agreement can be either a mortgage or deed of trust.

In a **mortgage**, the **mortgagor** (owner) borrows money from the **mortgagee** (lender), and the real estate purchased with the borrowed money is used as **security** for the debt.

Depending on state law, a **mortgage** on real property takes the form of a **lien** or **transfer of title**. In a **lien theory** state, a mortgage serves to place a lien on the specified property. In a **title theory** state, the mortgage conveys **legal title** to the mortgagee (or other designated individual) and the mortgagor retains **equitable title** and the **right of possession**.

A **deed of trust** transfers **title** from the **trustor** (property owner) to a **trustee,** who holds it on behalf of a **beneficiary** (lender).

The **borrower** under any mortgage or deed of trust must fulfill the terms of the promissory note, pay all real estate taxes on the secured property, maintain adequate property insurance, keep the property in good repair, and obtain the approval of the lender before making major alterations to the property.

When a mortgage loan is paid in full, a **defeasance clause** requires the lender to execute a **satisfaction (release** or **discharge)** that is **recorded** to clear title. If the borrower **defaults**, the lender can **accelerate** the due date of the remaining principal balance and all other payments and costs.

If the borrower continues in default, the lender can bring court action called **judicial foreclosure**.

A **deed of trust** executed by the borrower is **recorded** in the county in which property is located. The **trustor** transfers **legal title** to the **trustee** but retains equitable title and has the right to possession and use of the mortgaged property.

When the loan is paid in full, a **defeasance clause** requires the beneficiary to request the trustee to execute and deliver to the trustor a **deed of reconveyance** (release deed) to return legal title to the trustor.

If the borrower **defaults**, the lender can **accelerate** the due date of the remaining principal balance and all overdue costs. If the borrower continues in default, a **deed of trust with power of sale** allows the beneficiary (lender) to ask the trustee to conduct the **trustee's sale** without court action. A **mortgage with power of sale** also enables a sale without court action.

An **impound (escrow) account** may be required to create a reserve fund to ensure that future tax, property insurance, and other payments are made. **The lender** makes tax, insurance, and other payments on the **borrower's behalf**.

The **National Flood Insurance Reform Act of 1994** imposes obligations on lenders and loan servicers to set aside escrow funds for flood insurance on new loans for property in flood-prone areas.

When property with an outstanding mortgage or deed of trust is conveyed, the new owner may **take title** in one of two ways, if allowed by the loan document:

1. **"Subject to"** —the **new owner** makes payments on existing loans but is **not personally liable** if the property is sold on default and proceeds of the sale do not satisfy debt. "Subject to" is no longer in use.
2. **Assuming** the existing mortgage or deed of trust and agreeing to pay the debt—the **new owner** takes personal responsibility for existing loans and is subject to a **deficiency judgment** if the property is sold on default and proceeds of the sale do not satisfy the debt.

An **alienation clause (due-on-sale clause)** in a loan document requires full payment on the sale of the property and can prevent future purchasers of the property from assuming the loan.

Priority of mortgages and other liens is determined by the order in which they were recorded. **Priority** may be changed by **subordination agreement**.

Most forms of real estate financing provide for **amortization** of the loan payments so that the principal of the loan is paid off by the end of the loan term. A **straight loan** is an interest-only loan. With an **adjustable-rate mortgage (ARM)**, the interest rate changes over the term of the loan according to an identified economic indicator—the **index**. A **margin** is added to the index to determine the rate the borrower will pay and a **rate cap** sets the highest interest rate that can be charged at any point over the life of the loan. Rate **adjustments** are made monthly, quarterly, or annually, as agreed between borrower and lender. The loan might have a **conversion** option that allows it to be converted to a fixed-rate loan.

With a **growing-equity mortgage**, payments of principal are increased each month to pay off the loan more quickly. A **balloon payment** typically is a final loan payment that is at least twice as much as any other payment.

A **reverse mortgage** can be used by someone age 62 or older to receive one or more payments that result in a claim by the lender on the equity in the mortgaged property when the homeowner moves from the property, dies, defaults on one of the loan terms, or sells the property. The funds paid out by the lender accrue interest at the rate specified in the mortgage documents, all of which is repaid from the borrower's equity.

If a **judicial foreclosure** is granted, the **judge** orders the property sold. A **public sale** is advertised and the real estate is sold to the **highest bidder**.

The borrower has **equitable right of redemption** within a time period (before and/or after sale) allowed by state law. No court action is necessary to begin the sale process if the mortgage or deed of trust has a **power-of-sale** clause.

The mortgagee may have the right to a **deficiency judgment** against the borrower for an unpaid balance, **when allowed by state law**, if the sale proceeds are less than the amount owed. The court can **award title** to the **lender** and no sale occurs in a **strict foreclosure**. The lender may accept a **deed in lieu of foreclosure** from a defaulting borrower, but title is **subject to junior liens** that are eliminated in a foreclosure.

In a **short sale**, the lender agrees to accept less than the amount of the remaining indebtedness in order to allow the property to be sold. Recent federal legislation has allowed the homeowner subject to a short sale to avoid taxation on the amount of debt forgiven by the lender, but continuation of this benefit is uncertain. The Consumer Financial Protection Bureau has issued rules for mortgage lenders to follow to insure that borrowers in default receive adequate notice and assistance throughout the foreclosure process.

Homeowners insurance, which will be required by a mortgage lender, will protect against loss due to natural disasters, accidents, theft, and fire. Additional coverage can also be obtained. The **Comprehensive Loss Underwriting Exchange (CLUE)** database allows insurers to share information on a consumer's claims history. The **Federal Emergency Management Agency (FEMA)** administers the National Flood Insurance Program. Flood insurance is required for properties located in identified areas prone to flooding, and should be considered in many areas even when it is not required.

UNIT 14 QUIZ

1. A charge of three discount points on a $120,000 loan equals
   a. $450.
   b. $3,600.
   c. $4,500.
   d. $116,400.

2. A prospective buyer needs to borrow money to buy a house. The buyer applies for and obtains a real estate loan from a mortgage company. Then the buyer signs a note and a mortgage. In this example, the buyer is called the
   a. mortgagor.
   b. beneficiary.
   c. mortgagee.
   d. vendor.

3. A prospective buyer needs to borrow money to buy a house. The buyer applies for and obtains a real estate loan from a mortgage company. Then the buyer signs a note and a mortgage. In this example, the mortgage company is the
   a. mortgagor.
   b. beneficiary.
   c. mortgagee.
   d. vendor.

4. The borrower under a deed of trust is known as the
   a. trustor.
   b. trustee.
   c. beneficiary.
   d. vendee.

5. A loan in which the borrower makes only interest payments is called a(n)
   a. fixed-rate loan.
   b. adjustable-rate mortgage.
   c. straight loan.
   d. reverse mortgage.

6. A state law prohibits lenders from charging more than 24% interest on any loan. This kind of law is called
   a. trustee law.
   b. a usury law.
   c. the statute of frauds.
   d. contract law.

7. After a foreclosure sale, the borrower who has defaulted on the loan may seek to pay off the mortgage debt plus any accrued interest and costs under what right?
   a. Equitable redemption
   b. Defeasance
   c. Usury
   d. Statutory redemption

8. Which clause would give a lender the right to have all future installments become due upon default?
   a. Escalation
   b. Defeasance
   c. Alienation
   d. Acceleration

9. What document is available to the mortgagor when the mortgage debt is completely repaid?
   a. Satisfaction of mortgage
   b. Defeasance certificate
   c. Deed of trust
   d. Mortgage estoppel

10. Who is entitled to a reverse mortgage?
    a. A homeowner age 62 or older
    b. The owner of an unencumbered home
    c. A homebuyer who cannot qualify for a regular loan
    d. An investor who rents a home only to senior citizens

11. A loan that provides for the full payment of the principal over the life of the loan is a(n)
    a. reverse mortgage.
    b. indexed loan.
    c. amortized loan.
    d. balloon payment.

12. All the following clauses in a loan agreement enable the lender to demand that the entire remaining debt be paid immediately *EXCEPT*
    a. a due-on-sale clause.
    b. a defeasance clause.
    c. an acceleration clause.
    d. an alienation clause.

13. Which of the following allows a mortgagee to proceed to a foreclosure sale without going to court first?
   a. Waiver of redemption right
   b. Power of sale
   c. Alienation clause
   d. Possession rights

14. The mortgagee foreclosed on a property after the borrower defaulted on the loan payments. The unpaid balance of the loan at the time of the foreclosure sale was $140,000, but at the foreclosure sale, the house sold for only $129,000. What must the lender do to recover the $11,000 the borrower still owes?
   a. Sue for damages
   b. Sue for specific performance
   c. Seek a judgment by default
   d. Seek a deficiency judgment

15. Discount points on a mortgage are computed as a percentage of the
   a. selling price.
   b. loan amount.
   c. closing costs.
   d. down payment.

16. In one state, a mortgagee holds legal title to real property offered as collateral for a loan, and the mortgagor retains the rights of possession and use. If the borrower defaults, the lender is entitled to immediate possession and rents. This state can be *BEST* characterized as what kind of state?
   a. Lien theory
   b. Mortgage theory
   c. Intermediate theory
   d. Title theory

17. In one state, a lender holds a lien on real property offered as collateral for a loan. The borrower retains both legal and equitable title to real property. If the borrower defaults on the loan, the lender must go through formal foreclosure proceedings to recover the debt. This state can be *BEST* characterized as what kind of state?
   a. Lien theory
   b. Mortgage theory
   c. Intermediate theory
   d. Title theory

18. A homebuyer has a mortgage that provides for increasing payments over the life of the loan so that it can be paid off earlier than would be the case with a regular amortized loan. The homebuyer has a
   a. mortgage with power of sale.
   b. growing-equity mortgage.
   c. balloon payment loan.
   d. reverse mortgage.

19. A junior lien may become first in priority if the original lender agrees to execute a
   a. deed of trust.
   b. subordination agreement.
   c. second mortgage agreement.
   d. call clause.

20. A buyer purchased a home under an agreement that made the buyer personally obligated to continue making payments under the seller's existing mortgage. If the buyer defaults and the court sale of the property does not satisfy the debt, the buyer will be liable for making up the difference. The buyer has
   a. purchased the home subject to the seller's mortgage.
   b. assumed the seller's mortgage.
   c. benefited from the alienation clause in the seller's mortgage.
   d. benefited from the defeasance clause in the seller's mortgage.

UNIT 15

Government Involvement in Real Estate Financing

LEARNING OBJECTIVES *When you have finished reading this unit, you will be able to*

- **explain** the primary and secondary mortgage marketplaces, the roles of the parties in each, and the impact on the parties through government influence;
- **describe** the difference between conventional, government, and private loan programs available for real estate financing;
- **describe** the various alternative and special purpose loan programs which can meet a borrower's special needs;
- **explain** the primary government regulations which govern real estate lending and provide consumer protection against unfair lending practices; and
- **define** the following *key terms*:

blanket loan
buydown
certificate of reasonable value (CRV)
Community Reinvestment Act of 1977 (CRA)
construction loan
conventional loan
Equal Credit Opportunity Act (ECOA)
Fannie Mae
Farmer Mac
Federal Deposit Insurance Corporation (FDIC)
Federal Reserve System (Fed)
FHA-insured loan
Freddie Mac
Ginnie Mae
government-sponsored enterprises (GSEs)
home equity loan
mortgage insurance premium (MIP)
Office of the Comptroller of the Currency (OCC)
open-end loan
package loan
primary mortgage market
private mortgage insurance (PMI)
Real Estate Settlement Procedures Act (RESPA)
Regulation Z
sale-and-leaseback
secondary mortgage market
triggering terms
Truth in Lending Act (TILA)
VA-guaranteed loan
wraparound loan

OVERVIEW

As economic conditions change, the forces of supply and demand create a rapidly evolving mortgage market. The challenge for today's real estate professionals is to maintain a working knowledge of the available financing options, to help buyers and sellers reach their real estate goals.

You have already learned about the types of loans and security options available to consumers. Here, we consider the overall financial marketplace, and refer to any loan secured by either a mortgage or a deed of trust as a mortgage loan.

We will also look at the ways in which the federal government is involved in real estate financing. A mortgage that has no direct federal involvement (even though it may be made by a federally chartered lender) is called a *conventional* loan. Loans that have direct federal involvement include those insured by the Federal Housing Administration (FHA) or guaranteed by the U.S. Department of Veterans Affairs (VA).

INTRODUCTION TO THE REAL ESTATE FINANCING MARKET

The real estate financing market has the following three basic components:

- Government influences, primarily the Federal Reserve System
- The primary mortgage market
- The secondary mortgage market

Under the umbrella of the monetary policy set by the Federal Reserve System, lenders that are part of the primary mortgage market originate loans that are bought, sold, and traded in the secondary mortgage market. Now, we will look at the bigger picture: the financial marketplace in which those mortgages exist.

The Federal Reserve System

The role of the **Federal Reserve System** (the Fed) is to maintain sound credit conditions, help counteract inflationary and deflationary trends, and create a favorable economic climate. The Federal Reserve System divides the country into 12 federal reserve districts, each served by a federal reserve bank. All nationally chartered banks must join the Fed and purchase stock in its district reserve banks.

The Fed regulates the flow of money and interest rates in the marketplace through its member banks by controlling the rate charged for loans it makes to those banks, called the *discount* rate, as well their *reserve requirements*—the minimum level of funds that a bank must maintain.

When the discount rate rises, interest rates on all sorts of loans will rise, making funding harder to obtain. When the discount rate is lowered, interest rates will go down, making borrowed funds easier to obtain, an incentive to businesses as well as homebuyers. The Fed's reserve requirements place funds out of circulation; when reserve requirements are increased, lender solvency is improved but funding is harder to obtain.

The Fed acts on the open market to stimulate the economy at a time of recession by increasing the amount of money in circulation by buying Treasury securities.

The Fed can also act to control inflation by decreasing the amount of money in circulation by selling Treasury securities.

The Primary Mortgage Market

The **primary mortgage market** is made up of the lenders that originate mortgage loans. These lenders make money available directly to borrowers. From a borrower's point of view, a loan is a means of financing an expenditure; from a lender's point of view, a loan is an investment. All investors look for profitable returns on their investments. Income on a loan is realized from the following two sources:

- Finance charges collected at closing, such as loan origination fees and discount points
- Recurring income, the interest collected during the term of the loan

Lenders can sell mortgage loans, which produces income to make more loans, and some lenders derive income from servicing loans for investors who have purchased the loans, or servicing loans made by other mortgage lenders. Servicing a loan involves

- collecting payments (including taxes and insurance, if the borrower must maintain an impound account as part of the loan agreement),
- accounting,
- bookkeeping,
- preparing insurance and tax records,
- processing payments of taxes and insurance, and
- following up on loan payment and delinquency.

Major lenders of home mortgage and commercial property loans include the following:

www.occ.gov
www.fdic.gov

- *Savings associations* (also called *thrifts*) and *commercial banks*. These institutions are known as *fiduciary lenders* because of their fiduciary obligations to protect and preserve their depositors' funds. Mortgage loans are perceived as secure investments for generating income and enable these institutions to pay interest to their depositors. Fiduciary lenders are subject to the standards and regulations established by the **Office of the Comptroller of the Currency (OCC)**, www.occ.gov. Deposits in insured institutions are covered up to the specified limit, currently $250,000 per depositor, per account, by the **Federal Deposit Insurance Corporation (FDIC)**, www.fdic.gov.
- *Insurance companies*. Insurance companies accumulate large sums of money from the premiums paid by their policyholders. While part of this money is held in reserve to satisfy claims and cover operating expenses, much of it is free to be invested in profit-earning enterprises, such as large commercial real estate loans.

www.ncua.gov

- *Credit unions*. Credit unions are cooperative organizations whose members place money in savings accounts. In the past, credit unions made only short-term consumer and home improvement loans. Now, they routinely originate longer-term first and second mortgage and deed of trust loans. Federally chartered credit unions are regulated by the National Credit Union Association (NCUA), www.ncua.gov. NCUA insures deposits of up to $250,000 in all federal credit unions as well as the majority of state-chartered credit unions.

www.prea.org

- *Pension funds*. Pension funds usually have large amounts of money available for investment. Because of the comparatively high yields and low risks offered by mortgages, pension funds have begun to participate actively in financing real estate projects. Most real estate activity for pension funds is handled through mortgage bankers and mortgage brokers. The Pension Real Estate Association, www.prea.org, is a nonprofit organization of public and corporate pension funds, endowment funds, and other institutional real estate investors.

- *Endowment funds*. Many commercial banks and mortgage bankers handle investments for endowment funds. The endowments of hospitals, universities, colleges, charitable foundations, and other institutions provide a good source of financing for low-risk commercial and industrial properties.
- *Investment group financing*. Large real estate projects, such as highrise apartment buildings, office complexes, and shopping centers, are often financed as joint ventures through group financing arrangements like syndicates, limited partnerships, and real estate investment trusts.
- *Mortgage banking companies*. Mortgage banking companies originate mortgage loans with money belonging to insurance companies, pension funds, and individuals, as well as funds of their own. They make real estate loans with the intention of selling them to investors and receiving a fee for servicing the loans. Mortgage banking companies are generally organized as stock companies. As a source of real estate financing, they are subject to fewer lending restrictions than are commercial banks or savings associations. They are not mortgage brokers.
- *Mortgage brokers*. Mortgage brokers are not lenders, but they are mentioned here because they are intermediaries who bring borrowers and lenders together. Mortgage brokers locate potential borrowers, process preliminary loan applications, and submit the applications to lenders for final approval. They do not service loans once the loans are made. Mortgage brokers also may be real estate brokers who offer these financing services in addition to their regular real estate brokerage activities.

www.nmlsconsumeraccess.org

The Secure and Fair Enforcement for Mortgage Licensing Act of 2008 (SAFE Act) requires states to license mortgage loan originators according to national standards and also requires all state agencies to participate in the Nationwide Mortgage Licensing System and Registry (NMLS), www.nmlsconsumeraccess.org, as of January 1, 2011. All mortgage loan originators (MLOs) must register annually and meet other requirements. NMLS is the sole system of licensure for mortgage companies for 57 state agencies and the sole system of licensure for MLOs for 59 state and territorial agencies.

IN PRACTICE A growing number of consumers apply for mortgage loans via the internet, particularly for a loan refinancing. Many major lenders have websites that offer information to potential borrowers regarding their current loan programs and requirements. In addition, online brokerages link lenders with potential borrowers. The best sites allow comparison of loan terms across a variety of loan programs. New borrowers are cautioned to make sure that there is the opportunity for a phone or in-person consultation before making any mortgage decision.

The Secondary Mortgage Market

In addition to the primary mortgage market, where loans are originated, there is a **secondary mortgage market** in which loans are bought and sold only after they have been funded. The secondary mortgage market thus helps lenders raise capital to make additional mortgage loans and is especially useful when money is in short supply. By freeing capital for additional loans, the secondary market stimulates both the housing construction market and the mortgage market. The lender benefits, not only by raising additional capital, but also by avoiding interest rate risks on adjustable rate loans when interest rates fall, as well as on fixed rate loans if interest rates rise, and by making a profit on the sale. In addition, the lender may continue to service the loan and collect a fee for that service.

In the secondary market, a number of mortgage loans are assembled into blocks called *pools*. The mortgages can be pooled by the lender who sells them or, more frequently, by the organization that purchases them. Securities that represent shares in these pooled mortgages are then sold to investors or other organizations. The key players in the secondary mortgage market were created by the federal government in the decades following the Great Depression and World war II to help increase loan opportunities for homebuyers. They are referred to collectively as **government-sponsored enterprises (GSEs)**. (*See* Figure 15.1.)

Fannie Mae Originally the Federal National Mortgage Association, **Fannie Mae** was created as a government agency in 1938. It became a completely private shareholder-owned corporation in 1968, although it is still under congressional supervision. Fannie Mae buys from a lender a block or pool of mortgages that may then be used as collateral for *mortgage-backed securities* that are sold on the global market.

www.fhfa.gov

The housing collapse that was felt around the country starting in 2006 brought into question the value a great many of the mortgages that Fannie Mae had purchased and resold to investors. In September 2008, Fannie Mae was placed into the conservatorship of the Federal Housing Finance Agency (FHFA), www.fhfa.gov. Fannie Mae continues to operate and provide a secondary market for mortgage loans, although with massive federal investment to protect its investors. Fannie Mae deals in conventional as well as FHA-insured and VA-guaranteed loans.

www.fanniemae.com
www.fanniemae.com/singlefamily

One of the most important features of the GSEs has been their development of standardized loan application, credit report, appraisal and other forms that are required for loans they purchase, as well as detailed guidelines for the lending process. Fannie Mae has a consumer-oriented site at www.fanniemae.com, and a site for lenders that provides access to its forms and guides at www.fanniemae.com/singlefamily.

FIGURE 15.1: Government-Sponsored Enterprises (GSEs)

Institution	Secondary Market Function
Fannie Mae	Conventional, FHA-insured, VA-guaranteed loans
Freddie Mac	Mostly conventional loans
Ginnie Mae	Special assistance loans

Freddie Mac Originally called the Federal Home Loan Mortgage Corporation, **Freddie Mac** was created in 1970 as a privately owned corporation but is also now under government conservatorship. Freddie Mac continues to provide a secondary market for mortgage loans, primarily conventional loans.

www.freddiemac.com

Many lenders use the standardized forms and follow the guidelines issued by Fannie Mae and Freddie Mac. More information on Freddie Mac is available at www.freddiemac.com.

Farmer Mac The Federal Agricultural Mortgage Corporation (**Farmer Mac**) is privately owned and publicly traded, and was established by Congress in 1988 to create a secondary market for agricultural mortgage and rural utilities loans and the portions of agricultural and rural development loans guaranteed by the U.S. Department of Agriculture (USDA). Farmer Mac is part of the Farm Credit System and is regulated by the Farm Credit Administration. Farmer Mac guarantees payment of principal and interest on the loans it purchases and pools those loans for sale. Farmer Mac has not had the financial difficulties that have plagued Fannie Mae and Freddie Mac in recent years, primarily because market values in rural areas have not gone through the wide swings that most urban areas have experienced. Information on Farmer Mac is at www.farmermac.com; Farmer Mac has a subsidiary, Farmer Mac II, LLC, found at www.farmermac2.com.

www.farmermac.com
www.farmermac2.com

Ginnie Mae The Government National Mortgage Association, **Ginnie Mae**, was created in 1968 and has always been a governmental agency. Information on this agency can be found at www.ginniemae.gov. Ginnie Mae is a division of the Department of Housing and Urban Development (HUD), organized as a corporation without capital stock. Ginnie Mae does not buy or sell loans or issue mortgage-backed securities. Instead, Ginnie Mae administers special-assistance programs and guarantees investment securities issued by private offerors (such as banks, mortgage companies, and savings and loan associations) and backed by pools of FHA-insured and VA-guaranteed mortgage loans. The *Ginnie Mae pass-through certificate* is a security interest in a pool of mortgages that provides for a monthly pass-through of principal and interest payments directly to the certificate holder. Such certificates are guaranteed by Ginnie Mae.

www.ginniemae.gov

LOAN PROGRAMS

Mortgage loans can be classified based on their loan-to-value ratio (LTV). The LTV is the ratio of debt to the value of the property, where the value is the sales price or appraised value, whichever is less. The *lower* the ratio of debt to value, the *higher* the down payment by the borrower. For the lender, the higher down payment means a more secure loan, which minimizes the lender's risk.

IN PRACTICE If the appraised value of a property is less than the sales price, the buyer/borrower will renegotiate the contract with the seller so that the sales price is reduced to the appraised value, or the buyer will make an additional down payment (the difference between the sales price and the appraised value). If appraised value is higher than the sales price, the sales price is considered the property value. The buyer does not get a financial "bonus" from the lender for negotiating a price that is lower than the property's appraised value.

MATH CONCEPTS

Determining LTV

If a property has an appraised value of $200,000, secured by an $180,000 loan, the LTV is 90%:

$180,000 ÷ $200,000 = 90%

Conventional Loans

Conventional loans are viewed as the most secure loans because their loan-to-value ratios are often lowest. The ratio may be 80% of the value of the property or less because the borrower may make a down payment of at least 20%. Because the payment of the debt rests on the ability of the borrower to pay, the lender carefully evaluates both the property and the prospective borrower. In determining the amount of the loan, the lender relies primarily on its appraisal of the property. To decide the buyer's willingness and ability to pay, information from credit reports, the buyer's credit score, and other factors, such as qualifying ratios and work history, are very important. Usually with a 20% down payment and a conventional loan, no additional insurance or guarantee on the loan is necessary to protect the lender's interest. A loan with less than a 20% down payment usually will require *private mortgage insurance*, which is discussed later. A conventional loan is not government insured or guaranteed, unlike FHA-insured and VA-guaranteed loans.

IN PRACTICE A foreclosure can be a long, messy proposition that has a negative effect on the borrower, the borrower's family, and the neighborhood in which the property is located. Even after a foreclosure, the lender can sue a defaulting borrower on the promissory note when it is a "recourse" loan that allows the lender to obtain a deficiency judgment against the borrower's assets. Lenders usually do not want to take this route unless it is absolutely necessary. Making sure that both property and borrower are qualified for the requested financing is the best protection against an unsuccessful loan.

Today, the secondary mortgage market has a significant impact on borrower qualifications, standards for the collateral, and documentation procedures followed by lenders. Loans must meet strict criteria to be sold to Fannie Mae and Freddie Mac. Lenders still can be flexible in their lending decisions, but they may not be able to sell unusual loans in the secondary market. To qualify for a conventional loan under Fannie Mae guidelines, for instance, the borrower's monthly housing expenses, including PITI (principal, interest, taxes, and insurance), must not exceed 28% of total monthly gross income. Also, the borrower's total monthly obligations, including housing costs plus other regular monthly payments, must not exceed 36% of total monthly gross income (80% LTV loans). The maximum for total monthly obligations can be as high as 45% or 50% if the borrower meets higher credit score and reserve requirements (borrower's available cash or other liquid assets). Loans that meet these criteria are called *conforming loans* and are eligible to be sold in the secondary market.

The Federal Housing Finance Agency (FHFA) publishes the maximum loan limits for loans sold to Fannie Mae and Freddie Mac. Through December 31, 2015, the maximum loan limit for a single-family home was set from $417,000 to $625,500 in high-cost areas. Specific loan limits are established for each county (or equivalent), and the loan limit may be lower for each specific high-cost area.

Loans that exceed the stated limits are called *nonconforming loans* or *jumbo loans* and are not marketable, but they may be held in the lender's investment portfolio, along with other loans the lender may have made that don't meet the underwriting guidelines of FHA, VA, or Fannie Mae/Freddie Mac. A real estate professional who is aware that such portfolio loans are possible may find this knowledge valuable when working with a borrower in unusual circumstances and a lender who is flexible.

Low LTV = *High* down payment

High down payment = *Low* lender risk

MATH CONCEPTS

Loan Qualification

Following is the qualifying math for a $260,000 loan at 4.5% interest for 30 years with payments of $1,318.20 per month in principal and interest, which we will round to $1,318:

Combined monthly gross income	$8,000
Monthly housing expenses:	
Principal and interest	$1,318
Property taxes	400
Hazard insurance	50
PMI insurance	90
Homeowners association dues	+ 30
Total housing expense	$1,888
	$1,888 ÷ 8,000 = 23.6%
Debt expenses:	
Installment payments	$200
Revolving charges	80
Auto loan	250
Child care	300
Other	+ 100
Total debt expense	$930
Plus housing	+ $1,888
Grand total	$2,818
	$2,818 ÷ 8,000 = 35%

These borrowers will qualify for this loan under conventional loan guidelines of 28% and 36%.

Private Mortgage Insurance

One way a borrower can obtain a conventional mortgage loan with a down payment that is less than 20% of the purchase price is by obtaining **private mortgage insurance (PMI)**. The borrower purchases an insurance policy that provides the lender with funds in the event of borrower default on the loan. This allows the lender to assume more risk so that the loan-to-value ratio can be higher than for other conventional loans. PMI protects the top portion of a loan, usually 20% to 30%, against borrower default. This means that, if the property is sold at a foreclosure sale for less than the outstanding balance of the loan, the PMI usually is enough to make up the difference.

The borrower pays a monthly premium or fee while PMI is in force, which may be made part of the loan payment. The Homeowner's Protection Act of 1998 (HPA) requires that the lender automatically terminate the PMI payment if the borrower has accrued at least 22% equity in the home and is current on mortgage payments.

IN PRACTICE The 22% of equity that HPA has set as the point at which PMI can be canceled is based on the purchase price of the home. If market appreciation or improvements made by the borrower have increased the value of the home, the lender is not required by HPA to consider those factors but may be willing to do so. The borrower must contact the lender to find out how to proceed. The lender may require an appraisal, at the borrower's expense, to document the increase in value.

FHA-Insured Loans

portal.hud.gov/hudportal/HUD?src=/buying/loans
www.hud.gov

The Federal Housing Administration (FHA), which operates under HUD, neither builds homes nor lends money. The term *FHA loan* actually refers to a loan that is *insured* by the agency. An **FHA-insured loan** must be made by an FHA-approved lending institution. The FHA insurance provides additional security to the lender. As with private mortgage insurance, the FHA insures lenders against loss from borrower default. Information on FHA programs can be found at the HUD site, portal.hud.gov/hudportal/HUD?src=/buying/loans. Another way to reach the FHA site is to go to www.hud.gov and enter "FHA Resource Center" in the search box at the top of the page.

https://entp.hud.gov/idapp/html/hicostlook.cfm

The most popular FHA program covers fixed-rate loans for 10 to 30 years on one- to four-family residences. FHA does not set interest rates, but it does limit lender fees and specifies how closing costs and down payment may be paid and by whom, and regulates rate increases and caps on adjustable-rate loans. FHA-insured loans are competitive with other types of loans, often because an FHA-insured loan can be made even when the borrower makes a relatively low down payment, resulting in a high LTV. The maximum loan amounts that FHA will insure, by state and county, are available at https://entp.hud.gov/idapp/html/hicostlook.cfm. By law, FHA loans cannot charge prepayment penalties.

Other types of FHA-insured loans include adjustable-rate mortgages, home improvement and rehabilitation loans, and loans for the purchase of condominiums. Specific standards for condominium complexes and the ratio of owner-occupants to renters must be met for a loan on a condominium unit to be insured by FHA.

Currently, a borrower can obtain an FHA-insured loan with a down payment as low as 3.5% of the purchase price on a one- to four-unit structure, and certain closing costs can be included in the loan amount. A lower down payment may be possible with one of the special programs discussed later in this section. The borrower is charged a **mortgage insurance premium (MIP)** for all FHA loans. The up-front premium is charged at closing and can be financed into the mortgage loan. The borrower is also responsible for paying an annual premium that is usually charged monthly. The up-front premium is charged on all FHA loans, except those for the purchase of a condominium, which require only a monthly MIP.

The mortgaged real estate must be appraised by an approved FHA appraiser, and the borrower must meet standard FHA credit qualifications. Financing for manufactured homes and factory-built housing is also available, both for those who own the land that the home is on and also for manufactured homes that are, or will be, located on another plot of land.

If the purchase price exceeds the FHA-appraised property value, the buyer may pay the difference in cash as part of the down payment, although some exceptions are made for special programs.

Discount Points The lender of an FHA-insured loan may charge discount points in addition to a loan origination fee. The payment of points is a matter of negotiation between the seller and the buyer. As of November 2009, if the seller pays more than 6% of the costs normally paid by the buyer (such as discount points, the loan origination fee, the mortgage insurance premium, buydown fees (prepaid interest), other prepaid items, and impound or escrow amounts), the lender will treat the payments as a reduction in sales price and recalculate the mortgage amount accordingly.

Assumption Rules A qualified buyer may assume an existing FHA-insured loan. The application consists of a credit check to demonstrate whether the person assuming the loan is financially qualified. The process is quicker and less expensive than applying for a new loan. Sometimes, the older loan has a lower interest rate and no appraisal is required.

The assumption rules for FHA-insured loans vary, depending on the date the loan was originated. For loans originated on December 15, 1989, and later, an assumption is not permitted without complete buyer qualification.

HUD Home Sales Foreclosures of FHA-insured homes by HUD provide opportunities for both homebuyers and investors. HUD accepts bids on foreclosed properties only from real estate professionals who are registered with HUD and does not deal with the general public directly. Properties are sold in "as-is" condition, which means that HUD will not make repairs prior to the sale. Some homes can need extensive work, which also means that minimum bids can be set quite low, making a purchase of such a property a good investment for a buyer willing to make the required renovations.

www.hud.gov/hudhomes
www.hudhomestore.com

HUD allows an early bidding period for those who intend to be owner-occupants; properties are made available to investors only after that period has elapsed, if the property remains unsold. HUD has special programs that may offer a reduced down payment on property that is purchased with an FHA-insured loan. HUD's Good Neighbor Next Door program is intended to help revitalize certain areas by allowing law enforcement officers, firefighters, emergency medical technicians, and pre-kindergarten through grade 12 teachers to purchase eligible property in those areas at a 50% discount off the list price. The buyer must occupy the property as the buyer's sole residence for a minimum of 36 months. Property listings and more information on HUD property sales and programs can be found at www.hud.gov/hudhomes or www.hudhomestore.com.

VA-Guaranteed Loans

www.va.gov

www.benefits.va.gov/homeloans/

The U.S. Department of Veterans Affairs (VA) is authorized to guarantee loans used to purchase or construct homes for eligible veterans and their spouses (including unremarried spouses of veterans whose deaths were service-related). The VA also guarantees loans to purchase manufactured homes and the lots on which to place them. Information on the VA can be found at www.va.gov, and the **VA-guaranteed loan** program is explained at www.benefits.va.gov/homeloans/.

A veteran who meets any of the following time-in-service criteria is eligible for a VA-guaranteed loan:

- 90 days of active service for service people currently on active duty and veterans of at least 90 days of active service during World War II, the Korean War, the Vietnam conflict, and the Gulf War (which extends to the present time)
- A minimum of 181 days of active service during interconflict periods between July 26, 1947, and September 6, 1980
- Two full years of service during any peacetime period since 1980 (since 1981 for officers) or the full period (at least 181 days) for which the veteran was called or ordered to active duty
- Six or more years of continuous duty as a reservist in the Army, Navy, Air Force, Marine Corps, or Coast Guard, or as a member of the Army or Air National Guard

The VA assists veterans in financing the purchase of homes with little or no down payment at market interest rates. The VA issues rules and regulations that set forth the qualifications, limitations, and conditions under which a loan may be guaranteed. The owner must live on the property. The veteran must apply for a certificate of eligibility. This certificate sets forth the maximum guarantee to which the veteran is entitled, but the veteran must still qualify for the loan with the lender. For individuals with full eligibility, no down payment is required for a loan up to the maximum guarantee limit.

There is no VA dollar limit on the amount of the loan a veteran can obtain; this limit is determined by the lender and the qualification of the buyer. The VA limits the amount of the loan it will guarantee, however. For 2015, the guarantee limit was 25% of a loan of up to $417,000 on a one-unit property for most of the country, with a higher loan limit for some areas of Alaska, California, Colorado, District of Columbia, Florida, Guam, Hawaii, Idaho, Maryland, Massachusetts, New Hampshire, New Jersey, New York, Pennsylvania, Rhode Island, Tennessee, Utah, Virginia, Virgin Islands, Washington, West Virginia, and Wyoming.

IN PRACTICE The VA loan guarantee is tied to the current conforming loan limit for Fannie Mae and Freddie Mac. On a conforming loan of $417,000, the VA guarantee is $417,000 × 25%, or $104,250.

The VA also issues a **certificate of reasonable value (CRV)** for the property being purchased. The CRV states the property's current market value based on a VA-approved appraisal. The CRV places a ceiling on the amount of a VA-guaranteed loan allowed for the property. If the purchase price is greater than the amount cited in the CRV, the veteran may pay the difference in cash.

VA regulations allow only one active VA-guaranteed loan at a time, and a veteran may own only two properties that were acquired using VA-guaranteed loan benefits. The right to the VA-guaranteed loan benefit will never expire as long as any prior VA-guaranteed loan has been paid in full.

The VA borrower pays a loan origination fee to the lender, as well as a funding fee to the U.S. Department of Veterans Affairs. For the period from November 22, 2011, through September 30, 2016, the funding fee ranges from 1.25% to 2.15%, depending on the down payment amount. For a second or subsequent use of the VA guarantee, the fee ranges from 1.25% to 3.30%. The fee paid by Reservists or

National Guard veterans is 0.25% higher in most categories. For an interest rate reduction refinancing or loan assumption, all veterans pay a VA funding fee of 0.50%. There is *no* funding fee for

- a veteran who is receiving VA compensation for a service-connected disability,
- a veteran who would be entitled to receive compensation for a service-connected disability if the veteran did not receive retirement or active duty pay, or
- the surviving spouse of a veteran who died in service or from a service-connected disability.

Other Loan Costs The lender sets the loan interest rate, discount points, and closing costs. Closing costs such as the VA's property appraisal, the credit report, state and local taxes, and recording fees may be paid by the veteran purchaser, the seller, or shared by both. The veteran is not allowed to pay for the termite report, unless the loan is a refinance. No commissions, brokerage fees, or buyer broker fees may be charged to the veteran buyer.

The seller is allowed to pay for some closing costs, up to 4% of the loan amount, including prepaid closing costs, the VA funding fee, payoff of credit balances or judgments for the veteran, and temporary interest buydowns. Reasonable discount points may be charged on a VA-guaranteed loan, and either the veteran or the seller may pay them. Discount points are not included in the 4% limit.

Prepayment Privileges As with an FHA-insured loan, the borrower under a VA-guaranteed loan can prepay the debt at any time without penalty.

Assumption Rules VA-guaranteed loans made before March 1, 1988, are freely assumable, although an assumption processing fee will be charged. For loans made on or after March 1, 1988, the VA must approve the buyer and the assumption agreement. The original veteran borrower remains personally liable for the repayment of the loan unless the VA approves a *release of liability*. The release of liability will be issued by the VA only if

- the buyer assumes all the veteran's liabilities on the loan, and
- the VA or the lender approves both the buyer and the assumption agreement.

Releases are also possible if veterans use their own entitlement in assuming another veteran's loan.

IN PRACTICE A release of liability issued by the VA does not release the veteran's liability to the lender. This must be obtained separately from the lender. Real estate professionals should contact their local mortgage lenders for specific requirements for obtaining or assuming VA-guaranteed loans. The programs change from time to time.

Agricultural Loan Programs

www.fsa.usda.gov

The Farm Service Agency (FSA) is a federal agency of the Department of Agriculture. The FSA offers programs to help families purchase or operate family farms and has taken over the functions of the former Farmers Home Administration (FmHA). Through the Rural Housing and Community Development Service (RHCDS), FSA also provides loans to help families purchase or improve single-family homes in rural areas (generally areas with populations of fewer than 10,000 people). FSA loan programs fall into two categories: guaranteed loans that are made and serviced by private lenders and guaranteed for a specific percentage by the FSA, and loans made directly by the FSA. More information on FSA programs can be found at www.fsa.usda.gov.

www.farmcreditnetwork.com

The Farm Credit System (Farm Credit) provides loans to farmers, ranchers, rural homeowners, agricultural cooperatives, rural utility systems, and agribusinesses. Unlike commercial banks, Farm Credit banks and associations do not take deposits. Instead, loanable funds are raised through the system-wide sale of bonds and notes in capital markets. More information is at www.farmcreditnetwork.com.

OTHER FINANCING TECHNIQUES

Because borrowers often have different needs, a variety of financing techniques have been created that apply to various types of property. We have already discussed the owner-financed transaction that can be secured by means of a purchase money mortgage. There are also ways of structuring financing in a variety of situations.

Package Loan

A **package loan** includes real and personal property. In recent years, these kinds of loans have been very popular with developers and purchasers of unfurnished condominiums. Package loans usually include furniture, drapes, the kitchen range, microwave oven, refrigerator, dishwasher, washer, dryer, and other appliances as part of the sales price of the home.

Blanket Loan

A **blanket loan** covers more than one parcel or lot. It is usually used by a developer to finance a subdivision, but it can also be used to finance the purchase of improved properties or to consolidate multiple loans on a single property. A blanket loan usually includes a provision known as a *partial release clause*. This clause permits the borrower to obtain the release of any one lot or parcel from the blanket lien by repaying a certain amount of the loan. The development lender issues a partial release from the mortgage lien on the entire property for each parcel sold. The release form from the lender will include a provision that the lien will continue to cover all other unreleased lots. In this way, the lender retains a security interest in the unsold property for the remaining development loan balance, yet each purchaser of an improved or unimproved lot can obtain secured financing on that parcel.

IN PRACTICE Developer M has obtained financing for Shady Acres, a residential development, under the terms of a blanket loan issued by First State Bank. M grades the property, brings in utility lines, builds roads, and then markets the buildable lots to construction companies. As each lot or group of lots is sold, First State Bank is paid a proportionate share of its development loan by the developer and releases its lien rights as to that parcel. This allows each of the purchasers to obtain financing that will cover building construction costs. The purchaser of more than one lot may obtain a blanket loan that will release that lender's lien as to individual properties when construction is completed and properties are sold to home buyers. Each homebuyer can then obtain a mortgage loan secured by the property.

Wraparound Loan

A **wraparound loan** enables a borrower with an existing mortgage loan to obtain additional financing from a second lender without paying off the first loan. The second lender gives the borrower a new, increased loan at a higher interest rate and assumes payment of the existing loan. The total amount of the new loan includes the existing loan as well as the additional funds needed by the borrower. The borrower makes payments to the new lender on the larger loan. The new lender makes payments on the original loan out of the borrower's payments.

A wraparound mortgage can be used to refinance real property or to finance the purchase of real property when an existing mortgage cannot be prepaid. The buyer executes a wraparound mortgage to the seller or lender, who collects payments on the new loan and continues to make payments on the old loan. It also can finance the sale of real estate when the buyer wishes to invest a minimum amount of initial cash. A wraparound loan is possible only if the original loan permits it. For instance, an acceleration and alienation or a due-on-sale clause in the original loan documents may prevent a sale under a wraparound loan.

IN PRACTICE To protect against a seller's default on a previous loan, the buyer should require that protective clauses be included in any wraparound document to grant the buyer the right to make payments directly to the original lender.

Open-End Loan

An **open-end loan** provides a security interest when a *note* is executed by the borrower to the lender, but also secures any future *advances* of funds made by the lender to the borrower. The interest rate on the initial amount borrowed is fixed, but interest on future advances may be charged at the market rate in effect at that time. An open-end loan is often a less costly alternative to a home improvement loan. It allows the borrower to increase the debt to its original amount, or the maximum amount stated in the note, after the debt has been reduced by payments over a period of time. The note will include the terms and conditions under which the loan can be opened, and the provisions for repayment.

Construction Loan

A **construction loan** is made to finance the construction of improvements on real estate such as homes, apartments, and office buildings. The lender commits to the full amount of the loan but disburses the funds in payments during construction. These payments are also known as *draws*. Draws are made to the general contractor or the owner for that part of the construction work that has been completed since the previous payment. Before each payment, the lender inspects the work. The general contractor must provide the lender with adequate waivers that release all mechanics' lien rights for the work covered by the payment.

Construction loans are generally short-term *or* interim financing. The borrower pays interest only on the monies that have actually been disbursed. The borrower is expected to arrange for a permanent loan, also known as an end loan *or* take-out loan, which will pay off (take out) the construction financing lender when the work is completed by paying the principal owed on the construction loan.

Sale-and-Leaseback

Sale-and-leaseback arrangements, while not loans, are used to finance large commercial or industrial properties. The land and the building, usually used by the seller for business purposes, are sold to an investor. The real estate then is leased back by the investor to the seller, who continues to conduct business on the property as a tenant. The buyer becomes the landlord, and the original owner becomes the tenant. This enables a business to free money tied up in real estate to be used as working capital.

Buydown

A **buydown** is a way to temporarily (or permanently) lower the interest rate on a mortgage or deed of trust loan. Perhaps a homebuilder wishes to stimulate sales by offering a lower-than-market rate. Or a first-time residential buyer may have trouble qualifying for a loan at the prevailing rates. The buyer's relatives or the sellers might want to help the buyer qualify. In any case, a lump sum is paid in cash to the lender at the closing. The payment offsets (and so reduces) the interest rate and monthly payments during the mortgage's first few years. Typical buydown arrangements reduce the interest rate by 1% to 2% over the first one to two years of the loan term. After that, the rate rises. The hope is that the borrower's income will also increase, making it more likely that the borrower will be able to pay the increased monthly payments. In a permanent buydown, a larger up-front payment reduces the effective interest rate for the life of the loan.

IN PRACTICE As recent history has shown, a borrower should not overestimate the ability to meet future payment obligations. Holding onto employment—with or without an increase in income—may be the best that can be managed. The risk of incurring a property foreclosure should be carefully considered.

Home Equity Loan

A **home equity loan** is a source of funds that takes advantage of the equity built up in a home. The original mortgage loan remains in place; the home equity loan is junior to the original lien. Although the home equity line of credit will carry a higher interest rate than a purchase loan, it is an alternative to refinancing because only the amount borrowed will be subject to the higher rate. As an added benefit, the interest paid on a home equity loan of up to $100,000 is deductible from federal income tax. A home equity loan can be used for a variety of financial needs, such as to

- finance the purchase of an expensive item, such as a boat;
- consolidate existing installment loans or credit card debt; and
- pay medical, education, home improvement, or other expenses.

A home equity loan can be taken out as a fixed loan amount or as a line of credit. With the *home equity line of credit*, called a *HELOC*, the lender extends a line of credit that the borrower can use at will. One downside to a HELOC is that the full amount of the line of credit will appear on the borrower's credit report, even though it is not being used. On the upside, the home equity loan could eventually lead to a new first mortgage loan. The homeowner could refinance all outstanding mortgage loans at some point with a single new loan at an attractive interest rate, in which case the original mortgage loan and the home equity loan would be paid off.

IN PRACTICE The decision to borrow against the equity in a home should not be made lightly. Using the funds to make home improvements should at least result in a higher property value, building up additional equity to replace some or all of that encumbered. The prospect of paying off other kinds of debts (particularly, credit card and auto loans) may be enticing, but those debts probably won't result in the possible loss of one's home.

FINANCING LEGISLATION

The federal government regulates the lending practices of mortgage lenders through the Truth in Lending Act (TILA), Equal Credit Opportunity Act (ECOA), Community Reinvestment Act of 1977 (CRA), and Real Estate Settlement Procedures Act (RESPA). Recent legislation to assist property owners during the economic downturn is also discussed.

Truth in Lending Act and Regulation Z

Regulation Z, enacted by the Federal Reserve Board to enforce the **Truth in Lending Act (TILA)**, requires that credit institutions inform borrowers of the true cost of obtaining credit. With proper disclosures, borrowers can compare the costs of various lenders to avoid the uninformed use of credit. Regardless of the amount, *Regulation Z generally applies when a credit transaction is secured by a residence*. The regulation does *not* apply to business or commercial loans or to agricultural loans of any amount.

www.consumerfinance.gov

The Dodd-Frank Wall Street Reform and Consumer Protection Act of 2010 (Dodd-Frank) transferred most of the Federal Reserve's responsibilities for enforcing TILA in July, 2011, to the new Consumer Financial Protection Bureau (CFPB). Information on the reasons why CFPB was created, including mortgage loan abuses by lenders, can be found at www.consumerfinance.gov.

Under the Truth in Lending Act, a consumer must be fully informed of all finance charges and the true cost of the financing before a transaction is completed. The finance charge disclosure must include any loan fees, finder's fees, service charges, and points, as well as interest. In the case of a mortgage loan made to finance the purchase of a dwelling, the lender must compute and disclose the *annual percentage rate (APR)*.

www.federalreserve.gov/boarddocs/supmanual/cch/til.pdf

In 2009, the Helping Families Save Their Homes Act amended TILA by requiring that consumers be notified of the sale or transfer of their mortgage loans. The party acquiring the loan, whether a purchaser or assignee, must provide the required disclosures no later than 30 days after the date on which the loan was acquired. The Consumer Compliance Handbook for Regulation Z, which is updated regularly, can be found at www.federalreserve.gov/boarddocs/supmanual/cch/til.pdf.

Creditor A *creditor*, for purposes of Regulation Z, is any person who extends consumer credit more than 25 times each year or more than 5 times each year if the transactions involve dwellings as security. The credit must be subject to a finance charge or payable in more than four installments by written agreement.

Three-Business-Day Right of Rescission In the case of most consumer credit transactions covered by Regulation Z, the borrower has three business days in which to rescind (cancel) the transaction by notifying the lender. *This right of* *rescission does not apply to owner-occupied residential purchase-money or first mortgage or deed of trust loans*. It does, however, apply to refinancing a home mortgage or to a home equity loan.

Advertising Regulation Z provides strict regulation of real estate advertisements (in all media, including newspapers, flyers, signs, billboards, websites, radio or television ads, and direct mailings) that refer to mortgage financing terms. General phrases like "flexible terms available" may be used, but if details are given, they must comply with the act. The APR—which is calculated based on all charges rather than the interest rate alone—must be stated.

Advertisements for buydowns or reduced-rate mortgages must show both the limited term to which the interest rate applies and the annual percentage rate. If a variable-rate mortgage is advertised, the advertisement must include

- the number and timing of payments,
- the amount of the largest and smallest payments, and
- a statement of the fact that the actual payments will vary between these two extremes.

Specific credit terms, such as down payment, monthly payment, dollar amount of the finance charge, or term of the loan, are called **triggering terms**. These terms may not be advertised unless the advertisement includes the following information:

- Cash price
- Required down payment
- Number, amounts, and due dates of all payments
- Annual percentage rate
- Total of all payments to be made over the term of the mortgage (unless the advertised credit refers to a first mortgage or deed of trust to finance the acquisition of a dwelling)

Penalties A creditor who fails to comply with any requirements of TILA, other than certain advertising provisions, may be held liable to the consumer for actual damage and the cost of any legal action together with reasonable attorney's fees. In other actions, a creditor may be liable to a consumer for twice the amount of the finance charge, for a minimum of $100 and a maximum of $1,000, plus court costs, attorney's fees, and any actual damages. Alternatively, a successful class action alleging that a creditor understated the APR and/or finance charge could make the creditor liable for punitive damages of the lesser of $500,000 or 1% of the creditor's net worth, plus attorney's fees and court costs. In addition, a willful violation is a misdemeanor punishable by a fine of up to $5,000, one year's imprisonment, or both.

The Equal Credit Opportunity Act (ECOA) prohibits discrimination in granting credit based on

- race,
- color,
- religion,
- national origin,
- sex,
- marital status,
- age, and
- receipt of public assistance.

Equal Credit Opportunity Act

The federal **Equal Credit Opportunity Act (ECOA)** prohibits discrimination in the lending process based on the credit applicant's race, color, religion, national origin, sex, marital status, age (provided the applicant is of legal age), or receipt of public assistance. The ECOA requires that credit applications be considered only on the basis of income, the stability of the source of that income, net worth (total assets and liabilities), and credit rating.

The protections offered by ECOA are both similar (race, color, religion, and national origin) and different from those of the Fair Housing Act; ECOA includes age, marital status, and receipt of public assistance. Real estate professionals should be aware of the protections offered by this law because their clients should not face discrimination when applying for a loan to buy a property or when applying to rent one.

A creditor may not consider age unless the applicant is too young to legally sign a contract, which is usually 18, although the creditor may consider age if determining if income will drop due to retirement. Lenders are prohibited from discriminating against recipients of public assistance programs such as food stamps and rent subsidies. Lenders may not ask questions about a spouse, unless the spouse is also applying for credit; they may not discount a woman's income or assume that she will leave the workforce to raise children.

If a loan application is rejected, the federal Fair Credit Reporting Act (FCRA) requires that the lender detail the reasons for the rejection in a statement that must be provided to the loan applicant within 30 days. The loan applicant also has the right to a free copy of any credit report that was considered in the loan application process. Additional state protections may also apply.

The agency that enforces ECOA depends on the type of financial institution. The ECOA is enforced by the Federal Trade Commission (FTC) and the Department of Justice as well as other agencies.

Community Reinvestment Act of 1977 (CRA)

www.federalreserve.gov/communitydev/cra_about.htm

Community reinvestment refers to the responsibility of financial institutions to help meet their communities' needs for low-income and moderate-income housing. Under the **Community Reinvestment Act of 1977 (CRA)**, updated in 1995 and 2005, financial institutions are expected to meet the deposit and credit needs of their communities; participate and invest in local community development and rehabilitation projects; and participate in loan programs for housing, small businesses, and small farms. Information on the Community Reinvestment Act and other programs is at www.federalreserve.gov/communitydev/cra_about.htm.

The law requires any federally regulated financial institution to prepare a statement containing

- a definition of the geographic boundaries of its community;
- an identification of the types of community reinvestment credit offered, such as residential housing loans, housing rehabilitation loans, small-business loans, commercial loans, and consumer loans; and
- comments from the public about the institution's performance in meeting its community's needs.

Financial institutions are periodically reviewed by one of three federal financial regulatory agencies: the Comptroller of the Currency, the Federal Reserve's Board of Governors, or the Federal Deposit Insurance Corporation. The institutions must post a public notice that their community reinvestment activities are subject to federal review, and they must make the results of these reviews public.

Real Estate Settlement Procedures Act

The federal **Real Estate Settlement Procedures Act (RESPA)** applies to any residential real estate transaction involving a new first mortgage loan. RESPA is designed to ensure that the buyer and the seller are both fully informed of all costs related to closing the transaction. The disclosures required by TILA and RESPA have been combined into two new disclosure forms created by the Consumer Financial Protection Bureau. These disclosures and the new forms will be discussed later.

Computerized Loan Origination Thanks to the use of electronic databases and telecommunications, a real estate professional can use a desktop, laptop, or tablet computer, or even a smartphone to call up a menu of mortgage lenders, interest rates, and loan terms. All of this can be done from the brokerage office, the buyer's home, or any location that provides wireless internet service. Consumers can also make use of a variety of internet sites to shop for a loan, comparing features and costs, and even apply for a loan online.

In states that allow brokerage involvement in the mortgage loan process, a broker is permitted by RESPA to earn a fee of up to one-half point of the loan amount for providing a borrower access to a lender available through the brokerage's *computerized loan origination system (CLO)* and assisting the borrower in completing a loan application. The borrower pays the fee, which can be financed. The borrower must always be informed that there are lenders other than those that are available on the CLO.

Automated Underwriting and Scoring On the lenders' side, new *automated underwriting* procedures can shorten loan approvals from weeks to minutes. Automated underwriting also tends to lower the cost of loan application and approval by reducing a lender's time spent on the approval process by as much as 60%. Freddie Mac uses a system called *Loan Prospector*. As of June 1, 2015, Freddie Mac no longer charges lenders a fee (previously $20 per transaction) to use its automated underwriting service, to encourage its use. Fannie Mae has a system called *Desktop Underwriter*, which reduces approval time to minutes, based on the borrower's credit report, a paycheck stub, and a drive-by appraisal of the property. Complex or difficult mortgages can be processed in less than 72 hours. Through automated underwriting, one of a borrower's biggest headaches in buying a home—waiting for loan approval—is eliminated. In addition, prospective buyers can strengthen their purchase offer by including proof of loan approval.

When used in automated underwriting systems, the application of credit scores has become somewhat controversial. Critics of scoring are concerned that the scores may not be accurate or fair, and in the absence of human discretion, they could result in making it more difficult for low-income and minority borrowers to obtain mortgages.

Freddie Mac has the following to say about automated underwriting:

> Whether using traditional or automated methods, underwriters must consider all three areas of underwriting—collateral, credit reputation, and capacity. When reviewing collateral, underwriters look at house value, down payment, and property type. Income, debt, cash reserves, and product type are considered when underwriters are looking at capacity. Credit scores are simply one consideration when underwriters are reviewing credit reputation. Even lenders who use an automated underwriting system such as Loan Prospector, still rely on human judgment when the scoring system indicates that the loan application is a higher risk.

KEY POINT REVIEW

The **Federal Reserve System (Fed)** consists of 12 federal reserve district banks. The Fed regulates the flow of money and interest rates.

The **primary mortgage market** consists of lenders that originate mortgage loans and receive income based on finance charges collected at loan closing, including loan origination fees and discount points; the recurring income from the interest collected during the terms of a loan, if kept; and funds generated by the sale of loans on the secondary mortgage market. In addition, lenders can earn fees for servicing loans for other mortgage lenders or investors who have purchased the loans.

The **primary mortgage market** includes **fiduciary lenders**—savings associations and commercial banks—subject to the Office of the Comptroller of the Currency (OCC), **insurance companies**, **credit unions**, **pension funds**, **endowment funds** of universities, colleges, and other institutions, **investment groups** (joint ventures, syndicates, limited partnerships, and real estate investment trusts (REITs)), **mortgage banking companies**, and **mortgage brokers**.

The **secondary mortgage market**, where loans are bought and sold after being funded, provides **additional income** to lenders and **frees up funds** to make more loans, with lenders often retaining servicing functions for a fee, and purchases mortgage loans through agencies, assembles them into packages called **pools**, and sells them as **shares (securitized)** to investors or other agencies.

Fannie Mae has shareholders but is under the conservatorship of the Federal Housing Finance Agency (FHFA). It creates **mortgage-backed securities** using pool of mortgages as collateral; and deals in conventional, FHA, and VA loans.

Freddie Mac also has shareholders and is under the conservatorship of FHFA. It has authority to purchase mortgages, pool them, and use them as security for **bonds** sold on the open market.

Ginnie Mae (Government National Mortgage Association) is entirely a government agency, a division of the **Department of Housing and Urban Development (HUD)**, organized as a corporation but without corporate stock, that administers **special-assistance programs**, and guarantees **mortgage-backed securities** using FHA and VA loans as collateral.

Conventional loans are the most secure loans. The **loan-to-value ratio (LTV)** is often lowest for these loans—traditionally 80%—meaning the down payment is 20%, but the LTV may be as high as 100%. Conventional loans are **not** government-insured or guaranteed. Conventional loans meet all the requirements of the secondary market, set by Fannie Mae and Freddie Mac, for **conforming loans**. **Nonconforming loans** (jumbo loans) must be retained in the lender's investment portfolio.

Private mortgage insurance (PMI) may be required for LTVs higher than 80% (i.e., down payments of less than 20%). Federal law requires PMI to **automatically** terminate if the borrower has accumulated 22% equity in the home (based on purchase price or original appraised value, whichever is less) *and* is current on mortgage payments. **Fannie Mae** and **Freddie Mac** have extended the automatic termination option to all loans that are in good standing and have had no additional financing added to the original loan.

FHA-insured loans are backed by the **Federal Housing Administration (FHA)**, which is part of HUD. FHA does not make loans but insures loans made by an FHA-approved lending institution. The FHA **mortgage insurance premium (MIP)** has an up-front fee along with monthly installments. The premium can be financed within the loan.

VA-guaranteed loans are backed by the **U.S. Department of Veterans Affairs** and are available to eligible veterans and spouses.

The **Farm Service Agency (FSA)**, formerly **Farmers Home Administration (FmHA)**, is part of the Department of Agriculture and has programs to help families purchase or operate family farms, including the Rural Housing and Community Development Service (RHCDS) and the **Farm Credit System (Farm Credit)**.

The **package loan** includes all personal property and appliances as well as real estate.

A **blanket loan** covers more than one parcel or lot, and a **partial release clause** allows a borrower to pay off part of a loan to remove the liens from one parcel or lot at a time.

A **wraparound loan** allows a borrower to obtain additional financing while retaining the first loan on the property.

An **open-end loan** secures the current loan to the borrower and future advances made by the lender to the borrower.

Construction loans are used to finance construction of property improvements.

A sale-and-leaseback arrangement can be used to finance large commercial or industrial properties. A **buydown** is a payment made at closing to reduce the interest rate on the loan.

A **home equity loan (home equity line of credit** or **HELOC)** is junior to the original lien.

The **Truth in Lending Act** is implemented by **Regulation Z**, now enforced by the Consumer Financial Protection Bureau, and requires that, when a loan is secured by a residence, the lender must inform the borrower of the true cost of obtaining credit. The borrower has a **three-business-day right of rescission**. **Advertising** is strictly regulated, using **triggering terms** to mandate what must be disclosed, and there are civil and criminal penalties for violations.

The **Equal Credit Opportunity Act (ECOA)** prohibits **discrimination** in granting or arranging credit on the basis of race, color, religion, national origin, sex, marital status, age (as long as the applicant is not a minor), or receipt of public assistance.

The **Fair Credit Reporting Act (FCRA)** requires that reasons for a loan application rejection be provided to the applicant within 30 days and that the applicant be given the right to a free copy of any credit report that was considered in the loan application process.

The **Community Reinvestment Act (CRA)** requires financial institutions to help meet the need for affordable housing in their communities.

The **Real Estate Settlement Procedures Act (RESPA)**, which covers loan closings, also includes provisions that govern brokerage involvement in the loan process by means of a **computerized loan origination (CLO) system**, when permitted by state law. CLO allows real estate professionals to assist loan applicants in surveying lenders and providing information.

Automated underwriting (loan processing) programs provide loan approvals quickly and include Fannie Mae's *Desktop Underwriter* and Freddie Mac's *Loan Prospector*. A credit score may be used as part of a loan application evaluation process.

UNIT 15 QUIZ

1. The buyers purchased a residence for $195,000. They made a down payment of $25,000 and agreed to assume the seller's existing mortgage, which had a current balance of $123,000. The buyers financed the remaining $47,000 of the purchase price by executing a mortgage and note to the seller. This type of loan, by which the seller becomes a mortgagee, is called a
   a. wraparound mortgage.
   b. package mortgage.
   c. balloon note.
   d. purchase money mortgage.

2. A buyer purchased a new residence from a builder for $350,000. The buyer made a down payment of $30,000 and obtained a $320,000 mortgage loan. The builder of the house paid the lender 3% of the loan balance for the first year and 2% for the second year. This represented a total savings for the buyer of $16,000. What type of mortgage arrangement is this?
   a. Wraparound
   b. Package
   c. Blanket
   d. Buydown

3. Which of the following is *NOT* a participant in the secondary mortgage market?
   a. Fannie Mae
   b. Ginnie Mae
   c. Credit union
   d. Freddie Mac

4. The law providing that a loan applicant who is rejected must be provided with a statement of the reasons for the rejection within 30 days is the
   a. Real Estate Settlement Procedures Act.
   b. Community Reinvestment Act.
   c. Fair Credit Reporting Act.
   d. Equal Credit Opportunity Act.

5. If buyers seek a mortgage on a single-family house, they would be *LEAST* likely to obtain the mortgage from a
   a. mutual savings bank.
   b. life insurance company.
   c. credit union.
   d. commercial bank.

6. The conservatorship of Fannie Mae and Freddie Mac is the responsibility of the
   a. Federal Housing Finance Agency.
   b. Federal Housing Authority.
   c. Office of the Comptroller of the Currency.
   d. Federal Reserve System.

7. What legislation includes provisions that govern the use of computerized loan origination?
   a. Equal Credit Opportunity Act
   b. Fair Lending Act
   c. Community Reinvestment Act
   d. Real Estate Settlement Procedures Act

8. A developer received a loan that covers five parcels of real estate and provides for the release of the mortgage lien on each parcel when certain payments are made on the loan. This type of loan arrangement is called a
   a. purchase money loan.
   b. blanket loan.
   c. package loan.
   d. wraparound loan.

9. Funds for FHA-insured loans are usually provided by
   a. the FHA.
   b. the Federal Reserve.
   c. approved lenders.
   d. the seller.

10. The provisions of Regulation Z require all of the following to be disclosed to a residential buyer *EXCEPT*
    a. discount points.
    b. brokerage commissions.
    c. a loan origination fee.
    d. the loan interest rate.

11. The acronym HELOC stands for
    a. home equality lender of credit.
    b. home equity line of credit.
    c. healthy environment lender of cash.
    d. home energy lien or credit.

12. The buyers purchased a model home and all its furnishings and appliances by using a
    a. package loan.
    b. blanket loan.
    c. wraparound loan.
    d. buydown.

13. The primary activity of Freddie Mac is to
    a. guarantee mortgages with the full faith and credit of the federal government.
    b. buy and pool blocks of conventional mortgages.
    c. act in tandem with Ginnie Mae to provide special assistance in times of tight money.
    d. buy and sell VA and FHA mortgages.

14. The federal Equal Credit Opportunity Act allows lenders to discriminate against potential borrowers on the basis of
    a. race.
    b. sex.
    c. country of national origin.
    d. amount of income.

15. The buyers of a residence in Happy Hollow have a mortgage that allows them to borrow additional funds that will be secured by the home at any time. They have a(n)
    a. closed-end loan.
    b. open-end loan.
    c. provisional loan.
    d. fully adjustable loan.

16. Programs to help families purchase or operate family farms are provided by
    a. Ginnie Mae
    b. the Farm Service Agency.
    c. Fannie Mae
    d. Freddie Mac.

17. If a lender agrees to make a loan based on an 80% LTV, what is the amount of the loan if the property appraises for $114,500 and the sales price is $116,900?
    a. $83,200
    b. $91,300
    c. $91,600
    d. $92,900

18. The document that sets forth the maximum loan guarantee to which a veteran is entitled is the
    a. funding statement.
    b. certificate of eligibility.
    c. certificate of reasonable value.
    d. certificate of discharge.

19. The law that requires lenders to find ways to help meet the housing needs of those of low and moderate incomes is the
    a. Dodd-Frank Act.
    b. Equal Credit Opportunity Act.
    c. Community Reinvestment Act.
    d. Real Estate Settlement Procedures Act.

20. Which of the following requires that all advertising that references mortgage financing terms contain certain disclosures?
    a. Equal Credit Opportunity Act
    b. Fair Housing Act
    c. Community Reinvestment Act
    d. Truth in lending Act (Regulation Z)

16

UNIT

Real Estate Appraisal

LEARNING OBJECTIVES *When you have finished reading this unit, you will be able to*

- **explain** appraisal concepts and the process employed by the appraiser;
- **describe** the characteristics of value and price and explain how they differ;
- **describe** the three approaches to value; and
- **define** the following *key terms:*

accrued depreciation
anticipation
appraisal
Appraiser Independence Requirements (AIR)
assemblage
broker's price opinion (BPO)
capitalization rate
change
competition
conformity
contribution
cost approach
depreciation
economic life
external obsolescence
functional obsolescence
gross income multiplier (GIM)
gross rent multiplier (GRM)
highest and best use
income approach
law of diminishing returns
law of increasing returns
market data approach
market value
net operating income (NOI)
physical deterioration
plottage
progression
reconciliation
regression
sales comparison approach
sales price
substitution
supply and demand
Uniform Standards of Professional Appraisal Practice (USPAP)
value

OVERVIEW

Appraisal is a distinct area of specialization within the world of real estate professionals. Most real estate transactions require an appraisal by a licensed or certified real estate appraiser to provide a clearer understanding of the market's response to a subject property. Real estate professionals also must be aware of the fundamental principles of valuation in order to complete an accurate and effective comparative market analysis (CMA) that assists seller clients in arriving at a reasonable asking price and buyer clients to make appropriate offers based on current market conditions. In addition, knowledge of the appraisal process allows the real estate professional to recognize a questionable appraisal.

APPRAISING

An **appraisal** is an opinion of value based on supportable evidence and approved methods. An *appraisal report* is an opinion of market value on a property given to a lender or client with detailed market information. An *appraiser* is an independent professional trained to provide an *unbiased* opinion of value in an impartial and objective manner, following an identified appraisal process. Appraising is a professional service performed for a fee; it is a breach of ethics and accepted practice to collect a commission for an appraisal based on the value of the property appraised.

https://www.fanniemae.com/content/fact_sheet/appraiser-independence-requirements.pdf

An accurate, objective appraisal is an important part of a real estate transaction, as well as a safeguard against a fraudulent transaction. The Dodd-Frank Act required changes to the Truth in Lending Act and other legislation to prohibit the coercion and other activities that influenced appraisals in many cases of fraud that occurred during the housing crisis of the past decade. Fannie Mae initiated **Appraiser Independence Requirements (AIR)** that took effect October 15, 2010. A copy of the AIR can be found at https://www.fanniemae.com/content/fact_sheet/appraiser-independence-requirements.pdf.

Regulation of Appraisal Activities

Title XI of the Financial Institutions Reform, Recovery, and Enforcement Act of 1989 (FIRREA) requires that any appraisal used in connection with a federally related transaction be performed by a competent individual who is licensed or certified by the state in which the appraiser practices. Every state now has an appraiser licensing agency, which is required by FIRREA to be separate from the agency that licenses real estate professionals.

A federally related transaction is any real estate-related financial transaction in which a federal financial institution or regulatory agency is engaged. These transactions involve the sale, lease, purchase, investment, or exchange of real property. They also include the financing, refinancing, or use of real property as security for a loan or an investment, including mortgage-backed securities. Appraisals of residential property valued at $250,000 or less are exempt and need not be performed by licensed or certified appraisers. Nonresidential properties valued at more than $250,000 require a certified appraiser.

State licensing and certification criteria for appraisers must conform to the requirements of the Appraisal Subcommittee of the Federal Financial Institutions Examination Council, as recommended by the Appraiser Qualifications Board (AQB)

of the Appraisal Foundation. The Appraisal Foundation is a not-for-profit organization composed of representatives of the major appraisal and related groups. In conducting an appraisal, an appraiser must follow the ***Uniform Standards of Professional Appraisal Practice (USPAP)*** established by the Appraisal Standards Board (ASB) of the Appraisal Foundation. Members of the AQB meet regularly to review and make recommendations for changes to the level of education and experience required of appraisers. Members of the ASB also meet often to discuss revisions and updates to *USPAP*. Both of these boards are composed of practicing appraisers, state officials, and educators. The Appraisal Foundation has also created the Appraisal Practices Board (APB), which "offers voluntary guidance to appraisers, regulators and users of appraisal services on recognized valuation methods and techniques for all valuation disciplines."

www.appraisalfoundation.org
www.uspap.org

More information about the Appraisal Foundation and links to all of the Appraisal Foundation boards can be found at www.appraisalfoundation.org. USPAP undergoes review and revision in a two-year cycle starting with an even-numbered year; the current update can be read at www.uspap.org.

Organizations for Appraisers

Most appraisers work as independent contractors, even when they are employed by a large appraisal management company, but appraisers are also employed by public agencies. Numerous trade associations are available for appraisers and are valuable sources of education, legal updates, and networking opportunities. Some of the largest are the following:

www.appraisers.org
www.asfmra.org
www.appraisalinstitute.org
www.www.iaao.org
www.irwaonline.org
www.naifa.com

- American Society of Appraisers www.appraisers.org
- American Society of Farm Managers and Rural Appraisers, Inc. www.asfmra.org
- Appraisal Institute www.appraisalinstitute.org
- International Association of Assessing Officers www.www.iaao.org
- International Right of Way Association www.irwaonline.org
- National Association of Independent Fee Appraisers www.naifa.com

Comparative Market Analysis

Not all estimates of value are made by professional appraisers. As you have already learned, real estate professionals often prepare a comparative market analysis (CMA) for a seller or buyer. A CMA is distinctly different from an appraisal report offered by a licensed or certified appraiser. An appraisal is based on a detailed analysis of market conditions, the features of the subject property and comparable properties in the neighborhood, recent sales and listings, land value and current construction cost—all the elements that a lender wants to consider in determining whether or not to make a loan and accept the property as security for the debt. The CMA focuses on properties similar to the subject property in size, location, and amenities for the purpose of deriving a likely listing price or offering price. The CMA analysis is based on

- recently closed properties (solds),
- properties currently on the market (competition for the subject property), and
- properties that did not sell (expired listings in the area).

Broker's Price Opinion (BPO)

www.fanniemae.com/singlefamily

A **broker's price opinion (BPO)** is a less-expensive alternative of evaluating property that is often used by lenders working with home equity lines, refinancing, portfolio management, loss mitigation, and collections. Both Fannie Mae and Freddie Mac provide forms that are used by real estate professionals who perform BPOs for a fee. Although some BPOs are more extensive, including information about the neighborhood and an interior analysis, many are simply "drive bys" that verify the existence of the property, along with a listing of comparable sales. A BPO should not be confused with an appraisal, which consists of more in-depth analysis of gathered information and which may be performed only by a licensed or certified appraiser. A BPO cannot be used if the matter involves a federally related transaction that requires an appraisal and/or the transaction occurs in a state that requires one. Information on how a BPO is used in certain Fannie Mae programs can be obtained by entering "BPO" in the search box at www.fanniemae.com/singlefamily.

The Appraisal Process

The key to an accurate appraisal lies in the methodical collection and analysis of data. The appraisal process is an orderly set of procedures used to collect and analyze data to arrive at a justifiable conclusion of value. The value sought most often is market value, though an appraisal also can be made to determine a different value, such as a property's insurance value, salvage value, or assessment value. The data needed by the appraiser can be divided into two basic classes:

1. General data, which covers the nation, region, city, and neighborhood. The appraiser researches the physical, economic, social, and political influences that affect the value and potential of the subject property.
2. Specific data, which covers the type and features of improvements to the subject property as well as comparable properties that are similar to and competitive with the subject property.

Figure 16.1 outlines the steps an appraiser takes in carrying out an appraisal assignment.

Once the approaches have been reconciled and an opinion of value has been reached, the appraiser prepares a report for the client. The report should

- identify the real estate and real property interest being appraised;
- state the purpose and intended use of the appraisal;
- define the value sought;
- state the effective date of the value and the date of the report;
- state the extent of the process of collecting, confirming, and reporting the data;
- list all assumptions and limiting conditions that affect the analysis, opinion, and conclusions of value;
- describe the information considered, the appraisal approaches used, and the reasoning that supports the report's conclusions (if an approach was excluded, the report should explain why);
- describe the appraiser's opinion of the highest and best use of the real estate;
- describe any additional information that may be appropriate to show compliance with the specific guidelines established in *USPAP* or to clearly identify and explain any departures from those guidelines; and
- include a signed certification, as required by *USPAP*.

FIGURE 16.1: The Appraisal Process

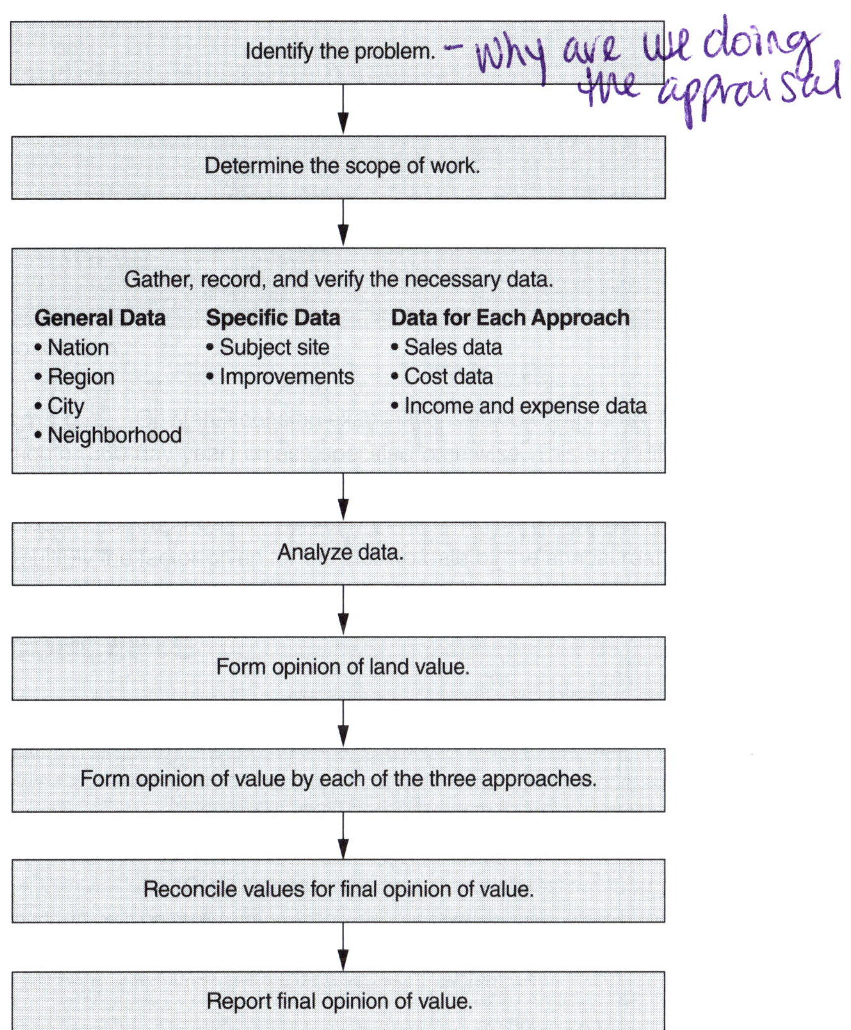

https://www.fanniemae.com/content/guide_form/1004.pdf

Uniform Residential Appraisal Report Figure 16.2 shows the *Uniform Residential Appraisal Report (URAR)*, which is the form required by many government agencies. It illustrates the types of detailed information required of an appraisal of residential property. It also highlights the extensive list of certifications required of the appraiser and is accompanied by a page of instructions. A copy of the form can also be found at https://www.fanniemae.com/content/guide_form/1004.pdf.

IN PRACTICE Technology has come to the appraisal office, just as it has to the real estate office. Software can be used to make completing the URAR more efficient; the completed electronic form can be attached to a transmittal letter and sent electronically to the client along with digital copies of any exhibits, such as maps and photos.

FIGURE 16.2: Uniform Residential Appraisal Report (URAR)

Uniform Residential Appraisal Report

File #

The purpose of this summary appraisal report is to provide the lender/client with an accurate, and adequately supported, opinion of the market value of the subject property.

SUBJECT

Property Address | City | State | Zip Code
Borrower | Owner of Public Record | County
Legal Description
Assessor's Parcel # | Tax Year | R.E. Taxes $
Neighborhood Name | Map Reference | Census Tract
Occupant ☐ Owner ☐ Tenant ☐ Vacant | Special Assessments $ | ☐ PUD | HOA $ | ☐ per year ☐ per month
Property Rights Appraised ☐ Fee Simple ☐ Leasehold ☐ Other (describe)
Assignment Type ☐ Purchase Transaction ☐ Refinance Transaction ☐ Other (describe)
Lender/Client | Address
Is the subject property currently offered for sale or has it been offered for sale in the twelve months prior to the effective date of this appraisal? ☐ Yes ☐ No
Report data source(s) used, offering price(s), and date(s).

CONTRACT

I ☐ did ☐ did not analyze the contract for sale for the subject purchase transaction. Explain the results of the analysis of the contract for sale or why the analysis was not performed.

Contract Price $ | Date of Contract | Is the property seller the owner of public record? ☐ Yes ☐ No | Data Source(s)
Is there any financial assistance (loan charges, sale concessions, gift or downpayment assistance, etc.) to be paid by any party on behalf of the borrower? ☐ Yes ☐ No
If Yes, report the total dollar amount and describe the items to be paid.

NEIGHBORHOOD

Note: Race and the racial composition of the neighborhood are not appraisal factors.

Neighborhood Characteristics	One-Unit Housing Trends	One-Unit Housing	Present Land Use %
Location ☐ Urban ☐ Suburban ☐ Rural	Property Values ☐ Increasing ☐ Stable ☐ Declining	PRICE AGE	One-Unit %
Built-Up ☐ Over 75% ☐ 25–75% ☐ Under 25%	Demand/Supply ☐ Shortage ☐ In Balance ☐ Over Supply	$ (000) (yrs)	2-4 Unit %
Growth ☐ Rapid ☐ Stable ☐ Slow	Marketing Time ☐ Under 3 mths ☐ 3–6 mths ☐ Over 6 mths	Low	Multi-Family %
Neighborhood Boundaries		High	Commercial %
		Pred.	Other %

Neighborhood Description

Market Conditions (including support for the above conclusions)

SITE

Dimensions | Area | Shape | View
Specific Zoning Classification | Zoning Description
Zoning Compliance ☐ Legal ☐ Legal Nonconforming (Grandfathered Use) ☐ No Zoning ☐ Illegal (describe)
Is the highest and best use of the subject property as improved (or as proposed per plans and specifications) the present use? ☐ Yes ☐ No If No, describe

Utilities	Public	Other (describe)		Public	Other (describe)	Off-site Improvements—Type	Public	Private
Electricity	☐	☐	Water	☐	☐	Street	☐	☐
Gas	☐	☐	Sanitary Sewer	☐	☐	Alley	☐	☐

FEMA Special Flood Hazard Area ☐ Yes ☐ No | FEMA Flood Zone | FEMA Map # | FEMA Map Date
Are the utilities and off-site improvements typical for the market area? ☐ Yes ☐ No If No, describe
Are there any adverse site conditions or external factors (easements, encroachments, environmental conditions, land uses, etc.)? ☐ Yes ☐ No If Yes, describe

IMPROVEMENTS

General Description		Foundation		Exterior Description materials/condition		Interior materials/condition
Units ☐ One ☐ One with Accessory Unit		☐ Concrete Slab ☐ Crawl Space		Foundation Walls		Floors
# of Stories		☐ Full Basement ☐ Partial Basement		Exterior Walls		Walls
Type ☐ Det. ☐ Att. ☐ S-Det./End Unit		Basement Area sq. ft.		Roof Surface		Trim/Finish
☐ Existing ☐ Proposed ☐ Under Const.		Basement Finish %		Gutters & Downspouts		Bath Floor
Design (Style)		☐ Outside Entry/Exit ☐ Sump Pump		Window Type		Bath Wainscot
Year Built		Evidence of ☐ Infestation		Storm Sash/Insulated		Car Storage ☐ None
Effective Age (Yrs)		☐ Dampness ☐ Settlement		Screens		☐ Driveway # of Cars
Attic	☐ None	Heating ☐ FWA ☐ HWBB ☐ Radiant		Amenities	☐ Woodstove(s) #	Driveway Surface
☐ Drop Stair	☐ Stairs	☐ Other	Fuel	☐ Fireplace(s) #	☐ Fence	☐ Garage # of Cars
☐ Floor	☐ Scuttle	Cooling ☐ Central Air Conditioning		☐ Patio/Deck	☐ Porch	☐ Carport # of Cars
☐ Finished	☐ Heated	☐ Individual	☐ Other	☐ Pool	☐ Other	☐ Att. ☐ Det. ☐ Built-in

Appliances ☐ Refrigerator ☐ Range/Oven ☐ Dishwasher ☐ Disposal ☐ Microwave ☐ Washer/Dryer ☐ Other (describe)
Finished area **above** grade contains: | Rooms | Bedrooms | Bath(s) | Square Feet of Gross Living Area Above Grade
Additional features (special energy efficient items, etc.)

Describe the condition of the property (including needed repairs, deterioration, renovations, remodeling, etc.).

Are there any physical deficiencies or adverse conditions that affect the livability, soundness, or structural integrity of the property? ☐ Yes ☐ No If Yes, describe

Does the property generally conform to the neighborhood (functional utility, style, condition, use, construction, etc.)? ☐ Yes ☐ No If No, describe

Freddie Mac Form 70 March 2005 | Page 1 of 6 | Fannie Mae Form 1004 March 2005

FIGURE 16.2: Uniform Residential Appraisal Report (URAR) (continued)

Uniform Residential Appraisal Report

File #

There are comparable properties currently offered for sale in the subject neighborhood ranging in price from $ to $.

There are comparable sales in the subject neighborhood within the past twelve months ranging in sale price from $ to $.

FEATURE	SUBJECT	COMPARABLE SALE # 1		COMPARABLE SALE # 2		COMPARABLE SALE # 3	
Address							
Proximity to Subject							
Sale Price	$		$		$		$
Sale Price/Gross Liv. Area	$ sq. ft.	$ sq. ft.		$ sq. ft.		$ sq. ft.	
Data Source(s)							
Verification Source(s)							
VALUE ADJUSTMENTS	DESCRIPTION	DESCRIPTION	+(-) $ Adjustment	DESCRIPTION	+(-) $ Adjustment	DESCRIPTION	+(-) $ Adjustment
Sale or Financing Concessions							
Date of Sale/Time							
Location							
Leasehold/Fee Simple							
Site							
View							
Design (Style)							
Quality of Construction							
Actual Age							
Condition							
Above Grade	Total | Bdrms. | Baths	Total | Bdrms. | Baths		Total | Bdrms. | Baths		Total | Bdrms. | Baths	
Room Count							
Gross Living Area	sq. ft.	sq. ft.		sq. ft.		sq. ft.	
Basement & Finished Rooms Below Grade							
Functional Utility							
Heating/Cooling							
Energy Efficient Items							
Garage/Carport							
Porch/Patio/Deck							
Net Adjustment (Total)		☐ + ☐ -	$	☐ + ☐ -	$	☐ + ☐ -	$
Adjusted Sale Price of Comparables		Net Adj. % Gross Adj. %	$	Net Adj. % Gross Adj. %	$	Net Adj. % Gross Adj. %	$

SALES COMPARISON APPROACH

I ☐ did ☐ did not research the sale or transfer history of the subject property and comparable sales. If not, explain

My research ☐ did ☐ did not reveal any prior sales or transfers of the subject property for the three years prior to the effective date of this appraisal.

Data source(s)

My research ☐ did ☐ did not reveal any prior sales or transfers of the comparable sales for the year prior to the date of sale of the comparable sale.

Data source(s)

Report the results of the research and analysis of the prior sale or transfer history of the subject property and comparable sales (report additional prior sales on page 3).

ITEM	SUBJECT	COMPARABLE SALE # 1	COMPARABLE SALE # 2	COMPARABLE SALE # 3
Date of Prior Sale/Transfer				
Price of Prior Sale/Transfer				
Data Source(s)				
Effective Date of Data Source(s)				

Analysis of prior sale or transfer history of the subject property and comparable sales

Summary of Sales Comparison Approach

Indicated Value by Sales Comparison Approach $

RECONCILIATION

Indicated Value by: Sales Comparison Approach $ Cost Approach (if developed) $ Income Approach (if developed) $

This appraisal is made ☐ "as is", ☐ subject to completion per plans and specifications on the basis of a hypothetical condition that the improvements have been completed, ☐ subject to the following repairs or alterations on the basis of a hypothetical condition that the repairs or alterations have been completed, or ☐ subject to the following required inspection based on the extraordinary assumption that the condition or deficiency does not require alteration or repair:

Based on a complete visual inspection of the interior and exterior areas of the subject property, defined scope of work, statement of assumptions and limiting conditions, and appraiser's certification, my (our) opinion of the market value, as defined, of the real property that is the subject of this report is $, as of , which is the date of inspection and the effective date of this appraisal.

Freddie Mac Form 70 March 2005 Page 2 of 6 Fannie Mae Form 1004 March 2005

FIGURE 16.2: Uniform Residential Appraisal Report (URAR) (continued)

Uniform Residential Appraisal Report

File #

ADDITIONAL COMMENTS

COST APPROACH

COST APPROACH TO VALUE (not required by Fannie Mae)

Provide adequate information for the lender/client to replicate the below cost figures and calculations.

Support for the opinion of site value (summary of comparable land sales or other methods for estimating site value)

ESTIMATED ☐ REPRODUCTION OR ☐ REPLACEMENT COST NEW	OPINION OF SITE VALUE ..... = $
Source of cost data	Dwelling Sq. Ft. @ $ ..... =$
Quality rating from cost service Effective date of cost data	Sq. Ft. @ $ ..... =$
Comments on Cost Approach (gross living area calculations, depreciation, etc.)	
	Garage/Carport Sq. Ft. @ $ ..... =$
	Total Estimate of Cost-New ..... = $
	Less Physical | Functional | External
	Depreciation =$( )
	Depreciated Cost of Improvements..... =$
	"As-is" Value of Site Improvements..... =$
Estimated Remaining Economic Life (HUD and VA only) Years	Indicated Value By Cost Approach ..... =$

INCOME

INCOME APPROACH TO VALUE (not required by Fannie Mae)

Estimated Monthly Market Rent $ X Gross Rent Multiplier = $ Indicated Value by Income Approach

Summary of Income Approach (including support for market rent and GRM)

PUD INFORMATION

PROJECT INFORMATION FOR PUDs (if applicable)

Is the developer/builder in control of the Homeowners' Association (HOA)? ☐ Yes ☐ No Unit type(s) ☐ Detached ☐ Attached

Provide the following information for PUDs ONLY if the developer/builder is in control of the HOA and the subject property is an attached dwelling unit.

Legal name of project

Total number of phases Total number of units Total number of units sold

Total number of units rented Total number of units for sale Data source(s)

Was the project created by the conversion of an existing building(s) into a PUD? ☐ Yes ☐ No If Yes, date of conversion

Does the project contain any multi-dwelling units? ☐ Yes ☐ No Data source(s)

Are the units, common elements, and recreation facilities complete? ☐ Yes ☐ No If No, describe the status of completion.

Are the common elements leased to or by the Homeowners' Association? ☐ Yes ☐ No If Yes, describe the rental terms and options.

Describe common elements and recreational facilities

Freddie Mac Form 70 March 2005 Page 3 of 6 Fannie Mae Form 1004 March 2005

FIGURE 16.2: Uniform Residential Appraisal Report (URAR) (continued)

Uniform Residential Appraisal Report

File #

This report form is designed to report an appraisal of a one-unit property or a one-unit property with an accessory unit; including a unit in a planned unit development (PUD). This report form is not designed to report an appraisal of a manufactured home or a unit in a condominium or cooperative project.

This appraisal report is subject to the following scope of work, intended use, intended user, definition of market value, statement of assumptions and limiting conditions, and certifications. Modifications, additions, or deletions to the intended use, intended user, definition of market value, or assumptions and limiting conditions are not permitted. The appraiser may expand the scope of work to include any additional research or analysis necessary based on the complexity of this appraisal assignment. Modifications or deletions to the certifications are also not permitted. However, additional certifications that do not constitute material alterations to this appraisal report, such as those required by law or those related to the appraiser's continuing education or membership in an appraisal organization, are permitted.

SCOPE OF WORK: The scope of work for this appraisal is defined by the complexity of this appraisal assignment and the reporting requirements of this appraisal report form, including the following definition of market value, statement of assumptions and limiting conditions, and certifications. The appraiser must, at a minimum: (1) perform a complete visual inspection of the interior and exterior areas of the subject property, (2) inspect the neighborhood, (3) inspect each of the comparable sales from at least the street, (4) research, verify, and analyze data from reliable public and/or private sources, and (5) report his or her analysis, opinions, and conclusions in this appraisal report.

INTENDED USE: The intended use of this appraisal report is for the lender/client to evaluate the property that is the subject of this appraisal for a mortgage finance transaction.

INTENDED USER: The intended user of this appraisal report is the lender/client.

DEFINITION OF MARKET VALUE: The most probable price which a property should bring in a competitive and open market under all conditions requisite to a fair sale, the buyer and seller, each acting prudently, knowledgeably and assuming the price is not affected by undue stimulus. Implicit in this definition is the consummation of a sale as of a specified date and the passing of title from seller to buyer under conditions whereby: (1) buyer and seller are typically motivated; (2) both parties are well informed or well advised, and each acting in what he or she considers his or her own best interest; (3) a reasonable time is allowed for exposure in the open market; (4) payment is made in terms of cash in U. S. dollars or in terms of financial arrangements comparable thereto; and (5) the price represents the normal consideration for the property sold unaffected by special or creative financing or sales concessions* granted by anyone associated with the sale.

*Adjustments to the comparables must be made for special or creative financing or sales concessions. No adjustments are necessary for those costs which are normally paid by sellers as a result of tradition or law in a market area; these costs are readily identifiable since the seller pays these costs in virtually all sales transactions. Special or creative financing adjustments can be made to the comparable property by comparisons to financing terms offered by a third party institutional lender that is not already involved in the property or transaction. Any adjustment should not be calculated on a mechanical dollar for dollar cost of the financing or concession but the dollar amount of any adjustment should approximate the market's reaction to the financing or concessions based on the appraiser's judgment.

STATEMENT OF ASSUMPTIONS AND LIMITING CONDITIONS: The appraiser's certification in this report is subject to the following assumptions and limiting conditions:

1. The appraiser will not be responsible for matters of a legal nature that affect either the property being appraised or the title to it, except for information that he or she became aware of during the research involved in performing this appraisal. The appraiser assumes that the title is good and marketable and will not render any opinions about the title.

2. The appraiser has provided a sketch in this appraisal report to show the approximate dimensions of the improvements. The sketch is included only to assist the reader in visualizing the property and understanding the appraiser's determination of its size.

3. The appraiser has examined the available flood maps that are provided by the Federal Emergency Management Agency (or other data sources) and has noted in this appraisal report whether any portion of the subject site is located in an identified Special Flood Hazard Area. Because the appraiser is not a surveyor, he or she makes no guarantees, express or implied, regarding this determination.

4. The appraiser will not give testimony or appear in court because he or she made an appraisal of the property in question, unless specific arrangements to do so have been made beforehand, or as otherwise required by law.

5. The appraiser has noted in this appraisal report any adverse conditions (such as needed repairs, deterioration, the presence of hazardous wastes, toxic substances, etc.) observed during the inspection of the subject property or that he or she became aware of during the research involved in performing this appraisal. Unless otherwise stated in this appraisal report, the appraiser has no knowledge of any hidden or unapparent physical deficiencies or adverse conditions of the property (such as, but not limited to, needed repairs, deterioration, the presence of hazardous wastes, toxic substances, adverse environmental conditions, etc.) that would make the property less valuable, and has assumed that there are no such conditions and makes no guarantees or warranties, express or implied. The appraiser will not be responsible for any such conditions that do exist or for any engineering or testing that might be required to discover whether such conditions exist. Because the appraiser is not an expert in the field of environmental hazards, this appraisal report must not be considered as an environmental assessment of the property.

6. The appraiser has based his or her appraisal report and valuation conclusion for an appraisal that is subject to satisfactory completion, repairs, or alterations on the assumption that the completion, repairs, or alterations of the subject property will be performed in a professional manner.

Freddie Mac Form 70 March 2005 Page 4 of 6 Fannie Mae Form 1004 March 2005

FIGURE 16.2: Uniform Residential Appraisal Report (URAR) (continued)

Uniform Residential Appraisal Report

File #

APPRAISER'S CERTIFICATION: The Appraiser certifies and agrees that:

1. I have, at a minimum, developed and reported this appraisal in accordance with the scope of work requirements stated in this appraisal report.

2. I performed a complete visual inspection of the interior and exterior areas of the subject property. I reported the condition of the improvements in factual, specific terms. I identified and reported the physical deficiencies that could affect the livability, soundness, or structural integrity of the property.

3. I performed this appraisal in accordance with the requirements of the Uniform Standards of Professional Appraisal Practice that were adopted and promulgated by the Appraisal Standards Board of The Appraisal Foundation and that were in place at the time this appraisal report was prepared.

4. I developed my opinion of the market value of the real property that is the subject of this report based on the sales comparison approach to value. I have adequate comparable market data to develop a reliable sales comparison approach for this appraisal assignment. I further certify that I considered the cost and income approaches to value but did not develop them, unless otherwise indicated in this report.

5. I researched, verified, analyzed, and reported on any current agreement for sale for the subject property, any offering for sale of the subject property in the twelve months prior to the effective date of this appraisal, and the prior sales of the subject property for a minimum of three years prior to the effective date of this appraisal, unless otherwise indicated in this report.

6. I researched, verified, analyzed, and reported on the prior sales of the comparable sales for a minimum of one year prior to the date of sale of the comparable sale, unless otherwise indicated in this report.

7. I selected and used comparable sales that are locationally, physically, and functionally the most similar to the subject property.

8. I have not used comparable sales that were the result of combining a land sale with the contract purchase price of a home that has been built or will be built on the land.

9. I have reported adjustments to the comparable sales that reflect the market's reaction to the differences between the subject property and the comparable sales.

10. I verified, from a disinterested source, all information in this report that was provided by parties who have a financial interest in the sale or financing of the subject property.

11. I have knowledge and experience in appraising this type of property in this market area.

12. I am aware of, and have access to, the necessary and appropriate public and private data sources, such as multiple listing services, tax assessment records, public land records and other such data sources for the area in which the property is located.

13. I obtained the information, estimates, and opinions furnished by other parties and expressed in this appraisal report from reliable sources that I believe to be true and correct.

14. I have taken into consideration the factors that have an impact on value with respect to the subject neighborhood, subject property, and the proximity of the subject property to adverse influences in the development of my opinion of market value. I have noted in this appraisal report any adverse conditions (such as, but not limited to, needed repairs, deterioration, the presence of hazardous wastes, toxic substances, adverse environmental conditions, etc.) observed during the inspection of the subject property or that I became aware of during the research involved in performing this appraisal. I have considered these adverse conditions in my analysis of the property value, and have reported on the effect of the conditions on the value and marketability of the subject property.

15. I have not knowingly withheld any significant information from this appraisal report and, to the best of my knowledge, all statements and information in this appraisal report are true and correct.

16. I stated in this appraisal report my own personal, unbiased, and professional analysis, opinions, and conclusions, which are subject only to the assumptions and limiting conditions in this appraisal report.

17. I have no present or prospective interest in the property that is the subject of this report, and I have no present or prospective personal interest or bias with respect to the participants in the transaction. I did not base, either partially or completely, my analysis and/or opinion of market value in this appraisal report on the race, color, religion, sex, age, marital status, handicap, familial status, or national origin of either the prospective owners or occupants of the subject property or of the present owners or occupants of the properties in the vicinity of the subject property or on any other basis prohibited by law.

18. My employment and/or compensation for performing this appraisal or any future or anticipated appraisals was not conditioned on any agreement or understanding, written or otherwise, that I would report (or present analysis supporting) a predetermined specific value, a predetermined minimum value, a range or direction in value, a value that favors the cause of any party, or the attainment of a specific result or occurrence of a specific subsequent event (such as approval of a pending mortgage loan application).

19. I personally prepared all conclusions and opinions about the real estate that were set forth in this appraisal report. If I relied on significant real property appraisal assistance from any individual or individuals in the performance of this appraisal or the preparation of this appraisal report, I have named such individual(s) and disclosed the specific tasks performed in this appraisal report. I certify that any individual so named is qualified to perform the tasks. I have not authorized anyone to make a change to any item in this appraisal report; therefore, any change made to this appraisal is unauthorized and I will take no responsibility for it.

20. I identified the lender/client in this appraisal report who is the individual, organization, or agent for the organization that ordered and will receive this appraisal report.

Freddie Mac Form 70 March 2005 | Page 5 of 6 | Fannie Mae Form 1004 March 2005

FIGURE 16.2: Uniform Residential Appraisal Report (URAR) (continued)

Uniform Residential Appraisal Report

File #

21. The lender/client may disclose or distribute this appraisal report to: the borrower; another lender at the request of the borrower; the mortgagee or its successors and assigns; mortgage insurers; government sponsored enterprises; other secondary market participants; data collection or reporting services; professional appraisal organizations; any department, agency, or instrumentality of the United States; and any state, the District of Columbia, or other jurisdictions; without having to obtain the appraiser's or supervisory appraiser's (if applicable) consent. Such consent must be obtained before this appraisal report may be disclosed or distributed to any other party (including, but not limited to, the public through advertising, public relations, news, sales, or other media).

22. I am aware that any disclosure or distribution of this appraisal report by me or the lender/client may be subject to certain laws and regulations. Further, I am also subject to the provisions of the Uniform Standards of Professional Appraisal Practice that pertain to disclosure or distribution by me.

23. The borrower, another lender at the request of the borrower, the mortgagee or its successors and assigns, mortgage insurers, government sponsored enterprises, and other secondary market participants may rely on this appraisal report as part of any mortgage finance transaction that involves any one or more of these parties.

24. If this appraisal report was transmitted as an "electronic record" containing my "electronic signature," as those terms are defined in applicable federal and/or state laws (excluding audio and video recordings), or a facsimile transmission of this appraisal report containing a copy or representation of my signature, the appraisal report shall be as effective, enforceable and valid as if a paper version of this appraisal report were delivered containing my original hand written signature.

25. Any intentional or negligent misrepresentation(s) contained in this appraisal report may result in civil liability and/or criminal penalties including, but not limited to, fine or imprisonment or both under the provisions of Title 18, United States Code, Section 1001, et seq., or similar state laws.

SUPERVISORY APPRAISER'S CERTIFICATION: The Supervisory Appraiser certifies and agrees that:

1. I directly supervised the appraiser for this appraisal assignment, have read the appraisal report, and agree with the appraiser's analysis, opinions, statements, conclusions, and the appraiser's certification.

2. I accept full responsibility for the contents of this appraisal report including, but not limited to, the appraiser's analysis, opinions, statements, conclusions, and the appraiser's certification.

3. The appraiser identified in this appraisal report is either a sub-contractor or an employee of the supervisory appraiser (or the appraisal firm), is qualified to perform this appraisal, and is acceptable to perform this appraisal under the applicable state law.

4. This appraisal report complies with the Uniform Standards of Professional Appraisal Practice that were adopted and promulgated by the Appraisal Standards Board of The Appraisal Foundation and that were in place at the time this appraisal report was prepared.

5. If this appraisal report was transmitted as an "electronic record" containing my "electronic signature," as those terms are defined in applicable federal and/or state laws (excluding audio and video recordings), or a facsimile transmission of this appraisal report containing a copy or representation of my signature, the appraisal report shall be as effective, enforceable and valid as if a paper version of this appraisal report were delivered containing my original hand written signature.

APPRAISER

Signature ______________________
Name ______________________
Company Name ______________________
Company Address ______________________
____
Telephone Number ______________________
Email Address ______________________
Date of Signature and Report ______________________
Effective Date of Appraisal ______________________
State Certification # ______________________
or State License # ______________________
or Other (describe) ____________ State # ____________
State ______________________
Expiration Date of Certification or License ______________________

ADDRESS OF PROPERTY APPRAISED
____
____

APPRAISED VALUE OF SUBJECT PROPERTY $ ____________

LENDER/CLIENT
Name ______________________
Company Name ______________________
Company Address ______________________
____
Email Address ______________________

SUPERVISORY APPRAISER (ONLY IF REQUIRED)

Signature ______________________
Name ______________________
Company Name ______________________
Company Address ______________________
____
Telephone Number ______________________
Email Address ______________________
Date of Signature ______________________
State Certification # ______________________
or State License # ______________________
State ______________________
Expiration Date of Certification or License ______________________

SUBJECT PROPERTY

☐ Did not inspect subject property
☐ Did inspect exterior of subject property from street
Date of Inspection ______________________
☐ Did inspect interior and exterior of subject property
Date of Inspection ______________________

COMPARABLE SALES

☐ Did not inspect exterior of comparable sales from street
☐ Did inspect exterior of comparable sales from street
Date of Inspection ______________________

Freddie Mac Form 70 March 2005 Page 6 of 6 Fannie Mae Form 1004 March 2005

While the appraiser does not determine value, neither is value determined by what the seller wants to receive, what the buyer wants to pay, or what the real estate professional suggests. The appraiser, relying on experience and expertise in valuation theories, develops an objective report that supports the value indicated by the market. Sellers and real estate professionals may not agree with the appraiser's value, and may argue that it is lower than they think that it should be. Since the appraisal is most often ordered by a lender, who will make a loan decision based on the property's appraised value, the appraiser must be able to back up the appraisal report with quantifiable data. It is the lender who will want to know, "If there is a loan default, at what price can the property probably be sold to recover the remaining loan balance?" The lender is relying on the skill of the appraiser to answer this question.

VALUE

The characteristics of value

Demand

Utility

Scarcity

Transferability

To have **value** in the real estate market—that is, monetary worth based on desirability—a property must have the following characteristics, which can be remembered as DUST:

- *Demand*—the need or desire for possession or ownership backed by the financial means to satisfy that need
- *Utility*—the property's usefulness for its intended purposes
- *Scarcity*—a finite supply
- *Transferability*—the relative ease with which ownership rights are transferred from one person to another

Market Value

The goal of an appraiser most often is to estimate or express an opinion of a property's market value. **Market value** generally is considered the most probable price that a property should bring in a competitive and open market under all conditions requisite to a fair sale. The buyer and the seller are both assumed to be acting prudently and knowledgeably and the price is not affected by undue stimulus. The property's most probable price is not the average price for such properties, or the highest price possible.

A determination of market value thus requires that

- the buyer and the seller are unrelated and acting without undue pressure;
- both the buyer and the seller are well informed of the property's use and potential, including both its defects and its advantages;
- a reasonable time is allowed for exposure of the property in the open market;
- payment is made in cash or its equivalent; and
- the price paid for the property is a normal market price, unaffected by special financing amounts or terms, services, fees, costs, or credits incurred in the market transaction.

Market value—an opinion of a property's worth

Market price—the asking, offer, or sales price of a property

Market Price *Market value* is an opinion of value based on an analysis of data. The data may include not only an analysis of comparable sales but also an analysis of potential income, expenses, and replacement costs. *Market price*, on the other hand, is a property's asking, offer, or sales price.

Cost One of the most common misconceptions about valuing property is that its cost represents its market value. Cost and market value may be the same. In fact, when the improvements on a property are new, cost and value are likely to be equal. But more often, cost does not equal market value. For example, a homeowner may install a swimming pool for $30,000; however, the cost of the improvement may not add $30,000 to the value of the property.

Basic Principles of Value

A number of economic principles can affect the value of real estate. The most important are defined here.

Anticipation According to the principle of **anticipation**, value is created by the expectation that certain events will occur. For instance, the value of a house may be affected if rumors circulate that a major employer in the area will be going out of business. In the same way, a neighborhood may see an increase in property values if a major employer announces that it is moving to the area. The income approach to value is based on the principle of anticipation.

Change No physical or economic condition remains constant; this is the principle of **change**. Real estate is subject to natural phenomena such as tornadoes, fires, and routine wear and tear. The real estate business is subject to market demands, like any other business. An appraiser must be knowledgeable about both the past and the predictable future effects of natural phenomena and the behavior of the marketplace.

Competition The interaction of supply and demand creates **competition**. Profitable businesses tend to attract competition. For example, the success of a retail store may cause investors to open similar stores in the area. This tends to mean less profit for all stores concerned unless the purchasing power in the area substantially increases.

Conformity The principle of **conformity** means that maximum value is created when a property is in harmony with its surroundings. Maximum value is realized if the use of land conforms to existing neighborhood standards. In a single-family residential neighborhood, for instance, buildings should be similar in design, construction, size, and age. Many parts of the country have experienced the "teardown" phenomenon in which a large, expensive new home replaces a smaller, mid-century home that is more typical of others in the neighborhood. The new home will not realize its maximum value because it has violated the principle of conformity—at least, until a significant number of such conversions has taken place.

Contribution Under the principle of **contribution**, the value of any part of a property is measured by its effect on the value of the whole parcel. Installing a swimming pool, greenhouse, or private bowling alley may not add value to the property equal to its cost, but remodeling an outdated kitchen or bathroom might.

Highest and Best Use The most profitable single use of a property is its **highest and best use**. The use must be

- physically possible,
- legally permitted,
- economically or financially feasible, and
- the most profitable or maximally productive.

The highest and best use of a site can change with social, political, and economic forces. A parking lot in a busy downtown area, for example, may not maximize the land's profitability to the same extent that an office building would. On the other hand, if the downtown area has an oversupply of office space but is short of parking areas, the parking lot may be the most profitable current use of the land.

Increasing and Diminishing Returns The addition of improvements to land and structures tends to increase the property's market value, but only up to a certain point. Beyond that point, additional improvements no longer affect a property's value because buyers or renters in the market cannot be expected to pay more for the property. As long as money spent on improvements produces an increase in income or value, the **law of increasing returns** applies. At the point where additional improvements do not increase income or value, the **law of diminishing returns** applies. No matter how much money is spent on the property, the property's value does not keep pace with the expenditures. A remodeled kitchen or bathroom might increase the value of a house; adding restaurant-quality appliances and hand-crafted wood floors, however, could be costs that the owner would not be able to recover.

IN PRACTICE The law of diminishing returns sometimes creates an awkward situation during a listing appointment. The owner is proud of all the improvements that have been made to the property and may produce a box filled with receipts for all the additions that have been made to the property over the years. When the real estate professional presents the carefully prepared CMA, however, it becomes clear that the probable market value of the property will not cover the cost of the improvements. The real estate professional must be prepared to explain why it would be foolhardy for the owner to set a listing price high enough to cover all of those costs. The real estate professional must also know how to react if the owner chooses to ignore the evidence presented by the CMA. A property listing that languishes on the market because the listing price is too high is bad for everyone.

Plottage: The individual value of two adjacent properties may be greater if they are combined in an assemblage than if each is sold separately.

Plottage The principle of **plottage** is in evidence when the consolidation of adjacent lots into a single larger one produces a greater total land value than the sum of the two sites valued separately. For example, two adjacent lots valued at $35,000 each might have a combined value of $90,000 if consolidated. The process of merging two separately owned lots under one owner is known as **assemblage**. *Plottage* is the amount that the value of the combined properties is increased by successful assemblage.

Regression and Progression In general, the worth of a better-quality property is adversely affected by the presence of a lesser-quality property. This is known as the principle of **regression**. Thus, in a neighborhood of modest homes, a structure that is larger, better maintained, or more luxurious would tend to be valued in the same range as the less lavish homes. Conversely, under the principle of **progression**, the value of a modest home would be higher if it were located among larger, fancier properties.

Substitution According to the principle of **substitution**, the maximum value of a property tends to be set by how much it would cost to purchase an equally desirable and valuable substitute property. Substitution is the foundation of the sales comparison approach to appraising that is discussed later.

Supply and Demand The principle of **supply and demand** operates in the real estate market just as it does in the market for any product. The value of a product depends on the supply—the number of such products available in the marketplace. When the supply of similar properties increases, their value decreases and when demand for such properties increases, their value increases.

IN PRACTICE The factors of supply and demand tend to operate in a cycle and point out how the immovability of real estate is a critical part of that cycle. When there is a high demand for homes and relatively few properties available for sale, prices will go up. This could be caused by a number of factors, from business expansion in the area to a natural disaster that destroys part of the housing supply. At the same time, another area may be experiencing a glut of properties on the market, usually because of dismal economic conditions that force companies to close or downsize. Some residents will choose to move to where the work is, putting even more properties on the market and also placing additional pressure on businesses that struggle to survive as a declining, and less prosperous, population reduces the demand for their products and services.

THE THREE APPROACHES TO VALUE

To arrive at an accurate opinion of value, an appraiser traditionally uses one or more of three basic valuation techniques: the sales comparison approach, the cost approach, and the income approach. The three methods serve as checks against each other and using more than one approach helps the appraiser narrow the range of the final conclusion of value. Each approach is most useful with a specific type of property.

The Sales Comparison Approach

In the **sales comparison approach** (also known as the **market data approach**), value is obtained by comparing the property being appraised—the subject property—with recently sold comparable properties—properties similar to the subject in location and features. Because no two parcels of real estate are exactly alike, each comparable property must be analyzed for differences and similarities between it and the subject property. This approach is a good example of the principle of substitution, discussed above. The **sales price** of a comparable is adjusted to reflect the impact on value of any differences between the subject and comparable. The elements of comparison for which adjustments must be made include the following:

- *Property rights*. An adjustment must be made when less than fee simple—the full legal bundle of rights—is involved. An adjustment could be made because of the presence of a land lease, ground lease, life estate, easement, deed restriction, and/or encroachment.
- *Financing concessions*. The financing terms under which a property was sold must be considered, including mortgage loan terms and owner financing or an interest rate buydown by a builder-developer.
- *Market conditions*. Interest rates, supply and demand, and other economic indicators must be analyzed.
- *Conditions of sale*. Adjustments must be made for motivational factors that would affect the sale, such as foreclosure, a sale between family members, or some nonmonetary incentive.

- *Market conditions since the date of sale*. An adjustment must be made if economic changes occur between the date of sale of the comparable property and the date of the appraisal.
- *Location or area preference*. Similar properties might differ in price from neighborhood to neighborhood or even between locations within the same neighborhood.
- *Physical features and amenities*. Physical features, such as the structure's age, size, and condition when compared to the subject property, may require adjustments.

The sales comparison approach is usually considered the most reliable of the three approaches in appraising single-family homes, where the intangible benefits of home ownership may be difficult to measure otherwise. Figure 16.3 is an abbreviated version of the information that an appraiser will provide a client, but it illustrates the kind of comparisons and value adjustments that are made.

The Cost Approach

The **cost approach** to value also is based on the principle of substitution. The cost approach consists of five steps:

1. Estimate the value of the land as though it were vacant and available to be put to its highest and best use.
2. Estimate the current cost of constructing buildings and improvements.
3. Estimate the amount of **accrued depreciation** (loss in value) resulting from the property's physical deterioration, external depreciation, and functional obsolescence.
4. Deduct the accrued depreciation estimated in Step 3 from the construction cost estimated in Step 2.
5. Add the estimated land value from Step 1 to the depreciated cost of the building and site improvements derived in Step 4 to arrive at the total property value.

For example:

Value of the land	=	$50,000
Current cost of construction	=	$180,000
Accrued depreciation	=	$20,000
$180,000 – $20,000	=	$160,000
$50,000 + $160,000	=	$210,000

In this case, the total property value is $210,000.

An example of the cost approach to value, applied to the same property as in Figure 16.3 is shown in Figure 16.4.

FIGURE 16.3: Sales Comparison Approach to Value

		Comparable Properties		
	Subject Property	**A**	**B**	**C**
Sales price		**$262,000**	**$252,000**	**$265,000**
Financing concessions	none	none	none	none
Date of sale		current	current	current
Location	good	same	poorer +4,500	same
Age	6 years	same	same	same
Size of lot	60' × 135'	same	same	larger –5,000
Landscaping	good	same	same	same
Construction	brick	same	same	same
Style	ranch	same	same	same
No. of rooms	8	same	same	same
No. of bedrooms	4	same	poorer +4,500	same
No. of baths	2½	same	same	better –500
Sq. ft. of living space	2,500	same	same	better –2,000
Other space (basement)	full basement	same	same	same
Condition—exterior	average	better –2,500	poorer +2,000	better –2,500
Condition—interior	good	same	same	better –1,500
Garage	3-car attached	same	same	same
Other improvements	none	none	none	none
Net adjustments		–2,500	+11,000	–11,000
Adjusted value		$259,500	$263,000	$254,000

Note: The value of a feature that is present in the subject but not in the comparable property is added to the sales price of the comparable. The value of a feature that is present in the comparable but not in the subject property is subtracted from the sales price of the comparable. A good way to remember this is as follows: CBS stands for "comp better, subtract"; and CPA stands for "comp poorer, add." The adjusted sales prices of the comparables represent the probable range of value of the subject property. From this range, a single market value estimate can be selected.

Depreciation In a real estate appraisal, **depreciation** is a loss in value for any reason. It refers to a condition that adversely affects the value of an improvement to real property. Land is not considered a depreciating asset; it retains its value indefinitely, except in such rare cases as an urban parcel that is rezoned, improperly developed land, or misused farmland. Depreciation is the result of a negative condition that affects real property.

IN PRACTICE Depreciation for appraisal purposes is not the same as depreciation for tax reporting purposes. Depreciation for appraisal purposes represents the actual loss in value caused by property deterioration, damage, or obsolescence. Depreciation for tax purposes is an annual deduction from taxable income for a term of years, as permitted by IRS regulations, which may even allow the term of years to be shortened so that accelerated depreciation can be taken.

FIGURE 16.4: Cost Approach to Value

Subject Property		
Land valuation: Size 60' × 135' @ $450 per front foot		$ 27,000
Plus site improvements: driveway, walks, landscaping, etc.		10,000
Total		$ 37,000
Building valuation: replacement cost		
2,500 sq. ft. @ $75 per sq. ft.	$187,500	
Less depreciation:		
Physical depreciation		
Curable		
(items of deferred maintenance) exterior painting	$4,000	
Incurable (structural deterioration)	9,750	
Functional obsolescence	0	
External obsolescence	0	
Total depreciation	$13,750	
Depreciated value of building		$173,750
Indicated value by cost approach		$210,750

Depreciation is considered curable or incurable, depending on whether it can be corrected economically. For appraisal purposes, depreciation is divided into three classes, according to cause:

- **Physical deterioration.** A curable item is one in need of repair, such as painting (deferred maintenance), that would result in an increase in value equal to or exceeding its cost. An item is incurable if it is a defect caused by physical wear and tear and its correction would not be economically feasible or contribute a comparable value to the building, such as an extensive crack in the foundation. The cost of a major repair may not warrant the financial investment.
- **Functional obsolescence.** Obsolescence means a loss in value from the market's response to the item. Outmoded or unacceptable physical or design features that are no longer considered desirable by purchasers are considered curable if they can be replaced or redesigned at a cost that would be offset by the anticipated increase in ultimate value. Outmoded plumbing, for instance, is usually easily replaced. Room function may be redefined at no cost if the basic room layout allows for it. A bedroom adjacent to a kitchen, for example, may be converted to a family room. Currently undesirable physical or design features that cannot be easily remedied because the cost of the cure would be greater than its resulting increase in value are considered incurable. A four-bedroom home with only one bathroom is likely to suffer from incurable functional obsolescence.
- **External obsolescence.** If depreciation is caused by negative factors not on the subject property, such as environmental, social, or economic forces, it is always incurable. The loss in value cannot be reversed by spending money on the property. For example, close proximity to a polluting factory is a factor that cannot be cured by the owner of the subject property.

The easiest but least precise way to determine depreciation is the straight-line method, also called the economic age-life method. Depreciation is assumed to occur at an even rate over a structure's **economic life**, the period during which it is expected to remain useful for its original intended purpose. The property's cost is divided by the number of years of its expected economic life to derive the amount of annual depreciation.

For instance, a $420,000 property may have a land value of $90,000 and an improvement value of $330,000. If the improvement is expected to last 60 years, the annual straight-line depreciation would be $5,500 ($330,000 divided by 60 years). Such depreciation can be calculated as an annual dollar amount or as a percentage of a property's improvements.

The cost approach is most useful in the appraisal of newer or special-purpose buildings such as schools, churches, and public buildings. Such properties are difficult to appraise using other methods because there are seldom enough local sales to use as comparables and because the properties do not ordinarily generate income.

Much of the functional obsolescence and all the external obsolescence can be evaluated only by considering the actions of buyers in the marketplace.

The Income Approach

Income Approach

Gross
Income
Vacancy
Expenses
Net operating income

The **income approach** to value is based on the present value of the right to future income. It assumes that the income generated by a property will determine the property's value. The income approach is used for valuation of income-producing properties such as apartment buildings, office buildings, retail stores, and shopping centers and is based on anticipation. A simplified version of the computations used in applying to income approach is shown in Figure 16.5. In estimating value using the income approach, an appraiser must take the following five steps:

1. Estimate the property's annual potential gross income. An estimate of economic rental income must be made based on market studies. Current rental income may not reflect the current market rental rates, especially in the case of short-term leases or leases about to terminate. Potential income also includes income to the property from such sources as vending machines, parking fees, and laundry machines.
2. Deduct an appropriate allowance for vacancy and rent loss, based on the appraiser's experience, and arrive at the effective gross income.
3. Deduct the annual operating expenses from the effective gross income to arrive at the annual **net operating income (NOI)**. Management costs are always included, even if the current owner manages the property. Mortgage payments (principal and interest) are debt service and are not considered operating expenses. Capital expenditures are not considered expenses; however, an allowance can be calculated representing the annual usage of each major capital item.
4. Estimate the price a typical investor would pay for the income produced by this particular type and class of property. This is done by estimating the rate of return (or yield) that an investor will demand for the investment of capital in this type of building. This rate of return is called the **capitalization rate** (or "cap" rate) and is determined by comparing the relationship of net operating income with the sales prices of similar properties that have sold in the current market. For example, a comparable property that is producing an

annual net income of $15,000 is sold for $187,500. The capitalization rate is $15,000 divided by $187,500, or 8%. If other comparable properties sold at prices that yielded substantially the same rate, it may be concluded that 8% is the rate that the appraiser should apply to the subject property.

5. Apply the capitalization rate to the property's annual net operating income to arrive at the estimate of the property's value.

FIGURE 16.5: Income Capitalization Approach to Value

Potential gross annual income		$60,000
Market rent (100% capacity)		
Income from other sources (vending machines and pay phones)	+600	
	$60,600	
Less vacancy and collection losses (estimated) @ 4%		–2,424
Effective gross income		$58,176
Expenses:		
Real estate taxes	$9,000	
Insurance	1,000	
Heat	2,500	
Maintenance	6,400	
Utilities, electricity, water, gas	800	
Repairs	1,200	
Decorating	1,400	
Replacement of equipment	800	
Legal and accounting	600	
Advertising	300	
Management	3,000	
Total		$27,000
Annual net operating income		$31,176

Capitalization rate = 10% (overall rate)
Capitalization of annual net income: $31,176 ÷ 0.10 = $311,760
Market value by income approach = $311,760

With the appropriate capitalization rate and accurate projected annual net operating income, the appraiser can obtain an estimate of value by applying the income approach.

This formula and its variations are important in dealing with income property:

Income ÷ rate = value
Income ÷ value = rate
Value × rate = income

For example:

Net operating income ÷ capitalization rate = value
$18,000 income ÷ 9% cap rate = $200,000 value or
$18,000 income ÷ 8% cap rate = $225,000 value

Note the relationship between the rate and the value. As the rate goes down, the value increases.

Gross Rent or Gross Income Multipliers If a buyer is interested in purchasing a one- to four-unit residential rental property, the **gross rent multiplier (GRM)** based on monthly rental income could be used for a rough approximation of value. If the buyer is interested in purchasing five or more units, a **gross income multiplier (GIM)** based on annual income could be used.

The formulas are as follows:

- For a property with one to four residential units that has no income from other sources:
  Sales price ÷ monthly gross rent = gross rent multiplier (GRM)
- For a property with five or more units and commercial properties with income from a variety of sources:
  Sales price ÷ annual gross income = gross income multiplier (GIM)

For example, if a home recently sold for $155,000 and its monthly rental income was $1,250, the GRM for the property would be

$155,000 ÷ $1,250 = 124 GRM

If a commercial property recently sold for $155,000 and its annual rental income was $15,000, the GIM for the property would be

$155,000 ÷ $15000 = 10.33 GIM

To establish an accurate GRM, an appraiser must have recent sales and rental data from at least four properties that are similar to the subject property. The resulting GRM can then be applied to the estimated fair market rental of the subject property to arrive at its market value. The formula would be as follows:

Rental income × GRM = Estimated market value

Figure 16.6 shows some examples of GRM comparisons.

Reconciliation

When the three approaches to value are applied to the same property, they normally produce three separate indications of value. (Compare Figure 16.3 with Figure 16.4.) **Reconciliation** is the act of analyzing and effectively weighing the findings from the three approaches. In reconciliation, an appraiser explains not only the appropriateness of each approach but also the relative reliability of the data within each approach in line with the type of value sought. The appraiser should also explain how the data reflect the current market.

FIGURE 16.6: Gross Rent Multiplier

Comparable No.	Sales Price	Monthly Rent	GRM
1	$280,000	$1,800	155.56
2	243,000	1,350	180.00
3	287,000	2,000	143.50
4	262,500	1,675	156.72
Subject	?	1,750	?

Note: Based on an analysis of these comparisons, comparables 1 and 3 show extremes. Based on monthly rent between comparables 1 and 4, a GRM of 156.72 seems reasonable for homes in this area. In the opinion of an appraiser, the estimated value of the subject property would be $1,750 × 156.72, or $274,260.

The process of reconciliation is not simply taking the average of the three estimates of value. An average implies that the data and logic applied in each of the approaches are equally valid and reliable and should, therefore, be given equal weight. In fact, however, certain approaches are more valid and reliable with some kinds of properties than with others.

For example, in appraising a home, the income approach is rarely valid, and the cost approach is of limited value unless the home is relatively new. Therefore, the sales comparison approach is usually given greatest weight in valuing single-family residences. In the appraisal of income or investment property, the income approach normally is given the greatest weight. In the appraisal of churches, libraries, museums, schools, and other special-use properties, where little or no income or sales revenue is generated, the cost approach usually is assigned the greatest weight. From this analysis, or reconciliation, a single opinion of market value is produced.

KEY POINT REVIEW

An **appraisal** provides the appraiser's opinion of **value** based on supportable evidence and appraisal methods, as defined by the ***Uniform Standards of Professional Appraisal Practice (USPAP)*** established by the Appraisal Foundation's **Appraisal Standards Board**.

An **appraiser** must be state-licensed or certified for an appraisal performed as part of a **federally related transaction**. The **Appraiser Qualifications Board** sets minimum education and experience requirements for licensing or certification and the **Appraisal Practices Board** recommends acceptable business practices.

The **Uniform Residential Appraisal Report (URAR)** is required by Fannie Mae and Freddie Mac.

A **comparative market analysis (CMA)** is a report by a real estate professional of market statistics, but it is not an appraisal.

A **broker's price opinion (BPO)** may be used in a nonfederally related transaction: home equity lines, refinancing, portfolio management, loss mitigation, and collections.

Value is created by **demand**, **utility**, **scarcity**, and **transferability** of property (DUST). **Market value** is the most probable price that property should bring in a fair sale, but not necessarily the same as the **price** asked or paid or the **cost** to construct.

The basic principles of value include **anticipation** of certain events, **change** that can be physical or economic, **competition** for clients and customers, **conformity** of properties in a neighborhood, and **contribution** to a property's value of any individual improvement. A property's **highest and best use** is the use that is physically possible, legally permitted, economically or financially feasible, and the most profitable or maximally productive. The **law of increasing and diminishing returns** is in evidence when additional property improvements no longer bring a comparable increase in property value.

Plottage is the increase in value that can result when two or more parcels of land are combined in the process called **assemblage**. The principle of **progression** is in evidence when a property's value is enhanced because of more valuable properties in the vicinity; the opposite is true and the principle of **regression** is in effect when a property's value is lower because of less valuable properties in the vicinity.

The principle of **substitution** is the foundation of the sales comparison approach. A buyer will not want to pay more for a property than it would cost to purchase an equally desirable and suitable property. The principle of **supply and demand** dictates that prices will rise when demand is high relative to supply, and prices will fall when supply is high relative to demand.

The **sales comparison approach (market data approach)** makes use of sales of properties comparable to the property that is the subject of the appraisal by adding or subtracting from the sales price of each comp the value of a feature present or absent in the subject property versus the comparable.

The **cost approach** uses the current **cost** of constructing building and other property improvements and an estimate of **accrued depreciation** using the **straight-line method (economic age-life method)**, or an estimate of individual items of **physical deterioration, functional obsolescence**, or **external obsolescence**.

The **income approach** is based on the present value of the right to future income arrived at by these steps:

1. Estimating annual potential **gross income**
2. Deducting an allowance for **vacancy and rent loss** to find **effective gross income**
3. Deducting **annual operating expenses** to find **net operating income (NOI)**
4. Estimating the **rate of return (capitalization rate** or **cap rate)** for the subject by analyzing cap rates of similar properties
5. Deriving an estimate of the subject's market value by applying the cap rate to the property's annual NOI using this formula: **net operating income ÷ capitalization rate = value**

Reconciliation is the process by which the validity and reliability of the results of the approaches to value are weighed objectively to determine the appraiser's final opinion of value.

UNIT 16 QUIZ

1. Which appraisal method uses a rate of investment return?
   a. Sales comparison approach
   b. Cost approach
   c. Income approach
   d. Gross income multiplier method
2. The characteristics of value include which of the following?
   a. Competition
   b. Scarcity
   c. Anticipation
   d. Balance
3. There are two vacant adjacent lots, each worth approximately $50,000. If their owner sells them as a single lot, however, the combined parcel will be worth $120,000. What principle does this illustrate?
   a. Substitution
   b. Plottage
   c. Regression
   d. Progression
4. The amount of money a property is likely to command in the marketplace is its
   a. intrinsic value.
   b. market price.
   c. subjective value.
   d. book value.
5. A homeowner constructs a five-bedroom brick house with an indoor pool in a neighborhood of modest two-bedroom and three-bedroom frame houses on narrow lots. The value of this house is *MOST* likely to be affected by what principle?
   a. Progression
   b. Assemblage
   c. Change
   d. Regression
6. The owners of a modest ranch house in a neighborhood of larger, more expensive homes may find that the value of their home is affected by what principle?
   a. Progression
   b. Increasing returns
   c. Competition
   d. Regression
7. For appraisal purposes, accrued depreciation is *NOT* caused by
   a. functional obsolescence.
   b. physical deterioration.
   c. external obsolescence.
   d. accelerated depreciation.
8. The term *reconciliation* refers to which of the following?
   a. Loss of value due to any cause
   b. Separating the value of the land from the total value of the property to compute depreciation
   c. Analyzing the results obtained by the different approaches to value to form an opinion of value
   d. The process by which an appraiser determines the highest and best use for a parcel of land
9. If a property's annual net income is $24,000 and it is valued at $300,000, what is its capitalization rate?
   a. 8%
   b. 10.5%
   c. 12%
   d. 15%
10. Which of the following is *NOT* used by an appraiser applying the income approach to value?
    a. Annual net operating income
    b. Capitalization rate
    c. Accrued depreciation
    d. Annual gross income

11. An appraiser asked for an opinion of the value of an existing shopping center would probably give the *MOST* weight to which approach to value?

a. Cost approach
b. Sales comparison approach
c. Income approach
d. Index method

12. The market value of a parcel of real estate is

a. an estimate of its future benefits.
b. the amount of money paid for the property.
c. an estimate of the most probable price it should bring.
d. its value without improvements.

13. Capitalization is the process by which annual net operating income is used to

a. determine cost.
b. estimate value.
c. establish depreciation.
d. determine potential tax value.

14. From the reproduction or replacement cost of a building, the appraiser deducts depreciation, which represents

a. the remaining economic life of the building.
b. remodeling costs to increase rentals.
c. loss of value due to any reason.
d. costs to modernize the building.

15. All of the following factors would be important in comparing properties under the sales comparison approach to value *EXCEPT*

a. differences in dates of sale.
b. differences in financing terms.
c. differences in appearance and condition.
d. differences in original cost.

16. A building was purchased new five years ago for $240,000. It currently has an estimated remaining useful life of 55 years. What is the property's total depreciation to date for appraisal purposes?

a. $14,364
b. $20,000
c. $48,000
d. $54,000

17. A building was purchased new five years ago for $240,000. It currently has an estimated remaining useful life of 55 years. What is the current market value of the building if its construction cost has not increased?

a. $235,636
b. $220,000
c. $192,000
d. $186,000

18. The appraised value of a residence with four bedrooms and one bathroom would probably be reduced because of

a. external obsolescence.
b. functional obsolescence.
c. curable physical deterioration.
d. incurable physical deterioration.

19. Which principle of value indicates that a developer's very profitable real estate project will attract others to engage in similar activity in the same area and thus drive down profits?

a. Anticipation
b. Competition
c. Value
d. Progression

20. Change, contribution, plottage, and substitution are some of the basic principles that affect what aspect of real estate?

a. Demand
b. Depreciation
c. Value
d. Supply

Closing the Real Estate Transaction

■ **LEARNING OBJECTIVES** *When you have finished reading this unit, you will be able to*

- **describe** the specific steps and processes involved in order to achieve conveyance of clear and marketable title, including compliance with all applicable laws;
- **describe** the closing procedures and the respective roles of all parties;
- **explain** the provisions of the Real Estate Settlement Procedures Act (RESPA) and the Mortgage Disclosure Improvement Act (MDIA);
- **describe and explain** all buyer and seller charges and credits contained in the closing statement;
- **explain** the financial entries and mathematical calculations contained in the closing statement;
- **review** and confirm the accuracy of a closing statement; and
- **define** the following *key terms:*

accrued items
affiliated business arrangement (ABA)
closing
Closing Disclosure
closing statement
credit
debit
escrow accounts
escrow closing
impound accounts
Loan Estimate
Mortgage Disclosure Improvement Act (MDIA)
mortgage servicing transfer statement
prepaid items
prorations
Real Estate Settlement Procedures Act (RESPA)
survey

OVERVIEW

The conclusion of the real estate transaction is the **closing**, when title to the real estate is transferred in exchange for payment of the purchase price. Until closing preparations begin, a real estate professional's relationship is primarily with the buyer or the seller. During the closing period, new players come on the scene: appraisers, inspectors, loan officers, insurance agents, and lawyers. Negotiations may continue, sometimes right up until the property is finally transferred. A thorough knowledge of the closing process is the best defense against the risk of a transaction failing.

PRECLOSING PROCEDURES

Closing is the point at which ownership of a property is transferred in exchange for the payment of the purchase price.

Closing involves two major events. First, the promises made in the sales contract are fulfilled; second, the mortgage funds are distributed to the buyer. Before the property changes hands, however, each party—buyer and seller—usually will have specific concerns that must be addressed. As emphasized previously, the closing process is based on the provisions of the sales contract, making it important that the parties treat the negotiation for the purchase of the property—the process of offer and accept—very seriously.

Many real estate professionals maintain a list of events that must take place prior to the actual closing in order to avoid surprises that might lead to delays.

Buyer's Issues

Both the buyer and the buyer's lender must be sure that the seller can deliver the title that was promised in the purchase agreement and that the property is now in essentially the same condition it was in when the buyer and the seller agreed to the sale. This involves examination of

- the results of any inspections, such as termite or structural inspections, or required repairs;
- the survey;
- the title evidence, including the seller's deed and any documents demonstrating the removal of undesired liens and encumbrances; and
- any lease, if a tenant resides on the premises.

Final Property Inspection In the real estate contract, the buyer usually reserves the right to make a *final inspection*, often called a *walk-through*, shortly before the closing takes place. The buyer, accompanied by the real estate professional, verifies that necessary repairs have been made, that the property has been well maintained, that all fixtures are in place, and that no unauthorized removal or alteration of any part of the improvements has taken place. It is not a time to reopen negotiations, but to verify that the condition of the property is in compliance with the terms of the contract. *See* Figure 17.1.

FIGURE 17.1: For Your Protection, Get a Home Inspection

CAUTION

U.S. Department of Housing
and Urban Development
Federal Housing Administration (FHA)

OMB Approval No: 2502-0538
(exp. 07/31/2009)

For Your Protection: Get a Home Inspection

Why a Buyer Needs a Home Inspection

A home inspection gives the buyer more detailed information about the overall condition of the home prior to purchase. In a home inspection, a qualified inspector takes an in-depth, unbiased look at your potential new home to:

- Evaluate the physical condition: structure, construction, and mechanical systems;
- Identify items that need to be repaired or replaced; and
- Estimate the remaining useful life of the major systems, equipment, structure, and finishes.

Appraisals are Different from Home Inspections

An appraisal is different from a home inspection. Appraisals are for lenders; home inspections are for buyers. An appraisal is required to:

- Estimate the market value of a house;
- Make sure that the house meets FHA minimum property standards/requirements; and
- Make sure that the property is marketable.

FHA Does Not Guarantee the Value or Condition of your Potential New Home

If you find problems with your new home after closing, FHA can not give or lend you money for repairs, and FHA can not buy the home back from you. That is why it is so important for you, the buyer, to get an independent home inspection. Ask a qualified home inspector to inspect your potential new home and give you the information you need to make a wise decision.

Radon Gas Testing

The United States Environmental Protection Agency and the Surgeon General of the United States have recommended that all houses should be tested for radon. For more information on radon testing, call the toll-free National Radon Information Line at 1-800-SOS-Radon or 1-800-767-7236. As with a home inspection, if you decide to test for radon, you may do so before signing your contract, or you may do so after signing the contract as long as your contract states the sale of the home depends on your satisfaction with the results of the radon test.

Be an Informed Buyer

It is your responsibility to be an informed buyer. Be sure that what you buy is satisfactory in every respect. You have the right to carefully examine your potential new home with a qualified home inspector. You may arrange to do so before signing your contract, or may do so after signing the contract as long as your contract states that the sale of the home depends on the inspection.

HUD-92564-CN (6/06)

CAUTION

Survey A **survey** provides information about the exact location and size of the property. Typically, the survey indicates the location of all buildings, driveways, fences, and other improvements located on the premises. The survey should also indicate any existing easements and encroachments. The cost of the survey is negotiated in the sales contract. The survey is important in verifying the legal description of the property.

IN PRACTICE Relying on an old survey is not a good idea; the property should be resurveyed prior to closing, even in the rare instance that it is not required by the title company or lender. A current survey confirms that the property purchased is exactly what the buyer wants and that no encroachments have arisen since the last transfer of title.

The *title* or *opinion of title* discloses all liens, encumbrances, easements, conditions, and restrictions on the property.

Title Evidence The buyer and the buyer's lender will require that the seller's title comply with the terms of the real estate contract. Although practices vary from state to state, most require that the seller produce a current abstract of title or title commitment from a title insurance company. When an abstract of title is used, the purchaser's attorney examines it and issues an opinion of title. The attorney's opinion of title is a statement of the quality of the seller's title, and it lists all liens, encumbrances, easements, conditions, and restrictions that appear in the record and to which the seller's title is subject. The attorney's opinion is not a guarantee of title. You previously learned about how ownership is proven and the importance of examining the chain of title for various defects.

When the purchaser pays cash or obtains a new loan to purchase the property, the seller's existing loan is paid in full and satisfied on the record. The exact amount required to pay the existing loan is provided in a current *payoff statement* from the lender, effective the date of closing. The payoff statement notes the unpaid amount of principal, the interest due through the date of the proposed payment, the fee for issuing the certificate of satisfaction or *release deed*, credits to the seller (if any) for tax and insurance reserves, and the amount of any prepayment penalty. The same procedure is followed for any other liens, such as a second mortgage or home equity loan, that must be released before the buyer takes title.

If the buyer assumes the seller's existing mortgage loan, the buyer needs to know the exact balance of the loan as of the closing date. Usually, the lender is required to provide the buyer with a mortgage reduction certificate, which certifies the amount owed on the mortgage loan, the interest rate, and the date and amount of the last interest payment.

The closing agent examines the title commitment or the abstract that was issued several days or weeks before the closing. Because liens may have been filed during the interval, two searches of the public record are often made. The first search shows the status of the seller's title on that date. The second search, known as a *bring down*, is made after the closing and before any new documents are filed.

As part of the later search, the seller may be required to execute an *affidavit of title*, a sworn statement in which the seller assures the title insurance company (and the buyer) that no other defects in the title have occurred since the date of the title examination (e.g., judgments, bankruptcies, divorce, unrecorded deeds or contracts, unpaid repairs or improvements that might lead to mechanics' liens). The affidavit gives the title insurance company a basis on which to sue the seller should the statements in the affidavit be incorrect.

In areas in which real estate sales transactions are customarily closed through an escrow, the escrow instructions usually provide for an extended coverage policy to be issued to the buyer effective the date of closing. The seller then has no need to execute an affidavit of title.

IN PRACTICE Real estate professionals often assist in preclosing arrangements as part of their service to customers. In some states, real estate professionals are required to advise the parties of the approximate expenses involved in closing when a real estate sales contract is signed. In other states, real estate professionals have a statutory duty to coordinate and supervise closing activities. Aside from state laws on this issue, a real estate professionals without a specific role in the closing may still be the person with the greatest knowledge of the details of the transaction. Because of this, many real estate professionals feel it is part of their fiduciary duty to be present at a face-to-face closing.

Seller's Issues

Obviously, the seller's main interest is to receive payment for the property, so the seller will want assurance that the buyer has obtained the necessary financing and will have sufficient funds to complete the sale. In turn, the seller should review the purchase agreement to ensure that she has completed the required tasks. Unless the seller owns the property free and clear of any mortgage debt, there must also be a payoff statement from the seller's lender(s), noting the amount owed that will be paid out of the sale proceeds. Both parties, along with their attorneys or real estate professionals, will want to inspect the disclosure statement made prior to closing to make sure that all monies involved in the transaction have been accounted for properly.

Real Estate Professional's Role at Closing

Depending on local practice, the real estate professional's role at closing can vary from simply collecting the commission to conducting the proceedings. In the states that require an attorney's participation, a real estate professional's responsibility is essentially finished as soon as the real estate contract is signed. Even so, most real estate professionals continue to be involved all the way through closing on behalf of their clients because it is also in a real estate professional's best interest that the transaction moves successfully and smoothly to a conclusion. This may mean actively arranging for title evidence, surveys, appraisals, and inspections or repairs related to structural conditions, water supplies, sewerage facilities, or toxic substances.

Although real estate professionals do not always conduct closing proceedings, they usually attend. Often, the parties look to their real estate professionals for guidance, assistance, and information during what can be a stressful experience. Real estate professionals must be thoroughly familiar with the procedures involved in preparing the disclosure statement provided prior to closing, including the proration of costs involved in closing the transaction, which will be discussed later.

IN PRACTICE Even in a state that does not require an attorney at closing, the real estate professional should never discourage the seller's or the buyer's use of an attorney, before and/or at closing. The real estate professional can, however, provide guidance on the importance of selecting a competent, experienced real estate attorney. The attorney must be knowledgeable about real estate documents and closing practices in order for the transaction to close smoothly.

Lender's Interest in Closing

Whether a buyer obtains new financing or assumes the seller's existing loan, the lender wants to protect its security interest in the property and ensure that its mortgage lien has priority over other liens. The lender may require a survey, a pest control or another inspection report, or a certificate of occupancy (for a newly constructed building). In order to ensure that the buyer takes good and marketable title at closing, lenders generally require that the buyer obtain a mortgagee's title insurance policy.

The buyer must also provide a fire and hazard insurance policy (along with a receipt for the premium). Usually, the homeowners insurance policy the buyer purchases combines the required hazard insurance on the structure, as well as insurance on the buyer's personal property.

The lender typically will request that a reserve account be established for tax and insurance payments so that the buyer sets aside funds for these large expenses of homeownership. The lender may even require representation by its own attorney at closing.

Internal Revenue Service Reporting Requirements

Certain real estate closings must be reported to the Internal Revenue Service (IRS) on Form 1099-S. The affected properties include a sale or exchange of

- land (improved or unimproved), including air space;
- an inherently permanent structure, including any residential, commercial, or industrial building;
- a condominium unit and its appurtenant fixtures and common elements (including land); or
- shares in a cooperative housing corporation.

Information to be reported includes the sales price, the amount of property tax reimbursement credited to the seller, and the seller's Social Security number. If the closing agent does not notify the IRS, the responsibility for filing the form falls on the mortgage lender, although the real estate professionals or the parties to the transaction ultimately could be held liable.

CONDUCTING THE CLOSING

Closing is known by different names in different areas. In some areas, for instance, closing is called *settlement and transfer*. The closing process also takes different forms, depending on state law, local custom, or the convenience of the parties. In some parts of the country, the parties to a transaction sit around a table and exchange copies of documents as they are executed, a process known as *passing papers*. ("We passed papers on the new house Wednesday morning.") In other regions, the buyer and the seller never meet; the paperwork is handled by an escrow agent in a process known as *closing escrow*. ("We'll close escrow on our house next week.") The main concerns are always that the buyer receive marketable title and the seller receive the purchase price.

Face-to-Face Closing

In a *face-to-face closing*, the parties may meet for the first time.

A face-to-face closing may be held at the office of the title company, the lending institution, an attorney for one of the parties, the real estate professional, the county recorder, or the escrow company. In many cases, this is the first and only time the buyer and the seller will meet. Those attending a closing may include

- the buyer;
- the seller;
- the real estate professionals (both the buyer's and the seller's representatives);
- the seller's and the buyer's attorneys;
- a representative of the lending institution involved with the buyer's new mortgage loan, the buyer's assumption of the seller's existing loan, or the seller's payoff of an existing loan; and
- a representative of the title insurance company.

Closing Agent or Closing Officer The closing agent may be a representative of the title company or lender, the real estate professional representing one of the parties, or the buyer's or the seller's attorney. Some title companies and law firms employ paralegal assistants who conduct closings for their firms.

The closing agent orders and reviews the title insurance policy or title certificate, survey, property insurance policy, and other items. After the sales contract is reviewed, the disclosure statement that indicates the division of income and expenses between the parties is prepared. Finally, the time and place of closing is arranged.

The Exchange The exchange is made when the parties are satisfied that everything is in order. After the buyer and the seller have signed all the necessary paperwork, the seller delivers the signed deed to the buyer, who accepts it. All pertinent documents are then recorded in the correct order to ensure continuity of title. For instance, if the seller pays off an existing loan and the buyer obtains a new loan, the seller's satisfaction of mortgage must be recorded before the seller's deed to the buyer. Because the buyer cannot pledge the property as security for the new loan until ownership has been transferred, the buyer's new mortgage or deed of trust is recorded only after the seller's deed to the buyer is recorded.

IN PRACTICE A face-to-face or roundtable closing can be challenging and may not be the best approach to use if there has been friction between buyer and seller leading up to the closing. In addition, there may be a confidentiality or privacy concern in having all parties present to hear all discussions, questions asked, or concerns raised. Having the closing agent ferry documents between separate rooms in which each of the parties and their representatives are sequestered may be the best way to avoid any risk of conflict at such a stressful moment.

Closing in Escrow

In an *escrow closing*, a third party coordinates the closing activities on behalf of the buyer and the seller.

In an **escrow closing**, a disinterested third party is authorized to act as *escrow agent*, or *escrow holder*, and coordinate the closing activities. The selection of the escrow agent is determined by negotiation, custom, or state law. The escrow agent may be an attorney, a title company, a trust company, an escrow company, or the escrow department of a lending institution. Although a few states do not permit certain transactions to be closed in escrow, escrow closings are used to some extent in most states.

Escrow Procedure After the sales contract is signed, the buyer and seller execute escrow instructions to the escrow agent. Once the escrow instructions are received by the escrow agent, they can be changed only at the written direction of both buyer and seller. The real estate professional who is holding the earnest money turns it over to the escrow agent, who deposits it in a special trust, or escrow, account.

The buyer and the seller deposit all pertinent documents and other items with the escrow agent before the specified date of closing.

The seller deposits

- the deed conveying the property to the buyer;
- title evidence (abstract and attorney's opinion of title, certificate of title, title insurance, or Torrens certificate);
- existing hazard insurance policies;
- a letter or mortgage reduction certificate from the lender stating the exact principal remaining (if the buyer is assuming the seller's loan);
- affidavits of title (if required);
- a payoff statement (if the seller's loan is to be paid off); and
- other instruments or documents necessary to clear the title or to complete the transaction.

The buyer deposits

- the balance of the cash needed to complete the purchase, usually in the form of a certified check;
- loan documents (if the buyer secures a new loan);
- proof of hazard insurance, including (where required) flood insurance; and
- other necessary documents, such as inspection reports required by the lender.

The escrow agent has the authority to examine the title evidence. When marketable title is shown in the name of the buyer, all other conditions of the escrow agreement have been met, and the parties have received the disclosure statement, the agent is authorized to disburse the purchase price to the seller, minus all charges and expenses. The agent then records the deed and, if a new loan has been obtained by the buyer, the mortgage or deed of trust.

If the escrow agent's examination of the title discloses liens, a portion of the purchase price can be withheld from the seller. The withheld portion is used to pay the liens to clear the title.

If the seller cannot clear the title, or if for any reason the sale cannot be consummated, the escrow instructions usually provide that the parties be returned to their former status, as if no sale occurred. The escrow agent returns the documents of title to the seller and returns the purchase money to the buyer.

LEGISLATION RELATED TO CLOSING

The **Real Estate Settlement Procedures Act (RESPA)** is a federal law that requires certain disclosures about the mortgage and settlement process and prohibits certain practices that increase the cost of settlement services, such as kickbacks and referral fees. The **Mortgage Disclosure Improvement Act (MDIA)** has changed how buyers, sellers, lenders, mortgage brokers, title agents, and real estate professionals prepare for a closing. The Consumer Financial Protection Bureau (CFPB) issued the TILA-RESPA Integrated Disclosure rule (TRID) to implement provisions of the Dodd-Frank Act intended to combine and clarify financing disclosures to consumers. This rule applies to transactions originating on or after October 3, 2015.

Real Estate Settlement Procedures Act (RESPA)

RESPA regulations apply to a first-lien residential mortgage loan made to finance the purchase of a one- to four-family home, cooperative, or condominium, for either investment or occupancy, as well as second or subordinate liens for home equity loans when a purchase is financed by a federally related mortgage loan. A federally related loan is one made by a bank, savings association, or other lender whose deposits are insured by a federal agency; a loan insured by the FHA or guaranteed by the VA; a loan administered by HUD; and a loan intended to be sold by the lender to Fannie Mae, Ginnie Mae, or Freddie Mac. RESPA is administered by HUD.

RESPA does not apply to the following:

- Loans on large properties (i.e., more than 25 acres)
- Loans for business or agricultural purposes
- Construction loans or other temporary financing
- Vacant land (unless a dwelling will be placed on the property within two years)
- A transaction financed solely by a purchase-money mortgage taken back by the seller
- An installment contract (contract for deed)
- A buyer's assumption of a seller's existing loan—but if the terms of the assumed loan are modified, or if the lender charges more than $50 for the assumption, the transaction is subject to RESPA regulations

RESPA prohibits certain practices that increase the cost of settlement services:

- Section 8 prohibits kickbacks and fee-splitting for referrals of settlement services, and unearned fees for services not actually performed. Violators are subject to criminal and civil penalties, including a fine up to $10,000 and/or imprisonment up to one year. The consumer may privately pursue a violator in court; the violator may be liable for an amount up to three times the amount of the charge paid for the service.
- Section 9 prohibits the home seller from requiring that the buyer purchase title insurance from a particular company. The buyer may sue the seller for such a violation; the violator is liable for up to three times the amount paid for the title insurance.
- Section 10 prohibits the lender from requiring excessive escrow account deposits for such items as taxes and hazard insurance.

Affiliated Business Arrangement (ABA) To streamline the settlement process, a real estate firm, title insurance company, mortgage broker, home inspection company, or even a moving company may agree to offer a package of services to consumers, a system known as an **affiliated business arrangement** (ABA). RESPA permits an ABA between a real estate brokerage and a mortgage company or other settlement service provider when

- there is a 1% or more common ownership between the companies, as long as the consumer is clearly informed of the relationship among the service providers,
- participation is not required,
- other providers are available, and
- the only thing of value received from the arrangement, in addition to permitted payments for services provided, is a return on the ownership interest.

Fees must be reasonably related to the value of the services provided and must not be fees exchanged among the affiliated companies simply for referring business to one another.

Other RESPA Requirements RESPA prohibits the lender from requiring the borrower to deposit funds in an escrow account for taxes and insurance that exceed certain limits, thus preventing the lender from taking advantage of the borrower. While RESPA does not require that an escrow account be set up, certain government loan programs and some lenders require that an escrow account be established as a condition of a loan. RESPA places limits on the amount that a lender may require: on a monthly basis, the lender may require only one-twelfth of the total of the disbursements for the year, plus an amount necessary to cover a shortage in the account. No more than one-sixth of the year's total disbursements may be held as a cushion (a cushion is not required). Once a year, the lender must perform an escrow account analysis and return any amount over $50 to the borrower.

A **mortgage servicing transfer statement** is required if the lender intends to sell or assign the right to service the loan to another loan servicer. The loan servicer must notify the borrower 15 days before the effective date of the loan transfer, including in the notice the name and address of the new servicer, toll-free telephone numbers, and the date the new servicer will begin accepting payments. If the borrower makes a timely payment to the old servicer within 60 days of the loan transfer, the borrower cannot be penalized.

TILA-RESPA Integrated Disclosure Rule

The **TILA-RESPA Integrated Disclosure rule** (also called the "Know Before You Owe" mortgage disclosure rule or TRID) replaces the four previous disclosure forms with two new forms: the Loan Estimate and the Closing Disclosure. The Consumer Financial Protection Bureau (CFPB) prepared these forms to make it easier for consumers to understand the costs involved in closing. The new forms are required for transactions originating on or after October 3, 2015. The forms apply to most consumer mortgage transactions, but not to home equity lines of credit, reverse mortgages, or mortgages secured by a mobile home or a dwelling that is not attached to land. The forms also do not apply to a creditor who makes five or fewer mortgages in a year. Although the burden of implementing these reforms is the responsibility of the lender, real estate professionals should be aware of current requirements because failure to meet the standards can and will delay closings.

Loan Estimate Form The **Loan Estimate** form replaces the initial Truth in Lending statement (TIL) and the Good Faith Estimate (GFE). This form highlights the information that historically has been the most important to consumers. Interest rate, monthly payment, and total closing costs are clearly presented on the first page. The Loan Estimate form must be provided to the consumer three business days after a loan application is submitted to the lender. The Loan Estimate must contain the exact language specified by the CFPB, making it easier for borrowers to compare loan conditions from one lender to another.

The only fee that the lender may collect before the loan applicant receives the Loan Estimate is the fee for a credit report. Once the Loan Estimate is issued, the lender is committed to making the loan on the indicated terms and may only modify the Loan Estimate in certain specific instances. If certain information or circumstances change after the original Loan Estimate is issued, a new Loan Estimate must be issued.

Some closing costs or fees may or may not change prior to settlement.

The fees are divided into three categories:

- No tolerance—fees that may not increase before closing: lender charges for taking, underwriting, and processing the loan application, including points, origination fee, and yield spread premium
- 10% tolerance—fees that cannot increase by more than 10% in any given category: settlement services for which the lender selects the provider or for which the borrower selects the provider from the lender's list, title services and title insurance if the lender selects the provider, and recording fees
- Unlimited tolerance—fees for services that are out of the lender's control: services for which the borrower chooses the provider (such as escrow and title insurance), impounds for taxes, mortgage interest, and the cost of homeowners insurance

The last page of the Loan Estimate is a summary of the loan terms that the consumer can use to compare different loans and terms to aid in price shopping. The lender is responsible for the accuracy of the Loan Estimate as well as the actual costs that the lender charges, which are shown on the Closing Disclosure form.

http://www.consumerfinance.gov/regulatory-implementation/tila-respa/

The new form is shown in Figure 17.2. Additional sample forms can be found at http://www.consumerfinance.gov/regulatory-implementation/tila-respa/.

FIGURE 17.2: Loan Estimate

Save this Loan Estimate to compare with your Closing Disclosure.

Loan Estimate

DATE ISSUED
APPLICANTS

PROPERTY
SALE PRICE

LOAN TERM
PURPOSE
PRODUCT
LOAN TYPE ☐ Conventional ☐ FHA ☐ VA ☐ ____________
LOAN ID #
RATE LOCK ☐ NO ☐ YES, until
Before closing, your interest rate, points, and lender credits can change unless you lock the interest rate. All other estimated closing costs expire on

Loan Terms

Loan Terms	Can this amount increase after closing?
Loan Amount	
Interest Rate	
Monthly Principal & Interest *See Projected Payments below for your Estimated Total Monthly Payment*	
	Does the loan have these features?
Prepayment Penalty	
Balloon Payment	

Projected Payments

Payment Calculation	
Principal & Interest Mortgage Insurance Estimated Escrow *Amount can increase over time*	
Estimated Total Monthly Payment	
Estimated Taxes, Insurance & Assessments *Amount can increase over time*	**This estimate includes** **In escrow?** ☐ Property Taxes ☐ Homeowner's Insurance ☐ Other: *See Section G on page 2 for escrowed property costs. You must pay for other property costs separately.*

Costs at Closing

Estimated Closing Costs	Includes in Loan Costs + in Other Costs – in Lender Credits. *See page 2 for details.*
Estimated Cash to Close	Includes Closing Costs. *See Calculating Cash to Close on page 2 for details.*

Visit **www.consumerfinance.gov/mortgage-estimate** for general information and tools.

LOAN ESTIMATE PAGE 1 OF 3 • LOAN ID #

FIGURE 17.2: Loan Estimate (continued)

Closing Cost Details

Loan Costs

A. Origination Charges

% of Loan Amount (Points)

B. Services You Cannot Shop For

C. Services You Can Shop For

D. TOTAL LOAN COSTS (A + B + C)

Other Costs

E. Taxes and Other Government Fees

Recording Fees and Other Taxes
Transfer Taxes

F. Prepaids

Homeowner's Insurance Premium (months)
Mortgage Insurance Premium (months)
Prepaid Interest (per day for days @)
Property Taxes (months)

G. Initial Escrow Payment at Closing

Homeowner's Insurance per month for mo.
Mortgage Insurance per month for mo.
Property Taxes per month for mo.

H. Other

I. TOTAL OTHER COSTS (E + F + G + H)

J. TOTAL CLOSING COSTS

D + I
Lender Credits

Calculating Cash to Close

Calculating Cash to Close	
Total Closing Costs (J)	
Closing Costs Financed (Paid from your Loan Amount)	
Down Payment/Funds from Borrower	
Deposit	
Funds for Borrower	
Seller Credits	
Adjustments and Other Credits	
Estimated Cash to Close	

Adjustable Payment (AP) Table

Adjustable Payment (AP) Table	
Interest Only Payments?	
Optional Payments?	
Step Payments?	
Seasonal Payments?	
Monthly Principal and Interest Payments	
First Change/Amount	
Subsequent Changes	
Maximum Payment	

Adjustable Interest Rate (AIR) Table

Adjustable Interest Rate (AIR) Table	
Index + Margin	
Initial Interest Rate	
Minimum/Maximum Interest Rate	
Change Frequency	
First Change	
Subsequent Changes	
Limits on Interest Rate Changes	
First Change	
Subsequent Changes	

LOAN ESTIMATE PAGE 2 OF 3 • LOAN ID #

FIGURE 17.2: Loan Estimate (continued)

Additional Information About This Loan

LENDER
NMLS/___ LICENSE ID
LOAN OFFICER
NMLS/___ LICENSE ID
EMAIL
PHONE

MORTGAGE BROKER
NMLS/___ LICENSE ID
LOAN OFFICER
NMLS/___ LICENSE ID
EMAIL
PHONE

Comparisons	Use these measures to compare this loan with other loans.
In 5 Years	Total you will have paid in principal, interest, mortgage insurance, and loan costs. Principal you will have paid off.
Annual Percentage Rate (APR)	Your costs over the loan term expressed as a rate. This is not your interest rate.
Total Interest Percentage (TIP)	The total amount of interest that you will pay over the loan term as a percentage of your loan amount.

Other Considerations

Appraisal We may order an appraisal to determine the property's value and charge you for this appraisal. We will promptly give you a copy of any appraisal, even if your loan does not close. You can pay for an additional appraisal for your own use at your own cost.

Assumption If you sell or transfer this property to another person, we
☐ will allow, under certain conditions, this person to assume this loan on the original terms.
☐ will not allow assumption of this loan on the original terms.

Homeowner's Insurance This loan requires homeowner's insurance on the property, which you may obtain from a company of your choice that we find acceptable.

Late Payment If your payment is more than ___ days late, we will charge a late fee of ______________

Refinance Refinancing this loan will depend on your future financial situation, the property value, and market conditions. You may not be able to refinance this loan.

Servicing We intend
☐ to service your loan. If so, you will make your payments to us.
☐ to transfer servicing of your loan.

Confirm Receipt

By signing, you are only confirming that you have received this form. You do not have to accept this loan because you have signed or received this form.

Applicant Signature   Date   Co-Applicant Signature   Date

LOAN ESTIMATE   PAGE 3 OF 3 • LOAN ID #

Closing Disclosure Form The **Closing Disclosure form** itemizes all charges that are normally paid by a borrower and a seller in connection with settlement, whether required by the lender or another party, or paid by the lender or any other person. The Closing Disclosure form replaces the HUD-1 Settlement Statement and the final TIL. The form provides more information about the costs of taxes and insurance and how the interest rate and payments may change in the future. It also warns consumers about things they may want to avoid such as prepayment penalties. The borrower must receive a completed Closing Disclosure at least three business days before the closing. If a new Closing Disclosure is required because a creditor has made a significant change to the loan terms (such as an increase in the APR greater than 0.125%, a different loan product, or the addition of a prepayment penalty), a new three-day waiting period begins.

http://www.consumerfinance.gov/regulatory-implementation/tila-respa/

A completed sample form is shown in Figure 17.3. For more information and updates from the Consumer Financial Protection Bureau (CFPB) regarding this rule, visit the CFPB website.

FIGURE 17.3: Closing Disclosure

Closing Disclosure

This form is a statement of final loan terms and closing costs. Compare this document with your Loan Estimate.

Closing Information

Date Issued	4/15/2013
Closing Date	4/15/2013
Disbursement Date	4/15/2013
Settlement Agent	Epsilon Title Co.
File #	12-3456
Property	456 Somewhere Ave Anytown, ST 12345
Sale Price	$180,000

Transaction Information

Borrower	Michael Jones and Mary Stone 123 Anywhere Street Anytown, ST 12345
Seller	Steve Cole and Amy Doe 321 Somewhere Drive Anytown, ST 12345
Lender	Ficus Bank

Loan Information

Loan Term	30 years
Purpose	Purchase
Product	Fixed Rate
Loan Type	☒ Conventional ☐ FHA ☐ VA ☐ ___________
Loan ID #	123456789
MIC #	000654321

Loan Terms

		Can this amount increase after closing?
Loan Amount	$162,000	**NO**
Interest Rate	3.875%	**NO**
Monthly Principal & Interest *See Projected Payments below for your Estimated Total Monthly Payment*	$761.78	**NO**
		Does the loan have these features?
Prepayment Penalty		**YES** • **As high as $3,240** if you pay off the loan during the first 2 years
Balloon Payment		**NO**

Projected Payments

Payment Calculation	**Years 1-7**	**Years 8-30**
Principal & Interest	$761.78	$761.78
Mortgage Insurance	+ 82.35	+ —
Estimated Escrow *Amount can increase over time*	+ 206.13	+ 206.13
Estimated Total Monthly Payment	$1,050.26	$967.91

		This estimate includes	In escrow?
Estimated Taxes, Insurance & Assessments *Amount can increase over time* *See page 4 for details*	$356.13 a month	☒ Property Taxes	**YES**
		☒ Homeowner's Insurance	**YES**
		☒ Other: Homeowner's Association Dues	**NO**
		See Escrow Account on page 4 for details. You must pay for other property costs separately.	

Costs at Closing

Closing Costs	$9,712.10	Includes $4,694.05 in Loan Costs + $5,018.05 in Other Costs – $0 in Lender Credits. *See page 2 for details.*
Cash to Close	$14,147.26	Includes Closing Costs. *See Calculating Cash to Close on page 3 for details.*

CLOSING DISCLOSURE PAGE 1 OF 5 • LOAN ID # 123456789

FIGURE 17.3: Closing Disclosure (continued)

Closing Cost Details

Loan Costs	Borrower-Paid		Seller-Paid		Paid by Others
	At Closing	Before Closing	At Closing	Before Closing	
A. Origination Charges	**$1,802.00**				
01 0.25 % of Loan Amount (Points)	$405.00				
02 Application Fee	$300.00				
03 Underwriting Fee	$1,097.00				
04					
05					
06					
07					
08					
B. Services Borrower Did Not Shop For	**$236.55**				
01 Appraisal Fee to John Smith Appraisers Inc.					$405.00
02 Credit Report Fee to Information Inc.		$29.80			
03 Flood Determination Fee to Info Co.	$20.00				
04 Flood Monitoring Fee to Info Co.	$31.75				
05 Tax Monitoring Fee to Info Co.	$75.00				
06 Tax Status Research Fee to Info Co.	$80.00				
07					
08					
09					
10					
C. Services Borrower Did Shop For	**$2,655.50**				
01 Pest Inspection Fee to Pests Co.	$120.50				
02 Survey Fee to Surveys Co.	$85.00				
03 Title – Insurance Binder to Epsilon Title Co.	$650.00				
04 Title – Lender's Title Insurance to Epsilon Title Co.	$500.00				
05 Title – Settlement Agent Fee to Epsilon Title Co.	$500.00				
06 Title – Title Search to Epsilon Title Co.	$800.00				
07					
08					
D. TOTAL LOAN COSTS (Borrower-Paid)	**$4,694.05**				
Loan Costs Subtotals (A + B + C)	$4,664.25	$29.80			

Other Costs	Borrower-Paid At Closing	Borrower-Paid Before Closing	Seller-Paid At Closing	Seller-Paid Before Closing	Paid by Others
E. Taxes and Other Government Fees	**$85.00**				
01 Recording Fees Deed: $40.00 Mortgage: $45.00	$85.00				
02 Transfer Tax to Any State			$950.00		
F. Prepaids	**$2,120.80**				
01 Homeowner's Insurance Premium (12 mo.) to Insurance Co.	$1,209.96				
02 Mortgage Insurance Premium (mo.)					
03 Prepaid Interest ($17.44 per day from 4/15/13 to 5/1/13)	$279.04				
04 Property Taxes (6 mo.) to Any County USA	$631.80				
05					
G. Initial Escrow Payment at Closing	**$412.25**				
01 Homeowner's Insurance $100.83 per month for 2 mo.	$201.66				
02 Mortgage Insurance per month for mo.					
03 Property Taxes $105.30 per month for 2 mo.	$210.60				
04					
05					
06					
07					
08 Aggregate Adjustment	– 0.01				
H. Other	**$2,400.00**				
01 HOA Capital Contribution to HOA Acre Inc.	$500.00				
02 HOA Processing Fee to HOA Acre Inc.	$150.00				
03 Home Inspection Fee to Engineers Inc.	$750.00			$750.00	
04 Home Warranty Fee to XYZ Warranty Inc.			$450.00		
05 Real Estate Commission to Alpha Real Estate Broker			$5,700.00		
06 Real Estate Commission to Omega Real Estate Broker			$5,700.00		
07 Title – Owner's Title Insurance (optional) to Epsilon Title Co.	$1,000.00				
08					
I. TOTAL OTHER COSTS (Borrower-Paid)	**$5,018.05**				
Other Costs Subtotals (E + F + G + H)	$5,018.05				
J. TOTAL CLOSING COSTS (Borrower-Paid)	**$9,712.10**				
Closing Costs Subtotals (D + I)	$9,682.30	$29.80	$12,800.00	$750.00	$405.00
Lender Credits					

FIGURE 17.3: Closing Disclosure (continued)

Calculating Cash to Close Use this table to see what has changed from your Loan Estimate.

	Loan Estimate	Final	Did this change?
Total Closing Costs (J)	$8,054.00	$9,712.10	**YES** • See **Total Loan Costs (D)** and **Total Other Costs (I)**
Closing Costs Paid Before Closing	$0	– $29.80	**YES** • You paid these Closing Costs **before closing**
Closing Costs Financed (Paid from your Loan Amount)	$0	$0	**NO**
Down Payment/Funds from Borrower	$18,000.00	$18,000.00	**NO**
Deposit	– $10,000.00	– $10,000.00	**NO**
Funds for Borrower	$0	$0	**NO**
Seller Credits	$0	– $2,500.00	**YES** • See Seller Credits in **Section L**
Adjustments and Other Credits	$0	– $1,035.04	**YES** • See details in **Sections K and L**
Cash to Close	$16,054.00	$14,147.26	

Summaries of Transactions Use this table to see a summary of your transaction.

BORROWER'S TRANSACTION

K. Due from Borrower at Closing				**$189,762.30**
01 Sale Price of Property				$180,000.00
02 Sale Price of Any Personal Property Included in Sale				
03 Closing Costs Paid at Closing (J)				$9,682.30
04				
Adjustments				
05				
06				
07				
Adjustments for Items Paid by Seller in Advance				
08 City/Town Taxes		to		
09 County Taxes		to		
10 Assessments		to		
11 HOA Dues	4/15/13	to	4/30/13	$80.00
12				
13				
14				
15				
L. Paid Already by or on Behalf of Borrower at Closing				**$175,615.04**
01 Deposit				$10,000.00
02 Loan Amount				$162,000.00
03 Existing Loan(s) Assumed or Taken Subject to				
04				
05 Seller Credit				$2,500.00
Other Credits				
06 Rebate from Epsilon Title Co.				$750.00
07				
Adjustments				
08				
09				
10				
11				
Adjustments for Items Unpaid by Seller				
12 City/Town Taxes	1/1/13	to	4/14/13	$365.04
13 County Taxes		to		
14 Assessments		to		
15				
16				
17				
CALCULATION				
Total Due from Borrower at Closing (K)				$189,762.30
Total Paid Already by or on Behalf of Borrower at Closing (L)				– $175,615.04
Cash to Close ☒ From ☐ To Borrower				**$14,147.26**

SELLER'S TRANSACTION

M. Due to Seller at Closing				**$180,080.00**
01 Sale Price of Property				$180,000.00
02 Sale Price of Any Personal Property Included in Sale				
03				
04				
05				
06				
07				
08				
Adjustments for Items Paid by Seller in Advance				
09 City/Town Taxes		to		
10 County Taxes		to		
11 Assessments		to		
12 HOA Dues	4/15/13	to	4/30/13	$80.00
13				
14				
15				
16				
N. Due from Seller at Closing				**$115,665.04**
01 Excess Deposit				
02 Closing Costs Paid at Closing (J)				$12,800.00
03 Existing Loan(s) Assumed or Taken Subject to				
04 Payoff of First Mortgage Loan				$100,000.00
05 Payoff of Second Mortgage Loan				
06				
07				
08 Seller Credit				$2,500.00
09				
10				
11				
12				
13				
Adjustments for Items Unpaid by Seller				
14 City/Town Taxes	1/1/13	to	4/14/13	$365.04
15 County Taxes		to		
16 Assessments		to		
17				
18				
19				
CALCULATION				
Total Due to Seller at Closing (M)				$180,080.00
Total Due from Seller at Closing (N)				– $115,665.04
Cash ☐ From ☒ To Seller				**$64,414.96**

FIGURE 17.3: Closing Disclosure (continued)

Additional Information About This Loan

Loan Disclosures

Assumption
If you sell or transfer this property to another person, your lender

- ☐ will allow, under certain conditions, this person to assume this loan on the original terms.
- ☒ will not allow assumption of this loan on the original terms.

Demand Feature
Your loan

- ☐ has a demand feature, which permits your lender to require early repayment of the loan. You should review your note for details.
- ☒ does not have a demand feature.

Late Payment
If your payment is more than *15* days late, your lender will charge a late fee of *5% of the monthly principal and interest payment.*

Negative Amortization (Increase in Loan Amount)
Under your loan terms, you

- ☐ are scheduled to make monthly payments that do not pay all of the interest due that month. As a result, your loan amount will increase (negatively amortize), and your loan amount will likely become larger than your original loan amount. Increases in your loan amount lower the equity you have in this property.
- ☐ may have monthly payments that do not pay all of the interest due that month. If you do, your loan amount will increase (negatively amortize), and, as a result, your loan amount may become larger than your original loan amount. Increases in your loan amount lower the equity you have in this property.
- ☒ do not have a negative amortization feature.

Partial Payments
Your lender

- ☒ may accept payments that are less than the full amount due (partial payments) and apply them to your loan.
- ☐ may hold them in a separate account until you pay the rest of the payment, and then apply the full payment to your loan.
- ☐ does not accept any partial payments.

If this loan is sold, your new lender may have a different policy.

Security Interest
You are granting a security interest in
456 Somewhere Ave., Anytown, ST 12345

You may lose this property if you do not make your payments or satisfy other obligations for this loan.

Escrow Account
For now, your loan

☒ will have an escrow account (also called an "impound" or "trust" account) to pay the property costs listed below. Without an escrow account, you would pay them directly, possibly in one or two large payments a year. Your lender may be liable for penalties and interest for failing to make a payment.

Escrow		
Escrowed Property Costs over Year 1	$2,473.56	Estimated total amount over year 1 for your escrowed property costs: *Homeowner's Insurance* *Property Taxes*
Non-Escrowed Property Costs over Year 1	$1,800.00	Estimated total amount over year 1 for your non-escrowed property costs: *Homeowner's Association Dues* You may have other property costs.
Initial Escrow Payment	$412.25	A cushion for the escrow account you pay at closing. See Section G on page 2.
Monthly Escrow Payment	$206.13	The amount included in your total monthly payment.

☐ will not have an escrow account because ☐ you declined it ☐ your lender does not offer one. You must directly pay your property costs, such as taxes and homeowner's insurance. Contact your lender to ask if your loan can have an escrow account.

No Escrow		
Estimated Property Costs over Year 1		Estimated total amount over year 1. You must pay these costs directly, possibly in one or two large payments a year.
Escrow Waiver Fee		

In the future,
Your property costs may change and, as a result, your escrow payment may change. You may be able to cancel your escrow account, but if you do, you must pay your property costs directly. If you fail to pay your property taxes, your state or local government may (1) impose fines and penalties or (2) place a tax lien on this property. If you fail to pay any of your property costs, your lender may (1) add the amounts to your loan balance, (2) add an escrow account to your loan, or (3) require you to pay for property insurance that the lender buys on your behalf, which likely would cost more and provide fewer benefits than what you could buy on your own.

FIGURE 17.3: Closing Disclosure (continued)

Loan Calculations

Total of Payments. Total you will have paid after you make all payments of principal, interest, mortgage insurance, and loan costs, as scheduled.	$285,803.36
Finance Charge. The dollar amount the loan will cost you.	$118,830.27
Amount Financed. The loan amount available after paying your upfront finance charge.	$162,000.00
Annual Percentage Rate (APR). Your costs over the loan term expressed as a rate. This is not your interest rate.	4.174%
Total Interest Percentage (TIP). The total amount of interest that you will pay over the loan term as a percentage of your loan amount.	69.46%

Questions? If you have questions about the loan terms or costs on this form, use the contact information below. To get more information or make a complaint, contact the Consumer Financial Protection Bureau at **www.consumerfinance.gov/mortgage-closing**

Other Disclosures

Appraisal
If the property was appraised for your loan, your lender is required to give you a copy at no additional cost at least 3 days before closing. If you have not yet received it, please contact your lender at the information listed below.

Contract Details
See your note and security instrument for information about
- what happens if you fail to make your payments,
- what is a default on the loan,
- situations in which your lender can require early repayment of the loan, and
- the rules for making payments before they are due.

Liability after Foreclosure
If your lender forecloses on this property and the foreclosure does not cover the amount of unpaid balance on this loan,

☒ state law may protect you from liability for the unpaid balance. If you refinance or take on any additional debt on this property, you may lose this protection and have to pay any debt remaining even after foreclosure. You may want to consult a lawyer for more information.

☐ state law does not protect you from liability for the unpaid balance.

Refinance
Refinancing this loan will depend on your future financial situation, the property value, and market conditions. You may not be able to refinance this loan.

Tax Deductions
If you borrow more than this property is worth, the interest on the loan amount above this property's fair market value is not deductible from your federal income taxes. You should consult a tax advisor for more information.

Contact Information

	Lender	Mortgage Broker	Real Estate Broker (B)	Real Estate Broker (S)	Settlement Agent
Name	Ficus Bank		Omega Real Estate Broker Inc.	Alpha Real Estate Broker Co.	Epsilon Title Co.
Address	4321 Random Blvd. Somecity, ST 12340		789 Local Lane Sometown, ST 12345	987 Suburb Ct. Someplace, ST 12340	123 Commerce Pl. Somecity, ST 12344
NMLS ID					
ST License ID			Z765416	Z61456	Z61616
Contact	Joe Smith		Samuel Green	Joseph Cain	Sarah Arnold
Contact NMLS ID	12345				
Contact ST License ID			P16415	P51461	PT1234
Email	joesmith@ ficusbank.com		sam@omegare.biz	joe@alphare.biz	sarah@ epsilontitle.com
Phone	123-456-7890		123-555-1717	321-555-7171	987-555-4321

Confirm Receipt

By signing, you are only confirming that you have received this form. You do not have to accept this loan because you have signed or received this form.

Applicant Signature Date Co-Applicant Signature Date

Your Home Loan Toolkit

http://files.consumerfinance.gov/f/201503_cfpb_your-home-loan-toolkit-web.pdf

The CFPB developed an information booklet called ***Your Home Loan Toolkit***, which must be provided by a creditor to a mortgage applicant as part of the loan application process, although other real estate professionals, such as brokers, are encouraged to make the booklet available to prospective borrowers. The booklet provides the borrower with general information about settlement (closing) and how to find the best mortgage. It provides numerous resources for further information, as well as a line-by-line description of the Loan Disclosure form. More information on *Your Home Loan Toolkit* is available from the CFPB at http://files.consumerfinance.gov/f/201503_cfpb_your-home-loan-toolkit-web.pdf. Effective October 3, 2015, *Your Home Loan Toolkit* replaced the previously mandated *Settlement Cost Booklet.*

Kickbacks and Referral Fees

RESPA prohibits the payment of kickbacks, or unearned fees, in any real estate settlement service.

It prohibits a referral fee when no services are actually rendered. The payment or receipt of a fee, a kickback, or anything of value for a referral for settlement services includes activities such as mortgage loans, title searches, title insurance, attorney services, surveys, credit reports, and appraisals.

IN PRACTICE Although RESPA's requirements are aimed primarily at lenders, real estate professionals fall under RESPA when they refer buyers to particular lenders, title companies, attorneys, or other providers of settlement services. Real estate professionals who offer computerized loan origination are also subject to regulation. Remember: Buyers have the right to select their own providers of settlement services.

Mortgage Disclosure Improvement Act

The **Mortgage Disclosure Improvement Act** (MDIA), which took effect July 31, 2009, changed how buyers and sellers, lenders, mortgage brokers, title agents, and real estate professionals prepare for a closing. The intent of this law is to prevent the consumer from receiving an enticingly low interest rate at the initial loan application and then learning at settlement that the lender is charging more in fees.

The requirements of the MDIA are now incorporated into the CFPB disclosure requirements. Until the applicant/borrower receives the Loan Estimate, the lender may collect only a reasonable fee for accessing the applicant's credit history. In addition, the lender must provide a statement to the loan applicant indicating that the applicant is not obligated to complete the transaction simply because disclosures were provided or because the individual applied for a loan. Generally, if the APR increases more than 0.125% from that stated in the Closing Disclosure, the creditor must provide a new disclosure with a revised APR and wait an additional three business days before closing the loan. The consumer is permitted to accelerate the process if a personal emergency, such as a foreclosure, exists.

Before closing, everyone involved in the real estate transaction should check and double-check that the Loan Estimate and Closing Disclosure forms are consistent with the original application.

PREPARATION OF CLOSING STATEMENTS

A typical real estate transaction requires accounting for the expenses incurred by either party, generally on the Closing Disclosure, which is required for any federally related closing. All expenses must be itemized to arrive at the exact amount of cash required from the buyer and the net proceeds that will be paid to the seller. These include prorated items—those prepaid by the seller for which the seller must be reimbursed (such as taxes) and expenses the seller has incurred but for which the buyer will be billed (such as mortgage interest paid in arrears when a loan is assumed).

How the Closing Statement Works

The **closing statement** is an accounting of the parties' debits and credits. A **debit** is a charge—an amount that a party owes and must pay at closing. A **credit** is an amount entered in a person's favor—an amount that has already been paid, an amount being reimbursed, or an amount the buyer promises to pay in the form of a loan.

A **debit** is an amount to be paid by the buyer or the seller.

A **credit** is an amount payable to the buyer or the seller.

To determine the amount a buyer must bring to closing, any buyer expenses and prorated amounts for items prepaid by the seller are added to the purchase price. Then the buyer's credits are totaled. Credits to the buyer include the earnest money (already paid), the balance of the loan the buyer obtains or assumes, and the seller's share of any prorated items the buyer will pay in the future.

Finally, the total of the buyer's credits is subtracted from the total of the buyer's debits to arrive at the actual amount of cash the buyer must bring to closing. The buyer usually brings a cashier's or certified check.

A similar procedure is followed to determine the net proceeds to the seller. The seller's debits are subtracted from the seller's credits. Seller credits include the purchase price plus the buyer's share of any prorated items that the seller has prepaid. The seller's debits include expenses to be paid by the seller, the seller's share of prorated items to be paid by the buyer, and the balance of any mortgage loan or other lien that the seller must satisfy. (*See* Figure 17.3.)

Broker's Commission The responsibility for paying a real estate broker's commission will have been determined by previous agreement. If the broker represents the seller, the seller is normally responsible for paying the commission. If a representation agreement exists between a broker and the buyer or if two representatives are involved, one for the seller and one for the buyer, the commission *may* be distributed as an expense between both parties or according to some other arrangement.

Attorney's Fees If either of the parties' attorneys will be paid from the closing proceeds, that party will be charged with the expense in the closing statement. This expense may include fees for the preparation or review of documents or for representing the parties at settlement.

Recording Expenses The seller usually pays for any recording charges (filing fees) necessary to clear all defects and furnish the purchaser with a marketable title. Items customarily charged to the seller include the recording of any release deed or satisfaction of mortgage, quitclaim deed, affidavit, or satisfaction of a mechanic's lien. The buyer pays for recording charges that arise from the actual transfer of title. Usually, such items include the recording of the deed that conveys title to the purchaser and a mortgage or deed of trust executed by the buyer for the benefit of the lender.

Transfer Tax Most states, counties, and local municipalities require some form of transfer tax, conveyance fee, or tax stamps on real estate conveyances. Responsibility for this charge varies according to local practice and the terms of the sales contract.

Title Expenses Responsibility for title expenses varies according to local custom. In most areas, the seller is required to furnish evidence of good title and pay for the title search. If the buyer's attorney inspects the evidence or if the buyer purchases title insurance policies, the buyer is charged for the expense.

Loan Fees For a new loan, the lender generally charges an origination fee and could possibly charge discount points, particularly if the borrower wants a below-market interest rate.

Tax Reserves and Insurance Reserves (Escrow or Impound Accounts) Most mortgage lenders require that borrowers provide funds to pay future real estate taxes and insurance premiums. These funds are held in an **escrow account** or **impound account**. A borrower starts the account at closing by depositing funds to cover at least the amount of unpaid real estate taxes from the date of the lien to the end of the current month. (The buyer receives a credit from the seller at closing for any unpaid taxes.) Afterward, an amount equal to one month's portion of the estimated taxes is included in the borrower's monthly mortgage payment.

The borrower is responsible for maintaining adequate property insurance as a condition of the mortgage loan. The first year's premium is paid in full at closing if it has not been paid earlier by the buyer, effective on the date of closing. The borrower's monthly loan payment typically will include principal and interest on the loan (unless the payment is interest-only), plus one-twelfth of the estimated taxes and insurance (PITI) that will be owed at the end of the coming year. The taxes and insurance are held by the lender in an escrow account until the bills are due.

IN PRACTICE RESPA permits lenders to maintain a cushion equal to one-sixth of the total estimated amount of annual taxes and insurance. However, if state law or mortgage documents allow for a smaller cushion, the lesser amount prevails.

Appraisal Fee Either the seller or the purchaser pays the appraisal fee, depending on who orders the appraisal. When the buyer obtains a mortgage, it is customary for the lender to require an appraisal, in which case, the buyer usually bears the cost, although this is always a negotiable item. If the fee is paid at the time of the loan application, it is reflected on the closing statement as having been paid before closing.

Survey Fee The purchaser who obtains new mortgage financing customarily pays a survey fee. The sales contract may require that the seller furnish a survey.

Additional Fees If the borrower's loan is insured by FHA, the borrower owes a lump sum for payment of the mortgage insurance premium (MIP) if it is not financed as part of the loan. The borrower of a VA-guaranteed loan pays a funding fee directly to the Department of Veterans Affairs at closing. If a conventional loan carries private mortgage insurance (PMI), the buyer prepays one year's mortgage insurance premium at closing.

Accounting for Expenses

Expenses paid out of the closing proceeds are debited only to the party making the payment. Occasionally, an expense item (e.g., an escrow fee, a settlement fee, or a transfer tax) may be shared by the buyer and the seller. In that case, each party is debited for that individual's share of the expense.

PRORATIONS

Most closings involve the division of financial responsibility between the buyer and the seller for such items as loan interest, taxes, rents, fuel, and utility bills. These allowances are allocated between the parties in the required proportions, or **prorations**. Prorations are necessary to ensure that expenses and credits are divided fairly between the seller and the buyer.

General Rules for Prorating

The rules or customs governing the computation of prorations for the closing of a real estate sale vary widely from state to state. The following are some general guidelines for preparing the closing statement:

- In most states, the seller owns the property on the day of closing, and prorations or apportionments are usually made up to and including the day of closing. A few states specify that the buyer owns the property on the closing date. In that case, adjustments are made as of the day preceding the day on which title is closed.
- Mortgage interest, general real estate taxes, water taxes, insurance premiums, and similar expenses are usually computed by using 360 days in a year and 30 days in a month. In some areas, however, prorations are computed on the basis of the actual number of days in the calendar month of closing. The agreement of sale should specify which method will be used.
- On almost every mortgage loan, the interest is paid in arrears. A mortgage payment due on June 1, for example, includes interest due for May. The buyer who places a new mortgage loan on May 31 may be pleasantly surprised to learn that the first mortgage payment is not due for another month.
- Accrued or prepaid general real estate taxes are usually prorated at the closing. In some states, real estate taxes are paid in advance; that is, if the tax year runs from January 1 to December 31, taxes for the coming year are due on January 1. In this case, the seller, who has prepaid a year's taxes, should be reimbursed for the portion of the year remaining after the buyer takes ownership of the property. In other areas, taxes are paid in arrears, on December 31 for the year just ended. In that case, the buyer should be credited by the seller for the time the seller occupied the property. When the amount of the current real estate tax cannot be determined definitely, the proration is usually based on the last obtainable tax bill, often with a percentage increase—say, 10%—to account for a likely reassessment.
- Special assessments for municipal improvements such as sewers, water mains, or streets are usually paid in annual installments over several years, with

annual interest charged on the outstanding balance of future payments. The seller normally makes the current payments, and the buyer assumes all future payments. The special assessment installment generally is not prorated at the closing. A buyer may insist that the seller allow the buyer a credit for the seller's share of the interest to the closing date. The agreement of sale may address the manner in which special assessments will be handled at closing.

- Rent is usually adjusted on the basis of the actual number of days in the month of closing. The seller customarily receives the rents for the day of closing and pays all expenses for that day. If any rents for the current month are uncollected when the sale is closed, the buyer often agrees by a separate letter to collect the rents, if possible, and remit the prorated share to the seller.
- A security deposit made by a tenant to cover the cost of repairing damage caused by the tenant, or the last month's rent which has been collected in advance, are generally transferred by the seller to the buyer without prorating. The only exception would be if the property were being transferred in the last month of the lease; thus, the last month's rent would be prorated.

Accrued items = Buyer credits
Prepaid items = Seller credits

Accrued items are expenses to be prorated (such as water bills and interest on an assumed mortgage) that are owed by the seller but will be paid after the sale by the buyer. The seller pays for these items by giving the buyer credits for them at closing.

Prepaid items are expenses to be prorated (such as fuel oil in a tank) that have been prepaid by the seller but not fully used up, so they become credits to the seller.

The Arithmetic of Prorating

The computation of a proration involves identifying a yearly charge for the item to be prorated, then dividing by 12 to determine a monthly charge for the item. Also, it is usually necessary to identify a daily charge for the item by dividing the monthly charge by the number of days in the month. These smaller portions are then multiplied by the number of months or days in the prorated period to determine the accrued or unearned amount that will be figured in the settlement.

Using this general principle, there are two methods of calculating a proration:

- The yearly charge is divided by a 360-day year (called a banking or statutory year), or 12 months of 30 days each.
- The yearly charge is divided by 365 (a calendar year) to determine the daily charge, and the actual number of days in the proration period is determined, with this number multiplied by the daily charge.

The final proration figure will vary slightly, depending on which computation method is used. The final figure also will vary according to the number of decimal places to which the division is carried. All the proration calculations here are computed by carrying the division to three decimal places and then rounding to the nearest cent only after the final proration figure is determined.

Accrued Items

When the real estate tax is levied for the calendar year and is payable during that year or in the following year, the accrued portion is for the period from January 1 to the date of closing (or to the day before the closing in states where the sale date is excluded). If the current tax bill has not yet been issued, the parties must agree on an estimated amount based on the previous year's bill and any known changes in assessment or tax levy for the current year. If the assessment for the current year is not known, the parties may agree to add an estimated amount, say 10%, to the amount of the last assessment.

Sample Proration Calculation Assume that a sale is to be closed on September 17. Using a 360-day year, prorate the current real estate taxes of $3,600 for the accrued period of 8 months, 17 days. First determine the prorated cost of the real estate tax per month and day:

$3,600 ÷ 12 months = $300 per month
$300 ÷ 30 days = $10 per day

Next, multiply these figures by the accrued period and add the totals to determine the prorated real estate tax:

$300 × 8 months = $2,400
$10 × 17 days = $170
$2,400 + 170 = $2,570

Thus, the accrued real estate tax for 8 months and 17 days is $2,570. This amount represents the seller's accrued earned tax. It will be a credit to the buyer and a debit to the seller on the closing statement.

FIGURE 17.4: Credits and Debits

Item	Credit to Buyer	Debit to Buyer	Credit to Seller	Debit to Seller	Prorated
Principal amount of new mortgage	√				
Payoff of existing mortgage				√	
Unpaid principal balance if assumed mortgage	√			√	
Accrued interest on existing assumed mortgage	√			√	√
Tenant's security deposit	√			√	
Purchase money mortgage	√			√	
Unpaid water and other utility bills	√			√	√
Buyer's earnest money	√				
Selling price of property		√	√		
Fuel oil on hand (valued at current market price)		√	√		√
Prepaid insurance and tax reserve for mortgage assumed by buyer		√	√		√
Refund to seller of prepaid water charges and similar utility expenses		√	√		√
Prepaid general real estate taxes		√	√		√

Note: This chart is based on generally applicable practices. Closing practices may be different in your state or county.

To compute this proration using the actual number of days in the accrued period, the following method is used:

The accrued period from January 1 to September 17 runs 260 days (January's 31 days plus February's 28 days and so on, plus the 17 days of September).

$3,600 ÷ 365 days = $9.863 per day
$9.863 × 260 days = $2,564.38

Although these examples show proration as of the date of settlement, the agreement of sale may indicate otherwise. For instance, if the buyer's possession date does not coincide with the settlement date, the parties could prorate according to the date of possession.

IN PRACTICE On state licensing examinations, tax prorations are usually based on a 30-day month (360-day year) unless specified otherwise. This may differ from local custom regarding tax prorations. Many title insurance companies provide proration charts that detail tax factors for each day in the year. To determine a tax proration using one of these charts, multiply the factor given for the closing date by the annual real estate tax.

MATH CONCEPTS

Computing Interim Interest

Interim interest is charged by a lender when a borrower obtains a new loan. This interest is called *interim* because it is for the interim period of time from the day of closing through the end of the closing month. Most real estate loan interest is paid in arrears, but interim interest is an example of interest paid in advance.

If closing on a loan on June 12, the borrower will owe interim interest for 19 days. The first full payment (PI) will be due August 1; this payment will include interest for July. If the closing is September 21, interim interest for 10 days will be paid at closing, and the first full payment will be due November 1 (paying interest for October).

FOR EXAMPLE A borrower is closing on a $114,300 loan with an interest rate of 4.75% on November 18. How much interim interest will be due at closing? The first full payment is due January 1.

30 days in November – 18 (days until closing) = 12 days + 1 (day of closing) = 13 days

$114,300 × 4.75% = 5,429.25 annual interest

$5,429.25 ÷ 360 = $15.081 interest per day

$15.081 × 13 days = $196.053 interim interest due at closing

$196.05 interim interest due at closing is the answer (rounded to the nearest cent).

Prepaid Items

A tax proration might be a prepaid item. Because real estate taxes may be paid in the early part of the year, a tax proration calculated for a closing that will take place later in the year must reflect the fact that the seller has already paid the tax. For example, in the preceding problem, suppose that all taxes had been paid. The buyer would then have to reimburse the seller; the proration would be credited to the seller and debited to the buyer.

In figuring the tax proration, the number of future days, months, and years for which taxes have been paid must be ascertained. The formula commonly used for this purpose is as follows:

	Years	**Months**	**Days**
Taxes paid to (Dec. 31, end of tax year)	20XX	12	30
Date of closing (Sept. 17, 20XX)	20XX	– 9	– 17
Period for which tax must be paid		3	13

This formula will calculate the amount the buyer will reimburse the seller for the unearned portion of the real estate taxes. The prepaid period determined by the formula for prepaid items is three months and 13 days. Three months at $300 per month equals $900, and 13 days at $10 per day equals $130. Add these two figures to determine that the proration is $1,030 credited to the seller and debited to the buyer.

Sample Prepaid Item Calculation One example of a prepaid item is a water bill. Assume that the unmetered water is billed in advance by the city. The six months' billing is $480 for the period ending October 31 ($480 ÷ 6 = $80 per month). The sale is to close on August 3. Because the water bill is paid through October 31, the prepaid time must be computed. Using a 30-day basis, the prepaid period is the 27 days left in August plus two full months. To compute one day's cost, divide $80 by 30, which equals $2.667 per day. The computation is as follows:

27 × $2.667 per day =	$72.009
2 months × $80 =	$160.000
	$232.009 or $232.01

This is a prepaid item; it is credited to the seller and debited to the buyer on the closing statement.

To figure this proration based on the actual days in the month of closing, the following process would be used:

$80 per month ÷ 31 days in August	=	$2.581 per day
August 4 through August 31	=	28 days
28 days × $2.581	=	$72.268
2 months × $80	=	$160.000
$72.268 + $160	=	$232.268 or $232.27

SAMPLE CLOSING STATEMENT

Settlement computations take many possible forms. The elements of a sample transaction follow, and you are to compute the charges paid by the buyer and the seller. Because customs differ in various parts of the country, the way certain expenses are charged in some locations may be different from the illustration. The charges to be made to the parties, and the computations involved, are shown at the end of the example.

Basic Information of Offer and Sale

A couple lists a property at 3045 North Racine Avenue in Riverdale, East Dakota, for sale with a real estate brokerage. The listing price is $237,000, and possession will take place within two weeks after all parties have signed the contract. Under the terms of the listing agreement, the sellers agree to pay the listing agent a commission of 6% of the sales price.

The Offer to Purchase On May 18, the real estate brokerage company submits a contract offer to the seller from the buyer, who resides at 22 King Court, Riverdale. The buyer offers $230,000, with earnest money and down payment of $46,000. The buyer expects to obtain a conventional 30-year fixed-rate mortgage for 80% of the purchase price and, therefore, will not need private mortgage insurance (PMI). The seller accepts the buyer's offer on May 29, with a closing date of June 15.

In this real estate transaction, taxes are paid in arrears. Taxes for this year, estimated at last year's figure of $3,450, have not been paid. According to the contract, prorations will be made on the basis of 30 days in a month.

The Buyer's Loan Application The buyer's new loan is for $184,000. The buyer's locked-in rate of 5% is good until 4 pm June 20, 20XX. The buyer will pay interest on the loan for the remainder of the month of closing: 15 days at $25.56 per day ($383.40). The first full payment, including July's interest, will be due on August 1. The loan origination fee is 1.25%, or $2,300. In connection with this loan, the buyer must provide a flood certification ($12), a survey ($395), and a pest inspection ($65).

The buyer will be charged $500 to have the property appraised. The buyer is only charged for the credit report at the time of loan application, but the appraisal fee must be paid upon loan approval and before closing.

The cost of a one-year hazard insurance policy is $3 per $1,000 of appraised value ($230,000 ÷ 1,000 × 3 = $690) and will be paid at closing to the insurance company. The lender requires a reserve account for property taxes and insurance. The buyer's initial deposit is 7⁄12 of the anticipated county real estate tax of $3,450 ($2,012.50) and two months of the insurance policy ($115). The lender requires that 1⁄12 of the annual insurance premium ($57.50) and taxes ($287.50) be included in the monthly payment.

Closing Costs The unpaid balance of the seller's mortgage as of June 1, 20XX, will be $115,500. Payments are $825 per month, with interest at 7% per year on the unpaid balance.

The seller submits evidence of title in the form of a title insurance binder at a cost of $30. The title insurance policy, to be paid by the buyer at the time of closing, costs an additional $540, which includes $395 for the lender's coverage and $145 for the owner's coverage. The seller must pay $20 for the recording of two instruments to clear defects in the seller's title. The seller must also pay an attorney's fee of $600 for preparing the deed and for legal representation, which will be paid from the closing proceeds.

The buyer has agreed to pay for the state transfer tax stamps in the amount of $230 ($0.50 per $500 of the sales price or fraction thereof). The buyer must pay an attorney's fee of $500 for examining the title evidence and for legal representation. The buyer must pay $20 to record the deed and $50 to record the mortgage.

Computing the Prorations and Charges The following list illustrates the various steps in computing the prorations and other amounts that are part of this transaction:

- Closing date: June 15
- Commission: 6% (0.06) × $230,000 sales price = $13,800
- Seller's mortgage interest: 7% (0.07) × $115,400 principal due after June 1 payment = $8,078 interest per year; $8,078 ÷ 360 days = $22.44 interest per day; 15 days of accrued interest to be paid by the seller × $22.44 = $336.60 interest owed by the seller; $115,400 + $336.60 = $115,736.60 payoff of seller's mortgage
- Real estate taxes (estimated at $3,450): $3,450 ÷ 12 months = $287.50 per month; $287.50 ÷ 30 days = $9.58 per day
- The earned period, from January 1 to and including June 15 (5 months, 15 days): $287.50 × 5 months = $1,437.50; $9.58 × 15 days = $143.70; $1437.50 + $143.70 = $1,581.20 seller owes buyer
- Transfer tax ($0.50 per $500 of consideration, or fraction thereof): $230,000 ÷ $500 = $460; $460 × $0.50 = $230 transfer tax paid by buyer
- Buyer's tax reserve payment: $2,012.50 paid to separate account (7⁄12 of the anticipated county real estate taxes of $3,450)
- Buyer's one-year hazard insurance payment: $3 per $1,000 of appraised value ($230,000 ÷ 1,000 × 3 = $690 paid in advance to insurance company)
- Buyer will pay 15 days of interest for June (15 × $25.56 = $383.40) at closing
- Buyer's first full payment will be due on August 1

The seller's loan payoff is $115,736.60. The seller must pay an additional seller's fee of $25 to record the mortgage release, as well as $100 for a pest inspection and $200 for a survey, as negotiated between the parties.

KEY POINT REVIEW

Closing (settlement and transfer) is the point at which ownership of a property is transferred in exchange for the selling price.

To complete the transaction, the buyer requires the survey; title evidence; results of necessary inspections; an affidavit of title from the seller and, where applicable, documents showing the removal of prior encumbrances; the deed from the seller; and the lease, if a tenant resides on the premises. The buyer will expect to make a successful final property inspection (walk-through) and to receive a closing statement showing the amount and distribution of funds.

To complete the transaction, the seller will need the payoff statement from the seller's lender noting the amount owed; evidence that the buyer has the necessary funds; and a closing statement showing the distribution of funds.

The lender will want assurance that its lien rights will have priority and will want the buyer to obtain a mortgagee's title insurance policy.

The **Internal Revenue Service (IRS)** may require completion and submission of the Form 1099-S statement of income to the seller showing the seller's Social Security number. Form 1099-S is filed by a closing agent or the mortgage lender, with the real estate professionals or the parties being ultimately liable for the filing.

Depending on state law and local custom, closing may take place at a face-to-face meeting of the parties at the escrow company, title company, lender's office, or attorney's office, or the parties may execute documents separately and never meet.

An **escrow holder (escrow agent)** is a disinterested third party authorized to coordinate the closing activities.

The **Real Estate Settlement Procedures Act (RESPA)** is a federal law enacted to protect consumers in the settlement process by requiring accurate and timely information about the actual costs of a transaction, eliminating **kickbacks** and other referral fees, prohibiting the seller from requiring the buyer to buy title insurance from a particular company, and prohibiting lenders from requiring excessive escrow account deposits.

RESPA does not apply to a transaction financed solely by a purchase-money mortgage taken back by a seller, installment contracts (contract for deed), or a buyer's assumption of a seller's existing loan.

The CFPB has produced *Your Home Loan Toolkit*, a booklet that must be provided by a lender to every person from whom they receive or for whom they prepare a loan application (except for refinancing).

The **Loan Estimate form** must be provided to the borrower no later than three business days after receiving a loan application. The **Closing Disclosure** given to the borrower and the seller itemizes all charges to be paid in connection with closing.

The Loan Estimate and Closing Disclosure forms developed by the CFPB are required for transactions originating on or after October 3, 2015.

Affiliated business arrangements (ABA) that make use of companies with a shared ownership require notice to clients.

A **mortgage servicing transfer statement** must be given by the lender to the borrower if the lender intends to sell or assign the servicing rights to the borrower's loan.

A **closing statement** involves an accounting of the amounts paid by or received by the parties.

A **debit (give)** is a charge that must be paid by the buyer or the seller at closing. A **credit (receive)** is the amount entered in favor of the buyer or the seller. In most instances, a debit to one party is a credit to the other party.

Certain charges are **prorated**, divided between the buyer and the seller, in one of two ways. A yearly charge can be divided by a **360-day year** (banking year), or 12 months of 30 days each. A yearly charge could be divided by a **365-day year** (366 days in leap year) to determine the daily charge, the actual number of days in the proration period is determined, and the number of days is multiplied by the daily charge. In most states, the charges are prorated as of the date of closing, with the seller being responsible for the date of closing.

UNIT 17 QUIZ

1. Which statement is *TRUE* of real estate closings in most states?
   a. Closings are generally conducted by real estate professionals.
   b. The buyer usually receives the rent for the day of closing.
   c. The buyer must reimburse the seller for any title evidence provided by the seller.
   d. The seller usually pays the expenses for the day of closing.
2. All encumbrances and liens shown on the report of title, other than those waived or agreed to by the purchaser and listed in the contract, must be removed so that the title can be delivered free and clear. The removal of such encumbrances is typically the duty of the
   a. buyer.
   b. seller.
   c. real estate professional.
   d. title company.
3. Legal title *ALWAYS* passes from the seller to the buyer
   a. on the date of execution of the deed.
   b. when the closing statement has been signed.
   c. when the deed is placed in escrow.
   d. when the deed is delivered and accepted.
4. Which item would a lender generally require at the closing?
   a. Title insurance commitment
   b. Market value appraisal
   c. Application
   d. Credit report
5. A buyer purchases a home in an area where closings are traditionally conducted in escrow. Which item would a buyer deposit with the escrow agent before the closing date?
   a. Deed to the property
   b. Title evidence
   c. Estoppel certificate
   d. Cash needed to complete the purchase
6. The Closing Disclosure must be used to illustrate all settlement charges for
   a. every real estate transaction.
   b. transactions financed by VA and FHA loans only.
   c. residential transactions financed by federally related mortgage loans.
   d. all transactions involving commercial property.
7. A mortgage reduction certificate is executed by a(n)
   a. abstract company.
   b. attorney.
   c. lending institution.
   d. grantor.
8. At closing, the principal amount of a purchaser's new mortgage loan is a
   a. credit to the seller.
   b. credit to the buyer.
   c. debit to the seller.
   d. debit to the buyer.
9. At closing, the earnest money left on deposit with a real estate professional is a
   a. credit to the seller.
   b. credit to the buyer.
   c. balancing factor.
   d. debit to the buyer.
10. The annual real estate taxes on a property amount to $1,800. The seller has paid the taxes in advance for the calendar year. If the closing is set for June 15, which statement is *TRUE*?
    a. Credit the seller $825; debit the buyer $975.
    b. Credit the seller $1,800; debit the buyer $825.
    c. Credit the buyer $975; debit the seller $975.
    d. Credit the seller $975; debit the buyer $975.

11. If a seller collected rent of $900 from the buyer, payable in advance, on August 1, which statement is *TRUE* at the closing on August 15, if the closing date is an expense to the seller? (Use a 30-day month)
  a. The seller owes the buyer $900.
  b. The buyer owes the seller $900.
  c. The seller owes the buyer $450.
  d. The buyer owes the seller $450.

12. Security deposits should be listed on a closing statement as a credit to the
  a. buyer.
  b. seller.
  c. lender.
  d. real estate professional.

13. A building was purchased for $850,000, with 10% down and a loan for the balance. If the lender charged the buyer two discount points, how much cash did the buyer need at closing if the buyer incurred no other costs?
  a. $17,000
  b. $85,000
  c. $100,300
  d. $102,000

14. Which charge noted on the Closing Disclosure must be the same or less than the charge noted on the Loan Estimate form?
  a. Cost of settlement services when the lender selects the provider
  b. Lender charges for taking and underwriting the loan
  c. Cost of settlement services when the borrower selects the provider from the list provided by the lender
  d. Cost of homeowners insurance

15. At closing, the listing agent's commission is usually shown as a
  a. credit to the seller.
  b. credit to the buyer.
  c. debit to the seller.
  d. debit to the buyer.

16. At the closing of a real estate transaction, the person performing the settlement gave the buyer a credit for certain accrued items. These items were
  a. bills relating to the property that had already been paid by the seller.
  b. bills relating to the property that the buyer needed to pay.
  c. all of the seller's real estate bills.
  d. all of the buyer's real estate bills.

17. At closing, a prepaid item by the seller is
  a. debited to the seller.
  b. evenly divided between the buyer and the seller.
  c. credited to the buyer.
  d. credited to the seller.

18. The purpose of the Real Estate Settlement Procedures Act (RESPA) is to
  a. make sure buyers do not borrow more than they can repay.
  b. make real estate professionals more responsive to buyers' needs.
  c. help buyers know how much money is required.
  d. ensure that buyers know all settlement costs that will be charged to them.

19. The document that provides the borrower with general information about settlement costs, RESPA provisions, and what happens at settlement is
  a. the loan application.
  b. *Your Home Loan Toolkit.*
  c. the Closing Disclosure form.
  d. the Loan Estimate form.

20. Under the TILA-RESPA Integrated Disclosure rule (TRID), a lender must extend the closing how many days if the annual percentage rate (APR) has changed more than 0.125% before closing?
  a. Two business days
  b. Three business days
  c. Four business days
  d. Five business days

UNIT 18

Leases

■ LEARNING OBJECTIVES

When you have finished reading this unit, you will be able to

- **explain** the essential elements of leasehold interests;
- **describe** the essential terms of a lease agreement;
- **distinguish** the various types of leases;
- **explain** the means by which the lease may be terminated and discharged and the remedies available to the parties for its breach; and
- **define** the following *key terms*:

actual eviction	ground lease	percentage lease
assignment	holdover tenancy	purchase option
constructive eviction	lease	renewal option
estate (tenancy) at sufferance	lease purchase	rent
estate (tenancy) at will	leasehold estate	reversionary right
estate (tenancy) for years	lessee	right of first refusal
estate (tenancy) from period to period	lessor	sale-and-leaseback
gross lease	month-to-month tenancy	security deposit
	net lease	sublease
	nondisturbance clause	

OVERVIEW

Although some owners of rental units manage their own properties (a real estate license is not required to do so), most rental properties are professionally managed. In many states, property managers are required to hold a real estate broker's or property manager's license. As with all real estate services, a real estate sales associate can only manage property with the consent of the employing broker and in the broker's name.

Real estate professionals should be knowledgeable about the local rental market to better assist prospective buyers who may need temporary housing, those who prefer to rent a home or cannot afford to purchase one, or investor-buyers, or to manage their own portfolios. In any case, anyone with an interest in rental property should be aware of the basic provisions of leases and management agreements, and other landlord-tenant issues.

LEASING REAL ESTATE

www.census.gov

The recent record number of property foreclosures has been accompanied by an increase in the number of residential rental properties, both because foreclosed owners have become renters and because investors have taken advantage of the decline in market values to increase their portfolios. There has been a drop in the rate of home ownership in the first decade of this century, from 66.2% in 2000 to 65.1% in 2010, and a corresponding increase in the number of households residing in rental units. Additional statistics on the housing market are available from the U.S. Census Bureau, www.census.gov.

The foundation of the relationship between a property owner and tenant is the lease. A **lease** is a contract between a **lessor** (the owner of real estate, or landlord) and a **lessee** (the tenant). A lease transfers the lessor's rights to exclusive possession and use of the property to the tenant for a specified period of time and establishes the consideration the lessee is to pay **rent** for use of the property. Rent is a fixed, periodic payment made by a tenant of a property to the owner for possession and use, usually by prior agreement of the parties. Other rights and obligations of the parties are also set forth. The landlord retains a **reversionary right** to possession after the lease term expires.

The statute of frauds in most states requires lease agreements for more than one year to be in writing to be enforceable. In general, oral leases for one year or less that can be performed within a year of their making are enforceable. A written lease should be executed (signed) by both the lessor and the lessee.

IN PRACTICE Even though an oral lease, such as a lease for one year commencing from the day of agreement, may be enforceable, it is always better practice to put a lease agreement in writing. A written lease signed by both landlord and tenant provides concrete evidence of the terms and conditions to which the parties have agreed.

Leasehold Estates

A tenant's right to possess real estate for the term of the lease is called a **leasehold (less-than-freehold) estate**. A leasehold is generally considered personal property. When the tenant assumes many of the landowner's obligations under a lease for life or for more than 49 years, certain states give the tenant some of the benefits and privileges of ownership, such as the right to use the leasehold interest as security for a loan.

Just as there are several types of freehold (ownership) estates, there are different kinds of leasehold estates. (*See* Figure 18.1.)

FIGURE 18.1: Leasehold Estates

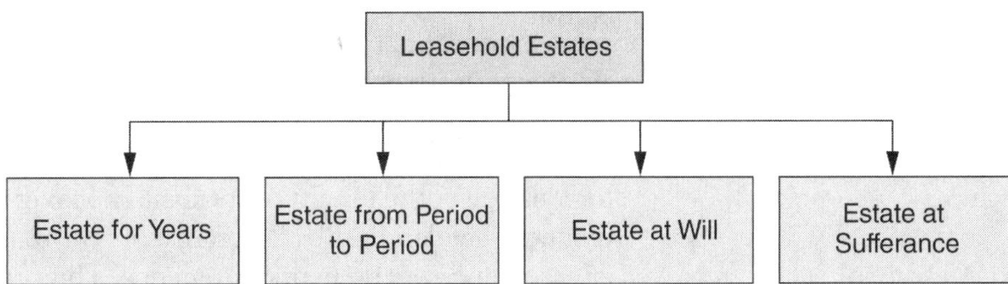

Estate (tenancy) for years
- *Any definite period*

Estate for Years An **estate** (tenancy) **for years** is a leasehold estate that continues for a definite period. That period may be years, months, weeks, or even days. An estate for years (sometimes called an *estate for term*) always has specific starting and ending dates. When the estate expires, the lessee is required to vacate the premises and surrender possession to the lessor. No notice is required to terminate the estate for years because the lease agreement states a specific expiration date. When the date comes, the lease expires, and the tenant's rights are extinguished.

If both parties agree, the lease for years may be terminated before the expiration date. Otherwise, neither party may terminate without showing that the lease agreement has been breached. Any extension of the tenancy requires that a new contract be negotiated.

As is characteristic of all leases, a tenancy for years gives the lessee the right to occupy and use the leased property according to the terms and covenants contained in the lease agreement. A lessee has the right to use the premises for the entire lease term and that right is unaffected by the original lessor's death or the sale of the property, unless the lease states otherwise. If the original lease provides for an option to renew, no further negotiation is required; the tenant merely exercises the option.

Estate from period to period (periodic tenancy):
- *Indefinite term*
- *Automatically renewing*

Estate From Period to Period An **estate (tenancy) from period to period**, or *periodic tenancy*, is created when the landlord and tenant enter into an agreement for an indefinite time—that is, the lease does not contain a specific expiration date. Such a tenancy is created initially to run for a definite amount of time—for instance, month to month, week to week, or year to year—but the tenancy continues indefinitely until proper notice of termination is given. Rent is payable at definite intervals. A periodic tenancy is characterized by *continuity* because it is automatically renewable under the original terms of the agreement until one of the parties gives notice to terminate. In effect, the payment and acceptance of rent extend the lease for another period. A **month-to-month tenancy**, for example, is created when a tenant takes possession with no definite termination date and pays monthly rent. Periodic tenancy is often used in residential leases.

IN PRACTICE A landlord and a tenant who is unsure how long the apartment will be needed have agreed that an apartment can be rented by the month without specifying the number of months the lease will run. The lease simply continues until either the landlord or the tenant gives proper notice to terminate.

If the original agreement provides for the conversion from an estate for years to a periodic tenancy, no negotiations are necessary; the tenant simply exercises the option.

An estate from period to period also might be created when a tenant with an estate for years remains in possession, or holds over, after the lease term expires. If no new lease agreement has been made, a **holdover tenancy** is created. The landlord may evict the tenant or treat the holdover tenant as one who holds a periodic tenancy. The landlord's acceptance of rent usually is considered conclusive proof of acceptance of the periodic tenancy. The courts customarily rule that a tenant who holds over can do so for a term equal to the term of the original lease, provided the period is for one year or less. For example, a tenant with a lease for six months would be entitled to a new six-month tenancy, but if the original lease were for five years, the holdover tenancy could not exceed one year. Some leases stipulate that in the absence of a renewal agreement, a tenant who holds over does so as a month-to-month tenant.

To terminate a periodic estate, either the landlord or the tenant must give proper notice. The form and timing of the notice may be established by state statute. Normally, the notice must be given at least one period in advance. For example, to terminate an estate from week to week, one week's notice is required; to terminate an estate from month to month, one month's notice is required. For an estate from year to year, however, the notice requirements vary from two months to six months. Many states have statutory notice requirements.

Estate (tenancy) at will:

- *Indefinite term*
- *Possession with landlord's consent*

Estate at Will An **estate** (tenancy) **at will** gives the tenant the right to possess property with the landlord's consent for an unspecified or uncertain term. An estate at will is a tenancy of indefinite duration; it continues until it is terminated by either party giving proper notice. No initial period of occupancy is specified, as is the case in a periodic tenancy. An estate at will is automatically terminated by the death of either the landlord or the tenant. It may be created by express agreement or by operation of law. During the existence of a tenancy at will, the tenant has all the rights and obligations of a lessor-lessee relationship, including the duty to pay rent at regular intervals. As a practical matter, tenancy at will is rarely used in a written agreement and is viewed skeptically by the courts.

IN PRACTICE A landlord tells a tenant that at the end of the lease someone else will be moving into the apartment. The landlord gives the tenant the option to continue to rent until the new tenant is ready to move in. If the tenant agrees, an estate (tenancy) at will is created.

Estate (tenancy) at sufferance:

- *Tenant's previously lawful possession continues without landlord's consent*

Estate at Sufferance An **estate** (tenancy) **at sufferance** arises when a tenant who lawfully took possession of real property continues in possession of the premises without the landlord's consent after the right of possession has expired. This estate can arise when a tenant for years fails to surrender possession at the lease's expiration.

When a tenant fails to surrender possession, or *holds over*, the tenant is responsible for the payment of monthly rent at the existing terms and rate. A lease may contain a holdover clause, in which case that provision will govern the rights of both the landlord and the tenant. If a lease does not contain such a clause, then state law will govern and will typically offer three options:

- The landlord can accept rent offered by the tenant, thereby creating a new tenancy under conditions of the original lease, a *holdover tenancy*. If the original lease term was greater than one year, generally the new tenancy is limited to one year.
- The landlord can treat the tenant as a *tenant at sufferance* by either objecting to the tenant holding over or informing the tenant of such treatment, thus creating a month-to-month or periodic tenancy. The landlord receives rent, and both parties have to provide notice within a certain period of terminating the arrangement.
- The landlord can treat the tenant as a trespasser and proceed with an eviction and damages action. Under this situation, the landlord must comply with the *notice to quit* requirements in the lease as well as state law regarding the landlord-tenant relationship.

LEASE AGREEMENTS

Most states require no special wording to establish the landlord-tenant relationship. The lease may be written, oral, or implied, depending on the circumstances and the requirements of the statute of frauds. The law of the state where the real estate is located must be followed to ensure the validity of the lease.

Requirements of a Valid Lease

A lease is a contract between the **lessor** (landlord) and the **lessee** (tenant). To be valid, a lease must meet the following requirements, which are essentially the same as in any other contract:

- *Capacity to contract*. The parties must have the legal capacity to contract; that is, be of legal age and sound mind.
- *Legal objective*. The objective of the lease must be legal.
- *Offer and acceptance*. The parties must reach a mutual agreement (meeting of the minds) on all the terms of the contract.
- *Consideration*. The lease must be supported by valid consideration, an exchange of promises. The landlord promises to provide occupancy and the tenant promises to pay rent. Rent is typically monetary, although the tenant could provide agreed-upon labor in maintaining or fixing up the property. Because a lease is a contract, the rent and other terms may not be changed unless both parties agree to the changes in a writing that is executed in the same manner as the original lease.

The leased premises should be clearly described. For most residential leases, the street address or the street address and the apartment number is usually sufficient. If supplemental space is part of the rental, it should be clearly identified. If the lease covers land, such as a ground lease, then a legal description should be used. There should be no ambiguity.

Preprinted lease agreements are usually better suited to residential leases. Commercial leases are generally more complex, have different legal requirements, and may include complicated calculations of rent and maintenance costs. Drafting a commercial lease—or even a complex residential lease, for that matter—may constitute the practice of law. Unless the real estate professional is also an attorney, legal counsel should be sought.

IN PRACTICE For a complex lease, the professional can use a two- or three-page form to facilitate a preliminary agreement on the basic terms of the lease, subject to approval of a final draft prepared by an attorney (usually, the attorney for the landlord). The final document would then require execution by both parties.

Possession of Premises

The lessor, as the owner of the real estate, is usually bound by the *covenant of quiet enjoyment* that the lessee can occupy the premises without interference from the owner or anyone else. Quiet enjoyment does not have anything to do with barking dogs or late-night motorcycles. The lease usually stipulates the conditions under which the landlord may enter the property to perform maintenance, to make repairs, or for other stated purposes. Except in emergencies, the tenant's permission is usually required, which may be stipulated in the lease or by state law.

Use of Premises

A lessor may restrict a lessee's use of the premises through provisions included in the lease. For example, the property is leased only to the lessee "and shall be used strictly as a residence and for no other purpose." Use restrictions are particularly common in leases for stores or commercial space. For example, a lease may provide that the leased premises are to be used only as a real estate office and for no other purpose. In the absence of such clear limitations, a lessee may use the premises for any lawful purpose.

Term of Lease

The term of a lease, the period for which the lease will run, should be stated precisely, including the beginning and ending dates together with a statement of the total period of the lease. For instance, a lease might run "for a term of 30 years beginning June 1, 2010, and ending May 31, 2040." A perpetual lease for an inordinate amount of time or an indefinite term usually will be ruled invalid, but if the language of the lease and the surrounding circumstances clearly indicate that the parties intended such a term, the lease will be binding on the parties. Some states prohibit leases that run for 100 years or more.

Security Deposit

Tenants are often required to provide a **security deposit**, which is held by the landlord during the lease term. The security deposit is used if the tenant defaults on payment of rent or destroys the premises. Real estate professionals should be aware of state laws that govern security deposits: how they may be held, maximum amounts, whether interest must be paid, and how and when they are returned. To safeguard against nonpayment of rent, landlords may require an advance rental payment or a contract for a lien on the tenant's property or may require the tenant to have a third person guarantee payment.

IN PRACTICE A lease should specify whether a payment is a security deposit or an advance on rent. If it is a security deposit, the tenant is usually not entitled to apply it to the final month's rent. If it is an advance on rent, the landlord must treat it as income for tax purposes.

Improvements

Neither the landlord nor the tenant is required to make any improvements to the leased property. The tenant may, however, make improvements with the landlord's permission or as required to make the rented premises accessible, as discussed in the next paragraph. In most residential properties, any alterations become the property of the landlord. In many commercial leases, however, the tenant is permitted to install trade fixtures, those articles attached to a rental space that are required to conduct the tenant's business. Trade fixtures may be removed before the lease expires, provided the tenant restores the premises to the previous condition, with allowance for the wear and tear of normal use.

Accessibility

The federal Fair Housing Act makes it illegal to discriminate against a prospective tenant on the basis of the tenant's real or perceived disability. A tenant with a disability must be permitted to make reasonable modifications to a property at the tenant's own expense. If the modifications would interfere with a future tenant's use, the landlord may require that the premises be restored to their original condition at the end of the lease term. The Americans with Disabilities Act (ADA) will also affect a landlord's obligations when a commercial property or place of public accommodation is being leased.

Maintenance of Premises

Most states require a lessor of residential property to maintain dwelling units in a habitable condition. The landlord must make any necessary repairs to common areas, such as hallways, stairs, and elevators, and maintain safety features, such as fire sprinklers and smoke alarms. Residential tenants do not have to make any repairs, but they must return the premises in the same condition they were received, with allowances for ordinary wear and tear. Lessees of commercial and industrial properties usually maintain the premises and are often responsible for making their own repairs.

Destruction of Premises

The obligation to pay rent for damaged or destroyed premises differs depending on the type of property and the lease. Usually, residential tenants are permitted to reduce their rent payments in proportion to the amount of space they are unable to use. Likewise, tenants who lease only part of a building, such as office or commercial space, generally are not required to continue to pay rent after the leased premises are destroyed. In some states, if the property was destroyed as a result of the landlord's negligence, the tenant can recover damages.

On the other hand, tenants who have constructed buildings on leased land, often agricultural or industrial land, are still obligated for the payment of rent even if the improvements are damaged or destroyed. If the buildings are destroyed, these tenants must turn to their insurance companies to deal with their loss of the improvement.

Assignment and Subleasing

In an **assignment** of a lease, a tenant transfers the entire leasehold interest to another person. The new tenant is legally obligated to comply with all of the promises the original tenant made in the lease.

Under a **sublease**, a tenant transfers less than the entire leasehold interest by *subletting* the premises to a new tenant. The original tenant remains responsible for rent being paid by the new tenant and for any damage done to the rental during the lease term. The new tenant is responsible only to the original tenant to pay the rent due. The sublessor's (original lessee's) interest in the real estate is known as a *sandwich lease*.

Assignment and subleasing are allowed only when a lease specifically permits them. In both an assignment and a sublease, details of the arrangement should be in writing.

In most cases, the sublease or assignment of a lease does not relieve the original lessee of the obligation to pay rent. The landlord may, however, agree to waive the former tenant's liability. Most leases prohibit a lessee from assigning or subletting without the lessor's consent. This permits the lessor to retain control over the occupancy of the leased premises. As a rule, the lessor must not unreasonably withhold consent.

Recording a Lease

Anyone who inspects a leased property receives actual notice of the tenant's occupancy. For this reason, it is usually considered unnecessary to record a lease, although most states allow a lease to be recorded in the county in which the property is located. Furthermore, leases of three years or longer often are recorded as a matter of course. Some states require that a long-term lease be recorded, especially when the lessee intends to mortgage the leasehold interest.

A lease will typically run with the land; a change in the ownership of the leased fee estate doesn't affect the leasehold unless there is a provision in the lease providing for termination of an existing tenancy under specified circumstances or as provided by state law. Existing tenants usually have the right to remain in possession until the lease expires. A prospective buyer of property, especially an occupied single-family home, should inquire about the status of the occupants. The title records are searched for any recorded leases as part of the purchase transaction.

Nondisturbance Clause

A **nondisturbance clause** is included in the financing instrument used to mortgage leased premises. By accepting this provision, the mortgagee agrees not to terminate the tenancy of the lessee(s), so long as the lessee is current in payment of the required rent, should the mortgagee foreclose on the mortgagor's building.

Options

A lease may contain a clause that grants the lessee the privilege of renewing the lease (called a **renewal option**). The lessee must, however, give notice of intent to exercise the option. Some leases grant the lessee the option to purchase the leased premises (called a **purchase option**). This option normally gives the tenant the right to purchase the property at a predetermined price within a certain period, possibly the lease term. The lease might also contain a **right of first refusal** that allows the tenant the opportunity to buy the property before the owner accepts an offer from another party. The lease option may stipulate that the tenant is to be given credit toward the purchase price for some percentage of the rent paid, as the parties negotiate.

IN PRACTICE All the general statements concerning provisions of a lease are controlled largely by the terms of the agreement and state law. Landlord-tenant laws also vary from state to state. Great care must be exercised in reading the entire lease document before signing it because every clause in the lease has an economic and legal impact on either the landlord or the tenant. Although preprinted lease forms are available, there is no such thing as a standard lease. When complicated lease situations arise, legal counsel should be sought.

TYPES OF LEASES

A lease can be characterized by the manner in which rent payments are determined as well as the type of property being leased. There are three basic forms of lease payments: the gross lease, the net lease, and the percentage lease. (*See* Figure 18.2.) A variable lease will combine one of these forms of payment with adjustments in the amount of rent to be paid.

Gross Lease

In a **gross lease**, the tenant pays a fixed rent and some or all of the utility expenses, while the landlord pays all taxes, insurance, repairs, any other utility expenses, and maintenance connected with the property (usually called *property charges* or *operating expenses*). Residential and commercial office leases are most often gross leases.

IN PRACTICE The landlord may pay for water, trash collection, and sewerage fees, while the tenant pays for items such as electricity, gas, and cable or other access to phone, television, and internet services.

Net Lease

In a **net lease**, the tenant pays all or most of the property expenses, such as hazard insurance, property taxes, and/or common area maintenance (CAM) charges, in addition to the rent. The monthly rental is net income for the landlord after operating costs have been paid. Leases for entire commercial and industrial buildings and the land on which they are located, ground leases, and long-term leases are usually net leases.

Percentage Lease

Either a gross lease or a net lease may be a **percentage lease**. This type of lease is generally used for retail business leases. The rent is based on a minimum fixed rental fee plus a percentage of the gross income received by the tenant doing business on the leased property. The percentage charged is negotiable and varies depending on the nature of the business, location of the property, and general economic conditions.

FIGURE 18.2: Types of Leases

Type of Lease	Lessor	Lessee
Gross lease	Pays property charges (taxes, repairs, insurance, maintenance, some or all utilities)	Pays basic rent plus some utility costs
Net lease	May pay some property charges	Pays basic rent plus all or most property charges
Percentage lease (commercial and industrial)	Often pays property charges (taxes, repairs, insurance, maintenance, some utilities)	Pays basic rent plus percentage of gross sales (may pay property costs, such as utilities)

Variable Lease A lease may allow for increases in the rental charges during the lease term. A *graduated lease* provides for specified rent increases at set future dates. An *index lease* allows rent to be increased or decreased periodically based on changes in the consumer price index or some other indicator.

Other Types of Leases

Ground Lease When a landowner leases unimproved land to a tenant who agrees to erect a building on the land, the lease is usually called a **ground lease**. It is most often used in commercial and industrial property development. Ground leases typically involve separate ownership of the land and the buildings. These leases must be long enough to make the transaction desirable to the tenant investing in the building. They often run for terms of 50 to 99 years.

Ground leases are generally *net leases*: the lessee must pay rent on the ground, as well as real estate taxes, insurance, upkeep, utilities, and repairs. At the end of the lease term, any tenant-built structures on the property usually become the property of the landlord.

Oil and Gas Lease When an oil company leases land to explore for oil and gas, a special lease agreement must be negotiated. Except for enough surface space to conduct extraction operations, the lease covers subsurface rights. Usually, the landowner receives a cash payment for executing the lease. If no well is drilled within the period stated in the lease, the lease expires, although most oil and gas leases permit the oil company to continue its rights for another year by paying another flat rental fee. Such rentals may be paid annually until a well is produced. If oil or gas is found, the landowner usually receives a percentage of its value as a royalty. As long as oil or gas is obtained in significant quantities, the lease continues indefinitely. Oil and gas leases, even after they have expired, are often listed as exclusions in title insurance policies.

Lease Purchase A **lease purchase** is used when a tenant wants to purchase the property but is not yet able to do so. Perhaps the tenant cannot obtain favorable financing or clear title, or the tax consequences of a purchase are currently unfavorable. The terms of the sale are negotiated and agreed to at the time that the lease is signed. A down payment is paid, which may or may not be refundable, and part of the periodic rent may be applied toward the purchase price of the property. Both parties hope that, by the time the lease expires, the tenant's issues have been resolved and financing can be obtained or the tenant can purchase the property outright.

Sale-and-leaseback In a **sale-and-leaseback**, the property owners sell the property and then lease it back for an agreed period and rental. The original owners pull out their equity to use on other projects and are also able to reduce their taxable income when they pay rent to the new owner. The new owner has a reliable source of rental income for an extended time.

IN PRACTICE The sale-and-leaseback is often used by a company that owns its own office building but is in need of capital, perhaps for business expansion. The building can be sold to obtain funds, but the company will be allowed to remain in the building as a tenant and pay rent to the new owners.

DISCHARGE OF A LEASE

As with any contract, a lease is discharged when the contract terminates. Termination can occur either when all parties have fully performed their obligations under the agreement, or when the parties agree to cancel the lease. If the tenant, for instance, offers to surrender the leasehold interest, and if the landlord accepts the tenant's offer, the lease is terminated. A tenant who simply abandons leased property, however, remains liable for the terms of the lease—including the rent. The terms of the lease will usually indicate whether the landlord is obligated to try to re-rent the space. If the landlord intends to sue for unpaid rent, however, most states require an attempt to mitigate damages by re-renting the premises to limit the amount owed.

The lease does not terminate if the parties die or if the property is sold. There are two exceptions to this general rule. First, a lease from the owner of a life estate ends with the death of the person on whose life the estate is measured. Second, the death of either party terminates a tenancy at will. In all other cases, the heirs of a deceased landlord are bound by the terms of existing valid leases.

If leased real estate is sold or otherwise conveyed, the new landlord takes the property subject to the rights of the tenants. A lease agreement may contain language that permits a new landlord to terminate existing leases, although this is much more common in commercial properties than in residential properties. The clause, known as a *sale clause*, requires that the tenant be given some period of notice before the termination. Because the new owner takes title subject to the rights of the tenant, the sale clause enables the new landlord to claim possession and negotiate a new lease under new terms and conditions.

A tenancy may also be terminated by operation of law, as in a bankruptcy, foreclosure, or condemnation proceeding in an eminent domain action.

Breach of Lease

When a tenant breaches (violates) any lease provision, the landlord may sue the tenant to obtain a judgment to cover past-due rent, damages to the premises, or other defaults. Likewise, when a landlord breaches any lease provision, the tenant is entitled to certain remedies. The rights and responsibilities of the landlord-tenant relationship are governed by state law.

Suit for Possession—Actual Eviction When a tenant breaches a lease or improperly retains leased premises, the landlord may regain possession through a legal process known as **actual eviction**. The landlord must serve notice on the tenant before commencing the lawsuit. Most lease terms require at least a 10-day notice in the case of default. In many states, however, only a five-day or three-day notice is necessary when the tenant defaults in the payment of rent. When a court issues a judgment for possession to a landlord, the tenant must vacate the property. If the tenant fails to leave, the landlord can have the judgment enforced by a court officer, who forcibly removes the tenant and the tenant's possessions. The landlord then has the right to re-enter and regain possession of the property. In some states, in cases of nonpayment of rent, a landlord also has the right to *distrain*, that is, to seize the tenant's property for rent in arrears, generally by changing the locks and giving notice. Most states require a court order to pursue the remedy of *distraint*.

Tenants' Remedies—Constructive Eviction If a landlord breaches any clause of a lease agreement, the tenant has the right to sue and recover damages against the landlord. If the leased premises become unusable for the purpose stated in the lease, the tenant may have the right to abandon them. This action, called **constructive eviction**, terminates the lease agreement. The tenant must prove that the premises have become unusable because of the conscious neglect of the landlord. To claim constructive eviction, the tenant must leave the premises while the conditions that made the premises uninhabitable exist.

FOR EXAMPLE A tenant's lease requires that the landlord furnish heat. The landlord fails to repair a defective furnace, and no heat is provided to the tenant's apartment during the winter months. The tenant is forced to abandon the apartment. Because the lack of heat was due to the landlord's negligence, the tenant has been constructively evicted.

Protenant Legislation

www.uniformlaws.org

For the most part, leases are drawn up primarily for the benefit of the landlord. However, due to tenants' rights movements and increased consumer awareness, many states have adopted all or part of the Uniform Residential Landlord and Tenant Act that was created in 1972 by what is now the National Conference of Commissioners on Uniform State Laws, www.uniformlaws.org. The model law, which is currently undergoing revision, addresses the need for both parties to a lease to fulfill certain basic obligations. The act addresses such issues as

- the landlord's right of entry,
- maintenance of the premises,
- the tenant's protection against retaliation by the landlord for complaints, and
- the disclosure of the property owner's name and address to the tenant.

The act further establishes the specific remedies available to both the landlord and the tenant if a breach of the lease agreement occurs.

Fair Housing and Civil Rights Laws

The federal fair housing and civil right laws that were previously covered affect landlords and tenants just as they do sellers and purchasers. All persons must have access to housing of their choice without any differentiation in terms and conditions based on race, color, religion, national origin, sex, disability, or familial status. State and local municipalities have their own fair housing laws that add protected classes such as age and sexual orientation. Withholding an apartment that is available for rent, segregating certain people in separate sections of an apartment complex or parts of a building, and charging people in the protected classes different amounts for rent or security deposits all constitute violations of the law.

IN PRACTICE The fair housing laws require that the same tenant criteria be applied to families with children that are applied to adults. A landlord cannot charge a different amount of rent or security deposit because one of the tenants is a child. While landlords have historically argued that children are noisy and destructive, the fact is that many adults are also noisy and destructive.

It is important to remember that a violation of federal or state fair housing laws can occur even without deliberate intent to discriminate—and even if a prospective tenant asks for the kind of assistance that would make a real estate professional guilty of discrimination.

IN PRACTICE The Manero family from Thailand moved to Oakton and contacted a real estate professional for assistance in finding a rental property. The real estate professional asked a number of questions to determine what kind of housing the family sought, their budget, and what part of town they preferred. Mrs. Manero insisted that she wanted to live in a part of town that they had heard about where a number of Thai families lived. She asked the real estate professional to find them a house in that part of town. The real estate professional complied but was subsequently disciplined by the state's real estate licensing agency and also fined by the fair housing division of the state's attorney general's office. The real estate professional learned, the hard way, that he should have informed the Maneros that he could show them properties in any part of town they requested that were within their budget but could not direct them to a neighborhood based on the nationality of the residents.

KEY POINT REVIEW

A **lease** is a contract between the **lessor** (the owner of real estate, also called the **landlord**) and the **lessee** (the **tenant**) that transfers possession and use of the property, lasts for a specified period, and is made in return for consideration (possession and payment).

The **statute of frauds** in most states requires that leases for more than one year be **in writing to be enforceable**. The lessor has a **reversionary right** to possession of property when a lease expires.

The **leasehold estate** of the lessee can be one of the following:

- An **estate for years (tenancy for years)** continues for a definite period. A **holdover tenancy** may be created when a tenant with an estate for years stays on after the lease term expires and the landlord accepts rent payment.
- An **estate from period to period (periodic tenancy)** has no specific expiration date, but rent is payable at definite intervals and the lease term has continuity because it automatically renews. A **month-to-month tenancy** is a common form of residential lease.
- An **estate at will (tenancy at will)** has no specified initial term, is created by **express agreement** or **operation of law**, and can be **terminated** by the landlord or the tenant at any time on proper notice.
- An **estate at sufferance (tenancy at sufferance)** is created when the tenant stays on without the landlord's consent after termination. The landlord's acceptance of rent creates a holdover tenancy, or the landlord can treat the tenant as a trespasser and begin eviction proceedings and an action for damages under state law.

A **valid lease** requires parties with **CLOAC** (**C**apacity to contract, **L**egal objectives, **O**ffer and **A**cceptance, and valid **C**onsideration). A lease typically includes a **description** of leased premises; implied **covenant of quiet enjoyment** and a **nondisturbance clause** ; limitations on tenant's **use** of the property and the **term** (length) of the lease; **security deposit**, which must comply with state law; and a statement as to whether **improvements** may be made by the tenant.

Fixtures generally become the landlord's property unless they are removable **trade fixtures**. Federal fair housing law requires the landlord to allow a tenant with a disability to make **reasonable modifications** to the premises. The **Americans with Disabilities Act (ADA)** requires that commercial nonresidential property be free of barriers or that reasonable accommodations be provided.

A typical lease will also include a provision that **maintenance** of premises will be performed by the landlord in compliance with state law; whether or not an **assignment** of the lease will be permitted, and if so, whether the assignment will relieve the tenant of further obligation to the landlord; and whether or not a **sublease** will be permitted and under what terms. **Recording** of the lease may be required by state law. An **option** may give the tenant the right to renew the lease, the right to purchase the leased property, or the right of first refusal if the landlord decides to sell the property.

A **gross lease** requires the tenant to pay rent and the landlord to pay the expenses of ownership, such as taxes, insurance, and maintenance. A **net lease** requires the tenant to pay rent plus all or most property expenses, with the landlord also paying some property expenses. In a **percentage lease**, the tenant pays rent plus a percentage of gross sales and may pay property expenses.

A **variable lease** allows an increase in rent during the lease period. A **graduated lease** states specific rent increases. An **index lease** allows rent changes (up or down) based on the consumer price index or other indicator.

A **ground lease** involves separate ownership of land and buildings. An **oil and gas lease** allows exploration for and removal of oil and gas. In a **lease purchase**, part of the rent may be applied to the purchase price. A **sale-and-leaseback** allows the original owner to use the property as a tenant while freeing up capital for other business purposes.

The remedies for **breach** of a lease are governed by state law. The landlord may bring **suit for possession** (actual eviction), or the tenant may claim a **constructive eviction** if the premises are uninhabitable.

The **Uniform Residential Landlord and Tenant Act** has been adopted by many states in whole or in part and a revision is underway.

Federal fair housing and **civil right laws** affect landlords and tenants just as they do sellers and purchasers.

UNIT 18 QUIZ

1. Which transaction is *BEST* described as involving a ground lease?
   a. A landowner agrees to let a tenant drill for oil on a property for 75 years.
   b. The tenant agrees to pay a proportionate, increased rental based on annual appraisals of the rented property.
   c. A landlord charges a commercial tenant separate amounts for the land and the leased building.
   d. The tenant pays a base amount for the property plus a percentage of business-generated income.
2. A tenant enters into a commercial lease that requires a monthly rent of a minimum fixed amount, plus an additional amount determined by a percentage of the tenant's gross receipts exceeding $5,000. This type of lease is called a
   a. standard lease.
   b. gross lease.
   c. percentage lease.
   d. net lease.
3. If a tenant moved out of a rented store building because access to the building was blocked as a result of the landlord's negligence, the
   a. tenant might have no legal recourse against the landlord.
   b. landlord may be liable for the rent until the expiration date of the lease.
   c. landlord may have to provide substitute space.
   d. tenant may be entitled to recover damages from the landlord.
4. A tenant moves a pet into an apartment community that has a no-pets policy. The landlord wishes to remove the tenant due to the breach. The legal process to remove a tenant is known as
   a. constructive eviction.
   b. eminent domain.
   c. actual eviction.
   d. partial eviction.
5. A tenant still has five months remaining on a one-year apartment lease. When the tenant moves to another city, he transfers possession of the apartment to a friend for the entire remaining term of the lease. The friend pays rent directly to the tenant. In this situation, the tenant has become a(n)
   a. assignor.
   b. sublessor.
   c. sublessee.
   d. lessor.
6. Which of the following is *TRUE* about a holdover tenant?
   a. The landlord must accept additional rent if the tenant remains on the premises.
   b. The tenant must give the landlord a 30-day notice to vacate.
   c. The tenant may continue to occupy the premises without permission of the landlord.
   d. The landlord may evict the tenant.
7. A tenant's tenancy for years will expire in two weeks. The tenant plans to move to a larger apartment across town when the current tenancy expires. In order to terminate this agreement, the tenant must
   a. give the landlord immediate notice or the lease will automatically renew.
   b. give the landlord one week's prior notice or the lease will automatically renew.
   c. do nothing because the agreement will terminate automatically at the end of the current term.
   d. sign a lease for the new apartment, which will automatically terminate the existing lease.
8. When a tenant holds possession of a landlord's property without a current lease agreement and without the landlord's approval, the
   a. tenant is maintaining a gross lease.
   b. landlord can file suit for possession.
   c. tenant has no obligation to pay rent.
   d. landlord may be subject to a constructive eviction.

9. Under the negotiated terms of a certain residential lease, the landlord is required to maintain the water heater. If the tenant is unable to get hot water because of a faulty water heater that the landlord has failed to repair after repeated notification, the tenant could do all of the following *EXCEPT*

a. sue the landlord for damages.
b. order a new water heater and send the bill to the landlord.
c. abandon the premises claiming constructive eviction.
d. terminate the lease agreement.

10. A person has a one-year leasehold interest in a house. The interest automatically renews itself at the end of each year. The person's interest is referred to as a tenancy

a. for years.
b. from period to period.
c. at will.
d. at sufferance.

11. Rent would *BEST* be described as

a. contractual consideration to a third party.
b. consideration for the use of real property.
c. all monies paid by the lessor to the lessee.
d. the total balance owed under the terms of a lease.

12. Which of the following would automatically terminate a residential lease?

a. Total destruction of the property
b. Sale of the property
c. Failure of the tenant to pay rent
d. Death of the tenant

13. Which of the following describes a net lease?

a. An agreement in which the tenant pays a fixed rent and the landlord pays all taxes, insurance, and expenses related to the property
b. A lease in which the tenant pays rent, plus some—or most—of the operating expenses related to the property
c. A lease in which the tenant pays the landlord a percentage of the monthly income derived from the property
d. An agreement granting an individual a leasehold interest in fishing rights for shoreline properties

14. A tenancy in which the tenant continues in possession after the lease has expired, without the landlord's permission, is a

a. tenancy for years.
b. periodic tenancy.
c. tenancy at will.
d. tenancy at sufferance.

15. A percentage lease calls for a minimum rent of $1,200 per month plus additional annual rent of 4% of the year's gross business exceeding $150,000. If the business generated $270,000, how much annual rent does the tenant owe?

a. $10,800
b. $14,400
c. $19,200
d. $25,200

16. Which of the following describes a gross lease?

a. An agreement in which the tenant pays a fixed rent and some or all of the utilities and the landlord pays all taxes, insurance, and expenses related to the property
b. A lease in which the tenant pays rent plus some of the operating expenses related to the property
c. A lease in which the tenant pays the landlord a percentage of the monthly income derived from the property
d. An agreement allowing the tenant to terminate the lease if certain conditions near the premises become unbearable

17. A tenant signs a lease that includes a schedule of rent increases on specific dates over the course of the lease term. What kind of lease has this tenant signed?

a. Percentage
b. Net
c. Graduated
d. Index

18. A tenant signs a lease that includes the following clause: "The stated rent under this agreement will be increased or decreased every three months based on the percentage increase in the consumer price index (CPI) for that period." What kind of lease has this tenant signed?

a. Percentage
b. Net
c. Graduated
d. Index

19. The death of either the landlord or the tenant will terminate the lease and the parties' heirs will *NOT* be bound by its terms under which of the following tenancies?

a. Tenancy for years
b. Periodic tenancy
c. Tenancy at will
d. Tenancy at sufferance

20. The tenant leases a heated apartment, but the landlord fails to provide heat because of a defective central heating plant. The tenant vacates the premises and refuses to pay any rent. This is an example of

a. abandonment.
b. actual eviction.
c. constructive eviction.
d. lessor negligence.

Property Management

LEARNING OBJECTIVES

When you have finished reading this unit, you will be able to

- **describe** the various property management specialties available in the property management field and the role of the property manager in each;
- **explain** the essential elements of the property management agreement;
- **list and explain** the primary responsibilities of the property manager;
- **describe** the various federal laws with which the property manager must be knowledgeable and comply with in the performance of his or her duties;
- **describe** the implementation of risk management procedures to insure the safety and security of the property's tenants as well as protecting the landlord from liability and loss; and
- **define** the following *key terms*:

budget comparison statement
cash flow report
corrective maintenance
management agreement
management plan
multiperil policies
operating budget
preventive maintenance
profit and loss statement
property manager
risk management
routine maintenance
surety bonds
tenant improvements
workers' compensation acts

OVERVIEW

As a specialized field, property management is one of the fastest growing areas of real estate practice. Property management involves the leasing, managing, marketing, and overall maintenance of real estate owned by others, usually rental property. Many mortgage lenders require that investors hire a professional property manager to manage their properties.

THE PROPERTY MANAGER

A property manager must
- achieve the goals of the owners,
- generate income, and
- preserve and/or increase the value of the property.

The role of the **property manager** is complex, requiring the manager to wear many hats. It is not unusual for a property manager to be a market analyst, salesperson, accountant, advertising specialist, and maintenance person—all in the same day. In addition, the property manager frequently interacts with people in various professions, including lawyers, environmental engineers, and accountants. The three principal responsibilities of the property manager are to

- achieve the objectives of the property owners,
- generate income for the owners, and
- preserve and/or increase the value of the investment property.

The property manager carries out the goals of the property owners. In the process, the property manager is responsible for maintaining the owner's investment and making sure the property earns income. These goals can be accomplished in several ways. The physical property must be maintained in good condition. Suitable tenants must be found, rent must be collected, and employees must be hired and supervised. The property manager is responsible for budgeting and controlling expenses, keeping proper accounts, and making periodic reports to the owner. In all of these activities, the manager's primary goal is to operate and maintain the physical property in such a way as to preserve and enhance the owner's capital investment.

Some property managers work for property management companies. These firms manage properties for a number of owners under management agreements. A property manager in a general agency relationship with the property owner could be an independent contractor with great authority and discretion in management decisions. A property manager or an owner may employ building managers to supervise the daily operations of a building. In some cases, these individuals might be residents of the building.

IN PRACTICE In most states, licensed real estate professionals are permitted to manage properties for others. Some states have separate property management licenses. When directly employed by the owner, nonlicensed individuals are permitted by some states to manage properties. While some states require licensing in order to manage condominium or cooperative homeowners associations, others do not. Some states require an on-site manager for residential income-producing properties having more than a certain number of units; for example, California requires a manager on-site for residential properties of 16 or more units.

Securing Management Business

Possible clients of a property management business include

- corporate owners,
- apartment buildings,
- owners of small rental residential properties,
- homeowners associations,
- investment syndicates,
- trusts, and
- owners of office buildings.

A good reputation is often the manager's best advertising. A manager who consistently demonstrates the ability to increase property income over previous levels, while meeting legal requirements and enhancing the property's attractiveness to tenants, should have little difficulty finding new business.

Before contracting to manage any property, the professional property manager should be certain that the building owner has realistic income expectations. Necessary maintenance, unexpected repairs, and effective marketing all take time and money. In addition, most states have landlord-tenant laws that require the landlord-owner to keep the property repaired and make sure it complies with building codes. Through the agency relationship with the owner, the property manager becomes responsible for repairs and the building's condition.

New Opportunities

Specialization has opened a range of new opportunities. Well-trained specialists are needed to manage shopping centers, commercial buildings, and industrial parks, in addition to the more visible management of residential properties. The following are just a few of the specialties that have an ongoing need for competent managers.

Community Association Management The prevalence of homeowners and condominium associations combined with complex planning and development codes have placed new demands on property managers. Working as part of a team, property managers assist in providing a comprehensive array of services to volunteer boards. Many states now require at least a real estate license or an association management license for those who specialize in managing associations.

Housing for Seniors Opportunities abound in managing housing for those age 55 and older, including federally assisted housing programs. In addition to marketing, managers of senior housing are often responsible for the operation of the facility, as well as housekeeping, meal service, social event planning, and medical emergency planning. When subsidized housing is involved, the property manager needs to be familiar with state and federal rules pertaining to eligibility requirements and income verification.

Manufactured Homes Homes built in factories meeting HUD specifications are called manufactured homes or HUD-code homes. These homes may be placed on individually owned land, but more than a third are sited in communities. A tenant may rent only the "pad," the land on which the home is sited, or the home itself. Many communities, especially those in the sun belt states, are geared toward seniors; managers at these communities must be effective at building community spirit.

Resort Housing Managing second-home and resort rentals presents specific challenges. A resort manager must be able to care for and maintain often-vacant properties and be able to attract and manage short-term tenants. Many such properties are located in high-risk areas for natural disasters such as hurricanes, so the manager must be able to prepare for an emergency as well as to work with insurance adjusters.

Concierge Services A new area for property managers to specialize in is the training and managing of concierge staff for office buildings and other settings. Concierge staff are responsible for anything from arranging for taxi rides to assisting with internet-enabled equipment for a conference.

Asset Management An asset manager monitors a portfolio of properties similar to a securities portfolio by analyzing the performance of the properties and making recommendations to the owners of the properties. Real property asset management helps clients decide what type of real estate to invest in—commercial, residential, industrial, or agricultural—and which property is best to purchase, the best financial sources for a real estate purchase, and when to dispose of property.

Corporate Property Manager Hiring a corporate property manager allows a corporation to invest in real estate and increase its capital, even if the corporation is not necessarily knowledgeable about property management. Typically, the corporate property manager is an employee of the corporation and not an independent contractor.

Leasing Agent A leasing agent is usually an independent contractor working on a commission basis. Leasing agents are usually in high demand because of their skill in securing lessees.

Professional Associations

Most metropolitan areas have local associations of building and property owners and managers that are affiliates of regional and national associations. Many of these professional organizations provide information and contacts for all aspects of property management. Many also provide well-respected designations that help open doors for the property manager who is willing to fulfill the educational and/or experience requirements that a designation requires. The better-known associations include the following:

www.boma.org
www.bomi.org
www.caionline.org
www.irem.org
www.icsc.org
www.naahq.org
www.nahb.org
www.narpm.org

- Building Owners and Managers Association International (BOMA)—commercial real estate, www.boma.org
- Building Owners and Managers Institute International (BOMI)—education programs for commercial property and facility management industries, www.bomi.org
- Community Associations Institute (CAI)—homeowners associations, condominiums, and other planned communities, www.caionline.org
- Institute of Real Estate Management (IREM)—multifamily and commercial real estate designation, www.irem.org
- International Council of Shopping Centers (ICSC)—shopping centers worldwide, www.icsc.org
- National Apartment Association (NAA)—multifamily housing industry, www.naahq.org
- National Association of Home Builders (NAHB)—all aspects of home building, www.nahb.org
- National Association of Residential Property Managers (NARPM)—single-family and small residential properties, www.narpm.org

THE MANAGEMENT AGREEMENT

The first step in taking over the management of any property is to enter into a **management agreement**, a contract creating a general agency relationship between the owner and the property manager. The management agreement defines the duties and responsibilities of each party; it is a guide used in operating the property, as well as a reference in case of any future disputes.

The Property Manager's Role

The property manager is typically considered a *general agent*. As an agent, the property manager is charged with the fiduciary responsibilities of care, obedience, accounting, loyalty, and disclosure. Property managers are usually empowered to make many more decisions on behalf of the owner than a real estate professional can make in the real estate professional's representation of a seller or a buyer. After entering into an agreement with a property owner, a manager handles the property the same way the owner would. In all activities, the manager's first responsibility is to realize the highest return on the property in a manner consistent with the owner's instructions and applicable law. As in any other contract in which the duties and responsibilities of the parties are specified, the management agreement should be in writing, and it should include the following points:

- *Description* of the property.
- *Time period* the agreement covers and specific provisions for termination.
- *Definition of the management's responsibilities*. All the manager's duties should be specifically stated in the contract. Any limitations or restrictions on what the manager may do should be clearly stated.
- *Statement of the owner's purpose and responsibilities*. The owner should clearly state what the manager is to accomplish. One owner may want to maximize net income, while another may want to increase the capital value of the investment. What the manager does depends on the owner's long-term goals for the property. The agreement should list the owner's responsibilities for management expenses, such as payroll, advertising, insurance, and management fees.
- *Extent of the manager's authority*. This provision should state what authority the manager is to have in matters such as hiring, firing, and supervising employees; fixing rental rates for space; and making expenditures and authorizing repairs. Repairs that exceed a certain expense limit may require the owner's written approval.
- *Reporting*. The frequency and detail of the manager's periodic reports on operations and financial position should be agreed on. These reports serve as a means for the owner to monitor the manager's work. They also form a basis for both the owner and the manager to spot trends that are important in shaping management policy. The state real estate commission usually will have regulations concerning reporting.
- *Compensation*. The management fee or other form of compensation may be based on a percentage of gross or net income, a fixed fee, or some combination of these and other factors. The compensation provision of the agreement should state the base fee, as well as any leasing fees, supervision fees, or other commissions or compensations.
- *Allocation of costs*. The agreement should state which of the property manager's expenses—such as office rent, office help, telephone, advertising, and association fees—will be paid by the manager. Other costs will be paid by the owner.
- *Liability*. The agreement should require that the manager be included as an additional insured on the property liability policy.
- *Antitrust provisions*. Management fees are subject to the same antitrust considerations as sales commissions. They cannot be standardized in the marketplace, because standardization would be considered price-fixing. The fee must be negotiated between the agent and the principal. In addition,

the property manager may be entitled to a commission on new rentals and renewed leases.

- *Equal opportunity statement.* Residential property management agreements should include a statement that the property will be shown, rented, and otherwise made available to all persons, regardless of race, color, religion, sex, disability, national origin, or family status, and to any class of person protected by local, state or federal law.

MATH CONCEPTS

Rental Commissions

Residential property managers often earn commissions when they find tenants for a property. Rental commissions are usually based on the annual rent from a property. For example, if an apartment unit rents for $1,200 per month and the commission payable is 8%, the commission is calculated as follows:

$1,200 per month × 12 months = $14,400

$14,400 × 0.08 = $1,152

THE PROPERTY MANAGER'S RESPONSIBILITIES

Property management begins with a **management plan** prepared by the property manager. A management plan outlines the details of the owner's objectives with the property, as well as what the property manager expects to accomplish and how, including all financial objectives.

The Management Plan

In preparing a management plan, a property manager analyzes three factors: the owner's objectives, the regional and neighborhood market, and the specific property. Occupancy, absorption rates, and new starts are critical indicators. The plan also includes a budgetary section on sources of revenue and anticipated expenses. While the management plan is a document for the present, it is forward-looking in determining the feasibility of a property owner's long-term goals for a specific property.

Financial Reports

One of the primary responsibilities of a property manager is maintaining financial reports, including an operating budget, cash flow report, profit and loss statement, and budget comparison statement. While there are no standard formats for these reports, there is some similarity among the reports, and it is important for the property manager to adapt a report to meet an owner's needs. The reports are sent to the property owner at the agreed-upon intervals, by mail or email, but the property manager should meet the client at least once a year to go over the property's financial status in detail. Not only is this helpful to the owner's understanding of the property's performance, it is an excellent way for the property manager to demonstrate the levels of service and expertise that are being provided to the client.

Operating Budget The projection of income and expense for the operation of a property over a one-year period is called an **operating budget**. This budget, developed before attempting to rent property, is based on anticipated revenues and expenses and provides the owner the amount of expected profit. The property uses the operating budget as a guide for the property's financial performance in the present and future.

Once a property manager has managed a property for a length of time, an operating budget may be developed based on the results of the profit and loss statement in comparison to the original budget (actual versus projected). After making the comparison, a new operating budget is prepared for a new time period in the future.

Cash Flow Report A **cash flow report** is a monthly statement that details the financial status of the property. Sources of income and expenses are noted, as well as net operating income and net cash flow. The cash flow report is the most important financial report because it provides a picture of the current financial status of a property.

Income Income includes gross rentals collected, delinquent rental payments, utilities, vending machine proceeds, contracts, late fees, and storage charges. In some properties, there is space that is not income producing, such as the property manager's office. The rental value of the property that is not producing income is subtracted from the gross rental income to equal the gross collectible, or billable, rental income.

Any losses from uncollected rental payments or evictions are deducted from total gross income to arrive at net operating income.

Expenses A property will incur both fixed and variable expenses. Fixed expenses are those that remain fairly predictable, even though they may increase or decrease somewhat, such as employee wages and other administrative expenses, utilities, and other basic operating costs. Variable expenses may be recurring or nonrecurring and can include capital improvements, building repairs, and landscaping.

Cash Flow *Cash flow* is derived as shown below. The entry for "debt service" in the third equation includes any mortgage payments on the property.

Gross rental income + other income – losses incurred = total income

Total income – operating expenses = net operating income

Net operating income – debt service – reserves = cash flow

Profit and Loss Statement A **profit and loss statement** is a financial picture of revenues and expenses used to determine whether a business has made money or suffered a loss. It may be prepared monthly, quarterly, semiannually, or annually. The statement is created from the monthly cash flow reports and does not include itemized information. A formula for a profit and loss statement is as follows:

Gross receipts – operating expenses – total mortgage payment + mortgage loan principal = net profit

Budget Comparison Statement The **budget comparison statement** compares actual results with the original budget, often giving either percentages or a numerical variance of actual versus projected income and expenses. Budget comparisons are especially helpful in identifying trends in order to help with future budget planning.

Renting the Property

Effective rental of the property being managed is essential to ensure its long-term financial health. A property manager may use the services of a leasing agent. The real estate professional acting as leasing agent will be concerned solely with renting space and will not be responsible for maintaining and managing the property.

Setting Rental Rates While some municipalities control rent increases for residential tenants, most communities allow the market to determine the amount of rent that a tenant should pay. Because rental rates are influenced primarily by supply and demand, property managers should conduct a detailed survey of the competitive space available in the neighborhood, emphasizing similar properties. In establishing rental rates, property managers must consider the following:

- The rental income must be sufficient to cover the property's fixed charges and operating expenses.
- The rental income must provide a return on the owner's investment.
- The rental rate should be comparable with prevailing rates in comparable buildings in the area; it may be slightly higher or slightly lower, depending on the desirability of the property.
- The current vacancy rate in the property is a good indicator of how much of a rent increase might be possible. A building with a low vacancy rate is a better candidate for an increase than one with a high vacancy rate.

A rental rate for residential space is usually stated as the monthly rate *per unit.* Commercial leases—including office, retail, and industrial space rentals—are usually stated according to either annual or monthly rates *per square foot.*

An elevated level of vacancy may indicate poor management, a defective or undesirable property, or rental rates that are too high for the market or the property. A high occupancy rate may mean that rental rates are too low. Before adjusting the rental rates, the manager should investigate the rental market to determine whether a rent increase is warranted.

Marketing To ensure that a property generates income, the property manager must attract the best tenants. The marketing strategy must take into consideration the property itself, the supply and demand in the area where the property is located, and the amount of money available for advertising.

Advertising All advertising and promotional activities must comply with federal, state, and local nondiscrimination laws. The content cannot market to one protected class, such as race, color, religion, sex, national origin, familial status, or disability. To ensure that a property generates income, the property manager must attract the best tenants.

Advertising methods are numerous and include internet sites and social media, newspapers, brochures, radio, television, and direct mail.

Management Activities Because property management firms are often known by reputation, it is important for a firm to maintain good public relations. One way to cultivate public relations is through community involvement and charitable giving.

Firms can also write and issue public service announcements (PSAs) or press releases regarding special projects. These announcements can attract the attention of the media and, ultimately, prospective tenants.

Marketing and Advertising Costs A cost-benefit analysis helps a property manager assess whether a particular advertising method worked to attract new tenants. Property marketing expenses are usually figured on a cost-per-prospect-per-lease basis. For example, if a three-bedroom apartment rents for $1,500, is typically viewed by 10 prospects before it is leased, and a single newspaper advertisement is the only marketing, an $800 newspaper ad would cost $80 per prospect.

www.apartmentfinder.com
www.apartmentguide.com
www.craigslist.com
www.forrent.com
www.realtor.com
www.trulia.com
www.zillow.com

The internet has significantly expanded a property manager's ability to reach consumers. Online apartment vacancy listing sites include www.apartmentfinder.com, www.apartmentguide.com, www.craigslist.com, www.forrent.com, www.realtor.com, www.trulia.com, and www.zillow.com.

Selecting Tenants Proper selection is the first step in establishing and maintaining sound, long-term relationships with tenants. The manager should be sure that the premises are suitable for the tenant in terms of size, location, and amenities, and that the tenant can afford the space. A commercial tenant's business should be compatible not only with the building but also with the businesses of the other tenants. Managers should always ask commercial tenants about the potential for expansion. Because the property may not have enough room for expansion, the manager could soon lose the tenant to a larger space.

IN PRACTICE Some commercial leases prohibit the introduction of similar businesses. In any event, introduction of competitors into the same property should be undertaken with care because competitors in the same location will often decrease the activity of both businesses and soon one or the other will seek to move.

The residential property manager must be sure to comply with all federal, state, and local fair housing laws in selecting tenants. Although fair housing laws do not apply to commercial properties, commercial property managers need to be aware of federal, state, and local antidiscrimination and equal opportunity laws that may govern industrial or retail properties, including the Americans with Disabilities Act, which is discussed later.

Most states have strict requirements as to how security deposits should be handled by the property manager: how soon they must be deposited, into what kind of account, and when they must be refunded. In general, funds belonging to others, such as security deposits and collected rents, should be placed into a trust or escrow account. Property managers should not use any of these funds personally (conversion) or mix the funds into personal accounts (commingling).

Collecting Rents A property manager should accept only those tenants who can be expected to meet their financial obligations. The manager should investigate financial references, check with local credit bureaus, and when possible, interview a prospective tenant's former landlord to ensure the tenant is able to meet financial obligations. Financial qualification standards must be applied in a similar fashion to all applicants to avoid even the appearance of a discriminatory practice.

MATH CONCEPTS

Calculating Monthly Rent per Square Foot (Commercial)

1. Determine the total square footage of the rental premises (generally floor space only).

   50 feet × 30 feet = 1,500 square feet
2. Find the total annual rent.
   $2,500 per month × 12 months = $30,000 per year
3. Divide the total annual rent by the total square feet to determine the annual rate per square foot.
   $30,000 ÷ 1,500 square feet = $20 per square foot
4. Convert the annual rate to a monthly rate.
   $20 ÷ 12 months = $1.67 per square foot (rounded to nearest cent)

The terms of rental payment should be spelled out in the lease agreement, including

- time and place of payment,
- provisions and penalties for late payment and returned checks, and
- provisions for cancellation and damages in case of nonpayment.

The property manager should establish a firm and consistent collection plan. The plan should include a system of notices and records that complies with state and local law.

Every attempt must be made to collect rent without resorting to legal action. Legal action is costly and time consuming, and does not contribute to good tenant relations. In some cases, however, legal action is unavoidable. In these instances, a property manager must be prepared to initiate and follow through with the necessary legal steps. Obviously, legal action must be taken in cooperation with the property owner's or management firm's legal counsel.

Maintaining Good Relations With Tenants The ultimate success of a property manager depends on the ability to maintain good relations with tenants. Dissatisfied tenants are more likely to vacate the property early. A high tenant turnover rate results in greater expenses for advertising and redecorating and less profit for the owner due to uncollected rents. Empty units and storefronts can also damage a property's reputation—and its perceived desirability.

An effective property manager establishes a good communication system with tenants—and prospective tenants. An internet site that highlights property features and solicits new tenants can also have a section limited to residents that posts activities, maintenance updates, and other news to keep tenants informed and involved. Email notices, printed and electronic newsletters, and posted memoranda, especially when updated on a regular basis, are also useful.

Above all, maintenance and service requests must be attended to promptly, and all lease terms and building rules must be enforced consistently and fairly. A manager who fails to treat all tenants the same in terms of rent collection and enforcement of lease terms or rules and regulations will create ill will among tenants and might even be violating fair housing laws. A good manager is tactful and decisive, and acts to benefit both owner and occupants.

The property manager must be able to address residents who do not pay rent on time or who violate building regulations. When one tenant fails to follow the rules, the other tenants often become frustrated and dissatisfied. Careful recordkeeping shows whether rent is remitted promptly and in the proper amount. Records of all lease renewal dates should be kept so that the manager can anticipate a lease expiration and retain a good tenant who might otherwise move when the lease term ends.

Maintaining the Property One of the most important functions of a property manager is the supervision of property maintenance. A manager must learn to balance the services provided with their cost—that is, to satisfy tenants' needs while keeping operating expenses within budget.

To maintain the property efficiently, the manager must be able to assess the building's needs and how best to meet those needs. Because staffing and scheduling requirements vary with the type, size, and geographic location of the property, the owner and the manager usually agree in advance on maintenance objectives. In some cases, the best plan may be to operate a low-rent property with minimal expenditures for services and maintenance. Another property may be more lucrative if kept in top condition and operated with all possible tenant services. A well-maintained, high-service property can command premium rental rates.

Types of maintenance
- Preventive
- Repair or corrective
- Routine

A primary maintenance objective is to protect the physical integrity of the property over the long term. For example, preserving the property by repainting the exterior or replacing the heating system helps decrease long-term maintenance costs. Keeping the property in good condition involves the following three types of maintenance:

- Preventive
- Repair or corrective
- Routine

Preventive maintenance includes regularly scheduled activities such as painting and seasonal servicing of appliances and systems. Preventive maintenance preserves the long-range value and physical integrity of the building. This is both the most critical and the most neglected maintenance responsibility. Failure to perform preventive maintenance invariably leads to greater expense in other areas of maintenance.

Repair or **corrective maintenance** involves the actual repairs that keep the building's equipment, utilities, and amenities functioning. Repairing a toilet, fixing a leaky faucet, and replacing a broken air-conditioning unit are acts of corrective maintenance.

A property manager also must supervise the **routine maintenance** of the building. Routine maintenance includes such day-to-day duties as performing minor carpentry and plumbing repairs, and providing regularly scheduled upkeep of heating, air-conditioning, and landscaping.

IN PRACTICE One of the major decisions a property manager faces is whether to contract for maintenance services from an outside firm or to hire on-site employees. The property manager will make the decision on what is most cost-effective for the owner. This decision should be based on a number of factors, including the

- size of the building,
- complexity of the tenants' requirements,
- time and expense involved, and
- availability of suitable labor.

Construction involves making a property meet a tenant's needs.

A commercial or industrial property manager often is called on to make **tenant improvements** (*or build-outs*). These are construction alterations to the interior of the building to meet a tenant's particular space needs. Such alterations range from simply repainting or recarpeting to completely gutting the interior and redesigning the space by erecting new walls, partitions, and electrical systems. Tenant improvements are especially important when renting new buildings. In new construction, the interiors are usually left incomplete so that they can be adapted to the needs of individual tenants. One matter that must be clarified is which improvements will be considered trade fixtures (personal property belonging to the tenant) and which will belong to the owner of the real estate.

Modernization or renovation of buildings that have become functionally obsolete and thus unsuited to today's building needs is also important. The renovation of a building often enhances its marketability and increases its potential income. At the same time, federal and state regulations regarding lead-based paint, asbestos, and other hazardous substances that may be found in or around a structure can entail expensive remediation efforts.

Environmental Concerns The environment is an increasingly important property management issue. A variety of environmental issues, from waste disposal to air quality, must be addressed by the property manager. Tenant concerns, as well as federal, state, and local regulations, determine the extent of the manager's environmental responsibilities. Property managers are not expected to be experts in all of the disciplines necessary to operate a property; they are expected to be knowledgeable in many diverse subjects, most of which are technical in nature. Environmental concerns are one such subject.

Recycling facilities may be required by law, but even if they are not, the manager may want to provide them for tenants, which can benefit the environment, as well as make the property more marketable. Hazardous wastes produced by employees or tenants must be properly disposed of. Even the normally nonhazardous waste of an office building must be controlled to avoid violation of laws requiring segregation and recycling of types of waste. Residential property managers of buildings constructed before 1978 must provide lead-based paint disclosure forms to all new tenants. Environmental audits also identify issues relating to asbestos, radon, and mold.

Air quality issues are a key concern for those involved in property management and design. *Building-related illness (BRI)* and *sick building syndrome (SBS)* are illnesses that are more prevalent today because of energy efficiency standards used in construction that make buildings more airtight with less ventilation. BRI is a clinically diagnosed condition that can be attributed directly to airborne building contaminants. Symptoms include asthma, hypersensitivity, and some allergies. SBS is more typical in an office building, and symptoms include fatigue, nausea, dizziness, headache, and sensitivity to odors. Often, increasing ventilation or replacing interior features, such as carpeting, can solve air quality problems.

FEDERAL LAWS PROHIBITING DISCRIMINATION

Federal laws prohibiting discrimination in the provision of housing, accommodations, services, and access to credit affect the property management profession. The Americans with Disabilities Act, the Equal Credit Opportunity Act, and the Fair Housing Act all help to ensure that consumer rights are not violated.

The Americans with Disabilities Act

www.ada.gov

The Americans with Disabilities Act (ADA), www.ada.gov, has had a significant impact on the responsibilities of the property manager, in both building amenities and employment issues.

ADA Title I provides that any employer of 15 or more employees must adopt nondiscriminatory employment procedures. In addition, an employer must make reasonable accommodations to enable an individual with a disability to perform essential job functions.

Property managers also must be familiar with ADA Title III, which prohibits discrimination in commercial properties and public accommodations. ADA requires that companies ensure that people with disabilities have full and equal access to facilities and services. (*See* Figure 19.1).

IN PRACTICE A prospective tenant is visually impaired. The property manager should be prepared to provide a lease agreement that is in large, easy-to-read type or that is printed in Braille, as required.

FIGURE 19.1: Reasonable Modifications to Public Facilities or Services

Provide doors with automatic opening mechanisms

Provide menus (and real estate listings) in a large-print or braille format

Install an intercom so customers can contact a second-floor business in a building without an elevator

Lower public telephones

Add grab bars to public restroom stalls

Permit guide dogs to accompany customers

Provide a shopper's assistant to help disabled customers

Provide ramps in addition to entry stairs

To protect owners of existing structures from the massive expense of extensive remodeling, the ADA recommends reasonably achievable accommodations to provide access to the facilities and services. New construction and remodeling, however, must meet higher standards of accessibility and usability because it costs less to incorporate accessible features in the design than to retrofit. Though the law intends to provide for people with disabilities, many of the accessible design features and accommodations benefit everyone.

The property manager typically is responsible for determining whether a building meets ADA accessibility requirements. The property manager also must prepare a plan for retrofitting a building that is not in compliance when removal of existing barriers is readily achievable and can be performed without much difficulty or expense. Some tax advantages may be available to help offset the expense of ADA compliance. ADA experts may be consulted, as well as architectural designers who specialize in accessibility issues.

IN PRACTICE The U.S. Department of Justice has ADA specialists available to answer general information questions about compliance issues. The ADA Information Line is 800-514-0301 (TTY: 800-514-0383).

Existing barriers must be removed when this can be accomplished in a readily achievable manner with little difficulty and at reasonable cost. The following are typical examples of readily achievable modifications:

- Ramping or removing an obstacle from an otherwise accessible entrance
- Lowering wall-mounted public telephones
- Adding raised letters and Braille markings on elevator buttons
- Installing auditory signals in elevators
- Reversing the direction in which doors open

Alternative methods can be used to provide reasonable accommodations if extensive restructuring is impractical or if retrofitting is unduly expensive. For example, installing a cup dispenser at a water fountain that is too high for a person in a wheelchair may be more practical than installing a lower water fountain.

IN PRACTICE Federal, state, and local laws may provide additional requirements for accommodating people with disabilities. Real estate professionals should be aware of the full range of laws to ensure that their practices are in compliance.

Equal Credit Opportunity Act

Guiding principle: what you do for one, do for all.

www.fdic.gov/regulations/laws/rules/6500-1200.html

The Equal Credit Opportunity Act (ECOA) prohibits a lender from denying a loan based on a person's race, color, religion, national origin, sex, marital status, age, or receipt of public assistance. The ECOA affects the property manager in several ways. A manager should use the same lease application for every applicant. If a manager requires a credit report from one applicant, the manager should require credit reports from all applicants. The manager should be consistent in evaluating the income and debt of applicants and in determining whether to rent to an applicant. A complete copy of the law can be found at www.fdic.gov/regulations/laws/rules/6500-1200.html.

Fair Housing Act

www.justice.gov/crt/about/hce/housing_coverage.php

The federal Fair Housing Act and its amendments prohibit discrimination in the sale, rental, or financing of housing based on race, color, religion, national origin, sex, familial status, or disability. Property managers need to ensure that their marketing practices do not violate fair housing laws. For example, blockbusting and steering are prohibited. *Blockbusting* is encouraging people to rent or to sell a property by claiming that the entry of a protected class of people into the neighborhood will have a negative impact on property values. *Steering* is the channeling of protected class members to certain buildings or neighborhoods. The Department of Justice has information on fair housing issues at www.justice.gov/crt/about/hce/housing_coverage.php.

IN PRACTICE Many fair housing complaints are related to property management issues that could have been avoided by treating all rental applicants with the same courtesy and respect. A fair housing training program can be useful at any stage of a real estate professional's career and is often a requirement for license renewal.

RISK MANAGEMENT

Enormous monetary losses can result from unexpected or catastrophic events. As a result, one of the most critical areas of responsibility for a property manager is **risk management**.

Risk Management Techniques

Memory Tip

The four alternative risk management techniques:

Avoid

Control

Transfer

Or

Retain

Risk management involves answering the question, What happens if something goes wrong? The perils of any risk must be evaluated in terms of options. In considering the possibility of a loss, the property manager must decide whether it is better to

- *avoid it* by removing the source of risk (e.g., a swimming pool may pose an unacceptable risk);
- *control it* by preparing for an emergency before it happens (by installing sprinklers, fire doors, and security systems);
- *transfer it* by shifting the risk onto another party (by taking out an insurance policy); or
- *retain it* by deciding that the chances of the event occurring are too small to justify the expense of any other response (an alternative might be to take out an insurance policy with a large deductible, which usually is considerably less expensive).

Security of Tenants

Recent court decisions in several states have held owners and their agents responsible for physical harm that was inflicted on tenants by intruders. These decisions have prompted property managers and owners to think about how to protect tenants and secure apartments from intruders. After the terror attacks of September 11, 2001, managers of commercial properties also have increased awareness of security issues. A professional security analysis can help identify areas of concern and suggest possible remedies.

There is also concern caused by wrongdoing or criminal behavior inflicted by tenants on other tenants in a building. Many leases now have a crime-free provision that makes criminal activity, such as drug use or assault, grounds for eviction.

Types of Insurance

Just as it is for homeowners, insurance is a first line of defense in risk management for other real property owners and managers. Numerous forms of insurance policies are available, covering a wide range of possible events that might result in devastating loss. A single policy may cover risks in one or more categories.

Tenant's Insurance The property manager should notify tenants that they must obtain renter's insurance, known as HO-4, in order to protect their personal belongings. The real estate owner can only insure what is owned (i.e., the building); the owner of the building cannot insure the personal property of tenants. Residential tenants need an HO-4 or renter's policy to insure their personal property. Business tenants can obtain their own business or commercial policy.

Commercial Insurance An insurance audit should be performed by a competent, reliable insurance agent who is familiar with insurance issues for the type of property involved. The audit will indicate areas in which greater or lesser coverage is recommended and will highlight particular risks. The final decision, however, is made by the property owner.

Common types of coverage available to income property owners and managers include the following:

- *Fire and hazard.* Fire insurance policies provide coverage against direct loss or damage to property from a fire on the premises. Standard fire coverage can be extended to include other hazards, such as windstorm, hail, smoke damage, or civil insurrection.
- *Flood.* Flood insurance is always a separate policy from home, rental, or building insurance policies. A flood insurance policy is available to any property located in a community participating in the National Flood Insurance Program (NFIP). It covers flooding caused by heavy rains, melting snow, inadequate drainage systems, or failed levees or dams. Consult www.fema.gov/national-flood-insurance-program.

www.fema.gov/national-flood-insurance-program

- *Consequential loss, use, and occupancy.* Also known as *loss of rent* or *business interruption insurance*, consequential loss insurance covers the results, or consequences, of a disaster. Consequential loss can include the loss of rent or revenue to a business that occurs if the business's property cannot be used.
- *Contents and personal property.* This type of insurance covers building contents and personal property during periods when they are not actually located on the premises.
- *Liability.* Public liability insurance covers the risks an owner assumes whenever the public enters the building. A claim paid under this coverage is used for medical expenses incurred by a person who is injured in the building or on the property as a result of the owner's negligence. Claims for medical or hospital payments for injuries sustained by building employees hurt in the course of their employment are covered by state laws known as **workers' compensation acts**.

- *Casualty*. Casualty insurance policies include coverage against theft, burglary, vandalism, and machinery damage, as well as health and accident insurance.
- *Surety bonds*. **Surety bonds** cover an owner against financial losses resulting from an employee's criminal acts or negligence while performing assigned duties.

Many insurance companies offer **multiperil policies** for apartment buildings. Such a policy offers an insurance package that includes standard types of commercial coverage, such as fire, hazard, public liability, and casualty. Special coverage for terrorism, earthquakes, and floods is also available. Remember that flood insurance is always a separate policy.

Condominium associations carry insurance on all the *common elements*, and cooperatives carry insurance on the building. Condominium owners and proprietary lease owners must carry their own casualty and liability insurance, as well as insurance to cover the destruction of their unit's contents by fire or other hazard. If condominium owners rent out space to tenants, the tenants must carry their own personal property insurance.

The property manager may also want to carry insurance to cover the management office and its contents, as well as professional malpractice claims. For example, a property manager may want to consider purchasing errors and omissions (E&O) insurance to protect against any financial management mistakes.

Insurance Claims

Two methods are used to determine the amount of a claim under an insurance policy. One method considers the *depreciated* or *actual cash value* of the damaged property; the property is not insured for what it would cost to replace it but rather for what it was originally worth, less the depreciation in value that results from use and the passage of time. The other method considers *current replacement cost*—the building or property is insured for what it would cost to rebuild or replace today. When purchasing insurance, the property manager must act on the owner's decision as to whether the property should be insured at full replacement cost or at depreciated cost. Full replacement cost coverage is generally more expensive than depreciated cost coverage.

As with homeowners insurance policies, commercial policies include *coinsurance clauses* that require the insured to carry fire coverage, usually in an amount equal to 80% of a building's replacement value.

Property managers can encounter legal issues with insurance claims. For example, if the property owner is not available to file an insurance claim, the property manager must have proper authorization, such as a power of attorney.

KEY POINT REVIEW

A **property manager**, whether an individual or a company, acts as the **general agent** of the investment property owner in administering the property to achieve the **objectives** of the owner, generate **income**, and preserve and/or increase the property's **value**.

Property management functions may require a real estate or property management **license**, as provided by state law.

Property managers may undertake **asset management** by helping the owner to decide the **type** of real estate in which to invest (residential or commercial), the **best** property to purchase, the **financial resources** necessary to fund the purchase, and the best time to **dispose** of the property.

A **leasing agent** is usually a state-licensed real estate professional working as an **independent contractor** or property manager on a commission basis.

A **corporate property manager** is usually an **employee** of the corporation.

A **management plan** and **management agreement** should

- describe the property;
- define the term of the agreement and how it can be terminated;
- define the manager's responsibilities, including the extent of the manager's authority;
- state the owner's responsibility for management expenses;
- indicate the manager's compensation;
- list the financial reports that the manager must make;
- require that there be compliance with all applicable federal, state, and local laws by all parties; and
- provide an operating budget, which is a one-year projection of income and expenses.

A **cash flow report** will summarize income and expenses.

Periodic **profit and loss statements** provide general financial information. **Net profit** is determined by computing **gross receipts**, then subtracting operating expenses and interest paid on a mortgage loan. A **budget comparison statement** compares actual results with the original budget.

The building manager **sets rents** that are sufficient to cover fixed charges and operating expenses and a **fair return** on the owner's investment, in line with the **prevailing rates** in comparable buildings, and a reflection of the current **vacancy rate** of the property. Rents are determined at a **monthly rate per unit** for residential property and at a **monthly rate per square foot** for commercial property.

A building manager **selects tenants** within certain parameters, while complying with all applicable federal, state, and local fair housing, antidiscrimination, and equal opportunity laws.

Commercial tenant considerations typically include **the suitability** of the building in terms of size, location, and amenities; **compatibility** of the prospective tenant with the building and other tenants; and the **availability** of space for expansion, if necessary.

The building manager should establish a firm and consistent **collection plan** for rents. Lease agreements should spell out the **time and place** of payment, **penalties** for late payment and bounced checks, and **cancellation procedures** and **damages** in case of nonpayment.

Building managers maintain **good relations with tenants** with tact and uniformity expressed in effective **communications**, fair and consistent **enforcement** of rules, prompt attention to **maintenance and service** requests, and careful **recordkeeping**, with attention to **lease renewal dates**.

To find and retain reliable tenants, a building manager must devise an **effective marketing strategy**.

Adequate property maintenance includes **preventive** maintenance, timely **repairs** or corrective actions, and the **routine** activities that help preserve the property and enhance its desirability to tenants.

The **environmental concerns** that require the attention of the property manager include the **disposal of hazardous wastes**, the **lead-based paint disclosure** for residential property constructed before 1978, **building-related illness (BRI)**, and **sick building syndrome (SBS)**.

Federal laws affecting property management include the following:

- **Americans with Disabilities Act (ADA)**, which includes
  - **Title I**, which applies to **employers** with 15 or more employees and provides for employment of qualified job applicants, regardless of disability, with reasonable accommodations
  - **Title III**, which prohibits discrimination in **commercial properties and public accommodations** and requires that access to facilities and services be provided when reasonably achievable in existing buildings, with a higher standard for new construction or remodeling
- **Equal Credit Opportunity Act (ECOA)**, which prohibits lenders from denying a loan based on a person's race, color, religion, national origin, sex, marital status, age, or receipt of public assistance; additional protections may be added by state or local laws
- Federal **Fair Housing Act**, which prohibits discrimination in the sale, rental, or financing of housing based on race, color, religion, national origin, sex, familial status, or disability; additional protected individuals may be added by state or local laws

Risk management includes treatment of risk by deciding whether to **avoid** it, **control** it, **transfer** it, **or retain** it (ACTOR) and focuses on tenant security and types of insurance available. The renter's insurance policy that covers the renter's personal property is the HO-4 policy.

UNIT 19 QUIZ

1. Which type of insurance coverage insures an employer against *MOST* claims for job-related injuries?
   a. Consequential loss
   b. Workers' compensation
   c. Casualty
   d. Surety bond
2. Avoid, control, transfer, or retain are the four alternative techniques of
   a. tenant relations.
   b. acquiring insurance.
   c. risk management.
   d. property management.
3. Adaptations of property specifications to suit tenant requirements are
   a. tax-exempt improvements.
   b. tenant improvements.
   c. prohibited by most nonresidential leases.
   d. generally not a good idea.
4. A guest slips on an icy apartment building stair and is hospitalized. A claim against the building owner for medical expenses may be paid under which of the following policies held by the owner?
   a. Workers' compensation
   b. Casualty
   c. Liability
   d. Fire and hazard
5. All of the following should be included in a management agreement *EXCEPT*
   a. a description of the property.
   b. compensation.
   c. restrictions regarding ages of children.
   d. the extent of the manager's authority.
6. A property manager is offered a choice of three insurance policies with different deductibles. If the property manager selects the policy with the highest deductible, which risk management technique is being used?
   a. Avoiding risk
   b. Retaining risk
   c. Controlling risk
   d. Transferring risk
7. Asbestos, sick building syndrome (SBS), and lead-based paint are all examples of
   a. issues beyond the scope of a property manager's job description.
   b. problems found only in newly constructed properties.
   c. issues that arise under the Americans with Disabilities Act (ADA).
   d. environmental concerns that a property manager may have to address.
8. The manager of a commercial building has many responsibilities in connection with the operation and maintenance of the structure. The manager would normally be considered the agent of
   a. the building's owner.
   b. the building's tenants.
   c. both the owner and the tenants.
   d. neither the owner nor the tenants.
9. Which of the following would be considered a variable expense when a manager develops an operating budget?
   a. Employee wages
   b. Utilities
   c. Building repairs
   d. Basic operating costs
10. In *MOST* market areas, rents are determined by
    a. supply and demand factors.
    b. the local apartment owners' association.
    c. HUD.
    d. a tenants' union.
11. A highrise apartment building burns to the ground. What type of insurance covers the landlord against the resulting loss of rent?
    a. Fire and hazard
    b. Liability
    c. Consequential loss, use, and occupancy
    d. Casualty

12. A property manager hires a full-time maintenance person. While repairing a faucet in one of the apartments, the maintenance person steals a laptop computer and the tenant sues the owner. The property manager could protect the owner against this type of loss by purchasing
    a. liability insurance.
    b. workers' compensation insurance.
    c. a surety bond.
    d. casualty insurance.

13. Residential leases are usually expressed as a(n)
    a. annual or monthly rate per square foot.
    b. percentage of total space available.
    c. monthly rate per unit.
    d. annual rate per room.

14. A property manager repairs a leaking sink. This is classified as which type of maintenance?
    a. Preventive
    b. Corrective
    c. Routine
    d. Construction

15. A property manager who enters into a management agreement with an owner is usually a
    a. special agent.
    b. general agent.
    c. universal agent.
    d. designated agent.

16. A statement sent to an owner that does not reflect the entire debt service as an expense is called a(n)
    a. cash flow report.
    b. profit and loss statement.
    c. budget comparison statement.
    d. operating budget statement.

17. An insurance policy package that includes standard commercial property coverage such as fire, hazard, public liability, and casualty is called what kind of policy?
    a. Coinsurance
    b. Multiperil
    c. Universal
    d. Surety

18. Removing existing barriers when readily achievable in public buildings, such as adding Braille markings to elevator buttons, is a requirement of which law?
    a. Fair Housing Act
    b. Equal Credit Opportunity Act
    c. Americans with Disabilities Act
    d. Regulation Z

19. Title III of the Americans with Disabilities Act (ADA) impacts which type of property?
    a. Residential
    b. Industrial
    c. Commercial and public accommodations
    d. Privately owned

20. In evaluating rental applications, it is important for the property manager to establish consistent criteria for acceptable debt and income ratios in order to be in compliance with
    a. federal antitrust laws.
    b. the Americans with Disabilities Act.
    c. Regulation Z.
    d. the Equal Credit Opportunity Act.

Land-Use Controls and Property Development

■ **LEARNING OBJECTIVES** *When you have finished reading this unit, you will be able to*

- **explain** the concept of police power and the provisions under which it protects the public health, safety, and welfare;
- **explain** zoning, ordinances, permits, and property use;
- **define** building codes as they relate to the requirements and restrictions placed on construction standards;
- **explain** the issues and regulations involved in subdivisions;
- **explain** non-governmental (private) land use restrictions: covenants, conditions, and restrictions (CC&Rs);
- **describe** the various laws and agencies which regulate land sales; and
- **define** the following *key terms*:

buffer zone
building code
certificate of occupancy
comprehensive plan
conditional-use permit
covenants, conditions, and restrictions (CC&Rs)
deed restrictions
density zoning
developer
enabling acts
Interstate Land Sales Full Disclosure Act (ILSA)
nonconforming use
planned unit development (PUD)
plat map
restrictive covenants
subdivider
subdivision
variance
zoning ordinances

OVERVIEW

Over the years, the government's policy has been to encourage private ownership of land, but this does not always mean that owners can do whatever they want with their properties. In most areas of the United States, local governments have developed comprehensive planning that restricts how land may be used, with the goal of orderly and planned growth.

Real estate professionals must be knowledgeable about local land-use restrictions in order to avoid showing a buyer a property that is not suitable for the buyer's intended use, especially when a buyer is looking for a property to develop for a specific commercial or residential use. The buyer of a home within a subdivision or planned unit development that is subject to a residential community association will also be subject to limitations that appear in the property deed or specific rules that are created and enforced by the association. Even an individual parcel of real estate may be subject to restrictions that a prior owner has included in the deed or a document that has been made part of the property's chain of title. While no one expects real estate professionals to become experts in land use, they should be aware of these issues and be able to direct their clients to appropriate sources of additional information.

LAND-USE CONTROLS

www.ers.usda.gov/media/250065/eib14j_1_.pdf

Land use is controlled through public and private limitations as well as through the direct ownership of land by federal, state, and local governments. According to the U.S. Department of Agriculture (USDA), over 60% of the land area of the United States is privately owned. The federal government owns more than 28% of the land, state and local governments own 9%, and over 2% is Indian trust land. These percentages change very little over time, although in Alaska a large portion of federal land has been transferred to the state or placed in native (private) ownership. A complete report by the USDA on major uses of land in the United States can be found at www.ers.usda.gov/media/250065/eib14j_1_.pdf. Here, you will learn about how property development and use is regulated at every level.

Government Ownership

Government-owned land is used for national parks and forests, military bases, federal office buildings, schools, museums, state parks, government buildings, and municipal parks and buildings, as well as streets, highways, and bridges. Beyond direct ownership of land, government controls on property use range from regulation of the use and disposal of hazardous materials by the federal government to the design, construction, and type of buildings that are permitted at the local level.

The *police power* of government is the source of its authority to create regulations needed to protect the public health, safety, and welfare. Through **enabling acts**, states delegate to counties and local municipalities the authority to enact ordinances in keeping with general laws. The degree to which governmental bodies seek to regulate land uses varies and is often a reflection of the priorities of local residents. While there may be little objection anywhere to regulations that control noise, air, and water pollution, the topic of population density can elicit strong reactions.

The Comprehensive Plan

Local governments, municipalities, and counties establish development goals by creating a **comprehensive plan**. The comprehensive plan, also known as a *master plan*, is not a regulatory document, but a guide that tries to anticipate changing needs. The comprehensive plan usually is long term, perhaps 20 years or longer, and often includes (a) a general plan that can be revised and updated more frequently, (b) plans for specific areas, and (c) strategic plans. Systematic planning for orderly growth usually considers the following elements:

- Land use—determining how much land may be proposed for residence, industry, business, agriculture, traffic and transit facilities, utilities, community facilities, parks and recreational facilities, floodplains, and areas of special hazards
- Housing needs of present and anticipated residents, including rehabilitation of declining neighborhoods, as well as new residential developments
- Movement of people and goods, including highways and public transit, parking facilities, and pedestrian and bikeway systems
- Community facilities and utilities such as schools, libraries, hospitals, recreational facilities, fire and police stations, water resources, sewerage, waste treatment and disposal, storm drainage, and flood management
- Energy conservation to reduce energy consumption and promote the use of renewable energy sources

The preparation of a comprehensive plan involves surveys, studies, and analyses of housing, demographic, and economic characteristics and trends. The plan typically is drafted by a *planning commission* and approved by the city council or other governing body following a period for public comment at hearings held for that purpose. A municipality's planning activities may be coordinated with other government bodies and private interests to achieve orderly growth and development.

IN PRACTICE After the Great Chicago Fire of 1871 reduced most of the city's downtown to rubble and ash, the city engaged planner Daniel Burnham to lay out a design for Chicago's future. The resulting Burnham Plan of orderly boulevards linking a park along Lake Michigan with other large parks and public spaces throughout the city established an attractive and workable urban space. The plan is still being implemented today.

ZONING

Zoning ordinances implement the comprehensive plan and regulate and control the use of land and structures within designated land-use districts, in part by separating conflicting land uses. If the comprehensive plan is the big picture, zoning provides the details that carry out the comprehensive plan.

Although no nationwide or statewide zoning ordinances exist, the federal government and the states regulate land use through coastal management, environmental laws, and scenic easements.

Zoning affects such things as

- permitted uses of each parcel of land,
- lot sizes,
- types of structures,
- building heights,

- setbacks (the minimum distance from property boundaries that structures may be built),
- style and appearance of structures,
- density (the ratio of land area to structure area), and
- protection of natural resources.

www.nyc.gov/planning

http://pittsburghpa.gov/dcp/zoning/

www.portlandoregon.gov/bps/31612

Zoning ordinances should conform to the comprehensive plan, but both must remain flexible to meet the changing needs of society. Extensive information on how the zoning process works can be found at the websites for New York City, www.nyc.gov/planning; Pittsburgh, http://pittsburghpa.gov/dcp/zoning/; and Portland, www.portlandoregon.gov/bps/31612.

IN PRACTICE The changing nature of the U.S. economy has resulted in areas of vacant factories and warehouses in many cities. Some cities have revised zoning ordinances to permit new residential or commercial developments in areas once zoned strictly for industrial use. Coupled with tax incentives, the changes have lured developers back into the cities. The resulting housing is often stylishly contemporary, conveniently located, and affordable. In some cities, rundown waterfront areas have become attractive recreational spaces that revitalize surrounding commercial and residential areas.

Zoning Classifications

Zoning ordinances have traditionally designated land for residential, commercial, industrial, and agricultural uses. These land-use areas are further divided into subclasses. For example, a residential area may be subdivided to provide for detached single-family dwellings, semidetached structures containing not more than four dwelling units, lowrise apartment buildings without elevators (walkups), and highrise apartment buildings.

A **planned unit development (PUD)** is a development where land is set aside for mixed-use purposes, such as residential, commercial, and public areas. Zoning regulations may be modified for PUDs. PUDs tend to also be heavily regulated by private restrictions.

Zoning Ordinances

To meet both the growing demand for a variety of housing types and the need for innovative residential and nonresidential development, municipalities have adopted ordinances for subdivisions and planned residential developments. Some municipalities also use **buffer zones** to ease the transition from one use to another. A buffer zone is typically a strip of land separating land dedicated to one use from land dedicated to another use. For example, landscaped parks, playgrounds, and hiking trails may be used to screen residential areas from nonresidential zones. Certain types of zoning that focus on special land-use objectives are used in some areas. These include

- *bulk zoning* to control density and avoid overcrowding by imposing restrictions such as setbacks, building heights, and percentage of open area or by restricting new construction projects;
- *aesthetic zoning* to specify certain types of architecture for new buildings; and
- *incentive zoning* to ensure that certain uses are incorporated into developments, such as requiring the street floor of an office building to house retail establishments.

Constitutional Issues Zoning can be a highly controversial issue and often raises questions of constitutional law. The Fourteenth Amendment to the U.S. Constitution prevents the states from depriving "any person of life, liberty, or property, without due process of law." The ongoing question is, How can a local government enact zoning ordinances that protect the public safety and welfare without violating the constitutional rights of property owners? Due process of law means that citizens can discuss zoning ordinances before they are enacted in public hearings. Those affected by the proposed change are provided notice of such hearings and have the opportunity to attend and be heard.

Any land-use legislation that is destructive, unreasonable, arbitrary, or confiscatory usually is considered void. Furthermore, zoning ordinances must not violate the various provisions of the state's constitution. Commonly applied tests in determining the validity of ordinances require that

- power be exercised in a reasonable manner;
- provisions be clear and specific;
- ordinances be nondiscriminatory;
- ordinances promote the public health, safety, and general welfare under the government's police power; and
- ordinances apply to all property in a similar manner.

Zoning Permits

Compliance with zoning can be monitored by requiring that a property owner obtain a permit before beginning any development. A permit will not be issued unless the proposed development conforms to the permitted zoning, among other requirements. A *zoning permit* is usually required before a *building permit* will be issued.

Nonconforming Use Frequently, a lot or an improvement does not conform to the zoning use because it existed before the enactment or amendment of the zoning ordinance. Such a **nonconforming use** may be allowed to continue legally as long as it complies with the regulations governing nonconformities in the local ordinance, until the improvement is destroyed or torn down, or until the current use is abandoned. If the nonconforming use is allowed to continue indefinitely, it is considered to be grandfathered into the new zoning.

Real estate professionals should never assume, nor allow their clients to assume, that an existing nonconforming use will be allowed to continue. A prospective buyer should verify with the local zoning authorities the conditions under which the use is allowed to remain or whether changes are permitted.

IN PRACTICE Under a city's original zoning ordinances, a small grocery store was well within a commercial zone. When the zoning map was changed to accommodate an increased need for residential housing, the grocery store was grandfathered into the new zoning.

Zoning Hearing Board Most communities have a zoning hearing board (or zoning board of appeal) to hear testimony about the effects a zoning ordinance may have on specific parcels of property. A petition for an exception to the zoning law may be presented to the appeals board, as described next.

A conditional-use permit allows a nonconforming but related land use.

A variance permits a prohibited land use to avoid undue hardship.

Variances and Conditional-Use Permits Once a plan or zoning ordinance is enacted, property owners and developers know what they can and cannot do on their property. Nevertheless, a property owner may want to use the property in a way that differs to some degree from what the zoning would allow. Generally, the property owner in such a situation may request either a *conditional-use permit* or a *variance* to allow a use that does not meet current zoning requirements.

A **conditional-use permit** (also known as a special-use permit) is usually granted to a property owner to allow a special use of property that is defined as an allowable conditional use within that zone, such as a house of worship or daycare center in a residential district. For a conditional-use permit to be appropriate, the intended use must meet certain standards set by the municipality.

A **variance** will provide relief if a zoning regulation deprives an owner of the reasonable use of the property. To qualify for a variance, the owner must demonstrate the unique circumstances that make the variance necessary. In addition, the owner must prove that the regulation has caused harm or created a burden. A variance might also be sought to provide relief if an existing zoning regulation creates a physical hardship for the development of a specific property. For example, if an owner's lot is level next to a road but slopes steeply 30 feet away from the road, the zoning board may allow a variance so the owner can build closer to the road than the setback allows.

Both variances and conditional-use permits are issued by zoning boards only after public hearings. Owners of nearby properties must be given an opportunity to voice their opinions.

A property owner also can seek a change in the zoning classification of a parcel of real estate by obtaining an amendment to the district map or zoning ordinance for that area; that is, the owner can attempt to have the zoning changed to accommodate an intended use of the property.

BUILDING CODES AND CERTIFICATES OF OCCUPANCY

www.iccsafe.org

Most municipalities have enacted ordinances to specify construction standards that must be met when repairing or erecting buildings. These are called **building codes**, and they set many requirements for such things as materials and standards of workmanship, sanitary equipment, electrical wiring, and fire prevention. Not all building codes are local. Florida has adopted a statewide building code as a way to help protect properties against the massive destruction caused by hurricanes. California requires specific building standards to help protect structures and fixtures from damage that can be caused by earthquakes. Many communities in the United States have adopted the International Building Code that was developed by the International Code Council, www.iccsafe.org and is regularly reviewed and updated.

Permits

A property owner who wants to build a structure or alter or repair an existing building usually must obtain a building permit. Through the permit requirement, municipal officials are made aware of new construction or alterations and can verify compliance with building codes and zoning ordinances. An inspector will closely examine the plans and conduct periodic inspections of the work to ensure that the construction complies with relevant ordinances and codes. Once the completed structure has been inspected and found satisfactory, the building official will issue a **certificate of occupancy** or occupancy permit.

The certificate of occupancy indicating that the property is suitable for habitation must be issued before anyone moves in and usually before a lender will allow closing. Most municipalities allow for transfer of property ownership without the need to comply with the most current building codes. The exceptions are usually for safety reasons, such as the California requirement that a water heater be strapped in place for protection in an earthquake. Federal regulations may also be applicable, such as the design and construction requirements of the Americans with Disabilities Act (ADA).

If the construction of a building or an alteration violates a deed restriction, the issuance of a building permit will not cure this violation. A building permit is merely evidence of the applicant's compliance with municipal regulations.

Similarly, communities with historic districts, or those that are interested in maintaining a particular look or character, may have aesthetic ordinances. These laws require that all new construction or restorations be approved by a special board. The board ensures that the new structures will blend in with existing building styles. Owners of existing properties will need to obtain approval to have their homes painted or remodeled.

IN PRACTICE The subject of planning, zoning, and restricting the use of real estate is extremely technical, and the interpretation of the law is not always clear. Questions concerning any of these subjects in relation to real estate transactions should be referred to legal counsel. The prospective property owner should also be aware of the costs for various permits.

SUBDIVISION

Most communities have adopted **subdivision** and land development ordinances as part of their comprehensive plans. Just as no national zoning ordinance exists, no uniform planning and land development legislation affects the entire country. Laws governing subdividing and land planning are controlled by the state and local governing bodies where the land is located. Rules and regulations developed by state agencies may provide certain minimum standards. Many local governments have established standards that are higher than the minimum standards.

Subdivider and Developer

A **subdivider** segments land into parcels.

A **developer** constructs improvements on subdivided parcels.

A **subdivider** is a person who buys undeveloped acreage and divides it into smaller lots for sale to individuals or developers or for the subdivider's own use. A **developer**, who may also be a subdivider, improves the land, constructs homes or other buildings on the lots, and sells them. Developing is generally a more extensive activity than subdividing. A subdivision ordinance will include provisions for submitting and processing a proposed subdivision. A major advantage of subdivision ordinances is that they encourage flexibility, economy, and ingenuity in the use of land.

Land Development Plan

Before the actual subdividing can begin, the subdivider must go through the process of land planning. The resulting land development plan must comply with the municipality's comprehensive or master plan. Although comprehensive plans and zoning ordinances are not necessarily inflexible, a plan that requires a change to either must undergo a long, expensive, and frequently complicated process that will include public hearings and action by multiple governing bodies.

Subdivision Plan

In plotting out a subdivision according to local planning and zoning controls, a subdivider determines the size as well as the location of the individual lots. The maximum or minimum size of a lot is generally regulated by local ordinances and must be considered carefully. Most subdivisions are laid out by use of lots and blocks. An area of land is designated as a block, with the area making up the block then divided into individual building lots.

The land itself must be studied, usually in cooperation with a surveyor, so that the subdivision takes advantage of natural drainage and land contours. A subdivider should provide for utility easements, as well as easements for water and sewer mains. A developer is often required to submit an environmental impact report with the application for subdivision approval. This report explains what effect the proposed development will have on the surrounding area.

One negative aspect of subdivision development is the potential for increased tax burdens on all residents, both inside and outside the subdivision. To protect local taxpayers against the costs of a heightened demand for public services, many local governments strictly regulate nearly all aspects of subdivision development and may impose impact fees. *Impact fees* are charges made in advance to cover anticipated expenses involving off-site capital improvements such as expanding water and sewer facilities, additional roads, and school expansions.

Plat Map From the land development and subdivision plans, the subdivider draws the plat map. A **plat map** is a detailed map illustrating the geographic boundaries of individual lots. The plat map shows the lots, blocks, sections, streets, public easements, and monuments in the prospective subdivision. (*See* Figure 6.7 for an example of a subdivision plat map.) The plat map may also include engineering data and restrictive covenants. The plat map must be approved by the municipality before it can be recorded. Once a plat map is properly recorded, it may be used to describe the individual parcels of real property. A metes-and-bounds or government survey system description will pinpoint the location of the subdivision plat map on the surface of the earth, which will become part of its description.

Subdivision Density Zoning ordinances typically dictate minimum lot sizes, as well as population density requirements for subdivisions and land developments. For example, a zoning restriction may set the minimum lot area on which a subdivider can build a single-family housing unit at 10,000 square feet. This means that the subdivider can build four houses per acre. Many zoning authorities establish special **density zoning** standards for certain subdivisions. Density zoning ordinances restrict the average maximum number of houses per acre that may be built within a particular subdivision. If the area is density zoned at an average maximum of four houses per acre, for instance, the subdivider may choose to cluster building lots to achieve an open effect. Regardless of lot size or number of units, the subdivider will be in compliance with the ordinance as long as the average number of units in the development, called its *gross density*, remains at or below the maximum density allowed.

PRIVATE LAND-USE CONTROLS

Not all restrictions on the use of land are imposed by government bodies. As already mentioned, certain restrictions to control and maintain the desirable quality and character of a property or subdivision may be created by private parties, including the property owners themselves. These restrictions are separate from and in addition to the land-use controls exercised by the government, but a private restriction cannot violate a federal, state, or local law. Any restriction that would attempt to do so would be void.

Deed restrictions are limitations to the use of property imposed by a past owner or the current owner by inclusion in the deed to the property and are binding on future grantees.

Restrictive Covenants

Unlike deed restrictions, **restrictive covenants** or **covenants, conditions, and restrictions (CC&Rs),** are private rules set up by the developer that establish standards for all the parcels within the defined subdivision or PUD. The developer's restrictions may be imposed through a covenant in the deed or by a separate recorded declaration that is referenced in the deed. CC&Rs typically govern the type, height, and size of buildings that individual owners can erect, as well as land use, architectural style, construction methods, setbacks, and square footage. CC&Rs are enforced by the homeowners association (HOA) that is set up by the developer and turned over to the homeowners when a specified number of properties has been sold.

Unlike most deed restrictions, many CC&Rs have time limitations; for example, a restriction might state that it is "effective for a period of 25 years from this date." After the specified time, the restriction becomes inoperative or it may be extended if approved by the required number of owners. The rules of the HOA may also allow a specified number of homeowners to change a CC&R.

Restrictive covenants are usually considered valid if they are reasonable restraints that benefit all property owners in the subdivision; that is, they protect property values or safety. If a restriction is too broad, it may be construed as preventing the free transfer of property. If a restrictive covenant or condition is judged unenforceable by a court, the estate will stand free from the invalid covenant or condition. A restrictive covenant, just as with a deed restriction, cannot be used for an illegal purpose, such as the exclusion from a subdivision of members of certain races, nationalities, or religions.

Private land-use controls may be more restrictive of an owner's use than the local zoning ordinances. The rule is that the more restrictive of the two takes precedence. For example, local zoning ordinances may not address the use of a shed on a residential lot, but the CC&Rs in a particular subdivision may prohibit sheds, which means that a property owner in that subdivision may not place a shed on the property.

Private restrictions can be enforced in court when one lot owner or the HOA applies to the court for an injunction to prevent another lot owner from violating the recorded restrictions. The court injunction will direct the violator to stop or remove the violation. The court retains the power to punish the violator for failing to obey. If another lot owner or the HOA fails to take prompt action while a violation is occurring, the right to an injunction can be lost. The court might state that the right was lost through *laches*—that is, the legal principle that a right may be lost through undue delay or failure to assert it.

IN PRACTICE A real estate professional should consider inserting a contingency in a purchase contract whenever there is doubt about any public or private restrictions which may exist, especially when knowing this information is important to the buyer. Real estate professionals must also be careful to stay informed about publicized changes in zoning so that a misrepresentation charge cannot later be made against the real estate professional who "knew or should have known" this information.

REGULATION OF LAND SALES

Just as the sale and use of property within a state are controlled by state and local governments, the sale of property in one state to buyers in another state is subject to strict federal and state regulations.

Interstate Land Sales Full Disclosure Act

www.gpo.gov/fdsys/pkg/FR-2011-12-21/pdf/2011-31713.pdf

The U.S. Congress created the **Interstate Land Sales Full Disclosure Act (ILSA)** to prevent fraudulent marketing schemes that may arise when land is sold without being seen by the purchasers. The Act was amended by the Dodd-Frank Act in 2011 and its administration is now under the authority of the Consumer Financial Protection Bureau. A full copy of the revised law is at www.gpo.gov/fdsys/pkg/FR-2011-12-21/pdf/2011-31713.pdf. Under ILSA, the property seller is required to file a statement of record with CFPB before offering unimproved lots in interstate commerce by telephone or through the mail. The statement of record must contain numerous disclosures about the property.

A developer is also required to provide each purchaser or lessee of property with a printed report before the purchaser or lessee signs a purchase contract or lease. The report must disclose specific information about the property, including the

- type of title being transferred to the buyer,
- number of homes currently occupied on the site,
- availability of recreation facilities,
- distance to nearby communities,
- utility services and charges, and
- soil conditions and foundation or construction problems.

If the purchaser or lessee does not receive a copy of the report before signing the purchase contract or lease, the consumer may have grounds to void the contract.

The act provides a number of exemptions. For instance, it does not apply to subdivisions consisting of fewer than 25 lots or to those in which each lot is 20 acres or more. Lots offered for sale solely to developers also are exempt from the act's requirements, as are lots on which buildings exist or where a seller is obligated to construct a building within two years.

State Subdivided Land Sales Laws

Many states have enacted their own subdivided land sales laws. Some affect only the sale to state residents of land located outside the state. Other states' laws regulate sales of land located both inside and outside the state. These state land sales laws tend to be stricter and more detailed than the federal law. Real estate professionals should be aware of the law in their state, if any, and how it compares with federal law.

KEY POINT REVIEW

Land use is controlled and regulated through **public restrictions, such as** planning, zoning, building codes, and subdivision plans; **private restrictions** imposed by deed; and direct ownership of land by federal, state, and local governments.

The **police power** of the state is its authority to create regulations to protect the public health, safety, and welfare. State enabling acts allow the power to enact laws authorized by the state's police power to be passed down to municipalities and other local governing authorities. Such regulations must be exercised in a reasonable manner, clear and specific, nondiscriminatory, and applicable to all property in a similar manner.

A **comprehensive plan (master plan)** created by a local government usually covers land use, housing needs, movement of people and goods, community facilities and utilities, and energy conservation.

Zoning ordinances are local laws implementing the land uses designated in the comprehensive plan and typically cover items such as **permitted uses**, lot sizes, types of structures, building heights, setbacks, style and appearance of structures, density, and protection of natural resources.

Zoning classifies property by uses and types, such as **commercial**, **industrial**, **residential**, agricultural, and **planned unit developments (PUDs)**.

Other ways in which zoning is used include **buffer zones** separating residential from nonresidential areas, **bulk zoning** to control density, **aesthetic zoning** to specify certain types of architecture for new buildings, and **incentive zoning** to require certain uses in developments.

Zoning is enforced through the use of **permits**. An individual case may be considered by a **zoning hearing board (or zoning board of appeals)**, which may decide to allow a **nonconforming use** to continue, grant a **variance** from a zoning ordinance to permit a prohibited land use to avoid undue hardship, or grant a **conditional-use permit (special-use permit)**.

Building codes require permits for new construction and remodeling of or additions to existing construction. State and federal regulations may add additional requirements.

A **certificate of occupancy (occupancy permit)** is issued upon satisfactory completion of work for which a **building permit** was issued.

Subdivision and land development ordinances may be created by the state or may be made part of a local government's comprehensive plan. **A subdivider** buys undeveloped acreage and divides it into smaller lots for sale to individuals or developers. A **developer** improves the land, construct homes or other buildings, and sells them.

A **plat map (subdivision map)** shows geographic boundaries of separate land parcels, usually by showing **blocks** of land divided into individual **lots**. A **subdivision plan** describes subdivision features, including utility easements, and compliance with zoning and other laws.

Private land-use controls include **deed restrictions** that are placed in a deed and the **covenants, conditions, and restrictions (CC&Rs)** placed or referenced in deeds to all property owners in a subdivision. Deed restrictions and CC&Rs cannot impose an illegal covenant or condition. Restrictions may be enforced by an injunction obtained by a property owner or HOA against the property owner committing the violation. If private land-use controls are in conflict with local zoning, the **more restrictive** applies.

The **federal Interstate Land Sales Full Disclosure Act (ILSA)** regulates the interstate sale of unimproved lots in subdivisions of 25 or more lots of less than 20 acres each. The law does not apply to subdivisions sold solely to developers. **State subdivision laws** may also apply to sales within the state of subdivisions located either inside or outside the state.

UNIT 20 QUIZ

1. A subdivision declaration reads, "No property within this subdivision may be further subdivided for sale or otherwise, and no property may be used for other than single-family housing." This is an example of
   a. a restrictive covenant.
   b. an illegal reverter clause.
   c. R-1 zoning.
   d. a conditional-use clause.

2. A landowner who wants to use property in a manner that is prohibited by a local zoning ordinance but which would benefit the community can apply for which of the following?
   a. Conditional-use permit
   b. Prescriptive easement
   c. Occupancy permit
   d. Property allowance

3. What is *NOT* included in public land-use controls?
   a. Subdivision regulations
   b. Covenants, conditions, and restrictions
   c. Environmental protection laws
   d. Comprehensive plan specifications

4. Under its police powers, a municipality may regulate all of the following about housing in a development *EXCEPT*
   a. lot sizes.
   b. building heights.
   c. identity of ownership.
   d. type of structure.

5. The purpose of a building permit is to
   a. assert a deed's restrictive covenant.
   b. maintain municipal control over the volume of building.
   c. provide evidence of compliance with municipal regulations.
   d. show compliance with restrictive covenants.

6. Zoning powers are conferred on municipal governments in which of the following ways?
   a. By state enabling acts
   b. Through the master plan
   c. By popular local vote
   d. Through city charters

7. A town located near a small recreational lake enacts a new zoning code. Under the new code, commercial buildings are not permitted within 1,000 feet of the lake. A commercial building that is permitted to continue in its former use even though it is built on the lakeshore is an example of
   a. nonconforming use.
   b. variance.
   c. special use.
   d. adverse possession.

8. To determine whether a location can be put to future use as a retail store, one would examine the
   a. building code.
   b. list of permitted nonconforming uses.
   c. housing code.
   d. zoning ordinance.

9. All of the following are legal deed restrictions *EXCEPT*
   a. types of buildings that may be constructed.
   b. allowable ethnic origins of purchasers.
   c. activities that are not to be conducted at the site.
   d. minimum size of buildings to be constructed.

10. A restriction in a seller's deed may be enforced by which of the following?
    a. Court injunction
    b. Zoning board of appeal
    c. City building commission
    d. State legislature

11. A property owner owns a large tract of land. After an adequate study of all the relevant facts, the owner legally divides the land into 30 lots suitable for the construction of residences. In this situation, the property owner is acting as a(n)
   a. subdivider.
   b. developer.
   c. land planner.
   d. urban planner.

12. A map illustrating the sizes and locations of streets and lots in a subdivision is called a
   a. gridiron plan.
   b. survey.
   c. subdivision plat map.
   d. property report.

13. In one city, developers are limited by the zoning law to constructing no more than an average of three houses per acre in any subdivision. What does this restriction regulate?
   a. Clustering
   b. Gross density
   c. Out-lots
   d. Covenants

14. Which of the following is a variance?
   a. An exception to a zoning ordinance
   b. A court order prohibiting certain activities
   c. A reversion of ownership
   d. A nullification of an easement

15. Permitted land uses and set-asides, housing projections, transportation issues, and objectives for implementing future controlled development would all be found in a community's
   a. zoning ordinance.
   b. comprehensive plan.
   c. enabling act.
   d. land-control law.

16. Which of the following items would usually *NOT* be shown on the plat map for a new subdivision?
   a. Easements for sewer and water mains
   b. Land to be used for streets
   c. Numbered lots and blocks
   d. Prices of residential and commercial lots

17. A plat for a proposed subdivision is submitted to the
   a. municipality.
   b. property owners.
   c. developer.
   d. state.

18. Restrictive covenants
   a. are no longer effective when the title is transferred.
   b. apply only until the developer has conveyed the title.
   c. can be removed by a court of competent jurisdiction.
   d. apply to and bind successive owners of the property.

19. To protect the public from fraudulent interstate land sales, a developer involved in interstate land sales of 25 or more lots must
   a. provide each purchaser with a printed report disclosing details of the property.
   b. pay the prospective buyer's expenses to see the property involved.
   c. provide preferential financing.
   d. allow a 30-day cancellation period.

20. When is a certificate of occupancy issued?
   a. When the owner of a multifamily residential property wishes to limit the number of individuals who may live in a single unit
   b. At the time a property owner applies for a building permit
   c. After building construction work has been inspected and found satisfactory by the municipal inspector
   d. When an application for a variance or conditional-use permit has been granted by the zoning board

Environmental Issues and the Real Estate Transaction

LEARNING OBJECTIVES

When you have finished reading this unit, you will be able to

- **identify** the basic environmental hazards the real estate professional should be aware of for the protection of client interests as well as the personal risk of liability for nondisclosure;
- **define** *groundwater* and *water table* and describe the provisions of the Safe Drinking Water Act;
- **describe** the issues involved with underground storage tanks, and the associated legal requirements facing the property owner;
- **explain** the regulation involved in the creation and operation of waste disposal sites and in the control of brownfields;
- **list** the various federal laws which protect the public from uncontrolled hazardous waste, and the liability issues facing those who violate any of these laws;
- **explain** the responsibilities and duties of real estate professionals regarding environmental issues; and
- **define** the following *key terms*:

asbestos
brownfields
carbon monoxide (CO)
chlorofluorocarbons (CFCs)
Comprehensive Environmental Response, Compensation, and Liability Act (CERCLA)
encapsulation
environmental impact statement (EIS)
environmental site assessment (ESA)
formaldehyde
groundwater
hydraulic fracturing (fracking)
lead
Lead-Based Paint Hazard Reduction Act (LBPHRA)
mold
polychlorinated biphenyls (PCBs)
radon
Small Business Liability Relief and Brownfields Revitalization Act
Superfund Amendments and Reauthorization Act (SARA)
underground storage tanks (USTs)
urea-formaldehyde foam insulation (UFFI)
water table

OVERVIEW

Environmental issues are health issues, and health issues based on environmental hazards have become real estate issues. Although real estate professionals are not expected to have the technical expertise necessary to determine whether a hazardous substance is present on or near a property, they should be familiar with state and federal environmental laws and the regulatory agencies that enforce them. In that way, the real estate professional can help a prospective purchaser find authoritative information about hazardous substances in order to make an informed purchase decision.

HAZARDOUS SUBSTANCES

www.epa.gov
www.hud.gov

Pollution and hazardous substances in the environment are of interest to real estate professionals because they affect the attractiveness, safety, desirability, and market value of cities, neighborhoods, and backyards. No one wants to live in a toxic environment. (*See* Figure 21.1.) You will see various references to the Environmental Protection Agency (EPA), www.epa.gov, which is charged with federal regulation of numerous environmental hazards. Rules of the Department of Housing and Urban Development (HUD), www.hud.gov, also come into play.

FIGURE 21.1: Environmental Hazards

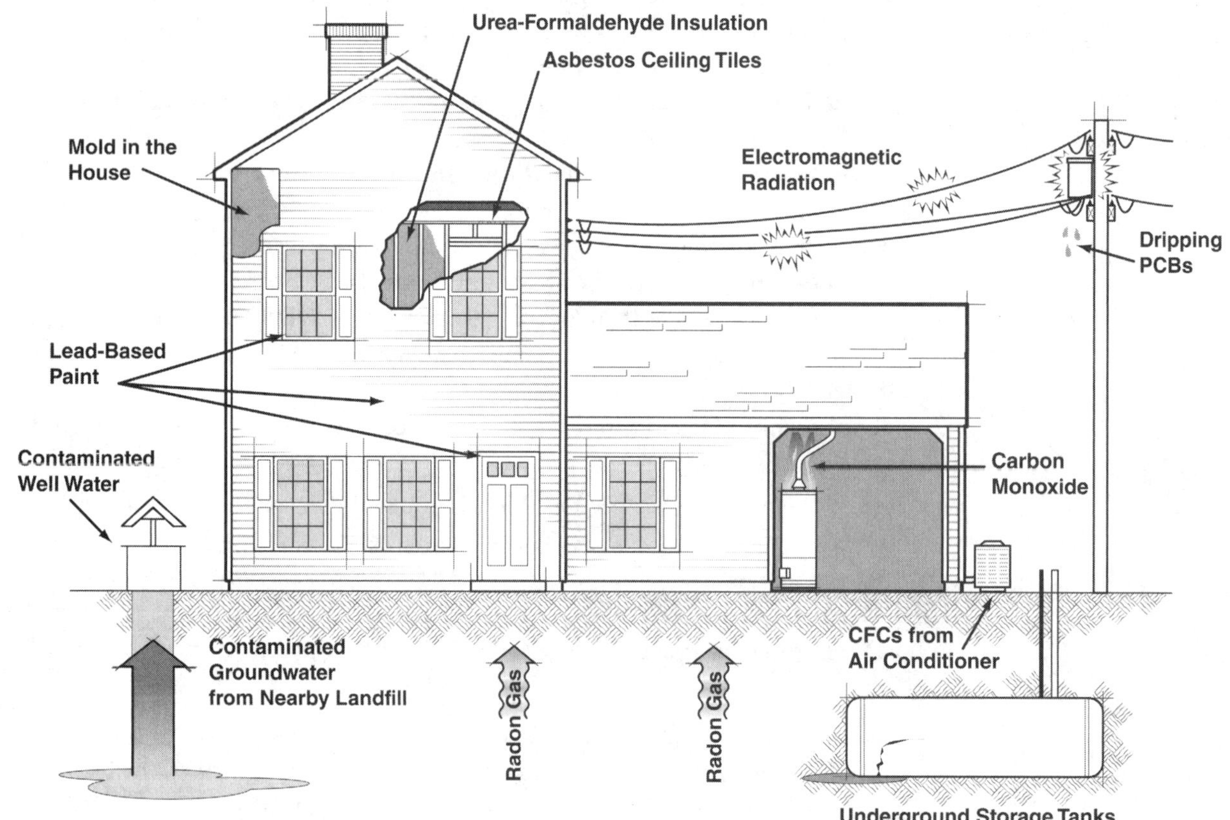

State laws are also of concern when discussing environmental hazards. A state-mandated disclosure about the condition of the property and any known environmental issues is usually required by a seller of property with one to four dwelling units. In the past, real estate professionals tended to accept seller-supplied disclosure forms without question, trusting that all was accurate and complete. Today that trust is risky business. In fact, some states impose a burden on the real estate professional to discover problems and ask questions. Similarly, real estate professionals should inform buyers of the need to ask and discover and not rely on disclosure forms as a warranty or guarantee. As a rule, sellers are to disclose what they are aware of, but buyers are put on notice to discover hazards they are concerned about.

IN PRACTICE It is important that real estate professionals and sellers provide property disclosures to prospective buyers when required by law. For example, in the 2003 South Dakota case of *Saiz v. Horn*, homebuyers found substantial defects in the home they purchased. The buyers learned that the seller had in the past given prospective buyers a disclosure statement revealing the defects but had not provided it to the buyers. The court found that the real estate professional should have told the homebuyers that the sellers had a legal duty to provide them with a disclosure statement.

Asbestos

Asbestos is a fire-resistant mineral that was once used extensively as insulation and to strengthen other materials. A component of more than 3,000 types of building materials, asbestos was first used in the early 1900s and is found in most construction, including residential, built from the early 1940s until 1978, when its use was banned. The EPA estimates that about 107,000 primary and secondary schools and 733,000 public and commercial building shave asbestos-containing materials (ACMs).

Asbestos was used to cover pipes, ducts, and heating and hot water units. Its fire-resistant properties made it a popular material for use in floor tile, exterior siding, roofing products, linoleum flooring materials, joint compounds, wallboard material, backing, and mastics. Though some ACMs are easy to identify (e.g., insulation around heating and water pipes), identifying asbestos may be more difficult when it is behind walls or under floors.

Asbestos-based products can create airborne contaminants that may result in respiratory diseases.

Asbestos is highly *friable*, meaning that as it ages, asbestos fibers easily break down into tiny, very light filaments that stay in the air a long time when it is disturbed or exposed, as often occurs during renovation or remodeling. Those who have inhaled asbestos fibers often develop serious and deadly respiratory diseases decades later. While federal regulations establish guidelines for owners of public and commercial buildings to test for asbestos-containing materials, there are no guidelines regarding the presence of asbestos in residential properties.

Because improper removal procedures may further contaminate the air within the structure, the process requires state-licensed technicians and specially sealed environments. The waste generated must be disposed of at a licensed facility, which further adds to the cost of removal. **Encapsulation**, or the sealing off of disintegrating asbestos, is an alternate method of asbestos control that may be preferable to removal in certain circumstances, provided the condition of the encapsulated asbestos is monitored periodically to make sure it is not disintegrating.

Only a certified asbestos inspector should perform an asbestos inspection of a structure to identify which building materials may contain asbestos. The inspector can also provide recommendations and costs associated with remediation. Buyers should be aware of where ACMs are located so that they are not disturbed during any repair, remodeling, demolition, or even routine use. Appraisers also should be aware of the possible presence of asbestos.

www.epa.gov

More information on asbestos-related issues can be found at www.epa.gov. Numerous publications that provide guidance, information, and assistance with asbestos issues are available.

Lead-Based Paint and Other Lead Hazards

Lead was used as a pigment and drying agent in alkyd oil-based paint. Lead-based paint may be on any interior or exterior surface, but it is particularly common on doors, windows, and other woodwork. The federal government estimates that lead is present in about 75% of all private housing built before 1978; that's approximately 57 million homes, ranging from apartments to mansions.

Children younger than six are the most vulnerable to damage from excessive lead levels, which can cause learning disabilities, developmental delays, reduced height, and poor hearing. Excessive exposure in adults can induce anemia and hypertension, trigger gallbladder problems, and cause reproductive problems in both men and women.

Lead from paint or other sources can result in damage to the brain, nervous system, kidneys, and blood. Children younger than six are particularly vulnerable.

Lead dust can be ingested from the hands of a crawling infant, inhaled by any occupant of a structure, or ingested from the water supply because of lead pipes or lead solder. Soil and groundwater may be contaminated by everything from lead plumbing in leaking landfills to discarded skeets and bullets from an old shooting range. High levels of lead have been found in the soil near waste-to-energy incinerators.

In 1996, the EPA and HUD issued final regulations under the **Lead-Based Paint Hazard Reduction Act (LBPHRA)** of 1992, requiring disclosure of the presence of any known lead-based paint hazards to potential buyers or renters. The federal law does not require that anyone test for the presence of lead-based paint, however. Under later regulations, EPA imposed training and certification requirements, which took effect June 23, 2008, for renovators of certain property containing lead-based paint.

The EPA now requires the following from sellers, landlords, and renovators of residential dwellings built before 1978:

- Landlords must disclose known information on lead-based paint and hazards before leases take effect. Leases must include a disclosure form regarding lead-based paint.
- Sellers have to disclose known information on lead-based paint and hazards prior to execution of a contract for sale. Sales contracts must include a completed disclosure form about lead-based paint. (*See* Figure 21.2.) This is the form for sellers and is slightly different from the form for landlords. Real estate professionals should use EPA-written disclosure forms rather than creating their own forms.
- Buyers must have up to 10 days to conduct a risk assessment or inspection for the presence of lead-based paint hazards.

- Real estate professionals must provide buyers and lessees with "Protect Your Family from Lead in Your Home," the pamphlet created by the EPA, HUD, and the U.S. Consumer Product Safety Commission.
- Anyone who is paid to perform work that disturbs paint in housing, schools, and child care facilities built before 1978 must be trained and certified in EPA lead-based work practices. This includes residential rental property owners/managers, general contractors, and special trade contractors (e.g., painters, plumbers, carpenters, electricians). The Renovation, Repair, and Painting (RR&P) program involves prerenovation education, including distribution of the pamphlet *Renovate Right* to the property owner before work commences. It can be found at www.epa.gov/lead/pubs/renovaterightbrochure.pdf. General information about the program is at www.epa.gov/getleadsafe/.
- Real estate professionals must ensure that all parties comply with the law.
- Sellers, lessors, and renovators are required to disclose any prior test results or any knowledge of lead-based paint hazards. With only a very narrow exception, all real estate professionals (subagent, buyer's representative, transaction facilitator) are required to advise sellers to make the required disclosures. Only buyer's representatives who are paid entirely by the buyer are exempt.

www.epa.gov/lead/pubs/renovaterightbrochure.pdf
www.epa.gov/getleadsafe/

IN PRACTICE The EPA and HUD are serious about enforcement of lead-based paint notification rules. In early 2008, a Boston property management company agreed to pay a $28,000 penalty and spend nearly $290,000 to replace windows containing lead-based paint. A year later, a large, nonprofit corporation that develops, finances, and manages affordable, mixed-income housing and nearly two dozen associated property owners agreed to pay a $200,000 penalty and to spend more than $2 million in lead-paint abatement at their residential properties. In fall 2009, a New York City property management company and 20 affiliated owners of federally assisted multifamily properties in Brooklyn agreed to pay a $20,000 penalty and perform lead-based paint hazard reduction work in 639 units in 17 properties.

A home can be inspected for lead hazards in the following ways:

- *Paint inspection.* A paint inspection will provide the lead content of every different type of painted surface in a home. This inspection will not indicate whether the paint is a hazard or how the homeowner should deal with it.
- *Risk assessment.* A risk assessment indicates whether there are any sources of serious lead exposure, such as peeling paint or lead dust. It also describes what actions can be taken to address the hazards.

EPA guidance pamphlets, a list of professionals qualified to inspect or assess for lead-based paint, and other information about lead-based hazards are available from the National Lead Information Center at 800-424-5323 and www.epa.gov/lead/nlic.html.

www.epa.gov/lead/nlic.html

FIGURE 21.2: Disclosure of Lead-Based Paint and Lead-Based Paint Hazards

Disclosure of Information on Lead-Based Paint and/or Lead-Based Paint Hazards

Lead Warning Statement

Every purchaser of any interest in residential real property on which a residential dwelling was built prior to 1978 is notified that such property may present exposure to lead from lead-based paint that may place young children at risk of developing lead poisoning. Lead poisoning in young children may produce permanent neurological damage, including learning disabilities, reduced intelligence quotient, behavioral problems, and impaired memory. Lead poisoning also poses a particular risk to pregnant women. The seller of any interest in residential real property is required to provide the buyer with any information on lead-based paint hazards from risk assessments or inspections in the seller's possession and notify the buyer of any known lead-based paint hazards. A risk assessment or inspection for possible lead-based paint hazards is recommended prior to purchase.

Seller's Disclosure

(a) Presence of lead-based paint and/or lead-based paint hazards (check (i) or (ii) below):

(i) ______ Known lead-based paint and/or lead-based paint hazards are present in the housing (explain).

____

(ii) _____ Seller has no knowledge of lead-based paint and/or lead-based paint hazards in the housing.

(b) Records and reports available to the seller (check (i) or (ii) below):

(i) ______ Seller has provided the purchaser with all available records and reports pertaining to lead-based paint and/or lead-based paint hazards in the housing (list documents below).

____

(ii) _____ Seller has no reports or records pertaining to lead-based paint and/or lead-based paint hazards in the housing.

Purchaser's Acknowledgment (initial)

(c) ________ Purchaser has received copies of all information listed above.

(d) ________ Purchaser has received the pamphlet *Protect Your Family from Lead in Your Home.*

(e) Purchaser has (check (i) or (ii) below):

(i) _____ received a 10-day opportunity (or mutually agreed upon period) to conduct a risk assessment or inspection for the presence of lead-based paint and/or lead-based paint hazards; or

(ii) _____ waived the opportunity to conduct a risk assessment or inspection for the presence of lead-based paint and/or lead-based paint hazards.

Agent's Acknowledgment (initial)

(f) ________ Agent has informed the seller of the seller's obligations under 42 U.S.C. 4852(d) and is aware of his/her responsibility to ensure compliance.

Certification of Accuracy

The following parties have reviewed the information above and certify, to the best of their knowledge, that the information they have provided is true and accurate.

Seller	Date	Seller	Date
Purchaser	Date	Purchaser	Date
Agent	Date	Agent	Date

Radon

Radon is a naturally occurring, colorless, odorless, tasteless, radioactive gas produced by the decay of other radioactive substances. Radon is measured in picocuries (a unit of radiation) contained in a liter of air (pCi/L). Radon is found in every state and territory with radon levels in the outdoor air averaging 0.4 pCi/L. Fans and thermal "stack effects" (i.e., rising hot air draws cooler air in from the ground through cracks in the basement and foundation walls) pull radon into buildings.

The potential for developing lung cancer from exposure to radon is a function of the extent and the length of a person's exposure to radon. Radon has been classified as a Class A known human carcinogen. Furthermore, smokers have a radon risk factor 15 times greater than nonsmokers.

Because neither the EPA nor current scientific consensus has been able to establish a "threshold" safe level of radon exposure, the EPA suggests an "action" level of 4 pCi/L. The action level of 4 was chosen because 95% of the time, current technology can bring the level below 4, and 75% of the time, levels can be reduced to 2 pCi/L. A radon mitigation system is less expensive when installed during construction. Mitigation consists of removing the radon before it seeps into the house by means of a fan installed in a pipe running from the basement to the attic to draw the radon up and out.

Home testing may be done with passive devices, such as alpha track detectors and a charcoal canister. Continuous monitors require electrical power and usually a trained technician. Test results are normally received within 10 days or so when using a passive device (immediately when using an electric continuous monitor). Although a 90-day testing period is most accurate, the EPA developed a 48-hour procedure that can be used in a real estate transaction. The 48-hour test can satisfactorily predict whether a home's annual average is at or above 4 pCi/L in 94% of cases.

www.epa.gov/radon/pubs/citguide.html

Because one out of every 15 homes probably needs mitigation, before looking at properties, real estate professionals should discuss radon concerns with their buyers. Real estate professionals can direct buyers to www.epa.gov/radon/pubs/citguide.html for the pamphlet *A Citizen's Guide to Radon* and additional information about testing and mitigation methods.

Formaldehyde

www.epa.gov/iaq/formaldehyde.html

Formaldehyde, a colorless chemical with a strong, pronounced odor, is used widely in the manufacture of building materials and many household products because of its preservative characteristics. Often emitted as a gas, formaldehyde is one of the most common and problematic volatile organic compounds (VOCs) and is one of the few indoor air pollutants that can be measured. Formaldehyde was listed as a hazardous air pollutant in the Clean Air Act Amendments of 1990. Its use and effects are described at www.epa.gov/iaq/formaldehyde.html.

Formaldehyde is classified as a "probable human carcinogen" (i.e., causing cancer in animals and probably in humans). For the 10 to 20% of the population that is "sensitive" to formaldehyde, formaldehyde may trigger respiratory problems (shortness of breath, wheezing, chest tightness, asthma), as well as eye and skin irritations (burning sensations in the eyes and throat). It is a major contributor to sick building syndrome (SBS) in commercial properties.

www.epa.gov/opptintr/chemtest/formaldehyde/

The largest source of formaldehyde in any building is likely to be the off-gassing from pressed-wood products made using adhesives that contain urea-formaldehyde (UF) resins. Pressed-wood products include particleboard, hardwood plywood paneling, and medium-density fiberboard. It is also used in carpeting and ceiling tiles. Since 1985, HUD has regulated the use of plywood and particleboard so that they conform to specified formaldehyde-emission levels in the construction of prefabricated homes and manufactured housing. New regulations that will be enforced by the EPA under the Formaldehyde Standards for Composite Wood Products Act, enacted in 2010, went into effect in 2013; more information can be found at www.epa.gov/opptintr/chemtest/formaldehyde/.

Urea-Formaldehyde Foam Insulation (UFFI), once popular, then banned, and now legal again, is rarely used. When incorrectly mixed, UFFI never properly cures, resulting in strong emissions shortly after installation. Studies have shown that formaldehyde emissions generally decrease over time, so homes where UFFI was installed many years ago are unlikely to still have high levels of formaldehyde unless the insulation is exposed to extreme heat or moisture. Real estate professionals should check their state's property disclosure form to see whether UFFI must be disclosed. Appraisers should also be aware of the presence of formaldehyde.

Carbon Monoxide

www.cpsc.gov

Carbon monoxide (CO) is a colorless, odorless, and tasteless gas that occurs as a by-product of burning fuels such as wood, oil, and natural gas, owing to incomplete combustion. Carbon monoxide is quickly absorbed by the body, where it inhibits the blood's ability to transport oxygen, resulting in dizziness and nausea. As CO concentrations increase, the symptoms become more severe, and death may occur within a short time. According to the Consumer Product Safety Commission, www.cpsc.gov, about 170 deaths from nonautomotive carbon monoxide poisoning occur in the United States each year. Thousands of other individuals require hospital emergency room care annually. Many cases arise from the use of portable generators in areas that have undergone a natural disaster.

www.epa.gov/iaq/co.html

In addition to portable generators, furnaces, water heaters, space heaters, fireplaces, and wood stoves all produce CO as a natural result of their combustion of fuel. When these units are functioning properly and are properly ventilated, their CO emissions are not a problem; however, improper ventilation or equipment malfunctions can allow large quantities of CO to be released into a residence or commercial structure in a very short amount of time. CO is a problem often encountered by property managers if tenants use kerosene heaters. More information is available at www.epa.gov/iaq/co.html.

IN PRACTICE Carbon monoxide detectors are available, sometimes in combination with smoke detectors, and their use is mandatory in some areas. Even if it is not, a property manager should discuss with the landlord the importance of installing a detector in any rental property that is equipped with an appliance or heater that might create a CO problem. Annual maintenance of heating systems also helps avoid CO exposure.

Polychlorinated Biphenyls

Polychlorinated biphenyls (PCBs) consist of more than 200 chemical compounds that are not found naturally in nature. Flame resistant, they were often used in electrical equipment, such as transformers, electrical motors in refrigerators, caulking compounds, and hydraulic oil in older equipment. The EPA has classified PCBs as reasonably carcinogenic, and these chemicals have been implicated in lower fertility and shortened life spans. Although the commercial distribution of PCBs was banned in 1979, PCBs remain in the environment because burning them at more than 2,400 degrees in a closed environment is the only known way to destroy them.

PCBs are most likely a concern for commercial and industrial property managers. These managers should ask the local utility company to identify and remove any type of transformer that might be a source of PCBs. If the PCBs leak into the environment, penalties and removal methods are expensive.

Chlorofluorocarbons

Chlorofluorocarbons (CFCs) are nontoxic, nonflammable chemicals used as refrigerants in air conditioners, refrigerators, and freezers. CFCs are also used in aerosol sprays, paints, solvents, and foam-blowing applications. Although CFCs are safe in most applications and are inert in the lower atmosphere, once CFC vapors rise to the upper atmosphere, where they may survive from 2 to 150 years, they are broken down by ultraviolet light into chemicals that deplete the ozone layer.

Global treaties have sought to reduce the production levels of CFCs. The manufacture of these chemicals ended for the most part in 1996, with exceptions for production in developing countries, medical products (e.g., asthma inhalers), and research.

Although newer air conditioners use a different product, older appliances may leak CFCs and should be properly disposed of to prevent further leakage. A buyer's representative may wish to advise the client to consider upgrading to newer, more energy-efficient and environmentally safe appliances.

Only EPA-certified technicians should do any work on a refrigeration system, especially the larger systems found in commercial and industrial buildings. Approved equipment should carry a label reading, "This equipment has been certified by ARI/UL to meet EPA's minimum requirements for recycling and recovery equipment."

Mold

Mold can be found almost anywhere and can grow on almost any organic substance, as long as moisture, oxygen, and an organic food source are present. Moisture feeds mold growth. If a moisture problem is not discovered or addressed, mold growth can gradually destroy what it is growing on. In addition, some molds can cause serious health problems, including allergic reactions and asthma attacks. Some molds are known to produce potent toxins and/or irritants.

Some moisture problems in homes and buildings have been directly linked to recent changes in construction practices. Some of these practices have resulted in buildings that are too tightly sealed, preventing adequate ventilation. Building materials, such as drywall, may not allow moisture to escape easily. The material used in drywall wicks moisture to the nutrition source of glue and paper. Vinyl wallpaper and exterior insulation finish systems (EIFS), also known as synthetic stucco, also do not allow moisture to escape. Other moisture problems include roof leaks, unvented combustion appliances, and landscaping or gutters that direct water to the building.

www.epa.gov/iedmold1/mold_remediation.html

www.epa.gov/iedmold1/index.html

The EPA has published guidelines for the remediation and/or cleanup of mold and moisture problems in schools and commercial buildings, available at www.epa.gov/iedmold1/mold_remediation.html. General mold information can be found at www.epa.gov/iedmold1/index.html.

Mold is an important issue for real estate professionals, particularly because homeowners insurance policies now generally exclude mold from coverage. Plaintiffs may name property sellers, landlords, property management companies, and real estate professionals as defendants in a case, in addition to construction and insurance companies.

IN PRACTICE In a 2005 Wisconsin case, *Eddy v. B.S.T.V., Inc.*, a couple sued a real estate company for failing to disclose mold contamination in the home they purchased. The real estate company's insurer refused to provide coverage, stating that the insurance policy had specific exclusion clauses that would not cover property damage arising out of a real estate professional's failure to render professional services. The couple bringing the lawsuit alleged that the real estate professionals breached the real estate company's professional-service responsibilities and that, therefore, the exclusions applied. The real estate company tried to argue that because its real estate agents were trained in identifying mold-related hazards, the claim did not fit the exclusion clause. The court did not agree, and the real estate company was held liable. The court held that the exclusion clauses in the policy prevented insurance coverage for the injuries.

In light of this case and other court decisions on this topic, real estate companies and professionals find it difficult to know what to do when mold is suspected or found on a property. There are no federal requirements to disclose mold contamination at this time, and only a few states require disclosure. Real estate professionals should remind buyers that sellers cannot disclose what they do not know. Also, real estate professionals should advise buyers that they have not only the right but also the burden to discover the presence of mold.

IN PRACTICE Real estate professionals may need to take extra steps to protect themselves from liability. Those who suspect that mold is present in a home should ask many questions about leaks, floods, and prior damage and remind the sellers to honestly and truthfully disclose any insurance claims regarding mold and other water issues. Any conversation with a seller should be followed up with a summary of the conversation in writing, even if just an email, particularly if the seller says that there has never been any instance of water damage to the property and the real estate professional suspects that this is not the truth. Copies of all emails and other communications with the seller should be kept in the office's records of the transaction, in case they are ever needed.

GROUNDWATER PROTECTION

Groundwater, water that exists under the earth's surface within the tiny spaces or crevices in geological formations, forms the **water table**, the natural level at which the ground is saturated. The water table may be several hundred feet underground or near the surface. When the earth's natural filtering systems are inadequate to ensure the availability of pure water, any contamination of underground water threatens the supply of pure, clean water for private wells or public water systems.

Numerous state and federal laws have been enacted to preserve and protect the water supply.

Groundwater can be contaminated from a number of sources, including runoff from waste disposal sites, leaking underground storage tanks, septic systems, dry wells, and storm drains, as well as the illegal disposal of hazardous materials and regular use of insecticides and herbicides. Because water flows from one place to another, contamination can spread far from its source. Once the contamination has been identified, its source can be eliminated. Although the water may eventually become clean, the process can be time consuming and extremely expensive.

The Safe Drinking Water Act

www.epa.gov/hfstudy/index.html

The Safe Drinking Water Act (SDWA) was passed in 1974 (and amended in 1986 and 1996) to protect public health by regulating the nation's public drinking water supply. The SDWA authorizes the EPA to set national health-based standards for drinking water. The amendments strengthened the law by increasing source water protection, operator training, funding for water system improvements, and public information. For example, the EPA now requires that water suppliers report any health risk situation within 24 hours, instead of the 72 hours mandated originally. One of the EPA's recent concerns is the effect on groundwater of the byproducts produced by **hydraulic fracturing (fracking)**, the process used to extract natural gas from the deep layers of rock in which it is embedded. A regularly updated report by the EPA can be found at www.epa.gov/hfstudy/index.html. In June 2015, the EPA issued a draft Executive Summary of its ongoing investigation that indicated there was no evidence that hydraulic fracturing had caused "widespread, systemic impacts on drinking water resources in the United States."

Most property disclosure forms require sellers to identify the property's water source, such as well water, municipal water supply, or some other source. Anything other than a municipal water supply should be tested. Also, sellers are generally required to identify the type and location of any septic system used on the property because an incorrectly placed or poorly functioning system can contaminate the water source.

IN PRACTICE Real estate professionals should educate their sellers about full and honest disclosure concerning the property's water supply and septic systems. Buyers should be educated about potential groundwater contamination sources both on and off a property. Real estate professionals should always recommend testing the water supply when it is not part of a municipal source.

UNDERGROUND STORAGE TANKS

Underground storage tanks (USTs) are commonly found on sites where petroleum products are used or where gas stations and auto repair shops are or were located. They also may be found in a number of other commercial and industrial establishments, including printing and chemical plants, wood treatment plants, paper mills, paint manufacturers, dry cleaners, food processing plants, and chemical storage or process waste plants. Military bases and airports are also common sites for underground tanks. In residential areas, tanks can be used to store heating oil.

Legal Requirements

Federal and state laws impose strict requirements on landowners whose property contains underground storage tanks. The federal UST program is regulated by EPA. The regulations apply to tanks that contain hazardous substances or liquid petroleum products and that store at least 10% of their volume underground. Some states also have adopted laws regulating underground storage tanks that are more stringent than the federal laws. UST owners are required to register their tanks and adhere to strict technical and administrative requirements that govern

- installation,
- maintenance,
- corrosion prevention,
- overspill prevention,
- monitoring, and
- recordkeeping.

Owners are also required to demonstrate that they have sufficient financial resources to cover any damage that might result from leaks.

The following types of tanks are among those that are exempt from the federal regulations:

- Tanks that hold less than 110 gallons
- Farm and residential tanks that hold 1,100 gallons or less of motor fuel used for noncommercial purposes
- Tanks that store heating oil burned on the premises
- Tanks on or above the floor of underground areas, such as basements or tunnels
- Septic tanks and systems for collecting storm water and wastewater

Most seller property disclosures are required only for residential properties. However, most of the problematic USTs are found in commercial and industrial properties, thereby placing the duty of discovery squarely on the buyer. Because many of the older tanks have never been registered and exempt tanks are not required to be registered, real estate professionals and their buyers should be particularly alert to the presence of fill pipes, vent lines, stained soil, and fumes or odors, any of which may indicate the presence of a UST. Detection, removal, and cleanup of surrounding contaminated soil can be expensive, so it is important to deal with these issues before, not after, closing.

IN PRACTICE Whenever a real estate professional is in doubt about whether or not a property contains USTs, a contingency should be added to the property buyer's offer allowing the buyer to have the property inspected for USTs.

WASTE DISPOSAL SITES AND BROWNFIELDS

Federal, state, and local regulations govern the location, construction, content, and maintenance of landfill sites built to accommodate the vast quantities of garbage produced every day in America. Additionally, legislation exits to govern the use of **brownfields**, which are defunct, derelict, or abandoned commercial or industrial sites, many of which are suspected to contain toxic waste.

Waste Disposal Sites

A landfill is an enormous hole, either excavated for the purpose of waste disposal or left over from surface mining operations. The hole is lined with clay or a synthetic liner to prevent leakage of waste material into the water supply. A system of underground drainage pipes permits the monitoring of leaks and leaching. Waste is laid on the liner at the bottom of the excavation, and a layer of topsoil is then compacted onto the waste. The layering procedure is repeated until the landfill is full, with the layers mounded up sometimes as high as several hundred feet.

Capping is the process of laying two to four feet of soil over the top of the site and then planting grass on it to enhance the landfill's aesthetic value and prevent erosion. A ventilation pipe runs from the landfill's base through the cap to vent off accumulated natural gases created by the decomposing waste. Test wells around landfill operations are installed to constantly monitor the groundwater in the surrounding area, and soil analyses test for contamination.

Capped landfills have been used as parks and golf courses. Rapid suburban growth has resulted in housing developments and office campuses being built on landfill sites. Most newer landfill sites are well documented, but the locations of many older landfill sites are no longer known.

Special hazardous waste disposal sites contain radioactive waste from nuclear power plants, toxic chemicals, and waste materials produced by medical, scientific, and industrial processes. Additional waste disposal sites used as on-site garbage dumps are located on rural property, such as farms, ranches, and residences. Some materials, such as radioactive waste, are sealed in containers buried deep underground and placed in *tombs* designed to last thousands of years. These disposal sites are usually limited to extremely remote locations, well away from populated areas or farmland.

www.epa.gov/osw/laws-regs/regs-haz.htm

Hazardous and radioactive waste disposal sites are subject to strict state and federal regulation to prevent the escape of toxic substances. For more information, EPA's website, www.epa.gov/osw/laws-regs/regs-haz.htm is a good place to start.

Brownfields

According to the U.S. General Accounting Office, several hundred thousand brownfields plague communities as eyesores and potentially dangerous and hazardous properties, often contributing to the decline of property values.

www.epa.gov/brownfields/laws/index.htm

The Brownfields Law The **Small Business Liability Relief and Brownfields Revitalization Act** (or Brownfields Law) was signed into law in 2002. The Brownfields Law provides funds to assess and clean up brownfields, clarifies liability protections, and provides tax incentives toward enhancing state and tribal response programs. The law is also important for property owners and developers because it shields innocent developers from liability for toxic wastes that existed at a site prior to the purchase of property. In effect, a property owner who neither caused nor contributed to the contamination is not liable for the cleanup. Significantly, the law encourages the development of abandoned properties, some of which are located in prime urban real estate areas. Information on the Brownfields Law can be found at www.epa.gov/brownfields/laws/index.htm.

ENVIRONMENTAL LEGISLATION

The EPA, which was created in 1970, works with other federal agencies to oversee and implement many of the laws passed since then to protect and improve the environment. Most federal laws encourage state and local governments to enact their own legislation.

Comprehensive Environmental Response, Compensation, and Liability Act

The **Comprehensive Environmental Response, Compensation, and Liability Act (CERCLA)** was created in 1980. It established a fund of $9 billion, called the Superfund, to clean up uncontrolled hazardous waste sites and to respond to spills. The act created a process for identifying potential responsible parties (PRPs) and for ordering them to take responsibility for the cleanup action. CERCLA is administered and enforced by EPA.

Liability A landowner is liable under CERCLA when a release or a threat of release of a hazardous substance has occurred on the landowner's property. Regardless of whether the contamination is the result of the landowner's actions or those of others, the owner can be held responsible for the cleanup. This liability includes the cleanup not only of the landowner's property but also of any neighboring property that has been contaminated. A landowner who is not responsible for the contamination can seek reimbursement for the cleanup costs from previous landowners, any other responsible party, or the Superfund. If other parties are not available, however, even a landowner who did not cause the problem could be solely responsible for the cleanup costs. This *strict liability* was modified somewhat by an amendment to the Superfund law that is described in the next part of this section.

Once the EPA determines that hazardous material has been released into the environment, the agency is authorized to begin remedial action. First, it attempts to identify the potentially responsible parties (PRPs). If the PRPs agree to cooperate in the cleanup, they must also agree about how to divide the cost. If the PRPs do not voluntarily undertake the cleanup, EPA may hire its own contractors to do the necessary work. The EPA then bills the PRPs for the cost. If the PRPs refuse to pay, the EPA can seek damages in court for up to three times the actual cost of the cleanup.

Liability under the Superfund is considered strict, joint and several, and retroactive. Strict liability means that the owner is responsible to the injured party without excuse. Joint and several liability means that each individual owner is personally responsible for the total damages. If only one of the owners is financially able to handle the total damages, that owner must pay the total and collect the proportionate shares from the other owners whenever possible. Retroactive liability means that the liability is not limited to the current owner but includes prior owners during the time the site was contaminated.

Superfund Amendments and Reauthorization Act

The **Superfund Amendments and Reauthorization Act (SARA)** created an "innocent landowner" immunity status. It recognized that, in certain cases, a landowner in the chain of ownership was completely innocent of all wrongdoing and therefore should not be held liable. The innocent landowner immunity clause established the criteria by which to judge whether a person or business could be exempted from liability. The criteria included the following:

- The pollution was caused by a third party.
- The property was acquired after the fact.
- The landowner had no actual or constructive knowledge of the damage.
- Due care was exercised when the property was purchased (the landowner made a reasonable search, called an environmental or Phase I site assessment) to determine that no damage to the property existed.
- Reasonable precautions were taken in the exercise of ownership rights.

The most serious effects on property value associated with environmental problems involve the presence of undisclosed landfills and hazardous waste sites. Real estate professionals can encourage buyers to consult www.epa.gov/superfund/sites/index.htm to determine whether a property of interest is located near a Superfund site. Buyers should also speak with neighbors about activities that have taken place on or near a property.

IN PRACTICE The buyer of commercial, industrial, and even some residential and agricultural properties should include a contingency in an offer to purchase that allows the buyer to hire an environmental engineer to conduct an environmental site assessment (discussed in the next section). A residential property located next to a dry cleaner or gas station, or a farm which uses overhead tanks that can spill and drip to pump fuel into farm machinery, can have hidden issues that may result in liability for the buyer. In other words, the parties should do everything possible to avoid surprises.

LIABILITY OF REAL ESTATE PROFESSIONALS

Although federal and state laws have defined many of the liabilities involved in environmental issues, common law (case law based on judicial precedent) is often used for further interpretation. The real estate professional and all others involved in a real estate transaction must be aware of both actual and potential liability.

A real estate professional can avoid liability with environmental issues by

- becoming familiar with common environmental problems in the licensee's area,
- looking for signs of environmental contamination,
- suggesting (and including as a contingency) an environmental audit if the licensee suspects contamination, and
- giving no advice on environmental issues.

Sellers often carry the most exposure to liability. Purchasers may be held liable even if they didn't cause the contamination. Lenders may end up owning worthless assets if owners default on loans rather than undertake expensive cleanup efforts. Real estate professionals could be held liable for improper disclosure; therefore, it is necessary to be aware of the potential environmental risks from neighboring properties, such as gas stations, manufacturing plants, or even funeral homes.

Additional exposure is created for individuals involved in other aspects of real estate transactions. For example, real estate appraisers must identify and adjust for environmental problems. Adjustments to market value typically reflect the cleanup cost plus a factor of the degree of panic and suspicion that exists in the current market. Although the sales price can be affected dramatically, the underlying market value might possibly remain relatively equal to others in the neighborhood. The real estate appraiser's greatest responsibility is to the lender, which depends on the appraiser to identify values affected by environmental hazards. Although the lender may be protected under certain conditions by virtue of the 1986 amendments to the Superfund act, the lender must be aware of any potential problems and may require additional environmental reports.

Insurance carriers also might be affected. Mortgage insurance companies protect lenders' mortgage investments and might be required to carry part of the ultimate responsibility in cases of loss. More important, a hazard insurance carrier might be directly responsible for damages if such coverage was included in the initial policy.

Discovery of Environmental Hazards

Real estate professionals are not expected to have the technical expertise necessary to discover the presence of environmental hazards. They are presumed by the public to have special knowledge about real estate, so real estate professionals must be aware of possible hazards and where to seek professional help.

The most appropriate people on whom a real estate professional can rely for sound environmental information are scientific or technical experts. Environmental auditors (or *environmental assessors*) are scientific or technical experts who can provide the most comprehensive studies. Developers and purchasers of commercial and industrial properties (and even purchasers of some agricultural and residential properties) often rely on an environmental assessment that includes the property's history of use, a current-use review, and an investigation into the existence of reported or known contamination sources in the subject area that may affect the property. Testing of soil, water, air, and structures can be conducted, if warranted.

Not only do environmental experts detect environmental problems, they can usually offer guidance about how best to resolve the conditions. Although an environmental audit or assessment may occur at any stage in a transaction, they are most frequently a contingency that must be satisfied before closing.

IN PRACTICE An environmental assessment and accompanying tests conducted by an environmental consultants can take time. The real estate professional should be aware of the time required and encourage the prospective property buyer to contact the environmental consultants as soon as it is known that such tests are needed, either before an offer to purchase is made or as a contingency in the offer. In some cases, the need for such an assessment may be enough to convince a prospective buyer to avoid the property entirely.

Environmental Site Assessments

An **environmental site assessment** (ESA) is often performed on a property to show that due care was exercised in determining whether any environmental impairments exist. The assessment can help prevent parties from becoming involved in contaminated property and work as a defense to liability. It is often requested by a lending institution, developer, or a potential buyer. The assessment is commonly performed in phases, such as Phase 1 or Phase 2. A Phase 1 ESA is requested first to determine whether any potential environmental problems exist at or near the subject property that may cause impairment. A Phase 2 ESA includes soil, water, and other testing, and is performed if warranted. There are no federal regulations that define what an environmental assessment must include.

Environmental Impact Statements

A federally funded project requires that an **environmental impact statement (EIS)** be performed. The statement details the impact the project will have on the environment. It can include information about air quality, noise, public health and safety, energy consumption, population density, wildlife, vegetation, and the need for sewer and water facilities. Increasingly, these statements are also being required for private development.

Disclosure of Environmental Hazards

Most state laws address the issue of disclosure of known material facts regarding a residential property of one to four units. In some states, real estate professionals may be liable if they should have known of a condition, even if the seller neglected to make the disclosure. Very few states require disclosure of environmental issues with commercial and industrial property. Real estate professionals specializing in these properties should emphasize to prospective buyers the importance of professional environmental audits in the absence of required disclosures.

KEY POINT REVIEW

Asbestos is a mineral composed of fibers that have fireproofing and insulating qualities. Asbestos is a health hazard when fibers break down (become **friable**) and are inhaled. Asbestos has been banned for use in insulation since **1978**. **Encapsulation** can prevent asbestos fibers from becoming airborne.

Lead can be found in pipes, pipe solder, paints, air, and soil. **Lead-based paint** is found in many of the housing units built before 1978. Lead accumulates in the body and can damage the brain, nervous system, kidneys, and blood.

The **Lead-Based Paint Hazard Reduction Act of 1992 (LBPHRA)** requires disclosure of known lead-based paint hazards to potential buyers or renters.

Real estate professionals must provide buyers and lessees with ***Protect Your Family from Lead in Your Home***, a pamphlet created by EPA, HUD, and the Consumer Product Safety Commission. Later regulations also require contractors and remodelers who disturb painted surfaces in homes, schools, and child care facilities built before 1978 to be trained and certified in the EPA's new lead-based work practices. The pamphlet *Renovate Right* must be given to the property owner before work begins.

Radon is an odorless, tasteless, **radioactive gas** produced by the natural decay of radioactive substances in the ground and is found throughout the United States. Radon gas may cause lung cancer. Testing for radon in buildings is not a federal requirement.

Formaldehyde, described as a hazardous air pollutant in the Clean Air Act Amendments of 1990, is used for building and household products, such as **urea-formaldehyde foam insulation (UFFI)**, and may cause respiratory problems, eye and skin irritations, and possibly cancer. Since 1985, it has been regulated by HUD for use in wood products.

Real estate professionals should check state formaldehyde disclosure requirements, and appraisers should note the presence of formaldehyde.

Carbon monoxide (CO) is a colorless, odorless gas that is by-product of fuel burning and is produced by portable generators, furnaces, water heaters, space heaters (including kerosene heaters), fireplaces, and wood stoves. Inhaling CO may cause carbon monoxide poisoning, which can result in death unless the gas is properly vented. CO is detectable with available carbon monoxide detectors, which may be required by state law.

Polychlorinated biphenyls (PCBs), which are suspected of causing health problems, may be found in electrical equipment. The manufacture and commercial distribution of PCBs has been banned since **1979**.

Chlorofluorocarbons (CFCs), used in refrigerators, aerosol sprays, paints, solvents, and foam applications, are no longer manufactured worldwide, for the most part since 1996, and have been replaced by available environmentally friendly substitutes for home appliances.

Mold is present in the air everywhere and grows in the presence of moisture, oxygen, and an organic food source. Some molds can cause serious health problems. The **EPA** has guidelines for remediation and/or cleanup of mold and moisture problems in schools and commercial buildings. Real estate professionals should recommend a **mold inspection** if mold is evident or suspected because of water problems.

Groundwater is found under the earth's surface and forms the water table. The **Safe Drinking Water Act (SDWA)** of 1974 regulates the public drinking water supply. On transfer of property, any water source other than a municipal supply should be tested, as should any septic system.

Underground storage tanks (USTs), which contain petroleum products, industrial chemicals, and other substances, are a concern because the leakage may imperil both public and private water sources. USTs are subject to federal law (regulated by EPA) and state law, which is sometimes stronger than federal law. When a purchase is being considered, a careful inspection of any property on which USTs are suspected should be conducted.

Waste disposal sites can be owned by municipalities, be part of commercial enterprises, or be found on farms and other rural properties. A landfill disposal site, whether excavated or making use of previously mined property, is **lined** to prevent seepage, **capped** with soil for aesthetic reasons, and **vented** to release gases created by decomposing waste.

Brownfields legislation encourages development of abandoned properties by shielding innocent developers from liability for toxic wastes that existed at a site prior to purchase.

The **Comprehensive Environmental Response, Compensation, and Liability Act (CERCLA)** is administered and enforced by EPA. CERCLA established a **Superfund** to clean up uncontrolled hazardous waste sites and identifies **potential responsible parties (PRPs)**.

Strict liability means that the landowner has no defense to the responsibility for cleanup; **joint and several liability** means that each of several landowners is responsible for the entire cleanup; and **retroactive liability** occurs when the present owner and previous owners are considered responsible for cleanup. CERCLA also defines when **innocent landowner immunity** applies.

Environmental liability issues for **real estate professionals** include discovery of environmental hazards by questioning the owner and recommending an **environmental site assessment (ESA)**. A **Phase 1 ESA** is a physical examination of the property and investigation of its history; a **Phase 2 ESA** includes sampling of soil and other materials, and is performed if it appears a problem may exist. An **environmental impact statement (EIS)** is required for federally funded projects and may be required by the state or locality.

State laws cover **disclosure of known material facts regarding property condition**, which may include environmental hazards.

UNIT 21 QUIZ

1. Regarding the federal Lead-Based Paint Hazard Reduction Act, which statement is *TRUE*?
   a. All residential housing built before 1978 must be tested for the presence of lead-based paint before being listed for sale or rent.
   b. A disclosure statement must be attached to all sales contracts and leases involving residential properties built before 1978.
   c. A lead-hazard pamphlet must be distributed to all prospective buyers but not to tenants.
   d. Purchasers of housing built before 1978 must be given five days to test the property for the presence of lead-based paint.

2. The term *encapsulation* refers to the
   a. process of sealing a landfill with three to four feet of topsoil.
   b. way in which insulation is applied to pipes and wiring systems.
   c. method of sealing disintegrating asbestos.
   d. way in which lead-based paint particles become airborne.

3. A real estate professional showed a pre-World War I house to a prospective buyer. The buyer has two toddlers and is worried about potential health hazards. Which of the following is *TRUE*?
   a. There is a risk that urea-formaldehyde foam insulation was used in the original construction.
   b. The real estate professional can offer to personally inspect for lead and remove any lead risks.
   c. Because of the age of the house, there is a good likelihood of the presence of lead-based paint.
   d. Removal of lead-based paint and asbestos hazards is covered by standard title insurance policies.

4. Which of the following is *TRUE* regarding asbestos?
   a. Improper removal of asbestos can cause further contamination of a building.
   b. Asbestos causes health problems only when it is eaten.
   c. The level of asbestos in a building is affected by weather conditions.
   d. HUD requires that all asbestos-containing materials be removed from all residential buildings.

5. All of the following may contribute to the growth of mold *EXCEPT*
   a. low humidity.
   b. presence of EIFS.
   c. roof leaks.
   d. improperly installed gutters.

6. Federal underground storage tank (UST) regulations require that
   a. home fuel oil tanks in basements be registered with the EPA.
   b. septic tanks be pumped every five years.
   c. liquid petroleum tanks that store at least 10% of their volume underground be in compliance.
   d. states not develop regulations more stringent than the federal requirements.

7. Which of the following describes the process of creating a landfill site?
   a. Waste is liquefied, treated, and pumped through pipes to tombs under the water table.
   b. Waste and topsoil are layered in a pit, mounded up, and then covered with dirt and plants.
   c. Waste is compacted and sealed in a container, then placed in a tomb designed to last several thousand years.
   d. Waste is buried in an underground concrete vault.

8. With the exception of the innocent landowner, liability under the Superfund is
   a. limited to the owner of record.
   b. joint and several and retroactive, but not strict.
   c. voluntary.
   d. strict, joint and several, and retroactive.

9. Radon poses the greatest potential health risk to people when it is
   a. contained in insulation material used in residential properties during the 1970s.
   b. found in high concentrations in unimproved land.
   c. trapped and concentrated in inadequately ventilated areas.
   d. emitted by malfunctioning or inadequately ventilated appliances.

10. What do urea-formaldehyde foam insulation (UFFI), lead-based paint, and asbestos have in common?
    a. They all pose a risk to humans because they may emit harmful gases.
    b. They all were banned in 1978.
    c. All three were used in insulating materials.
    d. They were all used at one time in residential construction.

11. A method of sealing off disintegrating asbestos is called
    a. *capping*.
    b. *encapsulation*.
    c. *containment*.
    d. *contamination closure*.

12. All of the following are true about lead-based paint *EXCEPT*
    a. it was commonly used in residences before 1978.
    b. renovation by a contractor of a residence that has lead-based paint requires education and certification.
    c. all residential buildings must be tested for lead-based paint.
    d. it is most dangerous when ingested.

13. The *MOST* common source of harmful lead in older residential properties is
    a. asbestos.
    b. basements.
    c. appliances.
    d. alkyd oil-based paint.

14. Urea-formaldehyde is found in residential properties in
    a. lead-based paints.
    b. insulating foam.
    c. home appliances.
    d. USTs.

15. In regulations regarding lead-based paints, HUD requires that
    a. homeowners test for its presence.
    b. paint be removed from surfaces before selling.
    c. known lead-based paint hazards be disclosed.
    d. only homeowners deal with its removal.

16. Radon is
    a. only found in the eastern United States.
    b. easy to detect because of its odor.
    c. a known human carcinogen.
    d. not found in older homes.

17. Contamination from underground storage tanks is
    a. found only in petroleum stations.
    b. addressed by EPA regulations.
    c. only caused by tanks currently in use.
    d. easily detected and eliminated.

18. All of the following are true about underground water contamination *EXCEPT*
    a. it is a minor problem in the United States.
    b. any contamination of underground water can threaten the supply of pure, clean water from private wells and public water systems.
    c. protective state and federal laws concerning water supply have been enacted.
    d. real estate professionals need to be aware of potential contamination sources.

19. CERCLA regulations for administration of the Superfund, which helps pay for cleanup of uncontrolled hazardous waste sites,

a. exempt from responsibility those sites that contaminate neighboring properties.
b. release from liability those owners of contaminated property who did not actually cause known contamination.
c. make no provision for recovering Superfund expenses incurred in cleanup operations.
d. impose strict, joint and several, and retroactive liability on potentially responsible parties.

20. Asbestos dust can cause

a. lung disease.
b. radiation sickness.
c. skin cancer.
d. AIDS.

22 UNIT

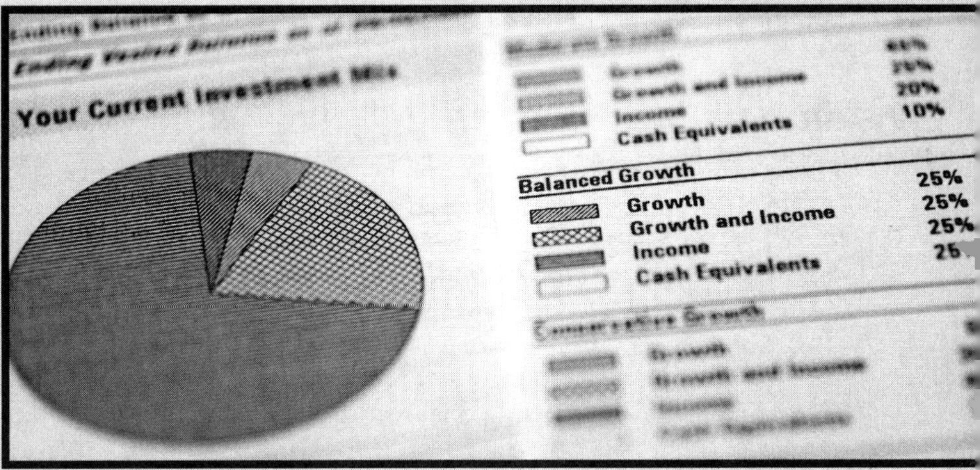

Investing in Real Estate

LEARNING OBJECTIVES *When you have finished reading this unit, you will be able to*

- **identify** the advantages and disadvantages of investing in real estate;
- **describe** the real estate investment objectives and the inherent financial concepts involved in the investment process;
- **explain** the essential benefits of leverage, including pyramiding, in the acquisition of real estate investments;
- **describe** the tax benefits inherent in real property investments;
- **describe** the mechanics of real estate investment syndicates, trusts, and mortgage conduits; and
- **define** the following *key terms*:

accelerated cost recovery system (ACRS)
adjusted basis
appreciation
basis
boot
capital gain
cash flow
cost recovery
depreciation
equity buildup
exchanges
income property
inflation
intrinsic value
leverage
liquidity
pyramiding
real estate investment trust (REIT)
real estate mortgage investment conduit (REMIC)
straight-line depreciation
syndicate

OVERVIEW

Real estate is a popular investment. Whichever way the overall market turns, the real estate investment market continues to initiate innovative and attractive investment strategies. These developments make it important for real estate professionals to have an elementary and up-to-date knowledge of real estate investment. A real estate professional should never act as an investment advisor but should instead refer investors to competent tax accountants, attorneys, or investment specialists.

WHY REAL ESTATE?

Real estate has always been an important part of an investment portfolio, but real estate, as any commodity, has good years and not-so-good years. In recent years, real estate values nationwide have gone through significant changes. The peaks in property valuations that were achieved in most areas at the beginning of this century were followed by the troughs that helped cause, and were exacerbated by, the recession years of 2006–2008. Some parts of the country, particularly on the coasts, proved fairly recession-proof in terms of real estate prices, but others still struggle to recoup the losses that have been sustained. As with any investment, real estate requires careful consideration of both its advantages and its disadvantages. The advantages and disadvantages of real estate as an investment are summarized in Figure 22.1 and discussed next.

FIGURE 22.1: Advantages and Disadvantages of Real Estate Investments

Advantages	Disadvantages
Generally, above-average rates of return	Investment is expensive
Use leverage of borrowed money to purchase real estate	Real estate is not highly liquid
Greater control over investment	Must actively manage investment
Tax benefits	High degree of risk

Advantages of Real Estate Investment

Over longer periods—10 to 20 years or more—real estate investments typically have shown above-average (or even high) *rates of return*. In some parts of the country, an impressive return can be received even after a relatively short period of ownership. In theory, this means that an investor can use borrowed money to finance a real estate purchase and feel relatively sure that the asset, if held long enough, will return more money than the cost to finance the purchase.

Real estate investments also offer more immediate advantages. Real estate offers investors a greater control over their investments than other options, such as stocks, bonds, or other securities. The real estate marketplace consists of buyers and sellers who deal directly with each other.

You have already learned about the tax benefits of home ownership. Real estate investors also receive certain tax benefits, which we will discuss here.

Disadvantages of Real Estate Investment

Real estate investments are expensive. Large amounts of capital are usually required, even when financing is available. Investing in real estate is difficult without expert advice. Investment decisions must be based on careful study of all facts, reinforced by a thorough knowledge of real estate and how it is affected by the marketplace.

Liquidity refers to how quickly an asset may be converted into cash. Unlike stocks and bonds, real estate is not highly liquid over the short term. For example, an investor who holds stocks can easily direct a stockbroker to sell stocks when funds are needed; the stockbroker sells the stock and the investor receives the cash. In contrast, a real estate investor may have to sell property at a substantially lower price than desired to bring about a quick sale. If market values are down, the investor who wants to refinance property to free up cash will have to settle for whatever the lender feels the market dictates.

Real estate requires active management. A real estate investor can rarely just sit and watch the money grow. The investor may choose to personally manage the property or hire a professional property manager, but management decisions still must be made. How much rent should be charged? How should repairs and tenant grievances be handled? What is the long-term goal of the property owner? Is the property manager working to achieve that goal?

IN PRACTICE Those who are new to investing or who are too busy to handle the details of property management should hire a professional property manager. While this will entail an additional expense that the property's income will need to absorb, it should be well worth it. As you have already learned, a property manager can screen and select tenants, handle the day-to-day issues that arise, provide an important conduit and buffer between landlord and tenant, add discipline to the process of allocating funds to maintain and preserve the asset, and increase the property's income potential. All of these will help the property owner achieve the long-term goal of owning the investment.

Finally, despite its popularity, a real estate investment does not guarantee profit. It involves a high degree of risk. The possibility that an investment property will decrease in value or not generate enough income to make it profitable is a sometimes volatile factor that the investor must consider.

THE INVESTMENT

Real estate investors anticipate various investment objectives. Their goals can be reached more effectively depending on the type of property and ownership they choose. The most prevalent form of real estate investment is *direct ownership*. Both individuals and corporations may own real estate directly and manage it as an investment income or cash flow (income). This type of real estate is known as **income property.**

Appreciation

Real estate is an avenue of investment open to those interested in holding property primarily for increasing value, which is known as **appreciation**. Two main factors affect appreciation: inflation and intrinsic value.

Inflation is the increase in the amount of money in circulation. When more money is available, its value declines. When the value of money declines, wholesale and retail prices rise. This is essentially an operation of supply and demand.

The **intrinsic value** of real estate is the result of a person's individual choices and preferences for a given geographic area. For example, property located in a pleasant neighborhood near attractive business and shopping areas has a greater intrinsic value to most people than similar property in a more isolated location. As a rule, the greater the intrinsic value, the more money a property commands on its sale.

Unimproved Land

Often, investors speculate in purchases of either agricultural land or undeveloped land located in what they expect to be a major path of growth. In such a case, however, the property's intrinsic value and potential for appreciation are not easy to determine. This type of investment carries many inherent risks. How fast will the area develop? Will it grow sufficiently for the investor to make a good profit? Will the expected growth occur? More important, will the profits eventually realized from the property be great enough to offset the costs of holding it, such as property taxes? Because these questions often cannot be answered with any degree of certainty, lending institutions may be reluctant to lend money for the purchase of raw land.

As will be discussed later, income tax laws do not allow for the depreciation of land because it is not considered a deteriorating asset, so that tax advantage is lost. Land also might not be liquid (salable) at certain times under certain circumstances because few people will purchase raw or agricultural land on short notice. Despite all the risks, land has historically been a good inflation hedge if it is held for the long term.

Investment in land ultimately is best left to experts, and even they frequently make bad land investment decisions.

Income

A person who wishes to buy and personally manage real estate may find that rental income property is the best investment.

Cash Flow The objective of directing funds into income property is to generate spendable income, called **cash flow**. Cash flow is the total amount of money remaining after all expenditures have been paid. These expenses include taxes, operating costs, and maintenance. The cash flow produced by any given parcel of real estate is determined by at least three factors: amount of rent received, operating expenses, and method of debt repayment.

Generally, the amount of rent (income) that a property may command depends on a number of factors, including the property's location, physical appearance, and amenities. If the cash flow from rents is not enough to cover all expenses, negative cash flow may result. At a time of high property appreciation, a minimal amount of negative cash flow may be acceptable; at other times, it can be disastrous for a cash-strapped property owner.

To keep cash flow high, an investor should attempt to keep operating expenses reasonably low. Such operating expenses include general building maintenance, repairs, utilities, and tenant services. At time same time, it is unwise to reduce operating expenses to the point at which building condition suffers significant deterioration, which is also likely to be reflected in its perceived desirability and treatment by tenants.

An investor often stands to make more money by investing with borrowed money, usually obtained through a mortgage loan or deed of trust loan. Low mortgage payments spread over a long period result in a higher cash flow because they allow the investor to retain more income each month. In turn, high mortgage payments contribute to a lower cash flow.

Investment Opportunities

Income-producing properties include apartment and office buildings, hotels, motels, shopping centers, and industrial properties, as well as single-family residences, including condominiums. When considering the purchase of a single-family residential property, the prospective investor's *due diligence* (exploration of the benefits and drawbacks of the investment) before making a purchase should always include finding out whether or not there are any limitations on property rental.

LEVERAGE

Leverage is the use of borrowed money to finance an investment. As a rule, an investor can receive a maximum return from the initial investment by making a small down payment, paying a low interest rate, and spreading mortgage payments over as long a period as possible.

Leveraging a purchase by financing it provides a return that reflects the result of market forces on the entire original purchase price but one that is measured only against the actual cash invested. For example, if an investor spends $400,000 for a rental property, makes an $80,000 down payment, and then sells the property five years later for $500,000, the return over five years is $100,000. Disregarding ownership expenses, the return is not 25% of the original amount invested ($100,000 compared with $400,000), but 125% of the original amount invested ($100,000 compared with $80,000).

Risk is *directly proportionate to leverage*. A high degree of leverage translates into greater risk for the investor, as well as for the lender, because of the high ratio of borrowed money to the value of the real estate. Lower leverage results in less risk. When property values drop in an area or vacancy rates rise, or both, the highly leveraged investor may be unable to pay even the financing costs of the property.

Equity Buildup

Equity buildup results from the addition to the amount paid as down payment on property of the principal portion of loan payments, plus any increase in property value due to appreciation. In a sense, equity buildup is like money in the investor's bank account. This accumulated equity is not realized as cash unless the property is sold, refinanced, or exchanged. And, of course, equity is lost when a property's market value decreases, even if the property is not sold.

Pyramiding

An effective method for real estate investors to increase their holdings without investing additional capital is through pyramiding. **Pyramiding** is the process of using one property to drive the acquisition of additional properties. Two methods of pyramiding can be used: pyramiding through sale and pyramiding through refinance.

In pyramiding through sale, an investor first acquires a property and then improves it for resale at a substantially higher price. The profit from the sale of the first property is used to purchase additional properties. The disadvantage of this method is that the proceeds from each sale are subject to taxation.

IN PRACTICE An investor bought a small, run-down, vacant commercial building for $125,000. The building was refurbished over the next three months, at a cost of $45,000. The investor then sold the property for $375,000. The investor used the $170,000 he cleared from the sale after remodeling costs and taxes to buy an almost-vacant, run-down, strip shopping center with eight units. He plans to spend $100,000 renovating the units and then sell each as a tenancy in common for at least $75,000.

The goal of pyramiding through refinancing is to use the value of the original property to drive the acquisition of additional properties while retaining all the properties acquired. The investor refinances the original property and uses the proceeds of the refinance to purchase additional properties. These properties are refinanced, enabling the investor to acquire further properties. By holding on to the properties, the investor may delay the capital gains taxes that would result from a sale.

IN PRACTICE An investor bought a single-family rental property for $340,000, making a down payment of $100,000. In 10 years, when the loan balance was $190,000, the investor refinanced the property for $600,000. She used the $410,000 she received after the first loan was paid off to buy three more investment properties. Without adding a single dollar to her original investment capital, she now owns four investment properties.

Note: The forms of pyramiding described here are not related to a *pyramid scheme*, which is an illegal enterprise.

TAX BENEFITS

www.irs.gov

Income tax laws change frequently, and some tax advantages of owning investment real estate are altered periodically by Congress. An investor can make a more educated and profitable real estate purchase with professional tax advice. The Internal Revenue Service (IRS), www.irs.gov, is the best place to start for federal tax information.

Depreciation (Cost Recovery)

Depreciation, or **cost recovery**, allows an investor to recover the cost of an income-producing asset through tax deductions over the asset's useful life. Though investors rarely purchase property without expecting it to appreciate over time, the tax laws recognize that all physical structures deteriorate (and lose value) over time. Cost recovery deductions may be taken only on personal property and improvements to land. Land is not depreciated because it is not considered a deteriorating asset.

www.irs.gov/publications/p527/ch02.html

Depreciation taken periodically in equal amounts over an asset's useful life is called **straight-line depreciation**. For certain property purchased before 1987, it was also possible to use an **accelerated cost recovery system (ACRS)** to claim greater deductions in the early years of ownership, gradually reducing the amount deducted in each year of useful life. The Taxpayer Relief Act of 1997 established specific rules governing holding periods and taxability of depreciation for real property. Currently, statutory depreciation for federal tax purposes is 27.5 years for residential real estate and 39 years for commercial real estate. See www.irs.gov/publications/p527/ch02.html for more information on depreciation.

Capital Gain

Capital gain is defined as the difference between the **adjusted basis** of property and its net selling price. At various times, the tax law has excluded a portion of capital gains from income tax and taxed various types of gains differently.

Basis A property's cost basis determines the amount of gain to be taxed. The **basis** of the property is the investor's initial cost of the real estate. The investor adds to the basis the cost of any physical improvements subsequently made to the property. The amount of any depreciation claimed as a tax deduction is subtracted from the basis. The result is the property's adjusted basis. When the investor sells the property, the amount by which the sales price exceeds the property's adjusted basis is the capital gain.

For example, consider an investor who purchased a single-family home for use as a rental property. The purchase price was $95,000. The investor now sells the property for $300,000. Shortly before the sale date, the investor makes $25,000 worth of capital improvements to the home by adding a garage to the property. Depreciation of $15,000 on the property improvements has been taken during the term of the investor's ownership. The investor will pay a broker's commission of 5% of the sales price. The investor's closing costs will be $1,800. The capital gain is computed as follows:

Selling price		$300,000
Less:		
5% commission	$ 15,000	
Closing costs	+ 1,800	
	$ 16,800	– 16,800
Net sales price		$283,200
Basis:		
Original cost	$ 95,000	
Improvements	+ 25,000	
	$120,000	
Less:		
Depreciation	– 15,000	
Adjusted basis	$ 105,000	– 105,000
Total capital gain		$178,200

Exchanges

Real estate investors can defer taxation of capital gains by making property **exchanges**. To qualify for a tax-deferred exchange, the properties involved must be of *like kind* as defined under Section 1031 of the Internal Revenue Code. One parcel of real estate is considered of like kind to another parcel of real estate, even when they have different uses (a shopping center and an industrial complex), as long as both are held for investment (not owner-occupied) and are not located in a foreign country. Real estate and personal property cannot be exchanged in a tax-deferred transaction because they are not of like kind.

Even property that has appreciated greatly since its initial purchase may be exchanged for other property, as long as both are of like kind. A property owner will incur tax liability on the transaction only if additional capital or property is also received; the additional capital or property, called **boot**, is taxed. The value of the boot is added to the basis of the property for which it is given. The tax that would have been paid on the property transferred is deferred, not eliminated. When the investor finally sells the acquired property, the capital gain will be taxed. In many states, state income taxes can also be deferred by using the exchange form of property transfer. Use of a qualified intermediary (also known as an *accommodator* or a *facilitator*) is considered a safe harbor by the IRS and is essential for a delayed exchange.

Tax-deferred exchanges are governed by strict federal requirements, and competent guidance from a tax professional is essential.

IN PRACTICE A person owns an apartment building with an adjusted basis of $225,000 and a market value of $375,000. That person exchanges the building plus $75,000 in cash for another apartment building having a market value of $450,000. That building has an adjusted basis of $175,000. The owner's basis in the new building is $300,000 (the $225,000 basis of the building exchanged plus the $75,000 cash boot paid), and there is no tax liability on the exchange. The previous owner of the new building must pay tax on the $75,000 boot received and has a basis of $175,000 (the same as the previous building) in the building now owned.

Deductions

www.irs.gov/publications/p925/index.html

In addition to tax deductions for depreciation, investors may be able to deduct losses from their real estate investments. Again, tax laws can be complex and must be strictly followed. The amount of loss that may be deducted depends on whether an investor actively participates in the day-to-day management of the rental property or makes management decisions. Other factors are the amount of the loss and the source of the income from which the loss is to be deducted. Investors who do not actively participate in the management or operation of the real estate are considered passive investors. Passive investors may not use losses to offset active income derived from active participation in real estate management, wages, or income from stocks, bonds, and the like. The tax code cites specific rules for active and passive income and losses and may be subject to changes. See www.irs.gov/publications/p925/index.html.

Certain tax credits are allowed for the renovation of older buildings, low-income housing projects, and historic property. A tax credit is a direct reduction in the tax due rather than a deduction from income before tax is computed. Tax credits encourage the revitalization of older properties and the creation of low-income housing.

Installment Sales

www.irs.gov/taxtopics/tc705.html

A taxpayer who sells real property and receives payment on an installment basis pays tax only on the profit portion of each payment received. Interest received is taxable as ordinary income. See www.irs.gov/taxtopics/tc705.html.

REAL ESTATE INVESTMENT OPTIONS

Various structures exist for real estate investment, including syndicates, trusts, and mortgage conduits.

Real Estate Investment Syndicate

A real estate investment **syndicate** is a business venture in which people pool their resources to own or develop a particular piece of property. This structure permits people with only modest capital to invest in large-scale operations. Typical syndicate projects include highrise apartment buildings and shopping centers. Syndicate members realize some profit from rents collected on the investment, but the main return usually comes when the syndicate sells the property.

Syndicate participation can take many legal forms. For instance, syndicate members may hold property as tenants in common or as joint tenants. Various kinds of partnership, corporate, and trust ownership options are possible.

Private syndication generally involves a small group of closely associated or experienced investors. Public syndication involves a much larger group of investors who may or may not be knowledgeable about real estate as an investment. Any pooling of individuals' funds raises questions of securities registration under federal and state securities laws, known as *blue-sky laws*. Both federal and state laws must be followed.

Real Estate Investment Trust

www.reit.com

By directing their funds into a **real estate investment trust (REIT)**, real estate investors take advantage of the same tax benefits as do mutual fund investors. A real estate investment trust does not have to pay corporate income tax as long as 90% of its income is distributed to its shareholders. Certain other conditions also must be met. To qualify as a REIT, at least 75% of the trust's income must come from real estate. Investors purchase certificates in the trust, which in turn invests in real estate or mortgages (or both). Profits are distributed to investors. The National Association of Real Estate Investment Trusts has an informative site at www.reit.com.

Real Estate Mortgage Investment Conduit

www.freddiemac.com/mbs/html/product/remics.html

A **real estate mortgage investment conduit (REMIC)** has complex qualification, transfer, and liquidation rules. The REMIC must satisfy the asset test, which requires that after a start-up period, almost all assets be qualified mortgages and permitted investments. In addition, investors' interests may consist of only one or more classes of regular interests and a single class of residual interests. Holders of regular interests receive interest or similar payments based on either a fixed rate or a variable rate. Holders of residual interests receive distributions (if any) on a pro rata basis. Find information on REMICs at www.freddiemac.com/mbs/html/product/remics.html.

KEY POINT REVIEW

Investment in real estate offers the **advantages** of

- the **leverage** enabled by the use of borrowed money,
- the possibility of an above-average **rate of return**,
- greater **control** than ownership of securities,
- **tax benefits** in certain situations,
- **income (cash flow)** production, and the
- possibility of property **appreciation** (increase in value over time).

Disadvantages of investment in real estate include its

- high cost to acquire;
- lack of liquidity;
- need for active management or hiring of a professional property manager; and
- a high degree of risk, although an investor's ability to hold into property long term tends to reduce risk.

The **cash flow** of income property, the amount remaining after all ownership expenses have been paid, tends to make it the safest form of real estate investment. **Rent** paid by tenants is a major source of property income and depends on the property's location, physical appearance, and available amenities, but when rent does not cover property expenses, **negative cash flow** results.

Pyramiding is a method of using the ownership of one property to drive the acquisition of additional properties. In **pyramiding through selling**, the investor acquires a property, improves it for resale at a substantially higher price, and then uses the profit from the sale to purchase another property. In **pyramiding through refinancing**, the investor uses the refinance proceeds of one property to purchase new properties.

The **tax benefits** of owning investment real estate depend on current tax law. **Capital gain** is the difference between the adjusted cost basis of a property and its net selling price, and it may be taxed at a more favorable rate than a taxpayer's earned income. **Adjusted cost basis** is the investor's acquisition cost, plus the cost of any physical improvements made to the property and less the amount of any **depreciation** claimed as a tax deduction.

Depreciation (cost recovery) allows an investor to recover the cost of an income-producing asset through tax deductions over the asset's useful life. **Losses** from the sale of a real estate investment may be deductible. **Tax credits** (direct reductions of tax owed) are available for the renovation of older buildings, low-income housing projects, and historic properties.

Exchanges offer investors the opportunity to **defer** the payment of taxes on profit indefinitely. Property may be **exchanged** for other **like-kind** property. The property owner is taxed only on additional capital or property received as part of the exchange (**boot**). Tax is **deferred** (not eliminated), with the capital gain taxed on the eventual sale.

A **real estate investment syndicate** is a business venture in which participants pool resources to own or develop property. Pooling of funds may involve **securities registration** under federal and state securities laws.

A **real estate investment trust (REIT)** does not pay corporate income tax as long as 90% of its income is distributed to its shareholders and other conditions are met. Restrictions and regulations on the formation and operation of REITs are complex.

A **real estate mortgage investment conduit (REMIC)** has qualification, transfer, and liquidation rules; it is notable because of the **asset test** requirement.

UNIT 22 QUIZ

1. A small multifamily property generates $50,000 in rental income, $10,000 in expenses, and $25,000 in debt service. The property appreciates about $25,000 each year. What is the cash flow on this property?
   a. $15,000
   b. $25,000
   c. $35,000
   d. $40,000

2. Cash flow is
   a. equivalent to operating expense.
   b. the total amount of spendable income left after expenses.
   c. the use of borrowed money to finance an investment.
   d. selling costs plus depreciation.

3. The primary source of tax shelters in real estate investments comes from which accounting concept?
   a. Recapture
   b. Boot
   c. Net operating income
   d. Depreciation

4. A man made an initial real estate investment of $245,000. He subsequently made $80,000 worth of improvements to the property. If the man subtracts depreciation from the initial cost and adds the cost of improvements, what will be the result?
   a. Adjusted basis
   b. Capital gain
   c. Basis
   d. Salvage value

5. All of the following are associated with a Section 1031 exchange *EXCEPT*
   a. boot.
   b. qualified intermediary.
   c. like kind.
   d. the elimination of capital gains tax.

6. A woman refinanced her house and used the proceeds to purchase two rental properties. This method of increasing her holdings is called
   a. exchanging.
   b. pyramiding.
   c. syndicating.
   d. depreciating.

7. Which statement is *TRUE* about a syndicate?
   a. Members must hold title as joint tenants.
   b. Most profit on the investment is realized from rents.
   c. It is a private or public business venture to own property.
   d. Blue-sky laws do not apply.

8. A real estate mortgage investment conduit (REMIC) has complex rules regarding
   a. qualification.
   b. transfer.
   c. liquidation.
   d. all of these.

9. A seller is selling an investment property. The original cost of the property was $80,000. The selling price is $225,000. The seller paid an 8% commission and $2,000 in closing costs. Two years ago, the seller made $10,000 worth of improvements to the property. Depreciation is $15,000. What is the seller's adjusted basis in the property?
   a. $65,000
   b. $75,000
   c. $80,000
   d. $90,000

10. A seller is selling an investment property. The original cost of the property was $800,000. The selling price is $1,250,000. The seller paid an 8% commission and $10,000 in closing costs. Two years ago, the seller made $100,000 worth of improvements to the property. Depreciation is $150,000. What is the seller's total capital gain?
   a. $390,000
   b. $450,000
   c. $800,000
   d. $900,000

11. Advantages of an investment in real estate include all of the following *EXCEPT*
   a. the possibility of a tax-deferred exchange.
   b. high liquidity.
   c. the use of leverage to increase rates of return.
   d. tax deductions.

12. The investor who sells property on an installment sale basis
   a. is taxed on all of the gain in the year the property is sold.
   b. is taxed on that part of the gain received in each year's installment payments.
   c. gives the buyer all the federal income tax liability.
   d. gives the buyer the privilege of deferring all the federal income tax liability.

13. One method a real estate investor may use to defer capital gains tax is to
   a. sell property for cash only.
   b. obtain the maximum amount of leverage.
   c. exchange property for like-kind property.
   d. build a reserve account for items that are likely to wear out.

14. As part of a Section 1031 exchange, an investor had to give the other party $111,500 and a 1957 Chevrolet. The cash and car are
   a. equity.
   b. boot.
   c. collateral.
   d. like kind.

15. Which situation would result in the highest degree of leverage?
   a. Using your own funds entirely
   b. Using more of your own funds than those you borrow
   c. Using more of the funds you borrow than your own funds
   d. Using borrowed funds entirely

16. Someone looking for a tax-advantaged investment similar to a mutual fund would probably invest in a
   a. real estate investment trust.
   b. general partnership.
   c. limited partnership.
   d. corporation.

17. When considering an investment in real estate, the prospective investor should consider all of the following *EXCEPT*
   a. anticipated appreciation of the property.
   b. possible effects of inflation on the property.
   c. assessed valuation of the property.
   d. intrinsic value of the property.

18. *Cash flow* is a term that refers to the
   a. amount of money flowing into and out of a property.
   b. bookkeeping function that accounts for the cash each day.
   c. taxes, operating expenses, and loan payments on the property.
   d. total amount of income left after all expenses have been paid.

19. Purchasing a property using leverage, refinancing it after it has appreciated, and using the cash from the refinancing to purchase additional property is one form of
   a. plottage.
   b. pyramiding.
   c. consolidation.
   d. contribution.

20. The type of real estate investment that is required by federal law to distribute 90% of its income to its shareholders is the
   a. general partnership.
   b. limited partnership.
   c. real estate investment trust.
   d. time-share estate.

GEORGIA REAL ESTATE PRACTICE

Unit 23 Ownership

LEARNING OBJECTIVES

When you have finished reading this unit, you will be able to

- **identify** the elements of real and personal property and what distinguishes one from the other;
- **recognize** the three primary components of zoning ordinances and the standards used for establishing these laws;
- **explain** the laws and legal requirements affecting title evidence and transfer; and
- **describe** the forms of ownership and how they may be held.

KEY TERMS

administrator's deed
adverse possession
assessment factor/rate
assessed value
bulk restrictions
certificate of permanent location
color of title
concurrent ownership (Georgia)
condition precedent and subsequent estates
condominium associations
condominium declaration
condominium ownership
corporate resolution
fee simple estate
forfeiture for crime statute
Georgia Condominium Act
Georgia Joint Tenancy Act
Georgia Land Sales Act
Georgia's little NEPA laws
Georgia's mechanic's lien law
Georgia Time-Share Act
Georgia Zoning Procedures Law
grantor/grantee index
headrights
impact fees
limited liability company (LLC)
limited warranty deed
millage rate
mills
metes and bounds
performance bond
police powers
power of attorney
prescriptive easement
public offering statement
regulated riparian state
sheriff's deed
short-form legal description
sole proprietorship
warranty deed
year's support

INTRODUCTION

Many general principles of real property ownership, which were discussed in previous units, also apply in Georgia. Statutes and codes in Georgia, though, impact certain common law principles to more clearly define real estate ownership in this state. By examining topics covering real property (legal descriptions, title rights and restrictions), land use and development, title evidence/transfer, and forms of ownership, this unit allows students and future licensees to look at real estate ownership from a Georgia perspective.

An excellent source for information on specific Georgia real estate practices and laws may be found at the online "Georgia Real Estate InfoBase," which is available through the Georgia Real Estate Commission's website.

DEFINITIONS

Strictly speaking, the terms *real estate* and *real property* differ somewhat in meaning. Real estate refers to a physical commodity consisting of land (its surface, the air above it, the ground below it) plus any permanent attachments to the land. More inclusively, real property's definition adds ownership rights to those land interests defined as real estate. In practice, though, the two terms are often used interchangeably. Consider the following from the Official Code of Georgia Annotated (§ OCGA 44-1-2):

a. the term "realty" or "real estate" means:
   1. All lands and the buildings thereon;
   2. All things permanently attached to land or to the buildings thereon; and
   3. Any interest existing in, issuing out of, or dependent upon land or the buildings thereon
b. The property right of the owner of real estate extends downward indefinitely and upward indefinitely.

Note this definition under the Code is technically describing real property, yet inserts the terms *real estate* and *realty* instead. Licensees practicing in Georgia should understand that the use of these terms rarely distinguishes the technical differences between them.

On the other hand, when describing personal property, the Georgia Code (§ OCGA 44-1-3a) is straightforward in its definition: "personal property defines all property which is movable in nature, and has inherent value not otherwise defined as Realty."

Personal Property

Simply put, personal property is anything that is mobile and not intended to be permanently affixed to land. Understanding this distinction becomes a practical concern for real estate licensees completing sales contracts in Georgia. Items considered real property—buildings, trees, landscaping, plumbing fixtures, permanently installed kitchen appliances such as stovetops and dishwashers—are all included in the sale and transferred by deed. On the other hand, items of personal property—furniture, potted plants, countertop microwave ovens, et cetera—are not a part of the deed transfer. If these and similar items are to be part of the sale, they should be itemized on a separate bill of sale document.

Georgia courts vary in their rulings as to the legal status of items such as chandeliers, drapery rods, and window treatments. Though real estate licensees in the state are free to rely on case law or even community custom, the best way to address any ambiguities regarding these issues is to specify the status of those items in the sales contract.

Manufactured Housing

One particular Georgia statute illustrates how real property and personal property definitions may even overlap. Manufactured housing, most commonly exemplified in Georgia as mobile homes, are inherently identified as personal property. But this statute also establishes conditions under which manufactured homes become real property. Specifically, if a mobile home in Georgia was sold on or after July 1, 2006, and the owner has not yet been issued a certificate of title from the commissioner of motor vehicles, the home can be classified as real property under the following conditions (§ OCGA 8-2-183-1):

- Owner of the mobile home also has ownership interest in the land on which the home is affixed
- Owner and all holders of security interests in the home file a **certificate of permanent location** in the county records where the property is located
- Manufactured homeowner must surrender any current certificate of title

Once the certificate of permanent location has been filed, for all legal purposes, the home becomes part of the real property on which it is located and is so noted in the property's legal description recorded in the county records.

LEGAL DESCRIPTIONS

An adequate legal description in Georgia is one that will be good enough to identify the property from any other property or clear enough that anyone could go on the land and point out the boundary lines. Every legal description in the state must always indicate that the property is located in Georgia and name the county where it can be found. Then, depending on the location in the state, the legal description will include districts, land lots, and headright areas or Georgia militia districts.

Some of the earliest property descriptions in Georgia use the **headrights** approach to describe property along the coastal areas of the state. These descriptions were in place before current state survey systems; the headrights system typically describes irregular-shaped property heavily dependent on natural boundaries such as rivers, streams, and trees. Moreover, some of the oldest headright districts in Georgia use antiquated line designations known as Georgia militia districts (GMDs) formed for common defense purposes, unrelated to county or contemporary survey lines.

These line designations would commonly be referenced by a **metes-and-bounds** property description, which has since become the legal controlling method of describing real property in Georgia, regardless of how irregular the land parcel may be shaped. With its linear measurements, boundary references, and compass directions, the metes-and-bounds description forms a near-perfect geometrically enclosed outline of the parcel that always ends at the point of beginning.

Georgia also recognizes a second form of real property description known by any one of the following names:

- lot-and-block system,
- recorded plat, and
- the **short-form legal description**.

In the 1800s, surveys divided much of Georgia into its present descriptions of districts and land lots with grid lines dividing areas into rectangles and squares. Land lots then divide the districts into smaller sections. This method of land description evolved into the creation of subdivision plats that are recorded in the county where the land is located to create the short-form legal description.

EXAMPLE Lot 71 Indian Valley Estates 2 located in land lot 217 of the 4th district of Fulton County, Georgia.

In addition to describing the land division, plat maps in Georgia should also include a surveyor's seal and info, state registration number, and date of survey.

The principal source of a property's legal description might be a homeowner's **warranty deed** or a security deed if the property has been secured by a loan. If a homeowner does not have a copy of the legal description, and assuming the property deed has been recorded into the public records of the county where the property is located, the legal description can be found in the real estate records at the clerk's office of superior court in the county where the property is located. The first step would be to check the **grantor/grantee index** book where the property owner's last name will be listed alphabetically in the grantee section. The line after the property owner's name in the index will reveal the deed book and page number where the warranty deed and legal description may be found. If there is no recorded deed of the property, a legal description might be found using the property's plat map.

IN PRACTICE To ensure the accuracy of a property's legal description, a prudent buyer of real property might want to make the contract for sale conditional on a new survey in case discrepancies exist between the existing survey and the updated one. In Georgia practice, the most recent survey from a certified professional supersedes any previous survey.

Additionally, there might be circumstances where an existing survey might not be acceptable. For example, owners might be selling only a part of their property, they might be reserving a personal easement right on the property as part of the sale, or they might have previously sold a portion of the property but have not yet updated the property's current legal description. In each of these situations, an updated survey to create a more precise legal description would be necessary.

TITLE RIGHTS AND RESTRICTIONS

The general bundle of rights afforded by real property ownership (possession, control, enjoyment, disposition) offers absolute title unqualified by any restrictions other than those imposed by government entities or covenants. Absolute ownership of real property in Georgia expands these common law principles to include the following rights:

- To sell

- To lease
- To devise by will
- To mortgage
- To encumber
- To build and destroy within the bounds of law
- To dedicate or give away

While common law often controls these rights, Georgia codes have impact as well. Real property rights in Georgia involving water usage illustrate this statutory influence.

Water Rights

Property owners are entitled to the natural flow of water across or adjacent to their land and are entitled to reasonable use of that water for domestic, agricultural, or manufacturing purposes. A landowner whose property adjoins nonnavigable waterways, such as rivers or streams, would own the land beneath the flowing water. If the water's dividing line borders two separate properties, each of the landowner's boundaries would extend to the center of the main current. For land adjacent to public access waterways affected by ocean tides and navigable for barge traffic, landowners have no ownership of the waterbeds beneath.

Though Georgia laws do not presume to interfere with private property water rights, the state under its **police powers** to protect the public interest does regulate private and public use of water. Landowners are prohibited from diverting water from its normal course, diminishing its natural flow, or interfering with the enjoyment of other adjacent landowners. Moreover, the Georgia Environmental Protection Division (EPD) regulates surface and groundwater for reasonable use. The withdrawal of more than 100,000 gallons of water per day from surface or groundwater requires permits from the EPD. Further regulations also address conflicts between competing water users and water shortage. These limitations of water rights in the state classify Georgia as a **regulated riparian** state.

In some instances, disputes over water rights may extend to conflicts between states. Since 1990, Georgia has engaged in an on-again, off-again water war with Alabama and Florida. In an effort to bolster its drinking water sources, Georgia has sought permits from the U.S. Army Corps of Engineers to create reservoirs on rivers that flowed through the three states. Alabama and Florida have responded with lawsuits claiming the reservoirs would be a threat to their own water supplies. Florida claimed that these reservoirs, if granted, would deplete the flow of water into bay areas that sustain the state's oyster industry. Alabama cited existing pollutants in water flows from Georgia, claiming any depletion of water flow would increase contamination.

As in most states, common law and government restrictions limit absolute ownership in Georgia. Three areas are addressed in some detail by Georgia statutes and court rulings:

- easements,
- mechanics' liens, and
- property taxes.

Easements in Georgia

As discussed in Unit 4, an easement gives the holder the right to use property of another for a specific purpose. Georgia establishes four ways of creating easements:

1. **Express grant.** Established by deed, contract, or other written agreement. Generally an expressed easement will set forth the location, dimensions, and permissible or intended use of the easement.
2. **Prescriptive easements**. Under Georgia law, a claimant must prove four elements before a court will ratify this type of permanent use of property by a non-title holder.
   - Use of improved land for an uninterrupted period of 7 or more years. For wild lands, the statutory period is 20 years.
   - The width of the easement is less than 20 feet.
   - The width of the easement has not deviated from its original width.
   - The easement has been kept open and in repair for seven uninterrupted years.
3. **Expressed reservation.** In many states, when a grantor conveys a parcel of land that is landlocked, public policy dictates that an easement for ingress and egress be implied—a principle predicated on the theory that a means of accessing a property falls under an owner's reasonable use and enjoyment rights. However, Georgia does not recognize an implied reservation of an easement. A landowner who fails to expressly reserve an easement for ingress and egress to his remaining land will not be rewarded for this negligence.
4. **Compulsory Purchase and Sale.** In instances where owners of adjoining land have boundary line or other easement disputes, Georgia courts may order the compulsory purchase and sale of the land over which the easement is claimed. A jury will typically determine the amount of compensation paid to the landowner by the claimant.

Easement disputes in Georgia often arise over the misuse of an easement or the location or dimensions of an easement, or both. Moreover, an easement dispute may revolve around the grantor's interference with the easement holder's use of the easement. Another common easement dispute in the state involves boundary lines and encroaching improvements. As for maintaining the easement parcel, documents creating an express easement should specify which party has the responsibility. Otherwise, Georgia courts normally assign that obligation to the dominant tenant, the party with the right of use.

Mechanics' Liens in Georgia

Generally speaking, someone who performs work on another person's property deserves payment for improving that property. **Georgia's mechanics' lien law** protects that party regarding compensation for work performed on the property. However, any claimant must follow precisely this lien's requirements because Georgia courts harshly punish missteps in the filing process by invalidating the lien as a result of any errors.

Mechanics' liens in Georgia attach to the property and take effect at the time when the first labor or materials are furnished—even before any document has been filed at the county courthouse.

There are generally two areas of dispute regarding this type of lien in Georgia.

The first area involves a service provider. Someone has provided services on or for a property, was not paid, and wants to file a lien on the property. Service providers might typically include contractors, subcontractors, and material providers, but the list might also include architects, engineers, and land surveyors.

The second area involves homeowners in some form of dispute over work quality or payment dispute for services provided to their property. The homeowners subsequently learn that a mechanic's lien has attached to their property and want the lien removed because it clouds the title to the property. Until it is removed, selling or refinancing the property would be extremely difficult.

The claimant (a service provider) must file the mechanic's lien at the clerk's office of the superior court in the Georgia county where the property is located within 90 days after completing the work or supplying materials for the work. No later than two days after filing the lien, the claimant must send a copy by registered or certified mail to the owner or the contractor acting as agent of the owner. Within 365 days of lien filing, unless receiving voluntary payment from the property owner or contractor agent, the claimant must perfect the lien by a lawsuit or some form of binding arbitration.

The homeowner or contractor agent may shorten this 365-day legal action period by filing a notice to contest the lien demanding that the claimant begin legal action within 60 days after the notice to contest has been filed. If the lien claimant does not comply with the notice to contest by starting legal action within 60 days, then the courts would extinguish the lien rights 90 days after the notice to contest was filed.

Another step that a homeowner or contractor may take to shorten the lien process would be to file a notice of commencement no later than 15 days after work on property has started. Once this notice is sent and posted on the property, any subcontractors or material providers are required to file a preliminary lien notice within 30 days. If this notice is not filed, the lien right would be waived.

IN PRACTICE The above-mentioned notices would not apply for any labor or services in which providers have contracted directly with property owners. In addition, to eliminate the threat of mechanics' liens, property owners or their contractor agent might obtain **performance bonds** for the work on the property. These bonds would ensure that everyone gets paid as long as workers make their claims within an allotted time period, usually 60 to 90 days after work completed.

REAL PROPERTY TAXES IN GEORGIA

Real property taxes in Georgia are based on the value of the property (ad valorem) and are paid in the calendar year (January 1 to December 31) for which they are levied. By state law, a property tax lien attaches to the property on January 1 of each year, the valuation date for the property, even though the due date for the taxes varies from county to county. The lien will be released when the homeowner pays the property taxes for that calendar year. On December 31 of each year, the tax commissioner issues a legal execution against all delinquent property tax payers, and these liens assume the highest legal priority against any other recorded claims against the property.

Real property owners whose property is their legal residence since January 1 of the calendar year may receive a state homestead property tax exemption of $2,000 if they file an application by the date property tax returns are due in the county—typically April 1. Some counties in Georgia have increased the amounts of exemptions for homesteads and up to 10 additional acres surrounding the home.

Georgia offers additional exemptions for citizens who are 65 years and older and whose annual retirement income does not exceed $10,000. Georgia residents who are age 62 and older may also receive school property tax exemptions if their adjusted gross income is less than $30,000.

Disabled veterans in Georgia, as well as their surviving, unremarried spouses, also receive substantial homestead exemptions. In 2006, Georgia passed special property tax exemptions covering full property value for the unremarried surviving spouse of a peace officer or firefighter killed in the line of duty, as long as the surviving spouse occupies the homestead.

Real property taxes in Georgia, though always a politically charged topic, is perhaps one the most misunderstood areas of public financing. In reality, the numbers used to determine these taxes are simply a function of basic math. The process begins when the taxing authority in the counties or municipalities decides how much revenue the district needs to provide necessary services for its government—known as setting the budget for the upcoming year. Next, the authority estimates how much money will be generated by ongoing sources of revenue, such as license fees, fines and penalties, traffic citations, et cetera. After these sums of money are deducted from the estimate of revenues needed for the yearly budget, whatever dollar amount remaining is the sum that must be collected from property taxes.

After arriving at this first key figure, the tax assessor then begins calculating a second, equally important number: the assessed value of all taxable property within the governing district. To arrive at this number, the fair market value of all real property in the district is estimated, and from that figure, the value of all tax-exempted property is subtracted to arrive at a value of all tax eligible properties.

Tax exempted properties include certain nonprofit corporations, places of religious worship, government buildings, historical buildings, and libraries.

Then, to most effectively assure that property owners in Georgia pay no more or no less to fully fund the budget, Georgia establishes an **assessment factor** of 40% throughout the state and this is levied on fair market values to arrive at the taxable **assessed value** of real property. Tax assessors multiply the 40% factor times the estimated fair market value of property in the district to arrive at an assessed value for all property in the district.

Finally, to determine the property tax or **millage rate** for the district, the money for the budget needed from property tax collection is divided by the assessed value of all property in the taxing jurisdiction.

FIGURE 23.1: Municipal Tax Calculation

The municipality of Golden Lake, Georgia
Budget revenues needed for upcoming year—$9,000,000
Anticipated revenues from ongoing collections—$4,000,000
Revenues needed from ad valorem taxes—$5,000,000

Estimated fair market value of all real property in Golden Lake $250,000,000
Real property exempted from ad valorem taxed—$25,000,000
Fair market value of all taxable real property—$225,000,000
Georgia standard equalization/assessment rate—40%
Assessed value of all taxable property—$90,000,000

Property tax rate/millage rate for Golden Lake
Tax revenue needed—$5,000,000
Divided by assessed value of taxable property—$90,000,000
Equals 0.0555

To calculate each individual parcel of real property's fair share of the cost of government, first multiply the home's fair market value by the Georgia equalization factor of 40% to find the property's assessed or taxable value. Next, subtract any eligible tax exemptions to arrive at the adjusted assessed value. Finally multiply that number by the tax rate to arrive at the dollar amount for the yearly property taxes.

FIGURE 23.2: Homestead Tax Calculation

Millicent's homestead in Golden Lake Georgia
Fair market value—$315,000
Equalization/assessment rate—40%
Assessed value—$126,000
State homestead exemption—$2,000
Local homestead exemption—$4,000
Adjusted assessed value—$120,000
Golden Lake tax/millage rate—0.0555
Millicent's ad valorem property tax—$6,660

Mills

Property tax rates in Georgia may also be expressed in **mills**. One mill is equal to one-tenth of a penny, or 0.001. Mills can be converted into a tax or millage rate by multiplying the number of mills by 0.001. As an example, consider a homeowner whose property taxes are levied by the county at a rate of 10 mills, by the city at a rate of 20 mills, and by the local school board at a rate 13.75 mills. So the property is taxed at a total of 43.75 mills. To convert this number of mills to a millage/tax rate, multiply 43.75 by 0.001 to calculate a millage rate of 0.04375 for each $1 of the property's assessed value.

Though property taxes in Georgia are assessed at the county level by a board of tax assessors, the state revenue inspector is responsible for the tax digest of each county to determine whether real property is assessed uniformly and equally between and within the counties. Property owners who do not agree with their assessments can file appeals with their county's board of equalization.

MATH CONCEPTS According to the county tax assessor, a property's fair market value is $287,500. The standard assessment rate in Georgia is 40%. If the millage rate is 3%, how much are the yearly ad valorem taxes?

1. Multiply the market value by the assessment rate to determine the assessed value of the property: $287,500 × 0.40 = $115,000
2. Multiply the assessed value of the property by the tax rate to calculate annual tax:

$115,000 assessed value
× 0.03 tax rate
$3,450 annual taxes

Assessed value	Annual taxes
Market value × assessment rate	Assessed value × tax rate

In some problems, the tax or millage rate is not stated as a percentage of the entire assessed value. Instead, it might be expressed as a dollar amount per $100 or per $1,000 of assessed value.

EXAMPLE 1 A property with an assessed value of $180,250 is taxed at a rate of $2.40 per hundred dollars of assessed value. How much are the annual taxes?

1. Divide $180,250 by 100 to determine how many $100 increments there are in the assessed value: $180,250 ÷ $100 = $1,802.50, or $1,803.
2. Multiply the number of $100 increments by the millage rate to calculate the annual taxes:

1,803 $100 increments
× $2.40 tax rate
$4,327.20 annual taxes

In other problems, the tax rate is expressed as a number of mills per $1 of assessed value. A mill = 0.001.

EXAMPLE 2 A property's market value is $350,000 and the assessment rate is 40%. The tax rate is 31 mills per $1 of assessed value. How much are the annual taxes?

1. Multiply the market value by the assessment rate to find the assessed value:

   $350,000 × 0.40 = $140,000

2. To determine the millage/tax rate for 31 mills, multiply this number by 0.001:

   31 × 0.001 = 0.031

3. Multiply the assessed value by the tax rate to determine the annual tax:

   $140,000 × 0.031 = $4,340

Also note that a millage rate may also be converted back to mills by dividing the rate by 0.001. Example: Millage rate of 0.056 ÷ 0.001 = 56 mills.

ZONING

Local governments in Georgia, enabled by the police power clause in the state's constitution, regulate private property land use through zoning laws. Generally, city and county zoning ordinances contain three distinct components:

- Land use
- Height restrictions
- Area or **bulk restrictions**.

Georgia zoning ordinances, within the community's jurisdiction, classify all parcels of land into four general categories of land use:

- Industrial
- Commercial
- Residential
- Agricultural

Though such land uses are often exclusionary, allowing only the specified use, Georgia sometimes recognizes special uses for property that fall outside of existing zoning regulations. A property owner in a residentially zoned area may be allowed to operate a business that serves the needs of that community. For such utility, zoning boards will issue a conditional use permit.

A second area addressed through zoning law is building height restrictions. Ordinances here would categorize height specifications of structures by land use, as well as by geographical location. For example, maximum heights for buildings in multifamily zoning categories may be different for those structures in detached, single-family communities. Moreover, height limitations on structures near municipal airports would be more restrictive than limitations in central business districts.

Bulk restrictions focus on the spatial issues between buildings and the land area on which the structure sits. Here common local ordinances might include

- size of buildings in relationship to lot size;
- setback lines defining space between the building and lot boundary lines; and
- requirements that structures be built near the front or back of parcel and whether parking should be in front or behind the building.

Even though the state enables local authorities to enact land use regulations, the Georgia legislature reserves the right to prescribe procedures by which local zoning boards evaluate rezoning issues and petitions for zoning variances and conditional uses.

Basically, the state requires local zoning authorities to adopt at least the following six standards in exercising their authority:

- Suitable use: the property fits in with adjacent and nearby properties
- No adverse impact on the existing land uses of neighboring properties
- Reasonable economic land use as currently zoned
- Whether a zoning proposal will result in excessive or burdensome use of existing streets, transportation facilities, utilities, or schools
- Whether a zoning proposal is consistent with the overall land use plan of community
- Any other condition affecting use and development of property that might support approval or denial of a proposal

Local governments might also include additional requirements to their evaluation process. An example might be ordinances that focus effects on forestry or tree preservation or the environmental impact of a proposal.

The Zoning Procedures Law in Georgia ensures that local governments give the general public a voice when making zoning decisions. This due process involves a public hearing before any zoning or conditional use decisions are made. Notice must be placed in local general circulation newspaper 15 to 45 days before a hearing. Additionally, signage advertising proposed zoning must be posted on the property no less than 15 days before the hearing. A written policy and procedures of the local government exercise of zoning powers must also be made available to the public.

Individuals in Georgia wishing to acquire a zoning variance must show why the variance is necessary for the preservation and enjoyment of property rights and does not merely serve as a convenience to the applicant. For example, local property setback guidelines might prevent a landowner from any reasonable construction on his oddly shaped lot, and without a variance to address this issue, his property might be virtually worthless. Moreover, an applicant must show how the variance, if granted, will be in harmony with the general intent of the local government's comprehensive land plan. Though most decisions on variances require public hearings, a few may be granted administratively under certain technical guidelines.

Examples might include a commercial property owner seeking a reduction of required parking spaces in order to preserve natural greenery or a landowner seeking a modification of land use to improve water runoff on the property.

Building Codes

Georgia has also adopted specialized building code classifications to set standards for construction methods and materials. Among these are construction codes for residential buildings, as well as codes for energy, fire, gas, and plumbing. Additional local ordinances might cover codes for swimming pools and spas, property maintenance, and green-building construction.

Local construction codes might further establish minimal acceptable standards that builders must follow, such as the adequacy and positioning of studs and floor joists, load-bearing walls, and roofing requirements, as well as electrical wiring outlets and switches.

Generally speaking, Georgia real estate licensees are not expected to know the requirements of state or local building codes in detail. However, a licensee may suggest to clients that a home inspector or contractor be hired to inspect a property if it is older, or if there are any concerns about its construction. A property that does not conform to building codes might delay or derail a buyer's obtaining a loan to finance the purchase of the property.

SUBDIVISION DEVELOPMENT

State land use regulations and construction codes in Georgia not only place limitations and restrictions on homeowners, but also regulate property developers. Community developments where individual lots are less than 5 acres may be subject to the **Georgia Land Sales Act**, which requires developers to provide written comprehensive property reports and disclosures to purchasers before written sales contracts are signed. If purchasers do not receive these documents within 48 hours of signing agreements, they have a seven-day right of cancellation from that time.

Even if property developments do not fall under the guidelines of this state law, police power statutes under the Georgia Constitution allow local governing bodies or planning commissions to review and approve building plans for residential developments within their jurisdiction. These subdivision regulations require developers to follow locally acceptable standards for street systems, building lot specifications, and block size. These standards could include

- street layout and design,
- frequency of intersections,
- street width,
- maximum slopes, and
- grades.

Other regulations might stem from health and safety concerns. For example, fire departments might require a minimum radius for *cul de sacs* to allow maneuvering of large trucks and equipment. Health departments might enforce standards for septic systems when public sewer is unavailable. Subdivision regulations might also discourage creating lots and blocks that have inefficient, irregular shapes.

Subdivision developers in Georgia must file with local governing authorities documents that geographically represent the subdivision's size and shape. This plat map includes the street systems, blocks, and building lots—all represented in scale. If approved, this subdivision map becomes part of the public record. Future buyers might then review these plats to verify shape and dimension of the parcels, as well as noting any restrictions on lot size, setbacks, and height requirements imposed on the subdivision as a condition for approval. Typically, property developers in Georgia will also file a declaration of covenants that will impose private limitations and restrictions on the community's homeowners.

As a further use of **police powers**, local governments in Georgia often impose **impact fees** on property developments to pay for future improvements and services necessitated by new developments. As these developments create demand for additional schools, sewer lines, power grids and recreational facilities, impact fees are a one-time charge to the property developers to defray some of the costs local governments incur in providing these benefits in the future. Impact fees in Georgia help ensure that new developments pay for their public requirements and services, rather than having taxpayers in the jurisdiction assume the financial burden.

Impact fees by local governments in Georgia are subject to the explicit requirements of the Georgia Development Impact Fee Act, which sets minimum standards for the establishment of these fees.

Private real property developments in Georgia requiring state or local approval that may significantly impact the environment would fall under **Georgia's "little NEPA" laws**. These are the state's equivalent to the federal National Environmental Policy Act (NEPA), which requires government to prepare environmental impact statements (EIS) for all appropriate projects.

CONDOMINIUM AND TIME SHARE DEVELOPMENTS

Statutes in Georgia covering real property developments are perhaps categorically most specific in the creation of condominiums and time-shares.

The **Georgia Condominium Act** of 1975 created a set of rules that govern the formation and operation of these type of properties. Condominiums created before 1975 are controlled by the Georgia Apartments Act. However, condo owners can bring a pre-1975 complex under jurisdiction of the Condominium Act by submitting the condominium documents in accordance with the provisions set for in the Act.

Under the Condominium Act, developers must record three documents in the public land records of the county where the project is located.

1. **Condominium declaration**—containing the legal boundaries of the units (in words); list of the legal common elements and the unit assignment for each; percentage of common element ownership for each unit; private encumbrances—lien rights, covenants (use restrictions, architectural control provisions and enforcement rights)
2. Floor plans—showing the interior of the condominium project, specifically the legal boundaries of the units (in drawings)
3. Plats—showing the exterior of the condominium project

Because virtually all condominiums in Georgia are subject to covenants, conditions, and restrictions, a developer would also be required to record these documents in the public record.

Because condominium homeowner associations in Georgia are created as nonprofit corporations, the Georgia Nonprofit Corporation Code would typically apply to these associations. This Code would requires that Articles of incorporation for the homeowners association be filed with the Georgia secretary of state and that bylaws be adopted to operate the incorporated association.

Timeshare estates in Georgia, whether offered as fee simple ownership or as leasehold right of use interest, fall under the regulation of the **Georgia Time-Share Act**. This law addresses the statewide promotion and sale of all time-share property located in or outside of Georgia.

Similar to condominium requirements, developers must file documents creating time-share programs in the superior court of the counties where time-share properties are to be located.

Before transferring time-share estates in Georgia, no later than the date of a sales agreement, time-share developers must issue purchasers a **public offering statement**, which is a written document containing all essential project information covering details on the management and operation of the program, including the buyer's right to cancel the contract within seven days without penalty.

IN PRACTICE The Georgia Time-Share Act also ensures that all advertising and promotional contests comply with the Fair Business Practices Act as administered in the state by the Office of Consumer Affairs.

As with the Georgia Condominium Act, the Georgia Real Estate Commission has no regulatory powers over time-shares. Enforcement of the law comes through private civil action and would be prosecuted by the state attorney general.

The Georgia Real Estate Commission does, however, require that only licensed real estate brokers and their sales affiliates may sell time-shares in the state.

TITLE TRANSFER BY DEED

As is the case throughout the United States, title to real property in Georgia establishes legal rights of ownership of the land and attachments, the minerals below the land, the airspace above the land, and the waters flowing on or through the land. Possession of a deed provides physical evidence of these rights for the property owner.

To ensure enforceability of their title against any subsequent claims, property owners in Georgia record their deeds in the public record of the county courthouse where their properties are located. Recording of the deed requires two witnesses: one official (a notary) and one unofficial.

Paying a deed transfer tax is another requirement for recording the deed in Georgia. Once owners record their deeds, their last names appear alphabetically under the grantee's index found in public records kept in the clerk of superior court's office. Under the most recent owner's name, the plat book number and the page number point to where the property's deed can be found.

In Georgia, the title is normally conveyed by a warranty deed that promises to new property owners (the grantees) that the title has been legally conveyed to them by the grantors, free from known adverse claims and unrecorded liens and easements. The grantors also promise to defend the title against any future outside claims. If the promise is to forever defend the title, to even the time before the grantors' ownership, then the grantees receive a warranty deed. If the grantors warrant only to defend the title against claims that arose during their ownership, the grantees will receive a **limited warranty deed** in Georgia.

IN PRACTICE When grantors in Georgia transfer title to grantees, they are promising good and marketable title that is legally sufficient and free from reasonable doubt or defects—in other words, a title that prudent buyers would accept as a basis for paying fair market value for a property.

Though a warranty deed in Georgia makes a promise of marketable title conveyance from grantor to grantee, these promises do not guarantee good title. Legally, it only means the grantor will be liable if the title is not good. We might infer that the promises a grantor makes in the warranty deed are only as good as the grantor's future financial capabilities. What if the grantor goes bankrupt or simply disappears? Any warranties of title become worthless—or at best uncertain of enforcement.

Consequently, even though on face value warranty deeds in Georgia provide legal recourse against the seller-grantor, a prudent buyer-grantee would require assurances of a satisfactory title. Because most real estate loans are secured by the purchased property, lenders would never approve loans without some guarantee or proof of good title.

The Title Search

Any such declaration typically begins with a formal title search. The examiner first compiles a history of the property ownership. As recommended by the State Bar of Georgia Title Standard, this history would cover a 50-year period, with the grantor/grantee index in the public records providing the necessary information.

Once the title examiner compiles this history or chain of title, the search continues with an examination of records that might identify easements, security or mechanics' liens, or any other documents that might affect the title. The examiner also searches county records for lawsuits, divorces, judgments, federal tax liens, past-due ad valorem taxes, pending litigations, and probate proceedings. When the search is complete, the examiner prepares a title report or abstract. A report finding the title free of serious defects or sufficiently marketable provides the grounds for an insurance company to issue a title policy, which provides evidence of good title for the grantee.

IN PRACTICE In Georgia, the responsibility and cost of the examination process needed for assurances of satisfactory title rests on the shoulders of the grantees. Though the grantees may initiate title searches themselves, typically they pay for a professional examiner.

The Warranty Deed

The warranty deed is the most common method of voluntary title transfer in Georgia. The deed must be in writing, signed by the maker of the deed, the grantor, and delivered to the grantee. Regarding married couples in Georgia, if the title is vested exclusively in one spouse, the other spouse need not sign the deed. Though when one spouse transfers title to the other, closing attorneys in Georgia may require both spouses to sign the deed in order to avoid any issues arising out of a title being vested in one spouse and only possession for the other spouse.

If a deed in Georgia is signed through a **power of attorney**, that legal document must be in writing and executed with the same formality required for a deed—that is, under seal and signed before two witnesses, one official and one unofficial.

TITLE TRANSFER BY WILLS

Georgia law also significantly impacts wills, another form of voluntary title transfer.

Contrary to most legal documents of conveyance in the state where the required legal age is 18, a testator (maker of will) need only be 14.

To transfer real property in Georgia, wills must be formalized in writing and witnessed by two legally competent parties. Georgia does not recognize handwritten or holographic wills to convey real property.

Oral wills (nuncupative) may be recognized in Georgia for real property transfer under the following strict guidelines: A testator in time of final illness may recite a last will and testament in front of two legally competent witnesses with no interest in the estate; these witnesses must then must formalize the declaration in writing within 30 days of hearing the testament.

The Probate Process

The probate process in Georgia to administer a decedent's estate begins with the court confirming the will's executor as named by the testator or appointing an administrator if the will has not named one. Within 60 days of appointment, the executor must publish probate proceedings in a local newspaper handling official notices. Any creditors then have three months after publication ends to make claims against the estate, though most creditors will just send any payment invoices directly to the estate. The executor makes an official inventory of the estate, settles claims against the estate, and then distributes any real property remaining according to the terms of the will by an executor's deed, which does not contain any warranty promises.

Because Georgia does not recognize community property laws or the legal life estates of dower and courtesy—all of which in certain states offer statutory real property rights to married couples even where one spouse is not an actual party to the deed—a decedent's estate for the most part would be transferred according to the terms of the will.

However, wills in Georgia may not supersede the **year's support statute**. This law addresses circumstances in which a surviving spouse claims the will does not provide sufficient inheritance for the family. The year's support statute allows the spouse to petition the court to set aside enough property or the value thereof from the estate to sustain an "accustomed standard of living" for 12 months. Effectively, the probate court's execution of the year's support petition constitutes an involuntary transfer of the decedent's real property assets.

Intestate Succession

Another instance where probate courts in Georgia might initiate a type of involuntary transfer occurs when a decedent with a real property estate did not have a will. An administrator, often a surviving spouse or another heir, is appointed by the court to dispose of the estate's property. If there are no outside claims against the estate and the heirs agree on how property will be distributed, the court, upon petition by the administrator, might allow the probate process to be skipped. Generally, the probate process unfolds following the state laws of intestate succession (descent and distribution). Typical distribution of property by the administrator might be the following:

- Surviving spouse and one child: equal split between the two
- Surviving spouse and one or more children: one-third to spouse; two-thirds to children
- Surviving spouse and no children: all to spouse
- No surviving spouse but are children: all divided among children
- No surviving spouse and no children: all to parents; from here distribution goes down the hereditary ladder, so to speak

All property from the estate would be transferred by **administrative deed** with no warranties.

TITLE TRANSFER BY FORECLOSURE

As in most states, unpaid title liens in Georgia may result in judgments against the property owner, initiating a court-ordered sale of the real property. Homestead protection statutes affecting unsecured creditors reserve for the property owner at least $5,000 from this type of sale. Furthermore, in court-ordered sales, Georgia bankruptcy laws allow homestead exemptions of $21,500 for a single homeowner and up to $43,000 for married couples.

Title transfers through foreclosures occur most frequently in Georgia through defaults associated with home loans and property taxes. A Georgia lender's security deed will outline the foreclosure process for loan default, but it is the property tax lien in the state, commanding the highest enforcement priority, that is most directly impacted by statutory codes.

Once the county tax commissioner executes legal action against a delinquent property owner on the last day of each calendar year, the legal process unfolds swiftly. Within 10 days and by certified mail, the owner receives notice of the pending foreclosure action. The county sheriff will advertise notice of the sale in the local legal newspaper for four consecutive weeks before the sale. Property tax auctions are generally held at noon on the first Tuesday of each month on the courthouse steps in the county where the property is located. The sales cover delinquent tax amounts, all penalties and fees, and any associated expenses—with the final price determined by competitive bidding. The successful bidder will receive a tax deed from the sheriff but has no immediate physical control over the property.

The delinquent taxpayer or any party with title rights or lien interests, may redeem the property anytime within 12 months from the date of the sale by paying the redemption price—the amount paid for the tax deed plus 20% of that amount for the first year or some fraction of that percentage if the redemption occurs in the first year between the tax sale and the 12-month redemption period. Moreover, at the end of this redemption period, the tax deed purchaser may begin to forever bar or foreclose any redemption right by serving proper notice on the delinquent owner and any other rights holders. Otherwise, the tax deed purchaser would be entitled to an extra 10% for each subsequent year or fraction until redemption might occur. Additionally, Georgia law requires a minimum time of one year plus 45 days to lapse between acquisition of the tax deed and actual physical control of the property.

NOTE The redemption period and process noted above applies only to a foreclosure due to a default on the payment of taxes, a foreclosure for tax sale. Georgia uses a non-judicial procedure process for the default on a property loan, in which the "power of sale" procedure gives a lender the right to advertise the property and then hold an auction to sell the property. Once the property has been foreclosed, there is no right of redemption for the borrower in default.

TITLE TRANSFER BY ADVERSE POSSESSION

Georgia codes on **adverse possession** further exemplify a type of involuntary title transfer in the state. Common law principles of adverse possession essentially allow those who continually trespass or take possession of an otherwise owner-neglected piece of real property to claim title if the true owner fails to acknowledge or take action against the trespasser.

Georgia law requires a 20-year statute of limitations period for any legal claim of general adverse possession. After this time, the true owner cannot legally remove the land squatter. Effectively, though involuntarily, the true owner has given up title to the property because the landowner's nonaction to remove a trespasser is akin to surrendering the property.

Specific requirements for the adverse possessor in Georgia are as follows:

1. Be in actual possession of property while physically using land as any owner would—such as maintaining, repairing, and improving property.
2. Possession is open and notorious—easily known by any others who look. Sneaking around or concealing use would disqualify any claims.
3. Hostile—without true owner's permission.
4. Continuous and uninterrupted—as opposed to claiming it but not sticking around for duration of a 20-year period.
5. Exclusive use—true owner does not use property during the statute of limitations period.

Adverse possession laws in Georgia may also apply when a presumed land owner's written evidence of title turns out to be flawed in some way that invalidates the deed.

For example, William White conveyed property to Fiona Evans by warranty deed. However, Evans subsequently discovered that when White originally received the title to the property, the grantor lacked legal capacity. As a result White's deed was invalidated by this flaw and the deed he transferred later to Evans was in turn also invalid. In effect Evans is an adverse possessor and holds what the law describes as **color of title**. In this circumstance, Georgia law would allow Evans to perfect her title (make it legal) after a prescriptive seven-year period of continuous possession and uninterrupted use of her home.

Finally, Georgia's RICO law (Racketeer Influenced and Corrupt Organizations Act) adds a rather lively postscript for involuntary real property transfer in the state. This statute's **forfeiture for crime** component allows the state to seize property used in or acquired as a consequence of criminally influenced activities.

LEGAL FORMS OF OWNERSHIP

Subject to limits imposed by the U.S. Constitution, the Georgia Constitution or state legislature, any person, natural or artificial (such as corporations or government entities), can own land in Georgia. Included on the list are the following:

- United States government
- Georgia state government
- Political subdivisions of the state (cities, counties, agencies such as the Georgia Port Authority)
- Individuals—citizens of Georgia and other states
- Aliens whose governments are at peace with the United States
- Corporations, including those in Georgia, other states, and foreign countries
- Trusts, LLCs, and limited partnerships
- Infants and mental incompetents—those these ownerships must be through legal guardianship.

Estates

Though the term *estate* generally refers to the ownership interest (freehold) held in land, it may sometimes refer to a rental interest (leasehold). Georgia considers an estate as an interest in real property that is possessory or may become possessory. An absolute freehold, or fee simple or **fee simple estate**, entitles the owner to the entire property with unconditional powers of disposition. (§ 44-6-20).

Freedom to dispose of the property in any way during the life of the owner and to decide who will inherit the land on the owner's death are the defining characteristics of an estate held in fee simple. This is the most commonly held ownership interest in Georgia.

A less common type of title held in Georgia is an estate that requires some kind of specific performance before ownership will be granted or vested. The conditions of ownership may be "precedent" requiring some kind of action performed by the grantee before the estate will vest or "subsequent," where performing or not performing a specific noted in the deed transfer may cause the forfeiture of an estate.

IN PRACTICE A woman is granted an estate for the family beach house conditioned upon her finishing law school. This would be a **condition precedent**, because she will not be granted ownership to the house until she finishes law school. On the other hand, if the young woman is first granted an estate to the beach house, but that estate will become vested (permanent) only if she finishes school, then her continued ownership is subject to this **condition subsequent**. If she does not complete law school, she loses the beach house.

If there are questions about whether a condition is precedent or subsequent, Georgia courts generally favor the finding of a condition subsequent. Furthermore, if the grantee fails to meet the terms of the subsequent condition, Georgia courts will typically cure the situation through payment of damages by grantee rather than rule for property forfeiture. This judicial preference of favoring conditions subsequent has evolved in Georgia because courts favor establishment of land ownership and are reluctant to disrupt that ownership when remedies other than loss of land are available.

Concurrent Ownership

Of course, any ownership of real property in Georgia may be held by one individual (in severalty). When it comes to co-ownership, though, the state law is more select in its recognition. Certain states legally establish forms of co-ownership for married couples, even though only one spouse actually holds title. Such is not the case in Georgia, where title is held only by whomever the deed identifies. If persons hold title together, married or not, they do so either as tenants in common or as joint tenants, the only two acceptable forms of **concurrent ownership** in the state.

Traditionally, Georgia laws have not favored joint tenancy. It was only as recently as 1976, with the passage of the **Joint Tenancy Act,** that the general assembly legislated that a true joint tenancy with the right of survivorship could even exist in the state. This statute requires that the words "joint tenancy" be used when creating this type of concurrent ownership and if these exact words are not used, the ownership will be as tenants in common. Moreover, all joint tenants must be natural persons, not artificial persons, such as corporations or LLCs.

Condominium Ownership

Not only does the Georgia Condominium Act create statutory guidelines for this type of property development, the codes under this statute also create special rights for homebuyers in these developments. Before signing sales contracts, the purchaser must receive specific documentation that includes

- the condominium declaration and amendments,
- a floor plan of the unit purchased,
- a description of all common elements, and
- the limited common elements of individual units.

If a condominium is part of a property conversion, these documents must also describe the condition of components and systems and the expected useful life of such components and systems. Additionally, a copy of the condominium association's articles of incorporation, bylaws, covenants, and an estimated annual budget of the association must be included. It is important for all the homeowners to understand that condo associations in Georgia exercise collective powers and responsibilities of all the owners by ensuring that bylaws, covenants, and restrictions are followed.

The sales contract signed by the purchaser would be voidable up to seven days after all the above-mentioned items have been delivered to the purchaser.

The Georgia Condominium Act was amended in 2008 to clarify rules regarding insurance requirements and liabilities. **Condominium associations** are required to obtain a casualty insurance policy to cover all structural elements and common elements within the condominium community, plus certain fixtures, and other portions of units.

IN PRACTICE Because condo owners pay regularly into an association fund which purchases an annual hazard insurance policy for the entire complex, unit owners are not required to purchase this type of policy separately for their own homes, as they would for individual standalone properties. Condominium homeowners have maintenance responsibilities for their own units, while repairs and maintenance responsibilities of the common areas belong to the association.

Ownership by a Business or Company

A business or company may own property in Georgia as a corporation, a **limited liability company (LLC)**, a partnership, or as a **sole proprietor**. Georgia law provides for real property ownership for each of these types of businesses.

When a corporation owns real property in Georgia, legal matters regarding the property, including title transfer on behalf of the company, must be exercised by the signatures of the duly authorized officers of the corporation. These individuals will be identified in the **corporate resolution** document, which also will issue corporate approval of any property transaction. In some circumstances, depending on which corporate officers have executed the document, the deed must bear the corporate seal.

The Georgia secretary of state's website is a reliable resource for confirming whether a corporate entity is in good standing and also for confirming whether the individuals executing the deed are indeed officers of the corporation. As for listing agreements, and purchase and sale contracts, with the corporate resolution attached to the contracts, only one duly authorized officer need sign if the corporate seal is affixed. Lacking the seal, two authorized signatures are necessary. A corporation lacking a readily available resolution may request that a closing attorney prepare the document for the officer(s) to execute. Because formalities of corporate authority can be complex, a closing attorney may require more than the minimum legal necessities.

Limited liability companies, a growing form of business organization in Georgia, are easier to set up and manage than corporations, yet they offer similar benefits and protections. Typically, the managing member of the LLC would have the authority to execute real property contracts. As for business entities organized as partnerships in Georgia, one general partner's signature may bind all the partners to the real property transaction.

In a sole proprietorship, the least complex method of owning a business in Georgia, one person owns the entire business and reports all profits and losses directly on a personal income tax return.

UNIT 23 QUIZ

1. Which of the following *BEST* describes how a manufactured home becomes real property in Georgia?
   a. The owner of a mobile home is granted a certificate of title.
   b. An owner of the manufactured home has permanently attached his home to a parcel of land leased for more than 10 years.
   c. Mobile home owner places manufactured home on a parcel of land she owns.
   d. Owner of mobile home files for a certificate of permanent location and permanently affixed home to land he owns.

2. A vacant lot sells in a new community in Georgia in which land parcels do not have recorded property deeds. Information to complete a short-form legal description *MOST* likely will be found from what source?
   a. Seller's warranty deed
   b. A property survey
   c. A security deed
   d. The recorded subdivision plat

3. A legal description in Georgia would *MOST* commonly be found in a
   a. security deed.
   b. search of the public records in the county where the property is located.
   c. survey.
   d. seller's warranty deed.

4. When real property is conveyed in Georgia, which of the following legal descriptions would take priority over all others?
   a. Recorded plat
   b. Street address
   c. Metes and bounds
   d. Government survey

5. The condominium declaration filed by property developers in Georgia must include which of the following?
   a. The amount of the monthly condo association fee
   b. The rental policy of the condo association
   c. The name of the building or complex using the word "condominium"
   d. The architectural style of the condominium

6. To ensure that adequate funds will be available for public facilities to serve new community development, local governing authorities in Georgia might impose which type of revenue?
   a. An ad valorem tax on existing homes surrounding new developments
   b. An improvement tax on any new home built in local jurisdiction
   c. An additional local sales tax for residents who live in the in the surrounding area
   d. An impact fee charged to developers as part of approval for their new subdivisions

7. A buyer signs a contract to acquire a real property interest in Georgia. Before signing this agreement, the buyer is given a public offering statement. This document provides the buyer with complete property information, as well as a seven-day right to cancel after receiving this info. This type of property would most likely be a
   a. townhome.
   b. residential condominium.
   c. time-share.
   d. commercial condominium.

8. A woman in Georgia buys a home in a subdivision zoned residential. She wants to open a day care center for the community on her property. To do so, she would need a
   a. variance.
   b. nonconforming use permit.
   c. zoning change.
   d. conditional use permit.

9. In a court-ordered sale of a decedent's real property estate in Georgia to satisfy creditors, which form of homestead protection would probably offer the highest benefit?
   a. Georgia bankruptcy law exemption
   b. Descent and distribution
   c. Year's support statute
   d. Homestead protection covering unsecured creditors

10. When deeds are transferred through the power-of-attorney law in Georgia, that legal document
   a. may only apply to title transfers involving residential property.
   b. will only apply to a married couple if one spouse is signing for the other.
   c. must be signed and sealed before two official witnesses.
   d. must be executed with the same formal requirements applied to the deed.

11. Which of the following statements is *TRUE* regarding tax deeds purchased through property auctions in Georgia?
   a. The purchaser may take control of the property upon receiving the tax deed.
   b. The purchasers will receive a warranty deed from the sheriff.
   c. The delinquent owner may redeem the property anytime within a 12-month period following the sale.
   d. The property tax sale may take place within 10 days from the date the delinquent owner receives notice of foreclosure action.

12. For a deed to be recorded in Georgia, it must be
   a. signed by the grantor and the grantee.
   b. delivered to the grantor by the grantee.
   c. signed by the grantor in front of an official and unofficial witness.
   d. signed by the actual grantor.

13. A court-appointed administrator for a probated estate in Georgia distributes the proceeds from the sale of real property in the following manner: one-third to the surviving spouse and two-thirds to the surviving children. The administrator would probably be following what statutory policy in the state?
   a. Year's support
   b. Probate court's interpretation of will
   c. Intestate succession
   d. Absolute controlling power of the will

14. Georgia recognizes which of the following forms of concurrent ownership?
   a. Joint tenancy only
   b. Joint tenancy and cooperatives
   c. Community property and joint tenancy
   d. Joint tenancy and tenancy in common

15. Corporations owning real property in Georgia may
   a. take title as tenants in common or joint tenants.
   b. designate any corporate shareholder to transact an agreement.
   c. buy and sell property as a sole proprietorship.
   d. only execute deeds and contracts through officers authorized by the corporate resolution.

16. In Georgia, which of the following forms of ownership must be created by written intent and identified precisely in words?
   a. Joint tenancy
   b. Fee simple
   c. Community property
   d. Tenancy in common

17. A company in Georgia operates a business of buying, selling, and exchanging real property. The profits and losses of the business are reported on a personal income tax return. This company would be organized as what form of ownership?
   a. Partnership
   b. Business trust
   c. Sole proprietorship
   d. Corporation

18. What is *TRUE* about zoning variances in Georgia?
    a. They may only be issued after a public hearing by the zoning board.
    b. Zoning commissions typically grant variances administratively rather than after public hearings.
    c. Property owners must show how acquiring the variance is necessary to the enjoyment of their bundle of rights granted as owners of real property.
    d. Variances generally are more difficult to acquire than conditional use permits.

19. Two corporations in Georgia purchase an apartment building together. Title to this real property would be held as
    a. an estate in severalty.
    b. an estate in tenancy in common.
    c. an estate in joint tenancy.
    d. as a corporate partnership estate.

20. A metes-and-bounds legal description
    a. may not be acceptable in some Georgia counties.
    b. may also be known as a short-form legal description.
    c. must always use natural monuments.
    d. must always begin and end at the same identifiable point.

UNIT 24 Brokerage Relationships in Real Estate Transactions Act (BRRETA)

LEARNING OBJECTIVES

When you have finished reading this unit, you will be able to

- **explain** the basis, intent, and scope of BRRETA;
- **identify** the duties, obligations, and disclosures BRRETA imposes on brokerage relationships; and
- **describe** the types of brokerage relationships regulated under BRRETA.

KEY TERMS

agency
brokerage
brokerage engagement
brokerage relationship
BRRETA
client
common source information company
"cooperation and compensation"
customer
designated agent
dual agent
Edina Realty
Georgia Stigmatized Property Act
imputed knowledge
informed consent
ministerial acts
ordinary skill and care
passive concealment
single agency
subagent
"timely"
transactional broker

INTRODUCTION

Enacted in 1994 and amended in 2000, the Brokerage Relationships in Real Estate Transactions Act (BRRETA) applies to any real estate broker or affiliated licensee providing brokerage services to consumers in Georgia. In identifying roles and obligations of real estate agents serving the public, BRRETA defines these relationships by statute rather than through the traditional common law rules of agency. This unit will review the turbulent conditions surrounding the real estate industry from which BRRETA emerged; examine how the duties and disclosures imposed by the law helped clarify agency roles in brokerage relationships, as well as limit broker liability; and finally look at how these duties and obligations for agents apply to specific types of brokerage relationships.

THE LAW

§ 10-6A-1[1]

The law is called the Brokerage Relationship in Real Estate Transaction Act.

IN PRACTICE The statute is commonly called BRRETA.

§ 10-6A-2

(a) The Georgia General Assembly determines that the common law of agency applied to real estate relationships between brokers and real property consumers (sellers, buyers, landlords, tenants) does not serve the best interests of the public. Moreover, because the real estate brokerage industry significantly impacts the state's economy, the Legislature concludes that in order to prevent "detrimental misunderstandings and misinterpretations" between real estate brokers and consumers of their services, Georgia codes must address these issues to provide stability to the real estate markets. These codes regulate the relationships between sellers, landlords, buyers, tenants, and brokers (including their affiliated licensees) to the extent that these relationships are not controlled by written agreements between and among the parties.

THE HISTORICAL CONTEXT

Throughout the decade before BRRETA's enactment in 1994, real estate agency law throughout the United States was in disarray. The actions of real estate licensees, uncertain and often confused over agency responsibilities and duties, resulted in increasing broker liability, misunderstandings, and expensive lawsuits.

The substance of this turmoil revolved around real estate multiple listing services (MLS), which traditionally required any brokerage company whose licensees showed buyer prospects property marketed in the MLS to always act as **subagents** representing sellers and their listing brokers.

Subagency actually developed before there were multiple listing services. When brokers first started to allow other brokers to show their listings, as well as share in the seller-paid commissions, they wanted to make sure that the other brokers

[1] The laws cited in this unit have been modified from the original wording of the statutes cited. The statutes are from the Official Code of Georgia Annotated (O.C.G.A.) (2015).

would also be agent advocates for the seller. So the MLS organizations simply ratified what had become the norm in real estate transactions.

Though this MLS blanket requirement of subagency clearly placed all real estate licensees' loyalty with the seller, reality often told a different story. Working together easily resulted in natural bonds between buyers and real estate licensees, creating an environment where buyers provided confidential information to the licensees, and the licensees provided advice to the buyers. Judicial rulings began finding that brokers and their licensee affiliates could inadvertently create agency relationships with buyers by simply advising them during negotiations or offering services that might lead buyers to believe they were being represented as buyers by licensees who were actually acting as agents or subagents of the sellers.

A Federal Trade Commission (FTC) study in the 1980s found that 71% of buyers thought that subagents were actually representing them; 73% of these buyers told the licensee subagents what they would be willing to offer as a final price on homes. Furthermore, the study revealed that sellers believed that real estate licensees working with buyers were agents of the buyer.

Subagency was in fact becoming undisclosed dual agency.

The evolving climate of litigation for broker liability led to a national change in policy regarding broker cooperation through the MLS. The requirement of cooperation through subagency was eliminated in 1993 and replaced by the words "**cooperation and compensation**," in which a broker from another company who finds a buyer would be paid regardless of whom they represented. At first, many brokers were reluctant to share compensation with other brokers who did not represent their seller-clients. These listing brokers argued that subagency was the only fair policy for cooperating brokers expecting to be paid by sellers. Moreover, the belief was that if licensees working with buyers chose not to be subagents, then their compensation should come from their buyers. Gradually, though, as buyers began to demand their own representation and courts increasingly found that sellers may have vicarious liability for the words and actions of subagents whom they rarely met, resistance to the new MLS reality diminished.

The multiple listing services were not alone in their evolution. The Georgia General Assembly concluded that traditional common-law agency no longer adequately served relationships between real estate licensees and the public in the state. As a response, the Legislature passed the Brokerage Relationships in Real Estate Transactions Act in 1994, which defined and regulated real estate relationships in Georgia between licensees and the general public. The law essentially provided guidance for brokers and their sales affiliates in two ways:

- By classifying and clarifying brokers' duties and obligations to all parties in a real estate transaction
- By requiring licensees to disclose to clients and customers whose interests they are protecting—in other words, which party in the transaction the licensee actually represents

Though statutory codes like BRRETA were certainly a positive step forward in defining working relationships between real estate agents and the public, these laws inadvertently added to another area of increasing litigation: heightened buyer awareness that buyers were lacking exclusive, independent representation in real estate transactions. A task force set up by the Georgia Real Estate Commission in 1999 found that after BRRETA became law, listing agents who formally worked with buyers as customers were now seeking to become buyers' agents, often creating what BRRETA defined as dual agency. Furthermore, this committee determined that BRRETA lacked guidance on how agents might avoid conflicts between the duty to disclose information and the duty to maintain confidentiality. The task force identified three problem areas:

1. Brokers struggling with office policies for dual agency
2. Numerous consumer complaints to the Real Estate Commission over unsatisfactory agency representation
3. Attorney reports regarding growing number of civil suits over dual agency

In response to these issues, the task force recommended specific changes and additions to BRRETA that not only would more precisely identify disclosures and duties for real estate agents but also would serve to limit the liability for brokers and their affiliate licensees. These recommendations became part of a Georgia senate bill in 2000, which amended BRRETA in five fundamental areas:

1. Established that client relationships between brokers and buyers, sellers, landlords, and tenants may only be formed through written contracts
2. Established the practice of designated agency as being separate from dual agency
3. Established the practice of transactional brokerage and identified duties for licensees acting in this capacity
4. Clarified the duties of real estate agents to disclose adverse offsite neighborhood conditions
5. Clarified the duty of real estate agents to keep information confidential

SCOPE OF THE LAW

§ 10-6A-2b

The General Assembly declares that the codes of this law "are not intended" to establish or regulate contracts between brokers and their affiliated licensees.

§ 10-6A-15

Absent a written agreement between the parties, a broker's membership in a common source information organization such as a multiple listing service may not create an agency agreement between the broker and the company. Furthermore, membership in these common source information companies does not make the broker a subagent of any client or another broker who is a member of that same organization.

§ 10-6A-16

BRRETA's codes do not change or limit the Georgia Real Estate Commission's authority under the license law statutes or the Commission's rules and regulations that regulate the practices of brokers and their licensee affiliates.

IN PRACTICE These codes highlight that BRRETA has always been limited to defining private circumstances in which specific services were provided by brokers to create both client and customer relationships. Moreover those duties and disclosures BRRETA identifies govern these relationships only to the extent that they are not contractually established between brokers and the public seeking these brokerage services. Furthermore, the authority of BRRETA was never intended to supersede or even alter the Georgia Real Estate Commission's powers under the Real Estate License Law to regulate practices of brokers and their licensee affiliates. As for multiple listing services, these organizations were set up as a kind of middleman through which brokers could market their listings to other brokers who were members of the same MLS. In this capacity, no agency connection between brokers and these services was ever intended.

§ 10-6A-2

> BRRETA may serve as a basis for private rights of legal actions and defenses by sellers, buyer, tenants, landlords, and real estate brokers.

As this code suggests, BRRETA is also intended as a resource document for judicial disputes involving real estate agency. As such, it is important to understand that the legal realities of the law are found in the wording of the statute, with no implications or assumptions of broader interpretations or authority. Some in the legal community argued that the 1994 legislation establishing BRRETA lowered the bar with regard to false information claims against real estate brokers. They have argued that the statute only requires a showing that a broker misrepresented a material fact for a client to maintain a claim of liability against a broker. This legal interpretation rested on the claim that on this matter, BRRETA had in fact changed traditional common law principles, which held that misrepresentation claims against real estate agents must be supported by elements of fraud. However in the 2000 revision of BRRETA, the General Assembly clarified that the statute was never intended to supersede common law requirements in this area and that the elements of fraud, including the need for claimants to show they exercised due diligence, must still be proven.

§ 10-6A-5b2; § 10-6A-6b2; § 10-6A7b; § 10-6A8b

> Real estate licensees who provide false information to any parties with whom the agents are working—or who fail to disclose known adverse material facts regarding the physical condition of the property or adverse physical conditions of the neighborhood up to 1 mile from the property—are in violation of BRRETA. However, these violations "shall not create liability on the part of the broker absent a finding of fraud on the part of the broker."

IN PRACTICE Even after these clarifying codes became part of BRRETA in 2000, the law continued to be incorrectly interpreted in actions of litigation. Consider the following example:

Buyers noticed water stains on the carpet of the house they were interested in buying. When the buyers asked about the stains, the real estate listing agent allegedly told them the stains were from overwatering houseplants. After closing on the home, the buyers discovered serious water and structural damage and sued the listing agent for fraudulent misrepresentation. A judicial ruling on the case noted that the buyers were aware of the water stains and should have independently inspected the carpet to determine what caused them. As the court saw it, the buyers' blind reliance on the alleged misrepresentation of the listing broker was not justified and barred them from any claim of fraud.

§ 10-6A-11

> Compensation paid or promises of such payments to brokers by sellers, landlords, buyers, or tenants do not determine whether a brokerage relationship has been created between any broker and these parties.

Aside from this code, which simply states that brokers do not have to represent whoever pays their commission, and Section 10-6A-10(3), in which brokers have a duty to disclose to clients the source of their compensation and whether this compensation may be shared with other brokers, BRRETA offers no guidance in legal disputes over commissions. Any assumptions that commissions are only earned when a written brokerage engagement or cooperating brokerage relationship exists is simply not supported by the language of the law. BRRETA is very clear that payment of a commission to a licensee does not determine or establish an agency relationship. Brokers participating in a real estate transaction may be compensated by any party in the transaction.

IN PRACTICE A Georgia real estate brokerage firm filed a lawsuit citing a failure to be compensated for substantial services the firm provided in helping a company acquire land for property development. Though lacking a written agreement, the broker claimed there was an expressed understanding that the firm would work to procure the transaction for the client and would be paid a 7% commission for these efforts. In its efforts to dismiss the lawsuit, the development company cited BRRETA, claiming the lack of a written agency contract with the broker barred any claim for compensation. In its ruling in favor of the broker, the court cited that nowhere in BRRETA was there any mention of when or under what circumstances real estate brokers might claim compensation; BRRETA's silence on this matter demonstrated that the law did not intend to regulate real estate commissions. Essentially, the court deferred to the common law of "procuring cause," where absent a written agreement for compensation, a broker may recover payment for services through an implied contract (*Killearn Partners, Inc. v. Southeast Properties, Inc., 279 Ga. 144,611 S.E.2nd 26 (2005)*).

THE LANGUAGE OF BRRETA

The following terms, many of which are found in real estate common law, generally assume more precise definitions when used in BRRETA.

§ 10-6A-3

> (1) **Agency**: all relationships in which a real estate broker acts for or represents another as a client by written authority in a real property transaction

Common law agency relationships created ostensibly and by implication through words and actions are not recognized under BRRETA.

> (2) **Broker**: any person or entity issued a broker's real estate license by the Georgia Real Estate Commission pursuant to license law statutes. The term "broker" may also refer to the broker's licensee affiliates, except where the context might otherwise indicate.

Because agency duties and disclosures required under BRRETA are identified primarily as broker obligations, the definition here clarifies that a broker's affiliate licensees assume the same responsibilities to clients and customers.

(3) **Brokerage**: the occupation or business of a real estate broker

(4) **Brokerage engagement**: a written agency contract in which a buyer, seller, tenant, or landlord becomes a client of the broker and promises either to compensate the broker or to allow the broker to be compensated by another party in consideration that the broker produces a seller, buyer, tenant, or landlord who is ready, willing, and able to sell, buy, or rent the property, or to perform other brokerage services. The contract is often called a "brokerage engagement agreement."

The brokerage engagement definition has been altered in the 2000 BRRETA revision. Under the original 1994 statute, a brokerage engagement could be created by an expressed oral or written agreement. The amended requirement that brokerage engagements be in writing minimizes the likelihood of disputes between the parties. This definition also introduces the principle that brokerage engagements do not require the broker's compensation to come from the client.

(5) **Brokerage relationship**: describes both client and customer relationships with the broker.

(6) **Client**: individual represented by a real estate broker pursuant to a brokerage engagement

(7) **Common source information company**: any person or company that compiles, supplies, or resources information regarding real estate for sale or lease, or other data including, but not limited to, multiple listing services

(8) **Customer**: person not represented by a real estate broker through a brokerage engagement and for whom a broker may only provide ministerial services in a real estate transaction. A brokerage relationship with a customer may be established by verbal or written agreement.

Though brokerage relationships with customers are not typically documented in writing, such agreements are increasingly used by brokerage companies to clarify for customers what duties and services the broker and licensee affiliates may and may not offer them.

(9) **Designated agent**: one or more broker licensee affiliates assigned by the broker to represent one client to the exclusion of all other clients in the same transaction, as well as to the exclusion of all other licensees affiliated with the broker.

Designated agency is a type of agency introduced in the 2000 revision of BRRETA. Designated agency allows brokers and their affiliated licensees to substantially reduce liabilities previously associated with dual agency transactions. Designated agency allows two different licensee affiliates of the same broker to exclusively represent two different broker clients with opposing interests in the same transaction. Designated agency is examined in detail in BRRETA in Section 10-6a-13.

(10) **Dual Agent**: a broker who simultaneously has a client relationship with both a seller and a buyer or both a landlord and a tenant in the same transaction. Dual agency is examined in detail in BRRETA in Section 10-6A-12.

(11) **Material facts**: information that a party would want to know, does not know, and could not reasonably discover for themselves

Though Georgia remains a caveat emptor (buyer beware) state, real estate licensees are obligated to inform all parties in a transaction of any adverse material fact known to be true.

> (12) **Ministerial acts**: services performed by real estate licensees that do not require professional judgment or skill on the part of the licensee

Acts such as these, examples of which are described in Section 10-6A-14, are the only services BRRETA allows real estate licensees to offer customers.

> (13) **Timely**: a reasonable time for performance under the circumstances of a particular situation
>
> (14) **Transactional broker**: a broker who does not have a client relationship with any of the parties to a particular real estate transaction and who offers only ministerial acts on behalf of these parties; the broker will be compensated by one or more of the parties to the transaction according to an express verbal or written agreement for performing the ministerial acts. A transaction broker has no agency relationship with any party to the transaction. Transactional brokerage is examined in detail within BRRETA Section 10-6A-14.

BROKER-CLIENT RELATIONSHIPS

§ 10-6A-4(a)

> A broker providing brokerage services for a client or customer owes the client or customer only the duties and obligations set forth in the statute, unless the parties agree otherwise in writing. A broker may not have a fiduciary relationship or fiduciary obligations and may only be responsible for exercising ordinary care in performing specified duties designated in the statute and, in the case of a client, designated in the brokerage engagement.

§ 10-6A-4(b)

> When a broker with an existing brokerage relationship with either a customer or client creates a new or different brokerage relationship with the customer or client, the broker must timely disclose the new brokerage relationships to all brokers, customers, or clients involved in potential real estate transactions.

Before the enactment of BRRETA, the national scope of agency relationships among brokers and those receiving brokerage services was typically random and lacking definition throughout the real estate industry. For the most part, what ruled were common law principles of agency in which agents were considered to have a fiduciary relationship with clients. An agent's fiduciary obligations included an absolute loyalty to the client, along with a requirement for the agent to exercise an extraordinary level of care in performing duties for the client. For years and in most states, court rulings assigned these broad fiduciary responsibilities to real estate brokers in their representation of clients, leaving the real estate industry uncertain and often bewildered as to its legal liabilities.

IN PRACTICE By replacing the all-encompassing fiduciary obligations of brokers with more precise descriptions of duties owed to clients, BRRETA helped clarify agency relationships for brokers and their affiliate licensees. The statute's intent is threefold:

- To ensure the broker promotes the best interests of the client
- To ensure fairness, honesty, and accuracy to all other parties in a transaction
- To limit the broker's legal liabilities in performing those duties imposed by BRETTA and by brokerage engagement agreements (agency contracts), thereby preventing courts from ruling that brokers have duties beyond those specified in the statute and in the brokerage engagement

Sometimes brokerage relationships change, thereby altering or creating new duties and obligations between the parties. When this occurs, BRRETA requires that the broker disclose any new brokerage relationship to all other brokers, customers, or clients who are parties to an existing or possible future transaction. This disclosure requirement can come into play at various times during the brokerage engagement, including for example when the relationship changes from customer to client or from client to customer. The statute does not specify a period within which this disclosure must be made nor does it state whether the disclosure must be in writing. It would be advantageous, however, for the broker to make the disclosure as soon as possible after the brokerage engagement is signed, and when possible, for the disclosure to be in writing.

IN PRACTICE Broker Carlos has shown a property listed by another real estate company several times to a prospective buyer who has not signed a buyer brokerage engagement with Carlos. Before making an offer on the property, the buyer asks Carlos to represent him in the transaction. Carlos explains that BRRETA allows the buyer to become a client only through a signed written agreement with the broker. When the buyer agrees and signs a buyer brokerage engagement with Carlos, their relationship has changed from broker-customer to broker-client. BRRETA now requires Carlos to disclose this new relationship to the listing broker and the seller, as well as to any other customer, client, or broker who may be involved in the transaction.

Though BRRETA sets out four separate sections of client level duties—one for sellers, one for buyers, one for landlords, and one for tenants—these duties are essentially the same. The discussion that follows will analyze these duties as such, noting those differences appropriate to the existing type of agency relationship.

DUTIES TO CLIENTS

§ 10-6A-5(a); § 10-6A-6(a); § 10-6A-7(a); § 10-6A-8(a)

A broker contracted by a seller, buyer, landlord, or tenant will (1) perform the terms of the brokerage engagement.

IN PRACTICE Brokers must look to the written brokerage engagement, either the seller/landlord listing agreement or the buyer/tenant brokerage agreement to determine what services they must perform for their client. The duties imposed by BRRETA may be changed, increased, or even eliminated by the written brokerage engagement. Though the brokerage engagement forms used in most transactions require compliance with BRRETA, the duties of the broker are drafted very narrowly to limit the potential legal liability of the broker.

(2) Promote the client's interests by

A. seeking a buyer or a tenant at the price and terms stated in the brokerage engagement or at a price and terms acceptable to the seller or the landlord; the broker may not, however, be obligated to seek additional offers to buy or lease the property while the property is subject to a contract for sale or lease (or letter of intent to lease), unless so indicated in the brokerage engagement; or in seeking a property to buy or lease at a price acceptable to the purchaser or the tenant, the broker may not, however, be obligated to seek other properties for the buyer or the tenant while the buyer is party to a contract to purchase property or the tenant is party to a contract to lease (or letter of intent to lease), unless the brokerage engagement so provides.

IN PRACTICE Depending on the type of client relationship, the broker will either be searching for a buyer, a tenant, or a property to be purchased or leased, all at prices and terms acceptable to the client. Though BRRETA does not require brokers to continue these searches once binding agreements are created for transactions, brokerage engagements may allow for the continuation of the search.

For example, if the purchase and sale contract gives the buyer a due diligence period or the contract requires the buyer to meet specific loan contingencies, the seller might typically want the listing broker to continue looking for purchasers to create backup contract positions in case the current contract does not survive the due diligence period or the current buyer under contract is unable to secure a loan.

(2) Promote the interests of the client by

B. timely presenting all offers to and from sellers, landlords, buyers, and tenants, even when the property is subject to a sale or lease or when the buyer or the tenant is subject to a contract for purchase or lease.

IN PRACTICE BRRETA is very clear that a broker must present all offers to and from clients as soon as reasonably possible, regardless of extenuating circumstances. For example, broker Ian is on his way to his seller-client's property closing, when he receives an offer on this same home. Ian's instinct is to ignore the offer because the property will be sold and transferred to the buyer within the next few hours. He then remembers BRRETA's requirement that all offers must be presented and that his obligation, notwithstanding the current circumstance, remains clear. Arriving at the closing attorney's office, Ian presents the offer to his seller-client.

This obligation to present all offers also extends to verbal offers, even though contracts for the purchase of real property must generally be in writing to be enforceable; notwithstanding the form of communication, any offer would still be a material fact for a client and thus would need to be disclosed.

[Promote the interests of the client by]

C. disclosing to sellers, landlords, buyers, and tenants adverse material facts concerning the transaction of which the broker has actual knowledge.

IN PRACTICE Because under BRRETA, the term *material fact* is limited to those facts that a client could not reasonably discover, the statute has significantly narrowed the broker's duty of disclosure from what it was under common law, where the scope of fiduciary duty may hold the broker to extraordinary yet often undefined levels of responsibility.

Whether a disclosure should be made under the "material fact" provision of BRRETA often requires examining the context of the situation.

For example, a broker in Atlanta lists the home of a seller he has recently met. A broker from another company shows the home to a prospective buyer. The buyer is actually the listing broker's cousin, a fact that the seller-client would reasonably want to know because it might affect the negotiations. Moreover, Atlanta is a big city in which the seller's discovery of this relationship without being told seems highly unreasonable. Thus, BRRETA would define the listing broker's familial relationship with the buyer as a material fact, one that the broker would need to disclose to his seller-client.

Consider another example illustrating how the circumstantial context determines if information would be material. A broker representing a buyer shows his client a home in which he knows that a murder occurred a few years ago. While this type of incident would normally be thought of as an adverse material fact under BRRETA, surprisingly, this is not the case in this context. **Georgia's Stigmatized Property Statute** protects real estate agents from liability for not disclosing that the seller's property was the site of a homicide, felony, or suicide. The law also applies to property that is or has been occupied by a person infected with a virus or any other disease that has determined by medical evidence to be highly unlikely to be transmitted through occupancy of a property presently or previously by such an infected person. (O.C.G.A. § 44-1-16) In other words, these occurrences would not be classified as a material fact under the state law. However, real estate licensees are required to answer truthfully to the best of their knowledge regarding homicides, felonies, or suicides on the property and are not protected from liability if they lie about the same.

> [Promote interests of the client by]
> D. advising all clients to obtain to obtain expert advice for material matters, which are beyond the expertise of the broker.

IN PRACTICE A married couple asks broker Fiona, who represents them as a buyer's agent, to explain the ways of taking title in Georgia to a home together. Fiona obligingly describes the differences between the couple taking title as tenants in common or as joint tenants, information she has learned in real estate education. But when the couple asks her which one of these ownership methods she might recommend, Fiona advises them that the question is a legal one beyond her area of professional expertise and that they should contact an attorney for advice.

To further protect themselves from potential liability in these matters, brokers should be reluctant in recommending to clients a specific individual or company for expert advice. The danger is that the recommended party may not serve the clients well and the broker may be blamed. A better approach for the broker might be to offer a list of names and let the client contact and choose whomever they prefer.

> [Promote the interests of the client by]
> E. timely accounting for all money and property received in which the client has or may have an interest.

IN PRACTICE In a real estate sales contract, this stipulation typically applies to the earnest money submitted by the purchaser as part of the contract creation. BRRETA assigns the responsibility of ensuring that these funds are handled appropriately to the brokers involved in the transaction. In real estate leasing contracts with similar broker responsibilities noted, this stipulation typically applies to security deposits submitted by the tenant to the landlord, pursuant to the lease.

[Brokers contracted by clients will]

(3) exercise **ordinary skill and care** in performing the duties noted in BRRETA, which promotes the client's interests, as well as any other duties as may be agreed upon by the parties in the brokerage engagement.

In the 1994 enactment of BRRETA, the statute lowered the fiduciary standard of care to one that required brokers to perform duties with "reasonable care." Under this standard, however, lawsuits began disputing the meaning of the word "reasonable," challenging that brokers were falling short of this standard in carrying out duties. Broker liabilities often were decided by the testimony of expert witnesses. In the 2000 revision of BRRETA, the term "reasonable care" was amended to read "ordinary care." Essentially, brokers and their licensee affiliates are expected to have the skills of a competent real estate professional and, in performing duties, exercise the care that a competent agent would use.

IN PRACTICE A broker shows his buyer-client a 30-year-old home. He submits an offer to purchase the property and it is accepted. The contract is not conditional upon a property inspection, even though the seller does not provide a property disclosure. After moving in, the buyer discovers that after heavy rains, there is water in the home's basement. The buyer sues the broker, claiming the broker was negligent and failed to perform his duties with reasonable care in not recommending that the buyer have the property inspected during the contract due diligence period. Before the 2000 revision of BRRETA, if the buyer's expert witness testified that any "reasonable" prudent buyer's agent would have advised the client to have the older home inspected, the broker may have been held liable for lack of reasonable care in performing this duty. However, the 2000 revision of the statute provides additional protection for the broker by lowering the standard of care from reasonable to ordinary. In this context, the decision to inspect the older property falls exclusively with the buyer.

In addition to narrowing the scope of duties owed to clients to only those set forth in BRRETA and in the written brokerage engagements, BRRETA also moderates the legal standard of care required of brokers representing their clients. The fiduciary responsibilities of absolute loyalty and performing duty with extraordinary care in common law agency are substantially limited under BRRETA. The statute in fact specifically states that unless the parties agree otherwise in a written agreement, the agency relationship is not fiduciary. However, the duty of "ordinary skill and care" brokers must exercise for their clients under BRRETA would assume the necessary professional skills to satisfactorily perform these obligations. Interestingly, there is at least one brokerage firm in Georgia that offers all clients a fiduciary brokerage engagement that the company markets as the only "true agency" in a brokerage relationship between real estate brokers and their clients

[Brokers contracted by clients will]

(4) comply with all BRRETA requirements and all other applicable statutes and regulations, including but not limited to fair housing and civil rights laws, and

(5) keep information confidential by express request from clients unless clients permit such disclosures or such disclosures are required by law; however, confidential information disclosed between a broker and any of the broker's affiliated licensees assisting the broker in representing the client will not be a breach of the confidentiality requirement.

IN PRACTICE In the course of representing Oliver, a client, in the purchase of a parcel of land, broker Deborah is told by Oliver that, in fact, he is acting as a straw buyer for a company that plans to build an entertainment complex on the land. As a straw buyer, Oliver is committing no illegal acts and as his buyer's agent, Deborah is obligated to keep this information confidential. She does not breach this confidentiality by revealing that her client is a straw buyer to affiliate licensee Keith who is assisting her with the transaction.

DISCLOSURES TO CLIENTS

§ 10-6A-10

All brokerage engagements must

1. advise the prospective client of the types of agency relationships offered by the brokerage company

§ 10-6A-12(f)

Every broker must develop and enforce an office brokerage relationship policy among affiliated licensees that either specifically permits or rejects the practice of disclosed dual agency. This office policy must be disclosed pursuant to Section 10-6A-10(1).

IN PRACTICE Though BRRETA does not require these disclosures until the brokerage engagement is created, it is a good practice for brokers and licensee affiliates to provide this information soon after meeting prospective clients. Knowing which real estate agency relationships permitted in Georgia are practiced by the brokerage company avoids confusion for the parties and provides some clarity as to how the brokerage company might best serve their needs. Real estate agents should also understand that BRRETA specifically requires that brokerage companies express in writing whether they practice or reject dual agency. Just leaving out dual agency in the list of agency relationships the brokerage firm practices is not sufficient. The company must affirmatively state that it does not practice dual agency.

[All brokerage engagements must]

(2) advise prospective clients of any brokerage relationships held by the broker with other parties that may conflict with any interests of perspective clients actually known to the broker. This stipulation would not apply to the fact that brokers may be representing other sellers and landlords in selling or leasing property or that the broker may be representing other buyers and tenants in buying or leasing other property.

IN PRACTICE Though this subsection of the statute imposes disclosures of possible conflicts of interest a broker might have with prospective clients, it does not provide any insight on what types of other brokerage relationships might present these conflicts of interest. The language, however, does limit the broker's disclosure to "other parties" within a single transaction and does not require the disclosure of how one agency relationship held by the broker might conflict with another agency relationship. Instead this part of the statute requires only the disclosure of specific conflicts between individuals, both of whom are represented by the same broker.

As an example, consider Theresa, a property developer who hires broker Vincent to represent her in efforts to acquire as many homes as possible in a certain section of town.

Her plan is to redevelop the area into an upscale mixed-use community. Theresa instructs Vincent to keep the negotiations as low key as possible because she believes that when the plans become public, it will be harder to negotiate price from a favorable position. At the same time, another homeowner in the area contacts Vincent. The homeowner is thinking of listing his home with Vincent but wants the agent's opinion as to whether he would be better off selling now or in a year.

If Vincent decided to sign a brokerage engagement with this homeowner, before doing so, he would have to disclose his agency relationship with the property developer. The problem here is that Vincent is already representing the developer in efforts to negotiate the lowest prices for property in that area; if he accepts the homeowner's listing, he would be working in that specific instance to negotiate the highest price possible for his seller-client. Of course, Vincent would also have to disclose his brokerage engagement with the homeowner to Theresa, his buyer-client. In effect, if Vincent accepts the homeowner as a seller-client, he would operate as a disclosed dual agent with serious conflicts of interest.

> [All brokerage engagements must]
>
> (3) advise prospective clients of the terms under which the broker's compensation will be paid, which must be so stated in the brokerage engagement, as well as stating whether the brokers will share such compensation with other brokers.

IN PRACTICE BRRETA does not require that the amount of the compensation to be paid to cooperating brokers be revealed to the parties in the transaction, only whether the commission will or will not be shared. Moreover, as indicated in BRRETA Section 10-A-11, compensation earned by brokers in a transaction may be paid to them by customers or clients.

> [All brokerage engagements must]
>
> (4) advise the prospective client of the broker's obligations under BRRETA to keep information confidential.

IN PRACTICE A previous discussion of this broker obligation to keep information confidential may be found in BRRETA under Section 10-6A-5(5). Referenced as a disclosure requirement above, the statute simply states that the brokers must inform clients of their right to confidentiality when entering a brokerage engagement with the parties.

TERMINATION OF BROKERAGE ENGAGEMENT

§ 10-6A-9

> (a) The relationships between brokers and clients set forth under BRRETA begin at the time the client engages the broker and continue until
>
> (1) performance of duties in brokerage engagement, or
>
> (2) until one of the following events takes place:
>
> A. Expiration date of the brokerage engagement
>
> B. Termination of agreement by any or all parties, as authorized in the brokerage engagement.
>
> C. Absent any provision for termination of the agreement and no termination having occurred, BRRETA will end the brokerage engagement after one year from its beginning

IN PRACTICE Generally, contract forms for brokerage engagements in Georgia offer brokers greater flexibility for early termination of an agreement than might be available for their clients. For example, a broker and a client are having difficulty getting along. Communication is becoming so problematic that the broker feels she cannot adequately represent her client and terminates the engagement as a result. In another instance, a broker wants to avoid a dual agency situation that would arise by showing a buyer-client one of the broker's own listings. Here the broker might choose to withdraw from the buyer agency situation and perhaps refer the purchaser to another agent. While buyer brokerage engagements may permit the buyer to terminate the agreement early if the contract language allows or if there is a material breach of the contract by the broker, the listing brokerage engagement is typically much more restrictive in a client's rights of early termination, imposing substantial financial penalties for such actions by the seller.

Within BRRETA, the sole regulation for ending broker contracts with clients occurs only if these agreements do not specify a termination date. Because the Georgia Real Estate Commission requires that all exclusive brokerage engagements include a termination date, BRRETA's actions to end an agency agreement one year from its start essentially apply to nonexclusive engagements, such as an open listing. In this agency relationship, expiration dates often are not a part of the agreement; moreover, the open listing may sometimes be a verbal understanding between multiple brokers and a real property seller, an agreement that surprisingly may be enforced under Georgia's statute of frauds.

§ 10-6A-9(b)

> Except as otherwise agreed in writing and as provided in subsection (a) of this section, a broker owes no further duties to the client after the engagement terminates except:
>
> (1) To to account for all monies relating to the engagement: , and
>
> (2) Tto keep confidential all information received during the brokerage engagement where confidentiality was requested by clients unless
>
> A. the client subsequently permits the disclosure,
>
> B. such disclosures are required by law, or
>
> C. the information becomes public from a source other than the broker.

IN PRACTICE Broker Felix had a client relationship with a seller that has recently ended. As the seller's agent, Felix was privy to personal information regarding the seller, including the fact that the seller was going through a divorce. The seller decided not to renew the listing with Felix's company and has since acquired another listing broker for his property. Felix now has a buyer-client who wants to see the property belonging to Felix's former client. Though Felix knows of the seller's impending divorce, Felix is still bound by the duty of confidentiality to his former client, and he may not reveal the fact to his current buyer-client.

BROKER-CUSTOMER RELATIONSHIP

In its definition of a customer as a person who is not represented by a broker pursuant to a brokerage engagement, BRRETA considers any seller, landlord, buyer, or tenant working with a broker without this written client agreement to be a customer. As such, under BRRETA, a broker's duties to customers are more limited than a broker's obligations to clients. A broker-customer relationship can arise in various situations. For example, before entering into a written brokerage engagement that forms a broker-client relationship, the individual with whom the broker is working would be a customer; when a broker represents one party in a transaction as a client, the broker typically treats other parties to the transaction as customers; and when a broker does not enter into a brokerage engagement with any party in a transaction, the broker has customer relationships with all parties to the transaction.

§ 10-6A-5c; 6c; 7c; 8c

> A broker engaged by clients in a real estate transaction may provide assistance to customers by performing ministerial acts of such types as described in Section 10-6A-14 of BRRETA, and performing such ministerial acts for customers will not be thought to create brokerage engagement between the brokers and customers.

IN PRACTICE Unlike client-level services that require a broker's professional judgment and skills, ministerial acts are simply administrative services that brokers may perform for customers. For example, a broker may not offer advice or negotiating strategies for customers submitting or receiving contract offers in a real estate transaction; however, a broker may act as a scribe and fill out a contract offer form for a customer who provides the numbers and language to be inserted in the appropriate spaces in this document. A broker might also print a list of properties for sale in a multiple listing service for a buyer as a ministerial service but could not evaluate those properties as investment or personal lifestyle decisions for these customers.

§ 10-6A-5d; § 10-6A-6d; § 10-6A-7d; § 10-6A-8d

> A broker engaged by sellers and landlords does not breach any duty or obligation to these clients by showing alternative properties to buyers and tenants; nor do brokers engaged by buyers and tenants breach any obligation to these clients by showing properties of interest to these clients to other prospective buyers and tenants.

IN PRACTICE Broker Ann represents seller Jones and is showing her client's home to customers Susan and Scott. Though they like seller Jones's home, Susan and Scott ask Ann to show them other properties for sale in the neighborhood. Ann may do so without violating her client obligations to Jones. Commercial real estate broker Sam is showing tenant-client Meghan properties for her leasing consideration to operate a restaurant. Sam also has tenant-customers to whom he is showing one of the properties in which Meghan has particular interest. Sam does not violate any client duties to Meghan by showing this property to other customers.

DUTY OF HONESTY

§ 10-6A-9c

> In the event a conflict arises between a broker's duty to keep the confidence of a client and the duty not to give customers false information, the broker's duty not to give false information to customers must prevail and govern the broker's actions. No parties may have claims against brokers or the broker's affiliated licensees for revealing information so stipulated in this paragraph of the statute.

IN PRACTICE Broker Susan has just signed a brokerage engagement with seller Dylan. She notices a water stain on the ceiling of the kitchen. Dylan says the stain occurred as a result of a shower pan leak in the upstairs bath. He further tells Susan that the shower pan has been replaced and that he is having the ceiling area repainted later that day. Because the problem is fixed, Dylan tells broker Susan he sees no reason for her to mention it to any prospective buyers or brokers working with them. She explains to her client that the issue with the ceiling would be a material fact that those parties would want to know and that she would need to disclose it even if the situation had been resolved. In this example, a broker's duty under BRRETA to reveal known information that would be material to prospective buyers supersedes following a client's instructions of confidentiality. If the agency relationship between Dylan and Susan were governed by common law fiduciary principle, then the broker's loyalty to the client would have taken precedence and Susan may very well have been liable for revealing any information that the client wanted to be kept confidential.

§ 10-6A-5b; § 10-6A-6b; § 10-6A-7b; § 10-6A-8b

> Brokers may not knowingly give customers false information; however, a broker is not liable to customers for providing false information to them if the broker did not have actual knowledge that the information was false and discloses to the seller the source of the information.

IN PRACTICE Brokers must tell the truth as they know it when dealing with customers. Though a broker may be gathering information for the benefit of a buyer or a seller-customer, the broker is essentially a messenger for delivery of the information, while not guaranteeing its accuracy. A broker has no liability under BRRETA for disclosing information to customers that turns out to be incorrect, as long as the broker is unaware that the information is false and discloses the basis for the information. If buyers or sellers know the source of the information, then they can decide whether the source is reliable or if further investigation on the buyer's part might be necessary.

As an example, a broker representing a developer in a new subdivision hands a prospective buyer-customer a pamphlet printed by the local chamber of commerce that identifies the local high school as having the highest performance scores in the county. After purchasing the home, the buyer discovers this claim is false. Though the listing broker passed on this inaccurate information to the buyer-customer, the broker did not know the claim was inaccurate and was not the source of the information. Under these circumstances, BRRETA would not hold the broker liable for the misrepresentation. In matters important to customers, the safest course of action for brokers is to encourage parties to do their own research.

DISCLOSURE OF ADVERSE MATERIAL FACTS: BUYER AND TENANT CUSTOMERS

§ 10-6A-5b(1); § 10-6A-6b(1)

> A broker must disclose to buyer and tenant customers all adverse material facts relating to a property's physical condition and improvements on such property, including but not limited to material defects in the property, environmental contamination, and any fact required by statute or regulation to be disclosed (i.e., all such facts known to be true by the broker and which could not be discovered by a reasonably diligent inspection of the property by the buyer and the tenant).

IN PRACTICE This stipulation revolves around two issues for brokers working with buyer or tenant customers: first, that under BRRETA, adverse material facts or defects concern those property details that a party does not know, could not reasonably discover, and would reasonably want to know; second, that brokers have to disclose such facts only if they are known by them. So, if a broker knows that a listed property's basement accumulates water after heavy storms, this is information that a buyer-customer does not know, could not reasonably discover unless the buyer happened to be in the basement after a heavy storm, and would reasonably want to know as part of the decision where or not to move ahead with an offer to purchase. In other words, it is a known adverse material fact pertaining to the physical condition of the property, information that the broker must disclose to the buyer-customer. On the other hand, if a listing broker failed to disclose a water stain on the ceiling in the living room to a buyer, BRRETA would not define this as a material fact requiring disclosure by the broker because a prospective buyer who exercised diligence in examining the home could more than reasonably discover it.

Furthermore, brokers have no legal obligations under BRRETA to investigate or conduct an inspection of a listed property to search for unknown adverse conditions. However, if brokers suspect or believe there is a likelihood that an adverse condition exists on the property, that belief may prudently trigger action to investigate. For example, if the roof on the property a broker is listing seems in obvious disrepair with a few shingles missing and others curling up, even if the seller has not noticed any water leaks in the home, the broker might still want to point these conditions out to prospective buyers. Even though the buyer could reasonably discover these adverse conditions by inspecting the property, if the listing broker remains silent on this matter, the lack of disclosure may lead to unpleasant accusations that the listing broker had knowledge but chose not to disclose, which may sour the entire transaction for all parties involved.

§§ 10-6A-5b(2); 10-6A-6b(2)

> A broker engaged by sellers or landlords must timely disclose to buyers and tenants all material facts relating to existing adverse physical conditions in the neighborhood, within 1 mile of the property, that are actually known to the listing broker and that could not reasonably be discovered by the buyer through a review of reasonably available governmental regulations, documents, maps, and statistics. Examples of these include land use maps and plans; zoning ordinances; floodplain maps; tax maps; school district boundary maps; transportation maps; and government jurisdiction boundary line maps. Nothing in this stipulation creates any duty for the broker to discover or seek to discover either adverse material facts pertaining to the physical condition of the property or to the existing neighborhood. Nothing in this stipulation limits sellers or landlords from obligations under any applicable law to disclose to prospective buyers and tenants all physical adverse material facts known by the seller concerning the physical condition of the property, nor does it limit the obligations of prospective buyers and tenants to familiarize themselves with potentially adverse conditions related to the property or neighborhood. No broker will be liable to disclose any matter other than those described in this section of the statute.

IN PRACTICE In its efforts to further limit the liability of real estate brokers in Georgia, the BRRETA revision of 2000 clarified what the original statute had not adequately addressed: what constitutes a reasonably diligent property inspection on the part of buyers and tenants. By inserting a list of statutory and regulatory documents that buyers and tenants might reasonably review as part of their due diligence process, BRRETA reinforced a long held "caveat emptor" (buyer beware) common law principle in Georgia.

Though BRRETA certainly limits broker liabilities to customers, sellers and landlords do not receive similar benefits of statutory protection. BRRETA does not in any way limit the obligation of sellers or landlords under any applicable law to disclose adverse material facts concerning the physical condition of their property. These obligations include the obligation of landlords to disclosure whether the property has a propensity to flood; certain disclosures regarding lead-based paint; and the sellers' obligations not to conceal from buyers specific information that might be important to the buyers and would probably affect a decision to purchase or not (**passive concealment**).

DISCLOSURE OF ADVERSE OFFSITE CONDITIONS

Another area in which the 2000 revision of BRRETA clarified broker disclosure obligations focused on a broker's duty to investigate and disclose adverse neighborhood conditions to prospective buyer or tenant customers. Fraud claims had long been brought against brokers with regard to brokers' failures to disclose or correctly represent adverse offsite conditions. Brokers wanting to avoid claims in this area found it difficult to come up with a clear course of action to avoid problems. BRRETA addressed the troubles surrounding three questions.

1. **How far away does a broker need to go to identify adverse off-site conditions?**

Disclosure was required only if the condition is within 1 mile of the property. Basically, the 1 mile represents a geographical boundary surrounding the property in the transaction. Though the statute does not describe how the 1-mile boundary is to be measured, presumably the distance would be a 1-mile radius from any point in the property. Adverse conditions within this radius would be disclosed even if the property was separated from the adverse condition by a physical barrier such as a body of water, a highway, or even a political border such as a city or county boundary line.

2. **What kind of neighborhood adverse condition should the broker be looking for?**

Only adverse conditions that currently exist. Potential adverse conditions are excluded in the disclosure requirement. For example, if the county had plans at an undisclosed future time to turn a two-lane road into a six-lane freeway, even if the broker knew of the plan, disclosure would not be required.

3. **Does a broker's legal exposure in this area potentially exist in every transaction?**

No. A broker is required to disclose offsite adverse conditions only if the broker knows about the condition. Moreover, a broker's obligation to disclose is only required for adverse offsite physical conditions. If a broker is listing a home in a neighborhood where other property owners often noisily entertain late into the night, this is not classified as a physical condition in the neighborhood. Finally, if buyers or renters could discover objectionable neighborhood conditions through a diligent inspection of the neighborhood or by reasonably reviewing available public documents, the broker would not be responsible for disclosure of these conditions.

DISCLOSURE OF ADVERSE MATERIAL FACTS: SELLERS AND LANDLORDS

§ 10-6A-7b(2)

A broker engaged by a buyer must timely disclose to a prospective seller with whom the broker is working as a customer and who is selling the property, which will be financed either by a loan assumption or by seller providing all or part of the financing, all material adverse facts known by the broker concerning the buyer's ability to perform the terms of the sale, and in the case of a residential transaction, the buyer's intent to occupy the property as a principal residence. Nothing in this stipulation limits any obligation of the prospective buyer under any applicable law to disclose the above material facts to the seller.

§ 10-6A-8b(2)

A broker engaged by a tenant must timely disclose to a prospective landlord with whom the broker is working as a customer all adverse material facts actually known by the broker concerning the tenant's financial ability to perform the terms of the lease or letter of intent to lease or intent to occupy the property. Nothing in this stipulation limits any obligation of the prospective tenant under any applicable law to disclose the above material facts to the landlord.

IN PRACTICE Material facts disclosed to customers vary under BRRETA, depending on which parties the broker is working with. For sellers and landlord customers, they would reasonably want to know the financial capabilities of the broker's buyer or tenant client. While the landlord is seeking some assurance that the tenant can pay the rent, the seller, who might be providing financing for the purchaser in the form of a loan or having the purchaser assume a seller's existing loan, would want an even more thorough look at a buyer's financial profile. On the other hand, for a buyer or tenant customer, what they would reasonably want to know involves the physical condition of the property they would be purchasing or leasing, as well as any neighborhood adverse conditions that might exist.

TYPES OF BROKER-CLIENT RELATIONSHIPS

Before the enactment of BRRETA in 1994, brokers in Georgia represented sellers in virtually all real estate transactions. The primary agency brokerage contract was the listing agreement between the broker and the seller. Furthermore, brokers working with prospective buyers and showing them properties listed by other brokerage companies almost exclusively practiced subagency, in which these brokers also represented the seller as a subagent of the listing broker. Essentially, prospective buyers were without representation. This environment changed after BRRETA's adoption as brokerage companies began to offer multiple agency choices, particularly buyer representation, which evolved out of a growing demand from consumers seeking brokerage services. Correspondingly, subagency has almost completely disappeared in Georgia.

Not only has the emergence of buyer agency led to the virtual disappearance of subagency in Georgia but also realizations by sellers that they may be vicariously liable for the words and actions of a subagent, a broker with whom the seller had little or no contact. BRRETA makes no direct comment on subagency, though this form of broker-client relationship is still permitted in the state. However, requirements under BRRETA that all agency agreements be in writing do apply here because the broker working with the buyer in a transaction may only become a subagent through a direct brokerage engagement with the seller of the property.

BRRETA permits three basic types of broker-client relationships:

- single agency, in which the broker only represents one party in a transaction;
- dual agency, in which the broker represents both parties as clients in the same transaction; and
- designated agency, in which the broker appoints one or more of affiliated licensees to exclusively represent different clients in the same transaction.

SINGLE AGENCY REPRESENTATION

IN PRACTICE As we recall from our study of Section 10-6A-5–8, BRRETA allows brokers to form client relationships independently through brokerage engagements with sellers, landlords, buyers, or tenants. While representing a seller or a landlord exclusively in a transaction, the broker will treat buyers or tenants, brokers and licensee affiliates from separate companies, and any other third parties in the transaction as customers.

Customarily, brokerage engagements in Georgia stipulate that compensation for brokers will be paid by the seller or the landlord to the listing broker and that this compensation may be shared by the listing broker with cooperating brokers working with buyers or tenants. BRRETA in no way regulates the terms or sources of broker compensation. The statute, as we recall, merely clarifies that payment of compensation does not in itself create a client-broker relationship between the parties giving and receiving the compensation. Additionally, BRRETA simply requires the broker to disclose to clients the terms of the compensation and whether it may be shared with cooperating brokers.

DUAL AGENCY

IN PRACTICE While defining dual agency as a brokerage practice in which one broker simultaneously represents both parties in the same transaction (§ 10-6A-10), BRRETA does not describe what is meant by the term "same transaction" in which dual agency may occur. As real estate transactions unfold, though, the circumstances will usually dictate when dual agency exists.

For example, if a broker has signed a brokerage engagement with both the buyer and the seller in the purchase and sale of a home, it is clearly the same transaction and dual agency exists. In other situations, whether a broker is involved with two clients in the same or in separate transactions might not be as clear.

EXAMPLE To illustrate, listing broker Eric receives a contract offer from buyer-customer Nancy to purchase his seller-client Steve's property. The offer, which is accepted, is conditional upon Nancy selling her existing home before closing on Steve's property. Nancy signs an engagement with Eric to represent her in finding a buyer for her current home. On first glance, since Eric now has a client relationship with both Steve and Nancy, who is buying Steve's property, we might assume that Eric is a dual agent.

A closer look at the circumstance reveals that Eric's client relationships with Steve and Nancy do not exist in the same transaction. In the purchase and sale of Steve's home, Nancy remains Eric's customer. Nancy is Eric's client in a separate transaction in which he represents her as a listing broker to help sell her home. Therefore, no dual agency exists in this situation. However, Eric's newly formed client relationship with Nancy in a separate transaction might well be considered as a material fact for Steve and should be disclosed to him by Eric.

§ 10-6A-12(a)

> A broker may act as a dual agent only with the written consent of all clients.

IN PRACTICE There are no exceptions to this regulation. Georgia real estate licensing law provides that a broker can be sanctioned by the Georgia Real Estate Commission for violating this regulation—sanctions that might very well include the loss of the broker's license.

This written consent disclosure for dual agency evolved out of a climate of liability claims and litigation that had afflicted the real estate brokerage industry for a number of years before the statute's enactment by the Georgia Legislature in 1994. The problem was simply that a broker acting as a subagent was often negligent in informing prospective buyers with whom he was working that the broker was not representing them but was actually working for the listing broker and seller.

A brokerage firm with several hundred licensee affiliates processes, on a monthly basis, a number of transactions in which one of the company's affiliates is identified as the buyer's agent and another is identified as the listing or the seller's agent. What remains undisclosed in these contracts is the fact that because both the buyers and the sellers are represented as clients by the same brokerage company (the broker), this relationship is in fact dual agency and the licensee affiliates of the broker identified in the contracts as exclusively representing either the buyer or the seller-client do in fact each assume that same dual agency status as the broker.

EXAMPLE A more systemic problem for the real estate profession in that pre-BRRETA period could be found internally within brokerage companies that were practicing undisclosed dual agency. This undisclosed dual agency played out on a national stage with a 1993 federal class action lawsuit against Minnesota-based **Edina Realty**, one of the largest brokerage firms in the country. This landmark court case had enormous impact on the actions of brokerage companies throughout the United States. The incident began with a specific client complaint against Edina Realty. A buyer represented by one of the firm's agent affiliates had bought a home listed for sale by another Edina Realty agent affiliate. After the home was sold, the buyer filed a lawsuit against Edina Realty claiming that her buyer's agent and the firm's listing agent appeared to be working together to pressure her into making a decision to buy the home.

As an example of this conspiracy, she alleged in her lawsuit that a garden hose spigot was misrepresented by both her buyer's agent and the listing agent as a sprinkler system. The buyer felt her agent was not looking after her interests and appeared more interested in coordinating a quick deal with the listing agent. The buyer's attorney argued that she was first informed of her agent's legal role when it was presented as a clause in the purchase contract she signed. The clause indicated that the Edina Realty agent with whom she was working was her buyer's agent.

In fact, as the buyer's attorney pointed out, because both the buyer's agent and the listing agent were affiliates of the same broker, the Edina agent working with the buyer was a dual agent—not exclusively representing the buyer as was presented in the contract. This misrepresentation of the firm's true agency status in the transaction turned out to be just the tip of the iceberg.

The consequences of this lawsuit and two other similar cases involving Edina Realty eventually concluded with a class action settlement involving thousands of undisclosed dual agency claims against the company resulting in judgments against the Minnesota brokerage firm for some $20 million.

In its comprehensive disclosure requirements included in the written consent that clients must provide for brokers to act as dual agents, many have reasonably concluded that BRRETA offered one of the most impactful responses of all statutory reactions to the Edina Realty judicial rulings.

§ 10-6A-12a

Such written consents for dual agency shall include the following:

(1) A description of the type of transactions in which the broker will serve as a dual agent

(2) A statement that, in serving as a dual agent, the broker represents two clients whose interests are or at times might be different or even adverse

(3) A statement that a dual agent will disclose all known adverse material facts relevant to the transaction to all parties in the transaction, except for confidential information made at the request of another client, which is not allowed to be disclosed under BRRETA nor required to be disclosed under the statute

(4) A statement that the broker or the broker's affiliated licensees will timely disclose to each client in a transaction any material relationship they might have with other clients in the transaction other than what is incidental to the transaction. BRRETA defines a material relationship as personal, familial, or business relationship known to the broker or affiliated licensees that might interfere with the ability of these agents to exercise fair and independent judgment with regard to another client.

(5) A statement that the client does not have to consent to dual agency

(6) A statement that the client has voluntarily given consent and that the client has read and understands the engagement.

IN PRACTICE As stated in disclosure (3) of the written consent form, a broker acting as a dual agent must disclose adverse material facts to both clients involved in the transaction. The only exception to this regulation is whether either client in the transaction instructs the dual agent to keep certain information confidential, and the law permits such information to be kept in confidence by the broker.

For example: A broker is representing a subdivision developer who has built a small community of 20 homes. Fifteen of the homes have been sold, and the broker is told by her client that even though he has construction loans on the property coming due in a month, this is information he wants kept in confidence. The broker also represents a prospective buyer who has expressed an interest in making an offer on one of the remaining homes in the builder-client's subdivision. The fact that the seller/builder has a loan payoff due soon on the property would certainly be of material interest to the broker's buyer-client because it may very well strengthen the buyer's negotiating position. But because the broker also represents the seller in this transaction and has been instructed not to reveal this potential material fact, the broker may not disclose it to the buyer-client.

Another example: A seller tells her listing broker that she does not want it revealed that the exterior on the backside of her home is constructed with a type of siding that has been the subject of lawsuits by homeowners in various parts of the country over the durability of the product. The client tells the broker she has owned the home for five years and has never had a problem with the siding. The broker has a buyer-client who wants this home. Here, though the dual-agent broker has been instructed by the seller-client not to reveal this information, BRRETA would classify this as a material fact regarding the physical condition of the property, a fact that must be disclosed to all clients, superseding any instructions to the contrary by the client.

§ 10-6A-12(b)

> When a client signs a written consent, including the requirements set forth in this section of the statute, the client is deemed to be informed and to have given consent for dual agency.

IN PRACTICE When clients sign a brokerage engagement with a broker that includes the disclosure statements found in Section 10-6A-12(a) 1–4, the clients effectively say they have been informed, understand the risks involved, and consent for the broker to practice dual agency. Just as effectively, these clients are barred by law from subsequently arguing that no consent was given or that it was not informed consent. Before this statutory protection, parties could file a lawsuit against a broker and argue that they did not understand dual agency or give **informed consent** to its practice.

The consent to dual agency must be obtained before the broker performs anything more than ministerial services that might change the brokerage relationship from customer to another client engagement in the same transaction. Brokers should never assume that consent to dual agency is not necessary until the parties sign a purchase and sale agreement or a tenant and landlord lease. The language of BRRETA mandates that the consent for dual agency must be given by all clients before the broker may act as a dual agent. If the consent is not given until parties are negotiating terms of the contract, more than likely the broker has already acted in the capacity of a dual agent.

It should also be pointed out that the dual agency disclosures in brokerage engagement forms do not assume that the broker will be acting as a dual agent in the transaction. The disclosures merely inform the client about dual agency and allow the client to either consent or reject its practice should the circumstance occur. So, at the point in which the broker actually shows a buyer-client property in which the broker is also representing the seller as a client, the broker must disclose that, in showing the property, the broker will be acting in the capacity of dual agent. This disclosure is necessary, because in Section 10-6A-4(b), BRRETA requires a broker with a brokerage relationship to disclose whether the brokerage relationship changes.

§ 10-6A-12(c)

> No persons may make claims or take action against a dual agent for making disclosures allowed or required by the statute, and the dual agent does not terminate any client agreement by making such disclosures.

§ 10-6A-12(d)

> In a dual agency situation, clients and brokers and their respective licensees possess only actual knowledge and information. There may be **no imputed knowledge** or information between and among clients, brokers, or their affiliate licensees.

IN PRACTICE Under the common law of agency, principals and their agents are considered to have knowledge of information that the other possesses, even if this information was never actually communicated between the two parties. The assumption here is that in some phenomenal, perhaps telepathic manner, information is somehow transferred between principal and agents. If this were the case in dual agency, it would be impossible for brokers to fulfill their duties of confidentiality to their clients. To eliminate the presumptions inherent in this imputed knowledge principle, BRRETA eliminates it and establishes that brokers, their licensee affiliates, and all clients possess and are responsible for disclosing only actual knowledge.

§ 10-6A-12(e)

> In any transaction, a broker may withdraw, without liability, from representing a client who has not agreed to dual agency at any time before the existence of the dual agency. In such a situation, the broker is permitted to continue to represent the client who gave consent to dual agency, as well as to represent the client who did not give consent in other transactions not involving dual agency. In withdrawing from representation of the client who did not give consent to dual agency, the broker may refer that party to another brokerage company and receive a fee for such a referral.

IN PRACTICE In referring a party to another brokerage company, Georgia licensing law requires that the broker get the client's agreement to the referral and inform the client whether the broker will receive any compensation for the referral from the other brokerage company.

§ 10-6A-12(f)

> Every broker must develop and enforce an office brokerage relationship policy for its affiliated licensees that either specifically permits or rejects the practice of disclosed dual agency. This policy must be disclosed pursuant to Section 10-6a-10(1)(a).

DESIGNATED AGENCY

Before the 2000 amendment to BRRETA, situations were considered dual agency when two different licensees affiliated with the same brokerage firm each represented her own client in the same transaction. As we have discussed, the words and actions of agents in these circumstances were in very few ways consistent with any recognized disclosed dual agency practices.

In the revision of its statute in 2000, BRRETA created designated agency, a new type of brokerage relationship that addressed the inherently complicated and risky conflicts of interests associated with dual agency. Moreover, designated agency provided a viable brokerage alternative to dual agency that significantly reduced disclosure issues surrounding dual agency that had burdened the real estate industry with litigation disasters like the Edina Realty case.

§ 10-6A-13(a)

> A broker may assign directly, or pursuant to a company policy, different licensees or other management-level personnel affiliated with the broker as designated agents to exclusively represent different clients in the same transaction. Any company policy adopted to offer designated agency must include provisions to ensure that clients are represented according to the requirements of BRRETA. A designated agent of a seller, landlord, buyer, or tenant owes the client the duties set forth respectively in Section 10-6A-5, 10-6A-6, 10-6A-7, or 10-6A-8 of this statute.

IN PRACTICE Generally, there are two sets of circumstances under which brokerage companies engage in designated agency. The most common application occurs when a real estate licensee affiliate has a client who wants to see a property listed by another licensee affiliate in the same brokerage firm. Before BRRETA's enactment of designated agency, if this property were shown to the prospective buyer-client, the broker and the two licensee affiliates would be practicing as dual agents.

If designated agency is one of the brokerage relationship options offered by the company, each licensee affiliate may be assigned or designated to exclusively represent the client with whom that agent is working. This assignment may be made directly by the broker or as is more commonly the case under the circumstances here, company policy may automatically allow each of the licensee affiliates to assume the exclusive representation of their respective clients.

EXAMPLE As a real estate agent affiliated with Acme Realty, licensee Phoebe enters into a buyer brokerage engagement with buyer Vincent. Over the course of several weeks, Phoebe shows Vincent several properties listed by various brokerage companies. Vincent expresses an interest in seller Baker's home, a property he has noticed while driving around. As it turns out, the property happens to be listed by Carey, another agent affiliated with Acme Realty.

Phoebe shows Vincent the home and he decides to make an offer on the property. Acme Realty has a company policy that when two of its agent affiliates represent two different clients in a potential transactional process involving a single property, each agent is automatically assigned by the company to exclusively represent the respective clients. So, Phoebe represents Vincent as a designated agent and Carey represents Baker as a designated agent.

In certain situations, circumstances may dictate that a real estate firm's broker directly assign designated agents.

EXAMPLE Returning to the previous scenario, suppose Vincent has an interest in seller Larkin's home, which happens to be listed by his buyer-agent Phoebe. This circumstance would change Phoebe's separate brokerage relationships with Vincent (buyer's agent) and with Larkin (seller's agent) into a common dual agency relationship with both clients. As a result, Phoebe would be required to obtain a signed consent form for dual agency from each client.

Before designated agency existed, if buyer-client Vincent, for example, rejected dual agency, to continue with this transaction, Acme Realty would have to refer the client to another brokerage company. Because Acme Realty now offers designated agency, agent Phoebe would consult with her broker, who may then designate another Acme Realty agent to exclusively represent client Vincent while agent Phoebe continues to exclusively represent seller Larkin. In other words, designated agency allows Acme Realty to maintain sole representation and compensatory interest in the transaction.

§ 10-6A-13(b)

> If a broker appoints different designated agents in accordance with subsection (a) of this Code section, neither the broker, the licensee affiliates, nor the real estate brokerage firm may be dual agents.

IN PRACTICE Because the same broker is still representing both buyer and seller (or landlord and tenant) in the same transaction, designated agency appears to be at odds with traditional common law principles of agency. However, the 2000 revision of BRRETA changed the law by separating designated agency from dual agency and establishing regulations to control designated agency. Here we see a classic example of a state legislature having the power to enact statutes that supersede common law. BRRETA explicitly states that in designated agency situations, no dual agency exists for the broker, the affiliated licensees, or the brokerage company.

The most readily apparent application of essentially carving designated agency out of dual agency is that real estate agents can practice designated agency without being subject to lengthy, written dual agency disclosure requirements. Furthermore, as each client is exclusively represented by an agent looking out for the client's interests, designated agency is a much safer form of brokerage practice: each agent owes his client the same duties as under a traditional single agency representation.

§ 10-6A-13(c)

> Designated agents are considered to possess only actual knowledge and information; there may be no imputed knowledge between and among the broker, designated agents, and the clients. Except to their broker, designated agents may not disclose information kept in confidence by express request or instruction from the client represented by the designated agent—other than information allowed or required to be disclosed within BRRETA. The broker of a designated agent may not reveal confidential information it receives from the designated agent or the client with whom the designated agent is working. BRRETA considers confidential information as information for which clients have not given consent to disclose and for which the negotiating position of the client may be harmed.

§ 10-6A-13(d)

> The broker or any of the broker's licensee affiliates acting as designated agents are not permitted to disclose information kept in confidence by express request or instruction by a party before the creation of designated agency. The broker and the licensee affiliates may continue to keep such information confidential unless expressly permitted to disclose by the party who gave the information, or if disclosure of such information is required by law.

IN PRACTICE Other than to their broker, designated agents cannot disclose confidential information from clients to any other agent in the firm, including of course the designated agent for the other party in the transaction. Moreover, if the designated agent for one party had previously represented the other party in the transaction, the designated agent would be required to maintain confidential information learned as a result of that brokerage relationship unless such confidentiality is expressly waived by the former client or the information is required to be disclosed by law.

EXAMPLE Agent Harry is representing buyer Maria as a client. As is often the case in a real estate agency relationship, Harry learns much about his client. Maria becomes very interested in a property that Harry has listed. To avoid the inherent conflicts of interest found in dual agency, Harry consults his broker and another licensee affiliate of the broker is assigned to represent Maria, to which she agrees. In these circumstances, Harry is now Maria's designated agent, representing her exclusively. He would not be permitted to disclose any information made confidential by Maria to any party other than his broker, unless Maria subsequently allows such disclosures or the disclosure is required by law.

In a designated agency transaction, the broker still acts in a supervisory capacity for any of the designated agents. The broker must make sure that information coming her way from each designated agent is not passed along to the other designated agent in the transaction unless this disclosure of information is expressly permitted by the respective client or its disclosure is required by law. BRRETA's limitations on the disclosure of confidential information by brokers and designated agents provides protection for real estate licensees by eliminating the conflicting duties inherent in a dual agency relationship. Thus designated agency allows a brokerage company to represent both sides of the transaction without as many of the risks associated with dual agency. Designated agency is also a good fit for buyers and sellers because the agent for each client represents them exclusively in the transaction.

NONAGENCY: TRANSACTION BROKERAGE

A transaction broker does not represent any of the parties in a transaction as clients but may treat all parties as customers by assisting them in administrative tasks. As originally enacted in 1994, BRRETA did not address transaction brokerage at all because this kind of brokerage practice was virtually nonexistent at that time in Georgia. Transaction brokerage relationships usually arise out of very specific circumstances. For example, a prospective buyer may need brokerage services only to identify and locate a special type of property in a certain area of town. The buyer does not wish to enter into a brokerage engagement with the broker because he feels confident in evaluating the properties found by a broker without the broker's assistance and also is comfortable in negotiating the contract without help. The buyer also understands that under BRRETA, a broker may receive compensation from any party without creating a broker-client relationship. As such, the buyer agrees to compensate the broker if the broker is not paid through a cooperating agreement with a listing broker or if the broker is not compensated from the seller of a FSBO (for sale by owner).

In either of these situations, the broker would be a transaction broker representing neither buyer nor seller in the brokerage process.

§ 10-16-14(a)

A broker acting as a transaction broker may provide assistance to buyers, sellers, tenants, and landlords by performing ministerial acts. Examples of these ministerial acts include, without limitation, the following:

(1) Identifying property for sale, lease, lease, or exchange

(2) Providing real estate statistics and information on property

(3) Providing preprinted real estate form contracts, leases, and related exhibits and addenda

(4) Acting as a scribe in the preparation of real estate contract forms and related exhibits and addenda

(5) Locating architects, engineers, surveyors, inspectors, lenders, insurance agents, attorneys, and other professionals

(6) Identifying schools, shopping facilities, places of worship, and other similar facilities on behalf of any of the parties in a real estate transaction

IN PRACTICE As we have discussed, ministerial services, as identified in BRRETA, do not require an agent's professional judgment or discretion to perform. Verbs used in the list such as ***locate***, ***identify***, and ***provide*** each suggest purely administrative acts of service. If we were to replace those words with verbs such as ***evaluate***, ***analyze***, ***advise***, and ***research***, we can see that these ministerial tasks evolve into client-level services.

BRETTA does not indicate a standard of care with which a broker must perform ministerial acts for customers. Georgia case law, though, has held that brokers must use reasonable and ordinary care when providing brokerage services for customers. An interesting note here is that BRRETA now only requires ordinary care from brokers when they are performing duties for customers, which is no greater than the level of care Georgia courts have typically assigned to brokerage services provided for customers.

§ 10-6A-14(b)

A broker acting as a transactional broker must do all of the following:

(1) Timely present all offers to and from the parties involved in the sale, lease, or exchange of real property

(2) Timely account for all monies and property received by the broker on behalf of a party in a real estate transaction

(3) Timely disclose the following to all buyers and tenants with whom the broker is working:

(A) Disclose all adverse material facts relevant to the physical condition of the property, environmental contamination, and facts required by statute or regulation to be disclosed that are actually known by the broker and that could not be discovered by the buyer or the tenant through a reasonable inspection of the property

(B) Disclose all material facts pertaining to adverse physical conditions in the immediate neighborhood within 1 mile of the property that are actually known by the broker and that could not be discovered by the buyer or the tenant through a diligent inspection of the neighborhood or thorough review of available public documents, such as governmental regulations, maps and statistics, zoning laws, and boundary lines of governmental jurisdiction

IN PRACTICE BRRETA gives a transaction broker many of the same duties that are given to a broker who represents a client:

- Presenting all offers
- Accounting for trust funds
- Disclosing adverse material facts concerning the property and the neighborhood of which the broker is aware

Also, just as a broker must exercise ordinary skill and care in performing duties imposed by BRRETA, so does a transaction broker. A transaction broker is not, however, charged with promoting the customer's interest in a way that a broker representing a client is expected to promote the client's interest.

§ 10-6A-14(c)

> Transaction brokers may not knowingly give any party in a real estate transaction false information, provided that the broker does not know the information is false and discloses the source of the information. Nothing under this subsection of BRRETA limits any obligation of a seller to disclose to prospective buyers all adverse material facts of which they are aware regarding the physical condition of the property and the neighborhood. Nor does this subsection of BRRETA limit the obligation of prospective buyers to familiarize themselves with potentially adverse conditions related to the physical conditions of the property or surrounding neighborhood. Violations of this subsection may not create liability on the part of the broker absent finding fraud on the part of the broker.

IN PRACTICE Here in this subsection (c) of the section, we find transaction brokers working with customers subject to the same disclosure requirements and afforded the same liability protection found in Section 10-6A- 5(b) that addressed regulation for those brokers with client relationships who are also working with customers.

UNIT 24 QUIZ

1. Concluding that the relationships between real estate brokers and the general public were not well served by the common laws of agency, the Georgia Legislature enacted BRRETA primarily to
   a. eliminate the common law principle of subagency.
   b. establish guidelines for contracts between brokers and consumers of brokerage services.
   c. identify which parties in a real estate transaction paid the broker.
   d. prevent harmful misunderstandings and misrepresentations between brokers and clients or customers.

2. In the early 1990s, multiple listing services throughout the country eliminated the requirement that brokers showing listings from the MLS to buyers represent the sellers and listing brokers for these properties because
   a. subagency was determined to be the fairest method of representation for MLS properties.
   b. buyer agency was determined to be the best method of representation for MLS properties.
   c. the requirement resulted in ever increasing litigation throughout the country.
   d. this change increased profitability for the multiple listing services.

3. In addition to requiring that all brokerage engagements between brokers and clients be in writing and more precisely identifying both duties and disclosures for real estate licensees, the 2000 revision of BRRETA
   a. replaced dual agency in Georgia with designated agency.
   b. limited liability for real estate brokers and their affiliated licensees.
   c. identified transactional brokerage as a new type of brokerage engagement.
   d. limited licensee disclosures to the real property alone.

4. As a basis for legal actions surrounding real estate agency in Georgia, BRRETA is intended to be used in what capacity?
   a. As a law that provides broad interpretation and authority in judicial rulings for real estate agency litigation
   b. As a law that eliminates common law influence over matters of real estate agency in Georgia
   c. As a law that may limit or alter rules and regulation of the Real Estate Commission in regulating actions of licensees
   d. As a law that is to be interpreted strictly by the wording of the statute alone

5. In its enactment of BRRETA, the Georgia General Assembly intended for the law to
   a. regulate all agency contracts, including the general agency agreements between brokers and their affiliated licensees.
   b. lower the bar with regard to false information claims against real estate brokers and their affiliate licensees.
   c. hold multiple listing organizations responsible for verifying property information given to the service by brokerage companies.
   d. uphold common law requirements regarding proof of fraud in claims of misrepresentation.

6. Broker Amy shows her listed property to a buyer-customer. According to BRRETA, what is *TRUE* regarding this situation?
   a. Broker Amy has a brokerage relationship only with the seller of the real property.
   b. Broker Amy may not collect a commission from her customer.
   c. Broker Amy has a brokerage engagement with the seller.
   d. A signed customer agreement would create a brokerage engagement between Broker Amy and her buyer-customer.

transaction broker - compensated by either party in the transaction

7. Under the Brokerage Relationships in Real Estate Transactions Act, a broker owes a client the duty of
   a. promoting the client's interest above all else.
   b. discovering material facts that might help a client make an informed decision.
   c. finding the best possible home inspector for a client.
   d. performing according to the terms of the brokerage engagement.

8. As defined by BRRETA, a ministerial act could involve which of the following services?
   a. Negotiating a lease for a tenant to operate a business in a shopping center
   b. Filling out a contract offer form for a buyer who requires no assistance in determining a monetary figure, as well as other details to include in the offer
   c. Disclosing adverse material facts for customers
   d. Analyzing what properties would best suit a buyer's investment goals

9. BRRETA requires that a broker make agency disclosures
   a. when first meeting a prospective client.
   b. to all prospective customers, as well as prospective clients.
   c. when first entering into a brokerage engagement.
   d. when first entering into any brokerage relationship.

10. A specific duty of disclosure that brokers owe to both clients and customers under BRETTA involves disclosing
    a. the types of agency relationships offered by the brokerage company.
    b. the terms of the broker's compensation and if the broker will share such compensation with cooperating brokers.
    c. adverse material facts known by the broker.
    d. the broker's obligation to keep information confidential.

11. BRRETA allows a transaction broker to
    a. represent only one party in a transaction.
    b. assist only one party in a transaction.
    c. be compensated by either party in a transaction.
    d. represent either party in a transaction.

12. Two real estate licensee affiliates for the same broker find themselves working on the same transaction. Licensee A is exclusively representing the buyer, and licensee B is exclusively representing the seller. Under BRRETA, what would be *TRUE* in these circumstances?
    a. Both licensees are dual agents in this transaction.
    b. Two agents of the same brokerage company may not represent separate clients of the broker in the same transaction.
    c. Both licensees are designated agents in this transaction.
    d. The licensees may not exchange client information held in confidence with any agent in their company, including their broker.

13. Which of the following disclosures is required of a broker acting as a dual agent?
    a. A statement that the client should seek legal advice before signing the disclosure consent
    b. A statement disclosing how the broker will be compensated in the transaction
    c. A statement that if the client rejects dual agency, the brokerage company may work with the client as a designated agent
    d. A statement that the broker represents two clients whose interests are, or at times, could be adverse

14. BRRETA allows a single agent in a real estate transaction to
    a. receive compensation from a client or customer in a transaction.
    b. only to be compensated through a written brokerage engagement.
    c. only perform ministerial acts in the transaction.
    d. represent a buyer and a seller in the same transaction.

15. Licensee affiliate Stan is acting as Susan's designated buyer's agent. If Susan instructs Stan to keep confidential that as soon as she closes on the property, she plans to tear down the existing home and build a new one, then as the designated agent, Stan
   a. may not disclose this information to anyone else.
   b. may not disclose this information to anyone else other than to the other designated agent in the transaction and to his broker.
   c. may disclose the information to his broker, but not to any other affiliated licensee of the broker, including the other designated agent.
   d. must disclose this information to all parties in the transaction because it is an adverse material fact.

16. Under BRRETA, transactional brokers may
   a. offer professional advice to all parties in the transaction.
   b. be compensated by either or both parties in the transaction.
   c. may have brokerage engagements with only one party in the transaction.
   d. may not have brokerage relationships in the transaction.

17. With regard to the termination of brokerage engagements, BRRETA
   a. has the authority under all circumstances to end the agreement within one year from its beginning date.
   b. will in all circumstances leave a termination decision to the discretion of the broker and client.
   c. states that the agreement will terminate in one year only if the engagement lacks a termination date and the parties do not end it by authority granted in the agreement.
   d. will terminate the agreement upon default by either the client or the broker.

18. Adverse material facts that brokers disclose to customers as identified in BRRETA will
   a. always describe physical conditions of the property and the neighborhood within 1 mile of the property.
   b. sometimes include information that BRRETA requires brokers to discover.
   c. vary in content, depending on whether the broker is disclosing to sellers and landlord customers or buyer and tenant customers.
   d. have no impact if these facts are disclosed after a contract for sale has been created between the parties.

19. Which of the following brokerage services might a transactional broker provide for the parties in a transaction?
   a. Evaluate how well a property might serve a buyer's investment goals
   b. Prequalify a perspective buyer before showing property to that individual
   c. Fill out an offer to purchase form for a buyer who provides all the necessary details to complete the contract offer
   d. Advise a buyer as to whether the asking price for a property is a reasonable one, or recommend that the buyer make a lower offer

20. The 2000 revision of BRRETA identified which of the following brokerage relationships as separate from dual agency?
   a. Both designated and transaction agency
   b. Single agency
   c. Designated agency
   d. Designated agency and single agency

Contract Forms for Real Estate Practice in Georgia

LEARNING OBJECTIVES

When you have finished reading this unit, you will be able to

- **describe** the duties and disclosures common to brokerage engagements;
- **identify** the basic components of real estate contracts for purchase and sale and the role of real estate licensees in these agreements; and
- **explain** how Georgia Code regulates residential leases and tenant-landlord relationships.

KEY TERMS

appraisal contingency
banking days
broker
buyer
buyer's broker
constructive eviction
contract
commission acknowledgment form
contract acceptance
contract exhibits
correlate/correlation
dispossessory affidavit
escrow agent
right of possession
exclusive buyer brokerage agreement
exclusive right-to-sell listing agreement
FSBO
general right to terminate
Georgia landlord-tenant Code
Georgia statute of frauds
inspection
landlord
latent defects
lease/purchase
offer
option to purchase leased property
party
qualified acceptance
retainer fee
safety/protection clause
self-help eviction
seller
seller's broker
seller's property condition disclosure
special stipulations
standard terms
survival clause
tenant
tenant at will
terminate or termination
time is of the essence

OVERVIEW

As is the case for almost all industries, contracts provide the lifeline for the real estate profession. Brokerage engagements create seller, buyer, landlord, or tenant clients for licensees. Contracts for purchase and sale determine the conditions under which a property is transferred from the seller to the buyer. Contracts for lease set forth the conditions for the renting of a property. For productive real estate professionals in Georgia, understanding the terms and language of such contract forms, along with a diligence in preparing these documents, remains paramount in providing superior service for clients and in realizing income goals for themselves.

This unit will examine residential real estate contract forms commonly used by brokers in Georgia, with a particular focus on how statutory laws and regulations impact the rights and obligations of all parties to these agreements. Specific contract forms used in this unit are published by Orthrus Real Estate Enterprises, LLC, and are available to use for members of Georgia Multiple Listing Service (GAMLS) and First Multiple Listing Service (FMLS).

Contract forms may vary slightly from year to year. The forms used in this unit are for training purposes only. Licensees should always use the forms approved by their broker, and brokers should use preprinted forms that have been reviewed and approved by attorneys. Forms available through a state association or from a multiple listing service are preferred because they have undergone thorough drafting and review by competent real estate attorneys.

BROKERAGE ENGAGEMENTS

As established in the Brokerage Relationships in Real Estate Transactions Act (BRRETA), the term *brokerage engagement* refers to any written real estate agency contract in Georgia in which a seller, buyer, landlord, or tenant either promises to compensate a broker or agrees that a broker may be compensated by another in exchange for the broker's producing a ready, willing, and able party to buy, sell, or rent a property or performing other brokerage services. Subject to the limitations of statutory laws and regulations, brokers and clients are free to contract for whatever relationship they wish and perform whatever duties and obligations to which the parties agree.

A brokerage engagement agreement (contract) must include some language indicating that the client engages the broker to perform specific brokerage services for the client (such as finding a property for a client to purchase or lease or finding a buyer or a tenant for an owner's property). The brokerage engagement may also provide for authorized termination by either party subject to the occurrence of specified events, or that either party has the right to terminate without cause.

This topic will examine the two most common brokerage engagements: the **exclusive right to sell listing agreement** and the **exclusive buyer brokerage agreement** Though not reviewed here, preprinted contract forms that establish brokerage engagements with tenants and landlords, as well as for property management agreements, are readily available for licensees as members of REALTOR® associations and of multiple listing services in Georgia.

IN PRACTICE Regardless of the party they represent in real estate transactions, brokers and their affiliated licensees most effectively serve the interests of clients through awareness of the ebb and flow in the real property marketplace. Advice for a seller client should focus on setting a listing price that will attract the attention of potential buyers. An overpriced listing will not likely attract serious buyers; an underpriced listing will probably attract a slew of buyers but will not bring the client fair market price for the property. Such intuitions are equally important for a buyer's agent providing advice to a client submitting a contract offer to purchase.

CMA: COMPARATIVE MARKET ANALYSIS

Whether assisting a seller in setting a listing price or advising a buyer on property offers, a competent real estate agent forms an opinion based on market evidence, which is best communicated to a client through the preparation of a comparative market analysis (CMA). (This is sometimes called a competitive marketing analysis.) This CMA displays relevant data that allows real estate agents to compare similar properties in the same general neighborhood in order to estimate fair market value for a subject property, whether for a listing or for an offer to purchase a listing. As a tool for helping clients market and acquire real property, the CMA borrows from the sales comparison method used by professional appraisers.

IN PRACTICE In 1991, Georgia passed a law requiring that any persons appraising real property in the state must first be classified as an appraiser by the Georgia Real Estate Appraisers Board. Only those classified as such may call themselves appraisers or refer to real estate property evaluations they have made as appraisals. Though the concepts of a CMA and of a professional appraisal may be similar, an appraiser adheres to far more stringent standards in arriving at an estimate of value than does a real estate licensee. Georgia Real Estate License Law will find a licensee guilty of an unfair trade practice for indicating that an opinion of real property valuations offered to parties is an appraisal unless the licensee holds such a classification in the state. In the same context, the license law allows agents to prepare CMAs for clients as long as licensees emphasize that their market analyses are offered as a guide for recommending a listing price or sales price offer. Moreover, the CMA should avoid appraisal terms such as "estimating market value" by substituting phrases such as "preparing a comparative market analysis (CMA)." The contents of the CMA, like an appraisal, will concentrate on recent property sales but, unlike the typical appraisal, might also include properties whose listing dates have expired, as well as active listings of properties.

Case Study Narrative

Real estate licensee Eric who is affiliated with Top Floor Realty prepares for an upcoming listing appointment with a prospective seller-client. The property involved is a four-bedroom, two-and-a-half bath fully renovated 1960s brick home in an established neighborhood of solidly built, well-maintained houses. Real estate activity in the area has been brisk over the past year, and Eric has identified 10 houses that have sold over this period that might serve as comparable properties to the subject home. To effectively narrow his initial search, Eric examines each property on the list as to size, construction style, specific features, and amenities to determine which ones appear most similar to the subject property. As part of this process, Eric consults his broker, who suggests that he limit use of the "comps" to those homes that have sold in the past four months. Following this advice, four properties remain on the list. To provide some guidance in balancing sales prices of these comparable homes based on property feature differences with the subject home, Eric's broker recommends the following price adjustments:

- Main dwelling square footage: $35 per square foot
- Finished basement: $17 per square foot
- Brick construction: $7,500
- Full bath: $6,000
- Half bath: $3,000
- Two-car garage: $8,000
- Two-car carport: $4,000
- Wood deck: $3,000
- Screen porch: $4,000
- Sunroom/enclosed patio/porch: $5,500

Eric now puts together a CMA as shown in Figure 25.1.

FIGURE 25.1: Sample CMA

Item	Subject Property	Comparable Property 1	Prop 1	Comparable Prop 2	Prop 2	Comparable Prop 3	Prop 3	Comparable Prop 4	Prop 4
Street Address	1103 Franklin Avenue	1950 Elfin Road		1300 Sycamore Lane		1060 Franklin Avenue		8 Golden Court	
List Price		$407,900	Sale-List	$399,500	Sale-List	$415,000	Sale-List	$409,500	List-Sale
Sales Price		$393,500	Ratio: 96.5%	$387,750	Ratio: 97%	$400,000	Ratio: 96.4%	$385,000	Ratio: 94.2%
Sale Date(months ago)		1.5 months ago		0.5 months ago		4 months ago		3 months ago	
Terms of Sale / Financing		Conventional Loan		Conven-tional Loan		Conven-tional Loan		Conven-tional Loan	
Distance from Subject		0.4 miles		0.5 miles		0.1 miles		0.3 miles	
Square Feet of Living Area	2,575 sq ft	2,625 sq ft	–$1,750	2,535 sq ft	$1,400	2,705 sq ft	–$4,550	2,675 sq ft	–$3,500
Age	48 years	47 years		same		same		46 years	
Construction	Brick	same		same		same		frame	$7,500
Condition	Good	same		same		same		same	
Number of Rooms	11	same		10		12		same	
Number of Bedrooms	4	4		3		4		4	
Number of Baths	2.5	same		3	–$3,000	3	–$3,000	3	–$3,000
Garage/Carport	2 Carport	same		2 car garage neg $4,000	–$4,000	2 car garage	–$4,000	same	
Decks/Porches/ Sunroom	sunroom	scrnd porch	$1,500	same		scrnd porch	$1,500	scrnd porch	$1,500
Basement/ Finished	900 sq ft finished	same		no basement $15,300	$15,300	finsh-750 sf $2,550	$2,550	same	
Landscaping	Good	same		same		same		same	
Total Net Adjustments			–$250		$9,700		–$7,500		$2,500
Comp Sale			$393,500		$387,750		$400,000		$385,000
Adjusted Sales Price			$393,250		$397,450		$392,500		$387,500

Correlation Of Adjusted Sales Prices

Comp 1: $393,250 × 0.40 = $157,300

Comp 2: $397,450 × 0.15 = $59,618

Comp 3: $392,500 × 0.20 = $78,500

Comp 4: $387,500 × 0.25 = $96,875

= $392,293

FIGURE 25.1: Sample CMA (continued)

EXPIRED LISTINGS									
Street Address	**Time on Market**	**Distance from Subject**	**Number Rooms**	**Number Bedrooms**	**Number Baths**	**Approx. Square Feet**	**Finished Basement**	**Deck/ Porch Sunroom**	**Garage/ Carport**
952 Franklin Avenue ($425,000)	120 days		11	4	2.5	2600	Yes	screen pch 2 car gar	2 car gar
1502 Sycamore Lane ($423,500)	120 days	0.4 miles	10	3	3	2500	yes	sunroom	2 car gar

ACTIVE LISTINGS									
Street Address	**Time on Market**	**Number Rooms**	**Number Bedrooms**	**Number Baths**	**Approx. Square Feet**	**Finished Basement**	**Deck/ Porch Sunroom**	**Garage/ Carport**	**Construct**
1250 Sycamore Lane ($405,000)	1 month	11	4	2	2450	unfinished	sunroom	2 carport	brick
615 Franklin Avenue ($412,500)	6 weeks	12	4	3	2700	yes	screen pch 2 car gar		brick
2350 Elfin Road ($410,750)	3 weeks	11	4	2.5	2600	yes	sunroom	2 car gar	frame
501 Golden Court ($408,500)	2 months	10	3	3	2400	unfinished	screen pch	2 carport	brick

Identified as the subject property, the seller's home, along with the four recently sold homes in the area serving as comparable properties, are found at the top of the CMA form. Also noted here are the list prices of the four "comps," as well as the percentage of the list price that the actual sales price represents. The first vertical column on the left identifies those items used to compare the subject property with the comparable homes. The next vertical column provides specific features of the seller's home. The remaining vertical columns provide the features present in each of the four comps.

Where differences in property elements exist between the seller's property and any of the sold properties, the CMA adjusts the sales prices of the comp so that each one becomes more similar to the seller's home. Using the feature "square feet of living space" as an example, the seller's property on Franklin Avenue has 2,575 square feet. The Elfin Road comp has 50 more square feet. So in order to make this comp more similar to the subject home, this difference in area between the two properties must be eliminated. The CMA accomplishes this process by establishing a dollar amount for the 50 square feet. Using the price adjustment of $35 per square foot suggested by the broker, the CMA multiplies 50 by $35 to calculate a $1,750 adjustment. Next, by subtracting this amount from the sales price of the comp, the CMA effectively accounts for differences in this feature between the two properties.

Note on the form, this negative $1,750 is inserted in the Elfin Road column next to the indicated square-footage feature. In the next vertical column covering comparable property 2 on Sycamore Lane, the square footage is 2,535, which is 40 square feet fewer than the subject home. Here we see that the difference is identified as a positive $1,400 [40 × $35] that must be added to the sales price in order to make this living area feature similar to the seller's home. The adjustment process for living area is repeated in the other two comparable vertical columns to arrive at the appropriate positive or negative dollar amount.

In examining other items of comparison in the CMA, necessary adjustments using the broker's price points continue to show up under each comparable home, where necessary. Note that no adjustments are ever performed on the subject property, only on the comparable sales. If no differences exist between the subject and the sold homes in comparing a specific feature, the CMA inserts the word "same."

After each item of comparison is completed, the CMA then totals the positive and negative adjustments in the separate vertical columns, creating a total net adjustment for each of the four comparable properties. Next, the net adjustment would either be added to or subtracted from its corresponding sales price to arrive at an adjusted sales price for each.

Real estate agent Eric notices that the adjusted sales prices of the four comparable properties used in his CMA have approximately a $10,000 range: from a low of $387,500 to a high of $397,450. After consulting his broker, Eric prioritizes the adjusted sales prices by examining the number of adjustments made for each property, as well as the dollar amount of the adjustments. With only two adjustments made for a net amount of only $–250, Eric decides that comp 1 on Elfin Road is clearly the most similar to the seller's home at 1103 Franklin Avenue and assigns a 40% reliability factor to it; with three adjustments totaling $2,500, comp 4 on Golden Court earns a 25% rating. On the same street as the seller's home, comp 3 has five adjustments for $7,500, though at a 20% factor, Eric rates it slightly higher than the 15% assigned to comp 2 on Sycamore Lane with four adjustments, but with the highest net adjustment of all the comps at $9,700.

Figure 25.1 demonstrates how the CMA correlates the four adjusted sales prices of the comparable properties. Each of these prices is multiplied by its assigned ratio of reliability. Once these four calculations are done, the resulting dollar values are added together to establish a fair market sales price for the subject property. Eric will emphasize to his perspective client that his CMA is an estimation of a reasonable sales price for the home and that a professional appraisal may differ somewhat in its opinion of the market value of the seller's home. As for helping the seller determine a marketing price for the home, Eric may refer to the ratios of sales price to list price for the comparable homes noted at the top of his CMA. Here, the data reveals that the actual sales prices of the four comps represents on average 96.2% of the price those sellers were asking for their properties. Applying this percentage to his CMA's fair market sales price estimate for the seller's home, Eric makes the following calculation to arrive at listing price suggestions for the seller's home.

$392,293 ÷ 96.3% = $407,365.

With this figure in hand, Eric might advise a listing price of somewhere between $407,000 and $410,000 for the property.

Figure 25.1 also shows that Eric's CMA includes two expired listings and four active listing of homes in the general area of the seller's property. The CMA suggests that the expired listings were priced outside of the range estimated by Eric's market analysis and having this data for the prospective client to see may serve to reinforce the validity of Eric's advice in effectively marketing the seller's home. Furthermore, the active listings shown on the CMA may help clarify for the seller the real estate activity in the vicinity, as well as identifying what may be the current competition.

Eric's listing appointment goes well. The sellers, Tabitha and Sean Yeats, are impressed with his presentation of Top Floor Realty's marketing plan for their home; moreover, they agree that the CMA Eric prepared for them provides a fair market pricing analysis, and they also approve of his suggested price range for the property offering, believing it will attract prospective buyers, as well as satisfy their financial expectations. The couple is ready to move forward with a brokerage agreement in which Top Floor Realty and licensee affiliate Eric will exclusively represent them in the marketing and sale of their home. Eric prints out a brokerage engagement contract for the sellers to review.

THE EXCLUSIVE RIGHT-TO-SELL LISTING AGREEMENT

Important Broker Disclosures

FIGURE 25.2: Important Broker Disclosures

Exclusive Right to Sell
Listing Agreement

Date: March 15, 20xx

IMPORTANT BROKER DISCLOSURES

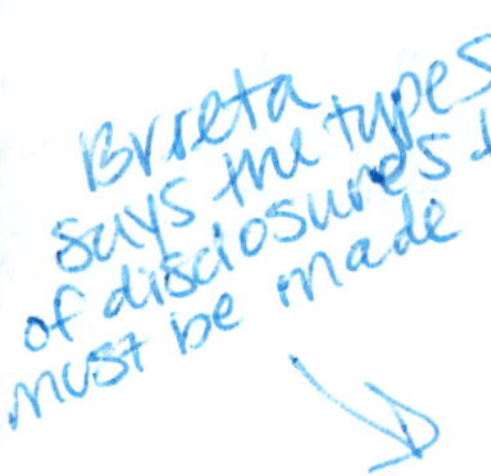

Prior to entering into this agreement with you, Georgia law requires that the undersigned Broker make certain disclosures to you, as follows:

(1) Advise you of the types of brokerage relationships available through Broker and Broker's office policy. These are set forth below.
(2) Advise you of any other brokerage relationships held by Broker which would conflict with any interest of yours actually known to Broker. While not legally considered to be a conflict, Broker and Broker's affiliated licensees represent other Sellers and Buyers regarding sales of property which may be in direct competition with the sale of your property.
(3) Advise you as to Broker's compensation and whether Broker will share such compensation with other brokers who may represent other parties to the transaction. Broker's compensation and sharing arrangements are set out below.
(4) Advise you of Broker's obligation to keep certain information confidential.

Broker as limited agent.
When you sign this agreement, the Broker's (and the Broker's affiliated licensees') relationship to you will be as an independent contractor and a limited agent and, as provided below, possibly a dual agent. "Limited agent" means that the Broker may, acting under the authority of this agreement, solicit offers to purchase, sell, lease, or exchange the property subject to this agreement without being subject to your control, except as to the result of the work. Broker, as a limited agent, shall not be deemed to have a fiduciary relationship or fiduciary obligation with you (or any party), except as may be expressly provided otherwise by law, nor shall Broker or Broker's affiliated licensees be considered your employees.

Broker will make disclosures to prospective Buyers about your Property in reliance on information you provide, and based on Broker's actual knowledge. Your obligation to disclose material adverse facts about the Property, particularly latent or hidden defects, is not changed by this agreement.
Broker shall treat all prospective buyers honestly and shall not knowingly give them false information. Broker shall keep confidential any information you expressly ask Broker to keep confidential unless specifically prohibited by law. Broker shall timely disclose to prospective buyers with whom Broker is working all material adverse facts pertaining to the physical condition of the Property, including, but not limited to, material defects in the Property, environmental contamination, and facts required by statute or regulation to be disclosed which are actually known by Broker, particularly if such defects could not be discovered by a reasonably diligent inspection of the Property by the buyer. Broker shall not be liable to a buyer for providing false information if the false information was provided to Broker by you and Broker did not have actual knowledge that the information was false. Nothing in this paragraph shall limit any of your obligations under any applicable law to disclose to prospective buyers all material adverse facts actually known by you pertaining to the physical condition of the Property, nor shall it limit the obligation of prospective buyers to inspect the physical condition of the Property. Georgia law provides that no cause of action shall arise on behalf of any person against Broker for revealing information in compliance with this paragraph.

Broker may provide assistance to prospective buyers without violating any duties to you.
Under Georgia law, Broker may provide assistance to buyers by performing such ministerial acts as preparing offers and presenting them to you; locating lenders, inspectors, attorneys, insurance agents, surveyors, schools, shopping facilities, places of worship, and all such other like or similar services; discussing other listed and sold properties. Performing such ministerial acts shall not be construed in such a manner as to violate this agreement, nor shall performing such ministerial acts for a buyer be construed in such a manner as to form a brokerage engagement with a buyer.

1 of 6

Form 151, *Exclusive Right to Sell Listing Agreement*
 Initials: ________ ________ ________ ________
R10312012

Instanet forms

FIGURE 25.2: Important Broker Disclosures (continued)

Broker may show alternative properties to buyers and provide information.
Under Georgia law, Broker does not breach any duty or obligation to you by showing alternative properties to prospective buyers. Broker may also provide information on other properties which may be in competition with your property.

Dual Agency is permitted by Georgia law if both buyer and seller consent in writing.
Dual Agency is permitted by Georgia law if both client parties consent. The following disclosures are made so that you will have full disclosure in choosing whether to give your consent and allow dual agency. **YOU DO NOT HAVE TO CONSENT TO DUAL AGENCY.** As a dual agent, Broker, will represent you in selling your Property and also represent a buyer with whom Broker has a brokerage engagement. In serving as a dual agent, Broker represents a buyer and seller whose interests are or at times could be different or even adverse. When Broker serves as dual agent, both you and the buyer will be clients of Broker. Broker, as a dual agent, may not disclose to you or the other client information made confidential by request or instructions from you or the other client, except information allowed or required to be disclosed by law. When dual agency exists, Georgia law provides that Broker may assign one affiliated licensee to you and another to buyer; this is known as Designated Agency. In that case, those licensees may not disclose, except to Broker, information made confidential by request or instructions of the client the licensee is representing, except information allowed or required to be disclosed under Georgia law. If Broker or Broker's affiliated licensees have a material relationship with the other client other than that incidental to the transactions, a disclosure of the nature of such a relationship must be provided to you. A material relationship shall mean any actually known personal, familial, or business relationship between Broker or Broker's affiliated licensees and a client which would impair the ability of Broker or the affiliated licensees to exercise fair and independent judgment relative to another client. The other party whom Broker may represent in the event of dual agency may or may not be identified at the time you enter into this agreement. If a party is not identified at such time, when such party is identified, if it is a party with whom either Broker or Broker's affiliated licensees has a material relationship, Broker shall promptly provide to you a disclosure of the nature of such relationship.

UNLESS EXPRESSLY SET FORTH TO THE CONTRARY IN THE SPECIAL STIPULATIONS BELOW, BROKER'S OFFICE BROKERAGE RELATIONSHIP POLICY IS TO PROVIDE SELLER AND LANDLORD AGENCY; BUYER AND TENANT AGENCY; DESIGNATED AGENCY; DUAL AGENCY; SUBAGENCY; OR TO ACT AS A TRANSACTION BROKER; AND BY SIGNING THIS AGREEMENT SELLER EVIDENCES SELLER'S CONSENT TO BROKER ACTING AS A DUAL AGENT AND DESIGNATED AGENT.

The Important Broker Disclosures form initially provides clients with a series of brokerage disclosures required by law before the parties enter into a real estate agency agreement. The first group of four disclosures comes directly from a broker's obligation to a client under BRRETA. This section of the engagement then defines the broker's agency relationship with the seller as one of a nonfiduciary, independent contractor whose authority is limited to the terms set forth in the exclusive right-to-sell listing agreement. Here, the primary responsibility of the broker or the affiliated licensee will be to solicit offers for the purchase of the sellers' home.

The disclosures continue by informing the client that because the broker or the licensee affiliate is bound to treat all third-party customers honestly, these agents will be relying on the accuracy of the property information provided by the sellers when disclosing material facts to prospective buyers. The clients are further informed that the real estate agents will not be liable for providing false information to prospective buyers if such false information provided to them by the seller-clients was unknown to the agents. This section goes on to remind the seller-clients of their particular obligation to disclose any **latent defects** they know of relating to the physical condition of the property to prospective buyers. Latent defects are defined here as those material facts concerning the physical condition of the property that buyers could not discover through a reasonably diligent inspection of the property.

The next section of the disclosures form explains those services that the broker and the licensee affiliates may provide for prospective buyer-customers without violating duties to their seller-clients. Included here are ministerial services that do not rely on the agents' judgment or discretion, as well as providing information about and showing properties to buyers that may be in competition with the property of the broker's client.

Last, the important broker disclosure focuses on dual and designated agency. Here, the information reveals that dual agency is permitted in Georgia only if the client parties in the transaction consent in writing. The section provides the full disclosures that brokers must provide for clients under BRRETA, so that clients might make an informed decision as to whether they would agree to dual agency in a real estate transaction. Clients are also informed that the other party whom the broker may represent in the event of dual agency may or may not be yet identified at the time the client agrees to dual agency. Furthermore, as this section explains, in a potential dual agency situation, BRRETA allows a broker to designate separate licensee affiliates to give exclusive representation to each client involved in the same transaction.

The series of disclosures at the front of this brokerage engagement form concludes with a statement to the clients regarding the broker's office policy as to which brokerage relationships the firm offers; an additional statement informs clients that unless indicated to the contrary in the special stipulations section of this agreement, the client signatures to this engagement consent to the broker acting as a dual and designated agent.

Agent Eric discloses to his seller-clients that his broker, Top Floor Realty, offers all types of agency relationships except subagency. The seller-clients decide to have Eric represent them as a designated agent, but not as a dual agent.

THE AGREEMENT BETWEEN BROKER AND SELLER

FIGURE 25.3: The Agreement Between Broker and Seller

EXCLUSIVE RIGHT TO SELL LISTING AGREEMENT

NOTICE TO SELLER: By signing this agreement, you acknowledge that you have read and understand all the above disclosures, which are incorporated herein by this reference, and have been advised of all of the foregoing prior to voluntarily entering into this agreement.

This **Exclusive Right to Sell Listing Agreement** is entered into on March 15, 20xx by and between Bernadette Joyce and Sean Joyce (the "Seller") and Top Floor Realty, Inc (the "Broker").

1. TERM

In consideration of the undersigned Broker's agreement to act as a limited agent for and on behalf of the undersigned Seller to use Broker's efforts to sell the Property within the terms of this agreement, the undersigned Seller does hereby authorize and grant to Broker the exclusive right and power from March 18, 20xx, until 12 o'clock midnight on August 14, 20xx (hereinafter referred to as the "Expiration Date"), to sell or exchange the Property described below at a price of US$ 409,500, or at such price or terms to which Seller may consent. Should a contract for the purchase of the Property be procured under the term of this agreement but fail to close until after the Expiration Date, this agreement shall automatically be extended through and including the date of closing, or through and including the date upon which the contract was terminated, as applicable.

2. PROPERTY

The property to be offered for sale is located in Bilbo County, Georgia, and is known as 1103 Franklin Avenue (the "Property"), and being more particularly described as all that tract or parcel of land lying and being in Land Lot 113 of the 9th District, 33rd Section, Bilbo County, Georgia, being Lot 51, Block 11, Phase n/a of ____________ Subdivision, as more particularly set out in Plat Book 343, Page 421, of the official records of Bilbo County, Georgia, Tax ID # 9-22-111B or, in the alternative, as set out on an Exhibit attached hereto and made a part hereof by this reference. Seller warrants that Seller has title to the Property described herein and has full authority to enter into this agreement

2 of 6

Form 151, *Exclusive Right to Sell Listing Agreement*
 Initials: ________ ________ ________ ________
R10312012

This exclusive-right-to-sell listing agreement contract form begins by giving notice that in signing the listing agreement, the sellers verify that they have read and understand all the preceding broker disclosures. The parties to the agreement are then identified as Bernadette and Sean Joyce, the sellers, and Top Floor Realty, the broker, with an agreement date of March 15.

IN PRACTICE Though real estate agency contracts in Georgia are between clients and brokers, in context, the term *broker* may also refer to the brokerage firm or to an affiliated licensee of the firm.

Item 1: Term

The sellers agree to a 150-day listing, begin on March 18 as day 1, then counting all days including weekends and holidays, ending at midnight on August 14. The sellers authorize Top Floor Realty (and Eric Cambridge as a licensee affiliate) to act on their behalf as a limited agent in order to find a buyer for their home at a price of $409,500, or any other price and terms acceptable to the sellers. Should a contract for the sale of the property occur under the terms of the engagement, but fails to close until after the agreement's expiration date, the agency engagement will be automatically extended through and including the date of closing.

IN PRACTICE Though the listing agreement typically identifies a sales price acceptable to a seller, the purchase and sale contract between the seller and a buyer may of course be established at any price acceptable to the two parties.

Item 2: Property

The sellers show Eric a copy of their warranty deed from which he is able to fill in a short-form legal description of the property. This section also allows the property tax ID number to be included, though it is not a requirement for a real property description in Georgia.

IN PRACTICE Rather than filling in the legal description, a copy of an acceptable legal description of the property in Georgia (either the short form or a metes-and-bounds survey) may simply be attached to the listing agreement. Also acceptable would be a specific reference to the deed book and page number in the county courthouse records where the property is located.

FIGURE 25.4: Broker Compensation

3. BROKER COMPENSATION

Seller agrees to pay to Broker a sales commission of [check one] ☒ ___6___% of the sales price, **or**
☐ US$_______n/a_______ in the event that during the term of this agreement:

3.1. Broker (or any other licensee) procures a person ready, willing and able to purchase the Property for a price not less than US$_______409,500_______; or

3.2. Seller enters into an enforceable contract for the sale or exchange of the Property with any buyer (without an exclusion set out in this agreement as to any buyer), whether by or through the efforts of Broker or any other person, including Seller.

IT IS UNDERSTOOD AND AGREED BY SELLER THAT THIS IS AN EXCLUSIVE RIGHT TO SELL AND THAT EVEN IF SELLER, DURING THE TERM OF THIS AGREEMENT, OR ANY EXTENSION HEREOF, SELLS THE PROPERTY, BROKER SHALL BE ENTITLED TO A COMMISSION AT THE RATE SPECIFIED HEREIN.

Seller acknowledges and agrees that Broker is providing a valuable service to Seller by marketing the Property and may incur significant costs and expenses in doing so. In order to partially compensate Broker for Broker's time in the event no commission is paid hereunder, Seller has paid to Broker a retainer fee in the amount of US$_______n/a_______, which fee shall be deposited into Broker's trust account. This fee shall be refundable to Seller only if Broker is paid the full commission as provided above. Upon the termination or expiration of this Agreement or the closing of the Property, Broker shall be authorized to transfer the retainer fee to Broker's general account. In the event the Property is sold and a commission is due to Broker, Seller shall at closing receive a credit against the commission due in the amount of the retainer fee actually paid.

Notwithstanding the payment of a retainer fee as provided above, Seller shall reimburse Broker or Broker's affiliated licensees for their costs and expenses incurred in marketing the Property (including, but not limited to, printing costs, advertising fees, mileage reimbursements and multiple listing fees) if Seller defaults hereunder. The right to collect reimbursement for these costs and expenses shall be in addition to, not in lieu of, any other claim or cause of action Broker may have hereunder, except that these costs and expenses may be offset against the commission paid to Broker, if any.

Item 3: Broker Compensation

The sellers agree to pay Top Floor Realty a commission of 6% of the property's sales price if during the term of the listing agreement, one of two events occurs:

1. The broker (or any licensee affiliate) procures an individual ready, willing, and able to purchase the property for not less than $409,500.
2. The seller enters into an enforceable contract for the sale of the property with any buyer through the efforts of the broker or any other party, including the seller.

IN PRACTICE The broker's commission is not earned through the actual sale of the property, but through the broker finding a buyer to purchase the property at terms acceptable to the seller. Typically, this situation occurs when an enforceable contract for sale is created between the seller and a buyer, but it is possible that a broker may earn the commission from the seller without the creation of a contract for sale. For example, if agent Eric presents his seller-clients with a contract offer on their home for $409,500 from a qualified purchaser who requests no seller contributions toward the buyer's closing costs, Top Floor Realty has performed the service for which it was hired. In other words, even if Sean and Bernadette Joyce decide, for whatever reason, not to accept this offer, the broker has still earned compensation from the sellers according to the terms of the listing agreement.

Top Floor Realty will also be entitled to a commission if during the term of the listing period or any agreed-upon extension of the period, an enforceable contract for sale is created for the listed property. Because this contract is an exclusive right-to-sell listing agreement, the broker earns this commission whether Top Floor Realty, another broker, or any other party (including the seller) procures the sale.

IN PRACTICE Within a brokerage engagement, some real estate firms generate another form of broker compensation through retainer fees. In a listing agreement, the seller-client might pay the broker a predetermined sum of money that would help offset some of the brokerage costs in marketing a property if no commission is earned through a contract for sale during the listing period. This **retainer fee** paid by the seller-client typically would be deposited in a broker's trust account when the agency contract is created. When the listing agreement terminates or expires, or when the property closes, the retainer fee will be transferred from a trust account into the broker's general account. If the sale has closed and the broker receives a commission, then normally at that time the seller will be credited the sum of the retainer fee against the commission paid to the listing broker. Because Top Floor Realty does not require retainer fees from listing clients, this compensation will not apply to this brokerage relationship.

This contract section concludes by disclosing the compensatory liabilities for a seller in default of this brokerage engagement. The seller would be liable for reimbursing the broker or affiliated licensee all marketing costs for the property, as well as any related expenses. These reimbursements would be in addition to any other claims the broker might make, such as a legal action to collect a commission.

FIGURE 25.5: Other Relationships

4. OTHER RELATIONSHIPS

Seller acknowledges and agrees that Broker may cooperate with another broker or compensate another broker, and that any commission hereunder may be disbursed or allocated in the sole discretion of Broker and may be allocated to other brokers who may or may not represent other parties to the transaction. The commissions payable for the sale, lease or management of property are not set in any manner other than between Broker and Seller. Broker agrees to use his or her best efforts to procure a person ready, willing and able to purchase the Property at the price and on the terms specified herein. Should Seller contract WITHOUT the services of Broker to make a direct sale, exchange, or lease with option to purchase the Property within ___60___ days after the Expiration Date, or any extension thereof, to a buyer to whom the Property was offered during the term of this agreement, or any extension hereof, by Broker, by Seller, or anyone else, Seller agrees to pay Broker a commission at the same rate of commission as specified herein. In this regard, Broker shall furnish Seller prior to the Expiration Date of this agreement or any extension hereof, a written list of names of all persons to whom the Property was offered, and such list shall be conclusive as to any commission rights due for any offerings made by Broker, or by persons authorized by Broker. It is agreed and understood that if and when Seller enters into any listing agreement for the Property with a subsequent broker, Broker's commission rights are enforceable only as a cooperating subagent of the new listing broker, EXCEPT under sales contracts or exchange contracts or lease with option to purchase contracts entered into prior to the Expiration Date or any extension thereof, wherein Broker shall be entitled to a commission at the same rate of commission specified herein.

Seller acknowledges that Broker is a member of ______GAMLS and FMLS______ ("MLS"), and Broker is bound to file this listing with said MLS according to the rules of the MLS service. Seller hereby acknowledges that any and all Multiple Listing Services involved are neither a party to this agreement, nor responsible for errors or omissions on the part of Seller or of Broker.

3 of 6

Form 151, *Exclusive Right to Sell Listing Agreement*

 Initials: ________ ________ ________ ________

R10312012

Item 4: Other Relationships

This section of the listing agreement begins by explaining to the seller-client that the broker/agent may cooperate with other brokers to locate perspective buyers for the listed property and may at the listing broker's discretion share the commission paid by the seller with the other brokers who may or may not represent the buyers with whom they are working.

The next part of this section concerns the broker's right to earn a commission from the seller after the listing agreement has expired, under the following conditions:

1. At the time of the listing expiration date, the agent presents the seller with a written list of names of individuals to whom the agent marketed the listed property.
2. Next, if within a specific number of days—as inserted into the blank space in this section—from the listing contract's expiration date, the seller without the services of a broker makes a direct sale of the property to one of the persons on this list, the seller agrees to pay the broker a commission at the same rate stipulated in the expired agreement.
3. If the seller subsequently enters into a listing agreement with another broker during this identified time period, the former broker's commission rights are only enforceable as a subagent of the new listing broker.

IN PRACTICE The commission right described here is sometimes referred to as a **"safety" or "protection" clause** for a broker's compensation. The clause and the time period for its enforcement will not automatically be a part of the listing engagement; rather, its insertion in the engagement between the broker and the seller is a matter of negotiation between the parties. In our listing agreement scenario, agent Eric does negotiate a 60-day period after the listing's expiration date for this commission protection or safety clause.

In the final part of this section, Top Floor Realty informs the sellers that the brokerage firm belongs to both Georgia MLS and First MLS and that the seller's home will be listed in both services. Neither of these services is a party to brokerage engagements or holds responsibility for any errors of information supplied by sellers and submitted by brokers.

FIGURE 25.6: Marketing

5. MARKETING

Broker is hereby authorized by Seller to advertise and market the Property for sale during this agreement or any extension hereof, to place Broker's "FOR SALE" sign on the Property, to remove all other "FOR SALE" signs and lockboxes, if any, to place a lockbox with house key on the Property, and to photograph the Property and use such photographs in promoting the sale. Seller agrees to refer all inquiries concerning the sale of the Property to Broker during the term of this agreement. Seller further agrees to consider Broker's recommendations to enable Broker to show the Property to its best advantage, to allow Broker to show it at all reasonable hours and otherwise cooperate with Broker. NOTICE: Whether or not a lockbox is used as a tool to market the Property, Broker and MLS recommend that valuables such as checks, money, and jewelry be removed by Seller to a secured place during the term of this listing. Seller acknowledges that isolated instances of burglaries of homes on which lockboxes have been placed and for which the lockbox has been alleged to have been used to access the home have been reported. Lockboxes should not be placed where they can be easily removed, such as on door handles that can be unscrewed from the outside.

Seller shall cooperate with Broker in marketing and showing the Property by making the Property available during reasonable times for viewing, and by being available during reasonable times to receive time sensitive communications from Broker. Seller and Broker shall abide by all federal, state and local laws, and shall assist one another in reporting any suspicious or unlawful activity such as mortgage fraud to appropriate law enforcement, mortgage company and title company personnel. The undersigned Seller and Broker, by their respective signatures, herein agree they will not discriminate against any prospective buyer because of race, color, sex, religion, handicap, familial status, or national origin of such person in accordance with applicable federal and state laws.

Seller agrees that members of MLS and other brokers may act in association with Broker in procuring or attempting to procure a buyer, and authorizes Broker to distribute listing and sales information to other members of MLS and the public. Seller agrees Broker is authorized to utilize any or all media and current technology available to advertise and market the Property for sale by providing information directly to the public, and further agrees to the publication of sales price information to all persons authorized to purchase such information.

Item 5. Marketing

In this section, the seller authorizes the broker to advertise and generally market the property for sale; this process may include placing For Sale signs on the property; taking photographs for flyers, brochures, and website presentations; and placing lockboxes with the house keys on the property. The seller is cautioned as to safety issues in relation to property showings and protection of valuables and the placement of lockboxes in secure places to minimize potential home intrusions. Additionally, the seller promises to consider the broker's advice on ways and times to show the property to its best advantage and to refer all inquiries about the sale to the broker.

IN PRACTICE The clients, Sean and Bernadette Joyce, agree to use a lockbox for showings of their home; however, the lockbox will not be displayed on the outside of the home. The sellers require a three-hour advance notice for any showing of the home and will place the lockbox on the porch near the front door after such notice.

This section acknowledges that the seller gives approval for the broker to use MLS organizations as a means to secure prospective buyers for the property; furthermore, the broker may utilize all media and current technology in advertising the property and in providing sales price information to the public.

IN PRACTICE The Joyces do not want the address of their home displayed on any general internet advertising by their broker regarding the offering for sale of the property. Additionally, they do not want third parties on internet sites to have the ability to comment on or offer reviews of their home, nor do they want hyperlinks to such information displayed on a broker's internet website.

The broker, licensee affiliates, and the seller also promise to abide by all federal, state, and local laws in the marketing of the property, and in accordance with fair housing regulations, not to discriminate against prospective buyers. Moreover, all parties promise to report suspicious or unlawful activities in the transactional process, such as mortgage or title fraud, to appropriate sources.

FIGURE 25.7: Property Disclosures

6. PROPERTY DISCLOSURES
Seller warrants and represents that the information with respect to the Property as set out in this agreement is true and correct and that Seller has fully revealed to Broker all pertinent information with respect to the Property, including defects therein, if any, and that Broker is authorized to convey all such information to prospective buyers. Seller agrees to provide Broker with a completed Seller's Property Condition Report. Seller acknowledges that Broker intends to rely upon the accuracy of all information furnished by Seller, and Seller agrees to indemnify and hold harmless broker and MLS, their agents and employees, from any and against all loss, costs, damages, or liabilities of any nature whatsoever resulting from Seller's withholding any information from Broker or, as a result of Seller's giving any information which is incorrect to Broker, or arising out of, directly or indirectly, Seller's failure to make such disclosures of any and all physical characteristics of the Property that may adversely affect the value of the Property, including but not limited to lead-based paint, radon gas, asbestos, water problems and/or structural defects. All defects in the Property which shall adversely affect its value shall be disclosed by the Seller in writing and shall be attached hereto and made a part of this Agreement by reference.

Seller acknowledges that Seller has received from Broker an information pamphlet disclosing the dangers of lead-based paint and Broker has informed Seller of the requirements for disclosure of lead-based paint in all homes built before 1978, as required under The Residential Lead-Based Paint Hazard Reduction Act of 1992, 42 U.S.C. §4851-4856 (the "Act"). Seller further agrees to make all such disclosures as required under the Act to all potential buyers of Seller's Property.

4 of 6

Form 151, *Exclusive Right to Sell Listing Agreement*
 Initials: ________ ________ ________ ________
R10312012

Item 6. Property Disclosures

Here the sellers warrant that all information provided for their home, including adverse property defects is, to the best of their knowledge, true and accurate. The sellers authorize the listing broker to communicate all such information to prospective buyers and their real estate agents. This information will typically be provided to the listing agent in the form of a **seller's property condition disclosure.** The sellers also will indemnify (hold harmless) the broker, affiliated licensees, the MLS, or any other parties from any liability for communication information that was incorrectly given from the seller to the broker. If a property structure was constructed before 1978, the seller acknowledges in this section that the listing agent has provided the seller an informational pamphlet regarding the dangers of lead-based paint and the necessary disclosure required from the homeowners.

IN PRACTICE Listing agent Eric Cambridge gives the sellers a property disclosure form to complete before the property listing will appear in the two multiple listing services on March 18. Eric asks the Joyces to be as thorough as possible in filling out the form, because he will rely on the document to communicate accurate property information to prospective buyers and their agents.

Because the sellers' home was built before 1978, he asks the clients if they have knowledge of any lead-based paint or hazards in their home and if they have any reports or records of such information. The Joyces do not have such information, and Eric gives them a statement to initial and sign, verifying their response.

FIGURE 25.8: Hold Harmless

7. HOLD HARMLESS

As to any matters not covered by Broker's duties in this agreement, Broker is not an expert and Seller is encouraged and advised to seek expert advice and to retain appropriate experts such as environmental engineers, termite inspectors, engineers, surveyors, plumbers, contractors, property inspectors, lawyers, accountants and the like, as Seller may deem appropriate. Seller expressly acknowledge that Broker is not an expert in matters relating to the condition or construction of the Property and the surrounding neighborhood, including, but not limited to, any structural, safety, title, environmental, financial, tax, legal or health concerns, or issues regarding the surrounding community, future or current real estate development, mortgage fraud or municipal services offered to local residents, and has given no advice nor made any representations in regard thereto upon which Seller has relied. Seller releases any Broker and any affiliated agent and employee from any cost, expense or liability that may result from Seller's reliance on any perceived advice given with respect to the foregoing. If liability is found to exist under the standard of care or conduct required of Broker or its affiliated licensee, their liability is limited to the amount of commission actually received in this particular transaction, less any amount paid to a cooperating broker, if any. If no commission is paid, Broker's liability shall be limited to one hundred US dollars (US$100.00).

Seller shall indemnify, hold harmless and defend Broker from and against any and all claims, demands, causes of action, liabilities, losses, costs, damages and expenses (including reasonable attorneys' fees and expenses and court costs incurred in defending any such claim or in enforcing this indemnity) that may be incurred by Broker arising out of or in connection with the acts or omissions of Seller and Seller's agents, representatives, contractors and consultants, or any of them, including but not limited to claims arising out of or in connection with personal injury or death of persons, loss, destruction or damage to property, the holding of any funds by anyone other than Broker, or any claim by third parties arising out of this agreement. Seller warrants and represents that Seller is not a party to any other listing agreement, and that if Seller owes a real estate commission to any other real estate licensee claiming under any other agreement, said commission shall be in addition to, not in lieu of, Seller's obligations under this agreement.

Item 7. Hold Harmless

Here, the listing contract informs the sellers that outside of duties specifically identified in this brokerage engagement, the broker and any affiliated licensees hold no professional expertise in other areas, and that the sellers should not rely on their agent's advice on issues relating to these areas. Rather, the clients are encouraged to seek independent expert advice regarding these matters. The sellers will also acknowledge in this section that they are releasing the broker and affiliated licensees from any liability over the sellers' claims of reliance on the agent's advice in these areas.

If the agent is found liable in performance or duties and standard care stipulated in the brokerage engagement, the sellers agree that this liability for the agent shall not exceed the amount of commission actually received in the particular transaction; absent any commission paid to the broker, the agent's liability is limited to $100.

As for claims against the listing agent for communicating false or inaccurate information given to them by the client, the sellers not only hold the agent harmless but also will incur the costs of defending the agent against such claims. This section concludes with the sellers warranting that they are not a party to any other current listing agreement and that any commissions owed by the sellers in previous engagements will not affect the sellers' obligation of compensation under this agreement.

FIGURE 25.9: Miscellaneous

8. **MISCELLANEOUS**

a) The provisions of this agreement shall extend to and be binding on the respective heirs, executors, administrators and successors of each party hereto;
b) If any provision of this agreement is determined by a court of competent jurisdiction to be invalid or unenforceable, the remainder of this agreement shall nonetheless remain in full force and effect;
c) This agreement, including any exhibits attached hereto, contain the entire agreement between the parties pertaining to the subject matter hereof and fully supersede all prior written or oral agreements and understandings between the parties pertaining to such subject matter;
d) This agreement shall be governed by and interpreted under the laws of the State of Georgia;
e) Time is of the essence of this agreement;
f) Any indemnity, hold harmless or obligation to pay commission contained herein shall survive the termination of this agreement;
g) Any notice, request or other communication required or permitted to be given hereunder shall be in writing and shall be delivered by hand or overnight courier (such as United Parcel Service or Federal Express), sent by facsimile, sent by electronic mail ("email") or mailed by United States registered or certified mail, return receipt requested, postage prepaid and addressed to each party at its address as set forth below. Any such notice shall be considered given on the date of such hand or courier delivery, confirmed facsimile transmission, deposit with such overnight courier for next business day delivery, or deposit in the United States mail, but the time period (if any is provided herein) in which to respond to such notice shall commence on the date of hand or overnight courier delivery or on the date received following deposit in the United States mail as provided above. Rejection or other refusal to accept or inability to deliver because of changed address of which no notice was given shall be deemed to be receipt of the notice. By giving at least five (5) banking days' prior written notice thereof, any party may from time to time and at any time change its mailing address hereunder. The parties' respective mailing and email addresses for notice purposes are indicated after the parties' signatures below. Telephone numbers are given for convenience of reference only. Notice by telephone shall not be effective; and
h) This document and any amendments thereto, may be executed in multiple counterparts by the parties, and such counterparts shall have the same legal enforceability and binding effect as though it were signed by all parties in original form.

5 of 6

Form 151, *Exclusive Right to Sell Listing Agreement*
 Initials: _________ _________ _________ _________
R10312012

Item 8. Miscellaneous

Here, a series of general matters of information pursuant to this listing brokerage engagement are set forth. Among these is the seller's acknowledgment of the following:

- This listing agreement serves as the sole and entire engagement between the broker and the client in this particular matter.
- The terms of the agreement will bind any heirs of the parties, as well as any executors and administrators of related probated documents.
- The agreement may be signed and executed in multiple counterparts and will be governed and interpreted by the state of Georgia.
- Any indemnity or commission promised will survive termination of the agreement.
- Time is of the essence: punctual performance will be recognized by the parties as an essential element of the contract.

Communications between the parties will be in writing and the acceptable methods of communication identified in the contract are as follows: by hand or overnight courier; by facsimile (fax); by electronic mail (e-mail); and by U.S. mail postage prepaid and addressed as set forth on the signature page of agreement. Such notices between the parties are considered "given" on the date of hand or courier delivery; deposited as such for next business day delivery; confirmed fax transmission; or deposited in the U.S. mail.

FIGURE 25.10: Special Stipulations

h) This document and any amendments thereto, may be executed in multiple counterparts by the parties, and such counterparts shall have the same legal enforceability and binding effect as though it were signed by all parties in original form.

Special Stipulations:

1.Top Floor Realty Inc. may not represent Bernadette and Sean Joyce as a duel agent in the sale of the client's home, but may represent the parties as a designated agent in the selling transaction.

2.Appointments to show property shall be made with seller at least 3 hours in advance. Seller will place lockbox with keys on porch next to front door when notice of showing is given

3.Internet marketing of the home shall not include the property's address, nor shall internet advertising allow third parties to comment on,offer reviews of, or display hyperlinks to such information on a broker's internet website.

4.Top Floor Realty does not offer Sub Agency

☐ Substantive provisions continued on additional page.

IN WITNESS WHEREOF, the parties have duly executed this agreement.

All Names should be both signed and printed.

Broker:

Top Floor Realty,Inc / TFR03
Name of Brokerage Firm / Broker Code

404 222-1111 / 404 222-4444
Brokerage Phone Number / Brokerage Fax Number

➢ ____________________

Eric Cambridge
Agent Printed Name

770 102-6543 / 404 222-4444
Agent Phone Number / Agent Fax Number

ericcom@comcast.net
Agent Email Address

Required License Number(s):

H-1999 / 987654
Broker's License Number / Agent's License Number

Seller:

➢ ____________________

Bernadette Joyce
Seller Printed Name

➢ ____________________

Sean Joyce
Seller Printed Name

678-4321 / 678 888-6666
Seller Phone Number / Seller Fax Number

s/b joyce@gmail.com
Seller Email Address

1103 Franklin Avenue
Seller Address

Atlanta GA 33333
Seller City State Zip

Form 151, *Exclusive Right to Sell Listing Agreement*

 Initials: 

R10312012

Special Stipulation

Under this section, the parties may insert conditional items pursuant to this engagement that are not preprinted in the contract form or include additional language that may alter, negate, or supersede existing preprinted items in the contract.

With regard to this contract narrative, three items are included as special stipulations:

- The sellers' rejection of the dual agency consent for their broker
- Property showing instructions regarding lockbox keys
- Limitations on the property's internet advertising

As a requirement noted in the Important Broker Disclosure section at beginning of contract, the fourth item noted in Special Stipulations discloses that Top Floor Realty does not offer subagency.

Signatures

The exclusive right-to-sell listing agreement concludes with the printed names and signatures of the parties in the brokerage engagement, including the required identification references, the legally appropriate addresses as referenced in item 8 of the agreement, and telephone numbers, as so indicated.

Under the Broker heading, the brokerage company name will be first identified. Next, the agent identified may be either the qualifying broker of the company or more typically the broker's licensee affiliate who is working directly with the seller-client. The sellers in the brokerage engagement are on the right-hand side of this page.

All paras p.508-522 put together for final completed contract

FIGURE 25.11: Completed Exclusive Right-to-Sell Listing Agreement

Exclusive Right to Sell Listing Agreement

Date: March 15, 20xx

IMPORTANT BROKER DISCLOSURES

Prior to entering into this agreement with you, Georgia law requires that the undersigned Broker make certain disclosures to you, as follows:

(1) Advise you of the types of brokerage relationships available through Broker and Broker's office policy. These are set forth below.
(2) Advise you of any other brokerage relationships held by Broker which would conflict with any interest of yours actually known to Broker. While not legally considered to be a conflict, Broker and Broker's affiliated licensees represent other Sellers and Buyers regarding sales of property which may be in direct competition with the sale of your property.
(3) Advise you as to Broker's compensation and whether Broker will share such compensation with other brokers who may represent other parties to the transaction. Broker's compensation and sharing arrangements are set out below.
(4) Advise you of Broker's obligation to keep certain information confidential.

Broker as limited agent.
When you sign this agreement, the Broker's (and the Broker's affiliated licensees') relationship to you will be as an independent contractor and a limited agent and, as provided below, possibly a dual agent. "Limited agent" means that the Broker may, acting under the authority of this agreement, solicit offers to purchase, sell, lease, or exchange the property subject to this agreement without being subject to your control, except as to the result of the work. Broker, as a limited agent, shall not be deemed to have a fiduciary relationship or fiduciary obligation with you (or any party), except as may be expressly provided otherwise by law, nor shall Broker or Broker's affiliated licensees be considered your employees.

Broker will make disclosures to prospective Buyers about your Property in reliance on information you provide, and based on Broker's actual knowledge. Your obligation to disclose material adverse facts about the Property, particularly latent or hidden defects, is not changed by this agreement.
Broker shall treat all prospective buyers honestly and shall not knowingly give them false information. Broker shall keep confidential any information you expressly ask Broker to keep confidential unless specifically prohibited by law. Broker shall timely disclose to prospective buyers with whom Broker is working all material adverse facts pertaining to the physical condition of the Property, including, but not limited to, material defects in the Property, environmental contamination, and facts required by statute or regulation to be disclosed which are actually known by Broker, particularly if such defects could not be discovered by a reasonably diligent inspection of the Property by the buyer. Broker shall not be liable to a buyer for providing false information if the false information was provided to Broker by you and Broker did not have actual knowledge that the information was false. Nothing in this paragraph shall limit any of your obligations under any applicable law to disclose to prospective buyers all material adverse facts actually known by you pertaining to the physical condition of the Property, nor shall it limit the obligation of prospective buyers to inspect the physical condition of the Property. Georgia law provides that no cause of action shall arise on behalf of any person against Broker for revealing information in compliance with this paragraph.

Broker may provide assistance to prospective buyers without violating any duties to you.
Under Georgia law, Broker may provide assistance to buyers by performing such ministerial acts as preparing offers and presenting them to you; locating lenders, inspectors, attorneys, insurance agents, surveyors, schools, shopping facilities, places of worship, and all such other like or similar services; discussing other listed and sold properties. Performing such ministerial acts shall not be construed in such a manner as to violate this agreement, nor shall performing such ministerial acts for a buyer be construed in such a manner as to form a brokerage engagement with a buyer.

Initials: ________ ________ ________ ________

FIGURE 25.11: Completed Exclusive Right-to-Sell Listing Agreement (continued)

Broker may show alternative properties to buyers and provide information.
Under Georgia law, Broker does not breach any duty or obligation to you by showing alternative properties to prospective buyers. Broker may also provide information on other properties which may be in competition with your property.

Dual Agency is permitted by Georgia law if both buyer and seller consent in writing.
Dual Agency is permitted by Georgia law if both client parties consent. The following disclosures are made so that you will have full disclosure in choosing whether to give your consent and allow dual agency. **YOU DO NOT HAVE TO CONSENT TO DUAL AGENCY.** As a dual agent, Broker, will represent you in selling your Property and also represent a buyer with whom Broker has a brokerage engagement. In serving as a dual agent, Broker represents a buyer and seller whose interests are or at times could be different or even adverse. When Broker serves as dual agent, both you and the buyer will be clients of Broker. Broker, as a dual agent, may not disclose to you or the other client information made confidential by request or instructions from you or the other client, except information allowed or required to be disclosed by law. When dual agency exists, Georgia law provides that Broker may assign one affiliated licensee to you and another to buyer; this is known as Designated Agency. In that case, those licensees may not disclose, except to Broker, information made confidential by request or instructions of the client the licensee is representing, except information allowed or required to be disclosed under Georgia law. If Broker or Broker's affiliated licensees have a material relationship with the other client other than that incidental to the transactions, a disclosure of the nature of such a relationship must be provided to you. A material relationship shall mean any actually known personal, familial, or business relationship between Broker or Broker's affiliated licensees and a client which would impair the ability of Broker or the affiliated licensees to exercise fair and independent judgment relative to another client. The other party whom Broker may represent in the event of dual agency may or may not be identified at the time you enter into this agreement. If a party is not identified at such time, when such party is identified, if it is a party with whom either Broker or Broker's affiliated licensees has a material relationship, Broker shall promptly provide to you a disclosure of the nature of such relationship.

UNLESS EXPRESSLY SET FORTH TO THE CONTRARY IN THE SPECIAL STIPULATIONS BELOW, BROKER'S OFFICE BROKERAGE RELATIONSHIP POLICY IS TO PROVIDE SELLER AND LANDLORD AGENCY; BUYER AND TENANT AGENCY; DESIGNATED AGENCY; DUAL AGENCY; SUBAGENCY; OR TO ACT AS A TRANSACTION BROKER; AND BY SIGNING THIS AGREEMENT SELLER EVIDENCES SELLER'S CONSENT TO BROKER ACTING AS A DUAL AGENT AND DESIGNATED AGENT.

EXCLUSIVE RIGHT TO SELL LISTING AGREEMENT

NOTICE TO SELLER: By signing this agreement, you acknowledge that you have read and understand all the above disclosures, which are incorporated herein by this reference, and have been advised of all of the foregoing prior to voluntarily entering into this agreement.

This **Exclusive Right to Sell Listing Agreement** is entered into on March 15, 20xx by and between Bernadette Joyce and Sean Joyce (the "Seller") and Top Floor Realty,Inc (the "Broker").

1. TERM
In consideration of the undersigned Broker's agreement to act as a limited agent for and on behalf of the undersigned Seller to use Broker's efforts to sell the Property within the terms of this agreement, the undersigned Seller does hereby authorize and grant to Broker the exclusive right and power from March 18, 20xx, until 12 o'clock midnight on August 12, 20xx (hereinafter referred to as the "Expiration Date"), to sell or exchange the Property described below at a price of US$ 409,500, or at such price or terms to which Seller may consent. Should a contract for the purchase of the Property be procured under the term of this agreement but fail to close until after the Expiration Date, this agreement shall automatically be extended through and including the date of closing, or through and including the date upon which the contract was terminated, as applicable.

Form 151, *Exclusive Right to Sell Listing Agreement*
 Initials: ________ ________ ________ ________
R10312012

FIGURE 25.11: Completed Exclusive Right-to-Sell Listing Agreement (continued)

2. PROPERTY
The property to be offered for sale is located in Bellville County, Georgia, and is known as 1103 Franklin Avenue (the "Property"), and being more particularly described as all that tract or parcel of land lying and being in Land Lot 113 of the 9th District, 33rd Section, Bellville County, Georgia, being Lot 51, Block 11, Phase n/a of ______ Subdivision, as more particularly set out in Plat Book 343, Page 421, of the official records of Bellville County, Georgia, Tax ID # 9-22-111B or, in the alternative, as set out on an Exhibit attached hereto and made a part hereof by this reference. Seller warrants that Seller has title to the Property described herein and has full authority to enter into this agreement

3. BROKER COMPENSATION
Seller agrees to pay to Broker a sales commission of [check one] ☒ six % of the sales price, **or** ☐ US$ n/a in the event that during the term of this agreement:

3.1. Broker (or any other licensee) procures a person ready, willing and able to purchase the Property for a price not less than US$ 409,500 ; or

3.2. Seller enters into an enforceable contract for the sale or exchange of the Property with any buyer (without an exclusion set out in this agreement as to any buyer), whether by or through the efforts of Broker or any other person, including Seller.

IT IS UNDERSTOOD AND AGREED BY SELLER THAT THIS IS AN EXCLUSIVE RIGHT TO SELL AND THAT EVEN IF SELLER, DURING THE TERM OF THIS AGREEMENT, OR ANY EXTENSION HEREOF, SELLS THE PROPERTY, BROKER SHALL BE ENTITLED TO A COMMISSION AT THE RATE SPECIFIED HEREIN.

Seller acknowledges and agrees that Broker is providing a valuable service to Seller by marketing the Property and may incur significant costs and expenses in doing so. In order to partially compensate Broker for Broker's time in the event no commission is paid hereunder, Seller has paid to Broker a retainer fee in the amount of US$ n/a , which fee shall be deposited into Broker's trust account. This fee shall be refundable to Seller only if Broker is paid the full commission as provided above. Upon the termination or expiration of this Agreement or the closing of the Property, Broker shall be authorized to transfer the retainer fee to Broker's general account. In the event the Property is sold and a commission is due to Broker, Seller shall at closing receive a credit against the commission due in the amount of the retainer fee actually paid.

Notwithstanding the payment of a retainer fee as provided above, Seller shall reimburse Broker or Broker's affiliated licensees for their costs and expenses incurred in marketing the Property (including, but not limited to, printing costs, advertising fees, mileage reimbursements and multiple listing fees) if Seller defaults hereunder. The right to collect reimbursement for these costs and expenses shall be in addition to, not in lieu of, any other claim or cause of action Broker may have hereunder, except that these costs and expenses may be offset against the commission paid to Broker, if any.

4. OTHER RELATIONSHIPS
Seller acknowledges and agrees that Broker may cooperate with another broker or compensate another broker, and that any commission hereunder may be disbursed or allocated in the sole discretion of Broker and may be allocated to other brokers who may or may not represent other parties to the transaction. The commissions payable for the sale, lease or management of property are not set in any manner other than between Broker and Seller. Broker agrees to use his or her best efforts to procure a person ready, willing and able to purchase the Property at the price and on the terms specified herein. Should Seller contract WITHOUT the services of Broker to make a direct sale, exchange, or lease with option to purchase the Property within sixty days after the Expiration Date, or any extension thereof, to a buyer to whom the Property was offered during the term of this agreement, or any extension hereof, by Broker, by Seller, or anyone else, Seller agrees to pay Broker a commission at the same rate of commission as specified herein. In this regard, Broker shall furnish Seller prior to the Expiration Date of this agreement or any extension hereof, a written list of names of all persons to whom the Property was offered, and such list shall be conclusive as to any commission rights due for any offerings made by Broker, or by persons authorized by Broker. It is agreed and understood that if and when Seller enters into any listing agreement for the Property with a subsequent broker, Broker's commission rights are enforceable only as a cooperating subagent of the new listing broker, EXCEPT under sales contracts or exchange contracts or lease

Form 151, *Exclusive Right to Sell Listing Agreement*
 Initials: ________ ________ ________ ________
R10312012

FIGURE 25.11: Completed Exclusive Right-to-Sell Listing Agreement (continued)

with option to purchase contracts entered into prior to the Expiration Date or any extension thereof, wherein Broker shall be entitled to a commission at the same rate of commission specified herein.

Seller acknowledges that Broker is a member of ______GAMLS and FMLS______ ("MLS"), and Broker is bound to file this listing with said MLS according to the rules of the MLS service. Seller hereby acknowledges that any and all Multiple Listing Services involved are neither a party to this agreement, nor responsible for errors or omissions on the part of Seller or of Broker.

5. MARKETING

Broker is hereby authorized by Seller to advertise and market the Property for sale during this agreement or any extension hereof, to place Broker's "FOR SALE" sign on the Property, to remove all other "FOR SALE" signs and lockboxes, if any, to place a lockbox with house key on the Property, and to photograph the Property and use such photographs in promoting the sale. Seller agrees to refer all inquiries concerning the sale of the Property to Broker during the term of this agreement. Seller further agrees to consider Broker's recommendations to enable Broker to show the Property to its best advantage, to allow Broker to show it at all reasonable hours and otherwise cooperate with Broker. NOTICE: Whether or not a lockbox is used as a tool to market the Property, Broker and MLS recommend that valuables such as checks, money, and jewelry be removed by Seller to a secured place during the term of this listing. Seller acknowledges that isolated instances of burglaries of homes on which lockboxes have been placed and for which the lockbox has been alleged to have been used to access the home have been reported. Lockboxes should not be placed where they can be easily removed, such as on door handles that can be unscrewed from the outside.

Seller shall cooperate with Broker in marketing and showing the Property by making the Property available during reasonable times for viewing, and by being available during reasonable times to receive time sensitive communications from Broker. Seller and Broker shall abide by all federal, state and local laws, and shall assist one another in reporting any suspicious or unlawful activity such as mortgage fraud to appropriate law enforcement, mortgage company and title company personnel. The undersigned Seller and Broker, by their respective signatures, herein agree they will not discriminate against any prospective buyer because of race, color, sex, religion, handicap, familial status, or national origin of such person in accordance with applicable federal and state laws.

Seller agrees that members of MLS and other brokers may act in association with Broker in procuring or attempting to procure a buyer, and authorizes Broker to distribute listing and sales information to other members of MLS and the public. Seller agrees Broker is authorized to utilize any or all media and current technology available to advertise and market the Property for sale by providing information directly to the public, and further agrees to the publication of sales price information to all persons authorized to purchase such information.

6. PROPERTY DISCLOSURES

Seller warrants and represents that the information with respect to the Property as set out in this agreement is true and correct and that Seller has fully revealed to Broker all pertinent information with respect to the Property, including defects therein, if any, and that Broker is authorized to convey all such information to prospective buyers. Seller agrees to provide Broker with a completed Seller's Property Condition Report. Seller acknowledges that Broker intends to rely upon the accuracy of all information furnished by Seller, and Seller agrees to indemnify and hold harmless broker and MLS, their agents and employees, from any and against all loss, costs, damages, or liabilities of any nature whatsoever resulting from Seller's withholding any information from Broker or, as a result of Seller's giving any information which is incorrect to Broker, or arising out of, directly or indirectly, Seller's failure to make such disclosures of any and all physical characteristics of the Property that may adversely affect the value of the Property, including but not limited to lead-based paint, radon gas, asbestos, water problems and/or structural defects. All defects in the Property which shall adversely affect its value shall be disclosed by the Seller in writing and shall be attached hereto and made a part of this Agreement by reference.

Seller acknowledges that Seller has received from Broker an information pamphlet disclosing the dangers of lead-based paint and Broker has informed Seller of the requirements for disclosure of lead-based paint in all homes built before 1978, as required under The Residential Lead-Based Paint Hazard Reduction Act of 1992, 42 U.S.C. §4851-4856 (the "Act"). Seller further agrees to make all such disclosures as required under the Act to all potential buyers of Seller's Property.

 Initials: ________ ________ ________ ________

FIGURE 25.11: Completed Exclusive Right-to-Sell Listing Agreement (continued)

7. HOLD HARMLESS

As to any matters not covered by Broker's duties in this agreement, Broker is not an expert and Seller is encouraged and advised to seek expert advice and to retain appropriate experts such as environmental engineers, termite inspectors, engineers, surveyors, plumbers, contractors, property inspectors, lawyers, accountants and the like, as Seller may deem appropriate. Seller expressly acknowledge that Broker is not an expert in matters relating to the condition or construction of the Property and the surrounding neighborhood, including, but not limited to, any structural, safety, title, environmental, financial, tax, legal or health concerns, or issues regarding the surrounding community, future or current real estate development, mortgage fraud or municipal services offered to local residents, and has given no advice nor made any representations in regard thereto upon which Seller has relied. Seller releases any Broker and any affiliated agent and employee from any cost, expense or liability that may result from Seller's reliance on any perceived advice given with respect to the foregoing. If liability is found to exist under the standard of care or conduct required of Broker or its affiliated licensee, their liability is limited to the amount of commission actually received in this particular transaction, less any amount paid to a cooperating broker, if any. If no commission is paid, Broker's liability shall be limited to one hundred US dollars (US$100.00).

Seller shall indemnify, hold harmless and defend Broker from and against any and all claims, demands, causes of action, liabilities, losses, costs, damages and expenses (including reasonable attorneys' fees and expenses and court costs incurred in defending any such claim or in enforcing this indemnity) that may be incurred by Broker arising out of or in connection with the acts or omissions of Seller and Seller's agents, representatives, contractors and consultants, or any of them, including but not limited to claims arising out of or in connection with personal injury or death of persons, loss, destruction or damage to property, the holding of any funds by anyone other than Broker, or any claim by third parties arising out of this agreement. Seller warrants and represents that Seller is not a party to any other listing agreement, and that if Seller owes a real estate commission to any other real estate licensee claiming under any other agreement, said commission shall be in addition to, not in lieu of, Seller's obligations under this agreement.

8. MISCELLANEOUS

a) The provisions of this agreement shall extend to and be binding on the respective heirs, executors, administrators and successors of each party hereto;
b) If any provision of this agreement is determined by a court of competent jurisdiction to be invalid or unenforceable, the remainder of this agreement shall nonetheless remain in full force and effect;
c) This agreement, including any exhibits attached hereto, contain the entire agreement between the parties pertaining to the subject matter hereof and fully supersede all prior written or oral agreements and understandings between the parties pertaining to such subject matter;
d) This agreement shall be governed by and interpreted under the laws of the State of Georgia;
e) Time is of the essence of this agreement;
f) Any indemnity, hold harmless or obligation to pay commission contained herein shall survive the termination of this agreement;
g) Any notice, request or other communication required or permitted to be given hereunder shall be in writing and shall be delivered by hand or overnight courier (such as United Parcel Service or Federal Express), sent by facsimile, sent by electronic mail ("email") or mailed by United States registered or certified mail, return receipt requested, postage prepaid and addressed to each party at its address as set forth below. Any such notice shall be considered given on the date of such hand or courier delivery, confirmed facsimile transmission, deposit with such overnight courier for next business day delivery, or deposit in the United States mail, but the time period (if any is provided herein) in which to respond to such notice shall commence on the date of hand or overnight courier delivery or on the date received following deposit in the United States mail as provided above. Rejection or other refusal to accept or inability to deliver because of changed address of which no notice was given shall be deemed to be receipt of the notice. By giving at least five (5) banking days' prior written notice thereof, any party may from time to time and at any time change its mailing address hereunder. The parties' respective mailing and email addresses for notice purposes are indicated after the parties' signatures below. Telephone numbers are given for convenience of reference only. Notice by telephone shall not be effective; and

Form 151, *Exclusive Right to Sell Listing Agreement*
 Initials: ________ ________ ________ ________
R10312012

FIGURE 25.11: Completed Exclusive Right-to-Sell Listing Agreement (continued)

h) This document and any amendments thereto, may be executed in multiple counterparts by the parties, and such counterparts shall have the same legal enforceability and binding effect as though it were signed by all parties in original form.

Special Stipulations:

1.Top Floor Realty Inc. may not represent Bernadette and Sean Joyce as a duel agent in the sale of the client's home, but may represent the parties as a designated agent in the selling transaction.

2.Appointments to show property shall be made with seller at least 3 hours in advance. Seller will place lockbox with keys on porch next to front door when notice of showing is given

3.Internet marketing of the home shall not include the property's address, nor shall internet advertising allow third parties to comment on,offer reviews of, or display hyperlinks to such information on a broker's internet website.

4.Top Floor Realty does not offer Sub Agency

☐ Substantive provisions continued on additional page.

IN WITNESS WHEREOF, the parties have duly executed this agreement.

All Names should be both signed and printed.

Broker:

Top Floor Realty,Inc / TFR03
Name of Brokerage Firm / Broker Code

404 222-1111 / 404 222-4444
Brokerage Phone Number / Brokerage Fax Number

➢ ______________________

Eric Cambridge
Agent Printed Name

770 102-6543 / 404 222-4444
Agent Phone Number / Agent Fax Number

ericcom@comcast.net
Agent Email Address

Required License Number(s):

H-1999 / 987654
Broker's License Number / Agent's License Number

Seller:

➢ ______________________

Bernadette Joyce
Seller Printed Name

➢ ______________________

Sean Joyce
Seller Printed Name

678-4321 / 678 888-6666
Seller Phone Number / Seller Fax Number

s/b joyce@gmail.com
Seller Email Address

1103 Franklin Avenue
Seller Address

Atlanta GA 33333
Seller City / State / Zip

 Initials: ________ ________ ________ ________

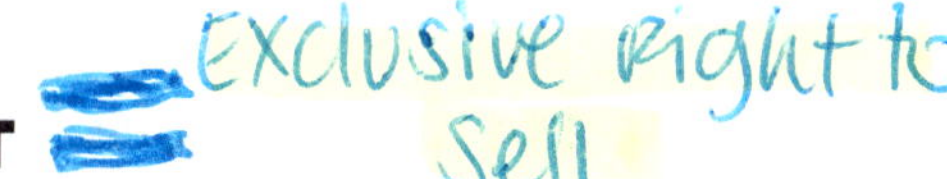

THE EXCLUSIVE BUYER BROKERAGE AGREEMENT

FIGURE 25.12: Important Broker Disclosures

Exclusive Buyer Brokerage Agreement

Date: March 20, 20xx

IMPORTANT BROKER DISCLOSURES

Prior to entering into this agreement with you, Georgia law requires that the undersigned Broker make certain disclosures to you, as follows:

(1) Advise you of the types of brokerage relationships available through Broker and Broker's office policy. These are set forth below.
(2) Advise you of any other brokerage relationships held by Broker which would conflict with any interest of yours actually known to Broker. While not legally considered to be a conflict, Broker and Broker's affiliated licensees represent other Sellers and Buyers regarding sales of property which may be in direct competition with the purchase of a specific property by you.
(3) Advise you as to Broker's compensation and whether Broker will share such compensation with other brokers who may represent other parties to the transaction. Broker's compensation and sharing arrangements are set out below.
(4) Advise you of Broker's obligation to keep certain information confidential.

Broker as limited agent.
When you sign this agreement, the Broker's (and the Broker's affiliated licensees') relationship to you will be as a limited agent and, as provided below, possibly a dual agent. "Limited agent" means that the Broker will, acting under the authority of this agreement, solicit offers to purchase, sell, lease, or exchange the property subject to this agreement without being subject to your control, except as to the result of the work. Broker, as a limited agent, shall not be deemed to have a fiduciary relationship or fiduciary obligation with you (or any party), except as may be expressly provided otherwise by law, nor shall Broker or Broker's affiliated licensees be considered your employees.

Broker may make disclosures to prospective sellers in reliance on information you provide, and based on Broker's actual knowledge, unless you expressly make such information confidential. Regardless, Broker may not knowingly give false information to prospective sellers.
Broker shall treat all prospective sellers honestly and shall not knowingly give them false information. Broker may disclose to prospective sellers with whom Broker is working, all information you do not make confidential AND information you do make confidential if such disclosure is required by law. Broker is not liable to a seller for providing false information if the false information was provided to Broker by you and Broker did not have actual knowledge that the information was false. Nothing in this paragraph shall limit any of your obligations under any applicable law to make required disclosures, if any, to prospective sellers. Georgia law provides that no cause of action shall arise on behalf of any person against Broker for revealing information in compliance with this paragraph.

Broker may provide assistance to prospective buyers without violating any duties to you.
Under Georgia law, Broker may provide assistance to the seller by performing such ministerial acts as preparing offers and presenting them to you; locating professionals to assist seller and all such other like or similar services; discussing other potential buyers. Performing such ministerial acts shall not be construed in such a manner as to violate this agreement, nor shall performing such ministerial acts for the seller be construed in such a manner as to form a brokerage engagement with the seller.

Broker may show other buyers property in which you have an interest and may provide them with information.
Under Georgia law, such action is not necessarily a breach any duty or obligation to you. Broker may also provide information on other buyers who may be in competition with you for a property.

Dual Agency is permitted by Georgia law if both buyer and seller consent in writing.
Dual Agency is permitted by Georgia law if both client parties consent. The following disclosures are made so that you will have full disclosure in choosing whether to give your consent and allow dual agency. **YOU DO NOT**

1 of 5

Form RE150, *Exclusive Buyer Brokerage Agreement*
 Initials: ________ ________ ________ ________
R10312012

FIGURE 25.12: Important Broker Disclosures (continued)

HAVE TO CONSENT TO DUAL AGENCY. As a dual agent, Broker, will represent a seller (with whom Broker has a brokerage engagement) in selling you property and also represent you in buying the property. In serving as a dual agent, Broker represents a buyer and seller whose interests are or at times could be different or even adverse. When Broker serves as dual agent, both you and the seller will be clients of Broker. Broker, as a dual agent, may not disclose to you or the other client information made confidential by request or instructions from you or the other client, except information allowed or required to be disclosed by law. When dual agency exists, Georgia law provides that Broker may assign one affiliated licensee to you and another to buyer; this is known as Designated Agency (and not Dual Agency). In that case, those licensees may not disclose, except to Broker, information made confidential by request or instructions of the client the licensee is representing, except information allowed or required to be disclosed under Georgia law. If Broker or Broker's affiliated licensees have a material relationship with the other client other than that incidental to the transactions, a disclosure of the nature of such a relationship must be provided to you. A material relationship shall mean any actually known personal, familial, or business relationship between Broker or Broker's affiliated licensees and a client which would impair the ability of Broker or the affiliated licensees to exercise fair and independent judgment relative to another client. The other party whom Broker may represent in the event of dual agency may or may not be identified at the time you enter into this agreement. If a party is not identified at such time, when such party is identified, if it is a party with whom either Broker or Broker's affiliated licensees has a material relationship, Broker shall promptly provide to you a disclosure of the nature of such relationship.

UNLESS EXPRESSLY SET FORTH TO THE CONTRARY IN THE SPECIAL STIPULATIONS BELOW, BROKER'S OFFICE BROKERAGE RELATIONSHIP POLICY IS TO PROVIDE SELLER AND LANDLORD AGENCY; BUYER AND TENANT AGENCY; DESIGNATED AGENCY; DUAL AGENCY; SUBAGENCY; OR TO ACT AS A TRANSACTION BROKER; AND BY SIGNING THIS AGREEMENT SELLER EVIDENCES SELLER'S CONSENT TO BROKER ACTING AS A DUAL AGENT AND DESIGNATED AGENT.

Important Broker Disclosures

Disclosures in this section are nearly identical to those discussed under the exclusive right-to-sell listing agreement. The differences center on which party the broker represents. Here, the buyer becomes the broker's client; therefore—absent dual agency—sellers, their agents, and any other third parties involved are treated as customers. Consequently, under the exclusive buyer brokerage agreement, the real estate agent will be relying on information provided by buyer-clients for making appropriate disclosures of material facts to sellers and their agents.

IN PRACTICE Examples of information provided by buyer-clients to their agents that may require disclosure to sellers as a material fact include the following:

- A prospective buyer's financial ability to purchase the property under the terms acceptable to the seller
- Whether the buyer intends to occupy the property
- If the buyer is currently under contract to purchase another property

This buyer agency agreement, as in the seller agency agreement, informs the client that the broker's representation is that of a limited agent; though, here, the buyer agent's primary duty is to find a suitable property for the client to purchase. Those ministerial services the agent might offer to third-party customers now may be performed for sellers without violating client duties. In addition, showing other buyer prospects property in which the broker's client also has an interest would not breach any obligations owed to that client. Finally, the exclusive buyer brokerage agreement includes the same guidelines and disclosures necessary for dual and designated agency set forth in the exclusive right-to-sell listing agreement.

IN PRACTICE When real property sellers interview agents to list their property, they generally expect to enter into a written engagement with the brokerage firm selected. This may not always be the case, though, in brokerage relationships with buyers. The prospective client, after reading these important broker disclosures, may not wish to become a client of the broker, but rather remain a customer. In this situation, a written engagement would not be required in Georgia to establish this relationship. Increasingly, though, if agreeing to work with a buyer as a customer, the brokerage firm will have the customer sign a form indicating a desire to be treated as such.

Narrative

Eureka Real Estate Services, a brokerage firm located in the metro Atlanta area specializes in working with prospective buyers who are relocating to the region. Lucy Gordon, a licensee affiliate with Eureka, meets with Sebastian Scott, whose company is transferring him to its Atlanta location in the next three to four months. Sebastian tells Lucy that she and her brokerage firm have been highly recommended, and that he and his wife, Miranda, need immediate help in locating the right neighborhood and home for their family. Friends living in the area have identified three or four neighborhoods that the couple may want to consider; however, because he and his wife will be extremely busy over the next few months with work and preparing for their move, they have little time to actually explore the market for homes in those areas. As he explains, the Scotts would like to provide some basic criteria and preferences regarding amenities and a price range for their ideal home and then rely on Gordon to handle the research and legwork required for the search. She would communicate her findings to the couple by e-mail. Once the Scotts have identified the homes that have drawn their greatest interest, the couple will travel to metro Atlanta and have Gordon show them the selected properties.

Gordon tells Sebastian Scott that she and Eureka Real Estate Services will gladly represent the couple in the search for the right home for their family. She explains that given the guidelines of service the couple requires, her broker's policy is to request a retainer fee of $1,500 dollars. After speaking with his wife, Sebastian agrees to this fee and the Scotts enters into the brokerage engagement for a period of 90 days with Eureka and Lucy Gordon on March 20.

FIGURE 25.13: Term and Compensation

EXCLUSIVE BUYER BROKERAGE AGREEMENT

NOTICE TO BUYER: By signing this agreement, you acknowledge that you have read and understand all the above disclosures, which are incorporated herein by this reference, and have been advised of all of the foregoing prior to voluntarily entering into this agreement.

This **Exclusive Buyer Brokerage Agreement** is entered into on March 20, 20xx by and between Sebastian Scott and Miranda Scott (the "Buyer") and Eureka Real Estate Services (the "Broker").

1. TERM

In consideration of the undersigned Broker's agreement to act as a limited agent for and on behalf of the undersigned Buyer to use Broker's efforts to locate property within the terms of this agreement, the undersigned Buyer, does hereby authorize and grant to Broker the exclusive right and power from March 20, 20xx, until 12 o'clock midnight on June 17, 20xx (hereinafter referred to as the "Expiration Date"), to locate property suitable for Buyer to purchase at a price of US$ $400,000, or such price or terms to which Buyer may consent. Should a contract for the purchase of property be procured under the term of this agreement but fail to close until after the Expiration Date, this agreement shall automatically be extended through and including the date of closing, or through and including the date upon which the contract was terminated, as applicable.

2. BROKER COMPENSATION

Buyer agrees to pay to Broker a sales commission of [check one] ☒ 4 % of the sales price, **or** ☐ $ n/a in the event that during the term of this agreement Buyer enters into an enforceable contract for the purchase or exchange of property with any seller (without an exclusion set out in this agreement as to any seller), whether by or through the efforts of Broker or any other person, including Buyer.

IT IS UNDERSTOOD AND AGREED BY BUYER THAT THIS IS AN EXCLUSIVE BUYER BROKERAGE AGREEMENT AND THAT IF BUYER, DURING THE TERM OF THIS AGREEMENT, OR ANY EXTENSION HEREOF, PURCHASES PROPERTY, BROKER SHALL BE ENTITLED TO A COMMISSION AT THE RATE SPECIFIED HEREIN. NOTWITHSTANDING THE ABOVE, IT IS CUSTOMARY IN GEORGIA THAT THE LISTING OR SELLER'S BROKER WILL SHARE ITS COMMISSION WITH THE BROKER. BUYER'S OBLIGATION TO PAY COMMISSION TO BROKER SHALL BE REDUCED BY THE AMOUNT OF COMMISSION RECEIVED BY BROKER FROM LISTING OR SELLER'S BROKER.

Buyer acknowledges and agrees that Broker is providing a valuable real estate brokerage service to Buyer and may incur significant costs and expenses in doing so. In order to partially compensate Broker for Broker's time in the event no commission is paid hereunder, Buyer has paid to Broker a retainer fee in the amount of US$ 1,500.00, which fee shall be deposited into Broker's trust account and refundable to Buyer only if Broker is paid the full commission as provided above. Upon the termination or expiration of this Agreement, Broker shall be authorized to transfer the retainer fee to Broker's general account.

2 of 5

Form RE150, *Exclusive Buyer Brokerage Agreement*
 Initials: ________ ________ ________ ________
R10312012

Item 1: Term

The term of the engagement is counted from March 20 for 90 consecutive days (including weekends and holidays), ending on June 18. The Scotts tell agent Gordon that they prefer that their purchase price not exceed $400,000.

IN PRACTICE Other buyer agency contract forms commonly used in Georgia may not have a blank space to insert a contract price as this one does, though the language here does make clear that the final contract price may be any to which the buyer might agree. The agent's insertion of $400,000 in the designated space simply indicates the preferred ceiling of her client's price range.

Item 2: Brokers Compensation

Just as the exclusive right-to-sell listing agreement protects the listing broker's commission during the term of the engagement should an enforceable contract for sale occur, the exclusive buyer brokerage agreement protects the compensation for the broker, who represents the purchaser in the same manner. Here, the buyer does promise to compensate the broker should the party enter into a contract to purchase real property during the agreement's term. An important addendum to this promise reveals a more common reality: that the custom in Georgia is for the listing broker to share the commission with the broker who is working with the purchaser. Consequently, the buyer's obligation to compensate the broker is typically either reduced by the amount of commission the buyer's broker receives from the listing broker or even eliminated altogether.

Narrative

The Scotts have agreed to pay Eureka Real Estate Services a sales commission of 4% of the sales price if they enter into an enforceable contract to buy a home during the term of the brokerage engagement. The most probable scenario is that the clients will purchase a home listed through an MLS in which the listing broker of the home will cooperate with Eureka and licensee affiliate Gordon by sharing compensation earned from the seller. If the Scotts happen to contract with a **FSBO** (for sale by owner) property, then agent Gordon will in most circumstances be able to negotiate her broker's commission through the seller of the home. The policy of Eureka is that if the firm receives at least 3% of the sales price as commission in a sales transaction, the firm will not require that the buyer-client make up any differences in the commission amount for which the brokerage agreement might create. So, notwithstanding Eureka receiving less than a 3% compensation from either of the above-mentioned sources, the Scotts will likely have no commission obligations.

The compensation section of this contract also reveals the client's consent to pay their broker a $1,500 retainer fee, which will be deposited in Eureka's trust account; this sum will be refunded to the Scotts if the broker receives at least 3% commission from the sales price of the property. The retainer fee will be kept by the broker if the brokerage engagement is terminated or expires.

FIGURE 25.14: Other Relationships, Duties, and Property Disclosures

3. OTHER RELATIONSHIPS

Buyer acknowledges and agrees that Broker may cooperate with another broker or compensate another broker, and that any commission hereunder may be disbursed or allocated in the sole discretion of Broker and may be allocated to other brokers who may or may not represent other parties to the transaction. The commissions payable for the purchase of property are not set in any manner other than between Broker and Buyer. Broker agrees to use his or her best efforts to procure a person ready, willing and able to sell property to buyer. Should Buyer contract WITHOUT the services of Broker to make a direct purchase, exchange, or lease with option to purchase the property within __60__ days after the Expiration Date, or any extension thereof, for a property offered during the term of this agreement, or any extension hereof, by Broker, by Buyer, or anyone else, Buyer agrees to pay Broker a commission at the same rate of commission as specified herein. It is agreed and understood that if and when Buyer enters into any Exclusive Buyer Brokerage Agreement for property with a subsequent broker, Broker's commission rights remain enforceable and Broker shall be entitled to a commission at the same rate of commission specified herein. Further, Buyer agrees to refer all properties "for sale by owner" that are of interest to Buyer to Broker during the term of this agreement.

Buyer acknowledges that Broker is a member of ____GaMLS and FMLS____ ("MLS"). Buyer agrees Broker is authorized to utilize any or all media and current technology available to locate property for sale.

4. DUTIES

Broker shall provide buyer brokerage services to Buyer and assist Buyer in attempting to locate property suitable for Buyer to purchase. Buyer shall cooperate with Broker in being available to view properties by providing Broker with accurate and truthful information regarding Buyer's ability to purchase property, and by being available during reasonable times to receive time sensitive communications from Broker. Buyer and Broker shall abide by all federal, state and local laws, and shall assist one another in reporting any suspicious or unlawful activity such as mortgage fraud to appropriate law enforcement, mortgage company and title company personnel.

5. PROPERTY DISCLOSURES

As to any matters not covered by Broker's duties in this agreement, Broker is not an expert and Buyer is encouraged and advised to seek expert advice and to retain appropriate experts such as environmental engineers, termite inspectors, engineers, surveyors, plumbers, contractors, property inspectors, lawyers, accountants and the like, as Buyer may deem appropriate. Buyer expressly acknowledges that Broker is not an expert in matters relating to the condition or construction of the Property and the surrounding neighborhood, including, but not limited to, any structural, safety, title, environmental, financial, tax, legal or health concerns, or issues regarding the surrounding community, future or current real estate development, mortgage fraud or municipal services offered to local residents, and has given no advice nor made any representations in regard thereto upon which Buyer has relied. Buyer releases any Broker and any affiliated agent and employee from any cost, expense or liability that may result from Seller's reliance on any perceived advice given with respect to the foregoing. If liability is found to exist under the standard of care or conduct required of Broker or its affiliated licensee, their liability is limited to the amount of commission actually received in a particular transaction, less any amount paid to a cooperating broker, if any. If no commission is paid, Broker's liability shall be limited to one hundred US dollars (US$100.00).

6. Buyer shall indemnify, hold harmless and defend Broker from and against any and all claims, demands, causes of action, liabilities, losses, costs, damages and expenses (including reasonable attorneys' fees and expenses and court costs incurred in defending any such claim or in enforcing this indemnity) that may be incurred by Broker arising out of or in connection with the acts or omissions of Buyer and Buyer's agents, representatives, contractors and consultants, or any of them, including but not limited to claims arising out of or in connection with personal injury or death of persons, loss, destruction or damage to property, the holding of any funds by anyone other than Broker, or any claim by third parties arising out of this agreement. Buyer warrants and represents that Buyer is not a party to any other buyer brokerage agreement, and that if Buyer owes a real estate commission to any other real estate licensee claiming under any other agreement, said commission shall be in addition to, not in lieu of, Buyer's obligations under this agreement.

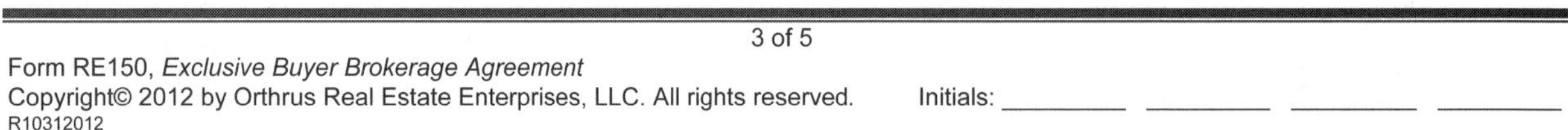

3 of 5

Form RE150, *Exclusive Buyer Brokerage Agreement*

 Initials: ______ ______ ______ ______

R10312012

Item 3: Other Relationships

Similar to acknowledgments by the seller in the listing engagement, in the buyer engagement, the purchaser(s) agree that the broker may cooperate with and be compensated by other brokers who may or may not represent the parties with whom they are working. Agent Gordon also negotiates a 60-day "safety clause" with her buyers that protects her broker's commission rights if within 60 days after the existing buyer brokerage agreement terminates or expires, the Scotts end up purchasing a property shown to them during the time frame of their agreement with Eureka. Unlike in the safety clause found in an exclusive listing agreement, the commission right here holds true even if the purchaser should enter into another buyer brokerage agreement during the 60-day period of the protection clause.

Item 4: Duties

The sole duties of both the buyer-clients and the broker/licensee affiliates under the limited agency relationship are summarized in this section. Eureka Real Estate Services will provide the Scotts with brokerage services and assist them in locating a suitable home to purchase. In turn, the Scotts will provide accurate information to the broker regarding their financial ability to purchase a property and timely respond to broker communications that affect the process of the agency engagement. Additionally, all parties agree to abide by applicable laws and to report suspicious or unlawful activities to the appropriate entities.

Item 5: Property Disclosures

The contract language here is common to all brokerage engagement in which clients are indemnifying or holding brokers and affiliated licensees harmless from liability evolving from incorrect information communicated to the broker from the client. All clients are also advised here that they should seek independent expert advice on issues that fall outside of the real estate agent's professional expertise. If brokers and affiliated licensees are in fact liable in any required standard of care, this brokerage agreement limits such liability to the amount of commission the broker actually receives in a transaction, or $100 if no commission has been paid. Finally, client(s) warrant in exclusive brokerage agreements that they are not a part of any other similar engagements and that commission owed to the broker is independent from any other compensation obligations for the client.

FIGURE 25.15: Miscellaneous

6. MISCELLANEOUS

6.1. The provisions of this agreement shall extend to and be binding on the respective heirs, executors, administrators and successors of each party hereto;

6.2. If any provision of this agreement is determined by a court of competent jurisdiction to be invalid or unenforceable, the remainder of this agreement shall nonetheless remain in full force and effect;

6.3. This agreement, including any exhibits attached hereto, contain the entire agreement between the parties pertaining to the subject matter hereof and fully supersede all prior written or oral agreements and understandings between the parties pertaining to such subject matter;

6.4. This agreement shall be governed by and interpreted under the laws of the State of Georgia;

6.5. Time is of the essence of this agreement;

6.6. Any indemnity, hold harmless or obligation to pay commission contained herein shall survive the termination of this agreement;

6.7. Any notice, request or other communication required or permitted to be given hereunder shall be in writing and shall be delivered by hand or overnight courier (such as United Parcel Service or Federal Express), sent by facsimile, sent by electronic mail ("email") or mailed by United States registered or certified mail, return receipt requested, postage prepaid and addressed to each party at its address as set forth below. Any such notice shall be considered given on the date of such hand or courier delivery, confirmed facsimile transmission, deposit with such overnight courier for next business day delivery, or deposit in the United States mail, but the time period (if any is provided herein) in which to respond to such notice shall commence on the date of hand or overnight courier delivery or on the date received following deposit in the United States mail as provided above. Rejection or other refusal to accept or inability to deliver because of changed address of which no notice was given shall be deemed to be receipt of the notice. By giving at least five (5) banking days' prior written notice thereof, any party may from time to time and at any time change its mailing address hereunder. The parties' respective mailing and email addresses for notice purposes are indicated after the parties' signatures below. Telephone numbers are given for convenience of reference only. Notice by telephone shall not be effective; and

6.8. This document and any amendments thereto, may be executed in multiple counterparts by the parties, and such counterparts shall have the same legal enforceability and binding effect as though it were signed by all parties in original form.

 Initials: ________ ________ ________ ________
R10312012

FIGURE 25.15: Miscellaneous (continued)

Special Stipulations:

EUREKA REAL ESTATE SERVICES DOES NOT OFFER SUBAGENCY

☐ Substantive provisions continued on additional page.

IN WITNESS WHEREOF, the parties have duly executed this agreement.

All Names should be both signed and printed.

Broker:

Eureka Real Estate Services / EKS-12
Name of Brokerage Firm / Broker Code

709 987654 / 709 123-4567
Brokerage Phone Number / Brokerage Fax Number

➢ ______________________

LUCY GORDON
Agent Printed Name

404 777-7777 / 709 123-4567
Agent Phone Number / Agent Fax Number

LG1@mindspring.com
Agent Email Address

Required License Number(s):

J-3456 / 34567
Broker's License Number / Agent's License Number

Buyer:

➢ ______________________

Sebastian Scott
Buyer Printed Name

➢ ______________________

Miranda Scott
Buyer Printed Name

1-878 222-0000 / n/a
Buyer Phone Number / Buyer Fax Number

sms@google.net
Buyer Email Address

352 Lakeside Way
Buyer Address

Greenpeace NE 72455
Buyer City / State / Zip

Form RE150, *Exclusive Buyer Brokerage Agreement*

 Initials: ________ ________ ________ ________

R10312012

Item 6: Miscellaneous

The section here is identical in the format and language covered in the exclusive right-to-sell listing agreement.

Special Stipulations: The only inserted item is the disclosure that Eureka Real Estate Services does not offer the brokerage relationship of subagency.

Signatures: As in any brokerage engagement, client and broker signatures confirm that the parties acknowledge and agree to all components of this exclusive buyer's brokerage agreement.

IN PRACTICE As no statement under special stipulations addresses any client concerns with dual agency, the Scotts' signatures here would confirm authorization for the broker to assume this brokerage relationship.

FIGURE 25.16: Completed Exclusive Buyer Brokerage Agreement

Exclusive Buyer Brokerage Agreement

Date: March 20, 20xx

IMPORTANT BROKER DISCLOSURES

Prior to entering into this agreement with you, Georgia law requires that the undersigned Broker make certain disclosures to you, as follows:

(1) Advise you of the types of brokerage relationships available through Broker and Broker's office policy. These are set forth below.
(2) Advise you of any other brokerage relationships held by Broker which would conflict with any interest of yours actually known to Broker. While not legally considered to be a conflict, Broker and Broker's affiliated licensees represent other Sellers and Buyers regarding sales of property which may be in direct competition with the purchase of a specific property by you.
(3) Advise you as to Broker's compensation and whether Broker will share such compensation with other brokers who may represent other parties to the transaction. Broker's compensation and sharing arrangements are set out below.
(4) Advise you of Broker's obligation to keep certain information confidential.

Broker as limited agent.
When you sign this agreement, the Broker's (and the Broker's affiliated licensees') relationship to you will be as a limited agent and, as provided below, possibly a dual agent. "Limited agent" means that the Broker will, acting under the authority of this agreement, solicit offers to purchase, sell, lease, or exchange the property subject to this agreement without being subject to your control, except as to the result of the work. Broker, as a limited agent, shall not be deemed to have a fiduciary relationship or fiduciary obligation with you (or any party), except as may be expressly provided otherwise by law, nor shall Broker or Broker's affiliated licensees be considered your employees.

Broker may make disclosures to prospective sellers in reliance on information you provide, and based on Broker's actual knowledge, unless you expressly make such information confidential. Regardless, Broker may not knowingly give false information to prospective sellers.
Broker shall treat all prospective sellers honestly and shall not knowingly give them false information. Broker may disclose to prospective sellers with whom Broker is working, all information you do not make confidential AND information you do make confidential if such disclosure is required by law. Broker is not liable to a seller for providing false information if the false information was provided to Broker by you and Broker did not have actual knowledge that the information was false. Nothing in this paragraph shall limit any of your obligations under any applicable law to make required disclosures, if any, to prospective sellers. Georgia law provides that no cause of action shall arise on behalf of any person against Broker for revealing information in compliance with this paragraph.

Broker may provide assistance to prospective buyers without violating any duties to you.
Under Georgia law, Broker may provide assistance to the seller by performing such ministerial acts as preparing offers and presenting them to you; locating professionals to assist seller and all such other like or similar services; discussing other potential buyers. Performing such ministerial acts shall not be construed in such a manner as to violate this agreement, nor shall performing such ministerial acts for the seller be construed in such a manner as to form a brokerage engagement with the seller.

Broker may show other buyers property in which you have an interest and may provide them with information.
Under Georgia law, such action is not necessarily a breach any duty or obligation to you. Broker may also provide information on other buyers who may be in competition with you for a property.

Dual Agency is permitted by Georgia law if both buyer and seller consent in writing.
Dual Agency is permitted by Georgia law if both client parties consent. The following disclosures are made so that you will have full disclosure in choosing whether to give your consent and allow dual agency. **YOU DO NOT**

FIGURE 25.16: Completed Exclusive Buyer Brokerage Agreement (continued)

HAVE TO CONSENT TO DUAL AGENCY. As a dual agent, Broker, will represent a seller (with whom Broker has a brokerage engagement) in selling you property and also represent you in buying the property. In serving as a dual agent, Broker represents a buyer and seller whose interests are or at times could be different or even adverse. When Broker serves as dual agent, both you and the seller will be clients of Broker. Broker, as a dual agent, may not disclose to you or the other client information made confidential by request or instructions from you or the other client, except information allowed or required to be disclosed by law. When dual agency exists, Georgia law provides that Broker may assign one affiliated licensee to you and another to buyer; this is known as Designated Agency (and not Dual Agency). In that case, those licensees may not disclose, except to Broker, information made confidential by request or instructions of the client the licensee is representing, except information allowed or required to be disclosed under Georgia law. If Broker or Broker's affiliated licensees have a material relationship with the other client other than that incidental to the transactions, a disclosure of the nature of such a relationship must be provided to you. A material relationship shall mean any actually known personal, familial, or business relationship between Broker or Broker's affiliated licensees and a client which would impair the ability of Broker or the affiliated licensees to exercise fair and independent judgment relative to another client. The other party whom Broker may represent in the event of dual agency may or may not be identified at the time you enter into this agreement. If a party is not identified at such time, when such party is identified, if it is a party with whom either Broker or Broker's affiliated licensees has a material relationship, Broker shall promptly provide to you a disclosure of the nature of such relationship.

UNLESS EXPRESSLY SET FORTH TO THE CONTRARY IN THE SPECIAL STIPULATIONS BELOW, BROKER'S OFFICE BROKERAGE RELATIONSHIP POLICY IS TO PROVIDE SELLER AND LANDLORD AGENCY; BUYER AND TENANT AGENCY; DESIGNATED AGENCY; DUAL AGENCY; SUBAGENCY; OR TO ACT AS A TRANSACTION BROKER; AND BY SIGNING THIS AGREEMENT SELLER EVIDENCES SELLER'S CONSENT TO BROKER ACTING AS A DUAL AGENT AND DESIGNATED AGENT.

EXCLUSIVE BUYER BROKERAGE AGREEMENT

NOTICE TO BUYER: By signing this agreement, you acknowledge that you have read and understand all the above disclosures, which are incorporated herein by this reference, and have been advised of all of the foregoing prior to voluntarily entering into this agreement.

This **Exclusive Buyer Brokerage Agreement** is entered into on March 20, 20xx by and between Sebastian Scott and Miranda Scott (the "Buyer") and Eureka Real Estate Services (the "Broker").

1. TERM

In consideration of the undersigned Broker's agreement to act as a limited agent for and on behalf of the undersigned Buyer to use Broker's efforts to locate property within the terms of this agreement, the undersigned Buyer, does hereby authorize and grant to Broker the exclusive right and power from March 20, 20xx, until 12 o'clock midnight on June 17, 20 xx (hereinafter referred to as the "Expiration Date"), to locate property suitable for Buyer to purchase at a price of US$ $400,000, or such price or terms to which Buyer may consent. Should a contract for the purchase of property be procured under the term of this agreement but fail to close until after the Expiration Date, this agreement shall automatically be extended through and including the date of closing, or through and including the date upon which the contract was terminated, as applicable.

2. BROKER COMPENSATION

Buyer agrees to pay to Broker a sales commission of [check one] ☒ four % of the sales price, **or** ☐ US$ n/a in the event that during the term of this agreement Buyer enters into an enforceable contract for the purchase or exchange of property with any seller (without an exclusion set out in this agreement as to any seller), whether by or through the efforts of Broker or any other person, including Buyer.

 Initials: ________ ________ ________ ________
R10312012

FIGURE 25.16: Completed Exclusive Buyer Brokerage Agreement (continued)

IT IS UNDERSTOOD AND AGREED BY BUYER THAT THIS IS AN EXCLUSIVE BUYER BROKERAGE AGREEMENT AND THAT IF BUYER, DURING THE TERM OF THIS AGREEMENT, OR ANY EXTENSION HEREOF, PURCHASES PROPERTY, BROKER SHALL BE ENTITLED TO A COMMISSION AT THE RATE SPECIFIED HEREIN. NOTWITHSTANDING THE ABOVE, IT IS CUSTOMARY IN GEORGIA THAT THE LISTING OR SELLER'S BROKER WILL SHARE ITS COMMISSION WITH THE BROKER. BUYER'S OBLIGATION TO PAY COMMISSION TO BROKER SHALL BE REDUCED BY THE AMOUNT OF COMMISSION RECEIVED BY BROKER FROM LISTING OR SELLER'S BROKER.

Buyer acknowledges and agrees that Broker is providing a valuable real estate brokerage service to Buyer and may incur significant costs and expenses in doing so. In order to partially compensate Broker for Broker's time in the event no commission is paid hereunder, Buyer has paid to Broker a retainer fee in the amount of US$ 1500.00, which fee shall be deposited into Broker's trust account and refundable to Buyer only if Broker is paid the full commission as provided above. Upon the termination or expiration of this Agreement, Broker shall be authorized to transfer the retainer fee to Broker's general account.

3. OTHER RELATIONSHIPS

Buyer acknowledges and agrees that Broker may cooperate with another broker or compensate another broker, and that any commission hereunder may be disbursed or allocated in the sole discretion of Broker and may be allocated to other brokers who may or may not represent other parties to the transaction. The commissions payable for the purchase of property are not set in any manner other than between Broker and Buyer. Broker agrees to use his or her best efforts to procure a person ready, willing and able to sell property to buyer. Should Buyer contract WITHOUT the services of Broker to make a direct purchase, exchange, or lease with option to purchase the property within 60 days after the Expiration Date, or any extension thereof, for a property offered during the term of this agreement, or any extension hereof, by Broker, by Buyer, or anyone else, Buyer agrees to pay Broker a commission at the same rate of commission as specified herein. It is agreed and understood that if and when Buyer enters into any Exclusive Buyer Brokerage Agreement for property with a subsequent broker, Broker's commission rights remain enforceable and Broker shall be entitled to a commission at the same rate of commission specified herein. Further, Buyer agrees to refer all properties "for sale by owner" that are of interest to Buyer to Broker during the term of this agreement.

Buyer acknowledges that Broker is a member of GaMLS and FMLS ("MLS"). Buyer agrees Broker is authorized to utilize any or all media and current technology available to locate property for sale.

4. DUTIES

Broker shall provide buyer brokerage services to Buyer and assist Buyer in attempting to locate property suitable for Buyer to purchase. Buyer shall cooperate with Broker in being available to view properties by providing Broker with accurate and truthful information regarding Buyer's ability to purchase property, and by being available during reasonable times to receive time sensitive communications from Broker. Buyer and Broker shall abide by all federal, state and local laws, and shall assist one another in reporting any suspicious or unlawful activity such as mortgage fraud to appropriate law enforcement, mortgage company and title company personnel.

5. PROPERTY DISCLOSURES

As to any matters not covered by Broker's duties in this agreement, Broker is not an expert and Buyer is encouraged and advised to seek expert advice and to retain appropriate experts such as environmental engineers, termite inspectors, engineers, surveyors, plumbers, contractors, property inspectors, lawyers, accountants and the like, as Buyer may deem appropriate. Buyer expressly acknowledges that Broker is not an expert in matters relating to the condition or construction of the Property and the surrounding neighborhood, including, but not limited to, any structural, safety, title, environmental, financial, tax, legal or health concerns, or issues regarding the surrounding community, future or current real estate development, mortgage fraud or municipal services offered to local residents, and has given no advice nor made any representations in regard thereto upon which Buyer has relied. Buyer releases any Broker and any affiliated agent and employee from any cost, expense or liability that may result from Seller's reliance on any perceived advice given with respect to the foregoing. If liability is found to exist under the standard of care or conduct required of Broker or its affiliated licensee, their liability is limited to the amount of commission actually received in a particular transaction, less any

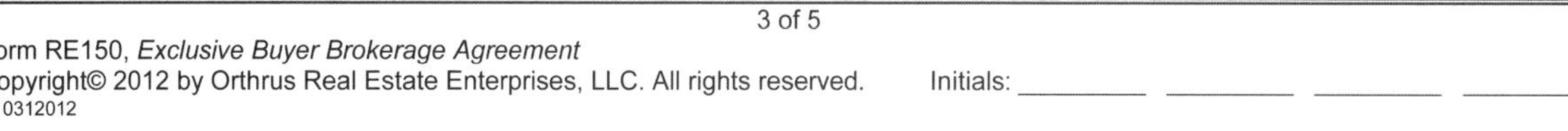

Form RE150, *Exclusive Buyer Brokerage Agreement*
 Initials: ________ ________ ________ ________
R10312012

FIGURE 25.16: Completed Exclusive Buyer Brokerage Agreement (continued)

amount paid to a cooperating broker, if any. If no commission is paid, Broker's liability shall be limited to one hundred US dollars (US$100.00).

Buyer shall indemnify, hold harmless and defend Broker from and against any and all claims, demands, causes of action, liabilities, losses, costs, damages and expenses (including reasonable attorneys' fees and expenses and court costs incurred in defending any such claim or in enforcing this indemnity) that may be incurred by Broker arising out of or in connection with the acts or omissions of Buyer and Buyer's agents, representatives, contractors and consultants, or any of them, including but not limited to claims arising out of or in connection with personal injury or death of persons, loss, destruction or damage to property, the holding of any funds by anyone other than Broker, or any claim by third parties arising out of this agreement. Buyer warrants and represents that Buyer is not a party to any other buyer brokerage agreement, and that if Buyer owes a real estate commission to any other real estate licensee claiming under any other agreement, said commission shall be in addition to, not in lieu of, Buyer's obligations under this agreement.

6. MISCELLANEOUS

6.1. The provisions of this agreement shall extend to and be binding on the respective heirs, executors, administrators and successors of each party hereto;

6.2. If any provision of this agreement is determined by a court of competent jurisdiction to be invalid or unenforceable, the remainder of this agreement shall nonetheless remain in full force and effect;

6.3. This agreement, including any exhibits attached hereto, contain the entire agreement between the parties pertaining to the subject matter hereof and fully supersede all prior written or oral agreements and understandings between the parties pertaining to such subject matter;

6.4. This agreement shall be governed by and interpreted under the laws of the State of Georgia;

6.5. Time is of the essence of this agreement;

6.6. Any indemnity, hold harmless or obligation to pay commission contained herein shall survive the termination of this agreement;

6.7. Any notice, request or other communication required or permitted to be given hereunder shall be in writing and shall be delivered by hand or overnight courier (such as United Parcel Service or Federal Express), sent by facsimile, sent by electronic mail ("email") or mailed by United States registered or certified mail, return receipt requested, postage prepaid and addressed to each party at its address as set forth below. Any such notice shall be considered given on the date of such hand or courier delivery, confirmed facsimile transmission, deposit with such overnight courier for next business day delivery, or deposit in the United States mail, but the time period (if any is provided herein) in which to respond to such notice shall commence on the date of hand or overnight courier delivery or on the date received following deposit in the United States mail as provided above. Rejection or other refusal to accept or inability to deliver because of changed address of which no notice was given shall be deemed to be receipt of the notice. By giving at least five (5) banking days' prior written notice thereof, any party may from time to time and at any time change its mailing address hereunder. The parties' respective mailing and email addresses for notice purposes are indicated after the parties' signatures below. Telephone numbers are given for convenience of reference only. Notice by telephone shall not be effective; and

6.8. This document and any amendments thereto, may be executed in multiple counterparts by the parties, and such counterparts shall have the same legal enforceability and binding effect as though it were signed by all parties in original form.

 Initials: ________ ________ ________ ________

FIGURE 25.16: Completed Exclusive Buyer Brokerage Agreement (continued)

Special Stipulations:

EUREKA REAL ESTATE SERVICES DOES NOT OFFER THE FOLLOWING BROKERAGE RELATIONSHIP:SUB AGENCY

1.EUREKA REAL ESTATE SERVICES DOES NOT OFFER SUB AGENCY

E

☐ Substantive provisions continued on additional page.

IN WITNESS WHEREOF, the parties have duly executed this agreement.

All Names should be both signed and printed.

Broker:

Eureka Real Estate Services / EKS-12
Name of Brokerage Firm / Broker Code

709 987654 / 709 123-4567
Brokerage Phone Number / Brokerage Fax Number

➢ ____________________

LUCY GORDON
Agent Printed Name

404 777-7777 / 709 123-4567
Agent Phone Number / Agent Fax Number

LG1@mindspring.com
Agent Email Address

Required License Number(s):

J-3456 / 34567
Broker's License Number / Agent's License Number

Buyer:

➢ ____________________

Sebastian Scott
Buyer Printed Name

➢ ____________________

Miranda Scott
Buyer Printed Name

1-878 222-0000 / n/a
Buyer Phone Number / Buyer Fax Number

sms@google.net
Buyer Email Address

352 Lakeside Way
Buyer Address

Greenpeace NE 72455
Buyer City / State / Zip

Form RE150, *Exclusive Buyer Brokerage Agreement*

 Initials: ______ ______ ______ ______

R10312012

STATUTE OF FRAUDS

Under the statute of frauds, to minimize fraud and abuse in the creation of binding agreements, Georgia law requires that any contract for sale of real estate or any interest in real estate must be in writing and signed by the person against whom the contract is being enforced or by someone authorized by that person. This written contract must also express all the agreement's essential terms, such as identifying the buyer and the seller, legally describing the property, stating the price to be paid for the property, and noting how that price is to be paid. **Georgia's statute of frauds** may allow a verbal real estate contract to be enforced if both parties admit there is a verbal contract and agree to its essential terms. Courts in Georgia have also ratified verbal real estate contracts if there has been substantial performance by the parties. Notwithstanding these particular circumstances, oral agreements for real estate transactions are rarely enforceable in Georgia.

FUNCTION OF LICENSEE

A primary responsibility for real estate licensees in Georgia centers on preparing offers that are enforceable by law, that reflect the wishes of buyers and sellers, as well as advise and guide these parties in the acceptance of offers and counteroffers, so that a legally binding contract for purchase and sale is created. Advice from licensees may not include guidance in ways to take title, in contractual investment strategies and resulting tax issues, or in the legal consequences of rescinding binding agreements. Composing the language for contracts falls under the practice of law, and so real estate agents are prohibited from drafting these documents. What the Real Estate License Law in Georgia does allow for, and indeed expects from licensees, is the competence to complete a contract form prepared by legal counsel by filling in blank spaces as provided. When blank spaces in the contract forms do not apply to the agreement between the parties, licenses should insert *n/a* into the blank space rather than leave it empty. When the preprinted language of the contract does not express the wishes or interests of the parties, the licensee should strike through the inappropriate material and have the parties initial this change, adding the time and date of the change to effectively identify the sequence of any such alterations.

CONTRACT FORM FOR RESIDENTIAL SALES

FIGURE 25.17: Contract for the Purchase and Sale of Residential Real Property

Contract for the Purchase and Sale of Residential Real Property

Offer Date: May 5, 20xx

This **Contract for the Purchase and Sale of Real Property** (the "Contract") is made by and between Sebastian Scott Miranda Scott, hereinafter called "Buyer" and Bernadette Joyce Sean Joyce, hereinafter called "Seller," for the hereinafter described Property, and in consideration of the mutual promises contained herein.

THIS CONTRACT INCORPORATES BY REFERENCE THOSE CERTAIN STANDARD TERMS FOR THE PURCHASE AND SALE OF GEORGIA REAL PROPERTY PUBLISHED BY ORTHRUS REAL ESTATE ENTERPRISES, LLC AT WWW.REFORMSGA.COM AND IN EFFECT AS OF THE OFFER DATE (THE "STANDARD TERMS"), WHICH STANDARD TERMS SHALL BECOME A PART HEREOF BY REFERENCE THERETO. EACH PARTY, BY AFFIXING HIS OR HER SIGNATURE HERETO, EXPRESSLY AGREES THAT HE OR SHE HAS READ THE STANDARD TERMS, AND THAT IT IS HIS OR HER INTENT THAT THE STANDARD TERMS SHALL BE INCORPORATED INTO AND ARE A PART OF THIS CONTRACT.

After identifying the parties to the agreement, this document informs the buyer and the seller that the contract not only consists of the nine sections numerically identified in the form but also incorporates by reference **standard terms** for the purchase and sale of real property in Georgia. This paragraph also indicates that by signing this contractual agreement, the parties are expressly intending that these terms are a part of the contract.

IN PRACTICE Contract forms commonly used by brokers in Georgia to create purchase and sale agreements typically include similar language referenced under the standard terms. Such language may be incorporated into the body of the contract form or, as in the form used here, included as a separate document. Extracting this terminology from the body of the contract form and establishing it as a separate yet inclusive part of the agreement, serves a dual purpose: To establish an essential contract framework that includes the necessary contractual details and to provide a "nuts and bolts" component that expands and clarifies for the buyer and the seller the full impact of the binding agreement between the parties.

Licensees may present a printed copy of the standard terms to buyers and sellers before either party signs the agreement, or the parties may acknowledge the sufficiency of accessing an online copy of the standard terms.

Note: In this topic's review of the contract form, incorporated references to standard terms under the corresponding basic contract item will be notated as SDTMS followed by the numerical designation found in the standard terms document.

Narrative

Returning to the scenarios created in the brokerage engagement section of this unit, our purchasers are Sebastian and Miranda Scott, who entered into a buyer agency agreement with Eureka Real Estate Services and the licensee affiliate Lucy Gordon. After several weeks of research and previewing homes for sale in the preferred neighborhoods identified by the Scotts, Gordon has assembled a portfolio of properties that she emails to her clients. After examining the list of homes, along with their agent's analysis and evaluations, the Scotts narrow their selection to five homes. They contact Gordon and set up a date to travel to Atlanta so that Gordon can show them the homes they have chosen to see.

They also email Gordon a letter from a lender in Atlanta with whom they have been working with in anticipation of their upcoming trip. The lender indicates that the Scotts are preapproved for a conventional loan up to $400,000. Their agent schedules showing appointments for the Scotts over a two-day period. After viewing all the homes, the clients identify two homes they would like to revisit. Gordon arranges these appointments, after which the Scotts inform her they are ready to make an offer on a home.

As it turns out, the home that the Scotts identify for an offer happens to be the same property used as the subject property in this unit's hypothetical CMA, subsequently listed in the same brokerage engagement unit topic. The sellers of that property, located at 1103 Franklin Avenue in metro Atlanta, are Bernadette and Sean Joyce, represented in the listing by Top Floor Realty, Inc., and its licensee affiliate, Eric Cambridge.

Informed of her clients' decision, Gordon arranges a meeting with the Scotts to assist in preparing a contract offer for 1103 Franklin Avenue.

FIGURE 25.18: Property Description and Purchase Price

1. PROPERTY DESCRIPTION

Seller agrees to sell, and Buyer agrees to purchase from Seller, the land, described as follows: [check all that apply]

- ☑ property address: 1103 Franklin Avenue , Bellville ; GA 33333
- ☐ more particularly described on the Legal Description Exhibit attached hereto;
- ☐ identical to the legal description for the property contained in the deed recorded in Deed Book ________, Page ________, et seq., ________ County, Georgia records;
- ☑ Land Lot(s) 113 of the 9th District, 33rd Section/ GMD, Lot(s) 51, Block(s) 11, Unit(s) n/a, Phase/Section(s) n/a of Golden Subdivision /Development, Bellville County, Georgia according to the plat recorded in Plat Book 343, Page 421, et seq., Bellville County, Georgia records;

together with all permits, privileges, rights, members, and appurtenances thereto and together with all improvements, fixtures, personal property, trees, timber and other crops and plants located thereon (the "Property").

2. PURCHASE PRICE

Buyer covenants that Buyer has adequate financial resources to purchase the Property. The Purchase Price shall be Three Hundred Ninety-Seven Thousand US Dollars (US$ 397,000.00).

Item 1: Property Description

(Here, and in the rest of the unit, "item" refers to the actual purchase and sale agreement [contract] inserted throughout the unit.) In preparing the contract offer, agent Gordon inserts the legal description found in the MLS marketing of the property.

SDTMS 1. (Standard Terms) Expanding on this first item in the purchase and sale contract form, the sellers promise to deliver good and marketable title for 1103 Franklin Avenue to the buyer by a limited warranty deed. Notwithstanding the property tax obligations yet due, zoning ordinances, and any encumbrances, easements, and restrictions recorded as of the contract acceptance date, the title delivered will be free and clear of any liens and mortgages. Moreover, the good and marketable title delivered to the buyer is one for which a title insurance company licensed in Georgia will provide a standard policy. (Remember that the notation SDTMS refers to the actual language provided in the standard terms for the purchase and sale of Georgia real property, and the language may or may not appear exactly as stated in those terms in an actual purchase contract).

Item 2: Purchase Price

The purchase price stated in an offer and in any subsequent contract between a buyer and a seller must be a definite amount or be stated in a manner that can lead to the calculation of a definite amount.

IN PRACTICE Absent a definite, stated monetary amount, two possible ways of calculating a legally enforceable contract price are as follows:

1. The contract price will not exceed $275,000, and it will be determined by a state-certified appraiser who is acceptable to all parties.
2. The price will be $2,500 per acre with the acreage to be determined by a survey performed by a licensed surveyor acceptable to all parties.

After consulting with Gordon, the Scotts make a contract offer of $397,000 for the home that represents approximately 97% of the $409,500 the Joyces are asking.

IN PRACTICE In support of her clients' financial resources statement, Gordon submits to the sellers and their listing broker a preapproval letter from a lender verifying the Scotts' ability to obtain a loan necessary to complete their purchase of the Joyces' home.

FIGURE 25.19: Earnest Money

3. EARNEST MONEY

A good faith deposit of ______Four Thousand______ US Dollars (US$__4,000.00__) (the "Earnest Money") shall be payable to __Eureka Real Estate Services__ (the "Escrow Agent") in the form of a ☑ check; ☐ certified funds; ☐ money order; or, ☐ cash. The amount of the good faith Earnest Money deposit identified above, if any, shall be applied toward the Purchase Price at closing.

3.1. Payment of Earnest Money - [check one]

☑ Buyer has remitted the Earnest Money to Escrow Agent, and Escrow Agent shall deposit same into a trust account within three (3) banking days from the date Escrow Agent receives an original or copy of the Accepted (as hereinafter defined) Contract; or

☐ Buyer has not remitted the Earnest Money to Escrow Agent, but shall remit same to Escrow Agent within ______ days from the date of Acceptance of this contract and Escrow Agent shall deposit same into a trust account within three (3) banking days from the date of receipt of the deposit and a copy or original of the Accepted Contract. In the event said payment is not timely remitted, Seller shall be promptly notified by Escrow Agent and Seller shall have the rights and remedies set out in this section.

Item 3: Earnest Money

The contract form provides space for any "good faith deposit" the purchaser wishes to include as part of the contract offer. While earnest money is customarily offered as part of a real estate transaction, it is not a legal requirement in Georgia, and is not identified as the consideration necessary to create a valid real estate contract.

IN PRACTICE The Scotts will submit a $4,000 earnest money check made out to their broker, Eureka Real Estate Services, which by depositing these funds in the firm's trust account will serve as the escrow agent for the good-faith funds. The earnest money will apply toward the buyers' purchase price. As a practical matter, earnest money deposits in Georgia real estate transactions will commonly be held by the broker working with the buyer, though circumstances sometimes dictate that the listing broker, the closing attorney, or even the seller may serve as an escrow agent for these funds.

Item 3.1: Payment of Earnest Money

The contract form provides two scenarios for the payment of these funds. The first notes the buyer has submitted the check to the escrow agent at the time of a contract offer, as is the case in the contract narrative. The escrow agent (commonly, a broker involved in the transaction) will then have three banking days from receipt of this deposit and a copy of the accepted contract to deposit these funds into a trust account. The other circumstance for payment of earnest money identifies the number of days after the contract acceptance date by which the buyer will submit the earnest money check to the escrow agent. On the day the escrow agent receives the money and a copy of the accepted offer, the funds must be deposited in the escrow agent's trust account. In the event the good-faith money is not timely submitted as promised, the escrow agent must notify the seller, who then may respond according to any rights and remedies set forth in the contract.

SDTMS 3.1: Escrow Agent's Trust Account—If the escrow agent's trust account in which earnest money funds are held pays interest on this money, the escrow agent is entitled to such interest.

SDTMS-3.2: Seller's Account—If the seller holds the earnest money or a nonrefundable builder's deposit, the funds may be held in the seller's general operating account. Unless otherwise required by Georgia law to deposit these funds in a trust account, the seller has discretion to use such money for whatever purpose the seller deems appropriate. Seller also is entitled to any interest generated by the account in which earnest money is deposited. If the seller holds earnest money, the broker will have no responsibility or control over the funds and will be released from any liability regarding the funds by all parties in the transaction.

SDTMS—3.2: Non-Refundable Builder Deposit (may be applicable for New Construction)—Unlike earnest money, which provides an incentive for buyers to perform contract terms, the deposit covers the estimated costs of any upgrades or options selected by the buyers and approved by the seller with regard to the newly constructed property.

SDTMS—3.3: Buyer's Failure to Remit Earnest Money—Regardless of whether earnest money is submitted before or after contract acceptance, if the check is not honored by the bank, the escrow agent will notify the buyers and the seller and the deposit amount agreed to in the contract will be paid by certified check or other collected funds to the escrow agent within three days of notice from the agent.

If the earnest money is not paid to the escrow agent as set forth in the contract, the earnest money is no longer a part of the contract and seller may do as follows:

- 3.3.1: Unilaterally terminate the contract within seven days of receiving notice from the escrow agent, releasing the buyers and the seller from any further contract responsibilities and obligations
- 3.3.2: If the seller holds earnest money, unilaterally terminate the contract within three days' notice to the buyers, thereby releasing all parties from any further contract responsibilities and obligations toward each other
- 3.3.3: Demand full performance of all other terms and conditions of the contract and proceed to closing

SDTMS—3.4: Disbursement of Earnest Money if Held by Escrow Agent— After ensuring that the earnest money has been credited to the trust account where it was deposited, the escrow agent may proceed in one of the following ways:

- Disburse the earnest money to the buyer if the contract is not accepted and is not in dispute
- Disburse the earnest money for credit to the buyers at closing
- Disburse the earnest money to the buyers at closing if it is not credited toward the purchase price at closing
- Disburse the earnest money pursuant to a separate written agreement signed by the parties agreeing to terms of disbursement
- Disburse the earnest money upon court order or arbitrator decision, either of which have jurisdiction over the disputed issue
- If the escrow agent has received notice from either party that the contract has been terminated or the closing has failed to occur, the escrow agent will notify all parties no more than 30 days after receiving such notice of the escrow agent's decision for disbursement of the earnest money

Furthermore, if the earnest money is in dispute, the escrow agent may file a judicial action to interplead the matter and allow the court of jurisdiction to decide how the funds are to be disbursed. In this circumstance, the escrow agent may deduct from the earnest money proceeds the costs and expenses for filing such an action. The parties also agree, absent willful default or gross negligence, to release the escrow agent from liabilities associated with the duties described in the contract.

IN PRACTICE As the language of this contract section reveals, disbursement of earnest money funds follow a specific set of rules. Moreover, as brokers are the most common holders of these deposits, their conduct in any disbursement of earnest money is highly regulated by the Georgia Real Estate Commission. Consequently, when serving as an escrow agent, regardless of which party the agent may represent in a transaction, the broker is also expected to make a reasonable interpretation of the contract in an unbiased manner to determine a proper disbursement of funds. Finally, if the escrow agent receives no disbursement objections before distributing the earnest money, the parties acknowledge that all rights of objection after disbursement are considered waived.

FIGURE 25.20: Closing and Closing Costs

4. CLOSING
Unless amended mutually by the parties, the closing of this transaction shall take place on June 15 20xx, 20___, at a mutually agreed upon time (the "Closing"). Said Closing shall be at the office of ________________ William Colon Esq. located at/in Bellville, Georgia (the "Closing Attorney"). If Closing Attorney is unavailable or unacceptable to Buyer's lender or title insurance company, then Buyer shall have the right to select a different Closing Attorney. Possession of the Property shall be granted [check one] ☑ at Closing **or** ☐________ days after the Closing at _______ o'clock _____.m.

5. CLOSING COST ALLOWANCE FOR BUYER
Seller shall contribute a maximum of [check one] ☐ n/a % of the purchase price, **or** ☑ US$ 5,000 toward costs associated with Buyer's purchase of the Property (the "Closing Cost Allowance").

Item 4: Closing

Here the purchaser indicates in the contract offer a date on which to close the transaction and identifies the attorney who will conduct the closing. Because the closing attorney in Georgia represents the lender who provides financing for the buyer's purchase, the chosen attorney will need to be acceptable to the buyer's lender, as well as to the title insurance company involved in the property transfer. The buyers will also indicate the date on which they expect to take possession of the property.

IN PRACTICE Sebastian and Miranda Scott wish to close the transaction for 1103 Franklin Avenue on June 15 and also take possession of the home on that date. On the recommendation of agent Lucy Gordon, they wish to close the transaction with the law firm of William Colon, Esq. If the buyers and/or the agent working with the buyers are uncertain as to a closing attorney preference, an acceptable option might be to indicate in the contract offer that the identity of the closing attorney will be determined at a later time. In fact, the selection of the closing attorney can be negotiated between the parties. If the sellers are paying most of the closing costs, or if there are any extenuating circumstances attached to the transfer of the title, the sellers may want to choose the closing attorney. More often though, because lenders commonly assign the cost of the closing attorney to the borrowers, common practice in Georgia allows the buyers to make that selection.

On occasion, particular circumstances might result in a seller agreeing to allow the buyer occupancy of the property before the closing. For example, a buyer may have closed on the sale of an existing home before the closing date of the newly purchased property. Realistically, this right for the buyer might be granted only if the seller has already vacated the property before closing. More commonly, residential contracts for purchase and sale may allow a seller to continue occupancy of a property for a period after the home's closing. This circumstance might arise out of a contingency, within the contract for sale of the seller's home, being satisfied only days before the closing date. Consequently, the seller was unwilling to commit to the move prior before that time and, as a result, requires additional time to organize and conduct the move-out process. Signed, written agreements between the parties are required in either of the above situations, and specific points acknowledged should include the following:

- Dates of occupancy outside of the specified closing date
- Any compensation for such occupancy
- Neither of the occupancies to be considered a tenant-landlord relationship
- Maintenance responsibility during occupancy

SDTMS-4.1: Closing Documents—The parties to the contract will execute and deliver all necessary documents to fulfill the terms of the contract, comply with all laws regulating the agreement, and meet those requirements related to the loan and title insurance companies involved in the transaction.

SDTMS-4.2: Obligations to Complete and ILSA Compliance—this section only applies to property under construction as of the contract acceptance date, or if the Seller has agreed to construct a home on the property before closing. The seller agrees to comply with appropriate provisions under the Interstate Land Sales Act (ILSA), which regulates the sale of unimproved land and pending construction on that land.

Item 5: Closing Cost Allowances for Buyer

IN PRACTICE The Scotts' lender has estimated their closing costs for this transaction to be around $8,000; in their contract offer, acting again on advice from Gordon, they ask the sellers to contribute $5,000 of that sum towards these costs. Agent Gordon explains to her clients that unlike in some states where costs associated with the buyer's loan are customarily paid by that party, the acceptable practice in Georgia is that these closing costs are open for negotiation between the buyer and the seller.

SDTMS 5. Expenses Related To Closing

SDTMS 5.1: Clearance of: "Title Defects"—The seller has the responsibility and related financial costs to clear the owner's property title of liens and other defects required to be remedied before title insurance companies agree to issue policies for buyers and lenders. Furthermore, the seller must bear any other costs related to obligations in transferring a marketable title to the purchaser.

SDTMS 5.2: Prorations—Absent any prohibition from a buyer's lender—Taxes, homeowner association dues, and other property utility costs will be prorated as of the date of closing, unless the parties agree in writing that said items will not be prorated or that the proration will be based on the date of possession rather than the date of closing. The parties also agree that should estimations of these prorations prove inaccurate, the parties will prorate again between themselves for any differences.

SDTMS 5.3: Buyer Expenses—The buyer will be responsible for all other costs, fees, and expenses related to the closing, if not otherwise provided for in the contract, including but not limited to the transfer tax, deed recording fees, and title insurances.

SDTMS 5.4: Seller Closing Costs—The seller will bear the costs of the attorney's fees if the attorney is representing the seller; if the attorney represents the lender, then the seller will be assigned only those costs indicated by the contractual agreement or those rendered directly to the seller from customary services provided by a closing attorney.

SDTMS 5.5: Closing Cost Allowance for Buyer—Any monies the seller agrees to contribute towards the buyers' closing costs is subject to the lender's underwriting criteria for such allowances. The buyers may use such funds to offset any costs incurred in the closing of the transaction, including but not limited to the cost of financing, title insurance, and homeowner association dues. If the buyers' lender does not allow the seller to contribute the full amount indicated in the contract, then the closing allowance will be amended to reflect the actual allowance and the seller will have no further obligation to the buyer.

FIGURE 25.21: Contingencies

6. CONTINGENCIES

In consideration of the covenants contained herein and other good and valuable consideration, the receipt and sufficiency whereof is hereby acknowledged, the Seller grants to the Buyer the following contingencies, as the same are defined in the Standard Terms: [Check all that are applicable]

6.1. ☑ **Buyer's General Right to Terminate** - *This contingency shall expire at 11:59 p.m. on the day that is* 15 *days after the Acceptance Date.* Due Diligence

6.2. ☑ **Appraisal Contingency** - *This contingency shall expire at 11:59 p.m. on the day that is* 30 *days after the Acceptance Date.*

6.3. ☑ **Financing Contingency -** *This contingency shall expire at 11:59 p.m. on the day that is* 21 *days after the Acceptance Date.* If Buyer and Seller agree to a financing contingency involving financing other than a new first or second mortgage from a third party institutional lender under the terms described below, such as a loan assumption or seller financing, an additional exhibit or special stipulation shall be attached hereto providing the additional terms of that financing. If Buyer chooses FHA or VA financing, a FHA or VA Exhibit shall be attached hereto.

[In the event the Financing Contingency is selected, check all of the following that are applicable:]

☐ **First Mortgage Loan Proceeds**: This Contract is contingent upon Buyer's ability to obtain a third party first mortgage loan to be secured by the Property, in a principal amount of no less than [check one] ☑ US$ n/a or ☐ 90 % of the purchase price, being amortized over a term of 30 years, at an interest rate per annum that is [check one] ☑ fixed at a rate not to exceed 5 %; **or** ☐ adjustable beginning at a rate not to exceed n/a % with the interest rate never to exceed n/a %, pursuant to an institutional lender's standard and customary underwriting criteria. The balance of the purchase price shall be paid by Buyer in cash, or in such other form as may be required by the Closing Attorney listed below, at time of Closing.

☐ **Second Mortgage Loan Proceeds:** This Contract is contingent upon Buyer's ability to obtain a third party second mortgage loan to be secured by the Property, in a principal amount of no less than [check one] ☐ US$ n/a or ☐ n/a % of the purchase price, being amortized over a term of n/a years, at an interest rate per annum that is [check one] ☐ fixed at a rate not to exceed _____%; **or** ☐ adjustable beginning at a rate not to exceed n/a % with the interest rate never to exceed n/a %, pursuant to an institutional lender's standard and customary underwriting criteria . The balance of the purchase price shall be paid by Buyer in cash, or in such other form as may be required by the Closing Attorney listed below, at time of Closing.

Item 6: Contingencies

The contract form here includes three fundamental contingency references (as also defined in the standard terms), which when checked by the buyer, will constitute a contingency or condition upon which the buyer's contract offer is based.

Item 6.1 and SDTMS 6.1: Buyer's General Right to Terminate—By checking this box in the contract form, the buyers are essentially making this offer conditional on a "due diligence" time period that is identified in the blank space. If accepted by the seller as such, the buyers will have this defined time period after the contract acceptance date to terminate the contract for any reason by delivering written notice to the seller and receiving a full refund of any earnest money. Before this contingency's expiration date, the buyers may also propose to the seller an amendment to the contract addressing any concerns the buyers might have regarding the property. If the seller does not accept the buyers' proposed amendment, then the buyers may either terminate the contract before the expiration of the contingency or accept the property "as is." If the seller does not receive timely written notice of the buyers' contract termination, the contingency will be deemed waived. If the buyers provide a timely written notice of termination, they will also provide the seller with any reports, tests, surveys, or other written documents the buyers have obtained regarding the property.

IN PRACTICE As a component of their offer on 1103 Franklin Avenue, the Scotts request a 15-day general right to terminate after the date of any contract acceptance. During this due diligence period, they may have the property inspected, more closely evaluate conditions of the neighborhood, verify the details of their loan commitment, or present an amendment in which they may ask the sellers to make certain repairs to the property or to renegotiate the sale price. The key is that until the expiration of their general right to terminate, the Scotts are not legally obligated to purchase the Joyces' home. On the other hand, if the Scotts do not negotiate an amendment to the contract or terminate the agreement by the expiration date of the time period, they are indeed legally obligated to purchase the home.

Item 6.2 and SDTMS 6.2: Appraisal Contingency—When checked as a condition for an agreement between the parties, if a certified appraisal of the property does not show a value equal to or greater than the contract price, the buyers have the right to terminate the contract. In doing so, the buyers will provide the seller with a copy of the appraisal and written notice of buyers' intent to terminate the contract before the expiration date of this contingency noted in contract section 6.2. Furthermore, if the property fails to appraise for a minimum of the purchase price, the buyers may, before the contingency's expiration, propose to the seller an amendment to the contract reducing the purchase price. The contingency will be waived if the seller does not receive notice of the buyers' termination of the contract before the contingency's expiration date.

IN PRACTICE The Scotts would like to include an appraisal contingency in their offer to purchase 1103 Franklin Avenue; to establish a reasonable time frame for this contract condition, their agent suggests that they consult the lender, who recommends a period of 30 days for the appraisal contingency.

Item 6.3 and SDTERMS-6.3: Financial Contingency—If this contingency is not checked on the contract form, no loan is considered as part of the agreement, effectively making it a cash transaction. In most real estate transactions, though, the buyers promise to pay cash from personal resources and to obtain the remaining cash for the transaction from a third party through a new loan secured by the property. In this situation, the buyer will typically make the purchase contract contingent on the ability to obtain financing. When noted as such on the contract form, the contingency gives the buyers the right to terminate the contract if the buyer is unable to secure financing under the terms set forth in this section of the form.

IN PRACTICE If a financial contingency clause only refers to the buyers "obtaining" a properly described loan, the buyers would be able to withdraw from the contract before obtaining the loan, refuse the loan offered, or not even attempt to secure the loan. In the contract form here, though, the financial contingency clause refers to the buyers' "ability to obtain" the loan; consequently, the buyers must make a good-faith effort to secure the loan. The buyers cannot withdraw from the search to secure the loan identified in the contract or reject the loan if it is offered by a lender.

The terms for the buyers' loan, as stipulated by Georgia courts, must be indicated in a "definite and complete" manner. Specification of the loan terms as shown in section 6.3 of the contract form include

- a clear statement of the loan amount or the loan amount as a percentage of the purchase price,
- a clear statement of the loan term,
- a clear statement of either a fixed interest rate applied yearly, or
- an adjustable interest rate noting the bottom-to-top range of the rate.

IN PRACTICE The buyers in our contract narrative, Sebastian and Miranda Scott, are preapproved for a conventional loan with a 90% LTV at a fixed interest rate not to exceed 5% per annum. These are the conditional terms upon which the couple's loan in the contract for purchase applies. Though the Scotts are ultimately free to secure a different loan for the purchase, their ability to obtain a loan with the precise terms identified in this section of the contract form will be the sole factor for satisfying the financial contingency of the agreement. The expiration date for the buyers' financial contingency is 21 days, a period suggested by the agent and supported by her clients' lender.

If the financing contingency involves a loan not secured from a third-party institutional lender under terms identified in this contract section, such as a loan assumption or seller financing, an additional exhibit must be attached to the contract.

If the buyers choose FHA or VA financing, FHA or VA loan exhibits must be attached to the contract.

SDTMS-6.3.1: If the buyers terminate the contract based on an inability to obtain financing according to the terms identified in contract item 6.3, the buyers must give the seller written notice of the contract termination, along with a written statement from the buyers' lender indicating lender's reason for denying the loan. The buyers will lose this contingency right under either of the following circumstances:

- 6.3.1.1: Buyer fails to provide proof of lender's denial or approval of loan before deadline set forth in contract item 6.3
- 6.3.1.2: Lender's denial of loan is based on buyer's lack of sufficient funds for down payment and closing costs; lack of timely loan application; buyer's failure to sell or lease current home; buyer's conduct after the contract acceptance date but before the contingency expiration date.

IN PRACTICE Here the standard terms relating to the financial contingency reinforce a "time is of the essence" component of the contract for purchase and sale. The agent, Lucy Gordon, emphasizes to the Scotts the importance of providing the lender with the necessary loan documentation as soon as possible so that buyers' ability to obtain the loan described in the contract can be verified within the 21-day contingency period. She also cautions her clients against altering their financial ability before the closing because it relates to cash assets for down payment and closing costs, and she advises them not to make any additional major purchases; such actions could jeopardize the buyers' capacity to secure a final loan approval within the contractually established time frame.

SDTMS-6.3.2: If the concessions made by the buyers or the sellers in the contractual agreement are not in compliance with the guidelines established by the underwriters of the buyers' loan, then the underwriter's guidelines prevail. For example, if a loan underwritten within the Department of Veterans Affairs (VA) or Federal Housing Administration (FHA) guidelines limit a buyer's closing costs contributions and the existing contract calls for the buyer to contribute more than the underwriting allowance, then the loan for that transaction will not be made unless the seller agrees to pay the difference between the contractual amount and the allowable amount for the buyer. If the seller does not agree to this change in closing costs contributions, then the contract allows the seller to unilaterally terminate the contract within three days of receiving notice of the changes in closing cost allowances.

IN PRACTICE Licensees can avoid the unpleasant realities described here by familiarizing themselves with current concession guidelines allowed for buyers and sellers in the three primary types of real property residential loans: conventional, FHA, and VA. For example, knowing that sellers may be allowed to contribute up to 6% of the contract sales price toward the buyer's FHA loan or up to 4% of a VA loan provides strategic guidance for licensees in drafting offers and counteroffers for clients. By the same token, a licensee's awareness that allowable seller concessions on conventional loans may vary from 3% to 6%, depending on the buyer's down payment, can minimize unnecessary negotiating obstacles. Note that these percentages may change over time, so it is very important for licensees to be familiar with the current allowances on seller concessions for the various types of loans in their marketplaces.

FIGURE 25.22: Inspection of Property

7. INSPECTION OF PROPERTY
Buyer has the right and obligation, with reasonable notice to Seller, to inspect the property (and all improvements located thereon) for defects and other issues including, but not limited to: air conditioning, electrical, fireplace, heating, lead/lead-based paint, mold, plumbing, radon, roof, structure, wood destroying organisms, environmental hazards, or other similar issues at any time and from time to time, after the time and date of Acceptance of the Contract, through and including the Closing, from the hours of [check one] ☑ 9:00 a.m. to 7:00 p.m. **or** ☐ ______n/a______. In order to facilitate the inspection of the Property [check one] ☐ Buyer **or** ☑ Seller shall make all required utilities operational and available on the Property through and including the day of Closing.

Item 7. Inspection of Property

The contract form acknowledges that a property inspection is a right of, as well as an obligation for, the buyer. A buyer's inspection for defects and other property issues listed in the contract form may occur at various points in the period between contract acceptance and the closing; particular time periods for actual inspections are identified in this section of the contract form.

A buyer's agent should always recommend that the buyer hire an independent, qualified professional home inspector to do a thorough inspection of the property. The inspector's official report will detail any problems with the property and may be the basis for the buyers' request that sellers perform repairs to the property or the buyers' explanations about the problems or defects discovered during the inspection.

IN PRACTICE The Scotts tell Gordon that if and when an agreement with the sellers can be reached, they plan to return to Atlanta within 10 days from the acceptance date to conduct a general inspection of the property. The exact time for the inspection will be determined.

SDTMS-7: Condition Of Property

7.1: Duty to Inspect—The parties to the contract expressly acknowledge an obligation to conduct a thorough investigation of the property and neighborhood conditions, and to secure independent professional advice regarding any issues that arise from the inspection, as well as any concerns they might have with the contract for purchase and sale.

IN PRACTICE Notwithstanding Georgia law that requires property owners to disclose adverse material facts known to be true regarding the property and neighborhood to perspective buyers, caveat emptor ("buyer beware") is the guiding principal inferred regarding the purchasers' concerns about a home, the surrounding community, and the contract for purchase document they are signing. Clients are advised to seek independent professional expertise for these issues. Though a client may reasonably expect a licensee to help them understand the contract form to be signed, the agent may not provide contract advice or strategy requiring legal interpretation or application.

7.2: For New Construction Only—Notwithstanding changes and improvements made to the property pursuant to the contract, the seller warrants that the newly constructed property will be in the same condition as on the contract acceptance date (normal wear and tear excepted) and "broom clean."

IN PRACTICE As represented by the standard terms that follow, contractual language for the purchase and sale of new construction establishes substantial protections for a seller's existing investment in such construction. Absent proof of seller negligence or fraud, a buyer's failure or refusal to close will, as a rule, constitute a breach of performance. Consequently, exercising due diligence through a careful reading of new construction contracts for purchase and sale becomes essential for buyers and should be reinforced by real estate licensees working with these parties.

7.2.1: Punch List—Before closing, after substantial completion of new construction, the buyers' and the sellers' representative(s) will inspect the property and prepare an amendment to the contract specifying all items that fail to comply with the plans and specification as defined in the contract. The buyers acknowledge that the seller will make best effort to address all items on the punch list before closing. Any items on said list remaining to be addressed by closing will, however, not constitute valid reason for the buyers' failure or refusal to close, as long as a certificate of occupancy has been issued; nor shall proceeds due the seller at closing be withheld or placed in escrow. With respect to items on the punch list, the seller will option to replace items in need of repair or to compensate the buyers for the cost of repairing those items.

7.2.2: Insulation—The buyer acknowledges that R-values and thickness of insulation are based on manufacturer representations, and that the seller does not warrant that these elements of installed insulation are correct. The seller also has a right to make substitutions in the installed insulation unilaterally, as long there are no substantial changes in the R-value of insulation installed in a substantial portion of the home.

7.2.3: Warranty—The buyer agrees to accept any builder's warranty in the contract as the sole warranty given by the seller to the buyer.

7.2.4: Selection Period—The seller will have the right to approve or disapprove of the buyer selection for options and upgrades to the property if the contract provides a selection period for the buyer and the seller to finalize such selections and options. If the buyer's selections are not completed during this defined period, the seller has the right to make them on behalf of the buyer.

7.2.5: Change Orders—If the buyer requests any changes to the plans and specifications for the new construction as defined in the contract, the buyer will make the request to the seller in writing. The seller will have sole and absolute discretion in granting such changes. If agreeing to changes, the seller will amend the contract to provide the buyer with the resulting costs and any necessary changes in the closing date as a result. The buyer will have 48 hours to accept the change order amendment and related costs. Payment for the changes must accompany the fully executed final change order, and these monies are added to the original nonrefundable builder deposit amount, if any.

7.3: For Resales of Homes, Lots and Raw Land—Any repairs agreed to by the seller in a contract amendment or exhibit will be performed in a "**good and workmanlike**" manner and be completed no later than three days before closing.

IN PRACTICE As the language "good and workmanlike" suggests, the seller's performance of any repair obligations is subject to a broad interpretation. To minimize potential conflicts with sellers, licensees might remind clients that language used to request such property repairs needs to be direct and specific in conveying the buyer's intent in this matter. For example, if the buyers wants a seller to replace the rotting wood on an outdoor deck attached to a home, the buyers' written request should specifically identify the exact location of the designated wood on the deck, what type of wood they request for the repair/replacement, and what kind of finish they might expect for the wood.

7.4: Damage to Property Before Closing—The seller will maintain sufficient hazard insurance on the property until the sale of the property closes. If the property is materially damaged or destroyed before closing and the seller is unwilling or unable to restore the property to its prior condition, the buyer will have the following options: cancel the contract and receive a refund of the earnest money or accept the property in its damaged condition and have any insurance proceeds paid to the seller applied toward the purchase price or otherwise paid to the buyer. The buyer also indemnifies the seller against any damages resulting from personal injury or death claims caused by actions of the buyer or arising out of property damage or conditions not brought about through seller negligence.

7.5: Eminent Domain—If after the contract acceptance date and before closing, the seller receives notice of any eminent domain action against the property, the seller will give immediate notice to the buyer. Within 30 days of the notice, the buyer will have the right to terminate the contract and receive a full refund of the earnest money or have the right to close the transaction and have the seller assign the rights to any condemnation proceeds to the buyer.

7.6: Plans and Specifications—The buyer acknowledges that any floor plans renderings, or drawings supplied by the seller that intend to depict the home are just approximations and do not necessarily reflect the actual "as built" conditions. The buyer also acknowledges that certain items and home improvements, such as paint color, may vary from any samples that have been shown to the buyer by the seller.

FIGURE 25.23: Brokerage

8. **BROKERAGE**

By signing below, all parties represented by a Broker acknowledge that no Broker in this transaction shall owe any duty to Buyer or Seller greater than what is set forth in their brokerage engagements and the Brokerage Relationships in Real Estate Transactions Act, O.C.G.A. § 10-6A-1 *et seq.*, and further, that they have read and acknowledged and consent to the inclusion of all additional brokerage disclosures provided in the Standard Terms.

8.1. Material Relationships - Neither the Broker nor Broker's affiliated licensees have a material relationship with Seller or Buyer except as follows: n/a n/a.

8.2. Buyer's Broker - The Buyer's Broker identified on the signature page of this Contract is the Broker assisting the Buyer, regardless of whether the Buyer is a customer or a client as defined under Georgia law. It includes the agent or agents of the Broker who are involved in this particular transaction. The Buyer's Broker is [check one]:

i. ☑ representing the Buyer as a client under a written brokerage agreement; **or**
ii. ☐ representing the Buyer as a customer, performing only ministerial acts; **or**
iii. ☐ acting as a dual agent, with responsibilities to both Seller and Buyer; **or**
iv. ☐ acting as a designated agent, with responsibilities to both Seller and Buyer, as described more fully below.

8.3. Seller's Broker - The Seller's Broker identified on the signature page of this Contract shall refer collectively to all persons assisting the Seller, regardless of whether the Seller is a customer or client as defined under Georgia law. It includes the agent or agents of the Broker who are involved in this particular transaction. The Seller's Broker is [check one]:

i. ☑ representing the Seller as a client under a written brokerage agreement; **or**
ii. ☐ representing the Seller as a customer, performing only ministerial acts; **or**
iii. ☐ acting as a dual agent, with responsibilities to both Seller and Buyer; **or**
iv. ☐ acting as a designated agent, with responsibilities to both Seller and Buyer, as described more fully below.

8.4. By checking the designated agent box above, the parties acknowledge that they have consented to a designated agency and acknowledge that ________________ will work exclusively with Buyer as Buyer's designated agent and ________________ will work exclusively with the Seller as Seller's designated agent.

Item 8: Brokerage

All parties represented by a broker in the transaction acknowledge in their signed acceptance of the agreement that no broker will owe any duty to buyer greater than what it stated in the brokerage engagement and in BRRETA. Such acceptance further acknowledges that all parties have read and consent to the inclusion of all additional disclosures provided in the standard terms.

IN PRACTICE Here again, the nonfiduciary aspect of the brokerage engagement is emphasized to all parties. Also reconfirmed by the signatures of all parties to the agreement is an acknowledgment that all the disclosures in the standard terms are part of the contract.

Item 8.1: Material Relationships—Unless indicated in the space provided within this contract form section, no broker or affiliated licensee has a material relationship with either the seller or the buyer.

SDTMS 8.1—The buyer and the seller acknowledge that they may be represented by the broker only through a signed brokerage engagement and that, without such an agreement, they are fully responsible for protecting their own interests. Furthermore, the buyer and the seller warrant that they have no existing dealings with other brokers who may have compensation claims with respect to the current transaction between the parties.

Item 8.2: Buyer's Broker—as identified on the signature page of this contract form, the buyer's broker is the broker assisting the buyer, who may be a client or a customer of the broker and by extension of any licensee affiliate of the broker. Notation boxes in this section of the contract form indicate whether the broker

- represents the buyer as a client,
- represents the buyer as a customer,
- is acting as a dual agent, or
- is acting as a designated agent.

Item 8.3: Seller's Broker—As identified on the signature page of the contract form, the seller's broker refers collectively to all persons working with the seller, whether through a client engagement or as a customer. This includes agents of the broker. Notation boxes in this section of the contract form indicate whether the broker

- represents the seller as a client,
- represents the seller as a customer,
- is acting as a dual agent, or
- is acting as a designated agent.

Item 8.4: If the designated agency box in above section of the contract form is checked, all parties consent to designated agency and acknowledge that one of the licensees identified in this section will work exclusively with the seller as a designated agent and the other licensee identified in this section will work exclusively with the buyer as a designated agent.

IN PRACTICE Top Floor Realty, the broker working with Bernadette and Sean Joyce in the contract narrative represents these sellers as clients; Eureka Real Estate Services, the broker working with Sebastian and Miranda Scott, represents the buyer-clients.

SDTMS 8.2—The brokers' commission or other compensation in this transaction will be paid according to the terms of a separate agreement between the broker and the seller (the exclusive listing agreement); the broker and the buyer (the exclusive buyer brokerage agreement); or both.

IN PRACTICE Commonly, the broker(s) involved the transaction will sign a separate **commission acknowledgment** form, instructing the closing attorney as to the specific distribution of the commission funds. This form may also indicate to the closing attorney other payments pursuant to the contract for payment to third parties from closing funds.

Continuing our contract narrative, the 6% commission that Top Floor Realty earns from the sellers, Sean and Bernadette Joyce, in the transaction (as established in the exclusive right-to-sell listing agreement covered in the brokerage engagement topic of this unit) will be shared with Eureka Real Estate Services, the broker representing the buyers, the Scotts. The details of the commission split are noted in the commission acknowledgment form.

SDTMS 8.3: Disclaimers/Limits on Broker Liability—The buyer and the seller expressly acknowledge that the broker is not an expert in matters involving the condition of the property and neighborhood, including, but not limited to, structural, safety, title, environmental, tax, legal, or health concerns; issues surrounding community and municipal services offered to local residents; or future real estate development. As such, the broker has given no advice or representations in such matters upon which the buyers and the sellers have relied; all parties release the broker and affiliated licensees from any liabilities occurring from the parties' relying on any perceived advice from the broker on these matters. If liability is found to exist under the standard of care and conduct required of the broker the and affiliated licensee, their liability is limited to the amount of commission actually received in a particular transaction.

SDTMS 8.4: Dual Agent—By checking the dual agent box in sections 8.2 and 8.3 of the contract, the parties acknowledge that they have consented to dual agency and acknowledge that their interests may sometimes be adverse. If the parties agree to allow the broker to act as a dual agent, the broker will not disclose to another party any information a client has asked to be kept confidential or which would negatively affect that party's bargaining position, unless the disclosure is required by law.

SDTMS 8.5: Designated Agency—By checking the designated agency box in contract sections 8.2 and 8.3, the parties acknowledge they have consented to designated agency as defined under BRRETA.

FIGURE 25.24: Exhibits

9. EXHIBITS/Addendums

The following exhibits are attached to and made a part of this offer. The provisions of any exhibit attached to this contract and referenced below, shall prevail if in conflict with the provisions of the Contract:

☐ Legal Description	☐ FHA Exhibit
☑ Disclosure of Information on Lead-Based Paint and/or Lead Based Paint Hazards	☐ VA Exhibit
☐ Short Sale Exhibit	☐ Lease for Lease/Purchase Agreement Only
☑ Seller's Property Condition Disclosure	☑ Copy of Earnest Money Check for $4,000
☑ Bill of Sale	☐
	☐

Special Stipulations (provisions of any stipulation included in this contract shall prevail if in conflict with the provisions of this Contract, including any exhibit attached hereto):

Item 9: Exhibits

Referenced in this section of the agreement are attached documents that may support, add to, or alter existing preprinted language of the contract form. If any attached exhibit conflicts with any provisions in the body of the contract, the exhibit prevails.

Special Stipulations

In this section of the contract, the parties may add items or conditions to finalize and complete the purchase and sale agreement. In addition, language providing greater clarity to contract terms and obligations may be included here.

IN PRACTICE As a part of the legally enforceable contract between a buyer and a seller, a special stipulation requires clear, unambiguous language to effectively convey intent. The wording must be definite enough for the parties to decide whether or when the fulfillment of the condition or responsibility has occurred. Just as contracts used in this unit have been prepared with the advice of legal counsel, similarly, preprinted special stipulations are available to brokers and licensee affiliates through membership in Realtor® associations or multiple listing services.

SDTMS 9: Default—A party is in default upon breach of any term of the contract. Notwithstanding a party's failure to close, neither the seller nor the buyer is deemed to be in default, however, until such party has been given written notice of its failure to comply with the terms of the contract and who does not cure such failure within three banking days after receipt of such notice.

9.1: Buyer's Default—Buyer's default may result in a seller's termination of the contract, along with exercising all rights and remedies available under the law; such actions may include the buyer's forfeiture of earnest money deposits and lawsuits for damages. The seller may either accept the earnest money as full liquidated damages or bring suit for actual damages.

IN PRACTICE Georgia courts have held that the forfeiture of earnest money funds from the buyer to the seller is valid under the following circumstances:

- Actual damages must be difficult or impossible to estimate.
- Forfeiture of earnest money would not be considered a penalty rather than part of a mutual effort between parties to determine damages.
- The amount of earnest money must be a reasonable estimate of probable future loss.

9.2: Seller's Default—If transaction does not close due to the seller's default, the earnest money at the buyer's election, will be refunded to the buyer, at which time the contract will be null and void; or the buyer will have the right to sue for specific performance of the contract only if the buyer had fully satisfied contract obligations, including the buyer's obligation to deliver earnest money; and by delivering proof to the closing attorney and the seller that the buyer is ready, willing, and able to close this transaction. These options are the buyer's sole and exclusive remedy, and in no event may the buyer be entitled to damages.

9.3: Broker Commission—The terms of the contract between the buyer and the seller shall in no way alter the Broker's commission rights under a separate agreement between the broker and the seller or the broker and the buyer, or both. Even if a broker is not representing a defaulting party in the transaction, the broker will be entitled to collect from the defaulting party the full amount of the commission to which the broker would be entitled had the transaction closed.

SDTMS 10: Notices

All notices, requests, and other required communications between the parties must be in writing and delivered in the following manner: by hand or overnight courier, such as UPS or Federal Express; fax; email; U.S. registered or certified (return receipt requested), or regular mail, with postage prepaid and addressed to each party as set forth in contract. Notice will be considered given on the date of such hand or courier delivery, confirmed fax transmission, deposit with an overnight courier for next business day delivery, or deposit in the U.S. mail.

SDTMS 11: Miscellaneous

Mutual agreements warranted between the buyer and the seller include the following:

- 11.1: The contract is binding on respective heirs, executors, administrators, and successors of each party.
- 11.2: Any judicially determined unenforceable parts of the contract may not render the remainder of the contract unenforceable.
- 11.3: Section headings in the contract are for convenience of reference only and are not intended to limit or define the text of any section.
- 11.4: The contract, including any attached exhibits, contain the entire agreement between the parties.
- 11.5: The contract will be governed and interpreted by laws of Georgia.
- 11.6: Time is of the essence—Essentially this phrase indicates that all parties should perform the terms of the contract with all deliberate speed; time limits in contracts are not suggestions, but obligations and courts typically will strictly interpret dates and time limits.
- 11.7: **Survival clause**—Unless expressly agreed otherwise in the contract, or unless provided by another document executed by the buyer and the seller, performance of the provisions of the contract will survive the closing of the transaction.

IN PRACTICE Under the standard terms for the purchase and sale of Georgia real property, a closing may occur even if certain contractual obligations have yet to be performed by the parties. The responsibility for performance would remain and be extended by a designated time frame after the closing. In effect, the parties to the transaction may specifically address how contractual obligations and responsibilities will impact the closing.

For example, if it is clear to both parties that an obligation required in the contract, such as a property repair, cannot be performed by the closing date, the buyer and the seller may document in writing that the identified obligation may be performed within a specific period of time after the closing. On the other hand, the language of a contract might indicate that nonperformance of a specific contractual obligation constitutes a breach of responsibility and that the contract may not close until performance of the obligation is completed.

11.8: The form of the contract is provided as a convenience. All parties have an obligation to seek independent advice as to whether this form protects their rights and fulfills their expectations.

SDTMS 11.9: Definitions—The following capitalized terms when used in the contract form, if not otherwise defined in the standard terms, will have the meaning as described under this section.

11.9.1: **Acceptance** (Accepted)—Will only occur as follows: before an offer is withdrawn, revoked, or terminated; in writing and in accordance with any provision in the contract; if the receiver of the offer accepts it exactly as presented, without change; and provided acceptance is communicated, in writing, to the party making the offer

11.9.2: **Banking Days**—Monday through Friday, excluding federal holidays

11.9.3: **Broker**—Individual who holds a broker's real estate license as issued by the Georgia Real Estate Commission; the term "broker" includes the broker's affiliated licensees except where the context would indicate otherwise

11.9.4: **Buyer**—Term refers collectively to all persons named in the contract and signing the contract as the buyer, and the liability of each such person will be joint and several; notice given by the seller to any person named as the buyer, or by any such person to the seller, will bind all persons signing the contract as the buyer.

11.9.5: **Buyer's Broker**—The broker assisting the buyer whether the buyer is a customer or a client in accordance with Georgia law. The term also includes agent(s) of the broker who are involved in this particular transaction

11.9.6: **Contract**—An executed purchase and sale agreement between a buyer and a seller for the purchase of real property; the agreement includes and incorporates by reference the standard terms for contract for the purchase and sale of residential real property.

11.9.7: **Inspection**—Includes any and all inspections performed by the buyer or a licensed third-party inspector selected by the buyer

11.9.8: **Offer**—A proposal to purchase or sell the property that, upon acceptance, results in a binding contract. All offers include any counteroffers made as the result of an offer. Any counteroffer automatically terminates the offer being countered.

11.9.9: **Party**—Each person named in the contract as the buyer or the seller; does not include any broker or other third party named in the contract

11.9.10: **Seller**—Refers collectively to all persons named in the contract and signing the contract as the seller, as well as to their successors and/or assigns. Notice given by the buyer to any person named as the seller, or by any such person to the buyer, binds all persons signing the contract as the seller.

11.9.11: **Seller's Broker**—Brokers assisting the seller whether the seller is a customer or a client in accordance with Georgia law. It includes the agent or agents of the broker who are involved with this particular transaction.

11.9.12: **Terminate or Termination**—The termination of the contract pursuant to a right to do so as provided in the contract. Upon termination, the earnest money will be disbursed as provided in the contract, and the parties will have no further duties or rights under the contract except as expressly provided in the contract.

FIGURE 25.25: Offer, Counteroffer, and Acceptance

This ***Offer*** is open for ***Acceptance*** until 2 o'clock P m. on May 6, 20xx. An ***Acceptance*** after that time shall be considered a counteroffer.

The ***Offer*** is hereby ***Accepted***, with notice in the form of an executed contract being properly delivered to the party making the last offer, at _____ o'clock ___ m. on ____________________, 20____.

_____ _____ _____ _____ By initialing here, the parties acknowledge their receipt of a printed copy of the Standard Terms. Failure to initial this section shall indicate that the parties have declined a printed copy of and hereby acknowledge the sufficiency of the online copy of the Standard Terms.

All Names should be both signed and printed.

Buyer:

➢ ______________________

Sebastian Scott
Buyer Printed Name

➢ ______________________

Miranda Scott
Buyer Printed Name

1-878 222-0000 / n/a
Buyer Phone Number / Buyer Fax Number

sms@google.net
Buyer Email Address

352 Lakeside Way
Buyer Address

Greenpeace NE 76543
Buyer City State Zip

Seller:

➢ ______________________

Bernadette Joyce
Seller Printed Name

➢ ______________________

Sean Joyce
Seller Printed Name

______ / ______
Seller Phone Number / Seller Fax Number

____
Seller Email Address

____
Seller Address

____
Seller City State Zip

Buyer's Broker

Eureka Real Estate Services / EKS-12
Name of Brokerage Firm / Broker Code

709 987654 / 709 123-4567
Brokerage Phone Number / Brokerage Fax Number

➢ ______________________

Lucy Gordon
Agent Printed Name

404 777-7777 / 709 123-4567
Agent Phone Number / Agent Fax Number

LG1@mindspring.com
Agent Email Address

Required License Number(s):

J-3456 / 99999
Broker's License Number / Agent's License Number

Seller's Broker

Top Floor Realty,Inc / TFR03
Name of Brokerage Firm / Broker Code

404 222-1111 / 404 222-4444
Brokerage Phone Number / Brokerage Fax Number

➢ ______________________

Eric Cambridge
Agent Printed Name

770 102-6543 / 404 222-4444
Agent Phone Number / Agent Fax Number

Agent Email Address ericcom@comcast.net

Required License Number(s):

H-1999 / 987654
Broker's License Number / Agent's License Number

MLS Listing # 11387

Page 4 of 4
Form RE100, *Contract for the Purchase and Sale of Residential Real Property*
 Initials: ________ ________ ________ ________
R07152014

Instanet forms

OFFER, COUNTEROFFER, AND ACCEPTANCE

Narrative

The Scotts make their May 5 offer on 1103 Franklin Avenue open for acceptance by the sellers, Bernadette and Sean Joyce, until 2 pm on May 6. The buyers also initial in the space provided at the top of the contract page, indicating that they have received from the agent, Lucy Gordon, a printed copy of the standard terms for this contract for the purchase and sale of residential real property.

Under the Buyer heading on this page, Sebastian Scott and Miranda Scott print and sign their names and include their postal address, phone number, email address, and fax number (if applicable). As identified on this page, these are the contractually recognized means of communication with the buyers.

Under the Buyer's Broker heading, Lucy Gordon inserts the name of her brokerage firm, Eureka Real Estate Services, along with the Broker Code, phone and fax number. Next, she prints and signs her name, which legally makes the broker a part of this transaction, under the authority granted to her in the affiliation agreement with her broker. Also included is Gordon's real estate license number, along with her email address, phone number, and fax number.

Gordon gives the Scotts a copy of the contract offer, which she then sends by fax and email to Eric Cambridge, the licensee affiliate for the listing broker, Top Floor Realty. The completed offer includes the following items: the signatures of Gordon's buyer-clients on the contract form; the standard terms incorporated into the residential contract for purchase and sale; the seller's property condition disclosure and the lead-based paint disclosure, both signed on receipt by her clients; and a bill of sale signed by her clients, who are asking the sellers to include the outdoor patio furniture and gas grill as part of the contract offer. The Scotts' offer is open for acceptance by the sellers until 2 p.m. of the following day, May 6.

Gordon receives a response from the listing agent, Eric Cambridge, the following morning. His seller-clients are making a counteroffer of $399,000 for the contract sales price and offers to contribute $4,000 toward the buyers' closing costs. The sellers are willing to grant the buyers a 25-day appraisal contingency rather than the 30 days requested in the contract offer. The sellers agree to all other terms included in the buyers' offer.

IN PRACTICE The acceptance of a contract offer must be unconditional and identical in that it is a full agreement to the corresponding contact offer. A counteroffer occurs if one party makes an offer and the other party changes any term or creates a condition for an acceptance of an offer. A counteroffer effectively refuses the offer received, though in an effort to avoid appearing to outright reject an offer, parties often refer to their counteroffers as a **"qualified"** or **"conditional" acceptance**.

Call it what you will, though, the counteroffer not only rejects an offer but also terminates the offerers' ability to accept an original offer. Not realizing this fact of contract law can be frustrating, even disheartening to a party who might want to revisit a decision to counter rather than accept an earlier offer made in the negotiating process. Buyers and sellers should understand that every time they reject or counter an offer, the offer goes away with no guarantee that the other party will ever make another offer. Each counteroffer is, in effect, a new offer.

After discussing the sellers' counteroffer, the Scotts inform Gordon that they wish to accept it; she then sends her clients' signed counteroffer and acceptance to the listing agent, Eric Cambridge, who in turn notifies her of the receipt of said acceptance at 7 p.m. on May 6. Gordon also fills out a commission acknowledgment form, indicating the share of commission her broker will receive from the listing broker in the transaction and forwards the form to Cambridge.

Narrative

When listing agent Eric Cambridge notifies buyer's agent Lucy Gordon of the time he received the buyer's acceptance, a legally binding agreement was created between Sebastian and Miranda Scott and Bernadette and Sean Joyce for the purchase and sale of 1103 Franklin Avenue. As described, contract acceptance legally takes effect when the party or the agent of the party who receives an offer (offeree) communicates acceptance of such an offer to the party or the agent of the party (offeror) who sent the offer. Acceptable forms of communicating offer and acceptance are generally identified in the contract form.

If the contract form is silent as to acceptable methods of communicating an offer and an acceptance, courts have ruled that the medium for transmitting such notices should be one that is reasonable according to the circumstances. For example, if an offeror communicated an offer by registered mail, if the contract form provides no guidance in this matter, the offeree might reasonably communicate acceptance of that offer by registered mail.

After exercising due diligence obligations under their contract's general right to terminate a contingency, and before this condition's expiration date, the Scotts execute a contract amendment in which the seller will provide a home warranty for them. The seller agrees to the amendment, which is then incorporated into the purchase and sale agreement between the parties.

Completed Contract for the Purchase and Sale of Residential Real Property

Following are documents related to a completed contract for the purchase and sale of residential real property.

FIGURE 25.26: Purchase and Sale contract

Contract for the Purchase and Sale of Residential Real Property

Offer Date: May 5, 20xx

This **Contract for the Purchase and Sale of Real Property** (the "Contract") is made by and between Sebastian Scott Miranda Scott, hereinafter called "Buyer" and Bernadette Joyce Sean Joyce, hereinafter called "Seller," for the hereinafter described Property, and in consideration of the mutual promises contained herein.

THIS CONTRACT INCORPORATES BY REFERENCE THOSE CERTAIN STANDARD TERMS FOR THE PURCHASE AND SALE OF GEORGIA REAL PROPERTY PUBLISHED BY ORTHRUS REAL ESTATE ENTERPRISES, LLC AT WWW.REFORMSGA.COM AND IN EFFECT AS OF THE OFFER DATE (THE "STANDARD TERMS"), WHICH STANDARD TERMS SHALL BECOME A PART HEREOF BY REFERENCE THERETO. EACH PARTY, BY AFFIXING HIS OR HER SIGNATURE HERETO, EXPRESSLY AGREES THAT HE OR SHE HAS READ THE STANDARD TERMS, AND THAT IT IS HIS OR HER INTENT THAT THE STANDARD TERMS SHALL BE INCORPORATED INTO AND ARE A PART OF THIS CONTRACT.

1. PROPERTY DESCRIPTION

Seller agrees to sell, and Buyer agrees to purchase from Seller, the land, described as follows: [check all that apply]

- ☑ property address: 1103 Franklin Avenue , Bellville GA 33333 ;
- ☐ more particularly described on the Legal Description Exhibit attached hereto;
- ☐ identical to the legal description for the property contained in the deed recorded in Deed Book ________, Page ________, et seq., ________ County, Georgia records;
- ☑ Land Lot(s) 113 of the 9th District, 33rd Section/ GMD, Lot(s) 51, Block(s) 11, Unit(s) n/a, Phase/Section(s) n/a of Golden Subdivision /Development, Bellville County, Georgia according to the plat recorded in Plat Book 343, Page 421, Baggins et seq., Bellville County, Georgia records;

together with all permits, privileges, rights, members, and appurtenances thereto and together with all improvements, fixtures, personal property, trees, timber and other crops and plants located thereon (the "Property").

2. PURCHASE PRICE

Buyer covenants that Buyer has adequate financial resources to purchase the Property. The Purchase Price shall be Three Hundred Ninety-Seven Thousand US Dollars (US$ 397,000.00).

3. EARNEST MONEY

A good faith deposit of Four Thousand US Dollars (US$ 4,000.00) (the "Earnest Money") shall be payable to Eureka Real Estate Services (the "Escrow Agent") in the form of a ☑ check; ☐ certified funds; ☐ money order; or, ☐ cash. The amount of the good faith Earnest Money deposit identified above, if any, shall be applied toward the Purchase Price at closing.

3.1. Payment of Earnest Money - [check one]

☑ Buyer has remitted the Earnest Money to Escrow Agent, and Escrow Agent shall deposit same into a trust account within three (3) banking days from the date Escrow Agent receives an original or copy of the Accepted (as hereinafter defined) Contract; or

☐ Buyer has not remitted the Earnest Money to Escrow Agent, but shall remit same to Escrow Agent within ______ days from the date of Acceptance of this contract and Escrow Agent shall deposit same into a trust account within three (3) banking days from the date of receipt of the deposit and a copy or original of the Accepted Contract. In the event said payment is not timely remitted, Seller shall be promptly notified by Escrow Agent and Seller shall have the rights and remedies set out in this section.

 Initials: ________ ________ ________ ________

FIGURE 25.26: Purchase and Sale contract (continued)

4. CLOSING
Unless amended mutually by the parties, the closing of this transaction shall take place on June 15 20xx, 20___, at a mutually agreed upon time (the "Closing"). Said Closing shall be at the office of William Colon Esq. located at/in Bellville, Georgia (the "Closing Attorney"). If Closing Attorney is unavailable or unacceptable to Buyer's lender or title insurance company, then Buyer shall have the right to select a different Closing Attorney. Possession of the Property shall be granted [check one] ☑ at Closing **or** ☐_________ days after the Closing at _______ o'clock _____.m.

5. CLOSING COST ALLOWANCE FOR BUYER
Seller shall contribute a maximum of [check one] ☐ n/a % of the purchase price, **or** ☑ US$ 5000 toward costs associated with Buyer's purchase of the Property (the "Closing Cost Allowance").

6. CONTINGENCIES
In consideration of the covenants contained herein and other good and valuable consideration, the receipt and sufficiency whereof is hereby acknowledged, the Seller grants to the Buyer the following contingencies, as the same are defined in the Standard Terms: [Check all that are applicable]

6.1. ☑ **Buyer's General Right to Terminate** - *This contingency shall expire at 11:59 p.m. on the day that is* 15 *days after the Acceptance Date.*

6.2. ☑ **Appraisal Contingency** - *This contingency shall expire at 11:59 p.m. on the day that is* 30 *days after the Acceptance Date.*

6.3. ☑ **Financing Contingency -** *This contingency shall expire at 11:59 p.m. on the day that is* 21 *days after the Acceptance Date.* If Buyer and Seller agree to a financing contingency involving financing other than a new first or second mortgage from a third party institutional lender under the terms described below, such as a loan assumption or seller financing, an additional exhibit or special stipulation shall be attached hereto providing the additional terms of that financing. If Buyer chooses FHA or VA financing, a FHA or VA Exhibit shall be attached hereto.

[In the event the Financing Contingency is selected, check all of the following that are applicable:]
☐ **First Mortgage Loan Proceeds**: This Contract is contingent upon Buyer's ability to obtain a third party first mortgage loan to be secured by the Property, in a principal amount of no less than [check one] ☑ US$ n/a **or** ☐ 90 % of the purchase price, being amortized over a term of 30 years, at an interest rate per annum that is [check one] ☑ fixed at a rate not to exceed 5 %; **or** ☐ adjustable beginning at a rate not to exceed n/a % with the interest rate never to exceed n/a %, pursuant to an institutional lender's standard and customary underwriting criteria. The balance of the purchase price shall be paid by Buyer in cash, or in such other form as may be required by the Closing Attorney listed below, at time of Closing.
☐ **Second Mortgage Loan Proceeds:** This Contract is contingent upon Buyer's ability to obtain a third party second mortgage loan to be secured by the Property, in a principal amount of no less than [check one] ☐ US$ n/a **or** ☐ n/a % of the purchase price, being amortized over a term of n/a years, at an interest rate per annum that is [check one] ☐ fixed at a rate not to exceed _____%; **or** ☐ adjustable beginning at a rate not to exceed n/a % with the interest rate never to exceed n/a %, pursuant to an institutional lender's standard and customary underwriting criteria . The balance of the purchase price shall be paid by Buyer in cash, or in such other form as may be required by the Closing Attorney listed below, at time of Closing.

7. INSPECTION OF PROPERTY
Buyer has the right and obligation, with reasonable notice to Seller, to inspect the property (and all improvements located thereon) for defects and other issues including, but not limited to: air conditioning, electrical, fireplace, heating, lead/lead-based paint, mold, plumbing, radon, roof, structure, wood destroying organisms, environmental hazards, or other similar issues at any time and from time to time, after the time and date of Acceptance of the Contract, through and including the Closing, from the hours of [check one] ☑ 9:00 a.m. to 7:00 p.m. **or** ☐ ____________________________ . In order to facilitate the inspection of the Property [check one] ☐ Buyer **or** ☑ Seller shall make all required utilities operational and available on the Property through and including the day of Closing.

 Initials: ________ ________ ________ ________
R07152014

Instant Forms

FIGURE 25.26: Purchase and Sale contract (continued)

8. BROKERAGE

By signing below, all parties represented by a Broker acknowledge that no Broker in this transaction shall owe any duty to Buyer or Seller greater than what is set forth in their brokerage engagements and the Brokerage Relationships in Real Estate Transactions Act, O.C.G.A. § 10-6A-1 *et seq.*, and further, that they have read and acknowledged and consent to the inclusion of all additional brokerage disclosures provided in the Standard Terms.

8.1. Material Relationships - Neither the Broker nor Broker's affiliated licensees have a material relationship with Seller or Buyer except as follows: n/a
n/a.

8.2. Buyer's Broker - The Buyer's Broker identified on the signature page of this Contract is the Broker assisting the Buyer, regardless of whether the Buyer is a customer or a client as defined under Georgia law. It includes the agent or agents of the Broker who are involved in this particular transaction. The Buyer's Broker is [check one]:

i. ☑ representing the Buyer as a client under a written brokerage agreement; **or**
ii. ☐ representing the Buyer as a customer, performing only ministerial acts; **or**
iii. ☐ acting as a dual agent, with responsibilities to both Seller and Buyer; **or**
iv. ☐ acting as a designated agent, with responsibilities to both Seller and Buyer, as described more fully below.

8.3. Seller's Broker - The Seller's Broker identified on the signature page of this Contract shall refer collectively to all persons assisting the Seller, regardless of whether the Seller is a customer or client as defined under Georgia law. It includes the agent or agents of the Broker who are involved in this particular transaction. The Seller's Broker is [check one]:

i. ☑ representing the Seller as a client under a written brokerage agreement; **or**
ii. ☐ representing the Seller as a customer, performing only ministerial acts; **or**
iii. ☐ acting as a dual agent, with responsibilities to both Seller and Buyer; **or**
iv. ☐ acting as a designated agent, with responsibilities to both Seller and Buyer, as described more fully below.

8.4. By checking the designated agent box above, the parties acknowledge that they have consented to a designated agency and acknowledge that Lucy Gordon will work exclusively with Buyer as Buyer's designated agent and Eric Cambridge ____________ will work exclusively with the Seller as Seller's designated agent.

9. EXHIBITS

The following exhibits are attached to and made a part of this offer. The provisions of any exhibit attached to this contract and referenced below, shall prevail if in conflict with the provisions of the Contract:

☐ Legal Description
☑ Disclosure of Information on Lead-Based Paint and/or Lead Based Paint Hazards
☐ Short Sale Exhibit
☑ Seller's Property Condition Disclosure
☑ Bill of Sale
☐ FHA Exhibit
☐ VA Exhibit
☐ Lease for Lease/Purchase Agreement Only
☑ Copy of Earnest Money Check for $4000
☐ ____________
☐ ____________

Special Stipulations (provisions of any stipulation included in this contract shall prevail if in conflict with the provisions of this Contract, including any exhibit attached hereto):

☐ Substantive provisions continued on additional page.

 Initials: ________ ________ ________ ________

FIGURE 25.26: Purchase and Sale Contract (continued)

This ***Offer*** is open for ***Acceptance*** until 2 o'clock P m. on May 6, 20xx. An ***Acceptance*** after that time shall be considered a counteroffer.

The ***Offer*** is hereby ***Accepted***, with notice in the form of an executed contract being properly delivered to the party making the last offer, at _____ o'clock ___ m. on ____________________, 20____.

_____ _____ _____ _____ By initialing here, the parties acknowledge their receipt of a printed copy of the Standard Terms. Failure to initial this section shall indicate that the parties have declined a printed copy of and hereby acknowledge the sufficiency of the online copy of the Standard Terms.

All Names should be both signed and printed.

Buyer:

➢______________________

Sebastian Scott
Buyer Printed Name

➢______________________

Miranda Scott
Buyer Printed Name

1-878 222-0000 / n/a
Buyer Phone Number / Buyer Fax Number

sms@google.net
Buyer Email Address

352 Lakeside Way
Buyer Address

Greenpeace NE 76543
Buyer City / State / Zip

Seller:

➢______________________

Bernadette Joyce
Seller Printed Name

➢______________________

Sean Joyce
Seller Printed Name

______ / ______
Seller Phone Number / Seller Fax Number

Seller Email Address

Seller Address

Seller City / State / Zip

Buyer's Broker

Eureka Real Estate Services / EKS-12
Name of Brokerage Firm / Broker Code

709 987654 / 709 123-4567
Brokerage Phone Number / Brokerage Fax Number

➢______________________

Lucy Gordon
Agent Printed Name

404 777-7777 / 709 123-4567
Agent Phone Number / Agent Fax Number

LG1@mindspring.com
Agent Email Address

Required License Number(s):

J-3456 / 99999
Broker's License Number / Agent's License Number

Seller's Broker

Top Floor Realty,Inc / TFR03
Name of Brokerage Firm / Broker Code

404 222-1111 / 404 222-4444
Brokerage Phone Number / Brokerage Fax Number

➢______________________

Eric Cambridge
Agent Printed Name

770 102-6543 / 404 222-4444
Agent Phone Number / Agent Fax Number

ericcom@comcast.net
Agent Email Address

Required License Number(s):

H-1999 / 987654
Broker's License Number / Agent's License Number

MLS Listing # 11387

Form RE100, *Contract for the Purchase and Sale of Residential Real Property*
 Initials: 
R07152014

FIGURE 25.27: Seller's Property Disclosure Form

Seller's Property Condition Disclosure Statement

(Improved Property)

Name of Seller(s): Bernadette Joyce and Sean Joyce

Property Address: 1103 Franklin Avenue , Bellville, **Georgia,** 33333 **(the "Property")**

Purpose of Statement and Disclaimer:
This is a statement by the Seller pertaining to certain conditions and information concerning the Property known to the Seller. Unless otherwise indicated, the Seller does not possess any expertise in construction, architecture, engineering or any other specific area related to the construction or condition of the improvements on the Property or the land. Also, unless otherwise indicated, the Seller has not conducted any inspection of generally inaccessible areas such as underneath floor or wall coverings, under the foundation or on the roof. This Seller's Property Condition Disclosure Statement is not a warranty of any kind by the Seller, or by any agent representing the Seller. It is not a substitute for any inspections or tests to be conducted by the Buyer, and it is the Buyer's responsibility to obtain independent professional inspections, surveys, environmental tests, public records and any other information available pertaining to the Property. In no event shall the parties hold the Seller's Broker liable for any representations not directly made by the Broker or Broker's Agent.

Instructions to the Seller:
a. Answer all questions based upon your actual knowledge.
b. Attach additional pages with your signature if additional space is required.
c. Complete this form to the best of your ability.
d. If some items do not apply to the Property, check "N/A" (Non-applicable). If you do not know the answer, check "Unknown."

Seller's Statement:
The Seller makes the following representations to the Buyer based upon the Seller's actual knowledge at the time of signing this document. Unless otherwise indicated, the term "Property" includes the land and any enclosed structure on the land, including any sheds, outbuildings, garages or other detached structures, but not including any purely recreational or landscaping structures, such as swing sets, gazebos or arbors. The Seller acknowledges that a knowingly false or incomplete statement by the Seller on this form may subject the Seller to claims by the Buyer prior to or after the transfer of title. The Seller authorizes any agent acting on Seller's behalf, if any, to provide a copy of this statement to a prospective buyer of the residential real Property. The following are representations made by the Seller and are not the representations of the Seller's agent.

GENERAL INFORMATION/OWNERSHIP

1. When did you acquire the Property? 1990 (Year)
2. Since when have you occupied the Property? 10/1990 (Month/Year)
3. When was the dwelling built? 1967 (Year)

Have there been any major changes or renovations to the house or attached structures exceeding $1,000 since it was originally built? ☒**Yes** ☐**No**
If yes, please explain. Second Floor Addition in 1992;Basement finished in 1997;Bathroom/Kitchen Renovation in 1998
If yes, were all legally required permits, licenses and inspections related to the work obtained? ☒**Yes** ☐**No**

4. Was any part of the Property built before 1978? ☒**Yes** ☐**No**

If yes, which part? Main level of home
If yes, Seller must complete Lead Based Paint Disclosure and an investigation for the presence of lead-based paint is encouraged.

5. Is the house vacant? ☐**Yes** ☒**No** If yes, since when? ______ (Month/Year)

 Initials: ________ ________ ________ ________

FIGURE 25.27: Seller's Property Disclosure Form (continued)

6. Does anybody other than you have a lease, easement or any other right to use or occupy any part of the Property other than those stated in public record documents, such as rights to use a road or path or cut trees?
☐Yes ☒No ☐Unknown

If "Yes," explain: ______

7. Other than outstanding mortgages, are there any third party claims against the title to the Property such as contractor's liens, easements (other than general utility easements) or legal judgments? ☐Yes ☒No ☐Unknown

If "Yes," explain: ______

8. Are there any features of the Property shared in common with adjoining landowners or a homeowner's association, such as walls, fences or driveways? ☐Yes ☒No ☐Unknown

If "Yes," explain: ______

9. Is the Property encumbered by any covenants or restrictions, or governed by a homeowner's association?
☐Yes ☒No ☐Unknown

If "Yes," are there any special assessments, homeowner or other association fees that apply to the Property?
☐Yes ☐No ☐Unknown ☐N/A

If "Yes," explain **and attach Community Association Exhibit:**

______

10. Is any or all of the Property located in a designated floodplain or wetland? ☐Yes ☒No ☐Unknown

If "Yes," explain: ______

11. Is the Property located in an agricultural district? ☐Yes ☒No ☐Unknown

If "Yes," explain: ______

12. Has this Property ever been used as a landfill, had fuel storage tanks above or below the ground, or had motor fuel, motor oil, home heating fuel, lubricating oil or any other petroleum product, methane gas, or any hazardous or toxic substance spilled, leaked or otherwise released on the Property, or from the Property onto any other property? ☐Yes ☒No ☐Unknown

If "Yes," explain: ______

13. Is there now, or has there been, any evidence of erosion, settlement or other soil movement on the Property?
☐Yes ☐No ☒Unknown

If "Yes," explain: ______

14. At any time of the year, are there any springs, streams, ponds, dams or other water retention facilities on the Property? ☐Yes ☒No ☐Unknown

If "Yes," explain: ______

15. In which public school districts is the Property located? Elementary School Garden Springs

Middle School Horizon High School Dylan Thomas

STRUCTURAL

16. Is there now, or has there been, any wood rot or water damage to the main dwelling or any other enclosed structure located on the Property? ☒Yes ☐No ☐Unknown

If "Yes," explain: Water intrusion in basement prior to finished renovation; no problem since

Form RE130, *Seller's Property Condition Disclosure Statement*

 Initials: ______ ______ ______ ______

R10312012

FIGURE 25.27: Seller's Property Disclosure Form (continued)

17. Is there now, or has there been, any fire or smoke damage to the main dwelling or any other enclosed structure located on the Property? ☐Yes ☒No ☐Unknown

If "Yes," explain: ____________________

18. Is there now, or has there been, any storm or weather related damage to the main dwelling or any other enclosed structure located on the Property? ☒Yes ☐No ☐Unknown

If "Yes," explain: Some hail damage to roof prior to replacement of roof in 2002

19. Is there now, or has there been, any termite, insect, rodent or pest infestation or damage to the main dwelling or any other enclosed structure on the Property? ☐Yes ☒No ☐Unknown

If "Yes," explain: ____________________

20. Is the main dwelling or any other enclosed structure on the Property covered under a current termite bond? ☒Yes ☐No ☐Unknown

If "Yes," explain: Damage Repair Bond from Acme pest control

21. Is the main dwelling or any other enclosed structure on the Property currently being serviced by a pest control company? ☒Yes ☐No ☐Unknown

If "Yes," explain: Annual inspection by Acme pest control

22. Is there any portion of the exterior siding of the main dwelling or any other enclosed structure that consists of synthetic stucco? ☐Yes ☒No ☐Unknown

If "Yes," explain: ____________________

23. Are you aware of any asbestos or past asbestos remediation affecting the main dwelling or any other enclosed structure located on the Property? ☐Yes ☒No ☐Unknown

If "Yes," explain: ____________________

24. Has the Property been tested for radon? ☐Yes ☐No ☒Unknown

If "Yes," explain: ____________________

25. Has the main dwelling or any other enclosed structure been tested for lead-based paint? ☐Yes ☐No ☒Unknown

If "Yes," explain: ____________________

26. What is the type of roof/roof covering on the main dwelling (shingle, slate, asphalt, tile, other)?

____

27. Are there any known leaks or other material defects in the roof of the main dwelling or any other enclosed structure? ☐Yes ☒No ☐Unknown

If "Yes," explain: ____________________

28. When was the roof installed? 2002 (Year)

29. Is there a transferable warranty on the roof in effect now? ☐Yes ☒No ☐Unknown

If "Yes," explain: ____________________

If "Yes," when does the warranty expire? ____________________

 Initials: ________ ________ ________ ________

FIGURE 25.27: Seller's Property Disclosure Form (continued)

30. Are there any known material defects in the gutters or downspouts of the main dwelling or any other enclosed structure? ☐Yes ☒No ☐Unknown ☐N/A

If "Yes," explain: ____

31. Are there any known material defects in any of the following structural systems of the main dwelling or any other enclosed structure, including, but not limited to, footings, beams, girders, lintels, columns, partitions, retaining walls? ☐Yes ☒No ☐Unknown

If "Yes," explain: ____

MECHANICAL SYSTEMS AND OTHER

32. What is the source of water serving the Property? ☐Well ☐Private ☒Municipal ☐Other

If "Other," explain: ____

If a well, is the well shared with any other property? ☐Yes ☐No ☐Unknown ☒N/A

33. Are there any known issues with water quality and/or flow rate? ☐Yes ☒No ☐Unknown

If "Yes," explain: ____

34. What is the type of sewage system? ☒Public Sewer ☐Private Sewer ☐Septic Tank ☐Other

If "Other," explain: ____

35. If septic tank or other, when was it installed? ____ (Year) ☐Unknown Date last serviced? ____ (Month,/Year) ☐Unknown

36. What is the type of plumbing system? ☒Copper ☐PVC ☐Polybutylene ☐Galvanized Iron ☐Other ☐Unknown

If "Other," explain: ____

37. Are there any known material defects with the plumbing or sewage systems? ☐Yes ☒No ☐Unknown ☐N/A

If "Yes," explain: ____

38. What type of water heater services the main dwelling? ☐Gas ☒Electric ☐Solar ☐Other

If "Other," explain: ____

39. What size is the water heater? (In Gallons) ____ Is it tankless? ☒Yes ☐No ☐Unknown ☐N/A

40. When was the water heater installed? 2012 (Year)

41. Is there a transferable warranty on the water heater in effect now? ☐Yes ☐No ☒Unknown ☐N/A

If "Yes," explain: ____

If "Yes," when does it expire? ____

42. What type of heating system services the main dwelling? ☒Gas ☐Electric ☐Solar ☐Propane ☐Other

If "Other," explain: ____

43. Does the heating/air conditioning system have a high-efficiency filter? ☒Yes ☐No ☐Unknown

44. When was the heating/air conditioning system installed? 2008 (Year)

Form RE130, *Seller's Property Condition Disclosure Statement*
 Initials: ____ ____ ____ ____
R10312012

FIGURE 25.27: Seller's Property Disclosure Form (continued)

45. Is there a transferable warranty on the heating/air conditioning system in effect now? ☐Yes ☒No ☐Unknown

If "Yes," explain: ______

If "Yes," when does the warranty expire? ______

46. Are there any known material defects with the electrical system? ☐Yes ☒No ☐Unknown ☐N/A

If "Yes," explain: ______

47. Does the electrical system use fuses or circuit breakers? ☒Fuses ☐Circuit Breakers ☐Unknown ☐N/A

48. Have there been, or are there presently, any flooding, drainage or grading problems that have resulted in standing water on any portion of the Property? ☒Yes ☐No ☐Unknown

If "Yes," explain: Some in basement prior to finished renovation

49. Has the basement ever had seepage that resulted in standing water? ☒Yes ☐No ☐Unknown ☐N/A

If "Yes," explain: See #48

50. Have there been any major renovations of $500 or more done to the Property? ☒Yes ☐No ☐Unknown

If "Yes," explain: renovated finished basement;2nd floor addition;bathroom/kichen renovation

51. Does the Property have any special energy efficient features? ☒Yes ☐No ☐Unknown

If "Yes," explain: thermopane windows; tankless water system

52. Are there any fixtures or items permanently attached to the Property that are not included in the sale? ☐Yes ☒No

If "Yes," explain: ______

______

53. Have there been any prior professional inspections performed on the Property? ☒Yes ☐No ☐Unknown ☐N/A

If "Yes," explain: Inspections done prior to finished basement renovation

Have there been or are there any known material defects in any of the following?

54. Security Alarm system .... ☐Yes ☒No ☐Unknown ☐N/A
55. Carbon monoxide detector? .... ☐Yes ☒No ☐Unknown ☐N/A
56. Smoke detector? .... ☐Yes ☒No ☐Unknown ☐N/A
57. Fire sprinkler system? .... ☐Yes ☒No ☐Unknown ☐N/A
58. Foundation/slab? .... ☐Yes ☒No ☐Unknown ☐N/A
59. Interior walls/ceilings? .... ☐Yes ☒No ☐Unknown ☐N/A
60. Exterior walls or siding? .... ☐Yes ☒No ☐Unknown ☐N/A
61. Floors? .... ☐Yes ☒No ☐Unknown ☐N/A
62. Chimney/fireplace or stove? .... ☐Yes ☒No ☐Unknown ☐N/A
63. Patio/deck? .... ☐Yes ☒No ☐Unknown ☐N/A
64. Gas Grill? .... ☐Yes ☒No ☐Unknown ☐N/A
65. Lawn Sprinkling System? .... ☐Yes ☒No ☐Unknown ☐N/A
66. Oven/Range? .... ☐Yes ☒No ☐Unknown ☐N/A
67. Refrigerator? .... ☐Yes ☒No ☐Unknown ☐N/A
68. Dishwasher? .... ☐Yes ☒No ☐Unknown ☐N/A
69. Microwave Oven? .... ☐Yes ☒No ☐Unknown ☐N/A
70. Garbage Disposal? .... ☐Yes ☒No ☐Unknown ☐N/A

5 of 8

Form RE130, *Seller's Property Condition Disclosure Statement*
 Initials: ______ ______ ______ ______
R10312012

FIGURE 25.27: Seller's Property Disclosure Form (continued)

71. Trash Compactor? .... ☐Yes ☒No ☐Unknown ☐N/A
72. Attic Fan? .... ☐Yes ☒No ☐Unknown ☐N/A
73. Ceiling Fans? .... ☐Yes ☒No ☐Unknown ☐N/A
74. Intercom? .... ☐Yes ☒No ☐Unknown ☐N/A
75. Washer? .... ☐Yes ☒No ☐Unknown ☐N/A
76. Dryer? .... ☐Yes ☒No ☐Unknown ☐N/A
77. Sauna/Hot Tub? .... ☐Yes ☒No ☐Unknown ☐N/A
78. Pool/Pool Liner? .... ☐Yes ☒No ☐Unknown ☐N/A
79. Garage Doors? .... ☐Yes ☒No ☐Unknown ☐N/A
80. Garage Door Openers? .... ☐Yes ☒No ☐Unknown ☐N/A
81. Driveway? .... ☐Yes ☒No ☐Unknown ☐N/A
82. Walkways? .... ☐Yes ☒No ☐Unknown ☐N/A
83. Patio/Deck? .... ☐Yes ☒No ☐Unknown ☐N/A
84. Fence? .... ☐Yes ☒No ☐Unknown ☐N/A
85. Mailbox? .... ☐Yes ☒No ☐Unknown ☐N/A
86. TV Antenna? .... ☐Yes ☒No ☐Unknown ☐N/A
87. Sump Pump? .... ☐Yes ☒No ☐Unknown ☐N/A

If "Yes" to any of the above, explain:

☐ **Check here if additional pages are attached to this Seller's Property Condition Disclosure.**

Form RE130, *Seller's Property Condition Disclosure Statement*
 Initials: ________ ________ ________ ________
R10312012

FIGURE 25.27: Seller's Property Disclosure Form (continued)

NOTE TO SELLER: Seller ☐agrees ☐ does not agree to provide to Buyer a copy of any written report of prior professional inspections of the Property received by Seller. Seller acknowledges that any future inspections of the Property may necessitate a revision to the Seller's Property Condition Disclosure Statement.

Seller's Certification:
Seller certifies that the information in this Seller's Property Condition Disclosure Statement is true and complete to the best of Seller's actual knowledge as of the date signed by the Seller. If Seller acquires knowledge which renders the Seller's Property Condition Disclosure Statement provided previously materially inaccurate, the Seller shall deliver a revised Seller's Property Condition Disclosure Statement to the Buyer as soon as is practicable. In no event, however, shall Seller be required to provide a revised Seller's Property Condition Disclosure Statement after the transfer of title from the Seller to the Buyer or occupancy by the Buyer, whichever event comes first.

Seller:

➢ ______________________________ Date: March 18, 20xx

Bernadette Joyce
Seller Printed Name

➢ ______________________________ Date: March 18, 20xx

Sean Joyce
Seller Printed Name

Buyer's Acknowledgment:
Buyer acknowledges receipt of a copy of this statement, and Buyer understands that the information contained in this Seller's Property Condition Disclosure is a statement of certain conditions and information concerning the Property known to the Seller. It is not a warranty of any kind by the Seller or Seller's agent.

Buyer:

➢ ______________________________ Date: May 5, 20xx

Sebastian Scott
Buyer Printed Name

➢ ______________________________ Date: May 5, 20xx

Miranda Scott
Buyer Printed Name

 Initials: ________ ________ ________ ________

FIGURE 25.27: Seller's Property Disclosure Form (continued)

Additional Page(s) for Seller's Property Condition Disclosure Statement

☐ **Check here if additional pages are attached to this Seller's Property Condition Disclosure.**

 Initials: _________ _________ _________ _________
R10312012

FIGURE 25.28: Lead-Based Paint Disclosure

Disclosure of Information on Lead-Based Paint and/or Lead-Based Paint Hazards Lead Warning Statement

Every Buyer/Tenant of any interest in residential real property on which a residential dwelling was built prior to 1978 is notified that such property may present exposure to lead from lead-based paint that may place young children at risk of developing lead poisoning. Lead poisoning in young children may produce permanent neurological damage, including learning disabilities, reduced intelligence quotient, behavioral problems, and impaired memory. Lead poisoning also poses a particular risk to pregnant women. The Seller/Landlord of any interest in residential real property is required to provide the Buyer/Tenant with any information on lead-based paint hazards from risk assessments or inspections in the Seller's/Landlord's possession and notify the Buyer/Tenant of any known lead-based paint hazards. A risk assessment or inspection for possible lead-based paint hazards is recommended prior to purchase.

Seller's/Landlord's Disclosure (initial)

1. ________ Presence of lead-based paint and/or lead-based paint hazards (check (i) or (ii) below):

   (i) ______ Known lead-based paint and/or lead-based paint hazards are present in the housing (explain).

   (ii) __✗__ No knowledge of lead-based paint and/or lead-based paint hazards in the housing.

2. ________ Records and reports available to the Seller/Landlord (check (i) or (ii) below):

   (i) _____ Has provided the Buyer/Tenant with all available records and reports pertaining to lead-based paint and/or lead-based paint hazards in the housing (list documents below).

   (ii) __✗__ Has no reports or records pertaining to lead-based paint and/or lead-based paint hazards in the housing.

Buyer's/Tenant's Acknowledgment (initial)

1. ________ Has received copies of all information listed above.
2. ________ Has received the pamphlet ***Protect Your Family from Lead in Your Home***.
3. ________ Has (check (i) or (ii) below):

   (i) _____ received a ten (10) day opportunity (or mutually agreed upon period) to conduct a risk assessment or inspection for the presence of lead-based paint and/or lead-based paint hazards; or

   (ii) __✗__ waived the opportunity to conduct a risk assessment or inspection for the presence of lead-based paint and/or lead-based paint hazards.

Seller/Landlord Agent's Acknowledgment (initial)

________ Agent has informed the Seller/Landlord of the seller's obligations under 42 U.S.C. 4852(d) and is aware of his/her responsibility to ensure compliance.

Certification of Accuracy

The following parties have reviewed the information above and certify, to the best of their knowledge, that the information they have provided is true and accurate.

Seller/Landlord Signature	Date	Buyer/Tenant Signature	Date
Bernadette Joyce		Sebastian Scott	
Seller/Landlord Signature	Date	Buyer/Tenant Signature	Date
Sean Joyce		Miranda Scott	
Seller's/Landlord's Broker Signature	Date	Buyer's/Tenant's Broker Signature	Date
Eric Cambridge		LUCY GORDON	

1 of 1

Form RE140, *Disclosure of Information on Lead Based Paint*

R10312012

FIGURE 25.29: Bill of Sale

Bill of Sale

Date: May 5, 20xx

For and in consideration of the mutual covenants contained herein and other good and valuable consideration, the receipt and sufficiency of which is hereby acknowledged, the undersigned Buyer agrees to buy and the undersigned Seller agrees to sell the following items of personal property (the "Personalty') belonging to Seller free and clear of all liens:

Description of Personal Property	Price
Outdoor Patio Furniture:Table;4 chairs;2 recliner chairs;unbrella	$0.00
Gas Grill on Patio	$0.00
TOTAL:	$0.00

This Bill of Sale shall be contingent upon and effective as of the closing of that certain contract for the purchase and sale of real property (the Contract") with an acceptance date of: ________, 20___ and relating to the property located at: 1103 Franklin Avenue , , Bellville Georgia, 33333 (the "Property"). The Seller hereby warrants the Seller has the right to sell the Personalty but does not warrant the condition or workmanship of any Personalty described herein. Buyer acknowledges that a third party warranty for the Personalty may be available at an additional cost to Buyer.

In the event the Contract is terminated or expires prior to closing, this Bill of Sale shall become null and void, and any amounts paid by Buyer in consideration of this Bill of Sale shall be returned to the Buyer. All parties acknowledge that the consideration paid for the Personalty conveyed hereby shall be in addition to, and not included in, the purchase price of the Property.

☐ **Check here if additional pages are attached.**

This Bill of Sale is accepted by the party to whom it was presented on May 5, **20**xx.

All Names should be both signed and printed.

Buyer :	***Seller:***
➢ ________	➢ ________
Sebastian Scott	Bernadette Joynce
Buyer Printed Name	Seller Printed Name
➢ ________	➢ ________
Miranda Scott	Sean Joyce
Buyer Printed Name	Seller Printed Name

1 of 1

Form RE112, *Bill of Sale*

R10312012

Instanet forms

FIGURE 25.30: Counteroffer Form With Acceptance

Counteroffer # 1

Date: May 6, 20xx

This Counteroffer amends and is made a part of and is incorporated into the Georgia Contract for Purchase and Sale of Real Property offer dated May 5, 20xx for the sale of that entire tract or parcel of property located in Bilbo County, Georgia, and being known as 1103 Franklin Avenue Bellville, Georgia 33333 (Address).

The Offer is hereby countered as follows:

- ☒ Purchase Price is changed to Three Hundred Ninety-Nine Thousand US Dollars (US$ 399,000.00).
- ☐ Earnest Money is changed to ________ US Dollars (US$________).
- ☐ Earnest Money Holder is changed to ________.
- ☐ Closing Date is changed to ________, 20____.
- ☐ Possession Date is Changed to ________, 20____ by ______ o'clock __m.
- ☒ Seller contribution to closing costs is changed to ☐ ______ percent (______%) of the Purchase Price or is changed to ☒ Four Thousand US Dollars (US$ 4,000.00).
- ☐ The following items are excluded from the sale:
- ☐ The following items are included in the sale:

Other:
Seller grants to Buyer Appraisal Contingency for twenty five(25) days after the Acceptance Date of Contract

The original offer, executed by the party making said offer, as amended only by this final counteroffer, executed by all parties, shall constitute the full and entire agreement Other counteroffers are not a part of this contract.

☐ Substantive provisions continued on additional page.

Form RE110 *Counter Offer*
 Initials: ________ ________ ________ ________
R10312012

FIGURE 25.30: Counter Offer form with Acceptance (continued)

All other terms remain the same as the offer. The above Counteroffer, unless accepted, shall expire at 1 o'clock P m. on MAY 7, 20XX.

This Counteroffer is hereby Accepted, with notice being properly given to the party making the last offer, at 7 o'clock P m. on MAY 6, 20XX.

All Names should be both signed and printed.

Buyer:	***Seller:***
➢ ________________	➢ ________________
Sebastian Scott Buyer's Printed Name	Bernadette Joyce Seller's Printed Name
➢ ________________	➢ ________________
Miranda Scott Buyer's Printed Name	Sean Joyce Seller's Printed Name
Buyer's Broker:	***Seller's Broker:***
Eureka Real Estate Services Name of Brokerage Firm	Top Floor Realty, Inc Name of Brokerage Firm
➢ ________________	➢ ________________
Lucy Gordon Agent's Printed Name	Eric Cambridge Agent's Printed Name

Form RE110 *Counteroffer*

 Initials: ________ ________ / ________ ________

R10312012

FIGURE 25.31: Commission Acknowledgment Agreement

Commission Acknowledgement

Date: May 5, 20xx

This Commission Acknowledgment sets forth the commission amounts to be paid at time the closing of the contract for purchase and sale of real property with an Acceptance Date of May 6, 20xx between Bernadette Joyce and Sean Joyce Seller(s) and Sebastian Scott and Miranda Scott Buyer(s) for the sale of the property located at the following address: 1103 Franklin Avenue, Bellville,Georgia 33333.

Whereas the Seller has agreed per the terms of a separate Listing/Brokerage Agreement to pay a real estate commission to the undersigned Seller's Broker and said Seller's Broker has agreed per the terms of that Listing Agreement to share the commission with the undersigned Buyer's Broker, the gross commission to each shall be:

☒ ***Seller's Broker*** to receive a commission, which is equivalent to (3 %) of the purchase price of Three Hundred Ninety-Nine Thousand US Dollars ($ 399,000.00) **or** a flat fee commission of: ______ US Dollars ($______).

and

☒ ***Buyer's Broker*** to receive a commission, which is equivalent to (3 %) of the purchase price of Three Hundred Ninety-Nine Thousand US Dollars ($ 399,000.00) **or** a flat fee commission of: ______ US Dollars ($______).

Additional credits/debits to be noted on the HUD-1 Closing Statement to/from Seller's Broker:

☐ Seller's Broker to ☐ pay outside of closing, **or** ☐ funds to be disbursed by closing attorney from Broker's Commission in the amount of ______ US Dollars ($______) for the purpose of: ______ and paid to:
Company Name: ______
Company Address: ______

☐ Seller's Broker to ☐ pay outside of closing, **or** ☐ funds to be disbursed by closing attorney from Broker's Commission in the amount of ______ US Dollars ($______) for the purpose of: ______ and paid to:
Company Name: ______
Company Address: ______

☐ Seller's Broker to receive payment in the amount of ______ US Dollars ($______) for the purpose of ______ from:
Company Name: ______
Company Address: ______

☐ Seller's Broker to receive payment in the amount of ______ US Dollars ($______) for the purpose of ______ from:
Company Name: ______
Company Address: ______

Additional credits/debits to be noted on the HUD-1 Closing Statement to/from Buyer's Broker:

☒ Buyer's Broker to ☐ pay outside of closing, **or** ☒ funds to be disbursed by closing attorney from Broker's Commission in the amount of One Thousand Five Hundred US Dollars ($ 1,500.00) for the purpose of: refunding of retainer fee to Buyer pursuant to Brokerage Engagement and paid to:
Company Name: Sebastian Scott
Company Address: ______

Form RE115, *Commission Acknowledgment*
 Initials: ______ ______ ______ ______
R10312012

FIGURE 25.31: Commission Acknowledgment Agreement (continued)

☐ Buyer's Broker to ☐ pay outside of closing, **or** ☐ funds to be disbursed by closing attorney from Broker's Commission in the amount of__________________ US Dollars ($__________) for the purpose of:________________________ and paid to:
Company Name:____________________
Company Address: ____________________

☐ Buyer's Broker to receive payment in the amount of __________________US Dollars ($__________) for the purpose of____________________ from:
Company Name:____________________
Company Address: ____________________

☐ Buyer's Broker to receive payment in the amount of __________________US Dollars ($__________) for the purpose of____________________ from:
Company Name:____________________
Company Address: ____________________

☐ Special Stipulations:

All Names should be both signed and printed.

Buyer's Broker:	***Seller's Broker:***
Eureka Real Estate Services / _____	Top Floor Realty,Inc / _____
Name of Brokerage Firm / Broker Code	Name of Brokerage Firm / Broker Code
709 987654 / 709 123-4567	404 222-1111 / 404 222-4444
Brokerage Phone Number / Brokerage Fax Number	Brokerage Phone Number / Brokerage Fax Number
➢________________	➢________________
LUCY GORDON	Eric Cambridge
Agent Printed Name	Agent Printed Name
404 777-7777 / 709 123-4567	770 102-6543 / 404 222-4444
Agent Phone Number / Agent Fax Number	Agent Phone Number / Agent Fax Number
LG1@mindspring.com	ericcom@comcast.net
Agent Email Address	Agent Email Address
Required License Number(s):	Required License Number(s):
J-3456 / 99999	H-1999 / 987654
Broker's Number / Agent's Number	Broker's Number / Agent's Number

Form RE115, *Commission Acknowledgment*
 Initials: _____ _____ _____ _____
R10312012

FIGURE 25.32: Amendment Regarding General Right to Terminate

Amendment During Buyer's Right to Terminate Period

Date: MAY 17, 20XX

Amendment to that certain contract for purchase and sale of real property (the "Contract") with an Acceptance Date of MAY 6, 20XX **relating to Property known as** 1103 Franklin Avenue, Bellville, **Georgia** 33333.

For and in consideration of the mutual covenants and conditions contained herein, the payment of ten US dollars (US$10.00), and other good and valuable consideration, each paid to the other, the receipt and sufficiency of which is hereby acknowledged the undersigned Buyer(s) and Seller(s) amend the above referenced Contract as follows:
AT THE TIME OF CLOSING, SELLER SHALL PROVIDE BUYER A HOME WARRANTY ISSUED BY ACME HMS AT A COST TO SELLER NOT TO EXCEED $500.THE TERM OF THE WARRANTY SHALL BE FOR AT LEAST ONE YEAR FROM THE DATE OF CLOSING.

This amendment [check one] ☐ SHALL **or** ☒ SHALL NOT act as a unilateral notice of termination of the above referenced Contract if it is not accepted by the Seller and delivered back to Buyer prior to the end of the Buyer's right to terminate period or due diligence period, as defined in the Contract.

☐ Substantive provisions continued on additional page.

This Amendment is accepted by the party to whom it was presented on MAY 18, 20XX.

All Names should be both signed and printed.

Buyer:	*Seller:*
➢	➢
Sebastian Scott	Bernadette Joyce
Buyer Printed Name	Seller Printed Name
➢	➢
Miranda Scott	Sean Joyce
Buyer Printed Name	Seller Printed Name

Form RE262 *Amendment During Buyer's Right to Terminate Period*

R10312012

FIGURE 25.33: Standard Terms for Contract for Purchase Sale of Residential Real Property

Standard Terms for the Purchase and Sale of Georgia Real Property

THESE STANDARD TERMS FOR CONTRACT FOR THE PURCHASE AND SALE OF RESIDENTIAL REAL PROPERTY AS PUBLISHED BY ORTHRUS REAL ESTATE ENTERPRISES, LLC ARE TO BE USED IN CONJUNCTION WITH AN EXECUTED CONTRACT FOR THE PURCHASE AND SALE OF REAL PROPERTY AS PUBLISHED BY ORTHRUS REAL ESTATE ENTERPRISES, LLC AND ARE NOT INTENDED, ABSENT AN EXECUTED CONTRACT, TO BE BINDING ON ANY PARTY UNLESS EXPRESSLY INCORPORATED THEREIN.

1. PROPERTY DESCRIPTION
Seller shall convey to Buyer good and marketable title to the Property by limited warranty deed, free and clear of all mortgages and liens, except the Property shall be subject to the taxes not yet due and payable and all other encumbrances, zoning ordinances, easements and restrictions of record as of the Acceptance date of the Contract. Good and marketable title as used in the Contract shall mean title which a title insurance company licensed to do business in Georgia will insure at its regular rates, subject only to standard exceptions.

2. PURCHASE PRICE
Buyer covenants that Buyer has adequate financial resources to purchase the Property. The Purchase Price, as adjusted by the prorations and adjustments provided in the Contract, shall be payable in full at Closing in cash by wire transfer of immediately available United States currency to a bank account designated by Closing Attorney (as defined in the Contract).

3. EARNEST MONEY/NONREFUNDABLE BUILDER DEPOSIT

3.1. Escrow Agent's Trust Account – If the Earnest Money funds shall be held by Escrow Agent, and not Seller, the Earnest Money funds shall be deposited into Escrow Agent's trust account as set out in the Contract. If the trust account is an interest bearing account, Escrow Agent shall be entitled to the interest.

3.2. Seller's Account- If Earnest Money and/or Nonrefundable Builder Deposit are to be held by Seller, said funds may be deposited into Seller's general operating account, not segregated or set apart in any manner, and Seller shall have the right to use the Earnest Money for whatever purpose Seller deems appropriate, unless Seller is otherwise required under Georgia law to deposit funds into Seller's trust account. If Seller's General Operating Account is an interest bearing account, the interest earned thereon shall be retained by Seller. Buyer and Seller acknowledge and agree that: Broker has no responsibility for, or control over any funds deposited with Seller. Buyer has not relied upon the advice or recommendation of Broker as to the financial condition or stability of Seller. The parties agree to release Broker from liability for any costs, fees, or damages resulting from Seller's handling of any funds described herein.

3.3. Buyer's Failure to Remit Earnest Money - Regardless of whether the payment was remitted prior to Acceptance or on or before an agreed upon date thereafter, if the method of presentation is not honored by the institution upon which it was drawn, Escrow Agent shall promptly notify Buyer and Seller, and the amount of the agreed upon Earnest Money deposit shall be paid by certified check or other collected funds to Escrow Agent within three (3) days of notice from Escrow Agent. If Buyer fails to do so, Seller shall have the rights and remedies set out in the Contract. Notwithstanding the above, in the event the Earnest Money is not remitted to Escrow Agent as set out in the Contract, the Earnest Money is no longer a part of the Contract and Seller may:

3.3.1. Unilaterally terminate the Contract within seven (7) days of receipt of notice from Escrow Agent, thereby releasing Buyer and Seller from any further obligations or responsibilities to the other;

3.3.2. If Seller holds Earnest Money, unilaterally terminate this contract within three (3) days of notice to Buyer, thereby releasing Buyer and Seller from any further obligations or responsibilities to the other; or,

3.3.3. Demand full performance of all other terms and conditions of the Contract and proceed to Closing.

3.4. Disbursement of Earnest Money if Held by Escrow Agent - After receiving reasonable assurance that the bank has credited the deposit to the account where the Earnest Money is being held, the Escrow Agent may (i) disburse the Earnest Money to Buyer if contract is not accepted, unless that issue is disputed; (ii) disburse the Earnest Money for credit to Buyer at Closing; (iii) disburse the Earnest Money to Buyer at time of Closing if it is not credited towards the purchase price at Closing; (iv) disburse the Earnest Money pursuant to a separate written agreement signed by the parties, agreeing to the terms of disbursement of the

FIGURE 25.33: Standard Terms for Contract for Purchase Sale of Residential Real Property (continued)

Earnest Money; (v) disburse the Earnest Money upon order of a court or arbitrator which has jurisdiction over the matter; or (vi) if Escrow Agent has received notice from any party that the Contract has been terminated or Closing has failed to occur, no more than thirty (30) days after said notice has been received Escrow Agent shall notify all parties of Escrow Agent's disbursement decision. Upon receipt of Escrow Agent's notification of disbursement, a party shall have ten (10) days to object to the disbursement. After receipt of a party's objection, Escrow Agent may change its decision or proceed according to Escrow Agent's original notification, but shall, in any event, notify the parties of said final disbursement.

In addition, if the disbursement of the Earnest Money is in dispute, Escrow Agent may file an action to interplead the Earnest Money to allow a court of competent jurisdiction to decide how it is to be disbursed, and Escrow Agent may disburse Earnest Money as part of the required procedures related to this filing. Additionally, Escrow Agent may deduct any attorney's fees, court costs and other related expenses from the Earnest Money as necessary to reimburse Escrow Agent for costs related to the interpleader action, and Escrow Agent shall be entitled to recover additional costs as described above if Escrow Agent's expenses exceed the amount of the Earnest Money. The party that the court deems to be entitled to the Earnest Money may seek to recover its attorney's fees, court costs and the amount deducted by the Escrow Agent from the party that was not deemed to be entitled to the Earnest Money. In performing any of its duties under this Agreement, Escrow Agent shall not be liable for any loss, cost or damage which may incur as a result of serving as Escrow Agent hereunder, except for any loss, cost or damages arising out of its willful default or gross negligence. The parties agree to release Broker from liability for any costs, fees, or damages resulting from Escrow Agent's duties described in the Contract.

If no objection to the disbursement of the Earnest Money is received by Escrow Agent prior to the disbursement of the Earnest Money, the right to object to said disbursement shall be deemed waived by the parties.

3.2. Non-Refundable Builder Deposit (may be applicable when Property is New Construction)- The purpose of the Non-Refundable Builder Deposit is not to secure Buyer's performance under the Contract, but to cover the estimated cost of any upgrades, selections or options selected by Buyer and agreed to by Seller.

4. **CLOSING**

4.1. Closing Documents- At Closing each party shall execute and deliver such deeds, certifications, affidavits, and statements as are required to fulfill the terms of the Contract, comply with federal and state law, and meet the requirements of any title insurance company or lender involved in this transaction. These documents shall include, but not be limited to, those necessary to effectuate a party's IRS §1031 exchange, if applicable, consent to which is hereby given by each party to the other.

4.2. Obligation to Complete and ILSA Compliance - If Property is under construction as of the date of the Acceptance Date, or if Seller has agreed to construct a home on the Property prior to Closing, and in order to ensure compliance with the Interstate Land Sales Full Disclosure Act ("ILSA"), Seller covenants that, in all events, the Seller will complete the Home within two (2) years from the date of Buyer's execution of this Contract; provided that, the date for completion may also be extended beyond two years in the event of delays incurred by circumstances beyond Seller's control that are recognized under Georgia contract law as impossibility or frustration of performance. The Home shall be deemed substantially complete upon the issuance of a certificate of occupancy by the applicable local building jurisdiction or when the space can be used for its intended purpose ("Substantial Completion"), and a certificate of occupancy from the local building jurisdiction shall satisfy the Seller's obligation to complete hereunder. This paragraph is intended to require the unconditional completion of the Home pursuant to ILSA, and shall not waive Buyer's right to enforce the Closing date stated in the Contract. Notwithstanding any limitation on remedies set forth elsewhere in the Contract, this obligation to complete is unconditional and may not be abridged and in the event Seller breaches its covenant to complete as set forth in this paragraph, Buyer may exercise all remedies available to it under the Contract at law or in equity.

5. **EXPENSES RELATING TO CLOSING**

5.1. Clearance of "Title Defects" - "Title defects" are those defects required to be remedied by the title insurance company insuring title to the Lender, if any, or to the Buyer, if an owner's policy is requested by Buyer. Seller shall be responsible for the removal of any liens encumbering the title and any legal fees, recording or other costs associated with title curative work. Seller shall also bear the cost of any other document, instrument, advice, or other services rendered primarily for the benefit of the Seller, including, but

Form RE1, *Standard Terms for the Purchase and Sale of GeorgiaReal Property*

R06152014

FIGURE 25.33: Standard Terms for Contract for Purchase Sale of Residential Real Property (continued)

not limited to: powers-of-attorney, costs associated with a mail-out or multiple counterpart closing, the preparation of corporate resolutions for Seller, or other similar expenses.

5.2. Prorations - Unless prohibited by any Buyer's lender, taxes, homeowner's dues, utilities, garbage or other solid waste disposal fees, rent, and other similar costs, fees or amounts shall be prorated as of the date of closing, unless the parties expressly agree in writing (i) that said item or items shall not be prorated or (i) that the proration of an item or items shall be based on the date of possession (or some other date) and not the date or closing. If the estimate upon which the prorations were based is found to be inaccurate after closing because the actual amount of the charge exceeded or was less than the estimate, the parties agree to re-prorate, between themselves, any difference resulting from said change.

5.3. Buyer Expenses - Buyer shall be responsible for payment of all other costs, fees, and expenses if not otherwise provided for in the Contract, including, but not limited to Georgia transfer tax, deed recording fees and title insurance.

5.4. Seller Closing Costs - Seller shall bear the cost of Seller's attorney's fees and expenses, unless said attorney is also acting in the capacity of Closing Attorney representing a Lender. If Seller's attorney is acting in such a capacity, then Seller's obligation relates only to the charges and/or fees for services rendered directly to the Seller or not otherwise incurred as a result of (or as it relates to) usual and customary services provided by a Closing Attorney for a closing.

5.5. Closing Cost Allowance for Buyer- The Closing Cost Allowance agreed to by Seller in the Contract, if any, shall be subject to FNMA/FHLMC, FHA, USDA, VA or other Lender's underwriting criteria as may be applicable, and may be used for any purpose whatsoever to offset closing costs incurred by Buyer, such as title insurance, costs of financing, homeowners association dues, etc. (regardless of whether said cost is required by law, the Lender, or merely at the discretion of the Buyer) to close this transaction. In the event the Buyer's lender does not allow the Seller to contribute the full amount of the Closing Cost Allowance on the closing statement, this paragraph shall be deemed amended to reflect the actual closing cost allowance allowed by the Lender, and the Seller shall have no further obligation to Buyer therefor.

6. DEFINED CONTINGENCIES

6.1. Buyer's General Right to Terminate – *This contingency shall only be granted by the Seller if the appropriate box related thereto is checked within the body of the Contract and is thereby selected by the parties. If this contingency is not selected, this Section shall not be deemed a part of the Contract.* Subject to any expiration date expressed in writing in the Contract, the Buyer's General Right to Terminate is defined as Seller's grant to Buyer of the right to terminate the Contract by delivering written notice to Seller and receiving a full refund of the Earnest Money for any reason whatsoever. Buyer shall also have the right, but not the obligation, prior to the expiration of this contingency to propose to Seller an amendment to the Contract addressing any concerns Buyer has regarding the Property; provided, however, that Seller shall have no obligation to accept Buyer's proposed amendment. If Seller fails to accept Buyer's proposal to amend the Contract, if any, prior to the expiration of this contingency, Buyer shall have the option to either terminate the Contract prior to the expiration of this contingency, or accept the property "as is." If Seller does not receive timely written notice of Buyer's termination of the Contract as provided hereunder, this contingency shall be deemed waived. If Buyer does give Notice of Termination, the Earnest Money shall be refunded to Buyer, and Buyer shall promptly provide to Seller, without charge, copies of any reports, surveys, drawings, tests or other written documents obtained by Buyer with respect to the Property.

6.2. Appraisal Contingency-*This contingency shall only be granted by the Seller if the appropriate box related thereto is checked within the body of the Contract and is thereby selected by the parties. If this contingency is not selected, this Section shall not be deemed a part of the Contract.* Subject to any expiration date expressed in writing in the Contract, the Appraisal Contingency is defined as Seller's grant to Buyer of the right to terminate the Contract if Buyer does not receive an appraisal of the Property, performed by a licensed Georgia real estate appraiser, showing the value of the Property to be equal to or greater than the Purchase Price. If the Property does not appraise for a minimum of the Purchase Price, Buyer, at Buyer's sole discretion, shall have the right to terminate the Contract and receive a full refund of the Earnest Money by providing Seller a copy of the appraisal and written notice of Buyer's intent to terminate the Contract prior to the expiration of this contingency. If the Property fails to appraise for a minimum of the Purchase Price, either party shall also have the right, but not the obligation, prior to the expiration of this contingency to propose to the other an amendment to the Contract reducing the Purchase Price; provided, however, that neither party shall have the obligation to accept said proposed amendment. If Seller does not receive notice of Buyer's termination of the Contract as provided hereunder, this contingency shall be deemed waived.

Page 3 of 8

Form RE1, *Standard Terms for the Purchase and Sale of GeorgiaReal Property*

R06152014

FIGURE 25.33: Standard Terms for Contract for Purchase Sale of Residential Real Property (continued)

6.3. Financing Contingency-*This contingency shall only be granted by the Seller if the appropriate box related thereto is checked within the body of the Contract and is thereby selected by the parties. If this contingency is not selected, this Section shall not be deemed a part of the Contract.* Subject to any expiration date expressed in writing in the Contract, the Financing Contingency is defined as Seller's grant to Buyer of the right to terminate the Contract in the event the Buyer is unable to procure financing under the terms expressed in the Contract. The following conditions shall also apply:

6.3.1. If Buyer chooses to terminate the Contract based on an inability to obtain financing as described hereunder, Buyer must give Seller written notice of termination of the Contract along with a written statement from Buyer's lender (or lenders, if applicable), indicating the reason for the lender's denial of loan approval. This contingency shall be deemed waived by Buyer under the following circumstances:

6.3.1.1. If Buyer fails to provide proof of a lender's denial of loan approval prior to the deadline set forth in the Contract; or

6.3.1.2. If the lender's denial of loan approval is based on Buyer's lack of sufficient funds to pay for the down payment and closing costs, lack of timely loan application, Buyer's failure to sell or lease Buyer's current home, or Buyer's conduct after the Acceptance Date but prior to the expiration of this contingency.

6.3.2. If FNMA/FHLMC, FHA, USDA, or VA underwriting guidelines mandate compliance with any underwriting criteria expressly contrary to the provisions of the Contract, those provisions shall prevail and be binding upon the parties hereto, provided, however, that if any of these guidelines result in an increase in costs or expenses to the Seller, or affect the date of closing, then Seller, at Seller's sole discretion, shall have the right to unilaterally terminate the Contract within three (3) days of receipt of notice, thereby releasing Buyer and Seller from any further obligations or responsibilities to the other. If Seller does not terminate the Contract, Seller is deemed to consent to those changes that are mandated by the underwriting guidelines.

7. **CONDITION OF PROPERTY**

7.1. Duty to Inspect - Seller and Buyer have been advised and expressly acknowledge their obligation to conduct a thorough investigation, or to obtain independent professional advice, with respect to any concerns they may have regarding the Contract or the condition of the Property and the surrounding neighborhood, including, but not limited to, any structural, safety, title, environmental, financial, tax, legal or health concerns, or issues regarding the surrounding community, future or current real estate development, or municipal services offered to local residents.

7.2. For New Construction Only- If Property is under construction as of the date of the Acceptance Date, or if Seller has agreed to construct a home on the Property prior to Closing, then, except for changes and improvements made to the condition of Property pursuant to the Contract, Seller warrants and represents that, at Closing, Property shall be in the same condition on date of Closing as it is on date of Acceptance, normal wear and tear excepted and "broom clean."

7.2.1. Punchlist: Whether or not Buyer has inspected the Property during construction, Buyer and Seller's representative(s) shall inspect the Property prior to Closing and after construction of Property is substantially complete. If applicable, Buyer and Seller shall prepare and sign an amendment to the Contract (the "Punchlist") specifying all items, including any noted in previous inspections that fail to comply with the Plans and Specifications (as defined in the Contract). Buyer acknowledges that Seller will make its best efforts to address all of the items specified in the Punchlist on a timely basis as soon as reasonably possible before Closing. However, the fact that any such items remain to be addressed as of the Closing shall not constitute a valid reason for Buyer's failure or refusal to close, as long as a certificate of occupancy has been issued, and none of the proceeds due to Seller at Closing shall be withheld from Seller or placed in escrow. In lieu of repairing any item specified on the Punchlist, Seller shall have the option of replacing such item or paying a reasonable sum to Buyer for the cost of the repair

7.2.2. Insulation: Notwithstanding the thickness and R-values stated in the Contract, insulation may be of a lesser thickness and R-value in certain limited areas where the design of the home does not permit greater thickness, such as in locations where studs are placed in walls, at corners and at windows. The R-values and thickness stated are based on representations of the manufacturers and/or the installer of the insulation and Seller does not warrant or represent that these R-values or thickness are correct. Seller has the right to make substitutions as to the type, thickness and R-value of the insulation installed in the home without obtaining the consent of the Buyer as long as there are no substantial changes in the R-values of the insulation installed in a substantial portion of the home.

FIGURE 25.33: Standard Terms for Contract for Purchase Sale of Residential Real Property (continued)

7.2.3. Warranty: Buyer agrees to accept any builder's warranty described in the Contract (the "Warranty") as the sole warranty being given by the Seller to the Buyer. Seller disclaims any and all implied warranties of merchantability and fitness or habitability as to the Property and in the place of such warranties, whether arising from implication, custom, usage, course of trade, statutory or case law, or otherwise, is the Warranty described in the Contract as the sole warranty being given by Seller to Buyer. Buyer agrees that Seller shall not be liable for any defects not specifically provided for in the Warranty. The provisions of this paragraph shall survive the Closing and delivery of the deed to the Buyer, and without further documentation, all warranties which by their terms are transferable shall be deemed transferred to Buyer.

7.2.4. Selection Period: If the Contract provides for a selection period during which Buyer and Seller may finalize selections for options and/or upgrades to the Property, Seller has the right to approve or disapprove Buyer's selection of upgrades and options. Buyer understands and agrees materials used for all upgrades and options may vary somewhat from any samples provided and actual as-built conditions may also vary. Such variations are inherent in manufacturing and shall not be grounds for any refusal by Buyer to accept the home. If all option selections are not completed by Buyer within the specified timeframe indicated in the Contract, Seller shall have the right to make such selections on behalf of Buyer, which selections shall be deemed accepted and agreeable to Buyer.

7.2.5. Change Orders: Should Buyer request a change to the Plans and Specifications (as defined in the Contract) of the improvements on the Property (a "Change Order") after the initial selection period, if any, the request must be made to Seller in writing. Seller shall not be obligated to grant Buyer's Change Order request. At Seller's sole and absolute discretion, Seller may amend the Change Order request by providing the Buyer in writing with the additional cost for the change and any necessary extensions of the Closing date caused thereby. Buyer must approve and accept the cost for any additional options and/or changes by signing and returning the amended Change Order form to Seller within 48 hours of receipt, or the Change Order request shall be deemed denied and not a part of this Contract. Payment for the additional monies required for the change must accompany the fully executed final Change Order. The total amount of any monies actually paid for the Change Order shall be added to the original Non-Refundable Builder Deposit amount, if any.

7.3. For Resales of Homes, Lots and Raw Land: If Property is not under construction as of the date of the Acceptance Date, and Seller has not agreed to construct a home on the Property prior to Closing, and if the Seller has agreed in writing, by Contract amendment, exhibit or otherwise, to perform any repairs to the Property, any repairs performed by Seller shall be done in a "good and workmanlike" manner and shall be completed no later than three (3) days prior to Closing.

7.4. Damage to Property Before Closing - Seller shall keep in force sufficient hazard insurance on the property to protect all interests until this sale is closed and the deed delivered. If the Property is destroyed or materially damaged between the date hereof and the Closing and Seller is unable or unwilling to restore it to its previous condition prior to closing, Buyer shall have the option of canceling the Contract and receiving back the Earnest Money, or accepting the Property in its damaged condition, any insurance proceeds otherwise payable to Seller by reason of such damage shall be applied to the balance of the purchase price or otherwise be payable to Buyer. Buyer shall indemnify, hold harmless and defend Seller from and against any and all claims, demands, causes of action, liabilities, losses, costs, damages and expenses (including reasonable attorneys' fees and expenses and court costs incurred in defending any such claim or in enforcing this indemnity) that may be incurred by Seller arising out of or in connection with the acts or omissions of Buyer and its agents, representatives, contractors and consultants, or any of them (the "Claims"). The Claims shall include, but not be limited to, claims arising out of or in connection with personal injury or death of persons, loss, destruction or damage to property, or liens or claims of lien filed against the Property, excluding, however, any claims to the extent such claims arise out of the discovery of, or the non-negligent, accidental or inadvertent actual or threatened release or movement of, any Hazardous Materials resulting from Buyer's inspections and other activities (unless the Hazardous Materials are brought onto the Property by Buyer or Buyer's authorized agents, employees, consultants or contractors).

7.5. Eminent Domain- If, after the Acceptance Date of the Contract and prior to Closing, Seller receives notice of the commencement or threatened commencement of eminent domain or other like proceedings against the Property or any portion thereof, Seller shall immediately give Notice thereof to Buyer. Within thirty (30) days of Seller's notification to Buyer, Buyer shall elect by Notice to Seller either (i) to Terminate the Contract, in which event the Earnest Money shall be refunded to Buyer, or (ii) to close the transaction in accordance with the terms of the Contract but subject to such proceedings, in which event the Purchase Price

FIGURE 25.33: Standard Terms for Contract for Purchase Sale of Residential Real Property (continued)

shall not be reduced but Seller shall assign to Buyer Seller's rights in any condemnation award or proceeds. If Buyer does not give Notice timely, Buyer shall be deemed to have elected to close the transaction in accordance with this paragraph.

7.6. Plans and Specifications – Buyer hereby acknowledges and agrees that any floor plans, renderings, drawings, and the like, furnished by Seller to Buyer and which purport to depict the home, or any portion thereof, or the building containing the same, are merely approximations, and do not necessarily reflect the actual "as-built" conditions of the same. Illustrations in sales brochures and other marketing materials are artists' representations and are not actual construction plans or exact depictions of the Home. The Buyer further acknowledges and agrees that the decorations, furniture, furnishings, wallpaper, appliances and fixtures contained in any model home are for demonstrative purposes only and are not included in the sale of the Property. Buyer acknowledges that during the course of construction certain changes, substitutions of materials, deviations or omissions may be required by governmental authorities having jurisdiction over the Property, design changes, or availability of labor or materials. All such changes, deviations and omissions are hereby authorized by Buyer. Certain items and improvements to the Home such as paint color, tile cabinets, and appliances furnished by Seller may be subject to design change by the manufacturer or subject to shading in color or graduation and may vary from any samples that any have been shown to Buyer by Seller.

8. BROKERAGE

All parties represented by a Broker acknowledge that no Broker in this transaction shall owe any duty to Buyer or Seller greater than what is set forth in their brokerage engagements and the Brokerage Relationships in Real Estate Transactions Act, O.C.G.A. § 10-6A-1 et. seq and further:

8.1. Seller and Buyer each hereby represents and warrants to the other that he/she/they have not dealt with any real estate Broker, agent or salesperson (other than Seller's Broker or Buyer's Broker, as defined in the Contract) so as to create any legal right or claim in any such Broker, agent or salesperson for a commission or similar fee or compensation with respect to the negotiation and/or consummation of the Contract. Buyer and Seller acknowledge that they are not represented by a Broker unless they have signed a brokerage agreement with said Broker. If any party hereto is not represented by a Broker, that party acknowledges full responsibility for protecting his/ her/their own interests.

8.2. Any commission or other compensation due to a Broker shall be paid according to the terms of a separate agreement between Broker and Buyer, Broker and Seller, or both.

8.3. Buyer and Seller expressly acknowledge that Broker is not an expert in matters relating to the condition of the Property and the surrounding neighborhood, including, but not limited to, any structural, safety, title, environmental, financial, tax, legal or health concerns, or issues regarding the surrounding community, future or current real estate development, or municipal services offered to local residents, and has given no advice nor made any representations in regard thereto upon which Buyer or Seller have relied. All parties hereby release any Broker and any affiliated agent and employee from any cost, expense or liability that may result from their reliance on any perceived advice given with respect to the foregoing. If liability is found to exist under the standard of care or conduct required of Broker or its affiliated licensee, their liability is limited to the amount of commission actually received in this particular transaction.

8.4. Dual Agent - "Dual agent" means a Broker who simultaneously has a client relationship with both Seller and Buyer in the same real estate transaction. O.C.G.A. §10-6A-3(10). By checking the dual agent box in the Contract, the parties acknowledge that they have consented to a dual agency and acknowledge that their interests may sometimes be adverse. If the parties have agreed to allow a Broker to act as a dual agent, that Broker will not disclose to another party any information a client has asked the Broker to keep confidential, or which would negatively affect that party's bargaining position, unless the disclosure is required by law.

8.5. Designated Agent - "Designated agent" means one or more licensees affiliated with a Broker who are assigned by the Broker to represent solely one client to the exclusion of all other clients in the same transaction and to the exclusion of all other licensees affiliated with the Broker. O.C.G.A. §10-6A-3(9). By checking the designated agent box in the contract, the parties acknowledge that they have consented to a designated agency.

9. DEFAULT

A party shall be in default if he or she breaches any term of the Contract. Except in the event of a party's failure to close or as otherwise stated in the Contract, neither Seller nor Buyer shall be deemed to be in default hereunder,

FIGURE 25.33: Standard Terms for Contract for Purchase Sale of Residential Real Property (continued)

however, until and unless such party has been given written notice of its failure to comply with the terms of the Contract and thereafter does not cure such failure within three (3) banking days after receipt of such notice.

9.1. Buyer's Default - Buyer's default under any of the terms of the Contract may result in Seller's termination of the Contract, together with Seller's exercise of all rights and remedies available under the law, including, but not limited to, Buyer's forfeiture of earnest money deposits and law suits for damages. Seller may either accept the Earnest Money as full liquidated damages or bring legal action for actual damages, it being agreed by the parties that the actual damages are impossible to calculate. Seller's right to retain the Earnest Money is intended not as penalty, but as full liquidated damages pursuant to Official Code of Georgia Annotated, §13-6-7.

9.2. Seller's Default - If this transaction shall not be closed because of default of Seller, the Earnest Money shall, at Buyer's election, be refunded to Buyer, and, after repayment of the Earnest Money to Buyer, the Contract shall be null and void and neither Seller nor Buyer shall have any further rights or obligations hereunder; or Buyer shall have the right to sue for specific performance of the Contract, provided that such specific performance remedy shall be available to Buyer only upon Buyer's full satisfaction of each of Buyer's obligations under the Contract, including without limitation Buyer's obligation to deliver the Earnest Money and delivering sufficient proof to the Closing Attorney and Seller that Buyer is ready, willing and able to close this transaction. The option selected by Buyer shall be Buyer's sole and exclusive remedy, and in no event shall Buyer be entitled to damages.

9.3. Broker's Commission - By signing the Contract Buyer and Seller acknowledge and agree that Broker has performed a valuable third party service to Buyer and Seller. The terms of the Contract shall in no way alter or amend the terms of any separate written brokerage or other agreement between a Broker and Seller or Broker and Buyer, and Broker's remedy against a defaulting party with whom Broker has a separate written agreement shall be governed by the terms of that agreement. If, however, a defaulting party does not have a written agreement with a Broker, and that Broker is involved in this transaction as evidenced by a signed written agreement between Broker and the party they represent, each such Broker shall be entitled to collect from the defaulting party the full amount of commission to which the Broker would have been entitled had the Closing taken place. The defaulting party's payment of commission is intended not as penalty, but as full liquidated damages pursuant to Official Code of Georgia Annotated, §13-6-7.

10. NOTICES

Any notice, request or other communication required or permitted to be given hereunder shall be in writing and shall be delivered by hand or overnight courier (such as United Parcel Service or Federal Express), sent by facsimile, sent by electronic mail ("email") or mailed by United States registered or certified mail, return receipt requested, postage prepaid and addressed to each party at its address as set forth in the Contract. Any such notice shall be considered given on the date of such hand or courier delivery, confirmed facsimile transmission, deposit with such overnight courier for next business day delivery, or deposit in the United States mail, but the time period (if any is provided in the Contract) in which to respond to such notice shall commence on the date of hand or overnight courier delivery or on the date received following deposit in the United States mail as provided above. Rejection or other refusal to accept or inability to deliver because of changed address of which no notice was given shall be deemed to be receipt of the notice. By giving at least five (5) banking days' prior written notice thereof, any party may from time to time and at any time change its mailing address hereunder. Any notice of any party may be given by or to such party's counsel or Broker as long as it is signed by the appropriate party. The parties' respective mailing and email addresses for notice purposes are indicated after the parties' signatures in the Contract. Telephone numbers are given for convenience of reference only. Notice by telephone shall not be effective.

11. MISCELLANEOUS

The Buyer and Seller covenant and agree with each other that:

11.1. The provisions of the Contract shall extend to and be binding on the respective heirs, executors, administrators and successors of each party hereto;

11.2. If any provision of the Contract is determined by a court of competent jurisdiction to be invalid or unenforceable, the remainder of the Contract shall nonetheless remain in full force and effect;

11.3. The section headings appearing in the Contract are for convenience of reference only and are not intended, to any extent and for any purpose, to limit or define the text of any section or any subsection hereof;

FIGURE 25.33: Standard Terms for Contract for Purchase Sale of Residential Real Property (continued)

11.4. The Contract, including any Exhibits attached hereto, contain the entire agreement between the parties pertaining to the subject matter hereof and fully supersede all prior written or oral agreements and understandings between the parties pertaining to such subject matter;
11.5. The Contract shall be governed by and interpreted under the laws of the State of Georgia;
11.6. Time is of the essence of the Contract.
11.7. Unless expressly agreed otherwise in the Contract or unless provided otherwise in any other document executed by Seller and Buyer at or prior to closing, the provisions of the Contract shall survive closing.
11.8. The form of the Contract is provided as a convenience. All parties to the Contract have the obligation to seek independent legal advice as to whether this form protects their rights and fulfills their expectations.
11.9. Definitions:
Any capitalized or defined term, if not otherwise defined in these Standard Terms, shall have the meaning ascribed to it elsewhere in the Contract.

11.9.1. Acceptance (Accepted): "Acceptance" or "Accepted" shall mean the acceptance of the Contract pursuant to a right to do so provided in the Contract. Acceptance shall occur only prior to an Offer being withdrawn, revoked or terminated, in writing and in accordance with any provision of the Contract, if the receiver of an Offer accepts it exactly as presented, without modification, provided Acceptance is communicated, in writing, to the party making the Offer;
11.9.2. Banking Days: Monday through Friday, excluding federal holidays;
11.9.3. Broker: Any individual or entity issued a broker's real estate license by the Georgia Real Estate Commission pursuant to O.C.G.A. § 43-40. The term "Broker" includes the Broker's affiliated licensees except where the context would otherwise indicate;
11.9.4. Buyer: The term “Buyer” used in the Contract shall refer collectively to all persons named in the Contract and signing the Contract as Buyer, and the liability of each such person shall be joint and several. Notice given by Seller to any person named as Buyer, or by any such person to Seller, shall bind all persons signing the Contract as Buyer;
11.9.5. Buyer's Broker: Broker assisting the Buyer regardless of whether the Buyer is a customer or a client in accordance with Georgia law. It includes the agent or agents of the Broker who are involved with this particular transaction;
11.9.6. Contract: An executed purchase and sale agreement between a Buyer and Seller for the purchase of real property, which agreement shall include and incorporate by reference these Standard Terms for Contract for the Purchase and Sale of Residential Real Property.
11.9.7. Inspection: Includes any and all inspections regardless of whether by the Buyer individually or by a licensed (where required by law) or other third party inspector selected by Buyer; it includes all types of land surveys relating to real property; and, it includes any and all other types of borings, examinations, samplings, testings, and other reviews;
11.9.8. Offer: A proposal to purchase or sell the Property which, upon Acceptance, will result in a binding contract. An Offer includes any counteroffer made in result of an Offer. Any counteroffer automatically terminates the Offer being countered;
11.9.9. Party: Each person named in the Contract as Buyer or Seller and shall not include any Broker or other third party named in the Contract.
11.9.10. Seller: The term “Seller” used in the Contract shall refer collectively to all persons named in the Contract and signing the Contract as Seller, and their successors and/or assigns. Notice given by Buyer to any person named as Seller, or by any such person to Buyer, shall bind all persons signing the Contract as Seller;
11.9.11. Seller's Broker: Brokers assisting the Seller regardless of whether the Seller is a customer or client in accordance with Georgia law. It includes the agent or agents of the Broker who are involved with this particular transaction.
11.9.12. Terminate or **Termination**: "Terminate" or "Termination" shall mean the termination of the Contract pursuant to a right to do so provided in the Contract. Upon Termination, the Earnest Money shall be disbursed as provided in the Contract, and the Parties shall have no further rights or duties under the Contract except as expressly provided in the Contract.

GEORGIA RESIDENTIAL LANDLORD-TENANT ACT

While the terms of a contract for lease control the rights and duties in a landlord-tenant relationship, such actions are commonly regulated by statutory guidelines. Though not addressing contractual details in rental agreements, Georgia Code 44-7 does set forth general rights and responsibilities for the parties. Moreover, because most leases are written to protect landlords, laws in Georgia offer protections for the tenant. As such, leases for residential dwellings are prohibited from using language that

- seeks to limit, weaken, or waive landlord responsibility for any damages caused by failure to keep the property in good repair;
- attempts to avoid compliance with local ordinances;
- seeks to exempt landlords from complying with Georgia regulations regarding security deposits;
- allows landlords to regain possession of property from a delinquent or holdover tenant without first going through the judicial process as legally required; or
- requires tenants to pay a landlord's attorney fees as a result of a contract breach unless the lease also requires the landlord to pay the tenant's legal costs for a contract breach by the landlord.

IN PRACTICE A lease with any of above language is still valid, but the prohibited language is void and unenforceable.

tenant law is only if parties can't come to terms on their own

No governmental agency in Georgia has the authority to intervene in a dispute between a landlord and a tenant that cannot be resolved by the parties. To enforce legal rights in these situations, the parties must find a resolution through the court system. The basis for judicial decisions that decide landlord-tenant disputes in Georgia comes from two sources: the legislative codes of the Landlord-Tenant Act and case law in which the Georgia Supreme Court and state courts of appeal decide cases that clarify application of this statutory law.

OCGA 44-7-1

The relationship of landlord and tenant is created when the owner of real estate grants to another person, who accepts such grant, the right to possess, use, and enjoy the use of such real estate either for a fixed time or at will.

IN PRACTICE A tenant's right to occupy real property is called a **leasehold estate**. The estate may be a **periodic estate** or an **estate for years**. A periodic estate has a definite period with an automatic renewal if it is not terminated by the landlord or the tenant. An estate for years is a lease with a specific starting date and a specific ending date stated in the lease, with no automatic renewal.

If, as is common practice, the rental contract indicates a fixed time for the term of the lease, the lease will terminate at midnight on the final day of the term. Sometimes, the language of the lease provides for an automatic extension of the rental term, absent notice of termination from the tenant or a renewal option for the tenant subject to proper notice identified in the lease. A **tenant at will**, as identified in the code section, is a party who occupies rental property with the landlord's consent and makes rental payments without a written lease for an indefinite period. In this type of rental agreement, Georgia landlord-tenant codes, including eviction and security deposit laws, still apply. If this lease does not state an expiration date, as is often the case when the agreement is not in writing, Section 44-7-7 of the Georgia Code specifies that the tenant at will must be given a 60-day notice by the landlord before terminating the lease; the tenant is required to provide 30 days' notice for such termination. When a tenant at will fails to pay rent, the landlord is not required to give such notice of termination and can demand possession through dispossessory judicial action. Even though this type of lease is verbal, notices to terminate are always best served in writing to protect legal interests.

When a tenant stays beyond the legal tenancy without consent of the landlord, a **tenancy at sufferance** occurs; the tenant is commonly called a holdover tenant, and the landlord is not required to give any advance notice of eviction.

Verbal leases for a year or less, such as those created at will in Georgia, are enforceable by law. Rental agreements for more than one year must be in writing and include an adequate legal description of the property to be enforced legally.

CONTRACT FOR THE LEASE OF RESIDENTIAL REAL PROPERTY

Although many contracts for lease are similar in format and language, there is no such thing as a 'standard' lease provided or approved by any governmental agency or court. Leases may differ from landlord to landlord, but as is the case with any enforceable contract, the agreement is a legal document that defines the relationship between those persons who are party to the agreement. As such, real estate licensees are prohibited from drafting such contracts but are expected to provide assistance to landlord and tenant clients in the preparation of contracts for the rental of real property. As identified in a previous discussion of brokerage engagements and contacts for purchase and sale, the contract forms used here for leases are those commonly available for use by Georgia Multiple Listing Service (GAMLS) and First Multiple Listing Service (FMLS).

As a salesperson and affiliate licensee, be sure to check with your brokerage firm's management or your broker to ensure that you are using a proper lease form. Many firms use lease forms provided through the Georgia Association of REALTORS® (GAR). GAR contracts are typically updated yearly to reflect any changes in laws or real estate practice. To sharpen your skills in filling in contract forms properly, many salesperson postlicense and continuing education courses in Georgia teach licensees how to use the most recent contract forms available for Georgia transactions.

Narrative

Two years ago, Sebastian and Miranda Scott purchased a home at 1103 Franklin Avenue in Bellville, Georgia, a suburb of metropolitan Atlanta. The high-tech firm that employs the couple has recently established a global presence and, in the next few months, needs both Scotts to oversee an important company project in Europe. The project will require the Scotts to temporarily relocate for at least one year. The Scotts have made an appointment with agent Lucy Gordon, a licensee affiliate of Eureka Real Estate Services, who represented the couple two years ago in their purchase of the 1103 Franklin Avenue residence. They now want the brokerage firm to represent them in finding a tenant to lease their home for a year.

Because Eureka's office policy allows affiliate licensees to work with both landlords and tenants, Gordon agrees to assist the Scotts and enters into a 120-day exclusive lease procurement listing agreement with the couple on June 18, 20xx. The property will be offered for a 12-month lease at a monthly rent of $2,500. Upon finding a person(s) ready, willing, and able to rent the property for no less than $2,500 a month or any other price acceptable to the landlord, Eureka Realty will earn a commission equal to the first month's full rent. Receipt of the commission will be paid to the broker by the landlord upon receipt of first month's rent.

After marketing the rental listing for a month, Gordon locates a tenant for the Scotts' home on July 20. Erin Barker and Amanda Jones agree to a 12-month lease beginning on September 1, 20xx; the Scotts agree to the couple's monthly rental offer of $2,350.

FIGURE 25.34: Residential Lease Form, Items 1–6

Contract for the Lease Of Residential Real Property

Offer Date: July 20, 20 xx

This **Contract for the Lease of Residential Real Property** (the "Lease") is made on the Acceptance Date described herein by and between Sebastian Scott and Miranda Scott, hereinafter called "Landlord" and Erin Barker and Amanda Jones, hereinafter called "Tenant," for the hereinafter described Property, and in consideration of the mutual promises contained herein. It is expressly understood and agreed that this Lease creates the relationship of Landlord and Tenant. This Lease is not intended to create an estate for years or transfer any ownership interest in the Property to Tenant.

1. PROPERTY LEASED

Landlord hereby Leases to Tenant and the latter lets from the former, premises including a residential dwelling located at: 1103 Franklin Avenue Bellville, Georgia 33333 or, if this box is checked, ☒ as described on the attached Legal Description Exhibit, incorporated herein by this reference, hereinafter called the "Property," to which Landlord claims title.

2. TERM OF LEASE

The initial term of the Lease shall be 12 months, beginning on September 1,20xx and ending on August 31,20xx.

3. RENEWAL OF LEASE

At the expiration of the Lease term, and unless otherwise terminated pursuant to the terms of this Lease, this Lease will be automatically renewed [check one] ☒ on a month to month basis, or ☐ for a term of n/a days. At that time, the rental rate shall increase by 10 % of the most recent rental rate, or US$ n/a per month. All other terms of this Lease shall remain the same. If either the Landlord or the Tenant does not wish to renew this Lease at the end of the initial or extended Lease term, the party not wishing to renew shall notify the other party in writing of such intent not to renew, no less than thirty (30) days before the expiration of this Lease.

Hold over → In the event the Lease has been terminated by either party and Tenant has not vacated the Property at the end of the term, Tenant may be deemed a tenant at sufferance and shall pay a hold over fee, which shall not be regarded as rent, in the amount of US$ 200.00 per day until the Property has been vacated.

4. DELIVERY OF POSSESSION BY LANDLORD

If the Property is not ready for occupancy at the beginning of the Lease term, this Lease shall nevertheless remain in effect, but the rent shall be abated proportionately until Landlord is able to deliver possession of the Property. If Landlord has not delivered possession within 7 days after the commencement of this Lease, Tenant shall have the right to cancel this Lease by written notice delivered to Landlord or Property Manager, as hereinafter defined. Tenant's remedy shall be limited to such right of cancellation and the return of any rent or deposit prepaid to Landlord, and on such cancellation neither party shall have any further right against the other.

If Tenant takes occupancy of the Property prior to the beginning of the Lease term, such occupancy shall be subject to the terms of this Lease, and Tenant shall pay an additional prorated rental amount to Landlord for the period beginning on Tenant's actual date of occupancy and ending on the stated date of beginning of the Lease term.

Landlord shall timely satisfy all monetary obligations concerning the Property at all times to prevent the foreclosure of any liens or claims that could interfere with Tenant's possession of the Property, including, but not limited to the lien of any mortgage lender, tax authority and/or homeowner's or condominium association.

5. PROPERTY MANAGEMENT

From time to time, and at the Landlord's sole discretion, Landlord may engage the services of an agent or property manager ("Property Manager"), the terms of whose relationship with Landlord shall be set forth in a separate Property Management Agreement, to assist in the enforcement of Landlord's rights under this Lease, including, but not limited to the collection of rents, processing rental applications, assisting with repairs, holding security

FIGURE 25.34: Residential Lease Form, Items 1–6 (continued)

deposits, etc. Landlord shall provide Tenant with written notice, within no less than five (5) banking days, of the engagement of any such Property Manager or of any change in the designated Property Manager.

The Property [check one]:

☐ IS currently managed by the Property Manager designated on the signature page of this Lease. The Property Manager, by signing this Lease, certifies that he/she/it is authorized to sign this Lease on behalf of the Landlord, and to enforce the terms of this Lease on behalf of Landlord; **or**

☒ IS NOT currently managed by a Property Manager.

6. RENT

Tenant agrees to tender to Landlord a monthly rental payment, without any deduction or set-off whatsoever, in the amount of US$ 2,350.00, payable in advance on the 1st day of each month until the termination of this tenancy. The rental payments are payable to Miranda Scott at the following address: 5300 Unfathomable Boulevard Bellville,Georgia 33334 or to such other address as Landlord or the Property Manager may from time to time provide to Tenant by five (5) banking days' written notice.

If the Lease begins on any day of the month other than the payment date expressed in this section, the rent will be prorated until the next regularly scheduled payment date.

IN PRACTICE The contract form indicates that the lease established with Sebastian and Miranda Scott as the landlords and Erin Barker and Amanda Jones as the tenants is not intended to create an **estate for years** or transfer any ownership interest in the property to the tenant. While common law defines an estate for years simply as a tenancy for a specified period, under Georgia law, this type of lease (generally established for commercial purposes) does not create a landlord-tenant relationship but actually conveys an estate that gives the grantee the rights and powers of ownership for a defined period—typically greater than five years. As such, the owner of an estate for years commonly will record the estate identifying title interests, as well as pay property taxes. The Georgia Residential Landlord-Tenant Act identifies residential leases, like the one here, not as an estate for years, but as a leasehold estate, conveying only rights of possession from the landlord to the tenant for a particular use within a period specified in the contract between the parties.

Item 1: Property Leased

The location of the leased property is identified here. If the rental agreement includes the entire property, as it does in this contract narrative, Georgia courts require a complete legal description in the lease.

Item 2: Term of Lease

The rental agreement is for 12 months, beginning on September 1 and ending at midnight on August 31 of the following year.

Item 3: Renewal of Lease

This lease form provides that the rental agreement may be renewed automatically at the end of the current term either on a month-to-month basis or for a designated period identified in this section of the agreement. Also identified are any rent increases for this renewal option. If either party does not wish to renew the lease, notice to the other party will be given within a designated time frame before expiration of the lease term.

If either party terminates the lease before it expires and the tenant has yet to vacate, that person has created a tenancy at sufferance and will pay a holdover fee, not to be regarded as rent, for a sum agreed to by the parties.

Narrative

Unless either party gives at least 30 days' notice before the end of the rental term, the Scotts and their tenants agree that the Lease will be automatically renewed on a month-to-month basis with a 10% increase in the rent. The tenant will be at sufferance and charged a nonrental fee of $200 a day, should the tenant not vacate property by a mutually agreed termination date.

Item 4: Delivery of Possession by Landlord

Here the contract form indicates that if the property is not ready for occupancy at the start of the rental term, the lease will nevertheless remain in force but the rent will be reduced proportionately until the day the landlord is able to deliver possession of the property. After a contractually designated number of days from the start of the lease term, if the landlords still have not delivered possession of the property, the tenants may cancel the lease and be reimbursed any rents or deposits prepaid to landlords. Any such action will end all rights that either party has against the other.

Also addressed in this section is a policy for prorated rental payments from a tenant who occupies a property before the beginning of the rental term.

This section of the lease agreement concludes with acknowledgment of the landlords' responsibility to satisfy all monetary obligations connected to any liens or mortgages on the leased property that might interfere with tenants' possession.

Narrative

If the Scotts have not delivered possession of the property to Barker and Jones within seven days of the beginning of the lease term, the tenants may cancel the lease and have any and all prepaid deposits and rents returned.

IN PRACTICE Residential leases in Georgia typically provide tenants with a **right of possession** at the beginning of the lease term rather than a guarantee of actual possession on that date. Though such contract forms suggest an implied warranty by the landlords that the property will be available to the tenants on the date stated in the lease, the language of the agreement indicates no legal duty to provide actual possession. Notwithstanding this reality, the landlords make other guarantees to the tenants as set forth in this section of the contract form: a reduction of rent proportioned on a daily basis until possession is received, as well as a right of cancellation for the tenants should the property not be ready for occupancy by a designated date.

Item 5: Property Management

At the landlords' discretion, a property manager may be engaged to assist in the enforcement of the landlords' rights under the lease. Within five banking days of such an engagement or any change in such engagements, the landlords will provide tenants with written notice. The Scotts, in our narrative, are not using a property manager.

Item 6: Rent

Narrative

Erin Barker or Amanda Jones, or both, will pay rent of $2,350 in advance on the first day of each month payable to Miranda Scott. The rental check shall be mailed to Eureka Real Estate Services, c/o Lucy Gordon, 5300 Unfathomable Blvd., Bellville, GA 33334. At the time of signing the lease agreement on July 20, the tenant pays to the Scotts a security deposit of $2,350, equal to one month's rent, which will be deposited in the landlords' general bank account.

FIGURE 25.35: Security Deposit

7. **SECURITY DEPOSIT**

7.1. Deposit of Funds- Tenant [check one] ☒ HAS **or** ☐ HAS NOT paid a refundable security deposit as of the date of this Lease, and if not, then Tenant shall pay the refundable security deposit in the amount of US$ 2,350.00 (the "Security Deposit") within n/a days of the execution of this Lease, which Security Deposit shall be deposited within five (5) banking days in the interest bearing or non-interest bearing account of [check one] ☒ Landlord, **or** ☐ Other: ____________________ (the "Escrow Agent"). If deposited into an interest bearing account, the holder of the security deposit shall be entitled to retain any interest accrued. If the Escrow Agent is a Georgia real estate licensee, the Security Deposit shall be deposited into a trust account that is registered with the Georgia Real Estate Commission and is in compliance with the rules and regulations of the Georgia Real Estate Commission.

7.2. Transfer of Funds- Landlord shall have the right, after ten (10) banking days' written notice to Tenant and Escrow Agent, to transfer the Security Deposit to another holder and designate a new Escrow Agent, provided the Tenant agrees in writing.

7.3. No Offset of Rental Payments - Tenant shall not have the right to offset any rental payment or any other fee due under this Lease against the Security Deposit.

7.4. Return of Funds-The Security Deposit shall be returned to Tenant at the Tenant's last known mailing address via first class U.S. mail, postage prepaid, within thirty (30) days following the expiration of this Lease if all monies due Landlord have been paid, the Tenant has vacated the Property, and Tenant is not in default under the terms of this Lease. Landlord shall be entitled to withhold from the Security Deposit any sums still owed under this Lease, including, but not limited to, final rent payments, amounts owed for repairs (normal wear and tear excepted), amounts paid by Landlord to remove Tenant's personal property, delinquent utility bills paid on behalf of Tenant, or cleaning fees due to Tenant's failure to return the Property to Landlord in the same degree of cleanliness it was in when Tenant took occupancy of the Property (normal wear and tear excepted). The Security Deposit shall become the property of the Landlord ninety (90) days after the letter is mailed if the letter is returned as undeliverable, and if Landlord's reasonable attempts to locate the Tenant have failed.

7.5. Liability of Escrow Agent- It is agreed that the duties of Escrow Agent are herein specifically provided and are purely ministerial in nature, and that Escrow Agent, so long as Escrow Agent is acting in good faith, shall incur no liability whatsoever with respect to the Security Deposit except for willful misconduct or negligence. Landlord and Tenant do each hereby release Escrow Agent from any liability for any error of judgment or for any act done or omitted to be done by Escrow Agent in the good faith performance of its duties hereunder and do each hereby indemnify Escrow Agent against, and agree to hold, save, and defend Escrow Agent harmless from, any costs, liabilities, and expenses incurred by Escrow Agent in serving and faithfully

Page 2 of 12

Form RE120, *Contract for the Lease of Residential Real Property*

 Initials: ________ ________ ________ ________

R10312012

Item 7: Security Deposit

7.1. Deposit of Funds: Here, the contract form indicates the amount of the security deposit, the account in which the funds will be deposited, and whether the sum is paid when the rental agreement is created or in a designated number of days from the date the agreement is created.

IN PRACTICE Georgia law allows a landlord who is a natural person to hold a security deposit in a general bank account rather than a trust account, if that landlord and landlord's spouse and minor children own 10 or fewer rental units. In such circumstance, at the landlord's discretion, these funds may be used for general purposes. This exception does not apply if the landlord engages a third party to collect rent(s) and manage the property. These third parties would function as **escrow agents** for the security deposits and must deposit the funds in a trust account, the location of which must be provide in writing to the tenant. Moreover, as the contract form points out, if the holder of security deposits is a Georgia real estate licensee, the trust account holding the funds must be registered with the Georgia Real Estate Commission.

As a substitute for establishing escrow accounts for security deposits, Georgia law allows landlords to post bond with the superior court in the county where the property is located.

7.2: Transfer of Funds—With proper notice to, and agreement from, the tenant, the landlord may transfer the security deposit to another holder and designate a new escrow agent.

7.3: No Offset of Rental Payments—Tenants may not apply security deposits to offset any rental payments.

7.4: Return of Funds—Language of this section in the contract form explicitly follows that of Georgia's Residential Landlord-Tenant Act. Security deposits must be returned to tenants at that party's last known mailing address within 30 days of the Lease expiration. If such mailing is returned as undeliverable and if a landlord's reasonable attempts to locate the tenant have failed, the security deposit will become the property of the landlord 90 after mailing. The full sum will be returned to the tenant, provided that all monies due the landlord have been paid, the tenant has vacated the property, and the tenant is not in default under lease terms. Landlords are entitled to withhold from security deposits any sums under the lease, including but not limited to the following:

- Final rental payment
- Amounts owed for repairs (normal wear and tear excepted)
- Amounts paid by the landlord to remove a tenant's personal property
- Delinquent utility bills paid on behalf of a tenant
- Cleaning fees due to a tenant's failure to return property to the same degree of cleanliness present when the tenant took occupancy (normal wear and tear excepted)

IN PRACTICE If a landlord breaches these requirements for the return of a tenant's security deposit, Georgia law may hold the landlord liable for three times the amount of the improperly handled funds, as well any associated legal fees. If the landlord can show that the mishandling was a bona fide error and not intentional, liability would only be for the exact amount of funds.

7.5: Liability of Escrow Agent—Here, the escrow agent's duties are described as purely ministerial. Absent willful misconduct or negligence on the part of the escrow agent, the landlord and the tenant release this party from any liability involving errors and mistakes in judgment evolving from the escrow agent's good-faith performance of duties.

If a dispute arises between the parties over disbursement of the security deposit, the escrow agent may, upon written notice to parties,

- *(7.5.1)* disburse the funds upon a reasonable interpretation of the lease; or
- *(7.5.2)* interplead to a court of jurisdiction for ruling on the disbursement of earnest money less costs incurred for filing of action and attorney's fees. The escrow agent must give the parties 10 banking days' advance written notice of interpleader action.

FIGURE 25.36: Other Charges

8. OTHER CHARGES

In addition to any other rent, security deposit, utility fee or cost of repair herein described, Tenant shall be assessed a charge payable to Landlord within five (5) banking days of notice thereof in the following amounts and under the following circumstances:

8.1. Late Payment- If any rent payment due hereunder is not received by Landlord within ____5____ days of the date it is due, Tenant shall pay a late charge in an amount equal to n/a % of the amount of such payment, or US$____150.00____.

8.2. Dishonored Check- If any check tendered by Tenant or on behalf of Tenant to Landlord or Property Manager is returned to Landlord or Property Manager for insufficient funds or any other reason, Tenant shall pay to the party to whom the check was tendered a service charge in the amount of US$____100.00____. Landlord reserves the right to thereafter request that all future payments be made by money order or certified funds.

8.3. Re-keying- Landlord may charge a re-key fee in the amount of US$____75.00____ for the replacement of any keys during the term of the Lease or not returned to Landlord at the termination of this Lease.

8.4. Utility Re-connect Fee- In the event Tenant fails to maintain any utility or service required hereunder through the end of the Lease term, Tenant shall pay Landlord the cost of reconnecting said utility, as well as a one time charge in the amount of US$____100.00____.

8.5. Costs of Enforcement of Landlord's Rights- Should any payment due hereunder not be paid within ____15____ days of the date it is due, Landlord shall be entitled to take legal action to dispossess Tenant. Tenant shall be responsible for paying the court costs of such action, regardless of whether or not a court order is issued, or whether or not Tenant is allowed by Landlord to cure and reinstate by paying all amounts owed, unless the action is dismissed due to Landlord default hereunder. An additional administrative fee in the amount of US$____350.00____ shall be payable by Tenant to Landlord to cover attorney fees and other administrative costs incurred by Landlord for each such dispossessory action filed.

8.6. Pet Fee- Tenant agrees to pay a non-refundable pet fee in the amount of US$____250.00____ if pets are allowed to occupy the Property. This fee shall be in addition to the cost of any damage caused by Tenant's pet and shall not be used to offset any charges for the repair of said damage.

Item 8: Other Charges

The list of miscellaneous charges here are those commonly assessed by landlords in contracts for lease in Georgia. Aside from service fee limitations on dishonored checks received from tenants, statutory regulations do not address the following items:

8.1: Late Payment—The Scotts will assess a late charge to the tenants' monthly lease payment of $150 if the rental payment is not received at the designated mailing address within five days of its due date.

8.2: Dishonored Check—The Scotts will assess a service charge of $100 for a returned rental payment check. In such circumstances, the landlords reserve the right to request that future rental payments be made by certified funds or money order.

IN PRACTICE Georgia law allows this service charge to be up to $30 or 5% of the rental payment, whichever amount is greater.

8.3: Re-keying—The Scotts will charge a re-key charge of $75 for replacement of existing house keys or in the event such keys are not returned at the end of the lease.

8.4: Utility Re-connect Fee—If the tenants fail to maintain any utility service through the end of the lease term as stipulated by the contract, the Scotts require that the tenants pay them for the cost of reconnecting such utility service, as well as a one-time charge of $100.

8.5: Costs of Enforcement of Landlord's Rights—If any payments due the Scotts from the tenants are not received within 15 days of the due date, the landlords will be entitled to take legal dispossessory action against the tenants, who will be responsible for court costs for such action regardless of whether the tenant are subsequently allowed by the landlords to cure the default by paying all amounts owed. Furthermore the tenants will pay the landlords $350 as an additional administrative fee for costs incurred by dispossessory actions.

8.6: Pet Fee—As included in this contract form, this is a nonrefundable fee paid by the tenants solely for the right to have a pet occupy the leased property. Damages caused by any pet would be a separate expense for the tenants. The tenants in this lease, Barker and Jones have a dog for which they will pay the Scotts a $250 dollar pet fee.

FIGURE 25.37: Early Termination

9. **EARLY TERMINATION**

9.1. By Tenant- Tenant [check one] ☒ MAY **or** ☐ MAY NOT terminate this Lease prior to the end of the Lease term.

Provided the Landlord has consented to Tenant's right of early termination by so indicating hereinabove, Tenant may exercise that right by [check all that apply]:

☒ Providing Landlord with no less than 60 days' prior written notice of Tenant's intent to terminate early, signed by all Tenants.

☒ Paying an early termination fee in an amount equal to one month's rent.

☐ Paying an early termination fee in an amount equal to n/a % of the total rent due through the end of the original lease term, or US$ n/a.

All other terms of this Lease shall remain in full force and effect, including, but not limited to, Tenant's obligation to pay any rents or fees due through the date of Tenant's early termination of this Lease.

Page 3 of 12

Form RE120, *Contract for the Lease of Residential Real Property*

 Initials: ________ ________ ________ ________

R10312012

FIGURE 25.37: Early Termination (continued)

Exception for Members of the United States Military Service: *The terms of this section regarding early termination may not apply, and the provisions of the Service Members' Civil Relief Act of 2003, as amended, may control if Tenant provides Landlord with a copy of Tenant's official orders proving that Tenant has been called to active duty with the United States Armed Services during the term of this Lease; or, Tenant is on active duty with the United States military and Tenant or an immediate family member of Tenant occupying Property has received, during the term of this Lease, permanent change of station orders or temporary duty orders for a period not less than ninety (90) days.*

9.2. By Landlord- Landlord may terminate this Lease prior to the end of the Lease term by:

9.2.1. Providing Tenant with no less than sixty (60) days prior written notice of Landlord's intent to terminate the Lease early; and

9.2.2. Provided Tenant has paid all rents and fees due under this Lease at time of Lease termination and is otherwise not in default under this Lease, paying Tenant an early termination fee in the amount of US$ 2,350.00 , which shall be paid to Tenant within thirty (30) days after the early expiration of this Lease. Tenant hereby acknowledges that this early termination fee shall serve as full liquidated damages for any damages Tenant may suffer due to Landlord's early termination of this Lease.

All other terms of this Lease shall remain in full force and effect, including, but not limited to, Tenant's obligation to pay any rents or fees due through the date of Landlord's early termination of this Lease.

Item 9: Early Termination

9.1: By Tenant—The Scotts will allow the tenants to terminate the lease before its expiration date with a minimal 60-day notice by paying an early termination fee of $2,350, equal to one month's rent.

Exceptions for Military Service Members: As applicable under both federal and Georgia law, a lease of an active duty member of the regular or reserve component of the U.S. armed forces, the U.S. Coast Guard, the Georgia National Guard, or the Georgia Air National Guard may be terminated on ordered federal duty for a period of 90 days or longer.

IN PRACTICE Under the military exceptions to early termination of a lease, the tenant must provide the landlord with an official copy of orders proving that the tenant has been called to active duty during the term of the lease or that the tenant or an immediate family member of the tenant occupying the property has received a change of station or a temporary duty order for 90 days or longer. Georgia law also limits the tenant's liability for rent to 30 days after the landlord receives written notice of proof of the assignment.

9.2: By Landlord—The contract form also gives the Scotts the right to terminate the lease before the end of the term by

(9.2.1) providing the tenant with a notice no less than 60 days before termination; and

(9.2.2) paying the tenant an early termination fee of $2,350, provided that tenant has paid all rents and otherwise is not in default under lease. Fees will be paid to the tenant within 30 days after the early expiration of the lease.

FIGURE 25.38: Use of Property

10. USE OF PROPERTY

10.1. People- The Tenant agrees to use the Property as a residential dwelling and for no other purpose. The Tenant agrees to abide by the covenants, agreements, rules and regulations of this Lease, as well as all posted rules and regulations regarding the use of any recreational facilities, common areas, streets, driveways or sidewalks on the Property. It is the responsibility of the Tenant to familiarize himself with and abide by all federal, state, county and local laws, regulations and ordinances, and the rules, regulations and by-laws of any homeowners association or condominium association governing the use of the Property. It is understood that, in addition to the Tenant, ONLY the following people may occupy the rented Property:

Katherine Barker-Jones and Felix Barker-Jones

Tenant agrees not to do or to permit any act or practice injurious to the Property, or which may be otherwise prohibited by law.

10.2. Pets- Pets [check one] ☒ ARE **or** ☐ ARE NOT allowed under this Lease.

Provided Landlord has consented to pets to occupying the Property by so indicating hereinabove, this consent is limited by the following:

10.2.1. Only __1__ individual pet(s) is (are) allowed on the Property and are specifically described as follows:

breed	max. predicted weight	breed	max. predicted weight
Siberian Husky	/ 55 lb		/
	/		/

10.2.2. Tenant shall, at all times, abide by all applicable local laws, the requirements of Landlord's insurance carrier and association rules and regulations with respect to the keeping of animals or pets, including, but not limited to, leash laws, licensing laws, and laws regarding vaccinations and inoculations. Tenant shall, upon request and within five (5) banking days' notice, provide Landlord with proof of any current vaccinations applicable to the pet's species which are required by local law, including, but not limited to, rabies vaccinations.

10.2.3. Tenant shall keep pet confined or on a leash when out of doors. Tenant is responsible for all acts of pet or injuries caused by Tenant having a pet on the Property, including, but not limited to, proper cleanup and disposal of pet droppings; flea, tick or other pet related pest infestation within the dwelling; damage to the Property indoors and/or out of doors; and public disturbance or nuisance created by Tenant's pet. 10.2.4. If, in the sole discretion of Landlord or Property Manager, Tenant's pet becomes an annoyance to the public, then Landlord or Property Manager may, with five (5) days written notice to Tenant, demand the removal of the pet from the Property. If, in the sole discretion of Landlord or Property Manager, Tenant's pet becomes a threat to public health or safety, then Landlord or Property Manager may demand the removal of the pet from the Property immediately.

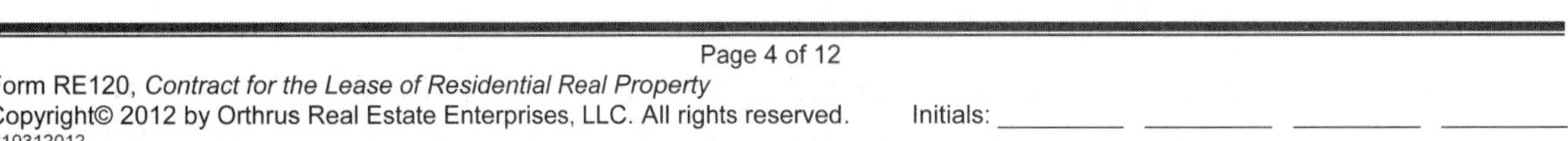
Page 4 of 12

Form RE120, *Contract for the Lease of Residential Real Property*

 Initials: ______ ______ ______ ______

R10312012

Item 10: Use of Property

10.1: People—Here the tenant agrees that the property will be used only as a residence and that the tenant will abide by all covenants, rules, and regulation of the lease as well as applicable federal, state, and local ordinances. As noted in this section of the contract form, occupants of the property will be restricted to Erin Barker, Amanda Jones, and their two children, Katherine and Felix.

10.2: Pets—The Scotts are allowing the tenants to keep their dog on the property.

10.2.1.—This consent is limited to the one Siberian husky who weighs 55 pounds.

10.2.2.—Regarding the dog, the tenants agree to abide by all leash, licensing, and inoculation laws; and upon the landlords' request, within five banking days provide proof of any vaccinations required by local law.

10.2.3.—The tenants agree to keep the pet confined or on leash when outdoors and are responsible for all acts or injuries caused by having a pet on the property, including cleanup and disposal of pet droppings and public disturbance or nuisance caused by the pet.

10.2.4.—At the sole discretion of the landlords, if the tenant's pet becomes an annoyance to the public, the landlord may with five days written notice to the tenant, demand the pet's removal from the property; if the pet becomes a threat to public safety or health, immediate removal may be demanded.

FIGURE 25.39: Condition of Property

11. CONDITION OF PROPERTY

Tenant shall, at all times, maintain the Property in a clean and orderly condition so as not to create waste of or damage to the Property, and shall return the Property to the Landlord in the same condition at the end of the Lease term as it was in at the beginning of the Lease term, normal wear and tear excepted.

11.1. Initial Inspection of the Property- Prior to commencement of this Lease and Tenant's occupancy of the Property, Landlord and Tenant shall each, separately or together, conduct an initial walk-through of the Property and complete the attached Rental Property Condition Report. It shall be the responsibility of the Tenant to note any damage to the Property observed during said walk-through if not already indicated on the report by Landlord, and Tenant expressly acknowledges that failure to do so may create liability on the part of the Tenant for any Property damage noted at the end of the Lease term. By taking possession of the Property, Tenant acknowledges that the Property has been received in clean condition and in good order with the exception of any matters noted in the Rental Property Condition Report. Except as otherwise indicated in this Lease, Tenant shall take possession of the Property "as is," and has not relied upon any promise or representation by Landlord to repair, improve or otherwise alter the Property.

11.2. Landlord Responsibility for Repairs- It is the Tenant's responsibility to notify Landlord of any condition or defect which would render the Property unsafe or unfit for use as a residential dwelling, or which, if left unrepaired, could lead to severe damage to the Property. Such conditions shall include, but are not limited to, nonfunctioning smoke detectors, rodent or termite infestation, roof or plumbing leaks, and severe erosion. Landlord shall, within a reasonable amount of time after receiving notice from Tenant, repair any defect which would create a safety or health hazard to the occupants of the Property, would render the Property untenable, or is required under federal, state or local law. Landlord shall not be responsible for any routine maintenance of the Property, except as otherwise indicated herein.

11.3. Tenant's Maintenance Responsibilities- Tenant agrees to be responsible for, and to make, at Tenant's expense, all routine maintenance of the Property. Tenant's maintenance responsibilities shall include, but not be limited to the following:

11.3.1. Unless other indicated herein, and except for Property separately maintained by a condominium or homeowner's association, all yard maintenance is the responsibility of the Tenant, and the grounds shall be kept neatly mowed and free of debris.

11.3.2. It is specifically understood that Tenant will, at Tenant's expense, keep sinks, lavatories, and commodes in good working order, reporting any initial malfunction within five (5) days of occupancy.

11.3.3. Tenant shall replace all broken windows and burned-out light bulbs, repairing any damage to screens, interior walls and doors.

11.3.4. Tenant shall be responsible for taking reasonable precautions in extreme cold weather to protect the pipes from freezing.

11.3.5. Tenant agrees to report to Landlord any malfunction of, or damage to, electrical, plumbing, heating or air conditioning systems. Tenant is responsible for changing air filters in heating and air conditioning systems every ___6___ months and reporting any water leaks immediately. Prior to reporting any herein described malfunction, however, the Tenant shall take reasonable steps to confirm that the malfunction is not due to a tripped circuit breaker or blown fuse. Failure to do so may result in a charge to Tenant in the amount of US$___100.00___ for the service call.

11.3.6. Tenant agrees to pay for the cost of all repairs made necessary by negligent or careless use of the Property, including repairs to electrical, plumbing, heating and cooling system, as well as floor coverings, wall coverings and appliances.

11.3.7. Tenant agrees to take reasonable precautions to prevent losses resulting from theft, malicious mischief, or vandalism.

11.4. Final Inspection of the Property- Within five (5) days after the Tenant ceases to occupy the Property (or within a reasonable time, if Tenant vacates the Property without notifying the Landlord), Landlord shall furnish Tenant with a copy of the completed Rental Property Condition Report, indicating any damage to the Property not noted at the initial inspection of the Property for which Tenant shall be held responsible. Tenant shall have the right to inspect the Property within three (3) banking days of receipt of the completed Rental Property Condition Report to confirm or dispute Landlord's assessment of the Property's condition. In the event Tenant disputes the accuracy of Landlord's Rental Property Condition Report, Tenant shall have five (5) banking days from the receipt of the Rental Property Condition Report to notify the Landlord in writing of which specific items Tenant disputes. All notices delivered as a result of this section shall be delivered in a manner consistent with the section of this Lease entitled "Notices."

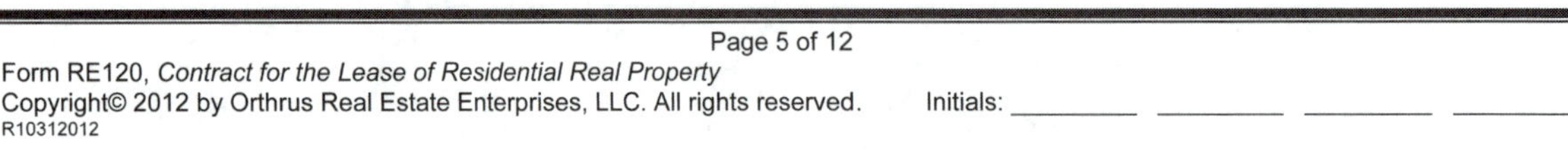
Page 5 of 12

Form RE120, *Contract for the Lease of Residential Real Property*

 Initials: ________ ________ ________ ________

R10312012

Item 11: Condition of Property

The tenants must at all times keep the property in clean and orderly condition to avoid any damage to the residence and must return the property in the same condition at end of lease term, normal wear and tear excepted.

11.1: Initial inspection of the Property—Either separately or together, the landlords and the tenants will conduct an initial walk-through of the property and complete a property condition report that will be attached to the lease. It is the tenants' responsibility to note any damage to the property observed during initial walk-through if it was not already noted on the landlords' report; the tenants expressly acknowledge that failure to do so may create liability on the part of the tenants for any property damages noted at the end of the lease term. Except as otherwise noted in the lease, the tenants take possession of the property "as is" and have not relied on any representation by the landlord to repair, improve, or otherwise alter the property.

11.2: Landlord Responsibility for Repairs—Though not responsible for any routine maintenance of the property, the landlords will, within a reasonable time after receiving notice from the tenants, repair any defect that would create a safety or health hazard to the occupants of the property. It is the tenants' responsibility to notify the landlords of any condition or defect that would render the property unsafe or unfit for a residential dwelling.

IN PRACTICE Local governing bodies in Georgia are given powers to order repairs, close, or demolish structures dangerous or detrimental to health and safety; these conditions may be identified under the law as follows:

- Defects that increase the hazard of fire, accidents, or other calamities
- Lack of adequate ventilation, light or sanitary facilities
- Disrepair and structural defects
- Uncleanliness

Furthermore, Georgia law allows tenants to vacate and suspend rental payments if the landlord allows the property to become uninhabitable; though to exercise this right, known as **constructive eviction**, the tenants must show conclusively that a landlord's failure to repair has made the property an unfit place for the tenants to live and that the property cannot be restored within a reasonable time by ordinary repairs to a fit condition. Consequently, for conditions in a residential property to constitute constructive eviction, which would release the tenants from the obligation to pay rent, there must be a failure by the landlord to make repairs, which leaves the property unfit to live in and not just uncomfortable to live in. A limited number of constructive eviction rulings in Georgia appear to offer no set guidelines as to what constitutes "inhabitable"; rather, determinations are made on a case-by-case interpretation of the facts.

Finally, though a lease may not waive a landlord's legal obligation to keep a property and its improvements in good repair, it is not uncommon for the lease to limit a landlord's personal responsibility and potential liability; to achieve this, it is not uncommon for a landlord to assign substantial maintenance responsibilities to the tenants as described in this contract form narrative.

11.3: Tenant's Maintenance Responsibilities—Tenants are responsible for, at the tenants' expense, all routine maintenance of the property, including the following:

11.3.1.—All yard maintenance and keeping grounds neatly mowed and free of debris

11.3.2.—Keeping sinks, lavatories, and commodes in good working order, reporting any malfunctions within five days of occupancy

11.3.3.—Replacing all broken windows and burned-out light bulbs, repairing any damage to screens, interior walls, and doors

11.3.4.—Taking reasonable precautions in extreme cold weather to protect pipes from freezing

11.3.5.—Reporting any malfunctions of or damage to electrical, plumbing, heating, and air-conditioning systems. Changing air filters in heating and air-conditioning systems every six months and reporting water leaks immediately. Before reporting any malfunctions of these systems, the tenants will take reasonable steps to confirm that the malfunction is not caused by a tripped circuit breaker or a blown fuse; failure to do so may result in a $100 charge to the tenant for the cost of a service call.

11.3.6.—Paying for all repairs made necessary by negligent or careless use of property by the tenants, including repairs to electrical, plumbing, heating, and cooling systems, as well as floor coverings, wall coverings, and appliances.

11.3.7.—Taking reasonable precautions to prevent losses from theft and malicious mischief and vandalism.

11.4: Final Inspection of the Property—As prescribed in Georgia law and incorporated into the contract form, within five days after the tenants no longer occupy the property, the landlord will furnish the tenants a copy of a completed rental property condition report, indicating those damages not noted on the initial property inspection for which the tenants will be held responsible. The tenants have the right to inspect the property within three banking days of receipt of the report to confirm or dispute the landlord's assessment. The tenants will have five banking days from receipt of the property condition report to notify the landlord in writing of any disputed items.

IN PRACTICE Georgia law exempts landlords from initial walk-through inspections with tenants to complete a property condition report, as well as the inspection after termination of the lease to complete the final assessment of property condition in the following circumstances:

- The landlord is a naturalized citizen.
- The landlord, the spouse, and minor children do not own more than 10 rental properties.
- The landlord does not engage a third party to manage properties.

Such is the case with Sebastian and Miranda Scott in the contract narrative; yet the contract form used in their lease includes walk-through inspections and property condition reports. Though not required by law, the inspection process allows both landlords and tenants protections. Absent this property assessment, any disputes between the parties regarding property conditions before and after the lease term would lack a basis for enforcement. The argument would essentially pit one verbal opinion against another. Landlords would have little support for making claims in this area against a tenant's security deposit, and tenants would have no way of showing that a defect existed before the lease term.

FIGURE 25.40: Damage to Property

12. RIGHT OF ENTRY

Tenant agrees that Landlord may enter the Property during reasonable hours for the purpose of inspecting the Property and Tenant's compliance with the terms of this Lease, making repairs, alterations, improvements or additions as Landlord may deem appropriate and showing the Property to prospective purchasers or tenants. Landlord will give Tenant twenty four (24) hours' advance notice before entering Property, except for in the event of an emergency. Landlord shall have the right to display "For Sale" or "For Rent" signs upon the Property within the last ___30___ days of the Lease term, and to market the Property for sale or for lease throughout the entire Lease term.

Within the last ___30___ days of the Lease term, Landlord [check one] ☐ SHALL **or** ☐ SHALL NOT have the right to place a lock box on the Property, during which time Tenant shall continue to be solely responsible for securing Tenant's valuables. Tenant shall cooperate with Landlord to make the Property available to prospective purchasers and tenants during reasonable hours.

13. ALTERATIONS TO THE PROPERTY

Tenant may not make any alterations or additions to the Property without the prior written consent of Landlord. Tenant is forbidden from changing, adding or removing any locks without prior written consent of Landlord. Tenant shall not paint, mark or otherwise deface walls, ceilings, floors, windows, cabinets, woodwork, stone, ironwork, or any other part of the Property, inside or out. Tenant specifically agrees not to damage the walls with screws, nails, glue or tape, though standard picture hooks and curtain or shade brackets shall be allowed. Any alterations or improvements made by Tenant, including fixtures, carpeting, painting, wallpaper, and landscaping, shall become a part of the Property unless otherwise consented to by Landlord in writing. Upon termination of this lease Tenant shall restore the property to its original condition, safety and appearance, ordinary wear and tear excepted, except as to the fixtures, carpeting, painting, wallpaper, shrubs or any other plants which Landlord has accepted. If Tenant fails to do so, Tenant will promptly reimburse Landlord for any expenses required to restore the Property.

14. DAMAGE TO THE PROPERTY NOT CAUSED BY TENANT

If the Property is damaged by fire, flood, toxic environmental hazard, extreme weather or other casualty not due to the negligence of Tenant, Tenant's invitees, licensees or guests, Landlord shall repair the damage within a reasonable time and rent shall continue unabated unless the casualty renders the Property fully untenable, in which case either party may terminate this Lease and Tenant, on payment of all rent due through the date Property is surrendered, shall not be liable for any further rent but shall be reimbursed the Security Deposit. In the event the Property is rendered only partially untenable by the above described casualty, Tenant shall be entitled to a reduction in the amount of rent proportionate to the amount of Property so damaged until such time as Property has been repaired; provided, however, that this shall not relieve the Landlord of the obligation to complete repairs within a reasonable time.

This Property [check one] ☐ HAS **or** ☒ HAS NOT been flooded by natural forces, such as excessive rain or an overflow of an established water source, within the five (5) years preceding the date of this Lease. The term "flood" as used in this paragraph shall mean the inundation of water over land or structures not usually covered by it, and shall not include water intrusion caused by a failure of plumbing.

This Property [check one] ☒ WAS **or** ☐ WAS NOT built prior to 1978. If the Property or any part thereof was built prior to 1978, Tenant acknowledges receipt of the Lead Based Paint Exhibit attached hereto and by this reference made a part hereof and the EPA brochure entitled "Protect Your Family From Lead In Your Home."

Tenant acknowledges that it is Tenant's responsibility to insure Tenant's personal property through a comprehensive policy of renter's hazard insurance. Neither Landlord, nor Property Manager nor Broker shall be liable to Tenant or any party claiming by, through or under Tenant for any damage to personal property stored on the Property, and Tenant does hereby indemnify Landlord, Property Manager and Broker against, and agrees to hold, save, and defend Landlord, Property Manager and Broker harmless from, any costs, liabilities, and expenses incurred as a result of damage to personal property stored on the Property.

Page 6 of 12

Form RE120, *Contract for the Lease of Residential Real Property*

R10312012

Item 12: Right of Entry

The tenants acknowledge the right of the landlords to enter the property, with 24-hour advance notice (except in case of emergency), to inspect the property for purposes of tenant compliance with the lease, as well as to make repairs and improvements as the landlords deem necessary and to show the property to perspective purchasers or tenants. Within the last 30 days of the lease, the landlords also have the right to market the property for sale or lease throughout the lease term and, within the last 30 days of the lease, display For Sale or For Lease signs on the property. The tenants agree to cooperate with the landlords in making property available to perspective purchasers and tenants during reasonable hours.

Item 13: Alterations to The Property

The tenants may make alterations or improvements to the property only with prior written consent of the landlords. The tenants specifically agree not to damage walls with screws, nails, glue, or tape; standard picture hooks and curtain and shade brackets are allowed. Absent a written agreement with the landlords to the contrary, improvements made by the tenants become part of the property. Notwithstanding improvements and alterations accepted by landlords, the tenants are to restore the property to its original condition (normal wear and tear excepted) upon termination of the lease. Failure to do so will require that the tenants promptly reimburse the landlords for expenses to restore the property.

Item 14: Damage to the Property Not Caused by Tenant

If the property is damaged by natural causes, fire, or environmental hazards, the landlords will repair the damage within a reasonable time and the tenants will continue paying rent unless the casualty renders the property untenable, in which case either party may terminate the lease and the tenants, in good standing regarding rental payments, will be reimbursed their security deposit. If the property is partially untenable, the tenants are entitled to a reduction in rent proportionate to amount of property damaged until such time as the property is fully repaired.

This section of the contract form also includes disclosures from the landlords, required by Georgia law, as to whether the property has been flooded by natural forces at least three times within the past five years, as well as lead-based paint disclosure information applicable for properties built before 1978. A further acknowledgment by the tenant refers to renter's hazard insurance, which is needed to protect the tenant's personal property and that the landlord, property manager, and broker would not be liable for any loss of such personal property.

Narrative

The Scotts disclose that the property has not been flooded by natural forces during their two-year ownership nor in its previous five years, as disclosed to them by the previous owners when the property was sold to them.

Because the Scotts' home was built before 1978, the tenants acknowledge receiving, along with an Environmental Protection Agency (EPA) brochure on lead-based paint, an exhibit indicating that the Scotts have no knowledge of lead-based paint on their property.

FIGURE 25.41: Utilities and Services

15. UTILITIES AND SERVICES
Tenant understands and agrees that the cost of utilities and services shall be paid as follows: [check all that apply]

Utility or Service	Paid by Tenant	Paid by Landlord	Optional or Not Required
Electricity	✘		
Gas	✘		
Water	✘		
Sewer	✘		
Waste removal	✘		
Telephone	✘		
Yard and Lawn Maintenance	✘		
Cable	✘		
Pest (other than termite or rodents) Control	✘		
Other: ______________________			
Other: ______________________			

Any utilities or services required to be maintained by Tenant must be transferred or connected in Tenant's name within ____3____ days of commencement of this Lease.

16. USE OF PARKING
Tenant shall park motor vehicles in areas designated by Landlord and no other areas. Any vehicle parked on the Property shall bear evidence of current license and registration, and no recreational vehicle, boat, motor home, trailer or inoperable vehicle of any kind shall be permitted to be parked on the Property. Any vehicle not in compliance with this section may be towed at Tenant's expense.

17. ADDITIONAL USE RESTRICTIONS
The following rules apply to Tenant and Tenant's invitees, guests and licensees:

17.1. Tenant shall not operate heavy equipment, play loud music or create any other condition which may constitute a nuisance or disrupt the quiet enjoyment of neighbors in the surrounding area.

17.2. Tenant shall not make use of portable heaters or air conditioning units without the written permission of Landlord.

17.3. Tenant will neither store nor dump any environmentally hazardous or combustible substances on the Property, except that Tenant may store normal household goods in amounts necessary for normal household use.

17.4. The possession of any illegal substance, stolen goods or other contraband on the Property is strictly forbidden.

Item 15: Utilities and Services

During the term of the lease, all utilities will be paid by the tenants, Erin Barker and Amanda Jones. The lease will require the tenants to transfer these services in the tenants' names within three days of the beginning of the lease term.

Item 16: Use of Parking

The Scotts are allowing the tenants to park motor vehicles in the garage attached to the property or in the driveway of the property.

Item 17: Additional Use Restrictions

The following rules apply to the tenants and the tenants' guests:

17.1—The tenants may not create neighborhood nuisances or disrupt the quiet enjoyment of neighbors.

17.2—The tenants may not use portable heaters or air conditioners without written permission of the landlords.

17.3—Except for normal household goods in amounts necessary for normal household use, the tenants may not store environmentally hazardous or combustible substances on the property.

17.4—Possession of any illegal substance or contraband on the property is strictly prohibited.

FIGURE 25.42: Landlord Liability

18. SUBORDINATION
This Lease is subject and subordinate to the lien of all mortgages now or at any time hereafter placed on any part of Landlord's property which includes the Property, to extensions or renewals thereof, and to all advances now or hereafter made on the security thereof. Tenant agrees, upon request, to execute such further instruments

Page 7 of 12
Form RE120, *Contract for the Lease of Residential Real Property*
 Initials: ________ ________ ________ ________
R10312012

FIGURE 25.42: Landlord Liability (continued)

evidencing such subordination as Landlord may request, and if Tenant fails to do so, Landlord is empowered to do so in the name of the Tenant.

19. LIMITATION OF LANDLORD'S LIABILITY
The term "Landlord," as used in this Lease, so far as covenants or obligations on the part of Landlord are concerned, shall be limited to mean and include only the Landlord or Landlords, who, at the time in question, own the Property. In the event of any transfer or transfers of ownership of the Property, the Landlord herein named (and in case of any subsequent transfers or conveyances, the then Landlord) shall be, from and after the date of such transfers and conveyances, freed and relieved of all liability with respect to the performance of any covenants or obligations on the part of Landlord contained in this Lease to be performed after the transfer. Without further agreement, the new owner of the Property shall be deemed to have assumed and agreed to observe and perform any and all obligations in this Lease. Landlord may transfer his interest in the Property without the consent of Tenant and such transfer or subsequent transfer shall not be deemed a violation on Landlord's part of any of the terms and conditions of this Lease. Landlord or transferor shall remain and continue to be liable for any performance or payment which shall have accrued or become owing during such Landlord's or transferor's tenure as Landlord hereunder.

20. INDEMNIFICATION OF LANDLORD
The Tenant shall not do or permit any act upon the Property which may subject the Landlord to any liability by reason of any illegal business or conduct upon the Property, or by reason of any violation of law or of any legal requirement of public authority, but shall exercise such control over the Property as to fully protect the Landlord. Notwithstanding that joint or concurrent liability may be imposed upon the Landlord by statute, ordinance, rule, regulations, or order, the Tenant shall indemnify the Landlord against any liability or expense of any nature due to the following:

20.1. Any breach of any covenant in this Lease required to be performed by the Tenant;
20.2. Any damage to person or property occasioned by the Tenant's use and occupancy of the Property or by any use or occupancy of the Property which the Tenant may permit its guests, invitees and/or licensees; and
20.3. Injury to any person, including death resulting at any time therefrom, occurring in or about the Property and on the sidewalks adjacent to the Property. If the Tenant is required to defend any action or proceeding pursuant to any such occurrence to which the Landlord is made a party, the Landlord shall be entitled to appear, defend, or otherwise take part in the matter involved, at its election, by counsel of its own choosing, providing such action by the Landlord does not limit or make void any liability of any insurer of the Landlord or Tenant hereunder in respect to the claim or matter in question. The Tenant's liability under this section shall be reduced by the net proceeds collected from any insurance taken out by the Tenant to cover losses from the events herein described.

Item 18: Subordination

Here the tenants acknowledge that the lien of any mortgage existing on the property or any placed on the property during the term of the lease will prevail over the tenants' right to lease the property.

IN PRACTICE Effectively for the tenants, this clause means that if the landlords default on a loan that secures the property, the lienholder decides whether the tenants' lease continues or under what conditions it may continue.

Item 19: Limitations of Landlord's Liability

The landlords are free to transfer interest in the property without the tenants' consent, relieving the landlords of all liability with respect to lease obligations and performance of any duties after the transfer. Notwithstanding further agreement between the parties, the new owners/landlords will assume performance for any and all obligations of the lease.

Item 20: Indemnification of Landlord

Notwithstanding any liability imposed by law on the landlords, the tenants will hold the landlords harmless (indemnify) against any liability or expense due to following:

20.1.—Any covenant breach in this lease required to be performed by the tenants

20.2.—Any damage to person or property caused by the tenants' occupancy and use of the property, including damage caused by the use and occupancy of guests of the tenants

20.3.—Injury, including death, to any person occurring in or about the property and on sidewalks adjacent to the property

FIGURE 25.43: Default

21. DEFAULT
A party shall be in default if he or she breaches any term of this Lease. Except as otherwise stated herein, neither Landlord nor Tenant shall be deemed to be in default hereunder, however, until and unless such party has been given written notice of its failure to comply with the terms of this Lease and thereafter does not cure such failure within three (3) banking days after receipt of such notice.

21.1. Tenant's Default- Tenant's default under any of the terms of this Lease may result in Landlord's termination of this Lease, together with Landlord's exercise of all rights and remedies available under the law, including, but not limited to, dispossessory actions, Tenant's forfeiture of security deposits and law suits for damages. Tenant covenants that Tenant has adequate financial resources to lease the Property. Tenant does not contemplate the filing of any bankruptcy, reorganization, arrangement, insolvency or liquidation proceedings, or any other proceeding for the relief of debtors in general, and Tenant acknowledges that Tenant's filing of a bankruptcy petition shall constitute an additional event of default hereunder, at which time this Lease shall immediately and automatically terminate with no right to cure.

21.2. Landlord's Default- If the Landlord should default on any of the provisions of this Lease, due to no fault of the Tenant, then Tenant shall be entitled, as Tenant's sole and exclusive remedy, to terminate this Lease, be reimbursed for Tenant's initial Security Deposit, and be paid a fee equal to the early termination fee (if any) described herein as full liquidated damages.

21.3. Waiver- All rights accorded to Landlord by this Lease shall be cumulative and in addition to any laws which currently exist or may exist in the future. Any failure by Landlord to exercise any rights under this Lease

Page 8 of 12
Form RE120, *Contract for the Lease of Residential Real Property*
 Initials: _________ _________ _________ _________
R10312012

FIGURE 25.43: Default (continued)

shall not act as waiver of those or any other rights, and shall not act as a bar to Landlord's future enforcement of those rights. No statement or promise by Landlord as to tenancy, repairs, and amount of rent to be paid, or any other terms shall be binding unless it is put in a writing signed by Landlord and made a specific part of this Lease.

Item 21: Default

Though a party may be in default upon a breach of any term of this lease, absent any statements otherwise included in the lease, neither the landlords nor the tenants will be deemed in default until and unless such party has been given written notice of the specific breach, and thereafter does not cure such failure of performance within three banking days after receipt of notice.

21.1: Tenant's Default—By entering into this rental agreement, the tenants acknowledge sufficient financial resources to lease the property and do not anticipate filing bankruptcy or any other proceeding for debt relief; moreover, the tenants acknowledge that filing a bankruptcy petition will constitute default, at which time the lease will immediately terminate, with no rights to cure. Any tenant default under this lease may result in the landlords' termination of the lease, as well as the landlords' exercise of all rights and remedies under the law, including dispossessory actions, the tenants' forfeiture of security deposits, and lawsuits for damages.

IN PRACTICE Landlords are prohibited in Georgia from engaging the **self-help eviction** when seeking to recover possession of a property from a tenant in default. A tenant may file a lawsuit against a landlord as the result of wrongful conduct in this matter. The landlord/tenant statutory code identifies specific guidelines for landlords who take eviction actions against a tenant in default of a lease. [O.C.G.A 44-7-50]

1. By written notice, the landlord demands possession of a property from a tenant who is in breach of lease.
2. If the tenant refuses to give up possession, the landlord (or landlord's agent/attorney) files a dispossessory affidavit at the courthouse in the county where the property is located.
3. The court charges the sheriff to deliver or "serve" notice to the tenant, who is required to answer the summons verbally or in writing within seven days from the date of the summons. Notice may also be received by another party occupying the property. If no person is found at the property, the sheriff may post a copy of the summons to the door and mail it to the tenant's last known address.
4. If the tenant fails to respond at the end of the seventh day, the lawsuit is in default. The court can then grant a writ of possession allowing the sheriff to remove the tenant immediately.
5. If the tenant answers the summons, a trial is held, typically in magistrate's court if the sum is less than $15,000. The tenant is allowed to occupy the property until a final outcome of the case, and the landlord is prohibited from suspending the utilities on the property before final disposition.

IN PRACTICE Though the filing for dispossessory actions can be accomplished through municipal, civil, or state court, it is usually filed in magistrate court—a.k.a. small claims court—because it is easier for non-lawyers to navigate. The focus of judges in these courts is on making equitable decisions rather than on technical readings of the law.

Georgia's landlord/tenant law also outlines a procedure for a landlord's right to claim the personal property of a tenant who is in breach of the rental payments. Referred to as "**distraint**," the legal guidelines allow a landlord to seize a tenant's personal property only after a grant by court order.

21.2: Landlord's Default—Upon the landlord's default through no cause of the tenant, this contract form entitles tenant to a sole and exclusive remedy as follows: termination of the lease, reimbursement of the security deposit, and the receipt of a fee equal to the early termination fee if stipulated in Lease.

21.3: Waiver—The landlord's rights in this lease are in addition to any granted by law. The landlord's failure to execute said rights do not constitute a waiver of these rights. Promises made by the landlord as to the terms of the lease are only be binding when put in writing and signed by the landlord and made a specific part of the lease.

FIGURE 25.44: Brokerage

22. BROKERAGE

By signing below, all parties represented by a Broker acknowledge that no Broker in this transaction shall owe any duty to Tenant or Landlord greater than what is set forth in their brokerage engagements and the Brokerage Relationships in Real Estate Transactions Act, O.C.G.A. § 10-6A-1 et. seq and further:

22.1. Landlord and Tenant each hereby represents and warrants to the other that he/she/they have not dealt with any real estate Broker, agent or salesperson (other than Property Manager, Landlord's Broker or Tenant's Broker, as hereinafter defined) so as to create any legal right or claim in any such Broker, agent or salesperson for a rental commission or similar fee or compensation with respect to the negotiation and/or consummation of this Lease. Tenant and Landlord acknowledge that they are not represented by a Broker unless they have signed a brokerage agreement with said Broker. If any party hereto is not represented by a Broker, that party acknowledges full responsibility for protecting his/ her/their own interests.

22.2. Any commission or other compensation due to a Broker shall be paid according to the terms of a separate agreement between Broker and Tenant, Broker and Landlord, or both.

22.3. Landlord and Tenant have been advised and expressly acknowledge their obligation to conduct a thorough investigation, or to obtain independent professional advice, with respect to any concerns they may have regarding the condition of the Property and the surrounding neighborhood, including, but not limited to, any structural, safety, environmental, financial, tax, legal or health concerns, or issues regarding the surrounding community, future or current real estate development, or municipal services offered to local residents. Tenant and Landlord expressly acknowledge that Broker is not an expert in any of these areas and has given no advice nor made any representations in regard thereto upon which Tenant or Landlord have relied. All parties hereby release any Broker and any affiliated agent and employee from any cost, expense or liability that may result from their reliance on any perceived advice given with respect to the foregoing.

22.4. Material Relationships- Neither the Broker nor Broker's affiliated licensees have a material relationship with Landlord or Tenant except as follows: N/A ____

____.

22.5. Tenant's Broker- The Tenant's Broker identified on the signature page of this Lease is the Broker assisting the Tenant, regardless of whether the Tenant is a customer or a client as defined under Georgia law. It includes the agent or agents of the Broker who are involved in this particular transaction. The Tenant's Broker is [check one]:

- **22.5.1.** ☐ representing the Tenant as a client under a written brokerage agreement; **or**
- **22.5.2.** ☒ representing the Tenant as a customer, performing only ministerial acts; **or**
- **22.5.3.** ☐ acting as a dual agent, with responsibilities to both Landlord and Tenant, as described more fully below; **or**
- **22.5.4.** ☐ acting as a designated agent, with responsibilities to both Landlord and Tenant, as described more fully below.

22.6. Landlord's Broker- The Landlord's Broker identified on the signature page of this Lease shall refer collectively to all persons assisting the Landlord, regardless of whether the Landlord is a customer or client as defined under Georgia law. It includes the agent or agents of the Broker who are involved in this particular transaction. The Landlord's Broker is NOT the Property Manager unless Landlord's Broker has also signed as Property Manager. The Landlord's Broker is [check one]:

- **22.6.1.** ☒ representing the Landlord as a client under a written brokerage agreement; **or**
- **22.6.2.** ☐ representing the Landlord as a customer, performing only ministerial acts; **or**
- **22.6.3.** ☐ acting as a dual agent, with responsibilities to both Landlord and Tenant, as described more fully below; **or**
- **22.6.4.** ☐ acting as a designated agent, with responsibilities to both Landlord and Tenant, as described more fully below.

22.7. Dual Agent- "Dual agent" means a Broker who simultaneously has a client relationship with both landlord and tenant in the same real estate transaction. O.C.G.A. §10-6A-3(10). By checking the dual agent box above, the parties acknowledge that they have consented to a dual agency and acknowledge that their interests may sometimes be adverse. If the parties have agreed to allow a Broker to act as a dual agent, that

Page 9 of 12

Form RE120, *Contract for the Lease of Residential Real Property*

 Initials: ________ ________ ________ ________

R10312012

Instant Forms

FIGURE 25.44: Brokerage (continued)

Broker will not disclose to another party any information a client has asked the Broker to keep confidential, or which would negatively affect that party's bargaining position, unless the disclosure is required by law.
22.8. Designated Agent- "Designated agent" means one or more licensees affiliated with a Broker who are assigned by the Broker to represent solely one client to the exclusion of all other clients in the same transaction and to the exclusion of all other licensees affiliated with the Broker. O.C.G.A. §10-6A-3(9). By checking the designated agent box above, the parties acknowledge that they have consented to a designated agency and acknowledge that ____ will work exclusively with Tenant as Tenant's designated agent and ____ will work exclusively with the Landlord as Landlord's designated agent.
22.9. Landlord [check one] ☐ IS **or** ☒ IS NOT a Georgia real estate licensee.

Item 22: Brokerage

In signing this lease, all parties represented by a broker acknowledge that no broker in the transaction owes any duty to the tenant or the landlord greater than what is set forth in their brokerage engagements and in BRRETA.

22.1.—The tenant and the landlord acknowledge that the broker may represent them only through a signed brokerage engagement without which the parties are fully responsible for protecting their own interests. The parties also acknowledge they have no existing dealings with other brokers who may have compensation claims with respect to this lease.

22.2.—The broker's commission or any other compensation in the transaction will be paid according to the terms of a separate agreement between the broker and the landlord or the broker and the tenant, or both.

22.3.—The landlord and the tenant expressly acknowledge that the broker is not an expert in areas and on matters that fall outside the training, education, and professional skills commonly associated with real estate brokerage. As such, the parties acknowledge no liability on the part of the broker or affiliated licensees for landlord or tenant reliance on advice or representations made by the brokers or affiliated licensees in these matters.

22.4: Material Relationships—Any material relationships for the broker or affiliated licensees that exist in the transaction are identified here.

22.5: Tenant's Broker—As identified on the signature page of the contract form, the tenant's broker is assisting the buyer either as a customer or a client. In the contract narrative, Eureka Real Estate Services and agent Lucy Gordon are working with tenants Erin Barker and Amanda Jones as customers.

22.6: Landlord's Broker—As identified on the signature page of this contract form, the landlords, Sebastian and Miranda Scott, are represented by and are clients of Eureka Real Estate Services and agent Lucy Gordon.

22.7: Dual Agency—There is no dual agency present in this lease transaction.

22.8: Designated Agency—There is no designated agency present in this lease transaction.

22.9.—The landlord is not a Georgia real estate licensee in this lease transaction.

FIGURE 25.45: Sublease and Notices

23. ASSIGNMENT/SUBLEASE
The Tenant covenants not to assign or sublet the Property without permission of the Landlord. No additional occupants other than those noted above are allowed without Landlord's express written permission.

24. NOTICES
Any notice, request or other communication required or permitted to be given hereunder shall be in writing and shall be delivered by hand or overnight courier (such as United Parcel Service or Federal Express), sent by facsimile, sent by electronic mail ("email") or mailed by United States registered or certified mail, return receipt requested, postage prepaid and addressed to each party at its address as set forth below. Any such notice shall be considered given on the date of such hand or courier delivery, confirmed facsimile transmission, deposit with such overnight courier for next business day delivery, or deposit in the United States mail, but the time period (if any is provided herein) in which to respond to such notice shall commence on the date of hand or overnight courier delivery or on the date received following deposit in the United States mail as provided above. Rejection or other refusal to accept or inability to deliver because of changed address of which no notice was given shall be deemed to be receipt of the notice. By giving at least five (5) banking days' prior written notice thereof, any party may from time to time and at any time change its mailing address hereunder. Any notice of any party may be given by or to such party's counsel or Broker. The parties' respective mailing and email addresses for notice purposes are indicated after the parties' signatures below. Telephone numbers are given for convenience of reference only. Notice by telephone shall not be effective.

Item 23: Assignment/Sublease

The contract form indicates that the tenant may only sublet or assign property with permission of the landlord. Occupants of the property are limited to those parties identified within the lease, unless otherwise agreed to in writing by the landlord.

Item 24: Notices

All notices, requests, and other required communication between the parties will be in writing and delivered in the following manner: by hand or overnight courier, such as Federal Express or UPS; fax; email; U.S. registered or certified mail (return receipt requested); or regular mail, postage prepaid and addressed to each party as set forth on the contract's signature page. Notice will be considered delivered on the date of the hand or courier delivery, confirmed fax transmission, deposit with the overnight courier for next day delivery, or deposit in the U.S. mail.

FIGURE 25.46: Miscellaneous Provisions

25. MISCELLANEOUS PROVISIONS

The Tenant and Landlord covenant and agree with each other that:

25.1. The provisions of this Lease shall extend to and be binding on the respective heirs, executors, administrators and successors of each party hereto;

25.2. If any provision of this Lease is determined by a court of competent jurisdiction to be invalid or unenforceable, the remainder of this Lease shall nonetheless remain in full force and effect;

25.3. Time is of the essence of this Lease;

25.4. The section headings appearing in this Lease are for convenience of reference only and are not intended, to any extent and for any purpose, to limit or define the text of any section or any subsection hereof;

25.5. This Lease, including any Exhibits attached hereto, contain the entire agreement between the parties pertaining to the subject matter hereof and fully supersede all prior written or oral agreements and understandings between the parties pertaining to such subject matter;

25.6. Tenant waives all rights of homestead exemption in the Property;

25.7. This Lease shall be governed by and interpreted under the laws of the State of Georgia;

25.8. Definitions:

25.8.1. Banking Days: Monday through Friday, excluding federal holidays;

25.8.2. Broker: "Broker" means any individual or entity issued a broker's real estate license by the Georgia Real Estate Commission pursuant to O.C.G.A. § 43-40. The term "Broker" includes the Broker's affiliated licensees except where the context would otherwise indicate;

25.8.3. Inspection: Includes any and all inspections regardless of whether by the Tenant individually or by a licensed (where required by law) or other third party inspector selected by Tenant;

25.8.4. Landlord: The term “Landlord” used herein shall refer collectively to all persons named above and signing this Lease as Landlord, and their successors and/or assigns if property shall be sold. Any acts

Page 10 of 12

Form RE120, *Contract for the Lease of Residential Real Property*

 Initials: ________ ________ ________ ________

R10312012

FIGURE 25.46: Miscellaneous Provisions (continued)

to be performed by the Landlord may be performed by the Property Manager or employees of the Landlord or Property Manager;

25.8.5. Tenant: The term “Tenant” used herein shall refer collectively to all persons named above and signing this Lease as Tenant, and the liability of each such person shall be joint and several. Notice given by Landlord to any person named as Tenant, or by any such person to Landlord, shall bind all persons signing this Lease as Tenant;

Item 25: Miscellaneous Provisions

Mutual agreements between the landlord and the tenant include the following:

25.1.—The contract is binding on respective heirs, executors, administrators, and successors of each party.

25.2.—Any judicially unenforceable parts of the contract will not render the remainder of the contract unenforceable.

25.3.—Time limits in the contract are strictly enforced, and the parties are bound to perform terms of agreement with all deliberate speed.

25.4.—Sections headings in the contract form are for convenience of reference only and are not intended to define or limit the text of any section.

25.5.—The contract form, including any attached exhibits, contain the entire agreement between the parties.

25.6.—The tenant waives all right to homestead exemptions extended to the owner-occupants of a residential property.

25.7.—The laws of Georgia govern the lease and are applied for interpreting the contract.

25.8—Definitions:

25.8.1.—Banking days: Monday through Friday, excluding federal holidays

25.8.2.—Broker: Individual holding a broker's license as issued by the Georgia Real Estate Commission; the term "broker" includes the broker-affiliated licensees, except where context indicates otherwise.

25.8.3.—Inspection: Includes any and all inspections performed by the tenant or a licensed inspector selected by the purchaser.

25.8.4.—**Landlord**: Refers collectively to all persons named in the lease and signing the lease as the landlord, and their successors and/or assigns if the property is sold.

Any acts to be performed by the landlord may be performed by the property manager or employees of the landlord or property manager.

25.8.5.—The term "**tenant**" refers collectively to all persons named in the lease and signing the lease as the tenant, and the liability of each such person is joint and several. Notice given by the landlord to any person named as the tenant, or by any such person to the landlord, binds all persons signing the lease as the tenant.

FIGURE 25.47: Exhibits and Special Stipulations

26. EXHIBITS
The followings exhibits are attached hereto and are by this reference made a part hereof:
☒ Rental Property Condition Report
☒ Legal Description Exhibit
☒ Lead Based Paint Exhibit
☒ EPA brochure "*Protect Your Family From Lead In Your Home*"
☐ Other: ____
☐ Other: ____
☐ Other: ____

27. SPECIAL STIPULATIONS:
NONE

Item 26: Exhibits

Referenced in this section of the agreement are attached documents that may support, add to, or alter the existing preprinted language of the contract form. If any attached exhibit conflicts with any provisions in the body of the contract, the exhibit prevails.

IN PRACTICE With respect to the lease narrative, included as exhibits to the contract form are the following: a rental property condition report signed by Sebastian and Miranda Scott as landlords and Erin Barker and Amanda Jones as tenants; a legal description exhibit; a lead-based paint exhibit; and the EPA brochure ***Protect Your Family from Lead in Your Home***.

Item 27: Special Stipulations

None are included in this lease narrative.

Acceptance and Signature Page

The lease offer is accepted, with notice properly given at 3 p.m. on July 20.

Erin Barker and Amanda Jones sign as tenants and Sebastian and Miranda Scott sign as landlords. Agent Lucy Gordon signs for Eureka Real Estate Services, as both the tenants' and the landlords' broker.

IN PRACTICE No dual or designated agency exists in this transaction because Eureka Realty and its affiliated licensee, Lucy Gordon, while working with both parties, represent only the Scotts, as an agent. The tenants work with Eureka Realty and Gordon as customers.

FIGURE 25.48: Completed Contract for Lease Of Residential Property

Contract for the Lease Of Residential Real Property

Offer Date: July 20, 20 xx

This **Contract for the Lease of Residential Real Property** (the "Lease") is made on the Acceptance Date described herein by and between Sebastian Scott and Miranda Scott, hereinafter called "Landlord" and Erin Barker and Amanda Jones, hereinafter called "Tenant," for the hereinafter described Property, and in consideration of the mutual promises contained herein. It is expressly understood and agreed that this Lease creates the relationship of Landlord and Tenant. This Lease is not intended to create an estate for years or transfer any ownership interest in the Property to Tenant.

1. PROPERTY LEASED

Landlord hereby Leases to Tenant and the latter lets from the former, premises including a residential dwelling located at: 1103 Franklin Avenue Bellville, Georgia 33333 or, if this box is checked, ☒ as described on the attached Legal Description Exhibit, incorporated herein by this reference, hereinafter called the "Property," to which Landlord claims title.

2. TERM OF LEASE

The initial term of the Lease shall be 12 months, beginning on September 1,20xx and ending on August 31,20xx.

3. RENEWAL OF LEASE

At the expiration of the Lease term, and unless otherwise terminated pursuant to the terms of this Lease, this Lease will be automatically renewed [check one] ☒ on a month to month basis, or ☐ for a term of n/a days. At that time, the rental rate shall increase by 10 % of the most recent rental rate, or US$ n/a per month. All other terms of this Lease shall remain the same. If either the Landlord or the Tenant does not wish to renew this Lease at the end of the initial or extended Lease term, the party not wishing to renew shall notify the other party in writing of such intent not to renew, no less than thirty (30) days before the expiration of this Lease.

In the event the Lease has been terminated by either party and Tenant has not vacated the Property at the end of the term, Tenant may be deemed a tenant at sufferance and shall pay a hold over fee, which shall not be regarded as rent, in the amount of US$ 200.00 per day until the Property has been vacated.

4. DELIVERY OF POSSESSION BY LANDLORD

If the Property is not ready for occupancy at the beginning of the Lease term, this Lease shall nevertheless remain in effect, but the rent shall be abated proportionately until Landlord is able to deliver possession of the Property. If Landlord has not delivered possession within 7 days after the commencement of this Lease, Tenant shall have the right to cancel this Lease by written notice delivered to Landlord or Property Manager, as hereinafter defined. Tenant's remedy shall be limited to such right of cancellation and the return of any rent or deposit prepaid to Landlord, and on such cancellation neither party shall have any further right against the other.

If Tenant takes occupancy of the Property prior to the beginning of the Lease term, such occupancy shall be subject to the terms of this Lease, and Tenant shall pay an additional prorated rental amount to Landlord for the period beginning on Tenant's actual date of occupancy and ending on the stated date of beginning of the Lease term.

Landlord shall timely satisfy all monetary obligations concerning the Property at all times to prevent the foreclosure of any liens or claims that could interfere with Tenant's possession of the Property, including, but not limited to the lien of any mortgage lender, tax authority and/or homeowner's or condominium association.

5. PROPERTY MANAGEMENT

From time to time, and at the Landlord's sole discretion, Landlord may engage the services of an agent or property manager ("Property Manager"), the terms of whose relationship with Landlord shall be set forth in a separate Property Management Agreement, to assist in the enforcement of Landlord's rights under this Lease, including, but not limited to the collection of rents, processing rental applications, assisting with repairs, holding security

 Initials: ________ ________ ________ ________

FIGURE 25.48: Completed Contract for Lease Of Residential Property (continued)

deposits, etc. Landlord shall provide Tenant with written notice, within no less than five (5) banking days, of the engagement of any such Property Manager or of any change in the designated Property Manager.

The Property [check one]:

☐ IS currently managed by the Property Manager designated on the signature page of this Lease. The Property Manager, by signing this Lease, certifies that he/she/it is authorized to sign this Lease on behalf of the Landlord, and to enforce the terms of this Lease on behalf of Landlord; **or**

☒ IS NOT currently managed by a Property Manager.

6. RENT

Tenant agrees to tender to Landlord a monthly rental payment, without any deduction or set-off whatsoever, in the amount of US$ 2,350.00, payable in advance on the 1st day of each month until the termination of this tenancy. The rental payments are payable to Miranda Scott at the following address: 5300 Unfathomable Boulevard Bellville,Georgia 33334 or to such other address as Landlord or the Property Manager may from time to time provide to Tenant by five (5) banking days' written notice.

If the Lease begins on any day of the month other than the payment date expressed in this section, the rent will be prorated until the next regularly scheduled payment date.

7. SECURITY DEPOSIT

7.1. Deposit of Funds- Tenant [check one] ☒ HAS **or** ☐ HAS NOT paid a refundable security deposit as of the date of this Lease, and if not, then Tenant shall pay the refundable security deposit in the amount of US$ 2,350.00 (the "Security Deposit") within n/a days of the execution of this Lease, which Security Deposit shall be deposited within five (5) banking days in the interest bearing or non-interest bearing account of [check one] ☒ Landlord, **or** ☐ Other: ______________________ (the "Escrow Agent"). If deposited into an interest bearing account, the holder of the security deposit shall be entitled to retain any interest accrued. If the Escrow Agent is a Georgia real estate licensee, the Security Deposit shall be deposited into a trust account that is registered with the Georgia Real Estate Commission and is in compliance with the rules and regulations of the Georgia Real Estate Commission.

7.2. Transfer of Funds- Landlord shall have the right, after ten (10) banking days' written notice to Tenant and Escrow Agent, to transfer the Security Deposit to another holder and designate a new Escrow Agent, provided the Tenant agrees in writing.

7.3. No Offset of Rental Payments - Tenant shall not have the right to offset any rental payment or any other fee due under this Lease against the Security Deposit.

7.4. Return of Funds-The Security Deposit shall be returned to Tenant at the Tenant's last known mailing address via first class U.S. mail, postage prepaid, within thirty (30) days following the expiration of this Lease if all monies due Landlord have been paid, the Tenant has vacated the Property, and Tenant is not in default under the terms of this Lease. Landlord shall be entitled to withhold from the Security Deposit any sums still owed under this Lease, including, but not limited to, final rent payments, amounts owed for repairs (normal wear and tear excepted), amounts paid by Landlord to remove Tenant's personal property, delinquent utility bills paid on behalf of Tenant, or cleaning fees due to Tenant's failure to return the Property to Landlord in the same degree of cleanliness it was in when Tenant took occupancy of the Property (normal wear and tear excepted). The Security Deposit shall become the property of the Landlord ninety (90) days after the letter is mailed if the letter is returned as undeliverable, and if Landlord's reasonable attempts to locate the Tenant have failed.

7.5. Liability of Escrow Agent- It is agreed that the duties of Escrow Agent are herein specifically provided and are purely ministerial in nature, and that Escrow Agent, so long as Escrow Agent is acting in good faith, shall incur no liability whatsoever with respect to the Security Deposit except for willful misconduct or negligence. Landlord and Tenant do each hereby release Escrow Agent from any liability for any error of judgment or for any act done or omitted to be done by Escrow Agent in the good faith performance of its duties hereunder and do each hereby indemnify Escrow Agent against, and agree to hold, save, and defend Escrow Agent harmless from, any costs, liabilities, and expenses incurred by Escrow Agent in serving and faithfully

 Initials: ________ ________ ________ ________

FIGURE 25.48: Completed Contract for Lease Of Residential Property (continued)

discharging its duties and obligations hereunder.

In the event a dispute arises between the parties regarding the final disbursement of the Security Deposit, the Escrow Agent may, upon written notice to the parties:

7.5.1. disburse the funds based upon a reasonable interpretation of this Lease; or

7.5.2. bring an appropriate action or proceeding in a court of competent jurisdiction for leave to deposit the Security Deposit, less the costs and expenses of the interpleader action actually incurred by Escrow Agent, including reasonable attorney fees. If Escrow Agent elects to interplead the Security Deposit, the Escrow Agent shall first give the parties ten (10) banking days' advance written notice.

8. OTHER CHARGES

In addition to any other rent, security deposit, utility fee or cost of repair herein described, Tenant shall be assessed a charge payable to Landlord within five (5) banking days of notice thereof in the following amounts and under the following circumstances:

8.1. Late Payment- If any rent payment due hereunder is not received by Landlord within ___5___ days of the date it is due, Tenant shall pay a late charge in an amount equal to _n/a_ % of the amount of such payment, or US$___150.00___.

8.2. Dishonored Check- If any check tendered by Tenant or on behalf of Tenant to Landlord or Property Manager is returned to Landlord or Property Manager for insufficient funds or any other reason, Tenant shall pay to the party to whom the check was tendered a service charge in the amount of US$___100.00___. Landlord reserves the right to thereafter request that all future payments be made by money order or certified funds.

8.3. Re-keying- Landlord may charge a re-key fee in the amount of US$___75.00___ for the replacement of any keys during the term of the Lease or not returned to Landlord at the termination of this Lease.

8.4. Utility Re-connect Fee- In the event Tenant fails to maintain any utility or service required hereunder through the end of the Lease term, Tenant shall pay Landlord the cost of reconnecting said utility, as well as a one time charge in the amount of US$___100.00___.

8.5. Costs of Enforcement of Landlord's Rights- Should any payment due hereunder not be paid within ___15___ days of the date it is due, Landlord shall be entitled to take legal action to dispossess Tenant. Tenant shall be responsible for paying the court costs of such action, regardless of whether or not a court order is issued, or whether or not Tenant is allowed by Landlord to cure and reinstate by paying all amounts owed, unless the action is dismissed due to Landlord default hereunder. An additional administrative fee in the amount of US$___350.00___ shall be payable by Tenant to Landlord to cover attorney fees and other administrative costs incurred by Landlord for each such dispossessory action filed.

8.6. Pet Fee- Tenant agrees to pay a non-refundable pet fee in the amount of US$____________ if pets are allowed to occupy the Property. This fee shall be in addition to the cost of any damage caused by Tenant's pet and shall not be used to offset any charges for the repair of said damage.

9. EARLY TERMINATION

9.1. By Tenant- Tenant [check one] ☒ MAY **or** ☐ MAY NOT terminate this Lease prior to the end of the Lease term.

Provided the Landlord has consented to Tenant's right of early termination by so indicating hereinabove, Tenant may exercise that right by [check all that apply]:

☐ Providing Landlord with no less than ___60___ days' prior written notice of Tenant's intent to terminate early, signed by all Tenants.

☒ Paying an early termination fee in an amount equal to ___one___ month's rent.

☐ Paying an early termination fee in an amount equal to _n/a_ % of the total rent due through the end of the original lease term, or US$___n/a___.

All other terms of this Lease shall remain in full force and effect, including, but not limited to, Tenant's obligation to pay any rents or fees due through the date of Tenant's early termination of this Lease.

 Initials: ________ ________ ________ ________

FIGURE 25.48: Completed Contract for Lease Of Residential Property (continued)

Exception for Members of the United States Military Service: *The terms of this section regarding early termination may not apply, and the provisions of the Service Members' Civil Relief Act of 2003, as amended, may control if Tenant provides Landlord with a copy of Tenant's official orders proving that Tenant has been called to active duty with the United States Armed Services during the term of this Lease; or, Tenant is on active duty with the United States military and Tenant or an immediate family member of Tenant occupying Property has received, during the term of this Lease, permanent change of station orders or temporary duty orders for a period not less than ninety (90) days.*

9.2. By Landlord- Landlord may terminate this Lease prior to the end of the Lease term by:

9.2.1. Providing Tenant with no less than sixty (60) days prior written notice of Landlord's intent to terminate the Lease early; and

9.2.2. Provided Tenant has paid all rents and fees due under this Lease at time of Lease termination and is otherwise not in default under this Lease, paying Tenant an early termination fee in the amount of US$ 2,350.00, which shall be paid to Tenant within thirty (30) days after the early expiration of this Lease. Tenant hereby acknowledges that this early termination fee shall serve as full liquidated damages for any damages Tenant may suffer due to Landlord's early termination of this Lease.

All other terms of this Lease shall remain in full force and effect, including, but not limited to, Tenant's obligation to pay any rents or fees due through the date of Landlord's early termination of this Lease.

10. USE OF PROPERTY

10.1. People- The Tenant agrees to use the Property as a residential dwelling and for no other purpose. The Tenant agrees to abide by the covenants, agreements, rules and regulations of this Lease, as well as all posted rules and regulations regarding the use of any recreational facilities, common areas, streets, driveways or sidewalks on the Property. It is the responsibility of the Tenant to familiarize himself with and abide by all federal, state, county and local laws, regulations and ordinances, and the rules, regulations and by-laws of any homeowners association or condominium association governing the use of the Property. It is understood that, in addition to the Tenant, ONLY the following people may occupy the rented Property:
Katherine Barker-Jones and Felix Barker-Jones

Tenant agrees not to do or to permit any act or practice injurious to the Property, or which may be otherwise prohibited by law.

10.2. Pets- Pets [check one] ☒ ARE **or** ☐ ARE NOT allowed under this Lease.
Provided Landlord has consented to pets to occupying the Property by so indicating hereinabove, this consent is limited by the following:

10.2.1. Only 1 individual pet(s) is (are) allowed on the Property and are specifically described as follows:

breed	max. predicted weight	breed	max. predicted weight
Siberian Husky	55 lb		

10.2.2. Tenant shall, at all times, abide by all applicable local laws, the requirements of Landlord's insurance carrier and association rules and regulations with respect to the keeping of animals or pets, including, but not limited to, leash laws, licensing laws, and laws regarding vaccinations and inoculations. Tenant shall, upon request and within five (5) banking days' notice, provide Landlord with proof of any current vaccinations applicable to the pet's species which are required by local law, including, but not limited to, rabies vaccinations.

10.2.3. Tenant shall keep pet confined or on a leash when out of doors. Tenant is responsible for all acts of pet or injuries caused by Tenant having a pet on the Property, including, but not limited to, proper clean

 Initials: _________ _________ _________ _________
R10312012

FIGURE 25.48: Completed Contract for Lease Of Residential Property (continued)

up and disposal of pet droppings; flea, tick or other pet related pest infestation within the dwelling; damage to the Property indoors and/or out of doors; and public disturbance or nuisance created by Tenant's pet.

10.2.4. If, in the sole discretion of Landlord or Property Manager, Tenant's pet becomes an annoyance to the public, then Landlord or Property Manager may, with five (5) days written notice to Tenant, demand the removal of the pet from the Property. If, in the sole discretion of Landlord or Property Manager, Tenant's pet becomes a threat to public health or safety, then Landlord or Property Manager may demand the removal of the pet from the Property immediately.

11. CONDITION OF PROPERTY

Tenant shall, at all times, maintain the Property in a clean and orderly condition so as not to create waste of or damage to the Property, and shall return the Property to the Landlord in the same condition at the end of the Lease term as it was in at the beginning of the Lease term, normal wear and tear excepted.

11.1. Initial Inspection of the Property- Prior to commencement of this Lease and Tenant's occupancy of the Property, Landlord and Tenant shall each, separately or together, conduct an initial walk-through of the Property and complete the attached Rental Property Condition Report. It shall be the responsibility of the Tenant to note any damage to the Property observed during said walk-through if not already indicated on the report by Landlord, and Tenant expressly acknowledges that failure to do so may create liability on the part of the Tenant for any Property damage noted at the end of the Lease term. By taking possession of the Property, Tenant acknowledges that the Property has been received in clean condition and in good order with the exception of any matters noted in the Rental Property Condition Report. Except as otherwise indicated in this Lease, Tenant shall take possession of the Property "as is," and has not relied upon any promise or representation by Landlord to repair, improve or otherwise alter the Property.

11.2. Landlord Responsibility for Repairs- It is the Tenant's responsibility to notify Landlord of any condition or defect which would render the Property unsafe or unfit for use as a residential dwelling, or which, if left unrepaired, could lead to severe damage to the Property. Such conditions shall include, but are not limited to, nonfunctioning smoke detectors, rodent or termite infestation, roof or plumbing leaks, and severe erosion. Landlord shall, within a reasonable amount of time after receiving notice from Tenant, repair any defect which would create a safety or health hazard to the occupants of the Property, would render the Property untenable, or is required under federal, state or local law. Landlord shall not be responsible for any routine maintenance of the Property, except as otherwise indicated herein.

11.3. Tenant's Maintenance Responsibilities- Tenant agrees to be responsible for, and to make, at Tenant's expense, all routine maintenance of the Property. Tenant's maintenance responsibilities shall include, but not be limited to the following:

11.3.1. Unless other indicated herein, and except for Property separately maintained by a condominium or homeowner's association, all yard maintenance is the responsibility of the Tenant, and the grounds shall be kept neatly mowed and free of debris.

11.3.2. It is specifically understood that Tenant will, at Tenant's expense, keep sinks, lavatories, and commodes in good working order, reporting any initial malfunction within five (5) days of occupancy.

11.3.3. Tenant shall replace all broken windows and burned-out light bulbs, repairing any damage to screens, interior walls and doors.

11.3.4. Tenant shall be responsible for taking reasonable precautions in extreme cold weather to protect the pipes from freezing.

11.3.5. Tenant agrees to report to Landlord any malfunction of, or damage to, electrical, plumbing, heating or air conditioning systems. Tenant is responsible for changing air filters in heating and air conditioning systems every ___6___ months and reporting any water leaks immediately. Prior to reporting any herein described malfunction, however, the Tenant shall take reasonable steps to confirm that the malfunction is not due to a tripped circuit breaker or blown fuse. Failure to do so may result in a charge to Tenant in the amount of US$___100.00___ for the service call.

11.3.6. Tenant agrees to pay for the cost of all repairs made necessary by negligent or careless use of the Property, including repairs to electrical, plumbing, heating and cooling system, as well as floor coverings, wall coverings and appliances.

11.3.7. Tenant agrees to take reasonable precautions to prevent losses resulting from theft, malicious mischief, or vandalism.

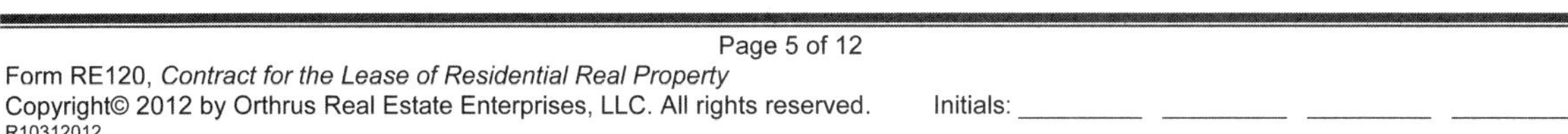

 Initials: ________ ________ ________ ________

FIGURE 25.48: Completed Contract for Lease Of Residential Property (continued)

11.4. Final Inspection of the Property- Within five (5) days after the Tenant ceases to occupy the Property (or within a reasonable time, if Tenant vacates the Property without notifying the Landlord), Landlord shall furnish Tenant with a copy of the completed Rental Property Condition Report, indicating any damage to the Property not noted at the initial inspection of the Property for which Tenant shall be held responsible. Tenant shall have the right to inspect the Property within three (3) banking days of receipt of the completed Rental Property Condition Report to confirm or dispute Landlord's assessment of the Property's condition. In the event Tenant disputes the accuracy of Landlord's Rental Property Condition Report, Tenant shall have five (5) banking days from the receipt of the Rental Property Condition Report to notify the Landlord in writing of which specific items Tenant disputes. All notices delivered as a result of this section shall be delivered in a manner consistent with the section of this Lease entitled "Notices."

12. RIGHT OF ENTRY

Tenant agrees that Landlord may enter the Property during reasonable hours for the purpose of inspecting the Property and Tenant's compliance with the terms of this Lease, making repairs, alterations, improvements or additions as Landlord may deem appropriate and showing the Property to prospective purchasers or tenants. Landlord will give Tenant twenty four (24) hours' advance notice before entering Property, except for in the event of an emergency. Landlord shall have the right to display "For Sale" or "For Rent" signs upon the Property within the last ____30____ days of the Lease term, and to market the Property for sale or for lease throughout the entire Lease term.

Within the last ____30____ days of the Lease term, Landlord [check one] ☐ SHALL **or** ☐ SHALL NOT have the right to place a lock box on the Property, during which time Tenant shall continue to be solely responsible for securing Tenant's valuables. Tenant shall cooperate with Landlord to make the Property available to prospective purchasers and tenants during reasonable hours.

13. ALTERATIONS TO THE PROPERTY

Tenant may not make any alterations or additions to the Property without the prior written consent of Landlord. Tenant is forbidden from changing, adding or removing any locks without prior written consent of Landlord. Tenant shall not paint, mark or otherwise deface walls, ceilings, floors, windows, cabinets, woodwork, stone, ironwork, or any other part of the Property, inside or out. Tenant specifically agrees not to damage the walls with screws, nails, glue or tape, though standard picture hooks and curtain or shade brackets shall be allowed. Any alterations or improvements made by Tenant, including fixtures, carpeting, painting, wallpaper, and landscaping, shall become a part of the Property unless otherwise consented to by Landlord in writing. Upon termination of this lease Tenant shall restore the property to its original condition, safety and appearance, ordinary wear and tear excepted, except as to the fixtures, carpeting, painting, wallpaper, shrubs or any other plants which Landlord has accepted. If Tenant fails to do so, Tenant will promptly reimburse Landlord for any expenses required to restore the Property.

14. DAMAGE TO THE PROPERTY NOT CAUSED BY TENANT

If the Property is damaged by fire, flood, toxic environmental hazard, extreme weather or other casualty not due to the negligence of Tenant, Tenant's invitees, licensees or guests, Landlord shall repair the damage within a reasonable time and rent shall continue unabated unless the casualty renders the Property fully untenable, in which case either party may terminate this Lease and Tenant, on payment of all rent due through the date Property is surrendered, shall not be liable for any further rent but shall be reimbursed the Security Deposit. In the event the Property is rendered only partially untenable by the above described casualty, Tenant shall be entitled to a reduction in the amount of rent proportionate to the amount of Property so damaged until such time as Property has been repaired; provided, however, that this shall not relieve the Landlord of the obligation to complete repairs within a reasonable time.

This Property [check one] ☐ HAS **or** ☒ HAS NOT been flooded by natural forces, such as excessive rain or an overflow of an established water source, within the five (5) years preceding the date of this Lease. The term "flood" as used in this paragraph shall mean the inundation of water over land or structures not usually covered by it, and shall not include water intrusion caused by a failure of plumbing.

 Initials: ________ ________ ________ ________
R10312012

FIGURE 25.48: Completed Contract for Lease Of Residential Property (continued)

This Property [check one] ☒ WAS **or** ☐ WAS NOT built prior to 1978. If the Property or any part thereof was built prior to 1978, Tenant acknowledges receipt of the Lead Based Paint Exhibit attached hereto and by this reference made a part hereof and the EPA brochure entitled "Protect Your Family From Lead In Your Home."

Tenant acknowledges that it is Tenant's responsibility to insure Tenant's personal property through a comprehensive policy of renter's hazard insurance. Neither Landlord, nor Property Manager nor Broker shall be liable to Tenant or any party claiming by, through or under Tenant for any damage to personal property stored on the Property, and Tenant does hereby indemnify Landlord, Property Manager and Broker against, and agrees to hold, save, and defend Landlord, Property Manager and Broker harmless from, any costs, liabilities, and expenses incurred as a result of damage to personal property stored on the Property.

15. UTILITIES AND SERVICES
Tenant understands and agrees that the cost of utilities and services shall be paid as follows: [check all that apply]

Utility or Service	**Paid by Tenant**	**Paid by Landlord**	**Optional or Not Required**
Electricity	✘		
Gas	✘		
Water	✘		
Sewer	✘		
Waste removal	✘		
Telephone	✘		
Yard and Lawn Maintenance	✘		
Cable	✘		
Pest (other than termite or rodents) Control	✘		
Other: ______________			
Other: ______________			

Any utilities or services required to be maintained by Tenant must be transferred or connected in Tenant's name within ___3___ days of commencement of this Lease.

16. USE OF PARKING
Tenant shall park motor vehicles in areas designated by Landlord and no other areas. Any vehicle parked on the Property shall bear evidence of current license and registration, and no recreational vehicle, boat, motor home, trailer or inoperable vehicle of any kind shall be permitted to be parked on the Property. Any vehicle not in compliance with this section may be towed at Tenant's expense.

17. ADDITIONAL USE RESTRICTIONS
The following rules apply to Tenant and Tenant's invitees, guests and licensees:

17.1. Tenant shall not operate heavy equipment, play loud music or create any other condition which may constitute a nuisance or disrupt the quiet enjoyment of neighbors in the surrounding area.

17.2. Tenant shall not make use of portable heaters or air conditioning units without the written permission of Landlord.

17.3. Tenant will neither store nor dump any environmentally hazardous or combustible substances on the Property, except that Tenant may store normal household goods in amounts necessary for normal household use.

17.4. The possession of any illegal substance, stolen goods or other contraband on the Property is strictly forbidden.

18. SUBORDINATION
This Lease is subject and subordinate to the lien of all mortgages now or at any time hereafter placed on any part of Landlord's property which includes the Property, to extensions or renewals thereof, and to all advances now or hereafter made on the security thereof. Tenant agrees, upon request, to execute such further instruments

 Initials: ________ ________ ________ ________

FIGURE 25.48: Completed Contract for Lease Of Residential Property (continued)

evidencing such subordination as Landlord may request, and if Tenant fails to do so, Landlord is empowered to do so in the name of the Tenant.

19. LIMITATION OF LANDLORD'S LIABILITY
The term "Landlord," as used in this Lease, so far as covenants or obligations on the part of Landlord are concerned, shall be limited to mean and include only the Landlord or Landlords, who, at the time in question, own the Property. In the event of any transfer or transfers of ownership of the Property, the Landlord herein named (and in case of any subsequent transfers or conveyances, the then Landlord) shall be, from and after the date of such transfers and conveyances, freed and relieved of all liability with respect to the performance of any covenants or obligations on the part of Landlord contained in this Lease to be performed after the transfer. Without further agreement, the new owner of the Property shall be deemed to have assumed and agreed to observe and perform any and all obligations in this Lease. Landlord may transfer his interest in the Property without the consent of Tenant and such transfer or subsequent transfer shall not be deemed a violation on Landlord's part of any of the terms and conditions of this Lease. Landlord or transferor shall remain and continue to be liable for any performance or payment which shall have accrued or become owing during such Landlord's or transferor's tenure as Landlord hereunder.

20. INDEMNIFICATION OF LANDLORD
The Tenant shall not do or permit any act upon the Property which may subject the Landlord to any liability by reason of any illegal business or conduct upon the Property, or by reason of any violation of law or of any legal requirement of public authority, but shall exercise such control over the Property as to fully protect the Landlord. Notwithstanding that joint or concurrent liability may be imposed upon the Landlord by statute, ordinance, rule, regulations, or order, the Tenant shall indemnify the Landlord against any liability or expense of any nature due to the following:

20.1. Any breach of any covenant in this Lease required to be performed by the Tenant;

20.2. Any damage to person or property occasioned by the Tenant's use and occupancy of the Property or by any use or occupancy of the Property which the Tenant may permit its guests, invitees and/or licensees; and

20.3. Injury to any person, including death resulting at any time therefrom, occurring in or about the Property and on the sidewalks adjacent to the Property. If the Tenant is required to defend any action or proceeding pursuant to any such occurrence to which the Landlord is made a party, the Landlord shall be entitled to appear, defend, or otherwise take part in the matter involved, at its election, by counsel of its own choosing, providing such action by the Landlord does not limit or make void any liability of any insurer of the Landlord or Tenant hereunder in respect to the claim or matter in question. The Tenant's liability under this section shall be reduced by the net proceeds collected from any insurance taken out by the Tenant to cover losses from the events herein described.

21. DEFAULT
A party shall be in default if he or she breaches any term of this Lease. Except as otherwise stated herein, neither Landlord nor Tenant shall be deemed to be in default hereunder, however, until and unless such party has been given written notice of its failure to comply with the terms of this Lease and thereafter does not cure such failure within three (3) banking days after receipt of such notice.

21.1. Tenant's Default- Tenant's default under any of the terms of this Lease may result in Landlord's termination of this Lease, together with Landlord's exercise of all rights and remedies available under the law, including, but not limited to, dispossessory actions, Tenant's forfeiture of security deposits and law suits for damages. Tenant covenants that Tenant has adequate financial resources to lease the Property. Tenant does not contemplate the filing of any bankruptcy, reorganization, arrangement, insolvency or liquidation proceedings, or any other proceeding for the relief of debtors in general, and Tenant acknowledges that Tenant's filing of a bankruptcy petition shall constitute an additional event of default hereunder, at which time this Lease shall immediately and automatically terminate with no right to cure.

21.2. Landlord's Default- If the Landlord should default on any of the provisions of this Lease, due to no fault of the Tenant, then Tenant shall be entitled, as Tenant's sole and exclusive remedy, to terminate this Lease, be reimbursed for Tenant's initial Security Deposit, and be paid a fee equal to the early termination fee (if any) described herein as full liquidated damages.

21.3. Waiver- All rights accorded to Landlord by this Lease shall be cumulative and in addition to any laws which currently exist or may exist in the future. Any failure by Landlord to exercise any rights under this Lease

 Initials: ________ ________ ________ ________

FIGURE 25.48: Completed Contract for Lease Of Residential Property (continued)

shall not act as waiver of those or any other rights, and shall not act as a bar to Landlord's future enforcement of those rights. No statement or promise by Landlord as to tenancy, repairs, and amount of rent to be paid, or any other terms shall be binding unless it is put in a writing signed by Landlord and made a specific part of this Lease.

22. BROKERAGE

By signing below, all parties represented by a Broker acknowledge that no Broker in this transaction shall owe any duty to Tenant or Landlord greater than what is set forth in their brokerage engagements and the Brokerage Relationships in Real Estate Transactions Act, O.C.G.A. § 10-6A-1 et. seq and further:

22.1. Landlord and Tenant each hereby represents and warrants to the other that he/she/they have not dealt with any real estate Broker, agent or salesperson (other than Property Manager, Landlord's Broker or Tenant's Broker, as hereinafter defined) so as to create any legal right or claim in any such Broker, agent or salesperson for a rental commission or similar fee or compensation with respect to the negotiation and/or consummation of this Lease. Tenant and Landlord acknowledge that they are not represented by a Broker unless they have signed a brokerage agreement with said Broker. If any party hereto is not represented by a Broker, that party acknowledges full responsibility for protecting his/ her/their own interests.

22.2. Any commission or other compensation due to a Broker shall be paid according to the terms of a separate agreement between Broker and Tenant, Broker and Landlord, or both.

22.3. Landlord and Tenant have been advised and expressly acknowledge their obligation to conduct a thorough investigation, or to obtain independent professional advice, with respect to any concerns they may have regarding the condition of the Property and the surrounding neighborhood, including, but not limited to, any structural, safety, environmental, financial, tax, legal or health concerns, or issues regarding the surrounding community, future or current real estate development, or municipal services offered to local residents. Tenant and Landlord expressly acknowledge that Broker is not an expert in any of these areas and has given no advice nor made any representations in regard thereto upon which Tenant or Landlord have relied. All parties hereby release any Broker and any affiliated agent and employee from any cost, expense or liability that may result from their reliance on any perceived advice given with respect to the foregoing.

22.4. Material Relationships- Neither the Broker nor Broker's affiliated licensees have a material relationship with Landlord or Tenant except as follows: N/A ____.

22.5. Tenant's Broker- The Tenant's Broker identified on the signature page of this Lease is the Broker assisting the Tenant, regardless of whether the Tenant is a customer or a client as defined under Georgia law. It includes the agent or agents of the Broker who are involved in this particular transaction. The Tenant's Broker is [check one]:

- **22.5.1.** ☐ representing the Tenant as a client under a written brokerage agreement; **or**
- **22.5.2.** ☒ representing the Tenant as a customer, performing only ministerial acts; **or**
- **22.5.3.** ☐ acting as a dual agent, with responsibilities to both Landlord and Tenant, as described more fully below; **or**
- **22.5.4.** ☐ acting as a designated agent, with responsibilities to both Landlord and Tenant, as described more fully below.

22.6. Landlord's Broker- The Landlord's Broker identified on the signature page of this Lease shall refer collectively to all persons assisting the Landlord, regardless of whether the Landlord is a customer or client as defined under Georgia law. It includes the agent or agents of the Broker who are involved in this particular transaction. The Landlord's Broker is NOT the Property Manager unless Landlord's Broker has also signed as Property Manager. The Landlord's Broker is [check one]:

- **22.6.1.** ☒ representing the Landlord as a client under a written brokerage agreement; **or**
- **22.6.2.** ☐ representing the Landlord as a customer, performing only ministerial acts; **or**
- **22.6.3.** ☐ acting as a dual agent, with responsibilities to both Landlord and Tenant, as described more fully below; **or**
- **22.6.4.** ☐ acting as a designated agent, with responsibilities to both Landlord and Tenant, as described more fully below.

22.7. Dual Agent- "Dual agent" means a Broker who simultaneously has a client relationship with both landlord and tenant in the same real estate transaction. O.C.G.A. §10-6A-3(10). By checking the dual agent box above, the parties acknowledge that they have consented to a dual agency and acknowledge that their interests may sometimes be adverse. If the parties have agreed to allow a Broker to act as a dual agent, that

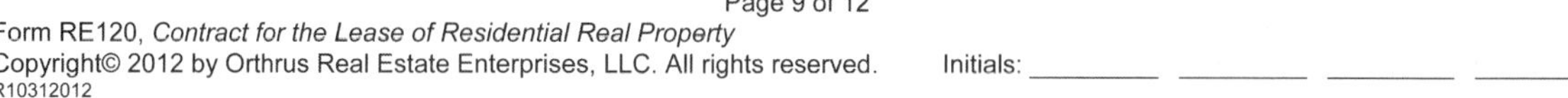

 Initials: ________ ________ ________ ________

FIGURE 25.48: Completed Contract for Lease Of Residential Property (continued)

Broker will not disclose to another party any information a client has asked the Broker to keep confidential, or which would negatively affect that party's bargaining position, unless the disclosure is required by law.
22.8. Designated Agent- "Designated agent" means one or more licensees affiliated with a Broker who are assigned by the Broker to represent solely one client to the exclusion of all other clients in the same transaction and to the exclusion of all other licensees affiliated with the Broker. O.C.G.A. §10-6A-3(9). By checking the designated agent box above, the parties acknowledge that they have consented to a designated agency and acknowledge that ______N/A______ will work exclusively with Tenant as Tenant's designated agent and ____________ will work exclusively with the Landlord as Landlord's designated agent.
22.9. Landlord [check one] ☐ IS **or** ☒ IS NOT a Georgia real estate licensee.

23. ASSIGNMENT/SUBLEASE
The Tenant covenants not to assign or sublet the Property without permission of the Landlord. No additional occupants other than those noted above are allowed without Landlord's express written permission.

24. NOTICES
Any notice, request or other communication required or permitted to be given hereunder shall be in writing and shall be delivered by hand or overnight courier (such as United Parcel Service or Federal Express), sent by facsimile, sent by electronic mail ("email") or mailed by United States registered or certified mail, return receipt requested, postage prepaid and addressed to each party at its address as set forth below. Any such notice shall be considered given on the date of such hand or courier delivery, confirmed facsimile transmission, deposit with such overnight courier for next business day delivery, or deposit in the United States mail, but the time period (if any is provided herein) in which to respond to such notice shall commence on the date of hand or overnight courier delivery or on the date received following deposit in the United States mail as provided above. Rejection or other refusal to accept or inability to deliver because of changed address of which no notice was given shall be deemed to be receipt of the notice. By giving at least five (5) banking days' prior written notice thereof, any party may from time to time and at any time change its mailing address hereunder. Any notice of any party may be given by or to such party's counsel or Broker. The parties' respective mailing and email addresses for notice purposes are indicated after the parties' signatures below. Telephone numbers are given for convenience of reference only. Notice by telephone shall not be effective.

25. MISCELLANEOUS PROVISIONS
The Tenant and Landlord covenant and agree with each other that:
25.1. The provisions of this Lease shall extend to and be binding on the respective heirs, executors, administrators and successors of each party hereto;
25.2. If any provision of this Lease is determined by a court of competent jurisdiction to be invalid or unenforceable, the remainder of this Lease shall nonetheless remain in full force and effect;
25.3. Time is of the essence of this Lease;
25.4. The section headings appearing in this Lease are for convenience of reference only and are not intended, to any extent and for any purpose, to limit or define the text of any section or any subsection hereof;
25.5. This Lease, including any Exhibits attached hereto, contain the entire agreement between the parties pertaining to the subject matter hereof and fully supersede all prior written or oral agreements and understandings between the parties pertaining to such subject matter;
25.6. Tenant waives all rights of homestead exemption in the Property;
25.7. This Lease shall be governed by and interpreted under the laws of the State of Georgia;
25.8. Definitions:
25.8.1. Banking Days: Monday through Friday, excluding federal holidays;
25.8.2. Broker: "Broker" means any individual or entity issued a broker's real estate license by the Georgia Real Estate Commission pursuant to O.C.G.A. § 43-40. The term "Broker" includes the Broker's affiliated licensees except where the context would otherwise indicate;
25.8.3. Inspection: Includes any and all inspections regardless of whether by the Tenant individually or by a licensed (where required by law) or other third party inspector selected by Tenant;
25.8.4. Landlord: The term "Landlord" used herein shall refer collectively to all persons named above and signing this Lease as Landlord, and their successors and/or assigns if property shall be sold. Any acts

 Initials: ________ ________ ________ ________
R10312012

FIGURE 25.48: Completed Contract for Lease Of Residential Property (continued)

to be performed by the Landlord may be performed by the Property Manager or employees of the Landlord or Property Manager;

25.8.5. Tenant: The term "Tenant" used herein shall refer collectively to all persons named above and signing this Lease as Tenant, and the liability of each such person shall be joint and several. Notice given by Landlord to any person named as Tenant, or by any such person to Landlord, shall bind all persons signing this Lease as Tenant;

26. EXHIBITS

The followings exhibits are attached hereto and are by this reference made a part hereof:

☒ Rental Property Condition Report
☒ Legal Description Exhibit
☒ Lead Based Paint Exhibit
☒ EPA brochure "*Protect Your Family From Lead In Your Home*"
☐ Other: ______________________________
☐ Other: ______________________________
☐ Other: ______________________________

27. SPECIAL STIPULATIONS:

NONE

☐ Substantive provisions continued on additional page.

 Initials: ________ ________ ________ ________

FIGURE 25.48: Completed Contract for Lease Of Residential Property (continued)

The **Lease** is hereby **Accepted**, with notice being properly given to the party making the last offer, at _____ o'clock 3P m. _________________.

All Names should be both signed and printed.

Tenant:

➢ ______________________

Erin Barker
Tenant Printed Name

➢ ______________________

Amanda Jones
Tenant Printed Name

777-2222 / ______
Tenant Phone Number / Tenant Fax Number

EB@comcast.net
Tenant Email Address

PO Box 767899
Tenant Address

Stockdale	Ga	98989
Tenant City	State	Zip

[Check one] ☐ Landlord or ☐ Property Manager:

➢ ______________________

Miranda Scott
Landlord or Property Manager Printed Name

➢ ______________________

Sebastian Scott
Landlord or Property Manager Printed Name

878 222-0000 / ______
Landlord or Property Mgr Phone / Landlord or Property Mgr Fax

sms@google.net
Landlord or Property Manager Email Address

1103 Franklin Avenue Bellville, Ga. 33333
Landlord or Property Manager Address

Landlord or Property Manager City	State	Zip

Tenant's Broker:

Eureka Real Estate Services / EKS-12
Name of Brokerage Firm / Broker Code

709 987-6541 / 709 123-4567
Brokerage Phone Number / Brokerage Fax Number

➢ ______________________

Lucy Gordon
Agent Printed Name

404 777-7777 / 709 123-4567
Agent Phone Number / Agent Fax Number

LGI@mindspring.com
Agent Email Address

Required License Number(s):

J-3456 / 99999
Broker's License Number / Agent's License Number

MLS Listing # 10345

Landlord's Broker:

Eureka Real Estate Services / EKS-12
Name of Brokerage Firm / Broker Code

709 987-6541 / 709 123-4567
Brokerage Phone Number / Brokerage Fax Number

➢ ______________________

Lucy Gordon
Agent Printed Name

404 777-7777 / 709 123-4567
Agent Phone Number / Agent Fax Number

LGI@minspring.com
Agent Email Address

Required License Number(s):

J-3456 / 99999
Broker's License Number / Agent's License Number

MLS Listing # 10345

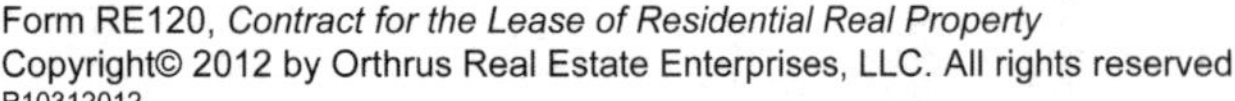

Initials: ________ ________ ________ ________

LEASE/PURCHASE AGREEMENT

Lease contract forms in Georgia may also be used for transactions where the tenant and the landlord mutually agree that at the end of the lease term, the tenant will purchase the property as buyer and the landlord, as seller, will transfer title to the tenant. Commonly called a lease/purchase agreement, this transaction is set forth by attaching two enforceable contracts: a rental agreement and an agreement for purchase and sale. The property sales contract form may be identical to the one reviewed earlier under this topic; the property lease contract, though, typically alters a few elements of the commonly used preprinted document in order to establish an enforceable connection with a second contract, the purchase and sale agreement. What follows here are excerpts from this particular type of lease establishing the lease/purchase contract between a tenant and a landlord. Other than said excerpts, remaining portions of the lease are identical to the contract for the lease of residential real property.

FIGURE 25.49: Lease/Purchase Agreement

Lease for Lease/Purchase Agreement Only Exhibit

(To be used with a residential purchase and sale agreement)

THIS LEASE AGREEMENT ("Lease") between the undersigned is for the property commonly known as ________________, ____________ , Georgia _________ , (the "Property") which is more particularly described in that certain contract for the purchase and sale of real property (the "Contract") to which this Lease, made on the Acceptance Date herinafter defined by and between ______________________________ ____, hereinafter called "Landlord" and ____, hereinafter called "Tenant," is an exhibit, the terms of which are incorporated herein by reference. It is expressly understood and agreed that this Lease creates the relationship of Landlord and Tenant, and this Lease constitute a separate agreement between the parties.

1. PROPERTY LEASED

Landlord hereby Leases to Tenant and the latter lets from the former, the Property, to which Landlord claims title.

2. TERM OF LEASE

The term of this Lease shall begin on the ____ day of _____________, 20___ and end on the Closing date of the sale of the Property as defined in the Contract, or any extension thereto, unless earlier terminated as provided herein. In the event the Contract and/or Lease has been terminated by either party and Tenant has not vacated the Property at the end of the term, Tenant may be deemed a tenant at sufferance and shall pay a hold over fee, which shall not be regarded as rent, in the amount of US$_________ per day until the Property has been vacated.

IN PRACTICE The contract form begins with the property's address followed by a statement that the legal description of the property may be found in the already established contract for purchase and sale between the parties of this lease. This paragraph goes on to indicate that this lease constitutes a separate agreement between the parties and will be attached to the sales contract as an exhibit. In effect, the lease added as an exhibit to the contract for purchase and sale will establish the lease/purchase binding agreement between the parties.

Item 2: Term of Lease

As is customary, the beginning date of the rental agreement is identified here. But because this is a lease form to be used specifically for a lease/purchase, the ending date of the lease is determined to be the closing date as defined in the separate contract for purchase and sale between the parties. Also, if either the sales contract or this lease contract is terminated by either party and the tenant has not vacated the property at the time of termination, the tenant may be deemed "at sufferance" and must pay a holdover fee per diem until vacating, for an amount identified in the contract form.

FIGURE 25.50: Security Deposit

6. **SECURITY DEPOSIT**

6.1. Deposit of Funds- THE SECURITY DEPOSIT DESCRIBED HEREUNDER IS SEPARATE AND DISTINCT FROM ANY EARNEST MONEY REFERRED TO OR DESCRIBED IN THE CONTRACT. Tenant [check one] ☐ HAS **or** ☐ HAS NOT paid a refundable security deposit as of the date of this Lease, and if not, then Tenant shall pay the refundable security deposit in the amount of US$____________ (the "Security Deposit") within ____ days of the execution of this Lease, which Security Deposit shall be deposited within five (5) banking days in the interest bearing or non-interest bearing account of [check one] ☐ Landlord, or ☐ Other: ____ (the "Escrow Agent"). If deposited into an interest bearing account, the holder of the security deposit shall be entitled to retain any interest accrued. If the Escrow Agent is a Georgia real estate licensee, the Security Deposit shall be deposited into a trust account that is registered with the Georgia Real Estate Commission and is in compliance with the rules and regulations of the Georgia Real Estate Commission.

6.2. Transfer of Funds- Landlord shall have the right, after ten (10) banking days' written notice to Tenant and Escrow Agent, to transfer the Security Deposit to another holder and designate a new Escrow Agent, provided the Tenant agrees in writing.

6.3. No Offset of Rental Payments- Tenant shall not have the right to offset any rental payment or any other fee due under this Lease against the Security Deposit.

6.4. Return of Funds-

6.4.1. Credit at Closing – The Security Deposit shall be applied to the Purchase Price at Closing.

6.4.2. Termination of the Contract – In the event the parties terminate the sale of the Property pursuant to the Contract, and Tenant is not in default of any term of the Contract or this Lease, the Security Deposit shall be returned to Tenant at Tenant's last known mailing address via first class U.S. mail, postage prepaid, within thirty (30) days following the termination of this Lease if all monies due Landlord have been paid, the Tenant has vacated the Property. Landlord shall be entitled to withhold from the Security Deposit any sums still owed under this Lease, including, but not limited to, final rent payments, amounts owed for repairs (normal wear and tear excepted), amounts paid by Landlord to remove Tenant's personal property, delinquent utility bills paid on behalf of Tenant, or cleaning fees due to Tenant's failure to return the Property to Landlord in the same degree of cleanliness it was in when Tenant took occupancy of the Property (normal wear and tear excepted). The Security Deposit shall become the property of the Landlord ninety (90) days after the letter is mailed if the letter is returned as undeliverable, and if Landlord's reasonable attempts to locate the Tenant have failed.

Item 6: Security Deposit

6.1: Deposit of Funds—Here it is indicated in bold print that any security deposit described in this section of the lease is separate and distinct from any earnest money referred to or described in the contract for purchase and sale. This statement is not found in the common rental agreement.

6.4.1: Credit at Closing—Upon the closing of the contract for purchase and sale between the parties, the security deposit attached to this lease will be applied to the purchase price.

6.4.2: Termination of Contract—Here, this particular lease form indicates that if either party terminates the contract for purchase and sale, according to the terms of that agreement, and the tenant is not in default of that contract or the lease, the tenant will be reimbursed the security deposit by first class U.S. mail within three days of termination.

FIGURE 25.51: Early Termination

8. EARLY TERMINATION

8.1. Tenant MAY NOT terminate this Lease prior to the end of the Lease term.

> ***Exception for Members of the United States Military Service:*** *The terms of this section regarding early termination may not apply, and the provisions of the Service Members' Civil Relief Act of 2003, as amended, may control if Tenant provides Landlord with a copy of Tenant's official orders proving that Tenant has been called to active duty with the United States Armed Services during the term of this Lease; or, Tenant is on active duty with the United States military and Tenant or an immediate family member of Tenant occupying Property has received, during the term of this Lease, permanent change of station orders or temporary duty orders for a period not less than 90 days.*

8.2. Contract Earnest Money - The Earnest Money deposit, as defined in and tendered pursuant to the Contract, shall be disbursed according to the terms of the Contract if the Contract is still in effect at the time of Lease termination and neither party is in default of any term of this Lease.

Item 8: Early Termination

8.1—Because this lease functions as an exhibit of the purchase and sale contract between the parties, performance of full lease term is a necessary component to the closing of the purchase and sale contract. Consequently, the tenant is prohibited from ending the lease term early.

8.2—If the contract for purchase and sale is still in effect at the time of Lease termination and neither party is in default of the lease, the earnest money as defined in the sales contract will be disbursed according to the terms of that contract.

FIGURE 25.52: Default

19. DEFAULT

A party shall be in default of this Lease if he or she breaches any term hereof or any term of the Contract. Likewise, a default under the Lease shall be considered a default under the Contract. Except as otherwise stated herein, neither Landlord nor Tenant shall be deemed to be in default hereunder, however, until and unless such party has been given written notice of its failure to comply with the terms of this Lease and thereafter does not cure such failure within three (3) banking days after receipt of such notice.

Default

A default by either party of the lease or the contract for purchase and sale will be considered a default of both contracts.

OPTION CONTRACT TO PURCHASE LEASED PROPERTY

An option contract is entirely different from the contract described above. While a lease/purchase contractual agreement mutually commits the tenant to the purchase of the property and the landlord to its sale at the end of the rental term, an option to purchase leased property simply establishes a right for the tenant to purchase, while committing the landlord to sell only if the tenant decides to buy the property. This unilateral option agreement, in effect, turns into a bilateral contract for purchase and sale of residential property if and when the tenant exercises that option or right to purchase. What follows here are the essential terms of this particular real estate transaction, as set forth on the first page of the contract form.

FIGURE 25.53: Option to Purchase

Option to Purchase Leased Property

This Option shall become a Contract for Purchase and Sale of Residential Property if and when the Option contained herein is exercised.

Offer Date: _____________________, 20____

This **Option to Purchase Leased Property** (the "Option," or, if the Option Right is exercised, the "Contract") is made on _______________, 20___ by and between ____, hereinafter called "Buyer" and ____, hereinafter called "Seller," for the hereinafter described Property, and in consideration of the mutual promises contained herein. If and when the Option Right is exercised by Buyer, all of the terms and conditions hereinafter set forth shall be deemed by the parties hereto to constitute, and be, a binding contract of sale and purchase of the Property for the Purchase Price (as hereinafter defined).

1. THE PROPERTY

The Buyer hereunder may also be known as "Tenant" and the Seller hereunder may also be known as "Landlord" under that certain lease agreement attached hereto for the lease of real property dated __________________ and executed by the parties hereto (the "Lease"), said property being located in _______________________ County, Georgia, and being known as ____ _______________ (the "Property"), and being more particularly described as that tract or parcel of land lying and being in Land Lot _________ of the _________ District, _____ Section, _____________ County, Georgia, being Lot _____, Block _____, Phase ___ of ______________________ Subdivision, as more particularly set out in Plat Book _____, Page _____, of the official records of ______________ County, Georgia, Tax ID # ______________ ______ **or, in the alternative, as set out on an Exhibit attached hereto and made a part hereof by this reference**. In the event of any conflict between the terms of this Option and the Lease, the terms of this Option shall control.

2. OPTION

2.1. The Seller hereby grants the Buyer the option to purchase the Property (the "Option Right") under the terms described below. In consideration of the right to exercise the Option Right, Buyer agrees to pay to Seller the nonrefundable sum of ____ US Dollars (US$______________________) (the "Option Fee"). All parties agree that the Option Fee shall not be applied as Earnest Money or credited against the Purchase Price, as described herein, or to any amounts due under the Lease.

2.2. The term of the Option Right shall begin on the Acceptance Date and shall remain open for exercise by Buyer until 11:59 p.m. on the day that is _____ days after the Acceptance Date, or upon expiration of the Lease, whichever is sooner.

2.3. The date upon which the Buyer exercises the Option Right shall be known as the Date of Option Exercise.

2.4. Buyer shall not have the right to exercise the Option if Buyer (as Tenant) is in default under the Lease as of the date of Buyer's attempted exercise of the Option.

3. AGREEMENT TO PURCHASE

Upon exercise of the Option, the undersigned Seller agrees to sell and the undersigned Buyer agrees to buy the Property. BUYER SHALL NOT BE OBLIGATED TO PURCHASE THE PROPERTY UNLESS AND UNTIL THE OPTION HAS BEEN EXERCISED AS SET FORTH ABOVE. Seller shall convey to Buyer good and marketable title to the Property by general warranty deed, free and clear of all mortgages and liens, except the Property shall be subject to the taxes not yet due and payable and all other encumbrances, zoning ordinances, easements and restrictions of record as of the Date of Option Exercise. Good and marketable title as used herein shall mean title which a title insurance company licensed to do business in Georgia will insure at its regular rates, subject only to standard exceptions.

This contract form, known as an option to purchase leased property, begins by identifying the parties to the transaction, the date the agreement is created, and the exact nature of this particular agreement. What is made clear is that a binding contract for purchase and sale will occur only if and when the party known as the buyer chooses to exercise the option or the right to purchase the property at a price identified within the document.

Item 1:The Property

Here the contract form identifies the buyer and the seller, respectively, as the tenant and the landlord, both of whom are parties to a lease for a property whose address and legal description are included in this section of the option agreement, with the lease attached to the contract form as an exhibit.

Item 2: Option

2.1.—Because this option agreement is a contract, as such it requires an exchange of consideration between the parties. For the seller, granting the buyer the option to purchase the property at terms described in this section satisfies that obligation; for the buyer, such consideration in the contract form is identified as a sum of money to be paid to the seller in exchange for giving buyer the option/right. This option fee paid by the buyer is nonrefundable and may not be applied as earnest money or credited against the purchase price, or to any amounts due under the lease between the parties.

2.2.—The term of the option right begins on the acceptance date of the agreement and remains open until 11:59 pm on the day that is a designated number of days from the acceptance date, and is so indicated in the space allowed in this section of the form.

IN PRACTICE The above terms satisfy the necessary components of an enforceable option contract: a designated purchase price, consideration paid for the option right, and an expiration date for the option right.

2.3.—The date on which the buyer exercises the option right will be known as the date of the option exercise.

2.4.—If the buyer (as tenant) is in default under the lease as of the date the buyer attempts to exercise the option to buy the property, the buyer is prohibited from exercising that right.

Item 3: Agreement to Purchase

Here, a statement in capitalized letters reiterates that under this particular contract, the buyer is not obligated to purchase the property unless and until the option has been exercised as set forth in the described terms.

IN PRACTICE While setting forth the terms of the option sales agreement for real property, contract forms commonly used by brokers in this particular transaction also provide all the essential elements for the purchase and sale agreement should the tenant choose to buy the property before the expiration of the option. As such, performance time frames in these contract forms are typically generated from the date the option to purchase is exercised. Additionally, if and when the tenant exercises this option, it's common for the lease expiration date to be automatically extended or shortened to coincide with the closing date of the sale between the parties. All terms of the lease remain in full force and the rent is prorated through and including the closing date. Also typically present in lease/option agreements is an acknowledgment from both parties that the property is being sold "as is" and that the seller's duty for repairs is limited to those specified in the lease within a role as landlord. Finally, as the tenant's exercise of the option turns the agreement into a contract for purchase and sale, any appropriate exhibits or stipulations common to this transaction would be included in or attached to the document. One exception may be the buyer's general right to terminate because the lease/option contract already allows the tenant a defined period in which to decide whether to actually buy the property.

UNIT 25 QUIZ

1. Which of the following statements *BEST* explains why important broker disclosures might be found at the beginning of agency-engagement contract forms?
   a. Separating these disclosures from the actual terms and specific details of the agreement makes it easier for the client to read and understand the contract.
   b. Statutory regulations require that disclosures must be set forth at the beginning of all real estate agency contract forms.
   c. Inserting disclosures at the beginning of the contract form for prospective clients to read more effectively ensures an "informed consent" on their part before committing to the engagement.
   d. Placing disclosures at the beginning creates a shorter, more concise contract form.

2. When presenting a CMA to a client, a real estate licensee might *BEST* describe this document as
   a. an analysis that estimates the market value for a particular property.
   b. a tool to help clients determine a fair market price for listing a property or for a sales price offer.
   c. a modified, noncertified appraisal.
   d. an evaluation of all recently sold properties in a specific market area.

3. The brokerage engagement allows for an agent to negotiate a "safety clause" with a client that serves to protect the broker's commission. Which of the following circumstances might activate such a clause in the contract?
   a. The client defaults on obligations defined in the brokerage engagement.
   b. A client does not agree to pay the broker a retainer fee.
   c. A buyer and a seller mutually terminate an existing purchase and sale contract.
   d. After an agency agreement expires, a buyer introduced to the property during the listing term purchases the property directly from the seller.

4. Which statement is *TRUE* about the agency relationship established by the brokerage engagement contract?
   a. The relationship is one of limited agency between the broker and the client.
   b. The relationship may only be one of single agency.
   c. The broker may represent the buyer or the seller as a transaction agent.
   d. The broker may not act as a dual agent.

5. Which of the following would be a violation of a broker's duties to a client?
   a. Showing property in which a buyer client has interest to other perspective buyers
   b. Giving a customer buyer prospect a copy of a county zoning map that includes the listed property of the broker's seller client
   c. Not informing a seller client that a prospective buyer-customer is a straw buyer for the true purchaser
   d. Disclosing to a seller customer that a buyer client does not plan to occupy the seller's property for which an offer has been submitted

6. The statute of frauds in Georgia minimizes fraud and abuse in real estate contracts by
   a. prohibiting real estate licensees from drafting contracts.
   b. requiring that a purchase and sale agreement for real estate be in writing.
   c. only enforcing real estate contracts that are in writing.
   d. creating a limited time period for the judicial enforcement of contracts.

7. A counteroffer might *BEST* be described as a(n)
   a. qualified or conditional acceptance.
   b. an offer that negatively affects contract negotiation.
   c. an offer that is indefinitely open for acceptance.
   d. rejection of an existing offer.

8. When the phrase "time is of the essence" is used in a purchase and sale contract form, it is important that all parties to the agreement understand what factor?
   a. That violations of time-specific performance will terminate the contract
   b. That the term applies mostly to a financial contingency
   c. That the term has considerable impact on contract default
   d. That parties to the contract must perform within a reasonable time frame

9. With regard to assisting buyers and sellers in creating purchase and sale contracts, real estate licensees may be expected to perform which of the following services?
   a. Prepare contract offers that may result in binding agreements between buyers and sellers
   b. Provide tax and investment strategies for clients in their purchase of a home
   c. Recommend the best attorney for a client who wants advice on the legal consequences of withdrawing from a contract agreement
   d. Help clients draft appropriate language for a special stipulation

10. A provision in the purchase and sale contract that would allow a closing to take place even if a term or a condition of the agreement has not been performed by the time of closing is commonly called a
   a. contingency clause.
   b. special stipulation.
   c. survival clause.
   d. termination of performance clause.

Survival clause

11. In disputes between landlords and tenants in Georgia, resolutions for the enforcement of either party's rights would *MOST* likely come
   a. from the Georgia agency that enforces the landlord-tenant statutory code.
   b. through arbitration by the Georgia Real Estate Commission.
   c. from judicial interpretations of case law and statutory code.
   d. from the Brokerage Relationships in Real Estate Transactions Act.

12. A tenant's right to withhold rent as an action taken under constructive eviction will generally be upheld by Georgia courts only if the
   a. tenant has taken on the costs of repairing the damage to the occupied property.
   b. landlord does not allow the tenant who made repairs to deduct that cost from the rent.
   c. tenant can document how the conditions in the property occupied violates their quiet enjoyment.
   d. tenant has moved out and shown that the property is unfit for habitability.

13. With regard to a tenant's security deposit for a residential lease in Georgia, which of the following statements is *TRUE*?
   a. Security deposits must be placed in a trust account.
   b. Only security deposits held by an escrow agent must be placed in a trust account.
   c. Any security deposit held by an escrow agent must be placed in a trust account.
   d. Landlords, and the spouse or minor children of a landlord, who own fewer than 10 rental units must place security deposits in a trust account.

14. Dispossessory actions taken by a landlord in Georgia with regard to residential leases
   a. are governed by the terms of the lease agreement with a tenant.
   b. are regulated by Georgia's landlord and tenant law.
   c. are part of the landlord's self-help eviction process.
   d. evolve out of common law principles applied to residential leases.

15. In Georgia, the right of possession granted by the landlord to the tenant on the day the lease term begins typically
    a. provides the tenant with a right to cancel the lease if actual possession is not given on that date.
    b. provides a guarantee of possession on that date to the tenant and holds the landlord in breach of contract if such possession is not given.
    c. does not guarantee actual possession for the tenant on that day but may offer a prorated rent reduction on a daily basis until possession is received.
    d. provides the tenant with a liquidated damage payment from the landlord if possession is not received on that date.

16. Information in a brokerage engagement that is not communicated by the preprinted contractual language and that may change or even eliminate preprinted language in the contract should
    a. be avoided wherever possible.
    b. be inserted as a special stipulation to the agreement.
    c. always be added as an amendment to the brokerage agreement.
    d. never supersede the intent of the preprinted contractual language.

17. Which of the following statements is *TRUE* regarding earnest money in a real estate transaction?
    a. Without earnest money, the contract lacks sufficient consideration.
    b. The earnest money may only be held by an escrow agent in a trust account.
    c. The earnest money may be distributed to the buyer if the contract is not accepted or is not in dispute.
    d. The escrow agent may only distribute earnest money through a written agreement signed by the parties agreeing on the terms of disbursement.

18. Under Georgia law, an enforceable real estate contract for purchase and sale must include
    a. a seller's property condition disclosure.
    b. an earnest money deposit.
    c. a contingency for a right to terminate the contract.
    d. at minimum a method to calculate a definite purchase price.

19. How do contract forms for the rental of residential property in Georgia generally address renewal of the lease?
    a. The tenant and the landlord must enter into a separate renewal agreement at the end of the current lease term.
    b. Absent a 60-day termination notice from either party before the end of the rental term, the lease will automatically renew as a tenancy at will.
    c. The lease may be renewed automatically at the end of the current term, either on a month-to-month basis or for a designated period identified in the lease.
    d. Renewal of leases must follow the guidelines established under the Georgia Residential Landlord-Tenant Act.

20. A person(s) who chooses *NOT* to sign a brokerage engagement
    a. may still work with an agent in a transactional brokerage relationship.
    b. must sign a customer election form to work with the broker.
    c. may receive no services from the broker.
    d. may not compensate brokers in a transaction.

26

UNIT

Financing and Closing Residential Transactions

LEARNING OBJECTIVES *When you have finished reading this unit, you will be able to*

- **identify** the three Georgia statutes that affect residential lending and the ways in which they influence financing options;
- **explain** the duties, documents, roles, and responsibilities involved in the closing process; and
- **describe** the costs associated with the settlement and how they are calculated.

KEY TERMS

back-end ratio
buyer's affidavit
deficiency judgment
equal dignities rule
equitable title
equitable right of redemption
front-end ratio
Georgia Fair Lending Act
Georgia Residential Mortgage Act
Georgia Residential Mortgage Fraud Act
in arrears
intangible tax
loan or credit underwriter
owner's affidavit
power of sale
security deed
settlement credits
settlement debits
transfer tax

OVERVIEW

Notwithstanding its primary function in the transference of property title between parties, or in the settlement of cash sales, the closing of residential real estate transactions involves a process that most often centers on the settlement of loans: primarily the new one for the qualified buyer, as well as any existing ones secured by the seller's home. Georgia is unique when it comes to real property financing because it is the only state that does not define a lender's security interest as a mortgage or a deed of trust but as a deed to secure debt or a security deed. Moreover, once a buyer receives title to the property from the seller at closing, that title is then transferred by security deed to the lender, who holds it until the borrower satisfies the debt. Georgia is also one of the few states that, by law, require a real estate closing to be conducted by an attorney. Real estate agents are very much part of this closing process in Georgia, monitoring a buyer's financing progress from preapproval and formal loan application through final underwriting acceptance. Licensees continue their service literally right up to closing day: providing progress reports regarding settlement issues, offering clients ongoing support for those inevitable anxieties, and preparing estimates of settlement costs for buyers and settlement proceeds for sellers.

GEORGIA STATUTES

O.C.G.A 7-1000 et seq.: Georgia Residential Mortgage Act

Administered through the Georgia Department of Banking and Finance, this law provides that all parties performing the acts of a mortgage lender or a broker are required to obtain a license, unless exempted under the Code. Licensing requirements will generally apply to businesses set up for brokering or directly making real estate loans, while exempting Federal Deposit Insurance Corporation (FDIC) depository institutions such as banks, saving and loan organizations, and credit unions. Also exempted from licensing are natural persons offering financing for the sale of owner-occupied property, provided that such parties make five or fewer such loans in a given year; this exemption is not granted to homesellers identified as corporations, LLCs, or trusts.

O.C.G.A. 7-6a-1-et seq.: Georgia Fair Lending Act (GAFLA)

This consumer protection law limits certain fees and charges for residential home loans and regulates aggressive lender activity in the refinancing market. Guidelines stipulate that penalties for late payments on loans may not exceed 5% of the amount of such payment and may not be assessed unless payment is 10 days late. Furthermore, lenders may not charge fees for transmitting balances for loan payoffs, and they may charge no more than $10 for processing transmittal requests for such balances occurring more than once in a 60-day period. With regard to "loan flipping" activities in which a lender aggressively targets homeowners for refinancing existing mortgages, the law does not allow lenders to knowingly "flip" loans for refinancing within five years of making the original loan at rates and costs that do not benefit the homeowner.

O.C.G.A. 16-8-100 et seq.: Georgia Residential Mortgage Fraud Act

In 2005, the Georgia General Assembly enacted the **Georgia Residential Mortgage Fraud Act**. The legislative body found that fraud involving residential mortgages was at an all-time high and that lending institutions and borrowers had lost hundreds of millions of dollars due to the fraud. Neighborhoods plagued by mortgage fraud had deteriorated. Property values that were fraudulently inflated resulted in substantial property tax increases for existing neighborhood homes.

As a result, Georgia passed the first mortgage fraud legislation of its kind in the country.

The law addressed the two basic categories of fraudulent activity: fraud for property committed by borrowers (providing false income or employment information) in order to qualify or receive better terms for a home loan; and fraud that occurs when professionals in the real estate and mortgage industry conspire to realize profits from misdeeds (sometimes called industry insider fraud or fraud for profit).

The Georgia Residential Mortgage Fraud Act not only makes mortgage fraud a felony, it also defines residential mortgage fraud racketeering activity under the Georgia RICO (Racketeer Influenced and Corrupt Organizations) Act. Specifically, the statute says that a person commits the offense of residential mortgage fraud when, and with the intent to defraud, the person

- knowingly makes false statements or omits relevant information during the loan process,
- knowingly uses or facilitates the use of documents containing such information during the lending process,
- receives any proceeds or other funds from a loan closing that results from violation of this law,
- conspires to violate any part of this law, or
- records or files a document known to contain such misstatements or omissions

IN PRACTICE The Residential Mortgage Fraud Act also applies to a real estate licensee who knowingly receives commission checks as part of a fraudulent closing process, even if the licensee did not actively participate in the illegal actions. Consequently, it is important for licensees to report any suspicious lending activity or potential mortgage fraud to their broker, local authorities, or the state attorney general. To avoid any perceived connections to mortgage fraud, licensees should be on the lookout for one or more of the following:

- Buyers paying substantially more at closing than indicated in the contract price
- Loan amounts for substantially more than the purchase price
- Settlement charges that were not listed in the lender's good-faith estimate for the buyer's loan
- Altered information in the original loan application
- Lenders or closing attorneys asking buyers or sellers to leave signature lines blank on closing forms
- Nondisclosed purchase money mortgages or second mortgages
- Buyers selling property shortly after closing for a substantially inflated price
- Any parties involved in the loan process receiving unusual payouts or kickbacks of any kind

Persons found in violation of the statute commit a felony and, upon conviction, may be punished by imprisonment of no less than 1 year nor more than 10 years, a fine not to exceed $5,000, or both. However, if the violation is part of a pattern of mortgage fraud or a conspiracy to commit such fraud, imprisonment may be for a period of 3 to 20 years, fines up to $100,000, or both.

LOAN SECURITY INSTRUMENTS

Mortgage vs. Deed to Secure Debt

Though the collateralized loan made to purchase real property in Georgia may commonly be called a mortgage, the instrument used by virtually all lenders in the state to secure such loans is legally defined as a deed to secure debt or **security deed**. Whereas a mortgage most often creates only a lien on the property for the lender, the title to that land, held by the borrower, remains subject to future judgment liens and other legal claims.

IN PRACTICE As far back as the 1800s, lenders in Georgia adopted the practice of getting an absolute conveyance from the borrower in the form of a warranty deed and giving back to the borrower a "bond for title," agreeing to reconvey the property to the borrower upon payoff of the debt. Later, the warranty deed and bond for title became a single instrument known as a deed to secure debt, or security deed. Georgia lenders favor this deed because it minimizes their risks and legal efforts should the borrower default, allowing for nonjudicial foreclosure that speeds up recovery of the real estate collateral for loans.

Current Georgia Code provides that the security deed is an absolute conveyance of title from the borrower to the lender (O.C.G.A.44-14-60). This conveyance effectively divides the title into two components: the legal title held by the lender to secure payment of the debt and **equitable title** held by the purchaser. Notwithstanding actions that interfere with the lender's legal title, the buyer retains the customary ownership rights, such as possession and use of the property, as well the responsibilities of paying taxes and insurance. The lender's security deed is filed in the land records of the county in which the property is located. The owner also retains a right of redemption: to reacquire the legal title from the lender when the debt is paid off. At that time, the lender marks the original security deed as paid and the owner may then have that deed marked as satisfied on all public records.

IN PRACTICE Because the security deed is the instrument of choice for lenders who make real property loans in the state, and this deed transfers legal title from buyer to lender at closing, Georgia is often classified as a "title theory" state. Though, in fact, the terms *title theory* and *lien theory* apply specifically to circumstances in which the financing of the securitized property is legally identified as a mortgage, which is not generally the case in Georgia. Lien theory covers situations in which the mortgage provides only a lien against the property for the lender; title theory applies when the mortgage also transfers title to the lender.

Though lenders in Georgia do commonly receive legal title from the borrower, the instrument of such conveyance is a security deed—not a mortgage—under which the terms *title* or *lien theory* exclusively apply. There is no law in Georgia that prohibits use of a mortgage for real estate financing, and if a lender should make this choice, only a lien against the property would occur—not a transfer of legal title from borrower to lender. Moreover, this mortgage would require a judicial foreclosure process for the lender to acquire legal title to real property. In other words, however unlikely, if a mortgage is used in this state, Georgia falls within the category of lien theory in that particular case.

The deed to secure debt in Georgia is a separate and distinct contract from the promissory note. While the note serves as contractual evidence of the borrower's personal obligations for the debt, the security deed provides the lender with a mechanism for recovering the property that serves as collateral for the loan. While typically identified as the property purchased by the borrower, the collateral to secure debt may also include personal property, as well as real property. Judicial rulings in Georgia have suggested that without an accompanying promissory note, a security deed may not be enforceable. Consequently, most lenders have the borrower execute both a promissory note and a deed to secure debt to most fully protect their interests.

As discussed previously, the promissory note clearly identifies the parties to the note as the payor and the payee, and it spells out the following: amount of the debt, the costs to the borrower, the terms of the repayment, any loan prepayment right, and the penalties for failure to fulfill loan terms. While the security deed in Georgia contains language and protection clauses for the lender similar to that in the mortgage and deed of trust, commonly used throughout the rest of the country, significant distinctions are present.

LANGUAGE AND PROVISIONS OF SECURITY DEED

Though mortgagor and mortgagee are often used generically to describe the borrower and lender, the deed to secure debt in Georgia identifies these parties as grantor and grantee. The borrower is the grantor of the security deed, because the borrower is the one transferring the property to secure the debt. The lender is the grantee of the security deed, because that party receives the absolute conveyance of the title to secure the debt. A valid and enforceable security deed has the following provisions:

- Identification of grantor and grantee
- Language that conveys property from grantor to grantee
- Valid legal description of property
- Proper execution of conveyance (signed by the owner of the property or another person under a valid power of attorney)
- Proper attestation (witnessing by an unofficial party and an official party such as a notary public, which allows the deed to be recorded; though lack of proper attestation will not affect the validity between grantor and grantee)
- An effective delivery of deed; the grantor (borrower) must put the deed in possession of the grantee (seller) or the grantee's agent with the intention that it must pass to the grantee. This requirement is normally fulfilled at closing when the attorney representing the lender takes possession of deed.

In Georgia, most security deeds contain a "**power of sale**" clause. This clause entitles the lender upon borrower default to call due the entire outstanding loan balance. For the most part, Georgia foreclosure laws are lender friendly in that the lender does not have to file a lawsuit in order to foreclose on the property. Rather, under Georgia statute, commonly referred to as nonjudicial foreclosure, the lender may bypass a court-ordered process. Under the power of sale in the security deed, the lender is authorized to sell the property serving as collateral for the loan upon default and apply the proceeds to the debt. Foreclosure sales in the state must meet minimum standards:

- The lender notifies the borrower of default and the time period for curing the default.

- If the default is not cured, the lender sends a demand letter to the borrower for payment of the loan, begins the advertisement of a foreclosure sale for four consecutive weeks in a newspaper considered the official "legal organ" in the county where the property is located. The ad must contain a complete legal description of the property, the name of the lender, and the name of the attorney who will conduct sale. Furthermore, the ad must indicate any application of the sale proceeds to pay taxes or other liens assessed against the property.
- The property is sold on the courthouse steps on the first Tuesday of the month (except if the day falls on a holiday) following the advertisement period. Though the terms of the sale are usually advertised as "cash," the highest bidder can make a deposit; however, a bidder who fails to provide cash can be passed over for a cash bidder. Parties bidding at the foreclosure sale can include third parties, members of the public, or the lender and the borrower, who have an interest in the proceedings and in the property.
- The party conducting the foreclosure sale is responsible for the proper distribution of the proceeds from the sale. The first payment goes to cover the costs of the sale, including attorney fees. The second payment goes to the lender holding the first lien on the property. If funds remain from the sale, junior lienholders will then receive payment. Finally, remaining funds, if any, go to the borrower who defaulted. If the foreclosure sale does not satisfy the debtor's outstanding balance, the lender may seek a **deficiency judgment** against the owner through the courts to collect the remaining portion of debt.

IN PRACTICE Georgia law follows an **equitable right of redemption** process that allows a defaulted borrower, before the foreclosure sale, to redeem the property by paying off the entire loan balance, interest, costs, and fees.

QUALIFYING FOR THE HOME LOAN

Preapproval

When a prospective homebuyer enters into a brokerage engagement with a real estate licensee, that party is placing trust in the agent's professional ability to locate and show properties that meet the client's needs, wants, and most importantly—financial capability. Presenting a home for sale to a prospective purchaser unqualified to buy that property not only reduces an agent's role to that of an unpaid tour guide but also may decrease the likelihood of any client enthusiasm for properties that are realistically affordable; in other words, everyone loses.

A winning scenario for all players in a real estate transaction realistically evolves only when a purchaser is financially qualified to meet the terms of a contract offer. Licensees most effectively reinforce this result by conducting property searches within a price range suggested by a client's preapproval letter from a lender. To get preapproved for a real property loan, a prospective buyer supplies a lender with some documentation of employment and income before starting the hunt for a home. After the lender verifies this information, as well as running a credit profile to confirm an acceptable borrowing capacity, the buyer may receive a preliminary approval for a specified maximum loan amount. Effectively, this preapproval lets buyers know in advance of the property search just how expensive a house they can afford. While sparing the buyer the disappointment of choosing a home that falls outside an affordability range, a lender's preapproval also helps streamline the closing process once the buyer has found the right house.

LOAN APPLICATION AND EVALUATION

Real estate financing, from the loan application to the available types of loans, operates in a somewhat changing environment, depending on such factors as the present economy and current federal and state regulations. This lesson provides information for teaching purposes only. Licensees, especially those working with buyer-clients, are expected to keep up with current financing trends and requirements through continuing education courses, relationships with lending professionals, and information available from state and federal resources. Real estate brokers and their affiliated licensees are not typically experts in real estate financing, and should refer their clients and customers to financing and mortgage professionals and institutions for accurate and complete information on the process of qualifying for a real estate loan.

As the first step in the loan process, prospective borrowers will provide detailed information about their finances by filling out an application form. Making a home loan is an investment for a lender and evaluating an applicant's financial profile estimates the potential profitability and risk of that investment. Most lenders use a standard residential loan application form generated by Fannie Mae or Freddie Mac, the two primary facilitators of residential loans in the secondary mortgage market.

Typically, the form requires the following information:

- Personal information, such as applicant's Social Security number, age, education, and marital status
- Current housing expense (monthly rent or house payment)
- Employment information, such as type of business, job title, duration of employment, and previous employment
- Income from all sources including employment (salary, commissions, and bonuses), investments (dividends and interest), and pensions
- Assets, including money in bank accounts, investment accounts, real estate, and retirement funds
- Liabilities, including credit card debts, car loans, real estate loans, alimony, child support payments, and unpaid taxes

Subsequently, the information provided about income, assets, and liabilities will be confirmed by the loan processor, who sends verification forms to the applicant's employer and account holders, as well gathering necessary W-2 forms and income tax returns from the prospective buyer(s).

Once all loan documentation has been collected and verified, the loan processor assembles a "loan package" that is now ready for underwriting: the process of determining whether the applicant and the property to be purchased meets the lender's minimum standards. The person conducting this evaluation is known as the **loan or credit underwriter**. Lenders who hold real estate loans in their own portfolios are free to set underwriting standards internally. In practice though, most home loans originated will not be kept in-house, but will sold in the secondary market place, primarily to major agencies such as Fannie Mae and Freddie

Mac; as such, most lenders apply underwriting standards and guidelines for loan decisions that are set by these two organizations.

In evaluating a loan applicant's financial capabilities, an underwriter wants answers for these questions: Does the prospective homebuyer have sufficient, verifiable funds to close the transaction, including the loan down payment and any assignable prepaid items? Second, can that same party afford the total monthly house payment associated with the loan? To answer these two essential questions, an underwriter considers three factors:

Stability of loan applicant's monthly income From an underwriter's standpoint, not all income is equal. Is the source of the income dependable. If so, how likely is this income to continue over a satisfactory period. The answers to both questions are factors that a prudent underwriter examines carefully. As an example, a regular salary from permanent employment counts as stable monthly income, as would Social Security retirement benefits; on the other hand, neither intermittent overtime pay from a permanent job nor income from a short-term temporary job would satisfy income stability requirements.

IN PRACTICE Self-employed loan applicants, as well as independent contractors, present certain challenges for underwriters. For these borrowers, lenders minimally require certified copies of tax returns for the previous two years and commonly ask for larger down payments. In recent years, underwriters have even started asking permanently employed borrowers to provide the previous year's tax return.

Once the underwriter determines the loan applicant's stable monthly income, the next step is to calculate whether such income is sufficient for the borrower to afford the loan's proposed monthly payment. Here the underwriter applies two income ratios:

1. The **front-end ratio**, or total house-payment-to-income ratio, measures the proposed monthly house note (includes principal and interest payment added to—if applicable—one month's property tax, one month's hazard insurance, one month's mortgage insurance, and any monthly home association dues) against the borrower's stable monthly income.
2. The **back-end ratio**, or debt-to-income ratio, measures the recurring monthly debt obligations (includes proposed house note, any revolving credit card payments, car payments, child support payment, school loan payment, etc.) against the borrower's stable monthly income.

IN PRACTICE Both the front-end and the back-end ratios are expressed as percentages. Over time, automated underwriting has allowed traditional qualifying percentages (such as 28%/36% front and back-end ratios for conventional loans and 29%/41% for FHA loans) to dramatically increase for borrowers. For example, a conventional loan conforming to Fannie Mae or Freddie Mac guidelines in which the down payment is 10% of the purchase price may now reach ratios as high as 38% on the front-end and near 50% on the back-end. Government-insured FHA loans that require only a 3.5% down payment from the borrower, may now allow front-end ratios up to 45% and back-end ratios to reach as high as 55%. Qualification ratios, though, may be adjusted upward or downward, depending on a lender's specific policy subject to factors, such as the amount of down payment and an applicant's credit score; broader influences generated by upheavals in real estate and financial marketplaces may also impact a lender's policy.

Remember that qualifying percentages, down payment allowances, and other loan features used in this course are current at the time of the writing of the course. Brokers and their affiliated licensees should always check with a mortgage professional on the current requirements for conventional, FHA, and VA loans before providing any general information on loan requirements to clients or customers. Taking periodic continuing education courses on real estate financing and mortgages is also an excellent way for licensees to remain current on loan types and requirements.

MATH CONCEPTS

Qualification Ratios

To calculate the front-end ratio, establish a maximally affordable house payment for the loan applicant and divide that total house payment by the applicant's gross monthly income.

total house payment ÷ gross monthly income = front-end ratio

To calculate the back-end ratio, establish the maximally reoccurring monthly debt for the loan applicant and divide that total reoccurring monthly debt by the applicant's gross monthly income.

total reoccurring monthly debt ÷ gross monthly income = back-end ratio

EXAMPLE A loan applicant wants to borrow 90% ($292,500) of the $325,000 purchase price for a home: $325,000 × 0.90 = $292,500. A lender has quoted the borrower a 4.5% interest rate for a conventional loan in this transaction, with a monthly principal and interest payment of $1,483. The lender will require the borrower to set up a budget mortgage payment that will also include the following monthly amounts:

P&I payment:	$1,483.00
Property tax:	+ $350.00
Hazard insurance:	+ $85.00
PMI:	+ $90.83
HOA:	+ $50
Total house payment:	$2,058.83

The loan applicant's recurring monthly debt is as follows:

Student loan:	+ $385.00
Car payment:	+ $360.00
Revolving credit:	+ $165.00

Total monthly recurring debt: $910.00 + $2,058.83 = $2,968.83

The borrower's gross household monthly income is $5,750.00.

MATH CONCEPTS

Income-to-Debt Ratio Calculations

$2,058.83 ÷ $5,750.00 = 35.80% for the front-end ratio

and

$2,968.33 ÷ $5,750.00 = 51.62% for the back-end ratio

Taking into account the borrower's down payment and credit score, the lender's automatic underwriting guidelines for this conventional loan allow a front-end ratio of up to 38% and a back-end ratio of up to 49 percent. While the borrower would qualify on the front-end, the back-end percentage is over 50%, beyond the range for lender acceptance.

In a further effort to qualify the borrower, the lender next applied guidelines for an FHA loan. In this circumstance, the applicant would borrow 96.5% ($313,625) of the $325,000 purchase price plus an additional up-front MIP fee of 1.75% ($5,488) for a total loan amount of $319,113. At a quoted interest rate of 4.25%, the borrower's principle and interest payment is $1,570. The necessary budget mortgage payment would then include the following:

P&I payment:	$1,570
Property tax:	+ $350
Hazard insurance:	+ $85
HOA:	+ $50
MIP:	+ $226
Total house payment:	$2,281
Recurring monthly debt:	+ $910 (car payment, student loan, revolving credit)

Total monthly reoccurring debt: $3,191

Front-end ratio: $2,281 ÷ $5,750 = 40%

Back-end ratio: $3,191 ÷ $5,750 = 55%

As the lender's automated underwriting FHA guidelines allows a front-end percentage up to 41% and back-end percentage to 55% for an applicant with good credit scores; the borrower may qualify for this loan.

Remember that these percentages are for training purposes only. The actual allowable front-end and back-end percentages for particular lenders and types of loan may be lower than those used in these examples.

Applicant's liquid assets: The loan underwriter needs to make sure that the borrower has adequate funds on hand to cover the down payment, closing costs assigned to that party, and any expenses incidental to the purchase of the property. Moreover, the loan applicant may need to show assets providing sufficient cash reserves to cover the first few house payments, as well as after- closing residual funds to handle other living expenses. Lenders may use a scoring system that averages or incorporates scores from the major credit reporting agencies in establishing their criteria for loan approvals.

Applicant's credit history: In addition to analyzing a loan applicant's income and financial assets, an underwriter examines the borrower's credit history, typically using information generated by major consumer credit reporting agencies, such as Equifax and Experian.

These credit reports indicate how reliably the borrower handles debt obligations and identifies any severe problems, such as foreclosure or bankruptcy. Lenders commonly use credit scores calculated by these agencies to assess risk in making loans to specific borrowers.

Qualifying the Property

Determining whether an applicant is an acceptable risk is one of two primary factors that lead to an underwriter's final decision on the home loan. Not only must the borrower be qualified but so must the property subject to purchase. Because this property will provide security for the lender, the underwriter must decide whether it's worth enough to serve as collateral for the loan in question. In other words, if foreclosure became necessary, would the property sell for enough money to satisfy the existing loan? To answer this question and effectively qualify the property, an underwriter relies on an appraisal report commissioned by the lender and provided by a state-licensed or certified appraiser to provide a professional estimate of the home's value. Remember that a CMA conducted by a real estate licensee may not be considered a professional estimate of a property's value (an appraisal) and as such is not used as a measure of a property's value for a lender's consideration of a specific loan.

CLOSING THE TRANSACTION

For buyers and sellers of real property, closing is the final step in the transactional process. All special stipulations and other contract obligations should be fulfilled by the time of closing, unless the contract terms provide for a later date of completion and such provisions survive the closing. At the closing, the seller signs the deed transferring title to the property, as well as affidavits required for title purposes, while the buyer pays the seller the agreed purchase price for the property; if a loan is involved in the purchase, the buyer will sign the promissory note, the deed to secure the debt, and any other lender-required documents.

Closing Attorney

The Georgia Supreme Court has confirmed that only a licensed attorney in the state is authorized to prepare or execute a deed to convey real property on behalf of another or to facilitate the signing of such a deed. Moreover, unlike in some other states, a title company in Georgia cannot close a real estate transaction without the participation of an attorney. The unauthorized practice of law is a criminal offense; anyone, other than an attorney licensed in the state, who conducts a real estate closing is guilty of a misdemeanor (O.C.G.A. 15-19-56).

IN PRACTICE If a buyer is getting a loan for the purchase, the closing attorney in Georgia will normally represent the lender. Shortly after a contractual agreement is created between a buyer and a seller, the closing attorney will arrange for a title examination of the purchased property. This examination may be conducted by the closing attorney's firm or by an agent of a title company associated with the attorney's firm. The title examiner issues a report or an abstract that is reviewed by the closing attorney to identify any irregularities or title defects that, if present, must be resolved before closing. A title judged free of such defects by the closing attorney is considered "marketable" and eligible to be insured by a title company in Georgia; such policies may be subsequently issued for both the buyer and the lender providing financing for the purchase. Once a clear title to the property is established, the closing attorney will begin preparing all the necessary documents to complete the transaction between the buyer and the seller.

Typically, the buyer and the seller will complete the closing transaction in person. Should either party be unable to physically attend the closing, the absent party(ies) may complete the transaction by either appointing an attorney-in-fact or by processing a closing through a mailing of the necessary signed documents.

IN PRACTICE In most situations, an absent party will use a power-of-attorney signature for documents at closing to complete the transaction. If using this method while working with a real estate licensee, the buyer or the seller should notify the agent that they have already signed a power of attorney that was prepared for them. To eliminate any last-minute issues, it is a good idea for licensees to have any power of attorney approved by the closing attorney before the closing date. Lenders and title companies often have specific requirements in order to insure a title based on power of attorney, and approval of the process may take some time particularly if the attorney-in-fact is not a spouse or immediate family member of the purchaser. In any case, the buyer's agent should follow up with the party and the closing attorney to ensure that the power of attorney has been approved. In Georgia, a power of attorney giving someone the authority to execute a real estate transaction for an absent party must be both in writing and notarized at the closing to be valid. The reasoning here is that since a deed to convey land or property must be witnessed and notarized at the closing, then the power of attorney should also be notarized to be valid—a legal concept identified as the **equal dignities rule**.

An absent buyer or seller may also complete the purchase and sale transaction in Georgia through a "mail away closing." In efforts to avoid identity theft and mortgage fraud, this process is often more complex than it sounds. The loan package may not be emailed or mailed directly to the other party. Most closing attorneys require the absent party to make arrangements with an attorney or the title company to receive the closing documents and to provide the closing attorney with the name, address, and phone number of this designated party. The closing attorney will then send the closing documents to this designated party, who will arrange a time with the absent party to meet and sign these documents in front of a notary. It is the responsibility of this designated attorney or title company to verify identification, witnessing, and notarizing of the closing documents, which are then returned to the closing attorney to complete the transaction. Licensees who have a buyer or a seller closing by mail need to make certain that the other party and any other licensee involved in the transaction are kept informed throughout this process.

CLOSING DOCUMENTS

In Georgia, because real estate closings must be conducted by an attorney, it is the responsibility of the attorney to be sure that all the appropriate documents are provided to the appropriate parties at the closing. Real estate licensees, however, should be knowledgeable about the following documents, so that they may explain their purpose before the closing to their clients, customers, or both:

- Warranty deed—The most common type of deed used in a Georgia residential real estate closing. Only the seller signs the warranty deed, which is then notarized by an authorized party (commonly the attorney or an employee of the attorney); an unofficial witness, who is not a party to the transaction, must also sign so that the deed may be recorded. Once the seller, the notary, and the unofficial witness have signed the deed, and the seller or the attorney delivers it to the buyer, the title is officially transferred. Standard practice has the attorney keep the original deed at closing for recording at the courthouse. The original deed is then mailed to the buyer after the recording.

- Security deed—As covered in the previous topic on residential lending, if a buyer takes out a new loan, the lender will require that party to sign this deed to secure debt. The security deed contains many of the same clauses as the warranty deed, but as the latter transfers title from seller to buyer, the former transfers title from buyer to lender. The security deed sets forth that the transfer of title to the lender only secures the loan. The buyer-borrower retains the right to possess and use the property, as well as the ownership obligations, such as paying property taxes. Like the warranty deed, the security deed must be notarized and witnessed before its recording.
- Promissory note—As the security deed provides security for the lender if the borrower does not repay the loan, the promissory note documents the borrower's promise to repay the loan. The note sets forth the terms under which the debt is to be repaid (interest rate, monthly payment, number of payments). These terms may also include the following:
  - — Prepayment penalty—a fee charged if the borrower pays off debt before end of the loan term (prohibited on FHA and VA loans)
  - — Late penalty—fee that the lender may charge if the borrower makes payment after due date
  - — Escalation clause—gives the lender the right to increase the interest rate if the buyer assumes the loan
  - — Acceleration clause—gives the lender the right to call the entire loan balance due upon borrower default in making loan payments
  - — Alienation clause (a.k.a. due-on-sale clause)—allows the existing lender to call the homeowner's entire loan note due in full if title to the property is transferred during the term of the loan
- Quitclaim deed—On occasion, the closing attorney will have someone sign the quitclaim deed before or at the closing. If the attorney shows the parties the quitclaim deed but does not ask them to sign, then the purpose is probably to indicate that someone else who had or might have had an interest in the property has released such interest so that the property may be transferred free and clear. If the closing attorney has a seller sign a quitclaim deed, that signatures serves to release some possible claim that seller might retain with regard to the property.

IN PRACTICE Attorneys use quitclaim deeds extensively to remove from the record possible conflicting property interests. Witnessed, notarized, and recorded, uses of such deeds may include correcting an error in a previously recorded deed, relinquishing a spouse's interest in the property when the seller's divorce is pending, transferring title between family members, and transferring title from an heir of a deceased prior owner.

- **Owner's affidavit**—The seller signs this document, swearing that there are no unpaid or unsatisfied liens, assessments, or encumbrances against the property, other than those identified by the title. The owner's affidavit protects the buyer, the lender, and the closing attorney because these parties may sue the seller for damages incurred by that party's fraudulent affidavit.
- **Buyer's affidavit**—Lenders will sometimes require a buyer to sign an affidavit at closing, in which the borrower swears there are no suits, judgments, or liens against or pending against that party. This affidavit assures the lender

that the loan has first priority and that there are no other claims on the borrower that make take precedence. Both a seller's and a buyer's affidavit are notarized but usually not recorded.

- **Miscellaneous closing documents and instruments**—Included among these are the property survey, the title policy, the occupancy affidavit, the truth-in-lending statement, sundry disclosures and disclaimers, and various FHA or VA forms, where appropriate.

While the closing attorney, representing the lender, may explain each document to the buyer and the seller as it comes their turn to sign, no legal advice may be offered to either party. Buyers and sellers are free to bring their own attorneys, though this is not a common occurrence in residential closings. In all cash transactions, the closing attorney may represent either the buyer or the seller.

Further duties of the closing attorney will include collecting all monies owed by the parties, including any wired sums from the purchaser's lender, into the law firm's escrow account. If the purchaser must pay more than $5,000 in closing costs, Georgia law requires that such funds be presented in the form of certified check(s), money orders, or wire transfers. The closing attorney also disburses checks from the escrow account to pay all closing costs, including the net proceeds check to the seller and the commission to the real estate brokers. One final duty of the attorney occurs after the closing when all appropriate documents are recorded in the deed records of the county in which the property is located.

A LICENSEE'S ROLE: CONTRACT TO CLOSING

The role of a Georgia real estate licensee in the transaction process hardly ends when the parties create a contract for purchase and sale. A substantial case might be made that an agent's true value is revealed by the professional care and service demonstrated in that period between the buyer and the seller in the contractual agreement and the execution of that agreement, the closing. A licensee's thorough understanding of the procedures and documents necessary to complete a closing, as well as provide assistance to both the buyer and the seller in the process leading up to closing, can make this inherently anxious routine a smoother experience for all involved. Between contract and closing (by custom and to the extent required under Georgia Real Estate License Law), whether working with or working for a seller or a buyer, there are duties for a licensee to fulfill, along with opportunities to assist both parties. Whether the transaction involves a property listed by another licensee of the same brokerage firm or a property listed by one firm and sold by another, all agents involved must coordinate their efforts.

While it's possible for a contract to close without the licensee's diligent assistance, an agent's persistent attention to the duties and responsibilities required of all parties to the agreement will go a long way toward avoiding delays and misunderstandings with regard to completing the transaction. Such attention to detail on a licensee's part may also reinforce for buyers and sellers the professional level of service expected of their agents..

IN PRACTICE The first job for a licensee involved in a newly created sales transaction is to deliver a complete signed copy of the agreement to the buyer and the seller, as well as to the agent's broker. Neglecting this step is a violation of Georgia Real Estate License Law. After fulfilling this initial responsibility, an agent may then turn attention to those areas of performance required from both the buyer and the seller that are essential to completing the sale and closing the transaction.

Compliance with contingencies: Unmet conditions or contingencies in a contract mean that the parties have not performed according to the terms of the agreement. Unless the parties agree otherwise, the transaction will not close until such obligations are completed. Contingencies tie up a property because it cannot be sold to someone else while performance of such conditions remain pending. Consequently, as a binding agreement is created, any contingencies included require the immediate and thorough attention of the licensees involved to ensure that buyer, the seller, or both take appropriate actions within the amount of time specified in the contract.

- Financing contingency—The financing contingency is the most common contingency in residential real estate contracts because the sale generally requires the buyer to secure a new loan in order to purchase. Because this contingency normally obligates the purchaser to formally apply for a specific loan within a specific number of days following contract creation, the licensee can serve the interests of all parties by urging the buyer to make such application as soon as possible and, within BRRETA guidelines, by providing the buyer with necessary appropriate information and assistance in this process.
- Appraisal contingency—Not only do lenders require appraisals as a condition of loan approval, many purchasers who do not require financing contingencies will nevertheless include an appraisal contingency in the contract offer. A purchaser may want a professional, independent opinion of the property's market value to guard against overpaying for the home. Like most contingencies, the condition for an appraisal is time sensitive, and licensees may facilitate the process by cooperating with the appraiser's efforts. This cooperation may be as basic as a listing agent making sure the house is unlocked for the appraiser or providing information to that party on comparable sales.
- Inspection contingency—If the contract is contingent on a timely inspection of the property by a qualified home inspector, the licensee might assist the buyer by supplying a list of several qualified inspectors and by accompanying the buyer to the property during such inspection.
- Sale of buyer's existing property—If the seller has accepted a contract from a purchaser that is contingent on the sale of the buyer's existing property, the licensee's responsibility is to assist the buyer in selling the property within the time specified in the purchase and sale agreement with the seller. Such assistance might involve listing the buyer's property if it is not already listed or referring the buyer to another broker if the licensee does not work in the area of the buyer's existing property. Listing the buyer's property would require the licensee to advise the seller-client in writing of this intent. Such disclosures are required under BRRETA because such actions might create conflicts of interests. If the buyer's property is already listed, the licensee might assist in that sale by actively looking for prospective purchasers.

LICENSEE'S DUTIES TO SELLER-CLIENT BEFORE CLOSING

Under the listing brokerage engagement, a licensee's obligations to the seller do not end with the acceptance of an offer to purchase. These responsibilities are twofold: keeping the seller informed of the buyer's financial ability to close the transaction and assisting the seller in complying with the terms of the contract. If the transaction is a cash sale or there is no financial contingency in the contract, the licensee might simply need to confirm the buyer's source of funds to complete the sale and communicate that information to the seller. However, because a substantial majority of residential real estate transactions involve a new loan for the purchaser, the licensee will need to update the seller regularly on that loan's progress.

IN PRACTICE A listing agent might update the seller accordingly as to the progress of the buyer's loan by following up in several areas:

- Has the buyer made a loan application according to the terms of the contract? The contract typically requires the buyer to apply for the loan within a certain amount of time, and it sometimes may require that the application be with a certain lender.
- Is the buyer making good-faith efforts to comply with the loan terms of the contract? If the lender is unable to acquire the necessary information from the buyer to complete the loan process, the buyer may not be applying for the loan in good faith.
- Has the property been appraised for the contract price, and is the lender requiring any additional repairs to the property? If the property does not appraise for the contract price or if there are unexpected repairs, the contract negotiations may have to be resumed.
- Has the lender approved the buyer for the loan? If the lender did not approve the buyer, the reasons for denial may be helpful in renegotiating the contract. As an example, the lender may approve the buyer for a 90% LTV, but not for the 95% LTV stated in the loan terms of the contract. In such cases, if permitted by the lender, the seller might decide to accept a purchase money mortgage from the buyer to cover the extra 5% needed for the down payment.

A listing agent also has a responsibility to assist the seller in complying with all the terms of the contract and in dealing with other issues that may arise before closing:

- The licensee may need to assist the seller in locating vendors and contractors to make repairs required by the contract or by the lender. While the licensee may offer assistance, any work orders should be initiated by the seller, so as to eliminate any liability to the broker for defects in the workmanship of the repairs.
- Contracts and statutes vary in requirements of certification against infestation and damage from termites and other wood-destroying organisms. Stipulations in this area may be imposed by the buyer, the lender, or a governmental agency, and as such, may require an inspection, clearance letter and/or a guarantee. Whatever requirements exist, the licensee should help the seller to understand and meet any certification requirements of the contract. Again, though, it the party who agreed in the contract to provide and pay for any certification who should order it and see that the appropriate party receives it.

- If, as part of the contract, the seller has agreed to furnish the buyer with a home warranty policy, the licensee should make sure that the seller complies with all necessary steps to supply such a policy to the buyer in time for closing.

LICENSEE'S DUTIES TO BUYER-CLIENT BEFORE CLOSING

Even though BRRETA does not define an agent's duties as fiduciary, highly professional, competent real estate licensees in Georgia will actively assist the buyer with any problems that arise before closing. If the property does not appraise for the contract price, the licensee may suggest alternatives for the buyer. If comparable sales in the area seem to indicate a greater value than estimated in the appraisal, the licensee might suggest that the buyer ask the lender to reconsider the appraisal. If a buyer decides that despite the appraiser's opinion, the property is worth the contract price to them, the licensee might suggest that the buyer, if able, pay the difference over the appraised value in cash. Otherwise, the licensee may assist the parties in renegotiating the contract price.

IN PRACTICE As for more proactive obligations, in representing a buyer (or even working with an unrepresented purchaser as a customer), a licensee has a responsibility to monitor that party's contractual obligations to best ensure the transaction's closing.

This monitoring process may include the following:

- Following up on the buyer's loan application—After a buyer takes a signed contract to a lender and makes formal application for the loan, the approval process begins. The lender will usually keep the buyer informed of the loan progress, and hopefully make some effort to communicate this progress to the real estate agents involved in the transaction. However, good business practice for a licensee dictates contacting the lender, minimally on a weekly basis, to monitor the loan's progress. If a problem arises, the lender may have a good suggestion for dealing with it and may request that the licensee assist in this matter by approaching either or both parties to the contract. If the lender is having difficulty getting necessary information from the buyer, a call from the licensee to the buyer may expedite the matter. Anytime requested information is not promptly supplied, the licensee should limit involvement to reminding the appropriate party to supply the information, while not becoming personally involved in securing such information for the lender.
- Following up on special stipulations—The buyer's agent should remind the buyer of any other contingencies or stipulations that the buyer is responsible for and should monitor the buyer's progress in complying. Besides the loan application, a matter generally demanding immediate attention after contract creation is the inspection of the property by the buyer or the buyer's inspector. Whether part of a due diligence clause or as a separate contingency, an inspection needs to occur within the time frame identified in the contract, and the licensee needs to work closely with the buyer to see that it happens on time. Often, the licensee will assume the responsibility of contacting the seller or the seller's tenants to arrange the inspection appointment, in addition to accompanying the buyer and the inspector to the property.
- Helping the buyer prepare for closing—A closing attorney expects the buyer to bring at least two things to closing: funds to meet the purchaser's cash obligations and a home hazard insurance policy if the purchase involves financing. Before

closing, the buyer's agent should make sure the purchaser has gathered sufficient funds in the payment form required by the attorney and Georgia statute. The closing attorney may also require any earnest money held by a broker to be wired or brought to closing in certified funds by the broker's licensee affiliate. When a loan is involved in the purchase, the buyer must arrange for a homeowners hazard insurance policy that includes the lender as a loss payee. Because some insurance companies require several days to deliver an original insurance policy, they may only be able to issue a binder at closing if not given sufficient notice before the closing date. Unless the closing attorney accepts such binders in lieu of the original policy, a delay of closing may occur. The licensee should therefore help the buyer understand the process for the insurance policies and the need to arrange for the policy in time in order to have an original to bring to closing.

- Informing the buyer of any changes in the property—A licensee also is responsible for informing the buyer of any substantial changes in the property before closing. For example, if the licensee should learn of a previous unknown property defect, such as a roof leak, the licensee should make the defect known to the buyer even though it may void the sales contract. Also, if the property should suffer damage beyond normal wear and tear before closing, the licensee should also make that known to the buyer.

Working With the Buyer, Representing the Seller

In a transaction in which the licensee represents only the seller, the licensee must treat the buyer as a customer. A licensee who works with a buyer while representing a seller in a transaction has an opportunity to develop a good rapport with that customer while also demonstrating a high level of professional competency. However, a licensee must remember in this circumstance that as an affiliated agent of the listing broker, the licensee remains legally responsible to the seller. Here the agent's actions should be guided by BRRETA, which allows a licensee who represents one party to perform ministerial acts for the other party without becoming an agent for that party. While such services allow a licensee to provide a buyer-customer with a list of inspectors, lenders, and attorneys from which to choose, recommending to the customer only one party from these categories may fall outside the scope of ministerial acts. Making such choices for a buyer-customer in the transaction could easily create a conflict of interest with the seller-client, as well as subject the licensee to a charge of undisclosed dual agency, a violation of BRRETA and license law.

IN PRACTICE While not interfering with a party's ultimate choice of a provider for a particular service, the licensee does have a responsibility to remind customers that services and fees of the selected vendor should not violate any corresponding terms of the purchase and sale contract. An example of this responsibility might involve a lender who only allows a seller to contribute up to 3% of the contract price toward the buyer's closing costs, while the sales contract indicates that the seller will contribute in excess of that sum. Helping a buyer understand this fact presents a possibility for reopening negotiations with the seller to address this particular issue and may lead to a workable solution for all parties.

Working With a Seller, Representing the Buyer

Under a buyer brokerage agreement, a licensee represents the buyer but needs to work closely with the other side in the sales agreement to effectively close the transaction. In this situation, it is the seller who is the customer of the licensee.

IN PRACTICE If the seller is represented by a listing agent, the buyer's agent will work directly with that licensee. If the property owner is unrepresented (FSBO), the licensee working for the buyer will work directly with the seller. In that circumstance, the licensee must be careful not to act in such a way that might imply or suggest an agency relationship with the seller. BRRETA requires that the buyer's agent treat the seller and the listing agent (if any) fairly, and the licensee may not knowingly give false information to these parties. Moreover, the buyer's agent must provide to the seller any known material facts concerning the purchaser's ability to complete the sale.

Working With the Closing Attorney

The closing attorney will need a true copy of the sales contract to do a title search, prepare the closing documents, and calculate the exact sums of money due from the buyer and to the seller. Common practice has the licensee providing the contract for the attorney. The closing attorney will also need the lender's copy of the buyer's home hazard insurance policy, a statement as to the cost of the policy if the buyer is to pay for it at closing, and, if required, a copy of the termite clearance letter. To facilitate transmittal if these documents, the closing attorney will often turn to the licensee.

IN PRACTICE When the lender approves the buyer's loan, the parties to the transaction will need to confirm a closing time, date, and place, according to the terms of the contract and the attorney's schedule and in cooperation with the buyer, the seller, and any cooperating agents. The licensee may need to coordinate this effort and verify that all parties are aware of the details. Usually the licensee affiliate of the broker representing the seller will be present at the closing to represent the broker. If a broker represents the buyer, that broker or her affiliate licensee may also attend the closing.

Unexpected developments often pop up during the contract-to-closing journey, and licensees who keep in close contact with the closing attorney's office are able to provide regular updates for clients and, as necessary, help them work through the anxieties that common to this often stressful process. Moreover, when working with first-time homebuyers, a licensee might want to discuss with the party what to expect as part of the actual closing procedure.

SETTLEMENT FORMS

Before October 3, 2015, those funds necessary to close a residential real estate transaction were identified and itemized on the settlement statement prepared by the closing attorney using a HUD-1 form as specified by the U.S. Department of Housing and Urban Development. The HUD-1 form displayed the amounts each party would pay out (**debits**) and receive (**credits**) at closing. Such items are commonly categorized as closing costs, prepaid and accrued sums, and payoffs of any existing property loans.

You may see HUD-1 forms in your real estate practice if you are reviewing any closing documents from transactions before October 2015. You may find that consumers who have been involved in previous real estate transactions have questions about how the new forms compare with forms, such as the HUD-1, that were used in past transactions.

Since October 3, 2015, two forms are being used to make the mortgage process clearer to consumers: the Loan Estimate (LE) and the Closing Disclosure (CD).

These forms are commonly called the TRID forms. The acronym TRID stands for TILA-RESPA Integrated Disclosures.

The Loan Estimate form provides information to consumers to make comparison shopping for mortgages clearer than it was before October 2015 and to ensure that consumers understand the loan and the closing costs involved with the loan. The LE replaces the Truth in Lending Statement (TIL) and the Good Faith Estimate (GFE) used before October 3, 2015. The lender must provide the LE to the consumer within three business days of the submission of a loan application, and the consumer must acknowledge receiving it.

The Closing Disclosure form replaces the HUD-1 form and the final TIL form that were used before October 3, 2015. The Closing Disclosure must be received by the consumer three business days before closing, and the lender must have proof that the consumer actually received the CD. The lender provides the CD to the borrower and to the closing attorney, but generally not to any brokers or agents involved in the transaction. Brokers and agents need to obtain the CD either from the lender or the borrower in order to review it in advance.

Note that the new forms and provisions of the TRID rules do not apply to

- home equity loans,
- mortgages on mobile homes or other dwellings not permanently attached to real estate, or
- reverse mortgages.

Brokers and their affiliated licensees should be familiar with the new forms, even though they are not responsible for preparing the forms. For additional information on the new TRID rules, consult the websites of the National Association of REALTORS® and the Consumer Finance Protection Bureau, both of which contain sample forms and additional information about the new TRID rule.

The disclosures required after October 3, 2015, changed the timing required for transactions that involve a mortgage. The potential for various delays to the closing is greater than in the past, and brokers and their affiliated licensees need to caution clients and customers not to delay in providing any information required by the lender.

Buyers' agents in particular have a responsibility to assist their clients in getting buyers to provide the lender all necessary information as early as possible, usually 10 to 14 days before the closing date to ensure that the Closing Disclosure can be delivered no later than three business days before closing. Brokers and agents on both sides of the transaction should be sure that the lender has information on any buyer-paid charges, seller-paid charges, and the license numbers of the real estate brokerage company and the individual licensee(s) handling the transaction (some of this information may appear in the purchase and sale contract provided to the lender).

The October 2015 TRID rules present some challenges for buyers, lenders, and brokers:

- Borrowers have 10 days to respond to whether they want to proceed with a loan once the LE is received from the lender. The lender is not permitted to verify or to document the borrower's claimed income before providing the LE. So, while brokers and buyers' agents, in particular, in the past encouraged prospective purchasers to be prequalified for a loan, that prequalification may be somewhat meaningless because the lender later actually verifies the borrower's income. At that point, the lender may determine that the borrower's "ratios" do not merit the type or amount of the loan the borrower is requesting. We will discuss ratios in some depth later in this lesson.

- In past years, Georgia purchase and sale contracts often specified a 30-day period between the acceptance of a contract and closing. Brokers may advise their clients or customers that adding an additional 15 days or so might be prudent. At any rate, before any particular closing date is set, borrowers should check with their lender to be sure the date is realistic.
- Last-minute negotiations and any significant change in loan terms or products triggers a new three-day waiting period for the Closing Disclosure, adding additional time between the contract and the closing.

The risk of delay in a transaction occurs when the sale of one property is contingent on the sale of another and when back-to-back closings for the properties are scheduled. Brokers and affiliated licensees may want to notify their clients or customers of this risk when drafting language for purchase and sale agreements.

IN PRACTICE Unless a diligent real estate agent has provided the seller with a written estimate of settlement costs, including some projection of the net proceeds to anticipate from the sale, the seller's first look at these items and numbers may come at the closing table. The buyer, though, is exposed to these monetary debits and credit during the loan approval procedure. Generally, the buyer will first see these costs itemized on the Loan Estimate form the lender is required by law to provide no later than three days after the submission of a loan application. Because the lion's share of settlement costs are associated with the buyer's new loan, it stands to reason that understanding the arithmetic of settlement usually presents a greater challenge to buyers than to sellers. To better understand the numbers, and as a matter of convenience and comfort, the buyer will often turn to the real estate licensee.

Being familiar with the applicable costs to complete the real estate transaction allows licensees not only to help buyers better understand the Loan Estimate but also to provide a basis for preparing both buyers and sellers to more confidently navigate through the numbers of the Closing Disclosure form that must be provided to the borrower three days before the closing of a transaction.

CLOSING COSTS

Closing costs are primarily those charges associated with closing the loan that are paid to the lender, the closing attorney, and the title insurance company, as well as any other costs to the parties as part of contractual agreement. Included among these items are the following:

- Loan origination fee
- Appraisal fee
- Title examination
- Underwriting fee
- Document preparation, processing, and courier fees
- Lender's and owner's (optional) title insurance policy
- Attorney's fee
- Flood certification fee

- Broker's commission
- New survey fee (optional)
- **Transfer tax**: An excise tax levied in Georgia on the sale of real property, which is paid to the clerk of superior court in the county where property is located. The deed to property may not be recorded without this tax being paid.
- **Intangible tax**: Required tax to be paid on any new loan for more than $1,500, with longer than a three-year term, secured to purchase real property in Georgia. Paid to the county in which the property is located, the intangible tax is a prerequisite for the recording of a security deed by a lender.

IN PRACTICE These last two settlement taxes required in Georgia are sometimes noted separately from the general closing costs on cost and net estimate forms provided for buyers and sellers. With the exception of the broker's fee (typically paid by the seller), estimate forms, as well as contract forms customarily used in Georgia, assign these costs to the purchaser, unless negotiated otherwise by the parties in the agreement for purchase and sale. Though not technically considered closing costs, the seller would be expected to pay for any back property taxes, liens, overdue homeowners association fees, or costs to correct any title problems.

PREPAID AND ACCRUED ITEMS

Not to be confused with the fixed sums identified as closing costs, though estimate forms sometimes include them as overall costs of the transaction, these charges are paid in advance, prorated, or escrowed at closing.

- Adjusted interest on the buyer's new loan—If the closing date is any day other than the first day of the month, the buyer will be required by the lender to prepay the loan interest at closing for the period beginning on closing day through the end of the closing month.
- Property taxes—Each city or county sets the due date for taxes on property located in its jurisdiction. Because property taxes in Georgia are assessed for the January-through-December calendar year, once billed, they automatically become a lien against the property, regardless of the due date. Consequently, once issued, the tax bill must be paid at closing in order for the seller to convey clear title to the property. The seller is responsible for payment of property taxes starting on January 1 through the day of closing, and the buyer is responsible for the taxes starting the day after closing through December 31.

IN PRACTICE If the closing takes place before the calendar tax bill has been issued, the closing attorney will normally prorate the taxes based on the previous year's tax bill. Most settlement statements provide that the buyer and the seller agree to make any financial adjustments for any differences between what is charge based on the previous year's tax bill and what is actually billed for the current calendar year.

Interestingly, though property tax proration is customarily stipulated in purchase and sale agreements, such proration is not required under Georgia law unless the contract so stipulates. Without this agreement, the seller is responsible for the full, calendar year tax bill, regardless of the date on which the closing occurred.

- Hazard insurance—The buyer pays in advance at closing for a one-year home hazard insurance policy. The buyer may bring the paid policy to closing or have the insurance company forward the policy to closing, the cost for which the attorney will debit the buyer. For an existing hazard insurance policy paid one year in advance, a seller is credited for the days on that policy beginning the day after closing and ending on the final day of that policy's annual term.
- Homeowners association fee—Generally assessed for condominium and townhome communities, and sometimes for single-family residence subdivisions. These fees will typically be prorated at closing, depending on the time intervals for which an HOA assesses its fees. New owners may also have to prepay initiation fees to the associations at closing.
- Escrow accounts—Required by lenders for a buyer who borrows in excess of 80% LTV (down payment less than 20%) to cover the following:
  - Property taxes—Set up to pay a buyer's future tax bills. The lender will generally require the borrower at closing to deposit a sufficient number of monthly tax payments to cover the next calendar tax bill when it comes due, plus an additional two months.
  - Hazard insurance—The lender requires two to four months of insurance premium to be escrowed at closing, in addition to the prepayment for a one-year policy.
  - Private mortgage insurance—Two months private mortgage insurance (PMI) (sometimes a mortgage insurance premium, or MIP) from the borrower is escrowed at closing.

IN PRACTICE Subject to lender guidelines, any negotiated seller contribution toward a purchaser's transactional costs may also include any of these prepaid items.

Payoff of Existing Property Loan(s)

If a seller has an existing loan(s) on the property, unless the loan is assumed by the buyer, as part of the overall purchase price, the closing attorney will pay the remaining portion of that loan from the seller's proceeds at the transaction's settlement. The total payoff will be itemized as the

- loan principal balance as of the seller's previous loan payment plus
- accrued loan interest built up from the day of the last payment through the closing day of the transaction.

PRORATING COSTS

Prorating Settlement Costs

Because the basic rules and arithmetic for prorating prepaid and loan payoff items for settlement are covered in Unit 17, the focus here will be on customary applications of such calculations in Georgia. Certain periodic expenses are connected with real property ownership, and in reviewing the process of prorating, three of these expenses are considered:

- Loan interest
- Annual property taxes
- Hazard insurance premiums

How proration works on the sale of a rental income-producing property will also be examined here. As a general custom in Georgia, the seller is responsible for the prorated expense of the closing day, but not beyond, and is entitled to income prorated for that closing day, though not beyond. The buyer's financial responsibility or benefits begin the day after closing, with the single exception of any new loan acquired to purchase the property. Here, the lender will charge the buyer interest for the closing day.

Prorating Loan Interest

IN PRACTICE Typically, the closing attorney will be prorating interest for two loans on the settlement form: the seller's existing loan and the buyer's new loan. Both calculations begin with an understanding that real property loan interest is always paid **in arrears**. Assume then that the settlement is for a closing that is to occur on September 18. In examining the seller's existing loan, the closing attorney sees that a loan payment was last made on September 1, which paid the loan interest for the month of August (in arrears).

Because the transaction is closing on September 18, obviously no future loan payments will be made—which begs the question: how will the seller account for the loan interest that has built up (accrued) from September 1 to September 18 (18 days)? The answer is quite simple: on the settlement statement, the closing attorney will debit the seller for that 18 days' interest owed to the seller's lender.

In this same transaction to be closed on September 18, the buyer of the property is acquiring a separate new-home loan. As is the custom with such a loan, the buyer does not have to make loan payment for the month that follows closing (October) but may wait until November 1 to make the initial payment. (The exception to this custom occurs only if a closing happens on the first day of a month. In that circumstance, the initial loan payment would be due on the first day of the month following closing).

So, when the buyer who is closing the loan on September 18 makes the first loan payment on November 1, the interest on that loan is paid for the month of October (in arrears). Once again a question is begged: if the buyer's first payment on the new loan begins November 1, which only pays the loan interest for October, how will the buyer account for the interest on the new loan from closing day to the end of September? Again, the answer is simple: on the transaction settlement form, the closing attorney will debit the buyer for 13 days of loan interest (September 18–September 30) owed to the buyer's lender.

MATH CONCEPTS

Prorating Loan Interest

Realizing that the interest portion of a real property loan payment is always paid for the previous month rather than the current month is central to understanding how such interest is prorated for settlement. The diagrams included with this lesson offer a visual application of this principle while allowing an accurate counting for days of loan interest at settlement owed by a seller for an existing loan and a buyer for a new loan. Brokers and licensees may create similar diagrams or graphs to accurately determine prorations related to costs for their clients or customers.

FIGURE 26.1: Accrued Interest and Interest Adjustment

4. For Accrued Interest—(Seller) Consider Payment Due Date (Usually 1st) Count Number of Days from Last Payment through the Closing Date (Debit to Seller)

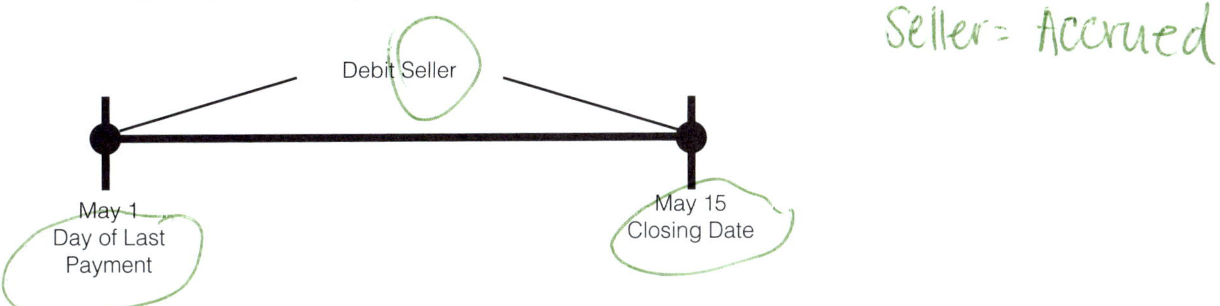

5. For Interest Adjustment—(Buyer) Consider Month of Closing Count Number of Days Including Closing Date through Eng of Month (Debit to Buyer)

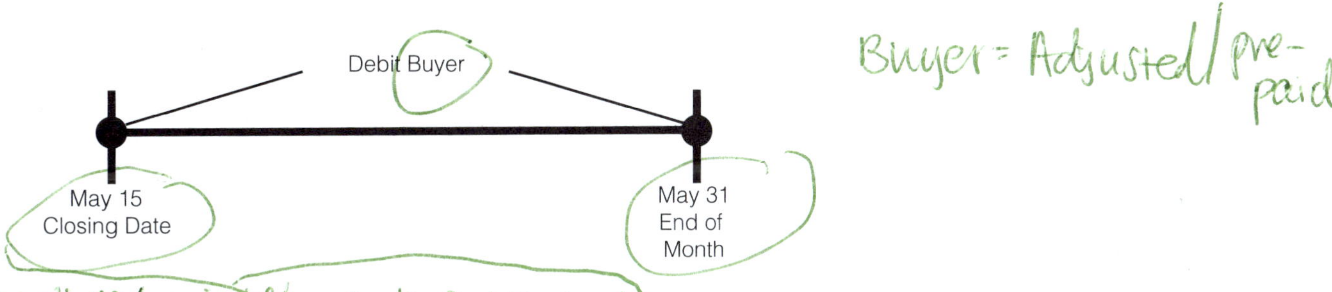

Regarding the seller's existing loan, the graph begins with the day the last loan payment was due and ends on the closing day of the sale. Assume that the transaction will close on May 15 and the last payment was made on May 1. That payment covered the loan interest in arrears from April 1 to April 30. Under normal circumstances, the seller's next loan payment would come on June 1, which would pay all of May's interest. But that will not happen because closing and the transference of title will occur on May 15. Consequently, at the settlement, the seller will owe the lender (debit the seller) 15 days of interest that, as the graph shows, has accrued (built up) beginning on the date of the last payment (May 1) and ending on Closing (May 15).

Now, let's examine the graph that allows the counting of prorated days for a buyer's new loan. Continuing with the same closing day of May 15, no loan payment will be due in June; rather the buyer will make the first payment for the new loan on July 1. That payment will pay loan interest in arrears for the month of June, but it will not cover interest, as shown in the graph, from closing day to the end of the closing month. At settlement, then, those 17 days (counting from May 15 to May 31), owed to the lender, will be debited to the buyer. Regarding the buyer's new loan, if the closing day occurs on the first day of the month, remember that is normally the only time the initial payment on that new loan will be due on the first day of the following month. For example, if a closing happens on September 1, the first payment will be on October 1—which pays loan interest in arrears for the entire month of October, including closing day. Therefore, in this particular circumstance, the buyer will owe the lender zero days of prorated interest at closing and will not be debited on the settlement statement.

Drawing graphs to visualize the process of counting days for accrued interest proration may be especially useful if the seller's existing loan payments are not due on the first day of a month. Assume, for example, that a closing will take place on February 10 and the seller's last payment due date was January 20. At first glance, these dates may cause some confusion, because the natural assumption is that such payments are customarily due on the first day of the month. But by setting up a graph for the seller's existing loan, it is a simple process to insert January 20 as the day of the last payment and February 10 as the closing date. This visual clue allows an accurate counting of 12 days from January 20 to January 31, and 10 days from Feb 1 to February 10, for a total of 22 days of prorated interest owed to the lender and debited to the seller at settlement.

FIGURE 26.2: Accrued Interest, Actual Dates

4. For Accrued Interest—(Seller) Consider Payment Due Date (Usually 1st) Count Number of Days from Last Payment through the Closing Date (Debit to Seller)

Debit Seller

January 20

February 10

IN PRACTICE If the seller directly provides financing for the buyer, the interest prorations for such loans (commonly called purchase money mortgages) would be handled at the closing exactly as though a private lender were making the loan for the purchaser. However, if the buyer were to assume a seller's existing loan as part of the purchase price, proration of loan interest would be handled somewhat differently. For example, a closing is to take place on July 18, with the buyer assuming a seller's existing loan balance of $100,000 as part of the transaction.

With a loan assumption, the buyer would continue to make the seller's next scheduled loan payment due on August 1. When the buyer makes that payment, interest will be paid in arrears for the entire month of July. However, because the buyer has only owned the property since the July 18 closing day, it is only fair that at closing the seller, who owned the property from July 1 to July 18, pay the loan's prorated interest for that period. Consequently, at the July 18 settlement, the seller will be debited and the buyer credited for 18 days of prorated loan interest.

Accurately counting the number of days for prorating mortgage interest on the seller's existing loan and the buyer's new loan is just the first of a two-step process to determine an exact dollar amount accounted for on the Closing Disclosure form. The other step involves calculating a per diem (daily) charge for the loan interest and then multiplying that sum by the number of prorated days.

PER DIEM CALCULATION

1. Loan amount (buyer's new loan) or loan balance (seller's existing loan) times the interest rate of the loan equals the annual interest for the loan.

   LA × IR = AI

2. Annual interest divided by 360 (unless the problem stipulates 365 days) equals daily/per diem interest.

   AI ÷ 360 = DI (per diem)

   If not provided, the buyer's new loan will have to be calculated using the sales price provided in the problem and the purchaser's loan-to-value ratio (LTV)

   sales price (SP) × loan-to-value ratio (LTV) = loan amount (LA)

EXAMPLES A homeowner's loan balance is $174,500, and the fixed interest rate is 5%; calculate the daily interest on the existing loan.

LA ($174,500) × IR (0.05) = AI ($8,725); AI ($8,725 ÷ 360 = DI ($24.2361) per diem

A buyer is purchasing a home for $265,000 with a new loan that is 90% of the purchase price and an interest rate of 4.5%. What is the per diem interest on this loan?

$265,000 (SP) × 0.90 (LTV) = $238,500 (LA)

$238,500 (LA) × 0.045 (IR) = $10,732.50 (AI)

$10,732.50 ÷ 360 = $29.8125 (per diem)

Summary

A buyer is approved for a loan with an interest rate of 5.25% to purchase a home for $325,000 using a 95% LTV. The seller's existing loan balance is $96,000 after the most recent monthly payment on October 1, and that loan carries an interest rate of 4.5%. If the property closes on October 28, what is the prorated interest charge for both the seller's existing loan and the buyer's new loan?

Accrued Interest/Seller

Step 1: Draw a graph inserting October 1 as the day of the seller's last payment and October 28 as the closing day.

FIGURE 26.3: Adjusted Interest, Actual Dates

4. For Accrued Interest—(Seller) Consider Payment Due Date (Usually 1st) Count Number of Days from Last Payment through the Closing Date (Debit to Seller)

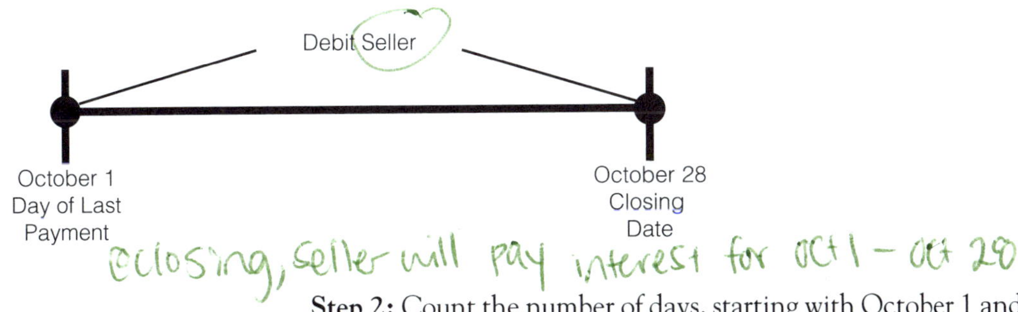

Step 2: Count the number of days, starting with October 1 and ending with October 28, for a total of 28 days of accrued loan interest owed by seller to the lender.

Step 3: Calculate the annual loan interest:

$96,000 (LA) × 0.045 (IR) = $4,320 (AI)

Step 4: Calculate the daily interest:

$4,320 (AI) ÷ 360 = $12 per diem

Step 5: Multiply 28 (days of interest owed) × $12 (interest per day) = $336 (accrued loan interest debited to seller at settlement).

Adjusted-Prepaid Interest/Buyer

Step 1: Draw a graph inserting October 28 as the closing day and October 31 as the last day of the closing month.

FIGURE 26.4: Adjusted Interest Proration, October 28 Closing

5. For Interest Adjustment—(Buyer) Consider Month of Closing Count Number of Days Including Closing Date through Eng of Month (Debit to Buyer)

Step 2: Count the number of days starting with October 28 and ending with October 31 for a total of four days of adjusted loan interest, prepaid by the buyer to the lender at closing.

Step 3: Calculate the loan amount:

$325,000 (SP) × 0.95 (IR) = $308,750 (LA)

Step 4: Calculate the annual loan interest:

$308,750 (LA) × 0.0525 (IR) = $16,209.375 (AI)

Step 5: Calculate the daily interest:

$16,209.375 ÷ 360 = $45.026 per diem

Step 6: Multiply 4 (days of adjusted interest/prepaid to lender) × $45.026 (interest per day) = $180.10 (adjusted/prepaid loan interest debited to buyer at settlement).

Reminder: Lenders always charge new loan buyer-customers and existing loan seller-customers for interest on closing day.

PRORATING PROPERTY TAX

IN PRACTICE As pointed out earlier in this unit, property taxes in Georgia are due on various dates during the year, depending on the county in which the property is located. Whatever the due date, the taxes are always applied to a calendar year. So, whether property taxes are due in May, August, or November, for example, the collected monies always pay for the period of January 1 to December 31.

Prorating these sums accurately requires two pieces of information: the date of closing and whether or not such taxes have been paid by the closing day. If the property taxes are unpaid as of closing, the seller is debited for the days beginning on January 1 and up to and including the settlement day. On the other hand, the proration process will credit the buyer of the property for the same number of days. The buyer is credited for these days at settlement to ensure that the seller's share will be in hand for the new owner when the property tax bill becomes due for the entire calendar year.

But what if, as of closing, the property taxes are prepaid for the calendar year? In that circumstance, the seller will be credited for the period starting the day after closing (remember, closing day belongs to seller, so they are charged for that day), up to and including the day of December 31. Conversely, as the new owner of the property, the buyer will then, rightfully, at settlement be debited for that period.

MATH CONCEPTS

Prorating Property Taxes

FIGURE 26.5: Property Taxes, Actual Dates

2. For Property Taxes—If property tax unpaid as of closing, count days from January 1 through closing day (debit to seller and credit to buyer). If tax has been prepaid as of closing, count from day after closing through December 31.

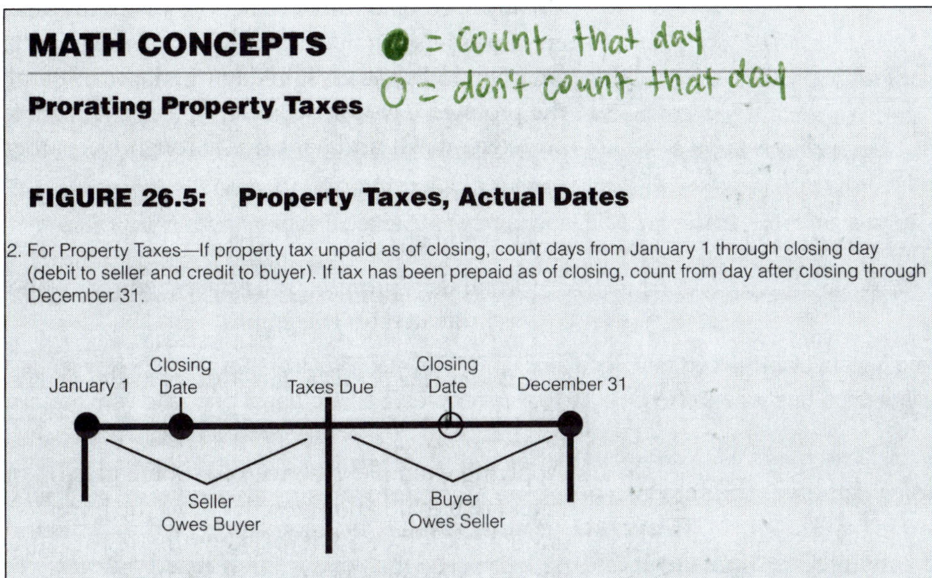

As identified in the graph, the beginning and ending dates for property taxes in Georgia always frame a natural calendar year. The graph also illustrates that if the closing occurs before the tax due date, the settlement for this proration will show a debit for the seller and a credit for the buyer. If property taxes are prepaid before the closing, the graph shows a credit for the seller and a debit to the buyer. Moreover, this graph assists in the counting process to accurately prorate the number of tax days to be debited and credited between the parties. Note that when the closing occurs before the tax due date, the days of January 1 and the closing are marked by a dark circle; this indicates that the counting of days will start on January 1 and end on closing day.

Example 1

The sale of a home is closing on March 11 and the property taxes have not been paid. How many days will be prorated for property taxes at settlement and how will these taxes be debited and credited? Inserting March 11 as the closing date on our graph visually indicates that the counting of days starts with January 1 and ends on March 11. Unless otherwise indicated, exact days of the month will be used to count.

January 1–31 = 31 days

February 1–28 = 28 days

March 1–11 = 11 days

Total days prorated = 70 debited to the seller and credited to the buyer, as indicated on the graph

Note again what the graph illustrates when the closing day occurs after the property taxes have been paid. Here, a plain circle shows up on the closing day, while December 31 has a shaded one. The plain circle reminds us not to begin the prorated count for crediting the seller on that day because the closing day remains the seller's responsibility. The starting point becomes the day after closing and the ending day for counting is December 31, which is indicated by a shaded circle.

Example 2

The sale of a home closes on October 31, and the taxes on the property have already been paid for the calendar year. How many days will be prorated for property taxes at settlement, and how will the taxes be debited and credited? Inserting October 31 as the closing day (marked with a plain circle) tells us that counting the prorated days for the seller's property tax credit will start the day after closing on November 1 and continue through December 31.

November 1–30 = 30 days

December 1–31 = 31 days

Total days prorated = 61 days credited to the seller and debited to the buyer as indicated on the graph.

To calculate the per diem for property taxes, simply divide the property's annual tax by 365 days.

Applying example 1 above of a home closing on March 11, where the property taxes are unpaid and the seller owes the buyer 70 prorated days of tax, now add an annual tax bill of $3,500. Then, divide this annual tax amount of $3,500 by 365 days to calculate a per diem of $9.589.

Next, multiply this daily tax amount of $9.589 by 70 to calculate a prorated figure of $671.23, debited to the seller and credited to the buyer at settlement.

Applying example 2 of a home closing on October 31, with prepaid property taxes and the buyer owing the seller for 61 days of prorated taxes, now add an annual tax bill of $5,200.

Then, divide this annual tax amount of $5,200 by 365 days to calculate a per diem of $14.2467.

Next, multiply this daily tax amount of $14.2467 by 61 to calculate a prorated figure of $869.04, credited to the seller and debited to the buyer at settlement.

Summary

The sale of a home with annual property taxes of $2,850 that are due every year on July 1 closes on May 18. Calculate the prorated property tax and indicate how this amount will be settled between the buyer and the seller.

Step 1: Draw graph for prorating the property taxes, indicating a calendar year, and insert a closing day of May 18 and a tax due date of July 1. Place a shaded circle at January 1 and another at closing day.

FIGURE 26.6: Prorating Property Taxes, May 18 Closing

2. For Property Taxes—If property tax unpaid as of closing, count days from January 1 through closing day (debit to seller and credit to buyer). If tax has been prepaid as of closing, count from day after closing through December 31.

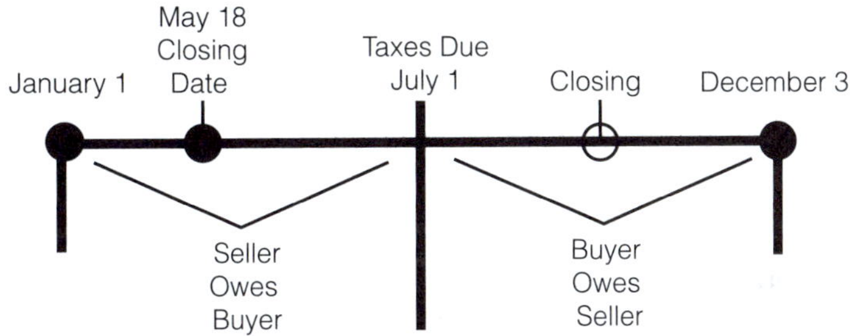

Step 2: Count the number of days starting with January 1 and ending with May 18.

Jan–31

Feb–28

Mar–31

Apr–30

May–18

Total = 138 days

Step 3: Divide $2,850 by 365 to calculate $7.81 for tax per diem.

Step 4: Multiply $7.81 by 138 to calculate $1,077.78, an amount that will be debited to the seller and credited to the buyer at settlement.

A homebuyer closes on August 15 on a property whose taxes of $4,500 have been prepaid for the calendar year. What portion of these taxes will be prorated between the parties and in what manner to each party?

Step 1: Draw an appropriate graph for prorating this sum with necessary insertions and markings.

FIGURE 26.7: Prorating Property Taxes, August 15 Closing

2. For Property Taxes—If property tax unpaid as of closing, count days from January 1 through closing day (debit to seller and credit to buyer). If tax has been prepaid as of closing, count from day after closing through December 31.

Step 2: Count the number of prorated days starting on the day after closing and ending on December 31.

August 16–31 = 16

September = 30

October = 31

November = 30

December = 31

Total = 138 days

Step 3: Divide $4,500 by 365 to calculate a tax per diem of $12.3288.

Step 4: Multiply $12.3288 by 138 to calculate $1,701.37, an amount that will be credited to the seller and debited to the buyer at settlement.

PRORATING HAZARD INSURANCE

IN PRACTICE Because a lender requires a homeowner to keep a hazard insurance policy for the property, the cost to maintain such protection will need to be prepaid annually by the owner. Cash buyers will commonly opt to purchase this type of insurance as well. A year's policy is initially paid for in advance by the buyer at closing, as mentioned earlier in this unit and then is renewed each year on that initial anniversary date.

The settlement practice of prorating the hazard insurance policy stems from the fact that, because the policy has been paid a year in advance, the closing of the sale happens before that policy's expiration date. Consequently, the seller will not own the property for the duration of the policy's term and deserves a partial refund for the period of that term.

In the past, when a purchaser might assume the seller's existing hazard insurance policy, such a refund would be represented on the settlement statement as a credit to the seller and a debit to the buyer. More typically today, a buyer acquires a separate hazard insurance policy at closing. Consequently, the seller's partial credit for the policy cost at settlement will come from the insurance company that issues the policy.

Unlike property taxes that are always paid for the existing calendar year, a hazard insurance policy's year will always begin on the date the policy was issued and end one year later, the day before the policy renews. As an example, if a policy's start date is September 29, it will end the following year on September 28, the day before it renews.

This same renewal date every year is commonly called the policy's ***anniversary date***. So if a property's anniversary date is indeed September 29, but the homeowner is closing the sale of the property earlier in the year on June 2, the seller would not own the property between June 2 and September 29. Because the seller's hazard insurance policy is paid through September 28, the seller would receive a credit from the insurance company for policy days beginning on June 3 (remember, the seller does not get a credit for closing day, June 2, because that day belongs to the seller) up to and including the last day of the policy on September 28.

MATH CONCEPTS

Prorating Hazard Insurance

FIGURE 26.8: Prorating Hazard Insurance

2. For Hazard Insurance—Count from Day after Closing Date through Ending Date of Policy

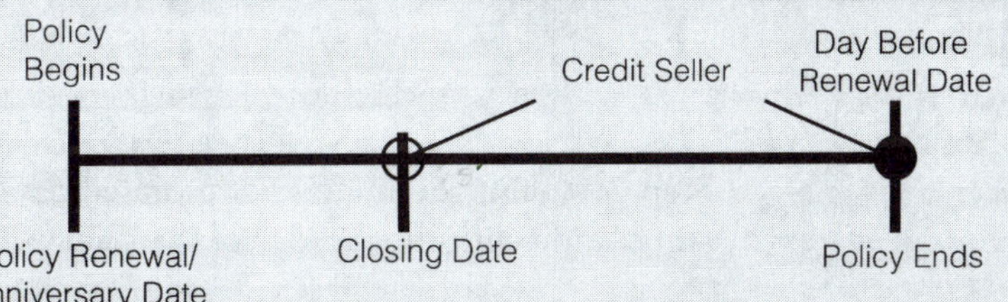

In contrast to a standard calendar year always present in prorating property taxes, note that this graph for hazard insurance proration starts when the policy begins and goes to the policy end date, which will always be one year later on the day before it renews. So, if February 28 is inserted as the date the policy begins, then February 27 (in the following year) must be inserted as the date the policy ends. If December 1 is the anniversary date of the policy, then November 30 must be inserted as the policy end date. And so forth.

Also, on this graph, note a plain circle marking the closing date and a shaded circle marking the policy end date. The plain circle provides visual instruction to begin counting the prorated period on the day after the closing, and the shaded circle at the policy end date indicates the final day to count.

EXAMPLE The closing date is August 31, and the seller's hazard insurance policy renews every year on February 5. So, in setting up the graph, the policy start date is February 5 and the end date, marked with a shaded circle, is February 4, a year later. The August 31 closing date is inserted and marked by a plain circle. Begin the count on September 1, the day after closing, as follows: September (30 days) plus October (31 days) plus November (30 days) plus December (31 days) plus January (31 days) plus February (4 days to the end of the policy) for a total of 157 days that will be prorated as a credit to the seller at settlement.

To calculate the per diem for the insurance proration, the annual premium is divided by 365 days. Applying this calculation to the above example, assume a hazard insurance annual premium of $900. Then, divide $900 by 365 to calculate a daily insurance proration of $2.4658. Next, multiply this per diem of $2.4658 by the 157 prorated days to calculate a policy proration credit to the seller for $387.13.

Summary

A seller's hazard insurance policy cost $850 and has an anniversary date of March 25. If the closing for the property's sale is June 29, the insurance proration will be for how many days and for what amount, and will this amount be a credit or a debit to the seller? Use 365 days for the daily proration.

Step 1: Draw the graph that sets the beginning date for the policy on March 25 and the end date for the policy, notated with a shaded circle, on March 24, a year later. Also insert the June 29 closing date on the graph, notating that date with a plain circle.

FIGURE 26.9: Prorating Hazard Insurance, Actual Dates

2. For Hazard Insurance—Consider Insurance Anniversary Date for Period Count from Day after Closing Date through Ending Date of Policy

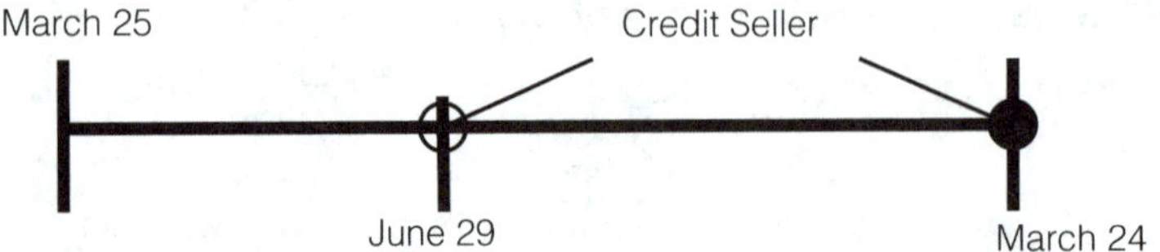

Step 2: Count the number of prorated days beginning with the day after closing and ending with the last day of the policy:

June 30 = 1
July = 31
August = 31
September = 30
October = 31
November = 30
December = 31
January = 31
February = 28
March 1–24 = 24
Total days = 268

Step 3: \$850 divided by 365 equals \$2.329 per diem.

Step 4: 268 multiplied by \$2.329 equals \$624.17.

The seller will be credited at settlement for a 268-day portion of the hazard insurance policy totaling \$624.17.

Reminder: Hazard insurance proration is always a credit to the seller.

PRORATING RENTAL INCOME

IN PRACTICE Because the owner of a leased property typically collects rent in advance on a monthly basis, when the rental property is sold, the seller gets to keep that portion of the rent through the closing day (that day belongs to the seller) but will credit the buyer of the property for that portion of the monthly rent beyond the closing day. For example, if the rent is paid in advance on the first day of every month and the sale of the property closes on June 20, the seller will keep the 20-day portion of the rent (through closing day) and credit the buyer of the property for the 10 remaining days of the month (June 21–30).

Sometimes, the rental month may not begin on that month's first day. For instance, when the rent is due every month on the 10th day, the rental month extends from that day until the 9th day of the following month. So, assume this leased property is sold and closes on November 5; because the rent was last paid on October 10, the seller gets to keep the portion of the monthly rent that pays for the October 10 to November 5 period (closing day) but would credit the new owner (buyer) for the four days of rent from November 6 to November 9 (the last day of rental month).

MATH CONCEPTS

Prorating Rental Income

FIGURE 26.10: Prorating Rental Income

3. For Rent—Determine Rent Period—Usually Monthly—Count from Day after Closing Date through Ending Date of Rent Period (Debit to Seller and Credit to Buyer If Rent Paid in Advance)

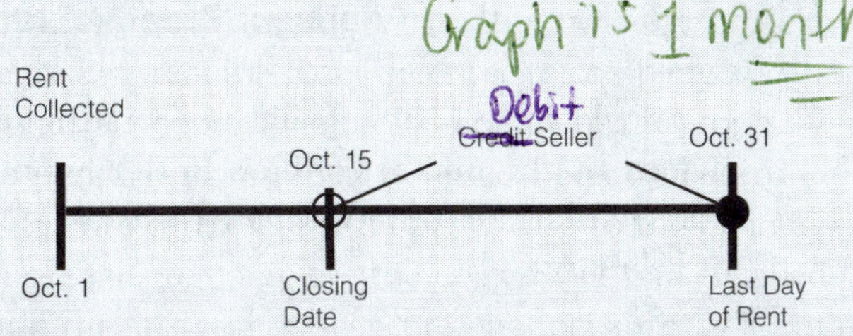

Because the graph covers the term of a rental month, it starts with the day the rent is collected and ends on the last day of the rental month. Note that the closing day is marked with a plain circle, indicating that the counting of prorated days starts on the day after closing and ends on the last day of the rental month (marked by a shaded circle). Also indicated is the number of days counted that are debited to seller (and credited to buyer). Remember why: the seller has collected a full month's rent in advance and must credit the buyer for the portion of full days in which the seller will no longer own the property.

EXAMPLE 1 On the graph, insert October 15 as closing day, October 1 as day the rent is collected, and October 31 as the last day of rent. (A rental month always ends the day before the rent becomes due again.) Visually, the plain circle marking the closing day indicates that counting of the prorated days (a debit to the seller) will begin on October 16 (the day after closing) and end on October 31, for a total of 16 days. *(Remember to include both the first and last day of the count.)*

EXAMPLE 2 On the graph, insert February 27 as closing day, February 15 as the day the rent is collected, and March 14 as the last day of rent. (A rental month always ends the day before rent becomes due again). The counting of the prorated days (a debit to the seller) begins on February 28 and continues through March 14, for a total of 15 days.

To calculate the daily amount for prorating rent, the sum of the monthly rent is divided by the number of days in the month that the rent was collected. Unless a problem indicates otherwise, use the exact number of days in the month (28 days for February).

FIGURE 26.11: Rental Income

3. For Rent—Determine Rent Period—Usually Monthly—Count from Day after Closing Date through Ending Date of Rent Period (Debit to Seller and Credit to Buyer If Rent Paid in Advance)

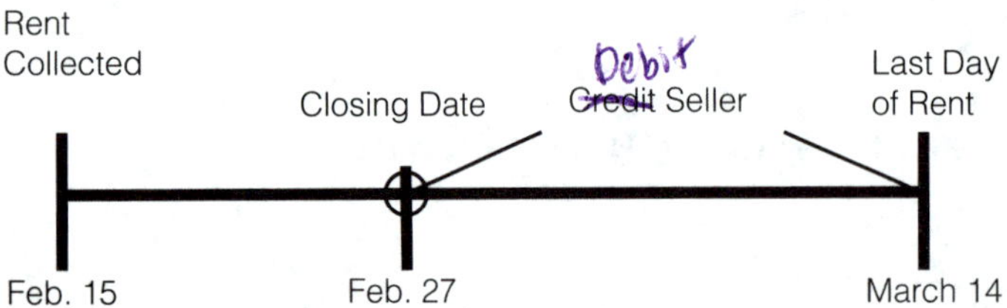

To calculate the daily amount of prorating rent, the sum of the monthly rent is divided by the number of days in that month the rent was collected. Unless a problem indicates otherwise, use the exact number of days in the month (28 days for February).

EXAMPLE 1 The monthly rent of $850 is collected on November 1. To prorate the daily rent, divide $850 by 30 days for per diem of $28.3333. If the same rent is collected on October 1, divide $850 by 31 for a per diem of $27.4194. If same rent is collected on February 1, divide $850 by 28 for a per diem of $30.3571.

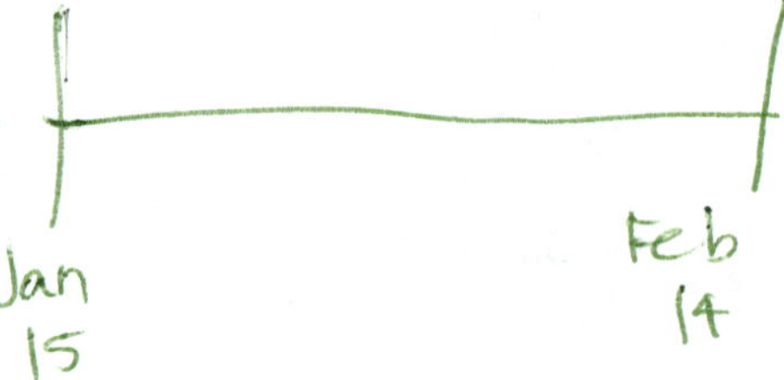

EXAMPLE 2 The monthly rent of $1,500 is collected on January 15, with the rental period ending on February 14. To prorate the daily rent, divide $1,500 by 31 (number of days of the month in which the rent is collected) for a per diem of $48.3871.

To calculate the prorated amount of rental income for settlement, multiply the number of prorated days times the daily rent.

Summary

A buyer closes April 9 on a rental property with leasing income totaling $3,500 a month. The rent is paid in advance on the first day of each month. At the settlement, how many rental income days are prorated between the buyer and the seller and for what prorated sum, and how is that amount debited and/or credited between the parties?

Step 1: Draw a graph for the proration of rental income showing April 1 as the day rent is collected, April 30 as the last day of the rental period (marked with shaded circle) and April 9 as the closing day (marked with plain circle).

FIGURE 26.12: Prorating Rental Income, Actual Dates

3. For Rent—Determine Rent Period—Usually Monthly—Count from Day after Closing Date through Ending Date of Rent Period (Debit to Seller and Credit to Buyer If Rent Paid in Advance)

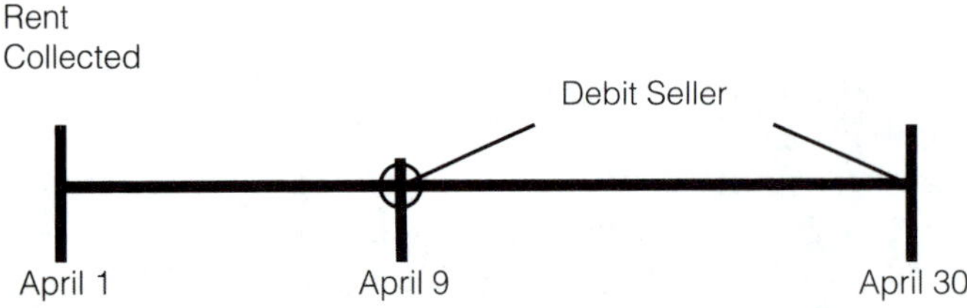

Step 2: Count prorated days for rental income starting on April 10 and ending on April 30 for a total of 21 days.

Step 3: Divide $3,500 by 30 days for a daily rental income of $116.6667.

Step 4: Multiply $116.6667 by 21 for a prorated rental income amount of $2,450 credited to the buyer and debited to the seller at settlement.

A rental property is sold and closed on July 7. The rent of $1,100 is due on the 10th day of each month. The rent would be prorated for how many days, for what amount, and settled in what manner between the seller and the purchaser.

Step 1: Draw the graph for proration of rental income indicating June 10 as the last day rent is collected, July 9 as the last day of the rental period (marked with a shaded circle), and July 7 as the closing day (marked with a plain circle).

FIGURE 26.13: Prorating Rental Income, July 7 Closing

3. For Rent—Determine Rent Period—Usually Monthly—Count from Day after Closing Date through Ending Date of Rent Period (Debit to Seller and Credit to Buyer If Rent Paid in Advance)

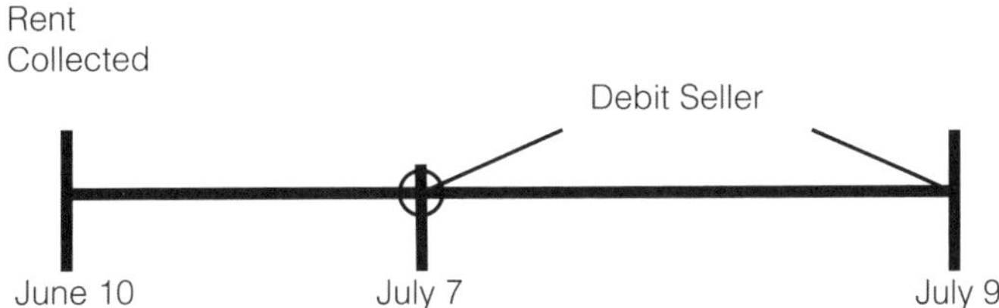

Step 2: Count the prorated days for the rental income, starting with July 8 and ending on July 9 for a total of two days.

Step 3: Divide $1,100 by 30 (number of days in June, the month the rent was last collected), for a daily proration of $36.6666.

Step 4: Multiply $36.6666 by 2 for a prorated amount of $73.33 debited to the seller and credited for the buyer at settlement.

Reminder Rental Income is also prorated as a debit to the seller and a credit to the buyer.

SETTLEMENT TAXES

Transfer Tax

IN PRACTICE Sometimes called a conveyance tax, the transfer tax is now commonly assigned to the purchaser at settlement, though as a required transaction cost, payment of the tax may be negotiated between the parties. The tax is calculated on the net sales price of a property (the sales price minus any assumable loan that may be part of sales price), at a rate of 10 cents per $100 of taxable sales price. So, if a property sells for a $250,000, the property would be taxed at 0.10 for each $100 of that $250,000. On the other hand, if this $250,000 sales price included a $150,000 existing loan on the property assumed by the purchaser, the transfer tax would be calculated on the net sales price of $150,000 ($250,000 minus the assumable loan of $100,000). Only an assumable loan would be subtracted from the sales price, not any new loan. The transfer tax is calculated as follows:

sales price (– assumable loan, if any) ÷ 100 × 0.10

Note: If after dividing by 100, the resulting number is not an even dollar amount, round up to the next dollar.

EXAMPLE $248,850 ÷ 100 = $2,488.50 (not an even dollar amount), so round it up to $2,489, then × 0.10 = $248.90 for transfer tax

Intangible Tax

Assessed on new loan(s) in the sales transaction at the rate of $1.50 per $500 of the loan amount. Commonly assigned to the buyer as a closing cost, payment is also negotiable between parties. There is no intangible tax on a loan assumption. Use this formula for calculating the intangible tax:

new loan amount ÷ 500 × $1.50

Note: If after dividing by 500, the answer is not an even dollar amount, round up to next dollar.

EXAMPLE $222,350 (LA) ÷ 500 = $447.50 (not even dollar amount); round up to $448 × 1.50 = $672 for intangible tax

MATH CONCEPTS

Calculating Transfer Tax

To calculate the transfer tax:

SP (sales price minus assumable loan) ÷ 100 (round up to next $, if necessary) × 0.10

1. If a property sells for $325,550, calculate the transfer tax:

   $325,550 ÷ 100 = $3,255.50, rounded up to $3,256 × 0.10 = $325.60

2. A property sells for $265,000 that includes a loan assumption of $165,000. Calculate the transfer tax:

   $265,000 – $165,000 (assumable loan) = $100,000 (taxable amount) ÷ 100 = $1,000 (an even $ amount, so no rounding up) × 0.10 = $100

MATH CONCEPTS

Calculating Intangible Tax

Use this formula to calculate the intangible tax:

LA (new loan amount) ÷ 500 (round up to next $, if necessary) × $1.50

1. A buyer purchases a home for $425,000, with a new loan for $340,000. Calculate the intangible tax:

   $340,000 ÷ 500 = $680 (even $, no rounding up) × $1.50 = $1,020.

2. A property is purchased for $200,000 that includes a new loan for $100,000, as well as an assumed loan for $75,000. Calculate the intangible tax:

   $100,000 ÷ $500 = 200 × 1.50 = $300

   Note: Only the new loan is used to figure the intangible tax.

Reminders After dividing by 100 on the transfer tax and 500 on the intangible tax, round up to next dollar if these applications equal an uneven dollar amount.

Transfer Tax

1. Calculated on all real property sales
2. Remember to subtract any assumable loan from the sales price to find the taxable amount
3. Ignore any new loan when calculating the transfer taxl

Intangible Tax

1. Calculated on new loans only, including purchase money mortgages from seller
2. Ignore any assumable loan when calculating this tax; no intangible tax on cash sales

Summary

A home is purchased for $355,250, and the buyer has acquired financing for 90% LTV. Calculate the transfer tax and the intangible tax on this sale.

Transfer Tax

Step 1: Divide $355,250 by 100 to calculate $3,552.50.

Step 2: Round $3,552.50 up to $3,553.

Step 3: Multiply $3,553 by 0.10 to calculate a transfer tax of $355.30.

Intangible Tax

Step 1: Multiply $355,250 (SP) by 0.90 (LTV) to calculate a loan amount of $319,725.

Step 2: Divide $319,725 by 500 to calculate $639.45.

Step 3: Round up $639.45 to $640.

Step 4: Multiply $640 by 1.50 to calculate the intangible tax of $960.

Withholding Tax

Georgia law requires withholding up to 3% of the purchase price on any sale or transfer of real property and related tangible personal property located in Georgia from nonresidents of the state who do not operate businesses in the state and do not file related Georgia income tax returns. The burden to withhold and pay this tax is placed on the buyer who must file the required tax return and remit payment on or before the last day of month after the month in which sale has occurred.

MONTHLY PAYMENT OF NEW LOAN

IN PRACTICE If a purchaser's loan down payment is 20% or larger, the total monthly payment will typically consist only of principal and interest or just interest. As an example, if an amortized loan payment is $1,250 a month or an interest-only loan payment is $1,000 a month, either of these amounts would comprise the buyer's total monthly loan obligation. Most home loans, though, consist of loan-to-value ratios (LTV) greater than 80%. Lenders consider these loans a higher risk and, as such, commonly require the buyer to add the following to the basic loan payment, thereby establishing the total monthly financial obligation:

- One month's property tax
- One month's hazard insurance
- One month's mortgage insurance (PMI or MIP)
- One month's HOA (if applicable)

This type of monthly loan payment is technically known as a budget mortgage, though in many real estate circles, it's often called the PITI (principal, interest, taxes, insurance) payment.

CALCULATION OF PRINCIPAL AND INTEREST LOAN PAYMENT

As reviewed previously, calculating a monthly principal and interest payment established by amortized loans requires two pieces of information: the *loan principal* (amount borrowed) and the *factor* (the dollar amount charged by the lender, depending on the interest rate, for each $1,000 borrowed). The amortized monthly payment is then calculated by dividing the loan principal by 1,000 and then multiplying that result by the factor:

loan ÷ 1,000 × factor = principal and interest payment

EXAMPLE A loan's principal is $275,000 with a 30-year loan factor of $4.77. Calculate an amortized principal and interest payment.

1. $275,000 ÷ 1,000 = 275
2. 275 × $4.77 = $1,311.75 principal and interest payment

If the borrower was purchasing a $345,000 home with this $275,000 loan, that represents a 79% LTV ($275,000 ÷ $345,000), in which case the $1,311.75 may constitute the complete monthly loan payment for the buyer (because the LTV is less than 80%, the DP is more than 20%).

But what if the buyer was using this $275,000 loan to purchase a $310,000 home? Now, the LTV is close to 90% ($275,000 ÷ $310,000), which represents a higher risk for a lender who would now require to borrower to set up a budget mortgage or PITI payment. So, the buyer would have to add a month's worth of property tax, hazard insurance, and mortgage insurance to the principal and interest payment of $1,311.75.

For the ***property tax and hazard insurance*** portions, the calculation is simply done by dividing the annual charge for these items by 12.

EXAMPLE $4,200 annual property tax ÷ 12 = $350 per month

$1,200 annual hazard insurance policy ÷ 12 = $100 per month

Private mortgage insurance (PMI)—A conventional loan (without government backing) with an LTV of more than 80% requires private mortgage insurance (PMI). The cost for this insurance varies depending on the loan's risk factor.

Typically, the higher the LTV, the higher the risk factor, and the higher the risk factor, the higher the cost for the PMI. Using a loan of $275,000 to purchase a $310,000 home produces an LTV of 89%. If this same loan were used to purchase a $290,000 home, the LTV would be almost 95% ($275,000 ÷ $290,000), putting this loan in a higher risk category. Calculating the monthly PMI is a two-step process.

First, the loan principal is multiplied by a certain percentage established by the insurance company and adjusted to the risk of a loan, to calculate an annual PMI premium. Second, the annual premium is divided by 12 in order to find the monthly PMI charge. As examples:

89% LTV (lower risk): $275,000 × .0040 = $1,100 ÷ 12 = $91.67

95% LTV (higher risk): $275,000 × .0069 = $1,897.50 ÷ 12 = $158.12

Mortgage insurance premium (MIP)—This insurance is required for all FHA loans because these loans are insured for private lenders by the government and offer extremely attractive LTVs of 96.5%, which inherently makes them a more risky venture. MIP in FHA loans is substantially more costly than PMI for conventional loans. Unlike PMI, which is only assessed monthly, MIP requires an up-front premium at settlement, which may be rolled into the buyer's overall loan amount, and a monthly premium for the borrower. The up-front premium is calculated as 1.75% of the loan principal, and the monthly assessment is currently 0.85% (0.0085) of the loan principal, which includes the rolled in up-front premium. As an example, let's continue to use a loan of $275,000.

First, to roll the up-front mortgage premium for FHA into the loan, use the following calculation:

$275,000 × 1.75% = $4,812.50 + $275,000 = $279,812.50 (total loan)

Then, calculate the annual MIP:

$279,812.50 × 0.0085 = $2,378.41

Next, calculate the monthly MIP:

$2,378.41 ÷ 12 = 198.20

NOTE To calculate an amortized payment of principal and interest for this FHA loan applying the same 30-year factor of $4.77:

$279,812.50 ÷ 1,000 = $279.8125 × $4.77 = $1,334.71

Summary

Here are calculations using the numbers from the above examples:

PITI: Conventional Loan

Principal and interest (P&I)	$1,311.75
Property tax	$350.00
Hazard insurance	$100.00
PMI	$91.67
Total payment	$1,853.42

PITI: FHA Loan (purchase price of $285,000 with 96.5% LTV)

Principal and interest (P&I)	$1,334.71
Property tax	$350.00
Hazard insurance	$100.00
MIP	$198.20
Total payment	$1,982.91

BUYER'S ESCROW AT SETTLEMENT

Through a budget mortgage, the homeowner's PITI payment allows the lender to accumulate monthly sums of property tax and hazard and mortgage insurance. These funds are held in the lender's escrow account and used to cover the borrower's ongoing financial obligations in these areas. This escrow is actually set up at the closing when the lender requires the new property owner to deposit additional monies in such an account. The Real Estate Settlement Procedures Act (RESPA) regulates the amount that the lender can collect in advance from the buyer to establish this escrow account.

Hazard insurance escrow: If the closing occurs on the first day of the month, and the borrower's first payment becomes due on the first day of the following month, the lender may collect two months of hazard insurance to establish the escrow account. If the closing occurs on any other day of the month, the buyer's first loan payment will skip a month, and at closing, the lender may collect three months of hazard insurance to deposit in the escrow account. FHA and VA loans typically may require four months of hazard insurance from the borrower at closing to establish the escrow.

Mortgage insurance escrow: This is equal to two months' escrow of PMI and MIP at closing, which the lender requires from the borrower, although sometimes this initial MIP deposit may be passed over.

Property tax escrow: At the time a property's annual taxes become due, RESPA provides that a lender may have on hand in an escrow account an amount equal to a full year's property tax plus an additional reserve of two months. This allowance or limitation (depending on your point of view), along with the due date of the borrower's first loan payment, determines the exact number of monthly tax payments the lender may require that party to deposit in escrow at closing.

IN PRACTICE Assume that taxes are due for the calendar year on September 1. That property is sold and closes on January 31, which means that the buyer's first budget loan payment (PITI) will be due on March 1. So, the new homeowner will make six payments before the September 1 property tax due date (March, April, May, June, July, August). RESPA, then, would allow the lender to collect eight monthly property tax payments from the buyer at closing on January 31 to establish the property tax escrow account. Why eight? Because as of September 1, the lender will have collected 6 such payments from the borrower's monthly PITI, and the 8 collected at closing adds up to the 14 such payments (a full year plus 2 reserve months) allowed the lender under the law.

MATH CONCEPTS

Calculating Property Tax Escrow

To determine how many months of property taxes a lender may require from the borrower to establish such an escrow account at closing first requires an understanding that because these taxes become due for the calendar year, federal law allows the lender to have deposited in an escrow account an amount equal to 14 monthly payments of this tax. Next, beginning with the month the borrower's initial loan payment is due, count the number of months up to, but not including, the month the taxes are due. Then, subtract that number of months from 14, and the resulting number of months will equal those the lender may collect from the buyer at settlement.

Math Principles

A closing for a property takes place October 15, and the taxes are due every year on July 1. In addition to the homebuyer's PITI payment, a lender may require the homebuyer to deposit how many months of property taxes in an escrow account at closing?

Step 1: Because the closing takes place on October 15, the buyer's first monthly payment is due on December 1. So count December, January, February, March, April, May, and June to determine that seven months of property taxes have been collected by the lender before the due date for these taxes on July 1.

Step 2: Subtract those 7 months from 14 to calculate the 7 months the lender may collect to establish the borrower's property tax escrow account at closing.

EXAMPLE The sale of property in which the annual taxes of $5,400 are due on May 1 of the calendar year closes on March 1. If the lender requires the buyer to set up a budget mortgage, how many months of property taxes must this borrower deposit in an escrow account at the settlement, and what will be the sum of such funds?

Step 1: Because the closing takes place on March 1, the buyer's first monthly payment is made on April 1. Count only May to determine that just 1 month of property tax will be collected before the May 1 due date for the annual tax.

Step 2: Subtract that 1 month from 14 to calculate the 13 months of property taxes the borrower will be required to deposit to establish the lender's escrow account at the settlement.

Step 3: Divide $5,400 by 12 to calculate a monthly tax amount of $450, and then multiple $450 by 13 months to calculate an escrow deposit sum of $5,850.

ESTIMATION FORMS: PURCHASER'S COST/SELLER'S NET

Unless a real estate licensee in Georgia is also a practicing attorney, a broker or an affiliated licensee will never conduct a closing in the state. Likewise, a licensee will not prepare a Loan Estimate or a Closing Disclosure, which allocates the costs of the transaction for and between the buyer and the seller. Nonetheless, an ability to apply those calculations that prorate prepaid and accrued sums, that assess the transfer and intangible tax, and that determine a buyer's monthly loan payment and escrow requirements allows the licensee to provide a superior level of service—that is, to prepare a form that realistically estimates for purchasers how much cash they will need to close the transaction and what the total monthly loan payment will be, and for sellers to reasonably estimate their net proceeds from the settlement. In representing a buyer or a seller, a real estate licensee may be called upon by the client to estimate the answers to these two questions on more than one occasion.

IN PRACTICE A seller-client may commonly ask the licensee to estimate the projected net proceeds from the property sale in the following circumstances:

1. **At the time of the listing agreement:** As discussed in the brokerage engagement section of the previous unit, presenting a comparative market analysis (CMA) during a listing presentation provides an objective credibility to a licensee's price suggestions for marketing the seller's home. That credibility may be further validated through the efforts of a licensee to prepare a Net Estimate form for the seller. At the end of the day, an acceptable home sale for that seller may depend on whether that contract price satisfies the "walk away cash" anticipated from the transaction.
2. **At the time the seller receives an offer:** An offer to purchase allows a Net Estimate form to be more accurate for the seller in its calculations. In preparing the form at this time, a licensee may better assist a seller in deciding whether to accept an offer or to prepare a counteroffer that may still satisfy the seller's monetary goal.
3. **Between contract and closing:** A licensee may prepare a final version of this form for a seller, once all contract contingencies have been satisfied, and the contract becomes a binding agreement. At this point the Net Estimate should come reasonably close to what will appear on the formal Closing Disclosure form.

   A licensee preparing an Estimated Purchaser Cost form provides the buyer with an idea of the out-of-pocket funds needed to close, as well as a look at the total monthly loan payment. These calculations help keep home purchasers grounded as to how much cash on hand they will actually need to close and confirm the reality of the sum needed to pay the reoccurring monthly loan note. Especially for first-time homebuyers, the numbers on this form often far exceed what they might expect. As is the case with the Net Estimate form for the seller, a licensee may prepare the Estimated Purchaser Cost form for a client in more than one circumstance.
4. **At the time of entering into a buyer brokerage engagement:** Before beginning a property search for a client, a licensee not only should know a purchaser's affordable price range but also make sure the buyer will be comfortable with how much money is needed to close and with what the actual monthly loan obligations demand. Even at this early stage before starting the home search, preparing an Estimated Purchaser Cost form can lessen the chance of buyers getting in over their heads.
5. **At the time of making an offer:** Though some costs are still unknown, with an offer at hand, the Estimated Purchaser's Cost form becomes more specific in showing the buyer how much cash may be needed for the commitment and what may be expected as to the monthly house payment.
6. **Between contract and closing:** After the purchaser makes formal application for a loan with a binding agreement on a specific property and has been given the Loan Estimate by the lender, a final Estimated Purchaser Cost form should come reasonably close to what will appear on the final settlement statement.

Whenever preparing seller net or purchaser cost forms, no matter at what stage of the brokerage engagement process, a licensee should continue to emphasize to clients that the forms are estimates only and that they may be subject to unanticipated changes in existing expenses or in the inclusion of additional costs. Inevitably, such exposure leaves the parties a little more relaxed and less overwhelmed when they actually take their seats at the closing table. Moreover, if possible, a licensee should ask for a copy of the Closing Disclosure before closing in order to review the numbers a final time. Avoiding, or at least minimizing, surprises at the closing table stabilizes blood pressure for all present.

Now we shall look at two typical estimation forms used by Georgia licensees in working with their seller-clients or buyer-clients. After reviewing the forms, we will review completed forms based on the sales transaction between the sellers (Bernadette and Sean Joyce) and the purchasers (Sebastian and Miranda Scott) that we studied in an earlier unit.

PREPARING NET TO SELLER FORM

All category and line references that follow refer to those in the Estimated Net to Seller form.

FIGURE 26.14: Estimated Net to Seller Form

ESTIMATED NET TO SELLER

Seller: ______________________ Date of Estimate: ____________
Property Address: ______________________ Estimated Closing Date: ________
______________________ Prepared By: ____________

1. **Estimated Purchase Price** ______________________ $ ______

SELLER'S LOAN/PAYOFF EXPENSES
2. First Loan Balance ____________
3. Accrued Interest On First ____________
4. Second Loan Balance ____________
5. Accrued Interest On Second ____________
6. Loan Penalty(s) ____________
7. Other ____________ ____________
8. Total Estimated Loan Expenses ______________________
9. Gross Equity ______________________

TRANSACTION COSTS
10. Closing Costs ____________
11. Unpaid Property Tax Proration ____________
12. Repairs ____________
13. Assessments/Other Liens ____________
14. Brokerage Fee ____________
15. Transfer Fee On Loan Assumption ____________
16. Survey ____________
17. Purchase Money Mortgage ____________
18: Other Home Warranty ____________ ____________
19. Total Estimated Transaction Costs ______________________

SUMMARY LINE
20. Gross Equity Less Costs ______________________

CREDITS
21. Seller's Escrow Refund ____________
22. Prepaid Property Tax Proration ____________
23. Homeowner's Insurance Refund ____________
24. Personal Property ____________
25. Other ____________
26. Total Estimated Credits to Seller ______________________

ESTIMATE SUMMARY
27. Estimated Cash To Seller ______________________

THIS ESTIMATE IS BASED ON INFORMATION AVAILABLE AT TIME OF PRESENTATION. NO REPRESENTATION, IMPLIED OR EXPRESSED, IS MADE TO THE ACCURACY OF THIS ESTIMATE.

______________________ ______________________

Seller's Signature Seller's Signature

Basic Data

This first section at the top of the form identifies the seller, the address of the property, the date of the estimate, and the licensee preparing the estimate. Also included are the projected closing date and the property tax due date, essential information for prorating accuracy.

Line 1: Estimated Purchase Price: All subsequent calculations for this estimate flow from this beginning number on line 1 of the form, which establishes a gross credit for the seller.

Seller's Loan Payoff Expenses: Items in this category are debited to the seller and deducted from the gross credit identified on line 1.

Line 2: The loan's principal balance as of the last payment made by the seller.

Line 3: Interest accrued on the loan from the day of the last payment through closing day (loan balance × interest rate = annual interest ÷ 360 or 365 = per diem × number of accrued days).

Note: Lines 2 and 3 are also applicable for a seller's existing loan to be assumed by the purchaser, because loan assumptions and any accrued interest on the loan from the last payment are debited to the seller as if the seller were paying if off from the proceeds of the sale.

Lines 4 and 5: Same as lines 2 and 3 if the seller's payoff also involves a second loan.

Line 6: Penalty assessments to the seller regarding loan payoff, such as a failure to notify the lender or a prepayment penalty that may or may not apply, depending on the terms of the promissory note between the lender and the borrower. Prepayment penalties are prohibited on FHA and VA loans.

Line 8: The total of lines 2–7 indicates the total loan payoff expense for the seller.

Line 9: The amount shows the existing gross credit for the seller after subtracting the payoff expenses on line 8 from the purchase price credit on line 1.

Transaction Costs

Items in this category identify any costs (debits) to the seller relating to the sale itself.

Line 10: The seller's contribution to closing costs as indicated in the purchase and Sale Contract. The sum may include any costs associated with the buyer's loan (including title insurance policies) and attorney fees (including title examination).

Line 11: A prorated amount debited to the seller for the calendar days beginning on January 1 through the day of closing (annual taxes ÷ 365 = per diem × number of prorated days).

Line 12: A debit that includes invoices from contractors and vendors who made repairs (or provided material for those repairs) as negotiated in the contract between the buyer and the seller, and who agreed to be paid for such work from funds at the sale's closing.

Line 13: Items that may currently represent a cloud on the property title and need to be taken care of by the seller before closing.

Line 14: The brokerage fee, typically calculated as a percentage of the contract sales price.

Line 15: Also referred to as an assumption fee that is assessed by the lender when the seller's existing loan is assumed. It is negotiable as to which party pays this fee.

Line 16: A new survey of property, if required by the lender or negotiated for by the purchaser. The cost may also be included as part of line 10, the seller's contribution to closing costs.

Line 17: Owner financing in which the seller is debited for any loans given directly to the purchaser so that party may complete the sales transaction. As such, a PMM is also credited to the buyer.

Line 18: Any additional cost for the seller.

Line 19: Add lines 10–18.

Summary Line

Line 20: Remaining credit for the seller after subtracting line 19 from line 9.

Credits

Line 21: Any leftover funds deposited by the seller into the lender-required escrow account to cover ongoing property expenses, including annual taxes, hazard insurance, and mortgage insurance.

Line 22: If the property taxes for the calendar year have already been paid, the seller is credited at closing (debit to purchaser) for prorated days beginning on the day after closing through December 31.

Line 23: Because this policy is paid a year in advance, the seller will be credited by the insurance company (or the buyer, if assuming seller's policy) for the prorated days beginning the day after closing and ending on the last day of the policy (annual policy ÷ 365 = per diem × number of days prorated = amount credited).

Line 24: If the transaction involves the buyer's purchasing any of the seller's personal property in the home, the seller is credited for that purchase amount.

Line 25: Any miscellaneous credit to the seller.

Line 26: Add lines 21–25.

Estimate Summary

Line 27: Add lines 20–26.

PREPARING ESTIMATED PURCHASER COSTS FORM

All category and line references that follow refer to the Estimated Purchaser Cost form.

FIGURE 26.15: Estimated Purchaser Costs Form

ESTIMATED PURCHASER COSTS

Seller: ______________________ Date of Estimate: __________
Property Address: ______________________ Estimated Closing Date: __________
______________________ Prepared By: __________

DOWN PAYMENT
1. Purchase Price ______
2. Amount of New Loan(s) And/Or Loans Assumed ______
3. Cash Down Payment (Line 1 minus Line 2) ______

FINANCING EXPENSES
4. Closing Costs ______
5. Loan discounts ______
6. Transfer Fee on Loan Assumption ______
7. Other (Intangible Tax)______ ______
8. Total Estimated Loan Expenses______

PREPAID ITEMS/MISCELLANEOUS COSTS
9. Prepaid Property Tax Proration ______
10. 1 Year Hazard Insurance or Insurance Proration ______
11. Interest Adjustment On New Loan ______
12. Personal Property ______
13. Other (Transfer Tax) ______ ______
14. **Total Estimated Prepaid/Miscellaneous Costs**______

ESCROW ITEMS
15. Purchase of Seller's Escrow Account (L /A Only) ______
16. Tax Escrow (___) Months ______
17. Hazard Insurance Escrow (__) Months ______
18. PMI Escrow (__) Months ______
19. **Total Estimated Escrow Items**______

SUMMARY LINE
20. **Estimated Funds Needed** ______

CREDITS
21. Earnest Money Deposit ______
22. Unpaid Property Tax Proration ______
23. Accrued Interest On Loan Assumed ______
24. Other ______ ______
25. **Total Estimated Credits**______

ESTIMATE SUMMARY
27. **Estimated Cash Needed to Close**______
A. Principal and Interest ______
B. Property Tax ______
C. Hazard Insurance ______
D. PMI ______
E. **Total Estimated Monthly Payment** ______

THIS ESTIMATE IS BASED ON INFORMATION AVAILABLE AT TIME OF PRESENTATION. NO REPRESENTATION, IMPLIED OR EXPRESSED, IS MADE TO THE ACCURACY OF THIS ESTIMATE.

______________________ ______________________

Purchaser's Signature Purchaser's Signature

Basic Data

The top of the form identifies the purchaser, the property address, the date of the estimate and the licensee preparing the estimate. Also included is the estimated closing date and the type of loan (including the terms of the loan) with which the property will be purchased.

Down Payment

Line 1: Contract price.

Line 2: The loan type impacts this calculation. For a conventional loan or PMM (purchase money mortgage from the seller), the buyer's purchase price will be multiplied by the loan-to-property-value ratio (SP × LTV = LA). For an FHA loan, the sales price is almost always multiplied by the maximum LTV for that loan, which is 96.5% (SP × 96.5% = LA). Commonly added to the initial loan amount is the 1.75% UFMIP, the up- front premium for the FHA loan (LA × 1.75% = UFMIP + LA = total FHA loan). A VA loan is calculated as 100% × SP. If the buyer is assuming the seller's loan, the exact balance as of the last payment will be shown on this line.

Line 3: The cash down payment (sales price – loan amount).

Financing Expenses

Line 4: This amount will be calculated by subtracting any seller contributions to the closing cost from the total sum of these costs.

Line 5: This is a prepaid fee to the lender in exchange for lowering the interest rate on the buyer's new loan. Each discount point amounts to 1% of the loan amount. The fee may be included in the line 4 closing costs and may be paid as part of the seller's contribution to the cost of the transaction.

Line 6: This amount may also be included as part of line 4 and negotiated for the seller to pay.

Line 7: This amount is assessed on all new loans (new loan(s) principal ÷ 500 (if not an even amount, round up to next dollar) × $1.50).

Line 8: Add lines 4–7.

Prepaid Items/Miscellaneous Costs

Line 9: An amount debited to the purchaser only if the seller has prepaid taxes for the calendar year. Count the number of days starting with day after closing through December 31. Then multiply this prorated number by the daily property tax to calculate the amount of debit to the purchaser.

Line 10: Amount prepaid at closing.

Line 11: Prorated days of Interest prepaid to the lender for the day of closing through the last day of the closing month. Next use this calculation:

> loan principal × interest rate = annual interest ÷ 360 (or 365) = per diem × number of days prorated = amount of prepaid/adjusted interest

Line 12: Non–real property items purchased from seller.

Line 13: The transfer tax, an amount assessed whenever title is transferred in a real property sale (sales price – any loan assumed ÷ 100, if uneven amount, round up to next dollar × 0.10).

Line 14: Add lines 9–13.

Escrow Items

Line 15: This amount is debited only if the purchaser assumes the seller's existing loan and purchases the remaining escrow account, along with the loan assumption.

Line 16: The number of months of prorated property tax the buyer is required to deposit in the lender escrow account at closing. That number, added to PITI payments the lender has collected before the tax due date, equals the 14 months of property tax the lender is allowed by law to have on hand in escrow when the property tax becomes due.

Line 17: This is 2–4 months depending on the loan type and the day of the first loan payment.

Line 18: Two months' mortgage insurance.

Line 19: Add lines 15–18.

Summary Line

Line 20: Estimated Funds Needed: line 3 + line 8 + line 14 + line 19.

Credits

Line 21: An amount as indicated in the contract.

Line 22: An amount credited here only if the calendar year property taxes have yet to be paid at closing. The count for the prorated tax days starts on January 1 and goes through closing day.

Line 23: If the purchaser is assuming the seller's existing loan, interest on that loan will be prorated from the last day the seller made a loan payment through closing day. The purchaser will be credited those days of loan interest, while the seller will be debited those same days.

Line 24: Any miscellaneous credits.

Line 25: Add lines 21–24.

Estimated Summary

Line 26: Estimated Cash Needed to Close: line 20 – line 25.

Estimated Monthly Payment

A. Loan principal ÷ 1,000 × factor ($ charge per $1,000 of loan)
B. Annual property tax ÷ 12
C. Annual hazard insurance ÷ 12
D. Loan principal × PMI % (given in problem ÷ 12
E. A + B + C + D

SELLER NET/PURCHASER COST EXERCISES

These first exercises uses information taken from the contract for the purchase and sale of residential real property reviewed in the previous unit.

Seller: Bernadette and Sean Joyce

Date of Estimated Net to Seller: May 10, 20xx

Prepared by: Eric Cambridge, licensee affiliate for Top Floor Realty

Property address: 1103 Franklin Avenue; Bellville, Georgia 33333

Purchaser: Sebastian and Miranda Scott

Date of Estimated Purchase Costs: May 13, 20xx

Prepared by: Lucy Gordon, licensee affiliate for Eureka Real Estate Services

Contract sales price: $399,000

Closing date: June 15, 20xx

Annual property tax: $4,800

Due date: October 1; use 365 days for proration

Brokerage fee: 6% of sales price

The Estimated Net to Seller Exercise

Seller's hazard insurance policy: $950

Anniversary date: November 1; use 365 days to compute prorated day of policy

Seller's existing loan balance: $225,000, as of last payment on June 1

Interest rate: 4.75%; use 360-day calendar to compute loan interest proration

Lender escrow account balance: $1,350

Seller contribution to closing: $4,000

Seller cost for new home warranty: $450

The Estimated Cost to Buyer Exercise

Buyer's earnest money: $4,000

Buyer's new loan: Conventional 90% LTV @ 4.25%; loan factor of $4.92 per $1,000

PMI % used is 0.0039 (.39%)

Buyer's annual hazard insurance: $1,200

Buyer closing costs: $2,500

Transfer tax and intangible tax: Paid by buyer

FIGURE 26.16: Completed Estimated Net to Seller Form

ESTIMATED NET TO SELLER

Seller: Bernadette/Sean Joyce Date of Estimate: May 10
Property Address: 1103 Franklin Ave. Estimated Closing Date: June 15
Bellville, GA 33333 Prepared By: Eric Cambridge

LOAN TYPE: Conventional Interest Rate: 4.75% Term: 30 Yrs
Property Tax: $4,800
Due Date: Oct. 1

1. **Estimated Purchase Price**		**$399,000.00**
SELLER'S LOAN/PAYOFF EXPENSES		
2. First Loan Balance	$225,000.00	
3. Accrued Interest On First	$ 445.31	
4. Second Loan Balance		
5. Accrued Interest On Second		
6. Loan Penalty(s)		
7. Other		
8. Total Estimated Loan Expenses		$225,445.31
9. Gross Equity		$173,554.69
TRANSACTION COSTS		
10. Closing Costs	$ 4,000.00	
11. Unpaid Property Tax Proration	$ 2,183.02	
12. Repairs		
13. Assessments/Other Liens		
14. Brokerage Fee	$ 23,940.00	
15. Transfer Fee On Loan Assumption		
16. Survey		
17. Purchase Money Mortgage		
18. Other Home Warranty	$450.00	
19. Total Estimated Transaction Costs		**$ 30,573.02**
SUMMARY LINE		
20. Gross Equity Less Costs		**$142,981.67**
CREDITS		
21. Seller's Escrow Refund	$ 1,350.00	
22. Prepaid Property Tax Proration		
23. Homeowners Insurance Refund	$ 359.18	
24. Personal Property		
25. Other		
26. Total Estimated Credits to Seller		**$ 1,709.18**
ESTIMATE SUMMARY		
27. Estimated Cash To Seller		**$144,690.85**

THIS ESTIMATE IS BASED ON INFORMATION AVAILABLE AT TIME OF PRESENTATION. NO REPRESENTATION, IMPLIED OR EXPRESSED, IS MADE TO THE ACCURACY OF THIS ESTIMATE.

Line 1: $399,000 is the contract purchase price

Line 2: $225,000 is the seller's loan balance as of the last payment

Line 3 calculation: $225,000 × 0.0475 = $10,687 ÷ 360 = $29.6875 × 15 (June 1–15) = $445.31

Line 8 calculation: $225,000 + $445.31 = $225,445.31

Line 9 calculation: $399,000 – $225,445.31 = $173,554.60

Line 10: $4,000 seller's contribution to closing costs

Line 11 calculation: \$4,800 ÷ 365 = \$13.1507 × 166 (days counted from January 1 to June 15) = \$2,183.02

Line 14 calculation: \$399,000 × 0.06 = \$23,940

Line 18: \$450 seller payment for buyer's home warranty

Line 19 calculation: \$4,000 + \$2,183.02 + \$23,940 + \$450 = \$30,573.02

Line 20 calculation: \$173,554.69 (line 9) – \$30,523.02 (line 19) = \$142,981.67

Line 21: \$1,350 represents the balance in the lender's escrow account that is credited to seller

Line 23 calculation: \$950 ÷ 365 = \$2.6027 × 138 (days counted from June16 through October 31, the last day of annual policy) = \$359.18

Line 26 calculation: \$1,350 + \$359.18 = \$1,709.18

Line 27 calculation: \$142,981.67 (line 20) + \$1,709.18 (line26) = \$144,690.85

The Estimated Purchaser Costs Exercise

FIGURE 26.17: Completed Estimated Purchaser Costs Form

ESTIMATED PURCHASER COSTS

Seller: Sebastian/Miranda Scott ____________ Date of Estimate: May 13 ______
Property Address: 1103 Franklin Ave. ____________ Estimated Closing Date: June 15 ___
Bellville, GA 33333 ____________ Prepared By: Lucy Gordon ______

LOAN TYPE: Conventional Interest Rate: 4.25% Term: 30 Yrs

DOWN PAYMENT		
1. Purchase Price	$399,000	
2. Amount of New Loan(s) And/Or Loans Assumed	$359,100	
3. Cash Down Payment (Line 1 minus Line 2)		$39,900
FINANCING EXPENSES		
4. Closing Costs	$2,500	
5. Loan discounts		
6. Transfer Fee on Loan Assumption		
7. Other (Intangible Tax)	$1,078.50	
8. Total Estimated Loan Expenses		$3,578.50
PREPAID ITEMS/MISCELLANEOUS COSTS		
9. Prepaid Property Tax Proration		
10. 1 Year Hazard Insurance or Insurance Proration	$1,200	
11. Interest Adjustment On New Loan	$678.30	
12. Personal Property		
13. Other (Transfer Tax)	$399	
14. **Total Estimated Prepaid/Miscellaneous Costs**		**$2,277.30**
ESCROW ITEMS		
15. Purchase of Seller's Escrow Account (L /A Only)		
16. Tax Escrow (12_) Months	$4,800	
17. Hazard Insurance Escrow (2_) Months	$200	
18. PMI Escrow (2_) Months	$233.42	
19. Total Estimated Escrow Items		**$5,233.42**
SUMMARY LINE		
20. Estimated Funds Needed		**$50,989.22**
CREDITS		
21. Earnest Money Deposit	$4,000	
22. Unpaid Property Tax Proration	$2,183.02	
23. Accrued Interest On Loan Assumed		
24. Other		
25. Total Estimated Credits		**$6,183.02**
ESTIMATE SUMMARY		
26. Estimated Cash Needed to Close		**$44,806.20**
A. Principal and Interest	$1,766.77	
B. Property Tax	$400	
C. Hazard Insurance	$100	
D. PMI	$116.71	
E. **Total Estimated Monthly Payment**	**$2,383.48**	

THIS ESTIMATE IS BASED ON INFORMATION AVAILABLE AT TIME OF PRESENTATION. NO REPRESENTATION, IMPLIED OR EXPRESSED, IS MADE TO THE ACCURACY OF THIS ESTIMATE.

Line 1: $399,000 contract purchase price

Line 2 calculation: $399,000 × 0.90 = $359,100

Line 3 calculation: $399,000 – $359,100 = $39,900

Line 4: $2,500 debit to the buyer for closing costs (remember the seller's contribution of $4,000 on the Estimated Net to Seller form)

Line 7 calculation: $359,100 ÷ $500 = $718.20, rounded up to $719 × $1.50 = $1,078.50

Line 8 calculation: $2,500 + $1,078.50 = $3,578.50

Line 10: Prepayment of $1,200 for the annual hazard insurance policy on the home

Line 11 calculation: $359,100 × 0.0425 = $15,261.75 ÷ 360 = $42.3938 × 16 (prorated days from June 15 to June 30) = $678.30

Line 13 calculation: $399,000 ÷ 100 = 3,990 × 0.10 = $399

Line 14 calculation: $1,200 + $678.30 + $399 = $2,277.30

Line 16 calculation: The purchaser's first loan payment is August 1, which means the purchaser will make only 2 escrow property tax payments (PITI) before the annual tax due date of October 1. Because the lender is allowed by law to collect 14 payments (1 year + 2 months in reserve) before the tax due date, the 2 payments already made as of October 1 are subtracted from the 14 allowed, which equals 12 months or 1 year for a total of $4,800 that may be collected for escrow at closing.

Line 17 calculation: $1,200 (annual) ÷ 6 = $200 or 2 months that may be collected for escrow at closing

Line 18 calculation: $359,100 × 0.0039 = $1,400.49 ÷ 12= $116.71 (1 month PMI) × 2 = $233.42

Line 19 calculation: $4,800 + $200 + $233.42 = $5,233.42

Line 20 calculation: $39,900 (line 1) + $3,578.50 (line 8) + $2,277.30 (line 14) + $5,233.40 (line 20) = $50,989.22

Line 21: $4,000 is buyer's earnest money deposit

Line 22 calculation: $4,800 ÷ 365 = $13.1507 × 166 (days counted from January 1 to June 15) = $2,183.02

Line 25 calculation: $4,000 + $2,183.02 = $6,183.02

Line 26 calculation: $50,989.22 – $6,183.02 = $44,806.20

Line A. calculation: $359,100 ÷ $1,000 = 359.1 × $4.92 (factor) = $1,766.77

Line B. calculation: $4,800 ÷ 12 = $400

Line C. calculation: $1,200 ÷ 12 = $100

Line D. calculation: $359,100 × 0.0039 = 1400.49 ÷ 12 = $116.71

Line E. calculation: $1,766.77 + $400 + $100 + $116.71= $2,383.48

The breakdown of numbers on the Estimated Net to Seller is not substantially altered if a purchaser uses an FHA or VA loan, rather than a conventional loan for the transaction. These government-backed loans do, however, allow and even anticipate larger contributions from the seller toward the transaction's costs, and that reality may somewhat impact the final net sum the seller will realize from the sale.

The cost estimate, though, for a purchaser using FHA or VA financing can look appreciably different from one involving a conventional loan. To illustrate this point, let's examine two Estimated Purchaser Costs forms: one in which the buyer is getting an FHA loan to purchase the home at 1103 Franklin Avenue for $399,000; the other in which a VA loan is used to buy the property for $399,000.

Note: On these two forms where the numbers are not impacted by the loan type, the figures remain the same as in the previous exercise. The interest rate for both types of loans will remain at 4.25%, with a loan factor of 4.92 per $1,000.

FIGURE 26.18: FHA Loan Completed

ESTIMATED PURCHASER COST

Purchaser: ______________________ Date of Estimate: ____________
Property Address: ______________________ Estimated Closing Date: __________
______________________ Prepared By: ______________

LOAN TYPE: FHA Interest Rate: 4.25% Term: 30 Yrs

DOWN PAYMENT
1. Purchase Price $399,000____________
2. Amount of New Loan(s) And/Or Loans Assumed $385,035 + $6,738 = $391,773
3. Cash Down Payment (Line 1 minus Line 2) **$ 13,965**

FINANCING EXPENSES
4. Closing Costs 0____________
5. Loan discounts ____________
6. Transfer Fee on Loan Assumption ____________
7. Other (Intangible Tax)____________ ____________
8. Total Estimated Loan Expenses____________0

PREPAID ITEMS/MISCELLANEOUS COSTS
9. Prepaid Property Tax Proration ____________
10. 1 Year Hazard Insurance or Insurance Proration $1,200____________
11. Interest Adjustment On New Loan $729.88____________
12. Personal Property ____________
13. Other (Transfer Tax) ____________ ____________
14. **Total Estimated Prepaid/Miscellaneous Costs**____________**$1,929.88**

ESCROW ITEMS
15. Purchase of Seller's Escrow Account (L /A Only) ____________
16. Tax Escrow (12_) Months $4,800____________
17. Hazard Insurance Escrow (4_) Months $400____________
18. PMI Escrow (_) Months ____________
19. Total Estimated Escrow Items____________**$5,200**

SUMMARY LINE
20. Estimated Funds Needed ____________**$21,094.88**

CREDITS
21. Earnest Money Deposit $4,000____________
22. Unpaid Property Tax Proration $2,183.02____________
23. Accrued Interest On Loan Assumed ____________
24. Other ____________ ____________
25. Total Estimated Credits____________**$6,183.02**

ESTIMATE SUMMARY
26. Estimated Cash Needed to Close____________**$14,911.86**
A. Principal and Interest $1,927.66____________
B. Property Tax $400____________
C. Hazard Insurance $100____________
D. PMI/MIP $277.50____________
E. **Total Estimated Monthly Payment** **$2,705.16**____________

THIS ESTIMATE IS BASED ON INFORMATION AVAILABLE AT TIME OF PRESENTATION. NO REPRESENTATION, IMPLIED OR EXPRESSED, IS MADE TO THE ACCURACY OF THIS ESTIMATE.

Line 2 calculation: $399,000 × 96.5% = $385,035. Remember, the FHA loan requires the borrower to pay an up-front MIP premium or 1.75% of loan, which is almost always financed into the basic loan amount, rather than paid in cash at closing. $385,035 × 1.75% = $6,738 + $385,035 = $391,773 (total loan amount)

Line 3 calculation: $399,000 – $385,035 = $13,965. Note that to calculate this down payment, the loan amount of $385,035 applies. From this point on, all other calculations involving the loan will use the full loan of $391,773, to which the UFMIP has been added.

Line 4: As mentioned above, as compared with transactions involving conventional loans, those with an FHA loan commonly find a seller making a greater financial contribution to the closing costs. Assume such is the case in this scenario, where the seller has agreed to pay all fixed closing costs for the transaction, as well as the transfer and intangible taxes. The buyer will cover all prepaid and escrow items.

Line 11 calculation: Here the interest adjustment is calculated on the buyer's full loan. $391,773 × 0.0425 = 16,650.352 ÷ 365 (365 days common for FHA) = 45.6174 × 16 (June 15–30) = $729.88

Line 14 calculation: $1,200 + $729.88 = $1,929.88

Line 20 calculation: $13,965 + $1,929.88 + $5,200 = $21,094.88

Line 26 calculation: $21,094.88 – 6,183.02= $14,911.86

Estimated Monthly Payment

A. $391,773 ÷ $1,000 = 391.8 × 4.92 (factor) = 1,927.66
B. $4,800 ÷ 12 = $400
C. $1,200 ÷ 12 = $100
D. $391,773 × 0.0085 (% for monthly MIP) = 3,330 ÷ 12 = $277.50
E. $1,927.66 + $400 + $100 + $277.50 = $2,705.16

IN PRACTICE Primarily because of the elevated cost of mortgage insurance, including the up-front MIP premium, note that the monthly payment to buy this home is approximately $320 more than in a conventional loan with the same interest rate. On the other hand, cash out of pocket to purchase this home with an FHA loan is some $30,000 less. Lower out-of-pocket costs make the FHA loan a prime financing option for first-time homebuyers. Because FHA loan limits vary depending on the overall property values in particular parts of the country, using this type of loan to purchase a $399,000 property, as in our scenario, applies to areas where general property values approach the higher ends of these government-backed loan limits.

FIGURE 26.19: VA Loan Completed

ESTIMATED PURCHASER COST

Purchaser: ________________ Date of Estimate: ________
Property Address: ________________ Estimated Closing Date: ________
________________ Prepared By: ________

LOAN TYPE: VA Interest Rate: 4.25% Term: 30 Yrs

DOWN PAYMENT

1. Purchase Price	$399,000	
2. Amount of New Loan(s) And/Or Loans Assumed	$399,000	
3. Cash Down Payment (Line 1 minus Line 2)		**0**

FINANCING EXPENSES

4. Closing Costs	0	
5. Loan discounts		
6. Transfer Fee on Loan Assumption		
7. Other (Intangible Tax)	$1,197	
8. Total Estimated Loan Expenses		$1,197

PREPAID ITEMS/MISCELLANEOUS COSTS

9. Prepaid Property Tax Proration		
10. 1 Year Hazard Insurance or Insurance Proration	$1,200	
11. Interest Adjustment On New Loan	$743.34	
12. Funding Fee	$8,500	
13. Personal Property		
14. Other		
15. **Total Estimated Prepaid/Miscellaneous Costs**		**$10,443.34**

ESCROW ITEMS

16. Purchase of Seller's Escrow Account (L /A Only)		
17. Tax Escrow (12_) Months	$4,800	
18. Hazard Insurance Escrow (2_) Months	$200	
19. PMI Escrow (_) Months		
20. Total Estimated Escrow Items		**$5,000**

SUMMARY LINE

21. Estimated Funds Needed		**$16,640.34**

CREDITS

22. Earnest Money Deposit	$4,000	
23. Unpaid Property Tax Proration	$2,183.02	
24. Accrued Interest On Loan Assumed		
25. Other		
26. Total Estimated Credits		**$6,183.02**

ESTIMATE SUMMARY

27. Estimated Cash Needed to Close		**$10,457.34**
A. Principal and Interest	$1,963.08	
B. Property Tax	$400	
C. Hazard Insurance	$100	
D. PMI		
E. **Total Estimated Monthly Payment**	**$2,463.08**	

THIS ESTIMATE IS BASED ON INFORMATION AVAILABLE AT TIME OF PRESENTATION. NO REPRESENTATION, IMPLIED OR EXPRESSED, IS MADE TO THE ACCURACY OF THIS ESTIMATE.

Lines 2 and 3: Because a VA loan allows a 100% LTV, the $399,000 loan amount is equal to the $399,000 sales price, resulting in a zero down payment. Remember though that this 100% LTV applies to the contract price or the appraised value, whichever is lower. So if the appraisal does not at least equal the contract price, the loan would be made on the lower appraised value. Consequently, unless the seller agreed to lower the price of the home, the borrower would have to come up with the difference in cash as a down payment.

Line 4: As in the scenario with FHA financing, the seller will pay all fixed transaction costs for the closing and the transfer tax, but not for the intangible tax.

Line 7 calculation: \$399,000 ÷ 500 = 798 × \$1.50= \$1,197

Item 11 calculation: \$399,000 (new loan) × 4.25% = 16,957.50 ÷ 365 (lender choice) = 46.4589 (daily interest) × 16 days (June 15–30) = \$743.34

Item 12: Fee paid by the borrower-veteran to the VA in turn for the VA guaranteeing the loan for the lender. The funding fee is calculated as a percentage of the loan, typically between 2% and 3% of that sum. With this loan, it is \$8,500.

Line 15 calculation: \$1,200 (line 10) + \$743.34 (line 11) + \$8,500 (line 12) = \$10,443.34

Line 17: \$400 × 12 months = \$4,800

Line 18: \$100 × 2 months = \$200

Line 21 calculation: \$1,197 (line 8) + \$ 10,443.34 (line 15) + \$5,000 (line 20) = \$16,640.34

Line 27 calculation: \$16,640.34 – \$6,183 = \$10,457.34

Estimated Monthly Payment

A. \$399,000 ÷ \$1,000 = 399 × 4.92 (factor) = \$1,963.08
B. \$400
C. \$100
D. None for a VA loan
E. \$2,463.08

The final scenario will exam the Estimated Purchaser Costs form and the Estimated Net to Seller form in a circumstance where the property owner becomes actively involved in the buyer's financing. In this case, 1103 Franklin Avenue is under contract for \$399,000 to a purchaser with a substantial sum of cash and whose financing consists of an assumption of the seller's existing loan, as well as a purchase money mortgage (PMM), a new loan given to the buyer from the seller. As before, the closing date, the property tax, and the hazard insurance, including due dates and prorations, remain the same.

FIGURE 26.20: Loan Assumption PMM

ESTIMATED PURCHASER COSTS

Purchaser: ______________________ Date of Estimate: ______________
Property Address: ______________________ Estimated Closing Date: __________
______________________ Prepared By: ______________

LOAN TYPE: Loan Assumption & PMM

DOWN PAYMENT

1. Purchase Price	$399,000	
2. Amount of New Loan(s) And/Or Loans Assumed	$225,000 & $100,000 = $325,000	
3. Cash Down Payment (Line 1 minus Line 2)	**$74,000**	
FINANCING EXPENSES		
4. Closing Costs	$2,500	
5. Loan discounts		
6. Transfer Fee on Loan Assumption	$750	
7. Other (Intangible Tax)	$300	
8. Total Estimated Loan Expenses		$3,550
PREPAID ITEMS/MISCELLANEOUS COSTS		
9. Prepaid Property Tax Proration		
10. 1 Year Hazard Insurance or Insurance Proration	$359.18	
11. Interest Adjustment On New Loan	$263.01	
12. Personal Property		
13. Other (Transfer Tax)	$174	
14. **Total Estimated Prepaid/Miscellaneous Costs**		**$796.19**
ESCROW ITEMS		
15. Purchase of Seller's Escrow Account (L /A Only)	$1,350	
16. Tax Escrow (12_) Months		
17. Hazard Insurance Escrow (2_) Months		
18. PMI Escrow (_) Months		
19. Total Estimated Escrow Items		**$1,350**
SUMMARY LINE		
20. Estimated Funds Needed		**$79,696.19**
CREDITS		
21. Earnest Money Deposit	$4,000	
22. Unpaid Property Tax Proration	$2,183	
23. Accrued Interest On Loan Assumed	$445.31	
24. Other		
25. Total Estimated Credits		**$6,628.31**
ESTIMATE SUMMARY		
26. Estimated Cash Needed to Close		**$73,067.88**
A. Principal and Interest	$1,435.50	
B. Property Tax	$400	
C. Hazard Insurance	$19.17	
D. PMI	$75.00	
E. **Total Estimated Monthly Payment**	**$1,989.67 + $600 (PMM) = $2,589.67**	

THIS ESTIMATE IS BASED ON INFORMATION AVAILABLE AT TIME OF PRESENTATION. NO REPRESENTATION, IMPLIED OR EXPRESSED, IS MADE TO THE ACCURACY OF THIS ESTIMATE.

Line 2: Two loans are involved: the seller's existing loan, with a balance of $225,000 as of the last payment on June 1, and the new loan, a purchase money mortgage for $100,000 given from the seller to the buyer. Added together, the loans total $325,000.

Line 3 calculation: $399,000 – $225,000 = $74,000

Line 4: $2,500 paid by the buyer; represents the total of closing costs for this transaction and is much lower than usual because this transaction does not include a loan from a private lender

Line 6: $750 lender fee for the buyer to assume the seller's loan

Line 7 calculation: There is one new loan in this transaction, the $100,000 PMM, so that is only amount subject to the intangible tax.

$100,000 ÷ 500 = 200 × 1.50 = $300

Line 8 Calculation: $2,500 + $750 + $300 = $3,550

Line 10 calculation: Along with the loan, the buyer will also assume the seller's current hazard insurance policy, which costs $950 and renews annually on November 1. To count the prorated days, begin the day after closing on June 16 and end on the last day of the policy, October 31, for a total of 138 days.

$950 ÷ 365 = $2.6027 daily × 138 days = $359.18

Line 11 calculation: Interest adjustment on the new loan of $100,000 from the seller, who is charging 6% simple interest for financing.

$100,000 × 0.06 = $6,000 ÷ 365 (seller's choice here) = $16.4384 × 16 days = $263.01

Note: The loan is prorated just as a new loan from a private lender would be.

Line 13 calculation: Remember the transfer tax is figured on the sales price less any assumable loan. So,

$399,000 – $225,000 = $174,000 ÷ 100 = 1,740 × 0.10 = $174

Line 14 calculation: $359.18 (line 10) + $263.01 (line 11) + $174 (line 13) = $796.19

Line 15: $1,350 escrow balance connected to the loan assumption of $225,000

Line 20 calculation: $74,000 (line 1) + $3,550 (line 2) + $796.19 (line 14) + $1,350 (line 19) = $79,696.19

Line 22 calculation: $4,800 ÷ 365 = $13.1507 per diem. Count January 1 to June 15 for 166 days. 166 × 13.1507 = $2,183.02

Line 23 calculation: The balance of the loan assumed as of the last payment is $225,000, which carries an interest rate of 4.75%.

$225,000 × 0.0475 = 10,687.50 ÷ 360 (lender's choice) = $29.6875 × 15 = $445.31

Remember, this a loan assumption, so the buyer will make that payment as normal on July 1 (no skipping a month). The July 1 payment includes interest in arrears for June. Because the seller owned the property through June 15, the seller will be debited for June 1–15 at the closing, which is a credit to the purchaser.

Line 26 calculation: $79,796.19 – $6,628.31 = $73,067.88

Estimated Monthly Payment

The seller's current loan payment was calculated on a principal borrowed of \$275,000 with a loan factor of \$5.22 per \$1,000 (based on 4.75% interest rate). So,

> \$275,000 ÷ 1,000 = 275 × \$5.22 (factor)= \$1435.50 as the P&I + \$400 (1 month property tax) + 79.17 (\$950 ÷ 12 = 1 month insurance) + \$75 (\$225,000 × 0.0040 PMI % = 900 ÷ 12 = \$75 for 1 month PMI) = \$1,989.67, assumed loan monthly payment
>
> PMM: \$100,000 ÷ 1000= 100 × \$6.00 per \$1,000 (factor for loan at 6% interest) = \$600 monthly payment (no PITI here for a PMM, just P&I).

So the total monthly payment for the buyer is \$1,989.67 + \$600= \$2,589.67

FIGURE 26.21: Estimated Net to Seller Loan Assumption PMM

ESTIMATED NET TO SELLER

Seller: ______________________ Date of Estimate: __________
Property Address: ______________________ Estimated Closing Date: __________
______________________ Prepared By: __________

1. **Estimated Purchase Price**		\$399,000
SELLER'S LOAN/PAYOFF EXPENSES		
2. First Loan Balance Assumption	\$225,000	
3. Accrued Interest On First	\$445.31	
4. Second Loan Balance		
5. Accrued Interest On Second		
6. Loan Penalty(s)		
7. Other ______		
8. Total Estimated Loan Expenses		\$225,445.31
9. Gross Equity		\$173.554.69
TRANSACTION COSTS		
10. Closing Costs		
11. Unpaid Property Tax Proration	\$2,183.02	
12. Repairs		
13. Assessments/Other Liens		
14. Brokerage Fee	\$23,940.00	
15. Transfer Fee On Loan Assumption		
16. Survey		
17. Purchase Money Mortgage	\$100,000	
18: Other ______		
19. Total Estimated Transaction Costs		**\$126,123**
SUMMARY LINE		
20. Gross Equity Less Costs		**\$47,431.69**
CREDITS		
21. Seller's Escrow Refund	\$1,350	
22. Prepaid Property Tax Proration		
23. Homeowner's Insurance Refund	\$359.18	
24. Personal Property		
25. Other Adjust Interest on PMN ______	\$263.01	
26. Total Estimated Credits to Seller		**\$1,972.19**
ESTIMATE SUMMARY		
27. Estimated Cash To Seller		**\$49,403.88**

THIS ESTIMATE IS BASED ON INFORMATION AVAILABLE AT TIME OF PRESENTATION. NO REPRESENTATION, IMPLIED OR EXPRESSED, IS MADE TO THE ACCURACY OF THIS ESTIMATE.

Line 2: $225,000 represents the loan assumption as a debit to the seller; effectively, treated the same as though the seller were paying off this sum to a lender. Instead, the seller is turning over this sum to the buyer to assume. Remember that on the Estimated Purchaser Cost form, the assumption was treated as a credit to the buyer because the sum was going toward the total purchase price.

Line 3 calculation: $225,000 × 0.0475 = 10,687.50 ÷ 360 = 29.6875 × 15 = $445.31. This is the same as though the seller were paying this accrued interest to the lender. Instead, the seller is paying it to buyer who is assuming the loan.

Line 8 calculation: $225,000 + $445.31 = $225,445.31

Line 9 calculation: $399,000 – $225,445.31 = $173,554.69

Line 11 calculation: $4,800 ÷ 265 = $13.1507 per diem. Count January 1 to June 15 for 166 days. 166 × $13.1507 = $2,183.02

Line 14 calculation: $399,000 × 0.06 = $23,940

Line 17: $100,000, new loan (PMM) the seller is giving to the buyer

Line 19 calculation: $2,183.02 + $23,940 + $100,000 + $126,123

Line 20 calculation: $173,554.69 (line 9) – $126,123 (line 19) = $47,431.69

Line 21: Escrow refund from buyer's purchase of this fund from seller

Line 23: $359.18, amount given to the seller as a refund for the insurance policy the buyer is assuming for the rest of the policy year. See the Estimated Purchaser Costs summary in this transaction for the calculation of this sum.

Line 25 calculation: Interest adjustment for the new loan of 100,000 at 6% interest that the buyer is receiving from the seller.

> $100,000 × 0.06 = $6,000 ÷ 365 (seller's choice) = $16.4385 × 16 (June15–30) = 263.01

Line 26 calculation: $1,350 + $359.18 + $263.01 = $1,972.19

Line 27 calculation: $47,431.69 (line 20) + $1,972.19 (line 26) = $49,403.88

UNIT 26 QUIZ

1. Which of the following statements is *TRUE* regarding the Georgia Residential Mortgage Fraud Act?
   a. Violations under this statute are considered misdemeanors, subject to fines of up to $10,000 for multiple convictions.
   b. Real estate licensees may be subject to this statute only if they actively participate in the fraudulent activities.
   c. Conspiracy to commit fraud must be proven for any violations under this law.
   d. Georgia law defines mortgage fraud as a racketeering activity by the parties involved.

2. Under Georgia's foreclosure laws, the sale of a defaulted borrower's property
   a. may not occur until a court order authorizes such a sale.
   b. may result in the defaulted borrower receiving funds from the proceeds of the sale.
   c. will effectively transfer equitable title to the party who makes the winning bid for the property at the auction sale.
   d. may take place only after the property is advertised for 14 days in the newspaper serving as the legal organ in the county where property is located.

3. In a loan underwriter's evaluation of a borrower's ability to afford the monthly loan payment, the front-end ratio for a budget mortgage is calculated by dividing the borrower's
   a. total monthly income by the monthly loan payment.
   b. principal and interest payment by that party's total monthly income.
   c. total PITI payment by that party's total monthly income.
   d. total monthly debt obligations by that party's total monthly income.

4. A valid and enforceable security deed in Georgia would require which of the following provisions?
   a. Identification of the borrower as the grantor and the lender as the grantee
   b. Proper witnessing by two official parties
   c. Identification of the borrower as the mortgagor and the lender as the mortgagee
   d. Effective delivery of the deed to the grantee, exclusively

5. In the period from contract to closing, a listing agent might provide which of the following services for a buyer who is a customer?
   a. Recommend a home inspector that the agent believes is the fairest and most professional in this line of work.
   b. Inform the buyer of previously unknown evidence of a termite issue that has developed on the property.
   c. Advise the buyer of the specific legal consequences if the buyer fails to perform one of the terms of the contract.
   d. Help the purchaser arrange for a homeowners hazard insurance policy required by the buyer's lender.

6. In updating a seller on the progress of a buyer's loan contingency, the listing agent might disclose to the client what specific type of information?
   a. That in addition to securing the loan with terms that match the contract's financial contingency, the buyer also is seeking another home loan for the property with more favorable terms
   b. That the buyer has decided to make loan application with two separate lenders
   c. That the buyer, though not required by the lender, has chosen to make a larger down payment to lower the monthly payment
   d. That the lender has approved the buyer for a 90% loan, not the 95% loan indicated in the terms of the contract's financial contingency

7. Commonly in Georgia, a licensee affiliate attends the closing in what primary capacity?
   a. To make certain that commission checks are distributed according to the terms of the contract exhibit form
   b. As the agent of the party in the transaction with whom they are working
   c. As a representative of the licensee's broker
   d. As an unofficial witness to sign the deed that transfers title

8. Which of the following closing documents would normally serve as evidence of the specific debt owed to the lender by the borrower?
   a. Security deed
   b. Mortgage
   c. Promissory note
   d. Warranty deed

9. The closing attorney will sometimes have a party sign a quitclaim deed before or at the closing. A common use of such a deed in Georgia may include
   a. adding a name to an existing deed that includes other grantee(s).
   b. indicating a claim, such as an easement, that the seller may retain upon the closing of the property.
   c. transferring property between family members by a document that does not have to be notarized or witnessed.
   d. relinquishing a spouse's interest in a property when the seller's divorce is pending.

10. When a binding agreement for the purchase and sale of real property is created, the MOST immediate concern for a licensee involved in the transaction would be to
   a. verify that the attorney identified in the contract is available to close the transaction on the date of settlement, as stipulated in that agreement.
   b. confirm that all parties subject to the transaction are clear on the time frames for any contract stipulations and conditions.
   c. deliver a complete signed copy of the agreement to the buyer and the seller, as well as to the licensee's broker.
   d. complete the commission conformation exhibit, verified and signed by all agents involved in the transaction.

11. After receiving a copy of the contract for purchase and sale, an attorney begins the closing process by
   a. verifying the source of funds for the transaction by contacting the buyer's lender or, absent a financial contingency, confirming such funds held by the buyer.
   b. arranging for the title examination of the property legally identified in the contract for purchase and sale.
   c. having the seller sign an owner's affidavit in which the property owner swears there are no unsatisfied liens, assessments, or encumbrances against the property other than those identified by the title.
   d. confirming that a title insurance policy will be purchased for the lender that the attorney will represent in the transaction.

12. The sale of a home closes on August 22, and the property taxes of $3,840 have already been paid for the calendar year of January 1 to December 31. How much of these prorated taxes would be credited to the seller and debited to the buyer at settlement? Use 365 days for prorating the days.
   a. $1,515.37
   b. $1,378.19
   c. $2,325.00
   d. $2,462.43

13. When a buyer assumes a property owner's existing loan as part of the purchase price, that loan balance appears on a settlement estimate form as
   a. a credit to the seller and a debit to the buyer.
   b. only a credit to the buyer.
   c. only a debit to the seller.
   d. a credit to the buyer and a debit to the seller.

14. A real estate transaction closes on November 30, and the seller prepays $1,000 annually for a hazard insurance policy. If the renewal date for that policy every year is May 10, what will be the prorated credit to the seller for that policy at settlement? Use 365 days for the proration.
   a. $435.61
   b. $441.09
   c. $443.83
   d. $438.36

15. Unpaid property taxes for the calendar year would show up on the Estimated Net to Seller form as a

a. credit to the seller.
b. debit to the buyer.
c. credit to the buyer.
d. debit to the seller.

16. Which of the following indicators of income would a lending underwriter generally classify as an acceptable source of income for determining a loan applicant's qualifying ratios?

a. A 1099 form showing self-employment income
b. A Social Security statement
c. A W-2 form showing a one-time company bonus payment
d. An inheritance of $5,000 from an estate

17. A homebuyer's purchase price includes a loan for $175,000, with an interest rate of 7%. If the property closes on March 17, how much prepaid/adjusted interest would the buyer owe the lender at closing? Use 360 for prorating days.

a. $510.42
b. $504.86
c. $477.75
d. $471.21

18. Which of the following statements is *TRUE* regarding a real estate closing in Georgia that involves a cash sale?

a. Because the closing attorney does not represent a lender, the attorney may give legal advice to either the buyer or the seller at the settlement.
b. The closing attorney will represent whichever party arranges the settlement day and time.
c. The closing attorney would not represent either buyer or seller.
d. The closing attorney may represent either party in the transaction.

19. A buyer paid $185,000 using a maximum LTV for an FHA loan. How much intangible tax would be due on this transaction?

a. $185.00
b. $555.00
c. $537.00
d. $535.57

20. If the annual property tax bill of $2,800 has not been paid as of settlement day on May 10, how much are the prorated taxes and how will this sum be assigned to the buyer and the seller? Use 365 days for prorations.

a. $989.58 will be debited to the seller and credited to the buyer
b. $989.58 will be credited to seller and debited to the buyer
c. $997.27 will be credited to the seller and debited to the buyer
d. $997.27 will be debited to the seller and credited to the buyer

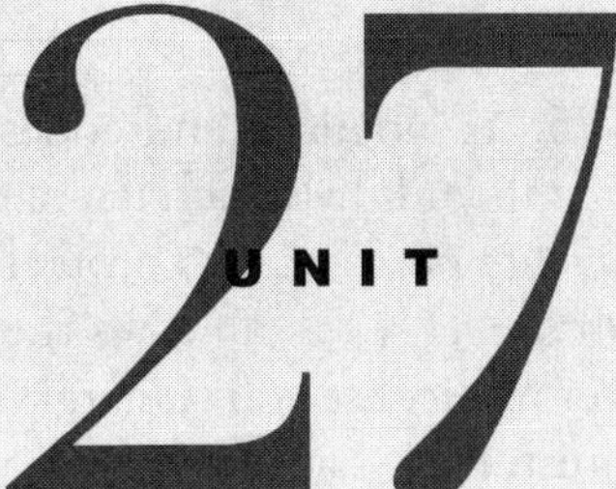

UNIT 27

Real Estate Commission and License Law

LEARNING OBJECTIVES

After successfully completing this course you will be able to

- **recognize** the terminology, rules, responsibilities and composition of the real estate commission;
- **describe** the regulations, procedures and processes for acquiring and maintain a real estate license;
- **explain** the business practices, operations, relationships needed to open and operate a real estate brokerage; and
- **describe** prohibited practices, disciplinary procedures and the role of the Real Estate Education, Research, and Recovery Fund.

KEY TERMS

affiliation agreement
associate broker
applicant
bank
blind ad
brokerage agreement
candidate for licensure
cease and desist order
citations
commission
commissioner
community association management license (CAM)
declaratory ruling
Disposition of Unclaimed Property Act
Fair Business Practice Act
fidelity bond insurance
firm
franchise name
franchisee
franchisor
Georgia Administrative Procedures Act
Georgia Criminal History Report (GCIC)
an instructional hour
lawful presence notarized affidavit
licensee
person
policy and procedures manual
property management services
qualifying broker
real estate (in Georgia)
Real Estate Education, Research, and Recovery Fund
reciprocity agreement
rules and regulations
salesperson
sanctions
sponsoring broker form
sole proprietorship
statutory overnight delivery
surrendering a license
unfair trade practices
Uniform Deceptive Trade Practice Act

DEFINITIONS: TERMINOLOGY OF LAWS AND RULES

43-40-1; 520.1-.02

As written and adopted by the state legislature in 1925, its language and codes revised over time, Georgia Real Estate License Law sets standards by which licensees perform their duties, as well as regulating the real estate profession to protect the public from unethical and incompetent agents. Statute 43-40 establishes the Real Estate **Commission** as the authoritative body over all licensees in Georgia, with the power to pass **rules and regulations** to administer the Law. In carrying out this legislative mandate, the Commission issues real estate licenses, sets fees, and, takes disciplinary action against licensees who violate the Laws and Rules. The Commission is not, however, empowered to intervene in the settlement of disputes between real estate licensees.

In this unit references to Georgia Real Estate License Law may be described as *Laws*, while references to the Commission's Rules and Regulations may be described as *Rules*.

The following terms, as used in this unit, provide in their definitions, a context that offers some insight into the spirit and intent of the License Law and the Commission Rules and Regulations.

An **associate broker**: A person acting on behalf of a real estate broker in performing any act authorized in this unit to be performed by a broker

An **applicant**: Any person who has completed all of the requirements for a license or an approval as set forth in O.C.G.A. 43-40 and in Commission Rules and Regulations (520-1), and who has submitted a complete application on the proper form accompanied by the correct fee.

A **bank**: Any financial institution regulated by a member of the federal financial institutions examination council, and authorized to provide federally insured checking accounts

Blind ad: Real estate advertisement placed by an affiliated licensee that fails to disclose the name of the employing broker as it is registered with the Commission

A broker: Any person who, for another, and who, for a fee, commission, or any other valuable consideration, or with the intent or expectation of receiving the same from another

- negotiates or attempts to negotiate, or assists in procuring prospects for the listing, sale, purchase, exchange, renting, lease, or option for any real estate or of the improvements thereon;
- holds himself or herself out as a referral agent for the purpose of securing prospects for the listing, sale, purchase, exchange, renting, lease, or option for any real estate; collects or attempts to collect rents, assessments, or other trust funds
- is employed by or on behalf of an owner(s) of lots, or other parcels of real estate at a salary, fee, or commission, or any other valuable consideration to sell such real estate or any part thereof;

- engages in the business of charging or contracting for the collecting of an advance fee, other than an advertising fee, in connection with any contract that undertakes primarily to promote the sale of real estate either through its listing in a publication issued primarily for such purpose, or for referral of information concerning such real estate to brokers, or both;
- auctions, offers to auction, or agrees to auction real estate;
- buys or offers to buy, sells or offers to sell, or otherwise deals in options to buy real estate;
- performs property management services or community association management services;
- provides or attempts to provide to any party to a real estate transaction consulting services designed to assist the party in the negotiations or procurement of prospects for the listing, sale, purchase, exchange, renting, lease, or option for any real estate thereon; or
- advertises or holds himself or herself out as engaged in any of the foregoing.

A **brokerage agreement**: An express written contract wherein the client promises to pay the real estate broker a valuable consideration, or agrees that the real estate broker may receive a valuable consideration from another as a result of the broker producing a seller, buyer, tenant, or landlord ready, able, and willing to sell, buy, or rent the property, or as a result of the broker performing property management or community association management services.

A brokerage engagement: As pertains to BRRETA (the Brokerage Relationship in Real Estate Transactions Act), the term in this unit identifies specific engagements including an exclusive listing contract, an open listing contract, a buyer's broker agreement, a property management agreement, a community association management agreement, and an exclusive tenant representation contract.

A brokerage relationship: Likewise defined under BRRETA, both agency and non-agency relationships formed by a broker; though the term used in this unit also makes reference to that fact that both these relationships occur as a consequence of the brokerage engagement.

A buyer: Purchaser, a person who acquires or attempts to acquire an interest in real estate

A **candidate for licensure**: Any person who has not yet successfully completed, but is in the process of completing, the requirement for licensure or approval as set forth in O.C.G.A. 43-40 and in Commission Rules and Regulations (520-1)

A client: Likewise as defined in BRRETA, a person who has entered into a brokerage engagement with a real estate broker

Commission: The Georgia Real Estate Commission

Commissioner: Hired by Commission members, the CEO of that government entity

Community association: An owner organization of a residential or mixed use common interest realty association in which membership is mandatory as a result of ownership within the development; such developments may include condominiums, cooperatives, homeowner associations, timeshares, lot divisions with restrictions in management, and other forms of common interest or planned development where a common management is present.

Community association manager: Person who acts on behalf of a real estate broker in providing only community association management services

Community association management services: Managerial or administrative services provided in exchange for valuable consideration, involving the operation of community association affairs, including but not limited to

- collecting, controlling and disbursing association funds;
- obtaining insurance;
- arranging for and coordinating maintenance to association property; and
- otherwise overseeing the day-to-day operations of the association.

A customer: Likewise as defined in BRRETA, a person who has not entered into a brokerage engagement with a broker but for whom a broker may perform ministerial acts

A dual agent: Likewise as defined in BRRETA, a broker who in the same real estate transaction simultaneously represents both the buyer and seller in a brokerage relationship

A **firm**: Any real estate business entity, including but not limited to a corporation, partnership, limited liability company, and sole proprietorship

A **franchise name**: Any name, the use of which requires permission from another who has an existing and continuing right in the trade name by virtues of any state or federal law

A **franchisee**: A firm licensee authorized to use a franchisor's trade name as part of or in conjunction with the licensee firm's name

A **franchisor**: A business entity owning a trade name whose use by others is controlled and authorized by the owner of the trade name

An **instructional hour**: A time period of instruction or other learning activity of at least 50 minutes in duration

A **licensee**: Any person who holds a real estate license as a broker, associate broker, salesperson, or community association manager

Ministerial acts: Those acts that the broker or an affiliated licensee performs for a person that do not require discretion or the exercise of judgment by the licensee

A person: Either an individual(s) or a firm

Property management services: In exchange for valuable consideration, marketing services provided to another including referring prospective tenants, leasing, physical, administrative, and financial maintenance, and overall management or supervision of these real property services pursuant to a property management agreement

Purchaser: see Buyer

Real Estate: An interest or estate in land, whether corporeal or incorporeal, freehold or non-freehold, in state or out of state, including condominiums, leaseholds, and mobile homes with the necessary service connections to be used as dwellings permanently attached to the land

A **salesperson**: Any person, other than an associate broker, who acts on behalf of a real estate broker in performing any act authorized to be performed by the broker in this unit

Statutory overnight delivery: Delivery of a document through the U. S. Postal Service or through a commercial firm which is regularly engaged in the business of document and/or package delivery in which the sender

- directs that the delivery be not later that the next business day following the day on which the document is received for delivery by the U.S. Postal Service or commercial firm, and
- receives a receipt acknowledging receipt of the document signed by addressee or an agent of the addressee.

Timely: A reasonable time under the particular circumstances

ORGANIZATION AND OPERATION OF COMMISSION

43-40-2 through 7 and 13; 520.1-.01; 520.1-.03

The Georgia Real Estate Commission (GREC) is comprised of six persons appointed by the governor and confirmed by the Georgia Senate. Commission members serve five-year staggered terms. Five of the six members must be actively licensed and residents of Georgia for the five years prior to appointment. The sixth member may have no connection to the real estate industry and serves on the Commission as a consumer advocate. If a vacancy on the Commission occurs, the governor fills that unexpired term, with no Senate confirmation required for that new member. Moreover, the governor has the authority to remove a Commission member for incompetence, dishonest conduct, and for an inability to perform duties, or negligence in that performance.

The Commission meets at least monthly and, at its first session of the year, will elect by secret ballot a chair and vice chair. Each commission member will receive a $25 stipend for each scheduled meeting, in addition to actual and necessary travel expenses to such meetings. As a Georgia governmental agency, the Real Estate Commission is set up as budget unit assigned to the office of the Secretary of State. However, the Commission receives no tax money from the state for its operational expenses. Furthermore, in its authorization to set fees for licensees, these charges must always approximate the total cost of the Commission's operation. Fees collected are deposited in the state treasury, and are used to pay the expenses of the Commission.

To serve as the Chief Executive Officer, (though not as a Commission member) the Commission hires a Real Estate **Commissioner** who conducts the day-to-day operations of the department, but has no voting interest in decisions made by commission members. The Commissioner is a full time government employee of good moral character, whose authority, delegated by the Commission, includes the hiring of a support staff. The Commissioner or any of that individual's staff are prohibited from holding an active real estate license, so any such licenses currently held must be placed on inactive status.

In its efforts to effectively administer License Law {O.C.G.A. 43-40}, the Rules and Regulations passed by the Commission may clarify or further explain the intent of this statute, though these authorized additions must always be based on the License Law, and may not conflict with that statute, nor create any new law. The Commission will utilize an official seal to authenticate written actions.

To certify a five-year license history, the Commission will maintain records on every licensee for that period of time and provide a copy of such records to any person making a written request. If disciplinary action has been taken against a licensee, such records may be available for the prior 15 years. Moreover, if formal discipline has been imposed including any payments made from the Commission's Recovery Fund, records for this licensee will be kept for 40 years.

Whenever an agent's license is surrendered, revoked, or suspended, the licensee must return the wall certificate and pocket license card to the Commission (absent any refundable license fees). If this licensee is a broker with affiliates, the licenses of those affiliates must be returned to the Commission as well.

By submitting a written, notarized application to the Commission, a person may request the following:

- To appear at a Commission meeting;
- That the Commission repeal or amend an existing Rule; the commission will respond within 30 days by either approving the petition, or showing cause for denial; and
- That the Commission issues a **declaratory ruling** as to whether some component of a Law or Rule applies to a particular situation

LICENSING LAWS

43-40-14 and 15

In its requirement for the licensing of real estate agents, the state of Georgia seeks to ensure that successful license applicants have the necessary professional competence and integrity to reliably serve the public. Moreover, this licensure serves as a basis for the Commission's enforcement of Laws, Rules and Regulations whose violations may result in the Commission censuring, suspending, or revoking that offending agent's license.

ACTING WITHOUT A LICENSE

43-40-31

Acting as a real estate broker, associate broker, salesperson, or community association manager without a real estate license undermines the basic intent of Laws and Rules. Notwithstanding any of the exemptions listed below as provided under 43-4-29, any person practicing a real estate related act as defined in paragraph (2) of Georgia Code 43-40-1, without a license, has committed a misdemeanor under the law. As such, the Real Estate Commission can issue a **cease and desist order** that becomes final ten days after issuance unless the party charged requests a hearing. The Commission is authorized to impose a fine up to $1,000 for each day such a violation continues.

EXCEPTIONS TO LICENSURE

43-40-29

The requirement for holding a broker, salesperson, or community association manager license does not apply to the following.

1. Property owners and their spouses, general partners in a limited partnership, a prospective buyer, landlord or tenant (or their full time employees) when any of the above mentioned buy, sell or lease property for their own purposes. A manager of a federally subsidized residential apartment complex, whose work began prior to 1989, is also included in this category.
2. An authorized attorney-in-fact, acting on behalf of the owner
3. An attorney at law, who, as part of regularly offered legal services, provides brokerage services
4. A person acting under court order or under the authority of a legal instrument, including a receiver, trustee in bankruptcy, executor, administrator, or guardian.
5. An government officer or employee performing official duties
6. A public or private utility company employee acting on behalf of that employer
7. Any person who as owner, employed full time by the owner, or as owner of a property management company that holds a controlling interest in the property, provides property management or community association management services.
8. A full time community association manager hired by that community's Homeowners Association
9. A person acting as a referral agent, as long as that party receives no referral fee from the party being referred; does not charge an advance fee; and does not act as a referral agent more than three times a year
10. A broker's unlicensed employee, hired to provide property management services under the authority of the broker, where such services are limited to:
    - delivering lease document;
    - receiving lease documents, security deposits, and rental payments;
    - showing rental units and under the broker's supervision, executing leases and rental agreement;
    - providing authorized information about a rental unit, lease application or lease;
    - giving a tenant information about the tenant's security deposit or rental payments; or
    - performing administrative acts authorized by the broker
11. The manager of a property with occupancy periods shorter than 90 days (aka, the innkeeper's exemption) as long as:
    - the manager has a written agreement with the owner
    - the manager does not execute any leases
    - applicable zoning laws permit short term occupancy
    - no deposit exceeds the rent for the minimum rental period
    - the guest pays all applicable taxes on the accommodations
    - the manager may specify rooms or units the guest will occupy
    - the manager does not impose an extra charge for utilities

— a guest need not give notice to vacate an accommodation
— the room or unit is not the guest's primary residence

12. The manager of a community association who is also a resident of the community, who does not manage any other properties
13. A person who only performs physical maintenance on the property
14. A CPA or accountant performing those duties relevant to that profession

LICENSE CATEGORIES AND REQUIREMENTS

43-40-8, 10 and 11; 520-1-.04(2)

A Broker may perform any real estate brokerage act that requires a real estate license in Georgia. The broker may operate independently in a **sole proprietorship** or as a **qualifying broker** of a firm that contracts with licensee affiliates. The Real Estate Commission will issue a broker's license in the name of the firm as well as one in the name of the qualifying broker. Qualifications for an applicant to receive a Broker's license are as follows:

- Be at least 21 years old (an applicant can take the broker's examination as early as the age of 20, but may not activate the license until age 21)
- Be a resident of Georgia unless the applicant qualifies for non-resident status
- Be a high school graduate or hold an equivalent certificate
- Satisfy all statutory requirements regarding any past criminal convictions
- Maintain an active real estate license for at least three of the last five years prior to filing an application
- Complete a Commission approved 60 instructional hours broker course, or furnish evidence of completion of an authorized educational equivalent (such as college real estate courses)
- Pass the real estate broker state examination

Licensing requirements for an **Associate Broker** are identical to those for a Broker's license. Though an associate broker may perform any service delegated to a broker, that licensee has not assumed the responsibilities of contracting directly with consumers, rather preferring to work as a licensee affiliate of another broker.

If an applicant for a Broker or Associate Broker license wants to use the licensure experience gained in another state, but is unable to produce a certified copy of such records in that state, the Commission may accept the following documentation in lieu of those records:

- A confirmation that the applicant obtained the necessary experience within ten years prior to making application in Georgia, and;
- A certification from the former licensing jurisdiction confirming that the applicant was licensed at some time during the prior ten years, Or
- The applicant produces affidavits related to transactions in which the applicant participated from a broker with whom the applicant was affiliated

A broker's affiliate who holds a license of a **salesperson**, may only act on behalf of a broker, and may perform in this capacity any real estate brokerage activity. Qualifications to receive the salesperson license are as follows:

- Be at least 18 years old,
- Be a resident of Georgia unless the applicant qualifies for non-resident status,
- Be a high school graduate or hold an equivalent certificate,

- Satisfy all statutory requirements regarding any past criminal convictions,
- Complete a Commission approved 75 instructional hours salesperson's course, or its authorized equivalent (such as college real estate courses), and
- Pass the real estate salesperson state examination.

A **Community Association Management license** (CAM license) does not permit the holder to assist in the sale or purchase of real property. Rather, this real estate license limits the holder, who works on behalf of a broker, to offering services particularly related to managing homeowner's associations, such as residential subdivisions or condominium complexes. Qualifications to receive this CAM license are as follows:

- Be at least 18 years old,
- Be a resident of Georgia unless the applicant qualifies for non-resident status,
- Be a high school graduate or hold an equivalent certificate,
- Satisfy all statutory requirements regarding any past criminal convictions
- Complete a Commission approved 25 instructional hours community association management course, or its authorized equivalent (such as a real estate college course), and
- Pass the real estate community association management state examination.

IN PRACTICE Only schools and instructors approved by the Real Estate Commission may offer and teach pre license courses for broker, salesperson, and community association management licenses.

The Commission will grant a broker's license to a corporation, partnership, or limited liability company under the following conditions:

- The firm must name a person who holds a broker's license as the Qualifying Broker
- Every person who acts as a licensee for the firm must hold a real estate license
- The Qualifying Broker must assure that the firm and its affiliated licensees comply with all Laws, Rules, and Regulations
- The Qualifying Broker must be authorized to bind the firm to any settlement of a contested lawsuit before the Commission.

Each real estate license is affixed with seal of the Real Estate Commission and will be delivered or mailed to the acting broker who has custody and responsibility for such licenses. The sales affiliate will receive a copy of the license in the form of a pocket card.

NONRESIDENT LICENSES

43-40-9; 520-1-.05(6)

The Real Estate Commission may grant nonresidents who do not hold a real estate license in their state, a Georgia license as long as that person meets the age, education, and examination required under Georgia License Law. That nonresident must also affiliate with a broker licensed in Georgia. A nonresident holding a real estate license in another state may also acquire a Georgia license by meeting requirements as determined by the Commission that include the following:

- Show proof of licensure in the applicant's state of residence, providing copies of records showing any disciplinary actions

- Pay any required fees
- Sign a statement confirming the applicant has read and agrees to follow Georgia License Law and the Commission's Rules and Regulations
- Sign an affiliation agreement with a resident or nonresident Georgia broker
- File a written statement with the Commission appointing the Real Estate Commissioner as the licensee's agent to receive service in legal matters on behalf of the applicant
- Sign a statement agreeing to cooperate with any investigation initiated by the Commission.

States whose educational requirements for licensure are similar to Georgia may have established **reciprocity agreements** with the Georgia Real Estate Commission. As such, Georgia may exempt nonresident applicants who hold licenses in those states from completing such requirements in Georgia.

IN PRACTICE With regard to real estate licensees who reside in Florida, and wish to obtain a non-resident license in Georgia, the Commission requires the Florida licensee to pass the state content portion of the qualifying license exam in Georgia along with submitting a certification of license history in Florida (no more than 1-year-old) from that state's real estate commission.

Absent a nonresident license in Georgia, a licensee from another state may still conduct real estate business in Georgia if that person first signs an affiliation agreement with a Georgia broker who agrees to be responsible for the transaction in which the nonresident participates. A separate agreement must be provided for each such transaction, and each contract must indicate:

- how the compensation for the transaction will be divided;
- that any listing or property management agreement will be in the name of the Georgia broker;
- that negotiations for any of these agreements will be conducted only with the express permission of the Georgia broker;
- that any advertisement for property will identify the Georgia broker as the listing agent;
- that all contracts identifying the Georgia broker will also identify that the out of state broker is not licensed in Georgia; and
- that all trust funds will be held in the Georgia's broker trust account unless all parties involved agree otherwise in writing.

A Georgia licensee moving to another state may qualify for a nonresident Georgia license, as long as that person applies to change the license status from resident to nonresident in accordance with 43-40-9. Rather than make this specific license change, a Georgia licensee moving to another state may also place the license on inactive status, in which case the licensee may not conduct real estate licensure business in Georgia, until they become residents again and reactivate the license, or change their license status to that of a nonresident licensee.

A nonresident broker may become licensed as a qualifying broker in Georgia, or for an out of state firm, as long as the brokerage firm is licensed by the Georgia Real Estate Commission and authorized to do business in Georgia.

When a nonresident's license lapses, it may be reactivated by paying the required fee for an original applicant, as long as the licensee has remained active in the home state of residence.

No Georgia real estate licensee may perform real estate activities in any other state unless properly licensed in that state.

ACQUIRING THE REAL ESTATE LICENSE

520-1-.04; 43-40-12, 15, and 16

Examinations After fulfilling the age, education, and in the case of the broker's license, experience requirements, the next step in the licensure process requires the candidate to pass the state qualifying examination. At the time application for this exam is submitted, the Commission will collect a fee from the candidate. If an applicant fails the exam, the candidate may take another exam upon submitting a new application and exam fee for each necessary retake.

IN PRACTICE Real estate licensing exams in Georgia are currently administered by Applied Measurement Professional, Inc. (AMP). Their website, www.goamp.com, allows access to a candidate handbook that includes topic outlines, procedures for establishing an examination appointment, as well as rules and scoring methods for the exam, sample test questions, and exam fees.

With evidence of such military service, applicants who are veterans with a minimum of 1-year served in the armed forces, 90 days of which were during an armed conflict, may be granted a 5-point credit on the real estate license-qualifying exam. If discharged due to injury or illness, with at least 10% disability, eligible Veterans may receive a 10-point credit on the exam. On the Broker's qualifying exam, credits for Veterans apply to the Information Gathering and Decision Making sections of that exam.

Examinations Out-of-state candidates for real estate licenses in Georgia may be exempted from both education and exam requirements if able to provide an original certification issued within the last 12 months that shows that in their state of residence, they

- passed a similar licensure exam,
- met all pre license and continuing education requirements for licensure in their home state,
- are currently licensed in good standing, and
- have no formal disciplinary action imposed by the real estate commission in their home state.

Applicants whose certifications fail to satisfy the above requirements must take and pass an appropriate Georgia licensing exam.

Actions by an applicant taking a licensing exam that involve supplying the contents of such an exam to other parties will constitute grounds for the Commission denying a license to that person.

LICENSURE APPLICATION

After successfully passing the state examination, a formal application for licensure must be made to the Georgia Real Estate Commission. Any such application, including license renewal, changes in license status, and any change in a brokerage firm's name must be submitted on current Commission-approved forms or online through the Commission's website at www.grec.state.ga.us. If applications or changes are mailed by the U.S. Postal Service, the effective filing date of these letters shall be the postmarked date. If otherwise transmitted, the acceptance date will be the date such letters are received. Applications may also be electronically submitted.

Submitted applications on authorized forms that lack the necessary information requested, or the required fees, will be considered incomplete. Failing to disclose on an application any required criminal convictions or disciplinary actions imposed in another state shall constitute falsification of the filing.

Persons who have completed the Commission authorized prelicense course (or authorized college credit(s) equivalent), and have passed the qualifying state exam, must subsequently apply for the Salesperson's or Community Association Manager's license within one year of the examination date. Those who fail to apply within these first three months must pay double the license fee. Waiting more than one year requires an individual to retake the state qualifying exam.

BROKERAGE FIRM LICENSURE

Broker candidates who have satisfied the educational requirements, passed the state qualifying exam, and have been active three of the last five years, must apply for the license within one year of the exam date—failure to do so would require the applicant to retake the exam. If a candidate was a broker in another state, the applicant must present an original certification (issued within 12 months of the current application) of this licensure, identifying the firm in which the applicant served as broker.

A broker may use his/her name as the firm's name, but whether or not this is the case, the brokerage firm may only conduct business in whatever name the license was issued. A brokerage firm will be granted two licenses: one in the name of the firm, the other in the name of the qualifying broker. A firm that is a sole proprietorship must submit the license application under the name in which the broker intends to conduct business. A firm that is organized as a corporation must submit the corporate charter as registered with the Secretary of State, along with the license application. In this case the Commission issues the corporate license in the name in which the company will do brokerage business.

If set up as a partnership, the brokerage firm must submit the partnership agreement along with the license application and a copy of this trade name certified by the County clerk, and as such that name will appear on the license. A license application for a limited liability company must include a certificate of authority to do business as issued by the Secretary of State, and may also show a plan to use a trade name as certified by the County Clerk. The trade name of a firm operating as a franchise must be either as it appears on ownership documents or as it is registered with the county in which it is doing business. Any time a brokerage firm plans to change its name, a new name certification for a new license must be submitted.

LICENSURE DOCUMENTATION

As of January 1, 2012, Georgia statute 50-36-1 requires any real estate licensure applicant to submit a signed **Lawful Presence Notarized Affidavit**, verifying the applicant's legal presence in the United States.

Applicants for all new real estate licenses must also submit a certified criminal history report from an appropriate law enforcement authority along with the application; this **GCIC report** may not be more that 60 days old at the time of application. If such records show a reportable criminal conviction, the licensee must also submit certified copies of the citation, accusation, or indictment that led to the conviction as well as a certified copy of the sentence. An applicant must also disclose any disciplinary sanctions that may have been imposed by licensing agencies, and provide certified copies of allegations preceding and after any sanctions by such agencies.

IN PRACTICE Subsequent to passing the qualifying state exam, if, along with the lawful presence document and a clean GCIC report, the applicant for a Salesperson or CAM license submits a **sponsoring broker form** (indicating with whom the licensee will affiliate), the candidate may be issued that real estate license on the same day the exam was completed.

GROUNDS FOR REFUSAL, SUSPENSION, OR REVOCATION OF A LICENSE

43-40-15

Under its mandate granted by License Law to protect the public from dishonest and untrustworthy agents, the Commission may deny a real estate license to any applicant with a prior criminal conviction, or with a disciplinary sanction imposed by an occupational licensing body in Georgia or any other state.

Georgia Senate Bill 114 passed in 2007 provides that no person who has a criminal conviction may apply for a real estate license unless that person has successfully completed all terms and conditions of any sentence imposed for the conviction. If that person has multiple convictions, at least five years must have passed after satisfying all the terms of the conviction before that person may apply for a real estate license—if that person has a single conviction, two years must have passed. In its definition of a conviction, the Commission includes: any plea or verdict of guilty, a sentencing regarding first offender treatment, or a plea of nolo contendere.

Pending criminal charges (including but not limited to theft, fraud, extortion, forgery, sex offenses) also prohibit persons from applying for a real estate license.

The Commission will not grant an applicant for a broker or associate broker's license with a felony conviction of crime or moral turpitude until:

- no criminal charges are pending against the applicant
- evidence of the applicant's good reputation for honesty, trustworthiness, integrity and competence has been shown
- at least 10 years have been passed since conviction, sentence, or release from incarceration

If an applicant has allowed a license to lapse or surrendered a license after an occupational licensing body has initiated an investigation or a disciplinary process, the Commission may issue an associate or broker's license only if (1) at least 10 years have passed since a revocation or surrender (2) no criminal charges are pending and (3) the applicant presents to the Commission evidence of being a trustworthy and honest person.

The Commission may also deny any license application or may impose a sanction on a licensed person for

- Making a false statement of material fact on his or her application, or causing a falsified application to be submitted to the Commission
- Violations of the federal fair housing law after any appeal for a conviction has been concluded
- Default on a guaranteed educational loan with no satisfactory repayment status (See GA Code 20-3-295 for more information on this subject.)
- Delinquent child support payments (See GA Code19-6-28.1 or 19-11-9.3 for more information on this subject.)

Georgia law requires state agencies responsible for monitoring payments on student loans and on child support to provide the Commission with certified lists, updated monthly, of persons who have defaulted on student loans and on persons who are delinquent in child support. The Commission may refuse a license or impose a sanction (such as a license suspension) on persons who have defaulted on loans or who are not current on child support payments. The Commission may grant a license or lift a sanction once the applicant or licensee has taken appropriate measures defined in Georgia law to correct those deficiencies.

Because of the time and expense involved in becoming an applicant for real estate licensure in Georgia, an applicant can request a preliminary decision from the Commission on any sanctions or convictions of record, before the applicant takes the required education and examination. As this preliminary decision is advisory, and not binding, an individual may still proceed with the prelicense education and exam requirements, and subsequently take the state qualifying exam.

If the Commission denies an application for licensure or license reinstatement, and the applicant has met all age, education, and exam requirements, as well as paying the applicable license fees, the applicant is entitled to a hearing and may also appeal for a judicial review if dissatisfied with the result of such a hearing. This right is provided under the **Georgia Administrative Procedures Act**. Under this statute, a candidate whose license application has been denied by the Commission has 60 days from the denial letter date to request a formal hearing. If no such request is made, or if the hearing affirms the license denial, the Commission may require the candidate to take a new exam and pay applicable fees again before making another license application.

The License Law requires any licensee convicted of a felony to immediately notify the Commission of that conviction. The licensee's license is automatically revoked within 60 days after the conviction unless the licensee makes a written request for a hearing during the 60-day period. After a hearing, the Commission may still impose a sanction against the licensee.

When a licensee who holds a school or instructor approval surrenders his or her license, the licensee's school or instructor approval may be revoked by the Commission. When the Commission revokes or suspends a licensee's license, then any school or instructor approval will also be revoked or suspended.

The License Law states in 43-40-15 that any grounds for suspension or revocation of a license set forth in the law are also grounds for the denial of a license. Conduct which relates to the denial of a real estate license by the Commission may also serve as grounds for sanctions upon a licensee when the conduct is that of a person already licensed by the Commission.

MAINTAINING THE LICENSE

43-40-8; 43-40-12; 520-1-.04; 520-1.05

Post-License Education In the first year of licensure as a salesperson, the License Law requires a new licensee to complete a 25-hour, Commission-approved post-license course. Failure to complete this course within this initial one year time period will result in a lapsed license, requiring the licensee to return the wall license certificate and pocket card to the Commission. If for any reason, the licensee fails to complete the course, but had enrolled in and paid for the course within the first year of licensure, that person may reinstate the license by completing the course work within six months. A salesperson who does not meet these requirements may reinstate the license by taking an approved 25 hour course, in addition to paying any penalties and fees as required by the Commission.

Notwithstanding those persons who have been actively licensed on or before January 1, 1980, all other licensees, at the time of license renewal, must furnish to the Commission evidence of the following: at least 36 course hours of completed, continuing education for each four year renewal period. Beginning July 1, 2016, three of these 36 hours of CE must cover some area of License Law, as identified by the Real Estate Commission. For first time licensees, the required 25 hour post license requirement will also count as 9 hours toward the first 4-year renewal CE requirement of 36 hours.

Commission approved real estate schools and instructors must also renew licenses, and Commission approved prelicense instructors must satisfy instructor continuing education requirements.

Reinstatement of Lapsed Licenses A license not renewed within the 4-year time period will lapse according to the following schedule: for an individual license, on the last day of the month of that person's birthday; for a brokerage firm, on the last day of the month of the fourth anniversary of its original licensure.

A person whose real estate license lapses because of nonpayment of fees or failure to satisfy all educational requirements cannot engage in real estate brokerage activities until the license is reinstated. As such, the licensee must return the wall license certificate and pocket card to the Commission.

A licensee who did not have to meet CE requirements (so-called "Grandfathered Licensees" who were licensed prior to 1980) and who allows a license to lapse for more than one year may reinstate it by paying the required fees, though that person will be issued a new license number and subsequently be required to complete the corresponding CE requirements.

A licensee may reinstate a lapsed license within two years by paying a reinstatement fee) and any other fee due, as long as CE requirements have been satisfied. If all CE requirements have not been satisfied, the licensee must take at least six hours of CE for each year of inactive license status. (All such education requirements by the Commission must be completed within one year.)

If a license has lapsed for more than two years, but less than five years, the Commission would require that the licensee, before reinstatement, pay all renewal fees, late charges, as well as a reactivation fee. Furthermore, within one year of application for reinstatement, the licensee must take and pass the prelicense course for salesperson, broker, or CAM.

The Commission requires that any person whose real estate license lapses for more than five years due to failure to pay renewal fees take and pass the state qualifying exam before applying for reinstatement.

Brokerage Affiliations Active Georgia associate brokers, salespersons, and community association managers must be affiliated with one active Georgia broker at a time. None of these licensees may conduct any brokerage activities until their employing, qualifying broker receives their wall certificate of licensure. Licensees affiliated with a broker in Georgia may also affiliate with an out-of-state broker if both brokers give written permission.

IN PRACTICE A person who holds a broker's license while acting as the qualifying broker of a firm, may also hold an associate broker's license and affiliate with a qualifying broker of another firm. If an associate broker changes license status to a qualifying broker, that person may not begin work until receiving a wall license certificate from the Commission indicating such change. A licensee who has been released by a broker may not conduct real estate activities until affiliated with a new broker or until the licensee has received a wall certificate as a qualifying broker.

Inactive Licensure Real estate licensees who decide they do not want to continue performing real estate activities at the current time may go on inactive status by returning the license to the Commission. The license may remain on inactive status indefinitely, though renewal fees must continue to be paid. If the inactive licensee does not keep up with CE requirements, reinstating the license to active status requires that individual to complete at least six hours of approved education for each year the license was inactive. This course work must be completed no later than one year prior to the reactivation date of the license. However, this requirement does not apply to an inactive licensee who can furnish evidence of meeting the educational requirement for each renewal period during license inactivity.

IN PRACTICE While on inactive status, the licensee may only conduct real estate business as it relates to the buying, selling, leasing or exchanging of personally owned property. Though an unlicensed person in Georgia may perform real estate services as a full time employee for an unlicensed property owner, this exception is unavailable to an inactive licensee. For example, an inactive licensee would be unable to go to work as an onsite sales agent for a subdivision developer who did not have a broker's license. In order to do so, the inactive licensee would have to give up the real estate license (aka: **surrender the license**). To surrender the license means it may not be reinstated, and to become licensed again, that person must re-qualify as an original candidate.

An active real estate licensee who is retiring after 20 years of such licensure, may, upon request to the Commission, keep the license certificate, a benefit also available to the family of a deceased licensee.

FIRM MANAGEMENT AND OVERSIGHT

43-40-18; 520.1-07

The broker or qualifying broker shall directly manage and supervise real estate brokerage activities of each firm, and shall be responsible for

- reviewing brokerage/sales contracts, trust account procedures, and advertising for legal compliance;
- ensuring that proper distributions are made from trust accounts;
- making sure that only property licensed affiliates perform activities that require licensure;
- maintaining reasonable safekeeping for all required records related to real estate transaction;
- giving all licensee affiliates a written **policy and procedures manual** for firm operations;
- having brokerage firm management reasonably available on a continual basis to assist licensees; and
- ensuring that all licensee affiliates have written **affiliation agreements** with the firm that identify compensation earned for work completed in employment as well as compensation for work begun, but not completed prior to termination of employment. The Commission does not regulate the content, nor enforce the terms of this agreement.

IN PRACTICE With regard to the written affiliation agreement required between the Broker and salesperson or associate broker, the Commission has no authority, nor makes any endorsement as to whether this agreement establishes the agent as an employee or independent contractor. That choice remains at the discretion of the licensees involved in that affiliation contract. {43-40-30.1}

While a broker or qualifying broker may choose to delegate responsibilities associated with running the business and managing licensee affiliates, the broker continues to assume responsibilities for the actions of all licensees and employees. As such, the broker or qualifying broker assumes liability when a licensee affiliate violates the License Law or Commission Rules unless that broker can prove that

- reasonable supervisory procedures were available to the affiliate licensee,
- the broker did not take part in the violation, and
- the broker did not ratify the violation.

It is the broker's obligation to instruct all licensee affiliates on compliance with the Law and Rules, and to notify the Commission of any violations by these affiliates.

A broker must conduct business in the name as shown on the license certificate. Within the business organization of a brokerage firm

- a **sole proprietorship** must be entirely owned by the qualifying broker;
- a partnership must be run by a qualifying broker who is a general partner in the firm;
- a corporation requires the qualifying broker to be an officer of that entity, though not a stockholder;
- in a limited liability company, the qualifying broker serves as a member or manager of the LLC; and
- regardless of the firm's structure, the broker or qualifying broker must have signatory power on all trusts accounts maintained.

Upon the death, resignation, or termination of a qualifying broker, the firm has 60 days to name a new qualifying broker.

A broker may serve as a qualifying broker for more than one firm. An associate broker may also serve as a qualifying broker for another firm. In such a circumstance, the qualifying broker holding the associate broker's license must be notified in writing.

Real Estate Assistants/Support Personnel

If permitted by the brokerage firm policy, an affiliated licensee may hire a licensed or unlicensed assistant to help conduct business. Both the licensee and the broker are accountable for ensuring that the assistant understands license law, that a licensed helper remains properly licensed, and that an unlicensed assistant only performs ministerial services.

The above rule does not prevent the unlicensed employee of a property manager broker from carrying out activities permitted under License Law 43-40-29(10).

Effective as of November 1, 2014, an active licensee affiliated at one firm is now allowed to perform ministerial duties as support personnel at another firm, with the written consent from the broker at each firm.

Any broker that permits licensee affiliates to hire support personnel as independent contractors must

- have a written agreement with the affiliate, identifying duties and compensation for the assistant;
- have a written agreement with the assistant identifying those duties which may be performed for the affiliated licensee; and
- ensure that the affiliate licensee and the assistant for that affiliate enter into a written agreement outlining duties and compensation.

Regarding services of unlicensed assistants, a list of duties that may be performed under the direct supervision of a broker's licensee affiliate, though not inclusive, might involve:

- Answering and forwarding phone calls to a licensee
- Submitting listing data to an MLS
- Sign placement and removal
- Computing commissions
- Checking the status of a loan
- As directed by the licensee affiliate, ordering routine repairs
- Making copies of keys
- Assembling closing documents
- Acting as a courier
- Scheduling appointments
- Setting up dates and times for inspections
- Putting together closing documents
- Courthouse and public information research
- Installing and removing lockboxes
- Placing advertisements as directed by the supervising broker
- Writing ads for the approval of a licensee affiliate and supervising broker
- Receiving, recording and depositing earnest money, security deposits, and advanced rents

- Property maintenance
- Scheduling an open house and going to open house for security
- Typing contract forms as directed by licensees and supervising broker
- Monitoring licensee personnel files

Unlicensed assistants may not perform the following services:

- Cold calls to secure listings or prospects for other real estate engagements
- Hosting open houses, kiosks, home show booths or fairs
- Preparing ads or promotional materials without review and approval by supervising parties
- Showing property
- Notwithstanding inquiries on time and place, answering questions about title, finance, or closing
- Answering listing questions, except those of price or amenities (if authorized in writing)
- Discussing or explaining any real estate contract or document with anyone outside the firm
- Negotiating or agreeing to any compensation on behalf of the licensee
- Discussing with a buyer or tenant prospect, the attributes or amenities of a property
- Discussing the terms and conditions of a real property listing with the owner of the property
- Collecting or holding money received from a property owner or prospect
- Providing property owners with advice, recommendations, or suggestions for perspective listings
- Posing as a real estate license holder

A licensed broker in Georgia is permitted to share real estate commissions as well as pay referral fees to a licensed broker in another state.

OFFICE LOCATIONS/TRANSFER OF LICENSES

43-40-19; 43-40-23; 520.1-07(5)

Change of Address If a brokerage office changes its address or place of business, the Real Estate Commission must be notified within 30 days of the change.

In county or city locations where a brokerage firm maintains a primary or branch office, that jurisdiction may charge the broker a fixed sum license, professional, or occupational tax. If a broker sells property outside the boundaries in which the broker maintains as office, that jurisdiction may not charge the broker such a license fee, but may impose a gross receipt sales tax on such a transaction.

Transfer Process When an affiliated licensee decides to leave a brokerage firm, the broker must sign a transfer form and immediately forward the license either to the Commission or to the new broker with whom the licensee will affiliate, notifying the Commission of such action in writing. When a broker releases an affiliate's license that licensee may not conduct any real estate brokerage activities until receiving a license wall certificate from the Commission, which then must be delivered to the affiliate's new employing broker.

A salesperson or community association manager is prohibited from acting as a licensee under any broker other than the broker who holds that party's license, notwithstanding the following exception. When transferring to a new broker, a licensee with any transaction(s) under the former broker may finish and receive compensation for such transactions from that former broker, provided

- both brokers agree in writing to those identified transactions;
- the former broker agrees in writing to assume full responsibility for the licensees' activities in those transactions; and
- the agreement expresses the terms of the compensation for those transactions.

When affiliating with a new firm, licensees must sign an agreement specifying how the agent will be compensated during such affiliation, as well as how the licensee will be paid for any unfinished business when leaving the firm. Other than requiring that such agreements be in writing, the Commission does not regulate contractual content nor enforce the terms of the contract, leaving that matter to the courts or other arbitrating bodies.

Only brokers, or an associate broker authorized in writing by the broker, may sign applications for sponsoring broker forms, transfers, or releases.

Brokers are prohibited from refusing to sign a release/transfer request from an affiliated licensee. Any disputes between a licensee and a broker over the terms of the existing affiliation agreement remain outside the jurisdiction of the Commission, and shall not impact a broker's obligation to sign a transfer form upon request from an affiliate. Upon signing the release, whether the broker forwards the license to the Commission, to the new broker with notification to the Commission, or hands over the wall license to the licensee for delivery to the agent's new broker, such action must be done as soon as practically possible.

If original certificates of licensure and/or pocket license cards are lost, replacements of such items will be issued upon satisfactory proof of loss.

As brokerage engagements belong to the broker, not the affiliated salesperson or associate broker, a transferring licensee may not take any listing or buyer agreements to another firm unless specifically authorized by the broker. Moreover, signs, keys, lockboxes, letterheads, and other materials provided by the broker must remain. A departing licensee's failure to follow this legal protocol, however, shall not give cause for the broker's refusal to sign a release, but may give cause for the broker to file with the Commission a formal written complaint against the licensee.

From the date of release, a licensee has one month to affiliate with a new brokerage firm or go inactive. If a licensee has been terminated involuntarily, and has failed to sign a release form with the broker, the firm mails a letter to the licensee indicating that party's license has been returned to the Commission, and that the licensee has one month to handle the matter appropriately.

Until existing contracts with clients the licensee served as an affiliate of a former brokerage firm expire, the licensee is prohibited from contacting any of those parties, unless authorized in writing by the former broker.

MANAGING TRUST FUNDS AND ESCROW ACCOUNTS

43-40-20; 43-40-21; 520.1-.08

Brokerage Trust Accounts In a real estate brokerage transaction, any broker or affiliated licensee who accepts down payments, earnest money deposits, security deposits, rents, association fees, or other trust funds must maintain a separate, federally insured bank checking account in Georgia designated as a trust or escrow account for the deposit of these funds. Secure from any garnishments or attachments, such trust accounts must be registered with the Real Estate Commission, identifying the bank name and account number, within one month of its establishment. Likewise, if maintaining more than one trust account, a brokerage firm must notify the commission of the location and account number of each within one month of its opening. Brokers who choose never to hold trust funds are excused from maintaining these accounts. Should a broker who does not have an escrow account decide to hold funds on behalf of a party, the broker must open this trust account within one business day of accepting these funds.

IN PRACTICE Multiple trust accounts are sometimes used as a matter of convenience by a brokerage firm operating branch offices throughout a metropolitan area. Furthermore, if a firm is active in property management as well as home sales, separate trust accounts may be kept for each transactional area. The number of trust accounts maintained for a brokerage firm remains at the sole discretion of the broker.

The Commission may allow a nonresident broker who accepts trust funds to maintain the escrow account in a bank of the nonresident broker's state of residence, providing that the Commission may examine the account.

A licensee affiliate is prohibited from holding monies or anything of value belonging to others, including such funds received while the affiliate is acting as a principal. Rather, these sums must be handed over to the broker as soon as practically possible. When licensees sell their own real property, funds received from other parties must be placed in the brokerage firm's trust account, or in the licensee's own such account approved by the broker and registered with the Commission. When receiving another party's money, unless otherwise directed by the contract, the broker must promptly deposit those funds in the firm's trust/escrow account. If such an account pays interest, the contract must indicate who receives that interest.

Money that is clearly designated as belonging to the brokerage firm may be deposited into a trust account only to cover bank service charges or to maintain any minimum balance required by the financial institution. Moreover, any commissions due the brokerage firm may remain in the trust account under provisions that

- the commission amounts are clearly designated as broker funds;
- the commission amounts not needed to maintain the account are removed once a month; and
- only checks made payable to the broker are used to withdraw funds designated as belonging the firm.

System Requirements Brokerage firms are required to maintain either a manual or electronic accounting systems for trust accounts that provides the following details:

- Name of buyer and seller; tenant and landlord; member of community association and member or broker
- Amount and date of deposit
- Identification of property involved
- Amount, payee, and each check drawn on trust account with connection to that deposit

For examination/auditing purposes, whatever accounting system used must

- include all legal components necessary for sound business practice;
- be readily accessible;
- be in an understandable format; and
- be reasonable available for inspection by a representative of the Commission.

Trust Fund Examination/Reconciliation Using its own investigators or the services of a hired CPA, the Commission may examine a brokerage firm's or licensee affiliate's trust account at any time with reasonable cause as well as during each broker's license renewal period. A broker must make available to trust account inspectors any contracts and related documents involving escrow account deposits and disbursements. In lieu of an examination, the commission may decide to accept a written report of the account from a certified public accountant. In lieu of a trust account examination required for a brokerage firm the broker may provide a data summary on a Commission form, so long as the data is complete and without irregularities, though the Commission is not obligated to accept this type of report.

Should a broker refuse to provide information regarding a trust account as requested by the commission, or act in a manner that appears to violate this section of Laws and Rules pertaining to trust accounts, the Commission may conclude that the trust account is in an unsafe or unsound condition. Consequently, the Commission will immediately submit a report of this matter to the Attorney General, who may issue an injunction or impound the account and appoint a receiver for the escrow funds.

Minimally, on a monthly basis, the broker must reconcile the trust account with the bank statement and these reconciliations must be kept on file for at least three years. A licensee affiliate who owns a trust/escrow account must provide the brokerage firm on a quarterly basis a written reconciliation statement comparing total trust liability with the reconciled bank balance of the licensee's trust account.

A broker who manages leased real property or community associations may maintain a designated rental or assessment trust account separate from other brokerage business trust accounts. The balance in these client's trust accounts must always be sufficient to cover the payment of the owner's or association's bills. Security deposits must be clearly identified as credited to the tenant, and there must always be a balance in the account equal to the total of security deposits. A licensee who manages and owns rental property must keep security deposits in designated trust accounts and may not post bond in lieu of keeping such funds in the required escrow account.

Only the broker is empowered to disburse trust account funds; any improper disbursement of such money by the broker is deemed under the Laws as an act of incompetence in safeguarding the public interest. Acceptable disbursement scenarios may be as follows:

- A purchaser's offer is rejected, entitling that party to a full refund of Earnest Money.
- Upon withdrawing an offer not yet accepted, the purchaser is entitled to a full refund of Earnest Money.
- At settlement, the Earnest Money is refunded by check or credited to the purchaser
- Upon a written agreement, separate from the contract for sale, signed by all parties to the transaction.
- Upon court's decision on an interpleader action filed by the holder of the Earnest Money to determine how such funds should be disbursed
- Upon a court order as a result of legal action taken by one of the parties to the transaction
- Upon a reasonable interpretation of the contract so directed by the contract to the broker holding the Earnest Money. In such a circumstance, the broker must notify all parties in writing of the dispersal decision.

The broker is prohibited from disbursing any funds from trust until an earnest money check has cleared and the funds are in the broker's trust account.

When claiming part or all of an earnest money trust deposit as commission earned, the broker must ensure that

- the sales transaction has closed
- In a rental agreement, the tenant is occupying the property
- In a lease/purchase transaction, the sale has either closed, or that the date on which the closing was to take place has passed.
- there is a written agreement confirming the broker's entitlement to the funds as commission signed by all parties to the transaction.

Any refunds of Earnest Money held in a broker's trust account must be conveyed by check or credited a closing. Absent any broker commission earned, trust account balances for each identified transaction must show a zero balance after settlement. Brokers or affiliated licensees who maintain a designated trust account while filing for bankruptcy must immediately notify the Commission in writing of that petition.

Licensees selling their own real property are required to deposit funds secured from the sale of such property in the broker's trust account necessary to meet current payment obligations such as existing mortgages, contracts for deed and escrow reserves for property taxes and insurance.

IN PRACTICE A licensee's existing home loan does not contain an alienation (due on sale) clause that allows the license to sell the home while offering financing for a perspective buyer. The licensee will subsequently use part of the purchaser's monthly loan payment to continue making payments on the loan that currently is secured by the home. Moreover, as required under Laws, the licensee will need to deposit that portion of the buyer's loan payment that covers the licensee's existing loan payment into the broker's trust account every month to ensure proper, on-time payment of that current loan.

If circumstances infer that some trust funds have been abandoned, the licensee may distribute these funds only if:

- the written authorization to hold these funds requires such disbursal

- the licensee has complied with the requirements set forth in the **Disposition of Unclaimed Property Act**
- the licensee has complied with particular statutory or court ordered requirements appropriate to the circumstance.

BROKERAGE RELATIONSHIPS

520.1-.06; 43-40-22.1

1. Brokerage Engagements
   - Each exclusive agency contract with clients must express the terms of the agreement and contain a definite expiration date.
   - Licensees must ensure that all parties signing a brokerage engagement agreement receive at that time a copy of the agreement.
   - The Commission prohibits net brokerage engagements, requiring the licensee to notify a client of the gross price of the property that includes brokerage fees and services.
2. Requirements for Property Management Engagements
   - Identify the property to be managed
   - Indicate all terms and conditions for management agreement
   - Specify the time frame and manner in which the broker will forward to the owner property income as well as statements accounting for such income and related property expenses
   - Specify those payments the broker/manager will make to third parties
   - State the amount of and time frame in which compensation will be paid to the broker/manager
   - Specify whether the broker/manager or owner will hold security deposits and prepaid rents
   - Identify the management contract's beginning and ending date
   - Provide terms and conditions under which either party to the agreement may terminate the brokerage engagement
   - Signatures of broker and owner, or respective authorized agents
3. Fidelity Bonds
4. Any broker who, in providing community association services, handles more than $60,000 in association funds, must be covered by an insurance bond or policy for each association under which such circumstances exist. A broker must keep a copy of each policy, as well as providing one to the association managed. This fidelity bond/policy must
   - be issued by a properly authorized insurance company;
   - insure the maximum amount the broker/manager collects or disburses at any time, and must cover at all times at least the total of 3 months association dues;
   - designate the association as an additional insured party;
   - insure the broker and all parties associated with the broker who handle such funds; and
   - provide a 30-day notice to the broker/manager and the association prior to cancellation of policy except under circumstance of non-payment in which a 10 day notice of policy cancellation would apply.

5. Disclosure of Brokerage Relationships

   Whether selling or leasing a property owned, or offering to buy or lease a property listed with an employing brokerage firm, a licensee must clearly disclose any such position as a principal in the transaction to the other party, including such disclosure in the contract with that other party.

   A licensee representing a client in a real property sale or lease transaction must disclose in writing and in a timely manner, to either client (or both clients) whom the licensee represents in the transaction and from whom the licensee will receive compensation for service. If not representing either party in the transaction, the licensee must disclose from whom the licensee will receive compensation in the transaction. Such disclosures must be made no later than at the time of the offer.

IN PRACTICE BRRETA requires a licensee to make such disclosure "when entering into a brokerage engagement"

   When a licensee compensates another licensee who is a party to the transaction, as is typical in a cooperating arrangement between brokers, written consent must be acknowledged by all parties to the transaction.

BROKERAGE ADVERTISING

520.1-.09; 43-40-25 (b)

The Commission defines advertising or advertisement as "any manner, method, or activity by which a licensee through the use of any media makes known to the general public real estate for sale, rent, lease, or exchange."

1. Media: Inclusive of all types of print, photographic, computer and broadcast media; applicable to business cards, billboards, property signs, newsletters, and the internet. Internet advertising includes websites, blogs, video blogs, property listing database services, email farming, news groups, discussion lists, bulletin boards, social networking and social media, instant text messages, multimedia advertising, banner ads, pop-ups, and similar media.
2. Misleading Ads: Inaccurate or misleading advertising in any material fact or in any way is prohibited. In addition, Rule 520-1-.09 (2) requires that a licensee take immediate steps to stop any inaccurate or misleading advertising by a principal with whom the firm has a brokerage engagement.
3. Advertising by Affiliate Licensee: all ads must be done in name of broker who holds affiliate's license and who is accountable for content of affiliate's ad. Such ads must include the name of the broker (firm) as it is registered with the Commission. A licensee affiliate's ad that ignores this requirement is identified as a **blind ad**.
4. Written Permission: A licensee may not advertise a property without the written permission of the owner, the owner's authorized agent, or the owner of a leasehold estate. A licensee must have written permission to place a sign on any property offering it for sale or lease, and must remove any sign within ten days after the expiration of a listing. When advertising a property listed by another broker, that fact must clearly be disclosed in the ad, unless the other broker has expressly agreed in writing to waive such disclosure.

5. Discriminatory Advertising: Ads directed at or referred to persons of any particular race, color, religion, sex, handicap, familial status or national origin are prohibited. Content of any property ad must be confined to information relative only to the property itself.
6. A licensee may not print, make, publish, or cause any advertisement to be printed, made, or published which indicates any preference, limitation, or discrimination because of race, color, religion, sex, disability, familial status, or national origin.
7. Internet Advertising: All internet advertising must comply with all Commission rules related to unfair trade practices. In addition, any viewable web page shall disclose the name and telephone number of the licensee's firm.
8. When a licensee advertises in electronic messages with limited space or characters, the licensee must provide a direct link to a display that is in compliance with Commission rules. A licensee must also provide a direct link to a display in compliance with Commission advertising rules when the licensee advertises real estate on a website not owned or controlled by the licensee or the licensee's firm.
9. Commission rules require that a licensee remove any information that is outdated on a website maintained by the licensee or update such information within 30 days of the information being outdated.

   When a licensee uses a website maintained by a third party (other than the licensee's firm or the franchisor's website), the licensee shall provide to the third party by a written notice of any updates or outdated information to be removed from the website. The Commission will not hold a licensee in violation of Commission rules if the third party does not comply with the licensee's written request.

   A licensee is not responsible for any information taken from the licensee's website or other advertising without the licensee's consent.
10. Trade and Franchise Names: When using a trade or franchise name, a broker must ensure that the firm's name as registered with the Commission is included on all signs, cards, documents, etc. The name of the firm shall appear in equal or greater size, prominence, and frequency than the name of any affiliated licensee or group of licensees. An ad that uses only the trade or franchise name violates Commission regulations.
11. Firm Names and Telephone Numbers: In advertising specific real property:

    The firm's name as registered with the Commission and the phone number of the firm must be included in the ad. This regulation does not apply if a covenant, local governmental ordinances, or any lawful restriction prohibits the use of the firm's name on a particular type of sign.

    The firm's name and telephone number must appear in equal or greater size, prominence, and frequency than any affiliated licensee.

    If a firm advertises multiple listings in a block ad, each listing agent's name may appear in the ad, as long as the brokerage firm's name is larger and more prominent than the name of any other licensee. The firm's name only need appear once.
12. Licensees Advertising as Principals: Ads written by a licensee acting as a principal in a transaction must identify the writer of the ad as a licensee. Associate brokers, salespersons, and community association managers may

only advertise another party's real property under the direct supervision of their broker and in the name of their firm.

- — When a licensee wants to advertise his or her own specific property that is not under any brokerage agreement, the licensee may advertise the property independent from the licensee's broker, provided that: the licensee affiliate's broker has been notified in writing of the particular property to be advertised; the broker gives written consent to advertising the specific real estate and approves the advertisement itself; and
- — the advertisement includes one of the following two legends:
  - "seller, buyer, landlord, tenant (select the appropriate name) holds a real estate license"; or
  - "Georgia Real Estate Licensee # (insert licensee's six digit number)," or "GA. R.E. Lic. (insert licensee's number)."

13. Licensees Advertising Approved Schools: a licensee may not advertise a school, or promote courses to be offered there without a Commission-approved license to operate such a school.
14. A licensee shall make every reasonable attempt in advertising to assure the public knows that they are being contacted by a licensee.

HANDLING REAL ESTATE TRANSACTIONS

520.1-.10; 43-40-24

Licensees must present offers received promptly to clients and customers. Preparation of an offer by a licensee must include the affiliate's license number as well as the license number of the brokerage firm.

A licensee must provide a copy to any party signing a real estate document; after acceptance of an offer, copies of the agreement must be given to all those signing in addition to all brokerage firm(s) involved in the transaction.

Any broker whose firm was involved in a transaction or required to maintain a trust account must retain all related transaction documents for at least three years. Upon a reasonable request from the Commission, true copies of such documents must be produced for review.

Licensees are prohibited from falsifying any document, or representing to any party:

- an amount different from the actual contract price,
- a down payment different from the actual down payment,
- an amount different from earnest money, security deposit, or trust funds actually tendered,
- a trust fund payment in cash while, in fact, some other method of payment was used, and
- intentionally deceptive information.

Any charge, rebate, commission, profit, referral fee, or other valuable consideration related to a real property transaction must be disclosed on the settlement form for that transaction, or in a related document given to the licensee's principal prior to closing. The term 'principal' in this regulation refers to either a client or customer of the licensee, not working under another broker. Specific elements of this requirement include the following:

- A licensee may disclose payment to a principal prior to actual payment as provided within the terms of any written agreement between the parties.
- When working with the principal, a licensee must disclose, no later than at the time of closing, if a referral fee is to be paid to any licensed entity.
- As long as it is disclosed on the settlement statement, a licensee may share commission or other compensation with a principal.
- A licensee is not required to disclose a gift or service given to the principal, as long as such offerings are not contingent upon that party's purchase, sale, or exchange of real property.

In an effort to establish the right to collect compensation for a real estate transaction, no person in Georgia may bring court action unless proving that party held an active Broker's license at the time of the transaction, Moreover, any person acting on behalf of the broker must likewise show proper licensure while performing brokerage services at the time of the transaction.

The Real Estate Commission, through its Commissioner, may bring court action for any violation of these regulations.

LICENSEES AS PRINCIPALS

520.1-.11

An affiliated licensee who intends to participate any real estate activity, whether in that person's own name, or in the name of another entity in which the licensee has an interest, must first notify the broker in writing.

If a licensee, with the purpose of acquiring a brokerage engagement to list, buy, lease, or sell, promises to buy a property from the principal, such a promise must be made in writing prior to any such binding agreement. When offering to purchase a seller's property if such property is not sold by an identified date, the licensee must enter into a written agreement to purchase the property before entering into the brokerage listing engagement with the owner. When offering to purchase a buyer's property to enable that party to purchase another property, a licensee must first set forth all the terms of purchasing the buyer's property within a written purchase and sale agreement, no later than at the time that buyer enters into a contract to purchase the new property.

When advertising their own property, licensees must comply with requirement of Commission Rule, 520-1-.09. All ads run by licensee affiliates must run in the name of the broker, or must comply with all the requirements for advertising in a licensee's own name.

BUSINESS BROKERAGE

520.1-.12

If the sale of a business involves the transfer of any interest in real property, and the fee of a participating broker is dependent on the transfer of such interests, this business brokerage requires a real estate license. An unlicensed party is prohibited from participation in business brokerage involving a real estate transaction and then afterwards acquiring a license with the intent to approve the prior transaction.

UNFAIR TRADE PRACTICES, SANCTIONS, AND CITATIONS

43-40-25; 520.1-.13 and .14

Identified as "**unfair trade practices**" under License Law, this list of violations includes, but is not limited to the following:

1. A licensee may not discriminate because of race, color, religion, sex, disability, familial status, or national origin. Discriminatory behavior includes
   — refusal to sell or rent, or refusal to negotiate for the sale or lease after receiving a bona fide offer; or otherwise making real estate unavailable to any person
   — discrimination against any person with regard to the terms, conditions, and privileges associated with the sale or lease of real estate, as well in the provisions or services connected with such real estate
   — indications or intentions as evidenced in printed or published statements, notices and advertisements that suggest discrimination through preferences or limitations
   — representation to any person that real property is not available for inspection, sale, or lease, when such property, in fact, is available; explicit or implicit representation that change has, will, or may occur in a neighborhood, in order to induce or discourage the listing, selling, purchasing, or renting of real property

IN PRACTICE Commission Rule 520.1-.13 further reinforces federal and state laws providing all citizens the equal right to buy or lease the home of their choice. This Rule identifies specific discriminatory statements a licensee might make regarding effects of protected classes moving into an area, such as a lowering of property values, social changes in the area, an increase of crime in the area, and a decline in the quality of schools

2. Intentionally misleading or inaccurate advertisements of real property, and of the terms, values, policies, or services of the business conducted
3. Failure to account for or remit escrow/trust funds collected by a licensee
4. Commingling client funds with licensee funds
5. Failure to maintain trust funds in an escrow account, unless all parties with an interest in such funds otherwise agree in writing
6. Failure to disclose in writing to a principal in a real estate transaction
   — receipt of any item of value when making a purchase on behalf of a principal who is reimbursing the licensee
   — payment of a referral fee to another broker
   — receipt of anything of value for a referral to the principal of any service or product
7. Representing another broker without the express knowledge and permission of broker who holds the agent's license
8. Absent consent of the broker holding the agent's license, accepting compensation from any other broker

9. Acting as an agent and an undisclosed principal in the same transaction (it is okay for licensees to represent themselves in transaction as long as licensure is disclosed in writing to all other parties involved)
10. Any guarantee to another party that a property will generate a profit in a future sale
11. Placement of a real estate sign on an owner's property without written permission, or failure to remove such a sign within ten days of the listing expiration
12. Offering property for sale or lease without the owner's knowledge, or on terms different from those authorized by the owner
13. Persuading someone to breaking a real estate contract so that a new one may be substituted
14. Negotiating directly with a property owner, prospective buyer or tenant, knowing that party has a brokerage engagement with another licensee
15. Indicating that an opinion of value is an "appraisal," unless the licensee is in fact a state licensed or certified appraiser
16. Acting as a real estate licensee in another state while failing to meet the licensing requirements in that state
17. Paying commission to an unlicensed person unless that person is an heir of a deceased licensee, or a citizen from a country that does not issue real estate licenses

IN PRACTICE Statute 43-40-25(b)(17) was amended in 2006 to allow a broker to pay an unlicensed company of a salesperson or associated broker. Under this change, the broker must have written instructions in order to pay these non-licensed corporation fees earned by a licensee, who must hold a least 20% stock in the corporation. The benefit for payments in this manner to licensees may result in both tax and liability advantages for those persons.

18. Failure to include an expiration date in a written listing agreement, or failure to leave a copy of such an agreement with the seller
19. Failure to deliver, within a reasonable time, a completed copy of any purchase agreement, or offer to buy or sell real estate, to the buyer and seller
20. Failure by broker (or licensed affiliate) to deliver a copy of the settlement statement at closing to both seller and buyer, as well a disclosure of all monies handled by a broker after the closing.
21. Making any substantial misrepresentations
22. Acting as a dual agent without express written consent of all parties to the transaction
23. Failure of the salesperson, associate broker, or community association manager to turn trust funds over to the broker as soon as practically possible
24. Without justification, filing a lien against a property that may cloud the title
25. Incompetent and dishonest actions by licensees
26. Entering into a listing, lease, or sales contract with a person, while knowing the same already exists for that party, unless the broker who has such an engagement gives written authorization
    — An exception here exists for a community association manager, a circumstance in which the broker may bid on HOA business when requested to do so in writing by the association's board of directors
27. Failure to keep, for a least three years, copies of sales contracts, closing statements, or other documents that involved the deposit of trust funds; or failure

to produce copies of such documents upon a reasonable request from the Commission

28. Falsifying any contract or document information as well as being a part to such actions
29. Depositing trust funds into an interest-bearing trust account absent a written agreement by all parties as to who receives such interest
30. Failure to timely disclose an agency relationship that a licensee has with all parties in a transaction
31. Performing acts as a CAM licensee that may only be performed by a broker or licenses affiliates
32. As a licensee providing community association management services, attempting to list, sell, or lease property within the HOA without first getting written authorization from the association
33. Upon the termination of a community association manager contract, failing to deliver within 30 days to the HOA, all records, documents and funds, received on behalf of the association, including those items not previously accounted for
34. Upon termination of a property management contract, failure to deliver within 30 days to the property owner, all records, documents and funds
35. While negotiating a contract, altering the amount of commission a cooperating licensee is to receive, without that licensee's written consent
36. Referring a prospect without that person's written consent, and failure to inform the referral prospect that the licensee will receive a referral fee for that action

IN PRACTICE Licensees are not considered to be practicing law without a law license (an Unfair Practice) while completing contract forms prepared by attorneys. Acceptable contract forms must include a satisfactory legal description of the property, a method of payment, any stipulations or exhibits (addenda) as required, and specific dates to determine if the parties have performed in a timely manner. (43-40-25.1)

There are two laws in Georgia, while not a part of License Law or Commission Rules, that impact a licensee's business activities: the **Fair Business Practice Act** (O.C.G.A. 10-1-390) and the **Uniform Deceptive Trade Practice Act** (O.C.G.A. 10-1-370). Commonly known as the FBPA and the UDPTA, these statutes address activities of licensees in Georgia that violate antitrust laws. Licensees may violate the FBPA when, in order to encourage consumer transactions, they advertise or market services in a misleading or fraudulent manner. For example, by indicating to prospective clients that the commission rate the broker charges is a 'standard' rate charged by all brokers in the area, the licensee violates the FBPA. Violations of this statute carry penalties up to $5,000 per incident. The UDTPA has a much broader application than the FBPA, in that the scope of the law goes beyond advertisements and marketing practices, to cover any violation of antitrust law; and, unlike the FBPA, no actual consumer transaction has to even occur for this law to be violated. As an example, if two or more brokerage firms conspire to 'fix' commission rates or to initiate a boycott of another brokerage firm, they would be in violation of the UDTPA.

License Law grants the Commission broad powers in imposing disciplinary actions when a licensee is found guilty of a violation. For a more serious offense of Laws and Rules, the Commission may impose a **sanction** on the license that would become part of the holder's public record. For a minor infraction, the Commission might issue a **citation** that may only be found on the Commission' records. The order in any citation, that may require some additional performance by the licensee, becomes final 30 days after the date the citation was served.

Disciplinary actions by the Commission may include, but are not limited to the following:

- Refusing to grant or renew a license
- Administering a reprimand
- Suspending a license for a specific time, or indefinitely, with a reinstatement condition attached
- Revoking any license or approval for such a license
- Revoking a Broker's license, while replacing it with a Salesperson's license
- Assessing the licensee for any legal costs of a hearing or investigation
- Imposing a fine for each violation found by the Commission: up to $1,000 per violation, and up to $5,000 for multiple violations
- Requiring completion of a real estate course or courses
- Requiring periodic reports by an independent accountant on the status of a broker's trust account
- Limiting or restricting any license or approval as the Commission deems necessary to protect the public

In determining the severity of any new sanction issued, the Commission may consider any sanctions previously imposed against the licensee in Georgia or in any other state. The Commission may furthermore sanction any licensee who is guilty of an Unfair Practice whether that person was acting as a principal or in any licensed capacity {43-40-25.2}

INVESTIGATION AND HEARING

520.1-.14; 43-40-26, 27, and 28

The Commission may initiate the investigative process of any licensee on its own motion, as a result of information that came to its attention; or as a result of a sworn, written complaint from a citizen. Unless the motion concerns the mishandling of funds, or involves a matter that has been judicially litigated, the problem must have occurred within three years prior to the investigation. The Commission employs investigators to question witnesses and subpoena documents. Persons who fail to comply with the investigation might be held in contempt of court. The results of all investigations are reported only to the Commission or Commissioner, and are held in confidence subject to any subsequent hearing. As part of the investigation, the Commission can compile data about any conviction the licensee might have had. *Conviction* is defined as a verdict of guilty, plea of guilty, or plea of nolo contendere in court. Minor convictions, such as traffic violations are not included here.

If the investigation finds no violation, the matter is closed. If the report determines that the licensee has violated the License Law or the Rules and Regulations, the Commission may then issue a citation for a minor offense, or for a more serious offence, initiate a hearing process prior to imposing any sanctions. Before a license is sanctioned, suspended, or revoked, the licensee is entitled to a hearing granted by the Georgia Administrative Procedures Act, a statute apart from the License Law. This act identifies for state governmental authorities, such as the Real Estate

Commission, the exact procedures to follow when imposing disciplinary powers and enforcing rules. The licensee may also choose to hire an attorney prior to the hearing, which will occur whether or not the licensee chooses to appear. After hearing the evidence, the hearing officer reports the findings to the Commission, which then decides what disciplinary actions to take.

For the more serious violations, the Commission will refer the case to the state Attorney General who might then file an injunction to prevent the licensee from engaging in further violations. For example, in the case of a broker intentionally mishandling trust account funds, the Commission may determine the account to be in an unsafe or unsound condition. As such, a report will immediately be submitted to the Attorney General, who can issue an injunction as well as impounding the account and appointing a receiver over the trust account.

If dissatisfied with the final decision of the hearing the licensee can appeal to the court for a judicial review.

Whenever the Commission revokes or suspends a license, the name of the license holder can be published on the Commission website.

THE REAL ESTATE EDUCATION, RESEARCH, AND RECOVERY FUND

43-40-22

Part of the initial activation fee paid by first time real estate licensees, currently $20 as determined by the Commission, goes into a fund with the primary purpose of compensating any citizen who suffers damages from a licensee and is not able to recover the full liability sum through normal legal channels. The Commission may invest the money in this fund to enhance its value. The fund may also be used to underwrite the costs in developing courses, as well as conducting seminars and research projects for the benefit of licensees and the general public. License Law requires that at a minimum, one million dollars must be maintained in the fund, and if at risk of falling below that amount, the Commission would require all licensees to contribute up to an additional $30 a year at the time of license renewal. A licensee acting a principal or agent in a real estate transaction has no claim against the Fund, nor does a spouse, parent, sibling, child, or personal representative of the violating licensees.

A claimant against this Fund must adhere to a specific process as outlined in License Law as follows:

- Begin a court action against the accused licensee within two years. If choosing to do so, the Commission may intervene and defend the court action.
- The court awards a judgment in favor of the claimant for a specific damage amount
- The claimant, through a writ of execution, makes diligent efforts as part of a general lien against the defendant to seize that person's real or personal property, in order to satisfy the judgment.
- Having exhausted all methods of recovery, including judicial appeals, the claimant may then, after providing the Commission with thirty days written notice, apply for payment from the Commission Recovery Fund.

The Commission limits payments from the Recovery Fund as follows:

- No more than $25,000 per transaction will be paid

- No individual may collect more than $25,000
- No more than $75,000 can be paid out as a result of one licensee's transgressions

A real estate agent's license is automatically revoked (with no appeal process) if the Commission pays any settlement sum from the Fund for a judgment against the licensee. If the judgment is against a firm, the brokerage license is revoked. A licensee is not eligible to receive a new license until that person has repaid in full, plus interest, the full amount paid from the Fund. If a bankruptcy discharge results from repaying the fund, the licensee is not relieved from any penalties provided for in the License Law or Commission Rules.

UNIT 27 QUIZ

1. In its capacity to administer the License Law as created by Georgia statute, the Real Estate Commission may
   a. pass legislative amendments to License Law.
   b. only pass rules and regulations based on License Law.
   c. settle disputes among licensees regarding brokerage compensation.
   d. only pass rules and regulations with the approval of the real estate Commissioner.
2. With regard to the organization and operation of the Georgia Real Estate Commission, which of the following is *TRUE?*
   a. As a Commission member, the Real Estate Commissioner serves as the chief executive officer.
   b. All commission members must place their real estate licenses on inactive status.
   c. Five of the six Commission members must have active real estate licenses for at least five years.
   d. All Commission members must have active real estate licenses for at least five years.
3. The Real Estate Commission operates as a budget unit of Georgia assigned to the office of the Secretary of State, and as such
   a. the Commission's operations are funded by the requisite state taxes for such governmental entities.
   b. the Commission's budget shall be subject to review by the Secretary of State.
   c. the costs to conduct the Commission's operations must be equal to those fees the Commission charges to and receives from licensees.
   d. the Commission must consult the Secretary of State before issuing sanctions against any licensees.
4. Standard requirements for a Broker's license in Georgia would include
   a. evidence that in the three years immediately prior to making application, the candidate has held an active real estate license.
   b. evidence that in three of the five years immediately prior to making application, the candidate has held an active or inactive real estate license.
   c. evidence that in three of the four years immediately prior to making application, the candidate has held an active real estate license.
   d. evidence that the candidate in three of the five years immediately prior to making application has held an active real estate license.
5. The Real Estate Commission would issue a brokerage license to a firm under the condition that
   a. if the firm is set up as a corporation, the qualifying broker must be the majority shareholder.
   b. if the firm is set up as a sole proprietorship, the qualifying broker must be the owner of the entire company.
   c. if the firm is set up as a limited liability company (LLC), the qualifying broker must be an officer of the LLC.
   d. if the firm is set up as a partnership, the qualifying broker may be a general or a limited partner

6. When a candidate for a salesperson licensure passes the qualifying state exam
   a. the candidate may make a formal license application within three months of the exam date, pay regular license fees, and then place the license on active or inactive status.
   b. the candidate may make a formal license application within one year of the exam date, pay regular license fees, and then affiliate with a brokerage firm.
   c. The candidate may not make a formal license application until they have a sponsoring form from the broker with whom the licensee intends to affiliate.
   d. The candidate will automatically receive the wall license certificate and pocket card to hold onto, until the licensee selects a broker with whom to affiliate.

7. Paul is hired by Broker Garcia, whose firm manages a small apartment complex in Georgia. Under the direct supervision of Garcia, Paul collects rent, receives rental applications, and executes leases with perspectives tenants. Under these circumstances, Paul
   a. must have a property management real estate license.
   b. must have a property management license as well as a salesperson's real estate license.
   c. need not have a real estate license.
   d. may be compensated by Garcia for referring tenants to the sales division of the broker's firm.

8. In order to renew a salesperson license after the first four-year license renewal period, a salesperson must satisfy what education requirements?
   a. Only 36 hours of continuing education course work
   b. 36 hours of continuing education plus the 25 hour post-license course required in year one of licensure
   c. 27 hours of continuing education plus the 25 hour post-license course required by the end of the first year of licensure
   d. 27 hours of continuing education plus the 25 hour post-license course required prior to the end of the first license renewal period

9. If, as an owner occupant, a licensee affiliate decides to sell his or her home, the Commission would require the affiliate's broker to
   a. be notified in writing.
   b. provide written permission for the transaction.
   c. advertise the property only in the broker's name.
   d. to list the property in the broker's name.

10. License Law and Commission Rules allow a broker to disburse trust account funds under which of the following circumstances?
   a. Only upon the closing of a transaction
   b. Upon a written request from a buyer who has provided earnest money held in trust account by the broker as part of the transactional agreement.
   c. Upon an interpleader court action filed by either the buyer or seller in the transaction
   d. Upon a broker's reasonable interpretation of the contract, with written notification to all parties

11. The Commission prohibits 'blind ads' in the marketing of real property for sale as these advertisements
   a. mislead the public as to the actual purchase price of the property.
   b. violate Fair Housing Laws with regard to handicap discrimination.
   c. fail to include the location of the property.
   d. fail to disclosure the real estate licensure of the advertiser.

12. The Real Estate Commission may impose disciplinary actions against a licensee for which of the following practices?
   a. Waiting 10 days after the termination of a listing engagement to remove the brokerage firm's sign from the owner's property
   b. Depositing earnest money funds into an licensee affiliate's trust account rather than in the broker's trust account
   c. Paying an unlicensed assistant a percentage of the licensee's commission split with the broker
   d. Receiving a share of the broker's compensation earned in a sales transaction

13. The liability of the Real Estate Education, Research, and Recovery Fund for the actions of one licensee would be terminated after the Fund pays out how much money on behalf of that individual?
   a. $75,000
   b. $45,000
   c. $25,000
   d. $100,000

14. For a licensee, which of the following actions would be considered an Unfair Practice under License Law?
   a. Acting in a disclosed dual capacity as both a principal and an agent in a real estate transaction
   b. Paying a referral fee to a broker in Florida
   c. Indicating that the a competitive market analysis done for a client is an appraisal estimation
   d. Receiving compensation from another broker even with the written authorization of the affiliate's broker

15. Rules and Regulations require that the Real Estate Commission maintain certifications of a licensee's history as well as investigative files relating to such history under what schedules?
   a. Upon written request, Commission must provide only up to a four year certification history of a licensee's record
   b. All investigative files on a licensee's record must be maintained 10 years.
   c. Investigative files on a licensee's record in which the Commission imposes formal disciplinary action must be maintained for 15 years
   d. Investigative files on a licensee's record in which the Commission imposes formal disciplinary action must be maintained for 40 years

16. Which of the following is true regarding the selection and status of the Real Estate Commission and the Commissioner?
   a. The Commission members and the Commissioner are appointed by the Governor and confirmed by the State Senate.
   b. Commission members are elected by the State Senate, and the Commissioner is then selected by the Commission.
   c. Unlike the Commission whose members, appointed by the governor and confirmed by the State Senate, the Commissioner becomes a state employee hired by the Commission.
   d. Both Commission members and the Commissioner are salaried employees within the Secretary of State's governmental budge unit.

17. With regard to the handling of trust funds, a broker engaging in property management must ensure that
   a. the firm is covered by a Fidelity Insurance Bond whenever managing community associations.
   b. security deposits held in escrow accounts must always reflect a balance equal to the total of all such deposits.
   c. trust fund accounts that hold rental payments be kept separate from those escrow accounts that hold security deposits.
   d. all trust fund accounts are at least reconciled on a quarterly basis.

18. Under Commission Rules, which of the following disclosures is a licensee required to make to both buyer and seller at the time of a contract offer?
   a. Disclose whether the licensee's brokerage firm practices dual agency and/or designated agency
   b. Disclose whether the licensee is the broker or an affiliated licensee representing the broker
   c. Disclose if the licensee's compensation for services in the transaction will come from a client or a customer
   d. Disclose who the licensee represents in the transaction and from whom the licensee will be compensated

19. The Commission has determined a broker to be guilty of commingling trust account funds as well as failing to keep copies of trust fund accounting records for three years. The Commission has the authority to

a. file an injunction to stop any further trust account activity on the part of the broker.
b. fine the broker up to $1,000 and suspend the broker's license.
c. fine the broker up to $5,000 and issue a salesperson's license in place of that person's existing broker license.
d. revoke the broker's license and fine the offending party up to $10,000.

multiple violations - up to $5000

20. What is true regarding the funding for the Commission's Education, Research and Recovery Fund?

a. If the fund is at risk of falling below $1,000,000, brokerage firms would share in the payment of a prorated tax to bring the Fund back to its required level.
b. A primary source of money for this fund comes from fees for first time real estate licensees.
c. The Commission is prohibited from investing the money with the intent of increasing the balance in the fund.
d. The fund may compensate any principal or agent in a real estate transaction as long as the aggrieved party follows the proper statutory guidelines under License Law.

APPENDIX

State Licensing Agencies and Statutes

Alabama
www.arec.alabama.gov
www.legislature.state.al.us/CodeofAlabama/1975/coatoc.htm

Alaska
www.commerce.state.ak.us/occ/prec.htm
www.dced.state.ak.us/occ/pub/RECregulations.pdf

Arizona
www.re.state.az.us
www.azleg.gov/ArizonaRevisedStatutes.asp

Arkansas
www.arec.arkansas.gov

California
www.dre.ca.gov
http://leginfo.legislature.ca.gov/faces/codes.xhtm

Colorado
http://cdn.colorado.gov/cs/Satellite/DORA-DRE/CBON/DORA/1251627670428
www.lexisnexis.com/hottopics/Colorado/

Connecticut
www.ct.gov/DCP/cwp/view.asp?a=1624&Q=276076&PM=1
www.cga.ct.gov/asp/menu/statutes.asp

Delaware
www.dpr.delaware.gov/boards/realestate/
http://delcode.delaware.gov/title24/c029/index.shtml

District of Columbia
www.pearsonvue.com/dc/realestate/
http://dc.gov/DC/Government/DC+Courts+&+Laws

Florida
www.myfloridalicense.com/dbpr/
www.leg.state.fl.us/statutes/

Georgia
www.grec.state.ga.us
www.grec.state.ga.us/about/relaw.html

Hawaii
cca.hawaii.gov/reb/
www.cca.hawaii.gov/reb/

Idaho
www.irec.idaho.gov
www.legislature.idaho.gov/idstat/TOC/IDStatutesTOC.htm

Illinois
www.idfpr.com/dpr/re/realmain.asp
www.ilga.gov/legislation/ilcs/ilcs.asp

Indiana
www.ai.org/pla/real.htm
www.in.gov/legislative/ic/code/

Iowa
www.state.ia.us/government/com/prof/sales/home.html
www.state.ia.us/government/com/prof/sales/law_index.html

Kansas
www.accesskansas.org/krec
www.kansas.gov/krec/legal.html

Kentucky
www.krec.ky.gov
www.lrc.ky.gov/krs/titles.htm

Louisiana
www.lrec.state.la.us
www.lrec.state.la.us/laws-and-rules/

Maine
www.maine.gov/pfr/professionallicensing/professions/real_estate/
www.mainelegislature.org/legis/statutes/

Maryland
www.dllr.state.md.us/license/mrec/
www.dllr.state.md.us/license/law/mreclaw.shtml

Massachusetts
www.mass.gov/ocabr/licensee/dpl-boards/re/
www.mass.gov/legis/laws/mgl/

Michigan
www.michigan.gov/lara/0,4601,7-154-35299_61343_35414_60647_35475---,00
.html
www.legislature.mi.gov/doc.aspx?chapterindex

Minnesota
www.mn.gov/commerce/licensees/Real-Estate-License/
www.revisor.mn.gov/pubs/

Mississippi
www.mrec.state.ms.us
www.michie.com/Mississippi/

Missouri
www.pr.mo.gov/realestate.asp
www.moga.mo.gov/statutes/C339.HTM

Montana
www.bsd.dli.mt.gov/license/bsd_boards/rre_board/board_page.asp

Nebraska
www.nrec.ne.gov
uniweb.legislature.ne.gov/laws/laws.php

Nevada
www.red.state.nv.us
www.leg.state.nv.us/law1.cfm

New Hampshire
www.nh.gov/nhrec/
www.gencourt.state.nh.us/rsa/html/indexes/

New Jersey
www.state.nj.us/dobi/division_rec/
lis.njleg.state.nj.us

New Mexico
www.rld.state.nm.us/boards/Real¬_Estate_Commission.aspx
www.rld.state.nm.us/boards/Real_Estate_Commission_rules_and_Laws.aspx

New York
www.dos.ny.gov/licensing/re_broker/re_broker.html
http://public.leginfo.state.ny.us/menugetf.cgi?COMMONQUERY=LAWS

North Carolina
www.ncrec.state.nc.us
www.ncga.state.nc.us/gascripts/Statutes/Statutes.asp

North Dakota
www.realestatend.org
www.legis.nd.gov/general-information/north-dakota-century-code

Ohio
www.com.state.oh.us/real/
http://codes.ohio.gov/orc/

Oklahoma
www.ok.gov/OREC/
www.ok.gov/OREC/documents/License%20Code%20and%20Rule%20Book%20
September%2012,%202014.pdf

Oregon
www.rea.state.or.us
www.leg.state.or.us/ors/

Pennsylvania
www.portal.state.pa.us/portal/server.pt/community/state_real_estate
_commission/12523
www.pacode.com

Rhode Island
www.dbr.state.ri.us/divisions/commlicensing/realestate.php
www.rilin.state.ri.us/statutes/

South Carolina
www.llr.state.sc.us/pol/rec/
www.scstatehouse.gov/code/t40c057.php

South Dakota
www.dlr.sd.gov/bdcomm/realestate/
http://legis.state.sd.us/statutes/

Tennessee
www.tn.gov/regboards/trec/
www.tn.gov/regboards/trec/law.shtml

Texas
www.trec.state.tx.us
www.statutes.legis.state.tx.us

Utah
www.realestate.utah.gov
www.le.state.ut.us/~code/code.htm

Vermont
www.vtprofessionals.org/opr1/real_estate
www.leg.state.vt.us/statutesMain.cfm

Virginia
www.dpor.virginia.gov/boards/real-estate/
www.leg1.state.va.us/cgi-bin/legp504.exe?000+cod+TOC5500000

Washington
www.dol.wa.gov/business/realestate/lawsrules.html
http://apps.leg.wa.gov/rcw/

West Virginia
www.wvrec.org
www.wvrec.org/Law.pdf

Wisconsin
www.dsps.wi.gov/Licenses-Permits/RealEstateBroker
www.wilawlibrary.gov/topics/realprop.php

Wyoming
http://realestate.state.wy.us
www.wyoming.gov/loc/02252011_1/realEstate/legal/Pages/statutes.aspx

MATH FAQs

Answers to Your Most Frequently Asked Real Estate Math Questions

MATH FAQs CONTENTS

MATH FAQs INTRODUCTION

Math is an integral part of the real estate profession. The amount and complexity of the math a real estate professional or consumer encounters will vary, depending on the area of real estate involved. Calculators and computers are great time-savers, but a solid, basic knowledge of math is still important. It is a matter of taking the math concepts and adapting them to the real estate profession.

This review covers the basics of real estate math in the real-world situations that will be encountered, as well as the math problems a prospective licensee will most likely find on the real estate licensing examination. Even those who are uncomfortable working with numbers will find that this clear and simple review will reinforce concepts that haven't been encountered for many years—and maybe alert you to a few tricks and shortcuts, too.

Study, review, and practice help overcome stress and anxiety so that everyone can become comfortable with math. With practice and review, your confidence and ability in real estate math will grow.

USING THIS MATH REVIEW

This math review is organized in a way that makes it easy to look up just the information needed. The subject matter is presented in a straightforward manner with a minimum of wordy explanations and a maximum of quick tips, examples, formulas, memory aids, and shortcuts to help you become confident in real estate math.

Divided into sections, the review is divided into the following five general subject areas:

1. Calculators
2. Measurement
3. Fractions
4. Percentages
5. Proration

Within each general subject heading are a series of frequently asked questions (FAQs) and brief, clear explanations. The Math FAQs provide a good, general review of real estate math principles, but can also be used for a last-minute review of difficult issues or even as a reference in daily real estate practice.

SPECIAL FEATURES

Some math concepts have been explained earlier in the text in pertinent units. In this review you will find general explanations of additional concepts, as well as **Math Tips** that offer insight into both real estate math in general and the real estate exam's math content in particular. The **For Example** feature applies formulas and concepts to practical situations to show how the concept works in the real world. Practice problems at the end of the review provide the opportunity to apply one's understanding in an exam-style context.

Introduction to Calculators

Basic calculators are permitted when taking most state licensing examinations. The rules usually require that the calculator be silent, handheld, battery-operated, and nonprinting. Many states will not allow test takers to use a real estate or financial calculator while taking the real estate exam. Check with your state regarding the appropriate calculator for your exam.

WHAT KIND OF CALCULATOR DO I NEED?

A basic calculator with functions for addition (+), subtraction (–), multiplication (×), and division (÷) is sufficient for licensing examinations. A calculator with a battery only or solar power with a battery backup is recommended over solar-powered only. Choose a calculator that is most comfortable for you; allow yourself time to learn to use it correctly and to become comfortable with it before you take the licensing examination.

CALCULATORS WITH SPECIFIC REAL ESTATE FUNCTIONS

Many business or financial calculators have additional functions that are very beneficial to the real estate professional. Some of the relevant information that can be provided or found is indicated by keys for "N" (number of interest compounding periods/number of payments), "I" (interest rate per period), "PV" (present value of money/loan), "PMT" (amount of payment), and "FV" (future value of money). Business or financial calculators vary according to brand and/or model; therefore, the user's manual should always be followed to use the calculator properly. For example, some calculators indicate "TERM" instead of "N"; therefore, the number of years of the term is entered instead of the number of payments or compounding periods. Some have "LOAN" instead of "PV." Some instruct the user to enter the interest rate as an annual rate instead of a monthly rate. A business or financial calculator that contains these extra functions may prove useful, but anyone taking a licensing examination should always check with the state real estate commission to find out if the calculator can be used during the exam. No matter which calculator is chosen, the user should always read the user's manual.

FIGURE M.1: Calculator Functions to Look For

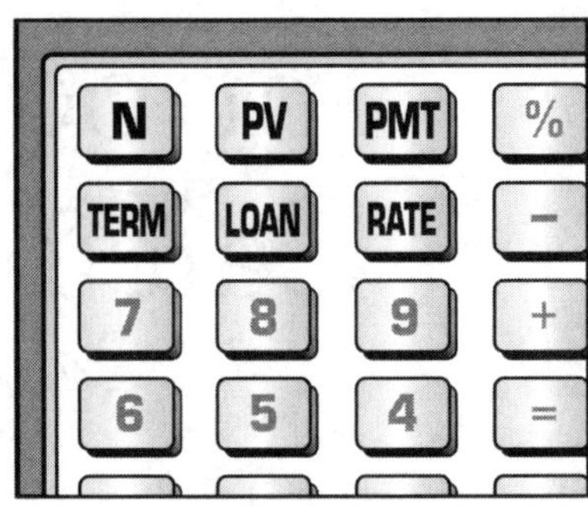

MATH TIP Be careful! Business or financial calculators often have been preset to round to two decimal places. The user's manual will indicate how to change any presettings to float or to display to a minimum of five decimal places. That change will provide an answer with enough decimal places to match multiple-choice answers on an exam. The calculations in this FAQ section are rounded to three decimal places except for those dealing with money. Those are rounded to the nearest cent. Proration problems are computed by carrying the division to three decimal places, and then rounding to the nearest cent only after the final proration figure is determined.

HOW DO I USE THE PERCENT KEY?

If you use the "%" key on calculators to solve percentage problems, read the user's manual for the key's proper use. Some calculators require the use of the "%" key or the "=" key *but never both in the same calculation*. Other calculators require the use of *both* the "%" key and the "=" key to get a correct answer. No matter which calculator you choose, read the user's manual.

FOR EXAMPLE If a property sold for $100,000 and a 7% commission was paid to the real estate professional, how much was the real estate professional paid?

The answer to this question can be determined two ways, as illustrated below.

Convert 7% to the decimal 0.07. (How to convert percentages to decimals is shown in Section 3.) Touch $100,000 into your calculator, then the × or multiplication key, then 0.07, then the = key to read $7,000.

Or, touch in $100,000, then the × or multiplication key, then 7, then the % key. If your calculator now reads $7,000, you've finished the question. If, when you touch the % key, it reads 0.07, then you must touch the = key to complete the calculation.

The use of the % key allows the calculator to convert to the proper decimal place, and there is no question about the placement of the decimal. The choice is yours: you can convert the percentage to a decimal or use the % key for the conversion.

Measurement Problems

WHAT ARE LINEAR MEASUREMENTS?

Linear measurement is line measurement. Linear measures are used for length or distance (e.g., length of a wall). Linear measures include feet, yards, inches, and miles. When the terms

- *foot,*
- *linear foot,*
- *running foot,* or
- *front foot*

are used, you are being asked to determine the *total length* of the dimension, whether measured in a straight line, crooked line, or curved line. The abbreviation for feet is '. Thus, 12 feet can be written as 12'. The abbreviation for inches is ". Thus, 12 inches can be written as 12".

WHAT DOES THE TERM *FRONT FOOT* REFER TO?

When the term *front foot* is used, you are dealing with the number of units on the **frontage** of a lot. The frontage is usually the street frontage, but it might be the water frontage if the lot is on a river, lake, or ocean. If two dimensions are given for a tract of land and they are not labeled, the first dimension is the frontage. The word *width* also refers to frontage; the length is the *depth* of the property.

HOW DO I CONVERT ONE KIND OF LINEAR MEASUREMENT TO ANOTHER?

12 inches = 1 foot

Inches ÷ 12 = feet (144 inches ÷ 12 = 12 feet)

Feet × 12 = inches (12 feet × 12 = 144 inches)

36 inches = 1 yard

Inches ÷ 36 = yards (144 inches ÷ 36 = 4 yards)

Yards × 36 = inches (4 yards × 36 = 144 inches)

3 feet = 1 yard

Feet ÷ 3 = yards (12 feet ÷ 3 = 4 yards)

Yards × 3 = feet (4 yards × 3 = 12 feet)

5,280 feet = 1 mile

Feet ÷ 5,280 = miles (10,560 feet ÷ 5,280 = 2 miles)

Miles × 5,280 = feet (2 miles × 5,280 = 10,560 feet)

16½ feet = 1 rod

Feet ÷ 16.5 = rods (82.5 feet ÷ 16.5 = 5 rods)

Rods × 16.5 = feet (5 rods × 16.5 = 82.5 feet)

320 rods = 1 mile

Rods ÷ 320 = miles (640 rods ÷ 320 = 2 miles)

Miles × 320 = rods (2 miles × 320 = 640 rods)

FOR EXAMPLE A rectangular lot is 50 feet by 150 feet. The cost to fence this lot is priced per linear/running foot. How many linear/running feet will be used to calculate the price of the fence?

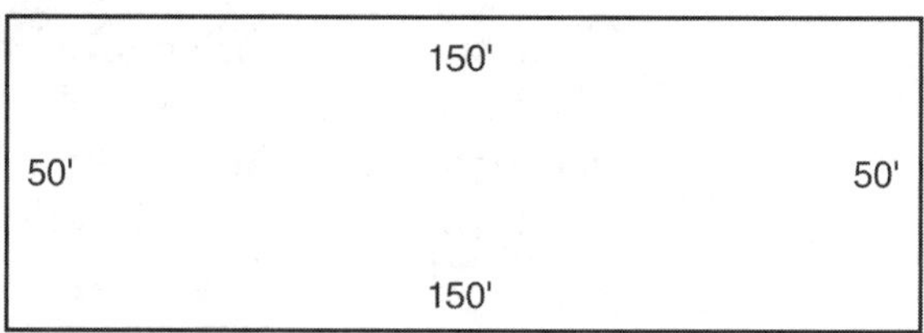

50 feet + 150 feet + 50 feet + 150 feet = 400 linear/running feet

400 linear/running feet is the answer.

FOR EXAMPLE A parcel of land that fronts on Interstate 45 in Houston, Texas, is for sale at $5,000 per front foot. What will it cost to purchase this parcel of land if the dimensions are 150 feet by 100 feet?

150 is the frontage because it is the first dimension given.

150 front feet × $5,000 = $750,000 cost

$750,000 is the answer.

HOW DO I SOLVE FOR AREA MEASUREMENT?

Area is the two-dimensional surface of an object. Area is quoted in *square units* or in *acres*. A linear measure multiplied by another linear measure always equals a square measure: feet times feet equals square feet; miles times miles equals square miles, yards times yards equals square yards, and so on. We will look at calculating the area of squares, rectangles, and triangles. Squares and rectangles are four-sided objects. All four sides of a square are the same length. Opposite sides of a rectangle are the same length. A triangle is a three-sided object. The three sides of a triangle can be the same length or two or three different lengths.

MATH TIP When two dimensions are given, assume they refer to a figure that is a rectangle unless told otherwise.

HOW DO I CONVERT ONE KIND OF AREA MEASUREMENT TO ANOTHER?

144 square inches = 1 square foot

Square inches ÷ 144 = square feet (14,400 square inches ÷ 144 = 100 square feet)

Square feet × 144 = square inches ÷ (100 square feet × 144 = 14,400 square inches)

1,296 square inches = 1 square yard

Square inches ÷ 1,296 = square yards (12,960 ÷ 1,296 = 10 square yards)

Square yards × 1,296 = square inches (10 square yards × 1,296 = 12,960 square yards)

9 square feet = 1 square yard

Square feet ÷ 9 = square yards (90 square feet ÷ 9 = 10 square yards)

Square yards × 9 = square feet (10 square yards × 9 = 90 square feet)

43,560 square feet = 1 acre

Square feet ÷ 43,560 = acres (87,120 ÷ 43,560 = 2 acres)

Acres × 43,560 = square feet (2 acres × 43,560 = 87,120 square feet)

640 acres = 1 section = 1 square mile

Acres ÷ 640 = sections (square miles) (1,280 acres ÷ 640 = 2 sections)

Sections (square miles) × 640 = acres (2 sections × 640 = 1,280 acres)

HOW DO I DETERMINE THE AREA OF A SQUARE OR RECTANGLE?

Length × width = **area of a square or rectangle**

FOR EXAMPLE How many square feet are in a room 15'6" × 30'9"? Remember, we must use like dimensions, so the inches must be converted to feet.

6" ÷ 12 = 0.5' + 15' = 15.5' wide

9" ÷ 12 = 0.75' + 30' = 30.75' long

30.75' × 15.5' = 476.625 square feet

476.625 square feet is the answer.

FOR EXAMPLE If carpet costs $63 per square yard to install, what would it cost to carpet the room in the previous example?

476.625 square feet ÷ 9 = 52.958333 square yards × $63 per square yard = $3,336.375, or $3,336.38 rounded

$3,336.38 is the answer.

FOR EXAMPLE How many acres are there in a parcel of land that measures 450' × 484'?

484' × 450' = 217,800 square feet ÷ 43,560 = 5 acres of land

5 acres is the answer.

HOW DO I DETERMINE THE AREA OF A TRIANGLE?

½ (base × height) = **area of a triangle**

or

(base × height) ÷ 2 = **area of a triangle**

FOR EXAMPLE How many square feet are contained in a triangular parcel of land that is 400 feet on the base and 200 feet high?

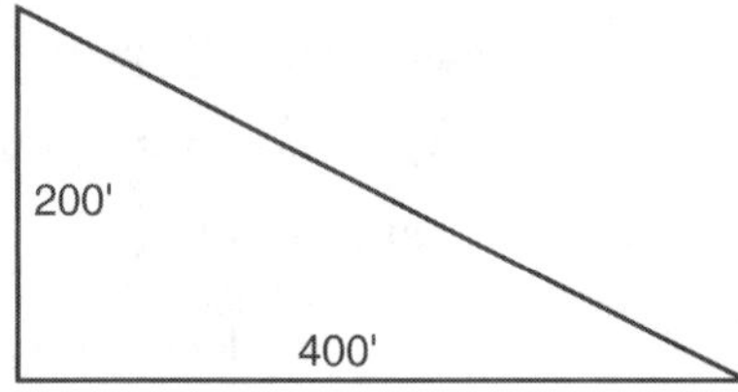

(400' × 200') ÷ 2 = 40,000 square feet

40,000 square feet is the answer.

FOR EXAMPLE How many acres are in a three-sided tract of land that is 300' on the base and 400' high?

(300' × 400') ÷ 2 = 60,000 square feet ÷ 43,560 = 1.377 acres

1.377 acres is the answer (rounded to three decimal places).

HOW DO I SOLVE FOR VOLUME?

Volume is the space inside a three-dimensional object. Volume is measured in *cubic units*. We will look at calculating the volume of boxes that have rectangular sides and triangular prisms. There are always three measures: length, width, and height. Multiplying the three measures expressed in the same kind of units results in cubic units—for example, feet times feet times feet equals cubic feet.

HOW DO I CONVERT FROM ONE KIND OF VOLUME MEASUREMENT TO ANOTHER?

1,728 cubic inches = 1 cubic foot

Cubic inches ÷ 1,728 = cubic feet
(17,280 cubic inches ÷ 1,728 = 10 cubic feet)

Cubic feet × 1,728 = cubic inches
(10 cubic feet × 1,728 = 17,280 cubic inches)

46,656 cubic inches = 1 cubic yard

Cubic inches ÷ 46,656 = cubic yards
(93,312 cubic inches ÷ 46,656 = 2 cubic yards)

Cubic yards × 46,656 = cubic inches
(2 cubic yards × 46,656 = 93,312 cubic inches)

27 cubic feet = 1 cubic yard

Cubic feet ÷ 27 = cubic yards (270 cubic feet ÷ 27 = 10 cubic yards)
Cubic yards × 27 = cubic feet (10 cubic yards × 27 = 270 cubic feet)

HOW DO I DETERMINE THE VOLUME OF A ROOM?

For purposes of determining volume, think of a room as though it were a box.

Length × width × height = **volume of a box**

FOR EXAMPLE A building is 500 feet long, 400 feet wide, and 25 feet high. How many cubic feet of space are in this building?

500' × 400' × 25' = 5,000,000 cubic feet

5,000,000 cubic feet is the answer.

FOR EXAMPLE How many cubic yards of concrete would it take to build a sidewalk measuring 120 feet long; 2 feet, 6 inches wide; and 3 inches thick?

6" ÷ 12' = 0.5' + 2' = 2.5' wide

3" ÷ 12' = 0.25' thick

120' × 2.5' × 0.25' = 75 cubic feet ÷ 27 = 2.778 cubic yards
(rounded to three decimal places)

2.778 cubic yards is the answer.

HOW DO I DETERMINE THE VOLUME OF A TRIANGULAR PRISM?

The terms *A-frame*, *A-shaped*, or *gable roof* on an exam describe a triangular prism.

½ (base × height × width) = **volume of a triangular prism**

or

(base × height × width) ÷ 2 = **volume of a triangular prism**

FOR EXAMPLE An A-frame cabin in the mountains is 50 feet long and 30 feet wide. The cabin is 25 feet high from the base to the highest point. How many cubic feet of space does this A-frame cabin contain?

50' × 30' × 25' ÷ 2 = 18,750 cubic feet

18,750 cubic feet is the answer.

FOR EXAMPLE A building is 40 feet by 25 feet with a 10-foot-high ceiling. The building has a gable roof that is 8 feet high at the tallest point. How many cubic feet are in this structure, including the roof?

40' × 25' × 10' = 10,000 cubic feet in the building

40' × 25' × 8' ÷ 2 = 4,000 cubic feet in the gable roof

10,000 cubic feet + 4,000 cubic feet = 14,000 cubic feet

14,000 cubic feet is the answer.

Section 3 Fractions, Decimals, and Percentages

WHAT ARE THE PARTS OF A FRACTION?

A fraction shows one number over another number. The **denominator** on the bottom of the fraction shows the number of equal parts in the whole or total. The **numerator** on the top of the fraction shows the number of those parts with which you are working. In the example below, the whole or total has been divided into eight equal parts, and you have seven of those equal parts.

$$\frac{\text{numerator}}{\text{denominator}} \qquad \frac{\text{(top number)}}{\text{(bottom number)}}$$

WHAT IS MEANT BY A *PROPER* AND AN *IMPROPER* FRACTION?

The value of a proper fraction is always less than one whole. $\frac{7}{8}$ is an example of a proper fraction. $\frac{7}{8}$ represents 7 parts out of 8 parts needed to make one whole. All proper fractions have a numerator smaller than the denominator. For example,

$\frac{5}{8}$ or $\frac{3}{4}$.

The fraction $\frac{11}{8}$ is an example of an **improper fraction**. The value of an improper fraction is always equal to or greater than one whole. The improper fraction $\frac{11}{8}$ states that you have 11 parts but only need 8 parts to make one whole. All improper fractions have a numerator larger than the denominator.

WHAT IS A MIXED NUMBER?

$11\frac{1}{2}$ is a **mixed number**. It consists of a whole number and a fraction.

HOW DO I MULTIPLY FRACTIONS?

When multiplying fractions, numerator is multiplied by numerator, and denominator by denominator. Let's start with an easy question. What is $\frac{1}{2} \times \frac{3}{4}$?

First multiply the numerators (top numbers), $1 \times 3 = 3$. Then, multiply the denominators (bottom numbers), $2 \times 4 = 8$. Thus, $\frac{1}{2} \times \frac{3}{4} = \frac{3}{8}$.

What is $4\frac{2}{3} \times 10\frac{5}{8}$? The first step is to convert the whole number 4 into thirds. This is done by multiplying the whole number 4 by the denominator of the fraction, which is 3, so that $4 \times 3 = 12$. Thus, the whole number 4 is equal to $\frac{12}{3}$ and $4\frac{2}{3}$ is equal to $\frac{12}{3} + \frac{2}{3}$ or $\frac{14}{3}$.

The next step is to convert the whole number 10 into eighths. This is done by multiplying the whole number 10 by the denominator of the fraction, 8. Thus, the whole number 10 is equal to $\frac{80}{8}$ and $\frac{80}{8} + \frac{5}{8} = \frac{85}{8}$.

So, what is $\frac{14}{3} \times \frac{85}{8}$? First, $14 \times 85 = 1{,}190$. Then, $3 \times 8 = 24$. Finally, $\frac{1{,}190}{24} = 49.583$.

An easier way to solve the problem is to convert the fractions to decimals.

$\frac{2}{3}$ is equal to $2 \div 3$ or 0.667 rounded to three decimal places.

$\frac{5}{8}$ is equal to $5 \div 8$ or 0.625.

$4.667 \times 10.625 = 49.587$ (rounded to three decimal places).

When working with fractions or decimal equivalents, you will find that the answers will be close but not exact, depending on how many places the answer is computed before rounding.

HOW DO I DIVIDE BY FRACTIONS?

Dividing by fractions is a two-step process. What is $\frac{3}{4} \div \frac{1}{4}$?

First, invert the second fraction by exchanging the numerator and denominator, then multiply the fractions and simplify the result. In this example, invert the $\frac{1}{4}$ to $\frac{4}{1}$. Then, $\frac{3}{4} \times \frac{4}{1} = \frac{12}{4}$. Finally, $12 \div 4 = 3$.

You may also convert $\frac{3}{4}$ to the decimal 0.75 and $\frac{1}{4}$ to the decimal 0.25.

$0.75 \div 0.25 = 3$. (There are three decimal parts of 0.25 in the figure 0.75.)

What is $100\ \frac{7}{8} \div \frac{3}{4}$?

$100 \times 8 = 800$.

$800 + 7 = \frac{807}{8}$.

$\frac{3}{4}$ is inverted to $\frac{4}{3}$.

$\frac{807}{8} \times \frac{4}{3} = 807 \times 4 = 3{,}228$; $8 \times 3 = 24$. $\frac{3{,}228}{24} = 3{,}228 \div 24 = 134.5$.

Or, $7 \div 8 = 0.875$ and $3 \div 4 = 0.75$.

$100.875 \div 0.75 = 134.5$.

HOW DO I CONVERT FRACTIONS TO DECIMALS?

Fractions will sometimes be used in real estate math problems. Because calculators may be used on most licensing examinations, it is best to convert fractions to decimals.

MATH TIP To convert a fraction to a decimal, divide the numerator (top number) by the denominator (bottom number).

For example:

$^{7}/_{8} = 7 \div 8 =$ **0.875**

$^{11}/_{8} = 11 \div 8 =$ **1.375**

$11\frac{1}{2} = 1 \div 2 = 0.5 + 11 =$ **11.5**

Once fractions have been converted to decimals, other calculations can be easily completed using the calculator. Note that many calculators automatically display the zero before the decimal point.

HOW DO I ADD OR SUBTRACT DECIMALS?

Line up the decimals, add or subtract, and bring the decimal down in the answer. You may add zeros if necessary as placeholders. For example, 0.5 is the same as 0.50, or .5.

$$\begin{array}{r} 0.50 \\ \underline{+\ 3.25} \\ =3.75 \end{array} \qquad \begin{array}{r} 8.20 \\ \underline{-\ 0.75} \\ =7.45 \end{array}$$

MATH TIP When you use a calculator, the decimal will be in the correct place in the answer (0.5 + 3.25 = 3.75, and 8.2 – 0.75 = 7.45).

HOW DO I MULTIPLY DECIMALS?

Multiply the numbers, then count the number of decimal places in each number. Next, start with the last number on the right and move the decimal the total number of decimal places to the left in the answer.

Multiply as you normally would to get the 1,500, then count the four decimal places in the numbers (0.20 and 0.75). In the 1,500, start at the last zero on the right and count four decimal places to the left. The decimal is placed to the left of the 1.

$$\begin{array}{r} 0.20 \\ \underline{\times\ 0.75} \\ 100 \\ \underline{140\ } \\ 0.1500 \text{ or } 0.15 \end{array}$$

MATH TIP When you use a calculator, the decimal will be in the correct place in the answer (0.2 × 0.75 = 0.15).

HOW DO I DIVIDE DECIMALS?

Divide the **dividend** (the number being divided) by the **divisor** (the number you are dividing by) and bring the decimal in the dividend straight up in the **quotient** (answer). If the divisor has a decimal, move the decimal to the right of the divisor and move the decimal the same number of places to the right in the dividend. Now divide as stated above.

$$\begin{array}{r} 0.75 \\ 2\overline{)1.50} \\ 1.4 \\ 10 \\ 10 \\ 0 \end{array} \qquad 0.5\overline{)15.5} = \begin{array}{r} 31. \\ 5\overline{)155.} \\ 15 \\ 05 \\ 5 \\ 0 \end{array}$$

MATH TIP When you use a calculator, you can have a decimal in the divisor and the decimal will be in the correct place in the answer ($1.5 \div 2 = 0.75$, and $15.5 \div 0.5 = 31$).

WHAT IS A PERCENTAGE?

Percent (%) means *per hundred* or *per hundred parts*. The whole or total always represents 100%.

5% = 5 parts of 100 parts, or $5 \div 100 = 0.05$ or $\frac{1}{20}$

75% = 75 parts of 100 parts, or $75 \div 100 = 0.75$ or $\frac{3}{4}$

120% = 120 parts of 100 parts, or $120 \div 100 = 1.2$ or $1\frac{1}{5}$

HOW CAN I CONVERT A PERCENTAGE TO A DECIMAL?

Move the decimal *two places* to the *left* and *drop* the % sign.

$20\% = 20 \div 100 = 0.20$ or 0.2

$1\% = 1 \div 100 = 0.01$

$12\frac{1}{4}\% = 12.25\%$, $12.25 \div 100 = 0.1225$

See Figure M.2.

HOW CAN I CONVERT A DECIMAL TO A PERCENTAGE?

Move the decimal *two places* to the *right* and *add* the % sign.

$0.25 = 25\%$

$0.9 = 90\%$

$0.0875 = 8.75\%$ or $8\frac{3}{4}\%$

See Figure M.2.

FIGURE M.2: Converting Decimal to Percentage and Percentage to Decimal

Decimal to Percentage	Percentage to Decimal
.10 ⟶ **10%**	**.10** ⟵ **10%**
Move decimal two places right to find the percentage	Move percentage two places left to find the decimal

HOW DO I MULTIPLY BY PERCENTAGES?

$500 \times 25\% = 500 \times {}^{25}/_{100} = {}^{12,500}/_{100} = \mathbf{125}$

or

$500 \times 25\% = 125$, or $500 \times 0.25 = \mathbf{125}$

HOW DO I DIVIDE BY PERCENTAGES?

$100 \div 5\% = 100 \div {}^{5}/_{100} = 100 \times {}^{100}/_{5} = {}^{10,000}/_{5} = \mathbf{2,000}$

or

$100 \div 5\% = \mathbf{2,000}$

or

$100 \div 0.05 = \mathbf{2,000}$

IS THERE ANY EASY WAY TO REMEMBER HOW TO SOLVE PERCENTAGE PROBLEMS?

The following three formulas are important for solving all percentage problems:

Total × rate = part
Part ÷ rate = total
Part ÷ total = rate

WHAT IS THE X-BAR METHOD?

The X-bar is another tool to use to solve percentage problems. For some people, the "three-formula method" is more difficult to remember than the visual image of an X-bar in which the horizontal line stands for a division and the x-brace supporting the horizontal line stands for a multiplication.

$$\frac{\text{part}}{\text{total} \times \text{rate}}$$

HOW DO I USE THE X-BAR?

The procedure for using the X-Bar is as follows:

1. Enter the two *known* items in the correct places.
2. If there is a multiplication sign between the two items, you *multiply* to equal the missing item.
3. If the line between the two items is *horizontal*, you *divide* to equal the missing item. When you divide, the top (**Part**) always goes into the calculator first and is divided by the bottom (**Total** or **Rate**).

The following examples show how the X-Bar can be used to solve percentage problems. These examples deal with discounts because everyone can relate to buying an item that is on sale. Later, we will see how the X-Bar can be used for many types of real estate problems.

FOR EXAMPLE John purchased a new suit that was marked $500. How much did John save if the suit was on sale for 20% off?

part
$500 X 20%

$500 × 20% = $100

$100 is the answer.

How much did John pay for the suit?

$500 total price – $100 discount = **$400 paid**

or

100% total price – 20% discount = 80% paid

part
$500 X 80%

$500 × 80% = $400

FOR EXAMPLE Richard paid $112.50 for a dress that was reduced 25%. How much was it originally marked?

100% original price – 25% discount = 75% paid

$112.50
total X 75%

$112.50 ÷ 75% = $150

FOR EXAMPLE Sols paid \$127.50 for a coat that was marked down from the original price of \$150. What percentage of discount did Sol receive?

\$150 original price – \$127.50 discount price = \$22.50 discount

$$\frac{22.50}{\$150 \times \text{rate}}$$

\$22.50 ÷ \$150 = 0.15, or 15%

Or

\$127.50 ÷ \$150 = 0.85, or 85%

85% was the percentage paid; therefore

100% original price – 85% paid = **15% discount**

HOW SHOULD I APPROACH TRICKY WORD PROBLEMS?

Five important steps must be taken to solve word problems.

1. **Read** the problem carefully and completely. Never touch the calculator until you have read the entire problem.
2. **Analyze** the problem to determine what is being asked, what facts are given that *will* be needed to solve for the answer, and what facts are given that *will not* be needed to solve for the answer. Eliminate any information and/or numbers given that are not needed to solve the problem. Take the remaining information and/or numbers and determine which will be needed first, second, and so on, depending on the number of steps it will take to solve the problem.
3. **Choose** the proper formula(s) and steps it will take to solve the problem.
4. **Insert** the known elements and calculate the answer.
5. **Check** your answer to be sure you keyed in the numbers and functions properly on your calculator. Be sure you finished the problem. For example, when the problem asks for the salesperson's or sales associate's share of a commission, do not stop at the broker's share of the commission and mark that answer just because it is one of the choices.

Percentage Problems

HOW DO I SOLVE COMMISSION PROBLEMS?

As it is used in a problem involving a real estate transaction, a full **commission** will be a percentage of the sales price, unless it is stated differently in the problem. Remember that full commission rates, commission splits between brokers, and commission shares between the broker and the sales associates are always negotiable. Always read a problem carefully to determine the correct rate(s).

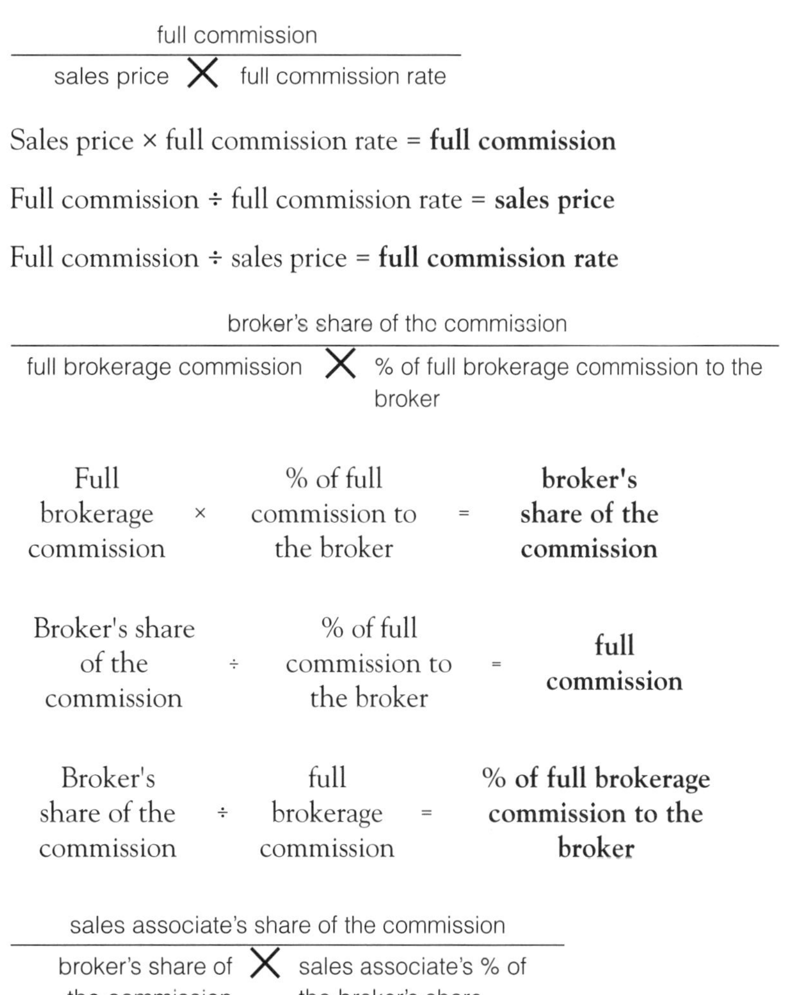

Broker's share of the commission × sales associate's % of the broker's share = **sales associate's share of the commission**

Sales associate's share of the commission ÷ sales associate's % of the broker's share = **broker's share of the commission**

Sales associate's share of the commission ÷ broker's share of the commission = **sales associate's % of the broker's share**

FOR EXAMPLE A seller listed a home for $200,000 and agreed to pay a commission of 5%. The home sold four weeks later for 90% of the list price. The listing broker agreed to give the selling broker 50% of the commission. The listing broker paid the listing sales associate 50% of her share of the commission, and the selling broker paid the selling sales associate 60% of his share of the commission. How much compensation did the selling sales associate receive?

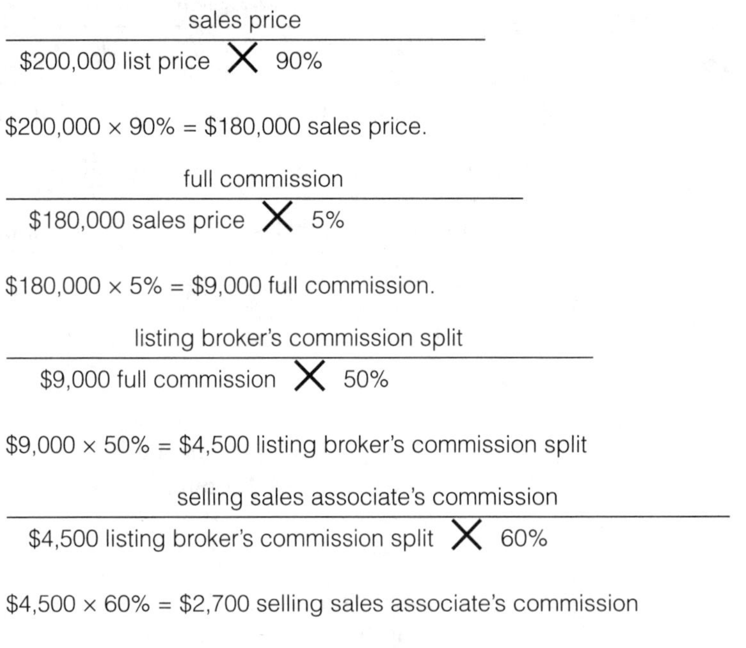

$2,700 selling salesperson's commission is the answer.

WHAT IS MEANT BY SELLER'S DOLLARS AFTER COMMISSION?

The first deduction from the sales price in a real estate transaction typically is the real estate commission. For example, if a house sold for $100,000 and a 5% commission was paid to the listing broker, that means the broker's compensation was $5,000. The seller still has 95% of the sales price, or $95,000. The seller's dollars after commission will be used to pay the seller's other expenses, including any outstanding mortgages secured by the property, and hopefully will leave some money for the seller. The sales price is 100%. Thus, 100% – commission % = percent after commission. The X-Bar can be applied to the sales price, seller's dollars after commission, and percentage after commission to provide the formulas shown below.

seller's dollars after commission

sales price × percentage after commission

Sales price × percentage after commission = **seller's dollars after commission**

Seller's dollars after commission ÷ percentage after commission = **sales price**

Seller's dollars after commission ÷ sales price = **percentage after commission**

FOR EXAMPLE After deducting $5,850 in closing costs and a 5% broker's commission, the sellers received their original cost of $175,000 plus a $4,400 profit. What was the sales price of the property?

$5,850 closing costs + $175,000 original cost + $4,400 profit =
$185,250 seller's dollars after commission

100% sales price – 5% commission = 95% after commission

$185,250 seller's dollars after commission

sales price × 95% after commission

$185,250 ÷ 95% = $195,000

$195,000 sales price is the answer.

HOW DO I DETERMINE INTEREST?

Interest is the cost of using money. The amount of interest paid is determined by the agreed annual interest rate, the amount of money borrowed (loan amount) or the amount of money still owed (loan balance), and the period of time the money is held. When a lender grants a loan for real estate, the loan-to-value ratio (LTV) is the percentage of the sales price or appraised value, whichever is less, that the lender is willing to lend.

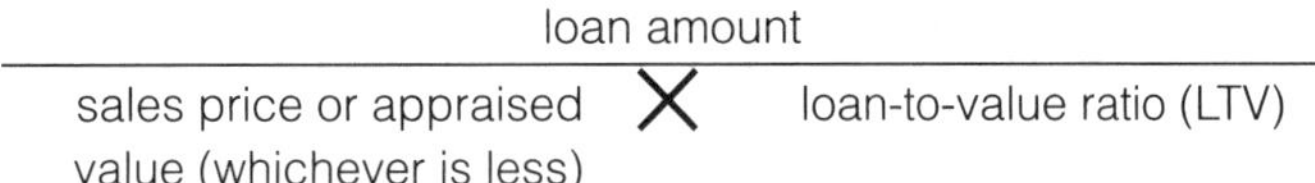

Loan amount ÷ sales price or appraised value (whichever is less) = **loan-to-value ratio (LTV)**

Sales price or appraised value (whichever is less) × loan-to-value ratio (LTV) = **loan amount**

Loan amount ÷ loan-to-value ratio (LTV) = **sales price or appraised value** (whichever is less)

annual interest

loan amount (principal) × annual interest rate

Loan amount (principal) × annual interest rate = **annual interest**

Annual interest ÷ annual interest rate = **loan amount (principal)**

Annual interest ÷ loan amount (principal) = **annual interest rate**

FOR EXAMPLE A parcel of rural land sold for $335,200. The lender approved a 90% loan at 4.5% for 30 years. The appraised value on this parcel was $335,500. How much interest is paid to the lender in the first monthly payment?

loan amount	
$335,200 sales price	× 90%

$335,200 × 90% = $301,680 loan amount

annual interest	
$301,680 loan amount	× 4.5%

$301,680 × 4.5% = $13,575.60 annual interest

$13,575.60 annual interest ÷ 12 months = $1,131.30 monthly interest

$1,131.30 interest in the first monthly payment is the answer.

HOW DO I DETERMINE MONTHLY PRINCIPAL AND INTEREST PAYMENTS?

A **loan payment factor** can be used to calculate the monthly principal and interest payment on a loan. The factor represents the monthly principal and interest payment to amortize a $1,000 loan and is based on the annual interest rate and the term of the loan.

(Loan amount ÷ $1,000) × loan payment factor = **monthly PI payment**

Monthly PI payment ÷ loan payment factor = **loan amount**

FOR EXAMPLE If a lender uses a loan payment factor of $6.99 per $1,000 of loan amount, what will be the monthly PI (principal and interest) payment?

($301,680 loan amount ÷ $1,000) × $6.99 = $2,108.74 monthly PI payment (rounded to the nearest cent)

$2,108.74 monthly PI payment is the answer.

HOW DO I SOLVE PROBLEMS ABOUT POINTS?

The word *point* means percent. One **point** equals 1% of the loan amount.

Two points mean 2%, or ½ point means ½%. A loan point is a percentage of the loan amount.

amount paid for points	
loan amount	× points as percentage of loan

Loan amount × points as percentage of loan = **amount paid for points**

Amount paid for points ÷ points as percentage of loan = **loan amount**

Amount paid for points ÷ loan amount = **points as percentage of loan**

FOR EXAMPLE The lender will charge 3½ discount points on an $800,000 loan. What will be the total amount paid as discount points at closing?

amount paid for points

$800,000 loan amount X 3.5%

$800,000 × 3.5% = $28,000

$28,000 paid for points is the answer.

HOW DO I DETERMINE PROFIT?

A **profit** is made when we sell something for more than we paid for it. If we sell something for less than we paid for it, we have suffered a **loss**.

Sales price – seller's cost = profit

When setting the X-Bar, the whole is the original investment or cost (i.e., the total amount paid by the seller, including the original purchase price and the cost of any improvements made after the purchase). The seller's cost must be the whole thing (the 100%) because percentages of profit or loss are percentages of the money invested. A 20% loss is 20% of the amount invested.

profit

seller's cost X percentage of profit

Seller's cost × percentage of profit = **profit**

Profit ÷ percentage of profit = **seller's cost**

Profit ÷ seller's cost = **percentage of profit**

The seller's cost plus the amount of the profit equals the sales price. Unfortunately, not every sale results in a profit to the seller. The seller's cost minus the amount of any loss equals the sales price. (100% cost ± % profit = % sales price)

sales price

seller's cost X percentage sold of cost

Seller's Cost × percentage sold of cost = **sales price**

Sales price ÷ percentage sold of cost = **seller's cost**

Sales price ÷ seller's cost = **percentage sold of cost**

FOR EXAMPLE A home listed for $285,000 and sold for $275,000, which gave the seller a 10% profit over the seller's cost. What was the seller's cost?

100% seller's cost + 10% profit = 110% sales price

$275,000 ÷ 110% = $250,000 seller's cost

$250,000 seller's cost is the answer.

FOR EXAMPLE Marco invested in a mountain cabin a few years ago and made no improvements to the property. He just sold the cabin for $80,640, losing 16% of his investment. What did the cabin cost Marco?

100% seller's cost – 16% loss = 84% today's value

$$\frac{\text{\$80,640 sales price}}{\text{seller's cost} \times 84\%}$$

$80,640 ÷ 0.84 = $96,000 seller's cost

$96,000 seller's cost is the answer.

HOW DO I ESTIMATE VALUE FOR INCOME-PRODUCING PROPERTIES?

When appraising income-producing property, an opinion of value can be formed by using the property's annual net operating income (NOI) and the current market rate of return or capitalization ("cap") rate. Annual scheduled gross income is adjusted for vacancies and credit losses to arrive at the annual effective gross income. The annual operating expenses are deducted from the annual effective gross income to arrive at the annual NOI.

Vacancy/credit loss is usually expressed as a percentage of the scheduled gross.

Scheduled gross income – vacancies and credit losses = **effective gross income**

Effective gross income – annual operating expenses = **NOI**

$$\frac{\text{NOI}}{\text{value} \times \text{capitalization rate}}$$

Value × capitalization rate = **NOI**

NOI ÷ capitalization rate = **value**

NOI ÷ value = **capitalization rate**

FOR EXAMPLE An office building produces $132,600 annual gross income. If the annual expenses are $30,600 and the appraiser uses an 8.5% cap rate, what is the estimated value?

$132,600 annual gross income – $30,600 annual expenses = $102,000 NOI

$$\frac{\text{\$102,000 NOI}}{\text{value} \times \text{8.5\% cap rate}}$$

$102,000 ÷ 8.5% = $1,200,000 value

$1,200,000 value is the answer.

The above formulas also can be used to calculate either the return on the real estate investment (ROI) or the monthly NOI. The total becomes *original cost* or *investment* instead of value.

FOR EXAMPLE An investor spends $335,000 for a property that should produce a 9% rate of return. What monthly NOI will the investor receive?

NOI
$335,000 investment × 9%

$335,000 × 9% = $30,150

$30,150 NOI ÷ 12 months = $2,512.50 monthly NOI

$2,512.50 monthly NOI is the answer.

HOW DO I SOLVE PROBLEMS INVOLVING PERCENTAGE LEASES?

When establishing the rent to be charged for retail space, a percentage lease may be used instead of a lease based simply on dollars per square foot. In a **percentage lease,** a base or minimum monthly rent is paid plus a percentage of the gross sales in excess of an amount set in the lease. The percentage lease also can be set up as a percentage of the total gross sales or of the base/minimum rent, whichever is larger. The discussion that follows considers the minimum plus percentage lease only.

Gross sales − gross sales not subject to the percentage = **gross sales subject to the percentage**

percentage rent
gross sales subject to the percentage × % in the lease

Gross sales subject to the percentage × % in the lease = **percentage rent**

Percentage rent ÷ % in the lease = **gross sales subject to the percentage**

Percentage rent ÷ gross sales subject to the percentage = **% in the lease**

Add the percentage rent and the base/minimum rent to find the total rent.

FOR EXAMPLE A lease calls for monthly minimum rent of $900 plus 3% of annual gross sales in excess of $270,000. What was the annual rent in a year when the annual gross sales were $350,600?

$900 monthly minimum rent × 12 months = $10,800 annual minimum rent

$350,600 annual gross sales – $270,000 annual gross sales not subject to the percentage = $80,600 annual gross sales subject to the percentage

percentage rent
$80,600 annual gross subject to the percentage × 3%

$80,600 × 3% = $2,418 percentage rent

$10,800 annual minimum rent + $2,418 percentage rent = $13,218 total annual rent

$13,218 total annual rent is the answer.

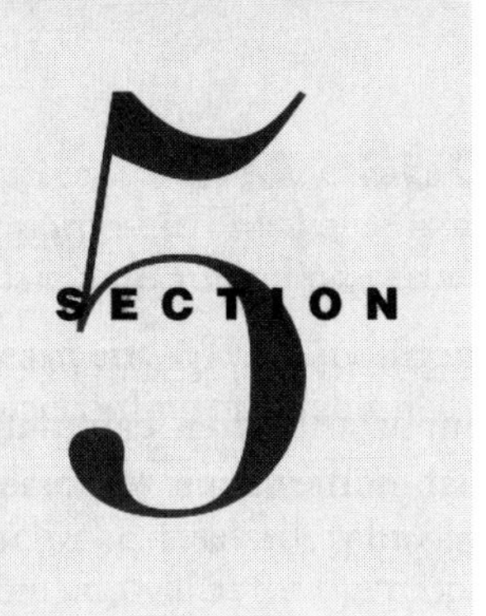

Proration Problems

To **prorate** means to divide proportionately. Some expenses and income may be prorated for the closing of a real estate transaction. We will look at prorating interest on a loan, ad valorem taxes on a property, homeowners insurance on a property, and rent on income-producing property. All the calculations in this section are carried to three decimal places and then rounded to the nearest cent in the final step.

WHAT ARE THE DIFFERENT CALENDARS USED FOR PRORATING?

When we prorate, we calculate the number of days owed for the expense or the rental income. The days may be calculated using a *banker's year*, *statutory year*, or *calendar year*. The **banker's year** and **statutory year** are the same because they both contain 12 months with 30 days in each month. The total number of days in both a banker's year and a statutory year is 360 days. The **calendar year** contains 12 months with 28 to 31 days in each month. The total number of days in a calendar year is 365. The total number of days in a calendar *leap* year (every fourth year) is 366. The following chart shows the days in each month.

	Banker's or Statutory Year	Calendar Year	Calendar Leap Year
January	30	31	31
February	30	28	29
March	30	31	31
April	30	30	30
May	30	31	31
June	30	30	30
July	30	31	31
August	30	31	31
September	30	30	30
October	30	31	31
November	30	30	30
December	30	31	31
Total days in a year	360	365	366

WHAT IS THE DIFFERENCE BETWEEN PRORATING *THROUGH* AND PRORATING *TO* THE DAY OF CLOSING?

In a proration problem, an examinee will be told whether to prorate *through* the day of closing or *to* the day of closing. **This is very important when calculating the days owed.** When prorating *through* the day of closing, the *seller* is responsible for the day of closing. When prorating *to* the day of closing, the *buyer* is responsible for the day of closing.

HOW DO I CALCULATE PRORATION PROBLEMS?

Once the number of days owed is known, the amount of the expense or income per day must be found. Either the annual amount is divided by the total days in the year to get the daily amount, or the monthly amount is divided by the total days in the month to get the daily amount.

MATH TIP The correct type of year (banker's or statutory year of 360 days, calendar year of 365 days, or calendar leap year of 366 days) must be used when computing the daily amount.

The final step is to multiply the amount per day by the number of days owed to get the prorated amount.

WHAT IS THE DIFFERENCE BETWEEN DEBIT AND CREDIT IN A PRORATION PROBLEM?

To calculate a proration problem, it is necessary to know how expenses and income are posted on the closing statement. **Debit** takes money from a person. **Credit** gives money to a person. (*See* Figure M.3.) When the prorated amount involves both the buyer and the seller, there will always be a double entry (i.e., the item appears twice, once as a debit to one party and once as a credit to the other party). If the seller owes the buyer, the prorated amount will be debited to the seller and credited to the buyer. If the buyer owes the seller, the prorated amount will be debited to the buyer and credited to the seller. When the prorated amount involves the buyer and someone other than the seller, there will be only a single entry. When the prorated amount involves the seller and someone other than the buyer, there will be only a single entry.

The five questions to ask when prorating are:

1. What calendar is to be used?
2. Is the expense paid in arrears or in advance?
3. Who has or will pay the expense?
4. Who has earned or received income?
5. When will the expense be paid?

FIGURE M.3: The Debit/Credit Flow

	Buyer	Seller
Sales Price	DEBIT	CREDIT
Tenants' Security Deposits	CREDIT	DEBIT
Fuel Oil (in tank)	DEBIT	CREDIT
Prorated Accrued Water Bill	CREDIT	DEBIT
Unearned Rents	CREDIT	DEBIT
Tax Reserve Account	DEBIT	CREDIT

Different items are treated differently as credits or debits to the buyer or the seller on a closing statement. Utility payments may not appear on the statement if the utility provider sends a final bill to the seller based on the date provided.

HOW DO I CALCULATE INTEREST IN A PRORATION PROBLEM?

When a loan is assumed or paid off, the accrued interest for the month of closing must be prorated. Interest is paid in arrears; therefore, the monthly payment made on the first day of the month pays interest for the entire previous month. The payment includes interest *up to but not including* the day of the payment unless specified otherwise. Not all payments are due on the first day of the month; therefore, attention must be paid to the stated day the interest has been paid through. The sellers owe unpaid interest (also called accrued, earned, or current interest) from the date of the last payment to or through the closing date.

If the prorations are to be calculated *through* the day of closing, the seller will owe payments *including* the day of closing. If the prorations are to be calculated *to* the day of closing, the seller will *owe up to but not including* the day of closing. Remember to use the correct type of year: the banker's or statutory year of 360 days, the calendar year of 365 days, or the calendar leap year of 366 days. When a loan is paid off, unpaid interest is calculated and added to the outstanding loan balance and is a **debit** *to the seller only*. Loan payoff is the sum of the principal balance and the accrued interest. On an assumption of the loan, the interest proration is a **debit** to the *seller* and a **credit** to the *buyer*.

FOR EXAMPLE A home was purchased on April 4 for $110,000, and the closing was set for the following May 8. The buyer assumed the seller's $93,600 loan balance on an original loan amount of $96,000 with 6.5% interest and monthly payments of $612.62 due on the first day of each month. How much will the interest proration be, using a banker's year and prorating through the day of closing? Who will be debited and who will be credited?

Banker's Year/Statutory Year

Step 1: Find the exact number of days of earned or accrued interest.

Seller owes 8 days (May 1 *through* May 8).

Note: It would be 7 days (8 days minus 1 day) if the problem had said prorate *to* the day of closing.

Step 2: Find the daily interest charge.

Outstanding loan balance × annual interest rate = annual interest

Annual interest ÷ 360 days per year = daily interest

$93,600 × 6.5% = $6,084 annual interest

$6,084 ÷ 360 days = $16.90 daily interest

Step 3: Compute the total amount of accrued interest.

Daily interest × days owed = interest proration

$16.90 daily interest × 8 days = $135.20

$135.20 debit seller, credit buyer is the answer.

Calendar Year (if the problem had said to use a calendar year)

Step 1: Find the exact number of days of earned or accrued interest.

Seller owes 8 days (May 1 *through* May 8).

Note: It would be 7 days (8 days minus 1 day) if the problem had said prorate *to* the day of closing.

Step 2: Find the daily interest charge.

Outstanding loan balance × annual interest rate = annual interest

Annual interest ÷ 365 days per year = daily interest

$93,600 × 6.5% = $6,084 annual interest

$6,084 ÷ 365 days = $16.668 daily interest

Step 3: Compute the total amount of accrued interest.

Daily interest × days owed = interest proration

$16.668 daily interest × 8 days = $133.344

$133.34 debit seller, credit buyer is the answer (rounded to the nearest cent).

HOW DO I PRORATE TAXES?

Real estate taxes are normally assessed from January 1 through December 31. The tax rate is *always* applied *to the assessed value of the property* instead of the market value, although some jurisdictions treat market value as the assessed value. Taxes are usually paid in arrears; therefore, the seller will owe the buyer for accrued taxes from January 1 *through* the day of closing or *to* the day of closing. The most recent tax bill is used to compute the proration, and this is usually the past year's tax bill. Remember to use the correct type of year: a banker's or statutory year has 360 days, a calendar year has 365 days, and a calendar leap year has 366 days.

If the taxes are paid in arrears, the tax proration will be a **debit** to the *seller* and a **credit** to the *buyer*. If the taxes are paid in advance, the tax proration will be a **debit** to the *buyer* and a **credit** to the *seller*.

FOR EXAMPLE The market value of a condominium is $115,000. For tax purposes, the property is assessed at 90% of the market value. The annual tax rate is $2.50 per $100 of assessed value. If the closing is on March 13, what is the prorated amount for the current tax year? Prorations are calculated through the day of closing and using a statutory year.

Banker's Year/Statutory Year

Step 1: Find the exact number of days of accrued taxes from the beginning of the tax period (January 1) up to and including the day of closing (March 13).

2 months (January and February) × 30 days per month = 60 days

60 + 13 days in March = 73 days

Note: It would be 72 days (73 days minus 1 day) if the problem had said prorate *to* the day of closing.

Step 2: Calculate the annual taxes.

Market value × assessment ratio = assessed value

(Assessed value ÷ $100) × tax rate per hundred = annual tax

$115,000 × 90% = $103,500

($103,500 ÷ $100) × $2.50 = $2,587.50 annual tax

Step 3: Find the tax amount per day.

Annual tax ÷ 360 days per year = daily tax

$2,587.50 ÷ 360 days = $7.188 daily tax

Step 4: Compute the prorated tax amount.

Daily tax × days owed = tax proration

$7.188 per day × 73 days = $524.724

$524.72 debit seller, credit buyer is the answer (rounded to the nearest cent).

Calendar Year (if the problem had said to use a calendar year)

Step 1: Find the exact number of days of accrued tax from the beginning of the tax period (January 1) up to and including the day of closing (March 13).

31 days in January + 28 days in February + 13 days in March = 72 days

Note: It would be 71 days (72 days minus 1 day) if the problem had said prorate *to* the day of closing.

Step 2: Calculate the annual tax.

Market value × assessment ratio = assessed value

(Assessed value ÷ \$100) × tax rate per hundred = annual tax

\$115,000 × 90% = \$103,500

(\$103,500 ÷ \$100) × \$2.50 = \$2,587.50 annual tax

Step 3: Find the tax amount per day.

Annual tax ÷ 365 days per year = daily tax

\$2,587.50 ÷ 365 days = \$7.089

Step 4: Compute the prorated tax amount.

Daily tax × days owed = tax proration

\$7.089 per day × 72 days = \$510.408

\$510.41 debit seller, credit buyer is the answer (rounded to the nearest cent).

HOW DO I PRORATE RENT?

When prorating rents, the amount of rent collected for the month of closing is the only amount prorated. The seller owes the buyer for the unearned rent starting with the day after closing through the end of the month if prorating *through* the day of closing. The seller owes the buyer for the unearned rent starting with the day of closing through the end of the month if prorating *to* the day of closing. If security deposits are being held by the seller, they are not prorated; therefore, the entire amount of the security deposits are transferred to the buyer. The actual number of days in the month of closing is always used for rent prorations, unless the problem provides differently. Both the rent proration and the security deposit amount will be a **debit** to the *seller* and a **credit** to the *buyer*.

FOR EXAMPLE A buyer is purchasing an apartment complex that contains 15 units that rent for \$450 per month each. A \$450 security deposit is being held on each unit. The sale is to close on March 14, and the March rent has been received for all 15 units. Compute the rent proration by prorating through the day of closing. Compute the security deposit.

Calendar Days (remember to use actual days in the month unless specified differently)

Step 1: Compute the unearned days of rent for the month of closing.

31	days in March
– 14	day of closing
17	days of unearned rent

Note: It would be 18 days (17 days plus 1 day) if the problem had said prorate *to* the day of closing.

Step 2: Compute the daily rent. Monthly rent × number of units paid = total rent collected ÷ number of actual days in the month of closing = daily rent.

$450 × 15 units = $6,750 monthly rent collected

$6,750 ÷ 31 days in March = $217.742 daily rent

Step 3: Compute the prorated rent amount.

Daily rent × days of unearned rent. $217.742 daily rent × 17 days = $3,701.614

Step 4: Compute the security deposit.

$450 per unit × 15 units = $6,750

$3,701.61 rent proration (rounded to the nearest cent) and **$6,750 security deposit** are the answers. They are both **debit seller** and **credit buyer**.

Real Estate Math Practice Problems

1. The value of a property is $91,000 today. What was the original cost if the property has lost 35% of its value over the past seven years?
   a. $67,407.41
   b. $95,789.47
   c. $122,850.00
   d. $140,000.00

2. What was the price per front foot for a 100' × 125' lot that sold for $125,000?
   a. $1,250
   b. $1,000
   c. $556
   d. $10

3. If the bank makes a 90% loan on a house valued at $88,500, how much additional cash is required as a down payment if the buyer has already paid $4,500 in earnest money?
   a. $3,500
   b. $4,000
   c. $4,350
   d. $8,850

4. What did the sellers pay for their home if they sold it for $298,672, which gave them a 12% profit over their original cost? Round your answer to the nearest cent.
   a. $243,671.43
   b. $266,671.43
   c. $312,512.64
   d. $334,512.64

5. What would be an estimate of value for a building producing $11,250 annual net income and showing a rate of return of 9%?
   a. $125,000
   b. $123,626
   c. $101,250
   d. $122,625

6. The sale of a home is to close on September 28. Included in the sale is a garage apartment that is rented for $350 per month. The tenant has paid the September rent. What is the rent proration, using actual days and prorating through the day of closing? Round your answer to the nearest cent.
   a. $325.67
   b. $23.33
   c. $350.00
   d. $175.00

7. What is the total cost of paving a driveway 15' wide, 40' long, and 4" thick if the concrete to be used costs $60.00 per cubic yard and labor costs $1.25 per square foot?
   a. $527.25
   b. $693.75
   c. $1,194.00
   d. $1,581.75

8. An owner agrees to list his property on the condition that he will receive at least $47,300 after paying a 5% broker's commission and paying $1,150 in closing costs. At what price must it sell?
   a. $48,450
   b. $50,815
   c. $50,875
   d. $51,000

9. A gift shop pays rent of $600 per month plus 2.5% of gross annual sales in excess of $50,000. What was the average monthly rent last year if gross annual sales were $75,000? Round your answer to the nearest cent.
   a. $1,125.00
   b. $756.25
   c. $600.00
   d. $652.08

10. A tenant's monthly rent is $825. What is the rent as a percentage of an annual income of $41,000? Round your answer to the nearest percent.

a. 18%
b. 24%
c. 33%
d. 40%

11. Two brokers split the 6% commission on the sale of a $324,000 home. The selling broker's sales associate was paid 70% of the selling broker's share. The listing broker's sales associate was paid 30% of the listing broker's share. How much did the listing broker's sales associate receive?

a. $2,916
b. $6,804
c. $19,440
d. $20,275

12. Find the number of square feet in a lot with a frontage of 75 feet, 6 inches, and a depth of 140 feet, 9 inches.

a. 10,626.625
b. 10,652.04
c. 216.25
d. 25,510.875

13. A 28-unit apartment house is being valued using the income approach. Each unit rents for $775 a month, an amount that is consistent with like rental units in the vicinity. For the past five years, the annual expenses of operation for the property have averaged $82,460 and the building has maintained a consistent vacancy rate of 5%. A potential investor is only interested if the cap rate is at least 9.5%. What is the property's likely value using these variables?

a. $2,741,100
b. $868,000
c. $1,736,000
d. $1,873,100

14. How much interest will the seller owe the buyer for a closing date of August 10 if the outstanding loan balance is $43,580? The interest rate on this assumable loan is 6%, and the last payment was paid on August 1. Prorations are to be done through the day of closing, using a statutory year.

a. $72.63
b. $145.20
c. $290.47
d. $508.20

15. The buyer has agreed to a $175,000 sales price, 2.5 loan discount points, and a 1% loan origination fee. If the buyer receives a 90% loan to value, how much will the buyer owe at closing for points and the origination fee?

a. $1,575.00
b. $3,937.50
c. $5,512.50
d. $6,125.00

16. Calculate eight months' interest on a $5,000 interest-only loan at 9.5%.

a. $475.00
b. $316.66
c. $237.50
d. $39.58

17. A 100-acre farm is subdivided into lots for homes. The streets require one-eighth of the entire property, and the remaining acreage is divided into 140 lots of approximately the same size. About how many square feet are in each lot?

a. 43,560
b. 35,004
c. 31,114
d. 27,225

18. The annual tax bill on a home was $1,282 and was paid in December. The home sold the following March and will close on April 23. How much will the tax proration be, using a calendar year and prorating to the day of closing?

a. $393.34
b. $402.41
c. $396.89
d. $427.33

19. What is the monthly net operating income on an investment of $115,000 if the rate of return is 12.5%? Round your answer to the nearest cent.

a. $1,150.00
b. $1,197.92
c. $7,666.67
d. $14,375.00

20. A sales associate sells a property for $258,500. The sales associate's employment agreement provides for a 60% share of the employing broker's commission. The commission due the selling broker is 2½%. What is the selling sales associate's share of the commission?

a. $2,106.00
b. $3,877.50
c. $6,462.50
d. $10,340.00

21. A developer buys 348,480 square feet of land at $0.75 per square foot and divides the land into half-acre lots. If the developer keeps three lots and sells the others for $24,125 each, what percentage of profit does the developer realize?

a. 47.4%
b. 32.2%
c. 20%
d. 16.7%

22. A landscaping contract for services for May 1 through October 31 totaling $2,500 has been paid in full for the current year. The house is sold and scheduled to close on July 16 and the buyers are assuming the sellers' landscaping agreement. What is the amount of the proration for this expense if a banker's year is used and all prorations are made through the day of closing? Round your answer to the nearest cent.

a. $1,444.46
b. $1,642.42
c. $1,785.50
d. $1,790.25

23. What is the interest rate on a $10,000 loan that requires a semiannual interest payment of $450?

a. 7%
b. 9%
c. 11%
d. 13.5%

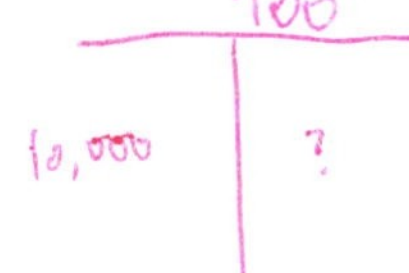

24. A warehouse is 80 feet wide and 120 feet long with ceilings 14 feet high. If 1,200 square feet of floor surface has been partitioned off, floor to ceiling, for an office, how many cubic feet of space will be left in the warehouse?

a. 151,200
b. 134,400
c. 133,200
d. 117,600

25. An office building produces $68,580 annual net operating income. What price would an investor pay for this property to show a minimum return of 12% on the investment?

a. $489,857
b. $571,500
c. $685,800
d. $768,096

26. A buyer is assuming the balance of a seller's second mortgage loan. The interest rate is 8%, and the last monthly payment of $578.16 was paid on April 1, leaving an outstanding balance of $18,450. Using a banker's year, compute the interest to be paid by the seller if the sale is to close on April 19. Prorate through the day of closing.

a. $110.83
b. $82.00
c. $77.90
d. $123.00

27. A lot purchased five years ago for $15,000 has appreciated a total of 17.5% since its purchase. What is it worth today?

a. $12,375
b. $15,525
c. $17,250
d. $17,625

28. A lot has a frontage of 100 feet and a depth of 150 feet. If the building line regulations call for a setback of 25 feet at the front, 10 feet at the back, and 6 feet on each side, how many square feet of usable space are left for the building?

a. 9,350
b. 10,120
c. 11,750
d. 15,000

29. A lease calls for rent of $1,000 per month plus 2% of annual sales in excess of $100,000. What is the annual rent if the annual sales are $150,000?

a. $12,000
b. $13,000
c. $14,000
d. $15,000

30. Taxes on a home for the current tax year amount to $6,468. The home was sold in July, and the sale closed on August 29. The seller had not paid any of the tax owed for the current year prior to the closing. What was the prorated tax amount using a calendar year if the proration was calculated to the day of closing?

a. $4,252.93
b. $4,607.34
c. $5,280.50
d. $6,468.00

31. A tract of land measures 1.25 acres. The lot is 150 feet deep. How much will the lot sell for at $65 per front foot?

a. $9,750
b. $8,125
c. $23,595
d. $25,420

32. If a 6.5% full brokerage commission was $5,200, what was the sales price of the house?

a. $80,400
b. $80,000
c. $77,200
d. $86,600

33. A buyer earns $60,000 per year and can qualify for a monthly PITI payment equal to 25% of monthly salary. If the annual tax and insurance on a prospective purchase is $678.24, what loan amount will the buyer qualify for if the monthly PI payment factor is $10.29 per $1,000 of loan amount?

a. $99,987
b. $108,965
c. $112,784
d. $115,980

34. Find the cost of building a house 29' × 34' × 17' with a gable roof 8' high at the highest point. The cost of construction is $2.25 per cubic foot.

a. $55,462.50
b. $46,588.50
c. $37,714.50
d. $27,731.25

35. An amount of $50,000 is invested at a rate of return of 12%. What is the net operating income?

a. $6,000
b. $5,600
c. $5,000
d. $4,167

36. Monthly interest on a loan with a 9.25% annual interest rate is $65.53. What is the loan amount rounded to the nearest hundred dollars?

a. $1,400
b. $2,800
c. $6,300
d. $8,500

37. What percentage of profit would Arun make if he paid $20,500 for a lot, built a home on the lot that cost $133,000, and then sold the lot and house together for $194,550? Round your answer to the nearest percent.

a. 13%
b. 23%
c. 27%
d. 45%

38. The buyer is purchasing a fourplex and closing on November 4. Each apartment rents for $875 per month. As of November 1, one apartment is vacant and the other tenants have paid their November rent. Compute the rent proration through the day of closing.

a. $345.00
b. $1,993.33
c. $2,275.00
d. $3,935.72

39. An income-producing property has $62,500 annual gross income and monthly expenses of $1,530. What is an estimate of the property's value using a 10% capitalization rate?

a. $441,400
b. $625,000
c. $183,600
d. $609,700

40. A new house and lot cost the buyer $565,000. Of this total price, the lot was estimated to be worth $130,000. The buyer held the property for eight years. If average market prices of comparable properties in the area increased by 32% over that period, what would be the total value of the property at the end of eight years?

a. $695,300
b. $745,800
c. $810,900
d. $925,800

41. The seller received a $121,600 check at closing after paying a 7% brokerage commission, $31,000 in other closing costs, and a $135,700 loan payoff. What was the total sales price?

a. $288,300
b. $306,300
c. $308,500
d. $310,000

42. A fence is being built to enclose a lot 125 feet by 350 feet. If there will be one 10-foot gate, how many running feet of fence will be needed?

a. 465
b. 600
c. 940
d. 960

43. A buyer pays $9,500 each for four parcels of land. He subdivides them into six parcels and sells each of the six parcels for $7,500. What is the buyer's percentage of profit? Round your answer to the nearest percent.

a. 16%
b. 18%
c. 22%
d. 38%

44. A property sells for $295,200. If it has appreciated for a total of 20% over the past five years, what did the owner pay for the property five years ago?

a. $175,000
b. $246,000
c. $286,000
d. $320,000

45. A teacher earns an annual income of $60,000, and the teacher's spouse earns $2,400 per month. How much can the couple pay monthly for their mortgage payment if the lender uses a 28% qualifying ratio?

a. $2,072
b. $1,400
c. $2,352
d. $672

46. If a buyer borrows $4,400, agreeing to pay back principal and interest in 18 months, what annual interest rate is the buyer paying if the total payback is $5,588?

a. 15%
b. 18%
c. 21.3%
d. 27%

47. If you purchase a lot that is 125' × 150' for $6,468.75, what price did you pay per front foot?

a. $23.52
b. $43.13
c. $51.75
d. $64.69

48. A buyer is granted a 90% loan for $340,500. How much will the monthly principal and interest payment be, using a loan payment factor of $7.16 per $1,000 of loan?

a. $2,194.18
b. $4,755.59
c. $2,437.98
d. $3,064.50

49. Calculate the amount of the total commission earned by a broker on a rural property selling for $61,000 if 6% is paid on the first $50,000 of the sales price and 3% is paid on the amount over $50,000.

a. $3,330
b. $3,830
c. $3,600
d. $3,930

50. A 50' × 100' lot has a 2,400-square-foot house on it that contains four bedrooms and three bathrooms. What percentage of the lot is not taken up by the house?

a. 21%
b. 48%
c. 50%
d. 52%

Answer Key for Real Estate Math Practice Problems

1. d **$140,000.00 original cost**

   100% original cost – 35% total depreciation = 65% today's value

   $91,000 today's value
   original cost × 65%

   $91,000 ÷ 65% = **$140,000 original cost**

2. a **$1,250 per front foot**

   $125,000 sales price ÷ 100 front feet = **$1,250 per front foot**

3. c **$4,350 due at closing**

   100% value – 90% LTV = 10% down payment

   $8,850 down payment
   $88,500 value × 10%

   $88,500 × 10% = $8,850

   $8,850 down payment – $4,500 earnest money = **$4,350 due at closing**

4. b **$266,671.43 original cost**

   100% original cost + 12% profit = 112% sales price

   $298,672 sales price
   original cost × 112%

   $298,672 ÷ 112% = **$266,671.43 original cost**

5. a **$125,000 value**

   $11,250 annual net income
   value × 9%

   $11,250 ÷ 9% = **$125,000 value**

6. b **$23.33 rent proration**

   30 days in September – 28 day of closing = 2 days due

   $350 monthly rent ÷ 30 days = $11.666667 per day × 2 days = **$23.33 rent proration**

7. c **$1,194.00 total cost**

   4" ÷ 12 = 0.333'

   Concrete: 40' × 15' × 0.333' = 199.8 cubic feet

   199.8 ÷ 27 = 7.4 cubic yards

   7.4 × $60 per cubic yard = $444

   Labor: 40' × 15' = 600 square feet

   600 × $1.25 per square foot = $750

   $444 concrete + $750 labor = **$1,194.00 total cost**

8. **d $51,000 sales price**

$47,300 net to seller + $1,150 closing costs = $48,450 seller's dollars after commission

100% sales price – 5% commission = 95% seller's percentage after commission

$$\frac{\text{\$48,450 seller's dollars after commission}}{\text{sales price} \times 95\%}$$

$48,450 ÷ 95% = **$51,000 sales price**

9. **d $652.08 average monthly rent**

$75,000 gross annual sales – $50,000 = $25,000 gross annual sales subject to 2.5%

$$\frac{\text{annual percentage rent}}{\text{\$25,000 gross sales subject to the percentage} \times 2.5\%}$$

$25,000 × 2.5% = $625 annual percentage rent

$625 annual percentage rent ÷ 12 months = $52.08 monthly percentage rent

$600 monthly minimum rent + $52.08 monthly percentage rent = **$652.08 average monthly rent**

10. **b 24%**

$825 monthly rent × 12 months = $9,900 annual rent

$$\frac{\text{\$9,900 annual rent}}{\text{\$41,000 annual income} \times \text{percent of annual income}}$$

$9,900 ÷ $41,000 = 0.241 or **24% (rounded to the nearest percent)**

11. **a $2,916 commission to listing broker's sales associate**

$$\frac{\text{full commission}}{\text{\$324,000 sales price} \times 6\%}$$

$324,000 × 6% = $19,440 full commission

$19,440 ÷ 2 brokers = $9,720 each broker's commission split

$$\frac{\text{listing broker's sales associate's commission}}{\text{\$9,720 broker's commission split} \times 30\%}$$

$9,720 × 30% = **$2,916 sales associate's commission**

12. **a 10,626.63 square feet**

6" ÷ 12 = 0.5'

0.5' + 75' = 75.5' frontage

9" ÷ 12 = 0.75'

0.75' + 140' = 140.75' depth

140.75' × 75.5' = **10,626.625 square feet**

13. c **$1,736,000 value**

$775 monthly rent × 28 units × 12 months = $260,400 annual scheduled gross income

$260,400 – 5% vacancy rate = $247,380 annual effective gross income

$247,380 – $82,460 annual expenses = $164,920 annual net operating income

$164,920 annual net operating income
property value X 9.5%

$164,920 ÷ 9.5% = **$1,736,000 property value**

14. a **$72.60 interest due**

Seller owes buyer 10 days (August 1 through August 10)

annual interest
$43,580 loan balance X 6%

$43,580 × 6% = $2,614.80 annual interest

$2,614.80 annual interest ÷ 360 days = $7.263 per day

$7.263 × 10 days = **$72.63 interest due**

15. c **$5,512.50 points and origination fee**

2.5 loan discount points + 1 point origination fee = 3.5 points

loan
$175,000 sales price X 90%

$175,000 × 90% = $157,500 loan

discount points and origination fee
$157,500 loan X 3.5%

$157,500 loan × 3.5% = **$5,512.50 points and origination fee**

16. b **$316.66 interest**

annual interest
$5,000 loan X 9.5%

$5,000 loan × 9.5% = $475 annual interest

$475 ÷ 12 months = $39.583 monthly interest

$39.583 × 8 months = **$316.664 interest or $316.66 (rounded to the nearest cent)**

17. d **27,225 square feet per lot**

⅛ = 1 ÷ 8 = 0.125 for streets

100 acres × 0.125 = 12.5 acres for streets

100 acres – 12.5 acres for streets = 87.5 acres for lots

87.5 × 43,560 square feet per acre = 3,811,500 square feet buildable land

3,811,500 ÷ 140 lots = **27,225 square feet per lot**

18. a $393.34 tax proration

Seller owes the buyer January 1 to April 23

31	January
+ 28	February
+ 31	March
+ 22	April
112	days due

$1,282 annual tax ÷ 365 days = $3.512 per day

$3.512 × 112 days = **$393.344 tax proration or $393.34 (rounded to the nearest cent)**

19. b $1,197.92 monthly NOI

annual NOI
$115,000 investment X 12.5%

$115,000 × 12.5% = $14,375 annual NOI

$14,375 ÷ 12 months = **$1,197.92 monthly NOI**

20. b $3,877.50 sales associate's commission

broker's commission
$258,500 sales price X 2½%

$258,500 × 2½ % = $6,462.50 broker's commission

sales associate's commission
$6,462.50 broker's commission X 60%

$6,462.50 × 60% = **$3,877.50 salesperson's commission**

21. c 20% profit

348,480 square feet × $0.75 per square foot = $261,360 cost

348,480 square feet ÷ 43,560 = 8 acres

8 acres × 2 lots per acre = 16 lots

16 lots – 3 lots = 13 lots sold

13 lots × $24,125 each = $313,625 total sales price

$313,625 sales price – $261,360 cost = $52,265 profit

$52,265 profit
$261,360 cost X **percentage profit**

$52,265 ÷ $261,360 = 0.199973 or **20% profit**

22. a $1,444.46 landscaping proration

May 1 through October 31 = 6 months or 180 days

30	July
– 16	closing date
14	days left in July
+ 30	August
+ 30	September
+ 30	October
104	days due

$2,500 landscaping expense ÷ 180 days = $13.889 per day

$13.889 × 104 days due = **$1,444.456 or $1444.46 landscaping proration (rounded to the nearest cent)**

23. b 9% interest rate

$450 semiannual interest × 2 = $900 annual interest

$900 annual interest
$10,000 loan × **interest rate**

$900 annual interest ÷ $10,000 loan = **0.09 or 9% interest rate**

24. d 117,600 cubic feet

120' × 80' = 9,600 square feet in building

9,600 – 1,200 square feet for office = 8,400 square feet left in warehouse

8,400 × 14-foot ceiling = **117,600 cubic feet left in warehouse**

25. b $571,500 price

$68,580 annual NOI
price × 12% cap rate

$68,580 ÷ 12% = **$571,500 price**

26. c $77.90 interest proration

Seller owes buyer 19 days (April 1 *through* April 19)

annual interest
$18,450 loan balance × 8%

$18,450 × 8% = $1,476

$1,476 annual interest ÷ 360 days = $4.10 per day

$4.10 × 19 days = **$77.90 interest proration**

27. d $17,625 today's value

100% cost + 17.5% total appreciation = 117.5% today's value

today's value
$15,000 original cost × 117.5%

$15,000 × 117.5% = **$17,625 today's value**

28. b 10,120 buildable square feet left

Front and back setbacks are 25' + 10' = 35'

150' depth – 35' setback = 115' left

Side setbacks are 6' + 6" = 12"

100' frontage – 12' = 88' left

115' × 88' = **10,120 buildable square feet left**

29. b $13,000 annual rent

$1,000 monthly minimum rent × 12 months = $12,000 annual minimum rent

$150,000 annual sales – $100,000 = $50,000 annual sales subject to 2%

annual percentage rent	
$50,000 annual sales ×	2%

$50,000 × 2% = $1,000

$12,000 annual minimum rent + $1,000 annual percentage rent = **$13,000 annual rent**

30. a $4,252.93 tax proration

Seller owes buyer January 1 to August 29

31	January
+ 28	February
+ 31	March
+ 30	April
+ 31	May
+ 30	June
+ 31	July
+ 28	August
240	days due

$6,468 annual tax ÷ 365 days = $17.72055 per day

$17.72055 × 240 days = **$4,252.93 tax proration**

31. c $23,595 sales price

1.25 acres × 43,560 = 54,450 square feet

54,450 ÷ 150' deep = 363' frontage

363' × $65 per front foot = **$23,595 sales price**

32. b $80,000 sales price

$5,200 full commission	
sales price ×	6.5%

$5,200 full commission ÷ 6.5% = **$80,000 sales price**

33. d $115,980 loan

$60,000 annual salary ÷ 12 months = $5,000 monthly salary

monthly PITI		
$5,000 monthly salary	X	25%

$5,000 × 25% = $1,250 monthly PITI

$678.24 annual taxes and insurance ÷ 12 months = $56.52 monthly TI

$1,250 monthly PITI – $56.52 monthly TI = $1,193.48 monthly PI

$1,193.48 monthly PI payment ÷ $10.29 = 115.9845 or 115.98 (rounded to the nearest cent)

115.98 × $1,000 = **$115,980 loan**

34. b $46,588.50 construction cost

29' × 34' × 17' = 16,762 cubic feet in house

29' × 34' × 8' ÷ 2 = 3,944 cubic feet in attic

16,762 cubic feet + 3,944 cubic feet = 20,706 cubic feet total

20,706 × $2.25 per cubic foot = **$46,588.50 construction cost**

35. a $6,000 NOI

NOI		
$50,000 investment	X	12% cap rate

$50,000 × 12% = **$6,000 NOI**

36. d $8,500 loan

$65.53 monthly interest × 12 months = $786.36 annual interest

$786.36 annual interest		
loan	X	9.25% interest rate

$786.36 ÷ 9.25% = **$8,501.19 (rounded to the nearest cent) = $8,500 loan rounded to the nearest hundred dollars.**

37. c 27%

$20,500 cost of lot + $133,000 cost of home = $153,500 total cost

$194,550 sales price – $153,500 total cost = $41,050 profit

$41,050 profit		
$153,500 total cost	X	% profit

$41,050 ÷ $153,500 = **0.267 or 27% profit (rounded to the nearest percent)**

38. c $2,275 rent proration

30	November
– 4	day of closing
26	days due

$875 monthly rent × 3 units = $2,625 monthly rent

$2,625 ÷ 30 days = $87.50 per day

$87.50 × 26 days = **$2,275 rent proration**

39. a **$441,400 estimated value**

$1,530 monthly expenses × 12 months = $18,360 annual expenses

$62,500 annual gross income – $18,360 annual expenses = $44,140 NOI

$44,140 NOI
estimated value X 10% cap rate

$44,140 ÷ 10% = **$441,400 estimated value**

40. b **$745,800 appreciated property value**

100% cost + 32% appreciation = 132% appreciated property value

appreciated property value
$565,000 cost of property X 132% appreciation

$565,000 cost × 132% = **$745,800 appreciated property value**

41. d **$310,000 sales price**

$121,600 seller's net + $31,000 closing costs + $135,700 loan payoff = $288,300 seller's dollars after commission

100% sales price – 7% commission = 93% seller's dollars after commission

$288,300 seller's dollars after commission
sales price X 93%

$288,300 ÷ 93% = **$310,000 sales price**

42. c **940 running feet**

125' + 350' + 125' + 350' – 10' gate = **940 running feet**

43. b **18% profit**

$9,500 cost × 4 parcels = $38,000 total cost

$7,500 sales price × 6 parcels = $45,000 sales price

$45,000 sales price – $38,000 cost = $7,000 profit

$7,000 profit
$38,000 cost X **percentage profit**

$7,000 ÷ $38,000 cost = 0.18421 or **18% profit (rounded to the nearest percent)**

44. b **$246,000 original cost**

100% cost + 20% total appreciation = 120% appreciated property value

$295,200 appreciated property value
original cost X 120%

$295,200 ÷ 120% = **$246,000 original cost**

45. a **$2,072 monthly payment**

$60,000 annual salary ÷ 12 months = $5,000 monthly salary

$5,000 + $2,400 monthly salary = $7,400 total monthly salary

monthly payment		
$7,400 monthly salary	X	28%

$7,400 × 28% = **$2,072 monthly payment**

46. b **18% annual interest rate**

$5,588 payback (principal + interest) – $4,400 loan (principal) = $1,188 interest for 18 months

$1,188 ÷ 18 months = $66 monthly interest

$66 × 12 months = $792 annual interest

$792 annual interest		
$4,400 loan	X	**annual interest rate**

$792 ÷ $4,400 = 0.18 or **18% annual interest rate**

47. c **$51.75 per front foot**

$6,468.75 price ÷ 125 front feet = **$51.75 per front foot**

48. c **$2,437.98 monthly principal and interest payment**

$340,500 loan ÷ $1,000 = 340.5

340.5 × $7.16 = **$2,437.98 monthly principal and interest payment**

49. a **$3,330 total commission**

commission		
first $50,000 of sales price	X	6%

$50,000 × 6% = $3,000 commission

$61,000 sales price – $50,000 sales price at 6% = $11,000 sales price at 3%

commission		
$11,000 of sales price above $50,000	X	3%

$11,000 × 3% = $330 commission

$3,000 commission + $330 commission = **$3,330 total commission**

50. d **52% not taken up by house**

50' × 100' = 5,000 square feet of lot – 2,400 square feet of house = 2,600 square feet not taken up by house

2,600 square feet not taken up by house		
5,000 square feet of lot	X	**percentage not taken up by house**

2,600 ÷ 5,000 = **0.52 or 52% not taken up by house**

Sample Examinations

PREVIEW: TESTING SERVICES

www.goamp.com
www.pearsonvue.com
www.prometric.com
www.psiexams.com

In some states, the real estate commission writes and administers the real estate licensing examinations. In others, a commercial testing service prepares two-part examinations that include both state-specific license law questions and questions on broader national issues and general principles. Most states use the examinations produced by one of the commercial testing services, which include Applied Measurement Professionals (AMP), www.goamp.com; Pearson VUE, www.pearsonvue.com; Prometric, www.prometric.com; and PSI Examination Services (PSI), www.psiexams.com; and others.

The sample examinations included here are not intended to be a review of *Modern Real Estate Practice* or your real estate course. Rather, they are designed to imitate real estate licensing exams, any one of which may emphasize some concepts and ignore others. The answer key for these sample examinations includes the relevant unit from which each question was drawn. Questions that involve mathematical calculations in addition to one or more real estate concepts will refer you to the math skills review in "Math FAQs." If your answer is not correct, it is advisable to restudy the suggested material. *Note that proration calculations here are based on a 30-day month unless otherwise stated. Additionally, decimals are rounded to two places, or the nearest cent.*

SAMPLE EXAM 1

1. Which of the following is a lien on real estate?
   a. Recorded easement
   b. Recorded mortgage
   c. Encroachment
   d. Deed restriction
2. A sales contract was signed by a minor. Which term describes this contract?
   a. Voidable
   b. Breached
   c. Discharged
   d. Void
3. A real estate professional receives a check for earnest money from a buyer and deposits the money in the real estate professional's personal interest-bearing checking account over the weekend. This action exposes the real estate professional to a charge of
   a. commingling.
   b. novation.
   c. subrogation.
   d. accretion.
4. A borrower takes out a mortgage loan that requires monthly payments of $875.70 for 20 years and a final payment of $24,095. This is what type of loan?
   a. Wraparound
   b. Accelerated
   c. Balloon
   d. Variable
5. If a borrower computed the interest charged for the previous month on a $260,000 loan balance as $1,300, what is the borrower's interest rate to the nearest half percent?
   a. 6%
   b. 6½%
   c. 5%
   d. 5½%
6. A real estate professional signs a contract with a buyer. Under the contract, the real estate professional agrees to help the buyer find a suitable property and to represent the buyer in negotiations with the seller. The buyer may not sign an agreement with any other real estate professional. What kind of agreement has this real estate professional signed?
   a. Exclusive buyer listing agreement
   b. Exclusive buyer representation agreement
   c. Open buyer agency agreement
   d. Option contract
7. A grantor conveys property by delivering a deed. The deed contains five covenants. This is *MOST* likely a
   a. general warranty deed.
   b. quitclaim deed.
   c. special warranty deed.
   d. deed in trust.
8. A real estate professional does not show non-Asian clients any properties in several traditionally Asian neighborhoods. The real estate professional bases this practice on the need to preserve the valuable cultural integrity of Asian immigrant communities. Which statement is *TRUE* regarding the real estate professional's policy?
   a. The real estate professional's policy is steering and violates federal and state fair housing laws regardless of motivation.
   b. Because the real estate professional is not attempting to restrict the rights of any single minority group, the practice does not constitute steering.
   c. The real estate professional's policy is steering, but it does not violate the fair housing laws because cultural preservation is the motive, not exclusion or discrimination.
   d. The real estate professional's policy has the effect, but not the intent, of steering.

9. A woman grants a life estate to her son-in-law and stipulates that, upon his death, the title to the property will pass to her grandson. The grandson's interest is known as a(n)
   a. remainder.
   b. reversion.
   c. estate at sufferance.
   d. estate for years.

10. A primary benefit of property held in joint tenancy is
   a. ownership by a maximum of two people.
   b. the fractional interests of the owners, which can be different.
   c. the fact that additional owners may be added later.
   d. the right of survivorship.

11. A licensed real estate sales associate has a written contract with the employing broker that specifies that the sales associate will not be treated as an employee for federal tax purposes. The sales associate's entire income is from sales commissions rather than an hourly wage. Based on these facts, the sales associate will be treated by the IRS as
   a. a real estate assistant.
   b. an employee.
   c. a subagent.
   d. a qualified real estate agent.

12. The states in which the owner gives up legal title of mortgaged real estate are known as
   a. title theory states.
   b. lien theory states.
   c. statutory title states.
   d. strict title forfeiture states.

13. The form of tenancy that will expire on a specific date is a
   a. joint tenancy.
   b. tenancy for years.
   c. tenancy at sufferance.
   d. tenancy by the entirety.

14. A large home that lacks sufficient indoor plumbing suffers from which condition?
   a. Functional obsolescence
   b. Curable physical deterioration
   c. Incurable physical deterioration
   d. External obsolescence

15. A developer built a structure that has six stories. Several years later, an ordinance was passed in that area banning any building six stories or higher. This building is a
   a. nonconforming use.
   b. situation in which the structure would have to be demolished.
   c. conditional use.
   d. violation of the zoning laws.

16. Assuming that the listing agent and the selling agent in a transaction split their commission equally, what was the sales price of the property if the commission rate was 5.5% and the listing agent received $12,584?
   a. $228,800
   b. $242,871
   c. $457,600
   d. $692,120

17. A real estate broker specializes in helping both buyers and sellers with the necessary paperwork involved in transferring property. Although not an agent of either party, the broker may not disclose either party's confidential information to the other. The broker is *BEST* described as a(n)
   a. buyer's broker.
   b. independent contractor.
   c. dual agent.
   d. transaction broker.

18. Three women owned a house as joint tenants. In the year 2009, one died. Last month, another died. Based on these facts, which of the following correctly describes the remaining woman's ownership interest in the house?
   a. Joint tenancy with the deceased women's heirs
   b. Tenancy in common with the deceased women's heirs
   c. Severalty
   d. Partitioned tenancy by the entirety

19. The listing and selling brokers agree to split a 7% commission 50-50 on a $295,900 land sale. The listing broker gives the listing sales associate 50% of the listing broker's share, and the selling broker gives the selling sales associate 65% of that share. How much does the selling sales associate earn from the sale after deducting expenses of $1,300? Round your answer to the nearest cent.

a. $5,431.73
b. $10,356.50
c. $5,178.00
d. $6,731.73

20. Police powers include all of the following *EXCEPT*

a. zoning.
b. deed restrictions.
c. building codes.
d. density requirements.

21. A seller wants to net $165,000 from the sale of a house after paying the broker's fee of 6% and other closing costs of $2,635. The seller's gross sales price will be

a. $152,623.
b. $174,900.
c. $152,465.
d. $178,335.

22. Three acres equals how many square feet?

a. 43,560
b. 130,680
c. 156,840
d. 27,878,400

23. A buyer is purchasing a condominium unit in a subdivision and obtains financing from a local bank. In this situation, which term *BEST* describes this buyer?

a. Vendor
b. Mortgagor
c. Grantor
d. Lessor

24. The current value of a property is $140,000. The property is assessed at 40% of its current value for real estate tax purposes, with an equalization factor of 1.5 applied to the assessed value. If the tax rate is $4 per $100 of assessed valuation, what is the amount of tax due on the property?

a. $840
b. $3,360
c. $2,240
d. $2,100

25. A building was sold for $260,000, with the purchaser putting 10% down and obtaining a loan for the balance. The lending institution charged a 1% loan origination fee. What was the total cash used for the purchase?

a. $2,340
b. $23,400
c. $28,340
d. $26,000

26. A parcel of vacant land has an assessed valuation of $274,550. If the assessment is 85% of market value, what is the market value?

a. $315,732
b. $320,000
c. $1,830,333
d. $323,000

27. Which of the following *BEST* describes a capitalization rate?

a. Amount determined by the gross rent multiplier
b. Rate of return an income property will produce
c. Mathematical value determined by a sales price
d. Rate at which the amount of depreciation in a property is measured

28. A parcel of land described as "the NW¼ and the SW¼ of Section 6, T4N, R8W of the Third Principal Meridian" was sold for $875 per acre. The listing agent will receive a 5% commission on the total sales price. How much will the agent receive?

a. $1,750
b. $5,040
c. $14,000
d. $15,040

29. If a house was sold for $360,000 and the buyer obtained a mortgage loan for $288,000, how much money would the buyer pay in discount points if the lender charged two points?

a. $7,200
b. $6,600
c. $6,000
d. $5,760

30. The commission rate is 7% on a sale of $250,000. What is the dollar amount of the commission?

a. $35,000
b. $17,500
c. $1,750
d. $3,571

31. A prospective buyer signs an offer to purchase a residential property. All the following circumstances would automatically terminate the offer *EXCEPT*

a. the buyer signed a written offer to buy a house and then died.
b. the buyer revoked the offer between the presentation and a possible acceptance.
c. the seller made a counteroffer.
d. the seller received a better offer from another buyer.

32. A buyer purchased a home under a land contract. Until the contract is paid in full, or the buyer meets statutory requirements, the buyer

a. holds legal title to the premises.
b. has no legal interest in the property.
c. possesses a legal life estate in the premises.
d. has equitable title in the property.

33. A buyer and a seller sign a contract for the sale of real property. A few days later, they decide to change many of the terms of the contract, while retaining the basic intent to buy and sell. The process by which the new contract replaces the old one is called

a. assignment.
b. novation.
c. assemblage.
d. rescission.

34. Using the services of a mortgage broker, a buyer borrowed $25,000 from a private lender. After the loan costs were deducted, the buyer received $24,255. What is the face amount of the note?

a. $24,255
b. $25,000
c. $4,255
d. $645

35. Whose signature is necessary for a signed offer to purchase real estate to become a contract?

a. Buyer's only
b. Buyer's and seller's
c. Seller's only
d. Seller's and seller's agent's

36. A borrower has just made the final payment on a mortgage loan. Regardless of this fact, the records will still show a lien on the mortgaged property until which event occurs?

a. A mortgage satisfaction document is recorded.
b. A reconveyance of the mortgage document is delivered to the mortgage holder.
c. A novation of the mortgage document takes place.
d. An estoppel of the mortgage document is filed with the clerk of the county in which the mortgagee is located.

37. If the annual net income from a commercial property is $75,000 and the capitalization rate is 8%, what is the property worth if the income approach is used?

a. $694,000
b. $600,000
c. $810,000
d. $937,500

38. A real estate professional enters into a listing agreement with a seller in which the seller will receive $120,000 from the sale of a vacant lot and the real estate professional will receive any sale proceeds exceeding that amount. This is what type of listing?

a. Exclusive agency
b. Net
c. Exclusive right to sell
d. Multiple

39. Under a cooperative form of ownership, an owner
   a. is a shareholder in the corporation.
   b. owns the unit outright and a share of the common areas.
   c. will have to take out a new mortgage loan on a newly acquired unit.
   d. receives a fixed-term lease for the unit.

40. A known defect or a cloud on the title to property may be cured by
   a. obtaining quitclaim deeds from all appropriate parties.
   b. recording the title after closing.
   c. paying cash for the property at the settlement.
   d. purchasing a title insurance policy at closing.

41. A seller signed an exclusive right-to-sell agreement with a real estate professional. If the seller finds a suitable buyer with no assistance, the real estate professional is entitled to
   a. full compensation from the buyer.
   b. no compensation from the seller.
   c. partial compensation.
   d. full compensation from the seller.

42. Under the terms of a net lease, a commercial tenant would usually be directly responsible for paying all the following property expenses *EXCEPT*
   a. maintenance expenses.
   b. mortgage debt service.
   c. fire and extended-coverage insurance.
   d. real estate taxes.

43. The Civil Rights Act of 1866 prohibits discrimination based on
   a. sex.
   b. religion.
   c. race.
   d. familial status.

44. What would it cost to put new carpeting in a room measuring 45 feet by 20 feet if the carpet costs $16.95 per square yard, plus a $250 installation charge?
   a. $1250
   b. $1945
   c. $1695
   d. $15,255

45. What is the difference between a general lien and a specific lien?
   a. A general lien cannot be enforced in court, while a specific lien can.
   b. A specific lien is held by only one person, while a general lien must be held by two or more people.
   c. A general lien is a lien against personal property, while a specific lien is a lien against real estate.
   d. A specific lien is a lien against a certain parcel of real estate or other property, while a general lien covers all of a debtor's property.

46. In an option to purchase real estate, which statement is *TRUE* of the optionee?
   a. The optionee must purchase the property but may do so at any time within the option period.
   b. The optionee is limited to a refund of the option consideration if the option is exercised.
   c. The optionee cannot obtain third-party financing on the property until after the option has expired.
   d. The optionee has no obligation to purchase the property during the option period.

47. A village board has decided that a parking lot near the central business district would enhance the beauty, safety, and vitality of the community by keeping cars from parking on the busiest streets. Unfortunately, a house is located on part of the land best suited for the new parking lot. Based on these facts, which statement is *TRUE*?

a. The homeowner's constitutional right to own property cannot be infringed by the village under any circumstances.
b. The village may tear down the house and build the parking lot without paying the homeowner any compensation, through the village's constitutional authority under the takings clause.
c. The village may tear down the house if it first pays the homeowner fair value after meeting legal requirements.
d. The village may not seize the house because it has insufficient reason to do so.

48. How many acres are there in the N½ of the SW¼ and the NE¼ of the SE¼ of a section?

a. 20
b. 40
c. 80
d. 120

49. A home is the smallest in a neighborhood of large, expensive houses. The effect of the other houses on the value of the small home is known as

a. regression.
b. progression.
c. substitution.
d. contribution.

50. A lien that arises as a result of a judgment, estate or inheritance taxes, a decedent's debts, or federal taxes is what type of lien?

a. Specific
b. General
c. Voluntary
d. Equitable

51. All of the following will terminate an offer to purchase real estate *EXCEPT*

a. failure to accept the offer within a prescribed period.
b. revocation by the offeror communicated to the offeree after acceptance.
c. a conditional acceptance of the offer by the offeree.
d. the death of the offeror or offeree.

52. Two men are joint tenants. One of the men sells his interest to another person. What is the remaining man's relationship to the new tenant regarding the property?

a. Joint tenants
b. Tenants in common
c. Tenants by the entirety
d. No relationship, because he cannot sell his joint tenancy interest

53. Two friends enter into a six-month oral lease. If one friend defaults, the other may

a. not bring a court action because leases must be in writing for a court to review them.
b. not bring a court action because the statute of frauds governs six-month leases.
c. bring a court action because six-month leases need not be in writing to be enforceable.
d. bring a court action because the statute of limitations does not apply to oral leases, regardless of their term.

54. On Monday, a prospective buyer offers to purchase a vacant lot for $25,000. On Tuesday, the owner counteroffers to sell the lot for $29,000. On Friday, the owner withdraws the counteroffer and accepts the buyer's original offer of $25,000. Under these circumstances, which statement is *TRUE*?

   a. A valid agreement exists because the seller accepted the buyer's offer exactly as it was made, regardless of the fact that it was not accepted immediately.
   b. A valid agreement exists because the seller accepted before the buyer provided notice that the offer was withdrawn.
   c. No valid agreement exists because the buyer's offer was not accepted within 72 hours of its having been made.
   d. No valid agreement exists because the seller's counteroffer was a rejection of the buyer's offer, and once rejected, it cannot be accepted later.

55. A man's neighbors use his driveway to reach their garage, which is on their property. The man's attorney explains that the neighbors have the right to use the driveway. The man's property is the

   a. dominant tenement.
   b. servient tenement.
   c. fee simple defeasible estate.
   d. fee simple determinable estate.

56. If the quarterly interest at 7.5% is $562.50, what is the principal amount of the loan?

   a. $7,500
   b. $15,000
   c. $30,000
   d. $75,000

57. A deed conveys ownership to the grantee "so long as the existing building is not torn down." What type of estate does this deed create?

   a. Fee simple determinable estate
   b. Homestead estate
   c. Fee simple absolute estate
   d. Life estate pur autre vie, with the measuring life being the building's expected structural lifetime

58. If the mortgage loan is 80% of the appraised value of a house and the interest rate of 6% amounts to $460 for the first month, what is the appraised value of the house?

   a. $115,000
   b. $92,000
   c. $73,600
   d. $55,200

59. Local zoning ordinances may regulate all of the following *EXCEPT*

   a. height of buildings in an area.
   b. density of population.
   c. appropriate use of buildings in an area.
   d. market value of a property.

60. A real estate professional took a listing and later discovered that the client had been declared incompetent by a court. What is the current status of the listing?

   a. The listing is unaffected because the real estate professional acted in good faith as the owner's agent.
   b. The listing is of no value to the real estate professional because the contract is void.
   c. The listing entitles the real estate professional to collect a commission from the client's guardian or trustee if the real estate professional produces a buyer.
   d. The listing must be renegotiated between the real estate professional and the client, based on the new information.

61. After a borrower's default on home mortgage loan payments, the lender obtained a court order to foreclose on the property. At the foreclosure sale, the property sold for $164,000; the unpaid balance on the loan at the time of foreclosure was $178,000. If state law permits, what must the lender do to recover the $14,000 that the borrower still owes?

   a. Sue for specific performance
   b. Sue for damages
   c. Seek a deficiency judgment
   d. Seek a judgment by default

62. Which activity is forbidden by the federal Fair Housing Act?
   a. Limitation by religion and nationality in the sale of a single-family home where the property is listed by a licensed real estate professional
   b. Limitation to members only in noncommercial lodgings of a private club
   c. Limitations against familial status and disability in the rental of a unit in an owner-occupied three-family dwelling when no discriminatory advertising is used
   d. Limitation by religion and sex in noncommercial housing in a convent or monastery

63. A buyer purchases a $137,000 property, depositing $3,000 as earnest money. The buyer obtains a 75% loan-to-value (LTV) loan with no additional items to be prorated and no closing costs to the buyer. How much more cash will the buyer need at the settlement?
   a. $37,250
   b. $34,250
   c. $33,500
   d. $31,250

64. A real estate professional arrives to present a purchase offer to a seller who is seriously ill and finds the seller's son and daughter-in-law also present. The son and daughter-in-law angrily urge the seller to accept the offer, even though it is much less than the asking price for the property. If the seller accepts the offer, she may not be bound by it because the
   a. real estate professional improperly presented an offer that was less than the asking price.
   b. real estate professional's failure to protect the seller from the son and daughter-in-law constituted a violation of the real estate professional's fiduciary duties.
   c. seller's rights under the ADA have been violated by the son and daughter-in-law.
   d. seller was under undue influence from the son and daughter-in-law, so the contract is voidable.

65. A property is sold. The deed of conveyance contained only the following guarantee: "This property was not encumbered during the time the seller owned it except as noted in this deed." What type of deed makes such a covenant?
   a. General warranty
   b. Special warranty
   c. Bargain and sale
   d. Quitclaim

66. An unmarried couple own a parcel of real estate. Each owns an undivided interest, with one owning one-third and the other owning two-thirds. The form of ownership under which the couple own their property is
   a. severalty.
   b. joint tenancy.
   c. tenancy at will.
   d. tenancy in common.

67. A buyer agrees to purchase a house for $184,500. The buyer pays $2,000 as earnest money and obtains a new mortgage loan for $167,600. The purchase contract provides for a March 15 settlement. The buyer and the sellers prorate the current year's real estate taxes of $1,880.96, which have been prepaid. The buyer has additional closing costs of $1,250, and the sellers have other closing costs of $850. How much cash must the buyer bring to the settlement?
   a. $16,389.09
   b. $17,639.10
   c. $17,839.09
   d. $19,639.10.

68. A real estate professional listed a house for $247,900. A member of a racial minority group saw the house and was interested in it. When the prospective buyer asked the real estate professional the price of the house, the real estate professional said that it was listed for $253,000 and that the seller was very firm on the price. Under the federal Fair Housing Act of 1968, such a statement is
   a. legal because the law requires only that the buyer be given the opportunity to buy the house.
   b. legal because the representation was made by the real estate professional and not directly by the owner.
   c. illegal because the difference in the offering price and the quoted price was greater than 10%.
   d. illegal because the terms of the potential sale were changed for the prospective buyer.

69. A woman placed a property in a trust. When she died, her will directed the trustee to sell the property and distribute the proceeds of the sale to her heirs. The trustee sold the property in accordance with the will. What type of deed was delivered at settlement?
   a. Trustee's deed
   b. Trustor's deed
   c. Deed of trust
   d. Reconveyance deed

70. An appraiser has been hired to prepare an appraisal report of a property for loan purposes. The property is an elegant old mansion that is now used as a restaurant. Which approach to value should the appraiser probably give the greatest weight when making this appraisal?
   a. Income
   b. Sales comparison
   c. Depreciated cost
   d. Functional obsolescence

71. A borrower applies for a mortgage, and the loan officer suggests that the borrower consider a term mortgage loan. Which statement *BEST* explains what the loan officer means?
   a. All the interest is paid at the end of the term.
   b. The debt is partially amortized over the life of the loan.
   c. The length of the term is limited by state law.
   d. The entire principal amount is due at the end of the term.

72. A condominium community has a swimming pool, sauna, and tennis courts. These facilities are *MOST* likely owned by the
   a. condominium board.
   b. corporation in which the unit owners hold stock.
   c. unit owners in the form of proportional divided interests.
   d. unit owners in the form of percentage undivided interests.

73. At closing for a typical real estate transaction, the buyer's earnest money deposit is a
   a. credit to the buyer only.
   b. credit to the seller, debit to the buyer.
   c. credit to the buyer and the seller.
   d. debit to the buyer only.

74. At closing for a typical real estate transaction, property tax not yet due is a
   a. credit to the buyer, debit to the seller.
   b. credit to the seller only.
   c. debit to the seller only.
   d. debit to the buyer, credit to the seller.

75. Real property can become personal property by the process known as
   a. annexation.
   b. severance.
   c. hypothecation.
   d. accretion.

76. A man and a woman are next-door neighbors. The man gives the woman permission to park a camper in his yard for a few weeks. He does not charge her rent for the use of the yard. The man has given the woman a(n)

a. revocable trust.
b. estate for years.
c. license.
d. permissive encroachment.

77. What is the cost of constructing a fence 6 feet, 6 inches, high around a lot measuring 90 feet by 175 feet, if the cost of erecting the fence is $1.25 per linear foot and the cost of materials is $0.825 per square foot of fence? Round your answer to the nearest cent.

a. $1,752.62
b. $2,054.63
c. $2,084.62
d. $3,504.63

78. A seller signs a listing agreement with a real estate professional. A second real estate professional from a different firm obtains a buyer for the property, and the first real estate professional does not receive a commission. The first real estate professional does not sue the seller, even though the seller compensated the second real estate professional. The listing agreement between the seller and the first real estate professional was probably which type?

a. Exclusive right to sell
b. Open
c. Exclusive agency
d. Dual agency

79. Antitrust laws do *NOT* prohibit real estate

a. companies agreeing on fees charged to sellers.
b. professionals allocating markets based on the value of homes.
c. companies from allocating markets based on the location of commercial buildings.
d. brokers from imposing a standard commission rate on all transactions handled by the sales associates employed by the office.

80. A tenant leased an apartment from a property owner. Because the owner failed to perform routine maintenance, the apartment building's central heating plant broke down in the fall. The owner neglected to have the heating system repaired, and the tenant had no heat for the first six weeks of winter. The tenant reported this problem repeatedly to the owner. Although eight months remained on his lease, the tenant moved out of the apartment and refused to pay any rent. If the owner sues to recover the outstanding rent, what would be the tenant's *BEST* defense?

a. Because the tenant lived in the apartment for more than 25% of the lease term, he was entitled to move out at any time without penalty.
b. The tenant was entitled to vacate the premises because the landlord's failure to repair the heating system constituted abandonment.
c. Because the apartment was made uninhabitable, the landlord's actions resulted in actual eviction.
d. The landlord's actions resulted in constructive eviction.

SAMPLE EXAM 2

1. A tenant's landlord plans to sell the building in which the tenant lives to the state so that a freeway can be built. The tenant's lease has expired, but the landlord permits the tenant to stay in the apartment until the building is torn down. The tenant continues to pay the rent as prescribed in the lease. What kind of tenancy does this tenant have?
   a. Holdover tenancy
   b. Month-to-month tenancy
   c. Tenancy at sufferance
   d. Tenancy at will

2. The owner of a house wants to fence the yard for the family pet. When the fence is erected, the fencing materials become real estate through
   a. severance.
   b. subrogation.
   c. annexation.
   d. attachment.

3. A seller is interested in selling a house as quickly as possible and believes that the best way to do this is to have several real estate professionals compete against each other for the commission. The listing agreements with four different real estate professionals specifically promise that if one of them finds a buyer for the property, the seller will be obligated to pay a commission to that real estate professional only. What type of agreement has the seller entered into?
   a. Executed
   b. Discharged
   c. Unilateral
   d. Bilateral

4. In some states, by paying the debt after a foreclosure sale, the delinquent borrower has the right to regain the property under which of the following?
   a. Novation
   b. Redemption
   c. Reversion
   d. Recovery

5. A country music singer who owns a cattle ranch enters into a sale-and-leaseback agreement with a local dentist. Which statement is *TRUE* of this arrangement?
   a. The singer retains title to the ranch.
   b. The dentist receives possession of the property.
   c. The dentist is the lessor.
   d. The singer is the lessor.

6. A real estate professional is employed by a buyer. When the real estate professional finds a property that the buyer might be interested in buying, she is careful to find out as much as possible about the property's owners and why their property is on the market. The real estate professional's efforts to keep the buyer informed of all facts that could affect a transaction is the duty of
   a. accounting.
   b. loyalty.
   c. confidentiality.
   d. disclosure.

7. A parcel of vacant land 80 feet wide and 200 feet deep was sold for $500 per front foot. How much money would a real estate professional receive as a 60% share of a 10% commission on the sale?
   a. $1,600
   b. $2,400
   c. $6,000
   d. $4,000

8. Which situation does *NOT* violate the federal Fair Housing Act?
   a. The refusal of a property manager to rent an apartment to a Muslim couple who are otherwise qualified
   b. The general policy of a loan company to avoid granting home improvement loans to individuals living in transitional neighborhoods
   c. The intentional neglect of a real estate professional to show an Asian family any property listings in neighborhoods other than those with a majority of Asian residents.
   d. A widow's insistence on renting her spare bedroom only to another widowed woman

9. If a storage tank that measures 12 feet by 9 feet by 8 feet is designed to store gas that costs $1.82 per cubic foot, what does it cost to fill the tank to one-half of its capacity? Round your answer to the nearest dollar.
   a. $685
   b. $786
   c. $864
   d. $1,572

10. A buyer bought a house for $225,000. The house, which had originally sold for $148,250, appraised for $210,500. Based on these facts, if the buyer applies for an 80% mortgage, what will be the amount of the loan?
    a. $118,600
    b. $168,400
    c. $180,000
    d. $196,750

11. A purchaser offers to buy a seller's property by signing a purchase contract. The seller accepts the offer. What kind of title interest does the buyer have in the property at this point?
    a. Legal
    b. Equitable
    c. Defeasible
    d. No title interest

12. Which federal law requires that finance charges be stated as an annual percentage rate?
    a. Truth in Lending Act
    b. Real Estate Settlement Procedures Act (RESPA)
    c. Equal Credit Opportunity Act (ECOA)
    d. Fair Housing Act

13. A seller signed a 90-day listing agreement with a real estate professional. Two weeks later, the seller was killed in an accident. What is the present status of the listing?
    a. The listing agreement is binding on the seller's estate for the remainder of the 90 days.
    b. Because the seller's intention to sell was clearly defined, the listing agreement is still in effect and the real estate professional may proceed to market the property on behalf of the seller's estate.
    c. The listing agreement is binding on the seller's estate only if the real estate professional can produce an offer to purchase the property within the remainder of the listing period.
    d. The listing agreement was terminated automatically when the seller died.

14. A woman conveys the ownership of an office building to a nursing home. The nursing home agrees that the rental income produced by the building will pay for the expenses of caring for the woman's parents. When both her parents have died, ownership of the office building will revert to the woman. The estate held by the nursing home is a
    a. remainder life estate.
    b. legal life estate.
    c. life estate pur autre vie.
    d. temporary leasehold estate.

15. A buyer signs a buyer representation agreement under which the real estate professional will help this client find a three-bedroom house in the $185,000 to $200,000 price range. A seller comes into the real estate professional's office and signs a listing agreement to sell a two-bedroom condominium for $170,000. Based on these facts, which statement is *TRUE*?
   a. The buyer is the real estate professional's client; the seller is the real estate professional's customer.
   b. The buyer is the real estate professional's customer; the seller is the real estate professional's client.
   c. While both the buyer and the seller are clients, the real estate professional owes the fiduciary duties of an agent only to the seller.
   d. Because both the buyer and the seller are the real estate professional's clients, the real estate professional owes the fiduciary duties of an agent to both.

16. In a township, which statement is *TRUE*?
   a. Section 31 lies to the east of Section 32.
   b. Section 18 is by law set aside for school purposes.
   c. Section 6 lies in the northeast corner of the township.
   d. Section 16 lies to the north of Section 21.

17. A real estate professional representing a seller is asked by the client to make sure that the deed to the buyer does not reveal the actual sales price. In this case, the real estate professional
   a. must inform the client that only the actual price of the real estate may appear on the deed.
   b. may ask that a deed be prepared that shows only nominal consideration of $10.
   c. should inform the seller that either the full price should be stated in the deed or all references to consideration should be removed from it.
   d. may show a price on the deed other than the actual price, provided that the variance is not greater than 10% of the purchase price.

18. A real estate professional obtained a listing agreement to act as the agent in the sale of a house. An unrepresented buyer has been found for the property, and all agreements have been signed. As agent of the seller, the real estate professional is responsible for which activity?
   a. Completing the buyer's loan application
   b. Making sure that the buyer receives copies of all documents the seller is required to deliver to the buyer
   c. Ensuring that the buyer is qualified for the new mortgage loan
   d. Scheduling the buyer's inspection of the property

19. A broker's employment agreement with a sales associate provides a commission share of 65% to the sales associate. What is the sales associate's compensation if the sales price of a property is $895,000, the broker is entitled to a 6½% commission, and there is no cooperating broker?
   a. $16,621.43
   b. $34,905.00
   c. $37,813.75
   d. $58,175.00

20. Which step is among those an appraiser would use in preparing a real property appraisal using the cost approach?
   a. Estimate the replacement cost of the improvements
   b. Deduct for the depreciation of the land and buildings
   c. Determine the original cost and adjust for depreciation
   d. Review the sales prices of comparable properties

21. When a mortgage lender provides the buyer with statements of all fees and charges the seller will incur, the lender is complying with requirements that originated under which federal law?
   a. Equal Credit Opportunity Act (ECOA)
   b. Truth in Lending Act (Regulation Z)
   c. Real Estate Settlement Procedures Act (RESPA)
   d. Fair Housing Act

22. The landlord of an apartment building neglected to repair the building's plumbing system. As a result, the apartments did not receive water. If a tenant's unit becomes uninhabitable, what is the *MOST* likely result?
   a. Suit for possession
   b. Claim of constructive eviction
   c. Tenancy at sufferance
   d. Suit for negligence

23. A man conveys a life estate to his son. Under the terms of the man's conveyance, the property will pass to the man's nephew on his son's death. Which interest in the property *BEST* describes that of the nephew's during the son's lifetime?
   a. Remainder
   b. Reversion
   c. Life estate pur autre vie
   d. Redemption

24. At closing, prorations for unpaid real estate taxes are shown as a
   a. credit to the seller and a debit to the buyer.
   b. debit to the seller and a credit to the buyer.
   c. credit to both the seller and the buyer.
   d. debit to both the seller and the buyer.

25. What type of lease establishes a rental payment and requires the lessor to pay for the taxes, insurance, and maintenance on the property?
   a. Percentage
   b. Net
   c. Expense only
   d. Gross

26. A conventional mortgage loan closed on July 1 for $165,000 at 3.75% interest amortized over 25 years at $857.06 per month. Using a 360-day year and interest paid in arrears, what would the principal amount be after the monthly payment was made August 1?
   a. $164,936.30
   b. $164,484.38
   c. $164,142.94
   d. $164,658.57

27. In the preceding question, what would the interest portion of the payment be?
   a. $17.19
   b. $257.81
   c. $515.63
   d. $618.75

28. A seller lists her home with a real estate professional for $220,000 but tells the real estate professional, who is acting as the seller's agent, "I've got to sell quickly because of a job transfer. If necessary, I can accept a price as low as $175,000." The real estate professional tells a prospective buyer to offer $180,000 "because the seller is desperate to sell." The seller accepts the buyer's offer. In this situation, which statement is *TRUE*?
   a. The real estate professional violated an established agency relationship with the seller.
   b. The real estate professional's action did not violate any agency relationship with the seller because the real estate professional did not actually reveal the seller's lowest acceptable price.
   c. The real estate professional acted properly to obtain a quick offer on the seller's property, in accordance with the seller's instructions.
   d. The real estate professional violated established fiduciary duties toward the buyer by failing to disclose that the seller would accept a lower price than the buyer offered.

29. Which of the following *BEST* describes the capitalization rate under the income approach to appraising real estate?
   a. Rate at which a property increases in value
   b. Rate of return a property earns as an investment
   c. Rate of capital required to keep a property operating most efficiently
   d. Maximum rate of return allowed by law on an investment

30. At closing, the cost of the lender's title insurance policy required for a new loan is usually shown as which of the following?

a. Credit to the seller
b. Credit to the buyer
c. Debit to the seller
d. Debit to the buyer

31. An FHA-insured loan in the amount of $157,500 at 4½% for 30 years closed on July 17. The first monthly payment is due on September 1. Using a 360-day year and assuming that interest is being paid for the day of closing, what was the amount of the interest payment the buyer had to make at the settlement?

a. $19.69
b. $275.63
c. $295.35
d. $315.04

32. If a home that cost $342,500 three years ago is now valued at 127% of its original cost, what is its current market value?

a. $364,750
b. $395,000
c. $424,500
d. $434,975

33. A buyer makes an offer on a property and the seller accepts. Three weeks later, the buyer announces that "the deal's off" and refuses to go through with the sale. If the seller is entitled to keep the buyer's earnest money deposit, there *MOST* likely is what kind of clause in the sales contract?

a. Liquidated damages clause
b. Contingent damages clause
c. Actual damages clause
d. Revocation clause

34. A search of the public record regarding title to a property is *MOST* likely to provide information about which item?

a. Encroachments
b. Rights of parties in possession
c. Inaccurate survey
d. Mechanics' liens

35. A rectangular lot is worth $193,600. This value is the equivalent of $4.40 per square foot. If one lot dimension is 200 feet, what is the other dimension?

a. 110 feet
b. 220 feet
c. 400 feet
d. 880 feet

36. A real estate professional listed an agricultural property at an 8% commission rate. After the sale of the property and the settlement had taken place, the seller discovered that the real estate professional had been listing other properties at a 6% commission rate. Based on this information, which statement is *TRUE*?

a. The real estate professional has done nothing wrong because a commission rate is always negotiable between the parties.
b. If the real estate professional inflated the usual commission rate for the area, the real estate professional may be subject to discipline by the state real estate commission.
c. The seller is entitled to rescind the transaction based on the principle of lack of reality of consent.
d. The seller is entitled to a refund from the real estate professional of 2% of the commission.

37. A renter has six months remaining on her apartment lease. The monthly rent is $875. The renter moves out of the apartment for four months, and a friend moves in. The friend pays the renter a monthly rental of $700, and the renter continues paying the full rental amount under her lease to the landlord. This is an example of

a. subletting.
b. assignment.
c. rescission and renewal.
d. surrender.

38. One real estate professional asked another, "Will I have to prove that I was the procuring cause in order to collect a commission if my seller sells the property without my help?" The other real estate professional answered, "No, not if you have an
   a. option listing."
   b. open listing."
   c. exclusive agency listing."
   d. exclusive right-to-sell listing."

39. The capitalization rate on a property reflects (among other things) which factor?
   a. Risk of the investment
   b. Replacement cost of the improvements
   c. Real estate taxes
   d. Debt service

40. An investment property now worth $180,000 was purchased seven years ago for $142,000. At the time of the purchase, the land was valued at $18,000. Assuming a 27½-year life for straight-line depreciation purposes, what is the present book value of the property?
   a. $95,071.00
   b. $108,071.25
   c. $110,436.37
   d. $126,000.78

41. After a buyer purchased a property from a seller, they both decided to rescind the recorded transfer. To do this, what must happen?
   a. The buyer must return the deed to the seller.
   b. The parties must record a notice of rescission.
   c. The parties must simply destroy the original deed in the presence of witnesses.
   d. The buyer must make a new deed to the seller.

42. A farmer owns the W½ of the NW¼ of the NW¼ of a section. The adjoining property can be purchased for $300 per acre. Owning all of the NW¼ of the section would cost the farmer
   a. $6,000.
   b. $12,000.
   c. $42,000.
   d. $48,000.

43. A real estate professional received a deposit, along with a written offer from a buyer. The offer stated: "The offeror will leave this offer open for the seller's acceptance for a period of 10 days." On the fifth day, and before acceptance by the seller, the offeror notified the real estate professional that the offer was withdrawn and demanded the return of the deposit. Which statement is *TRUE* in this situation?
   a. The offeror cannot withdraw the offer; it must be held open for the full 10-day period, as promised.
   b. The offeror has the right to withdraw the offer and secure the return of the deposit anytime before being notified of the seller's acceptance.
   c. The offeror can withdraw the offer, and the seller and the real estate professional will each retain one-half of the forfeited deposit.
   d. While the offeror can withdraw the offer, the real estate professional is legally entitled to declare the deposit forfeited and retain all of it in lieu of the lost commission.

44. A building's owner pays a property manager an 8½% commission based on the unit's annualized rent for each new tenant. Last year, the manager signed five new tenants—three at $795 per month, one at $1,200 per month, and one at $900 per month. What was the total amount of the property manager's new-tenant commissions for that year?
   a. $381.23
   b. $2,952.90
   c. $3,685.47
   d. $4,574.70

45. The monthly rent on a warehouse is $1 per cubic yard. Assuming the warehouse is 36 feet by 200 feet by 12 feet high, what is the annual rent?
   a. $3,200
   b. $9,600
   c. $38,400
   d. $115,200

46. If a veteran wishes to refinance a home by changing to a VA-guaranteed loan and the lender insists on 3½ discount points, which option is available to the veteran?

a. Refinance with a VA loan, provided the lender charges no discount points
b. Refinance with a VA loan, provided the lender charges no more than two discount points
c. Be required to pay a maximum of 1% of the loan as an origination fee
d. Proceed with the refinance loan and pay the discount points

47. A woman owned property that she conveyed to a man "so long as no real estate broker or salesperson ever sets foot on the property." If a broker or a salesperson visits the property, ownership will revert to the woman. Based on these two conveyances, which statement is *TRUE*?

a. The man holds the property in fee simple determinable.
b. The man holds the property in fee simple defeasible, subject to a condition subsequent.
c. The man may not transfer ownership of the property without the woman's permission.
d. The woman has retained a right of re-entry with regard to the property.

48. A real estate transaction has a closing date of November 15. The seller, who is responsible for costs up to and including the date of settlement, has already paid the property taxes of $11,160 for the calendar year. On the closing statement, the buyer will be

a. debited $1,395.
b. debited $9,765.
c. credited $1,395.
d. credited $9,765.

49. After a storeowner's spouse died, he could no longer maintain the store. A woman who wished to open a store agreed to move into the entire space and pay for the remaining seven years on the lease. The landlord agreed to the arrangement. This is known as a lease

a. assumption.
b. assignment.
c. surrender.
d. breach.

50. A purchaser buys a house for $234,500 by making a $25,000 cash down payment and taking out a $209,500 mortgage for 30 years. The lot value is $80,000. If the purchaser wants to depreciate the property over a period of 27½ years, what will be the annual depreciation amount using the straight-line method? Round your answer to the nearest cent.

a. $3,818.18
b. $4,709.09
c. $5,618.18
d. $7,444.44

51. A property manager leased a store for three years. The first year, the store's rent was $1,000 per month, and the rent was to increase 10% per year thereafter. The manager received a 7% commission for the first year, 5% for the second year, and 3% for the balance of the lease. What was the total commission earned by the property manager?

a. $840.40
b. $1,613.10
c. $1,935.60
d. $2,785.40

52. Against a recorded deed from the owner of record, the party with the weakest position is a

a. person with a prior unrecorded deed and who is not in possession.
b. person in possession with a prior unrecorded deed.
c. tenant in possession with nine months remaining on the lease.
d. painter who is half-finished painting the house at the time of the sale and who has not yet been paid.

53. A married couple files their income taxes jointly. Last year they sold their home for $340,000. Seven years ago, when they were first married, they bought the house for $250,000 and have lived in it ever since. Based on these facts, which statement is *TRUE*?
   a. Under current tax law, the couple will owe a capital gains tax this year on their $90,000 gain.
   b. Current tax law permits the couple to exclude up to $250,000 in capital gain from their income tax.
   c. Because their gain is less than $500,000, the couple will owe no capital gains tax this year.
   d. Under current tax law, the couple will be entitled to a penalty-free withdrawal of up to $10,000 from a 401(k) retirement account to use as a down payment.

54. A squatter moved into an abandoned home and lived there for some years. Ultimately, the squatter was granted title to the property by a court. Which element is *NOT* basic to acquiring title in this manner?
   a. Permission of the true owner
   b. Open and notorious use
   c. Occupancy for a period of time prescribed by state law
   d. Occupancy hostile to the best interests of the true owner

55. Maria, Frank, and Judy are joint tenants. Judy sells her interest to Laura, and then Frank dies. As a result, which statement is *TRUE*?
   a. Frank's heirs are joint tenants with Laura and Maria.
   b. Frank's heirs and Maria are joint tenants, but Laura is a tenant in common.
   c. Maria is a tenant in common with Laura and Frank's heirs.
   d. Maria and Laura are tenants in common.

56. At closing, the selling price is
   a. a debit to the buyer.
   b. a debit to the seller.
   c. a credit to the buyer.
   d. greater than the loan amount.

57. The state wants to acquire a strip of farmland to build a highway. Does the state have the right to acquire this land for public use?
   a. Yes, the state's right is called condemnation.
   b. Yes, the state's right is called eminent domain.
   c. Yes, the state's right is called escheat.
   d. No, under the U.S. Constitution, private property may never be taken by state governments or by the federal government.

58. A man died, and his estate was distributed according to his will as follows: 54% to his spouse, 18% to his children, 16% to his grandchildren, and the remainder to his college. The college received $79,000. How much did the man's children receive? Round your answer to the nearest dollar.
   a. $105,333
   b. $118,500
   c. $355,500
   d. $658,333

59. Which of the following is an example of external obsolescence?
   a. Numerous pillars supporting the ceiling in a store
   b. Leaks in the roof of a warehouse, making the premises unusable and, therefore, unrentable
   c. Coal cellar in a house with central heating
   d. Vacant, abandoned, and run-down buildings in an area

60. Which phrase, when placed in a print advertisement, would *MOST* nearly comply with the requirements of the Truth in Lending Act (Regulation Z)?
   a. "5½% interest"
   b. "5½% rate"
   c. "5½% annual interest"
   d. "5½% annual percentage rate"

61. Which statement is *FALSE* regarding a capitalization rate?

a. The rate increases when the risk increases.
b. An increase in rate, while other elements remain the same, means a decrease in value.
c. The net income is divided by the rate to estimate value.
d. A decrease in rate, while other elements remain the same, results in a decrease in value.

62. The Equal Credit Opportunity Act (ECOA) makes it illegal for lenders to refuse credit to or otherwise discriminate against which applicant?

a. Parent of twins who receives public assistance and cannot afford the monthly mortgage payments
b. New homebuyer who does not have a credit history
c. Single person who receives public assistance
d. Unemployed person with no job prospects and no identifiable source of income

63. When a man died, a deed was found in his desk drawer. Although the deed had never been recorded, it was signed, dated, and acknowledged. The deed gave the man's house to a local charity. The will, however, provided as follows: "I leave all of the real and personal property that I own to my beloved niece." In this situation, the house *MOST* likely will go to the

a. charity, because acknowledgment creates a presumption of delivery.
b. charity, because the man's intent was clear from the deed.
c. niece, because the deed was never delivered to or accepted by the charity.
d. niece, because the deed had not been recorded.

64. If a borrower takes out a $90,000 loan at 7½% interest to be repaid at the end of 15 years with interest paid annually, what is the total interest that the borrower will pay over the life of the loan?

a. $10,125
b. $80,000
c. $101,250
d. $180,000

65. After an offer is accepted, the seller finds that the real estate professional was the undisclosed agent for the buyer, as well as the agent for the seller. The seller may

a. withdraw without obligation to the real estate professional or the buyer.
b. withdraw but be subject to liquidated damages.
c. withdraw but only with the concurrence of the buyer.
d. refuse to sell but be subject to a suit for specific performance.

66. To net the owner $90,000 after a 6% commission is paid, what would the list price would have to be? Round your answer to the nearest dollar.

a. $95,400
b. $95,745
c. $95,906
d. $96,000

67. Which circumstance would *MOST* likely be legal under the provisions of the federal Fair Housing Act?

a. A lender refuses to make loans in areas where more than 25% of the population is Hispanic.
b. A private social club that discriminates against no protected group in granting membership refuses to rent a suite in its members-only vacation facility to a Nigerian family who are not members of the club.
c. A church excludes Middle Easterners from membership and rents its nonprofit housing to church members only.
d. A real estate professional directs prospective buyers away from areas where they are likely to feel uncomfortable because of their race.

68. It is discovered after a sale of a parcel of land that the land parcel is 10% smaller than the seller represented it to be. The real estate professional who passed this information on to the buyer is

a. not liable as long as the real estate professional only repeated the seller's data.
b. not liable if the misrepresentation was unintentional.
c. not liable if the buyer actually inspected the parcel.
d. liable if the real estate professional knew or should have known of the discrepancy.

69. An easement terminates

a. automatically.
b. when the owner of the servient tenement wishes to do so.
c. if the owners of the dominant and servient tenements become one and the same.
d. when a property owner dies.

70. Which activity is *NOT* a violation of the Real Estate Settlement Procedures Act (RESPA)?

a. Providing a Closing Disclosure to a borrower four days before the closing
b. Accepting a kickback on a loan subject to RESPA requirements
c. Requiring the buyer to use a particular title insurance company
d. Accepting a fee or charging for services that were not performed

71. The rescission provisions of the Truth in Lending Act (Regulation Z) apply to which transaction?

a. Home purchase loans
b. Construction lending
c. Business financing
d. Consumer credit

72. A property has a net income of $30,000. An appraiser decides to use a 12% capitalization rate rather than a 10% rate on this property. The use of the higher rate results in

a. a 2% increase in the appraised value.
b. a $50,000 increase in the appraised value.
c. a $50,000 decrease in the appraised value.
d. no change in the appraised value.

73. The section in a purchase contract that would provide for the buyer to forfeit any earnest money if the buyer fails to complete the purchase is known as a provision for

a. liquidated damages.
b. punitive damages.
c. hypothecation.
d. subordination.

74. In one commercial building, a tenant intends to start a small health food shop. An identical, adjacent building houses a showroom leased to a major national retailing chain. Both tenants have long-term leases with identical rents. If the appraiser uses a capitalization rate for the store leased to the national retailing chain that is lower than the rate for the other building, which statement is *TRUE*?

a. The indicated value of the chain's property will be lower than the indicated value of the food-shop property.
b. The indicated value of the chain's property will be higher than the indicated value of the food-shop property.
c. The appraiser would then be compelled to make use of the sales comparison approach to value.
d. It would indicate the appraiser believes a building occupied by a chain-store tenant is more valuable than an identical one occupied by a health food shop.

75. An insurance company agreed to provide a developer with financing for a shopping center at 7% interest plus an equity position. What type of loan is this?

a. Package
b. Participation
c. Open-end
d. Blanket

76. A $100,000 loan at 6% could be amortized with monthly payments of $644 on a 15-year basis or payments of $600 on a 30-year basis. The 30-year loan results in total payments of what percentage of the 15-year total payments? Round your answer to the nearest whole percentage.
   a. 106%
   b. 158%
   c. 186%
   d. 154%

77. According to an appraisal prepared for a loan approval, a property is worth $425,000. The previous homeowner bought the property for $290,000 and added $50,000 in improvements, for a total of $340,000. The property sold in foreclosure for $325,000. Which amount represents the property's market price?
   a. $290,000
   b. $325,000
   c. $425,000
   d. $340,000

78. What is the amount of tax payable if a property's assessed value is $185,000 and the tax rate is 40 mills in a community in which an equalization factor of 110% is used?
   a. $4,625.00
   b. $5,087.50
   c. $7,400.40
   d. $8,140.00

79. At closing, how will a proration of prepaid water, gas, and electric charges be reflected?
   a. Debit to the seller, credit to the buyer
   b. Debit to the buyer, credit to the seller
   c. Debit to the buyer only
   d. Credit to the seller only

80. An apartment manager decides not to purchase flood insurance. Instead, the manager installs raised platforms in the basement storage areas and has the furnace placed on eight-inch legs. This form of risk management is known as
   a. avoiding the risk.
   b. controlling the risk.
   c. retaining the risk.
   d. transferring the risk.

Glossary

Note: Most of the entries in this glossary reference specific pages in *Modern Real Estate Practice in Georgia Third Edition*. Page references are for where a term is defined or explained. Page references are not provided for terms that are included here because they are used in everyday professional practice or are of historical interest.

abstract of title The condensed history of the recorded ownership of a particular parcel of real estate, consisting of a summary of the original grant and all subsequent conveyances and encumbrances affecting the property and a certification by the abstractor that the history is complete and accurate. **122**

accelerated cost recovery system (ACRS) Method for claiming tax deductions for certain property purchased before 1987 in which it was possible to claim greater deductions in the early years of ownership, gradually reducing the amount deducted in each year of useful life. **431**

acceleration clause The clause in a mortgage or deed of trust that can be enforced to make the entire debt due immediately if the borrower defaults on an installment payment or other obligation. **245**

accession Acquiring title to additions or improvements to real property as a result of the annexation of fixtures or the accretion of alluvial deposits along the banks of streams. **24**

accretion The increase or addition of land by the deposit of sand or soil washed up naturally from a river, lake, or sea. **20**

accrued depreciation Loss in a property's value resulting from physical deterioration, external depreciation, and functional obsolescence. **304**

accrued items On a closing statement, items of expense that are incurred but not yet payable, such as interest on a mortgage loan or taxes on real property. **339**

acknowledgment A formal declaration made before a duly authorized officer, usually a notary public, by a person who has signed a document. **105**

acre A measure of land equal to 43,560 square feet, 4,840 square yards, 4,047 square meters, 160 square rods, or 0.4047 hectares. **89**

action to quiet title A court action that establishes ownership when ownership cannot be traced through an unbroken chain of title. **122**

actual eviction The legal process that results in a tenant's being physically removed from leased premises. **358**

actual notice Express information or fact; that which is known; direct knowledge. **121**

ad valorem tax A tax levied according to value, generally used to refer to real estate tax. Also called the *general tax*. **225**

addendum Any provision added to an existing contract without altering the content of the original. Must be signed by all parties. **213**

adjustable-rate mortgage (ARM) A loan characterized by a fluctuating interest rate, usually one tied to a bank or savings and loan association cost-of-funds index. **249**

adjusted basis *See* basis. **431**

administrative deed Deed by which court-appointed administrator distributes property from the estate of a decedent who died intestate.

administrative law judge (ALJ) The official who presides over a hearing involving a government agency and someone affected by a decision of that agency. The ALJ hears evidence, including the testimony of witnesses, and renders a decision. **43**

administrator A court-selected person who assists with the settlement of an estate of a person who died without leaving a will. A woman might be called an *administratrix*, although *administrator* is the term used most often to refer to either a man or a woman. **114**

adverse possession The actual, open, notorious, hostile, and continuous possession of another's land under a claim of title. Possession for a statutory period may be a means of acquiring title. **111**

adverse possession laws Georgia allows trespassers who occupy property of no visible ownership to make a general claim of title if, without the permission or interference of the true owner, they maintain open, continuously uninterrupted possession for 20 years.

affidavit of title A written statement, made under oath by a seller or grantor of real property and acknowledged by a notary public, in which grantors (1) identify themselves and indicate marital status, (2) certify that since the examination of the title, on the date of the contract no defects have occurred in the title, and (3) certify that they are in possession of the property (if applicable). **318**

affiliated business arrangement (ABA) Practice of one company offering a package of services to consumers. **323**

agency All relationships in which a real estate broker in Georgia acts for or represents another as a client by written authority in a real property transaction.

agency by ratification An agency relationship created after the fact.

agent One who acts or has the power to act for another. A fiduciary relationship is created under the *law of agency* when a property owner, as the principal, executes a listing agreement or management contract authorizing a licensed real estate broker to be his or her agent. A prospective property buyer may authorize a real estate broker to act as the buyer's agent to find a suitable property. **153**

air lots Designated airspace over a piece of land. An air lot, like surface property, may be transferred. **93**

air rights The right to use the open space above a property, usually allowing the surface to be used for another purpose. **19**

alienation The act of transferring property to another. Alienation may be voluntary, such as by gift or sale, or involuntary, as through eminent domain or adverse possession. **102, 110**

alienation clause The clause in a mortgage or deed of trust stating that the balance of the secured debt becomes immediately due and payable at the lender's option if the property is sold by the borrower. In effect, this clause prevents the borrower from assigning the debt without the lender's approval. **247**

allodial system A system of land ownership in which land is held free and clear of any rent or service due to the government; commonly contrasted to the feudal system. Land is held under the allodial system in the United States.

amendment A change to the existing content of a contract (i.e., if words or provisions are added to or deleted from the body of the contract). It must be initialed by all parties. **213**

American Land Title Association (ALTA) policy A title insurance policy that protects the interest in a collateral property of a mortgage lender who originates a new real estate loan. **125**

Americans with Disabilities Act (ADA) Act addresses rights of individuals with disabilities in employment and public accommodations. **38**

amortized loan A loan in which the principal, as well as the interest, is payable in monthly or other periodic installments over the term of the loan. **248**

annexation Process of converting personal property into real property. **22**

annual percentage rate (APR) The relationship of the total finance charges associated with a loan. This must be disclosed to borrowers by lenders under the Truth in Lending Act. **280**

anticipation The appraisal principle holding that value can increase or decrease based on the expectation of some future benefit or detriment produced by the property. **301**

antitrust laws Laws designed to preserve the free enterprise of the open marketplace by making illegal certain private conspiracies and combinations formed to minimize competition. Most violations of antitrust laws in the real estate business involve either *price-fixing* (real estate professionals conspiring to set fixed compensation rates) or *allocation of customers or markets* (real estate professionals agreeing to limit their areas of trade or dealing to certain areas or properties). **140**

appointed agency *See* designated agency. **165**

appraisal An estimate of the quantity, quality, or value of something. The process through which conclusions of property value are obtained; also refers to the report that sets forth the process of estimation and conclusion of value. **290**

appraisal report An opinion of a property's market value given to a lender or client with detailed market information. **290**

appraiser An independent person trained to provide an unbiased estimate of value. **2**

Appraiser Independence Requirements (AIR) Regulations issued by Fannie Mae that must be followed by appraisers to ensure accurate and objective appraisals. **290**

appreciation An increase in the worth or value of a property due to economic or related causes, which may prove to be either temporary or permanent; opposite of depreciation. **427**

appurtenance A right, privilege, or improvement belonging to, and passing with, the land; "runs with the land." **18**

appurtenant easement An easement that is annexed to the ownership of one parcel and allows the owner the use of the neighbor's land. **56**

area A level surface or piece of ground; the size of a surface; the amount of a two-dimensional object.

area preference People's desire for one area over another, based on a number of factors such as history, reputation, convenience, scenic beauty, and location. **25**

asbestos A mineral once used in insulation and other materials that can cause respiratory diseases. **405**

assemblage The combining of two or more adjoining lots into one larger tract to increase their total value. **302**

assessed value The value of real property for property tax purposes. This value is multiplied by the millage rate to calculate annual property taxes. 225

assessment The imposition of a tax, charge, or levy, usually according to established rates. 7

assessment equalization factor A factor (number) by which the assessed value of a property is multiplied to arrive at a value for the property that is in line with statewide tax assessments. The ad valorem tax would be based on this adjusted value. An equalization factor may be applied to raise or lower assessments in a particular district or county. 226

assessment factor Is 40% throughout Georgia. This factor is multiplied by the fair market value of real property to calculate taxable value of property. Also called *assessment rate*.

assigned agency *See* designated agency. 165

assignment The transfer in writing of interest in a bond, mortgage, lease, or other instrument. 206

associate licensee A licensed real estate **salesperson** who is employed by or associated with the broker to perform brokerage activities on behalf of or for the broker. 2

assumption of mortgage Acquiring title to property on which there is an existing mortgage and agreeing to be personally liable for the terms and conditions of the mortgage, including payments. 247

attachment The act of taking a person's property into legal custody by writ or other judicial order to hold it available for application to that person's debt to a creditor. 230

attorney's opinion of title An abstract of title that an attorney has examined and has certified to be, in the attorney's opinion, an accurate statement of the facts concerning the property's ownership. 124

automated underwriting Computer systems that permit lenders to expedite the loan approval process and reduce lending costs. 283

automatic extension clause A listing agreement clause stating that the agreement will continue automatically for a certain period of time after its expiration date. In many states, use of this clause is discouraged or prohibited. 179

avulsion The sudden tearing away of land, as by earthquake, flood, volcanic action, or the sudden change in the course of a stream. 21

back-end ratio Measures the borrower's revolving monthly debt obligations (including credit cards, car note, child support, school loan payment, etc.) against the borrower's stable monthly income. Calculation arrived at by dividing the monthly debt by the gross monthly income.

balance The appraisal principle stating that the greatest value in a property will occur when the type and size of the improvements are proportional to each other as well as the land.

balloon payment A final payment of a mortgage loan that is considerably larger than the required periodic payments because the loan amount was not fully amortized. 251

bargain and sale deed A deed that carries with it no warranties against liens or other encumbrances but that does imply that the grantor has the right to convey title. The grantor may add warranties to the deed. 107

base line The main imaginary line running east and west and crossing a principal meridian at a definite point; used by surveyors for reference in locating and describing land under the rectangular (government) survey system of legal description. 88

basis The financial interest that the Internal Revenue Service attributes to an owner of an investment property for the purpose of determining annual depreciation and gain or loss on the sale of the asset. If a property was acquired by purchase, the owner's basis is the cost of the property plus the value of any capital expenditures for improvements to the property, minus any depreciation allowable or actually taken. This new basis is called the *adjusted basis*. 431

benchmarks Permanent reference marks or points established for use by surveyors in measuring differences in elevation. 94

beneficiary (1) The person for whom a trust operates or in whose behalf the income from a trust estate is drawn. (2) A lender in a deed of trust loan transaction. 244

bilateral contract A legally enforceable promise or set of promises that must be performed and for which, if a breach of the promise occurs, the law provides a remedy. A contract may be either unilateral, by which only one party is bound to act, or bilateral, by which all parties to the instrument are legally bound to act as prescribed.

binder An agreement that may accompany an earnest money deposit for the purchase of real property as evidence of the purchaser's good faith and intent to complete the transaction. 210

blanket loan A mortgage covering more than one parcel of real estate, providing for each parcel's partial release from the mortgage lien upon repayment of a definite portion of the debt. 277

blockbusting The illegal practice of inducing homeowners to sell their properties by making representations regarding the entry or prospective entry of persons of a particular race or national origin into the neighborhood. 40

blue-sky laws Common name for those state and federal laws that regulate the registration and sale of investment securities. 433

boot Money or property given to make up any difference in value or equity between two properties in an *exchange*. 432

boycott When individuals or businesses withhold their patronage to a business as a protest or to reduce competition. 141

branch office A secondary place of business apart from the principal or main office from which real estate business is conducted. A branch office usually must be run by a licensed real estate professional. 134

breach of contract Violation of any terms or conditions in a contract without legal excuse; for example, failure to make a payment when it is due. 207

bring down A second title search that is made after the closing and before any new documents are filed. 318

broker Any person or entity issued a broker's real estate license by the Georgia Real Estate Commission pursuant to Real Estate License Law statutes. The term "broker" may also refer to the broker's licensee affiliates, except where the context might otherwise indicate. Though BRRETA identifies a licensee's duties and disclosures as broker obligations, affiliate licensees of the broker assume these same obligations.

broker protection clause Clause in a contract that protects a broker from losing a commission in the event a transaction is not completed or is intentionally delayed until after the listing expires. 179

brokerage The occupation or business of a real estate broker in Georgia. 133

brokerage engagement A written agency contract in which a buyer, a seller, a tenant, or a landlord becomes a client of the broker and promises to compensate the broker or allow the broker to be compensated by another party in consideration of the broker's producing a seller, a buyer, a tenant, or a landlord ready, willing, and able to buy, sell, or rent the property, or to perform other brokerage services.

brokerage relationship Describes both client and customer relationships with the broker.

broker's price opinion (BPO) An opinion of real estate value commissioned by a bank or an attorney and provided by a broker. 292

brownfields Defunct, derelict, or abandoned commercial or industrial sites; many have toxic wastes. 414

budget comparison statement Compares actual results with the original budget, often giving either percentages or a numerical variance of actual versus projected income and expenses. 373

buffer zone A strip of land, usually used as a park or designated for a similar use, separating land dedicated to one use from land dedicated to another use (e.g., residential from commercial). 392

building code An ordinance that specifies minimum standards of construction for buildings to protect public safety and health. 394

building permit Written governmental permission for the construction, alteration, or demolition of an improvement, showing compliance with building codes and zoning ordinances. 393

building-related illness (BRI) An illness due to air quality problems, typically toxic substances or pathogens; a clinically diagnosed condition. Symptoms include asthma, allergies, and hypersensitivity. 378

bulk restrictions Zoning laws that regulate appropriate distances and spatial relationships between property boundary lines and land improvements.

bulk transfer *See* Uniform Commercial Code.

bundle of legal rights The concept of land ownership that includes ownership of all legal rights to the land—possession, control within the law, enjoyment, exclusion, and disposition. 17

buydown A financing technique used to reduce the monthly payments for the first few years of a loan. Funds in the form of discount points are given to the lender by the builder or the seller to buy down or lower the effective interest rate paid by the buyer, thus reducing the monthly payments for a set time. 279

buyer representation agreement A principal-agent relationship in which the real estate professional acts on behalf of the buyer, usually as an agent, with fiduciary responsibilities to the buyer. 155

buyer's agent A real estate professional who is under contract to locate property for a buyer and represent the buyer's interests in a transaction. 156

buyer's broker A residential real estate professional who represents prospective buyers exclusively. 170

buyer's representative A residential real estate professional who represents the prospective purchaser in a transaction, often through a sales associate of the broker. The buyer's representative who acts as a buyer's agent owes the buyer-principal the common-law or statutory agency duties. 178

capital gain Profit earned from the sale of an asset. 431

capitalization A mathematical process for estimating the value of a property using a proper rate of return on the investment and the annual net operating income expected to be produced by the property. The formula is expressed as follows: income ÷ rate = value.

capitalization rate The rate of return a property will produce on the owner's investment. 307

capping The process of laying two to four feet of soil over the top of a landfill site and then planting grass on it to enhance the aesthetic value and prevent erosion. 415

carbon monoxide (CO) A colorless, odorless gas that occurs as a by-product of fuel combustion that may result in death in poorly ventilated areas. 410

cash flow The net spendable income from an investment, determined by deducting all operating and fixed expenses from the gross income. When expenses exceed income, a *negative cash flow* results. 428

cash flow report A monthly statement that details the financial status of the property. 373

caveat emptor A Latin phrase meaning "let the buyer beware." 3

CC&Rs *See* covenants, conditions, and restrictions. 397

certificate of occupancy Permission by the municipal inspector to occupy a completed building structure after being inspected and having complied with building codes. 395

certificate of reasonable value (CRV) A form indicating the appraised value of a property being financed with a VA loan. 275

certificate of sale The document generally given to the purchaser at a tax foreclosure sale. A certificate of sale does not convey title; normally, it is an instrument certifying that the holder received title to the property after the redemption period passed and that the holder paid the property taxes for that interim period. 227

certificate of title A statement of opinion on the status of the title to a parcel of real property based on an examination of specified public records. 123

chain of title The succession of conveyances, from some accepted starting point, whereby the present holder of real property derives title. 122

change The appraisal principle that holds that no physical or economic condition remains constant. 301

chattel *See* personal property. 21

chlorofluorocarbons (CFCs) Nontoxic, nonflammable chemicals containing atoms of carbon, chlorine, and fluorine, such as air conditioners and refrigerators. CFCs are safe in application but cause ozone depletion. 411

Civil Rights Act of 1866 An act that prohibits racial discrimination in the sale and rental of housing. 32

client Individual represented by a real estate broker pursuant to a brokerage engagement. 153

closing An event where promises made in a sales contract are fulfilled and mortgage loan funds (if any) are distributed to the buyer. 316

Closing Disclosure form Form required by the Consumer Financial Protection Bureau in specified real estate transactions. 329

closing escrow Process of settlement in which the buyer and the seller never meet; the paperwork is handled by an escrow agent. 320

closing statement A detailed cash accounting of a real estate transaction showing all cash received, all charges and credits made, and all cash paid out in the transaction. 336

cloud on the title Any document, claim, unreleased lien, or encumbrance that may impair the title to real property or make the title doubtful; usually revealed by a title search and removed by either a quitclaim deed or suit to quiet title. 108

code of ethics A written system of standards for ethical conduct. 5

codicil A supplement or an addition to a will, executed with the same formalities as a will, which normally does not revoke the entire will. 113

coinsurance clause A clause in insurance policies covering real property that requires the policyholder to maintain fire insurance coverage generally equal to at least 80% of the property's actual replacement cost. 257

collateral Something having value that is given to secure repayment of a debt. 222

color of title Invalid title help by a property owner/grantee who in good faith presumed valid title when property was transferred by grantor.

commingling The illegal act by a real estate professional of placing client or customer funds with personal funds. By law, real estate professionals are required to maintain a separate *trust* or *escrow account* for other parties' funds held temporarily by the real estate professional. 375

commission Payment to a real estate professional for services rendered, such as in the sale or purchase of real property; usually a percentage of the selling price of the property. 136

common elements Parts of a property that are necessary or convenient to the existence, maintenance, and safety of a condominium or are normally in common use by all the condominium residents. Each condominium owner has an undivided ownership interest in the common elements. 76

common law The body of law based on custom, usage, and court decisions. 152

common source information company Any person or company in Georgia that compiles, supplies, or resources information regarding real estate for sale or lease, or other data including but not limited to multiple listing services.

community association management Provides a team of property managers, accounting staff, office staff, and property consultants to manage property. **369**

community property A system of property ownership based on the theory that each spouse has an equal interest in the property acquired by the efforts of either spouse during marriage. A holdover of Spanish law found predominantly in the western U.S. states; the system was unknown under English common law. **72**

Community Reinvestment Act of 1977 (CRA) Under the act, which was revised most recently in 2008, financial institutions are expected to meet the deposit and credit needs of their communities; participate and invest in local community development and rehabilitation projects; and participate in loan programs for housing, small businesses, and small farms. **282**

comparables Properties used in an appraisal report that are substantially equivalent to the subject property.

comparative market analysis (CMA) A comparison of the prices of recently sold homes that are similar to a listing seller's home in terms of location, style, and amenities. **179**

competent party A person who has the capacity to be engaged in a legal contract; being of sound mind and body.

competition The appraisal principle stating that excess profits generate competition. **301**

Comprehensive Environmental Response, Compensation, and Liability Act (CERCLA) A federal law administered by the Environmental Protection Agency that establishes a process for identifying parties responsible for creating hazardous waste sites, forcing liable parties to clean up toxic sites, bringing legal action against responsible parties, and funding the abatement of toxic sites. *See also* Superfund. **416**

Comprehensive Loss Underwriting Exchange (CLUE) A database of consumer claims history that allows insurance companies to access prior claims information in the underwriting and rating process. **257**

comprehensive plan *See* master plan. **391**

computerized loan origination (CLO) An electronic network for handling loan applications through remote computer terminals linked to various lenders' computers. **283**

conciliation A form of alternative dispute resolution in which a conciliator meets with each of the parties separately to help them settle their differences voluntarily, without the formality of a hearing or trial. **43**

concurrent ownership Tenancy in common and joint tenancy are the two recognized forms of this type of ownership in Georgia.

condemnation A judicial or administrative proceeding to exercise the power of eminent domain, through which a government agency takes private property for public use and compensates the owner. **60**

conditional-use permit Written governmental permission allowing a use inconsistent with zoning but necessary for the common good, such as locating an emergency medical facility in a predominantly residential area. **394**

condition subsequent With condition subsequent, title will be forfeited if a condition is not fulfilled.

condominium The absolute ownership of a unit in a multiunit building based on a legal description of the airspace the unit actually occupies, or a separate dwelling unit in a multiunit development, plus an undivided interest in the ownership of the common elements in the building or development, which are owned jointly with the other condominium unit owners. **76**

condominium associations An association of condominium living space owners, the formation of which exercises collective powers and responsibilities of all the owners by ensuring that bylaws and covenants are followed.

condominium declaration Document containing the name of the complex, legal boundaries of all condominium units, and the common elements and percentage of ownership assigned to each unit. Required to be filed by developer before beginning project.

confession of judgment clause Permits judgment to be entered against a debtor without the creditor's having to institute legal proceedings.

conformity The appraisal principle holding that the greater the similarity among properties in an area, the better they will hold their value. **301**

consent Expressing or implying permission, approval, or agreement of an action or decision. **154**

consideration (1) That received by the grantor in exchange for the deed. (2) Something of value that induces a person to enter into a contract. **104, 204**

construction loan *See* interim financing. **278**

constructive annexation The combination of items into real property that are not fixed or fastened to the property. **24**

constructive eviction As interpreted in Georgia case law, a tenant's right to vacate property and cease rental payments if the tenant can show that the landlord's willful conduct or negligence has resulted in the property's becoming unsafe or unfit for habitability.

constructive notice Notice given to the world by recorded documents. All persons are charged with knowledge of such documents and their contents, whether or not they have actually examined them. Possession of property is also considered constructive notice that the person in possession has an interest in the property. 121

consumer An individual who purchases goods or services that are not for resale.

contingencies Provisions in a contract that require a certain act to be done or a certain event to occur before the contract becomes binding. 212

contract A legally enforceable promise or set of promises that must be performed and for which, if a breach of the promise occurs, the law provides a remedy. A contract may be either *unilateral*, by which only one party is bound to act, or *bilateral*, by which all parties to the instrument are legally bound to act as prescribed. 202

contract broker *See* nonagent. 153

contribution The appraisal principle stating that the value of any component of a property is what it gives to the value of the whole or what its absence detracts from that value. 301

controlled business arrangement An arrangement that offers consumers a package of services (e.g., a real estate firm, title insurance company, mortgage broker, and home inspection company).

conventional loan A loan that requires no federally sponsored insurance or guarantee. 270

conversion The illegal use of money received on behalf of the principal. 158

conveyance A term used to refer to any document that transfers title to real property. The term is also used in describing the act of transferring.

cooperating broker *See* listing broker. 178

cooperation and compensation In the early 1990s, these words replaced the unilateral offer of subagency language in MLS listings that had required all brokers showing property in the MLS to represent the sellers as subagents. With the new language, any broker who shows buyers property in the MLS can share in the listing broker's commission, regardless of whom these brokers represented.

cooperative A residential multiunit building whose title is held by a trust or corporation that is owned by and operated for the benefit of people living within the building who are the beneficial owners of the trust or shareholders of the corporation, each possessing a proprietary lease to a property unit. 78

co-ownership Title ownership held by two or more persons. 68

corporate resolution Document that gives authorization for real property transactions by the corporation and also designates corporate officers whose signatures are necessary for these transactions.

corporation An entity or organization, created by operation of law, whose rights of doing business are essentially the same as those of an individual. The entity has continuous existence until it is dissolved according to legal procedures. 75

corrective maintenance Correction of problems after they have occurred. 377

cost The total amount of money incurred for products or services.

cost approach The process of estimating the value of a property by adding to the estimated land value the appraiser's estimate of the reproduction or replacement cost of the building, less depreciation. 304

cost recovery An Internal Revenue Service term for *depreciation*. 430

counteroffer A new offer made in response to an offer received. It has the effect of rejecting the original offer, which cannot be accepted thereafter unless revived by the offeror. 210

covenant A written agreement between two or more parties in which a party or parties pledge to perform or not perform specified acts with regard to property; usually found in such real estate documents as deeds, mortgages, leases, and contracts for deed. 56, 106

covenant of quiet enjoyment The covenant implied by law by which a landlord guarantees that a tenant may take possession of leased premises and that the landlord will not interfere in the tenant's possession or use of the property. 107

covenants, conditions, and restrictions (CC&Rs) Private agreements that affect land use. They may be enforced by an owner of real estate that benefits from them and can be included in the seller's deed to the buyer. 56, 397

credit On a closing statement, an amount entered in a person's favor—either an amount the party has paid or an amount for which the party must be reimbursed. 336

curtesy A life estate, usually a fractional interest, given by some states to the surviving husband in real estate owned by his deceased wife. Most states have recognized other marital property rights and abolished curtesy. 54

customer Person not represented by a real estate broker in Georgia through a brokerage engagement and for whom a broker may only provide ministerial services in a transaction. Relationship may be established by verbal or written agreement.

datum A horizontal plane from which heights and depths are measured. 94

debit On a closing statement, an amount charged; that is, an amount that the debited party must pay. 336

debt to income (DTI) Information about an applicant's gross income and total debt that lenders generally look at as a percentage to determine qualification for a loan. 238

decedent A person who has died.

deed A written instrument that, when executed and delivered, conveys title to or an interest in real estate. 102

deed in lieu of foreclosure A deed given by the mortgagor to the mortgagee when the mortgagor is in default under the terms of the mortgage. If accepted by the mortgagee, this is a way for the mortgagor to avoid foreclosure. 253

deed in trust An instrument that grants a trustee under a land trust full power to sell, mortgage, and subdivide a parcel of real estate. The beneficiary controls the trustee's use of these powers under the provisions of the trust agreement. 108

deed of reconveyance A document that a trustee uses to transfer the title back to the trustor (borrower) when the note is repaid. 246

deed of trust An instrument used to create a mortgage lien by which the borrower conveys title to a trustee, who holds it as security for the benefit of the note holder (the lender); also called a trust deed.

deed of trust lien *See* trust deed lien.

deed restrictions Clauses in a deed limiting the future uses of the property. Deed restrictions may impose a vast variety of limitations and conditions—for example, they may limit the density of buildings, dictate the types of structures that can be erected, or prevent buildings from being used for specific purposes or even from being used at all. 56

default The nonperformance of a duty, whether arising under a contract or otherwise; failure to meet an obligation when due.

defeasance clause A clause used in leases and mortgages that cancels a specified right upon the occurrence of a certain condition, such as cancellation of a mortgage upon repayment of the mortgage loan. 246

defeasible fee estate An estate in which the holder has a fee simple title that may be divested upon the occurrence or nonoccurrence of a specified event. There are two categories of defeasible fee estates: fee simple on condition precedent (fee simple determinable) and fee simple on condition subsequent. 54

deficiency judgment Court-ordered ruling that allows the lender to seek a portion of a borrower's debt, not satisfied in the foreclosure sale, from the defaulted party's general assets. 254

delinquent taxes Taxes that are unpaid and past due.

delivery and acceptance When the title to property is delivered by the grantor and accepted by the grantee. 137

demand The amount of goods people are willing and able to buy at a given price; often coupled with *supply*. 8

demographics The study and description of a population. 10

denominator The number written below the line in a fraction. 457

density zoning Zoning ordinances that restrict the maximum average number of housing units per acre that may be built within a particular area, generally a subdivision. 396

Department of Housing and Urban Development (HUD) Federal agency that has established rules and regulations that further interpret the practices affected by federal law; for example, HUD distributes an equal housing opportunity poster. 34

depreciation (1) In appraisal, a loss of value in property due to any cause, including *physical deterioration*, *functional obsolescence*, and *external obsolescence*. (2) In real estate investment, a deduction for tax purposes taken over the period of ownership of income property, based on the property's acquisition cost. 305, 431

descent Acquisition of an estate by inheritance in which an heir succeeds to the property by operation of law. 111

designated agency A process that accommodates an *in-house* sale in which two different agents are involved. The broker designates one agent to represent the seller and one agent to represent the buyer. 165

designated agent One or more of a broker's licensee affiliates assigned by the broker to represent one client to the exclusion of all other clients in the same transaction, as well as to the exclusion of all other licensees affiliated with the broker. 165

determinable fee estate A fee simple estate providing that the property returns to the original grantor or heirs when a specified condition occurs, indicating that the property is no longer being used for the purpose prescribed.

developer One who attempts to put land to its most profitable use through the construction of improvements. 395

development The construction of improvements that benefit land. 3

devise A transfer of real property by will. The decedent is the devisor, and the recipient is the devisee. 112

discharge The act of terminating a contract or agreement; this may be done when it has been completely performed for by another party's breach or default. 206

disclaimer A statement indicating no legal responsibility for information; no warranties or representations have been made. 142

disclosure Relevant information or facts that are known or should have been known. **157**

discount point A unit of measurement used for various loan charges; one point equals 1% of the amount of the loan. **241**

discount rate The interest rate set by the Federal Reserve that member banks are charged when they borrow money through the Fed. **266**

distraint Legal guidelines that allow landlords to seize a tenant's personal property after a court order.

divisor A number or quantity divided into another. **460**

Do Not Call Registry A national registry, managed by the Federal Trade Commission, that lists the phone numbers of consumers who have indicated their preference to limit the telemarketing calls they receive. **145**

dominant tenement A property that includes in its ownership the appurtenant right to use an easement over another person's property for a specific purpose. **56**

dower The legal right or interest, recognized in some states, that a wife acquires in the property her husband held or acquired during their marriage. During the husband's lifetime, the right is only a possibility of an interest; upon his death, it can become an interest in land. **112**

dual agency Representing both parties to a transaction. This is unethical unless both parties agree to it, and it is illegal in some states. **163**

dual agent A broker who simultaneously has a client relationship with both seller and buyer or both landlord and tenant in the same transaction.

due-on-sale clause A provision in the mortgage stating that the entire balance of the note is immediately due and payable if the mortgagor transfers (sells) the property. **247**

duress Unlawful constraint or action exercised upon a person whereby the person is forced to perform an act against her will. A contract entered into under duress is voidable.

dwelling Any building or part of a building designed for occupancy as a residence by one or more families. **36**

earnest money Money deposited by a buyer under the terms of a contract, to be forfeited if the buyer defaults but to be applied to the purchase price if the sale is closed. **210**

easement A right to use the land of another for a specific purpose, such as for a right-of-way or utilities; an incorporeal interest in land because it does not include a right of possession. **56**

easement appurtenant An easement that follows along with the land. **56**

easement by implication An easement that occurs when a party's actions reflect the intention to create an easement.

easement by necessity An easement allowed by law as necessary for the full enjoyment of a parcel of real estate (e.g., a right of ingress and egress over a grantor's land). **58**

easement by prescription An easement acquired by open, notorious, continuous, hostile and adverse use of the property for the period of time prescribed by state law. **58**

easement in gross An easement that is not created for the benefit of any land owned by the owner of the easement but that attaches *personally to the easement owner*. For example, a right granted by a property owner to a friend to use a portion of the property for the rest of the friend's life would be an easement in gross. **57**

economic life The number of years during which an improvement will add value to land. **307**

Edina Realty Minnesota-based real estate company that was the subject of a landmark class action lawsuit against the firm over its practice of undisclosed dual agency. Litigation action affected the real estate industry throughout the country and led to statutory laws like BRRETA.

electronic contracting A process of integrating information electronically in a real estate transaction between clients, lender, and title and closing agents. **144**

Electronic Signatures in Global and National Commerce Act (E-Sign) An act that makes contracts (including signatures) and records legally enforceable regardless of the medium in which they are created. **144**

emblements Growing crops, such as corn, that are produced annually through labor and industry; also called *fructus industriales*. **22**

eminent domain The right of a government or municipal quasi-public body to acquire property for public use through a court action called *condemnation*, in which the court decides that the use is a public use and determines the compensation to be paid to the owner. **60**

employee For tax purposes, someone who works as a direct employee of an employer and has employee status. The employer is obligated to withhold income taxes and Social Security taxes from the compensation of employees. *See also* independent contractor. **135**

employment agreement *See* employment contract. **134**

employment contract A document evidencing formal employment between employer and employee or between principal and agent or representative. In the real estate business, this generally takes the form of the agreement between broker and sales associate, client representation agreement (including a listing agreement or buyer representation agreement), or property management agreement. **3, 155, 176**

enabling acts State legislation that confers zoning and other powers on municipal governments. **390**

encapsulation A method of controlling environmental contamination by sealing off a dangerous substance, such as asbestos. 405

encroachment A building or some portion of it—a wall or fence, for instance—that extends beyond the land of the owner and illegally intrudes on the land of an adjoining owner or a public street or alley. 59

encumbrance Anything—such as a mortgage, tax, or judgment lien; an easement; a restriction on the use of the land; or an outstanding dower right—that may diminish the value or use and enjoyment of a property. 55

enforceable contract A contract that meets all the elements of a valid contract, including compliance with any applicable statute of frauds or other law that requires it to be in writing and signed by the parties. 205

Environmental Impact Statement (EIS) A statement that details the impact a project will have on the environment. 419

environmental site assessment (ESA) An evaluation of property to show that due care was exercised in the determination of environmental impairments. 418

Equal Credit Opportunity Act (ECOA) The federal law that prohibits discrimination in the extension of credit because of race, color, religion, national origin, sex, age, marital status, or receipt of public assistance. 281

equal dignities rule Legal concept applied when a power of attorney is used to close a transaction. Because a deed to convey land or property must be witnessed and notarized at closing, the equal dignities rule requires that the power-of-attorney document likewise be witnessed and notarized.

equalization The raising or lowering of assessed values for tax purposes in a particular county or taxing district to make them equal to assessments in other counties or districts. 226

equalization factor A factor (number) by which the assessed value of a property is multiplied to arrive at a value for the property that is in line with statewide tax assessments. The *ad valorem tax* would be based on this adjusted value. 226

equitable lien *See* statutory lien. 222

equitable right of redemption Legal process that allows a defaulted borrower, before a foreclosure sale, to redeem the property by paying off the entire loan balance, including any interest, costs, and fees. 227

equitable title Property ownership rights held by the purchaser in conjunction with transferring legal title to the lender by a security deed. Owner retains a right of redemption to reacquire the legal title from the lender when the loan is paid off. 211

equity The interest or value that an owner has in property over and above any indebtedness. 238

equity buildup That portion of the loan payment directed toward the principal rather than the interest, plus any gain in property value due to appreciation. 429

erosion The gradual and sometimes imperceptible wearing away of the land by natural forces, such as wind, rain, and flowing water. 21

escheat The reversion of property to the state or county, as provided by state law, in cases in which a decedent dies intestate without heirs capable of inheriting, or when the property is abandoned. 62

escrow The closing of a transaction through a third party called an *escrow agent*, or *escrowee*, who receives certain funds and documents to be delivered upon the performance of conditions outlined in the escrow instructions. 321

escrow account The trust account established by a real estate professional under the provisions of the license law for the purpose of holding funds on behalf of the real estate professional's principal or some other person until the consummation or termination of a transaction; trust account established by an escrow agent to hold funds pending distribution at the closing of a transaction.

escrow agent Defined in the context of Orthrus contract forms as a third party in a real estate transaction; party who holds earnest money in trust for buyers and sellers and is responsible for disbursing these funds according to the terms of the contract.

escrow closing Occurs when a disinterested third party is authorized to act as escrow agent (escrow holder) and to coordinate the closing activities on behalf of the buyer and the seller. 321

escrow contract An agreement between a buyer, a seller, and an escrow holder setting forth rights and responsibilities of each. 246

escrow instructions A document that sets forth the duties of the escrow agent, as well as the requirements and obligations of the parties, when a transaction is closed through an escrow. 319

estate (tenancy) at sufferance The tenancy of a lessee who lawfully comes into possession of a landlord's real estate but who continues to occupy the premises improperly after the lease rights have expired. 352

estate (tenancy) at will An estate that gives the lessee the right to possession until the estate is terminated by either party; the term of this estate is indefinite. 352

estate for term *See* estate for years. 351

estate for years Contrary to its meaning under common law, this term in Georgia typically does not create a tenant-landlord relationship, but it actually conveys an estate that gives the grantee the rights and powers of owners for a defined period of time (typically for a period greater than five years).

estate (tenancy) from period to period An interest in leased property that continues from period to period—week to week, month to month, or year to year. 351

estate in land The degree, quantity, nature, and extent of interest a person has in real property. 52

estate tax Federal tax on a decedent's real and personal property. 230

estoppel Method of creating an agency relationship in which someone states incorrectly that another person is his agent and a third person relies on that representation.

estoppel certificate A document in which a borrower certifies the amount owed on a mortgage loan and the rate of interest.

ethics The system of moral principles and rules that becomes the standard for professional conduct. 5

eviction A legal process to oust a person from possession of real estate. 360

evidence of title Proof of ownership of property; commonly a certificate of title, an abstract of title with lawyer's opinion, title insurance, or a Torrens registration certificate. 106

exception The exclusion of a part of the property conveyed. 104

exchange A transaction in which all or part of the consideration is the transfer of *like-kind* property (e.g., real estate for real estate). 432

exclusive-agency listing A listing contract under which the owner appoints a real estate professional as her exclusive agent for a designated period of time to sell the specified property, on the owner's stated terms, for a commission. The owner reserves the right to sell the property without paying anyone a commission if the sale is to a prospect who has not been introduced or claimed by the real estate professional. 177

exclusive buyer representation agreement Agreement in which the buyer works with only one broker, although the broker is free to represent other buyer clients. 189

exclusive right-to-sell listing A listing contract under which the owner appoints a real estate professional as his exclusive agent for a designated period of time to sell the specified property on the owner's stated terms and agrees to pay the real estate professional a commission when the property is sold, whether by the real estate professional, the owner, or another real estate professional. 176

executed contract A contract in which all parties have fulfilled their promises and thus performed the contract. 203

execution The signing and delivery of an instrument. Also, a legal order directing an official to enforce a judgment against the property of a debtor.

executor An appointed person who carries out the directions of a will. A woman might be referred to as *executrix*, although executor is the term most commonly used to refer to either a man or a woman. 114

executory contract A contract under which something remains to be done by one or more of the parties. 203

express agency An agency relationship based on a formal agreement between the parties. 154

express agreement An oral or written contract in which the parties state the contract's terms and express their intentions in words. 154

express contract *See* express agreement. 202

external depreciation Reduction in a property's value caused by outside factors (i.e., those that are off the property). 304

external obsolescence Incurable depreciation caused by factors not on the subject property, such as environmental or economic factors. 307

facilitator An intermediary between a buyer and a seller, or a landlord and a tenant, who assists one or both parties with a transaction without representing either. Also known as a nonagent, transaction broker, transaction coordinator, and contract broker. 153

Fair Housing Act The federal law that prohibits discrimination in housing based on race, color, religion, sex, disability, familial status, and national origin. 34

Fair Housing Amendments Act of 1988 Expansion of the Fair Housing Act to include families with children and those with physical or mental disabilities. 34

familial status One or more individuals under age 18 living with a parent or guardian; also includes a woman who is pregnant and anyone who is in the process of assuming custody of a child under age 18. 36

Fannie Mae A government-supervised enterprise established to purchase any kind of mortgage loans in the secondary mortgage market from the primary lenders. 269

Farmer Mac The Federal Agricultural Mortgage Corporation—a privately owned and publicly traded company established by Congress to create a secondary market for agricultural mortgage and rural utilities loans and the portions of agricultural and rural development loans guaranteed by the U.S. Department of Agriculture (USDA). 269

Federal Deposit Insurance Corporation (FDIC) An independent federal agency established by Congress to examine and supervise financial institutions, manage receiverships, and insure deposits (currently up to $250,000 per depositor per financial institution). 267

Federal Emergency Management Agency (FEMA) A federal agency that is responsible for assisting the nation in preparing for, protecting against, responding to, and recovering from hazards. **257**

federal funds rate The rate recommended by the Federal Reserve for the member banks to charge each other on short-term loans. These rates form the basis on which the banks determine the percentage rate of interest they will charge their loan customers.

Federal Home Loan Mortgage Corporation *See* Freddie Mac. **269**

Federal National Mortgage Association *See* Fannie Mae. **269**

Federal Reserve System (Fed) The country's central banking system, which establishes the nation's monetary policy by regulating the supply of money and interest rates. **266**

fee-for-service Arrangement by which a consumer asks a real estate professional to perform specific real estate services for an agreed-upon fee. **139**

fee simple The highest interest in real estate recognized by the law; the holder is entitled to all rights to the property. **53**

fee simple absolute The maximum possible estate or right of ownership of real property, continuing forever. **53**

fee simple defeasible *See* defeasible fee estate. **53**

fee simple determinable A fee simple estate qualified by a special limitation. Language used to describe the limitation includes the words *so long as*, *while*, or *during*. **53**

fee simple estates Entitles owner to the entire property with unconditional powers of transferring the deed, including by will.

fee simple subject to a condition subsequent An estate carrying the limitation that, if it is no longer used for the purpose conveyed, it reverts to the original grantor by the right of reentry. **53**

feudal system A system of ownership usually associated with precolonial England, in which the king or other sovereign is the source of all rights. The right to possess real property was granted by the sovereign to an individual as a life estate only. Upon the death of the individual, title passed back to the sovereign, not to the decedent's heirs.

FHA-insured loan A loan insured by the Federal Housing Administration and made by an approved lender in accordance with FHA regulations. **273**

fiduciary One in whom trust and confidence is placed; a reference to a real estate professional employed under the terms of a listing contract or buyer representation agreement. **73**

fiduciary relationship A relationship of trust and confidence, as between trustee and beneficiary, attorney and client, or principal and agent. **156**

Financial Institutions Reform, Recovery, and Enforcement Act (FIRREA) This act restructured the savings and loan association regulatory system; enacted in response to the savings and loan crisis of the 1980s. **290**

financing The business of providing the funds that make real estate transactions possible.

first mortgage A mortgage that has priority over all other mortgages. **248**

fiscal policy The government's policy in regard to taxation and spending programs. The balance between these two areas determines the amount of money the government will withdraw from or feed into the economy, which can counter economic peaks and slumps.

fixture An item of personal property that has been converted to real property by being permanently affixed to the realty. **22**

forcible detainer Removal of a tenant from a rental property by the landlord if the tenant has breached one of the terms of the lease agreement, in compliance with statutory law.

foreclosure A legal procedure whereby property used as security for a debt is sold to satisfy the debt in the event of default in payment of the mortgage note or default of other terms in the mortgage document. The foreclosure procedure brings the rights of the parties to a conclusion and passes the title in the mortgaged property to either the holder of the mortgage or a third party who may purchase the realty at the foreclosure sale. Depending on the priority of the foreclosed mortgage, the property may be sold free of all other encumbrances incurred prior to the sale. **252**

forfeiture for crime Statute under the Georgia RICO Act that allows the state to seize property acquired by or used as a consequence of criminal activity.

formal will/witnessed will A document having written instructions of property disbursements upon the death of the owner. The document must be signed and witnessed.

formaldehyde An air pollutant that is a colorless chemical used to manufacture building materials and many household products, such as particleboard, hardwood plywood paneling, and urea-formaldehyde foam insulation. **409**

fraud Deception intended to cause a person to give up property or a lawful right. **166**

Freddie Mac A government-supervised enterprise established to purchase primarily conventional mortgage loans in the secondary mortgage market. **269**

freehold estate An estate in land in which ownership is for an indeterminate length of time, in contrast to a *leasehold estate*. 52

front-end ratio Percentage that measures the borrower's total monthly loan payment against the borrower's stable monthly income. Calculation arrived at by dividing the total house payment (P&I + 1 month's property tax,+ 1 month's hazard insurance + 1 month's mortgage insurance) by the borrower's gross monthly income.

front footage The measurement of a parcel of land by the number of feet of street or road frontage. 451

frontage The length of property along the street or waterfront. 451

FSBO A property that is not listed with a real estate broker but is being offered for sale directly by the owner of the property.

fully amortized loan A loan consisting of equal, regular payments satisfying the total payment of principal and interest by the due date. 248

functional obsolescence A loss of value to an improvement to real estate arising from problems of design or utility. 306

future interest A person's present right to an interest in real property that will not result in possession or enjoyment until sometime in the future, such as a reversion or right of reentry. 54

gap A defect in the chain of title of a particular parcel of real estate; a missing document or conveyance that raises doubt as to the present ownership of the land. 122

general agent One who is authorized by a principal to represent the principal in a specific range of matters. 159

general lien The right of a creditor to have all of a debtor's property—both real and personal—sold to satisfy a debt. 223

general partnership *See* partnership. 73

general real estate tax A tax that is made up of the taxes levied on the real estate by government agencies and municipalities. 225

general warranty deed A deed in which the grantor fully warrants good, clear title to the premises. Used in most real estate deed transfers, a general warranty deed offers the greatest protection of any deed. 106

Georgia Condominium Act Creates a set of regulations that govern the creation and operation of condominium projects in Georgia.

Georgia Land Sales Act Regulates community developments where individual lots are less than 5 acres. Requires full written property reports to be provided for all would-be purchasers before any contract execution, as well as a seven-day right of cancellation if a report is not provided 48 hours after signing a contract to purchase.

Georgia little NEPA laws State's equivalent of the federal Environmental Policy Act. Requires local governments to prepare environmental impact statements for projects seeking approval that may have significant impact on environment.

Georgia Residential Mortgage Fraud Act Statute that addresses intentional fraudulent statements and activities in the residential lending process, making such behavior a felony subject to imprisonment of up to 20 years and fines up to $100,000. Law applies to two basic categories of fraudulent activity: fraud for property, which is committed by borrowers who provide false income and employment information to qualify for a loan, or for better loan terms; and fraud for profit, which occurs when professionals in the real estate and mortgage industry conspire to realize profits from misdeeds.

Georgia statute of frauds Requires any contract for sale of real estate or any interest in real estate to be in writing and signed by the person against whom the contract is being enforced or by someone authorized by that person.

Georgia Stigmatized Property Act Statute that does not require real estate agents, sellers, or landlords to disclose if a property is or has been occupied by a person with a noncommunicable disease or if a property has been the site of a homicide or other felony, suicide, or death by accidental causes.

Georgia Time-Share Act Regulates developmental process of creating time-share properties in Georgia. Affords purchasers full documentation on a project, as well as a contract cancellation right.

Ginnie Mae A government agency that plays an important role in the secondary mortgage market. It guarantees mortgage-backed securities using FHA-insured and VA-guaranteed loans as collateral. 270

good and indefeasible title A title that cannot be annulled or rendered void.

good and workmanlike Language commonly used to describe the quality of the work expected of any party responsible for making repairs as part of contract obligations.

Good Faith Estimate (GFE) An estimate of all closing fees that was formerly provided to a borrower within three days of the loan application as was required by the Real Estate Settlement Procedures Act (RESPA).

Government National Mortgage Association *See* Ginnie Mae. 270

government survey system *See* rectangular (government) survey system. . 88, 396

government-sponsored enterprises (GSEs) Organizations created by the federal government (Fannie Mae, Freddie Mac, Farmer Mac, Ginnie Mae) to help increase loan opportunities for homebuyers. **269**

graduated-payment mortgage (GPM) A loan in which the monthly principal and interest payments increase by a certain percentage each year for a certain number of years and then level off for the remaining loan term.

grantee A person who receives a transfer of real property from a grantor. **102**

granting clause Words in a deed of conveyance that state the grantor's intention to convey the property at the present time. This clause is generally worded as "convey and warrant"; "grant"; "grant, bargain, and sell"; or the like. **104**

grantor The owner transferring title to or an interest in real property to a grantee. **103**

grantor/grantee index Public records located at office of clerk of superior court in county. Current titleholders of real property are listed alphabetically in the grantee index, while previous owners of same parcel are alphabetically listed in the grantor index.

gross income multiplier (GIM) A figure used as a multiplier of the gross annual income of a property to produce an estimate of the property's value; usually used for commercial property. **309**

gross lease A lease of property according to which a landlord pays all property charges regularly incurred through ownership, such as repairs, taxes, insurance, and operating expenses. Most residential leases are gross leases. **357**

gross rent multiplier (GRM) The figure used as a multiplier of the gross monthly income of a property to produce an estimate of the property's value; usually used for single-family residential property. **309**

ground lease A lease of land only, on which the tenant usually owns a building or is required to build as specified in the lease. Such leases are usually long-term net leases; the tenant's rights and obligations continue until the lease expires or is terminated through default. **358**

groundwater Water that exists under the earth's surface within the tiny spaces or crevices in geological formations. **412**

growing-equity mortgage A loan in which the monthly payments increase annually, with the increased amount being used to directly reduce the principal balance outstanding and thus shorten the overall term of the loan. **250**

habendum clause That part of a deed beginning with the words "to have and to hold," following the granting clause and defining the extent of ownership the grantor is conveying. **104**

habitability A property that is suitable for living in or on.

headrights The oldest form of real property description in Georgia used along the eastern coastal area of the state; depends on natural boundaries and markings describing land that is irregular in shape.

heir One who might inherit or succeed to an interest in land under the state law of descent when the owner dies without leaving a valid will. **53**

highest and best use The legally permitted and physically possible use of a property that would produce the greatest net income and, thereby, develop the highest value. **301**

holdover tenancy A tenancy in which a lessee retains possession of leased property after the lease has expired and the landlord, by continuing to accept rent, agrees to the tenant's continued occupancy as defined by state law. **352**

holographic will A will that is written, dated, and signed in the testator's handwriting. **113**

home equity loan A loan under which a property owner uses the property as collateral and can then draw funds up to a prearranged amount against the property. Also called a *home equity line of credit*, or *HELOC*. **279**

home inspection A thorough visual survey of a property's structure, systems, and site conditions conducted by a professional. **3**

Home Mortgage Disclosure Act A federal law, implemented at its creation by Regulation C of the Federal Reserve, that requires lenders to annually disclose the number of loan applications and loans made in certain areas to avoid the practice of redlining. On July 21, 2011, the rule-making authority of the law was transferred to the Consumer Financial Protection Bureau.

homeowners insurance Insurance that covers a residential real estate owner against financial loss from fire, theft, public liability, and other common risks. **256**

homestead Land that is owned and occupied as the family home. In many states, a portion of the area or value of this land is protected or exempt from judgments for debts other than those secured by the property. **55**

Housing for Older Persons Act of 1995 (HOPA) Amended the Fair Housing Act to provide that housing intended for persons aged 55 or older no longer needs to have significant facilities and services designed for the elderly. **34**

HUD-1 A form that was formerly used to itemize fees and services charged to a borrower and seller during a real estate transaction.

hydraulic fracturing (fracking) The process used to extract natural gas from the deep layers of rock in which it is embedded. **18, 413**

hypothecation To pledge property as security for an obligation or loan without giving up possession of it. 243

immobility The fact that property cannot be relocated to satisfy demand where supply is low, nor can buyers always relocate to areas with greater supply. 8

implied agency If the actions of the parties imply that they have mutually consented to an agency relationship, an implied agency relationship is formed. 155

implied agreement A contract under which the agreement of the parties is demonstrated by their acts and conduct. 155

implied contract *See* implied agreement. 202

implied warranty of habitability A theory in landlord/tenant law in which the landlord renting residential property implies that the property is habitable and fit for its intended use.

impound accounts An account that the mortgage lender may require a borrower to have to accumulate funds to pay future real estate taxes and insurance premiums. 337

improvement (1) Any structure, usually privately owned, erected on a site to enhance the value of the property (e.g., a building, fence, or driveway). (2) A publicly owned structure added to or benefiting land (e.g., a curb, sidewalk, street, or sewer). 24

imputed knowledge Principle of common law agency in which agents and principals are considered to have notice of information that each other possesses, even if such information was never communicated between the two parties. BRRETA does not recognize imputed knowledge, only actual knowledge possessed by a broker or a client.

in arrears Term that describes how the interest portion of a loan payment applies to the month before the month in which payment is made.

income approach The process of estimating the value of an income-producing property through capitalization of the annual net income expected to be produced by the property during its remaining useful life. 307

income property Property held for current income as well as a potential profit upon its sale. 427

incorporeal right A nonpossessory right in real estate (e.g., an easement or a right-of-way).

independent contractor Someone who is retained to perform a certain act but who is subject to the control and direction of another only as to the end result and not as to the way in which the act is performed. Unlike an employee, an independent contractor pays for all expenses and Social Security and income taxes and receives no employee benefits. Most real estate sales associates are independent contractors, meeting the Internal Revenue Service definition for a qualified real estate agent. 135

index An objective economic indicator to which the interest rate for an adjustable-rate mortgage is tied. 249

inflation The gradual reduction of the purchasing power of the dollar, usually related directly to increases in the money supply by the federal government. 428

informed consent Clients' written consent that they have read and understand disclosures concerning dual agency and agree to a broker's practice of this brokerage relationship.

inheritance taxes State-imposed taxes on a decedent's real and personal property. 230

installment sale A transaction in which the sales price is paid in two or more installments over two or more years. If the sale meets certain requirements, a taxpayer can postpone reporting such income until future years by paying tax each year only on the proceeds received that year. 433

intangible tax Required tax to be paid on any new loan of more than $1,500, with a longer than a three-year term, secured to purchase real property in Georgia. $1.50 is paid for every $500 borrowed.

interest A charge made by a lender for the use of money. 232

interest-only loan A loan that only requires the payment of interest for a stated period of time with the principal due at the end of the term. 248

interim financing A short-term loan usually made during the construction phase of a building project (often referred to as a *construction loan*). 278

intermediary *See* nonagent. 153

Internal Revenue Service tax lien A lien charged by the Internal Revenue Service for nonpayment of income taxes. 231

Internet Data Exchange (IDX) policy Policy that allows all multiple listing service (MLS) members to restrict internet access to MLS property listings. 142

Interstate Land Sales Full Disclosure Act (ILSA) A federal law that regulates the sale of certain real estate in interstate commerce. 398

intestate The condition of a property owner who dies without leaving a valid will. Title to the property will pass to the decedent's heirs, as provided in the state law of descent. 110

intrinsic value An appraisal term referring to the value of a property unaffected by a person's personal preferences. 428

inverse condemnation An action brought by a property owner seeking just compensation for diminished use and value of land because of an adjacent property's public use. 61

investment Money directed toward the purchase, improvement, and development of an asset in expectation of income or profits.

involuntary alienation *See* alienation. 110

involuntary lien A lien placed on property without the consent of the property owner. 222

joint tenancy Ownership of real estate between two or more parties who have been named in one conveyance as joint tenants. Upon the death of a joint tenant, the decedent's interest usually passes to the surviving joint tenant or tenants by the *right of survivorship*. 69

Joint Tenancy Act Created in Georgia, a true joint tenancy with the right of survivorship; also requires that this form of co-ownership be clearly indicated in any deed transfer.

judgment The formal decision of a court upon the respective rights and claims of the parties to an action or suit. After a judgment has been entered and recorded with the county recorder, it usually becomes a general lien on the property of the defendant. 55

judicial precedent In law, the requirements established by prior court decisions within the jurisdiction of the dispute. 417

jumbo loan *See* nonconforming loan. 271

junior lien An obligation, such as a second mortgage, that is subordinate in right or lien priority to an existing lien on the same property. 224

laches An equitable doctrine used by courts to bar a legal claim or to prevent the assertion of a right because of undue delay or failure to assert the claim or right. 398

land The earth's surface, extending downward to the center of the earth and upward infinitely into space, including things permanently attached by nature, such as trees. 16

land contract A transaction in which the sales price is paid in two or more installments over two or more years. If the sale meets certain requirements, a taxpayer can postpone reporting such income until future years by paying tax each year only on the proceeds received that year. Also called an installment sale. 214

landlord Refers collectively to all persons named in the lease and signing the lease as the landlord, as well as successors and assigns if the property is transferred or sold

land trust A trust in which property is conveyed, and in which real estate is the only asset. 74

latent defect A hidden structural defect that could not be discovered by ordinary inspection and that threatens a property's soundness or the safety of its inhabitants. Some states impose on property sellers and real estate professionals a duty to inspect for and disclose latent defects. 167

law of agency *See* agency. 153

law of diminishing returns Point at which additional property improvements do not increase the property's income or value. 302

law of increasing returns Applies as long as money being spent on property improvements produces an increase in the property's income or value. 302

lead Used as a pigment and drying agent in alkyd oil-based paint in about 75% of housing built before 1978. An elevated level of lead in the body can cause serious damage to the brain, kidneys, nervous system, and red blood cells. Children younger than six are most vulnerable. 406

Lead-Based Paint Hazard Reduction Act (LBPHRA) Federal legislation requiring disclosure of the presence of any known lead-based paint hazards to potential buyers or renters. The law does not require that anyone test for the presence of lead-based paint, however. 406

lease A written or oral contract between a landlord (the lessor) and a tenant (the lessee) that transfers the right to exclusive possession and use of the landlord's real property to the lessee for a specified period of time and for a stated consideration (rent). By state law, leases for longer than a certain period of time (generally one year) must be in writing to be enforceable. 350

lease option A lease under which the tenant has the right to purchase the property at an agreed-upon price either during the lease term or at its end. 356–357

lease purchase The purchase of real property, the consummation of which is preceded by a lease, usually long term, that is typically done for tax or financing purposes. 358

leasehold estate A tenant's right to occupy real estate during the term of a lease, generally considered a personal property interest, although a long-term lease may be eligible for treatment as real property for financing purposes. 351

legacy A disposition of money or personal property by will. 112

legal description A description of a specific parcel of real estate complete enough for an independent surveyor to locate and identify it. 85

legal life estate A form of life estate established by state law, rather than created voluntarily by an owner. It becomes effective when certain events occur. *See* dower, curtesy, and homestead for legal life estates used in some states. 54

legally competent parties People who are recognized by law as being able to contract with others; those of legal age and sound mind. 202

lessee *See* lease. 350

lessor *See* lease. 350

leverage The use of borrowed money to finance an investment. 429

levy To assess; to seize or collect. To levy a tax is to assess a property and set the rate of taxation. To levy an execution is to officially seize the property of a person in order to satisfy an obligation. 224

liability coverage Feature of homeowners insurance that covers injuries or losses sustained within the home. 257

license (1) In real estate practice, the privilege or right granted to a person by a state to operate as a real estate broker or salesperson. (2) The revocable permission for a temporary use of land—a personal right that cannot be sold. 26, 59

lien A right given by law to certain creditors to have their debts paid out of the property of a defaulting debtor, usually by means of a court sale. 56

lien theory Principle in which the mortgagor retains both legal and equitable title to property that serves as security for a debt. The mortgagee has a lien on the property, but the mortgage is nothing more than collateral for the loan. 243

life cycle costing In property management, comparing one type of equipment with another based on both purchase cost and operating cost over its expected useful lifetime.

life estate An interest in real or personal property that is limited in duration to the lifetime of its owner or some other designated person or persons. 54

life tenant A person in possession of a life estate. 54

limited agent *See* special agent. 159

limited liability company (LLC) A form of business organization that combines the most attractive features of limited partnerships and corporations. 75

limited partnership *See* partnership. 75

limited warranty deed Offers same warranties as warranty deed, except does not warrant forever, only for the time the grantor owned the property.

linear measurement Measurement in a straight line. 451

liquidated damages An amount predetermined by the parties to a contract as the total compensation to an injured party should the other party breach the contract. 211

liquidity The ability to sell an asset and convert it into cash, at a price close to its true value, in a short period of time. 427

lis pendens A recorded legal document giving constructive notice that an action affecting a particular property has been filed in either a state or a federal court. 59

listing agreement A contract between an owner (as principal) and a real estate professional (as representative of the owner) by which the real estate professional is employed to find a buyer for the owner's real estate on the owner's terms, for which service the owner agrees to pay a commission or other form of compensation. 155

listing broker The broker from whose office a listing agreement is initiated. 177

littoral rights (1) A landowner's claim to use water in large navigable lakes and oceans adjacent to her property. (2) The ownership rights to land bordering these bodies of water up to the high-water mark. 20

living trust A trust that is created during the trustor's lifetime. 73

Loan Estimate The form that must be provided to a consumer on loan application, as specified by the Consumer Financial Protection Bureau. 324–325

loan or credit underwriter Within the lending process, the party who makes the final decision on loan approval for borrower.

loan origination fee A fee charged to the borrower by the lender for making a mortgage loan. The fee is usually computed as a percentage of the loan amount. 241

loan-to-value (LTV) ratio The relationship between the amount of the mortgage loan and the value of the real estate being pledged as collateral. 270

lot-and-block (recorded plat) method A method of describing real property that identifies a parcel of land by reference to lot and block numbers within a subdivision, as specified on a recorded subdivision plat. 91

management agreement A contract between the owner of income property and a management firm or individual property manager that outlines the scope of the manager's authority. 370

management plan A highly detailed plan that lays out the owner's objectives for a property, as well as what the property manager wants to accomplish and how, including all budgetary information. 372

managing broker The real estate professional who is responsible for supervision of the real estate professionals who act on behalf of the brokerage; may also be called a supervising broker. 134

manufactured home A permanent installation built to federal specifications, providing a principal residence or a vacation home. 7

manufactured housing Dwellings that are built off site and trucked to a building lot where they are installed or assembled. 21

margin A premium added to the index rate representing the lender's cost of doing business. 249

market A place where goods can be bought and sold and a price established. **8**

market data approach Also known as the *sales comparison approach*. An estimate of value obtained by comparing property being appraised with recently sold comparable properties. **303**

market value The most probable price that a property would bring in an arm's-length transaction under normal conditions on the open market. **300**

marketable title Good or clear title, reasonably free from the risk of litigation over possible defects. **123**

master plan A comprehensive government plan to guide the long-term physical development of a particular area. **391**

master-planned community A planned combination of diverse land uses, such as housing, recreation, and shopping, in one contained development or subdivision; also called a planned unit development (PUD). **7**

material facts Information that a party would want to know, does not know, and could not reasonably discover for themselves.

mechanic's lien A statutory lien created in favor of contractors, laborers, material suppliers, and others who have performed work or furnished materials in the erection or repair of a building. **228**

Megan's Law Federal legislation that promotes the establishment of state registration systems to maintain residential information on every person who kidnaps children, commits sexual crimes against children, or commits sexually violent crimes. **168**

meridian One of a set of imaginary lines running north and south and crossing a base line at a definite point, used in the rectangular (government) survey system of property description. **88**

metes and bounds Controlling real property legal description in Georgia that surveys a property's boundaries to form a geometrically enclosed outline of the parcel, always ending up at its starting point.

metes-and-bounds method A method used to describe a parcel of land that begins at a well-marked point and follows the property's boundaries, using directions and distances around the tract, back to the place of beginning. **86**

mill One-tenth of one cent. Some states use a mill rate to compute real estate taxes; for example, a rate of 52 mills would indicate a tax of $0.052 for each dollar of assessed valuation of a property. **226**

millage rate The property tax rate for real property. Can be stated as an amount per $1 of assessed value, per $100 dollars of assessed value, per $1,000 of assessed value, or as a specific number of mills.

minimum level of services The services that real estate professionals must provide to clients, as prescribed differently by certain states; for example, assisting clients in negotiation and answering questions from clients about offers, counteroffers, and contingencies. **139**

ministerial acts Services provided by real estate licensees that do not require professional judgment or skill on the part of the licensee. Acts such as these examples of which are found in BRRETA Code Section 10-6A-14 are the only services that real estate licensees are allowed to offer customers. 165

minor A person who has not reached the age of majority and, therefore, does not have legal capacity to transfer title to real property. **103**

mixed use Property that accommodates more than one use, such as commercial use and residential use. **6**

Model Real Estate Time-Share Act An act that governs the management, use, and termination of time-share units. **79**

modular home A type of factory-built housing with components that are assembled at a building site on a prepared foundation. **8**

mold A form of fungus that can be found almost anywhere and can grow on almost any organic substance, so long as moisture and oxygen are present. Mold growth can gradually destroy what it is growing on, as well as cause serious health problems. **411**

monetary policy Governmental regulation of the amount of money in circulation through such institutions as the Federal Reserve Board. **9**

month-to-month tenancy A periodic tenancy under which the tenant rents for one month at a time. In the absence of a rental agreement (oral or written), a tenancy is generally considered to be month to month. **351**

monument A fixed natural or artificial object used to establish real estate boundaries for a metes-and-bounds description. **87**

mortgage A conditional transfer or pledge of real estate as security for the payment of a debt. Also, the document creating a mortgage lien. **3**

mortgage banker A mortgage loan company that originates, services, and sell loans to investors.

mortgage broker An agent of a lender who brings the lender and the borrower together. The broker receives a fee for this service.

Mortgage Disclosure Improvement Act (MDIA) Enacted in July 2008 as an amendment to the Truth in Lending Act (TILA) to require mortgage loan cost disclosures to consumers. Early disclosure (a good-faith estimate) of mortgage loan cost must be provided within three business days of receiving a consumer's application for a mortgage loan; a creditor must wait seven business days after providing the early disclosures before closing the loan; and a creditor must provide new disclosures and wait an additional three business days before closing the loan, if a change occurs that makes the annual percentage rate quoted in the early disclosure inaccurate beyond a specified tolerance. 335

mortgage insurance premium (MIP) An insurance policy premium used in FHA loans that the borrower is charged. The premium depends on the length of the loan and the loan-to-value (LTV) ratio. 273

mortgage lien A lien or charge on the property of a mortgagor that secures the underlying debt obligation. 228

mortgage servicing transfer statement Disclosure required by the lender if the lender intends to sell or assign the right to service the loan to another loan servicer. The loan servicer must notify the borrower 15 days before the effective date of the loan transfer, including in the notice the name and address of the new servicer, toll-free telephone numbers, and the date the new servicer will begin accepting payments. 324

mortgagee A lender in a mortgage loan transaction. 243

mortgagor A borrower in a mortgage loan transaction. 243

multiperil policies Insurance policies that offer protection from a range of potential perils, such as fire, hazard, public liability, and casualty. 383

multiple listing clause A provision in an exclusive listing for the authority and obligation on the part of the listing agent to distribute the listing to other real estate professionals in a multiple listing organization. 177

multiple listing service (MLS) A marketing organization composed of member real estate professionals who agree to share their listing agreements with one another in the hope of procuring ready, willing, and able buyers for their properties more quickly than they could on their own. Most multiple listing services accept exclusive right-to-sell or exclusive agency listings from their member real estate professionals. 136

mutual assent Requirement that there must be complete agreement between the parties about the purpose and terms of a contract. 204

National Association of REALTORS® (NAR) The largest real estate organization in the world; NAR members subscribe to a strict code of ethics. Active members are allowed to use the trademarked designation, REALTOR®. 4

National Do Not Call Registry A national registry, managed by the Federal Trade Commission, which lists the phone numbers of consumers who have indicated their preference to limit the telemarketing calls they receive. 145

negative amortization Process by which the amount of the loan increases. The mortgagor sets a payment cap, or maximum amount for payments, but the difference between the payment made and the full payment amount is added to the remaining mortgage balance. 249

negligent misrepresentation Occurs when the real estate professional should have known that a statement about a material fact was false. 166

negotiable instrument A written promise or order to pay a specific sum of money that may be transferred by endorsement or delivery. The transferee then has the original payee's right to payment. 239

net lease A lease requiring the tenant to pay not only rent but also costs incurred in maintaining the property, including taxes, insurance, utilities, and repairs. 357

net listing A listing based on the net price the seller will receive if the property is sold. Under a net listing, the real estate professional can offer the property for sale at the highest price obtainable to increase the commission. This type of listing is illegal in many states. 177

net operating income (NOI) The income projected for an income-producing property after deducting anticipated vacancy and collection losses and operating expenses. 307

niche marketing The target marketing of specific demographic populations, within the bounds of fair housing laws. 10

nonagent An intermediary between a buyer and a seller, or a landlord and a tenant, who assists one or both parties with a transaction without representing either. Also known as a *facilitator, transaction broker, transaction coordinator,* and *contract broker*. 155

nonconforming loan A loan that exceeds the Federal Housing Finance Agency (FHFA) loan limits; also called a *jumbo loan*. 271

nonconforming use A use of property that is permitted to continue after a zoning ordinance prohibiting it has been established for the area. 393

nondisturbance clause A mortgage clause stating that the mortgagee agrees not to terminate the tenancies of the lessees in the event the mortgagee forecloses on the mortgagor-lessor's building. 356

nonhomogeneity A lack of uniformity; dissimilarity. Because no two parcels of land are exactly alike, real estate is said to be nonhomogeneous. 25

notarization Certification by a notary or other authorized official of the validity of a signature on a document. 103

note A financing instrument that states the terms of the underlying obligation, is signed by its maker, and is negotiable (transferable to a third party). Also called a promissory note. **239**

novation Substituting a new obligation for an old one or substituting new parties to an existing obligation. **207**

numerator The number written above the line of a fraction representing the number to be divided by the denominator. **457**

nuncupative will An oral will declared by the testator in his final illness, made before witnesses and afterward reduced to writing; not permitted by all states. **113**

obsolescence The loss of value due to property features that are outmoded or less useful. Obsolescence may be functional or external. **306**

occupancy permit A permit issued by the appropriate local governing body to establish that the property is suitable for habitation by meeting certain safety and health standards. **395**

offer and acceptance Two essential components of a valid contract; a "meeting of the minds." An offer is a promise made by the offeror, requesting something in exchange for that promise. Acceptance is a promise by the offeree to be bound by the exact terms proposed by the offeror. **204**

offeror/offeree The person who makes the offer is the offeror. The person to whom the offer is made is the offeree. **204**

Office of the Comptroller of the Currency (OCC) Government agency which sets standards and regulations for fiduciary lenders. **267**

open-end loan A mortgage loan that is expandable by increments up to a maximum dollar amount, with the full loan being secured by the same original mortgage. **278**

open listing A listing contract under which the real estate professional's compensation is contingent on the real estate professional producing a ready, willing, and able buyer before the property is sold by the seller or another real estate professional. **177**

operating budget A property's anticipated financial performance in the present and future. It gives the owner a sense of expected profit. **372**

option An agreement to keep open for a set period an offer to sell or purchase property. **214**

ordinary skill and care Competent performance level required of real estate licenses under BRRETA in carrying out duties to both client and customer.

ostensible agency A form of implied agency relationship created by the actions of the parties involved rather than by written agreement or document.

owelty lien A lien created by the order of the court to make an equitable partition of property when otherwise an agreeable partition is impossible or impractical (i.e., in a divorce). The owelty lien allows the party acquiring the interest of a co-owner to place a lien on the entire property.

owner financing The seller is the primary lender, securing the property by means of a deed, note and mortgage, deed of trust, or contract for deed. In its traditional form, the buyer takes possession of the property and the seller retains legal title until paid in full, but some states have softened this outcome to provide that the buyer is entitled to legal title after a specified period of successful loan payments. **214**

P&I Principal and interest. **251**

package loan A real estate loan used to finance the purchase of both real property and personal property, such as in the purchase of a new home that includes carpeting, window coverings, and major appliances. **277**

panic peddling The illegal practice of soliciting people in a neighborhood to sell their homes because of fear or alarm; also referred to as blockbusting.

participation mortgage A mortgage loan wherein the lender has a partial equity interest in the property or receives a portion of the income from the property.

partition The division of cotenants' interests in real property when the parties do not all voluntarily agree to terminate the co-ownership; takes place through a court procedure. **71**

partnership An association of two or more individuals who carry on a continuing business for profit as co-owners. Under the law, a partnership is regarded as a group of individuals rather than as a single entity separate from the individual owners. A *general partnership* is a typical form of joint venture in which each general partner shares in the administration, profits, and losses of the operation. A *limited partnership* is a business arrangement whereby the operation is administered by one or more general partners and funded, by and large, by limited or silent partners, who are by law responsible for losses only to the extent of their investments. **75**

party wall An exterior wall of a building that straddles the boundary line between two lots, or a commonly shared partition wall between two connected properties. **57**

passing papers When parties to a transaction sit around a table and exchange copies of documents as the documents are executed. **320**

passive concealment Obligations of sellers and landlords to not conceal specific information regarding adverse physical conditions of property that might be of material importance to buyers and tenants in effecting a decision to buy or lease property.

patent A grant or franchise of land from the U.S. government.

payment cap The limit on the amount the monthly payment can be increased on an adjustable-rate mortgage when the interest rate is adjusted. **249**

payoff statement *See* reduction certificate. **318**

percent One part in a hundred. **460**

percentage lease A lease, commonly used for commercial property, whose rental is based on the tenant's gross sales at the premises; it usually stipulates a base monthly rental plus a percentage of any gross sales above a certain amount. **357**

percolation test A test of the soil to determine whether it will absorb and drain water adequately to use a septic system for sewage disposal.

performance bond May be purchased by a property owner or contractor agent when work to improve property is in progress. Because the bond assures that laborers and material suppliers will be paid for their work, it protects against mechanic's lien claims.

periodic tenancy *See* estate from period to period. **351**

personal property Items, called *chattels*, that do not fit into the definition of real property; movable objects. **21**

personalty Personal property. **21**

physical deterioration A reduction in a property's value resulting from a decline in physical condition; can be caused by action of the elements or by ordinary wear and tear. **306**

PITI The basic costs of owning a home—mortgage principal and interest, real estate taxes, and hazard insurance. **237**

PITT The four unities of tenants in a joint tenancy: possession, interest, time, and title. **70**

planned unit development (PUD) A planned combination of diverse land uses, such as housing, recreation, and shopping, in one contained development or subdivision. **7**

plat map A map of a town, section, or subdivision indicating the location and boundaries of individual properties. **91**

plottage The increase in value or utility resulting from the consolidation *(assemblage)* of two or more adjacent lots into one larger lot. **302**

point A term used for a percentage of the principal loan amount charged by the lender. Each point is equal to 1% of the loan amount. **241**

point of beginning (POB) In a metes-and-bounds legal description, the starting point of the survey, situated in one corner of the parcel; all metes-and-bounds descriptions must follow the boundaries of the parcel back to the point of beginning. **86**

police powers Enabled by the state constitution, these powers are passed down to municipalities to regulate property land use and development for the public welfare. **60**

polychlorinated biphenyls (PCBs) Used as an insulating material in dielectric oil. It can linger in the environment for long periods of time and can cause health problems. **410**

possession Owning or occupying a property. **17**

power of attorney Legal document that gives individuals the right to sign legal documents for another. In Georgia, document must be executed with the same formality required for a deed. **105**

power of sale Clause in security deed that authorizes lender upon borrower's default to bypass a court-ordered foreclosure process and sell the property serving as collateral for the loan. This process of property sale is identified by Georgia statute as nonjudicial foreclosure.

prepaid items On a closing statement, items that have been paid in advance by the seller, such as fuel costs and some real estate taxes, for which the seller must be reimbursed by the buyer. **339**

prepayment penalty A charge imposed on a borrower who pays off the loan principal early. This penalty compensates the lender for interest and other charges that would otherwise be lost. **242**

prescriptive easements Under Georgia law, open, continuous use of improved real property, uninterrupted by the landowner over a 7-year period may result in a legal permanent use of the property. The prescriptive period for wild land is 20 years in the state.

preventive maintenance Small repairs that help prevent bigger problems and expenses. **377**

price The amount of money paid for an item or service.

price-fixing Real estate professionals conspiring to set fixed compensation rates. **140**

primary mortgage market The mortgage market in which loans are originated, consisting of lenders such as commercial banks, savings associations, and mutual savings banks. **267**

principal A main party to a transaction—the person for whom an agent works. **153, 237, 429**

principal meridian The main imaginary line running north and south and crossing a base line at a definite point; used by surveyors for reference in locating and describing land under the rectangular (government) survey system of legal description. **88**

prior appropriation A concept of water ownership in which the landowner's right to use available water is based on a government-administered permit system. **21**

priority The order of position or time. The priority of liens is generally determined by the chronological order in which the lien documents are recorded; tax liens, however, have priority even over previously recorded liens. **121**

private mortgage insurance (PMI) Insurance provided by a private carrier that protects a lender against a loss in the event of a foreclosure and deficiency. **272**

probate A legal process by which a court determines who will inherit a decedent's property and what the estate's assets are. **112**

procuring cause The effort that brings about the desired result. Under an open listing, the real estate professional who is the procuring cause of the sale receives the commission. **137**

profit Making a gain from an investment after subtracting expenses.

profit and loss statement A general financial picture based on the monthly cash flow reports; does not include itemized information. **373**

progression An appraisal principle that the value of a lesser-quality property is favorably affected by the presence of a better-quality property. **302**

promissory note A financing instrument that states the terms of the underlying obligation, is signed by its maker, and is negotiable (transferable to a third party). **239**

property manager Someone who manages real estate for another person for compensation. Duties include collecting rents, maintaining the property, and keeping up all accounting. **368**

property reports The mandatory federal and state documents compiled by subdividers and developers to provide potential purchasers with facts about a property prior to a purchase.

proprietary lease A lease given by the corporation that owns a cooperative apartment building to a shareholder who has the right as a tenant to an individual unit. **7**

prorations Expenses, either prepaid or paid in arrears, that are divided or distributed between the buyer and the seller at the closing. **338**

protected class Any group of people designated as such by the Department of Housing and Urban Development (HUD) in consideration of federal civil rights legislation. Individual states and local jurisdictions provide such designation to additional groups as well. **34**

public offering statement Written documents providing a full property disclosure to purchasers of time-share developments, as required by Georgia law. Purchaser has seven-day right of cancellation from contract signing date.

public ownership Government-owned property.

puffing Exaggerated or superlative comments or opinions. **166**

pur autre vie "For the life of another." A life estate pur autre vie is a life estate that is measured by the life of a person or persons other than the grantee. **54**

purchase money mortgage A note secured by a mortgage or deed of trust given by a buyer, as borrower, to a seller, as lender, as part of the purchase price of the real estate. **214**

purchase option The right given by a lease to the tenant to purchase the property at a predetermined price within a certain period, possibly the lease term. **356**

pyramiding The process of acquiring additional property by refinancing property already owned and investing the loan proceeds in additional properties. **430**

quiet title A court action to remove a cloud on the title. **122**

quitclaim deed A conveyance that transfers whatever interest the grantor has in the specified real estate, without warranties or obligations. **107**

quotient The number resulting from dividing one number by another. **460**

radon A naturally occurring gas that is suspected of causing lung cancer. **409**

range A strip of land six miles wide, extending north and south and numbered east and west according to its distance from the principal meridian in the rectangular (government) survey system of legal description. **88**

rate cap The limit on the amount the interest rate can be increased at each adjustment period in an adjustable rate loan. The cap may also set the maximum interest rate that can be charged during the life of the loan. **249**

ratification Method of creating an agency relationship in which the principal accepts the conduct of someone who acted without prior authorization as the principal's agent.

ready, willing, and able buyer Person who is prepared to buy property on the seller's terms and is ready to take positive steps to consummate the transaction. **137**

real estate Land; a portion of the earth's surface extending downward to the center of the earth and upward infinitely into space, including all things permanently attached to it, whether naturally or artificially. **17**

real estate broker A person licensed to arrange the buying, selling, leasing, or exchange of real property for a fee. **2**

real estate investment syndicate *See* syndicate. **433**

real estate investment trust (REIT) Trust ownership of real estate by a group of individuals who purchase certificates of ownership in the trust, which in turn invests the money in real property and distributes the profits back to the investors free of corporate income tax. 433

real estate license law State law enacted to protect the public from fraud, dishonesty, and incompetence on the part of those they hire to represent them in the purchase and sale of real estate. 26

real estate licensee In real estate practice, a person who has the skills and knowledge to be licensed as a real estate broker or salesperson. 2

Real Estate Mortgage Investment Conduit (REMIC) A tax entity that issues multiple classes of investor interests (securities) backed by a pool of mortgages. 434

real estate recovery fund A fund established in some states from real estate license revenues to cover claims of aggrieved parties who have suffered monetary damage through the actions of a real estate professional.

Real Estate Settlement Procedures Act (RESPA) The federal law that requires certain disclosures to consumers about mortgage loan settlements. The law also prohibits the payment or receipt of kickbacks and certain kinds of referral fees. 282

real property The interests, benefits, and rights inherent in real estate ownership; often used as a synonym for real estate. 17

REALTOR® A registered trademarked term reserved for the sole use of active members of state and local REALTOR® associations affiliated with the National Association of REALTORS®. 4

reconciliation The final step in the appraisal process, in which the appraiser considers the estimates of value received from the sales comparison, cost, and income approaches to arrive at a final opinion of market value for the subject property. 309

reconveyance deed A deed used by a trustee under a deed of trust to return title to the trustor. 108

recorded plat A map of a subdivision filed as a public record showing the location and boundaries of the individual parcels. 91

recording The act of entering or recording documents affecting or conveying interests in real estate in the recorder's office established in each county. Until it is recorded, a deed or a mortgage ordinarily is not effective against subsequent purchasers or mortgagees. 120

rectangular (government) survey system A system established in 1785 by the federal government, providing for surveying and describing land by reference to principal meridians and base lines. 88

redemption The right of a defaulted property owner to recover property by curing the default. 227, 254

redemption period A period of time established by state law during which property owners have the right to redeem their real estate from a foreclosure or tax sale by paying the sales price, interest, and costs. Many states do not have mortgage redemption laws. 254

redlining The illegal practice by a lending institution of denying loans or restricting their number for certain areas of a community. 41

reduction certificate (payoff statement) The document signed by a lender indicating the amount required to pay a loan balance in full and satisfy the debt; used in the settlement process to protect both the seller's and the buyer's interests. 318

regression An appraisal principle that the value of a better-quality property is affected adversely by the presence of a lesser-quality property. 302

regulated riparian Classification given to state of Georgia where water rights are considered private property but are subject to police power state regulations to protect public welfare.

Regulation Z Implements the Truth in Lending Act, requiring credit institutions to inform borrowers of the true cost of obtaining credit. 280

release deed A document, also known as a *deed of reconveyance*, that transfers all rights given a trustee under a deed of trust loan back to the grantor after the loan has been fully repaid. 246

release of lien A lien on a property that is now free from a mortgage. 223

remainder interest The remnant of an estate that has been conveyed to take effect and be enjoyed after the termination of a prior estate, such as when an owner conveys a life estate to one party and the remainder to another. 54

renewal option A clause in a lease that grants the lessee the privilege of renewing the lease. 356

rent A fixed, periodic payment made by a tenant of a property to the owner for possession and use, usually by prior agreement of the parties. 350

rent schedule A statement of proposed rental rates, determined by the owner or the property manager or both, based on a building's estimated expenses, market supply and demand, and the owner's long-range goals for the property.

replacement cost The construction cost at current prices of a property that is not necessarily an exact duplicate of the subject property but serves the same purpose or function as the original. 257, 383

representation The role of a real estate professional acting on behalf of a client in a real estate transaction.

reproduction cost The construction cost at current prices of an exact duplicate of the subject property.

rescission The practice of one party canceling or terminating a contract, which has the effect of returning the parties to their original positions before the contract was made. 208

reservation Something that is retained by the seller (i.e., a life estate or an access easement). 103–104

Resolution Trust Corporation (RTC) Created in 1989 by the Financial Institutions Reform, Recovery, and Enforcement Act (FIRREA) to liquidate the assets of failed savings and loan associations. In 1995, the responsibilities of RTC were transferred to the Savings Association Insurance Fund of the Federal Deposit Insurance Corporation.

restrictive covenant A clause in a deed that limits the way the real estate ownership may be used. 397

reverse mortgage A loan by which a homeowner receives a lump sum, monthly payments, or a line of credit based on the homeowner's equity in the property secured by the mortgage. The loan must be repaid at a prearranged date, upon the death of the owner, or upon the sale of the property. 252

reversionary interest The remnant of an estate that the grantor holds after granting a life estate to another person. 54

reversionary right The return of the rights of possession and quiet enjoyment to the lessor at the expiration of a lease. 350

revocation Canceling or annulling licensed privileges or rights. 204

right of first refusal A clause allowing the tenant the opportunity to buy the property before the owner accepts an offer from another party. 77, 357

right of possession Customarily granted to the tenant from the landlord in a Georgia residential lease; here, a tenant is not guaranteed actual possession on the beginning date or the rental term but rather promised a right to possess the property on that date.

right of survivorship *See* joint tenancy. 69

right-of-way The right given by one landowner to another to pass over the land, construct a roadway, or use as a pathway, without actually transferring ownership. 57

riparian rights An owner's rights in land that borders on or includes a stream, river, or lake. These rights include access to and use of the water. 20

risk management Evaluation and selection of appropriate property and other insurance. 381

routine maintenance Day-to-day duties such as cleaning common areas, performing minor carpentry and plumbing adjustments, and providing regularly scheduled upkeep of heating, air-conditioning, and landscaping. 377

rules and regulations Real estate licensing authority orders that govern real estate professionals' activities, having the same force and effect as statutory law. 152

Safe Drinking Water Act An act to protect public health by authorizing the EPA to set national health-based standards for drinking water. 413

safety/protection clause A negotiable clause between broker and client that allows a broker to earn a commission after the term of the brokerage engagement expires. If a party designated in a list given to the client at the end of a listing agreement subsequently directly contracts with the seller during the time period established, the broker will earn a commission. Correspondingly, if after the term expires in a buyer brokerage engagement, the buyer directly contracts with the seller of the property shown to the buyer by the broker during the term of their agreement, the broker will earn a commission.

sale-and-leaseback A transaction in which the owner sells improved property and, as part of the same transaction, signs a long-term lease to remain in possession of the premises. 279

sales associate A person who performs real estate activities while employed by a licensed real estate broker. 2

sales comparison approach The process of estimating the value of a property by examining and comparing sales and listings of comparable properties. 303

sales price The amount of money paid to a seller for the product sold.

salesperson Any person, other than an associate broker, who acts on behalf of a real estate broker in performing any act authorized to be performed by the broker in this unit. 2

satisfaction Release or discharge when a note has been fully paid, returning to the borrower all interest in the real estate originally conveyed to the lender. Entering this release in the public record shows that the debt has been removed from the property. 108

satisfaction of mortgage A document acknowledging the payment of a mortgage debt. 243

secondary mortgage market A market for the purchase and sale of existing mortgages, designed to provide greater liquidity for mortgages. Mortgages are first originated in the *primary mortgage market*. 268

section A portion of a township under the rectangular (government) survey system. A township is divided into 36 sections, numbered 1 through 36. A section is a square with mile-long sides and an area of one square mile, or 640 acres. 89

security *See* collateral. 222

security agreement *See* Uniform Commercial Code. 243

security deed Loan security instrument of choice for residential lenders in Georgia that, unlike a mortgage or deed of trust, provides an absolute conveyance of title from borrower to lender. Borrower-purchaser identified as the grantor of the security deed, while lender is identified as the grantee of the security deed.

security deposit A payment by a tenant, held by the landlord during the lease term, and kept (wholly or partially) on default or on destruction of the premises by the tenant. **354**

self-help eviction Prohibited action in Georgia in which landlords might use their own methods to dispossess a delinquent tenant.

seller's broker The real estate broker who represents only the seller in transactions.

seller's disclosure notice Documents completed by the seller of a home listing any known issues of the property, including home improvements made.

seller's property condition disclosure Disclosure form the seller will typically complete for the listing agent that provide a summary of the property's physical condition, as well as identify any known property latent defects.

separate property Under community property law, property owned solely by either spouse before the marriage, acquired by gift or inheritance during the marriage, or purchased with separate funds after the marriage. **72**

servient tenement Land on which an easement exists in favor of an adjacent property, called the *dominant tenement*. **56**

setback The amount of space local zoning regulations require between a lot line and a building. **392**

settlement and transfer *See* closing. **320**

Settlement Statement (HUD-1) The special HUD form, recently replaced by a new form created by the Consumer Financial Protection Bureau, that itemized all charges to be paid by a borrower and a seller in connection with the settlement of a real estate transaction. Also called the HUD-1 form.

severalty Ownership of real property by one person only; also called *sole ownership*. **68**

severance Changing an item of real estate to personal property by detaching it from the land (e.g., cutting down a tree). **22**

shared appreciation mortgage (SAM) A mortgage loan in which the lender, in exchange for a loan with a favorable interest rate, participates in the profits (if any) the borrower receives when the property is eventually sold.

short-form legal description The second recognized real property legal description in Georgia; called lot-and-block system and subdivision plat map or recorded plat. Generally used in real estate contracts to identify property transferred.

short sale Sale of property in which the sales price is less than the remaining indebtedness. **108**

sick building syndrome (SBS) An illness caused by poor air quality, typically in large commercial buildings. Symptoms include fatigue, nausea, headache, and sensitivity to odors. **378**

single agency Agency relationship in which the agent represents only one party to a transaction. **162**

situs The location of land for legal purposes; the jurisdiction in which land is located. **25**

Small Business Liability Relief and Brownfields Revitalization Act Law that provides funds to assess and clean up brownfields, clarifies liability protections, and provides tax incentives toward enhancing state and tribal response programs (also known as Brownfields Law). **415**

sole proprietorship Business ownership by an individual in which all profits and losses are reported through personal tax returns.

special agent One who is authorized by a principal to perform a single act or transaction; a real estate professional is usually a special agent authorized to find a ready, willing, and able buyer for a particular property, when representing a seller, or a special agent authorized to find a suitable property, when representing a buyer. **159**

special assessment A tax or levy customarily imposed against only those specific parcels of real estate that will benefit from a proposed public improvement like a street or sewer. **227**

special warranty deed A deed in which the grantor warrants, or guarantees, the title only against defects arising during the period of the grantor's tenure and ownership of the property and not against defects existing before that time, generally using the language, "by, through, or under the grantor but not otherwise." **107**

specific lien A lien affecting or attaching only to a certain, identified parcel of land or piece of property. **223**

specific performance A legal action to compel a party to carry out the terms of a contract. **207**

spot survey A survey that shows the location, size, and shape of buildings on the lot, in addition to the lot's legal description. **93**

spot zoning Granting a particular parcel a classification that differs from the classification of other land in the immediate area; may be considered illegal.

statute of frauds That part of a state law that requires certain instruments, such as deeds, real estate sales contracts, and certain leases, to be in writing to be legally enforceable. **102**

statute of limitations That law pertaining to the period of time within which certain actions must be brought to court. **207**

statutory lien A lien imposed on property by statute—a tax lien, for example—in contrast to an *equitable lien*, which arises out of common law. **222**

statutory right of redemption The right of a defaulted property owner to recover the property after its sale by paying the appropriate fees and charges. **227**

statutory year A year composed of 12 months, with each month consisting of 30 days, for a total of 360 days in the year. Also called a *banker's year*. **339, 473**

steering The illegal practice of channeling home seekers to particular areas based on their race, national origin, religion, or other protected classification. **40**

stigmatized property A property that has acquired an undesirable reputation due to an event that occurred on or near it, such as violent crime, gang-related activity, illness, or personal tragedy. Some states restrict the disclosure of information about stigmatized properties. **168**

straight-line depreciation Depreciation taken periodically in equal amounts over an asset's useful life. **431**

straight loan A loan in which only interest is paid during the term of the loan, with the entire principal amount due with the final interest payment. **248**

subagent A broker working with a buyer who represents the seller and the listing broker of the real property shown to this buyer. **162**

subdivider One who buys undeveloped land, divides it into smaller, usable lots and sells the lots to potential users. **395**

subdivision A tract of land divided by the owner, known as the *subdivider*, into blocks, building lots, and streets according to a recorded subdivision plat, which must comply with local ordinances and regulations. **395**

subdivision and development ordinances Municipal ordinances that establish requirements for subdivisions and development.

subdivision plat *See* plat map. **91**

subject to Buyer takes title of property and makes payments on the existing loan but is not personally obligated to pay the debt in full. Original seller might continue to be liable for debt. **247, 260**

subjective value The perceived value of an item based on the benefits given to the owner. **356**

sublease *See* subletting. **356**

subletting The leasing of premises by a lessee to a third party for part of the lessee's remaining term. *See* also assignment. **224**

subordination Relegation to a lesser position, usually in respect to a right or security. **224**

subordination agreement A written agreement between holders of liens on a property that changes the priority of mortgage, judgment, and other liens under certain circumstances. **224**

subrogation The right acquired by the title company to any remedy or damages available to the insured when a title company makes a payment to settle a claim covered by a policy. **124**

substitution An appraisal principle that the maximum value of a property tends to be set by the cost of purchasing an equally desirable and valuable substitute property, assuming that no costly delay is encountered in making the substitution. **302**

subsurface rights Ownership rights in a parcel of real estate to the water, minerals, gas, oil, and so forth that lie beneath the surface of the property. **18**

suit for possession A court suit initiated by a landlord to evict a tenant from leased premises after the tenant has breached one of the terms of the lease or has held possession of the property after the lease's expiration. **360**

suit for specific performance *See* specific performance. **207**

suit to quiet title A court action intended to establish or settle the title to a particular property, especially when there is a cloud on the title. **126**

Superfund Popular name of the hazardous-waste cleanup fund established by the Comprehensive Environmental Response, Compensation, and Liability Act (CERCLA). **416**

Superfund Amendments and Reauthorization Act (SARA) An amendatory statute that contains stronger cleanup standards for contaminated sites, increased funding for Superfund, and clarifications of lender liability and innocent landowner immunity. *See* Comprehensive Environmental Response, Compensation, and Liability Act (CERCLA). **416–417**

supply The amount of goods available for sale in the market. The term is often coupled with *demand*. **8**

supply and demand The appraisal principle that follows the interrelationship of the supply of and demand for real estate. Because appraising is based on economic concepts, this principle recognizes that real property is subject to the influences of the marketplace as with any other commodity. **8**

surety bonds An agreement by an insurance or bonding company to be responsible for certain possible defaults, debts, or obligations incurred by an insured party; in essence, a policy insuring one's personal and/or financial integrity. In the real estate business, a surety bond is generally used to ensure that a particular project will be completed at a certain date or that a contract will be performed as stated. 383

surface rights Ownership rights in a parcel of real estate that are limited to the surface of the property and do not include the space above it *(air rights)* or the substances below the surface *(subsurface rights)*. 18

survey The process by which boundaries are measured and land areas are determined; the on-site measurement of lot lines, dimensions, and position of a house on a lot, including the determination of any existing encroachments or easements. 93

survival clause A clause in the contract for purchase and sale that, unless otherwise expressly agreed to in writing by the buyer and the seller, allows certain contractual obligations to be performed after closing.

syndicate A combination of people or firms formed to accomplish a business venture of mutual interest by pooling resources. In a *real estate investment syndicate*, the parties own and/or develop property, with the main profit generally arising from the sale of the property. 433

tacking Concept providing that successive periods of continuous occupation by different parties may be combined to reach the required total number of years needed to establish a claim for a prescriptive easement. 58

taking Process of land being taken from a property owner for public use through eminent domain with the requirement that the owner be compensated fairly. 61

tax basis The point from which gains and losses are figured for tax purposes. 431

tax credit An amount by which tax owed is reduced directly. 433

tax deed An instrument, similar to a certificate of sale, given to a purchaser at a tax sale. *See also* certificate of sale. 227

tax levy The formal action taken to impose a tax, usually by vote of a taxing district's governing body. 226

tax lien A charge against property, created by operation of law. Tax liens and assessments take priority over all other liens. 222

tax sale A court-ordered sale of real property to raise money to cover delinquent taxes. 227

taxation The process by which a government body raises monies to fund its operation. 62

tenancy by the entirety The joint ownership, recognized in some states, of property acquired by husband and wife during marriage. Upon the death of one spouse, the survivor becomes the owner of the property. 72

tenancy in common (TIC) A form of co-ownership by which each owner holds an undivided interest in real property as if each were sole owner. Each individual owner has the right to partition. Unlike joint tenants, tenants in common have the right of inheritance. 68

tenant Refers collectively to all persons named in a lease and signing the lease as the tenant, and the liability of each such person is joint and several.

tenant at will Defined under Georgia Residential Landlord-Tenant Act as a party who occupies rental property with the landlord's consent and makes rental payments without a written lease.

tenant improvements Alterations to the interior of a building to meet the functional demands of the tenant. Also known as *build-outs*. 378

tenant's insurance Insurance on the personal belongings of tenants. 382

testamentary trust A trust that is established by will after one's death. 74

testate Having made and left a valid will. 111

testator A person who has made a valid will. A woman might be referred to as a *testatrix*, although *testator* can be used for either a man or a woman. 112

tie-in agreement Agreement to sell one product only if the buyer purchases another product as well; also called a *tying agreement*. 141

tiers Strips of land that are six miles wide, extending east and west and numbered north and south according to their distance from the base line in the rectangular (government) survey system of legal description. 88

"time is of the essence" A phrase in a contract that requires the performance of a certain act within a stated period of time. 206

timely A reasonable time for performance under the circumstances of a particular situation.

time-share A form of ownership interest that may include an estate interest in property and that allows use of the property for a fixed or variable time period. 79

title (1) The right to ownership or the ownership of land. (2) The evidence of ownership of land. 102

title insurance A policy insuring a property owner or mortgagee against loss by reason of defects in the title to a parcel of real estate, other than encumbrances, defects, and matters specifically excluded by the policy. 124

title search The examination of public records relating to real estate to determine the current state of the ownership. **122**

Title VIII of Civil Rights Act of 1968 (Fair Housing Act) As since amended, the Fair Housing Act prohibits discrimination in housing based on race, color, religion, national origin, sex, familial status, or disability. **34**

Torrens system A method of evidencing title by registration with the proper public authority, generally called the *registrar*; named for its founder, Sir Robert Torrens. **86, 125**

town house A type of residential dwelling with two floors that is connected to one or more dwellings by a common wall or walls. Title to the unit and lot vest in the owner who shares a fractional interest with other owners in any common areas. **77**

township The principal unit of the rectangular (government) survey system. A township is a 6-mile square of 36 square miles. **89**

township lines All the lines in a rectangular survey system that run east and west, parallel to the base line and six miles apart. **88**

township strips *See* tier. **88**

trade fixture An article installed by a tenant under the terms of a lease that is removable by the tenant before the lease expires. **23**

transaction broker Helps both the buyer and the seller with paperwork and formalities in transferring ownership of real property, but who is not an agent of either party. **165**

transaction coordinator *See* nonagent. **165**

transfer tax An excise tax on the sale of real property in Georgia. Levied at the rate of 0.10 for every $100 of net sales price (sales price less any assumable loan). **109**

triggering terms Specific credit terms, such as down payment, monthly payment, and amount of finance charge or term of loan. **281**

trust A fiduciary arrangement whereby property is conveyed to a person or an institution, called a *trustee*, to be held and administered on behalf of another person, called a *beneficiary*. The one who conveys the trust is called the *trustor*. **73**

trust deed An instrument used to create a mortgage lien by which the borrower conveys title to a trustee, who holds it as security for the benefit of the note holder (the lender); also called a *deed of trust*. **108**

trustee One to whom something is entrusted and who holds legal title to property and administers the property for the benefit of a beneficiary. Can also be a member of a board entrusted with the administration of an institution or organization, such as a cooperative. **73**

trustee's deed A deed executed by a trustee conveying land held in a trust. **107**

trustor A borrower in a deed of trust loan transaction; one who places property in a trust. Also called a grantor or settler. **73**

Truth in Lending Act (TILA) Federal government regulates the lending practices of mortgage lenders through this act. **280**

unbundling services Offering only the real estate services that a client requires. **139**

underground storage tanks (USTs) Commonly found on sites where petroleum products are used or where gas stations and auto repair shops are located, and subject to federal and state regulations. In residential areas, tanks are used to store heating oil. Over time, neglected tanks may leak hazardous substances into the environment. **413**

undivided interest *See* tenancy in common. **68**

unenforceable contract A contract that has all the elements of a valid contract, yet neither party can sue the other to force performance of it. For example, an unsigned contract is generally unenforceable. **206**

Uniform Commercial Code (UCC) A codification of commercial law, adopted in most states, that attempts to make uniform all laws relating to commercial transactions, including chattel mortgages and bulk transfers. Security interests in chattels are created by an instrument known as a *security agreement*. To give notice of the security interest, a *financing statement* must be recorded. Article 6 of the code regulates *bulk transfers*—the sale of a business as a whole, including all fixtures, chattels, and merchandise.

Uniform Electronic Transactions Act (UETA) Sets forth rules for entering into an enforceable contract using electronic means. **144**

Uniform Partnership Act Law that provides for the continuation of an existing business if a partner in a general partnership dies, withdraws, or goes bankrupt. **75**

Uniform Residential Appraisal Report (URAR) The appraisal form created by Fannie Mae and Freddie Mac that is required for most residential real estate transactions. **293**

Uniform Standards of Professional Appraisal Practice (USPAP) A set of standards developed by the Appraisal Foundation that details information required for a property appraisal. **291**

unilateral contract A one-sided contract wherein one party makes a promise so as to induce a second party to do something. The second party is not legally bound to perform; however, if the second party does comply, the first party is obligated to keep the promise. 203

uniqueness The idea that no matter how identical they may appear, no two parcels of real estate are ever exactly alike. 8

unity of ownership The four unities that are traditionally needed to create a joint tenancy—unity of title, time, interest, and possession. 73

unity of possession Co-owners of a tenancy in common are each entitled to possession and use of the entire property, even though each hold only a fractional ownership interest. 70

universal agent A person empowered to do anything the principal could do personally. 158

urea-formaldehyde foam insulation (UFFI) Insulating foam that can release harmful formaldehyde gases. Formaldehyde causes some individuals to suffer respiratory problems, as well as eye and skin irritations. 410

usury Charging interest at a higher rate than the maximum rate established by state law. 241

VA-guaranteed loan A mortgage loan on approved property made to a qualified veteran by an authorized lender and guaranteed by the U.S. Department of Veterans Affairs in order to limit the lender's possible loss. 274

valid contract A contract that complies with all the essentials of a contract and is binding and enforceable on all parties to it. 205

value The power of a good or service to command other goods in exchange for the present worth of future rights to its income or amenities.

variable rate mortgage A mortgage loan in which the interest rate varies depending on market conditions. 281

variance Permission obtained from zoning authorities to build a structure or conduct a use that is expressly prohibited by the current zoning laws; an exception from the zoning ordinances. 394

vendee A buyer, usually under the terms of a land contract. 214

vendor A seller, usually under the terms of a land contract. 214

vendor's lien A lien that belongs to a vendor for the unpaid purchase price of land, where the vendor has not taken any other lien or security beyond the personal obligation of the purchaser. 223

void contract A contract that has no legal force or effect because it does not meet the essential elements of a contract. 205

voidable contract A contract that seems to be valid on the surface but may be rejected or disaffirmed by one or both of the parties. 205

volume The amount of space of a three-dimensional object. 454

voluntary alienation *See* alienation. 102

voluntary lien A lien placed on property with the knowledge and consent of the property owner. 222

warranty clause A part of the deed in which the seller warrants the title conveyed to the buyer.

warranty deed Most common deed used in Georgia to transfer real property. Makes promise of marketable title conveyance from grantor to grantee, as well as grantor's promise to warrant the title forever.

waste An improper use or an abuse of a property by a possessor who holds less than fee ownership, such as a tenant, life tenant, or vendee. Such waste ordinarily impairs the value of the land or the interest of the person holding the title or the reversionary rights.

water rights Common law rights held by owners of land adjacent to rivers, lakes, or oceans; includes restrictions on those rights and land ownership. 19

water table The natural level at which the ground is saturated. The water table may be several hundred feet underground or near the surface. 412

will A written document, properly witnessed, providing for the transfer of title to property owned by the deceased, called the *testator*. 112

workers' compensation acts State laws that require an employer to obtain insurance coverage to protect employees who are injured in the course of their employment. 382

wraparound loan A method of refinancing in which the new mortgage is placed in a secondary, or subordinate, position; the new mortgage includes both the unpaid principal balance of the first mortgage and whatever additional sums are advanced by the lender. In essence, it is an additional mortgage in which another lender refinances a borrower by lending an amount over the existing first mortgage amount without disturbing the existence of the first mortgage. 278

writ of attachment A document ordered by the court to have a sheriff enter a leased property to give possession back to the owner. 230

X-bar method A math tool used to solve percentage problems, indicating what values to multiply or divide to arrive at the unknown value. 461

year's support statute Allows surviving spouse and minor children to petition the court to hold back funds from decedent spouse's estate to provide an "accustomed standard" of living for 12 months.

zoning A regulatory tool that helps communities regulate and control how land is used. **391**

zoning board of appeals A board that must be formed when the local legislature adopts a new zoning law, to provide for property owners to object to the application of the law to their property. **393**

zoning ordinance An exercise of police power by a municipality to regulate and control the character and use of property. **391**

Answer Key

To access the student question bank—to create customized quizzes and exams from the hundreds of questions in the *Modern Real Estate Practice* text—go to the website: www.modernrealestatepractice.com.

Following are the correct answers to the review questions included in each unit of the text. In parentheses following the correct answers are references to the pages where the question topics are discussed or explained. If you have answered a question incorrectly, be sure to go back to the page or pages noted and restudy the material until you understand the correct answer.

Unit 1 Quiz Answers

Introduction to the Real Estate Business

1. **b** (2)
2. **b** (8)
3. **d** (9)
4. **c** (10)
5. **b** (2–3)
6. **d** (4)
7. **b** (9–10)
8. **a** (4)
9. **d** (2, 4)
10. **a** (6)
11. **b** (8)
12. **b** (2)
13. **a** (8–9)
14. **b** (6)
15. **d** (10)
16. **c** (8–9)
17. **d** (3)
18. **a** (8)
19. **c** (3)
20. **b** (10)

Unit 2 Quiz Answers

Real Property and the Law

1. **c** (17, 22)
2. **b** (23)
3. **c** (25)
4. **c** (21)
5. **c** (21)
6. **b** (16–18)
7. **a** (23)
8. **a** (25)
9. **a** (22)
10. **a** (23)
11. **c** (18–19)
12. **b** (22–24)
13. **c** (23)
14. **d** (18)
15. **a** (24)
16. **c** (20)
17. **b** (17–18)
18. **c** (23–24)
19. **b** (25)
20. **d** (21–23)

Unit 3 Quiz Answers

Fair Housing

1. **c** (34)
2. **a** (43)
3. **d** (33)
4. **b** (40)
5. **c** (40)
6. **a** (41)
7. **b** (37–38)
8. **b** (40)
9. **a** (43)
10. **b** (38)
11. **a** (33)
12. **b** (34)
13. **d** (43)
14. **c** (34, 36)
15. **d** (40–41)
16. **a** (43)
17. **d** (34)
18. **b** (38–39)
19. **d** (38–39)
20. **a** (34, 43)

Unit 4 Quiz Answers

Interests in Real Estate

1. **b** (60)
2. **a** (53)
3. **c** (53)
4. **c** (56)
5. **c** (59)
6. **d** (56–57)
7. **c** (60)
8. **a** (60)
9. **b** (56)
10. **c** (54)
11. **b** (54)
12. **b** (59)
13. **c** (55)
14. **d** (59)
15. **b** (55)
16. **b** (56)
17. **a** (57)
18. **a** (62)
19. **a** (58)
20. **d** (59)

Unit 5 Quiz Answers
Forms of Real Estate Ownership

1. d (70)
2. b (68–69)
3. a (69–70)
4. b (76)
5. c (73)
6. d (72)
7. b (68–69)
8. a (73)
9. d (78)
10. c (75)
11. c (75)
12. d (68)
13. d (72)
14. b (78)
15. b (71)
16. c (78)
17. b (79)
18. b (69–70, 72)
19. b (73)
20. a (70)

Unit 6 Quiz Answers
Land Description

1. b (90–91)
2. d (88)
3. d (90–91)
4. b (86)
5. c (90)
6. c (90)
7. a (90)
8. a (90)
9. a (90–91)
10. b (95)
11. a (90–91)
12. d (95)
13. c (91)
14. b (95)
15. b (86–88)
16. b (95)
17. b (95)
18. b (90)
19. b (90)
20. c (85)

Unit 7 Quiz Answers
Transfer of Title

1. a (102, 111)
2. a (104)
3. d (103)
4. a (105)
5. b (106)
6. a (107)
7. d (107)
8. b (107)
9. c (105)
10. b (105)
11. c (110)
12. b (111)
13. d (110)
14. a (106)
15. a (107)
16. c (110)
17. d (112)
18. c (113)
19. c (114)
20. d (104)

Unit 8 Quiz Answers
Title Records

1. a (119)
2. a (120)
3. c (121)
4. a (121)
5. a (123)
6. d (123)
7. d (123–124)
8. a (122)
9. c (123)
10. a (122)
11. c (120)
12. c (125)
13. b (125)
14. c (122)
15. c (125)
16. a (124)
17. c (120–121, 123)
18. a (121)
19. b (124–125)
20. c (124–125)

Unit 9 Quiz Answers
Real Estate Brokerage

1. b (137)
2. c (134–135)
3. b (134–135)
4. b (134–135)
5. a (136)
6. d (135)
7. d (141–142)
8. a (140–141)
9. c (132)
10. b (134)
11. d (140–141)
12. a (138)
13. c (138)
14. b (138)
15. d (144)
16. c (137)
17. c (140)
18. b (137)
19. b (134–135
20. d (134–135)

Unit 10 Quiz Answers
Real Estate Agency

1. d (153, 156)
2. a (159)
3. a (157)
4. b (166)
5. c (163–164)
6. b (165)
7. d (165)
8. d (157)
9. c (165)
10. c (158)
11. c (163–164)
12. c (152)
13. c (153)
14. a (156)
15. d (166)
16. b (157–158)
17. a (163–164)
18. c (153, 156)
19. a (156)
20. d (163–164)

Unit 11 Quiz Answers
Client Representation Agreements

1. a (176)
2. c (176–177)
3. c (178–179)
4. a (177)
5. b (187)
6. d (177)
7. a (177)
8. c (179)
9. a (176)
10. d (187)
11. c (177)
12. b (176)
13. c (189)
14. b (189)
15. c (176)
16. b (179)
17. b (177)
18. c (176)
19. b (177)
20. b (191)

Unit 12 Quiz Answers
Real Estate Contracts

1. c (203)
2. b (206)
3. d (203)
4. b (203)
5. c (204–205)
6. d (207)
7. d (213)
8. a (211)
9. a (212)
10. d (210–211)
11. b (214)
12. d (214)
13. d (214)
14. c (202–203)
15. d (204, 210)
16. b (210–211)
17. a (205)
18. b (204)
19. d (206)
20. b (214)

Unit 13 Quiz Answers
Real Estate Taxes and Other Liens

1. d (223)
2. b (224)
3. b (227–228)
4. c (223)
5. b (225)
6. d (226)
7. c (225)
8. c (228–229)
9. d (226)
10. c (223)
11. d (229)
12. d (230)
13. c (227)
14. b (222, 228)
15. b (228–229)
16. d (228–229)
17. d (227)
18. a (223)
19. b (225)
20. d (225)

Unit 14 Quiz Answers
Real Estate Financing

1. b (241–242)
2. a (243)
3. c (243)
4. a (244)
5. c (248)
6. b (241)
7. d (254)
8. d (245)
9. a (246)
10. a (252)
11. c (249)
12. b (246)
13. b (253)
14. d (255)
15. b (241)
16. d (244)
17. a (243)
18. b (250)
19. b (248
20. b (247)

Unit 15 Quiz Answers
Government Involvement in Real Estate Financing

1. d (277)
2. d (279)
3. c (268–270)
4. c (282)
5. b (267)
6. a (269)
7. d (282–283)
8. b (277)
9. c (273)
10. b (280–281)
11. b (279)
12. a (277)
13. b (269)
14. d (281–282)
15. b (279)
16. b (276)
17. c (272)
18. b (275)
19. c (282)
20. d (280–281)

Unit 16 Quiz Answers
Real Estate Appraisal

1. c (307)
2. b (300)
3. b (302)
4. b (300)
5. d (302)
6. a (302)
7. d (304–305)
8. c (309)
9. a (308–309)
10. c (307)
11. c (307)
12. c (300)
13. b (307–308)
14. c (305)
15. d (303–304)
16. b (304–307)
17. b (304–307)
18. b (306)
19. b (301)
20. c (301–303)

Unit 17 Quiz Answers
Closing the Real Estate Transaction

1. d (338)
2. b (316, 318)
3. d (318)
4. a (320)
5. d (321–322)
6. c (336)
7. c (318)
8. b (340)
9. b (340)
10. d (343)
11. c (343)
12. a (340)
13. c (342–344)
14. b (329)
15. c (340)
16. b (339)
17. d (339)
18. d (323)
19. b (335)
20. b (329)

Unit 18 Quiz Answers
Leases

1. c (358)
2. c (357)
3. d (360)
4. c (360)
5. b (356)
6. d (352–353)
7. c (351)
8. b (360)
9. b (360)
10. b (351)
11. b (350, 353)
12. a (359–360)
13. b (357)
14. d (352–353)
15. c (357)
16. a (357)
17. c (358)
18. d (358)
19. c (359)
20. c (360)

Unit 19 Quiz Answers
Property Management

1. b (382)
2. c (381)
3. b (378)
4. c (382)
5. c (371–372)
6. b (381)
7. d (378)
8. a (371)
9. c (373)
10. a (374)
11. c (382)
12. c (383)
13. c (374)
14. b (377)
15. b (371)
16. b (373)
17. b (383)
18. c (379–380)
19. c (379)
20. d (380)

Unit 20 Quiz Answers
Land-Use Controls and Property Development

1. a (397)
2. a (394)
3. b (397)
4. c (391–392)
5. c (394–395)
6. a (390)
7. a (393)
8. d (392)
9. b (397)
10. a (398)
11. a (394)
12. c (396)
13. b (397)
14. a (394)
15. b (391)
16. d (396)
17. a (396)
18. d (397)
19. a (398)
20. c (395)

Unit 21 Quiz Answers
Environmental Issues and the Real Estate Transaction

1. b (406–407)
2. c (405)
3. c (406–407)
4. a (405–406)
5. a (411–412)
6. c (414)
7. b (415)
8. d (416)
9. c (409)
10. d (405–407, 410)
11. b (405)
12. c (406–407)
13. d (406)
14. b (410)
15. c (406–407)
16. c (409)
17. b (413–415)
18. a (412–413)
19. d (416)
20. a (405)

Unit 22 Quiz Answers
Investing in Real Estate

1. a (428)
2. b (428)
3. d (430)
4. a (431)
5. d (432)
6. b (430)
7. c (433)
8. d (434)
9. b (431)
10. a (431)
11. b (426)
12. b (433)
13. c (432)
14. b (432)
15. d (429)
16. a (433)
17. c (427–429)
18. d (428)
19. b (430)
20. c (433)

Unit 23 Quiz Answers

Ownership

1. d (443)
2. d (444)
3. d (444)
4. c (443)
5. c (454)
6. d (453)
7. c (454)
8. d (451)
9. c (457)
10. d (456)
11. c (458))
12. c (455)
13. c (457)
14. d (460)
15. d (461)
16. a (460)
17. c (462)
18. c (452)
19. b (460)
20. d (443)

Unit 24 Quiz Answers

Brokerage Relationships in Real Estate Transactions Act (BRRETA)

1. d (468)
2. c (469)
3. b (470)
4. d (471)
5. d (471)
6. c (473)
7. d (473, 475)
8. b (495)
9. c (479)
10. c (476)
11. c (474)
12. c (492)
13. d (488)
14. a (472)
15. c (478)
16. b (474)
17. c (481)
18. c (483)
19. c (495)
20. c (470)

Answer Key for Unit 25 Exam

Contract Forms for Real Estate Practice in Georgia

1. c (510)
2. b (503)
3. d (515)
4. a (509)
5. c (508–509, 529–530)
6. b (544)
7. d (565)
8. c (562)
9. a (544)
10. c (562)
11. c (594)
12. d (609)
13. c (601)
14. b (595)
15. c (600)
16. b (522)
17. c (548)
18. d (547)
19. c (599)
20. a (474)

Answer Key for Unit 26 Exam

Financing and Closing Residential Transactions

1. d (649)
2. b (650)
3. c (655)
4. a (651)
5. b (662)
6. d (662)
7. c (665)
8. c (650)
9. d (659)
10. c (660)
11. b (657)
12. b (675)
13. d (711)
14. d (679)
15. d (692)
16. b (654)
17. a (673)
18. d (662)
19. c (684)
20. d (675)

Answer Key for Unit 27 Exam

Real Estate Commission and License Law

1. b (716)
2. c (719)
3. c (719)
4. d (722)
5. b (731)
6. a (726)
7. c (732)
8. c (729)
9. a (733)
10. d (736)
11. d (739)
12. c (744)
13. a (748)
14. c (744)
15. d (720)
16. c (719)
17. b (736)
18. d (734)
19. c (745)
20. b (747)

Sample Exam 1 Answers

1. b (224)
2. a (207)
3. a (160)
4. c (253)
5. a (252)
6. b (191)
7. a (108)
8. a (42)
9. a (56)
10. d (71)
11. d (136–137)
12. a (246)
13. b (351)
14. a (308)
15. a (393)
16. c (465–466)
17. d (167)
18. c (72–73)
19. a (465–466)
20. b (62)
21. d (189)
22. b (97, 453)
23. b (245)

24. b (228)
25. c (243, 468–469)
26. d (228–229, 477–478)
27. b (309–310)
28. c (92–93, 453, 465–466)
29. d (468–469)
30. b (465–466)
31. d (206, 211–212)
32. d (216)
33. b (209)
34. b (241)
35. b (211–212)
36. a (245)
37. d (310–311)
38. b (179)
39. a (9)
40. a (110)
41. d (181)
42. b (357)
43. c (34–35)
44. b (453–454)
45. d (225)
46. d (216, 356)
47. c (62–63)
48. d (92–93)
49. b (304)
50. b (225)
51. b (208–209)
52. b (71–72)
53. c (350)
54. d (211–213)
55. b (58)
56. c (467–468)
57. a (55)
58. a (272, 467–468)
59. d (391–392)
60. b (207)
61. c (256)
62. a (36)
63. d (335–344)
64. d (207)
65. b (109)
66. d (70–71)
67. b (336–344)
68. d (36)
69. a (110–111)
70. a (309)
71. d (250)
72. d (78)
73. a (337)
74. a (336–337)
75. b (24)
76. c (61)
77. d (451–452)
78. b (179)
79. d (142–143)
80. d (360)

Sample Exam 2 Answers

1. d (352)
2. c (24)
3. c (205)
4. b (256)
5. c (281)
6. d (158–259)
7. b (465–466, 451)
8. d (36, 41–43)
9. b (454–455)
10. b (272)
11. b (213)
12. a (282)
13. d (197)
14. c (56)
15. d (158–160)
16. d (92)
17. b (106)
18. b (178)
19. c (465–466)
20. a (306)
21. c (325)
22. b (360)
23. a (56)
24. b (336–337)
25. d (357)
26. d (467–468, 473–476)
27. c (467–468, 473–476)
28. a (158–160)
29. b (309–310)
30. d (343)
31. b (473–478)
32. d (460–461)
33. a (213)
34. d (230)
35. b (452–453)
36. a (138)
37. a (356)
38. d (139, 178)
39. a (309–310)
40. c (431)
41. d (104)
42. c (92–93)
43. b (206)
44. d (465–467)
45. c (455)
46. d (276–278)
47. a (55)
48. a (473–474, 476–478)
49. b (208, 356)
50. c (431)
51. c (465–466)
52. a (122–123)
53. c (241)
54. a (113)
55. d (71–73)
56. a (337)
57. b (62–63)
58. b (461)
59. d (308–309)
60. d (282)
61. d (309–310)
62. c (380)
63. c (107, 114–115)
64. c (467–468)
65. a (210)
66. b (189)
67. b (39–40)
68. d (169)
69. c (61)
70. a (324–327)
71. d (282)
72. c (309–310)
73. a (213)
74. b (309–311)
75. b (536)
76. c (252)
77. b (302)
78. d (228)
79. b (332–333)
80. b (381)

List of Figures

Index

G

H

I

Q

R

Notes

Notes

Notes

Notes

Notes

Notes

Notes

Notes

Notes